10828355

Prayer of the poor

Kabbalistic Shavuot Machzor

www.kabbalah.com™

The Kabbalah Centre
155 E. 48th St., New York, NY 10017
1062 S. Robertson Blvd., Los Angeles, CA 90035

First Edition
January 2012

Printed in the USA

ISBN13: 978-1-57189-860-9

TABLE OF CONTENTS

To the greatness of the value of the Ashurit font

And then you should open your mouth with wisdom and say *Keri'at Shema* with intention. This means you should understand the words you are saying and that when you recite the words of *Keri'at Shema* (from the Prayer Book) you should visualize in your mind the shape of each word and its letters. For example when you say the word "*Shema*" you should visualize the letters *Shin, Mem* and *Ayin* the way they are written in Ashurit font in front of your eyes. You should then visualize every word the same way until the end. You should visualize the vowels and the intonations that are above every letter, the same way as they are written in this Prayer Book and by doing so you should merit that each word will excel in its form to the Upper Worlds and every letter shall go to its place and to its root to activate miraculous actions and *tikkunim* (corrections) that are related to you. And by doing so (scanning the Ashurit font) on a daily basis, it will enable you (and it has been proven) to remove all negative thoughts and nonsense that interferes with the purity of our thought and intention in prayers. The more scanning of the Ashurit font a person does with the *Keri'at Shema* and any other part of the prayer will add purity to his thoughts during prayer. This meditation is a simple action and then you are promised to successfully educate yourself with your prayer and all will be desired by God just like the good scent. Amen so be it.

(*Seder HaYom* by Rav Yosef Chaim - The Ben Ish-Chai).

"When you go to sleep you should visualize the Tetragrammaton Name (יהוה), Blessed Be He, as if it was written capital Ashurit. The eyes should always turn to God and God will protect him falling into a trap".

(*Tziporen Shamir*, par. 68 v. 121 by Rav Chaim Yosef David Azulai - The Chida 1724-1806)

General guidance

According to Rav Isaac Luria (the Ari), and Rav Shalom Sharabi (the Rashash), all the words of intention, Holy Names and names of angels that are written in this book, even though they are a part of the text, should not be pronounced verbally. When you get to a word like this, you should scan it with your eyes and not say it.

IN THE MATTER OF SHAVUOT

(FROM THE *GATE OF MEDITATIONS* AND *PRI ETZ CHAIM*)

MEDITATIONS OF THE MIKVEH FOR THE EVE OF SHAVUOT

On the Eve of the Holiday you need to do *Mikveh*. And you should meditate on the Names: יוד הי ויו הי אלף הי יוד הי, which together have the numerical value of the word Holiday (*Regel* =233), and you should meditate that *Mikveh* has the numerical value of the Name: אלף הה יוד הה, which is 151. And you should say the following verse and meditate on the Names that are derived from it:

Vayikra וַיִּקְרָא

אלף למד הי יוד מם

ע"ב יוד הי ויו הי

Elohim אֱלֹהִים

אלף למד הי יוד מם

ס"ג יוד הי ואו הי

LayAbbasha לַיַּבָּשָׁה

אלף למד הה יוד מם

מ"ה יוד הא ואו הא

Eretz אֶרֶץ

אלף למד הא יוד מם

ב"ן יוד הה וו הה

ר"ת וּלְמִקְוֵה הַמַּיִם קָרָא יַמִּים

Ulemikveh Hamayim Kara Yamim

(with its nine letters =121) **יהוה אלהים**

Meditations of the Mikveh before the Dawn of Shavuot

Immerse in the early morning—a time that is called—*Ayelet HaShachar* (*Doe of the Dawn*) of *Shavuot* and meditate to be of the Entourage (*Shushvin*) of the Holy Queen Bride (*Matronita Malketa Kadisha*), *Rachel-Akeret Habayit* and to receive additional Holiness from the aspect of *Keter* of *Zeir Anpin* and to continue this illumination (in the secret of the Upper *Mikveh*, which is the 50th Gate of *Binah*, which is the source of *Keter* of *Zeir Anpin*) to the *Nukva* to cleanse and purify Her from the negativity of the 49 Gates of Impurity and to prepare Her for unification with *Zeir Anpin*.

לשם יהוה קודשא בריך הוא ושכינתיה (יאהדונהי), בדחילו ורחימו (יאההויהה), ורחימו ודחילו (איההיוהה) ליחדא שם יוד קי בואו קי (יהוה) ביחודא שלים, בשם כל ישראל, הנה אני מכין את עצמי להיות מן השושבינין דמטרוניתא מלכתא קדישא, רחל עקרת הבית, והנני בא עתה באשמורת הבוקר של יום חג השבועות, בעת הנקרא אילת השחר לטבול במקוה. לתקן את שרש טבילה זו במקום עליון ולהמשיך טהרה וטבילה ממקור כתר עליון הנמשך בלילה הזאת והוא נקרא שער החמישים. ככתוב: "וזרקתי עליכם מים טהורים". והריני מוכן לטבול ארבע הטבילות כנגד ארבע אותיות השם ברוך הוא בניקוד קמץ, ועוד הריני מוכן לטבול טבילה חמישית כנגד אור החסד העליון, שהוא הרצון העליון, המתגלה במזל השמיני הנקרא "נוצר חסד". ויהי נעם אדני אלהינו עלינו ומעשה ידינו כוננה עלינו ומעשה ידינו כוננהו.

Have the intention to build the *Keter* of *Nukva*. Meditate that *Chesed* (represented by the *Mikveh* water) of *Tiferet* of *Zeir Anpin* is divided into two aspects: The first part ascends and creates *Keter* of *Zeir Anpin* (as a completion for the all night study) and the second part goes to the back and starts to create *Keter* of *Nukva*.

Also meditate to draw illuminations for *Keter* of *Nukva*:

Yud Hei of ע"ב (=35) and *Yud Hei* of ס"ג (=35) and *Miluy* of ע"ב (=46) and *Miluy* of ס"ג (=37) equal 153, which is the numerical value of *Mikveh* (151= אלף הה יוד הה) and the two Names: ע"ב and ס"ג. And meditate that in this *Mikveh* the *Nukva* is purified and She is ready to start the elevation (for *Nukva*'s *Keter* to be equal) to *Zeir Anpin*'s *Keter* and for the final unification with *Zeir Anpin* in *Musaf*.

Then immerse yourself five times:

In the first immersion meditate on the letter *Yud* of the Tetragammaton in Kamatz יָ.
In the second immersion meditate on the first letter *Hei* of the Tetragammaton in Kamatz הָ.
In the third immersion meditate on the letter *Vav* of the Tetragammaton in Kamatz וָ.
In the fourth immersion meditate on the second letter *Hei* of the Tetragammaton in Kamatz הָ.
In the fifth immersion meditate to draw the illumination of the Upper *Chesed*, the Upper Desire – נוצר חסד (the Eighth *Mazal*).

THE ARI ON SHAVUOT

We explained before that in the seven weeks between *Pesach* and *Shavuot* the *Mochin* spreads in *Zeir Anpin* in its seven aspects, which are: *Chochmah* and *Binah*, and the *Chasadim* and *Gevurot* of *Da'at*, and *Chesed*, and *Gevurah*, and *Tiferet*, and also the *Malchut* is included with *Tiferet* since it is cleaved together with it back to back. And now in *Shavuot*, they spread also in Its *Netzach* and *Hod* (the secret of the two stone Tablets that were given in *Shavuot*, as was mentioned in the *Zohar*). And since they spread until there, then *Yesod* of *Zeir Anpin* unifies with *Malchut*—*Zivug* of *Gadlut*.

Also during the seven weeks of *Sefirat Ha'Omer*, *Zeir Anpin* grew to the level of Supernal *Chochmah* and *Binah* (*Gadlut Bet*, which is above *Yisrael Saba* and *Tevunah* that is called *Gadlut Alef*). So the only aspect of *Zeir Anpin* that is missing is the *Keter* (which is made from *Arich Anpin* itself), and therefore it is needed that *Zeir Anpin* will elevate in *Shavuot* until *Arich Anpin*.

This *Keter* that is given to *Zeir Anpin* starts to enter It in the beginning of the night of *Shavuot*, and it does not finish entering until dawn. Afterwards in the prayer of *Shacharit* and *Musaf* of the day of *Shavuot*, then *Nukva Rachel* is elevated in order to be unified with Him, like in *Shabbat* and Holidays. But, not like in *Shabbat* and Holidays, *Zeir Anpin* starts to be elevated towards *Arich Anpin* from dawn, (which happens later on *Shabbat* and the Holidays), and that is the greatness of *Shavuot*. Therefore, sexual relations are forbidden on the night of *Shavuot*, because there is no Unification in the Upper Worlds, as was mentioned. Furthermore, you need to be awake the entire night, and to be busy with the Torah.

A little earlier than before dawn, when the face of the sky turns dark in the East, called *Ayelet Hashachar*, you need to go to the *Mikveh*, and meditate to connect to the Supernal *Mikveh*, which is the Supernal *Keter* of *Zeir Anpin* and is also called the 50th Gate, and by this we receive the additional Holiness from the aspect of this *Keter*.

The reason is that on this night we do two things: One is to draw the Supernal *Keter* of *Zeir Anpin* by being busy with the Torah, and afterwards, at *Ayelet Hashachar*, we become bridesmaids of the Queen (*Rachel Nukva* of *Zeir Anpin*), and we escort the bride to the house of immersion, and she immerses in the Supernal *Mikveh* (She does not elevate to *Keter* of *Zeir Anpin*, but She receives purity and immersion from *Keter* of *Zeir Anpin*). Afterwards, through the prayer of *Shacharit* and *Musaf* of the day of *Shavuot*, She elevates like Him and then They unify, as was mentioned above.

Keter of *Zeir Anpin* and *Keter* of *Nukva* are done in one moment, as *Chesed* that spreads in *Tiferet* of *Zeir Anpin*, and divides into two, the first elevates towards *Keter* of *Zeir Anpin*, and the second comes out of the chest through the back of *Tiferet* and is given to *Rachel Nukva* of *Zeir Anpin* to create Her *Keter*. *Keter* of *Zeir Anpin* is the aspect of *Dikna* of *Arich Anpin* and descends through the lower half of *Tiferet* of *Ima* until the head of *Zeir Anpin*. We know that there are 50 Gates in *Ima*, which are the secret of Her five *Chassadim*, and when these five *Chassadim* complete to spread in *Zeir Anpin*, then half of *Tiferet* of *Ima* descends to be a crown (*Keter*) on Its head. It turns out that the *Keter* of *Zeir Anpin* is called the 50th Gate.

So from the half of *Chesed* of *Tiferet* of *Zeir Anpin* (that was divided and elevated upwards to the *Keter* of *Zeir Anpin*, and causes this *Keter* to descend to the head of *Zeir Anpin*), which is the aspect of water (mercy), this water continues to the *Nukva*, and She immerses in Them.

THE 24 ADORNMENTS OF THE BRIDE

As we explained above, throughout the night study we are preparing the Bride for her unification with *Zeir Anpin* in *Musaf*. By reading the 24 books of the Bible we meditate on 24 Names, one from each book. Each Name is derived from the first and last letters of the second word of the last verse of the book. The first letter has the vowel of *Kubutz* and the second letter has the vowel of *Kamatz*. For example: In the book of Beresheet, the second word in the last verse is Yosef יוסף, so we take the first letter which is *Yud* י and the last letter which is *Pei* פ with the vowels as follows: יֻפָּ.

It is important to meditate on the following Names during the *Kedusha* of *Keter* of *Musaf* (pg. 423) as it is written in the *Zohar* (Introduction verse 129): "During the year the *Nukva* has the Name: אל but now (during *Musaf* of *Shavuot* and also during *Shabbat*), the *Nukva* is elevated and receives a new Name: כבוד אל (=63 the secret of the inner *Da'at*).

THE RAV ON SHAVUOT

We learn from the *Zohar* that on the night of *Shavuot*, Rav Shimon and his students stayed awake and studied Torah. But for many people today, the true meaning of the holiday of *Shavuot* has been lost or forgotten. Few remember or understand the reason for the Creator's presentation of the Torah on Mount Sinai 3,400 years ago. According to the rule we learned from Rav Brandwein (my teacher), the fact that so many people ignore this event is proof of its importance. If it were not so important, the negative side would not bother to remove people's attention from it.

People have disconnected from the importance of the event on Mount Sinai because it is considered merely part of a religious tradition. And tradition, to most people, has only one purpose: To commemorate an event from the past. Yet what's the point in commemorating an event that occurred 3400 years ago if we cannot perceive the direct and immediate connection between that event and our life today?

Rav Shimon says, in effect, that every year on *Shavuot*, we can purchase life insurance. Whoever makes the right spiritual connection on *Shavuot* has been insured: They will not die or be hurt, and this insurance will last at least until the following *Rosh Hashanah*. But had Rav Shimon not stated this clearly in the *Introduction to the Zohar*, volume 1, verse 150, no one would believe such a thing possible. In a world where people don't know what will happen tomorrow, there is no price for this type of insurance Rav Shimon is offering us. From this, then, we can see that the reason for celebrating *Shavuot* is not religious or historical tradition, but rather pure self-interest.

So what exactly happened on Mount Sinai 3,400 years ago? What is the secret of this wonderful event? On Mount Sinai, the Israelites received the Torah and the Ten Utterances. We learn from the *Midrash* that before the Torah was given, the Creator offered it to all the nations of the world...and all refused to accept it. But when the Creator turned to the Israelites, they answered, "We will do and we will hear."

The *Talmud*, however, describes the event in a different and less ideal way. According to the *Talmud*, the Creator gave the Israelites an ultimatum. He elevated Mount Sinai in the air, collected the Israelites in the crater that lay underneath, and said to them, "Either accept the Torah or this will be your burial ground." Under these circumstances, the Israelites said what anyone would have said: "We will do and we will hear."

Today, as was the case then, most people are not excited about the Torah. So what is the point of *Shavuot*?

At the event of the giving of the Torah and every year on the holiday of *Shavuot*, the Creator gives us a very special opportunity that can be taken advantage of only if very specific energetic prerequisites are met. These prerequisites occur only once during the year: On the sixth day of the month of *Sivan*. It was not a coincidence that the Torah was given on this specific day. *Shavuot* is the only day of the year that is perfect for this mission. The *Zohar* reveals that timing has a decisive meaning in our world. *Shavuot* gives us the opportunity to connect with the consciousness of certainty and unity that is needed to reveal all the layers of reality. The message is simple: The secret of life is the connection to the Light. The secret of success in the world lies in our ability to connect to the Lightforce of the Creator and to channel it through us. Only in a month with this consciousness can the Torah be revealed.

THE RAV ON SHAVUOT

Every month, the Light of the Creator embodied in the Torah is revealed in the world, but the revelation is channeled through the negative aspects of separation and differentiation. During any other month, we would have looked at the Ten Utterances as laws—ten commands dictating that we shall not steal, we shall not kill, and so forth. Only in the month of *Sivan* can we grasp the inner, essential truth that will elevate our consciousness: We will not hurt another, not because it is the law but because the other is a part of us. The Ten Utterances don't describe a perfect social order or some kind of utopia, but rather the result of being in the right consciousness. When we connect to the Light, there will be no need for judge or legislator or policeman to make us follow laws imposed on us from without.

The combinations of Aramaic letters used to write the Ten Utterances is a communication channel that transmits both the Light of the Creator and the removal of death. This is the secret of the Ten Utterances; the content of the text is secondary in importance. If a person wants to reconnect to his spiritual self, he automatically understands "thou shalt not kill" because he would never do that to himself. We can take someone else's life only if we exist in separation. For this reason, the command is secondary. It was never the real purpose.

The *Zohar* says that the Revelation of *Shavuot*—the giving of the Torah on Mount Sinai—included not only the Ten Utterances but also life energy on such an enormous scale as to cancel completely the consciousness of death. There was, in other words, "removal of death." At that event, the correction was finished and freedom from the Angel of Death was achieved: Freedom from chaos, freedom from any manifestation of Satan-consciousness in the world. This freedom was a result of the illumination of the entire world with the Light of the Creator, a Light of life and perfection. This illumination enabled each person to see beyond time and space, from one end of the world to the other, and to achieve complete control and certainty regarding all aspects of his life, including future events.

Since there is no lack in the spiritual realm, energy does not disappear. Therefore, what happened 3400 years ago on Mount Sinai must happen again every year in the entire universe on the sixth day of *Sivan*. On *Shavuot*, all of us can connect to immortality. By taking the advice of Rav Shimon and the Ari, we can connect with this huge life energy. But there is a very specific way to establish this connection: We must draw the Light while practicing restriction. And it is the Ten Utterances that teach us how to practice restriction in our life. Whoever is exposed to the enormous Light of *Shavuot* without a proper spiritual vessel will be burned, was the message the Creator conveyed to the people. When that awesome Light is revealed in the world, either we connect to it through the consciousness explained in the Torah and thereby gain eternal life and the end of the correction process, or the immense Light will burn us. This is not a punishment but rather a physical result of an incompatibility between the vessel and the Light, just as an appliance built to conduct 110 volts of electricity will burn when it is fed 220 volts.

During the Exodus from Egypt, the Israelite nation was only a potential. When the Israelites said, "We will do," they created a new situation. On the individual level, the spiritual vessels were made compatible by revealing and connecting to the Ten Utterances—by learning the way to practice restriction. During the giving of the Torah on Mount Sinai, the cosmic energy protected them from the abundance of Light revealed by the Creator in the world. The Israelites became the channels for this awesome Lightforce, but only to provide a "community service" to the universe.

According to the *Zohar*, the Israelites are supposed to channel the Light of the Creator and pass it to all humankind. This concept was established at the cosmic level, too: On the sixth day of *Sivan*, the whole universe is able to receive the energy of the sun without being burned to a crisp.

At the Revelation event, therefore, we didn't receive ten commands, but rather ten levels of Light, health, love, continuity, and security. But at the moment of the Revelation itself, we couldn't contain the Light and reveal it in our everyday lives. The Light was in potential. Imagine, if you will, that we received an electric battery at the Revelation. After 40 days, Moses descended holding a Light bulb in his hands—an object that can reveal the potential in the battery. Thus, the Torah and the stone tablets are the physical appliances by which the Light of the Creator is revealed in the world.

By studying the Torah and the *Zohar* throughout the night of *Shavuot*, we connect to the channel that draws for us, in a controlled way, the spiritual plenitude revealed on Mount Sinai, in exactly the same manner as did the first Torah Scroll that Moses received during those 40 days on Mount Sinai. We are nourished by a life force that removes chaos and the Angel of Death from our midst, at least until the end of the year. This is what Rav Shimon teaches us.

The Light revealed on Mount Sinai is the same Light that will be revealed in the time of the Messiah in the Age of Aquarius. We must learn to optimize this energy and take care of it, or it might be too powerful for humans to handle and eventually cause a huge disaster, God forbid, that could affect all of us.

When the Israelites built the golden calf, they assumed that Moses would be the intermediary between them and the Light. They were not searching for a replacement for God, as we are often told, but rather a replacement for the Torah—for a different spiritual appliance to contain and reveal the potential Light received on *Shavuot*. Unfortunately, the Israelites didn't wait for Moses and thus lost the opportunity to finish the entire correction of humankind. Every year at *Shavuot*, however, we get a chance to correct part of that historical mistake. Rav Shimon suggests that we "keep busy" with the Torah for the whole night. "Being busy" with the Torah means investing the same effort that we put into our career or our business, where we toil from morning until night. Beyond that, just as we look at a business as a practical and useful undertaking, so, too, should we look at the Torah.

The Torah is nothing but a physical tool that contains Light in a coded form. We need the Torah—just as we need our physical body—to reveal Light in the material world. During *Shavuot*, the Light is revealed with tremendous force. To prepare for this, it is necessary to count the *Omer*. The Ari says that the holiday of *Shavuot* occurs seven weeks after Passover, not because that is how it is written in the Torah, but because *Shavuot* is the result of activity occurring in the spiritual world. Nothing in the physical world can be the cause of anything else. We count the *Omer*, according to all the kabbalistic meditations, to build a vessel that will enable us to deal successfully with the Revelation of *Shavuot*. There is no need for anything else. The Creator wants to bless all of Creation.

Another kabbalistic connection is to make *Kiddush* following the Morning Prayer and to have a dairy meal afterward. This is something that is done only on *Shavuot*, when *Malchut* (our physical world) reaches and touches the *Keter* of *Zeir Anpin*. This is a tremendous jump into the future.

By touching the point of origin, we can reach the future and accomplish the removal of death forever. This energy matches the energy of milk, which is connected to the Right Column—the emanation of *Chesed* (mercy), birth, and the life force that erupts and is realized in the world. By eating dairy products, we make a physical action that connects us with the events of *Shavuot* in the Upper Worlds. Just as flipping the switch turns on the Light in the room, the dairy meal draws the energy of *Shavuot* into our life. It is hard to believe that eating a cheese-filled pastry and drinking chocolate milk can offer us a life portion until the end of the year, but this is the natural law of the universe: Every physical action, even a small one, awakens similar actions in the spiritual world. And these actions, when done with the right timing, can create far-reaching results.

Kabbalah is not something new. It is 3,400 years old and was given to us on Mount Sinai. Kabbalah connects us with very old truths; it brings to our consciousness things we already know in our subconscious minds. Only the robotic influences of modern life prevent us from applying these truths with appropriate seriousness in our daily lives. To stop being robots, we must fundamentally change and renew our consciousness. The "life insurance" that we acquire during *Shavuot* must be accompanied by our decision that we can change the face of the world and ourselves. From now on, we will see other human beings as an integral part of ourselves, and we will treat them that way. In our efforts to change and elevate our consciousness, we will move forward until *Rosh Hashanah*, knowing that until then, we have been given life without limits.

Let us pray that with the revelation of the secret—the Kabbalah—on Mount Sinai, we ourselves can now become the real revelation. We must realize that through the power of the Revelation we are one with the Creator. There is no greater truth. At *Shavuot*, we have the opportunity to understand it with our minds, connect with it in our hearts, and act on it with every aspect of our being.

ERUV TAVSHILIN (MEALS MIX)

If the Holiday is followed by a Shabbat, we should do Eruv Tavshilin before the Holiday begins, in order to be able to cook during the Holiday for Shabbat – otherwise we can't. On the eve of the Holiday we take 2 kinds of cooked food (the best is a baked item such as bread/matzah - 2 ounces at least) and a cooked item such as meat, fish, or eggs (2 ounces at least). The Eruv maker should meditate to include the community with this blessing.

We put the 2 cooked items together and say the following blessing:

בָּרוּךְ baruch אַתָּה Ata יְהֹוָהאדניאהדונהי Adonai אֱלֹהֵינוּ Elohenu ילה
מֶלֶךְ melech הָעוֹלָם ha'olam אֲשֶׁר asher קִדְּשָׁנוּ kideshanu
בְּמִצְוֹתָיו bemitzvotav וְצִוָּנוּ vetzivanu עַל al מִצְוַת mitzvat עֵרוּב eruv:

And then say:

בְּדֵין beden עֵירוּבָא eruva יְהֵא yehe שָׁרֵא share לָנָא lana
לַאֲפוּיֵי la'afuyei וּלְבַשּׁוּלֵי ulvishulei וּלְאַטְמוּנֵי ulatmunei
וּלְתַקּוּנֵי ultakunei (וּלְמִשְׁחַט ulmishchat) וּלְאַדְלוּקֵי uladlukei
שְׁרָגָא sheraga וּלְמֶעֱבַד ulme'evad כָּל kol ילי צָרְכָנָא tzarchana
מִיּוֹם miyom ע"ה נגד, מזבח, זן, אל יהוה טוֹב tov והו לְשַׁבָּת leShabbat לָנָא lana
וּלְכָל ulchol יה אדני בְּנֵי benei הָעִיר ha'ir בוזפך, סנדלפון, ערי הַזֹּאת hazot:

After saying it in Aramaic a person should say it in a language that he understands (below in Hebrew and in English):

בעירוב זה יהיה מותר לנו לאפות ולבשל ולהדליק הנר ולעשות כל צרכינו מיו"ט לשבת:

"With this cooked and baked items should permit us to continue baking, cooking, lighting a flame from an existing fire and do all the necessary preparations from Yom Tov proper to Shabbat"

The Eruv will be eaten on *Shabbat*'s third meal (we should make sure it stays during the Holiday and *Shabbat* - if it disappears it could be a problem).

ERUV TAVSHILIN (MEALS MIX)

Blessed are You, Lord, our God, King of the world,
Who has sanctified us with His commandments and obliged us with concering the Mitzvah of Eruv.
"With this cooked and baked items should permit us to continue baking, cooking, lighting a flame from an existing fire and do all the necessary preparations from Yom Tov proper to Shabbat"

CANDLE LIGHTING

We light the candles to draw the spiritual Light into our personal lives. Every physical action in our world initiates a corresponding reaction in the Upper Worlds. By lighting the physical candles of *Pesach* with the consciousness and intent to connect to the energy of *Pesach* in the Upper Worlds, we arouse and draw spiritual Light into our physical world.

When a woman lights the candles, she is also helping to correct the sin of Eve, which was a Desire to Receive for the Self Alone. The action of lighting the candles becomes an act of sharing. Because the husband and children are closest to the woman, they receive the benefit of this action.

LESHEM YICHUD

לְשֵׁם leshem יִחוּד yichud קֻודְשָׁא kudsha בְּרִיךְ berich הוּא hu

וּשְׁכִינְתֵּיהּ ushchintei (יאהדונהי) בִּדְחִילוּ bid'chilu וּרְחִימוּ ur'chimu

(יאהדויהה), וּרְחִימוּ ur'chimu וּדְחִילוּ ud'chilu (איההויהה),

לְיַחֲדָא leyachda שֵׁם shem יוּ"ד yud קֵ"י kei בְּוָא"ו bevav קֵ"י kei

בְּיִחוּדָא beyichuda שְׁלִים shelim (יהוה) בְּשֵׁם beshem כָּל kol ילי

יִשְׂרָאֵל, Yisrael, הֲרֵינִי hareni בָּאָה va'a לְקַיֵּם lekayem

מִצְוַת mitzvat עֲשֵׂה ase שֶׁל shel הַצְּדָקָה hatzedakah ע"ה ריבוע אלהים

וַהֲרֵינִי vahareni נוֹתֶנֶת notenet שְׁתֵּי shetei פְּרוּטוֹת perutot

לִצְדָקָה litzdakah ע"ה ריבוע אלהים וְעוֹד ve'od הֲרֵינִי hareni נוֹתֶנֶת notenet

פְּרוּטָה peruta אַחַת achat לִצְדָקָה litzdakah ע"ה ריבוע אלהים לְתַקֵּן letaken

אֶת et שֹׁרֶשׁ shoresh מִצְוָה mitzva זוֹ zo וְכָל vechol ילי תַּרְיַ"ג taryag

מִצְווֹת mitzvot הַכְּלוּלוֹת hakelulot בָּהּ ba בְּמָקוֹם bemakom עֶלְיוֹן elyon.

It is good for a woman to give three coins for charity before lighting the candles and then continue,

וַהֲרֵינִי vahareni בָּאָה va'a לְקַיֵּם lekayem מִצְוַת mitzvat עֲשֵׂה ase

דְּרַבָּנָן derabanan לְהַדְלִיק lehadlik נֵרוֹת nerot לִכְבוֹד lichvod

---

CANDLE LIGHTING - LESHEM YICHUD

For the sake of unification between The Holy Blessed One and His Shechinah, with fear and love and with love and fear, in order to unify the Name Yud-Kei and Vav-Kei in perfect unity, and in the name of all Israel, I am hereby prepared to fulfill the obligatory precept of Tzedakah, and hereby I'm giving two coins for Tzedakah and another one for Tzedakah to correct the root of the precept of Tzedakah with all the 613 other precepts which are included in it, in the supernal place,

(It is good for a woman to give three coins for charity before lighting the candles and then continue).

And I hereby prepare to fulfill the obligatory precept from the sages of Lighting candles for the honor of Yom Tov

יוֹם yom ע״ה נגד, מזבח, זן, אל יהוה טוֹב tov והו • לְתַקֵּן letaken שֹׁרֶשׁ shoresh
מִצְוָה mitzva זוֹ zo בְּמָקוֹם bemakom עֶלְיוֹן elyon• וִיהִי vihi נֹעַם no'am
אֲדֹנָי Adonai ללה אֱלֹהֵינוּ Elohenu ילה עָלֵינוּ alenu וּמַעֲשֵׂה uma'ase יָדֵינוּ yadenu
כּוֹנְנָה konena עָלֵינוּ alenu וּמַעֲשֵׂה uma'ase יָדֵינוּ yadenu כּוֹנְנֵהוּ konenehu:

Then the woman should light the candles, close her eyes after all the candles are lit and recite the following blessing:

בָּרוּךְ baruch אַתָּה ata יְהֹוָהאדניאהדונהי Adonai אֱלֹהֵינוּ Elohenu ילה
מֶלֶךְ melech הָעוֹלָם haolam אֲשֶׁר asher קִדְּשָׁנוּ kidshanu
בְּמִצְוֹתָיו bemitzotav וְצִוָּנוּ vetzivanu לְהַדְלִיק lehadlik
נֵר ner יהוה אהיה יהוה אלהים יהוה אדני שֶׁל shel (On Shabbat add: שַׁבָּת shabbat וְשֶׁל veshel)
יוֹם yom ע״ה, נגד, מזבח, זן, אל יהוה טוֹב tov והו:

בָּרוּךְ baruch אַתָּה ata יְהֹוָהאדניאהדונהי Adonai אֱלֹהֵינוּ Elohenu ילה
מֶלֶךְ melech הָעוֹלָם haolam שֶׁהֶחֱיָנוּ shehecheyanu
וְקִיְּמָנוּ vekiyemanu וְהִגִּיעָנוּ vehigi'anu לַזְּמַן lazman הַזֶּה hazeh והו:

YEHI RATZON

The power of righteous children and a righteous husband is given to us through this blessing. A woman's greatest opportunity for sharing is with her family, which is closest to her in her daily life.The definition of sharing with one's child or spouse takes on a whole new meaning when understood from a Kabbalistic point of view. To help us understand what sharing genuinely means, we must first comprehend what is *not* deemed sharing. Kabbalist Rav Borg explains that when parents raise their kids, most acts of sharing are considered part of one's duty as a loving parent. In other words, there are no "merit points" in the Upper Worlds when we share with our loved ones. Real sharing occurs only when it's **difficult** for us to give, when we go outside of ourselves and leave our comfort zones. We ordinarily play with or give to our children when doing so pleases us. We derive as much pleasure as they do. If we can learn to share, and give our time and attention to them when it is difficult for us, we will reap far greater benefits. Lighting the Shabbat candles is considered to be a genuine act of sharing toward our family.

---

to correct the root of the precept in the Supernal Place. "May the pleasantness of the Lord, our God, be upon us and may He establish the work of our hands for us and may the work of our hands establish Him." (Psalms 90:17)

Blessed are You, Lord, our God, King of the world,
Who has sanctified us with His commandments and obliged us with lighting the candles of Yom Tov.

Blessed are You, Lord, our God, King of the world,
who has kept us alive, sustained us, and brought us to this time.

יְהִי yehi רָצוֹן ratzon מהש ע"ה, ע"ב בריבוע, קס"א ע"ה, אל שדי ע"ה

מִלְּפָנֶיךָ milfanecha ס"ג מ"ה ב"ן יְהֹוָה יאהדונהי Adonai אֱלֹהַי Elohai

מילוי דע"ב, דמב ; ילה וֵאלֹהֵי velohei לכב ; מילוי דע"ב, דמ"ב ; ילה אֲבוֹתַי avotai

שֶׁתָּחוּס shetachus וּתְרַחֵם utrachem ג"פ רי"ו ; וז"פ אל, רי"ו ול"ב נתיבות החכמה,

רמ"ח (אברים), עסמ"ב וט"ז אותיות פשוטות עָלַי alai, וְתַגְדִּיל vetagdil חֲסָדֶיךָ chasdecha

עִמָּדִי imadi לָתֵת latet לִי li זֶרַע zera אֲנָשִׁים anashim עוֹשֵׂי osei

רְצוֹנֶךָ retzonecha• וְעוֹסְקִים ve'oskim בְּתוֹרָתֶךָ betoratcha לִשְׁמָהּ lishma•

וְיִהְיוּ veyih'yu אל (יא"י מילוי דס"ג) מְאִירִים me'irim בַּתּוֹרָה batorah

בִּזְכוּת bizchut נֵרוֹת nerot יוֹם yom ע"ה נגד, מזבח, זן, אל יהוה טוֹב tov והו

הַלָּלוּ halalu, כְּמוֹ kemo שֶׁנֶּאֱמַר shene'emar: כִּי ki נֵר ner מִצְוָה mitzvah

וְתוֹרָה vetorah אוֹר or רז, א"ס וְגַם vegam תָּחוּס tachos וּתְרַחֵם utrachem

ג"פ רי"ו ; וז"פ אל, רי"ו ל"ב נתיבות החכמה, רמ"ח (אברים), עסמ"ב ט"ז אותיות פשוטות

עַל al בַּעֲלִי ba'ali

(A woman should meditate here and mention her husband's name and his father's name)

וְתִתֶּן vetiten ב"פ כהת לוֹ lo אֹרֶךְ orech יָמִים yamim נלך

וּשְׁנוֹת ushnot חַיִּים chayim אהיה אהיה יהוה, בינה ע"ה

עִם im בְּרָכָה beracha וְהַצְלָחָה vehatzlacha, וּתְסַיְּעֵהוּ ut'saye'ehu

לַעֲשׂוֹת la'asot רְצוֹנְךָ retzoncha בִּשְׁלֵמוּת bishlemut• כֵּן ken יְהִי yehi

רָצוֹן ratzon מהש ע"ה, ע"ב בריבוע וקס"א ע"ה, אל שדי ע"ה אָמֵן amen יאהדונהי•

(מ"ב אותיות בפסוק)

יִהְיוּ yih'yu אל (יא"י מילוי דס"ג) לְרָצוֹן leratzon מהש ע"ה, ע"ב בריבוע וקס"א ע"ה, אל שדי ע"ה

אִמְרֵי imrei פִי fi ר"ת אֱלֶף = אלף למד שין דלת יוד ע"ה וְהֶגְיוֹן vehegyon לִבִּי libi

לְפָנֶיךָ lefanecha ס"ג מ"ה ב"ן יְהֹוָה יאהדונהי Adonai צוּרִי tzuri וְגֹאֲלִי vego'ali:

YEHI RATZON

May it be pleasing before You, Lord, my God, and God of my forefathers, that You will take pity and be merciful to me, and may You increase Your compassion to meby granting me, for offspring, ones who do Your bidding and who occupy themselves in Your Torah for Its own sake. May they be resplendent in the Torah by virtue of these candles, as it was said: "Because the commandment is a candle and the Torah is Light." (Proverbs 6:23) *May You also take pity and be merciful to my husband* (woman should say here and mention - her husband's name and his father's name) *and may You grant him lengthy days and years of life, filled with blessings and success, and may You help him in doing Your bidding perfectly. May it so be Your desire, Amen. "May the words of my mouth and the thoughts of my heart be pleasing before You, God, my Rock and my Redeemer."* (Psalms 19:15)

MINCHAH OF EREV SHAVUOT

The purpose of the *Minchah* prayer is not simply to make a connection to the Light of the Creator, it is to quiet the energy of judgment in the world. The best time to do this is when the energy of judgment appears in its greatest number and intensity. Kabbalist Rav Isaac Luria (the Ari), would only recite *Minchah* when the sun was setting. He understood that the numerical value of the word *Minchah* (103) is also the number of sub-worlds (within the five major worlds), controlled by the Left Column energy of judgment.

The sin of the golden calf occurred during the time of *Minchah*, consequently becoming the seed that helped infuse the world with judgment in the late afternoon. Isaac the patriarch is our channel to overcome judgment. Isaac came to this world to create a path that would lead us to sweetening the judgment in our lives. We can choose to either continue creating difficult paths for ourselves or we can follow the path of sweetening judgment paved by Isaac.

LESHEM YICHUD

לְשֵׁם leshem יִחוּד yichud קוּדְשָׁא kudsha בְּרִיךְ berich הוּא hu

וּשְׁכִינְתֵּיהּ ush'chintei (יאהדונהי) בִּדְחִילוּ bid'chilu וּרְחִימוּ ur'chimu

(יאההויהה) וּרְחִימוּ ur'chimu וּדְחִילוּ ud'chilu (איההיוהה) לְיַחֲדָא leyachda

שֵׁם shem יוּ"ד yud קֵ"י kei בְּוָא"ו bevav קֵ"י kei בְּיִחוּדָא beyichuda

שְׁלִים shelim (יהוה) בְּשֵׁם beshem כָּל kol ילי יִשְׂרָאֵל Yisrael,

הִנֵּה hine אֲנַחְנוּ anachnu בָּאִים ba'im לְהִתְפַּלֵּל lehitpalel תְּפִלַּת tefilat

מִנְחָה mincha ע"ה ב"פ ב"ן שֶׁתִּקֵּן shetiken יִצְחָק Yitzchak ד"פ ב"ן אָבִינוּ avinu

עָלָיו alav הַשָּׁלוֹם hashalom עִם im כָּל kol ילי הַמִּצְוֹת hamitzvot

הַכְּלוּלוֹת hakelulot בָּהּ ba לְתַקֵּן letaken אֶת et שׇׁרְשָׁהּ shorsha

בְּמָקוֹם bemakom עֶלְיוֹן elyon לַעֲשׂוֹת la'asot נַחַת nachat רוּחַ ru'ach

לְיוֹצְרֵנוּ leyotzrenu וְלַעֲשׂוֹת vela'asot רְצוֹן retzon מהש ע"ה, ע"ב בריבוע וקס"א ע"ה,

אל שדי ע"ה בּוֹרְאֵנוּ bor'enu. וִיהִי vihi נֹעַם no'am אֲדֹנָי Adonai ללה

אֱלֹהֵינוּ Elohenu ילה עָלֵינוּ alenu וּמַעֲשֵׂה uma'ase יָדֵינוּ yadenu

כּוֹנְנָה konena עָלֵינוּ alenu וּמַעֲשֵׂה uma'ase יָדֵינוּ yadenu כּוֹנְנֵהוּ konenehu:

MINCHAH OF EREV SHAVUOT
LESHEM YICHUD

For the sake of unification of The Holy Blessed One and His Shechinah, with fear and love and with love and fear, in order to unify The Name Yud-Kei and Vav-Kei in perfect unity, and in the name of Israel, we have hereby come to recite the prayer of Minchah, established by Isaac, our forefather, may peace be upon him, With all its commandments, to correct its root in the supernal place, to bring satisfaction to our Maker, and to fulfill the wish of our Creator. "And may the pleasantness of the Lord, our God, be upon us and may He establish the work of our hands for us and may the work of our hands establish Him." (Psalms 90:17)

THE SACRIFICES – KORBANOT - THE TAMID – (DAILY) OFFERING

Moshe מֹשֶׁה el אֶל־ Adonai יְהֹוָהאדניאהדונהי ראה vaydaber וַיְדַבֵּר

benei בְּנֵי et אֶת־ פוי, אל אדני tzav צַו :lemor לֵּאמֹר מהש, ע״ב בריבוע וקס״א, אל שדי

korbani קָרְבָּנִי et אֶת־ alehem אֲלֵהֶם ve'amarta וְאָמַרְתָּ Yisrael יִשְׂרָאֵל

tishmeru תִּשְׁמְרוּ nichochi נִיחֹחִי re'ach רֵיחַ le'ishai לְאִשַּׁי lachmi לַחְמִי

lahem לָהֶם ve'amarta וְאָמַרְתָּ :bemo'ado בְּמוֹעֲדוֹ li לִי lehakriv לְהַקְרִיב

ladonai לַיהֹוָהאדניאהדונהי takrivu תַּקְרִיבוּ asher אֲשֶׁר ha'ishe הָאִשֶּׁה ze זֶה

shenayim שְׁנַיִם temimim תְמִימִם shana שָׁנָה benei בְנֵי־ kevasim כְּבָשִׂים

:ע״ה קס״א קנ״א קמ״ג tamid תָּמִיד ר״ת עשל ola עֹלָה ע״ה נגד, מזבח, זן, אל יהוה layom לַיּוֹם

vaboker בַבֹּקֶר ta'ase תַּעֲשֶׂה אהבה, דאגה echad אֶחָד hakeves הַכֶּבֶשׂ et אֶת־

ben בֵּין ta'ase תַּעֲשֶׂה hasheni הַשֵּׁנִי hakeves הַכֶּבֶשׂ ve'et וְאֵת

solet סֹלֶת ha'efa הָאֵיפָה va'asirit וַעֲשִׂירִית :ha'arbayim הָעַרְבָּיִם

beshemen בְּשֶׁמֶן belula בְּלוּלָה ב״ן ב״פ ע״ה lemincha לְמִנְחָה

אבגיתץ ,ישר olat עֹלַת :hahin הַהִין revi'it רְבִיעִת katit כָּתִית

(Meditate here to surrender the *klipa* named *Tola* using the Name: אבגיתץ)

ha'asuya הָעֲשֻׂיָה קמ״ג קנ״א קס״א ע״ה tamid תָּמִיד

nicho'ach נִיחֹחַ lere'ach לְרֵיחַ (ה׳ גבורות) הויות ה׳ ,נמם Sinai סִינַי behar בְּהַר

revi'it רְבִיעִת venisko וְנִסְכּוֹ :ladonai לַיהֹוָהאדניאהדונהי ishe אִשֶּׁה

bakodesh בַּקֹּדֶשׁ אהבה, דאגה ha'echad הָאֶחָד lakeves לַכֶּבֶשׂ hahin הַהִין

:ladonai לַיהֹוָהאדניאהדונהי ב״ן י״פ shechar שֵׁכָר nesech נֶסֶךְ hasech הַסֵּךְ

THE SACRIFICES – KORBANOT - THE TAMID – (DAILY) OFFERING

"And God spoke to Moses and said, Command the Children of Israel and say to them, My offering, the bread of My fire-offering, My pleasing fragrance, you shall take care to sacrifice to Me at its specified time. And you shall say to them: This is the fire-offering that you shall sacrifice to God, perfect one-year-old sheep, two per day, as a regular daily offering; one sheep you shall do in the morning and the second sheep you shall do in the late afternoon. And one tenth of ephahof fine flour, for a meal-offering, mixed with one quarter of a hin of pressed oil. This is a regular burnt-offering that is made at Mount Sinai as a pleasing fragrance and as a fire-offering before God. Its libation is one quarter of a hin for the one sheep in the Sanctuary, pour a libation of old wine before God.

וְאֶת ve'et הַכֶּבֶשׂ hakeves הַשֵּׁנִי hasheni תַּעֲשֶׂה ta'ase בֵּין ben

הָעַרְבָּיִם ha'arbayim כְּמִנְחַת keminchat הַבֹּקֶר haboker וּכְנִסְכּוֹ uchnisko

תַּעֲשֶׂה ta'ase אִשֵּׁה ishe (elevation to *Yetzirah*) רֵיחַ re'ach (elevation to *Beriah*)

נִיחֹחַ nicho'ach (elevation to *Atzilut*) לַיהֹוָהאדניאהדונהי ladonai (elevation to the Endless World):

The Incense

These verses from the *Torah* and the *Talmud* speak about the 11 herbs and spices that were used in the Temple. These herbs and spices were used for one purpose: to help us remove the force of death from every area of our lives. This is one of the few prayers whose sole goal is the eradication of death. The *Zohar* teaches us that whoever has judgment pursuing him needs to connect to this incense. The 11 herbs and spices connect to 11 Lights that sustain the *klipot* (shells of negativity). When we uproot the 11 Lights from the *klipot* through the power of the incense, the *klipot* lose their life-force and die. In addition to bringing the 11 spices to the Temple, the people brought resin, wine, and other items with metaphysical properties to help battle the Angel of Death.

It says in the *Zohar*: "Come and see, whoever is pursued by judgment is in need of incense and must repent before his master, for incense helps judgment to disappear from him." The 11 herbs and spices correspond to the 11 holy illuminations that revive the *klipa*. By elevating them, the *klipa* will die. Through these 11 herbs, the *klipot* are pushed away and the energy-point that was giving them life is removed. And since the Pure Side and its livelihood disappear, the *klipot* is left with no life. Thus the secret of the incense is that it cleanses the force of plague and cancels it. The incense kills the Angel of Death and takes away his power to kill.

אַתָּה Ata הוּא hu יְהֹוָהאדניאהדונהי Adonai אֱלֹהֵינוּ Elohenu ילה

שֶׁהִקְטִירוּ shehiktiru אֲבוֹתֵינוּ avotenu לְפָנֶיךָ lefanecha ס"ג מ"ה ב"ן

אֶת et קְטֹרֶת ketoret י"א פעמים אדני (הנבררים מהקליפות ע"י י"א הסממנים) ;

קטרת - הק' באתב"ש ד' = תרי"ג (מצוות) הַסַּמִּים hasamim ע"ה קנ"א, אדני אלהים

בִּזְמַן bizman שֶׁבֵּית shebet ב"פ ראה הַמִּקְדָּשׁ hamikdash קַיָּם kayam

כַּאֲשֶׁר ka'asher צִוִּיתָ tzivita אוֹתָם otam עַל־ al יַד yad מֹשֶׁה Moshe מהש,

ע"ב בריבוע וקס"א, אל שדי נְבִיאָךְ nevia'ch כַּכָּתוּב kakatuv בְּתוֹרָתָךְ betoratach:

The second sheep you shall do in the afternoon like the meal-offering of the morning; its libation you shall do as a fire-offering of a fragrance which is pleasing to God." (Numbers 28:1-8)

The Incense

It is You, Lord, our God, before whom our forefathers burned the incense spices, during the time when the Temple existed, as You had commanded them through Moses, Your Prophet, and as it is written in Your Torah:

THE PORTION OF THE INCENSE

To raise the *Sefirot* from all of *Nogah* of *Atzilut*, *Beriah*, *Yetzirah* and *Asiyah*.

וַיֹּאמֶר vayomer יְהֹוָהאדניאהדונהי Adonai אֶל־ el מֹשֶׁה Moshe

מהש, ע"ב בריבוע וקס"א, אל שדי קַח־ kach לְךָ lecha סַמִּים samim (*Tiferet, Netzach*)

ע"ה קנ"א, אדני אלהים נָטָף nataf | (*Hod*) וּשְׁחֵלֶת ushchelet (*Yesod*) וְחֶלְבְּנָה vechelbena

(*Malchut*) ע"ה פוי, אל אדני סַמִּים samim (*Keter, Chochmah, Binah, Chesed, Gevurah*)

ע"ה קנ"א, אדני אלהים וּלְבֹנָה ulvona זַכָּה zaka (**Surrounding Light**) בַּד bad בְּבַד bevad

יִהְיֶה yih'ye ייי: וְעָשִׂיתָ ve'asita אֹתָהּ ota קְטֹרֶת ketoret י"א פעמים אדני (הנבררים

מהקליפות ע"י י"א הסממנים); קטרת - הק' באתב"ש ד' = תרי"ג (מצוות) רֹקַח rokach מַעֲשֵׂה ma'ase

רוֹקֵחַ roke'ach שדי מְמֻלָּח memulach טָהוֹר tahor י"פ אכא קֹדֶשׁ kodesh

ס"ת רוחש בכוונו לגרש החיצונים ויועיל לזכירה: וְשָׁחַקְתָּ veshachakta מִמֶּנָּה mimena

הָדֵק hadek וְנָתַתָּה venatata מִמֶּנָּה mimena לִפְנֵי lifnei הָעֵדֻת ha'edut

בְּאֹהֶל be'ohel מוֹעֵד mo'ed אֲשֶׁר asher אִוָּעֵד iva'ed לְךָ lecha שָׁמָּה shama

קֹדֶשׁ kodesh קָדָשִׁים kadashim תִּהְיֶה tihye לָכֶם lachem. וְנֶאֱמַר vene'emar:

וְהִקְטִיר vehiktir עָלָיו alav אַהֲרֹן Aharon קְטֹרֶת ketoret י"א פעמים אדני

(הנבררים מהקליפות ע"י י"א הסממנים) ; קטרת - הק' באתב"ש ד' = תרי"ג (מצוות) סַמִּים samim

ע"ה קנ"א, אדני אלהים בַּבֹּקֶר baboker בַּבֹּקֶר baboker בְּהֵיטִיבוֹ behetivo

אֶת־ et הַנֵּרֹת hanerot יַקְטִירֶנָּה yaktirena: וּבְהַעֲלֹת uveha'alot

אַהֲרֹן Aharon אֶת־ et הַנֵּרֹת hanerot בֵּין ben הָעַרְבַּיִם ha'arbayim

ר"ת אהבה, דאגה, אחד יַקְטִירֶנָּה yaktirena קְטֹרֶת ketoret י"א פעמים אדני

(הנבררים מהקליפות ע"י י"א הסממנים) ; קטרת - הק' באתב"ש ד' = תרי"ג (מצוות) תָּמִיד tamid

ע"ה קס"א קנ"א קמ"ג לִפְנֵי lifnei יְהֹוָהאדניאהדונהי Adonai לְדֹרֹתֵיכֶם ledorotechem:

THE PORTION OF THE INCENSE

"And God said to Moses: Take for yourself spices, balsam sap, onycha, galbanum, and pure frankincense, each of equal weight. You shall prepare it as an incense compound: the work of a spice-mixer, well-blended, pure, and holy. You shall grind some of it fine and place it before the Testimony in the Tabernacle of Meeting, in which I shall meet with you. It shall be the Holy of Holies unto you." (Exodus 30:34-36) *And God also said: "Aaron shall burn upon the Altar incense spices early each morning when he prepares the candles. And when Aaron raises the candles at sundown, he shall burn the incense spices as a continual incense-offering before God throughout all your generations."* (Exodus 30:7-8)

THE WORKINGS OF THE INCENSE

The filling of the incense has two purposes: First, to remove the *klipot* in order to stop them from going up along with the elevation of the Worlds, and second, to draw Light to *Asiyah*. So meditate to raise the sparks of Light from all of the *Nogah* of *Azilut*, *Beriah*, *Yetzirah* and *Asiyah*.

Count the incense using your right hand, one by one, and don't skip even one, as it is said: "If one omits one of all the ingredients, he is liable to receive the penalty of death." And therefore, you should be careful not to skip any of them, because reciting this paragraph is a substitute for the actual burning of the incense.

תָּנוּ tanu רַבָּנָן rabanan פִּטּוּם pitum הַקְּטֹרֶת haketoret י״א פעמים אדני
(הנבררים מהקליפות ע״י י״א הסממנים) קטרת - הק׳ באתב״ש ד׳ = תרי״ג (מצוות);
פטום הקטרת = יְהֹוָה יֱהֹוִה מצפצ יה אדני אל אלהים מצפצ (ז׳ מרגלאין דשבת)׃
כֵּיצַד keitzad. שְׁלֹשׁ shelosh מֵאוֹת me'ot המספר = ש׳, אלהים דיודין
וְשִׁשִּׁים veshishim המספר = מילוי הש׳ (יו) וּשְׁמוֹנָה ushmona מָנִים manim הָיוּ hayu
בָהּ va. שְׁלֹשׁ shelosh מֵאוֹת me'ot המספר = ש׳, אלהים דיודין וְשִׁשִּׁים veshishim
המספר = מילוי הש׳ (יו) וַחֲמִשָּׁה vachamisha כְּמִנְיַן keminyan יְמוֹת yemot
הַחַמָּה hachama מָנֶה mane ע״ה פוי, אל אדני בְּכָל bechol ב״ן, לכב
יוֹם yom ע״ה נגד, מזבח, זן, אל יהוה. מַחֲצִיתוֹ machatzito בַּבֹּקֶר baboker
וּמַחֲצִיתוֹ umachatzito בָּעֶרֶב ba'erev. וּשְׁלֹשָׁה ushlosha מָנִים manim
יְתֵרִים yeterim קס״א, קנ״א וקמ״ג שֶׁמֵּהֶם shemehem מַכְנִיס machnis כֹּהֵן kohen מלה
גָּדוֹל gadol להח ; עם ד׳ אותיות = מבה, יזל, אום וְנוֹטֵל venotel מֵהֶם mehem
מְלֹא melo חָפְנָיו chofnav בְּיוֹם beyom ע״ה נגד, מזבח, זן, אל יהוה הַכִּפּוּרִים hakipurim
מַחֲזִירָן machaziran לַמַּכְתֶּשֶׁת lamachteshet בְּעֶרֶב be'erev
יוֹם yom ע״ה נגד, מזבח, זן, אל יהוה הַכִּפּוּרִים hakipurim כְּדֵי kedei לְקַיֵּם lekayem
מִצְוַת mitzvat דַּקָּה daka מִן min הַדַּקָּה hadaka. וְאַחַד ve'achad אהבה, דאגה
עָשָׂר asar סַמָּנִים samanim הָיוּ hayu בָהּ va. וְאֵלּוּ ve'elu הֵן hen׃

THE WORKINGS OF THE INCENSE

Our Sages have taught: How was the compounding of the incense done? Three hundred and sixty-eight portions were contained therein. These corresponded to the number of days in the solar year, one portion for each day: Half of it in the morning and half at sundown. As for the remaining three portions, the High Priest (Kohen Gadol), on Yom Kippur, filled both his hands with them. On the Eve of Yom Kippur, he would take them back to the mortar to fulfill the requirement that they should be very finely ground. Each portion contained eleven spices:

1) הַצֳּרִי haTzori (*Keter*) מצפצ, אלהים דיודין, י״פ ייי• 2) וְהַצִּפֹּרֶן vehaTziporen (*Yesod*)
יהוה אדני אהיה שדי• 3) וְהַחֶלְבְּנָה vehaChelbena (*Malchut*) ע״ה פוי, אל אדני•
4) וְהַלְּבוֹנָה vehaLevona (**Suronding Light** – שהוא אור לבן והוא יוזידי הנקרא אדון יוזיד)
מִשְׁקַל mishkal שִׁבְעִים shiv'im שִׁבְעִים shiv'im מָנֶה mane ע״ה פוי, אל אדני•
5) מוֹר Mor (*Chesed*)• 6) וּקְצִיעָה uKtzi'ah רהע (*Gevurah* – ״כי מצפון תפתח הרעה״,
והגבורה סוד רוח צפון)• 7) וְשִׁבֹּלֶת veShibolet נֵרְדְּ Nerd (*Tiferet*)•
8) וְכַרְכֹּם veCharkom (*Netzach*) בוזהך, סנדלפון, ערי• מִשְׁקַל mishkal שִׁשָּׁה shisha
עָשָׂר asar שִׁשָּׁה shisha עָשָׂר asar מָנֶה mane ע״ה פוי, אל אדני• 9) קֹשְׁטְ Kosht
(*Chochmah*) שְׁנֵים sheneim עָשָׂר asar• 10) קִלּוּפָה Kilufa (*Binah*) שְׁלֹשָׁה shelosha•
11) קִנָּמוֹן Kinamon (*Hod*) ר״ת ג״פ ק׳ (בסוד קדוש קדוש קדוש) תִּשְׁעָה tish'ah•
בּוֹרִית borit כַּרְשִׁינָא karshina תִּשְׁעָה tish'ah קַבִּין kabin• יֵין yen מיכ, י״פ האא
קַפְרִיסִין Kafrisin סְאִין se'in תְּלַת telat וְקַבִּין vekabin תְּלָתָא telata אהיה קבין
וְאִם ve'im יוהך, מ״א אותיות דפשוט, דמילוי ודמילוי דמילוי דאהיה ע״ה לֹא lo מָצָא matza
יֵין yen מיכ, י״פ האא קַפְרִיסִין Kafrisin מֵבִיא mevi חֲמַר chamar חִוָּר chivar
עַתִּיק atik• מֶלַח melach סְדוֹמִית Sedomit רוֹבַע rova• מַעֲלֶה ma'ale
עָשָׁן ashan כָּל kol ילי שֶׁהוּא shehu• רִבִּי Ribi נָתָן Natan הַבַּבְלִי haBavli
אוֹמֵר omer: אַף af מִכִּפַּת mikipat הַיַּרְדֵּן haYarden י׳ הויות וד׳ אותיות כָּל kol ילי
שֶׁהִיא shehi• אִם im יוהך, מ״א אותיות דפשוט, דמילוי ודמילוי דמילוי דאהיה ע״ה נָתַן natan
בָּהּ ba דְּבַשׁ devash שו׳ (דשופר) וי״ד (האוזו) = ש״ך דינין דגדלות פְּסָלָהּ pesala•
וְאִם ve'im יוהך, מ״א אותיות דפשוט, דמילוי ודמילוי דמילוי דאהיה ע״ה חִסֵּר chiser
אַחַת achat מִכָּל־ mikol ילי סַמְמָנֶיהָ samemaneha חַיָּב chayav מִיתָה mita:

---

1) Balsam. 2) Onycha. 3) Galbanum. 4) Frankincense; the weight of seventy portions each. 5) Myrrh. 6) Cassia. 7) Spikenard. 8) And Saffron; the weight of sixteen portions each. 9) Twelve portions of Costus. 10) Three of aromatic Bark 11) Nine of Cinnamon. Further, nine kavs of Lye of Carsina. And three kavs and three se'ehs of Cyprus wine. And if one should not find any Cyprus wine, he should bring an old white wine. And a quarter of the salt of Sodom. And a small measure of a smoke raising herb. Rabbi Natan, the Babylonian, advised also, a small amount of Jordan resin. If he added to it honey, he would make it defective. If he omits even one of all its herbs, he would be liable to death.

רַבָּן Raban שִׁמְעוֹן Shimon בֶּן ben גַּמְלִיאֵל Gamli'el אוֹמֵר omer:
הַצֳּרִי haTzori מצפצ, אלהים דיודין, י"פ ייי אֵינוֹ eno אֶלָּא ela שְׂרָף seraf
הַנּוֹטֵף hanotef מֵעֲצֵי me'atzei הַקְּטָף haketaf. בּוֹרִית borit
כַּרְשִׁינָא karshina לְמָה lema הִיא hee בָּאָה va'a. כְּדֵי kedei
לְשַׁפּוֹת leshapot בָּהּ ba אֶת et הַצִּפֹּרֶן haTziporen יהוה אדני אהיה שדי
כְּדֵי kedei שֶׁתְּהֵא shetehe נָאָה na'a. יֵין yen ע' (כנגד ע' אומות העולם התלויים בסמאל),
מ"כ, י"פ האא קַפְרִיסִין Kafrisin לְמָה lema הוּא hu בָּא va. כְּדֵי kedei
לִשְׁרוֹת lishrot בּוֹ bo אֶת et הַצִּפֹּרֶן haTziporen יהוה אדני אהיה שדי
כְּדֵי kedei שֶׁתְּהֵא shetehe עַזָּה aza. וַהֲלֹא vahalo מֵי mei ילי רַגְלַיִם raglayim
יָפִין yafin לָהּ la אֶלָּא ela שֶׁאֵין she'en מַכְנִיסִין machnisin מֵי mei ילי
רַגְלַיִם raglayim בַּמִּקְדָּשׁ bamikdash מִפְּנֵי mipenei הַכָּבוֹד hakavod לאו:
תַּנְיָא tanya. רִבִּי Ribi נָתָן Natan אוֹמֵר omer: כְּשֶׁהוּא keshehu
שׁוֹחֵק shochek אוֹמֵר omer הָדֵק hadek הֵיטֵב hetev. הֵיטֵב hetev
הָדֵק hadek. מִפְּנֵי mipenei שֶׁהַקּוֹל shehakol יָפֶה yafe לַבְּשָׂמִים labesamim.
פִּטְּמָהּ pitema לַחֲצָאִין lachatza'in כְּשֵׁרָה keshera. לִשְׁלִישׁ leshalish
וּלְרָבִיעַ ulravi'a לֹא lo שָׁמַעְנוּ shamanu. אָמַר amar רִבִּי Ribi
יְהוּדָה Yehuda: זֶה ze הַכְּלָל hakelal. אִם im יוהך, מ"א אותיות דפשוט, דמילוי
ודמילוי דמילוי דאהיה ע"ה כְּמִדָּתָהּ kemidata כְּשֵׁרָה keshera לַחֲצָאִין lachatza'in.
וְאִם ve'im יוהך, מ"א אותיות דפשוט, דמילוי ודמילוי דמילוי דאהיה ע"ה וְחִסֵּר chiser
אַחַת achat מִכָּל־ mikol ילי סַמָּמָנֶיהָ samemaneha וְחַיָּב chayav מִיתָה mita:

Rabban Shimon ben Gamliel says: The balsam was a sap that only seeped from the balsam trees. For what purpose was the lye of Carsina added? In order to rub the Onycha with it to make it pleasant looking. For what purpose was the Cyprus wine added? In order to steep in it the Onycha. Urine is more appropriate for this, but urine is not brought into the Temple out of respect. It was taught that Rabbi Natan said: When he ground, he said: 'Grind it fine, grind it fine.' This is because voice is beneficial to the spices. If he compounds half the amount it is still valid, yet regarding a third or a quarter, we have no information. Rabbi Yehuda said: This is the general rule: If it is in its correct proportions, then half is valid. Yet if he omits one of all its spices, he is liable to death.

תָּנֵי tanei בַּר Var קַפָּרָא Kapara: אַחַת achat לְשִׁשִּׁים leshishim אוֹ o
לְשִׁבְעִים leshiv'im שָׁנָה shana הָיְתָה hayta בָּאָה va'a שֶׁל shel
שִׁירַיִם shirayim לַחֲצָאִין lachatza'in. וְעוֹד ve'od תָּנֵי tanei בַּר Var
קַפָּרָא Kapara: אִלּוּ ilu הָיָה haya יהה נוֹתֵן noten אבגיתץ, ושר בָּהּ ba
קָרְטוֹב kortov שֶׁל shel דְּבַשׁ devash שו' (דשופר) וי"ד (האוזו) = ש"ך דינין דגדלות
אֵין en אָדָם adam מ"ה יָכוֹל yachol לַעֲמוֹד la'amod מִפְּנֵי mipenei
רֵיחָהּ recha. וְלָמָּה velama אֵין en מְעָרְבִין me'arvin בָּהּ ba דְּבַשׁ devash
שו' (דשופר) וי"ד (האוזו) = ש"ך דינין דגדלות מִפְּנֵי mipenei שֶׁהַתּוֹרָה shehatorah
אָמְרָה amra: כִּי ki כָל־ chol ילי שְׂאֹר se'or ג' מוזין דאלהים דקטנות
(ש' = אלהים דיודין ; א' כללות שם אלהים ; ר' = ריבוע אלהים) וְכָל־ vechol ילי דְּבַשׁ devash
שו' (דשופר) וי"ד (האוזו) = ש"ך דינין דגדלות לֹא־ lo תַקְטִירוּ taktiru מִמֶּנּוּ mimenu
שכן הם בוזינת דינין דקטנות ודגדלות לכן נאסרה הקרבתן אִשֶּׁה ishe לַיהֹוָהאדניאהדונהי ladonai:

Right

יְהֹוָהאדניאהדונהי Adonai צְבָאוֹת Tzeva'ot פני שכינה עִמָּנוּ imanu
ריבוע דס"ג, קס"א ע"ה וד' אותיות מִשְׂגָּב־ misgav משה, מהש, ע"ב בריבוע וקס"א, אל שדי,
ד"פ אלהים ע"ה לָנוּ lanu אלהים, אהיה אדני אֱלֹהֵי Elohei מילוי ע"ב, דמב ; ילה
יַעֲקֹב Yaakov ו' הויות, יאהדונהי אידהנויה סֶלָה sela:

Left

יְהֹוָהאדניאהדונהי Adonai צְבָאוֹת Tzeva'ot פני שכינה אַשְׁרֵי ashrei
אָדָם adam מ"ה ; יהוה צבאות אשרי אדם = תפארת בֹּטֵחַ bote'ach
בָּךְ bach אדם בוטח בך = אמן (יאהדונהי) ע"ה ; בוטח בך = מילוי ע"ב ע"ה:

Bar Kappara taught that once every sixty or seventy years the leftovers would accumulate to half the measure. Bar Kappara also taught that if one would add to it a Kortov of honey, no man would withstand its smell. Why is honey not mixed with it? Because the Torah had stipulated: Because any leaven or honey, you must not burn any of it as burnt-offering to God. (Kritut 6; Yerushalmi, Yoma: ch.4)
(Right) *"The Lord of Hosts is with us, our strength is the God of Jacob, Selah."* (Psalms 46:12)
(Left) *"The Lord of Hosts, joyful is one who trusts in You."* (Psalms 84:13)

Central

יְהֹוָֽהאדניאהדונהי Adonai הוֹשִׁיעָה hoshi'a יהוה וש״ע נהורין הַמֶּלֶךְ hamelech ר״ת יהה

יַעֲנֵנוּ ya'anenu בְּיוֹם veyom ע״ה נגד, מזבח, זן, אל יהוה

קָרְאֵנוּ kor'enu ר״ת יב״ק, אלהים יהוה, אהיה אדני יהוה ; ס״ת = ב״ן ועם כף דהמלך = ע״ב:

וְעָרְבָה ve'arva לַיהֹוָֽהאדניאהדונהי ladonai

מִנְחַת minchat יְהוּדָה Yehuda וִירוּשָׁלָ‍ִם virushalaim

כִּימֵי kimei עוֹלָם olam וּכְשָׁנִים uch'shanim קַדְמֹנִיּוֹת kadmoniyot:

ANA BEKO'ACH (to learn more about the *Ana Beko'ach* go to page 238)

The *Ana Beko'ach* is perhaps the most powerful prayer in the entire universe. Second-century Kabbalist Rav Nachunya ben HaKana was the first sage to reveal this combination of 42 letters, which encompass the power of creation.

Chesed, Sunday *(Alef Bet Gimel Yud Tav Tzadik)* אבג יתץ

אָנָּא ana בְּכֹחַ beko'ach• גְּדוּלַּת gedulat יְמִינְךָ yeminecha•

תַּתִּיר tatir צְרוּרָה tzerura:

Gevurah, Monday *(Kuf Resh Ayin Shin Tet Nun)* קרע שטן

קַבֵּל kabel רִנַּת rinat• עַמְּךָ amecha שַׂגְּבֵנוּ sagvenu•

טַהֲרֵנוּ taharenu נוֹרָא nora:

(Central) *"Lord save us. The King shall answer us the day we call."* (Psalms 20:10) *"May the Lord find the offering of Yehuda and Jerusalem pleasing as He had always done and as in the years of old."* (Malachi 3:4)

ANA BEKO'ACH

Chesed, Sunday אבג יתץ

We beseech You, with the power of Your great right, undo this entanglement.

Gevurah, Monday קרע שטן

Accept the singing of Your Nation. Strengthen and purify us, Awesome One.

Tiferet, Tuesday *(Nun Gimel Dalet Yud Kaf Shin)* נג"ד יכ"ש

נָא na גִּבּוֹר gibor♦ דוֹרְשֵׁי dorshei יִחוּדְךָ yichudecha♦

כְּבָבַת kevavat שָׁמְרֵם shomrem:

Netzach, Wednesday *(Bet Tet Resh Tzadik Tav Gimel)* בט"ר צת"ג

בָּרְכֵם barchem טַהֲרֵם taharem♦ רַחֲמֵי rachamei צִדְקָתְךָ tzidkatecha♦

תָּמִיד tamid גָּמְלֵם gomlem:

Hod, Thursday *(Chet Kuf Bet Tet Nun Ayin)* חק"ב טנ"ע

חֲסִין chasin קָדוֹשׁ kadosh♦ בְּרוֹב berov טוּבְךָ tuvcha♦

נַהֵל nahel עֲדָתֶךָ adatecha:

Yesod, Friday *(Yud Gimel Lamed Pei Zayin Kuf)* יג"ל פז"ק

יָחִיד yachid גֵּאֶה ge'e♦ לְעַמְּךָ le'amecha פְּנֵה pene♦

זוֹכְרֵי zochrei קְדֻשָּׁתֶךָ kedushatecha:

Malchut, Saturday *(Shin Kuf Vav Tzadik Yud Tav)* שק"ו צי"ת

שַׁוְעָתֵנוּ shav'atenu קַבֵּל kabel♦ וּשְׁמַע ushma צַעֲקָתֵנוּ tza'akatenu♦

יוֹדֵעַ yode'a תַּעֲלוּמוֹת ta'alumot:

BARUCH SHEM KEVOD

Whispering this final verse brings all the Light from the Upper Worlds into our physical existence.

(Whisper): יוהו אותיות בָּרוּךְ baruch שֵׁם shem כְּבוֹד kevod מַלְכוּתוֹ malchuto

לְעוֹלָם le'olam ריבוע ס"ג וי' אותיות דס"ג וָעֶד va'ed:

Tiferet, Tuesday נג"ד יכ"ש

Please, Mighty One, those who seek Your unity, guard them like the pupil of the eye.

Netzach, Wednesday בט"ר צת"ג

Bless them. Purify them. Your compassionate righteousness always grant them.

Hod, Thursday חק"ב טנ"ע

Invincible and Mighty One, with the abundance of Your goodness, govern Your congregation.

Yesod, Friday יג"ל פז"ק

Sole and proud One, turn to Your people, those who remember Your sanctity.

Malchut, Saturday שק"ו צי"ת

Accept our cry and hear our wail, You that knows all that is hidden.

BARUCH SHEM KEVOD

"Blessed is the Name of Glory. His Kingdom is forever and for eternity." (Pesachim 56a)

THE ASHREI

Twenty-one of the twenty-two letters of the Aramaic alphabet are encoded in the *Ashrei* in their correct order from *Alef* to *Tav*. King David, the author, left out the Aramaic letter *Nun* from this prayer, because *Nun* is the first letter in the Aramaic word *nefilah*, which means "falling." Falling refers to a spiritual decline, as in falling into the *klipa*. Feelings of doubt, depression, worry, and uncertainty are consequences of spiritual falling. Because the Aramaic letters are the actual instruments of Creation, this prayer helps to inject order and the power of Creation into our lives, without the energy of falling.

In this Psalm there are ten times the Name: יהוה for the Ten *Sefirot*. This Psalm is written according to the order of the *Alef Bet*, but the letter *Nun* is omitted to prevent falling.

אַשְׁרֵי ashrei (סוד הכתר) יוֹשְׁבֵי yoshvei בֵיתֶךָ vetecha ב"פ ראה

עוֹד od יְהַלְלוּךָ yehalelucha סֶּלָה sela: אַשְׁרֵי ashrei הָעָם ha'am

שֶׁכָּכָה shekacha מהש, משה, ע"ב בריבוע וקס"א, אל שדי, ד"פ אלהים ע"ה לוֹ lo

אַשְׁרֵי ashrei הָעָם ha'am ר"ת לאה שֶׁיְּהֹוָאדהֹנָי אהדונהי she'Adonai (*Keter*)

אֱלֹהָיו Elohav ילה: תְּהִלָּה tehila ע"ה אמת, אהיה פעמים אהיה, ז"פ ס"ג לְדָוִד leDavid

אֲרוֹמִמְךָ aromimcha אֱלוֹהַי Elohai הַמֶּלֶךְ hamelech וַאֲבָרְכָה va'avarcha

שִׁמְךָ shimcha לְעוֹלָם le'olam ריבוע ס"ג ו' אותיות ד"ס"ג וָעֶד va'ed:

בְּכָל־ bechol ב"ן, לכב יוֹם yom ע"ה נגד, מזבח, זן אל יהוה

אֲבָרְכֶךָּ avarcheka וַאֲהַלְלָה va'ahalela מ"ה יהוה שִׁמְךָ shimcha

לְעוֹלָם le'olam ריבוע ד"ס"ג ו' אותיות ד"ס"ג וָעֶד va'ed:

גָּדוֹל gadol להח ; יגם ד' אותיות = מבה, יזל, אום

יְהֹוָאדהֹנָי אהדונהי Adonai (*Chochmah*) וּמְהֻלָּל umhulal אדני, ללה

מְאֹד me'od וְלִגְדֻלָּתוֹ veligdulato והו אֵין en חֵקֶר cheker:

THE ASHREI

"Joyful are those who dwell in Your House, they shall praise You, Selah." (*Psalms 84:5*) *"Joyful is the nation that this is theirs and joyful the nation that the Lord is their God."* (*Psalms 145:15*) *"A praise of David:*

א *I shall exalt You, my God, the King, and I shall bless Your Name forever and for eternity.*

ב *I shall bless You every day and I shall praise Your Name forever and for eternity.*

ג *The Lord is great and exceedingly praised. His greatness is unfathomable.*

דּוֹר dor לְדוֹר ledor יְשַׁבַּח yeshabach מַעֲשֶׂיךָ ma'asecha ר"ת דלים

וּגְבוּרֹתֶיךָ ugvurotecha יַגִּידוּ yagidu ייז, כ"ב אותיות פשוטות (=אכא) וה' אותיות סופיות םןץףך:

הֲדַר hadar כְּבוֹד kevod הוֹדֶךָ hodecha וְדִבְרֵי vedivrei

נִפְלְאוֹתֶיךָ nifle'otecha ר"ת אלהים, אהיה אדני

אָשִׂיחָה asicha ר"ת הפסוק = פ"ז (בסוד כתם טהור פז):

וֶעֱזוּז ve'ezuz נוֹרְאוֹתֶיךָ no'rotecha יֹאמֵרוּ yomeru וּגְדוּלָּתְךָ ugdulatcha

(כתיב: וגדלותיך) ר"ת = ע"ב, ריבוע יהוה אֲסַפְּרֶנָּה asaperena ס"ת = ייא"י (מילוי דס"ג):

זֵכֶר zecher רַב־ rav טוּבְךָ tuvcha לאו יַבִּיעוּ yabi'u

וְצִדְקָתְךָ vetzidkatcha יְרַנֵּנוּ yeranenu ס"ת = ב"ן, יבמ, לכב ; ר"ת הפסוק = רי"ו יהוה:

חַנּוּן chanun וְרַחוּם verachum יְהֹוָהאדניאהדונהי Adonai (**Binah**)

חנון ורחום יהוה = עש"ל אֶרֶךְ erech ס"ת = ס"ג ב"ן אַפַּיִם apayim ר"ת = יהוה

וּגְדָל־ ugdal (כתיב: וגדול) חָסֶד chased ע"ב, ריבוע יהוה:

טוֹב־ tov והו יְהֹוָהאדניאהדונהי Adonai (***Chesed***) לַכֹּל lakol

יה אדני ; ס"ת ל"ו (מילוי דס"ג) וְרַחֲמָיו verachamav עַל־ al

כָּל kol ילי ; עמם ; ר"ת ריבוע ב"ן ע"ה מַעֲשָׂיו ma'asav ס"ת ע"ב, ריבוע יהוה:

ד *One generation and the next shall praise Your deeds and tell of Your might.*
ה *The brilliance of Your splendid glory and the wonders of Your acts, I shall speak of.*
ו *They shall speak of the might of Your awesome acts and I shall tell of Your greatness.*
ז *They shall express the remembrance of Your abundant goodness, and Your righteousness they shall joyfully proclaim.* ח *The Lord is merciful and compassionate, slow to anger and great in kindness.*
ט *The Lord is good to all, His compassion extends over all His acts.*

יוֹדוּךָ yoducha יְהֹוָאדֹנָיאהדונהי Adonai (*Gevurah*) כָּל־ kol ילי מַעֲשֶׂיךָ ma'asecha

וַחֲסִידֶיךָ vachasidecha ר"ת אלהים, אהיה אדני יְבָרְכוּכָה yevarchucha ס"ת = מ"ה:

כְּבוֹד kevod מַלְכוּתְךָ malchutcha יֹאמֵרוּ yomeru וּגְבוּרָתְךָ ugvuratcha

יְדַבֵּרוּ yedaberu ר"ת הפסוק = אלהים, אהיה אדני ; ס"ת = ב"ן, יבמ, לכב:

לְהוֹדִיעַ lehodi'a לִבְנֵי livnei הָאָדָם ha'adam ר"ת ללה, אדני

גְּבוּרֹתָיו gevurotav וּכְבוֹד uchvod הֲדַר hadar

מַלְכוּתוֹ malchuto ר"ת מ"ה וס"ת = רי"ו ; ר"ת הפסוק ע"ה = ק"כ צירופי אלהים:

מַלְכוּתְךָ malchutcha מַלְכוּת malchut כָּל־ kol ילי עֹלָמִים olamim

וּמֶמְשַׁלְתְּךָ umemshaltecha בְּכָל־ bechol ב"ן, לכב דּוֹר dor וָדֹר vador רי"ו:

סוֹמֵךְ somech ריבוע אדני יְהֹוָאדֹנָיאהדונהי Adonai (*Tiferet*)

לְכָל־ lechol יה אדני ; סומך אדני לכל ר"ת סאל, אמן (יאהדונהי) הַנֹּפְלִים hanoflim

וְזוֹקֵף vezokef לְכָל־ lechol יה אדני הַכְּפוּפִים hakefufim נמם:

עֵינֵי־ enei ריבוע דמ"ה כֹל chol ילי אֵלֶיךָ elecha יְשַׂבֵּרוּ yesaberu וְאַתָּה veAta

נוֹתֵן־ noten אבגיתץ, ושר לָהֶם lahem אֶת־ et אָכְלָם ochlam בְּעִתּוֹ be'ito:

י *All that You have made shall thank You, Lord, and Your pious ones shall bless You.*

כ *They shall speak of the glory of Your Kingdom and talk of Your mighty deeds.*

ל *His mighty deeds He makes known to man and the glory of His splendid Kingdom.*

מ *Yours is the Kingdom of all worlds and Your reign extends to each and every generation.*

ס *The Lord supports all those who fell and holds upright all those who are bent over.*

ע *The eyes of all look hopefully towards You, and You give them their food at its proper time.*

POTE'ACH ET YADECHA

We connect to the letters *Pei, Alef,* and *Yud* by opening our hands and holding our palms skyward. Our consciousness is focused on receiving sustenance and financial prosperity from the Light through our actions of tithing and sharing, our *Desire to Receive for the Sake of Sharing*. In doing so, we also acknowledge that the sustenance we receive comes from a higher source and is not of our own doing. According to the sages, if we do not meditate on this idea at this juncture, we must repeat the prayer.

פתוז (שע"ז נהורין למ"ה ולס"ה)

יוד הי ויו הי יוד הי ויו הי (וז' וזיוורתי)
אלף למד אלף למד (ש"ע)
יוד הא ואו הא (לז"א)
אדני (ולנוקבא)

פותוז את ידך ר"ת פאי
גימ' יאהדונהי וז"ן
וזכמה דז"א ו"ק
יסוד דנוק'

פּוֹתֵחַ pote'ach **אֶת** et **יָדֶךָ** yadecha ר"ת פאי וס"ת וזתך עם ג' אותיות = דִּיקָרְנוֹסָא

ובאתב"ש הוא סאל, פאי, אמן, יאהדונהי ; ועוד יכוין שם וזתך בשילוב יהוה – יְוָזְהָתְוָכָהָ

אלף למד הי יוד מם אלף למד הי יוד מם מוחין דפנים דאוזור **אלהים אלהים**
להמשיך פ"ו אורות לכל מילוי דכל

אוזור דפרצופי נה"י וזג"ת
דפרצוף וזג"ת דיצירה דז"א
לף מד י וד ם
אלף למד הי יוד מם

וזתך
סאל יאהדונהי

ואוזור דפרצופי נה"י וזג"ת
דיצירה דרוזל הנקראת לאה
לף מד י וד ם
אלף למד הי יוד מם

וּמַשְׂבִּיעַ umasbi'a וזתך עם ג' אותיות = דִּיקָרְנוֹסָא

ובא"ת ב"ש הוא סאל, אמן, יאהדונהי ; ועוד יכוין שם וזתך בשילוב יהוה – יְוָזְהָתְוָכָהָ

אלף למד הי יוד מם אלף למד הי יוד מם מוחין דפנים דאוזור **אלהים אלהים**
להמשיך פ"ו אורות לכל מילוי דכל

אוזור דפרצופי נה"י וזג"ת
דפרצוף נה"י דיצירה דז"א
לף מד י וד ם
אלף למד הי יוד מם

וזתך

ואוזור דפרצופי נה"י וזג"ת
דיצירה דרוזל הנקראת לאה
לף מד י וד ם
אלף למד הי יוד מם

לְכָל־ lechol יה אדני (להמשיך מוחין ד-יה אל הנוקבא שהיא אדני)

חַי chai כל וזי = אהיה אהיה יהוה, בינה ע"ה, וזיים

רָצוֹן ratzon מהש ע"ה, ע"ב בריבוע וקס"א ע"ה, אל שדי ע"ה ; ר"ת רוזל שהיא המלכות הצריכה לשפע

יוד יוד הי יוד הי ויו יוד הי ויו הי יסוד דאבא
אלף הי יוד הי יסוד דאימא
להמתיק **רוזל** וב' דמעין **שך פר**

We should also meditate to draw abundance and sustenance and blessing to all the worlds from the *ratzon* mentioned above. We should meditate and focus on this verse because it is the essence of prosperity, and meditate that God is intervening and sustaining and supporting all of Creation.

POTE'ACH ET YADECHA

פ *Open Your Hands and satisfy every living thing with desire.*

צַדִּיק tzadik יְהֹוָה Adonai יאהדונהי (*Yesod*) בְּכָל bechol ב"ן, לכב
דְּרָכָיו derachav וְחָסִיד vechasid בְּכָל bechol ב"ן, לכב מַעֲשָׂיו ma'asav יבמ, ב"ן:

קָרוֹב karov יְהֹוָה Adonai יאהדונהי (*Malchut*) לְכָל־ lechol יה אדני
קֹרְאָיו kor'av לְכֹל lechol יה אדני אֲשֶׁר asher
יִקְרָאֻהוּ yikra'uhu בֶאֱמֶת ve'emet אהיה פעמים אהיה, ז"פ ס"ג:

רְצוֹן retzon מהש ע"ה, ע"ב בריבוע וקס"א ע"ה, אל שדי ע"ה יְרֵאָיו yere'av יַעֲשֶׂה ya'ase
ר"ת ריי וְאֶת־ ve'et שַׁוְעָתָם shav'atam יִשְׁמַע yishma וְיוֹשִׁיעֵם veyoshi'em:

שׁוֹמֵר shomer כ"א הויות שבתפילין יְהֹוָה Adonai יאהדונהי (*Netzach*)
אֶת־ et כָּל־ kol ילי אֹהֲבָיו ohavav ר"ת אכא
וְאֵת ve'et כָּל־ kol ילי הָרְשָׁעִים haresha'im יַשְׁמִיד yashmid:

תְּהִלַּת tehilat יְהֹוָה Adonai יאהדונהי (*Hod*) יְדַבֶּר yedaber ראה פִּי pi
וִיבָרֵךְ vivarech ע"ב ס"ג מ"ה ב"ן, הברכה (למתק את ז' המלכים שמתו) כָּל kol ילי
בָּשָׂר basar שֵׁם shem קָדְשׁוֹ kodsho לְעוֹלָם le'olam ריבוע ס"ג וי' אותיות דס"ג
וָעֶד va'ed: וַאֲנַחְנוּ va'anachnu נְבָרֵךְ nevarech יָהּ Yah מֵעַתָּה me'ata
וְעַד־ ve'ad עוֹלָם olam הַלְלוּיָהּ haleluya אלהים, אהיה אדני ; ללה:

צ *The Lord is righteous in all His ways and virtuous in all His deeds.*
ק *The Lord is close to all who call Him, and only to those who call Him truthfully.*
ר *He shall fulfill the will of those who fear Him; He hears their wailing and saves them.*
ש *The Lord protects all who love Him and He destroys the wicked.*
ת *My lips utter the praise of the Lord and all flesh shall bless His Holy Name, forever and for eternity."*
(Psalms 145) "And we shall bless the Lord forever and for eternity. Praise the Lord!" (Psalms 115:18)

ר״ת הפסוק = נפש רוח נשמה חיה יחידה ע״ה

תִּכּוֹן tikon תְּפִלָּתִי tefilati קְטֹרֶת ketoret י״א פעמים אדני לְפָנֶיךָ lefanecha ס״ג מ״ה ב״ן

מַשְׂאַת mas'at כַּפַּי kapai מִנְחַת־ minchat עָרֶב arev: הַקְשִׁיבָה hakshiva

לְקוֹל lekol שַׁוְעִי shave'i מַלְכִּי malki וֵאלֹהָי velohai לכב ; מילוי ע״ב, דמ״ב ; ילה

כִּי־ ki אֵלֶיךָ elecha אֶתְפַּלָּל etpalal:

HALF KADDISH

יִתְגַּדַּל yitgadal וְיִתְקַדַּשׁ veyitkadash שדי ומילוי שדי ; י״א אותיות כמנין ו״ה

שְׁמֵיהּ shemei (שם י״ה דע״ב) רַבָּא raba קנ״א ב״ן, יהוה אלהים יהוה אדני,

מילוי קס״א וס״ג, מ״ה ברבוע וע״ב ע״ה ; ר״ת = ו״פ אלהים ; ס״ת = ג״פ יב״ק: אָמֵן amen אידהנויה.

בְּעָלְמָא be'alma דִּי di בְרָא vera כִּרְעוּתֵיהּ kir'utei.

וְיַמְלִיךְ veyamlich מַלְכוּתֵיהּ malchutei. וְיַצְמַח veyatzmach

פּוּרְקָנֵיהּ purkanei. וִיקָרֵב vikarev מְשִׁיחֵיהּ meshichei: אָמֵן amen אידהנויה.

בְּחַיֵּיכוֹן bechayechon וּבְיוֹמֵיכוֹן uvyomechon וּבְחַיֵּי uvchayei

דְכָל dechol ילי בֵּית bet ב״פ ראה יִשְׂרָאֵל Yisrael בַּעֲגָלָא ba'agala

וּבִזְמַן uvizman קָרִיב kariv וְאִמְרוּ ve'imru אָמֵן amen: אָמֵן amen אידהנויה.

The congregation and the *chazan* say the following:

28 words (until *be'alma*) – meditate: מילוי דמילוי דע״ב (יוד ויו דלת הי יוד ויו יוד ויו הי יוד)
28 letters (until *almaya*) – meditate: מילוי דמילוי דע״ב (יוד ויו דלת הי יוד ויו יוד ויו הי יוד)

יְהֵא yehe שְׁמֵיהּ shemei (שם י״ה דס״ג) רַבָּא raba קנ״א ב״ן,

יהוה אלהים יהוה אדני, מילוי קס״א וס״ג, מ״ה ברבוע וע״ב ע״ה מְבָרַךְ mevarach,

לְעָלַם le'alam לְעָלְמֵי le'almei עָלְמַיָּא almaya. יִתְבָּרַךְ yitbarach.

"Let my prayer be set before You
as the incense offering, the lifting up of my hand as the afternoon meal offering." (Psalms 141:2)
"Listen to the sound of my outcry, my King, My God for it is to You I am praying." (Psalms 5:3)

HALF KADDISH

May His great Name be more exalted and sanctified. (Amen)
In the world that He created according to His will, and may His kingdom reign. And may He cause His redemption to sprout and may He bring the Mashiach closer. (Amen) *In your lifetimes and in your days and in the lifetime of all the House of Israel, speedily and in the near future, and you should say, Amen.* (Amen) *May His great Name be blessed forever and for all eternity blessed*

Seven words with six letters each (שׁם בן מ״ב) meditate:

יהוה - יוד הי ויו הי - מילוי דמילוי דע״ב (יוד ויו דלת הי יוד ויו יוד ויו הי יוד)

Also, seven times the letter Vav (שׁם בן מ״ב) meditate:

יהוה - יוד הי ויו הי - מילוי דמילוי דע״ב (יוד ויו דלת הי יוד ויו יוד ויו הי יוד).

וְיִשְׁתַּבַּח veyishtabach י״פ ע״ב יהוה אל אבג יתץ.

וְיִתְפָּאַר veyitpa'ar הי נו יה קרע שטן. וְיִתְרוֹמַם veyitromam וה כוזו נגד יכש.

וְיִתְנַשֵּׂא veyitnase במוכסז בטר צתג. וְיִתְהַדָּר veyit'hadar כוזו יה וזקב טנע.

וְיִתְעַלֶּה veyit'ale וה יוד ה יגל פזק. וְיִתְהַלָּל veyit'halal א ואו הא שקו צית.

שְׁמֵיהּ shemei (שם י״ה דמ״ה) דְּקוּדְשָׁא dekudsha בְּרִיךְ berich הוּא hu:

אָמֵן amen אידהנויה.

לְעֵלָּא le'ela מִן min כָּל kol ילי בִּרְכָתָא birchata. שִׁירָתָא shirata.

תֻּשְׁבְּחָתָא tishbechata וְנֶחָמָתָא venechamata. דַּאֲמִירָן da'amiran

בְּעָלְמָא be'alma וְאִמְרוּ ve'imru אָמֵן amen: אָמֵן amen אידהנויה.

THE AMIDAH

When we begin the connection, we take three steps backward, signifying our leaving this physical world. Then we take three steps forward to begin the *Amidah*. The three steps are:

1. Stepping into the land of Israel – to enter the first spiritual circle.
2. Stepping into the city of Jerusalem – to enter the second spiritual circle.
3. Stepping inside the Holy of Holies – to enter the innermost circle.

Before we recite the first verse of the *Amidah*, we ask: "*God, open my lips and let my mouth speak,*" thereby asking the Light to speak for us so that we can receive what we need and not just what we want. All too often, what we want from life is not necessarily the desire of the soul, which is what we actually need to fulfill us. By asking the Light to speak through us, we ensure that our connection will bring us genuine fulfillment and opportunities for spiritual growth and change.

---

and lauded, and glorified and exalted, And extolled and honored,
and uplifted and praised, be the Name of the Holy Blessed One. (Amen) Above all blessings, songs, praises, and words of consolation that may be said in the world, and you shall say, Amen. (Amen)

> **When the eve of Shavuot (second day) falls on a Friday:**
> You should meditate to elevate *Nefesh* of *Asiyah* by the Name: (ב"ן) יוד הה ו הה,
> and then to the *Ruach* of the world of *Yetzirah* by the Name: (מ"ה) יוד הא ואו הא,
> and then to the *Neshamah* of *Beriah* by the Name: (ס"ג) יוד הי ואו הי,
> and then to elevate all the above mentioned to *Nefesh* of *Atzilut*: (ע"ב) יוד הי ויו הי.

yagid יַגִּיד ufi וּפִי tiftach תִּפְתָּח sefatai שְׂפָתַי (pause here) ללה Adonai אֲדֹנָי

בוכו = ס"ת tehilatecha תְּהִלָּתֶךָ (יוד (כ"ב אותיות פשוטות [=אכא] וה' אותיות סופיות במנצפך)

THE FIRST BLESSING - INVOKES THE SHIELD OF ABRAHAM.

Abraham is the channel of the Right Column energy of positivity, sharing, and mercy. Sharing actions can protect us from all forms of negativity.

Chesed that becomes *Chochmah*

In this section there are 42 words, the secret of the 42-Letter Name of God and therefore it begins with the letter *Bet* (2) and ends with the letter *Mem* (40).

Bend your knees at *'baruch'*, bow at *'Ata'* and straighten up at *'Adonai'*.

א baruch בָּרוּךְ ב Ata אַתָּה א–ת (אותיות הא"ב המסמלות את השפע המגיע) לה' המלכות

> **When the eve of Shavuot (second day) falls on a Friday:**
> **While bending** you should meditate on the Name: אלף הי יוד הי, in order to lower the *Neshamah* of the world of *Atzilut*, to be as *Mayin Nukvin* in order to elevate the *Shechinah*. And **while straightening up** you should meditate on the Name: יוד הי ויו הי, to elevate the *Shechinah* and to prepare the World of *Atzilut* to be able to receive the world of *Beriah*.

ג Adonai יְהֹוָהאדניאהדונהי (יא") י Elohenu אֱלֹהֵינוּ ילה

ת velohei וֵאלֹהֵי לכב ; מילוי ע"ב, דמב ; ילה צ avotenu אֲבוֹתֵינוּ

ק Elohei אֱלֹהֵי מילוי ע"ב, דמב ; ילה ר Avraham אַבְרָהָם (*Chochmah*)

וז"פ אל, רי"ו ול"ב נתיבות החכמה, רמ"ח (אברים), עסמ"ב וט"ז אותיות פשוטות

THE AMIDAH

"My Lord, open my lips, and my mouth shall relate Your praise." *(Psalms 51:17)*

THE FIRST BLESSING

Blessed are You, Lord,
our God and God of our forefathers: the God of Abraham,

ע ש

אֱלֹהֵי Elohei מילוי ע״ב, דמב ; ילה יִצְחָק Yitzchak (*Binah*) ד״פ ב״ן

ט נ

וֵאלֹהֵי velohei לכב ; מילוי ע״ב, דמב ; ילה יַעֲקֹב Yaakov (*Da'at*) ז׳ הויות, יאהדונהי אידהנויה

נ ג

הָאֵל haEl לאה ; ייא״י (מילוי דס״ג) הַגָּדוֹל hagadol האל הגדול = סיט ; גדול = להח

ד י

עם ד׳ אותיות = מבה, יזל, אום הַגִּבּוֹר hagibor ר״ת ההה וְהַנּוֹרָא vehanora.

כ ש

אֵל El ייא״י (מילוי דס״ג) ; ר״ת ע״ב, ריבוע יהוה עֶלְיוֹן elyon.

ב ט ר צ ת

גּוֹמֵל gomel חֲסָדִים chasadim טוֹבִים tovim. קוֹנֵה kone הַכֹּל hakol ילי

ג ח ק ב

וְזוֹכֵר vezocher חַסְדֵי chasdei אָבוֹת avot. וּמֵבִיא umevi

ט נ ע י

גּוֹאֵל go'el לִבְנֵי livnei בְנֵיהֶם venehem לְמַעַן lema'an

ג ל

שְׁמוֹ shemo מהש ע״ה, ע״ב בריבוע וקס״א ע״ה, אל שדי ע״ה בְּאַהֲבָה be'ahava אחד, דאגה:

When saying the word "*be'ahava*" you should meditate to devote your soul to sanctify the Holy Name and accept upon yourself the four forms of death.

---

the God of Isaac,
and the God of Jacob.
The great, mighty and awesome God.
The Supernal God, Who bestows beneficial kindness and creates everything. Who recalls the kindness of the forefathers and brings a Redeemer to their descendants for the sake of His Name, lovingly.

פ ז ק ש

מֶלֶךְ melech עוֹזֵר ozer וּמוֹשִׁיעַ umoshi'a וּמָגֵן umagen

ג״פ אל (יי״א מילוי דס״ג) ; ר״ת מיכאל גבריאל נוריאל:

Bend your knees at *'baruch'*, bow at *'Ata'* and straighten up at *'Adonai'*.

ק ו

בָּרוּךְ baruch אַתָּה Ata

When the eve of Shavuot (second day) falls on a Friday:
While bending your knees you should meditate: אלף הי יוד הי, in order to lower the *Neshamah* of *Beriah*, to be as *Mayin Nukvin* in order to elevate the *Shechinah*. And **while straightening up** you should meditate: יוד הי ואו הי, to elevate the *Shechinah* and to prepare the World of *Beriah* to be elevated to *Atzilut* and to be able to receive *Yetzirah*.

צ

יְהֹוָהאדניה(יְהֹוָהאֲדֹנָי)יאהדונהי Adonai (הד׳)

י ת

מָגֵן magen ג״פ אל (יי״א מילוי דס״ג) ; ר״ת מיכאל גבריאל נוריאל אַבְרָהָם Avraham

וז״פ אל, רי״ו ול״ב נתיבות החכמה, רמ״ח (אברים), עסמ״ב וט״ז אותיות פשוטות:

THE SECOND BLESSING

THE ENERGY OF ISAAC IGNITES THE POWER FOR THE RESURRECTION OF THE DEAD.

Whereas Abraham represents the power of sharing, Isaac represents the Left Column energy of judgment. Judgment shortens the *Tikkun* process and paves the way for our eventual resurrection.

Gevurah that becomes *Binah*.

In this section there are 49 words corresponding to the 49 gates of the Pure System in *Binah*.

אַתָּה Ata גִּבּוֹר gibor לְעוֹלָם le'olam ריבוע ס״ג וי׳ אותיות דס״ג אֲדֹנָי Adonai ללה

(ר״ת אַגְלָא והוא שם גדול ואמיץ, ובו היה יהודה מתגבר על אויביו. ע״ה אלד, בוכו).

מְחַיֵּה mechaye ס״ג מֵתִים metim אַתָּה Ata. רַב rav לְהוֹשִׁיעַ lehoshi'a.

King, Helper, Savior and Shield.
Blessed are You, Lord, the shield of Abraham.

THE SECOND BLESSING

You are mighty forever, Lord. You resurrect the dead and are very capable of redeeming.

מוֹרִיד morid הַטָּל hatal יוד הא ואו, כוזו, מספר אותיות דמילואי עסמ"ב ; ר"ת מ"ה:

If you mistakenly say "*Mashiv haru'ach*", and realize this before the end of the blessing ("*baruch Ata Adonai*"), you should return to the beginning of the blessing ("*Ata gibor*") and continue as usual. But if you only realize this after the end of the blessing, you should start the *Amidah* from the beginning.

מְכַלְכֵּל mechalkel חַיִּים chayim אהיה אהיה יהוה, בינה ע"ה בְּחֶסֶד bechesed

ע"ב, ריבוע יהוה. מְחַיֵּה mechaye ס"ג מֵתִים metim בְּרַחֲמִים berachamim

(במוכסז) מצפצ, אלהים דההין, י"פ ייי רַבִּים rabim (טלא דעתיק). סוֹמֵךְ somech

(אכדטם) כוק, ריבוע אדני נוֹפְלִים noflim (זו"ן). וְרוֹפֵא verofe חוֹלִים cholim

חולה = מ"ה וד' אותיות. וּמַתִּיר umatir אֲסוּרִים asurim. וּמְקַיֵּם umekayem

אֱמוּנָתוֹ emunato לִישֵׁנֵי lishenei עָפָר afar. מִי mi ילי כָּמוֹךְ chamocha

בַּעַל ba'al (you should enunciate the letter *Ayin* in the word *"ba'al"*) גְּבוּרוֹת gevurot

וּמִי umi ילי דּוֹמֶה dome לָּךְ lach. מֶלֶךְ melech מֵמִית memit

וּמְחַיֶּה umchaye ס"ג (יוד הי ואו הי) וּמַצְמִיחַ umatzmi'ach יְשׁוּעָה yeshu'a:

וְנֶאֱמָן vene'eman אַתָּה Ata לְהַחֲיוֹת lehachayot מֵתִים metim:

בָּרוּךְ baruch אַתָּה Ata יְהֹוָאֲדֹנָיאהדונהי Adonai

מְחַיֵּה mechaye ס"ג (יוד הי ואו הי) הַמֵּתִים hametim ר"ת מ"ה וס"ת מ"ה:

NAKDISHACH – THE KEDUSHA

The congregation recites this prayer together.

Lifting a heavy chest filled with vast treasures is impossible if you use just a single string: The string will snap because it is too weak. However, if we unite and combine numerous strings, we will eventually build a rope. A rope can easily lift the treasure chest. By combining and uniting the congregation's prayers, we become a united force, capable of pulling down the most valuable spiritual treasures. Furthermore, this unity helps people who are not well-versed or knowledgeable in the connections. By uniting and meditating as one soul, we all receive the benefit because of the power of unity, regardless of our knowledge and understanding. This prayer occurs in between the second and third blessings. It signifies the Central Column that unites the Left and Right Columns.

Who causes dew to fall.

You sustain life with kindness and resurrect the dead with great compassion. You support those who have fallen, heal the sick, release the imprisoned, and fulfill Your faithful words to those who are asleep in the dust. Who is like You, Master of might, and Who can compare to You, King, Who causes death, Who gives life, and Who sprouts salvation? And You are faithful to resurrecting the dead. Blessed are You, Lord, Who resurrects the dead.

In this prayer the angels speak to each other, saying: "*Kadosh, Kadosh, Kadosh*" ("Holy, Holy, Holy"). When we recite these three words, we stand with our feet stand together as one. With each utterance of *Kadosh*, we jump a little higher in the air. Jumping is an act of restriction and it defies the force of gravity. Spiritually, gravity has the energy of the Desire to Receive for the Self Alone. It is the reactive force of our planet, always pulling everything toward itself.

Saying the *Kedusha* (holiness) we meditate to bring the holiness of the Creator among us. As it says: "*Venikdashti betoch Benei Israel*" (God is hallowed among the children of Israel). You should meditate on the letters *Alef* א and *Bet* ב from the Name: אבגיתץ (the initials of the first verse of the *Ana Beko'ach*), which helps spiritual remembering.

נַקְדִּישָׁךְ nakdishach וְנַעֲרִיצָךְ vena'aritzach.

כְּנֹעַם keno'am שִׂיחַ si'ach סוֹד sod מי"כ, י"פ האא שַׂרְפֵי sarfei

קֹדֶשׁ kodesh הַמְשַׁלְּשִׁים hameshaleshim לְךָ lecha קְדֻשָּׁה kedusha.

וְכֵן vechen כָּתוּב katuv עַל al יַד yad נְבִיאָךְ nevi'ach. וְקָרָא vekara

זֶה ze אֶל־ el זֶה ze י"ב פרקין דיעקב מאירים ל"ב פרקין דרוז"ל וְאָמַר ve'amar:

קָדוֹשׁ kadosh | קָדוֹשׁ kadosh קָדוֹשׁ kadosh (סוד ג' רישין דעתיקא קדישא)

יְהֹוָהאדניאהדונהי Adonai צְבָאוֹת Tzeva'ot פני שכינה מְלֹא melo כָל־ chol ילי

הָאָרֶץ ha'aretz אלהים דההין ע"ה כְּבוֹדוֹ kevodo:

לְעֻמָּתָם le'umatam מְשַׁבְּחִים meshabechim וְאוֹמְרִים ve'omrim:

(או"א) בָּרוּךְ baruch כְּבוֹד־ kevod יְהֹוָהאדניאהדונהי Adonai ; כבוד ה' = יוד הי ואו הה

מִמְּקוֹמוֹ mimekomo עסמ"ב, הברכה (למתק את ז' המלכים שמתו) ; ר"ת ע"ב, ריבוע יהוה ; ר"ת מיכ:

וּבְדִבְרֵי uvdivrei קָדְשָׁךְ kodshach כָּתוּב katuv לֵאמֹר lemor:

(ז"ן) יִמְלֹךְ yimloch קדוש ברוך ימלך ר"ת יב"ק, אלהים יהוה, אהיה אדני יהוה

יְהֹוָהאדניאהדונהי Adonai לְעוֹלָם le'olam ריבוע ס"ג וי' אותיות דס"ג אֱלֹהַיִךְ Elohayich ילה

צִיּוֹן Tziyon יוסף, ו' הויות, קנאה לְדֹר ledor וָדֹר vador רי"ו ; ר"ת אצלו (מלכות אצל ז"א – ו)

הַלְלוּיָהּ haleluya אלהים, אהיה אדני ; ללה:

NAKDISHACH

We sanctify You and we revere You, according to the pleasant words of the counsel of the Holy Angels, who recite Holy before You three times, as it is written by Your Prophet: "And each called to the other and said: Holy, Holy, Holy, Is the Lord of Hosts, the entire world is filled with His glory." (Isaiah 6:3) Facing them they give praise and say: "Blessed is the glory of the Lord from His Place." (Ezekiel 3:12) And in Your Holy Words, it is written as follows: "The Lord, your God, shall reign forever, for each and for every generation. Zion, Praise the Lord!" (Psalms 146:10)

THE THIRD BLESSING

This blessing connects us to Jacob, the Central Column and the power of restriction. Jacob is our channel for connecting mercy with judgment. By restricting our reactive behavior, we are blocking our Desire to Receive for the Self Alone. Jacob also gives us the power to balance our acts of mercy and judgment toward other people in our lives.

Tiferet* that becomes *Da'at (14 words).

אַתָּה Ata קָדוֹשׁ kadosh וְשִׁמְךָ veshimcha קָדוֹשׁ kadosh ר"ת = אור, רז, אין סוף.

וּקְדוֹשִׁים ukdoshim בְּכָל bechol ב"ן, לכב יוֹם yom ע"ה נגד, מזבח, זן, אל יהוה

יְהַלְלוּךָ yehalelucha סֶּלָה sela:

בָּרוּךְ baruch אַתָּה Ata יְהֹוָאדהי(יְהֹוָאדהי)יאהדונהי Adonai

הָאֵל haEl לאה ; ייא"י (מילוי דס"ג) הַקָּדוֹשׁ hakadosh י"פ מ"ה (יוד הא ואו הא):

Meditate here on the Name: יאהדונהי, as it can help to remove anger.

THIRTEEN MIDDLE BLESSINGS

There are thirteen blessings in the middle of the *Amidah* that connect us to the Thirteen Attributes.

THE FIRST (FOURTH) BLESSING

This blessing helps us transform information into knowledge by helping us internalize everything that we learn.

Chochmah

In this blessing there are 17 words, the same numerical value as the word *tov* (good) in the secret of *Etz HaDa'at Tov vaRa*, (Tree of Knowledge Good and Evil), where we connect only to the *Tov*.

אַתָּה Ata חוֹנֵן chonen לְאָדָם le'adam מ"ה דַּעַת da'at.

וּמְלַמֵּד umlamed לֶאֱנוֹשׁ le'enosh בִּינָה bina ע"ה אהיה אהיה יהוה, חיים.

וְחָנֵּנוּ vechonenu מֵאִתְּךָ me'itecha חָכְמָה chochma במילוי = תרי"ג (מצוות)

בִּינָה bina ע"ה אהיה אהיה יהוה, חיים וָדָעַת vada'at ר"ת חבו:

בָּרוּךְ baruch אַתָּה Ata יְהֹוָאדהיאהדונהי Adonai חוֹנֵן chonen הַדָּעַת hada'at:

THE THIRD BLESSING

You are holy, and Your Name is holy, and the Holy Ones praise You every day, for you are God, the Holy King Selah. Blessed are You, Lord, the Holy God

THIRTEEN MIDDLE BLESSINGS - THE FIRST (FOURTH) BLESSING

You graciously grant knowledge to man and understanding to humanity. Graciously grant us, from Yourself, wisdom, understanding, and knowledge. Blessed are You, Lord, Who graciously grants knowledge.

THE SECOND (FIFTH) BLESSING

This blessing keeps us in the Light. Everyone at one time or another succumbs to the doubt and uncertainty that the Satan constantly implants in us. If we make the unfortunate mistake of stepping back and falling away from the Light, we do not want the Creator to mirror our actions and step away from us. Instead, we want Him to catch us. In the box below there are certain lines that we can recite and meditate on for others who may be stepping back. The war against the Satan is the oldest war known to man. And the only way to defeat the Satan is to unite, share, help and pray for each other.

Binah

In this blessing there are 15 words, as the powerful action of *Teshuva* (repentance) raises 15 levels on the way to *Kise Hakavod* (the Throne of Honor). It goes through seven *Reki'im* (firmaments), seven *Avirim* (air), and another firmament on top of the Holy Animals (together this adds up to 15). Also, there are 15 words in the two main verses of Isaiah the Prophet and King David that speak of *Teshuva* (*Isaiah 55:7*; *Psalms 32:5*). The number 15 is also the secret of the Name: יה.

הֲשִׁיבֵנוּ hashivenu אָבִינוּ avinu לְתוֹרָתֶךָ letoratecha (ווסד שבה - יְהֹוָאֲדֹנָיאהדונהי)✦

וְקָרְבֵנוּ vekarvenu מַלְכֵּנוּ malkenu לַעֲבוֹדָתֶךָ la'avodatecha✦

וְהַחֲזִירֵנוּ vehachazirenu בִּתְשׁוּבָה bitshuva שְׁלֵמָה shelema

לְפָנֶיךָ lefanecha ס״ג מ״ה ב״ן:

> If you want to pray for another and help them in their spiritual process say:
>
> יְהִי yehi רָצוֹן ratzon מהש ע״ה, ע״ב בריבוע וקס״א ע״ה, אל שדי ע״ה
> מִלְּפָנֶיךָ milfanecha ס״ג מ״ה ב״ן יְהֹוָאֲדֹנָיאהדונהי Adonai אֱלֹהַי Elohai מילוי ע״ב, דמב; ילה
> וֵאלֹהֵי velohei לכב ; מילוי ע״ב, דמב ; ילה אֲבוֹתַי avotai שֶׁתַּחְתּוֹר shetachtor
> וַחֲתִירָה chatira מִתַּחַת mitachat כִּסֵּא kise כְּבוֹדֶךָ kevodecha וּתְקַבֵּל utkabel
> בִּתְשׁוּבָה bitshuva אֶת et (*the person's name and his/her father's name*) כִּי ki יְמִינְךָ yemincha
> יְהֹוָאֲדֹנָיאהדונהי Adonai פְּשׁוּטָה peshuta לְקַבֵּל lekabel שָׁבִים shavim✦

בָּרוּךְ baruch אַתָּה Ata יְהֹוָאֲדֹנָיאהדונהי Adonai

הָרוֹצֶה harotze בִּתְשׁוּבָה bitshuva:

THE SECOND (FIFTH) BLESSING

Bring us back, our Father, to Your Torah,

and bring us close, our King, to Your service, and cause us to return with perfect repentance before You.

> *May it be pleasing before You, Lord, my God and God of my forefathers, that You shall dig deep beneath the Throne of Your glory and accept as repentant* (the person's name and his/her father's name) *because Your Right Hand, Lord, extends outwards to receive those who repent.*

Blessed are You, Lord, Who desires repentance.

THE THIRD (SIXTH) BLESSING

This blessing helps us achieve true forgiveness. We have the power to cleanse ourselves of our negative behavior and hurtful actions toward others through forgiveness. This blessing does not mean we plead for forgiveness and our slate is wiped clean. Forgiveness refers to the methodologies for washing away the residue that comes from our iniquities. There are two ways to wash away the residue: physical and spiritual. We collect physical residue when we are in denial of our misdeeds and the laws of cause and effect. We cleanse ourselves when we experience any kind of pain, whether it is financial, emotional, or physical. If we choose to cleanse spiritually, we forgo the physical cleansing. We do so by arousing the pain in ourselves that we caused to others. We feel the other person; and with a truthful heart, recite this prayer experiencing the hurt and heartache we inflicted on others. This form of spiritual cleansing prevents us from having to cleanse physically.

Chesed

In this blessing there are 21 words which is the numerical value of the Holy Name: אהיה.

סְלַח selach יהוה ע״ב לָנוּ lanu אלהים, אהיה אדני אָבִינוּ avinu ר״ת סאל, אמן (יאהדונהי)

כִּי ki וְחָטָאנוּ chatanu. מְחוֹל mechol לָנוּ lanu אלהים, אהיה אדני ; מחול לנו ע״ה =

קס״א וי׳ אותיות מַלְכֵּנוּ malkenu כִּי ki פָּשָׁעְנוּ fashanu. כִּי ki אֵל El ייא״י (מילוי דס״ג)

טוֹב tov והו וְסַלָּח vesalach יהוה ע״ב אָתָּה Ata: בָּרוּךְ baruch אַתָּה Ata

יְהֹוָהאדניאהדונהי Adonai וְחַנּוּן chanun הַמַּרְבֶּה hamarbe לִסְלוֹחַ lislo'ach:

THE FOURTH (SEVENTH) BLESSING

This blessing helps us achieve redemption after we are spiritually cleansed.

Gevurah

רְאֵה re'e ראה נָא na בְעָנְיֵנוּ ve'onyenu ר״ת רנ״ב (אברים באשה, כנגד הגבורה)

וְרִיבָה veriva רִיבֵנוּ rivenu. וּמַהֵר umaher לְגָאֳלֵנוּ lega'olenu

גְּאֻלָּה gc'ula מ״ה שְׁלֵמָה shelema לְמַעַן lema'an שְׁמֶךָ shemecha

כִּי ki אֵל El ייא״י (מילוי דס״ג) גּוֹאֵל go'el וְחָזָק chazak פהל אָתָּה Ata:

בָּרוּךְ baruch אַתָּה Ata יְהֹוָהאדניאהדונהי Adonai גּוֹאֵל go'el יִשְׂרָאֵל Yisrael:

THE FIFTH (EIGHTH) BLESSING

This blessing gives us the power to heal every part of our body. All healing originates from the Light of the Creator. Accepting and understanding this truth opens us to receive this Light. We should also think of sharing this healing energy with others.

THE THIRD (SIXTH) BBLESSING

Forgive us, our Father, for we have transgressed. Pardon us, our King, for we have sinned, because You are a good and forgiving God. Blessed are You, Lord, Who is gracious and forgives magnanimously.

THE FOURTH (SEVENTH) BLESSING

Behold our poverty and take up our fight; hurry to redeem us with a complete redemption for the sake of Your Name, because You are a powerful and a redeeming God. Blessed are You, Lord, Who redeems Israel.

Tiferet

רְפָאֵנוּ refa'enu יְהֹוָהאדניאהדונהי Adonai וְנֵרָפֵא venerafe ר"ת רי"ו.
הוֹשִׁיעֵנוּ hoshi'enu וְנִוָּשֵׁעָה venivashe'a כִּי ki תְהִלָּתֵנוּ tehilatenu
אַתָּה Ata ר"ת = ב"פ רי"ו. וְהַעֲלֵה veha'ale אֲרוּכָה arucha וּמַרְפֵּא umarpe
לְכָל־ lechol יה אדני תַּחֲלוּאֵינוּ tachalu'enu. וּלְכָל־ ulchol יה אדני
מַכְאוֹבֵינוּ mach'ovenu וּלְכָל־ ulchol יה אדני מַכּוֹתֵינוּ makotenu.

To pray for healing for yourself and/or others add the following, in the parentheses below, insert the names:

יְהִי yehi רָצוֹן ratzon מהש ע"ה, ע"ב בריבוע וקס"א ע"ה, אל שדי ע"ה
מִלְּפָנֶיךָ milfanecha ס"ג מ"ה ב"ן יְהֹוָהאדניאהדונהי Adonai אֱלֹהַי Elohai מילוי ע"ב, דמב ; ילה
וֵאלֹהֵי velohei לכב ; מילוי ע"ב, דמב ; ילה אֲבוֹתַי avotai שֶׁתִּרְפָּאֵנִי shetirpa'eni
(וְתִרְפָּא vetirpa (insert the person's name) בֶּן ben (Women: בַּת bat (insert their mother's name))
רְפוּאָה refu'a שְׁלֵמָה shelema רְפוּאַת refu'at הַנֶּפֶשׁ hanefesh
וּרְפוּאַת urfu'at הַגּוּף haguf, כְּדֵי kedei שֶׁאֶהְיֶה she'ehye וְחָזָק chazak פהל
(Women: וַחֲזָקָה chazaka פהל) בִּבְרִיאוּת bivri'ut, וְאַמִּיץ ve'amitz
(Women: וְאַמִּיצַת ve'amitzat) כֹּחַ ko'ach, בְּמָאתַיִם bematayim וְאַרְבָּעִים ve'arba'im
וּשְׁמוֹנָה ushmona רמ"ח (אברים), אברהם, וח"פ אל, רי"ו ול"ב נתיבות החכמה, עסמ"ב וט"ז אותיות
פשוטות (Women: בְּמָאתַיִם bematayim וַחֲמִשִּׁים vechamishim וּשְׁנַיִם ushnayim)
אֵבָרִים evarim וּשְׁלֹשׁ ushlosh מֵאוֹת me'ot המספר = ש = אלהים דיודין
וְשִׁשִּׁים veshishim המספר = מילוי השי' (ין) וַחֲמִשָּׁה vachamisha גִּידִים gidim שֶׁל shel
נִשְׁמָתִי nishmati וְגוּפִי vegufi, לְקִיּוּם lekiyum תּוֹרָתְךָ toratcha הַקְּדוֹשָׁה hakedosha.

כִּי ki אֵל El ייא"י (מילוי דס"ג) רוֹפֵא rofe רַחֲמָן rachaman וְנֶאֱמָן vene'eman
אַתָּה Ata: בָּרוּךְ baruch אַתָּה Ata יְהֹוָהאדניאהדונהי Adonai רוֹפֵא rofe
חוֹלֵי cholei חולה = מ"ה (יוד הא ואו הא) וד' אותיות עַמּוֹ amo יִשְׂרָאֵל Yisrael
ר"ת רפ"ו (להעלות הניצוצות שנפלו לקליפה דמשם באים התחלואים):

THE FIFTH (EIGHTH) BLESSING

Heal us, Lord, and we shall heal. Save us and we shall be saved.
For You are our praise. Bring cure and healing to all our ailments, to all our pains, and to all our wounds.

May it be pleasing before You, Lord, my God and God of my forefathers, that You would heal me (and the person's name and their mother's name*) completely with healing of the spirit and healing of the body, so that I shall be strong in health and vigorous in my strength in all 248 (*a woman says: *252) organs and 365 sinews of my soul and my body, so that I shall be able to keep Your Holy Torah.*

Because You are a healing,
compassionate, and trustworthy God, blessed are You, Lord, Who heals the sick of His People, Israel.

The Sixth (ninth) Blessing

This blessing draws sustenance and prosperity for the entire globe and provides us with personal sustenance. We would like all of our years to be filled with dew and rain, the sustaining lifeblood of our world.

Netzach

If you mistakenly say "*barech alenu*" instead of "*barchenu*", and realize this before the end of the *Amidah* ("*yihyu leratzon*" – the second one), then you should return and say "*barchenu*" and continue as usual. If you realize this later, you should start the *Amidah* from the beginning.

בָּרְכֵנוּ barchenu יְהֹוָהאדניאהדונהי Adonai אֱלֹהֵינוּ Elohenu ילה בְּכָל bechol
ב״ן, לכב מַעֲשֵׂי ma'asei יָדֵינוּ •yadenu וּבָרֵךְ uvarech שְׁנָתֵנוּ shenatenu
בְּטַלְלֵי betalelei רָצוֹן ratzon מהש ע״ה, ע״ב בריבוע וקס״א ע״ה, אל שדי ע״ה
בְּרָכָה beracha וּנְדָבָה undava בינה (וע״ה אהיה אהיה יהוה, וחיים)• וּתְהִי utehi
אַחֲרִיתָהּ acharita וְחַיִּים chayim אהיה אהיה יהוה, בינה ע״ה וְשָׂבָע vesava
וְשָׁלוֹם veshalom כַּשָּׁנִים kashanim הַטּוֹבוֹת hatovot לִבְרָכָה livracha•

To pray for sustenance for yourself and/or others add the following, in the parentheses below, insert the names:

יְהִי yehi רָצוֹן ratzon מהש ע״ה, ע״ב בריבוע וקס״א ע״ה, אל שדי ע״ה מִלְּפָנֶיךָ milfanecha
ס״ג מ״ה ב״ן יְהֹוָהאדניאהדונהי Adonai אֱלֹהֵינוּ Elohenu ילה וֵאלֹהֵי velohei
לכב ; מילוי ע״ב, דמב ; ילה אֲבוֹתֵינוּ avotenu שֶׁתִּתֵּן shetiten ב״פ כהת לִי li
(וְכֵן vechen לְ (insert the person's name) בֶּן ben (Women: בַּת bat) (insert their father's name))
וּלְכָל ulchol יה אדני הַסְּמוּכִים hasemuchim עַל al שׁוּלְחָנִי shulchani הַיּוֹם hayom
ע״ה נגד, מזבח, זן, אל יהוה וּבְכָל uvchol ב״ן, לכב יוֹם yom ע״ה נגד, מזבח, זן, אל יהוה
מְזוֹנוֹתַי mezonotai וּמְזוֹנוֹתֵיהֶם umzonotehem בְּכָבוֹד bcchavod בוכו וְלֹא velo
בְּבִזּוּי bevizui בְּהֶיתֵּר beheter וְלֹא velo בְּאִיסּוּר be'isur בִּזְכוּת bizchut
שִׁמְךָ shimcha הַגָּדוֹל hagadol להח ; עם ד׳ אותיות = מבה, יזל, אום
(Do not pronounce this name: דִּיקַרְנוֹסָא וזהך עם ג׳ אותיות - ובאתב״ש סאל, אמן, יאהדונהי)

The Sixth (ninth) Blessing

During the summer:

Bless us, Lord, our God, in all our endeavors, and bless our years with the dews of good will, blessing, and benevolence. May its conclusion be life, contentment, and peace, as with other years for blessing,

May it be pleasing before You, Lord, my God and God of my forefathers, that You would provide for me and for my household, today and everyday, mine and their nourishment, with dignity and not with shame, in a permissible but not a forbidden manner, by virtue of your great name

הַיּוֹצֵא hayotze מִפָּסוּק mipasuk: וַהֲרִיקֹתִי vaharikoti לָכֶם lachem
בְּרָכָה beracha עַד־ ad בְּלִי־ beli דָי dai וּמִפָּסוּק umipasuk: נְסָה nesa
עָלֵינוּ alenu אוֹר or רז, אין סוף פָּנֶיךָ panecha ס"ג מ"ה ב"ן יְהֹוָהאדהנויאהדונהי Adonai
וְאַל ve'al תַּצְרִיכֵנוּ tatzrichenu לִידֵי lidei מַתְּנוֹת matnot בָּשָׂר basar
וָדָם vadam כִּי ki אִם im יוהך, מ"א אותיות אהיה בפשוטו ומילואו ומילוי דמילואו ע"ה
מִיָּדְךָ miyadcha הַמְּלֵאָה hamele'a וּמֵאוֹצָר ume'otzar מַתְּנַת matnat וְחִנָּם chinam
תְּכַלְכְּלֵנִי techalkelni וְתַשְׁפִּיעֵנִי vetashpi'eni אָמֵן amen יאהדונהי סֶלָה sela.

כִּי ki אֵל El ייא"י (מילוי דס"ג) טוֹב tov והו וּמֵטִיב umetiv
אַתָּה Ata וּמְבָרֵךְ umvarech הַשָּׁנִים hashanim: בָּרוּךְ baruch
אַתָּה Ata יְהֹוָהאדהנויאהדונהי Adonai מְבָרֵךְ mevarech הַשָּׁנִים hashanim:

THE SEVENTH (TENTH) BLESSING

This blessing gives us the power to positively influence all of humanity. Kabbalah teaches that each individual affects the whole. We affect the world, and the rest of the world affects us, even though we cannot perceive this relationship with our five senses. We call this relationship quantum consciousness.

Hod

תְּקַע teka ב"פ מנזפך וי' אותיות בְּשׁוֹפָר beshofar גָּדוֹל gadol להוו ; עם ד' אותיות =
מבה, יזל, אום לְחֵרוּתֵנוּ lecherutenu. וְשָׂא vesa נֵס nes מ"ה אדני לְקַבֵּץ lekabetz
גָּלֻיּוֹתֵינוּ galuyotenu. וְקַבְּצֵנוּ vekabetzenu יַחַד yachad מֵאַרְבַּע me'arba
כַּנְפוֹת kanfot וזבו (בסגולתו להוציא ניצוצות מן הקליפות) ויכוין וַזָבֶן עם נקודותיו = ע"ב, ריבוע יהוה
הָאָרֶץ ha'aretz אלהים דההין ע"ה ; ר"ת = אדני לְאַרְצֵנוּ le'artzenu:

---

that comes from the verse: "pour down for you blessing until there be no room to suffice for it" (Malachi 3:10) and from the verse: "Raise up over us the light of Your countenance, Lord" (Psalms 4:7), and we will not require the gifts of flesh and blood, but only from your hand which is full, and from the treasure of the free gift you shall support and nurish me. Amen. Sela.

for You are a good and a beneficent God and You bless the years. Blessed are You, Lord, Who blesses the years.

THE SEVENTH (TENTH) BLESSING

Blow a great Shofar for our freedom and raise a banner to gather our exiles, and gather us speedily from all four corners of the Earth to our Land.

The following is recited throughout the entire year:

The following meditation helps us to release and redeem all the remaining sparks of Light we have lost through our irresponsible actions (especially sexual misconduct):

milfanecha מִלְּפָנֶיךָ מהש ע"ה, ע"ב בריבוע וקס"א ע"ה, אל שדי ע"ה ratzon רָצוֹן yehi יְהִי

ס"ג מ"ה ב"ן יְהֹוָהאדניאהדונהי Adonai אֱלֹהַי Elohai מילוי ע"ב, דמב ; ילה

tipa טִיפָּה ילי shekol שֶׁכָּל avotai אֲבוֹתַי ילה ; מילוי ע"ב, דמב ; לכב velohei וֵאלֹהֵי

levatala לְבַטָּלָה mimeni מִמֶּנִּי sheyatza שֶׁיָּצָא keri קֶרִי shel שֶׁל vetipa וְטִיפָּה

shelo שֶׁלֹּא uvifrat וּבִפְרַט bichlal בִּכְלָל Yisrael יִשְׂרָאֵל ילי umikol וּמִכָּל

beratzon בְּרָצוֹן ben בֵּין be'ones בְּאוֹנֶס ben בֵּין mitzva מִצְוָה bimkom בִּמְקוֹם

ben בֵּין beshogeg בְּשׁוֹגֵג ben בֵּין מהש ע"ה, ע"ב בריבוע וקס"א ע"ה, אל שדי ע"ה

,bema'ase בְּמַעֲשֶׂה uven וּבֵין behirhur בְּהִרְהוּר ben בֵּין ,bemezid בְּמֵזִיד

acher אַחֵר begilgul בְּגִלְגּוּל ben בֵּין ze זֶה begilgul בְּגִלְגּוּל ben בֵּין

hakelipot הַקְּלִיפּוֹת shetaki שֶׁתַּקִּיא ,bakelipot בַּקְּלִיפּוֹת venivla וְנִבְלַע

bizechut בִּזְכוּת ba בָּהּ shenivle'u שֶׁנִּבְלְעוּ keri קֶרִי hanitzotzot הַנִּיצוֹצוֹת

hayotze הַיּוֹצֵא מבה, יזל, אום = עם ד' אותיות ; להח hagadol הַגָּדוֹל shimcha שִׁמְךָ

ר"ת וזבו ו-ילי vayki'enu וַיְקִאֶנּוּ bala בָּלַע ומב chayil חַיִל :mipasuk מִפָּסוּק

uvizechut וּבִזְכוּת ס"ת וול ; (מילוי דס"ג) ייא"י El אֵל yorishenu יֹרִשֶׁנּוּ mibitno מִבִּטְנוֹ

יְוַהֲבָוֶהָ מבה, יזל, אום = עם ד' אותיות ; להח hagadol הַגָּדוֹל shimcha שִׁמְךָ

limkom לִמְקוֹם shetachazirem שֶׁתַּחֲזִירֵם (יְוַהֲבָוֶהָ :during the *Shovavim*)

.ase עֲשֵׂה ריבוע מ"ה ; קס"א ע"ה be'enecha בְּעֵינֶיךָ והו vehatov וְהַטּוֹב kedusha קְדוּשָׁה

You should meditate to correct the thought that caused the loss of the sparks of Light. Also meditate on the Names that control our thoughts for each of the six days of the week as follow:

Sunday	יְהֹוָה	על צבא כף ואו זין ואו טפטפיה א מן אהיה דמרגלא ושם:	*.Beriah*
Monday	יְהֹוִה	על מגן כף ואו זין ואו טפטפיה ה מן אהיה דמרגלא ושם:	*.Yetzirah*
Tuesday	מצפץ	צוה פוזד כף ואו זין ואו טפטפיה י מן אהיה דמרגלא ושם:	*.Asiyah*
Wednesday	אל	צוה פוזד כף ואו זין ואו טפטפיה י מן יהו דמרגלא ושם:	*.Asiyah*
Thursday	אלהים	על מגן כף ואו זין ואו טפטפיה ה מן יהו דמרגלא ושם:	*.Yetzirah*
Friday	מצפץ	על צבא כף ואו זין ואו טפטפיה ו מן יהו דמרגלא ושם:	*.Beriah*

Each of these Names (על צבא, כף ואו זין ואו, טפטפיה) adds up to 193, which is the same numerical value as the word *zokef* (raise). These Names raise the Holy Spark from the *Chitzoniyim*. Also, when you say the words "*mekabetz nidchei*" (in the continuation of the blessing), which adds up to 304 – the same numerical value of *Shin, Dalet* (demon), meditate to collect all the lost sparks and cancel out the power of the negative forces.

May it be pleasing before You, Lord, my God and God of my forefathers, that every single drop of keri that came out of me for vain, and from all of Yisrael in general, and especially not as a cause of precept, if it was coerced or willfully, with intention or without, by passing thought or by an action, in this lifetime or in previous, and it was swallowed by the klipa, that the klipa will vomit all the sparks of keri that was swollen by it, by virtue of your great name that comes from the verse: "He swallowed up wealth and vomited it out, and from his belly God will cast it." (Job 20:15), and by the virtue of your great name you will return them to the holy place, and do what is good in Your eyes.

בָּרוּךְ baruch אַתָּה Ata יְהֹוָהאדניאהדונהי Adonai ; יכוין וזבו בשילוב יהוה כזה: יְוַזְהְבֵוּוהְ

מְקַבֵּץ mekabetz ע"ב ס"ג מ"ה ב"ן, הברכה (למתק את ז' המלכים שמתו)

נִדְחֵי nidchei ע"ב, ריבוע יהוה עַמּוֹ amo וזבו יִשְׂרָאֵל Yisrael:

THE EIGHTH (ELEVENTH) BLESSING

This blessing helps us to balance judgment with mercy. As mercy is time, we can use it to change ourselves before judgment occurs.

Yesod

הָשִׁיבָה hashiva שׁוֹפְטֵינוּ shoftenu כְּבָרִאשׁוֹנָה kevarishona.

וְיוֹעֲצֵינוּ veyo'atzenu כְּבַתְּחִלָּה kevatechila ר"ת שכ"ה (דינים זכרים שביסוד) ויהוה (הממתקם).

וְהָסֵר vehaser מִמֶּנּוּ mimenu יָגוֹן yagon (סמאל) וַאֲנָחָה va'anacha (לילית).

וּמְלוֹךְ umloch עָלֵינוּ aleinu מְהֵרָה mehera אַתָּה Ata

יְהֹוָהאדניאהדונהי Adonai לְבַדְּךָ levadcha. בְּחֶסֶד bechesed ע"ב, ריבוע יהוה

וּבְרַחֲמִים uvrachamim מצפצ, אלהים דיודין, י"פ ייי ; להמתיק ברחמים דיני צדק ומשפט

בְּצֶדֶק betzedek וּבְמִשְׁפָּט uvmishpat ע"ה = ה"פ אלהים: בָּרוּךְ baruch אַתָּה Ata

יְהֹוָהאדניאהדונהי Adonai מֶלֶךְ melech אוֹהֵב ohev ממתיק דיני

צְדָקָה tzedaka ע"ה ריבוע אלהים וּמִשְׁפָּט umishpat ע"ה ה"פ אלהים:

THE NINTH (TWELFTH) BLESSING

This blessing helps us remove all forms of negativity, whether it comes from people, situations or even the negative energy of the Angel of Death [(**do not pronounce these names**) *Sa-ma-el* (male aspect) and*Li-li-th* (female aspect), which are encoded here], by using the Holy Name: *Shadai* שדי, which is encoded mathematically into the last four words of this blessing and also appears inside a *Mezuzah* for the same purpose.

Blessed are You, Lord, Who gathers the displaced of His Nation, Israel.

THE EIGHTH (ELEVENTH) BLESSING

Restore our judges, as at first, and our mentors, as in the beginning. Remove from us sorrow and moaning. Reign over us soon, You alone, Lord, with kindness and compassion, with righteousness and justice. Blessed are You, Lord, the King Who loves righteousness and justice.

Keter

לַמִּינִים laminim וְלַמַּלְשִׁינִים velamalshinim אַל al תְּהִי tehi תִקְוָה tikva

וְכָל vechol ילי הַזֵּדִים hazedim כְּרֶגַע kerega ג"פ אלהים עם ט"ו אותיות פשוטות

יֹאבֵדוּ yovedu• וְכָל־ vechol ילי אוֹיְבֶיךָ oyvecha (סמאל)

וְכָל־ vechol ילי שׂוֹנְאֶיךָ son'echa (לילית) מְהֵרָה mehera יִכָּרֵתוּ yikaretu•

וּמַלְכוּת umalchut הָרִשְׁעָה harish'a מְהֵרָה mehera תְעַקֵּר te'aker

וּתְשַׁבֵּר utshaber וּתְכַלֵּם utchalem וְתַכְנִיעֵם vetachni'em בִּמְהֵרָה bimhera

בְיָמֵינוּ veyamenu: בָּרוּךְ baruch אַתָּה Ata יְהֹוָאדנָי(יהואדני)יאהדונהי Adonai

שׁוֹבֵר shover אוֹיְבִים oyvim וּמַכְנִיעַ umachni'a זֵדִים zedim ר"ת = שדי:

THE TENTH (THIRTEENTH) BLESSING

This blessing surrounds us with total positivity to help us always be at the right place at the right time. It also helps attract only positive people into our lives.

Yesod

עַל al הַצַּדִּיקִים hatzadikim צדיק יסוד עולם וְעַל ve'al הַחֲסִידִים hachasidim

וְעַל ve'al שְׁאֵרִית she'erit עַמְּךָ amecha בֵּית bet ב"פ ראה יִשְׂרָאֵל Yisrael•

וְעַל ve'al פְּלֵיטַת peletat בֵּית bet ב"פ ראה סוֹפְרֵיהֶם sofrehem•

וְעַל ve'al גֵּרֵי gerei הַצֶּדֶק hatzedek וְעָלֵינוּ ve'alenu• יֶהֱמוּ yehemu

נָא na רַחֲמֶיךָ rachamecha יְהֹוָאדנָיאהדונהי Adonai אֱלֹהֵינוּ Elohenu ילה

וְתֵן veten שָׂכָר sachar י"פ ב"ן טוֹב tov והו לְכָל־ lechol יה אדני

הַבּוֹטְחִים habotchim בְּשִׁמְךָ beshimcha בֶּאֱמֶת be'emet אהיה פעמים אהיה, ז"פ ס"ג•

THE NINTH (TWELFTH) BLESSING

For the heretics and for the slanderers, let there be no hope. Let all the wicked perish in an instant. And may all Your foes and all Your haters be speedily cut down. And as for the evil government, may You quickly uproot and smash it, and may You destroy and humble it, speedily in our days. Blessed are You, Lord, Who smashes foes and humbles the wicked.

THE TENTH (THIRTEENTH) BLESSING

On the righteous, on the pious, on the remnants of the House of Israel, on the remnants of their writers' academies, on the righteous converts, and on us, may Your compassion be stirred, Lord, our God. And give good reward to all those who truly trust in Your Name.

וְשִׂים vesim וְחֶלְקֵנוּ chelkenu עִמָּהֶם imahem וּלְעוֹלָם ul'olam ריבוע ס"ג וי' אותיות דס"ג

לֹא lo נֵבוֹשׁ nevosh כִּי ki בְךָ vecha בָטָחְנוּ batachnu.

וְעַל ve'al חַסְדְּךָ chasdecha הַגָּדוֹל hagadol להחו ; עם ד' אותיות = מבה, יזל, אום

בֶּאֱמֶת be'emet אהיה פעמים אהיה, ז"פ ס"ג נִשְׁעָנְנוּ nish'anenu:

בָּרוּךְ baruch אַתָּה Ata יְהֹוָהאדניאהדונהי Adonai מִשְׁעָן mish'an

וּמִבְטָח umivtach לַצַּדִּיקִים latzadikim ר"ת ימול (כל מי שנימול נקרא צדיק):

THE ELEVENTH (FOURTEENTH) BLESSING

This blessing connects us to the power of Jerusalem, to the building of the Temple, and to the preparation for the *Mashiach*.

Hod

תִּשְׁכּוֹן tishkon בְּתוֹךְ betoch יְרוּשָׁלַיִם Yerushalayim עִירְךָ ircha

כַּאֲשֶׁר ka'asher דִּבַּרְתָּ dibarta ראה וְכִסֵּא vechise דָוִד David

עַבְדְּךָ avdecha פוי, אל אדני מְהֵרָה mehera בְּתוֹכָהּ vetocha תָּכִין tachin

Meditate here that *Mashiach Ben Yosef* shall not be killed by the wicked *Armilos* **(Do not pronounce).**

וּבְנֵה uvne אוֹתָהּ ota בִּנְיַן binyan עוֹלָם olam בִּמְהֵרָה bimhera

בְּיָמֵינוּ veyamenu: בָּרוּךְ baruch אַתָּה Ata יְהֹוָהאדניאהדונהי Adonai

בּוֹנֵה bone ס"ג יְרוּשָׁלָיִם Yerushalayim:

THE TWELFTH (FIFTEENTH) BLESSING

This blessing helps us achieve a personal state of *Mashiach* by transforming our reactive nature into becoming proactive. Just as there is a global *Mashiach*, each person has a personal *Mashiach* within. When enough people achieve their transformation, the way will be paved for the appearance of the global *Mashiach*.

---

and place our lot with them. And may we never be embarrassed, for it is in You that we place our trust; it is upon Your great compassion that we truly rely. Blessed are You, Lord, the support and security of the righteous.

THE ELEVENTH (FOURTEENTH) BLESSING

May You dwell in Jerusalem, Your City,

as You have promised. And may You establish the throne of David, Your servant, speedily within it and build it as an eternal structure, speedily in our days Blessed are You, Lord, Who builds Jerusalem.

Netzach

This blessing contains 20 words, which is the same number of words in *"Ki nicham Adonai Tzion nicham kol chorvoteha..." (Isaiah 51:3)*, a verse that speaks about the Final Redemption.

אֶת et צֶמַח tzemach יהוה אהיה יהוה אדני דָּוִד David
עַבְדְּךָ avdecha פוי, אל אדני מְהֵרָה mehera תַצְמִיחַ tatzmia'ch וְקַרְנוֹ vekarno
תָּרוּם tarum בִּישׁוּעָתֶךָ bishu'atecha. כִּי ki לִישׁוּעָתְךָ lishu'atcha
קִוִּינוּ kivinu כָּל־ kol ילי הַיּוֹם hayom ע"ה נגד, מזבח, זן, אל יהוה

You should meditate and ask here for the Final Redemption to occur right away.

בָּרוּךְ baruch אַתָּה Ata יְהֹוָאדהנהיאהדונהי Adonai
מַצְמִיחַ matzmi'ach קֶרֶן keren יְשׁוּעָה yeshu'a:

THE THIRTEENTH (SIXTEENTH) BLESSING

This blessing is the most important of all blessings, because here we acknowledge all of our reactive behavior. We make reference to our wrongful actions in general, and we also specify a particular incident. The section inside the box provides us with an opportunity to ask the Light for personal sustenance. The Ari states that throughout this prayer, even on fast days, we have a personal angel accompanying us. If we meditate upon this angel, all our prayers must be answered. The Thirteenth Blessing is one above the twelve zodiac signs, and it raises us above the influence of the stars and planets.

Tiferet

שְׁמַע shema קוֹלֵנוּ kolenu יְהֹוָאדהנהיאהדונהי Adonai (יוד הה וו הה)
אֱלֹהֵינוּ Elohenu ילה (אבג יתץ). אָב av הָרַחֲמָן harachaman רַחֵם rachem
אברהם, וז"פ אל, רי"ו ול"ב נתיבות החכמה, רמ"ח (אברים), עסמ"ב וט"ז אותיות פשוטות עָלֵינוּ alenu
(קרע שטן). וְקַבֵּל vekabel בְּרַחֲמִים berachamim מצפצ, אלהים דיודין, י"פ ייי
וּבְרָצוֹן uvratzon מהש ע"ה, ע"ב בריבוע וקס"א ע"ה, אל שדי ע"ה אֶת et
תְּפִלָּתֵנוּ tefilatenu (נגד יכש). כִּי ki אֵל El ייא"י (מילוי דס"ג)
שׁוֹמֵעַ shome'a תְּפִלּוֹת tefilot וְתַחֲנוּנִים vetachanunim אַתָּה Ata (בטר צתג).

THE TWELFTH (FIFTEENTH) BLESSING

The offspring of David, Your servant, may You speedily cause to sprout.
And may You raise their worth with Your salvation, because it is for Your salvation that we have hoped all day long. Blessed are You, Lord, Who sprouts out the worth of the salvation.

THE THIRTEENTH (SIXTEENTH) BLESSING

Hear our voice, Lord, our God. Merciful Father, have mercy over us.
Accept our prayer with compassion and favor, because You are God, Who hears prayers and supplications.

It is good for you to be aware, acknowledge and confess your prior negative actions and to ask for your livelihood here:

רִבּוֹנוֹ ribono שֶׁל shel עוֹלָם olam, חָטָאתִי chatati עָוִיתִי aviti
וּפָשַׁעְתִּי ufashati לְפָנֶיךָ lefanecha ס״ג מ״ה ב״ן יְהִי yehi רָצוֹן ratzon מהש ע״ה,
ע״ב בריבוע וקס״א ע״ה, אל שדי ע״ה מִלְּפָנֶיךָ milfanecha ס״ג מ״ה ב״ן שֶׁתִּמְחוֹל shetimchol
וְתִסְלַח vetislach יהוה ע״ב וּתְכַפֵּר utchaper לִי li עַל al כָּל kol ילי ; עמם
מַה ma מ״ה שֶׁחָטָאתִי shechatati וְשֶׁעָוִיתִי veshe'aviti וְשֶׁפָּשַׁעְתִּי veshepashati
לְפָנֶיךָ lefanecha ס״ג מ״ה ב״ן מִיּוֹם miyom ע״ה נגד, מזבח, זן, אל יהוה
שֶׁנִּבְרֵאתִי shenivreti עַד ad הַיּוֹם hayom ע״ה נגד, מזבח, זן, אל יהוה הַזֶּה haze והו
וּבִפְרַט uvifrat (mention here a specific negative action or behavior you have and ask for forgivness)
וִיהִי vihi רָצוֹן ratzon מהש ע״ה, ע״ב בריבוע וקס״א ע״ה, אל שדי ע״ה
מִלְּפָנֶיךָ milfanecha ס״ג מ״ה ב״ן יְהֹוָאֲדֹנָיאהדונהי Adonai אֱלֹהֵינוּ Elohenu ילה
וֵאלֹהֵי velohei לכב ; מילוי ע״ב, דמב ; ילה אֲבוֹתֵינוּ avotenu שֶׁתַּזְמִין shetazmin
פַּרְנָסָתֵנוּ parnasatenu וּמְזוֹנוֹתֵינוּ umzonotenu לִי li וּלְכָל ulchol יה אדני
אַנְשֵׁי anshei בֵּיתִי veti ב״פ ראה הַיּוֹם hayom ע״ה נגד, מזבח, זן, אל יהוה
וּבְכָל uvchol ב״ן, לכב יוֹם yom ע״ה נגד, מזבח, זן, אל יהוה
וָיוֹם vayom ע״ה נגד, מזבח, זן, אל יהוה בְּרֵיוַח berevach וְלֹא velo
בְּצִמְצוּם vetzimtzum, בְּכָבוֹד bechavod בוכו וְלֹא velo בְּבִזּוּי bevizui,
בְּנַחַת benachat וְלֹא velo בְּצַעַר vetza'ar, וְלֹא velo אֶצְטָרֵךְ etztarech
לְמַתְּנוֹת lematenot בָּשָׂר basar וָדָם vadam וְלֹא velo לְהַלְוָאָתָם lehalva'atam,
אֶלָּא ela מִיָּדְךָ miyadcha הָרְוָחָה harchava וְהַפְּתוּחָה vehapetucha
וְהַמְּלֵאָה vehamele'a וּבִזְכוּת uvizchut שִׁמְךָ shimcha הַגָּדוֹל hagadol
להוו; עם ד׳ אותיות = מבה, יזל, אום (Do not pronounce this Name: דִּיקַרְנוֹסָא וזהך עם ג׳ אותיות
– ובאתב״ש = סאל, אמן, יאהדונהי) הַמְּמוּנֶּה hamemune עַל al הַפַּרְנָסָה haparnasa:

Master of the World!

I have transgressed. I have committed iniquity and I have sinned before You. May it be Your will that You would pardon, forgive and excuse all my transgressions, and all the iniquities that I have committed, and all the sins that I have sinned before You, ever since the day I was created and until this day (and especially…). May it be pleasing before You, Lord, our God and God of my forefathers, that You would provide for my livelihood and sustenance, and that of my household, today and each and every day, with abundance and not with meagerness; with dignity and not with shame; with comfort and not with suffering; and that I may not require the gifts of flesh and blood, nor their loans, but only from Your Hand, which is generous, open, and full, and by virtue of Your great Name, which is responsible for livelihood.

וּמִלְּפָנֶיךָ umilfanecha ס"ג מ"ה ב"ן מַלְכֵּנוּ malkenu

רֵיקָם rekam אַל al תְּשִׁיבֵנוּ te'shivenu (וזקב טנע)

חָנֵּנוּ chonenu וַעֲנֵנוּ va'anenu וּשְׁמַע ushma תְּפִלָּתֵנוּ tefilatenu:

כִּי ki אַתָּה Ata שׁוֹמֵעַ shome'a תְּפִלַּת tefilat כָּל kol ילי פֶּה pe

(פה דו"א) מילה ; וע"ה אלהים, אהיה אדני (יגל פזק)

בָּרוּךְ baruch אַתָּה Ata יְהֹוָאדהנויה Adonai

You should meditate here on the Holy Name: **אראר"תא**

Rav Chaim Vital says: "I have found in the books of the kabbalists that the prayer of a person, who meditates on this Name in the blessing *shome'a tefila*, will never go unanswered."

שׁוֹמֵעַ shome'a תְּפִלָּה tefila (שקו צית) אתב"ש אֻכְצַ, ב"ן אדני וניקודה ע"ה = יוד הי וו הה:

The Final Three Blessings

Through the merit of Moses, Aaron and Joseph, who are our channels for the final three blessings, we are able to bring down all the spiritual energy that we aroused with our prayers and blessings.

The Seventeenth Blessing

During this blessing, referring to Moses, we should always meditate to try to know exactly what God wants from us in our life, as signified by the phrase, "Let it be the will of God." We ask God to guide us toward the work we came to Earth to do. The Creator cannot just accept the work that we want to do; we must carry out the work we were destined to do.

Netzach

You have made requests (of daily needs) to God. Now, after asking for your needs to be met, you should praise the Creator in the last three blessings. This is like a person who has received what he needs from his Master and departs from Him. You should say "*retze*" and meditate for the Supernal Desire (*Keter*) that is called *metzach haratzon* (the Forehead of the Desire).

And from before You, our King, do not turn us away empty-handed but be gracious, answer us, and hear our prayer. Because You hear the prayer of every mouth. Blessed are You, Lord, Who hears prayers.

רְצֵה retze אלף למד הה יוד מם

Meditate here to transform misfortune and tragedy (צרה) into desire and acceptance (רצה).

יְהֹוָואדהנויאהדונהי Adonai אֱלֹהֵינוּ Elohenu ילה בְּעַמְּךָ be'amecha יִשְׂרָאֵל Yisrael

וְלִתְפִלָּתָם velitfilatam שְׁעֵה she'e. וְהָשֵׁב vehashev הָעֲבוֹדָה ha'avoda

לִדְבִיר lidvir רי"ו בֵּיתֶךָ betecha ב"פ ראה. וְאִשֵּׁי ve'ishei יִשְׂרָאֵל Yisrael

וּתְפִלָּתָם utfilatam מְהֵרָה mehera בְּאַהֲבָה be'ahava אחד, דאגה

תְקַבֵּל tekabel בְּרָצוֹן beratzon מהש ע"ה, ע"ב בריבוע וקס"א ע"ה, אל שדי ע"ה.

וּתְהִי ut'hi לְרָצוֹן leratzon מהש ע"ה, ע"ב בריבוע וקס"א ע"ה, אל שדי ע"ה

תָּמִיד tamid ע"ה קס"א קנ"א קמ"ג עֲבוֹדַת avodat יִשְׂרָאֵל Yisrael עַמֶּךָ amecha:

וְאַתָּה veAta בְּרַחֲמֶיךָ verachamecha הָרַבִּים harabim. תַּחְפֹּץ tachpotz

בָּנוּ banu וְתִרְצֵנוּ vetirtzenu וְתֶחֱזֶינָה vetechezena עֵינֵינוּ enenu ריבוע מ"ה

בְּשׁוּבְךָ beshuvcha לְצִיּוֹן leTziyon יוסף, ו' הויות, קנאה בְּרַחֲמִים berachamim

מצפצ, אלהים דיודין, י"פ ייי: בָּרוּךְ baruch אַתָּה Ata יְהֹוָואדהנויאהדונהי Adonai

הַמַּחֲזִיר hamachazir שְׁכִינָתוֹ shechinato לְצִיּוֹן leTziyon יוסף, ו' הויות, קנאה:

THE EIGHTEENTH BLESSING

This blessing is our thank you. Kabbalistically, the biggest "thank you" we can give the Creator is to do exactly what we are supposed to do in terms of our spiritual work.

THE FINAL THREE BLESSINGS

THE SEVENTEENTH BLESSING

Find favor, Lord, our God,
in Your People, Israel, and turn to their prayer.

Restore the service to the inner sanctuary of Your Temple. Accept the offerings of Israel and their prayer with favor, speedily, and with love. May the service of Your People Israel always be favorable to You

And You in Your great compassion take delight in us and are pleased with us. May our eyes witness Your return to Zion with compassion. Blessed are You, Lord, Who returns His Shechinah to Zion.

Hod

Bow your entire body at '*modim*' and straighten up at '*Adonai*'.

מוֹדִים modim מאה ברכות שתיקן דוד לאמרם כל יום

When the eve of Shavuot (second day) falls on a Friday:
While bowing you should meditate: אלף הא יוד הא, in order to lower the *Ruach* of *Yetzirah*, to be as *Mayin Nukvin* in order to elevate the *Shechinah*. And **while straightening up** you should meditate: יוד הא ואו הא, to elevate the *Shechinah* and to prepare the World of *Yetzirah* to be elevated to *Beriah* and to be able to receive *Asiyah*.

אֲנַחְנוּ anachnu לָךְ lach שָׁאַתָּה sheAta הוּא hu יְהֹוָאדניאהדונהי Adonai (וג)
אֱלֹהֵינוּ Elohenu ילה וֵאלֹהֵי velohei לכב ; מילוי ע"ב, דמב ; ילה אֲבוֹתֵינוּ avotenu
לְעוֹלָם le'olam ריבוע ס"ג וי' אותיות דס"ג וָעֶד va'ed• צוּרֵנוּ tzurenu
צוּר tzur אלהים דההין ע"ה וְחַיֵּינוּ chayenu וּמָגֵן umagen ג"פ אל (ייא"י מילוי דס"ג) ;
ר"ת מיכאל גבריאל נוריאל יִשְׁעֵנוּ yish'enu אַתָּה Ata הוּא hu•
לְדוֹר ledor וָדוֹר vador רי"ו נוֹדֶה node לְּךָ lecha וּנְסַפֵּר unsaper
תְּהִלָּתֶךָ tehilatecha• עַל־ al חַיֵּינוּ chayenu הַמְּסוּרִים hamesurim
בְּיָדֶךָ beyadecha• וְעַל ve'al נִשְׁמוֹתֵינוּ nishmotenu הַפְּקוּדוֹת hapekudot
לָךְ lach• וְעַל־ ve'al נִסֶּיךָ nisecha שֶׁבְּכָל shebechol ב"ן, לכב
יוֹם yom ע"ה נגד, מזבח, זן, אל יהוה עִמָּנוּ imanu ריבוע ס"ג, קס"א ע"ה וד' אותיות וְעַל ve'al
נִפְלְאוֹתֶיךָ nifle'otecha וְטוֹבוֹתֶיךָ vetovotecha שֶׁבְּכָל shebchol ב"ן, לכב
עֵת et• עֶרֶב erev וָבֹקֶר vavoker וְצָהֳרָיִם vetzahorayim• הַטּוֹב hatov והו
כִּי־ ki לֹא־ lo כָלוּ chalu רַחֲמֶיךָ rachamecha• הַמְרַחֵם hamerachem
אברהם, ח"פ אל, רי"ו ול"ב נתיבות החכמה, רמ"ח (אברים), עסמ"ב וט"ז אותיות פשוטות כִּי־ ki לֹא lo
תַמּוּ tamu חֲסָדֶיךָ chasadecha כִּי ki מֵעוֹלָם me'olam קִוִּינוּ kivinu לָךְ lach:

THE EIGHTEENTH BLESSING

We give thanks to You, for it is You, Lord, Who is our God and God of our forefathers, forever and for all eternity. You are our Rock, the Rock of our lives, and the Shield of our salvation. From one generation to another, we shall give thanks to You and we shall tell of Your praise. For our lives that are entrusted in Your hands, for our souls that are in Your care, for Your miracles that are with us every day, and for Your wonders and Your favors that are with us at all times: evening, morning and afternoon. You are the good One, for Your compassion has never ceased. You are the compassionate One, for Your kindness has never ended, for we have always placed our hope in You.

MODIM DERABANAN

This prayer is recited by the congregation in the repetition when the *chazan* says "*modim*."

In this section there are 44 words which is the same numerical value as the Name: ריבוע אהיה (א אה אהי אהיה).

מוֹדִים modim מאה ברכות שתיקן דוד לאמרם כל יום אֲנַחְנוּ anachnu לָךְ lach

שָׁאַתָּה sheAta הוּא hu יְהֹוָה יאהדונהי Adonai אֱלֹהֵינוּ Elohenu ילה

וֵאלֹהֵי velohei לכב ; מילוי ע״ב, דמב ; ילה אֲבוֹתֵינוּ avotenu

אֱלֹהֵי Elohei מילוי ע״ב, דמב ; ילה כָל chol ילי בָּשָׂר basar• יוֹצְרֵנוּ yotzrenu

יוֹצֵר yotzer בְּרֵאשִׁית bereshit• בְּרָכוֹת berachot וְהוֹדָאוֹת vehoda'ot

לְשִׁמְךָ leshimcha הַגָּדוֹל hagadol להח ; עם ד׳ אותיות = מבה, יזל, אום

וְהַקָּדוֹשׁ vehakadosh עַל al שֶׁהֶחֱיִיתָנוּ shehecheyitanu וְקִיַּמְתָּנוּ vekiyamtanu•

כֵּן ken תְּחַיֵּנוּ techayenu וּתְחָנֵּנוּ utchonenu• וְתֶאֱסוֹף vete'esof

גָּלֻיּוֹתֵינוּ galuyotenu לְחַצְרוֹת lechatzrot קָדְשֶׁךָ kodshecha• לִשְׁמוֹר lishmor

וְחֻקֶּיךָ chukecha וְלַעֲשׂוֹת vela'asot רְצוֹנָךְ retzoncha• וּלְעָבְדְךָ ul'ovdecha

פוי, אל אדני בְּלֵבָב belevav בוכו שָׁלֵם shalem• עַל al שֶׁאֲנַחְנוּ she'anachnu

מוֹדִים modim לָךְ lach• בָּרוּךְ baruch אֵל El ייא״י (מילוי דס״ג) הַהוֹדָאוֹת hahoda'ot:

וְעַל ve'al כֻּלָּם kulam יִתְבָּרַךְ yitbarach וְיִתְרוֹמָם veyitromam

וְיִתְנַשֵּׂא veyitnase תָּמִיד tamid ע״ה קס״א קנ״א קמ״ג שִׁמְךָ shimcha

מַלְכֵּנוּ malkenu לְעוֹלָם le'olam ריבוע ס״ג ו״ אותיות דס״ג וָעֶד va'ed•

וְכָל־ vechol ילי הַחַיִּים hachayim אהיה אהיה יהוה, בינה ע״ה יוֹדוּךָ yoducha סֶּלָה sela:

MODIM DERABANAN

We give thanks to You, for it is You Lord,

our God and God of our forefathers, the God of all flesh, our Maker and the Former of all Creation. Blessings and thanks to Your great and Holy Name for giving us life and for preserving us. So may You continue to give us life, be gracious to us, and gather our exiles to the courtyards of Your Sanctuary, so that we may keep Your laws, fulfill Your will, and serve You wholeheartedly. For this, we thank You. Bless the God of thanksgiving.

And for all those things, may Your Name be always blessed,
exalted and extolled, our King, forever and ever, and all the living shall thank You, Selah.

וִיהַלְלוּ vihalelu וִיבָרְכוּ vivarchu יהוה ריבוע יהוה ריבוע מ"ה אֶת־ et

שִׁמְךָ shimcha הַגָּדוֹל hagadol להח ; עם ד' אותיות = מבה, יזל, אום בֶּאֱמֶת be'emet

אהיה פעמים אהיה, ז"פ ס"ג לְעוֹלָם le'olam ריבוע ס"ג ו' אותיות דס"ג כִּי ki טוֹב tov והו ;

כי טוב = יהוה אהיה, אום, מבה, יזל. הָאֵל haEl לאה ; ייא"י (מילוי דס"ג) יְשׁוּעָתֵנוּ yeshu'atenu

וְעֶזְרָתֵנוּ ve'ezratenu סֶלָה sela. הָאֵל haEl לאה ; ייא"י (מילוי דס"ג) הַטּוֹב hatov והו :

Bend your knees at *'baruch'*, bow at *'Ata'* and straighten up at *'Adonai'*.

בָּרוּךְ baruch אַתָּה Ata

> **When the eve of Shavuot (second day) falls on a Friday:**
> **While bending** you should meditate: אלף הה יוד הה, in order to lower the *Nefesh* of *Asiyah*, to be as *Mayin Nukvin* in order to elevate the *Shechinah*. And **while straightening up** meditate: יוד הה וו הה, to elevate the *Shechinah* and to prepare *Asiyah* to be elevated to *Yetzirah*.

יְהֹוָאדהנויאהדונהי Adonai (הי) הַטּוֹב hatov והו שִׁמְךָ shimcha

וּלְךָ ulcha נָאֶה na'e לְהוֹדוֹת lehodot ס"ת כהת, משיח בן דוד ע"ה :

The Final Blessing

We are emanating the energy of peace to the entire world. We also make it our intent to use our mouths only for good. Kabbalistically, the power of words and speech is unimaginable. We hope to use that power wisely, which is perhaps one of the most difficult tasks we have to carry out.

Yesod

שִׂים sim שָׁלוֹם shalom טוֹבָה tova אכא וּבְרָכָה uvracha

חַיִּים chayim אהיה אהיה יהוה, בינה ע"ה חֵן chen מילוי דמ"ה בריבוע, מוחי

וָחֶסֶד vachesed ע"ב, ריבוע יהוה צְדָקָה tzedaka ע"ה ריבוע אלהים

וְרַחֲמִים verachamim עָלֵינוּ alenu וְעַל־ ve'al כָּל־ kol ילי ; עמם

יִשְׂרָאֵל Yisrael עַמֶּךָ amecha וּבָרְכֵנוּ uvarchenu אָבִינוּ avinu כֻּלָּנוּ kulanu

כְּאֶחָד ke'echad אהבה, דאגה בְּאוֹר be'or רז, א"ס פָּנֶיךָ panecha ס"ג מ"ה ב"ן

And they shall praise and bless Your great Name, sincerely and forever, for It is good, the God of our salvation and our help, Selah, the good God. Blessed are You, Lord, whose Name is good and to You it is befitting to give thanks.

The Final Blessing

Place peace, goodness, blessing, life, grace, kindness, righteousness, and mercy upon us and upon all of Israel, Your People. Bless us all as one, our Father, with the Light of Your Countenance,

כִּי ki בְּאוֹר ve'or רז, א״ס פָּנֶיךָ panecha ס״ג מ״ה ב״ן נָתַתָּ natata לָנוּ lanu
אלהים, אהיה אדני יְהֹוָואדניאהדונהי Adonai אֱלֹהֵינוּ Elohenu ילה תּוֹרָה torah
וְחַיִּים vechayim אהיה אהיה יהוה, בינה ע״ה. אַהֲבָה ahava אחד, דאגה וָחֶסֶד vachesed
ע״ב, ריבוע יהוה. צְדָקָה tzedaka ע״ה ריבוע אלהים וְרַחֲמִים verachamim.
בְּרָכָה beracha וְשָׁלוֹם veshalom. וְטוֹב vetov והו בְּעֵינֶיךָ be'enecha
ע״ה קס״א ; ריבוע מ״ה לְבָרְכֵנוּ levarchenu וּלְבָרֵךְ ulvarech אֶת et כָּל kol ילי
עַמְּךָ amecha יִשְׂרָאֵל Yisrael בְּרוֹב berov י״פ אהיה עֹז oz וְשָׁלוֹם veshalom:

בָּרוּךְ baruch אַתָּה Ata יְהֹוָואדניאהדונהי Adonai
הַמְבָרֵךְ hamevarech אֶת et עַמּוֹ amo יִשְׂרָאֵל Yisrael
ר״ת = אלהים (אילההויהם = יב״ק) בַּשָּׁלוֹם bashalom. אָמֵן amen יאהדונהי.

When the eve of Shavuot (second day) falls on a Friday:
Meditate here to elevate the Name: יהוה, as follow:
The letter ה and the Name ב״ן to the letter ו and to the Name מ״ה.
The letter ו and the Name מ״ה to the letter ה and to the Name ס״ג.
The letter ה and the Name ס״ג to the letter י and to the Name ע״ב.

YIH'YU LERATZON

There are 42 letters in the verse in the secret of *Ana Beko'ach*.

יִהְיוּ yih'yu אל (ייא״י מילוי דס״ג) לְרָצוֹן leratzon מהש ע״ה, ע״ב בריבוע וקס״א ע״ה, אל שדי ע״ה
אִמְרֵי imrei פִי fi ר״ת אֶלֶף = אלף למד שין דלת יוד ע״ה וְהֶגְיוֹן vehegyon לִבִּי libi
לְפָנֶיךָ lefanecha ס״ג מ״ה ב״ן יְהֹוָואדניאהדונהי Adonai צוּרִי tzuri וְגֹאֲלִי vego'ali:

---

because it is with the Light of Your Countenance that You, Lord, our God, have given us Torah and life, love and kindness,righteousness and mercy, blessing and peace. May it be good in Your Eyes to bless us and to bless Your entire Nation, Israel, with abundant power and with peace.

Blessed are You, Lord, Who blesses His Nation, Israel, with peace, Amen.

YIH'YU LERATZON

"May the utterances of my mouth
and the thoughts of my heart find favor before You, Lord, my Rock and my Redeemer." (Psalms 19:15)

ELOHAI NETZOR

אֱלֹהַי Elohai מילוי ע"ב, דמב ; ילה נְצוֹר netzor לְשׁוֹנִי leshoni מֵרָע mera.
וּשְׂפָתוֹתַי vesiftotai מִדַּבֵּר midaber ראה מִרְמָה mirma. וְלִמְקַלְלַי velimkalelai
נַפְשִׁי nafshi תִדּוֹם tidom. וְנַפְשִׁי venafshi כֶּעָפָר ke'afar
לַכֹּל lakol יה אדני תִּהְיֶה tihye. פְּתַח petach לִבִּי libi בְּתוֹרָתֶךָ betoratecha.
וְאַחֲרֵי ve'acharei מִצְוֹתֶיךָ mitzvotecha תִּרְדּוֹף tirdof נַפְשִׁי nafshi.
וְכָל־ vechol ילי הַקָּמִים hakamim עָלַי alai לְרָעָה lera'a רהע. מְהֵרָה mehera
הָפֵר hafer עֲצָתָם atzatam וְקַלְקֵל vekalkel מַחְשְׁבוֹתָם machshevotam.
עֲשֵׂה ase לְמַעַן lema'an שְׁמָךְ shemach. עֲשֵׂה ase לְמַעַן lema'an
יְמִינָךְ yeminach. עֲשֵׂה ase לְמַעַן lema'an תּוֹרָתָךְ toratach. עֲשֵׂה ase
לְמַעַן lema'an קְדוּשָּׁתָךְ kedushatach. ר"ת הפסוק = מ"ה יהוה לְמַעַן lema'an
יֵחָלְצוּן yechaltzun יְדִידֶיךָ yedidecha ר"ת ילי הוֹשִׁיעָה hoshi'a יהוה וש"ע נהורין
יְמִינְךָ yemincha וַעֲנֵנִי va'aneni (כתיב: ועננו) ר"ת אל (ייא" מילוי דס"ג):

Before we recite the next verse ("*yih'yu leratzon*") we have an opportunity to strengthen our connection to our soul using our name. Each person has a verse in the *Torah* that connects to their name. Either their name is in the verse, or the first and last letters of the name correspond to the first or last letters of a verse. For example, the name Yehuda begins with a *Yud* and ends with a *Hei*. Before we end the *Amidah*, we state that our name will always be remembered when our soul leaves this world.

YIH'YU LERATZON (THE SECOND)

There are 42 letters in the verse in the secret of *Ana Beko'ach*.

יִהְיוּ yih'yu אל (ייא" מילוי דס"ג) לְרָצוֹן leratzon מהש ע"ה, ע"ב בריבוע וקס"א ע"ה, אל שדי ע"ה
אִמְרֵי־ imrei פִי fi ר"ת אֱלֶף = אלף למד שין דלת יוד ע"ה וְהֶגְיוֹן vehegyon לִבִּי libi
לְפָנֶיךָ lefanecha ס"ג מ"ה ב"ן יְהֹוָהאדניאהדונהי Adonai צוּרִי tzuri וְגֹאֲלִי vego'ali:

ELOHAI NETZOR

My God, guard my tongue from evil and my lips from speaking deceit. To those who curse me, let my spirit remain silent, and let my spirit be as dust for everyone. Open my heart toYour Torah and let my heart pursue Your commandments. All those who rise against me to do me harm, speedily nullify their plans and disturb their thoughts. Do so for the sake of Your Name. Do so for the sake of Your Right. Do so for the sake of Your Torah. Do so for the sake of Your Holiness, "So that Your loved ones may be saved. Redeem Your right and answer me." (Psalms 60:7)

YIH'YU LERATZON (THE SECOND)

"May the utterances of my mouth
and the thoughts of my heart find favor before You, Lord, my Rock and my Redeemer." (Psalms 19:15)

OSE SHALOM

We now take three steps backward to draw the Light of the Upper Worlds into our life. We bow to the Left, Right, and Center, and we should meditate that by taking these three steps backwards, that the Holy Temple that was destroyed should be built once again.

You take three steps backward;

Left
You turn to the left and say:

עֹשֶׂה ose שָׁלוֹם shalom
בִּמְרוֹמָיו bimromav ר״ת ע״ב, ריבוע יהוה

Right
You turn to the right and say:

הוּא hu בְּרַחֲמָיו verachamav יַעֲשֶׂה ya'ase
שָׁלוֹם shalom עָלֵינוּ aleinu ר״ת ש״ע נהורין

Center
You face the center and say:

וְעַל ve'al כָּל־ kol ילי ; עמם עַמּוֹ amo יִשְׂרָאֵל Yisrael
וְאִמְרוּ ve'imru אָמֵן amen יאהדונהי:

יְהִי yehi רָצוֹן ratzon מהש ע״ה, ע״ב בריבוע וקס״א ע״ה, אל שדי ע״ה מִלְּפָנֶיךָ milfaneicha ס״ג מ״ה ב״ן יְהוָֹאדניאהדונהי Adonai אֱלֹהֵינוּ eloheinu ילה וֵאלֹהֵי velohei לכב ; מילוי ע״ב, דמב ; ילה אֲבוֹתֵינוּ avoteinu, שֶׁתִּבְנֶה shetivne בֵּית bet ב״פ ראה הַמִּקְדָּשׁ hamikdash בִּמְהֵרָה bimhera בְּיָמֵינוּ veyameinu וְתֵן veten חֶלְקֵנוּ chelkenu בְּתוֹרָתְךָ betoratach לַעֲשׂוֹת la'asot חֻקֵּי chukei רְצוֹנָךְ retzonach וּלְעָבְדָךְ ul'ovdach פוי, אל אדני בְּלֵבָב belevav בוכו שָׁלֵם shalem.

You take three steps forward.

OSE SHALOM

He, Who makes peace in His high places, He, in His compassion, shall make peace upon us And upon His entire nation, Israel, and you shall say, Amen.

May it be pleasing before You,
Lord, our God and God of our forefathers, that You shall rebuild the Temple speedily, in our days, and place our lot in Your Torah, so that we may fulfill the laws of Your desire and serve You wholeheartedly.

YEHI SHEM

יְהִי yehi שֵׁם shem יְהֹוָֽאדהֹניאהדונהי Adonai מְבֹרָךְ mevorach ר"ת ריבוע ע"ב וריבוע ס"ג

יהוה מברך = רפ"ח (להעלות רפ"ח ניצוצות שנפלו לקליפה דמשם באים התולואים) מֵעַתָּה me'ata

וְעַד־ ve'ad עוֹלָם olam ילי: מִמִּזְרַח־ mimizrach שֶׁמֶשׁ shemesh עַד־ ad

ר"ת קדוש מְבוֹאוֹ mevo'o מְהֻלָּל mehulal שֵׁם shem יְהֹוָֽאדהֹניאהדונהי Adonai:

רָם ram עַל־ al כָּל־ kol ילי ; עמם גּוֹיִם goyim יְהֹוָֽאדהֹניאהדונהי Adonai עַל al

הַשָּׁמַיִם hashamayim י"פ טל, י"פ כוזו ; ר"ת וזשמל כְּבוֹדוֹ kevodo:

יְהֹוָֽאדהֹניאהדונהי Adonai אֲדֹנֵינוּ adonenu מָה־ ma מ"ה אַדִּיר adir הרי

שִׁמְךָ shimcha בְּכָל־ bechol ב"ן, לכב ; ומב הָאָרֶץ ha'aretz אלהים דההין ע"ה:

KADDISH TITKABAL

יִתְגַּדַּל yitgadal וְיִתְקַדַּשׁ veyitkadash שדי ומילוי שדי ; י"א אותיות כמנין ו"ה

שְׁמֵיהּ shemei (שם י"ה דע"ב) רַבָּא raba קנ"א ב"ן, יהוה אלהים יהוה אדני,

מילוי קס"א וס"ג, מ"ה ברבוע וע"ב ע"ה ; ר"ת = ו"פ אלהים ; ס"ת = ג"פ יב"ק: אָמֵן amen אידהנויה.

בְּעָלְמָא be'alma דִּי di בְרָא vera כִּרְעוּתֵיהּ chir'utei.

וְיַמְלִיךְ veyamlich מַלְכוּתֵיהּ malchutei. וְיַצְמַח veyatzmach

פּוּרְקָנֵיהּ purkanei. וִיקָרֵב vikarev מְשִׁיחֵיהּ meshichei: אָמֵן amen אידהנויה.

בְּחַיֵּיכוֹן bechayechon וּבְיוֹמֵיכוֹן uvyomechon וּבְחַיֵּי uvchayei

דְכָל dechol ילי בֵּית bet ב"פ ראה יִשְׂרָאֵל Yisrael בַּעֲגָלָא ba'agala

וּבִזְמַן uvizman קָרִיב kariv וְאִמְרוּ ve'imru אָמֵן amen: אָמֵן amen אידהנויה.

YEHI SHEM

"May the Name of the Lord be blessed from now till all eternity. From sunrise till sundown, may the Name of the Lord be praised and elevated. Above all nations is the Lord. His glory is above the Heavens." (Psalms 113:2-4) *"The Lord, our Master, how tremendous is Your Name in all the Earth."* (Psalms 8:10)

KADDISH TITKABAL

May His great Name be more exalted and sanctified. (Amen) *In the world that He created according to His will, and may His Kingdom reign. And may He cause His redemption to sprout and may He bring the Mashiach closer.* (Amen) *In your lifetimes and in your days and in the lifetime of all the House of Israel, speedily and in the near future, and you shall say, Amen.* (Amen)

The congregation and the *chazan* say the following:

28 words (until *be'alma*) – meditate:
מילוי דמילוי דע"ב (יוד ויו דלת הי יוד ויו יוד ויו הי יוד)
28 letters (until *almaya*) - meditate:
מילוי דמילוי דע"ב (יוד ויו דלת הי יוד ויו יוד ויו הי יוד)

יְהֵא yehe שְׁמֵיהּ shemei (שם י"ה דס"ג) רַבָּא raba קנ"א ב"ן,
יהוה אלהים יהוה אדני, מילוי קס"א וס"ג, מ"ה ברבוע וע"ב ע"ה מְבָרַךְ mevarach,
לְעָלַם le'alam לְעָלְמֵי le'almei עָלְמַיָּא almaya◆ יִתְבָּרַךְ yitbarach◆

Seven words with six letters each (שם בן מ"ב) – meditate:
יהוה ‑ יוד הי ויו הי ‑ מילוי דמילוי דע"ב (יוד ויו דלת הי יוד ויו יוד ויו הי יוד)
Also, seven times the letter Vav (שם בן מ"ב) – meditate:
יהוה ‑ יוד הי ויו הי ‑ מילוי דמילוי דע"ב (יוד ויו דלת הי יוד ויו יוד ויו הי יוד).

וְיִשְׁתַּבַּח veyishtabach י"פ ע"ב יהוה אל אבג יתץ◆

וְיִתְפָּאַר veyitpa'ar הי נו יה קרע שטן◆ וְיִתְרוֹמַם veyitromam וה כוזו נגד יכש◆

וְיִתְנַשֵּׂא veyitnase במוכסז בטר צתג◆ וְיִתְהַדָּר veyit'hadar כוזו יה וזקב טנע◆

וְיִתְעַלֶּה veyit'ale וה יוד ה יגל פזק◆ וְיִתְהַלָּל veyit'halal א ואו הא שקו צית◆

שְׁמֵיהּ shemei (שם י"ה דמ"ה) דְּקוּדְשָׁא dekudsha בְּרִיךְ verich הוּא hu⁝

אָמֵן amen אידהנויה◆

לְעֵלָּא le'ela מִן min כָּל kol ילי בִּרְכָתָא birchata◆ שִׁירָתָא shirata◆

תֻּשְׁבְּחָתָא tishbechata וְנֶחָמָתָא venechamata◆ דַּאֲמִירָן da'amiran

בְּעָלְמָא be'alma וְאִמְרוּ ve'imru אָמֵן amen⁝ אָמֵן amen אידהנויה.

תִּתְקַבַּל titkabal צְלוֹתָנָא tzelotana וּבָעוּתָנָא uva'utana

עִם im צְלוֹתְהוֹן tzelotehon וּבָעוּתְהוֹן uva'utehon דְּכָל dechol ילי

בֵּית beit ב"פ ראה יִשְׂרָאֵל Yisrael קֳדָם kadam אֲבוּנָא avuna

דְּבִשְׁמַיָּא devishmaya וְאִמְרוּ ve'imru אָמֵן amen⁝ אָמֵן amen אידהנויה◆

May His great Name be blessed forever and for all eternity. Blessed and lauded, and glorified, and exalted, and extolled, and honored, and uplifted, and praised be the Name of the Holy Blessed One. (Amen) Above all blessings, songs, praises, and words of consolation that may be said in the world, and you shall say, Amen. (Amen) May our prayers and pleas be accepted, together with the prayers and pleas of the entire House of Israel, before our Father in Heaven, and you say, Amen. (Amen)

יְהֵא yehe שְׁלָמָא shelama רַבָּא raba קנ"א ב"ן, יהוה אלהים יהוה אדני, מילוי קס"א וס"ג,

מ"ה ברבוע וע"ב ע"ה מִן min שְׁמַיָּא shemaya• וְחַיִּים chayim אהיה אהיה יהוה, בינה ע"ה

וְשָׂבָע vesava וִישׁוּעָה vishu'a וְנֶחָמָה venechama וְשֵׁיזָבָא vesheizava

וּרְפוּאָה urfu'a וּגְאֻלָּה ug'ula וּסְלִיחָה uslicha וְכַפָּרָה vechapara

וְרֵיוַח verevach וְהַצָּלָה vehatzala• לָנוּ lanu אלהים, אהיה אדני וּלְכָל ulchol יה אדני

עַמּוֹ amo יִשְׂרָאֵל Yisrael וְאִמְרוּ ve'imru אָמֵן amen: אָמֵן amen אידהנויה.

Take three steps backwards and say:

עוֹשֶׂה ose שָׁלוֹם shalom בִּמְרוֹמָיו bimromav ע"ב, ריבוע יהוה• הוּא hu

בְּרַחֲמָיו berachamav יַעֲשֶׂה ya'ase שָׁלוֹם shalom עָלֵינוּ alenu ר"ת ש"ע נהורין•

וְעַל ve'al כָּל kol ילי ; עמם עַמּוֹ amo יִשְׂרָאֵל Yisrael וְאִמְרוּ ve'imru אָמֵן amen:

אָמֵן amen אידהנויה•

LAMNATZE'ACH

By meditating upon the *Magen David* (Shield of David), we harness the power, strength, and valor of King David so that we can defeat our personal enemies. Our real enemies are not found in the outside world, regardless of what our ego tells us. Our real enemy is our *Desire to Receive for the Self Alone*. When we defeat the enemy within, external enemies suddenly disappear from our lives.

God revealed this Psalm to King David by Divine Inspiration. It was written on a golden plate made in the shape of the *Menorah* (shown on pg. 340). God also showed it to Moses. King David carried this Psalm written and engraved on the gold plate on his shield, the Shield of David. When King David went to war, he would meditate on the secrets of the *Menorah* and the seven sentences of this Psalm engraved in it, and his enemies would literally fall in defeat before him. By meditating upon it (reading the letters without turning the image upside down), we harness that power (*Midbar Kdemot*, by the Chida and also in *Menorat Zahav*, by Rav Zusha.)

May there be abundant peace from heaven. Life, contentment, salvation, consolation, deliverance, healing, redemption, pardon, atonement, comfort, and relief. For us and for His entire nation, Israel, and you shall say, Amen. (Amen) He, Who makes peace in His high places, He, in His compassion, shall make peace upon us And upon His entire nation, Israel, and you shall say, Amen. (Amen)

לַמְנַצֵּחַ lamnatze'ach בִּנְגִינֹת binginot מִזְמוֹר mizmor שִׁיר shir:

אֱלֹהִים Elohim אהיה אדני ; ילה יְחָנֵּנוּ yechonenu וִיבָרְכֵנוּ vivarchenu

יָאֵר ya'er כף ויו זין ויו פָּנָיו panav אִתָּנוּ itanu ר"ת פאי, אמן (יאהדונהי) סֶלָה sela:

לָדַעַת lada'at ר"ת סאל, אמן (יאהדונהי) בָּאָרֶץ ba'aretz דַּרְכֶּךָ darkecha

בְּכָל bechol ב"ן, לכב גּוֹיִם goyim יְשׁוּעָתֶךָ yeshu'atecha:

יוֹדוּךָ yoducha עַמִּים amim אֱלֹהִים Elohim אהיה אדני ; ילה יוֹדוּךָ yoducha

עַמִּים amim כֻּלָּם kulam: יִשְׂמְחוּ yismechu וִירַנְּנוּ viranenu

לְאֻמִּים le'umim ר"ת ע"ה = איההיוהה כִּי ki תִשְׁפֹּט tishpot עַמִּים amim

מִישֹׁר mishor וּלְאֻמִּים ul'umim בָּאָרֶץ ba'aretz תַּנְחֵם tanchem סֶלָה sela:

יוֹדוּךָ yoducha עַמִּים amim אֱלֹהִים Elohim אהיה אדני ; ילה יוֹדוּךָ yoducha

עַמִּים amim כֻּלָּם kulam: ר"ת יודוך ישמחו יודוך ארץ = ייא" (במילוי דס"ג)

ועם ר"ת אלהים לדעת יברכנו = ע"ב, ריבוע יהוה אֶרֶץ eretz נָתְנָה natna נתה, קס"א קנ"א קמ"ג

יְבוּלָהּ yevula ר"ת אני יְבָרְכֵנוּ yevarchenu אֱלֹהִים Elohim אהיה אדני ; ילה

אֱלֹהֵינוּ eloheinu ילה: יְבָרְכֵנוּ yevarchenu אֱלֹהִים Elohim אהיה אדני ; ילה

וְיִירְאוּ veyir'u אוֹתוֹ oto כָּל kol ילי אַפְסֵי afsei אָרֶץ aretz:

LAMNATZE'ACH

"For the Leader; with string-music: A Psalm, a Song. God be gracious unto us, and bless us; may He cause His face to shine toward us; Selah. That Your way may be known upon earth, Your salvation among all nations. Let the people give thanks to You, God; let the people give thanks to You, all of them. Let the nations be glad and sing for joy; for You will judge the people with equity, and lead the nations upon earth. Selah Let the people give thanks to You, God; let the people give thanks to You, all of them. The earth has yielded her increase; may God, our own God, bless us. May God bless us; and let all the ends of the earth fear Him." (Psalms 67)

זיט עלם מהש ללה אכא כהת הזי אלד לאו ההע

מנורת למנצח

דע לפני מי אתה עומד לפני מלך מל״ה הקב״ה

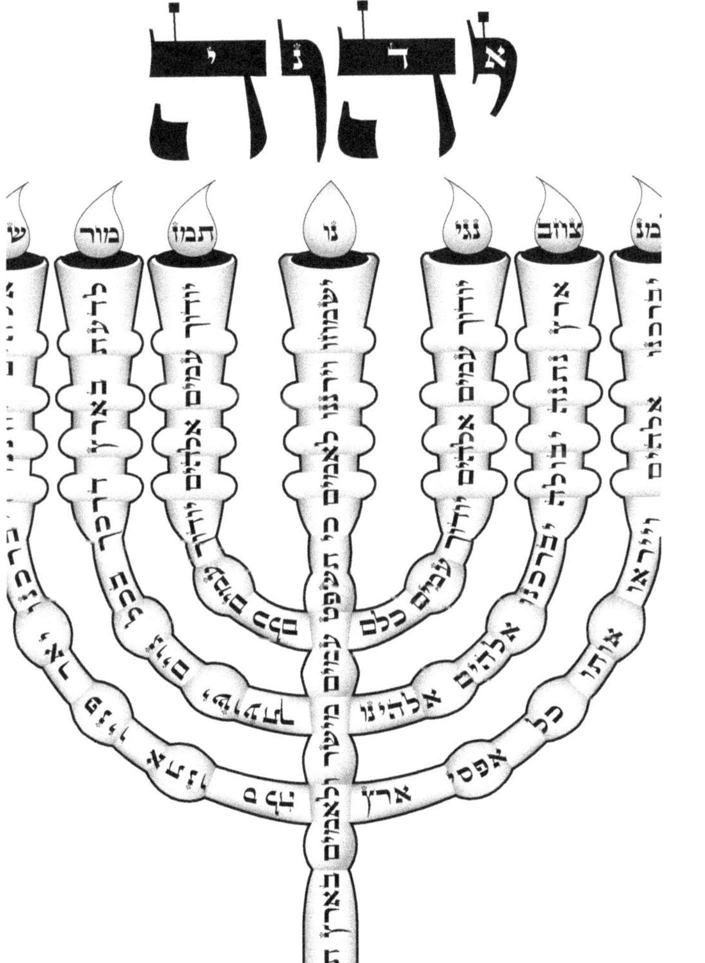

When the eve of Shavuot (second day) falls on a Friday the following is recited instead of "*lamnatze'ach binginot*":

יְהֹוָהאדני יאהדונהי Adonai מָלָךְ malach גֵּאוּת ge'ut לָבֵשׁ lavesh לָבֵשׁ lavesh

יְהֹוָהאדני יאהדונהי Adonai עֹז oz הִתְאַזָּר hit'azar אַף־ af ר"ת = אלהים, אהיה אדני

תִּכּוֹן tikon תֵּבֵל tevel ב"פ רי"ו בַּל־ bal תִּמּוֹט timot: נָכוֹן nachon כִּסְאֲךָ kis'acha

מֵאָז me'az ומב מֵעוֹלָם me'olam אָתָּה Ata ר"ת הפסוק קנ"א, אדני אלהים: נָשְׂאוּ nas'u

נְהָרוֹת neharot יְהֹוָהאדני יאהדונהי Adonai נָשְׂאוּ nas'u ר"ת = קין נְהָרוֹת neharot

קוֹלָם kolam יִשְׂאוּ yis'u נְהָרוֹת neharot דָּכְיָם dochyam ר"ת דני:

מִקֹּלוֹת mikolot מַיִם mayim רַבִּים rabim אַדִּירִים adirim הרי

מִשְׁבְּרֵי־ mishberei יָם yam ילי ; ר"ת אמי אַדִּיר adir הרי

בַּמָּרוֹם bamarom יְהֹוָהאדני יאהדונהי Adonai ; ר"ת אבי: עֵדֹתֶיךָ edoteicha

נֶאֶמְנוּ ne'emnu מְאֹד me'od ר"ת = קין לְבֵיתְךָ leveitcha ב"פ ראה

נַאֲוָה־ na'avah קֹּדֶשׁ kodesh יְהֹוָהאדני יאהדונהי Adonai לְאֹרֶךְ le'orech

יָמִים yamim נלך ; ר"ת ילי ; ס"ת = אדני ; יהוה לאורך ימים = ש"ע נהורין עם י"ג אותיות:

KADDISH YEHE SHELAMA

יִתְגַּדַּל yitgadal וְיִתְקַדַּשׁ veyitkadash שדי ומילוי שדי ; י"א אותיות כמנין ו"ה

שְׁמֵיהּ shemei (שם י"ה דע"ב) רַבָּא raba קנ"א ב"ן, יהוה אלהים יהוה אדני,

מילוי קס"א וס"ג, מ"ה ברבוע וע"ב ע"ה ; ר"ת = ו"פ אלהים ; ס"ת = ג"פ יב"ק: אָמֵן amen אידהנויה.

בְּעָלְמָא be'alma דִּי di בְרָא vera כִרְעוּתֵיהּ chir'utei.

וְיַמְלִיךְ veyamlich מַלְכוּתֵיהּ malchutei. וְיַצְמַח veyatzmach

פּוּרְקָנֵיהּ purkanei. וִיקָרֵב vikarev מְשִׁיחֵיהּ meshichei: אָמֵן amen אידהנויה.

"The Lord has reigned. He clothed Himself with pride. The Lord clothed Himself and girded Himself with might. He also established the world firmly, so that it would not collapse. Your Throne has been established. Ever since then, You have been forever. The rivers have lifted, Lord, the rivers have raised their voices. The rivers shall raise their powerful waves. More than the roars of many waters, and the powerful waves of the sea, You are immense in the high places, Lord. Your testimonies are extremely trustworthy. Your house is the holy sanctuary. The Lord shall be for the length of days." (Psalms 93)

KADDISH YEHE SHELAMA

May His great Name be more exalted and sanctified. (Amen)
In the world that He created according to His will, and may His kingdom reign.
And may He cause His redemption to sprout and may He bring the Mashiach closer. (Amen)

בְּחַיֵּיכוֹן bechayechon וּבְיוֹמֵיכוֹן uvyomechon וּבְחַיֵּי uvchayei

דְכָל dechol ילי בֵּית bet ב״פ ראה יִשְׂרָאֵל Yisrael בַּעֲגָלָא ba'agala

וּבִזְמַן uvizman קָרִיב kariv וְאִמְרוּ ve'imru אָמֵן amen: אָמֵן amen אידהנויה.

The congregation and the *chazan* say the following:

28 words (until *be'alma*) – meditate:

מילוי דמילוי דס״ג (יוד ויו דלת הי יוד ואו אלף ואו הי יוד)

28 letters (until *almaya*) - meditate:

מילוי דמילוי דמ״ה (יוד ואו דלת הא אלף ואו אלף ואו הא אלף).

יְהֵא yehe שְׁמֵיהּ shemei (שם י״ה דס״ג) רַבָּא raba קנ״א ב״ן,

יהוה אלהים יהוה אדני, מילוי קס״א וס״ג, מ״ה ברבוע וע״ב ע״ה מְבָרַךְ mevarach,

לְעָלַם le'alam לְעָלְמֵי le'almei עָלְמַיָּא almaya. יִתְבָּרַךְ yitbarach.

Seven words with six letters each (שם בן מ״ב) – meditate:

יהוה - יוד הי ואו הי - מילוי דמילוי דס״ג (יוד ויו דלת הי יוד ואו אלף ואו הי יוד) ;

Also, seven times the letter Vav (שם בן מ״ב) – meditate:

יהוה - יוד הא ואו הא - מילוי דמילוי דמ״ה (יוד ואו דלת הא אלף ואו אלף ואו הא אלף).

וְיִשְׁתַּבַּח veyishtabach י״פ ע״ב יהוה אל אבג יתץ.

וְיִתְפָּאַר veyitpa'ar הי נו יה קרע שטן. וְיִתְרוֹמַם veyitromam וה כוזו נגד יכש.

וְיִתְנַשֵּׂא veyitnase במוכסז בטר צתג. וְיִתְהַדָּר veyit'hadar כוזו יה וקב טנע.

וְיִתְעַלֶּה veyit'ale וה יוד ה יגל פזק. וְיִתְהַלָּל veyit'halal א ואו הא שקו צית.

שְׁמֵיהּ shemei (שם י״ה דמ״ה) דְּקוּדְשָׁא dekudsha בְּרִיךְ verich הוּא hu:

אָמֵן amen אידהנויה.

לְעֵלָּא le'ela מִן min כָּל kol ילי בִּרְכָתָא birchata. שִׁירָתָא shirata.

תֻּשְׁבְּחָתָא tishbechata וְנֶחָמָתָא venechamata. דַּאֲמִירָן da'amiran

בְּעָלְמָא be'alma וְאִמְרוּ ve'imru אָמֵן amen: אָמֵן amen אידהנויה.

In your lifetimes and in your days and in the lifetime of all the House of Israel, speedily and in the near future, and you shall say, Amen. (Amen) *May His great Name be blessed forever and for all eternity. Blessed and lauded, and glorified, and exalted, and extolled, and honored, and uplifted, and praised be the Name of the Holy Blessed One.* (Amen) *Above all blessings, songs, praises, and words of consolation that may be said in the world, and you shall say, Amen.* (Amen)

יְהֵא yehe שְׁלָמָא shelama רַבָּא raba קנ"א ב"ן, יהוה אלהים יהוה אדני, מילוי קס"א וס"ג,
מ"ה ברבוע וע"ב ע"ה מִן min שְׁמַיָּא shemaya. וְחַיִּים chayim אהיה אהיה יהוה, בינה ע"ה
וְשָׂבָע vesava וִישׁוּעָה vishu'a וְנֶחָמָה venechama וְשֵׁיזָבָא veshezava
וּרְפוּאָה urefu'a וּגְאֻלָּה uge'ula וּסְלִיחָה uslicha וְכַפָּרָה vechapara
וְרֵיוַח verevach וְהַצָּלָה vehatzala. לָנוּ lanu אלהים, אהיה אדני וּלְכָל ulchol יה אדני
עַמּוֹ amo יִשְׂרָאֵל Yisrael וְאִמְרוּ ve'imru אָמֵן amen: אָמֵן amen אידהנויה.

Take three steps backwards and say:

עוֹשֶׂה ose שָׁלוֹם shalom בִּמְרוֹמָיו bimromav ע"ב, ריבוע יהוה. הוּא hu
בְּרַחֲמָיו berachamav יַעֲשֶׂה ya'ase שָׁלוֹם shalom עָלֵינוּ alenu ר"ת ש"ע נהורין.
וְעַל ve'al כָּל kol ילי ; עמם עַמּוֹ amo יִשְׂרָאֵל Yisrael וְאִמְרוּ ve'imru אָמֵן amen:
אָמֵן amen אידהנויה.

ALENU

Alenu is a cosmic sealing agent. It cements and secures all of our prayers, protecting them from any negative forces such as the *klipot*. All prayers prior to *Alenu* drew down what the kabbalists call Inner Light. *Alenu*, however, attracts Surrounding Light, which envelops our prayers with a protective force-field to block out the *klipot*.

Drawing Surrounding Light in order to be protected from the *klipot* (negative side).

עָלֵינוּ alenu ריבוע דס"ג לְשַׁבֵּחַ leshabe'ach עלינו לשבח = אבג יתץ, ושר
לַאֲדוֹן la'adon אני ; ס"ת ס"ג ע"ה הַכֹּל hakol ר"ת ללה, אדני
לָתֵת latet גְּדֻלָּה gedula לְיוֹצֵר leyotzer בְּרֵאשִׁית bereshit ר"ת גלב (באך ב"י יג"ל)
שֶׁלֹּא shelo עָשָׂנוּ asanu כְּגוֹיֵי kegoyei הָאֲרָצוֹת ha'aratzot
וְלֹא velo שָׂמָנוּ samanu כְּמִשְׁפְּחוֹת kemishpechot הָאֲדָמָה ha'adama

---

May there be abundant peace from heaven, life, contentment, salvation, consolation, deliverance, healing, redemption, pardon, atonement, comfort, and relief. For us and for His entire nation, Israel, and you shall say, Amen. (Amen) *He, Who makes peace in His high places, with His compassion He shall make peace for us and for His entire nation, Israel. And you shall say, Amen.* (Amen)

ALENU

It is incumbent upon us to give praise to the Master of all and to attribute greatness to the Molder of Creation, for He did not make us like the nations of the lands. He did not place us like the families of the earth

vegoralenu וְגוֹרָלֵנוּ kahem כָּהֶם chelkenu וְחֶלְקֵנוּ sam שָׂם shelo שֶׁלֹּא
mishtachavim מִשְׁתַּחֲוִים shehem שֶׁהֵם .hamonam הֲמוֹנָם kechol כְּכָל
el אֶל el אֶל umitpalelim וּמִתְפַּלְּלִים varik וָרִיק lahevel לָהֶבֶל
(pause here, and when you say "*va'anchnu mishtachavim*" bow your entire body) .Yoshi'a יוֹשִׁיעַ lo לֹא
melech מֶלֶךְ lifnei לִפְנֵי mishtachavim מִשְׁתַּחֲוִים va'anachnu וַאֲנַחְנוּ
baruch בָּרוּךְ hakadosh הַקָּדוֹשׁ hamelachim הַמְּלָכִים malchei מַלְכֵי
י״פ אדני = ר״ת ; י״פ כוזו ,י״פ טל shamayim שָׁמַיִם note נוֹטֶה shehu שֶׁהוּא .hu הוּא
umoshav וּמוֹשַׁב .aretz אָרֶץ veyosed וְיוֹסֵד דו״א נוקבא של ספירות שבי׳
.עלם mima'al מִמַּעַל כוזו ,י״פ טל ,י״פ bashamayim בַּשָּׁמַיִם yekaro יְקָרוֹ
.meromim מְרוֹמִים begovhei בְּגָבְהֵי uzo עֻזּוֹ ush'chinat וּשְׁכִינַת
.acher אַחֵר od עוֹד ve'ein וְאֵין ילה eloheinu אֱלֹהֵינוּ hu הוּא
ve'efes וְאֶפֶס malkenu מַלְכֵּנוּ ס״ג ז״פ ,אהיה פעמים אהיה emet אֱמֶת
veyadata וְיָדַעְתָּ :batorah בַּתּוֹרָה kakatuv כַּכָּתוּב .zulato זוּלָתוֹ
el אֶל־ vahashevota וַהֲשֵׁבֹתָ יהוה אל ,זן ,מזבח ,נגד ע״ה hayom הַיּוֹם
hu הוּא Adonai יְהֹוָהאדניאהדונהי ki כִּי לאו ר״ת lvavecha לְבָבֶךָ
ע״ג ענו למנין עולה וכן יהה ר״ת ; ילה ; אדני אהיה haElohim הָאֱלֹהִים
; עלם mima'al מִמַּעַל כוזו ,י״פ טל ,י״פ bashamayim בַּשָּׁמַיִם
ע״ה דההין אלהים ha'aretz הָאָרֶץ ve'al וְעַל־ מלמעלה המתוזיל פנימי לאור רמז
:od עוֹד en אֵין מלמטה המתוזיל מקיף לאור רמז mitachat מִתָּחַת

He did not make our lot like theirs and our destiny like that of their multitudes, for they prostrate themselves to futility and emptiness and they pray to a deity that does not help. But we prostrate ourselves before the King of all Kings, the Holy Blessed One. It is He Who spreads the Heavens and establishes the earth. The Seat of His glory is in the Heaven above and the Divine Presence of His power is in the Highest of Heights. He is our God and there is no other. Our King is true and there is none beside Him. As it is written in the Torah: "And you shall know today and you shall take it to your heart that it is the Lord Who is God in the Heavens above and upon the Earth below, and there is none other". (Deuteronomy 4:39)

עַל al כֵּן ken נְקַוֶּה nekave לָּךְ lach יְהֹוָהאדניאהדונהי Adonai אֱלֹהֵינוּ Elohenu
ילה לִרְאוֹת lir'ot מְהֵרָה mehera בְּתִפְאֶרֶת betiferet עֻזָּךְ uzach ס"ת כהת, משיח
בן דוד ע"ה לְהַעֲבִיר leha'avir גִּלּוּלִים gilulim מִן min הָאָרֶץ ha'aretz אלהים דההין
ע"ה וְהָאֱלִילִים veha'elilim כָּרוֹת karot יִכָּרֵתוּן yikaretun. לְתַקֵּן letaken
עוֹלָם olam בְּמַלְכוּת bemalchut שַׁדַּי Shadai. וְכָל vechol ילי בְּנֵי benei
בָשָׂר vasar יִקְרְאוּ yikre'u בִשְׁמֶךָ vishmecha לְהַפְנוֹת lehafnot אֵלֶיךָ eleicha
כָּל kol ילי רִשְׁעֵי rish'ei אָרֶץ aretz. יַכִּירוּ yakiru וְיֵדְעוּ veyed'u כָּל kol ילי
יוֹשְׁבֵי yoshvei תֵבֵל tevel ב"פ רי"ו. כִּי ki לְךָ lecha תִּכְרַע tichra כָּל kol ילי
בֶּרֶךְ berech תִּשָּׁבַע tishava כָּל kol ילי לָשׁוֹן lashon. לְפָנֶיךָ lefanecha ס"ג מ"ה ב"ן
יְהֹוָהאדניאהדונהי Adonai אֱלֹהֵינוּ Elohenu ילה יִכְרְעוּ yichre'u וְיִפֹּלוּ veyipolu
וְלִכְבוֹד velichvod שִׁמְךָ shimcha יְקָר yekar יִתֵּנוּ yitenu. וִיקַבְּלוּ vikabelu
כֻלָּם chulam אֶת et עוֹל ol מַלְכוּתֶךָ malchutecha. וְתִמְלוֹךְ vetimloch
עֲלֵיהֶם alehem מְהֵרָה mehera לְעוֹלָם le'olam ריבוע ס"ג וי' אותיות דס"ג וָעֶד va'ed.
כִּי ki הַמַּלְכוּת hamalchut שֶׁלְּךָ shelcha הִיא hee. וּלְעוֹלְמֵי ul'olmei
עַד ad תִּמְלוֹךְ timloch בְּכָבוֹד bechavod בוכו. כַּכָּתוּב kakatuv
בְּתוֹרָתָךְ betoratach: יְהֹוָהאדניאהדונהי Adonai | יִמְלֹךְ yimloch לְעֹלָם le'olam
ריבוע ס"ג וי' אותיות דס"ג ; ר"ת ייל וָעֶד va'ed. וְנֶאֱמַר vene'emar: וְהָיָה vehaya יהוה ; יהה
יְהֹוָהאדניאהדונהי Adonai לְמֶלֶךְ lemelech עַל al כָּל kol ילי ; עמם
הָאָרֶץ ha'aretz אלהים דההין ע"ה בַּיּוֹם bayom ע"ה נגד, מזבח, זן, אל יהוה
הַהוּא hahu יִהְיֶה yih'ye ייי יְהֹוָהאדניאהדונהי Adonai אֶחָד echad אהבה, דאגה
וּשְׁמוֹ ushmo מהש ע"ה, ע"ב בריבוע וקס"א ע"ה, אל שדי ע"ה אֶחָד echad אהבה, דאגה:

Consequently, we place our hope in You, Lord, our God, that we shall speedily see the glory of Your might, when You remove the idols from the earth and the deities shall be completely destroyed to correct the world with the kingdom of the Almighty. And all mankind shall then call out Your Name and You shall turn back to Yourself all the wicked ones of the earth. Then all the inhabitants of the world shall recognize and know that, for You, every knee bends and every tongue vows. Before You, Lord, our God, they shall kneel and fall and shall give honor to Your glorious Name. And they shall all accept the yoke of Your Kingdom and You shall reign over them, forever and ever. Because the kingdom is Yours. and forever and for eternity, You shall reign gloriously. As it is written in the Torah: "The Lord shall reign forever and ever," (Exodus 15:18) and it is also stated: "The Lord shall be King over the whole world and, on that day, the Lord shall be One and His Name One." (Zechariah 14:9)

When the eve of Shavuot (second day) falls on a Friday we start here, otherwise we start on page 80.

KABBALAT SHABBAT

You should go out to the field and if it is not possible it is good to go outside to a courtyard to a place which is empty and clear. And you should stand in a high place and turn to the West. At the time of sunset, close your eyes and put your hands on your chest, right hand over the left and stand with awe and fear as you stand in front of the King to receive the Holiness of *Shabbat*.

You should meditate that *Chakal* חק"ל (field) which is the numerical value of 138 equals: הויה אהיה הויה אדני (יאהדונהי + יאההויהה). Also it has the same numerical value of the *Milui* of the four Names (וד י יו י + וד י או י + וד א או א + וד ה ו ה) with the ten letters. And also ס"ג (יוד הי ואו הי) with its ten letters and the Name אדני have the numerical value of 138.

Now in the field (*Sadeh* שדה) meditate that it is considered as the external part of the Four Worlds, and our goal, during *Kabbalat Shabbat* in the field, is to elevate this external part (the elevation is in the secret of the Internal Light of the external.)

You should visualize the Four Worlds in the following order, and meditate to elevate them as *Chochmah, Binah, Da'at* of the Lower World is going into *Netzach, Hod, Yesod* of the Upper World. And later (when saying the word "*havu*" in Psalm 29) meditate on the elevation of the three Upper Levels of *Asiya* into *Netzach, Hod, Yesod* of *Yetzirah*.

Atzilut יוד הי ויו הי

Beriah יוד הי ואו הי

Yetzirah יוד הא ואו הא

Asiyah יוד הה וו הה

Say the following with all your force and might and with happiness:

לְשֵׁם leshem יִחוּד yichud קוּדְשָׁא kudsha בְּרִיךְ berich הוּא hu
וּשְׁכִינְתֵּיהּ ush'chintei (יאהדונהי) בִּדְחִילוּ bid'chilu וּרְחִימוּ ur'chimu
(יאההויהה), וּרְחִימוּ ur'chimu וּדְחִילוּ ud'chilu (איההיוהה), לְיַחֲדָא leyachda
שֵׁם shem יו"ד yud קֵ"י kei בְּוָא"ו bevav קֵ"י kei בְּיִחוּדָא beyichuda
שְׁלִים shelim (יהוה) בְּשֵׁם beshem כָּל kol יכ"י יִשְׂרָאֵל Yisrael,
בּוֹאוּ bo'u וְנֵצֵא venetze לִקְרַאת likrat שַׁבָּת Shabbat מַלְכְּתָא malketa,
לַחֲקַל lachakal תַּפּוּחִין tapuchin קַדִּישִׁין kadishin.

KABBALAT SHABBAT
LESHEM YICHUD

For the sake of unification of the Holy Blessed One and His Shechinah with fear and love and with love and fear, in order to unify the Name Yud-Kei with Vav-Kei in perfect unity and in the name of all Israel, let us go out towards the Queen Shabbat, to the field of the holy apples.

MIZMOR LEDAVID

In this Psalm the word *Kol* קוֹל, which means voice, is used seven times.
The voice is the Voice of the Creator—*Kol Adonai.* These seven voices represent seven dimensions of the Light. These seven dimensions express themselves through the seven verses of the *Ana Beko'ach*, the 42-Letter Name of God. Whenever we make a connection to the 42-Letter Name of God, we are tapping the primordial force of Creation. This kind of energy brings new life, rejuvenation, and total positivity to our lives. This helps awaken us to receive the Light of Shabbat.

In this Psalm we also find the Name: יהוה eighteen times. Eighteen is the same numerical value as the Armaic word *Chai* חי meaning life. Accordingly, we have 72 letters (4x18). These equate to the numerical value of the Armaic word *Chesed* חסד. *Chesed* represents the energy of mercy. The reasoning behind this construction of the prayer is to give us the ability to surround ourselves with the energy of mercy that is now flowing into our world during *Shabbat.* Normally, at this time of day (sunset), the universe is filled with the energy of judgment. On Shabbat, however, we are connecting only to mercy, as Shabbat is a realm without judgment. But there is a prerequisite: We have to be careful not to stand in judgment of others during the period just before Shabbat. During this time, the Satan always tries to incite hostilities and arguments between husbands and wives, families and friends. If the Satan succeeds and we are judgmental, we cannot connect to the Light of mercy. We must put ourselves into a frame of total happiness.

In this Psalm there are 18 times יהוה that have 72 letters which is the numerical value of *Chesed*, for the mercy that descends from the Upper World. There are 11 verses which is the same numerical value as ו״ה and 91 words which is the numerical value for *Amen* אמן. Meditate that the three lower joints of the letter ל of *Tzelem* of *Abba* and *Ima* are entering *Zeir Anpin*.

מִזְמוֹר mizmor לְדָוִד leDavid

הָבוּ havu אח״ד, אהבה, דאגה

You should meditate to draw three times ב״ן from the Thirteen *Tikunei Dikna* of *Asiyah* to *Da'at* of *Asiyah* in order to elevate it to *Yesod* of *Yetzirah*.

לַיהֹוָהאדניאהדונהי ladonai בְּנֵי benei ר״ת הבל

You should meditate that your soul will be elevated with the soul of Abel during the night.

אֵלִים elim הבו יהוה בני אלים = יעקב

הָבוּ havu אח״ד, אהבה, דאגה

You should meditate to draw three times מ״ה from the Thirteen *Tikunei Dikna* of *Yetzirah* to *Binah* of *Asiyah* in order to elevate it to *Hod* of *Yetzirah*

לַיהֹוָהאדניאהדונהי la'donai כָּבוֹד kavod ר״ת כלה (ב״ן ג׳ ספירות) וָעֹז va'oz:

MIZMOR LEDAVID

A Psalm of David:
Render to the Lord, you sons of the powerful ones, render to the Lord honor and might.

הָבוּ havu אוזד, אהבה, דאגה

You should meditate to draw three times ס"ג from the Thirteen *Tikunei Dikna* of *Beriah* to *Chochmah* of *Asiyah* in order to elevate it to *Netzach* of *Yetzirah*. Also, three times הבו equal to יוד הא ואו (39), in which the last הא (*Nukva*) received from it.

לַיהֹוָה(אדני)אהדונהי ladonai כְּבוֹד kevod ר"ת כלה (ב"ן וג' ספירות) שְׁמוֹ shemo

ע"ב בריבוע וקס"א ע"ה, אל שדי ע"ה, מהש ע"ה ; הבו יהוה כבוד שמו = אדם דוד משיח

הִשְׁתַּחֲווּ hishtachavu

You should meditate to draw three times ע"ב from the Thirteen *Tikunei Dikna* of *Atzilut* to *Chochmah* of *Asiyah* in order for ס"ג to go to *Binah* and מ"ה and ב"ן will go to Da'at, as this is Their place in the secret of *Chasdim* and *Gevurot* as it is known.

לַיהֹוָה(אדני)אהדונהי ladonai בְּהַדְרַת־ behadrat ר"ת הבל

You should meditate that your soul will be elevated with the soul of Abel during the night.

קֹדֶשׁ kodesh ר"ת למפרע קבלה (שביום שבת צריך ללמוד קבלה):

Seven Voices – ז' קולות

קוֹל kol (*Chesed*) יְהֹוָה(אדני)אהדונהי Adonai (אבגיתץ – ו)

עַל־ al הַמָּיִם hamayim ר"ת = אלף למד (וחסד – ואל שני רמוז במילה בהמשך).

אֵל־ El י"א" (מילוי דס"ג) הַכָּבוֹד hakavod לאו הִרְעִים hir'im

ה"פ אדני (להמתיק שכ"ה דינים) יְהֹוָה(אדני)אהדונהי Adonai עַל־ al מַיִם mayim

רַבִּים rabim ר"ת הרעים (שכ"ה דינים – ושני השכ"ה דינים נמתקים ע"י שני שמות א"ל הרמוזים לעיל):

קוֹל־ kol (*Gevurah*) יְהֹוָה(אדני)אהדונהי Adonai (קרעשטן – ד)

בַּכֹּחַ bako'ach ר"ת יב"ק, אלהים יהוה, אהיה אדני יהוה

קוֹל kol (*Tiferet*) יְהֹוָה(אדני)אהדונהי Adonai (נגדיכש – א)

בֶּהָדָר behadar ר"ת יב"ק, אלהים יהוה, אהיה אדני יהוה:

Render to the Lord honor worthy of His Name, prostrate yourselves before the Lord in the glory of His Holiness. The voice of the Lord is upon the waters, The Lord of glory had thundered, the Lord is upon vast waters. The Voice of the Lord is powerful. The Voice of the Lord is majesty.

קוֹל kol (*Netzach*) יְהֹוָהאדנייאהדונהי Adonai (בטרצתג - א) שֹׁבֵר shover

אֲרָזִים arazim וַיְשַׁבֵּר vayeshaber יְהֹוָהאדנייאהדונהי Adonai אֶת־ et אַרְזֵי arzei

הַלְּבָנוֹן haLevanon ר"ת האא: וַיַּרְקִידֵם vayarkidem כְּמוֹ־ kemo עֵגֶל egel

לְבָנוֹן Levanon וְשִׂרְיוֹן veSiryon כְּמוֹ kemo בֶן־ ven רְאֵמִים re'emim:

קוֹל־ kol (*Hod*) יְהֹוָהאדנייאהדונהי Adonai (וְזִקְבְּטַנְעַ - ו) חֹצֵב chotzev

ס"ת הב"ל (כי עתה עולים בקדושה כל ניצוצות קין והבל שירדו בקליפות) לַהֲבוֹת lahavot אֵשׁ esh:

קוֹל kol (*Yesod*) יודהוואודניוואהדונהי Adonai (יוגלפזוקו - א)

יָחִיל yachil ס"ת ללה, אדני מִדְבָּר midbar יָחִיל yachil יְהֹוָהאדנייאהדונהי Adonai

מִדְבַּר midbar קָדֵשׁ kadesh ר"ת קין: קוֹל kol (*Malchut*) יְהֹוָהאדנייאהדונהי Adonai

(שְׁקוּצִית ויכוין לכלול בו כל שישה השמות האזורים - ודאאוא)

יְחוֹלֵל yecholel אַיָּלוֹת ayalot וַיֶּחֱשֹׂף vayechesof יְעָרוֹת ye'arot

וּבְהֵיכָלוֹ uvhechalo כֻּלּוֹ kulo אֹמֵר omer כָּבוֹד kavod:

יְהֹוָהאדנייאהדונהי Adonai לַמַּבּוּל lamabul יָשָׁב yashav ר"ת ילי וס"ת הבל

וַיֵּשֶׁב vayeshev יְהֹוָהאדנייאהדונהי Adonai מֶלֶךְ melech לְעוֹלָם le'olam

ריבוע ס"ג י' אותיות דס"ג: יְהֹוָהאדנייאהדונהי Adonai עֹז oz לְעַמּוֹ le'amo יִתֵּן yiten

יְהֹוָהאדנייאהדונהי Adonai יְבָרֵךְ yevarech עסמ"ב, הברכה (למתק את ז' המלכים שמתו)

אֶת־ et עַמּוֹ amo בַשָּׁלוֹם vashalom ר"ת ע"ב, ריבוע יהוה:

Meditate to raise *Chesed, Gevurah, Tiferet* to the place of *Chochmah, Binah, Da'at* and then to raise *Netzach, Hod, Yesod* to the place of *Chesed, Gevurah, Tiferet* and then to raise *Malchut* to the place of *Netzach, Hod, Yesod* by the seven voices (*kol*) and the seven יהוה.

The Voice of the Lord breaks cedars, the Lord breaks the cedars of Lebanon. He makes them dance around like a calf, Lebanon and Sirion like a wild young ox. The Voice of the Lord cleaves the flames of fire. The Voice of the Lord convulses the wilderness, the Lord convulses the wilderness of Kadesh. The Voice of the Lord frightens the hinds and strips the forests bare, and in His Temple all proclaim His glory. The Lord sat at the deluge, and the Lord sits as King forever. the Lord gives might to His people. The Lord will bless His people with peace. (Psalms 29)

ANA BEKO'ACH (See explanation and translation on pages 239-241)

Chesed, Sunday *(Alef Bet Gimel Yud Tav Tzadik)* אבג יתץ

•yeminecha יְמִינְךָ gedulat גְּדוּלַת •beko'ach בְּכֹחַ ana אָנָּא

:tzerura צְרוּרָה tatir תַּתִּיר

Gevurah, Monday *(Kuf Resh Ayin Sin Tet Nun)* קרע שטן

•sagevenu שַׂגְּבֵנוּ amecha עַמְּךָ •rinat רִנַּת kabel קַבֵּל

:nora נוֹרָא taharenu טַהֲרֵנוּ

Tiferet, Tuesday *(Nun Gimel Dalet Yud Kaf Shin)* נגד יכש

•yichudecha יִחוּדְךָ dorshei דוֹרְשֵׁי •gibor גִּבּוֹר na נָא

:shomrem שָׁמְרֵם kevavat כְּבָבַת

Netzach, Wednesday *(Bet Tet Resh Tzadik Tav Gimel)* בטר צתג

•tzidkatecha צִדְקָתְךָ rachamei רַחֲמֵי •taharem טַהֲרֵם barchem בָּרְכֵם

:gomlem גָּמְלֵם tamid תָּמִיד

Hod, Thursday *(Chet Kuf Bet Tet Nun Ayin)* חקב טנע

•tuvcha טוּבְךָ berov בְּרוֹב •kadosh קָדוֹשׁ chasin חֲסִין

:adatecha עֲדָתֶךָ nahel נַהֵל

Yesod, Friday *(Yud Gimel Lamed Pei Zayin Kuf)* יגל פזק

•pene פְּנֵה le'amecha לְעַמְּךָ •ge'e גֵּאֶה yachid יָחִיד

:kedushatecha קְדוּשָּׁתֶךָ zochrei זוֹכְרֵי

Malchut, Saturday *(Shin Kuf Vav Tzadik Yud Tav)* שקו צית

•tza'akatenu צַעֲקָתֵנוּ ushma וּשְׁמַע •kabel קַבֵּל shav'atenu שַׁוְעָתֵנוּ

:ta'alumot תַּעֲלוּמוֹת yode'a יוֹדֵעַ

BARUCH SHEM KEVOD

Whispering this final verse brings all the Light from the Upper Worlds into our physical existence.

malchuto מַלְכוּתוֹ kevod כְּבוֹד shem שֵׁם baruch בָּרוּךְ יוזו אותיות :(Whisper)

:va'ed וָעֶד ריבוע ס״ג וי׳ אותיות דס״ג le'olam לְעוֹלָם

LECHA DODI

This prayer was written by Kabbalist Rav Shlomo Elkabetz, and contains ten verses that connect us to the entire Ten *Sefirot*—the transmitters by which the Light of God animates our universe—including our souls. During the week, we encounter many challenges and opportunities that may disrupt and misalign these ten energy forces on both a personal and universal level. The level of disruption is based on our individual and collective actions. Consequently, the levels of energy in the world and in our soul can become disordered and in disarray. On a personal level this can manifest in overreacting and anger to situations to which we would normally respond with restraint and patience. Each of the ten verses in *Lecha Dodi* adjusts each level of the Ten *Sefirot*, rearranging them into their correct positions in the universe. It also realigns each *Sefira* within our body, putting us into proper emotional, physical, and spiritual balance.

The intention of *Lecha Dodi* is to elevate the ten *Sefirot* of *Yetzirah* to the Upper World (*Beriah*).

Keter

לְכָה lecha דּוֹדִי dodi לִקְרַאת likrat כַּלָּה kalah •

פְּנֵי penei חכמה בינה שַׁבָּת Shabbat נְקַבְּלָה nekabela :

Chochmah

שָׁמוֹר shamor וְזָכוֹר vezachor ע״ב קס״א, יהי אור ע״ה

(סוד המשכת השפע מן ד׳ שמות ליסוד הנקרא זכור) בְּדִבּוּר bedibur אֶחָד echad אהבה, דאגה •

הִשְׁמִיעָנוּ hishmi'anu אֵל El ייא״י (מילוי דס״ג) הַמְיֻחָד hameyuchad •

יְהֹוָאדהנויאהדונהי Adonai אֶחָד echad אהבה, דאגה וּשְׁמוֹ ushmo ע״ב בריבוע קס״א ע״ה,

אל שדי ע״ה, מהש ע״ה אֶחָד echad אהבה, דאגה • לְשֵׁם leshem

וּלְתִפְאֶרֶת ultiferet וְלִתְהִלָּה velit'hila ע״ה אמת, אהיה פעמים אהיה, ז״פ ס״ג : *Lecha*

Binah

לִקְרַאת likrat שַׁבָּת Shabbat לְכוּ lechu וְנֵלְכָה venelcha •

כִּי ki הִיא hee מְקוֹר mekor הַבְּרָכָה haberacha •

מֵרֹאשׁ merosh ריבוע אלהים אלהים דיודין ע״ה מִקֶּדֶם mikedem נְסוּכָה nesucha •

סוֹף sof מַעֲשֶׂה ma'ase בְּמַחֲשָׁבָה bemachashava תְּחִלָּה techila : *Lecha*

LECHA DODI

Keter *Go my beloved towards the bride, let us welcome the presence of the Shabbat!*

Chochmah *"Safeguard" and "remember" as one utterance. The unique God made us hear. God is One and His Name is One, for renown, for splendor and for praise.*

Binah *Come, let us go towards the Shabbat, for It is the source of blessing. From the beginning, from antiquity, It was honored. The end of deed was first in thought.*

Chesed

מִקְדַּשׁ mikdash מֶלֶךְ melech עִיר ir בוזרך, סנדלפון, ערי מְלוּכָה melucha.

קוּמִי kumi צְאִי tze'i מִתּוֹךְ mitoch הַהֲפֵכָה hahafecha.

רַב rav לָךְ lach שֶׁבֶת shevet בְּעֵמֶק be'emek הַבָּכָא habacha.

וְהוּא vehu יַחֲמוֹל yachmol עָלַיִךְ alayich חֶמְלָה chemla: *Lecha*

Gevurah

הִתְנַעֲרִי hitna'ari מֵעָפָר me'afar קוּמִי kumi. לִבְשִׁי livshi בִּגְדֵי bigdei

תִּפְאַרְתֵּךְ tifartech עַמִּי ami. עַל al יַד yad בֶּן ben יִשַׁי Yishai בֵּית bet

ב״פ ראה הַלַּחְמִי halachmi. קָרְבָה korva אֶל el נַפְשִׁי nafshi גְּאָלָהּ ge'ala: *Lecha*

Tiferet

הִתְעוֹרְרִי hit'oreri. הִתְעוֹרְרִי hit'oreri. כִּי ki בָא va אוֹרֵךְ orech קוּמִי kumi

אוֹרִי ori. עוּרִי uri עוּרִי uri שִׁיר shir דַּבֵּרִי daberi ראה. כְּבוֹד kevod

יְהֹוָהאדניאהדונהי Adonai ; כבוד יהוה = יוד הי ואו הה עָלַיִךְ alayich נִגְלָה nigla: *Lecha*

Netzach

לֹא lo תֵבוֹשִׁי tevoshi וְלֹא velo תִכָּלְמִי tikalmi.

מַה ma מ״ה תִּשְׁתּוֹחֲחִי tishtochachi וּמַה uma מ״ה תֶּהֱמִי tehemi.

בָּךְ bach יֶחֱסוּ yechesu עֲנִיֵּי aniyei ריבוע מ״ה עַמִּי ami.

וְנִבְנְתָה venivneta עִיר ir בוזרך, סנדלפון, ערי עַל al תִּלָּהּ tila: *Lecha*

Chesed *Sanctuary of the King! royal city! Arise and depart from amidst the upheaval. For too long you have dwelt in the valley of weeping. He will bestow His compassion upon you.*

Gevurah *Shake off the dust, arise. Don your clothes of splendor, my people. Through the son of Ishai, from Bet Lechem, will the redemption draw close to my soul.*

Tiferet *Wake up! Wake up! For your Light has come, rise and shine. Awaken, awaken, and utter a song. The glory of God is revealed upon you.*

Netzach *Feel no shame, do not be humiliated. Why are you downcast? Why are you disconsolate? In you will My people's afflicted find shelter, as the city is built upon its hilltop.*

Hod

וְהָיוּ vehayu לִמְשִׁסָּה limshisa שֹׁאסָיִךְ shosayich ♦ וְרָחֲקוּ verachaku כָּל kol ילי
מְבַלְּעָיִךְ meval'ayich ♦ יָשִׂישׂ yasis עָלַיִךְ alayich אֱלֹהָיִךְ Elohayich ילה ♦
כִּמְשׂוֹשׂ kimsos חָתָן chatan עַל al כַּלָּה kalah ♦: *Lecha*

Yesod

יָמִין yamin וּשְׂמֹאל usmol תִּפְרוֹצִי tifrotzi ♦ וְאֶת ve'et
יְהֹוָהאדניאהדונהי Adonai תַּעֲרִיצִי ta'aritzi ♦ עַל al יַד yad
אִישׁ ish בֶּן ben פַּרְצִי Partzi ♦ וְנִשְׂמְחָה venismecha וְנָגִילָה venagila ♦: *Lecha*

Malchut

בּוֹאִי bo'i בְשָׁלוֹם veshalom עֲטֶרֶת ateret בַּעְלָהּ ba'la ♦
גַּם gam בְּשִׂמְחָה besimcha בְּרִנָּה berina וּבְצָהֳלָה uv'tzahola ♦
תּוֹךְ toch אֱמוּנֵי emunei עַם am סְגֻלָּה segula ♦:

BO'I KALAH

When we utter the words *Bo'i Kalah*, which means "draw near bride," we receive an extra soul that comes to us every *Shabbat* to help us capture the extra energy that is being revealed. For example, an 8-ounce glass cannot contain ten ounces of water. The glass would need to be enlarged. When we receive the extra soul, this enlarges our soul, thereby, increasing its overall capacity to receive the additional Light of Shabbat. This is a golden opportunity to join our souls through the Light of *Shabbat*, with the Light of the Creator.

We learn from this verse, that to maximize our connection, we are supposed to treat the energy of *Shabbat* like a bride. After a man has been married for twenty years, he usually does not have the same feeling, passion, longing, and anticipation that he first had when his wife was still a bride, just a few brief moments before their wedding ceremony.

Hod *May your oppressors be downtrodden, and may those who devoured you be driven far away. Your God will rejoice over you as a groom rejoices over a bride.*

Yesod *To the right and to the left you shall spread, and you shall extol God through a man, a descendant of Perets. Then we shall be joyful and mirthful.*

Malchut *Come in peace, crown of her husband. Even in joy, in song, and in cheer. Among the faithful of the treasured nation.*

You should meditate to elevate the World of *Yetzirah* (which means: *Malchut* is elevated to *Netzach, Hod, Yesod*, then *Netzach, Hod, Yesod* are elevated to *Chesed, Gevurah, Tiferet*, then *Chesed, Gevurah, Tiferet* are elevated to *Chochmah, Binah, Da'at*, and then *Chochmah, Binah, Da'at,* are elevated to *Netzach, Hod, Yesod* of *Beriah.*) Indeed, the seven lower *Sefirot* of *Yetzirah* are elevated by the seven *Margela'in* and the Holy Names: **אהי"ה יה"ו**, which equal 42:

א יְהֹוָה, ה אל, י יֱהֹוִה, ה אלהים, י יה אדני, ה מצפצ, ו מצפצ

And the Three Upper *Sefirot* are elevated by the three times word *Bo'i* which is equal 13, like the words for love, unity and care (**אחד, אהבה, דאגה**), and also equals **יאאא** (13).

Bow to the Right
Chochmah - Speach

בּוֹאִי bo'i ג"פ באי = יוד הא ואו **כַּלָּה** kalah
בואי כלה = אכדטם (כי על ידי זה נמתקו הדינים)

Bow to the Left
Binah - Action

בּוֹאִי bo'i ג"פ באי = יוד הא ואו **כַּלָּה** kalah
בואי כלה = אכדטם (כי על ידי זה נמתקו הדינים)

תּוֹךְ toch **אֱמוּנֵי** emunei **עַם** am **סְגֻלָּה** segula:

Meditate to receive the extra soul called: *Nefesh*
from the aspect of the night of *Shabbat*

The third "*bo'i kalah*" should be said silently, as it corresponds to *Da'at* (and *Da'at* is not part of the Ten *Sefirot*).

Bow to the Center
Da'at - Thought

בּוֹאִי bo'i ג"פ באי = יוד הא ואו **כַּלָּה** kalah
ג"פ באי כלה = צדיק ; בואי כלה = אכדטם (כי על ידי זה נמתקו הדינים)

שַׁבָּת Shabbat **מַלְכְּתָא** malketa:
לְכָה lecha **דוֹדִי** dodi **לִקְרַאת** likrat **כַּלָּה** kalah.
פְּנֵי penei חכמה בינה **שַׁבָּת** Shabbat **נְקַבְּלָה** nekabela:

MIZMOR SHIR LEYOM HASHABBAT

The initials are of: *LeMoshe* (for Moses) connects us to quantum consciousness.

After we sing the *Lecha Dodi*, we recite two paragraphs that were recited by Adam during the first *Shabbat* in the Garden of Eden. Adam signifies all the souls of humanity. At the time of Creation, all these souls that were and ever will be were unified as one entity, we call Adam. The Garden of Eden is a realm of pure Light and immortality. The Aramaic letters that compose this paragraph represent specific energy forces that nourish and fulfill this unified soul called Adam. The letters are a formula that acts as an antenna to draw these forces into our lives, thereby giving us a taste of the Garden of Eden.

(We bow to the Right) *Come, bride,* (We bow to the Left) *Come bride.*
(We bow to the Center) *Among the faithful of the treasured nation, Come bride! Queen Shabbat!*
Go my beloved towards the bride; let us welcome the presence of the Shabbat!

מִזְמוֹר mizmor שִׁיר shir לְיוֹם leyom ע"ה נגד, מזבח, זן, אל יהוה הַשַּׁבָּת haShabbat

Initials of *LeMoshe* (למשה) –*Moshe* is a code name for the world of *Atzilut*, which is where we are now elevating *Beriah*, which gets illuminated from *Netzach, Hod, Yesod* of *Atzilut*. Also it is called *Moshe*, because now *Moshe* receives 1,000 illuminations (those he had lost because of the golden calf) and then gives us back what we lost. Also, *Moshe* with tens of thousands of righteous souls are descending in order to elevate all the Holy Sparks and the souls that are in the depths of the *klipa* and all the souls of the living and dead that cannot elevate on their own.

טוֹב tov והו לְהֹדוֹת lehodot ר"ת ט"ל (ג"פ באי וג"פ הבו דלעיל)

(טל = יוד הא ואו, שהם ג"ר (וזב"ד) דבריאה שיעלו כעת לאצילות)

Meditate to elevate the Three Upper *Sefirot* of *Beriah* to *Atzilut*

לַיהֹוָ(אדני)אהדונהי ladonai

Meditate on the Holy Name: יוד הי ויו הי which is *Malchut* of *Atzilut*.
Also meditate on the 42-Letter Name of *Mem Hei* of *Atzilut*:
יהוה, יוד הא ואו הא, יוד ואו דלת הא אלף ואו אלף ואו הא אלף
with this Name, the Seven Lower *Sefirot* of *Beriah* are going to be elevated to *Atzilut*.
Also meditate on the Holy Name: יוד הי ואו הי which is the secret of the world of *Beriah*
(which is now elevated to *Atzilut* by the 42-Letter Name mentioned above).

וּלְזַמֵּר ulzamer לְשִׁמְךָ leshimcha עֶלְיוֹן elyon: לְהַגִּיד lehagid בַּבֹּקֶר baboker

חַסְדֶּךָ chasdecha וֶאֱמוּנָתְךָ ve'emunat'cha בַּלֵּילוֹת balelot: עֲלֵי־ alei

עֲשׂוֹר asor וַעֲלֵי־ va'alei נָבֶל navel עֲלֵי alei הִגָּיוֹן higayon בְּכִנּוֹר bechinor:

כִּי ki שִׂמַּחְתַּנִי simachtani יְהֹוָ(אדני)אהדונהי Adonai בְּפָעֳלֶךָ befa'olecha

בְּמַעֲשֵׂי bema'asei יָדֶיךָ yadecha אֲרַנֵּן aranen: מַה־ ma מ"ה גָּדְלוּ gadlu

מַעֲשֶׂיךָ ma'asecha יְהֹוָ(אדני)אהדונהי Adonai מְאֹד me'od עָמְקוּ amku

מַחְשְׁב(וֹ)תֶיךָ machshevotecha (Superiour *Keter*) יהו: אִישׁ ish בַּעַר ba'ar

לֹא lo יֵדָע yeda וּכְסִיל uchsil לֹא־ lo יָבִין yavin אֶת־ et זֹאת zot:

בִּפְרֹחַ bifro'ach רְשָׁעִים resha'im כְּמוֹ kemo עֵשֶׂב esev כוונות הקדושה (ע"ב שמות)

The souls of the wicked are judged now to see if they are worthy of being elevated from *Gehenom*.

MIZMOR SHIR LEYOM HASHABBAT

"A Psalm, a song for the day of Shabbat!
It is good to say thanks to You, the Lord, and to sing Your Name, Exalted One, And to relate Your kindness in the morning and Your faithfulness in the evenings, upon a ten-stringed instrument and lyre, with singing accompanied by a harp. Because You have made me happy, Lord, with Your deeds, for the work of Your hands, I shall sing joyously. How great are Your deeds, Lord, and how greatly profound are Your thoughts. A boor cannot know nor can a fool understand this. When the wicked bloom like grass

וַיָּצִיצוּ vayatzitzu כָּל־ kol ילי פֹּעֲלֵי po'alei אָוֶן aven
(the *klipa* that wants to be elevated with the Holiness) לְהִשָּׁמְדָם lehishamdam
עֲדֵי־ adei עַד ad (but it is not allowed to go up): וְאַתָּה veAta מָרוֹם marom
לְעֹלָם le'olam ריבוע דס"ג י' אותיות דס"ג יְהֹוָהאדניאהדונהי Adonai: כִּי ki הִנֵּה hine
אֹיְבֶיךָ oyvecha יְהֹוָהאדניאהדונהי Adonai כִּי־ ki הִנֵּה hine אֹיְבֶיךָ oyvecha
יֹאבֵדוּ yovedu יִתְפָּרְדוּ yitpardu כָּל־ kol ילי פֹּעֲלֵי po'alei אָוֶן aven (the *klipa*):
וַתָּרֶם vatarem (the Holiness) כִּרְאֵים kir'em קַרְנִי karni בַּלֹּתִי baloti
בְּשֶׁמֶן beshemen רַעֲנָן ra'anan: וַתַּבֵּט vatabet עֵינִי eni ריבוע דמ"ה
בְּשׁוּרָי beshurai בַּקָּמִים bakamim עָלַי alai מְרֵעִים mere'im
תִּשְׁמַעְנָה tishmana אָזְנָי oznai יוד הי ואו הה: The souls of the righteous that are elevated now
צַדִּיק tzadik ג"פ באי כלה דלע"ל כַּתָּמָר katamar יִפְרָח yifrach ס"ת קרח
(meditate to elevate the soul of *Korach*) כְּאֶרֶז ke'erez בַּלְּבָנוֹן baLevanon יִשְׂגֶּה yisge:
שְׁתוּלִים shetulim בְּבֵית bevet ב"פ ראה יְהֹוָהאדניאהדונהי Adonai
בְּחַצְרוֹת bechatzrot אֱלֹהֵינוּ Elohenu ילה יַפְרִיחוּ yafrichu: עוֹד od
יְנוּבוּן yenuvun בְּשֵׂיבָה beseva דְּשֵׁנִים deshenim וְרַעֲנַנִּים vera'ananim
יִהְיוּ yih'yu אל (ייא" מילוי דס"ג): לְהַגִּיד lehagid כִּי־ ki יָשָׁר yashar
יְהֹוָהאדניאהדונהי Adonai צוּרִי tzuri וְלֹא־ velo עַוְלָתָה avlata (כתיב: עלתה) בּוֹ bo:

ADONAI MALACH

In this Psalm we have 45 words corresponding to the Holy Name: (מ"ה (יוד הא ואו הא

יְהֹוָהאדניאהדונהי Adonai (*Zeir Anpin*) מָלָךְ malach גֵּאוּת ge'ut
(410 cords of *Arich Anpin* - where *Zeir Anpin* is elevated on *Shabbat* and He is clothing them)
לָבֵשׁ lavesh לָבֵשׁ lavesh יְהֹוָהאדניאהדונהי Adonai עֹז oz הִתְאַזָּר hit'azar

---

and all doers of iniquity blossom in order to destroy them forever. And You are exalted forever, Lord. For behold, Your enemies, Lord! Your enemies shall perish and all the doers of iniquity shall be dispersed And You shall lift up my worth like an ox and I will be drenched with fresh oil. And my eyes will see my foes and my ears will hear those who rise up to harm me. A righteous man will flourish like a palm leaf, like a cedar in Lebanon he will grow tall. They are planted in the House of the Lord, they shall flourish in the courtyards of our God. They will still be fruitful in old age, vigorous and fresh they shall be to declare that the Lord is just, my Rock in whom there is no wrong." (Psalms 92)

ADONAI MALACH

"The Lord has reigned. He clothed Himself with pride. The Lord clothed and girded Himself with might.

אַף־ af ר"ת = אלהים, אהיה אדני תִּכּוֹן tikon תֵּבֵל tevel ב"פ רי"ו

בַּל־ bal תִּמּוֹט timot: נָכוֹן nachon כִּסְאֲךָ kis'acha מֵאָז me'az ומב

מֵעוֹלָם me'olam אַתָּה Ata ר"ת = קנ"א, אדני אלהים: נָשְׂאוּ nas'u נְהָרוֹת neharot

(410 cords of *Arich Anpin*
that draw Light from the sea of *Chochmah* -מוזא סתימא דא"א- on *Shabbat* to *Zeir Anpin*).

יְהֹוָהאדניאהדונהי Adonai

נָשְׂאוּ nas'u ר"ת = קין נְהָרוֹת neharot קוֹלָם kolam יִשְׂאוּ yis'u

(Backwards, initials of the name *Cain*, as when *Beriah* is elevated his sparks are being corrected)

נְהָרוֹת neharot דָּכְיָם dochyam ר"ת דני:

Meditate that we are now in the World of *Atzilut* – and with the 42-Letter Name (the seven voices) that comes from *Abba* and *Ima*, we are elevating to the World of *Beriah*.

מִקֹּלוֹת mikolot (410 cords) מַיִם mayim רַבִּים rabim ר"ת = מוזזך, סנדלפון, ערי

(*Ima* – לעשות בה מ"ן שהם ה"ג) אַדִּירִים adirim הרי מִשְׁבְּרֵי־ mishberei יָם yam ילי

Arich Anpin [has 221 *Ribo* (tens of thousands) illuminations],
He is giving 150 *Ribo* (tens of thousands) illuminations to *Zeir Anpin*.
Initials of אמי (my mother) because, *Zeir Anpin* first goes up and takes *Mochin* from *Ima* (mother).

אַדִּיר adir הרי בַּמָּרוֹם bamarom יְהֹוָהאדניאהדונהי Adonai

Initials of אבי (my father) because, *Zeir Anpin* later goes up and takes *Mochin* from *Abba* (father).

עֵדֹתֶיךָ edotecha נֶאֶמְנוּ ne'emnu מְאֹד me'od ר"ת = קין לְבֵיתְךָ levetcha

ב"פ ראה נַאֲוָה na'ava קֹדֶשׁ kodesh יְהֹוָהאדניאהדונהי Adonai לְאֹרֶךְ le'orech

יָמִים yamim נלך ; ר"ת ילי ; ס"ת אדני ; ה' לאורך ימים = שע' נהורים עם האותיות:

Meditate on the Name ילי to elevate the Name: אדני and the sparks of the souls of *Beriah* that are captured by the *klipa* and cannot elevate by the above mentioned 42-Letter Name. Then meditate on the Name: יֻוּדֻ הֵיֻ וֻיֻוֻ הֵיֻ, which is the *Atzilut* (where everything is being elevated).

He also established the world firmly, so that it would not collapse. Your Throne has been established. Ever since then, You have been forever. The rivers have lifted, Lord, the rivers have raised their voices. The rivers shall raise their powerful waves. More than the roars of many waters, and the powerful waves of the sea, You are immense in the high places, The Lord. Your testimonies are extremely trustworthy. Your House is the holy Sanctuary. The Lord shall be for the length of days." (*Psalms 93*)

BAR YOCHAI

Kabbalists throughout history agree that a human being cannot overcome the force of negativity alone, without the teachings and knowledge of the *Zohar* and the technology of *Kabbalah.* Why is it that when we know that something is bad for us, we still engage in it? Why is it that when we know something is good for us, we abstain or procrastinate? Why do we forego positive actions in favor of negative ones nine times out of ten? The reason, according to Kabbalah, is that we constantly battle an opponent in the Game of Life. This opponent is called Satan. It ignites all of our reactive negative thoughts and actions. For 5,000 years, it has been beating us at this game that hovers on the narrow edge of life and death, pain and suffering, good and evil. The kabbalistic insight as to why our opponent has been so successful is that Satan convinces humankind that Satan does not even exist. Through the Light of the *Zohar,* Satan is exposed and once we know who the opponent really is, we have a chance of beating it. The *Zohar* not only exposes and identifies the real enemy, it also gives us the power to overtake and defeat him.

It is incumbent upon us to connect to the seed and origin of the *Zohar* itself—its author, *Rav Shimon bar Yochai.* And so each *Shabbat* we sing the song of *Bar Yochai* to make this vital connection.

בַּר Bar יוֹחָאי Yochai נִמְשַׁחְתָּ nimshachta אַשְׁרֶיךָ ashrecha

שֶׁמֶן shemen שָׂשׂוֹן sason מֵחֲבֵרֶיךָ mechaverecha:

Malchut

בַּר Bar יוֹחָאי Yochai שֶׁמֶן shemen מִשְׁחַת mishchat קֹדֶשׁ kodesh,

נִמְשַׁחְתָּ nimshachta מִמִּדַּת mimidat הַקֹּדֶשׁ hakodesh

נָשָׂאתָ nasata צִיץ tzitz מנק נֵזֶר nezer הַקֹּדֶשׁ hakodesh,

חָבוּשׁ chavush עַל al רֹאשְׁךָ roshcha פְּאֵרֶךָ pe'erecha: ***Bar Yochai***

Yesod

בַּר Bar יוֹחָאי Yochai מוֹשַׁב moshav טוֹב tov והו יָשַׁבְתָּ yashavta,

יוֹם yom ע"ה נגד, מזבח, זן, אל יהוה נַסְתָּ nasta

יוֹם yom ע"ה נגד, מזבח, זן, אל יהוה אֲשֶׁר asher בָּרַחְתָּ barachta

בִּמְעָרַת bim'arat צוּרִים tzurim שֶׁעָמַדְתָּ she'amadeta שָׁם sham

קָנִיתָ kanita הוֹדְךָ hodcha וַהֲדָרֶךָ vahadarecha: ***Bar Yochai***

BAR YOCHAI

Bar Yochai, you are anointed and praises, drawing the oil of happiness from your friends.

Malchut *Bar Yochai holy oil anointed you from the holy tribute.*
You carried the tiara of the holy crown, on you head for beauty.

Yesod *Bar Yochai, you sat in good place, the day you run and escaped.*
In the cave of rock you stood, to obtain your majesty and glory.

Netzach Hod

בַּר Bar יוֹחָאי Yochai עֲצֵי atzei שִׁטִּים shitim עוֹמְדִים omdim,
לִמּוּדֵי limudei יְהֹוָהאדהּאהדונהי Adonai הֵם hem לוֹמְדִים lomdim. אוֹר or רז, א"ס
מֻפְלָא mufla אוֹר or רז, א"ס הַיְקוֹד hayekod הֵם hem יוֹקְדִים yokdim,
הֲלֹא halo הֵמָּה hema יוֹרוּךְ yorucha מוֹרֶךָ morecha: ***Bar Yochai***

Tiferet

בַּר Bar יוֹחָאי Yochai וְלִשְׂדֵה velisde תַּפּוּחִים tapuchim,
עָלִיתָ alita לִלְקוֹט lilkot בּוֹ vo מֶרְקָחִים merkachim.
סוֹד sod מיכ, י"פ האא תּוֹרָה torah כְּצִיצִים ketzitzim וּפְרָחִים ufrachim,
נַעֲשֶׂה na'ase אָדָם adam נֶאֱמַר ne'emar בַּעֲבוּרֶךָ ba'avurecha: ***Bar Yochai***

Gevurah

בַּר bar יוֹחָאי yochai נֶאֱזַרְתָּ ne'ezarta בִּגְבוּרָה bigvura רי"ו
וּבְמִלְחֶמֶת uvmilchemet אֵשׁ esh דָּת dat הַשְּׂעָרָה hasha'ra.
וְחֶרֶב vecherev רי"ו הוֹצֵאתָ hotzeta מִתַּעְרָהּ mita'ra,
שָׁלַפְתָּ shalafta נֶגֶד neged מזבח, זן, אל יהוה צוֹרְרֶיךָ tzorerecha: ***Bar Yochai***

Chesed

בַּר bar יוֹחָאי yochai לִמְקוֹם limkom אַבְנֵי avnei שַׁיִשׁ shayish,
הִגַּעְתָּ higata לִפְנֵי lifnei וחכמה בינה אַרְיֵה arye לַיִשׁ layish.
גַּם gam גֻּלַּת gulat כּוֹתֶרֶת koteret עַל al עַיִשׁ ayish,
תָּשׁוּרִי tashuri וּמִי umi ילי יְשׁוּרֶךָ yeshurecha: ***Bar Yochai***

Netzach Hod *Bar Yochai, the acacia wood stands for you to study God's teachings. A wonderful, shining light is a glow, as your teachers taught you.*

Tiferet *Bar Yochai, you came to a field of apples to gather potions. The secret of Torah is like buds and blossoms; "Let us create man" was stated with you in mind.*

Gevura *Bar Yochai, you take courage with vigor, and fight with fire. You drew a sword out of its sheath against your opponent.*

Chesed *Bar Yochai, to the place of marble stones, you arrived with lion's face. We will see even the headstone of lions, but who will see you?*

Binah

בַּר Bar יוֹחָאי Yochai בְּקֹדֶשׁ bekodesh הַקֳּדָשִׁים hakodashim,
קַו kav יָרוֹק yarok מְחַדֵּשׁ mechadesh י"ב הויות, קס"א קנ"א חֳדָשִׁים chodashim.
שֶׁבַע sheva שַׁבָּתוֹת shabatot סוֹד sod מ"כ, י"פ האא חֲמִשִּׁים chamishim,
קָשַׁרְתָּ kasharta קִשְׁרֵי kishrei שִׁי"ן shin קְשָׁרֶיךָ kesharecha: *Bar Yochai*

Chochmah

בַּר Bar יוֹחָאי Yochai יוּ"ד yod חָכְמָה chochmah במילוי = תרי"ג (מצוות)
קְדוּמָה keduma, הִשְׁקַפְתָּ hishkafta לִכְבוֹדוֹ lichvodo פְּנִימָה penima.
ל"ב lev נְתִיבוֹת netivot רֵאשִׁית reshit תְּרוּמָה teruma,
אַתְּ at כְּרוּב keruv מִמְשַׁח mimshach זִיו ziv אוֹרֶךָ orecha: *Bar Yochai*

Keter

בַּר bar יוֹחָאי yochai אוֹר or רז, א"ס מֻפְלָא mufla רוּם rom מַעְלָה ma'la,
יָרֵאתָ yareta מִלְּהַבִּיט milhabit כִּי ki רַב rav לָהּ la,
תַּעֲלוּמָה ta'aluma וְאַיִן ve'ayin קוֹרֵא kore לָהּ la,
נַמְתָּ namta עַיִן ayin ריבוע דמ"ה לֹא lo תְשׁוּרֶךָ teshurecha: *Bar Yochai*

בַּר Bar יוֹחָאי Yochai אַשְׁרֵי ashrei יוֹלַדְתֶּךָ yoladetecha,
אַשְׁרֵי ashrei הָעָם ha'am הֵם hem לוֹמְדֶךָ lomdecha.
וְאַשְׁרֵי ve'ashrei הָעוֹמְדִים ha'omdim עַל al סוֹדֶךָ sodecha מ"כ, י"פ האא
לְבוּשֵׁי levushci חֹשֶׁן choshen תֻּמֶּיךָ tumeicha וְאוּרֶךָ ve'urecha: *Bar Yochai*

בַּר bar יוֹחָאי yochai נִמְשַׁחְתָּ nimshachta אַשְׁרֶיךָ ashrecha,
שֶׁמֶן shemen שָׂשׂוֹן sason מֵחֲבֵרֶיךָ mechavereicha:

Binah *Bar Yochai, in the Holy of Holies, a green line renews the months. Seven Shabbats are the secret of fifty, the letter Shins for your own connections.*

Chochmah *Bar Yochai, the ancient Yud of Chochmah, you observed its inner honor. 32 paths are the beginning of offering; you are the Cherub from which brilliant light anoints.*

Keter *Bar Yochai, a wonderful light of highest greatness, you feared looking to her greatness. A mystery no one can read, you sleep, and no eye can see you.*

Bar Yochai, praised be those who gave birth to you, praised be the people who study your writings. And praised be the people who can understand your secret, dress with armor of your breastplate and of your Urim VeTumim. Bar Yochai, you are anointed and praises, drawing the oil of happiness from your friends.

KEGAVNA

Kegavna is a passage from the *Zohar* that the sages tell us to read after the song of *Bar Yochai*, because it reveals a secret of *Shabbat*. It helps remove us from this physical world, acting as a rocket booster and escape the "gravitational pull" of our planet.

כְּגַוְנָא kegavna דְּאִנּוּן de'inun מִתְיַחֲדִין mityachadin לְעֵילָּא le'ela
בְּאֶחָד be'echad אהבה, דאגה, אוּף of הָכִי hachi אִיהִי ihi אִתְיַחֲדַת ityachadat
לְתַתָּא letata בְּרָזָא beraza רז, א"ס דְּאֶחָד de'echad אהבה, דאגה, לְמֶהֱוֵי lemehevei
עִמְּהוֹן imehon לְעֵילָּא le'ela וְחַד chad לְקָבֵל lakavel וְחַד chad,
קוּדְשָׁא kudsha בְּרִיךְ berich הוּא hu אֶחָד echad אהבה, דאגה
לְעֵילָּא le'ela לָא la יָתִיב yativ עַל al כּוּרְסַיָּא kursaya דִּיקָרֵיהּ dikarei,
עַד ad דְּאִיהִי de'ihi אִתְעֲבִידַת it'avidat בְּרָזָא beraza רז, א"ס
דְּאֶחָד de'echad אהבה, דאגה כְּגַוְנָא kegavna דִּילֵיהּ dilei, לְמֶהֱוֵי lemehevei
אֶחָד echad אהבה, דאגה בְּאֶחָד be'echad אהבה, דאגה וְהָא veha אוּקִימְנָא ukimna
רָזָא raza רז, א"ס דַּיהֹוָהאדניאהדונהי dadonai אֶחָד echad אהבה, דאגה
וּשְׁמוֹ ushmo מהש ע"ה, ע"ב בריבוע קס"א ע"ה, אל שדי ע"ה אֶחָד echad אהבה, דאגה:
רָזָא raza רז, א"ס דְּשַׁבָּת deShabbat, אִיהִי ihi שַׁבָּת Shabbat,
דְּאִתְאַחֲדָא de'itachada בְּרָזָא beraza רז, א"ס דְּאֶחָד de'echad אהבה, דאגה
לְמִשְׁרֵי lemishrei עֲלָהּ ala רָזָא raza רז, א"ס דְּאֶחָד de'echad אהבה, דאגה
צְלוֹתָא tzelota דְּמַעֲלֵי dema'alei שַׁבַּתָּא shabeta, דְּהָא deha
אִתְאַחֲדַת itachadat כּוּרְסַיָּא kursaya יַקִּירָא yakira קַדִּישָׁא kadisha,
בְּרָזָא veraza רז, א"ס דְּאֶחָד de'echad אהבה, דאגה וְאִתְתַּקְּנַת ve'itetakanat
לְמִשְׁרֵי lemishrei עֲלָהּ ala מַלְכָּא malka קַדִּישָׁא kadisha עִלָּאָה ila'a.

KEGAVNA

She may join them above as one paralleling one. The Holy Blessed One is One above Who does not sit on the throne of glory until She also becomes as the secret of the one like Him so that She may be one within one. And we have established the secret of: The Lord is One and His Name is One. The secret of the Shabbat: She is called Shabbat when She is united in the secret of the one, so that He, being the secret of the one, may rest upon Her. This is the prayer of the evening of Shabbat, because then the holy Throne of Glory is unified in the secret of the one and is made prepared so that the supreme holy King may rest upon It.

כַּד kad עַיִּל ayil שַׁבַּתָּא shabeta, אִיהִי ihi אִתְיַיחֲדַת ityachadat
וְאִתְפַּרְשַׁת ve'itparshat מִסִּטְרָא misitra אָחֳרָא achara,
וְכָל vechol ילי דִּינִין dinin מִתְעַבְּרִין mit'aberin מִנָּהּ mina,
וְאִיהִי ve'ihi אִשְׁתְּאָרַת ishte'arat בְּיִחוּדָא beyichuda דִּנְהִירוּ dinhiru
קַדִּישָׁא kadisha, וְאִתְעַטְּרַת ve'itatrat בְּכַמָּה bechama עִטְרִין itrin
לְגַבֵּי legabei מַלְכָּא malka קַדִּישָׁא kadisha, וְכָל vechol ילי שׁוּלְטָנֵי shultanei
רוּגְזִין rugzin וּמָארֵי umarei דְּדִינָא dedina כֻּלְּהוּ kulhu עַרְקִין arkin,
וְלֵית velet שׁוּלְטָנָא shultana אָחֳרָא achara בְּכֻלְּהוּ bechulhu עָלְמִין almin.
וְאַנְפָּהָא ve'anpaha נְהִירִין nehirin בִּנְהִירוּ binhiru עִלָּאָה ila'a,
וְאִתְעַטְּרַת veitatrat לְתַתָּא letata בְּעַמָּא be'ama קַדִּישָׁא kadisha,
וְכֻלְּהוּ vechulhu מִתְעַטְּרִין mit'atrin בְּנִשְׁמָתִין benishmatin חַדְתִּין chadetin.
כְּדֵין keden שֵׁירוּתָא sheruta דִּצְלוֹתָא ditzlota, לְבָרְכָא levarcha
לָהּ la בְּחֶדְוָה bechedva, בִּנְהִירוּ binhiru דְּאַנְפִּין de'anpin.

Shabbat Candles connection

Look at the candles and meditate:

Abba* and *Ima

For the first candle:

The three *Yichudim* of *Abba* and *Ima* that add up to 250 which is the numerical value of *Ner* (candle).

יאהדויהה
יאהלוההים
יאהדונהי

Zeir* and *Nukva

For the second candle:

The three *Yichudim* of *Zeir* and *Nukva* that add up to 250 which is the numerical value of *Ner* (candle).

יאהדויהה
יאהלוההים
יאהדונהי

As they unite above to the One, so does She unite below in the secret of the One, so that When the Shabbat arrives, She unifies and divests herself of the other side and all the judgments are removed from Her and She remains in the oneness of the holy Light, and She crowns Herself with many crowns for the holy King. And all the wrathful dominions and the bearers of grievance flee together, and there remains no other power in all the worlds. And Her countenance shines with the supernal Light and She crowns Herself with the holy Nation below as they are all crowned with new souls. Then they begin by blessing her with joy and with radiant faces.

ARVIT OF SHAVUOT

In the evening prayer of *Arvit*, we connect to Jacob the Patriarch, who is the channel for Central Column energy. He helps us connect the two energies of Judgment and Mercy in a balanced way. It is said that the whole world was created only for Jacob, who embodies truth: "Give truth to Jacob" *(Michah 7:20)*. To activate the power of our prayer, and specifically the power of the prayer of *Arvit*, we must be truthful with others and, most importantly, with ourselves.

LESHEM YICHUD

leshem לְשֵׁם yichud יִחוּד kudsha קוּדְשָׁא berich בְּרִיךְ hu הוּא

ush'chintei וּשְׁכִינְתֵּיהּ (יאהדונהי) bid'chilu בִּדְחִילוּ ur'chimu וּרְחִימוּ

(יאהויהה) ur'chimu וּרְחִימוּ ud'chilu וּדְחִילוּ (איההיוהה) leyachda לְיַחֲדָא

shem שֵׁם yud יוּ"ד kei קֵ"י bevav בְּוָא"ו kei קֵ"י beyichuda בְּיִחוּדָא

shelim שְׁלִים (יהוה) beshem בְּשֵׁם kol כָּל ילי Yisrael יִשְׂרָאֵל, hine הִנֵּה

anachnu אֲנַחְנוּ ba'im בָּאִים lehitpalel לְהִתְפַּלֵּל tefilat תְּפִלַּת arvit עַרְבִית

shel שֶׁל (on Shabbat add: Shabbat שַׁבָּת kodesh קוֹדֶשׁ ve וְ) Shavuot שָׁבוּעוֹת

shetiken שֶׁתִּקֵּן Yaakov יַעֲקֹב ז׳ הויות, יאהדונהי אידהנויה avinu אָבִינוּ alav עָלָיו

hashalom הַשָּׁלוֹם im עִם kol כָּל ילי hamitzvot הַמִּצְוֹת hakelulot הַכְּלוּלוֹת

ba בָּהּ letaken לְתַקֵּן et אֶת shorsha שׁוֹרְשָׁהּ bemakom בְּמָקוֹם elyon עֶלְיוֹן

la'asot לַעֲשׂוֹת nachat נַחַת ru'ach רוּחַ leyotzrenu לְיוֹצְרֵנוּ vela'asot וְלַעֲשׂוֹת

retzon רְצוֹן מהש ע"ה, ע"ב בריבוע וקס"א ע"ה, אל שדי ע"ה bor'enu בּוֹרְאֵנוּ.

vihi וִיהִי no'am נֹעַם Adonai אֲדֹנָי ללה Elohenu אֱלֹהֵינוּ ילה

alenu עָלֵינוּ uma'ase וּמַעֲשֵׂה yadenu יָדֵינוּ konena כּוֹנְנָה

alenu עָלֵינוּ uma'ase וּמַעֲשֵׂה yadenu יָדֵינוּ konenehu כּוֹנְנֵהוּ:

ARVIT OF SHAVUOT - LESHEM YICHUD

*For the sake of unification of the Holy Blessed One and His Shechinah, with fear and love and with love and fear, in order to unify the Name Yud-Kei and Vav-Kei in perfect unity, and in the name of Israel, we have hereby come to recite the prayer of Arvit of (*on Shabbat add: *of the Holy Shabbat) Shavuot, established by Jacob, our forefather, may peace be upon him, With all its commandments, to correct its root in the supernal place, to bring satisfaction to our Maker,and to fulfill the wish of our Creator. "And may the pleasantness of the Lord, our God, be upon us and may He establish the work of our hands for us and may the work of our hands establish Him." (Psalms 90:17)*

HALF KADDISH

יִתְגַּדַּל yitgadal וְיִתְקַדַּשׁ veyitkadash שדי ומילוי שדי ; י"א אותיות כמנין ו"ה

שְׁמֵיהּ shemei (שם י"ה דע"ב) רַבָּא raba קנ"א ב"ן, יהוה אלהים יהוה אדני,

מילוי קס"א וס"ג, מ"ה ברבוע וע"ב ע"ה ; ר"ת = ו"פ אלהים ; ס"ת = ג"פ יב"ק: אָמֵן amen אידהנויה.

בְּעָלְמָא be'alma דִּי di בְרָא vera כִּרְעוּתֵיהּ kir'utei.

וְיַמְלִיךְ veyamlich מַלְכוּתֵיהּ mal'chutei. וְיַצְמַח veyatzmach

פּוּרְקָנֵיהּ purkanei. וִיקָרֵב vikarev מְשִׁיחֵיהּ meshichei: אָמֵן amen אידהנויה.

בְּחַיֵּיכוֹן bechayechon וּבְיוֹמֵיכוֹן uvyomechon וּבְחַיֵּי uvchayei

דְּכָל dechol ילי בֵּית bet ב"פ ראה יִשְׂרָאֵל Yisrael בַּעֲגָלָא ba'agala

וּבִזְמַן uvizman קָרִיב kariv וְאִמְרוּ ve'imru אָמֵן amen: אָמֵן amen אידהנויה.

The congregation and the *chazan* say the following:

28 words (until *be'alma*) and

28 letters (until *almaya*)

יְהֵא yehe שְׁמֵיהּ shemei (שם י"ה דס"ג) רַבָּא raba קנ"א ב"ן,

יהוה אלהים יהוה אדני, מילוי קס"א וס"ג, מ"ה ברבוע וע"ב ע"ה מְבָרַךְ mevarach

לְעָלַם le'alam לְעָלְמֵי le'almei עָלְמַיָּא almaya. יִתְבָּרַךְ yitbarach.

Seven words with six letters each (שם בן מ"ב) – and also,

seven times the letter Vav (שם בן מ"ב)

HALF KADDISH

May His great Name be more exalted and sanctified. (*Amen*)

In the world that He created according to His will, and may His Kingdom reign. And may He cause His redemption to sprout and may He bring the Mashiach closer. (*Amen*) *In your lifetimes and in your days and in the lifetime of all the House of Israel, speedily and in the near future, and you should say, Amen.* (*Amen*) *May His great Name be blessed forever and for all eternity blessed and lauded,*

וְיִשְׁתַּבַּח veyishtabach י״פ ע״ב יהוה אל אבג יתץ.

וְיִתְפָּאַר veyitpa'ar הי גו יה קרע שטן. וְיִתְרוֹמַם veyitromam וה כוזו נגד יכש.

וְיִתְנַשֵּׂא veyitnase במוכסז בטר צתג. וְיִתְהַדָּר veyit'hadar כוזו יה וזקב טנע.

וְיִתְעַלֶּה veyit'ale וה יוד ה יגל פזק. וְיִתְהַלָּל veyit'halal א ואו הא שקו צית.

שְׁמֵיהּ shemei (שם י״ה דמ״ה) דְּקוּדְשָׁא dekudsha בְּרִיךְ verich הוּא hu:

אָמֵן amen אידהנויה.

לְעֵלָּא le'ela מִן min כָּל kol יל״י בִּרְכָתָא birchata. שִׁירָתָא shirata.

תִּשְׁבְּחָתָא tishbechata וְנֶחָמָתָא venechamata. דַּאֲמִירָן da'amiran

בְּעָלְמָא be'alma וְאִמְרוּ ve'imru אָמֵן amen: אָמֵן amen אידהנויה.

BARCHU

The *chazan* says:

בָּרְכוּ barchu יהוה ריבוע יהוה ריבוע מ״ה אֶת et יְהֹוָהאדניאהדונהי Adonai

הַמְבוֹרָךְ: hamevorach ס״ת כהת, משיח בן דוד ע״ה:

If *Shavuot* (second day) falls on *Shabbat*:
Meditate to receive the extra soul called: *Ruach*
from the aspect of the night of *Shabbat*

First the congregation replies the following, and then the *chazan* repeats it:

Nefesh — *Ruach* — *Neshamah*

בָּרוּךְ baruch יְהֹוָהאדניאהדונהי Adonai הַמְבוֹרָךְ: hamevorach

Chayah — *Yechidah*

לְעוֹלָם le'olam ריבוע ס״ג וי׳ אותיות דס״ג וָעֶד va'ed:

---

and glorified and exalted,
and extolled and honored, and uplifted and praised be, the Name of the Holy Blessed One. (Amen) *Above all blessings, songs, praises, and words of consolation that may be said in the world, and you shall say, Amen.* (Amen)

BARCHU

Bless the Lord, the Blessed One.
Blessed be the Lord, the Blessed One, forever and for eternity.

HAMA'ARIV ARAVIM – FIRST CHAMBER – LIVNAT HASAPIR

In the time of *Arvit*, we have an opportunity to connect to four different "Chambers" in the House of the King - Chamber of Sapphire Stone (*Livnat Hasapir*), Chamber of Love (*Ahavah*), Chamber of Desire (*Ratzon*), and the Chamber of Holy of Holies (*Kodesh HaKodeshim*). Each Chamber connects us to another level in the spiritual plane. The blessing connecting us to the First Chamber, *Livnat Hasapir*, contains 53 words, which is also the numerical value of the word gan גן, meaning "garden," therefore connecting us to the Garden of Eden of our world.

Hechal Livnat Hasapir (the Sapphire Stone Chamber) of *Nukva* in *Beriah*.

בָּרוּךְ baruch אַתָּה Ata יְהֹוָהאדניאהדונהי Adonai אֱלֹהֵינוּ Elohenu ילה

מֶלֶךְ melech הָעוֹלָם ha'olam אֲשֶׁר asher בִּדְבָרוֹ bidvaro מַעֲרִיב ma'ariv

עֲרָבִים aravim בְּחָכְמָה bechochmah **(*Atzilut*)** במילוי = תרי"ג (מצוות).

פּוֹתֵחַ pote'ach שְׁעָרִים she'arim כתר בִּתְבוּנָה bitvuna **(*Beriah*)**.

מְשַׁנֶּה meshane עִתִּים itim **(*Yetzirah*)** וּמַחֲלִיף umachalif אֶת et

הַזְּמַנִּים hazemanim **(*Asiyah*)** וּמְסַדֵּר umsader אֶת et הַכּוֹכָבִים hakochavim

(*The Seven Planets*). בְּמִשְׁמְרוֹתֵיהֶם bemishmerotehem בָּרָקִיעַ baraki'a

כִּרְצוֹנוֹ kirtzono. בּוֹרֵא bore יוֹמָם yomam וָלָיְלָה valayla מלה. גּוֹלֵל golel

אוֹר or רז, אין סוף מִפְּנֵי mipenei חֹשֶׁךְ choshech שך נצוצות של וו' המלכים

וְחֹשֶׁךְ vechoshech שך נצוצות של וו' המלכים מִפְּנֵי mipenei אוֹר or רז, אין סוף.

הַמַּעֲבִיר hama'avir יוֹם yom ע"ה נגד, מזבח, זן, אל יהוה וּמֵבִיא umevi לָיְלָה layla

מלה. וּמַבְדִּיל umavdil בֵּין ben יוֹם yom ע"ה נגד, מזבח, זן, אל יהוה וּבֵין uven

לָיְלָה layla מלה. יְהֹוָהאדניאהדונהי Adonai צְבָאוֹת Tzeva'ot פני שכינה שְׁמוֹ shemo

מהש ע"ה, ע"ב בריבוע וקס"א ע"ה, אל שדי ע"ה יְהֹוָהאדניאהדונהי Adonai. בָּרוּךְ baruch

אַתָּה Ata יְהֹוָהאדניאהדונהי Adonai הַמַּעֲרִיב hama'ariv עֲרָבִים aravim:

HAMA'ARIV ARAVIM – FIRST CHAMBER – LIVNAT HASAPIR

Blessed are You, Lord, our God, King of the universe,

Who brings with His words evenings with wisdom. He opens gates with understanding. He changes the seasons and varies the times and arranges the stars in their constellations in the sky, according to His will. He creates day and night and rolls Light away from before darkness, and darkness from before Light. He is the One Who causes the day to pass and brings on night and separates between day and night. Lord of Hosts, His Name is the Lord. Blessed are You, Lord, who brings on evenings.

AHAVAT OLAM – SECOND CHAMBER - LOVE

This blessing connects us to the Second Chamber, *Ahavah* (Love) and its purpose is to inspire us with a renewed love for others and for the world.

Hechal Ahavah (the Love Chamber) of *Nukva* in *Beriah*.
The following paragraph has 50 words corresponding to the 50 Gates of *Binah*.

אַהֲבַת ahavat עוֹלָם olam בֵּית bet ב"פ ראה יִשְׂרָאֵל Yisrael עַמְּךָ amecha

אָהָבְתָּ ahavta. תּוֹרָה torah (*Atzilut*) וּמִצְוֹת umitzvot (*Beriah*) וְחֻקִּים chukim

(*Yetzirah*) וּמִשְׁפָּטִים umishpatim (*Asiyah*) אוֹתָנוּ otanu לִמַּדְתָּ limadeta.

עַל al כֵּן ken יְהֹוָה אהדונהי Adonai אֱלֹהֵינוּ Elohenu ילה

בְּשָׁכְבֵנוּ beshochvenu וּבְקוּמֵנוּ uvkumenu נָשִׂיחַ nasi'ach בְּחֻקֶּיךָ bechukecha

וְנִשְׂמַח venismach וְנַעֲלוֹז vena'aloz בְּדִבְרֵי bedivrei תַלְמוּד talmud

תּוֹרָתֶךָ toratecha וּמִצְוֹתֶיךָ umitzvotecha וְחֻקּוֹתֶיךָ vechukotecha

לְעוֹלָם le'olam ריבוע ס"ג ו' אותיות ס"ג וָעֶד va'ed. כִּי ki הֵם hem

חַיֵּינוּ chayenu וְאֹרֶךְ ve'orech יָמֵינוּ yamenu וּבָהֶם uvahem נֶהְגֶּה nehge

יוֹמָם yomam וָלָיְלָה valayla מלה. וְאַהֲבָתְךָ ve'ahavatcha לֹא lo תָסוּר tasur

מִמֶּנּוּ mimenu לְעוֹלָמִים le'olamim. בָּרוּךְ baruch אַתָּה Ata

יְהֹוָה אהדונהי Adonai אוֹהֵב ohev אֶת et עַמּוֹ amo יִשְׂרָאֵל Yisrael:

THE SHEMA (to learn more about the *Shema* go to pg. 346)

The *Shema* is one of the most powerful tools to draw the energy of healing to our lives. The true power of the *Shema* is unleashed when we recite this prayer while meditating on others who need healing energy.

1) In order to receive the Light of the *Shema*, you have to accept upon yourself the precept of: "Love your neighbor as yourself," and see yourself united with all the souls that comprise the Original Adam.
2) You need to meditate to connect to the precept of the Reciting of *Shema* twice a day.
3) Before saying the *Shema* you should cover your eyes with your right hand (saying the words "*Shema Yisrael … le'olam va'ed*".) And you should read the *Shema* with deep meditation, chanting it with the intonations. It is necessary to be careful with the pronunciation of all the letters.

(According to the Ramchal the elevation of the *Mochin* is as on the *Shema* of *Shacharit* on pg. 347.)

AHAVAT OLAM – SECOND CHAMBER - LOVE

With eternal love, You have loved Your Nation, the House of Israel.
Torah, commandments, statutes, and laws, You have taught us. Therefore, Lord, our God, when we lie down and when we rise up, we shall discuss Your statutes and we shall rejoice and exult in the words of the teachings of Your Torah, Your commandments, and Your statutes, forever and ever. They are our lifetimes and the length of our days; with them we shall direct ourselves day and night. And Your love, You shall never remove from us. Blessed are You, Lord, Who loves His Nation, Israel.

First, meditate in general, on the first *Yichud* of the four *Yichuds* of the Name: יהוה, and in particular, to awaken the letter ה, and then to connect it with the letter ו. Then connect the letter י and the letter ה together in the following order: *Hei* (ה), *Hei-Vav* (ה"ו), then *Yud-Hei* (י"ה), which adds up to 31, the secret of "יא"י" of the Name ס"ג. It is good to meditate on this *Yichud* before reciting any *Shema* because it acts as a replacement for the times that you may have missed reading the *Shema*. This *Yichud* has the same ability to create a Supernal connection like the reading of the *Shema* - to raise *Zeir* and *Nukva* together for the *Zivug* of *Abba* and *Ima*.

Shema – שְׁמַע

General Meditation: שם ע — to draw the energy from the seven lower *Sefirot* of *Ima* to the *Nukva*, which enables the *Nukva* to elevate the *Mayin Nukvin* (awakening from Below). **Particular Meditation:** שם = יהוה + שדי and five times the letters י and ד of ב"ן = ע [The letter *Hei* (ה) is formed by the letters *Dalet* (ד) and *Yud* (י), so in ב"ן we have four times the letter ה plus another time the letters י and ד from יוד of ב"ן.]. Also the three letters ו (18) - that are left from ב"ן, plus ב"ן itself (52) equals ע (70).

Yisrael – יִשְׂרָאֵל

General Meditation: שי"ר אל — to draw energy from *Chesed* and *Gevurah* of *Abba* to *Zeir Anpin*, to do his action in the secret of *Mayin Duchrin* (awakening from Above).

Particular Meditation: (the rearranged letters of the word *Yisrael*) – שר אלי

אלהים דיודין (אלף למד הי יוד מם) = ש',

רבוע אלהים (א אל אלה אלהי אלהים) = ר',

מ"א אותיות רבוע אלהים במילואו (אלף אלף למד אלף למד הי אלף למד הי יוד אלף למד הי יוד מם) = אל"י.

Also meditate to draw the Inner *Mochin* of *Abba* of *Katnut* into *Zeir Anpin*.

Adonai Elohenu Adonai - יהוה אלהינו יהוה

General Meditation: to draw energy to *Abba*, *Ima* and *Da'at* from *Arich Anpin*,

Particular Meditation: ע"ב (יוד הי ויו הי) קס"א (אלף הי יוד הי) ע"ב (יוד הי וי הי).

Echad – אֶחָד

(The secret of the complete *Yichud-Unification*)

The letters *Alef* א and *Chet* ח from *Echad* אחד are *Zeir Anpin* and the letter *Dalet* ד is *Nukva*. **You should meditate** to devote your soul for the sanctification of the Holy Name, thereby elevating your *Nefesh*, *Ruach*, *Neshamah* and *Neshamah* of *Neshamah* with *Zeir Anpin* and *Nukva* (using the Names: ע"ב and ס"ג) to *Abba* and *Ima* as the secret of *Mayin Nukvin*, and by that energy, *Abba* and *Ima* will be unified in the secret of the Name: יאהדונה"י. **Also meditate** to draw out the Inner Six Edges of *Gadlut* of *Ima* into *Zeir Anpin*. The Drop, which is ע"ב, is drawn out from the external of *Arich Anpin*, and descends to *Yesod* of *Ima*, where it becomes: ע"ב ס"ג מ"ה ב"ן, and the four spelled out אהיה (אלף הי יוד הי, אלף הא יוד הא, אלף הה יוד הה) become Her clothing. <u>As a result</u>, *Zeir Anpin* now has four spelled out יה"ו (יוד הי ויו, יוד הי ואו, יוד הא ואו, יוד הה וו), four spelled out אה"י (אלף הי יוד, אלף הי יוד, אלף הא יוד, אלף הה יוד) and the Inner Six Edges of *Gadlut* of *Ima*. **Also meditate** on the Name: אל"ף ה"י וי"ו ה"י, which is the entire *Mochin* in the secret of *Da'at*. **And also meditate** (according to the Ramchal) on the four spelled out *Alef* (אלף=111) of the Name: אהי"ה that is equal to the word *Midat (444)*, making the *Keter* for *Leah*.

Baruch Shem - בָּרוּךְ שֵׁם כְּבוֹד מַלְכוּתוֹ לְעוֹלָם וָעֶד

Baruch Shem Kevod – *Chochmah*, *Binah*, *Da'at* of *Leah;*

Malchuto – Her *Keter*; ***Le'olam*** – the rest of Her *Partzuf*;

Va'ed – the four היה (4 times 20 equal to *Va'ed*=80) will make the *Keter* for *Rachel*.

And the four spelled out היה (הי יוד הי, הי יוד הי, הא יוד הא, הה יוד הה) will make the rest of Her body.

שְׁמַע shema ע' רבתי יִשְׂרָאֵל Yisrael יְהֹוָה יאהדונהי Adonai

אֱלֹהֵינוּ Elohenu ילה יְהֹוָה יאהדונהי Adonai | אֶחָד echad ד' רבתי ; אהבה, דאגה:

(Whisper :) יוזו אותיות בָּרוּךְ baruch שֵׁם shem כְּבוֹד kevod מַלְכוּתוֹ malchuto,

לְעוֹלָם le'olam ריבוע דס"ג וי' אותיות דס"ג וָעֶד va'ed:

Yud, Chochmah, head – 42 words corresponding to the Holy 42-Letter Name of God.

א ב

וְאָהַבְתָּ ve'ahavta ב"פ אור, ב"פ רז, ב"פ אין סוף ; (יכוין לקיים מ"ע של אהבת ה') אֵת et

ג י

יְהֹוָה יאהדונהי Adonai אֱלֹהֶיךָ Elohecha ילה ; ס"ת כהת, משיח בן דוד ע"ה

ת צ ק ר

בְּכָל־ bechol ב"ן, לכב לְבָבְךָ levavcha וּבְכָל־ uvchol ב"ן, לכב נַפְשְׁךָ nafshecha

ע ש ט נ

וּבְכָל־ uvchol ב"ן, לכב מְאֹדֶךָ me'odecha: וְהָיוּ vehayu הַדְּבָרִים hadevarim

נ ג ד י כ

הָאֵלֶּה ha'ele אֲשֶׁר asher אָנֹכִי anochi מְצַוְּךָ metzavecha הַיּוֹם hayom

ש ב ט

ע"ה נגד, מזבח, זן, אל יהוה (pause here) עַל al לְבָבֶךָ levavecha: וְשִׁנַּנְתָּם veshinantam

ר צ ת ג

לְבָנֶיךָ levanecha וְדִבַּרְתָּ vedibarta בָּם bam מ"ב בְּשִׁבְתְּךָ beshivtecha

וז ק ב

בְּבֵיתֶךָ bevetecha ב"פ ראה וּבְלֶכְתְּךָ uvlechtecha בַדֶּרֶךְ vaderech

ט נ

ב"פ יב"ק, ס"ג קס"א וּבְשָׁכְבְּךָ uvshochbecha וּבְקוּמֶךָ uvkumecha:

ע י ג ל

וּקְשַׁרְתָּם ukshartam לְאוֹת le'ot עַל־ al יָדֶךָ yadecha

The Shema

"Hear Israel, the Lord our God. The Lord is One." (Deuteronomy 6:4)

"Blessed is the glorious Name, His Kingdom is forever and for eternity." (Pesachim 56a)

"And you shall love the Lord, your God, with all your heart and with all your soul and with all that you possess. Let those words that I command you today be upon your heart. And you shall teach them to your children and you shall speak of them while you sit in your home and while you walk on your way and when you lie down and when you rise. You shall bind them as a sign upon your hand

(פ ז ק ש)
וְהָיוּ vehayu לְטֹטָפֹת letotafot בֵּין ben עֵינֶיךָ enecha

ע"ה קס"א ; ריבוע מ"ה: (ק) וּכְתַבְתָּם uchtavtam (ו) עַל־ al

(צ) מְזֻזוֹת mezuzot ג"ת (זו מות) (י) בֵּיתֶךָ betecha ב"פ ראה (ת) וּבִשְׁעָרֶיךָ: uvish'arecha

VEHAYA IM SHAMO'A

***Hei, Binah,* arms and body** — 72 words corresponding to the 72 Names of God.

(והו) וְהָיָה vehaya יהוה ; יהה (ילי) אִם־ im יוה"ך, מ"א אותיות דפשוט, דמילוי ודמילוי דמילוי דאהיה ע"ה

(סיט) שָׁמֹעַ shamo'a (עלם) תִּשְׁמְעוּ tishme'u (מהש) אֶל־ el (ללה) מִצְוֹתַי mitzvotai (אכא) אֲשֶׁר asher

(כהת) אָנֹכִי anochi (הזי) מְצַוֶּה metzave (אלד) אֶתְכֶם etchem (לאו) הַיּוֹם hayom ע"ה נגד, מזבח, זן, אל יהוה

(pause here) (ההע) לְאַהֲבָה le'ahava אוזה, דאגה (יזל) אֶת־ et (מבה) יְהֹוָהאדניאהדונהי Adonai

(הרי) אֱלֹהֵיכֶם Elohechem ילה (enunciate the letter *Ayin* in the word *"ul'ovdo"*) (הקם) וּלְעָבְדוֹ ul'ovdo

(לאו) בְּכָל bechol ב"ן, לכב (כלי) לְבַבְכֶם levavchem (לוו) וּבְכָל־ uvchol ב"ן, לכב

(פהל) נַפְשְׁכֶם: nafshechem (נלך) וְנָתַתִּי venatati (ייי) מְטַר־ metar (מלה) אַרְצְכֶם artzechem

(חהו) בְּעִתּוֹ be'ito (נתה) יוֹרֶה yore (האא) וּמַלְקוֹשׁ umalkosh (ירת) וְאָסַפְתָּ ve'asafta (שאה) דְגָנֶךָ deganecha

(ריי) וְתִירֹשְׁךָ vetiroshcha (אום) וְיִצְהָרֶךָ: veyitz'harecha (לכב) וְנָתַתִּי venatati (ושר) עֵשֶׂב esev ע"ב שמות

---

and they shall be as frontlets between your eyes.
And you shall write them upon the doorposts of your house and your gates." (Deuteronomy 6:5-9)

VEHAYA IM SHAMO'A

"And it shall come to be that if you shall listen to My commandments that I am commanding you with today to love the Lord, your God, and to serve Him with all your heart and with all your soul, then I shall send rain upon your land in its proper time, both early rain and late rain. You shall then gather your grain and your wine and your oil. And I shall give grass

יוזו להוו כוק מנד

בְּשָׂדְךָ besadcha לִבְהֶמְתֶּךָ livhemtecha וְאָכַלְתָּ ve'achalta וְשָׂבָעְתָּ vesavata:

אני וזעם רהע ייז ההה

הִשָּׁמְרוּ hishamru לָכֶם lachem פֶּן־ pen יִפְתֶּה yifte לְבַבְכֶם levavchem

מיכ וול ילה סאל

וְסַרְתֶּם vesartem וַעֲבַדְתֶּם va'avadetem אֱלֹהִים elohim אֲחֵרִים acherim

ערי עשל

מושה (העומד נגד הקליפות) וְהִשְׁתַּחֲוִיתֶם vehishtachavitem לָהֶם lahem:

מיה והו דני הזש

וְחָרָה vechara (pause here) אַף־ af יְהֹוָהאדניאהדונהי Adonai בָּכֶם bachem

עמם ננא נית מבה

וְעָצַר ve'atzar אֶת־ et הַשָּׁמַיִם hashamayim י״פ טל, י״פ כוזו וְלֹא־ velo

פוי נמם ייל הרוז מצר

יִהְיֶה yihye ייי מָטָר matar וְהָאֲדָמָה veha'adama לֹא lo תִתֵּן titen ב״פ כהת

ומב יהה ענו מוזי דמב

אֶת־ et יְבוּלָהּ yevula וַאֲבַדְתֶּם va'avadetem מְהֵרָה mehera מֵעַל me'al עלם

מנק איע וזבו

הָאָרֶץ ha'aretz אלהים דההין ע״ה הַטֹּבָה hatova אֲשֶׁר asher

ראה יבמ היי

יְהֹוָהאדניאהדונהי Adonai נֹתֵן noten אבג יתץ, ושר לָכֶם lachem: ***Vav, Zeir Anpin***

מום א

וְשַׂמְתֶּם vesamtem **stomach** – 50 words corresponding to the 50 Gates of *Binah*

א ה י ה א

אֶת־ et דְּבָרַי devarai ראה אֵלֶּה ele עַל־ al לְבַבְכֶם levavchem

ה י ה א

וְעַל־ ve'al נַפְשְׁכֶם nafshechem וּקְשַׁרְתֶּם ukshartem אֹתָם otam

---

in your field for your cattle. And you shall eat and you shall be satiated. Be careful lest your heart be seduced and you may turn away and serve alien deities and prostrate yourself before them. And the wrath of the Lord shall be upon you and He shall stop the Heavens and there shall be no more rain and the earth shall not give forth its crop. And you shall quickly perish from the good land that the Lord has given you. And you shall place those words of Mine upon your heart and upon your soul and you shall bind them

ה י ה א

לְאוֹת le'ot ר"ת לאו עַל־ al יֶדְכֶם yedchem וְהָיוּ vehayu

ה י ה

לְטוֹטָפֹת letotafot בֵּין ben עֵינֵיכֶם enechem ריבוע מ"ה:

א ה י ה

וְלִמַּדְתֶּם velimadetem אֹתָם otam אֶת־ et בְּנֵיכֶם benechem

א ה י

לְדַבֵּר ledaber ראה בָּם bam שם בן מ"ב בְּשִׁבְתְּךָ beshivtecha

ה א ה

בְּבֵיתֶךָ bevetecha ב"פ ראה וּבְלֶכְתְּךָ uvlechtecha בַדֶּרֶךְ vaderech ב"פ יב"ק, ס"ג קס"א

י ה א ה

וּבְשָׁכְבְּךָ uvshochbecha וּבְקוּמֶךָ uvkumecha: וּכְתַבְתָּם uchtavtam עַל־ al

י ה א ה

מְזֻזוֹת mezuzot בֵּיתֶךָ betecha ב"פ ראה וּבִשְׁעָרֶיךָ uvish'arecha: לְמַעַן lema'an

י ה א ה

יִרְבּוּ yirbu יְמֵיכֶם yemechem ר"ת י"ל וִימֵי vimei בְנֵיכֶם venechem

י ה אהיה

עַל al הָאֲדָמָה ha'adama אֲשֶׁר asher (enunciate the letter *Ayin* in the word "*nishba*")

אהיה אהיה

נִשְׁבַּע nishba יכוין לשבועת המבול יְהֹוָהאדניאהדונהי Adonai

אהיה אהיה אהיה אהיה

לַאֲבֹתֵיכֶם la'avotechem לָתֵת latet לָהֶם lahem כִּימֵי kimei

אהיה אהיה אהיה

הַשָּׁמַיִם hashamayim י"פ טל, י"פ כוזו עַל־ al הָאָרֶץ ha'aretz אלהים דההין ע"ה:

---

as a sign upon your hands and they shall be as frontlets between your eyes. And you shall teach them to your children and speak of them while you sit at home and while you walk on your way and when you lie down and when you rise. You shall write them upon the doorposts of your house and upon your gates. This is so that your days shall be numerous and so shall the days of your children upon the Earth that the Lord had sworn to your fathers to give them as the days of the Heavens upon the Earth." (Deuteronomy 11:13-21)

VAYOMER

Hei, Malchut, legs and reproductive organs,

72 words corresponding to the 72 Names of God in direct order (according to the Ramchal).

ווו ייי סבט עאם

וַיֹּאמֶר vayomer יְהֹוָה(אדני)יאהדונהי Adonai אֶל־ el מֹשֶׁה Moshe

מבש ליה אנא

מהש, ע״ב בריבוע וקס״א, אל שדי, ד״פ אלהים ע״ה לֵּאמֹר lemor: דַּבֵּר daber ראה אֶל־ el

כמות הוזי אנד להו המע

בְּנֵי benei יִשְׂרָאֵל Yisrael וְאָמַרְתָּ ve'amarta אֲלֵהֶם alehem וְעָשׂוּ ve'asu

יצל מרה היי המם לוו

לָהֶם lahem צִיצִת tzitzit עַל־ al כַּנְפֵי kanfei בִגְדֵיהֶם vigdehem

כבי ליו פנל נמך

לְדֹרֹתָם ledorotam וְנָתְנוּ venatnu עַל־ al צִיצִת tzitzit

יחי מנה וזהו

הַכָּנָף hakanaf ע״ה קנ״א, אדני אלהים פְּתִיל petil י״פ ב״ן תְּכֵלֶת techelet:

ניה השא ירת שאה רלי

וְהָיָה vehaya יהוה ; יהה לָכֶם lachem לְצִיצִת letzitzit וּרְאִיתֶם ur'item אֹתוֹ oto

אום ליב והר ייי להוז

וּזְכַרְתֶּם uzchartem אֶת־ et כָּל־ kol ילי מִצְוֹת mitzvot יְהֹוָה(אדני)יאהדונהי Adonai

כעק מנד אני וזום רהע

וַעֲשִׂיתֶם va'asitem אֹתָם otam וְלֹא־ velo תָתוּרוּ taturu אַחֲרֵי acharei

יחז השה מככ

לְבַבְכֶם levavchem וְאַחֲרֵי ve'acharei עֵינֵיכֶם enechem ריבוע מ״ה

You should meditate on the precept:
"not to follow negative sexual thoughts of the heart and the sights of the eyes for prostitution."

VAYOMER

"And the Lord spoke to Moses and said,
Speak to the Children of Israel and say to them that they should make for themselves Tzitzit, on the corners of their garments, throughout all their generations. And they must place upon the Tzitzit, of each corner, a blue strand. And this shall be to you as a Tzitzit: you shall see it and remember the commandments of the Lord and fulfill them. And you shall not stray after your hearts and your eyes,

You should meditate to remember the exodus from *Mitzrayim* (Egypt).

lihyot לִהְיוֹת lachem לָכֶם lelohim לֵאלֹהִים ;

ani אֲנִי Adonai יְהוָה Elohechem אֱלֹהֵיכֶם:

Be careful to complete this paragraph together with the *chazan* and the congregation, and say the word "*emet*" out loud. The *chazan* should say the word "*emet*" in silence.

אֱמֶת emet

The congregation should be silent, listen and hear the words "*Adonai Elohechem emet*" spoken by the *chazan*. If you did not complete the paragraph together with the *chazan* you should repeat the last three words on your own. With these three words the *Shema* is completed.

יְהוָה Adonai אֱלֹהֵיכֶם Elohechem:

אֱמֶת emet

---

after which you adulterate. This is so that you shall remember to fulfill all My commandments and thereby be holy before your God. I am the Lord, your God, Who brought you out of the land of Egypt to be your God. I, the Lord, your God, Is true." (Numbers 15:37-41) *the Lord, your God, is true!*

VE'EMUNA – THIRD CHAMBER – RATZON

Ve'emuna connects us to the Third Chamber in the House of the King: *Ratzon*, or desire. Before we can connect to any form of spiritual energy, we need to feel a want or desire. Desire is the vessel that draws spiritual Light. A small desire draws a small amount of Light. A large desire draws a large amount.

Hechal Ratzon (the Desire Chamber) of *Nukva* in *Beriah*.

וֶאֱמוּנָה ve'emuna (בחינת לילה) כָּל kol ילי זֹאת zot וְקַיָּם vekayam עָלֵינוּ ,alenu

כִּי ki הוּא hu יְהֹוָהאדניאהדונהי Adonai אֱלֹהֵינוּ Elohenu ילה וְאֵין ve'en

זוּלָתוֹ •zulato וַאֲנַחְנוּ va'anachnu יִשְׂרָאֵל Yisrael עַמּוֹ •amo

הַפּוֹדֵנוּ hapodenu מִיַּד miyad מְלָכִים •melachim הַגּוֹאֲלֵנוּ hago'alenu

מַלְכֵּנוּ malkenu מִכַּף mikaf כָּל kol ילי עָרִיצִים •aritzim

הָאֵל haEl לאה ; ייא״ (מילוי דס״ג) הַנִּפְרָע hanifra לָנוּ lanu אלהים, אהיה אדני

מִצָּרֵינוּ •mitzarenu הַמְשַׁלֵּם hameshalem גְּמוּל gemul לְכָל lechol יה אדני

אוֹיְבֵי oyvei נַפְשֵׁנוּ :nafshenu הַשָּׂם hasam נַפְשֵׁנוּ nafshenu

בַּחַיִּים bachayim אהיה אהיה יהוה, בינה ע״ה וְלֹא velo נָתַן natan לַמּוֹט lamot

רַגְלֵנוּ •raglenu הַמַּדְרִיכֵנוּ hamadrichenu עַל al בָּמוֹת bamot

אוֹיְבֵינוּ •oyvenu וַיָּרֶם vayarem קַרְנֵנוּ karnenu עַל al כָּל kol ילי ; עמם

שׂוֹנְאֵינוּ •son'enu הָאֵל haEl לאה ; ייא״ (מילוי דס״ג) הָעוֹשֶׂה ha'ose

לָנוּ lanu אלהים, אהיה אדני נִסִּים nisim וּנְקָמָה unkama בְּפַרְעֹה •beFar'o

בְּאוֹתוֹת be'otot וּבְמוֹפְתִים uvmoftim בְּאַדְמַת be'admat בְּנֵי benei

חָם •Cham הַמַּכֶּה hamake בְעֶבְרָתוֹ ve'evrato כָּל kol ילי

בְּכוֹרֵי bechorei מִצְרָיִם Mitzrayim •מצר וַיּוֹצֵא vayotzi אֶת et

עַמּוֹ amo יִשְׂרָאֵל Yisrael מִתּוֹכָם mitocham לְחֵרוּת lecherut עוֹלָם •olam

---

VE'EMUNA – THIRD CHAMBER - RATZON

And trustworthy. All this and He are set upon us because He is the Lord, our God, and there is none other. And we are Israel, His Nation. He redeems us from the hands of kings. He is our King, Who delivers us from the reach of tyrants; The God, Who avenges us against our enemies. He pays our mortal enemies their due. He Who keeps us alive and does not allow our feet to falter; He Who lets us walk upon the plains of our foes. He Who raises our worth over all our enemies. He is God, Who wrought for us retribution against Pharaoh, with signs and wonders, in the land of the children of Cham. He Who struck down with His anger at the first-born of Egypt, and brought out His Nation, Israel, from amongst them to everlasting freedom.

הַמַּעֲבִיר hama'avir בָּנָיו banav

בֵּין ben גִּזְרֵי gizrei יַם yam ילי סוּף Suf. וְאֶת ve'et רוֹדְפֵיהֶם rodfehem

וְאֶת ve'et שׂוֹנְאֵיהֶם son'ehem בִּתְהוֹמוֹת bitehomot טִבַּע tiba. רָאוּ ra'u

בָנִים vanim אֶת et גְּבוּרָתוֹ gevurato שִׁבְּחוּ shibechu וְהוֹדוּ vehodu אהיה

לִשְׁמוֹ lishmo מהש ע"ה, ע"ב בריבוע וקס"א ע"ה, אל שדי ע"ה. וּמַלְכוּתוֹ umalchuto

בְּרָצוֹן beratzon מהש ע"ה, ע"ב בריבוע וקס"א ע"ה, אל שדי ע"ה קִבְּלוּ kibelu

עֲלֵיהֶם alehem. מֹשֶׁה Moshe מהש, ע"ב בריבוע וקס"א, אל שדי, ד"פ אלהים ע"ה

וּבְנֵי uvnei יִשְׂרָאֵל Yisrael ר"ת ע"ה נגד, מזבח, זן, אל יהוה לְךָ lecha עָנוּ anu

שִׁירָה shira בְּשִׂמְחָה besimcha רַבָּה raba וְאָמְרוּ ve'amru כֻלָּם chulam:

מִי־ mi ילי כָמֹכָה chamocha בָּאֵלִם ba'elim יְהֹוָהאדני יאהדונהי Adonai

ר"ת ע"ב, ריבוע יהוה; ס"ת מ"ה מִי mi ילי כָּמֹכָה kamocha נֶאְדָּר nedar

בַּקֹּדֶשׁ bakodesh ר"ת יב"ק, אלהים יהוה, אהיה אדני יהוה נוֹרָא nora תְהִלֹּת tehilot

עֹשֵׂה ose פֶלֶא fele: מַלְכוּתְךָ malchutcha יְהֹוָהאדני יאהדונהי Adonai

אֱלֹהֵינוּ Elohenu ילה רָאוּ ra'u בָנֶיךָ vanecha עַל־ al הַיָּם hayam ילי

יַחַד yachad כֻּלָּם kulam הוֹדוּ hodu אהיה וְהִמְלִיכוּ vehimlichu

וְאָמְרוּ ve'amru: יְהֹוָהאדני יאהדונהי Adonai | יִמְלֹךְ yimloch לְעֹלָם le'olam

ריבוע ס"ג וי' אותיות דס"ג; ר"ת ייל וָעֶד va'ed. וְנֶאֱמַר vene'emar: כִּי־ ki פָדָה fada

יְהֹוָהאדני יאהדונהי Adonai אֶת־ et יַעֲקֹב Yaakov ז' הויות, יאהדונהי אידהנויה

וּגְאָלוֹ ug'alo מִיַּד miyad חָזָק chazak פהל מִמֶּנּוּ mimenu: בָּרוּךְ baruch

אַתָּה Ata יְהֹוָהאדני יאהדונהי Adonai גָּאַל ga'al באתב"ש כתר יִשְׂרָאֵל Yisrael:

He Who caused His Children to pass between the sections of the Sea of Reeds, while their pursuers and their enemies, He drowned in the depths. The Children saw His might and they praised and gave thanks to His Name; they accepted His sovereignty over them willingly. Moses and the Children of Israel raised their voices in song to Him, with great joy, and they all said, as one "Who is like You among the gods, Lord? Who is like You, awesome in holiness, tremendous in praise and Who works wonders?" (Exodus 15:11) Our Children saw Your Kingdom, Lord, our God, upon the sea, and they all in unison gave thanks to You and accepted Your sovereignty and said: "The Lord shall reign forever and ever." (Exodus 15:18) And it is stated: "For the Lord has delivered Jacob and redeemed him from the hand of one that is stronger than he." (Jeremiah 31:10) Blessed are You, Lord, Who redeemed Israel.

HASHKIVENU – FOURTH CHAMBER – HOLY OF HOLIES

The Fourth Chamber is *Kodesh HaKodeshim*, the Holy of Holies, which is our link to the next level that we reach through the *Amidah*.

Hechal Kodesh HaKodashim (the Holy of Holies Chamber) of *Nukva* in *Beriah*.

הַשְׁכִּיבֵנוּ hashkivenu אָבִינוּ avinu לְשָׁלוֹם leshalom ר"ת לאה

וְהַעֲמִידֵנוּ veha'amidenu מַלְכֵּנוּ malkenu לְחַיִּים lechayim אהיה אהיה יהוה, בינה ע"ה

טוֹבִים tovim וּלְשָׁלוֹם ulshalom וּפְרוֹשׂ ufros עָלֵינוּ alenu

סֻכַּת sukat סוכה = סאל, אמן (יאהדונהי) שְׁלוֹמֶךָ shelomecha וְתַקְּנֵנוּ vetaknenu

מַלְכֵּנוּ malkenu בְּעֵצָה be'etza טוֹבָה tova אכא מִלְּפָנֶיךָ milfanecha ס"ג מ"ה ב"ן

וְהוֹשִׁיעֵנוּ vehoshi'enu מְהֵרָה mehera לְמַעַן lema'an שְׁמֶךָ shemecha

(we don't ask for protection, as there is no need for protection from the *klipa* on *Shabbat* – וְהָגֵן בַּעֲדֵנוּ)

Meditate to include *Hechal Kodesh HaKodashim* of *Beriah* in *Atzilut* so it becomes as *Atzilut* itself.

If *Shavuot* (second day) falls on *Shabbat*:
Meditate to receive the extra soul called: *Neshamah*
from the aspect of the night of *Shabbat*

וּפְרוֹשׂ ufros partitions of *Yesod* in *Ima* עָלֵינוּ alenu above *Yaakov* and *Rachel* וְעַל ve'al

יְרוּשָׁלַיִם Yerushalayim עִירָךְ irach סֻכַּת sukat סוכה = סאל = אמן (יאהדונהי)

שָׁלוֹם shalom• בָּרוּךְ baruch אַתָּה Ata יְהֹוָאדָהֹנָי יאהדונהי Adonai

הַפּוֹרֵשׂ hapores סֻכַּת sukat סוכה = סאל = אמן (יאהדונהי) ; ר"ת = אדני שָׁלוֹם shalom

And the partitions should become like the *Sukkah* roof in order to make room (inside *Zeir Anpin*) for the *Gevurot* to expand without going out to *Yaakov* and *Rachel*. So now They will receive Light from the *Chasadim* that were delayed from Their ascent.

עָלֵינוּ alenu ר"ת ש"ע נהורין וְעַל ve'al כָּל kol ילי ; עמם עַמּוֹ amo יִשְׂרָאֵל Yisrael

וְעַל ve'al יְרוּשָׁלַיִם Yerushalayim: אָמֵן יאהדונהי amen

HASHKIVENU – FOURTH CHAMBER – HOLY OF HOLIES

Lay us down in peace, Father, and stand us up, our King, for good life and for peace. Spread over us Your protection of peace. Set us straight, with good counsel from You and save us speedily, for the sake of Your Name. And spread over us and over Jerusalem, Your city, a shelter of mercy and peace. Blessed are You, Lord, Who spreads the shelter of peace over us and over His entire nation, Israel, and over Jerusalem, Amen!

When *Shavuot* (second day) falls on *Shabbat* we add:

VESHAMRU

We have the ability to unite Heaven and Earth through the power of the *Alef-Hei-Vav-Hei* אהיה.

וְשָׁמְרוּ veshamru בְנֵי־ venei יִשְׂרָאֵל Yisrael אֶת־ et הַשַּׁבָּת haShabbat

ר"ת ביאה לַעֲשׂוֹת la'asot אֶת־ et הַשַּׁבָּת haShabbat לְדֹרֹתָם ledorotam

ר"ת אהל (זו אשתו, למשוך נשמה קדושה ולא מסט"א) בְּרִית berit עוֹלָם olam: בֵּינִי beni

וּבֵין uven בְּנֵי benei יִשְׂרָאֵל Yisrael אוֹת ot הִוא hee ר"ת ביאה לְעֹלָם le'olam

ריבוע דס"ג י' אותיות דס"ג כִּי־ ki שֵׁשֶׁת sheshet יָמִים yamim נלך עָשָׂה asa

יְהֹוָהאדניאהדונהי Adonai אֶת־ et הַשָּׁמַיִם hashamayim י"פ טל, י"פ כוזו וְאֶת־ ve'et

הָאָרֶץ ha'aretz אלהים דההין ע"ה וּבַיּוֹם uvayom ע"ה נגד, מזבח, זן, אל יהוה

הַשְּׁבִיעִי hashevi'i שָׁבַת shavat וַיִּנָּפַשׁ vayinafash:

ELE MO'ADEI

אֵלֶּה ele מוֹעֲדֵי mo'adei יְהֹוָהאדניאהדונהי Adonai מִקְרָאֵי mikra'ei

קֹדֶשׁ kodesh אֲשֶׁר־ asher תִּקְרְאוּ tikre'u אֹתָם otam בְּמוֹעֲדָם bemo'adam:

וַיְדַבֵּר vaydaber ראה מֹשֶׁה Moshe מהש, ע"ב בריבוע וקס"א, אל שדי, ד"פ אלהים ע"ה

אֶת־ et מֹעֲדֵי mo'adei יְהֹוָהאדניאהדונהי Adonai אֶל־ el בְּנֵי benei יִשְׂרָאֵל Yisrael:

HALF KADDISH

יִתְגַּדַּל yitgadal וְיִתְקַדַּשׁ veyitkadash שדי ומילוי שדי ; י"א אותיות כמנין וה

שְׁמֵיהּ shemei (שם י"ה דע"ב) רַבָּא raba קנ"א ב"ן, יהוה אלהים יהוה אדני,

מילוי קס"א וס"ג, מ"ה ברבוע וע"ב ע"ה ; ר"ת = ו"פ אלהים ; ס"ת = ג"פ יב"ק: אָמֵן amen אידהנויה.

VESHAMRU

"And the Children of Israel shall keep the Shabbat, to make the Shabbat an eternal covenant for all their generations. Between Me and the Children of Israel, it is an eternal sign that in six days did the Lord make the Heavens and the Earth and on the Seventh day, He was refreshed." (Exodus 31:16-17)

ELE MO'ADEI

"Those are the holiday of the Lord, Holy covenant you shall call them, on their time. And Moses spoke the holidays of the lord to the children of Israel" (Leviticus 23:44)

HALF KADDISH

May His great Name be more exalted and sanctified. (Amen)

בְּעָלְמָא be'alma דִּי di בְרָא vera כִרְעוּתֵיהּ •kir'utei

וְיַמְלִיךְ veyamlich מַלְכוּתֵיהּ •malchutei וְיַצְמַח veyatzmach

פּוּרְקָנֵיהּ •purkanei וִיקָרֵב vikarev מְשִׁיחֵיהּ :meshichei אָמֵן amen אידהנויה•

בְּחַיֵּיכוֹן bechayechon וּבְיוֹמֵיכוֹן uvyomechon וּבְחַיֵּי uvchayei

דְכָל dechol ילי בֵּית bet ב"פ ראה יִשְׂרָאֵל Yisrael בַּעֲגָלָא ba'agala

וּבִזְמַן uvizman קָרִיב kariv וְאִמְרוּ ve'imru אָמֵן :amen אָמֵן amen אידהנויה•

The congregation and the *chazan* say the following:

28 words (until *be'alma*) and 28 letters (until *almaya*)

יְהֵא yehe שְׁמֵיהּ shemei (שם י"ה דס"ג) רַבָּא raba קנ"א ב"ן,

יהוה אלהים יהוה אדני, מילוי קס"א וס"ג, מ"ה ברבוע וע"ב ע"ה מְבָרַךְ mevarach

לְעָלַם le'alam לְעָלְמֵי le'almei עָלְמַיָּא •almaya יִתְבָּרַךְ •yitbarach

Seven words with six letters each (שם בן מ"ב) and also, seven times the letter Vav (שם בן מ"ב)

וְיִשְׁתַּבַּח veyishtabach י"פ ע"ב יהוה אל אבג יתץ•

וְיִתְפָּאַר veyitpa'ar הי נו יה קרע שטן• וְיִתְרוֹמַם veyitromam וה כוזו נגד יכש•

וְיִתְנַשֵּׂא veyitnase במוכסז בטר צתג• וְיִתְהַדָּר veyit'hadar כוזו יה וזקב טנע•

וְיִתְעַלֶּה veyit'ale וה יוד ה יגל פזק• וְיִתְהַלָּל veyit'halal א ואו הא שקו צית•

שְׁמֵיהּ shemei (שם י"ה דמ"ה) דְּקוּדְשָׁא dekudsha בְּרִיךְ verich הוּא hu:

אָמֵן amen אידהנויה•

לְעֵלָּא le'ela מִן min כָּל kol ילי בִּרְכָתָא •birchata שִׁירָתָא •shirata

תֻּשְׁבְּחָתָא tishbechata וְנֶחָמָתָא •venechamata דַּאֲמִירָן da'amiran

בְּעָלְמָא be'alma וְאִמְרוּ ve'imru אָמֵן :amen אָמֵן amen אידהנויה.

In the world that He created according to His will, and may His kingdom reign. And may He cause His redemption to sprout and may He bring the Mashiach closer. (Amen) *In your lifetimes and in your days and in the lifetime of all the House of Israel, speedily and in the near future, and you should say, Amen.* (Amen) *May His great Name be blessed forever and for all eternity blessed and lauded, and glorified and exalted, And extolled and honored, and uplifted and praised, be the Name of the Holy Blessed One.* (Amen) *Above all blessings, songs, praises, and words of consolation that may be said in the world, and you shall say, Amen.* (Amen)

THE AMIDAH - GENERAL

When we begin the connection, we take three steps backward, signifying our leaving this physical world. Then we take three steps forward to begin the *Amidah*. The three steps are:

1. Stepping into the land of Israel – to enter the first spiritual circle.
2. Stepping into the city of Jerusalem – to enter the second spiritual circle.
3. Stepping inside the Holy of Holies – to enter the innermost circle.

Before we recite the first verse of the *Amidah*, we ask: "*God, open my lips and let my mouth speak,*" thereby asking the Light to speak for us so that we can receive what we need and not just what we want. All too often, what we want from life is not necessarily the desire of the soul, which is what we actually need to fulfill us. By asking the Light to speak through us, we ensure that our connection will bring us genuine fulfillment and opportunities for spiritual growth and change.

If *Shavuot* falls on weekdays we skip the meditaions below and start the *Amidah* on the next page (98.)

If *Shavuot* (second day) falls on *Shabbat* we scan the meditaion below and continue the *Amidah* on the next page (98.)

The Format of the Ascention in *Arvit of Shabbat*

When saying "*Baruch*" meditate to draw *Netzach, Hod, Yesod* and *Chesed, Gevurah, Tiferet* of *Keter, Chochmah, Binah, Da'at* of *Netzach, Hod, Yesod* of *Chesed, Gevurah, Tiferet* of the Internal of *Tevunah* (that were drawn during the recitation of the "*Shema*" to *Keter, Chochmah, Binah, Da'at*. And *Chesed, Gevurah, Tiferet*) **to** *Chesed, Gevurah, Tiferet* and *Netzach, Hod, Yesod* of *Keter, Chochmah, Binah, Da'at* of *Netzach, Hod, Yesod* and *Chesed, Gevurah, Tiferet* of *Binah* of the Internal of *Zeir Anpin*.

When saying "*Ata*" meditate to draw *Keter, Chochmah, Binah* of *Keter, Chochmah, Binah* of *Tevuna* to *Keter, Chochmah, Binah* of *Zeir Anpin* and push down the Six Edges (of *Tevunah*) to the Six Edges of *Zeir Anpin*.

When saying "*Adonai*" meditate to draw *Netzach, Hod, Yesod* and *Chesed, Gevurah, Tiferet* of *Keter, Chochmah, Binah, Da'at* of *Netzach, Hod, Yesod* of *Chesed, Gevurah, Tiferet* of the Internal of *Israel Saba* **to** *Chesed, Gevurah, Tiferet* and *Netzach, Hod, Yesod* of *Zeir Anpin* **and then draw** *Keter, Chochmah, Binah* of *Israel Saba* to *Keter, Chochmah, Binah* of *Zeir Anpin* and push down the Six Edges (of *Israel Saba*) to the Six Edges of *Zeir Anpin*.

אֲדֹנָי Adonai ללה (pause here) שְׂפָתַי sefatai תִּפְתָּח tiftach וּפִי ufi יַגִּיד yagid

ייז (כ"ב אותיות פשוטות [=אכא] וה' אותיות סופיות מנצפך) תְּהִלָּתֶךָ tehilatecha ס"ת = בוכו:

THE FIRST BLESSING - INVOKES THE SHIELD OF ABRAHAM.

Abraham is the channel of the Right Column energy of positivity, sharing, and mercy. Sharing actions can protect us from all forms of negativity.

Chesed that becomes *Chochmah*

In this section there are 42 words, the secret of the 42-Letter Name of God and therefore it begins with the letter *Bet* (2) and ends with the letter *Mem* (40).

Bend your knees at *'baruch'*, bow at *'Ata'* and straighten up at *'Adonai'*.

א ב

בָּרוּךְ baruch אַתָּה Ata א–ת (אותיות הא"ב המסמלות את השפע המגיע) לה' המלכות

ג י

יְהֹוָאדנהי Adonai אהדונהי (יא) אֱלֹהֵינוּ Elohenu ילה

ת צ

וֵאלֹהֵי velohei לכב ; מילוי ע"ב, דמב ; ילה אֲבוֹתֵינוּ avotenu.

ק ר

אֱלֹהֵי Elohei מילוי ע"ב, דמב ; ילה אַבְרָהָם Avraham (*Chochmah*)

וז"פ אל, רי"ו ול"ב נתיבות החכמה, רמ"ח (אברים), עסמ"ב וט"ז אותיות פשוטות

ע ש

אֱלֹהֵי Elohei מילוי ע"ב, דמב ; ילה יִצְחָק Yitzchak (*Binah*) ד"פ ב"ן

ט נ

וֵאלֹהֵי velohei לכב ; מילוי ע"ב, דמב ; ילה יַעֲקֹב Yaakov (*Da'at*) ו' הויות, יאהדונהי אידהנויה

THE AMIDAH

"My Lord, open my lips, and my mouth shall relate Your praise." (Psalms 51:17)

THE FIRST BLESSING

Blessed are You, Lord,

our God and God of our forefathers: the God of Abraham, the God of Isaac, and the God of Jacob.

נ ג

הָאֵל haEl לאה ; ייא״ (מילוי דס״ג) הַגָּדוֹל hagadol האל הגדול = סיט ; גדול = להח

ד י

עם ד׳ אותיות = מבה, יזל, הום הַגִּבּוֹר hagibor ר״ת ההה וְהַנּוֹרָא vehanora •

כ ש

אֵל El ייא״ (מילוי דס״ג) ; ר״ת ע״ב, ריבוע יהוה עֶלְיוֹן elyon •

ב ט ר צ ת

גּוֹמֵל gomel חֲסָדִים chasadim טוֹבִים tovim • קוֹנֵה kone הַכֹּל hakol ילי

ג ח ק ב

וְזוֹכֵר vezocher חַסְדֵי chasdei אָבוֹת avot • וּמֵבִיא umevi

ט נ ע י

גּוֹאֵל go'el לִבְנֵי livnei בְנֵיהֶם venehem לְמַעַן lema'an

ג ל

שְׁמוֹ shemo מהש ע״ה, ע״ב בריבוע וקס״א ע״ה, אל שדי ע״ה בְּאַהֲבָה be'ahava אחד, דאגה:

When saying the word "*be'ahava*" you should meditate to devote your soul to sanctify the Holy Name and accept upon yourself the four forms of death.

פ ז ק ש

מֶלֶךְ melech עוֹזֵר ozer וּמוֹשִׁיעַ umoshi'a וּמָגֵן umagen

ג״פ אל (ייא״ מילוי דס״ג) ; ר״ת מיכאל גבריאל נוריאל:

Bend your knees at *'baruch'*, bow at *'Ata'* and straighten up at *'Adonai'*.

אהיה יהו אלף הי יוד הי (on *Shabbat*: יְהֹוָה)

ק ו צ

בָּרוּךְ baruch אַתָּה Ata יְה�ֹוָהאדני(יְהֹוָהאדני)יאהדונהי Adonai (הד)

י ת

מָגֵן magen ג״פ אל (ייא״ מילוי דס״ג) ; ר״ת מיכאל גבריאל נוריאל אַבְרָהָם Avraham

וח״פ אל, רי״ו ול״ב נתיבות החכמה, רמ״ח (אברים), עסמ״ב וט״ז אותיות פשוטות:

The great, mightyand awesome God. The Supernal God, Who bestows beneficial kindness and creates everything. Who recalls the kindness of the forefathers and brings a Redeemer to their descendants for the sake of His Name, lovingly. King, Helper, Savior and Shield. Blessed are You, Lord, the shield of Abraham.

The Second Blessing

THE ENERGY OF ISAAC IGNITES THE POWER FOR THE RESURRECTION OF THE DEAD.

Whereas Abraham represents the power of sharing, Isaac represents the Left Column energy of judgment. Judgment shortens the *Tikkun* process and paves the way for our eventual resurrection.

Gevurah that becomes *Binah*.

In this section there are 49 words corresponding to the 49 gates of the Pure System in *Binah*.

אַתָּה Ata גִּבּוֹר gibor לְעוֹלָם le'olam ריבוע ס"ג וי' אותיות דס"ג אֲדֹנָי Adonai ללה

(ר"ת אֲגְלָא והוא שם גדול ואמיץ, ובו היה יהודה מתגבר על אויביו. ע"ה אלד, בוכו).

מְחַיֶּה mechaye ס"ג מֵתִים metim אַתָּה Ata• רַב rav לְהוֹשִׁיעַ lehoshi'a•

מוֹרִיד morid הַטָּל hatal יוד הא ואו, כוזו, מספר אותיות דמילואי עסמ"ב ; ר"ת מ"ה:•

If you mistakenly say "*Mashiv haru'ach*", and realize this before the end of the blessing ("*baruch Ata Adonai*"), you should return to the beginning of the blessing ("*Ata gibor*") and continue as usual. But if you only realize this after the end of the blessing, you should start the *Amidah* from the beginning.

מְכַלְכֵּל mechalkel חַיִּים chayim אהיה אהיה יהוה, בינה ע"ה בְּחֶסֶד bechesed

ע"ב, ריבוע יהוה• מְחַיֶּה mechaye ס"ג מֵתִים metim בְּרַחֲמִים berachamim

(בְּמוּכסז) מצפצ, אלהים דההין, י"פ ייי רַבִּים rabim (טלא דעתיק)• סוֹמֵךְ somech

(אכדטם) כוק, ריבוע אדני נוֹפְלִים noflim (זו"ן)• וְרוֹפֵא verofe חוֹלִים cholim

חולה = מ"ה וד' אותיות• וּמַתִּיר umatir אֲסוּרִים asurim• וּמְקַיֵּם umekayem

אֱמוּנָתוֹ emunato לִישֵׁנֵי lishenei עָפָר afar• מִי mi ילי כָּמוֹךָ chamocha

גִּבּוֹרוֹת gevurot בַּעַל ba'al (you should enunciate the letter *Ayin* in the word "*ba'al*")

וּמִי umi ילי דּוֹמֶה dome לָּךְ lach• מֶלֶךְ melech מֵמִית memit

וּמְחַיֶּה umchaye ס"ג (יוד הי ואו הי) וּמַצְמִיחַ umatzmi'ach יְשׁוּעָה yeshu'a:•

The Second Blessing

You are mighty forever, Lord. You resurrect the dead and are very capable of redeeming.
Who causes dew to fall.

You sustain life with kindness and resurrect the dead with great compassion. You support those who have fallen, heal the sick, release the imprisoned, and fulfill Your faithful words to those who are asleep in the dust. Who is like You, Master of might, and Who can compare to You, King, Who causes death, Who gives life, and Who sprouts salvation?

וְנֶאֱמָן vene'eman אַתָּה Ata לְהַחֲיוֹת lehachayot מֵתִים metim:

אהיה יהו אלף הי יוד הי (on Shabbat: יְהֹוִה)

בָּרוּךְ baruch אַתָּה Ata יְהֹוָהאדני(יְהֹוֶהאדנִיה)יאהדונהי Adonai

מְחַיֵּה mechaye ס״ג (יוד הי ואו הי) הַמֵּתִים hametim ר״ת מ״ה וס״ת מ״ה:

THE THIRD BLESSING

This blessing connects us to Jacob, the Central Column and the power of restriction. Jacob is our channel for connecting mercy with judgment. By restricting our reactive behavior, we are blocking our Desire to Receive for the Self Alone. Jacob also gives us the power to balance our acts of mercy and judgment toward other people in our lives.

Tiferet* that becomes *Da'at (14 words).

אַתָּה Ata קָדוֹשׁ kadosh וְשִׁמְךָ veshimcha קָדוֹשׁ kadosh ר״ת = אור, רז, אין סוף.

וּקְדוֹשִׁים ukdoshim בְּכָל bechol ב״ן, לכב יוֹם yom ע״ה נגד, מזבח, זן, אל יהוה

יְהַלְלוּךָ yehalelucha סֶּלָה sela:

אהיה יהו אלף הא יוד הא (on Shabbat: מצפצ)

בָּרוּךְ baruch אַתָּה Ata יְהֹוָהאדני(יְהֹוָהאדנִיה)יאהדונהי Adonai

הָאֵל haEl לאה ; ייא״י (מילוי דס״ג) הַקָּדוֹשׁ hakadosh י״פ מ״ה (יוד הא ואו הא):

Meditate here on the Name: יאהדונהי, as it can help to remove anger.

THE MIDDLE BLESSING

The middle blessing connects us to the true essence of *Shavuot*. *Shavuot* is our connection to immortality and this blessing is our opportunity to choose the seed we wish to plant for immortality. The power of the letters in the Fourth Blessing is in their ability to automatically choose the correct seed we need and not necessarily the seed we want.

אַתָּה Ata בְּחַרְתָּנוּ vechartanu מִכָּל mikol ילי הָעַמִּים ha'amim.

אָהַבְתָּ ahavta אוֹתָנוּ otanu וְרָצִיתָ veratzita בָּנוּ banu.

And You are faithful to resurrecting the dead. Blessed are You, Lord, Who resurrects the dead.

THE THIRD BLESSING

You are holy, and Your Name is holy, and the Holy Ones praise You every day, for you are God, the Holy King Selah. Blessed are You, Lord, the Holy God.

THE MIDDLE BLESSING

You had chosen us from among all the nations. You had loved us and have found favor in us.

וְרוֹמַמְתָּנוּ veromamtanu מִכָּל mikol ילי הַלְּשׁוֹנוֹת haleshonot•
וְקִדַּשְׁתָּנוּ vekidashtanu בְּמִצְוֹתֶיךָ bemitzvotecha• וְקֵרַבְתָּנוּ vekeravtanu
מַלְכֵּנוּ malkenu לַעֲבוֹדָתֶךָ la'avodatecha• וְשִׁמְךָ veshimcha הַגָּדוֹל hagadol
להח ; ועם ד' אותיות = מבה, יזל, הום וְהַקָּדוֹשׁ vehakadosh עָלֵינוּ alenu קָרָאתָ karata:

When *Shavuot* falls on Saturday night then the following is said:

וַתּוֹדִיעֵנוּ vatodi'enu מִשְׁפְּטֵי mishpetei צִדְקֶךָ tzidkecha• וַתְּלַמְּדֵנוּ vatelamdenu
לַעֲשׂוֹת la'asot בָּהֶם bahem חֻקֵּי chukei רְצוֹנֶךָ retzonecha• וַתִּתֶּן vatiten ב"פ כהת
לָנוּ lanu אלהים, אהיה אדני יְהֹוָהאדניאהדונהי Adonai אֱלֹהֵינוּ Elohenu ילה
בְּאַהֲבָה be'ahava אחד, דאגה• מִשְׁפָּטִים mishpatim יְשָׁרִים yesharim•
וְתוֹרוֹת vetorot אֱמֶת emet אהיה פעמים אהיה, ו"פ ס"ג• חֻקִּים chukim וּמִצְוֹת umitzot
טוֹבִים tovim• וַתַּנְחִילֵנוּ vatanchilenu זְמַנֵּי zemanei שָׂשׂוֹן sason וּמוֹעֲדֵי umoadei
קֹדֶשׁ kodesh וְחַגֵּי vechagei נְדָבָה nedava• וַתּוֹרִישֵׁנוּ vatorishenu
קְדֻשַּׁת kedushat שַׁבָּת shabat וּכְבוֹד uchvod מוֹעֵד mo'ed וַחֲגִיגַת vachagigat
הָרֶגֶל haregel• בֵּין ben קְדֻשַּׁת kedushat שַׁבָּת shabat לִקְדֻשַּׁת likdushat
יוֹם yom ע"ה נגד, מזבח, זן, אל יהוה טוֹב tov והו הִבְדַּלְתָּ hivdalta•
וְאֶת ve'et יוֹם yom ע"ה נגד, מזבח, זן, אל יהוה הַשְּׁבִיעִי hashvi'i מִשֵּׁשֶׁת misheshet
יְמֵי yemei הַמַּעֲשֶׂה hama'ase קִדַּשְׁתָּ kidashta וְהִבְדַּלְתָּ vehivdalta•
וְקִדַּשְׁתָּ vekidashta אֶת et עַמְּךָ amcha יִשְׂרָאֵל Yisra'el בִּקְדֻשָּׁתָךְ bikdushatach:

וַתִּתֶּן vatiten ב"פ כהת לָנוּ lanu אלהים, אהיה אדני יְהֹוָהאדניאהדונהי Adonai
אֱלֹהֵינוּ Elohenu ילה בְּאַהֲבָה be'ahava אחד, דאגה
(On Shabbat add: שַׁבָּתוֹת shabbatot לִמְנוּחָה limnucha ו u) מוֹעֲדִים mo'adim
לְשִׂמְחָה lesimcha• חַגִּים chagim וּזְמַנִּים uzmanim לְשָׂשׂוֹן lesason•

You had exalted us above all the tongues and You had sanctified us with Your commandments. You drew us close, our King, to Your service and proclaimed Your great and Holy Name upon us.

You had informed us of Your righteous ordinances and You had taught us to do the decrees of Your will. May You give us, Lord, our God with love, fair ordinances and true teachings and good laws and commandments. And may You give us, as a heritage, seasons of joy and appointed festivals of Holiness and free willed festive-offerings. May You make us inherit the Shabbat Holiness and the glory of the Festival and the festive-offering of the Pilgrimage. You have distinguished between the sanctity of the Shabbat and the sanctity of the festival, and between the seventh day and the six working days, and had sanctified Your nation, Israel, with Your sanctity.

And may You give us, Lord, our God,
*with love (***on Shabbat add:** *Shabbat for rest and) holidays for happiness, festivals and time of joy,*

אֶת et יוֹם yom ע"ה נגד, מזבח, זן, אל יהוה (On Shabbat add: הַשַּׁבָּת hashabat
הַזֶּה hazeh והו. וְאֶת ve'et יוֹם yom ע"ה נגד, מזבח, זן, אל יהוה) וְחַג chag
הַשָּׁבוּעוֹת haShavuot הַזֶּה hazeh והו. אֶת et יוֹם yom ע"ה נגד, מזבח, זן, אל יהוה
טוֹב tov והו מִקְרָא mikra קֹדֶשׁ kodesh הַזֶּה hazeh והו. זְמַן zeman
מַתַּן matan תּוֹרָתֵנוּ toratenu. בְּאַהֲבָה be'ahava אחד, דאגה מִקְרָא mikra
קֹדֶשׁ kodesh. זֵכֶר zecher לִיצִיאַת litzi'at מִצְרָיִם Mitzrayim מצר.

אֱלֹהֵינוּ elhenu ילה וֵאלֹהֵי vElohei לכב ; מילוי ע"ב, דמב ; ילה אֲבוֹתֵינוּ avotenu
יַעֲלֶה ya'ale וְיָבֹא veyavo וְיַגִּיעַ veyagi'a וְיֵרָאֶה veyera'e ר"ו וְיֵרָצֶה veyeratze
וְיִשָּׁמַע veyishama וְיִפָּקֵד veyipaked וְיִזָּכֵר veyizacher ר"ת = מ"ב
זִכְרוֹנֵנוּ zichronenu וְזִכְרוֹן vezichron ע"ב קס"א ונש"ב אֲבוֹתֵינוּ avotenu.
זִכְרוֹן zichron ע"ב קס"א ונש"ב יְרוּשָׁלַיִם Yerushalayim עִירָךְ irach.
וְזִכְרוֹן vezichron ע"ב קס"א ונש"ב מָשִׁיחַ mashi'ach בֶּן ben דָּוִד David ע"ה כהת ;
בן דוד = אדני ע"ה עַבְדָּךְ avdach פוי, אל אדני. וְזִכְרוֹן vezichron ע"ב קס"א ונש"ב כָּל kol ילי
עַמְּךָ amecha בֵּית bet ב"פ ראה יִשְׂרָאֵל Yisra'el לְפָנֶיךָ lefanecha ס"ג מ"ה ב"ן
לִפְלֵיטָה lifleta לְטוֹבָה letova אכא. לְחֵן lechen מילוי דמ"ה בריבוע ; מוזי
לְחֶסֶד lechesed ע"ב, ריבוע יהוה וּלְרַחֲמִים ulrachamim.
לְחַיִּים lechayim אהיה אהיה יהוה, בינה ע"ה טוֹבִים tovim וּלְשָׁלוֹם ulshalom.
בְּיוֹם beyom ע"ה נגד, מזבח, זן, אל יהוה (On Shabbat add: הַשַּׁבָּת hashabat הַזֶּה hazeh והו.
וּבְיוֹם uvyom ע"ה נגד, מזבח, זן, אל יהוה) וְחַג chag הַשָּׁבוּעוֹת haShavuot הַזֶּה hazeh והו.

---

this day

(**on Shabbat add:** *of Shabbat and this day) of Shavuot holiday, and this good day of Holy Convocation, the time we received our Torah, with love, a Holy Convocation, a remembrance of the exit from Egypt.*

Our God and the God of our fathers,

may it rise and come and arrive and appear and find favor and be heard and be considered and be remembered, our remembrance and the remembrance of our fathers, the remembrance of Jerusalem, Your city, and the remembrance of Mashiach Ben David, Your servant, and the remembrance of Your entire Nation, the House of Israel, before You for deliverance, for good, for grace, kindness and compassion, for a good life and for peace on this Day of (**on Shabbat say:** *Shabbat and on this Day of) Shavuot holiday,*

בְּיוֹם beyom ע"ה נגד, מזבח, זן, אל יהוה טוֹב tov והו מִקְרָא mikra קֹדֶשׁ kodesh
הַזֶּה hazeh והו• לְרַחֵם lerachem אברהם, וו"פ אל, רי"ו ול"ב נתיבות החכמה, רמ"ח (אברים),
עסמ"ב וט"ז אותיות פשוטות בּוֹ bo עָלֵינוּ alenu וּלְהוֹשִׁיעֵנוּ ulhoshi'enu•
זָכְרֵנוּ zochrenu (from *Zeir Anpin*) יְהֹוָאדהנויאהדונהי Adonai אֱלֹהֵינוּ Elohenu ילה
בּוֹ bo לְטוֹבָה letova אכא• וּפָקְדֵנוּ ufokdenu (from *Nukva*) בוֹ vo
לִבְרָכָה livracha• וְהוֹשִׁיעֵנוּ vehoshi'enu (from *Da'at*) בוֹ vo לְחַיִּים lechayim
אהיה אהיה יהוה, בינה ע"ה טוֹבִים tovim• בִּדְבַר bidvar ראה יְשׁוּעָה yeshu'a
וְרַחֲמִים verachamim• חוּס chus וְחָנֵּנוּ vechanenu וַחֲמוֹל vachamol
וְרַחֵם verachem אברהם, וו"פ אל, רי"ו ול"ב נתיבות החכמה, רמ"ח (אברים), עסמ"ב וט"ז אותיות פשוטות
עָלֵינוּ alenu• וְהוֹשִׁיעֵנוּ vehoshi'enu כִּי ki אֵלֶיךָ elecha עֵינֵינוּ enenu ריבוע מ"ה•
כִּי ki אֵל El ייא"י מֶלֶךְ melech חַנּוּן chanun וְרַחוּם verachum אָתָּה Ata:
וְהַשִּׂיאֵנוּ vehashsyenu יְהֹוָאדהנויאהדונהי Adonai אֱלֹהֵינוּ Elohenu ילה•
אֶת et בִּרְכַּת birkat מוֹעֲדֶיךָ mo'adecha לְחַיִּים lechayim אהיה אהיה יהוה, בינה ע"ה
בְּשִׂמְחָה besimcha וּבְשָׁלוֹם uvshalom• כַּאֲשֶׁר ka'asher רָצִיתָ ratzita
וְאָמַרְתָּ ve'amarta לְבָרְכֵנוּ levarchenu• כֵּן ken תְּבָרְכֵנוּ tevarchenu
סֶלָה selah:

MEKADESH ISRAEL AND THE TIME

(On *Shabbat* add: אֱלֹהֵינוּ Elohenu ילה וֵאלֹהֵי veElohei לכב ; מילוי ע"ב, דמב ; ילה
אֲבוֹתֵינוּ avotenu רְצֵה retze נָא na בִמְנוּחָתֵנוּ vimnuchatenu)

---

on this good Day of Holy Convocation, to take pity on us and to save us.
Remember us, Lord,
our God, on it for good and consider us, on it, for blessing and deliver us on it for a good life with the words of deliverance and mercy. Take pity and be gracious to us and have mercy and be compassionate with us and save us, for our eyes turn to You, because You are God, King Who is gracious and compassionate.
And give us, Lord, our God Your blessing of Your holidays for happy and peaceful life.
As You desired and said to bless us. So You shall bless us Selah.

MEKADESH ISRAEL AND THE TIME

(**On *Shabbat*:** *Our God and the God of our forefathers, please desire our rest.)*

קַדְּשֵׁנוּ kadshenu בְּמִצְוֹתֶיךָ •vemitzvotecha תֵּן ten וְחֶלְקֵנוּ chelkenu

בְּתוֹרָתָךְ •vetoratach שַׂבְּעֵנוּ sabe'enu מִטּוּבָךְ mituvach לאו•

שַׂמֵּחַ same'ach נַפְשֵׁנוּ nafshenu בִּישׁוּעָתָךְ •bishu'atach

וְטַהֵר vetaher לִבֵּנוּ libenu לְעָבְדְּךָ le'ovdecha פוי, אל יהוה בֶּאֱמֶת ve'emet

אהיה פעמים אהיה, ו"פ ס"ג• וְהַנְחִילֵנוּ vehanchilenu יְהֹוָהאדניאהדונהי Adonai

אֱלֹהֵינוּ Elohenu ילה (On Shabbat add: בְּאַהֲבָה be'ahava אוזד, דאגה

וּבְרָצוֹן uvratzon מהש ע"ה, ע"ב בריבוע וקס"א ע"ה, אל שדי) בְּשִׂמְחָה vesimcha

וּבְשָׂשׂוֹן uvsason (On Shabbat add: שַׁבָּתוֹת shabatot ו) מוֹעֲדֵי mo'adei

קָדְשֶׁךָ, kodshecha וְיִשְׂמְחוּ veyismechu בְךָ vecha כָּל kol ילי יִשְׂרָאֵל Yisrael

מְקַדְּשֵׁי mekadshei שְׁמֶךָ •shemecha בָּרוּךְ baruch אַתָּה Ata

יְהֹוָהאדניאהדונהי Adonai

אהיה יהו אלף הה יוד הה (on Shabbat: יה אדני)

מְקַדֵּשׁ mekadesh (On Shabbat add: הַשַּׁבָּת hashabat וְ ve) יִשְׂרָאֵל Yisrael

וְהַזְּמַנִּים vehazemanim:

THE FINAL THREE BLESSINGS

Through the merit of Moses, Aaron and Joseph, who are our channels for the final three blessings, we are able to bring down all the spiritual energy that we aroused with our prayers and blessings.

THE FIFTH BLESSING

During this blessing, referring to Moses, we should always meditate to try to know exactly what God wants from us in our life, as signified by the phrase, "Let it be the will of God." We ask God to guide us toward the work we came to Earth to do. The Creator cannot just accept the work that we want to do; we must carry out the work we were destined to do.

Sanctify us with Your commandments and place
our lot in Your Torah and satiate us from Your goodness and gladden our spirits with Your salvation.
and purify our heart
so as to serve You truly. And grant us, Lord, our God, (**on Shabbat:** *with love and favor,*) *with happiness and joy* (**on Shabbat:** *Shabbatot and*) *the holidays, and all Yisrael, who sanctify Your Name will be joyful with You. Blessed are You, Lord, who sanctifies* (**on Shabbat:** *the Sabbath*) *and Israel and the Times.*

Netzach

Meditate for the Supernal Desire (*Keter*) that is called *metzach haratzon* (the Forhead of the Desire).

רְצֵה retze אלף למד הה יוד מם

Meditate here to transform misfortune and tragedy (צרה) into desire and acceptance (רצה).

יְהֹוָהאדניאהדונהי Adonai אֱלֹהֵינוּ Elohenu ילה בְּעַמְּךָ be'amecha יִשְׂרָאֵל Yisrael

וְלִתְפִלָּתָם velitfilatam שְׁעֵה she'e• וְהָשֵׁב vehashev הָעֲבוֹדָה ha'avoda

לִדְבִיר lidvir רי"ו בֵּיתֶךָ betecha ב"פ ראה• וְאִשֵּׁי ve'ishei יִשְׂרָאֵל Yisrael

וּתְפִלָּתָם utfilatam מְהֵרָה mehera בְּאַהֲבָה be'ahava אוזד, דאגה

תְקַבֵּל tekabel בְּרָצוֹן beratzon מהש ע"ה, ע"ב בריבוע וקס"א ע"ה, אל שדי ע"ה•

וּתְהִי ut'hi לְרָצוֹן leratzon מהש ע"ה, ע"ב בריבוע וקס"א ע"ה, אל שדי ע"ה

תָּמִיד tamid ע"ה קס"א קנ"א קמ"ג עֲבוֹדַת avodat יִשְׂרָאֵל Yisrael עַמֶּךָ amecha:

וְאַתָּה veAta בְּרַחֲמֶיךָ verachamecha הָרַבִּים harabim•

תַּחְפֹּץ tachpotz בָּנוּ banu וְתִרְצֵנוּ vetirtzenu וְתֶחֱזֶינָה vetechezena

עֵינֵינוּ enenu ריבוע מ"ה בְּשׁוּבְךָ beshuvcha לְצִיּוֹן leTziyon יוסף, ו' הויות, קנאה

בְּרַחֲמִים berachamim מצפצ, אלהים דיודין, י"פ ייי:

אהיה יהו אלף למד הי יוד מם (on *Shabbat*: אל)

בָּרוּךְ baruch אַתָּה Ata יְהֹוָהאדניאהדונהי Adonai

הַמַּחֲזִיר hamachazir שְׁכִינָתוֹ shechinato לְצִיּוֹן leTziyon יוסף, ו' הויות, קנאה:

THE FIFTH BLESSING

Find favor, Lord, our God,
in Your People, Israel, and turn to their prayer.
Restore the service to the inner sanctuary of Your Temple. Accept the offerings of Israel and their prayer with favor, speedily, and with love. May the service of Your People Israel always be favorable to You. And You in Your great compassion take delight in us and are pleased with us. May our eyes witness Your return to Zion with compassion. Blessed are You, Lord, Who returns His Shechinah to Zion.

THE SIXTH BLESSING

This blessing is our thank you. Kabbalistically, the biggest "thank you" we can give the Creator is to do exactly what we are supposed to do in terms of our spiritual work.

Hod

Bow your entire body at '*modim*' and straighten up at '*Adonai*'.

מוֹדִים modim מאה ברכות שתיקן דוד לאמרם כל יום אֲנַחְנוּ anachnu לָךְ lach

שָׁאַתָּה sheAta הוּא hu יְהֹוָאדניאהדונהי Adonai (ע"ב) אֱלֹהֵינוּ Elohenu ילה

וֵאלֹהֵי velohei לכב ; מילוי ע"ב, דמב ; ילה אֲבוֹתֵינוּ avotenu לְעוֹלָם le'olam

וָעֶד va'ed• ריבוע ס"ג וי' אותיות דס"ג צוּרֵנוּ tzurenu צוּר tzur אלהים דההין ע"ה

חַיֵּינוּ chayenu וּמָגֵן umagen ג"פ אל (ייא" מילוי דס"ג) ; ר"ת מיכאל גבריאל נוריאל

יִשְׁעֵנוּ yish'enu אַתָּה Ata הוּא hu• לְדֹר ledor וָדֹר vador רי"ו נוֹדֶה node

לְךָ lecha וּנְסַפֵּר unsaper תְּהִלָּתֶךָ tehilatecha• עַל־ al חַיֵּינוּ chayenu

הַמְּסוּרִים hamesurim בְּיָדֶךָ beyadecha• וְעַל ve'al נִשְׁמוֹתֵינוּ nishmotenu

הַפְּקוּדוֹת hapekudot לָךְ lach• וְעַל־ ve'al נִסֶּיךָ nisecha שֶׁבְּכָל shebechol

יוֹם לכב, ב"ן yom ע"ה נגד, מזבח, זן, אל יהוה עִמָּנוּ imanu ריבוע ס"ג, קס"א ע"ה וד' אותיות

וְעַל ve'al נִפְלְאוֹתֶיךָ nifle'otecha וְטוֹבוֹתֶיךָ vetovotecha שֶׁבְּכָל shebechol

עֵת לכב, ב"ן et• עֶרֶב erev וָבֹקֶר vavoker וְצָהֳרָיִם vetzahorayim• הַטּוֹב hatov

והו כִּי־ ki לֹא־ lo כָלוּ chalu רַחֲמֶיךָ rachamecha• הַמְרַחֵם hamerachem

אברהם, וז"פ אל, רי"ו ול"ב נתיבות החכמה, רמ"ח (אברים), עסמ"ב וט"ז אותיות פשוטות כִּי־ ki לֹא lo

תַמּוּ tamu חֲסָדֶיךָ chasadecha כִּי ki מֵעוֹלָם me'olam קִוִּינוּ kivinu לָךְ lach:

וְעַל ve'al כֻּלָּם kulam יִתְבָּרַךְ yitbarach וְיִתְרוֹמָם veyitromam

---

THE SIXTH BLESSING

We give thanks to You, for it is You, Lord, Who is our God and God of our forefathers, forever and for all eternity. You are our Rock, the Rock of our lives, and the Shield of our salvation. From one generation to another, we shall give thanks to You and we shall tell of Your praise. For our lives that are entrusted in Your hands, for our souls that are in Your care, for Your miracles that are with us every day, and for Your wonders and Your favors that are with us at all times: evening, morning and afternoon. You are the good One, for Your compassion has never ceased. You are the compassionate One, for Your kindness has never ended, for we have always placed our hope in You.

וְיִתְנַשֵּׂא veyitnase תָּמִיד tamid ע״ה קס״א קנ״א קמ״ג שִׁמְךָ shimcha

מַלְכֵּנוּ malkenu לְעוֹלָם le'olam ריבוע ס״ג וי׳ אותיות דס״ג וָעֶד va'ed.

וְכָל־ vechol ילי הַחַיִּים hachayim אהיה אהיה יהוה, בינה ע״ה יוֹדוּךָ yoducha סֶּלָה sela:

וִיהַלְלוּ vihalelu וִיבָרְכוּ vivarchu יהוה ריבוע יהוה ריבוע מ״ה אֶת־ et

שִׁמְךָ shimcha הַגָּדוֹל hagadol להח ; עם ד׳ אותיות = מבה, יזל, אום בֶּאֱמֶת be'emet

אהיה פעמים אהיה, ז״פ ס״ג לְעוֹלָם le'olam ריבוע ס״ג וי׳ אותיות דס״ג כִּי ki טוֹב tov והו ;

כי טוב = יהוה אהיה, אום, מבה, יזל. הָאֵל haEl לאה ; ייא״י (מילוי דס״ג) יְשׁוּעָתֵנוּ yeshu'atenu

וְעֶזְרָתֵנוּ ve'ezratenu סֶלָה sela. הָאֵל haEl לאה ; ייא״י (מילוי דס״ג) הַטּוֹב hatov והו:

Bend your knees at *'baruch'*, bow at *'Ata'* and straighten up at *'Adonai'*.

אהיה יהו אלף למד הה יוד מם (on *Shabbat*: אלהים)

בָּרוּךְ baruch אַתָּה Ata יְהֹוָהאדניאהדונהי Adonai (ה׳) הַטּוֹב hatov והו

שִׁמְךָ shimcha וּלְךָ ulcha נָאֶה na'e לְהוֹדוֹת lehodot ס״ת כהת, משיח בן דוד ע״ה:

THE FINAL BLESSING

We are emanating the energy of peace to the entire world. We also make it our intent to use our mouths only for good. Kabbalistically, the power of words and speech is unimaginable. We hope to use that power wisely, which is perhaps one of the most difficult tasks we have to carry out.

Yesod

שִׂים sim שָׁלוֹם shalom

טוֹבָה tova אכא וּבְרָכָה uvracha חַיִּים chayim אהיה אהיה יהוה, בינה ע״ה חֵן chen

מילוי דמ״ה בריבוע, מוזי וָחֶסֶד vachesed ע״ב, ריבוע יהוה צְדָקָה tzedaka ע״ה ריבוע אלהים

וְרַחֲמִים verachamim עָלֵינוּ alenu וְעַל־ ve'al כָּל־ kol ילי ; עמם

And for all those things, may Your Name be always blessed, exalted and extolled, our King, forever and ever, and all the living shall thank You, Selah. And they shall praise and bless Your Great Name, sincerely and forever, for It is good, the God of our salvation and our help, Selah, the good God. Blessed are You, Lord, whose Name is good, and to You it is befitting to give thanks.

THE FINAL BLESSING

Place peace, goodness, blessing, life, grace, kindness, righteousness, and mercy upon us and upon

יִשְׂרָאֵל Yisrael עַמֶּךָ amecha וּבָרְכֵנוּ uvarchenu אָבִינוּ avinu כֻּלָּנוּ kulanu

כְּאֶחָד ke'echad אהבה, דאגה בְּאוֹר be'or רז, א"ס פָּנֶיךָ panecha ס"ג מ"ה ב"ן כִּי ki

בְאוֹר ve'or רז, א"ס פָּנֶיךָ panecha ס"ג מ"ה ב"ן נָתַתָּ natata לָנוּ lanu אלהים, אהיה אדני

יְהֹוָה Adonai אֱלֹהֵינוּ Elohenu ילה תּוֹרָה torah וְחַיִּים vechayim

אהיה אהיה יהוה, בינה ע"ה. אַהֲבָה ahava אחד, דאגה וָחֶסֶד vachesed ע"ב, ריבוע יהוה.

צְדָקָה tzedaka ע"ה ריבוע אלהים וְרַחֲמִים verachamim. בְּרָכָה beracha

וְשָׁלוֹם veshalom. וְטוֹב vetov והו בְּעֵינֶיךָ be'enecha ע"ה קס"א ; ריבוע מ"ה

לְבָרְכֵנוּ levarchenu וּלְבָרֵךְ ulvarech אֶת et כָּל kol ילי עַמְּךָ amecha

יִשְׂרָאֵל Yisrael בְּרוֹב berov י"פ אהיה עֹז oz וְשָׁלוֹם veshalom:

אהיה יהו אלף למד הא יוד מם (*on Shabbat*: מצפצ)

בָּרוּךְ baruch אַתָּה Ata יְהֹוָה Adonai

הַמְבָרֵךְ hamevarech אֶת et עַמּוֹ amo יִשְׂרָאֵל Yisrael

ר"ת = אלהים (אילהויהם = יב"ק) בַּשָּׁלוֹם bashalom. אָמֵן amen יאהדונהי.

YIH'YU LERATZON

There are 42 letters in the verse in the secret of *Ana Beko'ach*.

יִהְיוּ yih'yu אל (ייא" מילוי דס"ג) לְרָצוֹן leratzon מהש ע"ה, ע"ב בריבוע וקס"א ע"ה, אל שדי ע"ה

אִמְרֵי imrei פִי fi ר"ת אֶלֶף = אלף למד שין דלת יוד ע"ה וְהֶגְיוֹן vehegyon לִבִּי libi

לְפָנֶיךָ lefanecha ס"ג מ"ה ב"ן יְהֹוָה Adonai צוּרִי tzuri וְגֹאֲלִי vego'ali:

---

all of Israel, Your People. Bless us all as one, our Father, with the Light of Your Countenance, because it is with the Light of Your Countenance that You, Lord, our God, have given us Torah and life, love and kindness, righteousness and mercy, blessing and peace. May it be good in Your Eyes to bless us and to bless Your entire Nation, Israel, with abundant power and with peace.

Blessed are You, Lord, Who blesses His Nation, Israel, with peace, Amen.

YIH'YU LERATZON

"May the utterances of my mouth
and the thoughts of my heart find favor before You, Lord, my Rock and my Redeemer." (Psalms 19:15)

ELOHAI NETZOR

אֱלֹהַי Elohai מילוי ע"ב, דמב ; ילה נְצוֹר netzor לְשׁוֹנִי leshoni מֵרָע mera•
וּשְׂפָתוֹתַי vesiftotai מִדַּבֵּר midaber ראה מִרְמָה mirma• וְלִמְקַלְלַי velimkalelai
נַפְשִׁי nafshi תִדּוֹם tidom• וְנַפְשִׁי venafshi כֶּעָפָר ke'afar
לַכֹּל lakol יה אדני תִּהְיֶה tih'ye• פְּתַח petach לִבִּי libi בְּתוֹרָתֶךָ betoratecha•
וְאַחֲרֵי ve'acharei מִצְוֹתֶיךָ mitzvotecha תִּרְדּוֹף tirdof נַפְשִׁי nafshi•
וְכָל־ vechol ילי הַקָּמִים hakamim עָלַי alai לְרָעָה lera'a רהע• מְהֵרָה mehera
הָפֵר hafer עֲצָתָם atzatam וְקַלְקֵל vekalkel מַחְשְׁבוֹתָם machshevotam•
עֲשֵׂה ase לְמַעַן lema'an שְׁמָךְ shemach• עֲשֵׂה ase לְמַעַן lema'an
יְמִינָךְ yeminach• עֲשֵׂה ase לְמַעַן lema'an תּוֹרָתָךְ toratach• עֲשֵׂה ase
לְמַעַן lema'an קְדוּשָּׁתָךְ kedushatach• ר"ת הפסוק = מ"ה יהוה לְמַעַן lema'an
יֵחָלְצוּן yechaltzun יְדִידֶיךָ yedidecha ר"ת ילי הוֹשִׁיעָה hoshi'a יהוה וש"ע נהורין
יְמִינְךָ yemincha וַעֲנֵנִי va'aneni (כתיב: ועננו) ר"ת אל (יא"י מילוי דס"ג):

Before we recite the next verse ("*yih'yu leratzon*") we have an opportunity to strengthen our connection to our soul using our name. Each person has a verse in the *Torah* that connects to their name. Either their name is in the verse, or the first and last letters of the name correspond to the first or last letters of a verse. For example, the name Yehuda begins with a *Yud* and ends with a *Hei*. Before we end the *Amidah*, we state that our name will always be remembered when our soul leaves this world.

YIH'YU LERATZON (THE SECOND)

There are 42 letters in the verse in the secret of *Ana Beko'ach*.

יִהְיוּ yih'yu אל (יא"י מילוי דס"ג) לְרָצוֹן leratzon מהש ע"ה, ע"ב בריבוע וקס"א ע"ה, אל שדי ע"ה
אִמְרֵי־ imrei פִי fi ר"ת אלף = אלף למד שין דלת יוד ע"ה וְהֶגְיוֹן vehegyon לִבִּי libi
לְפָנֶיךָ lefanecha ס"ג מ"ה ב"ן יְהֹוָאֲדֹנָהִי יאהדונהי Adonai צוּרִי tzuri וְגֹאֲלִי vego'ali:

ELOHAI NETZOR

My God, guard my tongue from evil and my lips from speaking deceit. To those who curse me, let my spirit remain silent, and let my spirit be as dust for everyone. Open my heart to Your Torah and let my heart pursue Your commandments. All those who rise against me to do me harm, speedily nullify their plans and disturb their thoughts. Do so for the sake of Your Name. Do so for the sake of Your Right. Do so for the sake of Your Torah. Do so for the sake of Your Holiness, "So that Your loved ones may be saved. Redeem Your right and answer me." (Psalms 60:7)

YIH'YU LERATZON (THE SECOND)

"May the utterances of my mouth
and the thoughts of my heart find favor before You, Lord, my Rock and my Redeemer." (Psalms 19:15)

OSE SHALOM

You take three steps backward;

עוֹשֶׂה ose שָׁלוֹם shalom

Left
You turn to the left and say:

בִּמְרוֹמָיו bimromav ר"ת ע"ב, ריבוע יהוה

הוּא hu בְּרַחֲמָיו verachamav יַעֲשֶׂה ya'ase

Right
You turn to the right and say:

שָׁלוֹם shalom עָלֵינוּ alenu ר"ת ש"ע נהורין

Center
You face the center and say:

וְעַל ve'al כָּל־ kol ילי ; עמם עַמּוֹ amo יִשְׂרָאֵל Yisrael

וְאִמְרוּ ve'imru אָמֵן amen יאהדונהי:

יְהִי yehi רָצוֹן ratzon מהש ע"ה, ע"ב בריבוע וקס"א ע"ה, אל שדי ע"ה מִלְּפָנֶיךָ milfanecha ס"ג מ"ה ב"ן יְהֹוָהאדניאהדונהי Adonai אֱלֹהֵינוּ Elohenu ילה וֵאלֹהֵי velohei לכב ; מילוי ע"ב, דמב ; ילה אֲבוֹתֵינוּ avotenu, שֶׁתִּבְנֶה shetivne בֵּית bet ב"פ ראה הַמִּקְדָּשׁ hamikdash בִּמְהֵרָה bimhera בְּיָמֵינוּ veyamenu וְתֵן veten חֶלְקֵנוּ chelkenu בְּתוֹרָתָךְ betoratach לַעֲשׂוֹת la'asot חֻקֵּי chukei רְצוֹנָךְ retzonach וּלְעָבְדָךְ ul'ovdach פוי, אל אדני בְּלֵבָב belevav בוכו שָׁלֵם shalem.

You take three steps forward.

When *Shavuot* (second day) falls on *Shabbat* we say "*Birkat Me'en Sheva*" (pg. 112-115), otherwise we continue *Kaddish Titkabal* (pg. 115)

OSE SHALOM

He, Who makes peace in His high places, He,
in His compassion, shall make peace upon us And upon His entire nation, Israel, and you shall say, Amen.
May it be pleasing before You,
Lord, our God and God of our forefathers, that You shall rebuild the Temple speedily, in our days, and place our lot in Your Torah, so that we may fulfill the laws of Your desire and serve You wholeheartedly.

When *Shavuot* (second day) falls on *Shabbat* we say here *Birkat Me'en Sheva*:

After the *Amidah*, the congregation should remain standing and say "*Vay'chulu*" out loud. And even when you pray alone you are obligated to say it. Since there is a deep secret about reciting it three times on Friday night (in the *Amidah*, here, and later in the *Kidush* over the wine.) Therefore you should not skip any of the three.

Do not speak while the congregation says "*Vay'chulu*" and not while the *chazan* says "*Birkat Me'en Sheva*".

VAY'CHULU

These verses from the *Torah* connect us to the very first *Shabbat* that occurred in the Garden of Eden. This *Shabbat* was the seed of the creation of our universe. By connecting ourselves to the original seed, we capture the force of Creation, bringing rejuvenation and renewal to our lives.

Meditate on the letter ק, from the Name: שׁקוֹצית

Also, meditate that the three upper parts of the Surrounding *Mochin* of the letter *Lamed* (ל) of the *Tzelem* (צל״ם) of *Ima* are entering *Zeir Anpin* (as the head of *Zeir Anpin* is expanding).

The *Mochin* from *Abba* will enter *Zeir Anpin* later in the *Kidush*.

וַיְכֻלּוּ vay'chulu ע״ב = ריבוע יהוה (י יה יהו יהוה) הַשָּׁמַיִם hashamayim י״פ טל, י״פ כוזו

וְהָאָרֶץ veha'aretz אלהים דההין ע״ה ; ר״ת והו וְכָל־ vechol צְבָאָם tzeva'am ס״ת צלם:

וַיְכַל vay'chal אֱלֹהִים Elohim אהיה אדני ; ילה בַּיּוֹם bayom ע״ה נגד, מזבח, זן, אל יהוה

הַשְּׁבִיעִי hashevi'i מְלַאכְתּוֹ melachto אֲשֶׁר asher עָשָׂה asa

וַיִּשְׁבֹּת vayishbot בַּיּוֹם bayom ע״ה נגד, מזבח, זן, אל יהוה

הַשְּׁבִיעִי hashevi'i מִכָּל־ mikol ילי מְלַאכְתּוֹ melachto אֲשֶׁר asher

עָשָׂה asa: וַיְבָרֶךְ vay'varech עסמ״ב, הברכה (למתק את ז׳ המלכים שמתו)

אֱלֹהִים Elohim אהיה אדני ; ילה אֶת־ et יוֹם yom ע״ה נגד, מזבח, זן, אל יהוה

הַשְּׁבִיעִי hashevi'i וַיְקַדֵּשׁ vay'kadesh אֹתוֹ oto כִּי ki בוֹ vo

שָׁבַת shavat מִכָּל־ mikol ילי מְלַאכְתּוֹ melachto אֲשֶׁר־ asher

בָּרָא bara קנ״א ב״ן, יהוה אלהים יהוה אדני, מילוי קס״א וס״ג, מ״ה ברבוע וע״ב ע״ה

אֱלֹהִים Elohim אהיה אדני ; ילה לַעֲשׂוֹת la'asot:

VAY'CHULU

"And the Heavens and the Earth were completed and all their hosts. And God completed, on the seventh day, His work that He had done. And He abstained, on the seventh day, from all His work which He had done. And God blessed the seventh day and He sanctified it, for on it He had abstained from all His work which God had created to do". (Genesis 2:1-3)

BIRKAT ME'EN SHEVA

We are connecting ourselves to the founding Patriarchs, Abraham, Isaac, and Jacob. This connection works like a mini-*Amidah* prayer that occurs on *Shabbat*. Usually there is no repetition of the *Amidah* during *Arvit* (the evening connection), because it is night, a time of darkness, which signifies a lack of available spiritual Light. But on *Shabbat*, the Light floods our plane of existence. The following connection is our tool for capturing this additional Light.

According to Kabbalah, "*Birkat Me'en Sheva*" has a great importance, as it's the secret of the Patriarchs - which means *Chesed, Gevurah* and *Tiferet* - that illuminate from Their places to the *Nukva* without Her going up to Them. That is why it's called "*Me'en Sheva*" (one blessing made from seven) and not a complete repetition (for all seven blessings). And therefore we say it even when praying in a place without a *Torah* scroll (like in the house of a groom or the house of a mourner).

בָּרוּךְ baruch אַתָּה Ata א-ת

(אותיות הא״ב המסמלות את השפע המגיע) לה׳ המלכות

יְהֹוָהאדניאהדונהי Adonai אֱלֹהֵינוּ Elohenu ילה

וֵאלֹהֵי velohei לכב ; מילוי ע״ב, דמב ; ילה אֲבוֹתֵינוּ avotenu◆

אֱלֹהֵי Elohei מילוי ע״ב = דמב ; ילה אַבְרָהָם Avraham וו״פ אל, רי״ו ול״ב נתיבות החכמה,

רמ״ח, עסמ״ב וט״ז אותיות פשוטות. אֱלֹהֵי Elohei מילוי ע״ב, דמב ; ילה יִצְחָק Yitzchak ד״פ ב״ן

וֵאלֹהֵי velohei לכב ; מילוי ע״ב, דמב ; ילה יַעֲקֹב Yaakov ז׳ הויות, יאהדונהי אידהנויה

הָאֵל haEl לאה ; יי״א״ (מילוי דס״ג) הַגָּדוֹל hagadol האל הגדול = סיט ;

להח ; עם ד׳ אותיות = מבה, יזל, אום הַגִּבּוֹר hagibor ר״ת ההה וְהַנּוֹרָא vehanora◆

אֵל El יי״א״ (מילוי דס״ג) ; ר״ת ע״ב, ריבוע יהוה עֶלְיוֹן elyon◆

קוֹנֵה kone בְּרַחֲמָיו verachamav שָׁמַיִם shamayim י״פ טל, י״פ כוזו וָאָרֶץ va'aretz:

If the *chazan* mistakenly continued the repetition as on weekdays, he should stop and return to the blessing of *Shabbat*.

BIRKAT ME'EN SHEVA

Blessed are You, Lord, our God and God of our forefathers:
The God of Abraham, the God of Isaac, and the God of Jacob. The great, mighty, and awesome God, the Supreme God, Who created with His compassion the Heavens and the Earth.

The congregation together with the *chazan*:

מָגֵן magen ג"פ אל (ייא"י מילוי דס"ג) ; ר"ת מיכאל גבריאל נוריאל

אָבוֹת avot בִּדְבָרוֹ bidvaro

אהיה יהו יְהֹוָה

מְחַיֶּה mechaye ס"ג מֵתִים metim בְּמַאֲמָרוֹ bema'amaro

אהיה יהו יְהֹוִה

הָאֵל haEl לאה ; אל (ייא"י מילוי דס"ג)

הַקָּדוֹשׁ hakadosh האל הקדוש = י"פ מ"ה שֶׁאֵין she'en כָּמוֹהוּ kamohu

אהיה יהו מצפצ

הַמֵּנִיחַ hameni'ach לְעַמּוֹ le'amo בְּיוֹם beyom ע"ה נגד, מזבח, זן, אל יהוה

שַׁבַּת Shabbat קָדְשׁוֹ kodsho

אהיה יהו יה אדני

כִּי ki בָם vam מ"ב רָצָה ratza לְהָנִיחַ lehani'ach לָהֶם lahem

אהיה יהו אל

לְפָנָיו lefanav נַעֲבוֹד na'avod בְּיִרְאָה beyir'a רי"ו וָפַחַד vafachad

וְנוֹדֶה venode לִשְׁמוֹ lishmo מהש ע"ה, ע"ב בריבוע וקס"א ע"ה, אל שדי ע"ה

בְּכָל bechol ב"ן, לכב יוֹם yom ע"ה נגד, מזבח, זן, אל יהוה תָּמִיד tamid ע"ה קס"א קנ"א קמ"ג

מֵעֵין me'en הַבְּרָכוֹת haberachot וְהַהוֹדָאוֹת vehahoda'ot

אהיה יהו אלהים

לַאֲדוֹן la'adon אני הַשָּׁלוֹם hashalom

אהיה יהו מצפצ

מְקַדֵּשׁ mekadesh הַשַּׁבָּת haShabbat וּמְבָרֵךְ umvarech הַשְּׁבִיעִי hashevi'i

וּמֵנִיחַ umeni'ach בִּקְדֻשָּׁה bikdusha לְעַם le'am עלם

מְדֻשְּׁנֵי medushenei עֹנֶג oneg ר"ת עדן נהר גן זֵכֶר zecher

לְמַעֲשֵׂה lema'ase בְרֵאשִׁית vereshit ר"ת מ"ב:

He Who had shielded the forefathers with His Word, Who resurrects the dead with His Utterance, The King, the Holy One Who has no equal, Who grants rest to His people on His Holy Shabbat day. For it is them that He desired in order to grant them rest. Before Him, we will serve with awe and dread and we shall give thanks to His Name everyday, forever with appropriate blessings and thanks to the Master of peace, Who sanctifies the Shabbat, blesses the seventh day, and gives rest with holiness to the people who are satiated with delight, in memory of the work of Creation.

The *chazan* continues alone:

אֱלֹהֵינוּ Elohenu יכה וֵאלֹהֵי velohei לכב ; מילוי דע"ב, דמב ; יכה אֲבוֹתֵינוּ avotenu
רְצֵה retze נָא na בִמְנוּחָתֵנוּ vimnuchatenu• קַדְּשֵׁנוּ kadeshenu
בְּמִצְוֹתֶיךָ bemitzvotecha שִׂים sim וְחֶלְקֵנוּ chelkenu בְּתוֹרָתָךְ betoratach•
שַׂבְּעֵנוּ sabe'enu מִטּוּבָךְ mituvach •לאו שַׂמֵּחַ same'ach נַפְשֵׁנוּ nafshenu
בִּישׁוּעָתָךְ bishu'atach• וְטַהֵר vetaher לִבֵּנוּ libenu לְעָבְדְּךָ le'ovdecha
פוי, אל אדני בֶּאֱמֶת be'emet אהיה פעמים אהיה, ז"פ ס"ג• וְהַנְחִילֵנוּ vehanchilenu
יְהֹוָהאדניאהדונהי Adonai אֱלֹהֵינוּ Elohenu ילה בְּאַהֲבָה be'ahava אחד, דאגה
וּבְרָצוֹן uvratzon מהש ע"ה, ע"ב בריבוע וקס"א ע"ה, אל שדי ע"ה
שַׁבַּת Shabbat קָדְשֶׁךָ kodshecha• וְיָנוּחוּ veyanuchu בָהּ va כָּל kol ילי
יִשְׂרָאֵל Yisrael מְקַדְּשֵׁי mekadshei שְׁמֶךָ shemecha• בָּרוּךְ baruch
אַתָּה Ata יְהֹוָהאדניאהדונהי Adonai מְקַדֵּשׁ mekadesh הַשַּׁבָּת haShabbat:

KADDISH TITKABAL

יִתְגַּדַּל yitgadal וְיִתְקַדַּשׁ veyitkadash שדי ומילוי שדי ; י"א אותיות כמנין ו"ה
שְׁמֵיהּ shemei (שם י"ה דע"ב) רַבָּא raba קנ"א ב"ן, יהוה אלהים יהוה אדני,
מילוי קס"א וס"ג, מ"ה ברבוע וע"ב ע"ה ; ר"ת = ו"פ אלהים ; ס"ת = ג"פ יב"ק: אָמֵן amen אידהנויה•
בְּעָלְמָא be'alma דִּי di בְרָא vera כִּרְעוּתֵיהּ kir'utei•
וְיַמְלִיךְ veyamlich מַלְכוּתֵיהּ malchutei• וְיַצְמַח veyatzmach
פּוּרְקָנֵיהּ purkanei• וִיקָרֵב vikarev מְשִׁיחֵיהּ meshichei: אָמֵן amen אידהנויה•

Our God and God of our forefathers,
may You please desire our rest, sanctify us with Your commandments, place our lot in Your Torah, satiate us with Your goodness, gladden our souls with Your salvation, and purify our hearts to serve You sincerely. And grant us, Lord, our God, with love and favor, Your Holy Shabbat as a heritage. And may they rest in it, all of Israel, those who sanctify Your Name. Blessed are You, Lord, Who sanctifies the Shabbat.

KADDISH TITKABAL

May His great Name be more exalted and sanctified. (Amen)
In the world that He created according to His will, and may His Kingdom reign. And may He cause His redemption to sprout and may He bring the Mashiach closer. (Amen)

בְּחַיֵּיכוֹן bechayechon וּבְיוֹמֵיכוֹן uvyomechon וּבְחַיֵּי uvchayei

דְּכָל dechol יל״י בֵּית bet ב״פ ראה יִשְׂרָאֵל Yisrael בַּעֲגָלָא ba'agala

וּבִזְמַן uvizman קָרִיב kariv וְאִמְרוּ ve'imru אָמֵן amen: אָמֵן amen אידהנויה.

The congregation and the *chazan* say the following:

28 words (until *be'alma*) and 28 letters (until *almaya*)

יְהֵא yehe שְׁמֵיהּ shemei (שם י״ה דס״ג) רַבָּא raba קנ״א ב״ן,

יהוה אלהים יהוה אדני, מילוי קס״א וס״ג, מ״ה ברבוע וע״ב ע״ה מְבָרַךְ mevarach

לְעָלַם le'alam לְעָלְמֵי le'almei עָלְמַיָּא almaya. יִתְבָּרַךְ yitbarach.

Seven words with six letters each (שם בן מ״ב) – and also, seven times the letter Vav (שם בן מ״ב)

וְיִשְׁתַּבַּח veyishtabach י״פ ע״ב יהוה אל אבג יתץ.

וְיִתְפָּאַר veyitpa'ar הי נו יה קרע שטן. וְיִתְרוֹמַם veyitromam וה כוזו נגד יכש.

וְיִתְנַשֵּׂא veyitnase במוכסז בטר צתג. וְיִתְהַדָּר veyit'hadar כוזו יה וקב טנע.

וְיִתְעַלֶּה veyit'ale וה יוד ה יגל פזק. וְיִתְהַלָּל veyit'halal א ואו הא שקו צית.

שְׁמֵיהּ shemei (שם י״ה דמ״ה) דְּקוּדְשָׁא dekudsha בְּרִיךְ verich הוּא hu:

אָמֵן amen אידהנויה.

לְעֵלָּא le'ela מִן min כָּל kol יל״י בִּרְכָתָא birchata. שִׁירָתָא shirata.

תֻּשְׁבְּחָתָא tishbechata וְנֶחֱמָתָא venechamata. דַּאֲמִירָן da'amiran

בְּעָלְמָא be'alma וְאִמְרוּ ve'imru אָמֵן amen: אָמֵן amen אידהנויה.

תִּתְקַבַּל titkabal צְלוֹתָנָא tzelotana וּבָעוּתָנָא uva'utana

עִם im צְלוֹתְהוֹן tzelotehon וּבָעוּתְהוֹן uva'utehon דְּכָל dechol יל״י

בֵּית bet ב״פ ראה יִשְׂרָאֵל Yisrael קֳדָם kadam אֲבוּנָא avuna

דְּבִשְׁמַיָּא devishmaya וְאִמְרוּ ve'imru אָמֵן amen: אָמֵן amen אידהנויה.

In your lifetimes and in your days and in the lifetime of all the House of Israel, speedily and in the near future, and you shall say, Amen. (Amen) May His great Name be blessed forever and for all eternity. Blessed and lauded, and glorified, and exalted, and extolled, and honored, and uplifted, and praised be the Name of the Holy Blessed One. (Amen) Above all blessings, songs, praises, and words of consolation that may be said in the world, and you shall say, Amen. (Amen) May our prayers and pleas be accepted, together with the prayers and pleas of the entire House of Israel, before our Father in Heaven, and you say, Amen. (Amen)

יְהֵא yehe שְׁלָמָא shelama רַבָּא raba קנ"א ב"ן, יהוה אלהים יהוה אדני, מילוי קס"א וס"ג, מ"ה ברבוע וע"ב ע"ה מִן min שְׁמַיָּא shemaya. וְחַיִּים chayim אהיה אהיה יהוה, בינה ע"ה וְשָׂבָע vesava וִישׁוּעָה vishu'a וְנֶחָמָה venechama וְשֵׁיזָבָא veshezava וּרְפוּאָה urfu'a וּגְאֻלָּה ug'ula וּסְלִיחָה uslicha וְכַפָּרָה vechapara וְרֵיוַח verevach וְהַצָּלָה vehatzala. לָנוּ lanu אלהים, אהיה אדני וּלְכָל ulchol יה אדני עַמּוֹ amo יִשְׂרָאֵל Yisrael וְאִמְרוּ ve'imru אָמֵן amen: אָמֵן amen אידהנויה.

Take three steps backwards and say:

עוֹשֶׂה ose שָׁלוֹם shalom

בִּמְרוֹמָיו bimromav ע"ב, ריבוע יהוה. הוּא hu בְּרַחֲמָיו berachamav

יַעֲשֶׂה ya'ase שָׁלוֹם shalom עָלֵינוּ alenu ר"ת ש"ע נהורין.

וְעַל ve'al כָּל kol ילי ; עמם עַמּוֹ amo יִשְׂרָאֵל Yisrael וְאִמְרוּ ve'imru אָמֵן amen:

אָמֵן amen אידהנויה.

When *Shavuot* (second day) falls on *Shabbat* we add *Mizmor LeDavid*:

MIZMOR LEDAVID

In "*Mizmor LeDavid*" there are 57 words as the numerical value of the word *Zan* זן (sustenance). Reciting it will prevent lacking in both spiritual and physical sustenance.

מִזְמוֹר mizmor לְדָוִד leDavid יְהֹוָֽאדניהֹאהדונהי Adonai רֹעִי ro'i לֹא lo אֶחְסָר echsar: בִּנְאוֹת bine'ot דֶּשֶׁא deshe יַרְבִּיצֵנִי yarbitzeni עַל־ al מֵי mei ילי מְנֻחוֹת menuchot ר"ת עמם יְנַהֲלֵנִי yenahaleni: נַפְשִׁי nafshi יְשׁוֹבֵב yeshovev יַנְחֵנִי yancheni בְמַעְגְּלֵי־ vema'gelei צֶדֶק tzedek לְמַעַן lema'an שְׁמוֹ shemo מהש ע"ה, ע"ב בריבוע וקס"א ע"ה, אל שדי ע"ה:

May there be abundant peace from heaven, life, contentment, salvation, consolation, deliverance, healing, redemption, pardon, atonement, comfort, and relief. For us and for His entire nation, Israel, and you shall say, Amen. (Amen) *He, Who makes peace in His high places, With His compassion He shall make peace for us and for His entire nation, Israel. And you shall say, Amen.* (Amen)

MIZMOR LEDAVID

"A Psalm of David: The Lord is my Shepherd, I shall not lack. In lush meadows He lays me down, beside tranquil waters He leads me. He restores my soul. He leads me on paths of justice for His Name's sake.

גַּם gam כִּי־ ki אֵלֵךְ elech בְּגֵיא begei צַלְמָוֶת tzalmavet לֹא־ lo אִירָא ira רָע ra
כִּי־ ki אַתָּה Ata עִמָּדִי imadi שִׁבְטְךָ shivtecha וּמִשְׁעַנְתֶּךָ umish'antecha
הֵמָּה hema יְנַחֲמֻנִי: yenachamuni תַּעֲרֹךְ ta'aroch לְפָנַי lefanai שֻׁלְחָן shulchan
נֶגֶד neged מזבח, זן, אל יהוה צֹרְרָי tzorerai דִּשַּׁנְתָּ dishanta בַשֶּׁמֶן vashemen
רֹאשִׁי roshi כּוֹסִי kosi רְוָיָה: revaya אַךְ ach אהיה טוֹב tov והו
וָחֶסֶד vachesed ע״ב, ריבוע יהוה (י יה יהו יהוה) ; ס״ת = יהוה יִרְדְּפוּנִי yirdefuni ר״ת = יהוה
כָּל־ kol ילי יְמֵי yemei חַיָּי chayai וְשַׁבְתִּי veshavti
בְּבֵית bevet ב״פ ראה יְהֹוָהאדניאהדונהי Adonai לְאֹרֶךְ: le'orech
יָמִים yamim נלך ; ר״ת ילי ; ס״ת = אדני ; יהוה לאורך ימים = שע׳ נהורים עם י״ג אותיות:

SHIR HAMA'ALOT LEDAVID

These verses connect us to the ancient Holy Temple. According to Kabbalah, the Holy Temple is the energy center and source of all spiritual Light for the whole world, similar to a nuclear power plant that provides electrical energy for an entire city. The land of Israel is the energy center of the planet; Jerusalem is the energy center of Israel; the physical Temple was the energy center of Jerusalem; and the Holy of Holies, inside the Temple, was the ultimate energy center for the Temple and thus for the entire physical world. When the Temple was standing, it acted as a generator that chugged along 24 hours a day to produce all the spiritual Light and energy we needed. With its destruction, the power lines were severed. The Aramaic letters in this connection re-establish the lines of communication with the spiritual essence of the Temple, giving us the ability to capture this energy for our personal lives.

This praise was said by King David for his kingdom, as everything was in one unification – "justice and peace kissed each other." And that's the meaning of: "I shall request good for you."

שִׁיר shir הַמַּעֲלוֹת hama'alot לְדָוִד leDavid שָׂמַחְתִּי samachti
בְּאֹמְרִים be'omrim לִי li בֵּית bet ב״פ ראה יְהֹוָהאדניאהדונהי Adonai נֵלֵךְ: nelech נלך:
עֹמְדוֹת omdot הָיוּ hayu רַגְלֵינוּ raglenu ר״ת רהע בִּשְׁעָרַיִךְ: bish'arayich
יְרוּשָׁלָםִ: Yerushalayim יְרוּשָׁלַםִ Yerushalayim הַבְּנוּיָה habenuya
כְּעִיר ke'ir בוזוך, סנדלפון, ערי שֶׁחֻבְּרָה־ shechubera לָּהּ la יַחְדָּו: yachdav

---

Though I walk in the valley overshadowed by death,
I will fear no evil for You are with me. Your rod and Your staff, they comfort me. You prepare a table for me in full view of my tormentors. You anointed my head with oil, my cup overflows. May only goodness and kindness pursue me all the days of my life, and may I dwell in the House of the Lord for long days." (Psalms 23)

SHIR HAMA'ALOT LEDAVID

"A Song of Ascents by David: I rejoiced when they said to me: Let us go to the House of the Lord. Our legs stood immobile within your gates, Jerusalem. The built-up Jerusalem is like a city that has been united together.

שֶׁשָּׁם shesham עָלוּ alu שְׁבָטִים shevatim שִׁבְטֵי־ shivtei יָהּ Yah עֵדוּת edut
לְיִשְׂרָאֵל leYisrael לְהֹדוֹת lehodot לְשֵׁם leshem יְהֹוָהאדניאהדונהי Adonai׃
כִּי ki שָׁמָּה shama יָשְׁבוּ yashvu כִסְאוֹת chis'ot לְמִשְׁפָּט lemishpat ע״ה ה״פ אלהים
כִּסְאוֹת kis'ot לְבֵית levet ב״פ ראה דָּוִיד David׃ שַׁאֲלוּ sha'alu שְׁלוֹם shelom
יְרוּשָׁלָםִ Yerushalayim יִשְׁלָיוּ yishlayu אֹהֲבָיִךְ ohavayich׃ יְהִי־ yehi
שָׁלוֹם shalom בְּחֵילֵךְ bechelech שַׁלְוָה shalva בְּאַרְמְנוֹתָיִךְ be'armenotayich׃
לְמַעַן lema'an אַחַי achai וְרֵעָי vere'ai אֲדַבְּרָה־ adabera נָּא na שָׁלוֹם shalom
בָּךְ bach׃ לְמַעַן lema'an בֵּית bet ב״פ ראה יְהֹוָהאדניאהדונהי Adonai
אֱלֹהֵינוּ Elohenu ילה אֲבַקְשָׁה avaksha טוֹב tov והו לָךְ lach׃

KADDISH YEHE SHELAMA

יִתְגַּדַּל yitgadal וְיִתְקַדַּשׁ veyitkadash שדי ומילוי שדי ; י״א אותיות כמנין ו״ה
שְׁמֵיהּ shemei (שם י״ה דע״ב) רַבָּא raba קנ״א ב״ן, יהוה אלהים יהוה אדני,
מילוי קס״א וס״ג, מ״ה ברבוע וע״ב ע״ה ; ר״ת = ו״פ אלהים ; ס״ת = ג״פ יב״ק׃ אָמֵן amen אידהנויה.
בְּעָלְמָא be'alma דִּי di בְרָא vera כִרְעוּתֵיהּ kir'utei.
וְיַמְלִיךְ veyamlich מַלְכוּתֵיהּ malchutei. וְיַצְמַח veyatzmach
פֻּרְקָנֵיהּ purkanei. וִיקָרֵב vikarev מְשִׁיחֵיהּ meshichei׃ אָמֵן amen אידהנויה.
בְּחַיֵּיכוֹן bechayechon וּבְיוֹמֵיכוֹן uvyomechon וּבְחַיֵּי uvchayei
דְכָל dechol ילי בֵּית bet ב״פ ראה יִשְׂרָאֵל Yisrael בַּעֲגָלָא ba'agala
וּבִזְמַן uvizman קָרִיב kariv וְאִמְרוּ ve'imru אָמֵן amen׃ אָמֵן amen אידהנויה.

For there the tribes ascend the tribes of God, who are testimony for Israel, to give thanks to the Name of the Lord. For there sat thrones of judgments, thrones of the House of David, they have prayed for the peace of Jerusalem, those who love you will be serene. May there be peace within your walls, and serenity within your palaces. For the sake of my brothers and my comrades, I shall speak of peace on your behalf. For the sake of the House of the Lord, I shall request good for you." (Psalms 122)

KADDISH YEHE SHELAMA

May His great Name be more exalted and sanctified. (Amen) *In the world that He created according to His will, and may His kingdom reign. And may He cause His redemption to sprout and may He bring the Mashiach closer.* (Amen) *In your lifetimes and in your days and in the lifetime of all the House of Israel, speedily and in the near future, and you shall say, Amen.* (Amen)

The congregation and the *chazan* say the following:

28 words (until *be'alma*) and 28 letters (until *almaya*)

יְהֵא yehe שְׁמֵיהּ shemei (שׁם י"ה דס"ג) רַבָּא raba קנ"א ב"ן,
יהוה אלהים יהוה אדני, מילוי קס"א וס"ג, מ"ה ברבוע וע"ב ע"ה מְבָרַךְ: mevarach
לְעָלַם le'alam לְעָלְמֵי le'almei עָלְמַיָּא almaya• יִתְבָּרַךְ: yitbarach•

Seven words with six letters each (שׁם בן מ"ב) and also, seven times the letter Vav (שׁם בן מ"ב)

וְיִשְׁתַּבַּח veyishtabach י"פ ע"ב יהוה אל אבג יתץ•

וְיִתְפָּאַר veyitpa'ar הי נו יה קרע שטן• וְיִתְרוֹמַם veyitromam וה כוזו נגד יכש•

וְיִתְנַשֵּׂא veyitnase במוכסז בטר צתג• וְיִתְהַדָּר veyit'hadar כוזו יה וזקב טנע•

וְיִתְעַלֶּה veyit'ale וה יוד ה יגל פזק• וְיִתְהַלָּל veyit'halal א ואו הא שקו צית•

שְׁמֵיהּ shemei (שׁם י"ה דמ"ה) דְּקוּדְשָׁא dekudsha בְּרִיךְ: verich הוּא hu:

אָמֵן amen אידהנויה•

לְעֵלָּא le'ela מִן min כָּל kol ילי בִּרְכָתָא birchata• שִׁירָתָא shirata•
תֻּשְׁבְּחָתָא tishbechata וְנֶחָמָתָא venechamata• דַּאֲמִירָן da'amiran
בְּעָלְמָא be'alma וְאִמְרוּ ve'imru אָמֵן amen: אָמֵן amen אידהנויה.

יְהֵא yehe שְׁלָמָא shelama רַבָּא raba קנ"א ב"ן, יהוה אלהים יהוה אדני, מילוי קס"א וס"ג,
מ"ה ברבוע וע"ב ע"ה מִן min שְׁמַיָּא shemaya• וְחַיִּים chayim אהיה אהיה יהוה, בינה ע"ה
וְשָׂבָע vesava וִישׁוּעָה vishu'a וְנֶחָמָה venechama וְשֵׁיזָבָא veshezava
וּרְפוּאָה urefu'a וּגְאֻלָּה uge'ula וּסְלִיחָה uslicha וְכַפָּרָה vechapara
וְרֵוַח verevach וְהַצָּלָה vehatzala• לָנוּ lanu אלהים, אהיה אדני וּלְכָל ulchol יה אדני
עַמּוֹ amo יִשְׂרָאֵל Yisrael וְאִמְרוּ ve'imru אָמֵן amen: אָמֵן amen אידהנויה.

May His great Name be blessed forever and for all eternity. Blessed and lauded, and glorified, and exalted, and extolled, and honored, and uplifted, and praised be the Name of the Holy Blessed One. (Amen) *Above all blessings, songs, praises, and words of consolation that may be said in the world, and you shall say, Amen.* (Amen) *May there be abundant peace from Heaven, life, contentment, salvation, consolation, deliverance, healing, redemption, pardon, atonement, comfort, and relief. For us and for His entire nation, Israel, and you shall say, Amen.* (Amen)

Take three steps backwards and say:

עוֹשֶׂה ose שָׁלוֹם shalom בִּמְרוֹמָיו bimromav ע״ב, ריבוע יהוה. הוּא hu

בְּרַחֲמָיו berachamav יַעֲשֶׂה ya'ase שָׁלוֹם shalom עָלֵינוּ alenu ר״ת ש״ע נהורין.

וְעַל ve'al כָּל kol ילי ; עמם עַמּוֹ amo יִשְׂרָאֵל Yisrael וְאִמְרוּ ve'imru אָמֵן amen:

אָמֵן amen אידהנויה.

BARCHU

The *chazan* (or a person who said the *Kaddish Yehe Shelama*) says:

רַבָּנָן rabanan: בָּרְכוּ barchu יהוה ריבוע יהוה ריבוע מ״ה אֶת et

יְהֹוָאדהנויאהדונהי Adonai הַמְּבוֹרָךְ: hamevorach ס״ת כהת, משיח בן דוד ע״ה:

First the congregation replies the following and then the *chazan* (or a person who said the *Kaddish Yehe Shelama*) repeats it:

Nefesh בָּרוּךְ: baruch *Ruach* יְהֹוָאדהנויאהדונהי Adonai *Neshamah* הַמְּבוֹרָךְ: hamevorach

Chayah לְעוֹלָם le'olam ריבוע ס״ג וי׳ אותיות דס״ג *Yechidah* וָעֶד va'ed:

ALENU

Alenu is a cosmic sealing agent. It cements and secures all of our prayers, protecting them from any negative forces such as the *klipot*. All prayers prior to *Alenu* drew down what the kabbalists call Inner Light. *Alenu*, however, attracts Surrounding Light, which envelops our prayers with a protective force-field to block out the *klipot*.

Drawing Surrounding Light in order to be protected from the *klipot* (negative side).

עָלֵינוּ alenu ריבוע דס״ג לְשַׁבֵּחַ leshabe'ach עלינו לשבח = אבג יתץ, ושר

לַאֲדוֹן la'adon אני ; ס״ת ס״ג ע״ה הַכֹּל hakol ר״ת ללה, אדני

לָתֵת latet גְּדֻלָּה gedula לְיוֹצֵר leyotzer בְּרֵאשִׁית bereshit ר״ת גלב (באר ב״י יג״ל)

He, Who makes peace in His high places, with His compassion
He shall make peace for us and for His entire nation, Israel. And you shall say, Amen. (Amen)

BARCHU

Masters: Bless the Lord, the Blessed One.
Blessed be the Lord, the Blessed One, forever and for eternity.

ALENU

It is incumbent upon us
to give praise to the Master of all and to attribute greatness to the Molder of Creation,

שֶׁלֹּא shelo עָשָׂנוּ asanu כְּגוֹיֵי kegoyei הָאֲרָצוֹת ha'aratzot וְלֹא velo

שָׂמָנוּ samanu כְּמִשְׁפְּחוֹת kemishpechot הָאֲדָמָה ha'adama שֶׁלֹּא shelo

שָׂם sam חֶלְקֵנוּ chelkenu כָּהֶם kahem וְגוֹרָלֵנוּ vegoralenu כְּכָל kechol

הֲמוֹנָם hamonam. שֶׁהֵם shehem מִשְׁתַּחֲוִים mishtachavim לָהֶבֶל lahevel

וָרִיק varik וּמִתְפַּלְּלִים umitpalelim אֶל el אֵל el לֹא lo יוֹשִׁיעַ Yoshi'a.

(pause here, and when you say "*va'anachnu mishtachavim*" bow your entire body)

וַאֲנַחְנוּ va'anachnu מִשְׁתַּחֲוִים mishtachavim לִפְנֵי lifnei מֶלֶךְ melech

מַלְכֵי malchei הַמְּלָכִים hamelachim הַקָּדוֹשׁ hakadosh בָּרוּךְ baruch:

הוּא hu. שֶׁהוּא shehu נוֹטֶה note שָׁמַיִם shamayim י"פ טל, י"פ כוזו ; ר"ת = י"פ אדני

שבי' ספירות של נוקבא דז"א וְיוֹסֵד veyosed אָרֶץ aretz. וּמוֹשַׁב umoshav

יְקָרוֹ yekaro בַּשָּׁמַיִם bashamayim י"פ טל, י"פ כוזו מִמַּעַל mima'al עלם.

וּשְׁכִינַת ush'chinat עֻזּוֹ uzo בְּגָבְהֵי begovhei מְרוֹמִים meromim.

הוּא hu אֱלֹהֵינוּ Elohenu ילה וְאֵין ve'en עוֹד od אַחֵר acher.

אֱמֶת emet אהיה פעמים אהיה, ז"פ ס"ג מַלְכֵּנוּ malkenu וְאֶפֶס ve'efes

זוּלָתוֹ zulato. כַּכָּתוּב kakatuv בַּתּוֹרָה batorah: וְיָדַעְתָּ veyadata

הַיּוֹם hayom ע"ה נגד, מזבח, זן, אל יהוה וַהֲשֵׁבֹתָ vahashevota אֶל־ el

לְבָבֶךָ levavecha ר"ת לאו כִּי ki יְהֹוָהאדניאהדונהי Adonai הוּא hu

הָאֱלֹהִים haElohim אהיה אדני ; ילה ; ר"ת יהה וכן עולה למנין ענו עג"כ

---

for He did not make us like the nations of the lands. He did not place us like the families of the Earth He did not make our lot like theirs and our destiny like that of their multitudes, for they prostrate themselves to futility and emptiness and they pray to a deity that does not help. But we prostrate ourselves before the King of all Kings, the Holy Blessed One. It is He Who spreads the Heavens and establishes the earth. The Seat of His glory is in the Heaven above and the Divine Presence of His power is in the Highest of Heights. He is our God and there is no other. Our King is true and there is none beside Him. As it is written in the Torah: "And you shall know today and you shall take it to your heart that it is the Lord Who is God

בַּשָּׁמַיִם bashamayim י"פ טל, י"פ כוזו מִמַּעַל mima'al עלם ;
רמז לאור פנימי המתוזיל מלמעלה וְעַל־ ve'al הָאָרֶץ ha'aretz אלהים דההין ע"ה
מִתָּחַת mitachat רמז לאור מקיף המתוזיל מלמטה אֵין en עוֹד od:

עַל al כֵּן ken נְקַוֶּה nekave לְּךָ lach יְהֹוָהאדניאהדונהי Adonai
אֱלֹהֵינוּ Elohenu ילה לִרְאוֹת lir'ot מְהֵרָה mehera בְּתִפְאֶרֶת betiferet
עֻזָּךְ uzach ס"ת כהת, משיוז בן דוד ע"ה לְהַעֲבִיר leha'avir גִּלּוּלִים gilulim
מִן min הָאָרֶץ ha'aretz אלהים דההין ע"ה וְהָאֱלִילִים veha'elilim כָּרוֹת karot
יִכָּרֵתוּן •yikaretun לְתַקֵּן letaken עוֹלָם olam בְּמַלְכוּת bemalchut
שַׁדַּי •Shadai וְכָל vechol ילי בְּנֵי benei בָשָׂר vasar יִקְרְאוּ yikre'u
בִשְׁמֶךָ vishmecha לְהַפְנוֹת lehafnot אֵלֶיךָ elecha כָּל kol ילי רִשְׁעֵי rish'ei
אָרֶץ •aretz יַכִּירוּ yakiru וְיֵדְעוּ veyed'u כָּל kol ילי יוֹשְׁבֵי yoshvei
תֵּבֵל tevel ב"פ רי"ו• כִּי ki לְךָ lecha תִּכְרַע tichra כָּל־ kol ילי בֶּרֶךְ •berech
תִּשָּׁבַע tishava כָּל kol ילי לָשׁוֹן •lashon לְפָנֶיךָ lefanecha ס"ג מ"ה ב"ן
יְהֹוָהאדניאהדונהי Adonai אֱלֹהֵינוּ Elohenu ילה יִכְרְעוּ yichre'u וְיִפֹּלוּ veyipolu
וְלִכְבוֹד velichvod שִׁמְךָ shimcha יְקָר yekar יִתֵּנוּ •yitenu
וִיקַבְּלוּ vikabelu כֻלָּם chulam אֶת et עוֹל־ ol מַלְכוּתֶךָ •malchutecha
וְתִמְלוֹךְ vetimloch עֲלֵיהֶם alehem מְהֵרָה mehera לְעוֹלָם le'olam
ריבוע ס"ג וי' אותיות דס"ג וָעֶד •va'ed כִּי ki הַמַּלְכוּת hamalchut שֶׁלְּךָ shelcha
הִיא •hee וּלְעוֹלְמֵי ul'olmei עַד ad תִּמְלוֹךְ timloch בְּכָבוֹד bechavod בוכו•

---

in the Heavens above and upon the Earth below, and there is none other." (Deuteronomy 4:39)

Consequently, we place our hope in You,

Lord, our God, that we shall speedily see the glory of Your might, when You remove the idols from the earth and the deities shall be completely destroyed to correct the world with the kingdom of the Almighty. And all mankind shall then call out Your Name and You shall turn back to Yourself all the wicked ones of the earth. Then all the inhabitants of the world shall recognize and know that, for You, every knee bends and every tongue vows. Before You, Lord, our God, they shall kneel and fall and shall give honor to Your glorious Name. And they shall all accept the yoke of Your Kingdom and You shall reign over them, forever and ever. Because the kingdom is Yours. and forever and for eternity, You shall reign gloriously.

כַּכָּתוּב kakatuv בְּתוֹרָתָךְ betoratach: יְהֹוָה אדני יאהדונהי Adonai | יִמְלֹךְ yimloch

לְעֹלָם le'olam ריבוע ס"ג וי' אותיות דס"ג ; ר"ת י"ל וָעֶד va'ed.

וְנֶאֱמַר vene'emar: וְהָיָה vehaya יהוה ; יהה יְהֹוָה אדני יאהדונהי Adonai

לְמֶלֶךְ lemelech עַל־ al כָּל־ kol ילי ; עמם הָאָרֶץ ha'aretz אלהים דההין ע"ה

בַּיּוֹם bayom ע"ה נגד, מזבח, זן, אל יהוה הַהוּא hahu

יִהְיֶה yih'ye ייי יְהֹוָה אדני יאהדונהי Adonai אֶחָד echad אהבה, דאגה

וּשְׁמוֹ ushmo מהש ע"ה, ע"ב בריבוע וקס"א ע"ה, אל שדי ע"ה אֶחָד echad אהבה, דאגה:

> If you prayed alone recite the following before you start *Arvit* and before "*Alenu*" instead of "*Barchu*":
>
> אָמַר amar רַבִּי Rabi עֲקִיבָא Akiva חַיָּה chaya אַחַת achat עוֹמֶדֶת omedet
>
> בָּרָקִיעַ baraki'a וּשְׁמָהּ ushma יִשְׂרָאֵל Yisrael וְחָקוּק vechakuk עַל al
>
> מִצְחָהּ mitzcha יִשְׂרָאֵל Yisrael. עוֹמֶדֶת omedet בְּאֶמְצַע be'emtza
>
> הָרָקִיעַ haraki'a וְאוֹמֶרֶת ve'omeret: בָּרְכוּ barchu יהוה ריבוע יהוה וריבוע מ"ה אֶת et
>
> יְהֹוָה אדני יאהדונהי Adonai הַמְבוֹרָךְ hamevorach ס"ת כהת, משיח בן דוד ע"ה וְכָל vechol
>
> ילי גְּדוּדֵי gedudei מַעְלָה mala עוֹנִים onim: בָּרוּךְ baruch יְהֹוָה אדני יאהדונהי Adonai
>
> הַמְבוֹרָךְ hamevorach לְעוֹלָם le'olam ריבוע ס"ג וי' אותיות דס"ג וָעֶד va'ed.

BLESSING FOR CHILDREN

After the *Kidush,* the kabbalists recommend that each father will bless his children because it is a time of favor and blessings are abundant. As children are unable to draw blessings upon themselves through their own action, doing so by an adult, will be very effective. As the Light of abundance comes down from Above to cling onto the children and embrace them because they have not yet sinned, and through children, the blessings can better spread (However, even grown up children can receive blessings from their fathers).

As it is written in the Torah:

"The Lord shall reign forever and ever," (Exodus 15:18) *and it is also stated: "The Lord shall be King over the whole world and, on that day, the Lord shall be One and His Name One."* (Zechariah 14:9)

> *Rabbi Akiva said: Standing in Heaven, there is one animal named Israel, and Israel is engraved on her forehead, and she is standing in mid-Heaven saying: Bless the Lord, the Blessed One, and all of Heaven's armies are answering: Blessed be the Lord, the Blessed One, forever and for eternity.*

For a son:

יְשִׂימְךָ yesimcha אֱלֹהִים Elohim אהיה אדני ; ילה
כְּאֶפְרַיִם keEfrayim וְכִמְנַשֶּׁה vechiMenashe. Continue "*yevarechecha*"

For a daughter:

יְשִׂימֵךְ yesimech אֱלֹהִים Elohim אהיה אדני ; ילה
כְּשָׂרָה keSara רִבְקָה Rivka רָחֵל Rachel וְלֵאָה veLeah.

Right

יְבָרֶכְךָ yevarechecha יְהֹוָהאדניאהדונהי Adonai וְיִשְׁמְרֶךָ veyishmerecha
ר"ת = יהוה ; וס"ת = מ"ה:

Left

יָאֵר ya'er כף ויו זין ויו יְהֹוָהאדניאהדונהי Adonai | פָּנָיו panav אֵלֶיךָ elecha
וִיחֻנֶּךָּ vichuneka מנד ; יהה אותיות בפסוק:

Center

יִשָּׂא yisa יְהֹוָהאדניאהדונהי Adonai | פָּנָיו panav אֵלֶיךָ elecha
וְיָשֵׂם veyasem לְךָ lecha שָׁלוֹם shalom האא תיבות בפסוק:

וְשָׂמוּ vesamu אֶת־ et שְׁמִי shemi עַל־ al בְּנֵי benei יִשְׂרָאֵל Yisrael
וַאֲנִי va'ani אני אֲבָרְכֵם avarchem:

הַמַּלְאָךְ hamal'ach פוי, אל אדני הַגֹּאֵל hago'el אֹתִי oti מִכָּל־ mikol ילי רָע ra
יְבָרֵךְ yevarech עסמ"ב, הברכה (למתק את ז' המלכים שמתו) אֶת־ et הַנְּעָרִים hane'arim
וְיִקָּרֵא veyikare עם ה' אותיות = ב"פ קס"א בָהֶם vahem שְׁמִי shemi וְשֵׁם veshem
אֲבֹתַי avotai אַבְרָהָם Avraham וז"פ אל, רי"ו ול"ב נתיבות החכמה, רמ"ח (אברים),
עסמ"ב וט"ז אותיות פשוטות וְיִצְחָק veYitzchak ד"פ ב"ן וְיִדְגּוּ veyidgu
לָרֹב larov בְּקֶרֶב bekerev הָאָרֶץ ha'aretz אלהים דההין ע"ה:
בֵּן ben פֹּרָת porat יוֹסֵף Yosef ציון, ו' הויות, קנאה בֵּן ben פֹּרָת porat עֲלֵי־ alei
עָיִן ayin ריבוע מ"ה בָּנוֹת banot צָעֲדָה tza'ada עֲלֵי־ alei שׁוּר shur ושר:

BLESSING FOR CHILDREN

For a son: *"May God make you as Ephraim and as Menashe."* (Genesis 48:20)
For a daughter: *May God make you as Sarah, Rivkah, Rachel and as Leah.*
(Right) *"May the Lord bless you and safeguard you.*
(Left) *May the Lord shine His countenance for you and be gracious to you.*
(Central) *May the Lord lift His countenance to you and set peace on you.*
And they placed My Name on the Children of Israel and I shall bless them." (Numbers 6:24-27)
"The angel who redeemed me from all evil
will bless the lads, and may my name and the name of my forefathers, Abraham and Isaac, be called upon them. And let them grow in multitude amidst the earth." (Genesis 48:16) *"A fruitful bough is Joseph. A fruitful bough by the well, and whose branches ran over the wall."* (Genesis 49:22)

KIDDUSH FOR THE EVE OF SHAVUOT

When *Shavuot* (second day) falls on Friday night then the following is said:

יוֹם yom ע״ה נגד, מזבח, זן, אל יהוה הַשִּׁשִּׁי hashishi:

וַיְכֻלּוּ vaychulu ע״ב, ריבוע יהוה (י יה יהו יהוה) הַשָּׁמַיִם hashamayim י״פ טל, י״פ כוזו
וְהָאָרֶץ veha'aretz אלהים דההין ע״ה ; ר״ת והו וְכָל־ vechol צְבָאָם tzeva'am ס״ת צלם:
וַיְכַל vaychal אֱלֹהִים Elohim אהיה אדני ; ילה בַּיּוֹם bayom ע״ה נגד, מזבח, זן, אל יהוה
הַשְּׁבִיעִי hashevi'i מְלַאכְתּוֹ melachto אֲשֶׁר asher עָשָׂה asa וַיִּשְׁבֹּת vayishbot
בַּיּוֹם bayom ע״ה נגד, מזבח, זן, אל יהוה הַשְּׁבִיעִי hashevi'i מִכָּל־ mikol ילי
מְלַאכְתּוֹ melachto אֲשֶׁר asher עָשָׂה asa: וַיְבָרֶךְ vayvarech עסמ״ב, הברכה (למתק
את ז׳ המלכים שמתו) אֱלֹהִים Elohim אהיה אדני ; ילה אֶת־ et יוֹם yom ע״ה נגד, מזבח, זן, אל
יהוה הַשְּׁבִיעִי hashevi'i וַיְקַדֵּשׁ vaykadesh אֹתוֹ oto כִּי ki בוֹ vo שָׁבַת shavat
מִכָּל־ mikol ילי מְלַאכְתּוֹ melachto אֲשֶׁר־ asher בָּרָא bara קנ״א ב״ן, יהוה אלהים יהוה
אדני, מילוי קס״א וס״ג, מ״ה ברבוע וע״ב ע״ה אֱלֹהִים Elohim אהיה אדני ; ילה לַעֲשׂוֹת la'asot:

אֵלֶּה ele מוֹעֲדֵי mo'adei יְהוָֹהאדניאהדונהי Adonai מִקְרָאֵי mikra'ei
קֹדֶשׁ kodesh אֲשֶׁר־ asher תִּקְרְאוּ tikre'u אֹתָם otam בְּמוֹעֲדָם bemo'adam:
וַיְדַבֵּר vaydaber ראה מֹשֶׁה Moshe מהש, ע״ב בריבוע וקס״א, אל שדי, ד״פ אלהים ע״ה
אֶת־ et מֹעֲדֵי mo'adei יְהוָֹהאדניאהדונהי Adonai אֶל־ el בְּנֵי benei יִשְׂרָאֵל Yisrael:

סַבְרִי savri מָרָנָן maranan

(and the others reply) לְחַיִּים lechayim אהיה אהיה יהוה, בינה ע״ה

בָּרוּךְ baruch אַתָּה Ata יְהוָֹהאדניאהדונהי Adonai אֱלֹהֵינוּ Elohenu ילה
מֶלֶךְ melech הָעוֹלָם ha'olam בּוֹרֵא bore פְּרִי peri הַגָּפֶן hagefen:

KIDDUSH FOR THE EVE OF SHAVUOT

VAY'CHULU

"And the Heavens and the Earth were completed and all their hosts. And God completed, on the seventh day, His work that He had done. And He abstained, on the seventh day, from all His work which He had done. And God blessed the seventh day and He sanctified it, for on it He had abstained from all His work which God had created to do". (Genesis 2:1-3)

"Those are the holiday of the Lord, Holy covenant you shall call them, on their time.
And Moses spoke the holidays of the lord to the children of Israel" (Levitcus 23:44)
By Your leave masters, **(and the others reply)** *for life!*
Blessed are You, Lord, our God, the King of the world, Who creates the fruit of the vine.

בָּרוּךְ baruch אַתָּה Ata יְהֹוָואדנהיאהדונהי Adonai אֱלֹהֵינוּ Elohenu ילה
מֶלֶךְ melech הָעוֹלָם ha'olam אֲשֶׁר asher בָּחַר bachar בָּנוּ banu
מִכָּל mikol ילי עָם am. וְרוֹמְמָנוּ veromemanu מִכָּל mikol ילי לָשׁוֹן lashon.
וְקִדְּשָׁנוּ vekidshanu בְּמִצְוֹתָיו vemitzotav. וַתִּתֶּן vatiten ב"פ כהת
לָנוּ lanu אלהים, אהיה אדני יְהֹוָואדנהיאהדונהי Adonai אֱלֹהֵינוּ Elohenu ילה
בְּאַהֲבָה be'ahava אחד, דאגה (On *Shabbat* add: שַׁבָּתוֹת shabbatot לִמְנוּחָה limnucha
ו u) מוֹעֲדִים mo'adim לְשִׂמְחָה lesimcha. חַגִּים chagim וּזְמַנִּים uzmanim
לְשָׂשׂוֹן lesason. אֶת et יוֹם yom ע"ה נגד, מזבח, זן, אל יהוה (On *Shabbat* add:
הַשַּׁבָּת hashabbat הַזֶּה hazeh והו. וְאֶת ve'et יוֹם yom ע"ה נגד, מזבח, זן, אל יהוה)
חַג chag הַשָּׁבוּעוֹת haShavuot הַזֶּה hazeh והו. אֶת et יוֹם yom ע"ה נגד, מזבח, זן,
אל יהוה טוֹב tov והו מִקְרָא mikra קֹדֶשׁ kodesh הַזֶּה hazeh והו. זְמַן zeman
מַתַּן matan תּוֹרָתֵנוּ toratenu. בְּאַהֲבָה be'ahava אחד, דאגה מִקְרָא mikra
קֹדֶשׁ kodesh. זֵכֶר zecher לִיצִיאַת litzi'at מִצְרָיִם Mitzrayim מצר.
כִּי ki בָנוּ banu בָחַרְתָּ bacharta וְאוֹתָנוּ ve'otanu קִדַּשְׁתָּ kidashta
מִכָּל mikol ילי הָעַמִּים ha'amim. (On *Shabbat* add: וְשַׁבָּתוֹת veshabbatot ו u)
מוֹעֲדֵי mo'adei קָדְשֶׁךָ kodshecha, (On *Shabbat* add: בְּאַהֲבָה be'ahava אחד, דאגה
וּבְרָצוֹן uvratzon מהש ע"ה, ע"ב בריבוע וקס"א ע"ה, אל שדי)
בְּשִׂמְחָה vesimcha וּבְשָׂשׂוֹן uvsason הִנְחַלְתָּנוּ hinchaltanu.
בָּרוּךְ baruch אַתָּה Ata יְהֹוָואדנהיאהדונהי Adonai מְקַדֵּשׁ mekadesh
(On *Shabbat* add: הַשַּׁבָּת hashabat וְ ve) יִשְׂרָאֵל Yisrael וְהַזְּמַנִּים vehazemanim:

When *Shavuot* falls on Saturday night we add the *Havdalah* connection (in the box on the next page), otherwise we continue with "*Shehechyanu*" on the next page.

Blessed are You, Lord our God, King of the universe, who has chosen us from among all nations, exalted us above all tongues, and sanctified us with its communications. And You, Lord our God, have lovingly given us: (**on Shabbat add:** *Sabbatot for rest) appointed times for gladness, feasts and times for joy,* (**on Shabbat add:** *this Sabbat and) this holiday of Shavuot, this good day of holy convocation, the time we received our Torah. With love, a holy convocation, a remembrance of the exit from Egypt. For You have chosen and sanctified us above all peoples,* (**on Shabbat add:** *and Sabbaths and) Your holy festivals* (**on Shabbat add:** *in love and favor) in gladness and joy have You granted us. Blessed are You, Lord, who sanctifies* (**on Shabbat add:** *the Sabbath and) Israel and the festive times.*

HAVDALAH

When *Shavuot* falls on Saturday night then the following is said:

בָּרוּךְ baruch אַתָּה Ata יְהֹוָהאדניאהדונהי Adonai אֱלֹהֵינוּ Elohenu ילה מֶלֶךְ melech
הָעוֹלָם ha'olam בּוֹרֵא bore מְאוֹרֵי me'orei הָאֵשׁ ha'esh שאה:

בָּרוּךְ baruch אַתָּה Ata יְהֹוָהאדניאהדונהי Adonai אֱלֹהֵינוּ Elohenu ילה מֶלֶךְ melech
הָעוֹלָם haolam הַמַּבְדִּיל hamavdil בֵּין ben קֹדֶשׁ kodesh לְחוֹל lechol וּבֵין uven
אוֹר or רז, א״ס לְחֹשֶׁךְ lechshech שך נצוצות של ז׳ המלכים וּבֵין uven יִשְׂרָאֵל Yisrael
לָעַמִּים la'amim, וּבֵין uven יוֹם yom ע״ה נגד, מזבח, זן, אל יהוה הַשְּׁבִיעִי hashvi'i
לְשֵׁשֶׁת lesheshet יְמֵי yemei הַמַּעֲשֶׂה hama'ase. בֵּין ben קְדֻשַּׁת kedushat
שַׁבָּת shabat לִקְדֻשַּׁת likdushat יוֹם yom ע״ה נגד, מזבח, זן, אל יהוה טוֹב tov והו
הִבְדַּלְתָּ hivdalta. וְאֶת ve'et יוֹם yom ע״ה נגד, מזבח, זן, אל יהוה הַשְּׁבִיעִי hashevi'i
מִשֵּׁשֶׁת misheshet יְמֵי yemei הַמַּעֲשֶׂה hama'ase הִקְדַּשְׁתָּ hikdashta.
וְהִבְדַּלְתָּ vehivdalta וְהִקְדַּשְׁתָּ vehikdashta אֶת et עַמְּךָ amcha יִשְׂרָאֵל Yisrael
בִּקְדֻשָּׁתָךְ bikdushatach: בָּרוּךְ baruch אַתָּה ata יְהֹוָהאדניאהדונהי Adonai
הַמַּבְדִּיל hamavdil בֵּין ben קֹדֶשׁ kodesh לְקֹדֶשׁ lekodesh:

SHEHECHEYANU

בָּרוּךְ baruch אַתָּה Ata יְהֹוָהאדניאהדונהי Adonai אֱלֹהֵינוּ Elohenu ילה
מֶלֶךְ melech הָעוֹלָם ha'olam שֶׁהֶחֱיָנוּ shehecheyanu
וְקִיְּמָנוּ vekiyemanu וְהִגִּיעָנוּ vehigi'anu לַזְּמַן lazeman הַזֶּה hazeh והו:

HAVDALAH

Blessed are You, Lord, our God, King of the world, Who creates the luminaries of fire.
Blessed are You, Lord, our God, King of the world, Who distinguishes between the sacred and the secular, between Light and darkness, and between Israel and the nations, and between the Day of Shabbat and the six days of action. You had distinguished and had sanctified Your Nation, Israel, with Your sanctity.
Blessed are You, Lord, Who distinguishes between holiness and holiness.

SHEHECHEYANU

Blessed are You, Lord, our God, King of the universe,
Who has kept us alive, sustained us, and brought us to this moment.

THE RAV ON TIKKUN LEL SHAVUOT

Rav Isaac Luria (the Ari) quotes the *Zohar,* saying: "*And you should know that whoever doesn't sleep in this night* [the night of Shavuot] *at all, not even for a moment, and deals with the Torah all night, is insured to complete his year and no harm will fall on him during this year.*"

This is an amazing passage. What it means is that on the night of *Shavuot*, we can connect to the power of the removal of death on a level that is sufficient for four months. If we are careful and stay awake the whole time to make a spiritual connection on the night of *Shavuot*, we are assured that we will not be forced to leave this world, at least until the end of the current year. Four months without chaos! Nothing in this world, with the exception of knowledge of Kabbalah, can supply us with such a treasure.

To better understand the connection between the month of *Sivan* and the holiday of *Shavuot*, we need to go back for a moment to the night of *Hoshanah Rabba*, which "seals" the holiday of *Sukkot*. After midnight, we can go out to check our shadow by the light of the moon. By checking our shadow, we can determine whether we have enough life-energy to sustain us for a whole year.

The light of the moon on this night is different from any other source of light at any other time. The shadow we check is different from any other shadow we have at any other time in life. It is a spiritual shadow that indicates the density of the life-energy in every area of our body. Like an x-ray, this special shadow reveals inner flaws in our body, but unlike an x-ray, the shadow also reveals the future. This shadow has a special name: *Tzelem* (*tzel* in Aramaic is shadow; *Tzelem* refers to an image, specifically "in God's image").

From the *Book of Genesis*, we learn that *Tzelem* is also a mold, an image. Humanity was created in the mold and image of the Creator, and we are a true copy of the original. The *Tzelem* actually represents a consciousness rather than any physical form. *Tzelem*-consciousness is that of unity and harmony. This same consciousness exists in all the physiological and psychological activities of the body at any given moment. If a person hurts his finger, the whole body immediately unites in the task of repairing and healing the wound. The attention, the position of the body, the level of activity, the blood pressure and pulse, the breathing rhythm, the metabolic rate, the oxygen supply at the site of the wound—all these indicate that every cell in the body is affected by the event and is working towards repairing and healing the wound.

According to *Tzelem*-consciousness, we can understand that all the people in the world are united at the spiritual level, which science calls the quantum level. We are all created in the image of God. All people have a similar mission at this level: To reveal the Light throughout the universe. All humankind is responsible for one another, and each one of us is needed to achieve the Final Correction and the redemption of the world. *Tzelem*-consciousness focuses individual identity and individual interest on one common need, just as no cell in the body rests until the wound has formed a scab. Thus, the individual identity of each cell is given a positive meaning: Every cell has a function, or "talents," that can help achieve the general mission. This consciousness of complete unity duplicates the Light because only in the Light is there no separation.

According to the Ari, the message and consciousness of the astrological sign of Gemini in general and the holiday of *Shavuot* specifically concentrate on one point: *Tzelem*. *Tzelem*-consciousness and its force can harmonize and unify everything in the universe at any level or aspect.

Recognizing this force and including it in our daily activities can revolutionize the quality of life for everyone all over the world. To some extent, achieving these goals is a matter of acquiring knowledge, but this intellectual aspect is secondary. Our path to the goal is the manifestation of ideas and the achievement of control over our destiny in a way that will enable us to finish our correction and complete the purpose of the entire Creation in full cooperation with the Creator.

Religion says: Pray to the Creator in times of hardship. The *Tzelem* says: You are the Creator. The Force of the Creator is within you. Let it flow through you, and the miracle will immediately take place. *Tzelem* is the life-force that beats within all of you, that gives you life and sustains it.

It is written in the Torah at the end of the portion of *Bamidbar* that for the Levites working in the Temple not to die, they had to comply with one specific rule. It was forbidden to look at the Ark of the Covenant with the naked eye, and whoever disobeyed this rule would die from the Force of the Light. There was an instruction that the Ark must always be covered. The Torah, however, uses the phrase "to swallow," rather than "to look" or "to see." It is as if someone would try to eat the Ark. It is true that if I swallow water or food, the moment either of them enters my body, no one is able to see it. But why use such an indirect expression to convey such a simple idea?

There is an essential difference between something that disappears inside me after I swallow it and something I cover with a mask or a handkerchief. With a mask or a handkerchief, it is still possible to see the shape of the thing it is concealing. By contrast, something that is swallowed disappears and cannot be identified—neither its shape nor its existence. The lesson the Torah is conveying is very special: When the Levites covered the Ark, the Ark simply disappeared, as if by magic. The covering was visible, but it was impossible to recognize the shape of the thing it was concealing.

Why? Because the Ark of the Covenant had lost its separate identity and only its *Tzelem* remained. After being covered, the Ark spread out from 1% consciousness to 99% consciousness. The Ark actually returned to its embryonic state. It became unidentifiable, just as an embryo's cells cannot be identified at the beginning of pregnancy and we cannot say which cell will develop into a heart and which will be the liver. The cells actually exist, but their essence is unseen. We can learn an important lesson from this: The unified cells develop into differentiated tissues, but the tissues themselves never lose the unified aspect from which they developed.

The closest thing to a physical expression of the *Tzelem* is the DNA in the nuclei of cells. Since DNA duplicates the body's cells in a manner that enables any wound to heal and all the cells to be replaced every seven years, why can't it tell the body of an amputee to grow a new leg? Physiologically it is possible; the physical infrastructure exists. Only doubt and negative consciousness prevent this kind of miracle from happening every day. The *Tzelem* is everywhere and in everything. All the cells of the body are 99% the same; cell differentiation is nothing more than an illusory effect. So who told a certain cell in the embryo to develop into an eye and another to become an ear? There must be a spiritual aspect beyond the physical one that established the reality. This spiritual aspect is the *Tzelem Elokim*—God's Image.

When we truly love people, we identify with them as with ourselves. We feel their feelings as if they were our own. This is the unity of the *Tzelem*. Separation from the *Tzelem* is what prevents us from creating miracles and revealing the complete Lightforce of the Creator in the world. The *Ari* teaches us that with the help of the astrological sign of Gemini and the holiday of *Shavuot*, we can reprogram our consciousness, exchanging our analytical, illusory consciousness for the reality of *Tzelem*-consciousness. In this way, spirit will rule matter, and we will materialize the Light within us and achieve control over the destiny of the universe.

The astrological sign of this month is Gemini, signified by twins, like the two angels on the Ark, which represent two aspects of one thing and thus expresses the unity of differences, the *Tzelem*-consciousness. The only reason we treat people as separate individuals is because of our illusory consciousness controlled by the negative side. *Tzelem*-consciousness makes it possible for us to rise above the illusion of separation. The level of our success depends on our level of certainty in the Light. With certainty, there is no need to turn to the Creator for help; we can just unite with the Creator. When we become like the Creator, we can create any miracle we need.

Once we achieve this level, however, there is only one more test to pass: The test of certainty. Every day, Satan will confront us with predicted and unpredictable challenges; he will provide us with reasons to get angry, to give up, to see the separation. But we can choose to continue to rise above all the illusions, to continue trusting in the Light, to be united with the Creator, and create solutions to all those illusory problems. We can command the car to start and drive, just as we would expect God to do. The *Tzelem* is capable of coordinating million of activities in the body because it is in certainty with regard to the Light. Our test is to be in unity with our unpleasant neighbor, with the IRS clerk, with the bank manager who made our check bounce, with our strict and inconsiderate boss. The level of our success depends on our level of certainty in the Light.

There is a connection between *Shavuot* and *Lag B'Omer*. *Shavuot* and *Lag B'Omer* are dates on which we can receive huge packages of life-energy. At *Lag B'Omer*, it is quite simple: Read the *Zohar* as much as possible throughout the night. At *Shavuot*, it is also simple, but there are a few more specific instructions. In order to connect to the *Keter* of *Zeir Anpin* and to establish the removal of death in our life, we must read a summary of the Torah. (For more information see pages I-VIII).

BERESHEET - GENESIS

בְּרֵאשִׁית בָּרָא קנ״א ב״ן אֱלֹהִים ילה אֵת הַשָּׁמַיִם י״פ טל, י״פ כוזו
וְאֵת הָאָרֶץ אלהים דההין ע״ה: וְהָאָרֶץ אלהים דההין ע״ה הָיְתָה תֹהוּ וָבֹהוּ
וְחֹשֶׁךְ ש״ך ניצוצות של ז׳ מלכים עַל־פְּנֵי חכמה בינה תְהוֹם וְרוּחַ אֱלֹהִים ילה, מום
מְרַחֶפֶת עַל־פְּנֵי חכמה בינה הַמָּיִם: וַיֹּאמֶר אֱלֹהִים ילה, מום יְהִי אוֹר רז, אין-סוף
וַיְהִי־אוֹר רז, אין-סוף: וַיַּרְא אֱלֹהִים ילה, מום אֶת־הָאוֹר רז, אין-סוף כִּי־טוֹב והו, אום
וַיַּבְדֵּל אֱלֹהִים ילה, מום בֵּין הָאוֹר רז, אין-סוף וּבֵין הַחֹשֶׁךְ ש״ך ניצוצות של ז׳ מלכים:
וַיִּקְרָא עם ה׳ אותיות = ב״פ קס״א אֱלֹהִים ילה, מום | לָאוֹר רז, אין-סוף יוֹם ע״ה = נגד, זן, מזבח
וְלַחֹשֶׁךְ ש״ך ניצוצות של ז׳ מלכים קָרָא לָיְלָה מלה וַיְהִי־עֶרֶב וַיְהִי־בֹקֶר
יוֹם ע״ה = נגד, זן, מזבח אֶחָד אהבה, דאגה: וַיֹּאמֶר אֱלֹהִים ילה, מום יְהִי רָקִיעַ בְּתוֹךְ
הַמָּיִם וִיהִי מַבְדִּיל בֵּין מַיִם לָמָיִם: וַיַּעַשׂ אֱלֹהִים ילה, מום אֶת־הָרָקִיעַ וַיַּבְדֵּל
בֵּין הַמַּיִם אֲשֶׁר מִתַּחַת לָרָקִיעַ וּבֵין הַמַּיִם אֲשֶׁר מֵעַל עלם לָרָקִיעַ וַיְהִי־כֵן:

וַיִּקְרָא עם ה׳ אותיות = ב״פ קס״א אֱלֹהִים ילה, מום לָרָקִיעַ שָׁמָיִם י״פ טל, י״פ כוזו וַיְהִי־
עֶרֶב וַיְהִי־בֹקֶר יוֹם ע״ה = נגד, זן, מזבח שֵׁנִי׃ וַיֹּאמֶר אֱלֹהִים ילה, מום יִקָּווּ הַמַּיִם
מִתַּחַת הַשָּׁמַיִם י״פ טל, י״פ כוזו אֶל־מָקוֹם אֶחָד אהבה, דאגה וְתֵרָאֶה הַיַּבָּשָׁה
וַיְהִי־כֵן׃ וַיִּקְרָא עם ה׳ אותיות = ב״פ קס״א אֱלֹהִים ילה, מום | לַיַּבָּשָׁה אֶרֶץ
וּלְמִקְוֵה קנ״א, אלהים אדני הַמַּיִם קָרָא יַמִּים נלך וַיַּרְא אֱלֹהִים ילה, מום
כִּי־טוֹב והו, אום׃ וַיֹּאמֶר אֱלֹהִים ילה, מום תַּדְשֵׁא הָאָרֶץ אלהים דההין ע״ה דֶּשֶׁא
עֵשֶׂב ע״ב שמות מַזְרִיעַ זֶרַע עֵץ פְּרִי עֹשֶׂה פְּרִי לְמִינוֹ אֲשֶׁר זַרְעוֹ־בוֹ
עַל־הָאָרֶץ אלהים דההין ע״ה וַיְהִי־כֵן׃ וַתּוֹצֵא הָאָרֶץ אלהים דההין ע״ה דֶּשֶׁא
עֵשֶׂב ע״ב שמות מַזְרִיעַ זֶרַע לְמִינֵהוּ וְעֵץ עֹשֶׂה־פְּרִי אֲשֶׁר זַרְעוֹ־בוֹ לְמִינֵהוּ
וַיַּרְא אֱלֹהִים ילה, מום כִּי־טוֹב והו, אום׃ וַיְהִי־עֶרֶב וַיְהִי־בֹקֶר יוֹם ע״ה = נגד, זן, מזבח
שְׁלִישִׁי׃ וַיֹּאמֶר אֱלֹהִים ילה, מום יְהִי מְאֹרֹת בִּרְקִיעַ הַשָּׁמַיִם י״פ טל, י״פ כוזו
לְהַבְדִּיל בֵּין הַיּוֹם ע״ה = נגד, זן, מזבח וּבֵין הַלָּיְלָה מלה וְהָיוּ לְאֹתֹת וּלְמוֹעֲדִים
וּלְיָמִים נלך וְשָׁנִים׃ וְהָיוּ לִמְאוֹרֹת בִּרְקִיעַ הַשָּׁמַיִם י״פ טל, י״פ כוזו לְהָאִיר
עַל־הָאָרֶץ אלהים דההין ע״ה וַיְהִי־כֵן׃ וַיַּעַשׂ אֱלֹהִים ילה, מום אֶת־שְׁנֵי הַמְּאֹרֹת
הַגְּדֹלִים להח, מבה, יזל, אום אֶת־הַמָּאוֹר הַגָּדֹל להח, מבה, יזל, אום לְמֶמְשֶׁלֶת
הַיּוֹם ע״ה = נגד, זן, מזבח וְאֶת־הַמָּאוֹר הַקָּטֹן לְמֶמְשֶׁלֶת הַלַּיְלָה מלה וְאֵת
הַכּוֹכָבִים׃ וַיִּתֵּן אֹתָם אֱלֹהִים ילה, מום בִּרְקִיעַ הַשָּׁמָיִם י״פ טל, י״פ כוזו לְהָאִיר
עַל־הָאָרֶץ אלהים דההין ע״ה׃ וְלִמְשֹׁל בַּיּוֹם ע״ה = נגד, זן, מזבח וּבַלַּיְלָה מלה וּלֲהַבְדִּיל
בֵּין הָאוֹר רז, אין־סוף וּבֵין הַחֹשֶׁךְ ש״ך ניצוצות של ז׳ מלכים וַיַּרְא אֱלֹהִים ילה, מום
כִּי־טוֹב והו, אום׃ וַיְהִי־עֶרֶב וַיְהִי־בֹקֶר יוֹם ע״ה = נגד, זן, מזבח רְבִיעִי׃
וַיֹּאמֶר אֱלֹהִים ילה, מום יִשְׁרְצוּ הַמַּיִם שֶׁרֶץ נֶפֶשׁ חַיָּה וְעוֹף יְעוֹפֵף
עַל־הָאָרֶץ אלהים דההין ע״ה עַל־פְּנֵי חכמה בינה רְקִיעַ הַשָּׁמָיִם י״פ טל, י״פ כוזו׃ וַיִּבְרָא
אֱלֹהִים ילה, מום אֶת־הַתַּנִּינִם הַגְּדֹלִים להח, מבה, יזל, אום וְאֵת כָּל־ ילי נֶפֶשׁ הַחַיָּה |
הָרֹמֶשֶׂת אֲשֶׁר שָׁרְצוּ הַמַּיִם לְמִינֵהֶם וְאֵת כָּל־ ילי עוֹף כָּנָף ע״ה קנ״א, אלהים אדני
לְמִינֵהוּ וַיַּרְא אֱלֹהִים ילה, מום כִּי־טוֹב והו, אום׃ וַיְבָרֶךְ עסמ״ב אֹתָם אֱלֹהִים ילה, מום
לֵאמֹר פְּרוּ וּרְבוּ וּמִלְאוּ אֶת־הַמַּיִם בַּיַּמִּים נלך וְהָעוֹף יִרֶב בָּאָרֶץ׃
וַיְהִי־עֶרֶב וַיְהִי־בֹקֶר יוֹם ע״ה = נגד, זן, מזבח חֲמִישִׁי׃ וַיֹּאמֶר
אֱלֹהִים ילה, מום תּוֹצֵא הָאָרֶץ אלהים דההין ע״ה נֶפֶשׁ חַיָּה לְמִינָהּ
בְּהֵמָה ב״ן, לכב וָרֶמֶשׂ וְחַיְתוֹ־אֶרֶץ לְמִינָהּ וַיְהִי־כֵן׃ וַיַּעַשׂ אֱלֹהִים ילה, מום
אֶת־חַיַּת הָאָרֶץ אלהים דההין ע״ה לְמִינָהּ וְאֶת־הַבְּהֵמָה ב״ן, לכב לְמִינָהּ
וְאֵת כָּל־ ילי רֶמֶשׂ הָאֲדָמָה לְמִינֵהוּ וַיַּרְא אֱלֹהִים ילה, מום כִּי־טוֹב והו:

וַיֹּאמֶר אֱלֹהִים ילה, מום נַעֲשֶׂה אָדָם מ״ה בְּצַלְמֵנוּ כִּדְמוּתֵנוּ וְיִרְדּוּ רי״ו
בִדְגַת הַיָּם ילי וּבְעוֹף הַשָּׁמַיִם י״פ טל, י״פ כוזו וּבַבְּהֵמָה ב״ן, לכב וּבְכָל־ לכב
הָאָרֶץ אלהים דההין ע״ה וּבְכָל־ לכב הָרֶמֶשׂ הָרֹמֵשׂ עַל־הָאָרֶץ אלהים דההין ע״ה:
וַיִּבְרָא אֱלֹהִים ילה, מום | אֶת־הָאָדָם מ״ה בְּצַלְמוֹ בְּצֶלֶם אֱלֹהִים ילה, מום
בָּרָא קנ״א ב״ן אֹתוֹ זָכָר וּנְקֵבָה בָּרָא קנ״א ב״ן אֹתָם: וַיְבָרֶךְ עסמ״ב אֹתָם
אֱלֹהִים ילה, מום וַיֹּאמֶר לָהֶם אֱלֹהִים ילה, מום פְּרוּ וּרְבוּ וּמִלְאוּ אֶת־
הָאָרֶץ אלהים דההין ע״ה וְכִבְשֻׁהָ וּרְדוּ בִּדְגַת הַיָּם ילי וּבְעוֹף הַשָּׁמַיִם י״פ טל, י״פ כוזו
וּבְכָל־ לכב חַיָּה הָרֹמֶשֶׂת עַל־ הָאָרֶץ אלהים דההין ע״ה: וַיֹּאמֶר אֱלֹהִים ילה, מום
הִנֵּה נָתַתִּי לָכֶם אֶת־כָּל־ ילי עֵשֶׂב ע״ב שמות | זֹרֵעַ זֶרַע אֲשֶׁר עַל־פְּנֵי חכמה בינה
כָל־ ילי הָאָרֶץ אלהים דההין ע״ה וְאֶת־כָּל־ ילי הָעֵץ אֲשֶׁר־בּוֹ פְרִי־ עֵץ זֹרֵעַ זָרַע
לָכֶם יִהְיֶה יי״ לְאָכְלָה: וּלְכָל־ יה אדני חַיַּת הָאָרֶץ אלהים דההין ע״ה וּלְכָל־ יה אדני
עוֹף הַשָּׁמַיִם י״פ טל, י״פ כוזו וּלְכֹל יה אדני | רוֹמֵשׂ עַל־הָאָרֶץ אלהים דההין ע״ה
אֲשֶׁר־בּוֹ נֶפֶשׁ חַיָּה אֶת־כָּל־ ילי יֶרֶק עֵשֶׂב ע״ב שמות לְאָכְלָה וַיְהִי־כֵן: וַיַּרְא
אֱלֹהִים ילה, מום אֶת־כָּל־ ילי אֲשֶׁר עָשָׂה וְהִנֵּה־טוֹב והו מְאֹד וַיְהִי־עֶרֶב וַיְהִי־
בֹקֶר יוֹם ע״ה = נגד, זן, מזבח הַשִּׁשִּׁי: וַיְכֻלּוּ ע״ב, ריבוע יהוה הַשָּׁמַיִם י״פ טל, י״פ כוזו
וְהָאָרֶץ אלהים דההין ע״ה וְכָל־ ילי צְבָאָם: וַיְכַל אֱלֹהִים ילה, מום
בַּיּוֹם ע״ה = נגד, זן, מזבח הַשְּׁבִיעִי מְלַאכְתּוֹ אֲשֶׁר עָשָׂה וַיִּשְׁבֹּת
בַּיּוֹם ע״ה = נגד, זן, מזבח הַשְּׁבִיעִי מִכָּל־ ילי מְלַאכְתּוֹ אֲשֶׁר עָשָׂה: וַיְבָרֶךְ עסמ״ב
אֱלֹהִים ילה, מום אֶת־יוֹם ע״ה = נגד, זן, מזבח הַשְּׁבִיעִי וַיְקַדֵּשׁ אֹתוֹ כִּי בוֹ שָׁבַת
מִכָּל־ ילי מְלַאכְתּוֹ אֲשֶׁר־בָּרָא קנ״א ב״ן אֱלֹהִים ילה, מום לַעֲשׂוֹת:

וַיַּרְא יְהֹוָאדנָיאהדונהי כִּי רַבָּה רָעַת הָאָדָם מ״ה בָּאָרֶץ וְכָל־ ילי יֵצֶר מַחְשְׁבֹת
לִבּוֹ רַק רַע כָּל־ ילי הַיּוֹם ע״ה = נגד, זן, מזבח: וַיִּנָּחֶם יְהֹוָאדנָיאהדונהי כִּי־עָשָׂה
אֶת־הָאָדָם מ״ה בָּאָרֶץ וַיִּתְעַצֵּב אֶל־לִבּוֹ: וַיֹּאמֶר יְהֹוָאדנָיאהדונהי אֶמְחֶה
אֶת־הָאָדָם מ״ה אֲשֶׁר־בָּרָאתִי מֵעַל עלם פְּנֵי חכמה בינה הָאֲדָמָה מֵאָדָם מ״ה
עַד־בְּהֵמָה ב״ן, לכב עַד־רֶמֶשׂ וְעַד־עוֹף הַשָּׁמָיִם י״פ טל, י״פ כוזו כִּי נִחַמְתִּי
כִּי עֲשִׂיתִם: וְנֹחַ מָצָא חֵן מוזי בְּעֵינֵי ריבוע מ״ה יְהֹוָאדנָיאהדונהי:

אֵלֶּה תּוֹלְדֹת נֹחַ נֹחַ אִישׁ צַדִּיק תָּמִים הָיָה יהה בְּדֹרֹתָיו אֶת־הָאֱלֹהִים ילה, מום
הִתְהַלֶּךְ־ מ״ה נֹחַ: וַיּוֹלֶד נֹחַ שְׁלֹשָׁה בָנִים אֶת־שֵׁם אֶת־חָם וְאֶת־יָפֶת: וַתִּשָּׁחֵת
הָאָרֶץ אלהים דההין ע״ה לִפְנֵי הָאֱלֹהִים ילה, מום וַתִּמָּלֵא הָאָרֶץ אלהים דההין ע״ה
חָמָס: וַיַּרְא אֱלֹהִים ילה, מום אֶת־הָאָרֶץ אלהים דההין ע״ה וְהִנֵּה נִשְׁחָתָה כִּי־
הִשְׁחִית כָּל־ ילי בָּשָׂר אֶת־דַּרְכּוֹ עַל־הָאָרֶץ אלהים דההין ע״ה:

וַיִּקַּח וזעם אַבְרָם וְנָחוֹר לָהֶם נָשִׁים שֵׁם אֵשֶׁת־אַבְרָם שָׂרָי וְשֵׁם אֵשֶׁת־נָחוֹר מִלְכָּה בַּת־הָרָן אֲבִי־מִלְכָּה וַאֲבִי יִסְכָּה׃ וַתְּהִי שָׂרַי עֲקָרָה אֵין לָהּ וָלָד׃ וַיִּקַּח וזעם תֶּרַח אֶת־אַבְרָם בְּנוֹ וְאֶת־לוֹט בֶּן־הָרָן בֶּן־בְּנוֹ וְאֵת שָׂרַי כַּלָּתוֹ אֵשֶׁת אַבְרָם בְּנוֹ וַיֵּצְאוּ אִתָּם מֵאוּר כַּשְׂדִּים לָלֶכֶת אַרְצָה כְּנַעַן וַיָּבֹאוּ עַד־חָרָן וַיֵּשְׁבוּ שָׁם׃ וַיִּהְיוּ יְמֵי־תֶרַח חָמֵשׁ שָׁנִים וּמָאתַיִם שָׁנָה וַיָּמָת תֶּרַח בְּחָרָן׃

וַיֹּאמֶר יְהוָה יאהדונהי אֶל־אַבְרָם **לֶךְ־לְךָ** מֵאַרְצְךָ וּמִמּוֹלַדְתְּךָ וּמִבֵּית ב״פ ראה אָבִיךָ אֶל־הָאָרֶץ אלהים דההין ע״ה אֲשֶׁר אַרְאֶךָּ׃ וְאֶעֶשְׂךָ לְגוֹי גָּדוֹל להח, מבה, יזל, אום וַאֲבָרֶכְךָ וַאֲגַדְּלָה שְׁמֶךָ וֶהְיֵה יהוה, יהה בְּרָכָה׃ וַאֲבָרְכָה מְבָרְכֶיךָ וּמְקַלֶּלְךָ אָאֹר וְנִבְרְכוּ יהוה ריבוע יהוה ריבוע מ״ה בְךָ כֹּל ילי מִשְׁפְּחֹת הָאֲדָמָה׃

וְאַבְרָהָם וז״פ אל, רמ״ח בֶּן־תִּשְׁעִים וָתֵשַׁע שָׁנָה בְּהִמֹּלוֹ בְּשַׂר עָרְלָתוֹ׃ וְיִשְׁמָעֵאל בְּנוֹ בֶּן־שְׁלֹשׁ עֶשְׂרֵה שָׁנָה בְּהִמֹּלוֹ אֵת בְּשַׂר עָרְלָתוֹ׃ בְּעֶצֶם הַיּוֹם ע״ה = נגד, זן, מזבח הַזֶּה והו נִמּוֹל אַבְרָהָם וז״פ אל, רמ״ח וְיִשְׁמָעֵאל בְּנוֹ׃ וְכָל־ ילי אַנְשֵׁי בֵיתוֹ ב״פ ראה יְלִיד בָּיִת ב״פ ראה וּמִקְנַת־כֶּסֶף מֵאֵת בֶּן־נֵכָר נִמֹּלוּ אִתּוֹ׃

וַיֵּרָא אֵלָיו יְהוָה יאהדונהי בְּאֵלֹנֵי מַמְרֵא וְהוּא יֹשֵׁב פֶּתַח־הָאֹהֶל כְּחֹם הַיּוֹם ע״ה = נגד, זן, מזבח׃ וַיִּשָּׂא עֵינָיו ריבוע מ״ה וַיַּרְא וְהִנֵּה שְׁלֹשָׁה אֲנָשִׁים נִצָּבִים עָלָיו וַיַּרְא וַיָּרָץ לִקְרָאתָם מִפֶּתַח הָאֹהֶל וַיִּשְׁתַּחוּ אָרְצָה אלהים דההין ע״ה׃ וַיֹּאמַר אֲדֹנָי (ווכל) אִם־ יוהך נָא מָצָאתִי חֵן מוזי בְּעֵינֶיךָ ע״ה קס״א אַל־נָא תַעֲבֹר מֵעַל עלם עַבְדֶּךָ פוי׃ יֻקַּח־ וזעם נָא מְעַט־מַיִם וְרַחֲצוּ רַגְלֵיכֶם וְהִשָּׁעֲנוּ תַּחַת הָעֵץ׃ וְאֶקְחָה פַת־לֶחֶם ג״פ יהוה וְסַעֲדוּ לִבְּכֶם אַחַר תַּעֲבֹרוּ כִּי־עַל־כֵּן עֲבַרְתֶּם עַל־עַבְדְּכֶם וַיֹּאמְרוּ כֵּן תַּעֲשֶׂה כַּאֲשֶׁר דִּבַּרְתָּ ראה׃

וַיְהִי אַחֲרֵי הַדְּבָרִים ראה הָאֵלֶּה וַיֻּגַּד לְאַבְרָהָם וז״פ אל, רמ״ח לֵאמֹר הִנֵּה יָלְדָה מִלְכָּה גַם־הִוא בָּנִים לְנָחוֹר אָחִיךָ׃ אֶת־עוּץ בְּכֹרוֹ וְאֶת־בּוּז אָחִיו וְאֶת־קְמוּאֵל אֲבִי אֲרָם׃ וְאֶת־כֶּשֶׂד וְאֶת־חֲזוֹ וְאֶת־פִּלְדָּשׁ וְאֶת־יִדְלָף וְאֵת בְּתוּאֵל׃ וּבְתוּאֵל יָלַד אֶת־רִבְקָה שְׁמֹנָה אֵלֶּה יָלְדָה מִלְכָּה לְנָחוֹר אֲחִי אַבְרָהָם וז״פ אל, רמ״ח׃ וּפִילַגְשׁוֹ וּשְׁמָהּ רְאוּמָה וַתֵּלֶד גַּם־הִוא אֶת־טֶבַח וְאֶת־גַּחַם וְאֶת־תַּחַשׁ וְאֶת־מַעֲכָה׃

ויהיו אל חיי שרה מאה שנה ועשרים שנה ושבע שנים שני חיי שרה:
ותמת שרה בקרית ארבע הוא חברון בארץ כנען ויבא
אברהם ח״פ אל, רמ״ח לספד לשרה ולבכתה: ויקם אברהם ח״פ אל, רמ״ח
מעל עלם פני חכמה בינה מתו וידבר ראה אל־בני־חת לאמר:

אלה הם בני ישמעאל ואלה שמתם בחצריהם ובטירתם שנים־עשר
נשיאם לאמתם: ואלה שני חיי ישמעאל מאת שנה ושלשים שנה
ושבע שנים ויגוע וימת ויאסף אל־עמיו: וישכנו מחוילה עד־
שור אבגיתץ, ושר, אהבת חנם אשר על־פני חכמה בינה מצרים מצר באכה אשורה
על־פני חכמה בינה כל־ ילי אחיו נפל:

ואלה תולדת יצחק ד״פ ב״ן בן־אברהם ח״פ אל, רמ״ח
אברהם ח״פ אל, רמ״ח הוליד את־יצחק ד״פ ב״ן: ויהי יצחק ד״פ ב״ן בן־ארבעים
שנה בקחתו את־רבקה בת־בתואל הארמי מפדן ארם אחות לבן
הארמי לו לאשה: ויעתר יצחק ד״פ ב״ן ליהוהאדני אהדונהי לנכח ג״פ יהוה אשתו
כי עקרה הוא ויעתר לו יהוהאדני אהדונהי ותהר רבקה אשתו:

וישמע יעקב יאהדונהי אידהנויה אל־אביו ואל־אמו וילך כלי פדנה ארם: וירא
עשו כי רעות בנות כנען בעיני ריבוע מ״ה יצחק ד״פ ב״ן אביו:
וילך כלי עשו אל־ישמעאל ויקח חעם את־מחלת | בת־ישמעאל בן־
אברהם ח״פ אל, רמ״ח אחות נביות על־נשיו לו לאשה:

ויצא יעקב יאהדונהי אידהנויה מבאר קנ״א ב״ן שבע וילך כלי חרנה:
ויפגע במקום וילן שם כי־בא השמש ויקח חעם מאבני המקום וישם
מראשתיו ריבוע אלהים ואלהים דיודין ע״ה וישכב במקום ההוא: ויחלם והנה סלם
מצב ארצה אלהים דההין ע״ה וראשו ריבוע אלהים ואלהים דיודין ע״ה מגיע השמימה
והנה מלאכי אלהים ילה, מום עלים וירדים ריי בו:

וישכם לבן בבקר וינשק לבניו ולבנותיו ויברך עסמ״ב אתהם
וילך כלי וישב לבן למקמו: ויעקב יאהדונהי אידהנויה הלך מ״ה לדרכו
ויפגעו־בו מלאכי אלהים ילה, מום: ויאמר יעקב יאהדונהי אידהנויה כאשר ראם
מחנה אלהים ילה, מום זה ויקרא עם ה׳ אותיות = ב״פ קס״א שם־המקום ההוא
מחנים:

וישלח יעקב יאהדונהי אידהנויה מלאכים לפניו אל-עשו אחיו ארצה אלהים דההין ע"ה שעיר שדה אדום: ויצו אתם לאמר כה היי תאמרון לאדני לעשו כה היי אמר עבדך פוי יעקב יאהדונהי אידהנויה עם-לבן גרתי ואחר עד-עתה: ויהי-לי שור אבגיתצ, ושר, אהבת חנם וחמור צאן ועבד ושפחה ואשלחה להגיד לאדני למצא-חן מוזי בעיניך ע"ה קס"א:

ואלה שמות אלופי עשו למשפחתם למקמתם בשמתם אלוף תמנע אלוף עלוה אלוף יתת: אלוף אהליבמה אלוף אלה אלוף פינן: אלוף קנז אלוף תימן אלוף מבצר: אלוף מגדיאל אלוף עירם אלה | אלופי אדום למשבתם בארץ אחזתם הוא עשו אבי אדום:

וישב יעקב יאהדונהי אידהנויה בארץ מגורי אביו בארץ כנען: אלה | תלדות יעקב יאהדונהי אידהנויה יוסף ציון, ו"פ יהוה בן-שבע-עשרה שנה היה יהה רעה רהע את-אחיו בצאן והוא נער את-בני בלהה ואת-בני זלפה נשי אביו ויבא יוסף ציון, ו"פ יהוה את-דבתם רעה רהע אל-אביהם: וישראל אהב את-יוסף ציון, ו"פ יהוה מכל- ילי בניו כי-בן-זקנים הוא לו ועשה לו כתנת פסים:

ויהי | ביום ע"ה = נגד, זן, מזבח השלישי יום ע"ה = נגד, זן, מזבח הלדת את-פרעה ויעש משתה לכל- יה אדני עבדיו וישא את-ראש | ריבוע אלהים ואלהים דיודין ע"ה שר המשקים ואת-ראש ריבוע אלהים ואלהים דיודין ע"ה שר האפים בתוך עבדיו: וישב את-שר המשקים על-משקהו ויתן הכוס אלהים, מום על-כף פרעה: ואת שר האפים תלה כאשר פתר להם יוסף ציון, ו"פ יהוה: ולא-זכר שר-המשקים את-יוסף ציון, ו"פ יהוה וישכחהו:

ויהי מקץ מנק שנתים ימים נלך ופרעה חלם והנה עמד על-היאר כף ויו זין ויו: והנה מן-היאר כף ויו זין ויו עלת אבגיתצ, ושר, אהבת חנם שבע פרות יפות מראה ובריאת בשר ותרעינה באחו: והנה שבע פרות אחרות עלות אבגיתצ, ושר, אהבת חנם אחריהן מן-היאר כף ויו זין ויו רעות מראה ודקות בשר ותעמדנה אצל הפרות על-שפת היאר כף ויו זין ויו: ותאכלנה הפרות רעות המראה ודקת הבשר את שבע הפרות יפת המראה והבריאת וייקץ פרעה:

וַיָּבֹא יְהוּדָה וְאֶחָיו בֵּיתָה ב"פ ראה יוֹסֵף ציון, ו"פ יהוה וְהוּא עוֹדֶנּוּ שָׁם וַיִּפְּלוּ לְפָנָיו אָרְצָה אלהים דההין ע"ה: וַיֹּאמֶר לָהֶם יוֹסֵף ציון, ו"פ יהוה מָה־ מ"ה הַמַּעֲשֶׂה הַזֶּה והו אֲשֶׁר עֲשִׂיתֶם הֲלוֹא יְדַעְתֶּם כִּי־נַחֵשׁ יְנַחֵשׁ אִישׁ אֲשֶׁר כָּמֹנִי: וַיֹּאמֶר יְהוּדָה מַה־ מ"ה נֹּאמַר לַאדֹנִי מַה־ מ"ה נְּדַבֵּר ראה וּמַה־ מ"ה נִּצְטַדָּק הָאֱלֹהִים ילה, מום מָצָא אֶת־עֲוֹן עֲבָדֶיךָ הִנֶּנּוּ עֲבָדִים לַאדֹנִי גַּם־אֲנַחְנוּ גַּם אֲשֶׁר־נִמְצָא הַגָּבִיעַ בְּיָדוֹ: וַיֹּאמֶר חָלִילָה לִּי מֵעֲשׂוֹת זֹאת הָאִישׁ אֲשֶׁר נִמְצָא הַגָּבִיעַ בְּיָדוֹ הוּא יִהְיֶה־ ייי לִּי עָבֶד וְאַתֶּם עֲלוּ לְשָׁלוֹם אֶל־אֲבִיכֶם:

וַיִּגַּשׁ אֵלָיו יְהוּדָה וַיֹּאמֶר בִּי אֲדֹנִי יְדַבֶּר־ ראה נָא עַבְדְּךָ פוי דָבָר ראה בְּאָזְנֵי יוד הי ואו הה אֲדֹנִי וְאַל־יִחַר אַפְּךָ בְּעַבְדֶּךָ פוי כִּי כָמוֹךָ כְּפַרְעֹה: אֲדֹנִי שָׁאַל אֶת־ עֲבָדָיו לֵאמֹר הֲיֵשׁ־לָכֶם אָב אוֹ־אָח: וַנֹּאמֶר אֶל־ אֲדֹנִי יֶשׁ־לָנוּ אלהים, מום אָב זָקֵן וְיֶלֶד זְקֻנִים קָטָן וְאָחִיו מֵת וַיִּוָּתֵר הוּא לְבַדּוֹ מ"ב לְאִמּוֹ וְאָבִיו אֲהֵבוֹ:

וַיֹּאמְרוּ הֶחֱיִתָנוּ נִמְצָא־חֵן מוזי בְּעֵינֵי ריבוע מ"ה אֲדֹנִי וְהָיִינוּ עֲבָדִים לְפַרְעֹה: וַיָּשֶׂם אֹתָהּ יוֹסֵף ציון, ו"פ יהוה לְחֹק עַד־הַיּוֹם ע"ה = נגד, זן, מזבח הַזֶּה והו עַל־אַדְמַת מִצְרַיִם מצר לְפַרְעֹה לַחֹמֶשׁ רַק אַדְמַת הַכֹּהֲנִים לְבַדָּם לֹא הָיְתָה לְפַרְעֹה: וַיֵּשֶׁב יִשְׂרָאֵל בְּאֶרֶץ מִצְרַיִם מצר בְּאֶרֶץ גֹּשֶׁן וַיֵּאָחֲזוּ בָהּ וַיִּפְרוּ וַיִּרְבּוּ מְאֹד:

וַיְחִי יַעֲקֹב יאהדונהי אידהנויה בְּאֶרֶץ מִצְרַיִם מצר שְׁבַע עֶשְׂרֵה שָׁנָה וַיְהִי יְמֵי־יַעֲקֹב יאהדונהי אידהנויה שְׁנֵי חַיָּיו שֶׁבַע שָׁנִים וְאַרְבָּעִים וּמְאַת שָׁנָה: וַיִּקְרְבוּ יְמֵי־יִשְׂרָאֵל לָמוּת וַיִּקְרָא עם ה' אותיות = ב"פ קס"א | לִבְנוֹ לְיוֹסֵף ציון, ו"פ יהוה וַיֹּאמֶר לוֹ אִם־ יוהך נָא מָצָאתִי חֵן מוזי בְּעֵינֶיךָ ע"ה קס"א שִׂים־נָא יָדְךָ תַּחַת יְרֵכִי וְעָשִׂיתָ עִמָּדִי חֶסֶד ע"ב, ריבוע יהוה וֶאֱמֶת אהיה פעמים אהיה, ז"פ ס"ג אַל־נָא תִקְבְּרֵנִי בְּמִצְרָיִם מצר: וְשָׁכַבְתִּי עִם־אֲבֹתַי וּנְשָׂאתַנִי מִמִּצְרַיִם מצר וּקְבַרְתַּנִי בִּקְבֻרָתָם וַיֹּאמַר אָנֹכִי איע אֶעֱשֶׂה כִדְבָרֶךָ ראה: וַיֹּאמֶר הִשָּׁבְעָה לִי וַיִּשָּׁבַע לוֹ וַיִּשְׁתַּחוּ יִשְׂרָאֵל עַל־רֹאשׁ ריבוע אלהים ואלהים דיודין ע"ה הַמִּטָּה:

וַיַּרְא יוֹסֵף ציון, ו״פ יהוה לְאֶפְרַיִם בְּנֵי שִׁלֵּשִׁים גַּם בְּנֵי מָכִיר בֶּן־מְנַשֶּׁה יֻלְּדוּ
עַל־בִּרְכֵּי יוֹסֵף ציון, ו״פ יהוה: וַיֹּאמֶר יוֹסֵף ציון, ו״פ יהוה אֶל־אֶחָיו אָנֹכִי איע מֵת
וֵאלֹהִים ילה, מום פָּקֹד יִפְקֹד אֶתְכֶם וְהֶעֱלָה אֶתְכֶם מִן־הָאָרֶץ אלהים דההין ע״ה
הַזֹּאת אֶל־הָאָרֶץ אלהים דההין ע״ה אֲשֶׁר נִשְׁבַּע לְאַבְרָהָם וז״פ אל, רמ״ח
לְיִצְחָק ד״פ ב״ן וּלְיַעֲקֹב יאהדונהי אידהנויה: וַיַּשְׁבַּע יוֹסֵף ציון, ו״פ יהוה אֶת־בְּנֵי יִשְׂרָאֵל
לֵאמֹר פָּקֹד יִפְקֹד אֱלֹהִים ילה, מום אֶתְכֶם וְהַעֲלִתֶם אֶת־עַצְמֹתַי מִזֶּה:

וַיָּמָת יוֹסֵף ציון, ו״פ יהוה (יָפָ־YUFA)
בֶּן־מֵאָה וָעֶשֶׂר שָׁנִים וַיַּחַנְטוּ אֹתוֹ וַיִּישֶׂם בָּאָרוֹן בְּמִצְרָיִם מצר:

SHEMOT - EXODUS

וְאֵלֶּה מ״ב שְׁמוֹת בְּנֵי יִשְׂרָאֵל הַבָּאִים מִצְרָיְמָה מצר אֵת יַעֲקֹב
ז״פ יהוה, יאהדונהי אידהנויה אִישׁ ע״ה קנ״א קס״א וּבֵיתוֹ בָּאוּ: רְאוּבֵן ג״פ אלהים שִׁמְעוֹן
לֵוִי דמב, מילוי ע״ב וִיהוּדָה: יִשָּׂשכָר י״פ אל י״פ ב״ן זְבוּלֻן וּבִנְיָמִן: דָּן וְנַפְתָּלִי גָּד
וְאָשֵׁר מלוי אהיה דיודין: וַיְהִי אל כָּל־ ילי נֶפֶשׁ רמ״ח ז׳ הויות יֹצְאֵי יֶרֶךְ־
יַעֲקֹב ז״פ יהוה, יאהדונהי אידהנויה שִׁבְעִים נָפֶשׁ רמ״ח ז׳ הויות וְיוֹסֵף ציון, קנאה, ו׳ הויות
הָיָה יהה בְמִצְרָיִם מצר: וַיָּמָת יוֹסֵף ציון, קנאה, ו׳ הויות וְכָל־ ילי אֶחָיו וְכֹל ילי הַדּוֹר
הַהוּא: וּבְנֵי יִשְׂרָאֵל פָּרוּ וַיִּשְׁרְצוּ וַיִּרְבּוּ וַיַּעַצְמוּ בִּמְאֹד מ״ה מְאֹד מ״ה
וַתִּמָּלֵא הָאָרֶץ אלהים דההין ע״ה אֹתָם:

וַיָּשָׁב מֹשֶׁה מהש, אל שדי אֶל־יְהֹוָאדני־אהדונהי וַיֹּאמַר אֲדֹנָי ללה לָמָה הֲרֵעֹתָה
לָעָם הַזֶּה והו לָמָּה זֶּה שְׁלַחְתָּנִי: וּמֵאָז ומב בָּאתִי אֶל־פַּרְעֹה לְדַבֵּר ראה
בִשְׁמֶךָ הֵרַע לָעָם הַזֶּה והו וְהַצֵּל לֹא־הִצַּלְתָּ אֶת־עַמֶּךָ ה׳ הויות, נמם: וַיֹּאמֶר
יְהֹוָאדני־אהדונהי אֶל־מֹשֶׁה מהש, אל שדי עַתָּה תִרְאֶה אֲשֶׁר אֶעֱשֶׂה לְפַרְעֹה כִּי
בְיָד חֲזָקָה יְשַׁלְּחֵם וּבְיָד חֲזָקָה יְגָרְשֵׁם מֵאַרְצוֹ:

וַיְדַבֵּר ראה אֱלֹהִים מום, אהיה אדני ; ילה אֶל־מֹשֶׁה מהש, אל שדי וַיֹּאמֶר אֵלָיו
אֲנִי אני, טדה״ד כוז״ו יְהֹוָאדני־אהדונהי: וָאֵרָא אֶל־אַבְרָהָם רמ״ח, וז״פ אל אֶל־
יִצְחָק ד״פ ב״ן וְאֶל־יַעֲקֹב ז״פ יהוה, יאהדונהי אידהנויה בְּאֵל יא״י שַׁדָּי רפ״ח יהוה
וּשְׁמִי רבוע ע״ב ורבוע ס״ג יְהֹוָאדני־אהדונהי לֹא נוֹדַעְתִּי לָהֶם: וְגַם יג״ל הֲקִמֹתִי אֶת־
בְּרִיתִי אִתָּם לָתֵת לָהֶם אֶת־אֶרֶץ אלהים דאלפין כְּנָעַן אֵת אֶרֶץ אלהים דאלפין
מְגֻרֵיהֶם אֲשֶׁר־גָּרוּ בָהּ: וְגַם יג״ל | אֲנִי אני, טדה״ד כוז״ו שָׁמַעְתִּי אֶת־נַאֲקַת בְּנֵי
יִשְׂרָאֵל אֲשֶׁר מִצְרַיִם מצר מַעֲבִדִים אֹתָם וָאֶזְכֹּר אֶת־בְּרִיתִי:

וַיֵּצֵא מֹשֶׁה מהש, אל שדי מֵעִם פַּרְעֹה אֶת־הָעִיר בוזוך, ערי, סנדלפון וַיִּפְרֹשׂ כַּפָּיו אֶל־יְהֹוָהאדניאהדונהי וַיַּחְדְּלוּ הַקֹּלוֹת וְהַבָּרָד ראה וּמָטָר רמ"ח ע"ה לֹא־נִתַּךְ אָרְצָה אלהים דההין: וַיַּרְא אלף למד יהוה פַּרְעֹה כִּי־חָדַל הַמָּטָר רמ"ח ע"ה וְהַבָּרָד ראה וְהַקֹּלֹת וַיֹּסֶף לַחֲטֹא וַיַּכְבֵּד לִבּוֹ הוּא וַעֲבָדָיו: וַיֶּחֱזַק לֵב פַּרְעֹה וְלֹא שִׁלַּח אֶת־בְּנֵי יִשְׂרָאֵל כַּאֲשֶׁר דִּבֶּר ראה יְהֹוָהאדניאהדונהי בְּיַד־מֹשֶׁה מהש, אל שדי:

וַיֹּאמֶר יְהֹוָהאדניאהדונהי אֶל־מֹשֶׁה מהש, אל שדי בֹּא אֶל־פַּרְעֹה כִּי־אֲנִי אני, טדה"ד כוו"ו הִכְבַּדְתִּי אֶת־לִבּוֹ וְאֶת־לֵב עֲבָדָיו לְמַעַן שִׁתִי אֹתֹתַי אֵלֶּה בְּקִרְבּוֹ: וּלְמַעַן תְּסַפֵּר בְּאָזְנֵי בִנְךָ וּבֶן־בִּנְךָ אֵת אֲשֶׁר הִתְעַלַּלְתִּי בְּמִצְרַיִם מצר וְאֶת־אֹתֹתַי אֲשֶׁר־שַׂמְתִּי בָם מ"ב וִידַעְתֶּם כִּי־אֲנִי אני, טדה"ד כוו"ו יְהֹוָהאדניאהדונהי: וַיָּבֹא מֹשֶׁה מהש, אל שדי וְאַהֲרֹן ע"ב רבוע ע"ב אֶל־פַּרְעֹה וַיֹּאמְרוּ אֵלָיו כֹּה הי אָמַר יְהֹוָהאדניאהדונהי אֱלֹהֵי דמב, ילה הָעִבְרִים עַד־מָתַי מֵאַנְתָּ לֵעָנֹת מִפָּנָי שַׁלַּח עַמִּי וְיַעַבְדֻנִי:

וְהָיָה יהוה כִּי־יְבִאֲךָ יְהֹוָהאדניאהדונהי אֶל־אֶרֶץ אלהים דאלפין הַכְּנַעֲנִי כַּאֲשֶׁר נִשְׁבַּע לְךָ וְלַאֲבֹתֶיךָ וּנְתָנָהּ לָךְ: וְהַעֲבַרְתָּ כָל־ ילי פֶּטֶר־ רפ"ח ע"ה רֶחֶם רמ"ח, ח"פ אל לַיהֹוָהאדניאהדונהי וְכָל־ ילי פֶּטֶר רפ"ח ע"ה | שֶׁגֶר בְּהֵמָה ב"ן, לכב, יבמ אֲשֶׁר יִהְיֶה יי לְךָ הַזְּכָרִים לַיהֹוָהאדניאהדונהי: וְכָל־ ילי פֶּטֶר רפ"ח ע"ה חֲמֹר תִּפְדֶּה בְשֶׂה וְאִם־ יוהך, ע"ה מ"ב לֹא תִפְדֶּה וַעֲרַפְתּוֹ וְכֹל ילי בְּכוֹר אָדָם מ"ה בְּבָנֶיךָ תִּפְדֶּה: וְהָיָה יהוה כִּי־יִשְׁאָלְךָ בִנְךָ מָחָר רמ"ח לֵאמֹר מַה־ מ"ה זֹּאת וְאָמַרְתָּ אֵלָיו בְּחֹזֶק פהל יָד הוֹצִיאָנוּ יְהֹוָהאדניאהדונהי מִמִּצְרַיִם מצר מִבֵּית ב"פ ראה עֲבָדִים: וַיְהִי אל כִּי־הִקְשָׁה פַרְעֹה לְשַׁלְּחֵנוּ וַיַּהֲרֹג יְהֹוָהאדניאהדונהי כָּל־ ילי בְּכוֹר בְּאֶרֶץ אלהים דאלפין מִצְרַיִם מצר מִבְּכֹר אָדָם מ"ה וְעַד־בְּכוֹר בְּהֵמָה ב"ן, לכב, יבמ עַל־כֵּן אֲנִי אני, טדה"ד כוו"ו זֹבֵחַ לַיהֹוָהאדניאהדונהי כָּל ילי פֶּטֶר־ רפ"ח ע"ה רֶחֶם רמ"ח, ח"פ אל הַזְּכָרִים וְכָל־ ילי בְּכוֹר בָּנַי אֶפְדֶּה: וְהָיָה יהוה לְאוֹת עַל־יָדְכָה וּלְטוֹטָפֹת בֵּין עֵינֶיךָ ע"ה קס"א כִּי בְּחֹזֶק פהל יָד הוֹצִיאָנוּ יְהֹוָהאדניאהדונהי מִמִּצְרָיִם מצר:

וַיְהִי אל, יא"י בְּשַׁלַּח פַּרְעֹה אֶת־הָעָם וְלֹא־נָחָם אֱלֹהִים מום, אהיה אדני ; ילה דֶּרֶךְ ב"פ יב"ק אֶרֶץ אלהים דאלפין פְּלִשְׁתִּים י"פ אלהים כִּי קָרוֹב הוּא כִּי | אָמַר אֱלֹהִים מום, אהיה אדני ; ילה פֶּן־יִנָּחֵם הָעָם בִּרְאֹתָם מִלְחָמָה וְשָׁבוּ מִצְרָיְמָה מצר:

וַיַּסֵּב אֱלֹהִים מום, אהיה אדני ; ילה | אֶת־הָעָם דֶּרֶךְ ב״פ יב״ק הַמִּדְבָּר יַם־ ילי סוּף
וַחֲמֻשִׁים עָלוּ בְנֵי־יִשְׂרָאֵל מֵאֶרֶץ אלהים דאלפין מִצְרָיִם מצר: וַיִּקַּח ועם
מֹשֶׁה מהש, אל שדי אֶת־עַצְמוֹת יוֹסֵף ציון, קנאה, ו״פ יהוה עִמּוֹ כִּי
הַשְׁבֵּעַ ע״ב ואלהים דיודין הִשְׁבִּיעַ אֶת־בְּנֵי יִשְׂרָאֵל לֵאמֹר פָּקֹד רבוע ע״ב
יִפְקֹד רבוע ע״ב אֱלֹהִים מום, אהיה אדני ; ילה אֶתְכֶם וְהַעֲלִיתֶם אֶת־עַצְמֹתַי
מִזֶּה אִתְּכֶם: וַיִּסְעוּ מִסֻּכֹּת וַיַּחֲנוּ בְאֵתָם בִּקְצֵה ה״פ טל, ג״פ אדני הַמִּדְבָּר:
וַיהֹוָאדניאהדונהי הֹלֵךְ מיה לִפְנֵיהֶם יוֹמָם בְּעַמּוּד עָנָן לַנְחֹתָם הַדֶּרֶךְ ב״פ יב״ק
וְלַיְלָה מלה בְּעַמּוּד אֵשׁ אלהים דיודין ע״ה לְהָאִיר לָהֶם לָלֶכֶת יוֹמָם וָלָיְלָה מלה:
לֹא־יָמִישׁ עַמּוּד הֶעָנָן יוֹמָם וְעַמּוּד הָאֵשׁ אלהים דיודין ע״ה לָיְלָה מלה לִפְנֵי הָעָם:

וַיֹּאמֶר יְהֹוָאדניאהדונהי אֶל־מֹשֶׁה מהש, אל שדי כְּתֹב זֹאת זִכָּרוֹן ע״ב קס״א נש״ב
בַּסֵּפֶר וְשִׂים בְּאָזְנֵי יְהוֹשֻׁעַ כִּי־מָחֹה אֶמְחֶה אֶת־זֵכֶר עֲמָלֵק ב״פ ק״ך מִתַּחַת
הַשָּׁמָיִם י״פ טל, י״פ כוזו: וַיִּבֶן וזיים, בינה ע״ה מֹשֶׁה מהש, אל שדי מִזְבֵּחַ זן, נגד
וַיִּקְרָא עם ה׳ אותיות = ב״פ קס״א שְׁמוֹ מהש ע״ה, אל שדי ע״ה יְהֹוָאדניאהדונהי | נִסִּי: וַיֹּאמֶר
כִּי־יָד עַל־כֵּס יָהּ מִלְחָמָה לַיהֹוָאדניאהדונהי בַּעֲמָלֵק ב״פ ק״ך מִדֹּר דֹּר:

וַיִּשְׁמַע יִתְרוֹ קס״א קס״א קנ״א קמ״ג כֹהֵן מלה מִדְיָן חֹתֵן מֹשֶׁה מהש, אל שדי אֵת
כָּל־ ילי אֲשֶׁר עָשָׂה אֱלֹהִים מום, אהיה אדני ; ילה לְמֹשֶׁה מהש, אל שדי וּלְיִשְׂרָאֵל
עַמּוֹ כִּי־הוֹצִיא יְהֹוָאדניאהדונהי אֶת־יִשְׂרָאֵל מִמִּצְרָיִם מצר: וַיִּקַּח ועם
יִתְרוֹ קס״א קס״א קנ״א קמ״ג חֹתֵן מֹשֶׁה מהש, אל שדי אֶת־צִפֹּרָה אֵשֶׁת
מֹשֶׁה מהש, אל שדי אַחַר שִׁלּוּחֶיהָ: וְאֵת שְׁנֵי בָנֶיהָ אֲשֶׁר שֵׁם יהוה שדי
הָאֶחָד אהבה, דאגה גֵּרְשֹׁם רבוע קס״א כִּי אָמַר גֵּר ב״ן קנ״א הָיִיתִי
בְּאֶרֶץ אלהים דאלפין נָכְרִיָּה:

בַּחֹדֶשׁ י״ב הוויות הַשְּׁלִישִׁי לְצֵאת ר״ת הבל בְּנֵי־יִשְׂרָאֵל מֵאֶרֶץ אלהים דאלפין
מִצְרָיִם מצר בַּיּוֹם ע״ה = נגד, זן, מזבח הַזֶּה והו בָּאוּ מִדְבַּר סִינָי נמם, ה״פ יהוה:
וַיִּסְעוּ מֵרְפִידִים וַיָּבֹאוּ מִדְבַּר סִינַי נמם, ה״פ יהוה וַיַּחֲנוּ בַּמִּדְבָּר רמ״ח, וח״פ אל
וַיִּחַן־שָׁם יִשְׂרָאֵל נֶגֶד זן, מזבח הָהָר רבוע אלהים + ה׳: וּמֹשֶׁה מהש, אל שדי
עָלָה אֶל־הָאֱלֹהִים מום, אהיה אדני ; ילה וַיִּקְרָא עם ה׳ אותיות = ב״פ קס״א אֵלָיו
יְהֹוָאדניאהדונהי מִן־הָהָר לֵאמֹר כֹּה היי תֹאמַר לְבֵית ב״פ ראה
יַעֲקֹב ז״פ יהוה, יאהדונהי אידהנויה וְתַגֵּיד לִבְנֵי יִשְׂרָאֵל: אַתֶּם רְאִיתֶם אֲשֶׁר
עָשִׂיתִי לְמִצְרָיִם מצר וָאֶשָּׂא אֶתְכֶם עַל־כַּנְפֵי נְשָׁרִים וָאָבִא אֶתְכֶם אֵלָי:

ועתה אם־ יוהך, ע"ה מ"ב שמוע תשמעו בקלי ושמרתם את־בריתי והייתם
לי סגלה מכל־ ילי העמים ע"ה קס"א כי־לי כל־ ילי הארץ אלהים דההין ע"ה׃
ואתם תהיו־לי ממלכת כהנים מלה וגוי קדוש אלה הדברים ראה אשר
תדבר ראה אל־בני ישראל׃ ויבא משה מהש, אל שדי ויקרא עם ה' אותיות = ב"פ קס"א
לזקני העם וישם לפניהם את כל־ ילי הדברים ראה האלה אשר צוהו
יהוהאדני אהדונהי׃ ויענו כל־ ילי העם יחדו ויאמרו כל ילי אשר־דבר ראה
יהוהאדני אהדונהי נעשה וישב משה מהש, אל שדי את־דברי ראה העם
אל־יהוהאדני אהדונהי׃ ויאמר יהוהאדני אהדונהי אל־משה מהש, אל שדי הנה מ"ה יה
אנכי איע בא אליך אני בעב הענן בעבור ישמע העם בדברי ראה
עמך ה' הויות, נמם וגם־ יג"ל בך יאמינו לעולם ויגד משה מהש, אל שדי
את־דברי ראה העם אל־יהוהאדני אהדונהי׃ ויאמר יהוהאדני אהדונהי
אל־משה מהש, אל שדי לך אל־העם וקדשתם היום ע"ה = נגד, זן, מזבח
ומחר רמ"ח וכבסו שמלתם׃ והיו נכנים ליום ע"ה = נגד, זן, מזבח השלישי כי
ביום ע"ה = נגד, זן, מזבח השלשי ירד יהוהאדני אהדונהי לעיני ריבוע מ"ה כל־ ילי העם
על־הר רבוע אלהים - ה' סיני נמם, ה"פ יהוה׃ והגבלת את־העם סביב לאמר
השמרו לכם עלות בהר אור, רז ונגע מלוי אהיה דאלפין בקצהו כל־ ילי
הנגע מלוי אהיה דאלפין בהר אור, רז מות יומת׃ לא־תגע בו יד כי־סקול יסקל
או־ירה יירה אם־ יוהך, ע"ה מ"ב בהמה ב"ן, לכב, יבמ אם־ יוהך, ע"ה מ"ב
איש ע"ה קנ"א קס"א לא יחיה במשך היבל המה יעלו בהר אור, רז׃ וירד רי"י
משה מהש, אל שדי מן־ההר אל־העם ויקדש את־העם ויכבסו שמלתם׃
ויאמר אל־העם היו נכנים לשלשת ימים נלך אל־תגשו אל־אשה׃
ויהי אל, ייא"י ביום ע"ה = נגד, זן, מזבח השלישי בהית הבקר ויהי אל, ייא"י קלת
וברקים וענן כבד על־ההר וקל נמם, רבוע מ"ה שפר חזק פהל מאד מ"ה
ויחרד כל־ ילי העם אשר במחנה׃ ויוצא משה מהש, אל שדי את־העם
לקראת האלהים מום, אהיה אדני ; ילה מן־המחנה ויתיצבו בתחתית ההר׃
והר רבוע אלהים - ה' סיני נמם, ה"פ יהוה עשן כלו מפני וחכמה בינה אשר ירד עליו
יהוהאדני אהדונהי באש אלהים דיודין ע"ה ויעל עשנו כעשן הכבשן ויחרד כל־ ילי
ההר מאד מ"ה׃ ויהי אל, ייא"י קול ע"ב ס"ג ע"ה השפר הולך וחזק פהל מאד מ"ה
משה מהש, אל שדי ידבר ראה והאלהים מום, אהיה אדני ; ילה יעננו בקול ע"ב ס"ג ע"ה׃

וירד ריי יהוהאדניאהדונהי על־הר רבוע אלהים + ה' סיני נמם, ה"פ יהוה אל־
ראש ריבוע אלהים ואלהים דיודין ע"ה ההר רבוע אלהים + ה' ויקרא עם ה' אותיות = ב"פ קס"א
יהוהאדניאהדונהי למשה מהש, אל שדי אל־ראש ריבוע אלהים ואלהים דיודין ע"ה ההר
ויעל משה מהש, אל שדי: ויאמר יהוהאדניאהדונהי אל־משה מהש, אל שדי רד העד
בעם פן־יהרסו אל־יהוהאדניאהדונהי לראות ונפל ממנו רב ע"ב ורבוע מ"ה: וגם יג"ל
הכהנים מלה הנגשים אל־יהוהאדניאהדונהי יתקדשו פן־יפרץ בהם
יהוהאדניאהדונהי: ויאמר משה מהש, אל שדי אל־יהוהאדניאהדונהי לא־יוכל העם
לעלת אל־הר רבוע אלהים + ה' סיני נמם, ה"פ יהוה כי־ אתה העדתה בנו לאמר
ר"ת הבל הגבל את־ההר וקדשתו: ויאמר אליו יהוהאדניאהדונהי לך־רד ועלית
אתה ואהרן ע"ב ורבוע ע"ב עמך ה' הויות, נמם והכהנים מלה והעם אל־יהרסו
לעלת אל־יהוהאדניאהדונהי פן־יפרץ־בם מ"ב: וירד ריי משה מהש, אל שדי אל־
העם ויאמר אלהם: וידבר ראה אלהים מום, אהיה אדני ; ילה את כל־ ילי
הדברים ראה האלה לאמר: (*Keter*) אנכי איע יהוהאדניאהדונהי אלהיך ילה
אשר הוצאתיך מארץ אלהים דאלפין מצרים מצר מבית ב"פ ראה עבדים
(*Chochmah*) לא־יהיה ייי לך אלהים מום, אהיה אדני ; ילה אחרים
על־פני וחכמה בינה: לא־תעשה לך פסל וכל־ ילי תמונה אשר בשמים
ממעל עלם ואשר בארץ אלהים דאלפין מתחת ואשר במים מתחת לארץ
אלהים דאלפין: לא־ תשתחוה להם ולא תעבדם כי אנכי איע יהוהאדניאהדונהי
אלהיך ילה אל ייא"י קנא קנ"א, מקוה פקד רבוע ע"ב עון ג"פ מ"ב אבת על־בנים
על־שלשים ועל־ רבעים לשנאי: ועשה חסד ע"ב, ריבוע יהוה לאלפים קס"א
לאהבי ולשמרי מצותי: (*Binah*) לא תשא את־שם־ יהוה שדי יהוהאדניאהדונהי
אלהיך ילה לשוא כי לא ינקה יהוהאדניאהדונהי את אשר־ישא את־
שמו מהש ע"ה, אל שדי ע"ה לשוא: (*Chesed*) זכור ע"ב קס"א את־יום ע"ה = נגד, זן, מזבח
השבת לקדשו: ששת ימים זלך תעבד ועשית כל־ ילי מלאכתך:
ויום ע"ה = נגד, זן, מזבח השביעי שבת ליהוהאדניאהדונהי אלהיך ילה לא־תעשה
כל־ ילי מלאכה אל אדני אתה | ובנך ובתך עבדך פוי ואמתך ובהמתך
וגרך אשר בשעריך: כי ששת־ימים זלך עשה יהוהאדניאהדונהי
את־השמים י"פ טל, י"פ כוזו ואת־הארץ אלהים דההין ע"ה את־הים ילי
ואת־כל־ ילי אשר־בם מ"ב וינח ביום ע"ה = נגד, זן, מזבח השביעי
על־כן ברך יהוהאדניאהדונהי את־יום ע"ה = נגד, זן, מזבח השבת ויקדשהו:

(*Gevurah*) כַּבֵּד אֶת־אָבִיךָ וְאֶת־אִמֶּךָ לְמַעַן יַאֲרִכוּן יָמֶיךָ עַל הָאֲדָמָה
אֲשֶׁר־יְהֹוָהאדניאהדונהי אֱלֹהֶיךָ ילה נֹתֵן אבגיתצ, ושר, אהבת חנם לָךְ׃
(*Tiferet*) לֹא תִּרְצָח (*Netzach*) לֹא תִּנְאָף (*Hod*) לֹא תִּגְנֹב
(*Yesod*) לֹא־תַעֲנֶה בְרֵעֲךָ עֵד שָׁקֶר׃ (*Malchut*) לֹא תַחְמֹד בֵּית ב״פ ראה
רֵעֶךָ לֹא־תַחְמֹד אֵשֶׁת רֵעֶךָ וְעַבְדּוֹ וַאֲמָתוֹ וְשׁוֹרוֹ וַחֲמֹרוֹ וְכֹל ילי אֲשֶׁר
לְרֵעֶךָ׃ וְכָל־ ילי הָעָם רֹאִים אֶת־הַקּוֹלֹת וְאֶת־הַלַּפִּידִם וְאֵת קוֹל ע״ב ס״ג ע״ה
הַשֹּׁפָר וְאֶת־הָהָר עָשֵׁן וַיַּרְא אלף למד יהוה הָעָם וַיָּנֻעוּ וַיַּעַמְדוּ מֵרָחֹק שדי׃
וַיֹּאמְרוּ אֶל־מֹשֶׁה מהש, אל שדי דַּבֵּר־ ראה אַתָּה עִמָּנוּ וְנִשְׁמָעָה וְאַל־יְדַבֵּר
ראה עִמָּנוּ אֱלֹהִים מום, אהיה אדני ; ילה פֶּן־נָמוּת׃ וַיֹּאמֶר מֹשֶׁה מהש, אל שדי אֶל־
הָעָם אַל־תִּירָאוּ כִּי לְבַעֲבוּר נַסּוֹת אֶתְכֶם בָּא הָאֱלֹהִים מום, אהיה אדני ; ילה
וּבַעֲבוּר תִּהְיֶה יִרְאָתוֹ עַל־פְּנֵיכֶם לְבִלְתִּי תֶחֱטָאוּ׃ וַיַּעֲמֹד הָעָם מֵרָחֹק שדי
וּמֹשֶׁה מהש, אל שדי נִגַּשׁ אֶל־הָעֲרָפֶל אֲשֶׁר־שָׁם הָאֱלֹהִים מום, אהיה אדני ; ילה׃
וַיֹּאמֶר יְהֹוָהאדניאהדונהי אֶל־מֹשֶׁה מהש, אל שדי כֹּה היי תֹאמַר אֶל־בְּנֵי יִשְׂרָאֵל
אַתֶּם רְאִיתֶם כִּי מִן־הַשָּׁמַיִם י״פ טל, י״פ כוזו דִּבַּרְתִּי ראה עִמָּכֶם׃ לֹא תַעֲשׂוּן
אִתִּי אֱלֹהֵי דמב, ילה כֶסֶף וֵאלֹהֵי דמב, ילה זָהָב לֹא תַעֲשׂוּ לָכֶם׃ מִזְבַּח זן, נגד
אֲדָמָה תַּעֲשֶׂה־לִּי וְזָבַחְתָּ עָלָיו אֶת־עֹלֹתֶיךָ וְאֶת־שְׁלָמֶיךָ אֶת־צֹאנְךָ
וְאֶת־בְּקָרֶךָ בְּכָל־ ב״ן, לכב, יבמ הַמָּקוֹם יהוה ברבוע, ו״פ אל אֲשֶׁר אַזְכִּיר אֶת־
שְׁמִי רבוע ע״ב ורבוע ס״ג אָבוֹא אֵלֶיךָ אני וּבֵרַכְתִּיךָ׃ וְאִם־ יוהך, ע״ה מ״ב מִזְבַּח זן, נגד
אֲבָנִים תַּעֲשֶׂה־לִּי לֹא־תִבְנֶה אֶתְהֶן גָּזִית כִּי חַרְבְּךָ הֵנַפְתָּ עָלֶיהָ פהל
וַתְּחַלְלֶהָ׃ וְלֹא־תַעֲלֶה בְמַעֲלֹת עַל־מִזְבְּחִי אֲשֶׁר לֹא־תִגָּלֶה עֶרְוָתְךָ עָלָיו׃

וְאֵלֶּה מ״ב הַמִּשְׁפָּטִים אֲשֶׁר תָּשִׂים לִפְנֵיהֶם׃ כִּי תִקְנֶה ג״פ אלף למד
עֶבֶד עִבְרִי שֵׁשׁ שָׁנִים יַעֲבֹד וּבַשְּׁבִעִת יֵצֵא לַחָפְשִׁי חִנָּם׃ אִם־ יוהך, ע״ה מ״ב
בְּגַפּוֹ יָבֹא בְּגַפּוֹ ר״ת אביב יֵצֵא אִם־ יוהך, ע״ה מ״ב בַּעַל אִשָּׁה הוּא
וְיָצְאָה אִשְׁתּוֹ עִמּוֹ׃ אִם־ יוהך, ע״ה מ״ב אֲדֹנָיו יִתֶּן־לוֹ אִשָּׁה וְיָלְדָה־לוֹ בָנִים
אוֹ בָנוֹת הָאִשָּׁה וִילָדֶיהָ תִּהְיֶה לַאדֹנֶיהָ וְהוּא יֵצֵא בְגַפּוֹ׃ וְאִם־ יוהך, ע״ה מ״ב
אָמֹר יֹאמַר הָעֶבֶד אָהַבְתִּי אֶת־אֲדֹנִי אֶת־אִשְׁתִּי וְאֶת־בָּנָי
לֹא אֵצֵא חָפְשִׁי׃ וְהִגִּישׁוֹ אֲדֹנָיו אֶל־הָאֱלֹהִים מום, אהיה אדני ; ילה וְהִגִּישׁוֹ
אֶל־הַדֶּלֶת אוֹ אֶל־הַמְּזוּזָה אדני, ללה וְרָצַע אֲדֹנָיו אֶת־אָזְנוֹ בַּמַּרְצֵעַ
וַעֲבָדוֹ לְעֹלָם ריבוע ס״ג ו״ אותיות׃

וְאֶל־מֹשֶׁה מהש, אל שדי אָמַר עֲלֵה אֶל־יְהֹוָה יאהדונהי אַתָּה וְאַהֲרֹן ע״ב ורבוע ע״ב
נָדָב ע״ה אהיה בוכ״ו וַאֲבִיהוּא וְשִׁבְעִים מִזִּקְנֵי יִשְׂרָאֵל וְהִשְׁתַּחֲוִיתֶם מֵרָחֹק שדי:
וְנִגַּשׁ מֹשֶׁה מהש, אל שדי לְבַדּוֹ מ״ב אֶל־יְהֹוָה יאהדונהי וְהֵם לֹא יִגָּשׁוּ וְהָעָם לֹא
יַעֲלוּ עִמּוֹ: וַיָּבֹא מֹשֶׁה מהש, אל שדי וַיְסַפֵּר לָעָם אֵת כָּל־ ילי דִּבְרֵי ראה
יְהֹוָה יאהדונהי וְאֵת כָּל־ ילי הַמִּשְׁפָּטִים וַיַּעַן כָּל־ ילי הָעָם קוֹל ע״ב ס״ג ע״ה
אֶחָד אהבה, דאגה וַיֹּאמְרוּ כָּל־ ילי הַדְּבָרִים ראה אֲשֶׁר־דִּבֶּר ראה יְהֹוָה יאהדונהי
נַעֲשֶׂה: וַיִּכְתֹּב מֹשֶׁה מהש, אל שדי אֵת כָּל־ ילי דִּבְרֵי ראה יְהֹוָה יאהדונהי
וַיַּשְׁכֵּם בַּבֹּקֶר וַיִּבֶן חיים, בינה ע״ה מִזְבֵּחַ זן, נגד תַּחַת הָהָר וּשְׁתֵּים עֶשְׂרֵה
מַצֵּבָה לִשְׁנֵים עָשָׂר שִׁבְטֵי יִשְׂרָאֵל: וַיִּשְׁלַח אֶת־נַעֲרֵי בְּנֵי יִשְׂרָאֵל
וַיַּעֲלוּ עֹלֹת וַיִּזְבְּחוּ זְבָחִים שְׁלָמִים לַיהֹוָה יאהדונהי פָּרִים: וַיִּקַּח חעם
מֹשֶׁה מהש, אל שדי חֲצִי הַדָּם רבוע אהיה וַיָּשֶׂם בָּאַגָּנֹת וַחֲצִי הַדָּם רבוע אהיה זָרַק
עַל־הַמִּזְבֵּחַ זן, נגד: וַיִּקַּח חעם סֵפֶר הַבְּרִית וַיִּקְרָא עם ה׳ אותיות = ב״פ קס״א בְּאָזְנֵי
הָעָם וַיֹּאמְרוּ כֹּל ילי אֲשֶׁר־דִּבֶּר ראה יְהֹוָה יאהדונהי נַעֲשֶׂה וְנִשְׁמָע: וַיִּקַּח חעם
מֹשֶׁה מהש, אל שדי אֶת־הַדָּם רבוע אהיה וַיִּזְרֹק עַל־הָעָם וַיֹּאמֶר הִנֵּה מ״ה יה
דַם־ רבוע אהיה הַבְּרִית אֲשֶׁר כָּרַת יְהֹוָה יאהדונהי עִמָּכֶם עַל כָּל־ ילי, עמם
הַדְּבָרִים ראה הָאֵלֶּה: וַיַּעַל מֹשֶׁה מהש, אל שדי וְאַהֲרֹן ע״ב ורבוע ע״ב
נָדָב ע״ה אהיה בוכ״ו וַאֲבִיהוּא וְשִׁבְעִים מִזִּקְנֵי יִשְׂרָאֵל: וַיִּרְאוּ אֵת אֱלֹהֵי דמב, ילה
יִשְׂרָאֵל וְתַחַת רַגְלָיו כְּמַעֲשֵׂה לִבְנַת הַסַּפִּיר וּכְעֶצֶם הַשָּׁמַיִם י״פ טל, י״פ כוזו
לָטֹהַר: וְאֶל־אֲצִילֵי בְּנֵי יִשְׂרָאֵל לֹא שָׁלַח יָדוֹ וַיֶּחֱזוּ אֶת־
הָאֱלֹהִים מום, אהיה אדני ; ילה וַיֹּאכְלוּ וַיִּשְׁתּוּ: וַיֹּאמֶר יְהֹוָה יאהדונהי אֶל־
מֹשֶׁה מהש, אל שדי עֲלֵה אֵלַי הָהָרָה וֶהְיֵה־ יהוה שָׁם וְאֶתְּנָה לְךָ אֶת־לֻחֹת
הָאֶבֶן יוד הה ואו הה וְהַתּוֹרָה וְהַמִּצְוָה אֲשֶׁר כָּתַבְתִּי לְהוֹרֹתָם: וַיָּקָם
מֹשֶׁה מהש, אל שדי וִיהוֹשֻׁעַ מְשָׁרְתוֹ וַיַּעַל מֹשֶׁה מהש, אל שדי
אֶל־הַר רבוע אלהים + ה׳ הָאֱלֹהִים מום, אהיה אדני ; ילה: וְאֶל־הַזְּקֵנִים אָמַר
שְׁבוּ־לָנוּ מום, אלהים, אהיה אדני בָזֶה עַד אֲשֶׁר־נָשׁוּב אֲלֵיכֶם וְהִנֵּה
אַהֲרֹן ע״ב ורבוע ע״ב וְחוּר עִמָּכֶם מִי־ ילי בַעַל דְּבָרִים ראה יִגַּשׁ אֲלֵהֶם:
וַיַּעַל מֹשֶׁה מהש, אל שדי אֶל־הָהָר וַיְכַס הֶעָנָן אֶת־הָהָר: וַיִּשְׁכֹּן
כְּבוֹד־ ל״ב יְהֹוָה יאהדונהי עַל־הַר רבוע אלהים + ה׳ סִינַי נמם, ה״פ יהוה
וַיְכַסֵּהוּ הֶעָנָן שֵׁשֶׁת יָמִים נלך וַיִּקְרָא עם ה׳ אותיות = ב״פ קס״א
אֶל־מֹשֶׁה מהש, אל שדי בַּיּוֹם ע״ה = נגד, זן, מזבח הַשְּׁבִיעִי מִתּוֹךְ הֶעָנָן:

וּמַרְאֵה כְּבוֹד ל״ב יְהֹוָאדניאהדונהי כְּאֵשׁ אלהים דיודין ע״ה אֹכֶלֶת בְּרֹאשׁ ריבוע אלהים ואלהים דיודין ע״ה הָהָר לְעֵינֵי ריבוע מ״ה בְּנֵי יִשְׂרָאֵל: וַיָּבֹא מֹשֶׁה מהש, אל שדי בְּתוֹךְ הֶעָנָן וַיַּעַל אֶל־הָהָר וַיְהִי אל, יא״י מֹשֶׁה מהש, אל שדי בָּהָר אור, רז אַרְבָּעִים יוֹם ע״ה = נגד, זן, מזבח וְאַרְבָּעִים לָיְלָה מלה:

וַיְדַבֵּר ראה יְהֹוָאדניאהדונהי אֶל־מֹשֶׁה מהש, אל שדי לֵּאמֹר: דַּבֵּר ראה אֶל־בְּנֵי יִשְׂרָאֵל וְיִקְחוּ־ וזעם לִי תְּרוּמָה מֵאֵת כָּל־ ילי אִישׁ ע״ה קנ״א קס״א אֲשֶׁר יִדְּבֶנּוּ לִבּוֹ תִּקְחוּ אֶת־תְּרוּמָתִי: וְזֹאת הַתְּרוּמָה אֲשֶׁר תִּקְחוּ מֵאִתָּם זָהָב וָכֶסֶף וּנְחֹשֶׁת:

כָּל־ ילי עַמּוּדֵי הֶחָצֵר סָבִיב מְחֻשָּׁקִים כֶּסֶף וָוֵיהֶם כָּסֶף וְאַדְנֵיהֶם נְחֹשֶׁת: אֹרֶךְ הֶחָצֵר מֵאָה דמב, מלוי ע״ב בָאַמָּה דמב, מלוי ע״ב וְרֹחַב | חֲמִשִּׁים בַּחֲמִשִּׁים וְקֹמָה חָמֵשׁ אַמּוֹת שֵׁשׁ מָשְׁזָר וְאַדְנֵיהֶם נְחֹשֶׁת: לְכֹל יה אדני כְּלֵי כלי הַמִּשְׁכָּן ב״פ רבוע אלהים + ה׳ בְּכֹל לכב, יבמ, ב״ן עֲבֹדָתוֹ וְכָל־ ילי יְתֵדֹתָיו וְכָל־ ילי יִתְדֹת הֶחָצֵר נְחֹשֶׁת:

וְאַתָּה תְּצַוֶּה | אֶת־בְּנֵי יִשְׂרָאֵל וְיִקְחוּ וזעם אֵלֶיךָ שֶׁמֶן י״פ טל, י״פ כוז״ו, ביט זַיִת אלהים אל מצפ״צ זָךְ כָּתִית לַמָּאוֹר לְהַעֲלֹת נֵר יהוה אהיה יהוה אלהים יהוה אדני תָּמִיד קס״א קנ״א קמ״ג: בְּאֹהֶל לאה מוֹעֵד מִחוּץ לַפָּרֹכֶת אֲשֶׁר עַל־הָעֵדֻת יַעֲרֹךְ אֹתוֹ אַהֲרֹן ע״ב ורבוע ע״ב וּבָנָיו מֵעֶרֶב רבוע יהוה ורבוע אלהים עַד־בֹּקֶר לִפְנֵי וזכמה בינה יְהֹוָאדניאהדונהי חֻקַּת עוֹלָם לְדֹרֹתָם מֵאֵת בְּנֵי יִשְׂרָאֵל: וְאַתָּה הַקְרֵב אֵלֶיךָ אני אֶת־אַהֲרֹן ע״ב ורבוע ע״ב אָחִיךָ וְאֶת־בָּנָיו אִתּוֹ מִתּוֹךְ בְּנֵי יִשְׂרָאֵל לְכַהֲנוֹ־לִי אַהֲרֹן ע״ב ורבוע ע״ב נָדָב ע״ה אהיה בוכ״ו וַאֲבִיהוּא אֶלְעָזָר וְאִיתָמָר בְּנֵי אַהֲרֹן ע״ב ורבוע ע״ב:

וּבְהַעֲלֹת אַהֲרֹן ע״ב ורבוע ע״ב אֶת־הַנֵּרֹת בֵּין הָעַרְבַּיִם ר״ת אהבה יַקְטִירֶנָּה קְטֹרֶת י״א אדני תָּמִיד ע״ה קס״א קנ״א קמ״ג לִפְנֵי וזכמה בינה יְהֹוָאדניאהדונהי לְדֹרֹתֵיכֶם: לֹא־תַעֲלוּ עָלָיו קְטֹרֶת י״א אדני זָרָה וְעֹלָה וּמִנְחָה וְנֵסֶךְ לֹא תִסְּכוּ עָלָיו: וְכִפֶּר מצפ״ץ אַהֲרֹן ע״ב ורבוע ע״ב עַל־קַרְנֹתָיו אַחַת בַּשָּׁנָה מִדַּם רבוע אהיה חַטַּאת הַכִּפֻּרִים אַחַת בַּשָּׁנָה יְכַפֵּר עָלָיו לְדֹרֹתֵיכֶם קֹדֶשׁ־קָדָשִׁים הוּא לַיהֹוָאדניאהדונהי:

וַיְדַבֵּר ראה יְהֹוָה יאהדונהי אֶל־מֹשֶׁה מהש, אל שדי לֵּאמֹר: כִּי תִשָּׂא אֶת־רֹאשׁ ריבוע אלהים ואלהים דיודין ע"ה בְּנֵי־יִשְׂרָאֵל לִפְקֻדֵיהֶם וְנָתְנוּ אִישׁ ע"ה קנ"א קס"א כֹּפֶר מצפ"ץ נַפְשׁוֹ לַיהֹוָה יאהדונהי בִּפְקֹד רבוע ע"ב אֹתָם וְלֹא־יִהְיֶה ייי בָהֶם נֶגֶף בִּפְקֹד רבוע ע"ב אֹתָם: זֶה | יִתְּנוּ כָּל־ ילי הָעֹבֵר רבוע יהוה ורבוע אלהים עַל־הַפְּקֻדִים מַחֲצִית הַשֶּׁקֶל בְּשֶׁקֶל הַקֹּדֶשׁ עֶשְׂרִים גֵּרָה ד"פ ב"ן הַשֶּׁקֶל מַחֲצִית הַשֶּׁקֶל תְּרוּמָה לַיהֹוָה יאהדונהי: כֹּל ילי הָעֹבֵר רבוע יהוה ורבוע אלהים עַל־הַפְּקֻדִים מִבֶּן עֶשְׂרִים שָׁנָה וָמָעְלָה יִתֵּן תְּרוּמַת יְהֹוָה יאהדונהי: הֶעָשִׁיר לֹא־יַרְבֶּה וְהַדַּל לֹא יַמְעִיט מִמַּחֲצִית הַשָּׁקֶל לָתֵת אֶת־תְּרוּמַת יְהֹוָה יאהדונהי לְכַפֵּר מצפ"ץ עַל־נַפְשֹׁתֵיכֶם: וְלָקַחְתָּ אֶת־כֶּסֶף הַכִּפֻּרִים מֵאֵת בְּנֵי יִשְׂרָאֵל וְנָתַתָּ אֹתוֹ עַל־עֲבֹדַת אֹהֶל לאה מוֹעֵד וְהָיָה יהוה, יהה לִבְנֵי יִשְׂרָאֵל לְזִכָּרוֹן ע"ב קס"א נש"ב לִפְנֵי יְהֹוָה יאהדונהי לְכַפֵּר מצפ"ץ עַל־נַפְשֹׁתֵיכֶם:

וַיֹּאמֶר יְהֹוָה יאהדונהי אֶל־מֹשֶׁה מהש, אל שדי כְּתָב־לְךָ אֶת־הַדְּבָרִים ראה הָאֵלֶּה כִּי עַל־פִּי | הַדְּבָרִים ראה הָאֵלֶּה כָּרַתִּי אִתְּךָ בְּרִית וְאֶת־יִשְׂרָאֵל: וַיְהִי־ אל, ייא" שָׁם עִם־יְהֹוָה יאהדונהי אַרְבָּעִים יוֹם ע"ה = נגד, זן, מזבח וְאַרְבָּעִים לַיְלָה מלה לֶחֶם ג"פ יהוה לֹא אָכַל וּמַיִם לֹא שָׁתָה וַיִּכְתֹּב עַל־הַלֻּחֹת אֵת דִּבְרֵי ראה הַבְּרִית עֲשֶׂרֶת הַדְּבָרִים ראה: וַיְהִי אל, ייא" בְּרֶדֶת מֹשֶׁה מהש, אל שדי מֵהַר סִינַי נמם, ה"פ יהוה וּשְׁנֵי לֻחֹת הָעֵדֻת בְּיַד־מֹשֶׁה מהש, אל שדי בְּרִדְתּוֹ מִן־הָהָר וּמֹשֶׁה מהש, אל שדי לֹא־יָדַע ב"פ מ"ב כִּי קָרַן עוֹר פָּנָיו בְּדַבְּרוֹ ראה אִתּוֹ: וַיַּרְא אלף למד יהוה אַהֲרֹן ע"ב ורבוע ע"ב וְכָל־ ילי בְּנֵי יִשְׂרָאֵל אֶת־מֹשֶׁה מהש, אל שדי וְהִנֵּה מ"ה יה קָרַן עוֹר פָּנָיו וַיִּירְאוּ מִגֶּשֶׁת אֵלָיו: וַיִּקְרָא עם ה' אותיות = ב"פ קס"א אֲלֵהֶם מֹשֶׁה מהש, אל שדי וַיָּשֻׁבוּ אֵלָיו אַהֲרֹן ע"ב ורבוע ע"ב וְכָל־ ילי הַנְּשִׂאִים בָּעֵדָה וַיְדַבֵּר ראה מֹשֶׁה מהש, אל שדי אֲלֵהֶם: וְאַחֲרֵי־כֵן נִגְּשׁוּ כָּל־ ילי בְּנֵי יִשְׂרָאֵל וַיְצַוֵּם אֵת כָּל־ ילי אֲשֶׁר דִּבֶּר ראה יְהֹוָה יאהדונהי אִתּוֹ בְּהַר אור, רז סִינָי נמם, ה"פ יהוה: וַיְכַל מֹשֶׁה מהש, אל שדי מִדַּבֵּר ראה אִתָּם וַיִּתֵּן י"פ מלוי ע"ב עַל־פָּנָיו מַסְוֶה מ"ה אדני ע"ה; אלף: וּבְבֹא מֹשֶׁה מהש, אל שדי לִפְנֵי חכמה בינה יְהֹוָה יאהדונהי לְדַבֵּר ראה אִתּוֹ יָסִיר אֶת־הַמַּסְוֶה מ"ה אדני ע"ה; אלף עַד־צֵאתוֹ וְיָצָא וְדִבֶּר ראה אֶל־בְּנֵי יִשְׂרָאֵל אֵת אֲשֶׁר יְצֻוֶּה: וְרָאוּ בְנֵי־יִשְׂרָאֵל אֶת־פְּנֵי חכמה בינה מֹשֶׁה מהש, אל שדי כִּי קָרַן עוֹר פְּנֵי חכמה בינה מֹשֶׁה מהש, אל שדי וְהֵשִׁיב מֹשֶׁה מהש, אל שדי אֶת־הַמַּסְוֶה מ"ה אדני ע"ה; אלף עַל־פָּנָיו עַד־בֹּאוֹ לְדַבֵּר ראה אִתּוֹ:

ויקהל קנ"א, מקוה משה מהש, אל שדי את־כל־ ילי עדת בני ישראל ויאמר
אלהם אלה הדברים ראה אשר־צוה פוי יהוהאדניאהדונהי לעשת אתם: ששת
ימים נלך תעשה מלאכה אל אדני וביום ע"ה = נגד, זן, מזבח השביעי יהיה ייי
לכם קדש שבת שבתון ליהוהאדניאהדונהי כל־ ילי העשה בו מלאכה אל אדני
יומת: לא־תבערו אש אלהים דיודין ע"ה בכל ב"ן, לכב, יבמ משבתיכם
ביום ע"ה = נגד, זן, מזבח השבת:

ומסך שער י"פ ז"ך החצר מעשה רקם תכלת וארגמן קנ"א קמ"ג
ותולעת שקוצי"ת שני ושש משזר ועשרים אמה דמב, מלוי ע"ב ארך וקומה
ברחב חמש אמות לעמת קלעי החצר: ועמדיהם ארבעה ואדניהם
ארבעה נחשת וויהם כסף וצפוי ראשיהם וחשקיהם כסף: וכל־ ילי
היתדת למשכן ב"פ רבוע אלהים - ה' ולחצר סביב נחשת:

אלה פקודי המשכן ב"פ רבוע אלהים - ה' משכן ב"פ (רבוע אלהים - ה') העדת
אשר פקד רבוע ע"ב על־פי משה מהש, אל שדי עבדת הלוים ביד איתמר בן־
אהרן ע"ב ורבוע ע"ב הכהן מלה: ובצלאל בן־אורי בן־חור למטה יהודה עשה
את כל־ ילי אשר־צוה פוי יהוהאדניאהדונהי את־משה מהש, אל שדי:
ואתו אהליאב בן־אחיסמך למטה־דן חרש וחשב ורקם בתכלת
ובארגמן קנ"א קמ"ג ובתולעת שקוצי"ת השני ובשש:

ויכס הענן את־אהל לאה מועד וכבוד ל"ב יהוהאדניאהדונהי מלא
את־המשכן ב"פ רבוע אלהים - ה': ולא־יכל משה מהש, אל שדי לבוא אל־אהל
לאה מועד כי־שכן ש"ע עליו הענן וכבוד ל"ב יהוהאדניאהדונהי מלא
את־המשכן ב"פ רבוע אלהים - ה': ובהעלות הענן מעל עלם
המשכן ב"פ רבוע אלהים - ה' יסעו בני ישראל בכל ב"ן, לכב, יבמ מסעיהם:
ואם־ יוהך לא יעלה הענן ולא יסעו עד־ יום ע"ה = נגד, זן, מזבח העלתו:

כי ענן (ענ–UNA)

יהוהאדניאהדונהי על־המשכן ב"פ רבוע אלהים - ה' יומם ואש אלהים דיודין ע"ה
תהיה לילה מלה בו לעיני ריבוע מ"ה כל־ ילי בית־ ב"פ ראה ישראל
בכל־ ב"ן, לכב, יבמ מסעיהם:

VAYIKRA - LEVITICUS

וַיִּקְרָא עם ה' אותיות = ב"פ קס"א אֶל־מֹשֶׁה מהש, אל שדי וַיְדַבֵּר ראה יְהֹוָהאדנ"יאהדונהי
אֵלָיו מֵאֹהֶל לאה מוֹעֵד לֵאמֹר: דַּבֵּר ראה אֶל־בְּנֵי יִשְׂרָאֵל וְאָמַרְתָּ אֲלֵהֶם
אָדָם מ"ה כִּי־יַקְרִיב מִכֶּם קָרְבָּן לַיהֹוָהאדנ"יאהדונהי מִן־הַבְּהֵמָה ב"ן, לכב, יבמ מִן־
הַבָּקָר וּמִן־הַצֹּאן מלוי אהיה דיודין ע"ה תַּקְרִיבוּ אֶת־קָרְבַּנְכֶם: אִם־ יוהך, ע"ה מ"ב
עֹלָה קָרְבָּנוֹ מִן־הַבָּקָר זָכָר תָּמִים יַקְרִיבֶנּוּ אֶל־פֶּתַח אֹהֶל לאה מוֹעֵד
יַקְרִיב אֹתוֹ לִרְצֹנוֹ לִפְנֵי וחכמה בינה יְהֹוָהאדנ"יאהדונהי:

אוֹ מִכֹּל ילי אֲשֶׁר־יִשָּׁבַע עָלָיו לַשֶּׁקֶר וְשִׁלַּם ב"פ רבוע ע"ב אֹתוֹ בְּרֹאשׁוֹ
וַחֲמִשִׁתָיו יֹסֵף עָלָיו לַאֲשֶׁר הוּא לוֹ יִתְּנֶנּוּ בְּיוֹם ע"ה = נגד, זן, מזבח אַשְׁמָתוֹ:
וְאֶת־אֲשָׁמוֹ יָבִיא לַיהֹוָהאדנ"יאהדונהי אַיִל תָּמִים מִן־הַצֹּאן מלוי אהיה דיודין ע"ה
בְּעֶרְכְּךָ לְאָשָׁם אֶל־הַכֹּהֵן מלה: וְכִפֶּר מצפצ עָלָיו הַכֹּהֵן מלה לִפְנֵי וחכמה בינה
יְהֹוָהאדנ"יאהדונהי וְנִסְלַח לוֹ עַל־אַחַת מִכֹּל ילי אֲשֶׁר־יַעֲשֶׂה לְאַשְׁמָה בָהּ:

וַיְדַבֵּר ראה יְהֹוָהאדנ"יאהדונהי אֶל־מֹשֶׁה מהש, אל שדי לֵּאמֹר: צַו פוי
אֶת־אַהֲרֹן ע"ב ורבוע ע"ב וְאֶת־בָּנָיו לֵאמֹר זֹאת תּוֹרַת הָעֹלָה הִוא הָעֹלָה עַל
מוֹקְדָה עַל־הַמִּזְבֵּחַ זן, נגד כָּל־ ילי הַלַּיְלָה מלה עַד־הַבֹּקֶר וְאֵשׁ אלהים דיודין ע"ה
הַמִּזְבֵּחַ זן, נגד תּוּקַד בּוֹ: וְלָבַשׁ הַכֹּהֵן מלה מִדּוֹ בַד וּמִכְנְסֵי־בַד יִלְבַּשׁ
עַל־בְּשָׂרוֹ וְהֵרִים אֶת־הַדֶּשֶׁן אֲשֶׁר תֹּאכַל הָאֵשׁ שאה אֶת־הָעֹלָה עַל־
הַמִּזְבֵּחַ זן, נגד וְשָׂמוֹ אֵצֶל הַמִּזְבֵּחַ זן, נגד: וּפָשַׁט אֶת־בְּגָדָיו וְלָבַשׁ בְּגָדִים
אֲחֵרִים וְהוֹצִיא אֶת־הַדֶּשֶׁן אֶל־מִחוּץ לַמַּחֲנֶה אֶל־מָקוֹם יהוה ברבוע, ו"פ אל
טָהוֹר י"פ אכא: וְהָאֵשׁ שאה עַל־הַמִּזְבֵּחַ זן, נגד תּוּקַד־בּוֹ לֹא תִכְבֶּה וּבִעֵר
עָלֶיהָ פהל הַכֹּהֵן מלה עֵצִים בַּבֹּקֶר בַּבֹּקֶר וְעָרַךְ עָלֶיהָ פהל הָעֹלָה וְהִקְטִיר
עָלֶיהָ פהל חֶלְבֵי הַשְּׁלָמִים: אֵשׁ אלהים דיודין ע"ה תָּמִיד ע"ה נתה, קס"א קנ"א קמ"ג תּוּקַד
עַל־הַמִּזְבֵּחַ זן, נגד לֹא תִכְבֶּה:

כַּאֲשֶׁר עָשָׂה בַּיּוֹם ע"ה = נגד, זן, מזבח הַזֶּה והו צִוָּה פוי יְהֹוָהאדנ"יאהדונהי לַעֲשֹׂת
לְכַפֵּר מצפצ עֲלֵיכֶם: וּפֶתַח אֹהֶל לאה מוֹעֵד תֵּשְׁבוּ יוֹמָם וָלַיְלָה מלה שִׁבְעַת
יָמִים נלך וּשְׁמַרְתֶּם אֶת־מִשְׁמֶרֶת יְהֹוָהאדנ"יאהדונהי וְלֹא תָמוּתוּ כִּי־כֵן צֻוֵּיתִי:
וַיַּעַשׂ אַהֲרֹן ע"ב ורבוע ע"ב וּבָנָיו אֵת כָּל־ ילי הַדְּבָרִים ראה אֲשֶׁר־צִוָּה פוי
יְהֹוָהאדנ"יאהדונהי בְּיַד־מֹשֶׁה מהש, אל שדי:

וַיְהִי אל בַּיּוֹם ע"ה = נגד, זן, מזבח הַשְּׁמִינִי קָרָא מֹשֶׁה מהש, אל שדי לְאַהֲרֹן ע"ב ורבוע ע"ב וּלְבָנָיו וּלְזִקְנֵי יִשְׂרָאֵל: וַיֹּאמֶר אֶל־אַהֲרֹן ע"ב ורבוע ע"ב קַח־לְךָ עֵגֶל בֶּן־בָּקָר לְחַטָּאת וְאַיִל לְעֹלָה תְּמִימִם וְהַקְרֵב לִפְנֵי חכמה בינה יְהֹוָהאדניאהדונהי: וְאֶל־בְּנֵי יִשְׂרָאֵל תְּדַבֵּר ראה לֵאמֹר קְחוּ שְׂעִיר־עִזִּים לְחַטָּאת וְעֵגֶל וָכֶבֶשׂ ב"פ קס"א בְּנֵי־שָׁנָה תְּמִימִם לְעֹלָה:

כִּי | אֲנִי אני, טדה"ד כוז"ו יְהֹוָהאדניאהדונהי הַמַּעֲלֶה אֶתְכֶם מֵאֶרֶץ אלהים דאלפין מִצְרַיִם מצר לִהְיֹת לָכֶם לֵאלֹהִים מום, אהיה אדני ; ילה וִהְיִיתֶם קְדֹשִׁים כִּי קָדוֹשׁ אָנִי אני, טדה"ד כוז"ו: זֹאת תּוֹרַת הַבְּהֵמָה ב"ן, לכב, יבמ וְהָעוֹף ג"פ ב"ן, יוסף, ציון וְכֹל ילי נֶפֶשׁ רמ"ח ז' הויות הַחַיָּה הָרֹמֶשֶׂת בַּמָּיִם וּלְכָל־ יה אדני נֶפֶשׁ רמ"ח ז' הויות הַשֹּׁרֶצֶת עַל־הָאָרֶץ אלהים דההין ע"ה: לְהַבְדִּיל בֵּין הַטָּמֵא וּבֵין הַטָּהֹר י"פ אכא וּבֵין הַחַיָּה הַנֶּאֱכֶלֶת וּבֵין הַחַיָּה אֲשֶׁר לֹא תֵאָכֵל:

וַיְדַבֵּר ראה יְהֹוָהאדניאהדונהי אֶל־מֹשֶׁה מהש, אל שדי לֵּאמֹר: דַּבֵּר ראה אֶל־בְּנֵי יִשְׂרָאֵל לֵאמֹר אִשָּׁה כִּי תַזְרִיעַ וְיָלְדָה זָכָר וְטָמְאָה שִׁבְעַת יָמִים נלך כִּימֵי נִדַּת דְּוֹתָהּ תִּטְמָא: וּבַיּוֹם הַשְּׁמִינִי יִמּוֹל בְּשַׂר עָרְלָתוֹ:

וְאִם־ יוהך, ע"ה מ"ב תֵּרָאֶה עוֹד בַּבֶּגֶד אוֹ־בַשְּׁתִי אוֹ־בָעֵרֶב רבוע יהוה ורבוע אלהים אוֹ בְכָל־ ב"ן, לכב, יבמ כְּלִי־ כלי עוֹר פֹּרַחַת הִוא בָּאֵשׁ אלהים דיודין ע"ה תִּשְׂרְפֶנּוּ אֵת אֲשֶׁר־בּוֹ הַנָּגַע מלוי אהיה דאלפין: וְהַבֶּגֶד אוֹ־הַשְּׁתִי אוֹ־הָעֵרֶב רבוע יהוה ורבוע אלהים אוֹ־כָל־ ילי כְּלִי כלי הָעוֹר אֲשֶׁר תְּכַבֵּס וְסָר י' הויות מֵהֶם הַנָּגַע מלוי אהיה דאלפין וְכֻבַּס שֵׁנִית וְטָהֵר י"פ אכא: זֹאת תּוֹרַת נֶגַע־ מלוי אהיה דאלפין צָרַעַת בֶּגֶד הַצֶּמֶר מצר | אוֹ הַפִּשְׁתִּים אוֹ הַשְּׁתִי אוֹ הָעֵרֶב רבוע יהוה ורבוע אלהים אוֹ כָּל־ ילי כְּלִי־ כלי עוֹר לְטַהֲרוֹ אוֹ לְטַמְּאוֹ:

וַיְדַבֵּר ראה יְהֹוָהאדניאהדונהי אֶל־מֹשֶׁה מהש, אל שדי לֵּאמֹר: זֹאת תִּהְיֶה תּוֹרַת הַמְּצֹרָע בְּיוֹם ע"ה = נגד, זן, מזבח טָהֳרָתוֹ וְהוּבָא אֶל־הַכֹּהֵן מלה: וְיָצָא הַכֹּהֵן מלה אֶל־מִחוּץ לַמַּחֲנֶה וְרָאָה הַכֹּהֵן מלה וְהִנֵּה מ"ה יה נִרְפָּא נֶגַע־ מלוי אהיה דאלפין הַצָּרַעַת מִן־הַצָּרוּעַ:

וְהִזַּרְתֶּם אֶת־בְּנֵי־יִשְׂרָאֵל מִטֻּמְאָתָם וְלֹא יָמֻתוּ בְּטֻמְאָתָם בְּטַמְּאָם אֶת־מִשְׁכָּנִי אֲשֶׁר בְּתוֹכָם: זֹאת תּוֹרַת הַזָּב וַאֲשֶׁר תֵּצֵא מִמֶּנּוּ שִׁכְבַת־זֶרַע לְטָמְאָה־בָהּ: וְהַדָּוָה בְּנִדָּתָהּ וְהַזָּב אֶת־זוֹבוֹ לַזָּכָר וְלַנְּקֵבָה וּלְאִישׁ אֲשֶׁר יִשְׁכַּב עִם־טְמֵאָה:

וידבר ראה יהוה יאהדונהי אל־משה מהש, אל שדי אחרי מות שני בני
אהרן ע״ב ורבוע ע״ב בקרבתם לפני־ וחכמה בינה יהוה יאהדונהי וימתו: ויאמר
יהוה יאהדונהי אל־משה מהש, אל שדי דבר ראה אל־אהרן ע״ב ורבוע ע״ב אחיך
ואל־יבא בכל־ ב״ן, לכב, יבמ עת י״פ אהיה י׳ הויות אל־הקדש מבית ב״פ ראה
לפרכת אל־פני וחכמה בינה הכפרת אשר על־הארן ע״ב ורבוע ע״ב ולא ימות כי
בענן אראה על־הכפרת: בזאת יבא אהרן ע״ב ורבוע ע״ב אל־הקדש
בפר סוזהר, ערי, סנדלפו״ן בן־בקר לחטאת ואיל לעלה:

ולא־תקיא הארץ אלהים דההין ע״ה אתכם בטמאכם אתה כאשר קאה את־
הגוי אשר לפניכם: כי כל־ ילי אשר יעשה מכל ילי התועבת האלה
ונכרתו הנפשות העשת מקרב עמם: ושמרתם את־משמרתי
לבלתי עשות מחקות התועבת אשר נעשו לפניכם ולא תטמאו בהם
אני אני, טדה״ד כוו״ו יהוה יאהדונהי אלהיכם ילה:

וידבר ראה יהוה יאהדונהי אל־משה מהש, אל שדי לאמר: דבר ראה
אל־כל־ ילי עדת בני־ישראל ואמרת אלהם קדשים תהיו כי קדוש
אני אני, טדה״ד כוו״ו יהוה יאהדונהי אלהיכם ילה: איש ע״ה קנ״א קס״א אמו ואביו
תיראו ואת־שבתתי תשמרו אני אני, טדה״ד כוו״ו יהוה יאהדונהי אלהיכם ילה:

והבדלתם בין־הבהמה ב״ן, לכב, יבמ הטהרה לטמאה ובין־
העוף ג״פ ב״ן, יוסף, ציון הטמא לטהר י״פ אכא ולא־ תשקצו את־נפשתיכם
בבהמה ב״ן, לכב, יבמ ובעוף ג״פ ב״ן, יוסף, ציון ובכל ב״ן, לכב, יבמ אשר תרמש
האדמה אשר־הבדלתי לכם לטמא: והייתם לי קדשים כי קדוש
אני אני, טדה״ד כוו״ו יהוה יאהדונהי ואבדל אתכם מן־העמים ע״ה קס״א להיות
לי: ואיש ע״ה קנ״א קס״א או־אשה כי־יהיה ייי בהם אוב או ידעני מות יומתו
באבן יוד הה ואו הה ירגמו אתם דמיהם בם מ״ב:

ויאמר יהוה יאהדונהי אל־משה מהש, אל שדי אמר אל־הכהנים מלה בני
אהרן ע״ב ורבוע ע״ב ואמרת אלהם לנפש רמ״ח וז׳ הויות לא־יטמא בעמיו: כי
אם־ יוהך, ע״ה מ״ב לשארו הקרב אליו לאמו ולאביו ולבנו ולבתו ולאחיו:
ולאחתו הבתולה הקרובה אליו אשר לא־היתה לאיש לה יטמא:

וספרתם לכם ממחרת השבת מיום ע"ה = נגד, זן, מזבח הביאכם
את־עמר י"ש (עולמות) התנופה שבע ע"ב ואלהים דיודין שבתות תמימת תהיינה:
עד ממחרת השבת השביעת תספרו חמשים יום ע"ה = נגד, זן, מזבח
והקרבתם מנחה חדשה ליהוהאדני אהדונהי: ממושבתיכם תביאו |
לחם ג"פ יהוה תנופה שתים שני עשרנים סלת תהיינה חמץ תאפינה
בכורים ליהוהאדני אהדונהי: והקרבתם על־הלחם ג"פ יהוה שבעת כבשים
תמימם בני שנה ופר פזר, ערי, סנדלפון בן־בקר אחד אהבה, דאגה ואילם שנים
יהיו אל עלה ליהוהאדני אהדונהי ומנחתם ונסכיהם אשה ריח־ניחח
ליהוהאדני אהדונהי: ועשיתם שעיר־עזים אחד אהבה, דאגה לחטאת ושני כבשים
בני שנה לזבח שלמים: והניף הכהן מלה | אתם על לחם ג"פ יהוה הבכרים
תנופה לפני חכמה בינה יהוהאדני אהדונהי על־שני כבשים קדש יהיו אל
ליהוהאדני אהדונהי לכהן מלה: וקראתם בעצם | היום ע"ה = נגד, זן, מזבח הזה והו
מקרא־ שם ע"ה, יהוה שדי קדש יהיה ייי לכם כל־ ילי מלאכת עבדה לא תעשו
חקת עולם אהיה דההין בכל־ ב"ן, לכב, יבמ מושבתיכם לדרתיכם: ובקצרכם
את־קציר ארצכם לא־תכלה נתה, קס"א קנ"א קמ"ג פאת שדך בקצרך ולקט
קצירך לא תלקט לעני ע"ה קס"א ולגר תעזב אתם אני אני, טדה"ד כוז"ו
יהוהאדני אהדונהי אלהיכם ילה:

ומכה בהמה ב"ן, לכב, יבמ ישלמנה ומכה אדם מ"ה יומת: משפט ע"ה ה"פ אלהים
אחד אהבה, דאגה יהיה ייי לכם כגר ב"ן קנ"א כאזרח יהיה ייי כי אני אני, טדה"ד כוז"ו
יהוהאדני אהדונהי אלהיכם ילה: וידבר ראה משה מהש, אל שדי אל־בני ישראל
ויוציאו את־המקלל אל־מחוץ למחנה וירגמו אתו אבן יוד הה ואו הה ובני־
ישראל עשו כאשר צוה פוי יהוהאדני אהדונהי את־משה מהש, אל שדי:

וידבר ראה יהוהאדני אהדונהי אל־משה מהש, אל שדי בהר אור, רז, אין סוף
סיני נמם, ה"פ יהוה לאמר: דבר ראה אל־בני ישראל ואמרת אלהם כי תבאו
אל־הארץ אלהים דההין ע"ה אשר אני אני, טדה"ד כוז"ו נתן אבג"ית"ץ, ושר, אהבת חנם לכם
ושבתה הארץ אלהים דההין ע"ה שבת ליהוהאדני אהדונהי: שש שנים תזרע שדך
ושש שנים תזמר כרמך ואספת את־תבואתה:

כי־לי בני־ישראל עבדים הם אשר־הוצאתי אותם
מארץ אלהים דאלפין ממצרים מצר אני אני, טדה"ד כוז"ו יהוהאדני אהדונהי אלהיכם ילה:

לֹא־תַעֲשׂוּ לָכֶם אֱלִילִם וּפֶסֶל וּמַצֵּבָה לֹא־תָקִימוּ לָכֶם וְאֶבֶן מַשְׂכִּית לֹא
תִתְּנוּ בְּאַרְצְכֶם לְהִשְׁתַּחֲוֺת עָלֶיהָ פהל כִּי אֲנִי אני, טדה״ד כוז״ו יְהֹוָאדניאהדונהי
אֱלֹהֵיכֶם ילה: אֶת־שַׁבְּתֹתַי תִּשְׁמֹרוּ וּמִקְדָּשִׁי תִּירָאוּ אֲנִי אני, טדה״ד כוז״ו
יְהֹוָאדניאהדונהי:

אִם־ יוהך, ע״ה מ״ב בְּחֻקֹּתַי תֵּלֵכוּ וְאֶת־מִצְוֺתַי תִּשְׁמְרוּ וַעֲשִׂיתֶם אֹתָם:
וְנָתַתִּי גִשְׁמֵיכֶם בְּעִתָּם וְנָתְנָה הָאָרֶץ אלהים דההין ע״ה יְבוּלָהּ וְעֵץ ע״ה קס״א
הַשָּׂדֶה שדי יִתֵּן פִּרְיוֹ: וְהִשִּׂיג לָכֶם דַּיִשׁ אֶת־בָּצִיר וּבָצִיר יַשִּׂיג אֶת־זָרַע
וַאֲכַלְתֶּם לַחְמְכֶם לָשֹׂבַע ע״ב ואלהים דיודין וִישַׁבְתֶּם לָבֶטַח בְּאַרְצְכֶם:

וְכָל־ ילי מַעְשַׂר ירת בָּקָר וָצֹאן מלוי אהיה דיודין ע״ה כֹּל ילי אֲשֶׁר־יַעֲבֹר
תַּחַת הַשָּׁבֶט הָעֲשִׂירִי יִהְיֶה־ ייי קֹּדֶשׁ לַיהֹוָאדניאהדונהי: לֹא יְבַקֵּר
בֵּין־טוֹב והו לָרַע י״פ ז״ך וְלֹא יְמִירֶנּוּ וְאִם־ יוהך, ע״ה מ״ב הָמֵר ב״פ ק״ך
יְמִירֶנּוּ וְהָיָה־ יהוה הוּא וּתְמוּרָתוֹ יִהְיֶה־ ייי קֹּדֶשׁ לֹא יִגָּאֵל:

אֵלֶּה הַמִּצְוֺת (הֵתָ–HuTa)

אֲשֶׁר צִוָּה פוי יְהֹוָאדניאהדונהי אֶת־מֹשֶׁה מהש, אל שדי אֶל־בְּנֵי יִשְׂרָאֵל
בְּהַר אור, רז, אין סוף סִינָי נמם, ה״פ יהוה:

BAMIDBAR - NUMBERS

וַיְדַבֵּר ראה יְהֹוָאדניאהדונהי אֶל־מֹשֶׁה מהש, אל שדי בְּמִדְבַּר אברהם, וז״פ אל, רמ״ח
סִינַי נמם, ה״פ יהוה בְּאֹהֶל לאה מוֹעֵד בְּאֶחָד אהבה, דאגה לַחֹדֶשׁ י״ב הוויות הַשֵּׁנִי
בַּשָּׁנָה הַשֵּׁנִית לְצֵאתָם מֵאֶרֶץ אלהים דאלפין מִצְרַיִם מצר לֵאמֹר: שְׂאוּ
אֶת־רֹאשׁ ריבוע אלהים ואלהים דיודין ע״ה כָּל־ ילי עֲדַת בְּנֵי־יִשְׂרָאֵל לְמִשְׁפְּחֹתָם
לְבֵית ב״פ ראה אֲבֹתָם בְּמִסְפַּר שֵׁמוֹת כָּל־ ילי זָכָר לְגֻלְגְּלֹתָם: מִבֶּן עֶשְׂרִים
שָׁנָה וָמַעְלָה כָּל־ ילי יֹצֵא צָבָא בְּיִשְׂרָאֵל תִּפְקְדוּ אֹתָם לְצִבְאֹתָם אַתָּה
וְאַהֲרֹן ע״ב ורבוע ע״ב:

וַיְדַבֵּר ראה יְהֹוָאדניאהדונהי אֶל־מֹשֶׁה מהש, אל שדי וְאֶל־אַהֲרֹן ע״ב ורבוע ע״ב לֵאמֹר:
אַל־תַּכְרִיתוּ אֶת־שֵׁבֶט מִשְׁפְּחֹת הַקְּהָתִי מִתּוֹךְ הַלְוִיִּם: וְזֹאת | עֲשׂוּ לָהֶם
וְחָיוּ וְלֹא יָמֻתוּ בְּגִשְׁתָּם אֶת־קֹדֶשׁ הַקֳּדָשִׁים אַהֲרֹן ע״ב ורבוע ע״ב וּבָנָיו יָבֹאוּ
וְשָׂמוּ אוֹתָם אִישׁ ע״ה קנ״א קס״א אִישׁ ע״ה קנ״א קס״א עַל־עֲבֹדָתוֹ וְאֶל־מַשָּׂאוֹ:
וְלֹא־יָבֹאוּ לִרְאוֹת כְּבַלַּע אֶת־הַקֹּדֶשׁ וָמֵתוּ:

וַיְדַבֵּר ראה יְהֹוָההאדניאהדונהי אֶל־מֹשֶׁה מהש, אל שדי לֵּאמֹר: נָשֹׂא אֶת־רֹאשׁ ריבוע אלהים ואלהים דיודין ע״ה בְּנֵי גֵרְשׁוֹן ע״ה ב״פ סוזפ״ך גַּם־ יג״ל הֵם לְבֵית ב״פ ראה אֲבֹתָם לְמִשְׁפְּחֹתָם: מִבֶּן שְׁלֹשִׁים שָׁנָה וָמַעְלָה עַד בֶּן־חֲמִשִּׁים שָׁנָה תִּפְקֹד אוֹתָם כָּל־ ילי הַבָּא לִצְבֹא צָבָא לַעֲבֹד עֲבֹדָה בְּאֹהֶל לאה (אלד ע״ה) מוֹעֵד:

זֹאת | חֲנֻכַּת הַמִּזְבֵּחַ זן, נגד בְּיוֹם ע״ה = נגד, זן, מזבח הִמָּשַׁח אֹתוֹ מֵאֵת נְשִׂיאֵי יִשְׂרָאֵל קַעֲרֹת כֶּסֶף שְׁתֵּים עֶשְׂרֵה מִזְרְקֵי־כֶסֶף שְׁנֵים עָשָׂר כַּפּוֹת זָהָב שְׁתֵּים עֶשְׂרֵה: שְׁלֹשִׁים וּמֵאָה דמב, מלוי ע״ב הַקְּעָרָה הָאַחַת כֶּסֶף וְשִׁבְעִים הַמִּזְרָק הָאֶחָד אהבה, דאגה כָּל ילי כֶּסֶף הַכֵּלִים אַלְפַּיִם קס״א וְאַרְבַּע־מֵאוֹת בְּשֶׁקֶל הַקֹּדֶשׁ: כַּפּוֹת זָהָב שְׁתֵּים־עֶשְׂרֵה מְלֵאֹת קְטֹרֶת עֲשָׂרָה עֲשָׂרָה הַכַּף בְּשֶׁקֶל הַקֹּדֶשׁ כָּל־ ילי זְהַב הַכַּפּוֹת עֶשְׂרִים וּמֵאָה דמב, מלוי ע״ב: כָּל־ ילי הַבָּקָר לָעֹלָה שְׁנֵים עָשָׂר פָּרִים אֵילִם שְׁנֵים־עָשָׂר כְּבָשִׂים בְּנֵי־שָׁנָה שְׁנֵים עָשָׂר וּמִנְחָתָם וּשְׂעִירֵי עִזִּים שְׁנֵים עָשָׂר לְחַטָּאת: וְכֹל ילי בְּקַר | זֶבַח הַשְּׁלָמִים עֶשְׂרִים וְאַרְבָּעָה פָּרִים אֵילִם שִׁשִּׁים עַתֻּדִים שִׁשִּׁים כְּבָשִׂים בְּנֵי־שָׁנָה שִׁשִּׁים זֹאת חֲנֻכַּת הַמִּזְבֵּחַ זן, נגד אַחֲרֵי הִמָּשַׁח אֹתוֹ: וּבְבֹא מֹשֶׁה מהש, אל שדי אֶל־אֹהֶל לאה (אלד ע״ה) מוֹעֵד לְדַבֵּר ראה אִתּוֹ וַיִּשְׁמַע אֶת־הַקּוֹל ע״ב ס״ג ע״ה מִדַּבֵּר ראה אֵלָיו מֵעַל עלם הַכַּפֹּרֶת אֲשֶׁר עַל־אֲרֹן הָעֵדֻת מִבֵּין שְׁנֵי הַכְּרֻבִים וַיְדַבֵּר ראה אֵלָיו:

וַיְדַבֵּר ראה יְהֹוָההאדניאהדונהי אֶל־מֹשֶׁה מהש, אל שדי לֵּאמֹר: דַּבֵּר ראה אֶל־אַהֲרֹן ע״ב ורבוע ע״ב וְאָמַרְתָּ אֵלָיו בְּהַעֲלֹתְךָ אֶת־הַנֵּרֹת אֶל־מוּל פְּנֵי וחכמה בינה הַמְּנוֹרָה יָאִירוּ שִׁבְעַת הַנֵּרוֹת: וַיַּעַשׂ כֵּן אַהֲרֹן ע״ב ורבוע ע״ב אֶל־מוּל פְּנֵי וחכמה בינה הַמְּנוֹרָה הֶעֱלָה נֵרֹתֶיהָ כַּאֲשֶׁר צִוָּה פוי יְהֹוָההאדניאהדונהי אֶת־מֹשֶׁה מהש, אל שדי:

וַיֹּאמֶר יְהֹוָההאדניאהדונהי אֶל־מֹשֶׁה מהש, אל שדי וְאָבִיהָ יָרֹק יָרַק בְּפָנֶיהָ הֲלֹא תִכָּלֵם שִׁבְעַת יָמִים נלך תִּסָּגֵר שִׁבְעַת יָמִים נלך מִחוּץ לַמַּחֲנֶה וְאַחַר תֵּאָסֵף: וַתִּסָּגֵר מִרְיָם מִחוּץ לַמַּחֲנֶה שִׁבְעַת יָמִים נלך וְהָעָם לֹא נָסַע עַד־הֵאָסֵף מִרְיָם: וְאַחַר נָסְעוּ הָעָם מֵחֲצֵרוֹת וַיַּחֲנוּ בְּמִדְבַּר אברהם, וז״פ אל, רמ״ח פָּארָן:

וַיְדַבֵּר ראה יְהֹוָה יאהדונהי אֶל־מֹשֶׁה מהש, אל שדי לֵּאמֹר: שְׁלַח־לְךָ אֲנָשִׁים וְיָתֻרוּ קס"א קס"א קנ"א קמ"ג אֶת־אֶרֶץ אלהים דאלפין כְּנַעַן אֲשֶׁר־אֲנִי אני, טדה"ד כוז"ו נֹתֵן אבגית"ץ, ושר, אהבת חנם לִבְנֵי יִשְׂרָאֵל אִישׁ ע"ה קנ"א קס"א אֶחָד אהבה, דאגה אִישׁ ע"ה קנ"א קס"א אֶחָד אהבה, דאגה לְמַטֵּה אֲבֹתָיו תִּשְׁלָחוּ כֹּל ילי נָשִׂיא בָהֶם: וַיִּשְׁלַח אֹתָם מֹשֶׁה מהש, אל שדי מִמִּדְבַּר פָּארָן עַל־פִּי יְהֹוָה יאהדונהי כֻּלָּם אֲנָשִׁים רָאשֵׁי בְנֵי־יִשְׂרָאֵל הֵמָּה:

וַיֹּאמֶר יְהֹוָה יאהדונהי אֶל־מֹשֶׁה מהש, אל שדי לֵּאמֹר: דַּבֵּר ראה אֶל־בְּנֵי יִשְׂרָאֵל וְאָמַרְתָּ אֲלֵהֶם וְעָשׂוּ לָהֶם צִיצִת עַל־כַּנְפֵי בִגְדֵיהֶם לְדֹרֹתָם וְנָתְנוּ עַל־צִיצִת הַכָּנָף ע"ה קנ"א, אלהים אדני פְּתִיל י"פ ב"ן תְּכֵלֶת: וְהָיָה יהוה, יהה לָכֶם לְצִיצִת וּרְאִיתֶם אֹתוֹ וּזְכַרְתֶּם אֶת־כָּל־ ילי מִצְוֹת יְהֹוָה יאהדונהי וַעֲשִׂיתֶם אֹתָם וְלֹא־תָתֻרוּ אַחֲרֵי לְבַבְכֶם וְאַחֲרֵי עֵינֵיכֶם ריבוע מ"ה אֲשֶׁר־אַתֶּם זֹנִים אַחֲרֵיהֶם: לְמַעַן תִּזְכְּרוּ וַעֲשִׂיתֶם אֶת־כָּל־ ילי מִצְוֹתָי וִהְיִיתֶם קְדֹשִׁים לֵאלֹהֵיכֶם ילה: אֲנִי אני, טדה"ד כוז"ו יְהֹוָה יאהדונהי אֱלֹהֵיכֶם ילה אֲשֶׁר הוֹצֵאתִי אֶתְכֶם מֵאֶרֶץ אלהים דאלפין מִצְרַיִם מצר לִהְיוֹת לָכֶם לֵאלֹהִים מום, אהיה אדני ; ילה אֲנִי אני, טדה"ד כוז"ו יְהֹוָה יאהדונהי אֱלֹהֵיכֶם ילה:

וַיִּקַּח ועם קֹרַח בֶּן־יִצְהָר בֶּן־קְהָת בֶּן־לֵוִי ע"ה יהוה אהיה וְדָתָן ע"ה קס"א קנ"א קמ"ג, ע"ה נתה וַאֲבִירָם בְּנֵי אֱלִיאָב וְאוֹן בֶּן־פֶּלֶת בְּנֵי רְאוּבֵן ג"פ אלהים ע"ה: וַיָּקֻמוּ לִפְנֵי חכמה בינה מֹשֶׁה מהש, אל שדי וַאֲנָשִׁים מִבְּנֵי־יִשְׂרָאֵל חֲמִשִּׁים וּמָאתָיִם נְשִׂיאֵי עֵדָה קְרִאֵי מוֹעֵד אַנְשֵׁי־שֵׁם יהוה שדי: וַיִּקָּהֲלוּ עַל־מֹשֶׁה מהש, אל שדי וְעַל־אַהֲרֹן ע"ב ורבוע ע"ב וַיֹּאמְרוּ אֲלֵהֶם רַב־ ע"ב ורבוע מ"ה לָכֶם כִּי כָל־ ילי הָעֵדָה כֻּלָּם קְדֹשִׁים וּבְתוֹכָם יְהֹוָה יאהדונהי וּמַדּוּעַ תִּתְנַשְּׂאוּ עַל־קְהַל ע"ב ס"ג יְהֹוָה יאהדונהי:

וְאָמַרְתָּ אֲלֵהֶם בַּהֲרִימְכֶם אֶת־חֶלְבּוֹ מִמֶּנּוּ וְנֶחְשַׁב לַלְוִיִּם כִּתְבוּאַת גֹּרֶן וְכִתְבוּאַת יָקֶב: וַאֲכַלְתֶּם אֹתוֹ בְּכָל־ ב"ן, לכב, יבמ מָקוֹם יהוה ברבוע, ו"פ אל אַתֶּם וּבֵיתְכֶם כִּי־שָׂכָר י"פ ב"ן הוּא לָכֶם חֵלֶף עֲבֹדַתְכֶם בְּאֹהֶל לאה (אלד ע"ה) מוֹעֵד: וְלֹא־תִשְׂאוּ עָלָיו חֵטְא בַּהֲרִימְכֶם אֶת־חֶלְבּוֹ מִמֶּנּוּ וְאֶת־קָדְשֵׁי בְנֵי־יִשְׂרָאֵל לֹא תְחַלְּלוּ וְלֹא תָמוּתוּ:

וַיְדַבֵּר ראה יְהֹוָהאדניאהדונהי אֶל־מֹשֶׁה מהש, אל שדי וְאֶל־אַהֲרֹן ע"ב ורבוע ע"ב לֵאמֹר׃ זֹאת חֻקַּת הַתּוֹרָה אֲשֶׁר־צִוָּה פוי יְהֹוָהאדניאהדונהי לֵאמֹר דַּבֵּר ראה | אֶל־בְּנֵי יִשְׂרָאֵל וְיִקְחוּ וזעם אֵלֶיךָ אני פָרָה אֲדֻמָּה עסמ"ב ורבוע עסמ"ב תְּמִימָה אֲשֶׁר אֵין־בָּהּ מוּם מום, אלהים, אהיה אדני אֲשֶׁר לֹא־עָלָה עָלֶיהָ פהל עֹל׃ וּנְתַתֶּם אֹתָהּ אֶל־אֶלְעָזָר הַכֹּהֵן מלה וְהוֹצִיא אֹתָהּ אֶל־מִחוּץ לַמַּחֲנֶה וְשָׁחַט אֹתָהּ לְפָנָיו׃

וַיֹּאמֶר יְהֹוָהאדניאהדונהי אֶל־מֹשֶׁה מהש, אל שדי אַל־תִּירָא אֹתוֹ כִּי בְיָדְךָ בוכ"ו נָתַתִּי אֹתוֹ וְאֶת־כָּל־ ילי עַמּוֹ וְאֶת־ אַרְצוֹ וְעָשִׂיתָ לּוֹ כַּאֲשֶׁר עָשִׂיתָ לְסִיחֹן מֶלֶךְ הָאֱמֹרִי אֲשֶׁר יוֹשֵׁב בְּחֶשְׁבּוֹן׃ וַיַּכּוּ אֹתוֹ וְאֶת־בָּנָיו וְאֶת־כָּל־ ילי עַמּוֹ עַד־בִּלְתִּי הִשְׁאִיר־לוֹ שָׂרִיד וַיִּירְשׁוּ אֶת־אַרְצוֹ׃ וַיִּסְעוּ בְּנֵי יִשְׂרָאֵל וַיַּחֲנוּ בְּעַרְבוֹת מוֹאָב יוד הא ואו הה מֵעֵבֶר רבוע יהוה ורבוע אלהים לְיַרְדֵּן י"פ יהוה וד' אותיות יְרֵחוֹ׃

וַיַּרְא בָּלָק בֶּן־צִפּוֹר אֵת כָּל־ ילי אֲשֶׁר־עָשָׂה יִשְׂרָאֵל לָאֱמֹרִי׃ וַיָּגָר קס"א ב"ן מוֹאָב יוד הא ואו הה מִפְּנֵי וחכמה בינה הָעָם מְאֹד מ"ה כִּי רַב־ ע"ב ורבוע מ"ה הוּא וַיָּקָץ מנק מוֹאָב יוד הא ואו הה מִפְּנֵי וחכמה בינה בְּנֵי יִשְׂרָאֵל׃ וַיֹּאמֶר מוֹאָב יוד הא ואו הה אֶל־זִקְנֵי מִדְיָן עַתָּה יְלַחֲכוּ הַקָּהָל ע"ב ס"ג אֶת־כָּל־ ילי סְבִיבֹתֵינוּ כִּלְחֹךְ הַשּׁוֹר אבגית"ץ, ושר, אהבת חנם אֵת יֶרֶק הַשָּׂדֶה שדי וּבָלָק בֶּן־צִפּוֹר מֶלֶךְ לְמוֹאָב יוד הא ואו הה בָּעֵת י"פ אהיה י' הויות הַהִוא׃

וַיַּרְא אלף למד יהוה פִּינְחָס בֶּן־אֶלְעָזָר בֶּן־אַהֲרֹן ע"ב ורבוע ע"ב הַכֹּהֵן מלה וַיָּקָם מִתּוֹךְ הָעֵדָה וַיִּקַּח וזעם רֹמַח אברהם, ח"פ אל, רמ"ח בְּיָדוֹ׃ וַיָּבֹא אַחַר אִישׁ־ ע"ה קנ"א קס"א יִשְׂרָאֵל אֶל־הַקֻּבָּה וַיִּדְקֹר אֶת־שְׁנֵיהֶם אֵת אִישׁ ע"ה קנ"א קס"א יִשְׂרָאֵל וְאֶת־הָאִשָּׁה אֶל־קֳבָתָהּ וַתֵּעָצַר הַמַּגֵּפָה מֵעַל עלם בְּנֵי יִשְׂרָאֵל׃ וַיִּהְיוּ מלוי ס"ג הַמֵּתִים בַּמַּגֵּפָה אַרְבָּעָה וְעֶשְׂרִים אָלֶף אלף למד שין דלת יוד ע"ה׃

וַיְדַבֵּר ראה יְהֹוָהאדניאהדונהי אֶל־מֹשֶׁה מהש, אל שדי לֵּאמֹר׃ פִּינְחָס בֶּן־אֶלְעָזָר בֶּן־אַהֲרֹן ע"ב ורבוע ע"ב הַכֹּהֵן מלה הֵשִׁיב אֶת־חֲמָתִי מֵעַל עלם בְּנֵי־יִשְׂרָאֵל בְּקַנְאוֹ אֶת־קִנְאָתִי בְּתוֹכָם וְלֹא־כִלִּיתִי אֶת־בְּנֵי־יִשְׂרָאֵל בְּקִנְאָתִי׃ לָכֵן אֱמֹר הִנְנִי נֹתֵן אבגית"ץ, ושר, אהבת חנם לוֹ אֶת־בְּרִיתִי שָׁלוֹם׃

וּבְיוֹם ע"ה = נגד, זן, מזבח הַבִּכּוּרִים בְּהַקְרִיבְכֶם מִנְחָה ע"ה ב"פ ב"ן חֲדָשָׁה
לַיהֹוָה אהדונהי בְּשָׁבֻעֹתֵיכֶם מִקְרָא־ שם ע"ה, יהוה שדי קֹדֶשׁ יִהְיֶה ייי לָכֶם
כָּל־ ילי מְלֶאכֶת עֲבֹדָה לֹא תַעֲשׂוּ: וְהִקְרַבְתֶּם עוֹלָה לְרֵיחַ אברהם, וו"פ אל, רמ"ח
נִיחֹחַ לַיהֹוָה אהדונהי פָּרִים בְּנֵי־בָקָר שְׁנַיִם אַיִל אֶחָד אהבה, דאגה שִׁבְעָה
כְבָשִׂים בְּנֵי שָׁנָה: וּמִנְחָתָם סֹלֶת בְּלוּלָה בַשָּׁמֶן י"פ טל, י"פ כוז"ו, ביט שְׁלֹשָׁה
עֶשְׂרֹנִים לַפָּר מוזחר, ערי, סנדלפון הָאֶחָד אהבה, דאגה שְׁנֵי עֶשְׂרֹנִים לָאַיִל
הָאֶחָד אהבה, דאגה: עִשָּׂרוֹן עִשָּׂרוֹן לַכֶּבֶשׂ ב"פ קס"א הָאֶחָד אהבה, דאגה לְשִׁבְעַת
הַכְּבָשִׂים: שְׂעִיר עִזִּים אֶחָד אהבה, דאגה לְכַפֵּר מצפצ עֲלֵיכֶם: מִלְּבַד
עֹלַת אבגיתץ, ושר, אהבת חנם הַתָּמִיד ע"ה נתה, קס"א קנ"א קמ"ג וּמִנְחָתוֹ תַּעֲשׂוּ תְּמִימִם
יִהְיוּ־ אל לָכֶם וְנִסְכֵּיהֶם:

בַּיּוֹם ע"ה נגד, זן, מזבח הַשְּׁמִינִי עֲצֶרֶת תִּהְיֶה לָכֶם כָּל־ ילי מְלֶאכֶת עֲבֹדָה לֹא
תַעֲשׂוּ: וְהִקְרַבְתֶּם עֹלָה אִשֵּׁה רֵיחַ נִיחֹחַ לַיהֹוָה אהדונהי פַּר מוזחר, ערי, סנדלפון
אֶחָד אהבה, דאגה אַיִל אֶחָד אהבה, דאגה כְּבָשִׂים בְּנֵי־שָׁנָה שִׁבְעָה תְּמִימִם:
מִנְחָתָם וְנִסְכֵּיהֶם לַפָּר מוזחר, ערי, סנדלפון לָאַיִל וְלַכְּבָשִׂים בְּמִסְפָּרָם
כַּמִּשְׁפָּט ע"ה ה"פ אלהים: וּשְׂעִיר חַטָּאת אֶחָד אהבה, דאגה מִלְּבַד
עֹלַת אבגיתץ, ושר, אהבת חנם הַתָּמִיד ע"ה נתה, קס"א קנ"א קמ"ג וּמִנְחָתָהּ וְנִסְכָּהּ: אֵלֶּה
תַּעֲשׂוּ לַיהֹוָה אהדונהי בְּמוֹעֲדֵיכֶם לְבַד מִנִּדְרֵיכֶם וְנִדְבֹתֵיכֶם לְעֹלֹתֵיכֶם
וּלְמִנְחֹתֵיכֶם וּלְנִסְכֵּיכֶם וּלְשַׁלְמֵיכֶם: וַיֹּאמֶר מֹשֶׁה מהש, אל שדי אֶל־בְּנֵי
יִשְׂרָאֵל כְּכֹל אֲשֶׁר־צִוָּה פוי יְהֹוָה אהדונהי אֶת־מֹשֶׁה מהש, אל שדי:

וַיְדַבֵּר ראה מֹשֶׁה מהש, אל שדי אֶל־רָאשֵׁי הַמַּטּוֹת לִבְנֵי יִשְׂרָאֵל לֵאמֹר זֶה
הַדָּבָר ראה אֲשֶׁר צִוָּה פוי יְהֹוָה אהדונהי: אִישׁ ע"ה קנ"א קס"א כִּי־יִדֹּר נֶדֶר
לַיהֹוָה אהדונהי אוֹ־הִשָּׁבַע ע"ב ואלהים דיודין שְׁבֻעָה לֶאְסֹר אִסָּר עַל־נַפְשׁוֹ לֹא
יַחֵל דְּבָרוֹ ראה כְּכָל־ ילי הַיֹּצֵא מִפִּיו יַעֲשֶׂה: וְאִשָּׁה כִּי־תִדֹּר נֶדֶר
לַיהֹוָה אהדונהי וְאָסְרָה אִסָּר בְּבֵית ב"פ ראה אָבִיהָ בִּנְעֻרֶיהָ:

וַיִּתֵּן י"פ מלוי ע"ב מֹשֶׁה מהש, אל שדי אֶת־הַגִּלְעָד לְמָכִיר בֶּן־מְנַשֶּׁה וַיֵּשֶׁב בָּהּ:
וְיָאִיר בֶּן־מְנַשֶּׁה הָלַךְ מיה וַיִּלְכֹּד אֶת־חַוֹּתֵיהֶם וַיִּקְרָא ב"פ קס"א עם ה' אותיות
אֶתְהֶן חַוֹּת יָאִיר: וְנֹבַח הָלַךְ מיה וַיִּלְכֹּד אֶת־קְנָת וְאֶת־בְּנֹתֶיהָ
וַיִּקְרָא ב"פ קס"א עם ה' אותיות לָה נֹבַח בִּשְׁמוֹ מהש ע"ה, אל שדי ע"ה:

אֵלֶּה מַסְעֵי בְנֵי־יִשְׂרָאֵל אֲשֶׁר יָצְאוּ מֵאֶרֶץ אלהים דאלפין מִצְרַיִם מצר לְצִבְאֹתָם בְּיַד־מֹשֶׁה מהש, אל שדי וְאַהֲרֹן ע״ב ורבוע ע״ב: וַיִּכְתֹּב מֹשֶׁה מהש, אל שדי אֶת־מוֹצָאֵיהֶם לְמַסְעֵיהֶם עַל־פִּי יְהֹוָהאדנייאהדונהי וְאֵלֶּה מ״ב מַסְעֵיהֶם לְמוֹצָאֵיהֶם: וַיִּסְעוּ מֵרַעְמְסֵס בַּחֹדֶשׁ י״ב הוויות הָרִאשׁוֹן בַּחֲמִשָּׁה עָשָׂר יוֹם ע״ה נגד, זן, מזבח לַחֹדֶשׁ י״ב הוויות הָרִאשׁוֹן מִמָּחֳרַת הַפֶּסַח יָצְאוּ בְנֵי־יִשְׂרָאֵל בְּיָד רָמָה לְעֵינֵי ריבוע מ״ה כָּל־ ילי מִצְרָיִם מצר:

וַתִּהְיֶינָה מַחְלָה תִרְצָה וְחָגְלָה וּמִלְכָּה ע״ה פוי, אל אדני וְנֹעָה בְּנוֹת צְלָפְחָד לִבְנֵי דֹדֵיהֶן לְנָשִׁים: מִמִּשְׁפְּחֹת בְּנֵי־מְנַשֶּׁה בֶן־יוֹסֵף ציון, ו״פ יהוה הָיוּ לְנָשִׁים וַתְּהִי נַחֲלָתָן עַל־מַטֵּה מִשְׁפַּחַת אֲבִיהֶן:

אֵלֶּה הַמִּצְוֹת (הֻתָּ–HuTA)

וְהַמִּשְׁפָּטִים אֲשֶׁר צִוָּה פוי יְהֹוָהאדנייאהדונהי בְּיַד־מֹשֶׁה מהש, אל שדי אֶל־בְּנֵי יִשְׂרָאֵל בְּעַרְבֹת מוֹאָב יוד הא ואו הה עַל יַרְדֵּן י״פ יהוה וד׳ אותיות יְרֵחוֹ:

DEVARIM - DEUTERONOMY

אֵלֶּה הַדְּבָרִים ראה אֲשֶׁר דִּבֶּר ראה מֹשֶׁה מהש, אל שדי אֶל־כָּל־ ילי יִשְׂרָאֵל בְּעֵבֶר רבוע יהוה ורבוע אלהים הַיַּרְדֵּן י״פ יהוה וד׳ אותיות בַּמִּדְבָּר אברהם, רמ״ח, וח״פ אל בָּעֲרָבָה מוֹל סוּף בֵּין־פָּארָן וּבֵין־תֹּפֶל וְלָבָן וַחֲצֵרֹת וְדִי זָהָב: אַחַד אהבה, דאגה עָשָׂר יוֹם ע״ה = נגד, זן, מזבח מֵחֹרֵב רבוע ס״ג ורבוע אהיה דֶּרֶךְ ב״פ יב״ק הַר־ רבוע אלהים - ה׳ שֵׂעִיר עַד קָדֵשׁ בַּרְנֵעַ: וַיְהִי אל בְּאַרְבָּעִים שָׁנָה בְּעַשְׁתֵּי־עָשָׂר חֹדֶשׁ י״ב הוויות בְּאֶחָד אהבה, דאגה לַחֹדֶשׁ י״ב הוויות דִּבֶּר ראה מֹשֶׁה מהש, אל שדי אֶל־בְּנֵי יִשְׂרָאֵל כְּכֹל ילי אֲשֶׁר צִוָּה פוי יְהֹוָהאדנייאהדונהי אֹתוֹ אֲלֵהֶם:

עַד אֲשֶׁר־יָנִיחַ יְהֹוָהאדנייאהדונהי | לַאֲחֵיכֶם כָּכֶם וְיָרְשׁוּ גַם־ יג״ל הֵם אֶת־הָאָרֶץ אלהים דההין ע״ה אֲשֶׁר יְהֹוָהאדנייאהדונהי אֱלֹהֵיכֶם ילה נֹתֵן אבגית״ץ, ושר, אהבת חנם לָהֶם בְּעֵבֶר רבוע יהוה ורבוע אלהים הַיַּרְדֵּן י״פ יהוה וד׳ אותיות וְשַׁבְתֶּם אִישׁ ע״ה קנ״א קס״א לִירֻשָּׁתוֹ אֲשֶׁר נָתַתִּי לָכֶם: וְאֶת־יְהוֹשׁוּעַ צִוֵּיתִי בָּעֵת י״פ אהיה י׳ הוויות הַהִוא לֵאמֹר עֵינֶיךָ ע״ה קס״א הָרֹאֹת אֵת כָּל־ ילי אֲשֶׁר עָשָׂה יְהֹוָהאדנייאהדונהי אֱלֹהֵיכֶם ילה לִשְׁנֵי הַמְּלָכִים הָאֵלֶּה כֵּן־יַעֲשֶׂה יְהֹוָהאדנייאהדונהי לְכָל־ יה אדני הַמַּמְלָכוֹת אֲשֶׁר אַתָּה עֹבֵר רבוע יהוה ורבוע אלהים שָׁמָּה מהש, משה, אל שדי: לֹא תִּירָאוּם כִּי יְהֹוָהאדנייאהדונהי אֱלֹהֵיכֶם ילה הוּא הַנִּלְחָם לָכֶם:

וָאֶתְחַנַּן אֶל־יְהֹוָה יאהדונהי בָּעֵת י"פ אהיה י' הויות הַהִוא לֵאמֹר: אֲדֹנָי ללה
יְהֹוִה יאהדונהי אַתָּה הַחִלּוֹתָ לְהַרְאוֹת אֶת־עַבְדְּךָ פוי אֶת־גָּדְלְךָ
וְאֶת־יָדְךָ בוכו הַחֲזָקָה אֲשֶׁר מִי־ ילי אֵל יי"א בַשָּׁמַיִם י"פ טל, י"פ כוזו
וּבָאָרֶץ אלהים דאלפין אֲשֶׁר־יַעֲשֶׂה כְמַעֲשֶׂיךָ וְכִגְבוּרֹתֶךָ: אֶעְבְּרָה־נָּא
וְאֶרְאֶה אֶת־הָאָרֶץ אלהים דההין ע"ה הַטּוֹבָה אכא אֲשֶׁר בְּעֵבֶר רבוע יהוה ורבוע אלהים
הַיַּרְדֵּן י"פ יהוה וד' אותיות הָהָר הַטּוֹב והו הַזֶּה והו וְהַלְּבָנֹן:

וַיִּקְרָא עם ה' אותיות = ב"פ קס"א מֹשֶׁה מהש, אל שדי אֶל־כָּל־ ילי יִשְׂרָאֵל וַיֹּאמֶר
אֲלֵהֶם שְׁמַע יִשְׂרָאֵל אֶת־הַחֻקִּים וְאֶת־הַמִּשְׁפָּטִים אֲשֶׁר אָנֹכִי איע דֹּבֵר
ראה בְּאָזְנֵיכֶם הַיּוֹם ע"ה = נגד, זן, מזבח וּלְמַדְתֶּם אֹתָם וּשְׁמַרְתֶּם לַעֲשֹׂתָם:
יְהֹוָה יאהדונהי אֱלֹהֵינוּ ילה כָּרַת עִמָּנוּ ריבוע ס"ג בְּרִית בְּחֹרֵב רבוע ס"ג ורבוע אהיה:
לֹא אֶת־אֲבֹתֵינוּ כָּרַת יְהֹוָה יאהדונהי אֶת־הַבְּרִית הַזֹּאת כִּי אִתָּנוּ אֲנַחְנוּ
אֵלֶּה פֹה מילה, ע"ה אלהים ע"ה מום הַיּוֹם ע"ה = נגד, זן, מזבח כֻּלָּנוּ חַיִּים בינה ע"ה:
פָּנִים ע"ב ס"ג מ"ה בְּפָנִים ע"ב ס"ג מ"ה | דִּבֶּר ראה יְהֹוָה יאהדונהי עִמָּכֶם
בָּהָר אור, רז, אין סוף מִתּוֹךְ הָאֵשׁ שאה: אָנֹכִי איע עֹמֵד בֵּין־יְהֹוָה יאהדונהי
וּבֵינֵיכֶם בָּעֵת י"פ אהיה י' הויות הַהִוא לְהַגִּיד לָכֶם אֶת־דְּבַר ראה יְהֹוָה יאהדונהי
כִּי יְרֵאתֶם מִפְּנֵי חכמה בינה הָאֵשׁ שאה וְלֹא־עֲלִיתֶם בָּהָר אור, רז, אין סוף לֵאמֹר:
(*Keter*) אָנֹכִי איע יְהֹוָה יאהדונהי אֱלֹהֶיךָ ילה אֲשֶׁר הוֹצֵאתִיךָ מֵאֶרֶץ אלהים דאלפין
מִצְרַיִם מצר מִבֵּית ב"פ ראה עֲבָדִים: (*Chochmah*) לֹא יִהְיֶה־ ייי לְךָ אֱלֹהִים ילה
אֲחֵרִים עַל־פָּנָי חכמה בינה לֹא תַעֲשֶׂה־לְךָ פֶסֶל | כָּל־ ילי תְּמוּנָה אֲשֶׁר
בַּשָּׁמַיִם י"פ טל, י"פ כוזו מִמַּעַל עלם וַאֲשֶׁר בָּאָרֶץ אלהים דאלפין מִתָּחַת וַאֲשֶׁר
בַּמַּיִם | מִתַּחַת לָאָרֶץ אלהים דאלפין לֹא־תִשְׁתַּחֲוֶה לָהֶם וְלֹא תָעָבְדֵם כִּי
אָנֹכִי איע יְהֹוָה יאהדונהי אֱלֹהֶיךָ ילה אֵל יי"א קַנָּא מקוה, קנ"א, אלהים אדני
פֹּקֵד רבוע ע"ב עֲוֹן ג"פ מ"ב אָבוֹת עַל־בָּנִים וְעַל־שִׁלֵּשִׁים וְעַל־רִבֵּעִים לְשֹׂנְאָי
וְעֹשֶׂה חֶסֶד ע"ב, ריבוע יהוה לַאֲלָפִים קס"א לְאֹהֲבַי וּלְשֹׁמְרֵי מִצְוֹתָי (כתיב: מצותו):
(*Binah*) לֹא תִשָּׂא אֶת־שֵׁם־ יהוה שדי יְהֹוָה יאהדונהי אֱלֹהֶיךָ ילה לַשָּׁוְא כִּי לֹא
יְנַקֶּה יְהֹוָה יאהדונהי אֵת אֲשֶׁר־יִשָּׂא אֶת־שְׁמוֹ מהש ע"ה, אל שדי ע"ה לַשָּׁוְא:
(*Chesed*) שָׁמוֹר אֶת־יוֹם ע"ה = נגד, זן, מזבח הַשַּׁבָּת לְקַדְּשׁוֹ כַּאֲשֶׁר צִוְּךָ |
יְהֹוָה יאהדונהי אֱלֹהֶיךָ ילה שֵׁשֶׁת יָמִים נלך תַּעֲבֹד וְעָשִׂיתָ כָּל־ ילי
מְלַאכְתֶּךָ וְיוֹם ע"ה = נגד, זן, מזבח הַשְּׁבִיעִי שַׁבָּת | לַיהֹוָה יאהדונהי אֱלֹהֶיךָ ילה

לֹא תַעֲשֶׂה כָל־ ילי מְלָאכָה אל אדני אַתָּה וּבִנְךָ־וּבִתֶּךָ וְעַבְדְּךָ־ פוי וַאֲמָתֶךָ
וְשׁוֹרְךָ וַחֲמֹרְךָ וְכָל־ ילי בְּהֶמְתֶּךָ וְגֵרְךָ אֲשֶׁר בִּשְׁעָרֶיךָ לְמַעַן יָנוּחַ עַבְדְּךָ פוי
וַאֲמָתְךָ כָּמוֹךָ אלהים, מום וְזָכַרְתָּ כִּי־עֶבֶד הָיִיתָ | בְּאֶרֶץ אלהים דאלפין מִצְרַיִם מצר
וַיֹּצִאֲךָ יְהֹוָה אהדונהי אֱלֹהֶיךָ ילה מִשָּׁם יהוה שדי בְּיָד חֲזָקָה פהל וּבִזְרֹעַ נְטוּיָה
עַל־כֵּן צִוְּךָ יְהֹוָה אהדונהי אֱלֹהֶיךָ ילה לַעֲשׂוֹת אֶת־יוֹם ע״ה = נגד, זן, מזבח הַשַּׁבָּת׃
(*Gevurah*) כַּבֵּד אֶת־אָבִיךָ וְאֶת־אִמֶּךָ כַּאֲשֶׁר צִוְּךָ יְהֹוָה אהדונהי אֱלֹהֶיךָ ילה
לְמַעַן | יַאֲרִיכֻן יָמֶיךָ וּלְמַעַן יִיטַב לָךְ עַל הָאֲדָמָה אֲשֶׁר־יְהֹוָה אהדונהי
אֱלֹהֶיךָ ילה נֹתֵן אבגית״ץ, ושר, אהבת חנם לָךְ׃ (*Tiferet*) לֹא תִּרְצָח׃
(*Netzach*) וְלֹא תִּנְאָף׃ (*Hod*) וְלֹא תִּגְנֹב׃ (*Yesod*) וְלֹא־תַעֲנֶה בְרֵעֲךָ
עֵד שָׁוְא׃ (*Malchut*) וְלֹא תַחְמֹד אֵשֶׁת רֵעֶךָ וְלֹא תִתְאַוֶּה בֵּית ב״פ ראה
רֵעֶךָ שָׂדֵהוּ וְעַבְדּוֹ וַאֲמָתוֹ שׁוֹרוֹ וַחֲמֹרוֹ וְכֹל ילי אֲשֶׁר לְרֵעֶךָ׃
אֶת־הַדְּבָרִים ראה הָאֵלֶּה דִּבֶּר ראה יְהֹוָה אהדונהי אֶל־כָּל־ ילי קְהַלְכֶם
בָּהָר אור, רז מִתּוֹךְ הָאֵשׁ שאה הֶעָנָן וְהָעֲרָפֶל קוֹל ע״ב ס״ג ע״ה
גָּדוֹל להח, מבה, יזל, הום וְלֹא יָסָף וַיִּכְתְּבֵם עַל־שְׁנֵי לֻחֹת אֲבָנִים וַיִּתְּנֵם אֵלָי׃
וַיְהִי אל כְּשָׁמְעֲכֶם אֶת־הַקּוֹל ע״ב ס״ג ע״ה מִתּוֹךְ הַחֹשֶׁךְ ש״ך ניצוצות של ח׳ מלכים
וְהָהָר בֹּעֵר בָּאֵשׁ אלהים דיודין ע״ה וַתִּקְרְבוּן אֵלַי כָּל־ ילי רָאשֵׁי שִׁבְטֵיכֶם
וְזִקְנֵיכֶם׃ וַתֹּאמְרוּ הֵן הֶרְאָנוּ יְהֹוָה אהדונהי אֱלֹהֵינוּ ילה אֶת־כְּבֹדוֹ וְאֶת־גָּדְלוֹ
וְאֶת־קֹלוֹ שָׁמַעְנוּ מִתּוֹךְ הָאֵשׁ שאה הַיּוֹם ע״ה = נגד, זן, מזבח הַזֶּה והו רָאִינוּ כִּי־
יְדַבֵּר ראה אֱלֹהִים מום, אהיה אדני ; ילה אֶת־הָאָדָם מ״ה וָחָי׃ וְעַתָּה לָמָּה מ״ה נָמוּת
כִּי תֹאכְלֵנוּ הָאֵשׁ שאה הַגְּדֹלָה הַזֹּאת אִם־ יוהך, ע״ה מ״ב יֹסְפִים | אֲנַחְנוּ לִשְׁמֹעַ
אֶת־קוֹל ע״ב ס״ג ע״ה יְהֹוָה אהדונהי אֱלֹהֵינוּ ילה עוֹד וָמָתְנוּ׃ כִּי מִי ילי כָל־ ילי
בָּשָׂר אֲשֶׁר שָׁמַע קוֹל ע״ב ס״ג ע״ה אֱלֹהִים מום, אהיה אדני ; ילה חַיִּים בינה ע״ה
מְדַבֵּר ראה מִתּוֹךְ־הָאֵשׁ שאה כָּמֹנוּ וַיֶּחִי׃ קְרַב אַתָּה וּשְׁמָע אֵת כָּל־ ילי אֲשֶׁר
יֹאמַר יְהֹוָה אהדונהי אֱלֹהֵינוּ ילה וְאַתְּ | תְּדַבֵּר ראה אֵלֵינוּ אֵת כָּל־ ילי אֲשֶׁר
יְדַבֵּר ראה יְהֹוָה אהדונהי אֱלֹהֵינוּ ילה אֵלֶיךָ אני וְשָׁמַעְנוּ וְעָשִׂינוּ׃ וַיִּשְׁמַע
יְהֹוָה אהדונהי אֶת־קוֹל ע״ב ס״ג ע״ה דִּבְרֵיכֶם ראה בְּדַבֶּרְכֶם ראה אֵלָי וַיֹּאמֶר
יְהֹוָה אהדונהי אֵלַי שָׁמַעְתִּי אֶת־קוֹל ע״ב ס״ג ע״ה דִּבְרֵי ראה הָעָם הַזֶּה והו אֲשֶׁר
דִּבְּרוּ ראה אֵלֶיךָ אני הֵיטִיבוּ כָּל־ ילי אֲשֶׁר דִּבֵּרוּ ראה׃ מִי־ ילי יִתֵּן וְהָיָה יהוה, יהה
לְבָבָם זֶה לָהֶם לְיִרְאָה רי״ו, גבורה אֹתִי וְלִשְׁמֹר אֶת־כָּל־ ילי מִצְוֹתַי
כָּל־ ילי הַיָּמִים נלך לְמַעַן יִיטַב לָהֶם וְלִבְנֵיהֶם לְעֹלָם ריבוע ס״ג וי׳ אותיות׃

לֵּךְ אֱמֹר לָהֶם שׁוּבוּ לָכֶם לְאָהֳלֵיכֶם: וְאַתָּה פֹּה מילה, ע"ה אלהים, ע"ה מום עֲמֹד עִמָּדִי וַאֲדַבְּרָה אֵלֶיךָ אני אֵת כָּל־ ילי הַמִּצְוָה וְהַחֻקִּים וְהַמִּשְׁפָּטִים אֲשֶׁר תְּלַמְּדֵם וְעָשׂוּ בָאָרֶץ אלהים דאלפין אֲשֶׁר אָנֹכִי איע נֹתֵן אבגית"ץ, ושר, אהבת חנם לָהֶם לְרִשְׁתָּהּ: וּשְׁמַרְתֶּם לַעֲשׂוֹת כַּאֲשֶׁר צִוָּה פוי יְהֹוָאדֹנָיאהדונהי אֱלֹהֵיכֶם ילה אֶתְכֶם לֹא תָסֻרוּ יָמִין וּשְׂמֹאל: בְּכָל־ ב"ן, לכב, יבמ הַדֶּרֶךְ ב"פ יב"ק אֲשֶׁר צִוָּה פוי יְהֹוָאדֹנָיאהדונהי אֱלֹהֵיכֶם ילה אֶתְכֶם תֵּלֵכוּ לְמַעַן תִּחְיוּן וְטוֹב והו לָכֶם וְהַאֲרַכְתֶּם יָמִים נלך בָּאָרֶץ אלהים דאלפין אֲשֶׁר תִּירָשׁוּן: וְזֹאת הַמִּצְוָה הַחֻקִּים וְהַמִּשְׁפָּטִים אֲשֶׁר צִוָּה פוי יְהֹוָאדֹנָיאהדונהי אֱלֹהֵיכֶם ילה לְלַמֵּד אֶתְכֶם לַעֲשׂוֹת בָּאָרֶץ אלהים דאלפין אֲשֶׁר אַתֶּם עֹבְרִים שָׁמָּה מהש, משה, אל שדי לְרִשְׁתָּהּ: לְמַעַן תִּירָא אֶת־יְהֹוָאדֹנָיאהדונהי אֱלֹהֶיךָ ילה לִשְׁמֹר אֶת־ כָּל־ ילי חֻקֹּתָיו וּמִצְוֹתָיו אֲשֶׁר אָנֹכִי איע מְצַוֶּךָ אַתָּה וּבִנְךָ וּבֶן־בִּנְךָ כֹּל ילי יְמֵי חַיֶּיךָ וּלְמַעַן יַאֲרִכֻן יָמֶיךָ: וְשָׁמַעְתָּ יִשְׂרָאֵל וְשָׁמַרְתָּ לַעֲשׂוֹת אֲשֶׁר יִיטַב לְךָ וַאֲשֶׁר תִּרְבּוּן מְאֹד מ"ה כַּאֲשֶׁר דִּבֶּר ראה יְהֹוָאדֹנָיאהדונהי אֱלֹהֵי דמב, ילה אֲבֹתֶיךָ לָךְ אֶרֶץ אלהים דאלפין זָבַת חָלָב וּדְבָשׁ: שְׁמַע יִשְׂרָאֵל יְהֹוָאדֹנָיאהדונהי אֱלֹהֵינוּ ילה יְהֹוָאדֹנָיאהדונהי | אֶחָד אהבה, דאגה: וְאָהַבְתָּ ב"פ רז, ב"פ אור, ב"פ א"ס אֵת יְהֹוָאדֹנָיאהדונהי אֱלֹהֶיךָ ילה בְּכָל־ ב"ן, לכב, יבמ לְבָבְךָ וּבְכָל־ ב"ן, לכב, יבמ נַפְשְׁךָ וּבְכָל־ ב"ן, לכב, יבמ מְאֹדֶךָ: וְהָיוּ הַדְּבָרִים ראה הָאֵלֶּה אֲשֶׁר אָנֹכִי איע מְצַוְּךָ הַיּוֹם ע"ה = נגד, זן, מזבח עַל־לְבָבֶךָ: וְשִׁנַּנְתָּם לְבָנֶיךָ וְדִבַּרְתָּ ראה בָּם מ"ב בְּשִׁבְתְּךָ בְּבֵיתֶךָ ב"פ ראה וּבְלֶכְתְּךָ בַדֶּרֶךְ ב"פ יב"ק וּבְשָׁכְבְּךָ וּבְקוּמֶךָ: וּקְשַׁרְתָּם לְאוֹת עַל־יָדֶךָ וְהָיוּ לְטֹטָפֹת בֵּין עֵינֶיךָ ע"ה קס"א: וּכְתַבְתָּם עַל־מְזֻזוֹת נית, זו מות בֵּיתֶךָ ב"פ ראה וּבִשְׁעָרֶיךָ:

וְיָדַעְתָּ כִּי־יְהֹוָאדֹנָיאהדונהי אֱלֹהֶיךָ ילה הוּא הָאֱלֹהִים מום, אהיה אדני ; ילה הָאֵל לאה (אלד ע"ה) הַנֶּאֱמָן שֹׁמֵר הַבְּרִית וְהַחֶסֶד ע"ב, ריבוע יהוה לְאֹהֲבָיו וּלְשֹׁמְרֵי מִצְוֹתָו לְאֶלֶף אל שדי במילוי ע"ה דּוֹר: וּמְשַׁלֵּם לְשֹׂנְאָיו אֶל־פָּנָיו לְהַאֲבִידוֹ לֹא יְאַחֵר לְשֹׂנְאוֹ אֶל־ פָּנָיו יְשַׁלֶּם־לוֹ: וְשָׁמַרְתָּ אֶת־הַמִּצְוָה וְאֶת־הַחֻקִּים וְאֶת־הַמִּשְׁפָּטִים אֲשֶׁר אָנֹכִי איע מְצַוְּךָ הַיּוֹם ע"ה = נגד, זן, מזבח לַעֲשׂוֹתָם:

וְהָיָה יהוה, הי"י | עֵקֶב תִּשְׁמְעוּן אֵת הַמִּשְׁפָּטִים הָאֵלֶּה וּשְׁמַרְתֶּם וַעֲשִׂיתֶם אֹתָם וְשָׁמַר יְהֹוָאדֹנָיאהדונהי אֱלֹהֶיךָ ילה לְךָ אֶת־הַבְּרִית וְאֶת־הַחֶסֶד ע"ב, ריבוע יהוה אֲשֶׁר נִשְׁבַּע לַאֲבֹתֶיךָ:

וַאֲהֵבְךָ וּבֵרַכְךָ וְהִרְבֶּךָ וּבֵרַךְ פְּרִי־ ע"ה אלהים דאלפין בִטְנְךָ וּפְרִי־ ע"ה אלהים דאלפין אַדְמָתֶךָ דְּגָנְךָ וְתִירֹשְׁךָ וְיִצְהָרֶךָ שְׁגַר־אֲלָפֶיךָ וְעַשְׁתְּרֹת צֹאנֶךָ עַל הָאֲדָמָה אֲשֶׁר־נִשְׁבַּע לַאֲבֹתֶיךָ לָתֶת לָךְ: בָּרוּךְ יהוה ע"ב ורבוע מ"ה תִּהְיֶה מִכָּל־ ילי הָעַמִּים ע"ה קס"א לֹא־יִהְיֶה ייי בְךָ עָקָר וַעֲקָרָה וּבִבְהֶמְתֶּךָ: וְהֵסִיר יְהֹוָה אדני יאהדונהי מִמְּךָ כָּל־ ילי חֹלִי וְכָל־ ע"ה קס"א מַדְוֵי מִצְרַיִם מצר הָרָעִים ה"פ אדני, שכ"ה אֲשֶׁר יָדַעְתָּ לֹא יְשִׂימָם בָּךְ וּנְתָנָם בְּכָל־ ב"ן, לכב, יבמ שֹׂנְאֶיךָ: וְאָכַלְתָּ אֶת־כָּל־ ילי הָעַמִּים ע"ה קס"א אֲשֶׁר יְהֹוָה אדני יאהדונהי אֱלֹהֶיךָ ילה נֹתֵן אבגית"ץ, ושר, אהבת חנם לָךְ לֹא־תָחוֹס עֵינְךָ ריבוע מ"ה עֲלֵיהֶם וְלֹא תַעֲבֹד אֶת־אֱלֹהֵיהֶם ילה כִּי־מוֹקֵשׁ הוּא לָךְ:

וְהָיָה יהוה, הוי אִם־ יוהך, ע"ה מ"ב שָׁמֹעַ תִּשְׁמְעוּ אֶל־מִצְוֹתַי אֲשֶׁר אָנֹכִי איע מְצַוֶּה אֶתְכֶם הַיּוֹם ע"ה = נגד, זן, מזבח לְאַהֲבָה אחד, דאגה אֶת־יְהֹוָה אדני יאהדונהי אֱלֹהֵיכֶם ילה וּלְעָבְדוֹ בְּכָל־ ב"ן, לכב, יבמ לְבַבְכֶם וּבְכָל־ ב"ן, לכב, יבמ נַפְשְׁכֶם: וְנָתַתִּי מְטַר־ אברהם ע"ה, רמ"ח ע"ה, וז"פ אל ע"ה אַרְצְכֶם בְּעִתּוֹ יוֹרֶה וּמַלְקוֹשׁ וְאָסַפְתָּ דְגָנֶךָ וְתִירֹשְׁךָ וְיִצְהָרֶךָ: וְנָתַתִּי עֵשֶׂב ע"ב שמות בְּשָׂדְךָ לִבְהֶמְתֶּךָ וְאָכַלְתָּ וְשָׂבָעְתָּ: הִשָּׁמְרוּ לָכֶם פֶּן יִפְתֶּה לְבַבְכֶם וְסַרְתֶּם וַעֲבַדְתֶּם אֱלֹהִים אֲחֵרִים וְהִשְׁתַּחֲוִיתֶם לָהֶם: וְחָרָה אַף־יְהֹוָה אדני יאהדונהי בָּכֶם ב"פ אל וְעָצַר אֶת־הַשָּׁמַיִם י"פ טל, י"פ כוזו וְלֹא־יִהְיֶה ייי מָטָר אברהם ע"ה, רמ"ח ע"ה, וז"פ אל ע"ה וְהָאֲדָמָה לֹא תִתֵּן ב"פ כהת אֶת־יְבוּלָהּ וַאֲבַדְתֶּם מְהֵרָה מֵעַל עלם הָאָרֶץ אלהים דההין ע"ה הַטֹּבָה אֲשֶׁר יְהֹוָה אדני יאהדונהי נֹתֵן אבגית"ץ, ושר, אהבת חנם לָכֶם: וְשַׂמְתֶּם אֶת־דְּבָרַי ראה אֵלֶּה עַל־לְבַבְכֶם וְעַל־נַפְשְׁכֶם וּקְשַׁרְתֶּם אֹתָם לְאוֹת עַל־יֶדְכֶם וְהָיוּ לְטוֹטָפֹת בֵּין עֵינֵיכֶם ריבוע מ"ה: וְלִמַּדְתֶּם אֹתָם אֶת־בְּנֵיכֶם לְדַבֵּר ראה בָּם מ"ב בְּשִׁבְתְּךָ בְּבֵיתֶךָ וּבְלֶכְתְּךָ בַדֶּרֶךְ ב"פ יב"ק וּבְשָׁכְבְּךָ וּבְקוּמֶךָ: וּכְתַבְתָּם עַל־מְזוּזוֹת בֵּיתֶךָ ב"פ ראה וּבִשְׁעָרֶיךָ: לְמַעַן יִרְבּוּ יְמֵיכֶם וִימֵי בְנֵיכֶם עַל הָאֲדָמָה אֲשֶׁר נִשְׁבַּע יְהֹוָה אדני יאהדונהי לַאֲבֹתֵיכֶם לָתֵת לָהֶם כִּימֵי הַשָּׁמַיִם י"פ טל, י"פ כוזו עַל־הָאָרֶץ אלהים דההין ע"ה: כִּי אִם־ יוהך, ע"ה מ"ב שָׁמֹר תִּשְׁמְרוּן אֶת־כָּל־ ילי הַמִּצְוָה הַזֹּאת אֲשֶׁר אָנֹכִי איע מְצַוֶּה אֶתְכֶם לַעֲשֹׂתָהּ לְאַהֲבָה אחד, דאגה אֶת־יְהֹוָה אדני יאהדונהי אֱלֹהֵיכֶם ילה לָלֶכֶת בְּכָל־ ב"ן, לכב, יבמ דְּרָכָיו וּלְדָבְקָה־בוֹ: וְהוֹרִישׁ יְהֹוָה אדני יאהדונהי אֶת־כָּל־ ילי הַגּוֹיִם הָאֵלֶּה מִלִּפְנֵיכֶם וִירִשְׁתֶּם גּוֹיִם גְּדֹלִים וַעֲצֻמִים מִכֶּם:

כָּל־ ילי הַמָּקוֹם יהוה ברבוע, ו״פ אל אֲשֶׁר תִּדְרֹךְ רבוע עסמ״ב כַּף־רַגְלְכֶם בּוֹ לָכֶם
יִהְיֶה ייי מִן־הַמִּדְבָּר וְהַלְּבָנוֹן מִן־הַנָּהָר נְהַר־פְּרָת וְעַד הַיָּם ילי הָאַחֲרוֹן
יִהְיֶה ייי גְּבֻלְכֶם: לֹא־יִתְיַצֵּב אִישׁ ע״ה קנ״א קס״א בִּפְנֵיכֶם פַּחְדְּכֶם וּמוֹרַאֲכֶם
יִתֵּן | יְהֹוָהאדניאהדונהי אֱלֹהֵיכֶם ילה עַל־פְּנֵי חכמה בינה כָּל־ ילי הָאָרֶץ אלהים דההין ע״ה
אֲשֶׁר תִּדְרְכוּ־בָהּ כַּאֲשֶׁר דִּבֶּר ראה לָכֶם:

רְאֵה ראה אָנֹכִי איע נֹתֵן אבג״ית״ץ, ושר, אהבת חנם לִפְנֵיכֶם הַיּוֹם ע״ה = נגד, זן, מזבח
בְּרָכָה וּקְלָלָה: אֶת־הַבְּרָכָה עסמ״ב אֲשֶׁר תִּשְׁמְעוּ אֶל־מִצְוֹת יְהֹוָהאדניאהדונהי
אֱלֹהֵיכֶם ילה אֲשֶׁר אָנֹכִי איע מְצַוֶּה אֶתְכֶם הַיּוֹם ע״ה = נגד, זן, מזבח: וְהַקְּלָלָה
אִם־ יוהך, ע״ה מ״ב לֹא תִשְׁמְעוּ אֶל־מִצְוֹת יְהֹוָהאדניאהדונהי אֱלֹהֵיכֶם ילה וְסַרְתֶּם
מִן־הַדֶּרֶךְ ב״פ יב״ק אֲשֶׁר אָנֹכִי איע מְצַוֶּה אֶתְכֶם הַיּוֹם ע״ה = נגד, זן, מזבח לָלֶכֶת
אַחֲרֵי אֱלֹהִים אֲחֵרִים אֲשֶׁר לֹא־יְדַעְתֶּם:

שִׁבְעָה שָׁבֻעֹת תִּסְפָּר־לָךְ מֵהָחֵל חֶרְמֵשׁ בַּקָּמָה תָּחֵל לִסְפֹּר שִׁבְעָה שָׁבֻעוֹת:
וְעָשִׂיתָ חַג שָׁבֻעוֹת לַיהֹוָהאדניאהדונהי אֱלֹהֶיךָ ילה מִסַּת נִדְבַת יָדְךָ בוכ״ו אֲשֶׁר
תִּתֵּן ב״פ כהת כַּאֲשֶׁר יְבָרֶכְךָ יְהֹוָהאדניאהדונהי אֱלֹהֶיךָ ילה: וְשָׂמַחְתָּ לִפְנֵי
חכמה בינה | יְהֹוָהאדניאהדונהי אֱלֹהֶיךָ ילה אַתָּה וּבִנְךָ וּבִתֶּךָ וְעַבְדְּךָ פוי וַאֲמָתֶךָ
וְהַלֵּוִי דמב, מלוי ע״ב אֲשֶׁר בִּשְׁעָרֶיךָ וְהַגֵּר ד״פ ב״ן וְהַיָּתוֹם יוסף, ציון, ו״פ יהוה
וְהָאַלְמָנָה כוק, רבוע אדני אֲשֶׁר בְּקִרְבֶּךָ בַּמָּקוֹם יהוה ברבוע, ו״פ אל אֲשֶׁר יִבְחַר
יְהֹוָהאדניאהדונהי אֱלֹהֶיךָ ילה לְשַׁכֵּן ש״ע שְׁמוֹ מהש ע״ה, אל שדי ע״ה שָׁם שדי יהוה:
וְזָכַרְתָּ כִּי־עֶבֶד הָיִיתָ בְּמִצְרָיִם מצר וְשָׁמַרְתָּ וְעָשִׂיתָ אֶת־הַחֻקִּים הָאֵלֶּה: חַג
הַסֻּכֹּת סאל תַּעֲשֶׂה לְךָ שִׁבְעַת יָמִים נלך בְּאָסְפְּךָ מִגָּרְנְךָ וּמִיִּקְבֶךָ: וְשָׂמַחְתָּ
בְּחַגֶּךָ אַתָּה וּבִנְךָ וּבִתֶּךָ וְעַבְדְּךָ פוי וַאֲמָתֶךָ וְהַלֵּוִי דמב, מלוי ע״ב וְהַגֵּר ד״פ ב״ן
וְהַיָּתוֹם יוסף, ציון, ו״פ יהוה וְהָאַלְמָנָה כוק, רבוע אדני אֲשֶׁר בִּשְׁעָרֶיךָ: שִׁבְעַת
יָמִים נלך תָּחֹג לַיהֹוָהאדניאהדונהי אֱלֹהֶיךָ ילה בַּמָּקוֹם יהוה ברבוע, ו״פ אל אֲשֶׁר־יִבְחַר
יְהֹוָהאדניאהדונהי כִּי יְבָרֶכְךָ יְהֹוָהאדניאהדונהי אֱלֹהֶיךָ ילה בְּכֹל ב״ן, לכב, יבמ תְּבוּאָתְךָ
וּבְכֹל ב״ן, לכב, יבמ מַעֲשֵׂה יָדֶיךָ וְהָיִיתָ אַךְ אהיה שָׂמֵחַ ס״ת חת״ך: שָׁלוֹשׁ פְּעָמִים |
בַּשָּׁנָה יֵרָאֶה רי״ו, גבורה כָל־ ילי זְכוּרְךָ אֶת־פְּנֵי חכמה בינה | יְהֹוָהאדניאהדונהי
אֱלֹהֶיךָ ילה בַּמָּקוֹם יהוה ברבוע, ו״פ אל אֲשֶׁר יִבְחָר בְּחַג הַמַּצּוֹת וּבְחַג הַשָּׁבֻעוֹת
וּבְחַג הַסֻּכּוֹת וְלֹא יֵרָאֶה רי״ו, גבורה אֶת־פְּנֵי חכמה בינה יְהֹוָהאדניאהדונהי רֵיקָם:
אִישׁ ע״ה קנ״א קס״א כְּמַתְּנַת יָדוֹ כְּבִרְכַּת יְהֹוָהאדניאהדונהי אֱלֹהֶיךָ ילה
אֲשֶׁר נָתַן־לָךְ:

שֹׁפְטִים וְשֹׁטְרִים תִּתֶּן־ ב"פ כהת לְךָ בְּכָל־ ב"ן, לכב, יבמ שְׁעָרֶיךָ אֲשֶׁר יְהֹוָ֣אדנה֣יאהדונהי אֱלֹהֶיךָ ילה נֹתֵן אבג"ית"ץ, ושר, אהבת חנם לְךָ לִשְׁבָטֶיךָ וְשָׁפְטוּ אֶת־הָעָם מִשְׁפַּט־ ע"ה ה"פ אלהים צֶדֶק: לֹא־תַטֶּה מִשְׁפָּט ע"ה ה"פ אלהים לֹא תַכִּיר פָּנִים ע"ב ס"ג מ"ה וְלֹא־תִקַּח רבוע אהיה דאלפין שֹׁחַד כִּי הַשֹּׁחַד יְעַוֵּר עֵינֵי ריבוע מ"ה חֲכָמִים וִיסַלֵּף דִּבְרֵי ראה צַדִּיקִם: צֶדֶק צֶדֶק תִּרְדֹּף לְמַעַן תִּחְיֶה וְיָרַשְׁתָּ אֶת־הָאָרֶץ אלהים דההין ע"ה אֲשֶׁר־יְהֹוָ֣אדנה֣יאהדונהי אֱלֹהֶיךָ ילה נֹתֵן אבג"ית"ץ, ושר, אהבת חנם לָךְ:

וְעָנוּ ג"פ מ"ב, רבוע אדני וְאָמְרוּ יָדֵינוּ יה אדני לֹא שָׁפְכוּ (כתיב: שפכה) אֶת־הַדָּם רבוע אהיה הַזֶּה והו וְעֵינֵינוּ ריבוע מ"ה לֹא רָאוּ: כַּפֵּר מצפצ לְעַמְּךָ ה' הויות, נמם יִשְׂרָאֵל אֲשֶׁר־פָּדִיתָ יְהֹוָ֣אדנה֣יאהדונהי וְאַל־תִּתֵּן ב"פ כהת דָּם רבוע אהיה נָקִי ע"ה קס"א בְּקֶרֶב קמ"ג קס"א עַמְּךָ ה' הויות, נמם יִשְׂרָאֵל וְנִכַּפֵּר לָהֶם הַדָּם רבוע אהיה: וְאַתָּה תְּבַעֵר הַדָּם רבוע אהיה הַנָּקִי ע"ה קס"א מִקִּרְבֶּךָ כִּי־תַעֲשֶׂה הַיָּשָׁר בְּעֵינֵי ריבוע מ"ה יְהֹוָ֣אדנה֣יאהדונהי:

כִּי־תֵצֵא לַמִּלְחָמָה עַל־אֹיְבֶיךָ וּנְתָנוֹ אבג"ית"ץ, ושר, אהבת חנם יְהֹוָ֣אדנה֣יאהדונהי אֱלֹהֶיךָ ילה בְּיָדֶךָ בוכ"ו וְשָׁבִיתָ שִׁבְיוֹ: וְרָאִיתָ בַּשִּׁבְיָה אֵשֶׁת יְפַת־תֹּאַר וְחָשַׁקְתָּ בָהּ וְלָקַחְתָּ לְךָ לְאִשָּׁה: וַהֲבֵאתָהּ אֶל־תּוֹךְ בֵּיתֶךָ ב"פ ראה וְגִלְּחָה אֶת־רֹאשָׁהּ וְעָשְׂתָה אֶת־צִפָּרְנֶיהָ: וְהֵסִירָה אֶת־שִׂמְלַת שִׁבְיָהּ מֵעָלֶיהָ פהל וְיָשְׁבָה בְּבֵיתֶךָ ב"פ ראה וּבָכְתָה אֶת־אָבִיהָ וְאֶת־אִמָּהּ יֶרַח יָמִים נלך וְאַחַר כֵּן תָּבוֹא אֵלֶיהָ וּבְעַלְתָּהּ וְהָיְתָה לְךָ לְאִשָּׁה: וְהָיָה יהוה, יהה אִם־ יוהך, ע"ה מ"ב לֹא חָפַצְתָּ בָּהּ וְשִׁלַּחְתָּהּ לְנַפְשָׁהּ וּמָכֹר י' הויות לֹא־תִמְכְּרֶנָּה בַּכָּסֶף לֹא־תִתְעַמֵּר בָּהּ תַּחַת אֲשֶׁר עִנִּיתָהּ:

זָכוֹר ע"ב קס"א אֵת אֲשֶׁר־עָשָׂה לְךָ עֲמָלֵק ב"פ ק"ך בַּדֶּרֶךְ ב"פ יב"ק בְּצֵאתְכֶם מִמִּצְרָיִם מצר: אֲשֶׁר קָרְךָ בַּדֶּרֶךְ ב"פ יב"ק וַיְזַנֵּב בְּךָ כָּל־ ילי הַנֶּחֱשָׁלִים אַחֲרֶיךָ וְאַתָּה עָיֵף וְיָגֵעַ וְלֹא יָרֵא אלף למד יהוה אֱלֹהִים מום, אהיה אדני ; ילה: וְהָיָה יהוה, יהה בְּהָנִיחַ יְהֹוָ֣אדנה֣יאהדונהי אֱלֹהֶיךָ ילה | לְךָ מִכָּל־ ילי אֹיְבֶיךָ מִסָּבִיב בָּאָרֶץ אלהים דאלפין אֲשֶׁר יְהֹוָ֣אדנה֣יאהדונהי אֱלֹהֶיךָ ילה נֹתֵן אבג"ית"ץ, ושר, אהבת חנם לְךָ נַחֲלָה לְרִשְׁתָּהּ תִּמְחֶה אֶת־זֵכֶר עֲמָלֵק ב"פ ק"ך מִתַּחַת הַשָּׁמָיִם י"פ טל, י"פ כוזו לֹא תִשְׁכָּח ע"ה קרעשטן:

וְהָיָה יהוה, הי"י כִּי־תָבוֹא אֶל־הָאָרֶץ אלהים דההין ע"ה אֲשֶׁר יְהֹוָה אהדונהי אֱלֹהֶיךָ ילה נֹתֵן אבגית"ץ, ושר, אהבת חנם לְךָ נַחֲלָה וִירִשְׁתָּהּ וְיָשַׁבְתָּ בָּהּ: וְלָקַחְתָּ מֵרֵאשִׁית | כָּל־ ילי פְּרִי ע"ה אלהים דאלפין הָאֲדָמָה אֲשֶׁר תָּבִיא מֵאַרְצְךָ אֲשֶׁר יְהֹוָה אהדונהי אֱלֹהֶיךָ ילה נֹתֵן אבגית"ץ, ושר, אהבת חנם לָךְ וְשַׂמְתָּ בַטֶּנֶא וְהָלַכְתָּ אֶל־הַמָּקוֹם יהוה ברבוע, ו"פ אל אֲשֶׁר יִבְחַר יְהֹוָה אהדונהי אֱלֹהֶיךָ ילה לְשַׁכֵּן ש"ע שְׁמוֹ מהש ע"ה, אל שדי ע"ה שָׁם שדי יהוה: וּבָאתָ אֶל־הַכֹּהֵן מלה אֲשֶׁר יִהְיֶה ייי בַּיָּמִים נלך הָהֵם וְאָמַרְתָּ אֵלָיו הִגַּדְתִּי הַיּוֹם ע"ה = נגד, זן, מזבח לַיהֹוָה אהדונהי אֱלֹהֶיךָ ילה כִּי־בָאתִי אֶל־הָאָרֶץ אלהים דההין ע"ה אֲשֶׁר נִשְׁבַּע יְהֹוָה אהדונהי לַאֲבֹתֵינוּ לָתֶת לָנוּ מום, אלהים, אהיה אדני:

וַתָּבֹאוּ אֶל־הַמָּקוֹם יהוה ברבוע, ו"פ אל הַזֶּה והו וַיֵּצֵא סִיחֹן מֶלֶךְ־חֶשְׁבּוֹן וְעוֹג מֶלֶךְ־הַבָּשָׁן לִקְרָאתֵנוּ לַמִּלְחָמָה וַנַּכֵּם: וַנִּקַּח אֶת־אַרְצָם וַנִּתְּנָהּ לְנַחֲלָה לָראוּבֵנִי וְלַגָּדִי וְלַחֲצִי שֵׁבֶט הַמְנַשִּׁי: וּשְׁמַרְתֶּם אֶת־דִּבְרֵי ראה הַבְּרִית הַזֹּאת וַעֲשִׂיתֶם אֹתָם לְמַעַן תַּשְׂכִּילוּ אֵת כָּל־ ילי אֲשֶׁר תַּעֲשׂוּן:

אַתֶּם נִצָּבִים הַיּוֹם ע"ה = נגד, זן, מזבח כֻּלְּכֶם לִפְנֵי חכמה בינה יְהֹוָה אהדונהי אֱלֹהֵיכֶם ילה רָאשֵׁיכֶם שִׁבְטֵיכֶם זִקְנֵיכֶם וְשֹׁטְרֵיכֶם כֹּל ילי אִישׁ ע"ה קנ"א קס"א יִשְׂרָאֵל: טַפְּכֶם נְשֵׁיכֶם וְגֵרְךָ אֲשֶׁר בְּקֶרֶב קמ"ג קס"א מַחֲנֶיךָ מֵחֹטֵב עֵצֶיךָ עַד שֹׁאֵב מֵימֶיךָ: לְעָבְרְךָ בִּבְרִית יְהֹוָה אהדונהי אֱלֹהֶיךָ ילה וּבְאָלָתוֹ אֲשֶׁר יְהֹוָה אהדונהי אֱלֹהֶיךָ ילה כֹּרֵת עִמְּךָ ה' הויות, נמם הַיּוֹם ע"ה = נגד, זן, מזבח:

הַעִדֹתִי בָכֶם ב"פ אל הַיּוֹם ע"ה = נגד, זן, מזבח אֶת־הַשָּׁמַיִם י"פ טל, י"פ כוזו וְאֶת־הָאָרֶץ אלהים דההין ע"ה הַחַיִּים בינה ע"ה וְהַמָּוֶת נָתַתִּי לְפָנֶיךָ סמ"ב הַבְּרָכָה עסמ"ב וְהַקְּלָלָה וּבָחַרְתָּ בַּחַיִּים בינה ע"ה לְמַעַן תִּחְיֶה אַתָּה וְזַרְעֶךָ: לְאַהֲבָה אחד, דאגה אֶת־יְהֹוָה אהדונהי אֱלֹהֶיךָ ילה לִשְׁמֹעַ בְּקֹלוֹ וּלְדָבְקָה־בוֹ כִּי הוּא חַיֶּיךָ וְאֹרֶךְ יָמֶיךָ לָשֶׁבֶת עַל־הָאֲדָמָה אֲשֶׁר נִשְׁבַּע יְהֹוָה אהדונהי לַאֲבֹתֶיךָ לְאַבְרָהָם רמ"ח, ח"פ אל לְיִצְחָק ד"פ ב"ן וּלְיַעֲקֹב ז"פ יהוה, יאהדונהי אידהנויה לָתֵת לָהֶם:

וַיֵּלֶךְ כלי מֹשֶׁה מהש, אל שדי וַיְדַבֵּר ראה אֶת־הַדְּבָרִים ראה הָאֵלֶּה אֶל־כָּל־ ילי יִשְׂרָאֵל: וַיֹּאמֶר אֲלֵהֶם בֶּן־מֵאָה דמב, מלוי ע״ב וְעֶשְׂרִים שָׁנָה אָנֹכִי איע הַיּוֹם ע״ה = נגד, זן, מזבח לֹא־אוּכַל עוֹד לָצֵאת וְלָבוֹא וַיהֹוָאדניה יאהדונהי אָמַר אֵלַי לֹא תַעֲבֹר אֶת־הַיַּרְדֵּן י״פ יהוה וד׳ אותיות הַזֶּה והו: יְהֹוָאדניה יאהדונהי אֱלֹהֶיךָ ילה הוּא | עֹבֵר רבוע יהוה ורבוע אלהים לְפָנֶיךָ סמ״ב הוּא־יַשְׁמִיד אֶת־הַגּוֹיִם הָאֵלֶּה מִלְּפָנֶיךָ סמ״ב וִירִשְׁתָּם יְהוֹשֻׁעַ הוּא עֹבֵר רבוע יהוה ורבוע אלהים לְפָנֶיךָ סמ״ב כַּאֲשֶׁר דִּבֶּר ראה יְהֹוָאדניה יאהדונהי: וְעָשָׂה יְהֹוָאדניה יאהדונהי לָהֶם כַּאֲשֶׁר עָשָׂה לְסִיחוֹן וּלְעוֹג מַלְכֵי הָאֱמֹרִי וּלְאַרְצָם אֲשֶׁר הִשְׁמִיד אֹתָם: וּנְתָנָם יְהֹוָאדניה יאהדונהי לִפְנֵיכֶם וַעֲשִׂיתֶם לָהֶם כְּכָל־הַמִּצְוָה אֲשֶׁר צִוִּיתִי אֶתְכֶם: חִזְקוּ וְאִמְצוּ אַל־תִּירְאוּ וְאַל־תַּעַרְצוּ מִפְּנֵיהֶם כִּי | יְהֹוָאדניה יאהדונהי אֱלֹהֶיךָ ילה הוּא הַהֹלֵךְ עִמָּךְ ה׳ הויות, נמם לֹא יַרְפְּךָ וְלֹא יַעַזְבֶךָּ:

הַקְהִילוּ אֵלַי אֶת־כָּל־ ילי זִקְנֵי שִׁבְטֵיכֶם וְשֹׁטְרֵיכֶם וַאֲדַבְּרָה ראה בְאָזְנֵיהֶם אֵת הַדְּבָרִים ראה הָאֵלֶּה וְאָעִידָה בָּם מ״ב אֶת־הַשָּׁמַיִם י״פ טל, י״פ כוזו וְאֶת־הָאָרֶץ אלהים דההין ע״ה: כִּי יָדַעְתִּי אַחֲרֵי מוֹתִי כִּי־הַשְׁחֵת תַּשְׁחִתוּן וְסַרְתֶּם מִן־הַדֶּרֶךְ ב״פ יב״ק אֲשֶׁר צִוִּיתִי אֶתְכֶם וְקָרָאת אֶתְכֶם הָרָעָה רהע בְּאַחֲרִית הַיָּמִים נלך כִּי־תַעֲשׂוּ אֶת־הָרַע בְּעֵינֵי ריבוע מ״ה יְהֹוָאדניה יאהדונהי לְהַכְעִיסוֹ בְּמַעֲשֵׂה יְדֵיכֶם: וַיְדַבֵּר ראה מֹשֶׁה מהש, אל שדי בְּאָזְנֵי כָּל־ ילי קְהַל ע״ב ס״ג יִשְׂרָאֵל אֶת־דִּבְרֵי ראה הַשִּׁירָה הַזֹּאת עַד תֻּמָּם:

הַאֲזִינוּ הַשָּׁמַיִם י״פ טל, י״פ כוזו וַאֲדַבֵּרָה ראה וְתִשְׁמַע הָאָרֶץ אלהים דההין ע״ה אִמְרֵי־פִי: יַעֲרֹף כַּמָּטָר רמ״ח ע״ה, ח״פ אל ע״ה לִקְחִי תִּזַּל כַּטַּל כוזו אִמְרָתִי י״פ אדני ע״ה כִּשְׂעִירִם עֲלֵי־דֶשֶׁא וְכִרְבִיבִים עֲלֵי־עֵשֶׂב ע״ב שמות: כִּי שֵׁם יהוה שדי יְהֹוָאדניה יאהדונהי אֶקְרָא ב״פ קנ״א הָבוּ אחד, אהבה, דאגה גֹדֶל להח, מבה, יזל, אום לֵאלֹהֵינוּ ילה:

וַיְדַבֵּר ראה יְהֹוָאדניה יאהדונהי אֶל־מֹשֶׁה מהש, אל שדי בְּעֶצֶם הַיּוֹם ע״ה = נגד, זן, מזבח הַזֶּה והו לֵאמֹר: עֲלֵה אֶל־הַר רבוע אלהים + ה׳ הָעֲבָרִים הַזֶּה והו הַר־ רבוע אלהים + ה׳ נְבוֹ אֲשֶׁר בְּאֶרֶץ אלהים דאלפין מוֹאָב יוד הא ואו הה אֲשֶׁר עַל־פְּנֵי חכמה בינה יְרֵחוֹ וּרְאֵה ראה אֶת־אֶרֶץ אלהים דאלפין כְּנַעַן אֲשֶׁר אֲנִי אני, טדה״ד כוז״ו נֹתֵן אבגית״ץ, ושר, אהבת חנם לִבְנֵי יִשְׂרָאֵל לַאֲחֻזָּה:

וּמֻ֗ת י"פ רבוע אהיה בָּהָר֙ אור, רז, אין סוף אֲשֶׁ֤ר אַתָּה֙ עֹלֶ֣ה שָׁ֔מָּה מהש, משה, אל שדי
וְהֵאָסֵ֖ף אֶל־עַמֶּ֑יךָ כַּאֲשֶׁר־מֵ֞ת י"פ רבוע אהיה אַהֲרֹ֤ן ע"ב ורבוע ע"ב אָחִ֙יךָ֙
בְּהֹ֣ר אור, רז, אין סוף הָהָ֔ר וַיֵּאָסֶ֖ף אֶל־עַמָּֽיו׃ עַל֩ אֲשֶׁ֨ר מְעַלְתֶּ֜ם בִּ֗י בְּת֙וֹךְ֙ בְּנֵ֣י
יִשְׂרָאֵ֔ל בְּמֵי־מְרִיבַ֥ת קָדֵ֖שׁ מִדְבַּר־צִ֑ן עַ֣ל אֲשֶׁ֤ר לֹא־קִדַּשְׁתֶּם֙ אוֹתִ֔י בְּת֖וֹךְ
בְּנֵ֥י יִשְׂרָאֵֽל׃ כִּ֥י מִנֶּ֖גֶד זן, מזבח תִּרְאֶ֣ה אֶת־הָאָ֑רֶץ אלהים דההין ע"ה
וְשָׁ֙מָּה֙ מהש, אל שדי לֹ֣א תָב֔וֹא אֶל־הָאָ֕רֶץ אלהים דההין ע"ה אֲשֶׁר־אֲנִ֥י אני, טדה"ד כוזו
נֹתֵ֖ן אבגית"ץ, ושר, אהבת חנם לִבְנֵ֥י יִשְׂרָאֵֽל׃

וְזֹ֣את הַבְּרָכָ֗ה עסמ"ב אֲשֶׁ֨ר בֵּרַ֥ךְ מֹשֶׁ֛ה מהש, אל שדי אִ֥ישׁ ע"ה קנ"א קס"א
הָאֱלֹהִ֖ים מום, אהיה אדני ; ילה אֶת־בְּנֵ֣י יִשְׂרָאֵ֑ל לִפְנֵ֖י חכמה בינה מוֹתֽוֹ׃ וַיֹּאמַ֗ר
יְהֹוָ֞ה יאהדונהי מִסִּינַ֥י בָּא֙ וְזָרַ֤ח רי"ו ע"ה, סמ"ב מִשֵּׂעִיר֙ לָ֔מוֹ הוֹפִ֙יעַ֙ מֵהַ֣ר פָּארָ֔ן
וְאָתָ֖ה מֵרִבְבֹ֣ת קֹ֑דֶשׁ מִֽימִינ֕וֹ אֵ֥שׁ דָּ֖ת (כתיב: אשדת) לָֽמוֹ׃ אַ֚ף חֹבֵ֣ב
עַמִּ֔ים ע"ה קס"א כָּל־ ילי קְדֹשָׁ֖יו בְּיָדֶ֑ךָ בוכו וְהֵם֙ תֻּכּ֣וּ לְרַגְלֶ֔ךָ יִשָּׂ֖א מִדַּבְּרֹתֶֽיךָ׃
תּוֹרָ֥ה צִוָּה־ פוי לָ֖נוּ מום, אלהים, אהיה אדני מֹשֶׁ֑ה מהש, אל שדי מוֹרָשָׁ֖ה קְהִלַּ֥ת
יַעֲקֹֽב ז"פ יהוה, יאהדונהי אידהנויה׃ וַיְהִ֥י אל בִישֻׁר֖וּן מֶ֑לֶךְ בְּהִתְאַסֵּף֙ רָ֣אשֵׁי עָ֔ם
יַ֖חַד כ"ב אתוון שִׁבְטֵ֥י ש"ך יִשְׂרָאֵֽל׃ יְחִ֥י רְאוּבֵ֖ן ג"פ אלהים, ע"ה קנ"א קס"א וְאַל־יָמֹ֑ת
וִיהִ֥י אל מְתָ֖יו מִסְפָּֽר׃

וְלֹא־קָ֨ם נָבִ֥יא ע֛וֹד בְּיִשְׂרָאֵ֖ל כְּמֹשֶׁ֑ה מהש, אל שדי אֲשֶׁר֙ יְדָע֣וֹ
יְהֹוָ֔ה יאהדונהי פָּנִ֖ים ע"ב ס"ג מ"ה אֶל־פָּנִֽים׃ ע"ב ס"ג מ"ה לְכָל־ יה אדני
הָאֹת֣וֹת וְהַמּוֹפְתִ֗ים אֲשֶׁ֤ר שְׁלָחוֹ֙ יְהֹוָ֔ה יאהדונהי לַעֲשׂ֖וֹת בְּאֶ֣רֶץ אלהים דאלפין
מִצְרָ֑יִם מצר לְפַרְעֹ֥ה וּלְכָל־ יה אדני עֲבָדָ֖יו וּלְכָל־ יה אדני אַרְצֽוֹ׃

וּלְכֹל֙ יה אדני הַיָּ֣ד (הַדָ–HuDa)

הַחֲזָקָ֔ה וּלְכֹ֖ל יה אדני הַמּוֹרָ֣א הַגָּד֑וֹל להח, מבה, יזל, אום
אֲשֶׁר֙ עָשָׂ֣ה מֹשֶׁ֔ה מהש, אל שדי לְעֵינֵ֖י ריבוע מ"ה כָּל־ ילי יִשְׂרָאֵֽל׃

Here we say *Kaddish Al Yisrael* (on pg. 444-446)

SHIR HASHIRIM – SONGS OF SONGS

שִׁיר הַשִּׁירִים אֲשֶׁר לִשְׁלֹמֹה: יִשָּׁקֵנִי מִנְּשִׁיקוֹת פִּיהוּ כִּי־טוֹבִים
דֹּדֶיךָ מִיָּיִן מ״כ, י״פ האא: לְרֵיחַ שְׁמָנֶיךָ טוֹבִים שֶׁמֶן תּוּרַק שְׁמֶךָ
עַל־כֵּן עֲלָמוֹת אֲהֵבוּךָ: מָשְׁכֵנִי אַחֲרֶיךָ נָּרוּצָה הֱבִיאַנִי הַמֶּלֶךְ חֲדָרָיו
נָגִילָה וְנִשְׂמְחָה בָּךְ נַזְכִּירָה דֹדֶיךָ מִיַּיִן מ״כ, י״פ האא מֵישָׁרִים אֲהֵבוּךָ:
כַּרְמִי שֶׁלִּי לְפָנָי חכמה, בינה הָאֶלֶף לְךָ שְׁלֹמֹה וּמָאתַיִם לְנֹטְרִים
אֶת־פִּרְיוֹ: הַיּוֹשֶׁבֶת בַּגַּנִּים חֲבֵרִים מַקְשִׁיבִים לְקוֹלֵךְ הַשְׁמִיעִנִי:

בְּרַח דּוֹדִי (דִּיָ–DuYA)

וּדְמֵה־לְךָ לִצְבִי אוֹ לְעֹפֶר הָאַיָּלִים עַל הָרֵי בְשָׂמִים כוזו, י״פ טל:

ESTER-ESTHER

וַיְהִי בִּימֵי אֲחַשְׁוֵרוֹשׁ הוּא אֲחַשְׁוֵרוֹשׁ הַמֹּלֵךְ מֵהֹדּוּ וְעַד־כּוּשׁ שֶׁבַע
וְעֶשְׂרִים וּמֵאָה מְדִינָה: בַּיָּמִים נלך הָהֵם כְּשֶׁבֶת הַמֶּלֶךְ אֲחַשְׁוֵרוֹשׁ עַל כִּסֵּא
מַלְכוּתוֹ אֲשֶׁר בְּשׁוּשַׁן הַבִּירָה: בִּשְׁנַת שָׁלוֹשׁ לְמָלְכוֹ עָשָׂה מִשְׁתֶּה
לְכָל יה אדני שָׂרָיו וַעֲבָדָיו חֵיל ומב פָּרַס וּמָדַי הַפַּרְתְּמִים וְשָׂרֵי הַמְּדִינוֹת
לְפָנָיו: וַיָּשֶׂם הַמֶּלֶךְ אֲחַשְׁרֵשׁ מַס עַל־הָאָרֶץ אלהים דההין וְאִיֵּי הַיָּם ילי:
וְכָל ילי מַעֲשֵׂה תָקְפּוֹ וּגְבוּרָתוֹ וּפָרָשַׁת גְּדֻלַּת מָרְדֳּכַי אֲשֶׁר גִּדְּלוֹ הַמֶּלֶךְ
הֲלוֹא־הֵם כְּתוּבִים עַל־סֵפֶר דִּבְרֵי הַיָּמִים נלך לְמַלְכֵי נלך מָדַי וּפָרָס:

כִּי מָרְדֳּכַי (מִיָּ–MuYA)

הַיְּהוּדִי אלד מִשְׁנֶה לַמֶּלֶךְ אֲחַשְׁוֵרוֹשׁ וְגָדוֹל להוז, מבה לַיְּהוּדִים מלה וְרָצוּי
לְרֹב אֶחָיו דֹּרֵשׁ טוֹב והו לְעַמּוֹ וְדֹבֵר ראה שָׁלוֹם לְכָל יה אדני, ילי זַרְעוֹ:

RUT-RUTH

וַיְהִי בִּימֵי שְׁפֹט הַשֹּׁפְטִים וַיְהִי רָעָב בָּאָרֶץ וַיֵּלֶךְ אִישׁ מִבֵּית ב״פ ראה
לֶחֶם ג״פ יהו״ה יְהוּדָה לָגוּר בִּשְׂדֵי מוֹאָב הוּא וְאִשְׁתּוֹ וּשְׁנֵי בָנָיו: וְשֵׁם הָאִישׁ
אֱלִימֶלֶךְ וְשֵׁם אִשְׁתּוֹ נָעֳמִי וְשֵׁם שְׁנֵי־בָנָיו מַחְלוֹן מנד וְכִלְיוֹן אֶפְרָתִים
מִבֵּית ב״פ ראה לֶחֶם ג״פ יהו״ה יְהוּדָה וַיָּבֹאוּ שְׂדֵי מוֹאָב וַיִּהְיוּ שָׁם:
וַיָּמָת אֱלִימֶלֶךְ אִישׁ נָעֳמִי וַתִּשָּׁאֵר הִיא וּשְׁנֵי בָנֶיהָ: וַיִּשְׂאוּ לָהֶם נָשִׁים
מֹאֲבִיּוֹת שֵׁם הָאַחַת עָרְפָּה וְשֵׁם הַשֵּׁנִית **רוּת** וַיֵּשְׁבוּ שָׁם כְּעֶשֶׂר שָׁנִים:
וַיָּמוּתוּ גַם־שְׁנֵיהֶם מַחְלוֹן מנד וְכִלְיוֹן וַתִּשָּׁאֵר הָאִשָּׁה מִשְּׁנֵי יְלָדֶיהָ וּמֵאִישָׁהּ:

וַתָּקָם הִיא וְכַלֹּתֶיהָ וַתָּשָׁב מִשְּׂדֵי מוֹאָב כִּי שָׁמְעָה בִּשְׂדֵה מוֹאָב כִּי־פָקַד
יְהֹוָה יאהדונהי אֶת־עַמּוֹ לָתֵת לָהֶם לָחֶם ג"פ יהו"ה: וַתֵּצֵא מִן־הַמָּקוֹם אֲשֶׁר
הָיְתָה־שָׁמָּה וּשְׁתֵּי כַלֹּתֶיהָ עִמָּהּ וַתֵּלַכְנָה בַדֶּרֶךְ לָשׁוּב אֶל־אֶרֶץ יְהוּדָה:
וַתֹּאמֶר נָעֳמִי לִשְׁתֵּי כַלֹּתֶיהָ לֵכְנָה שֹּׁבְנָה מלה אִשָּׁה לְבֵית ב"פ ראה אִמָּהּ יַעַשׂ
(כתיב: יעשה) יְהֹוָה יאהדונהי עִמָּכֶם חֶסֶד ע"ב, ריבוע יהוה כַּאֲשֶׁר עֲשִׂיתֶם עִם־
הַמֵּתִים וְעִמָּדִי: יִתֵּן יְהֹוָה יאהדונהי לָכֶם וּמְצֶאןָ מְנוּחָה אִשָּׁה בֵּית ב"פ ראה
אִישָׁהּ וַתִּשַּׁק לָהֶן וַתִּשֶּׂאנָה קוֹלָן וַתִּבְכֶּינָה: וַתֹּאמַרְנָה־לָּהּ כִּי־אִתָּךְ נָשׁוּב
לְעַמֵּךְ: וַתֹּאמֶר נָעֳמִי שֹׁבְנָה בְנֹתַי לָמָּה תֵלַכְנָה עִמִּי הַעוֹד־לִי בָנִים בְּמֵעַי
וְהָיוּ לָכֶם לַאֲנָשִׁים: שֹׁבְנָה בְנֹתַי לֵכְןָ כִּי זָקַנְתִּי מִהְיוֹת לְאִישׁ כִּי אָמַרְתִּי
יֶשׁ־לִי תִקְוָה גַּם הָיִיתִי הַלַּיְלָה מלה לְאִישׁ וְגַם יָלַדְתִּי בָנִים: הֲלָהֵן תְּשַׂבֵּרְנָה
עַד אֲשֶׁר יִגְדָּלוּ הֲלָהֵן תֵּעָגֵנָה לְבִלְתִּי הֱיוֹת לְאִישׁ אַל בְּנֹתַי כִּי־מַר־לִי
מְאֹד מִכֶּם כִּי־יָצְאָה בִי יַד־יְהֹוָה יאהדונהי: וַתִּשֶּׂנָה קוֹלָן וַתִּבְכֶּינָה עוֹד
וַתִּשַּׁק עָרְפָּה לַחֲמוֹתָהּ וְרוּת דָּבְקָה בָּהּ: וַתֹּאמֶר הִנֵּה שָׁבָה יְבִמְתֵּךְ אֶל־
עַמָּהּ וְאֶל־אֱלֹהֶיהָ שׁוּבִי אַחֲרֵי יְבִמְתֵּךְ: וַתֹּאמֶר רוּת אַל־תִּפְגְּעִי־בִי לְעָזְבֵךְ
לָשׁוּב מֵאַחֲרָיִךְ כִּי אֶל־אֲשֶׁר תֵּלְכִי אֵלֵךְ וּבַאֲשֶׁר תָּלִינִי אָלִין עַמֵּךְ עַמִּי
וֵאלֹהַיִךְ אֱלֹהָי דמב, ילה: בַּאֲשֶׁר תָּמוּתִי אָמוּת וְשָׁם אֶקָּבֵר כֹּה היי יַעֲשֶׂה
יְהֹוָה יאהדונהי לִי וְכֹה היי יֹסִיף כִּי הַמָּוֶת יַפְרִיד בֵּינִי וּבֵינֵךְ: וַתֵּרֶא כִּי־
מִתְאַמֶּצֶת הִיא לָלֶכֶת אִתָּהּ וַתֶּחְדַּל לְדַבֵּר ראה אֵלֶיהָ: וַתֵּלַכְנָה שְׁתֵּיהֶם
עַד־בּוֹאָנָה בֵּית ב"פ ראה לָחֶם ג"פ יהו"ה וַיְהִי כְּבוֹאָנָה בֵּית ב"פ ראה לֶחֶם ג"פ יהו"ה
וַתֵּהֹם כָּל ילי הָעִיר ערי, בוזוףר, סנדלפון עֲלֵיהֶן וַתֹּאמַרְנָה הֲזֹאת נָעֳמִי: וַתֹּאמֶר
אֲלֵיהֶן אַל־תִּקְרֶאנָה לִי נָעֳמִי קְרֶאןָ לִי מָרָא כִּי־הֵמַר שַׁדַּי לִי מְאֹד:
אֲנִי אני מְלֵאָה הָלַכְתִּי וְרֵיקָם הֱשִׁיבַנִי יְהֹוָה יאהדונהי לָמָּה תִקְרֶאנָה לִי נָעֳמִי
וַיהֹוָה יאהדונהי עָנָה בִי וְשַׁדַּי הֵרַע לִי: וַתָּשָׁב נָעֳמִי וְרוּת הַמּוֹאֲבִיָּה כַלָּתָהּ
עִמָּהּ הַשָּׁבָה מִשְּׂדֵי מוֹאָב וְהֵמָּה בָּאוּ בֵּית ב"פ ראה לֶחֶם ג"פ יהו"ה בִּתְחִלַּת
קְצִיר שְׂעֹרִים כתר: וּלְנָעֳמִי מוֹדַע (כתיב: מידע) לְאִישָׁהּ אִישׁ גִּבּוֹר חַיִל ומב
מִמִּשְׁפַּחַת אֱלִימֶלֶךְ וּשְׁמוֹ בֹּעַז: וַתֹּאמֶר רוּת הַמּוֹאֲבִיָּה אֶל־נָעֳמִי אֵלְכָה־
נָּא הַשָּׂדֶה וַאֲלַקֳטָה בַשִּׁבֳּלִים אַחַר אֲשֶׁר אֶמְצָא־חֵן מוזי בְּעֵינָיו וַתֹּאמֶר לָהּ
לְכִי בִתִּי: וַתֵּלֶךְ וַתָּבוֹא וַתְּלַקֵּט בַּשָּׂדֶה אַחֲרֵי הַקֹּצְרִים וַיִּקֶר מִקְרֶהָ חֶלְקַת
הַשָּׂדֶה לְבֹעַז אֲשֶׁר מִמִּשְׁפַּחַת אֱלִימֶלֶךְ: וְהִנֵּה־בֹעַז בָּא מִבֵּית ב"פ ראה
לֶחֶם ג"פ יהו"ה וַיֹּאמֶר לַקּוֹצְרִים יְהֹוָה יאהדונהי עִמָּכֶם וַיֹּאמְרוּ לוֹ יְבָרֶכְךָ
יְהֹוָה יאהדונהי: וַיֹּאמֶר בֹּעַז לְנַעֲרוֹ הַנִּצָּב עַל־הַקּוֹצְרִים לְמִי ילי הַנַּעֲרָה

הַזֹּאת: וַיַּעַן הַנַּעַר הַנִּצָּב עַל־הַקּוֹצְרִים וַיֹּאמַר נַעֲרָה מוֹאֲבִיָּה הִיא הַשָּׁבָה
עִם־נָעֳמִי מִשְּׂדֵה מוֹאָב: וַתֹּאמֶר אֲלַקֳטָה־נָּא וְאָסַפְתִּי בָעֳמָרִים אַחֲרֵי
הַקּוֹצְרִים וַתָּבוֹא וַתַּעֲמוֹד מֵאָז ומב הַבֹּקֶר וְעַד־עַתָּה זֶה שִׁבְתָּהּ
הַבַּיִת ב"פ ראה מְעָט: וַיֹּאמֶר בֹּעַז אֶל־רוּת הֲלוֹא שָׁמַעַתְּ בִּתִּי אַל־תֵּלְכִי
לִלְקֹט בְּשָׂדֶה אַחֵר וְגַם לֹא תַעֲבוּרִי מִזֶּה וְכֹה היי תִדְבָּקִין עִם־נַעֲרֹתָי:
עֵינַיִךְ בַּשָּׂדֶה אֲשֶׁר יִקְצֹרוּן וְהָלַכְתְּ אַחֲרֵיהֶן הֲלוֹא צִוִּיתִי אֶת־הַנְּעָרִים
לְבִלְתִּי נָגְעֵךְ וְצָמִת וְהָלַכְתְּ אֶל־הַכֵּלִים וְשָׁתִית מֵאֲשֶׁר יִשְׁאֲבוּן הַנְּעָרִים:
וַתִּפֹּל עַל־פָּנֶיהָ וַתִּשְׁתַּחוּ אָרְצָה וַתֹּאמֶר אֵלָיו מַדּוּעַ מָצָאתִי חֵן מוזי בְּעֵינֶיךָ
לְהַכִּירֵנִי וְאָנֹכִי איע נָכְרִיָּה: וַיַּעַן בֹּעַז וַיֹּאמֶר לָהּ הֻגֵּד הֻגַּד לִי כֹּל ילי
אֲשֶׁר־עָשִׂית אֶת־חֲמוֹתֵךְ אַחֲרֵי מוֹת אִישֵׁךְ וַתַּעַזְבִי אָבִיךְ וְאִמֵּךְ
וְאֶרֶץ מוֹלַדְתֵּךְ וַתֵּלְכִי אֶל־עַם אֲשֶׁר לֹא־יָדַעַתְּ תְּמוֹל שִׁלְשׁוֹם:
יְשַׁלֵּם יְהֹוָאדנֵי יאהדונהי פָּעֳלֵךְ וּתְהִי מַשְׂכֻּרְתֵּךְ שְׁלֵמָה מֵעִם יְהֹוָאדנֵי יאהדונהי
אֱלֹהֵי דמב, ילה יִשְׂרָאֵל אֲשֶׁר־בָּאת לַחֲסוֹת תַּחַת־כְּנָפָיו: וַתֹּאמֶר
אֶמְצָא־חֵן מוזי בְּעֵינֶיךָ אֲדֹנִי כִּי נִחַמְתָּנִי וְכִי דִבַּרְתָּ עַל־לֵב שִׁפְחָתֶךָ וְאָנֹכִי
איע לֹא אֶהְיֶה כְּאַחַת שִׁפְחֹתֶיךָ: וַיֹּאמֶר לָהּ בֹעַז לְעֵת הָאֹכֶל גֹּשִׁי הֲלֹם
וְאָכַלְתְּ מִן־הַלֶּחֶם ג"פ יהו"ה וְטָבַלְתְּ פִּתֵּךְ בַּחֹמֶץ וַתֵּשֶׁב מִצַּד הַקֹּצְרִים וַיִּצְבָּט־
לָהּ קָלִי וַתֹּאכַל וַתִּשְׂבַּע וַתֹּתַר: וַתָּקָם לְלַקֵּט וַיְצַו בֹּעַז אֶת־ נְעָרָיו לֵאמֹר
גַּם בֵּין הָעֳמָרִים תְּלַקֵּט וְלֹא תַכְלִימוּהָ: וְגַם שֹׁל־תָּשֹׁלּוּ לָהּ מִן־הַצְּבָתִים
וַעֲזַבְתֶּם וְלִקְּטָה וְלֹא תִגְעֲרוּ־בָהּ: וַתְּלַקֵּט בַּשָּׂדֶה עַד־הָעָרֶב וַתַּחְבֹּט אֵת
אֲשֶׁר־לִקֵּטָה וַיְהִי כְּאֵיפָה שְׂעֹרִים כתר: וַתִּשָּׂא וַתָּבוֹא הָעִיר ערי, בוזוזך, סנדלפון
וַתֵּרֶא חֲמוֹתָהּ אֵת אֲשֶׁר־לִקֵּטָה וַתּוֹצֵא וַתִּתֶּן ב"פ כהת לָהּ אֵת אֲשֶׁר־הוֹתִרָה
מִשָּׂבְעָהּ: וַתֹּאמֶר לָהּ חֲמוֹתָהּ אֵיפֹה לִקַּטְתְּ (כתיב: לקטתי) הַיּוֹם נגד, מזבח, זן
וְאָנָה עָשִׂית יְהִי מַכִּירֵךְ בָּרוּךְ וַתַּגֵּד לַחֲמוֹתָהּ אֵת אֲשֶׁר־עָשְׂתָה עִמּוֹ
וַתֹּאמֶר שֵׁם הָאִישׁ אֲשֶׁר עָשִׂיתִי עִמּוֹ הַיּוֹם נגד, מזבח, זן בֹּעַז: וַתֹּאמֶר נָעֳמִי
לְכַלָּתָהּ בָּרוּךְ הוּא לַיהֹוָאדנֵי יאהדונהי אֲשֶׁר לֹא־עָזַב חַסְדּוֹ אֶת־הַחַיִּים בינה
וְאֶת־הַמֵּתִים וַתֹּאמֶר לָהּ נָעֳמִי קָרוֹב לָנוּ הָאִישׁ מִגֹּאֲלֵנוּ הוּא: וַתֹּאמֶר רוּת
הַמּוֹאֲבִיָּה גַּם כִּי־אָמַר אֵלַי עִם־הַנְּעָרִים אֲשֶׁר־לִי תִּדְבָּקִין עַד אִם יוהך כִּלּוּ
אֵת כָּל ילי הַקָּצִיר אֲשֶׁר־לִי: וַתֹּאמֶר נָעֳמִי אֶל־רוּת כַּלָּתָהּ טוֹב והו בִּתִּי כִּי
תֵצְאִי עִם־נַעֲרוֹתָיו וְלֹא יִפְגְּעוּ־בָךְ בְּשָׂדֶה אַחֵר: וַתִּדְבַּק בְּנַעֲרוֹת בֹּעַז
לְלַקֵּט עַד־כְּלוֹת קְצִיר־הַשְּׂעֹרִים כתר וּקְצִיר הַחִטִּים וַתֵּשֶׁב אֶת־חֲמוֹתָהּ:
וַתֹּאמֶר לָהּ נָעֳמִי חֲמוֹתָהּ בִּתִּי הֲלֹא אֲבַקֶּשׁ לָךְ מָנוֹחַ אֲשֶׁר יִיטַב־לָךְ:

וְעַתָּה הֲלֹא בֹעַז מֹדַעְתָּנוּ אֲשֶׁר הָיִית אֶת־נַעֲרוֹתָיו הִנֵּה־הוּא זֹרֶה אֶת־גֹּרֶן
הַשְּׂעֹרִים כתר הַלָּיְלָה מלה: וְרָחַצְתְּ וָסַכְתְּ וְשַׂמְתְּ שִׂמְלֹתַיִךְ (כתיב: שמלתך) עָלַיִךְ
וְיָרַדְתְּ (כתיב: וירדתי) הַגֹּרֶן אַל־תִּוָּדְעִי לָאִישׁ עַד כַּלֹּתוֹ לֶאֱכֹל וְלִשְׁתּוֹת: וִיהִי
בְשָׁכְבוֹ וְיָדַעַתְּ אֶת־הַמָּקוֹם אֲשֶׁר יִשְׁכַּב־שָׁם וּבָאת וְגִלִּית מַרְגְּלֹתָיו
וְשָׁכָבְתְּ (כתיב: ושכבתי) וְהוּא יַגִּיד ייי לָךְ אֵת אֲשֶׁר תַּעֲשִׂין: וַתֹּאמֶר אֵלֶיהָ
כֹּל ילי אֲשֶׁר־תֹּאמְרִי אֵלַי אֶעֱשֶׂה: וַתֵּרֶד הַגֹּרֶן וַתַּעַשׂ כְּכֹל ילי אֲשֶׁר־צִוַּתָּה
חֲמוֹתָהּ: וַיֹּאכַל בֹּעַז וַיֵּשְׁתְּ וַיִּיטַב לִבּוֹ וַיָּבֹא לִשְׁכַּב בִּקְצֵה הָעֲרֵמָה וַתָּבֹא
בַלָּט וַתְּגַל מַרְגְּלֹתָיו וַתִּשְׁכָּב: וַיְהִי בַּחֲצִי הַלַּיְלָה מלה וַיֶּחֱרַד הָאִישׁ וַיִּלָּפֵת
וְהִנֵּה אִשָּׁה שֹׁכֶבֶת מַרְגְּלֹתָיו: וַיֹּאמֶר מִי ילי אָתְּ וַתֹּאמֶר אָנֹכִי איע רוּת
אֲמָתֶךָ וּפָרַשְׂתָּ כְנָפֶךָ עַל־אֲמָתְךָ כִּי גֹאֵל א״ת ב״ש - כתר אָתָּה: וַיֹּאמֶר בְּרוּכָה
אַתְּ לַיהֹוָהאדניאהדונהי בִּתִּי הֵיטַבְתְּ חַסְדֵּךְ הָאַחֲרוֹן מִן־הָרִאשׁוֹן לְבִלְתִּי־לֶכֶת
אַחֲרֵי הַבַּחוּרִים אִם יוהך דַּל וְאִם יוהך עָשִׁיר: וְעַתָּה בִּתִּי אַל־תִּירְאִי כֹּל ילי
אֲשֶׁר־ תֹּאמְרִי אֶעֱשֶׂה לָּךְ כִּי יוֹדֵעַ כָּל ילי שַׁעַר עַמִּי כִּי אֵשֶׁת חַיִל ומב אָתְּ:
וְעַתָּה כִּי אָמְנָם כִּי (אם כתיב ולא קרי) גֹאֵל א״ת ב״ש - כתר אָנֹכִי איע וְגַם יֵשׁ
גֹּאֵל א״ת ב״ש - כתר קָרוֹב מִמֶּנִּי: לִינִי הַלַּיְלָה מלה וְהָיָה יהוה, יהה בַבֹּקֶר אִם יוהך
יִגְאָלֵךְ טוֹב והו יִגְאָל וְאִם יוהך לֹא יַחְפֹּץ לְגָאֳלֵךְ וּגְאַלְתִּיךְ אָנֹכִי איע חַי־
יְהֹוָהאדניאהדונהי שִׁכְבִי עַד־הַבֹּקֶר: וַתִּשְׁכַּב מַרְגְּלוֹתָיו (כתיב: מרגלתו) עַד־הַבֹּקֶר
וַתָּקָם בְּטֶרֶם (כתיב: בטרום) יַכִּיר אִישׁ אֶת־רֵעֵהוּ וַיֹּאמֶר אַל יִוָּדַע כִּי־בָאָה
הָאִשָּׁה הַגֹּרֶן: וַיֹּאמֶר הָבִי הַמִּטְפַּחַת אֲשֶׁר־עָלַיִךְ וְאֶחֳזִי־בָהּ וַתֹּאחֶז בָּהּ
וַיָּמָד שֵׁשׁ־שְׂעֹרִים כתר וַיָּשֶׁת עָלֶיהָ וַיָּבֹא הָעִיר ערי, סחחך, סנדלפון: וַתָּבוֹא אֶל
חֲמוֹתָהּ וַתֹּאמֶר מִי ילי אַתְּ בִּתִּי וַתַּגֶּד־לָהּ אֵת כָּל ילי אֲשֶׁר עָשָׂה־לָהּ הָאִישׁ:
וַתֹּאמֶר שֵׁשׁ־הַשְּׂעֹרִים כתר הָאֵלֶּה נָתַן לִי כִּי אָמַר אֵלַי אַל־תָּבוֹאִי רֵיקָם
אֶל חֲמוֹתֵךְ: וַתֹּאמֶר שְׁבִי בִתִּי עַד אֲשֶׁר תֵּדְעִין אֵיךְ יִפֹּל דָּבָר ראה כִּי לֹא
יִשְׁקֹט הָאִישׁ כִּי־אִם יוהך כִּלָּה הַדָּבָר ראה הַיּוֹם נגד, מזבח, זן: וּבֹעַז עָלָה הַשַּׁעַר
וַיֵּשֶׁב שָׁם וְהִנֵּה הַגֹּאֵל א״ת ב״ש - כתר עֹבֵר אֲשֶׁר דִּבֶּר ראה בֹּעַז וַיֹּאמֶר סוּרָה
שְׁבָה־פֹּה מילה פְּלֹנִי אַלְמֹנִי וַיָּסַר וַיֵּשֵׁב: וַיִּקַּח חעם עֲשָׂרָה אֲנָשִׁים מִזִּקְנֵי
הָעִיר ערי, סחחך, סנדלפון וַיֹּאמֶר שְׁבוּ־פֹה מילה וַיֵּשֵׁבוּ: וַיֹּאמֶר לַגֹּאֵל א״ת ב״ש - כתר
חֶלְקַת הַשָּׂדֶה אֲשֶׁר לְאָחִינוּ לֶאֱלִימֶלֶךְ מָכְרָה נָעֳמִי הַשָּׁבָה מִשְּׂדֵה מוֹאָב:
וַאֲנִי אני אָמַרְתִּי אֶגְלֶה אָזְנְךָ לֵאמֹר קְנֵה נֶגֶד זן, מזבח הַיֹּשְׁבִים וְנֶגֶד זן, מזבח זִקְנֵי
עַמִּי אִם יוהך תִּגְאַל גְּאָל א״ת ב״ש - כתר וְאִם יוהך לֹא יִגְאַל הַגִּידָה לִּי וְאֵדְעָה
(כתיב: ואדע) כִּי אֵין זוּלָתְךָ לִגְאוֹל וְאָנֹכִי איע אַחֲרֶיךָ וַיֹּאמֶר אָנֹכִי איע אֶגְאָל:

וַיֹּאמֶר בֹּעַז בְּיוֹם נגד, מזבח, זן קְנוֹתְךָ הַשָּׂדֶה מִיַּד נָעֳמִי וּמֵאֵת רוּת הַמּוֹאֲבִיָּה
אֵשֶׁת־הַמֵּת קָנִיתָ (כתיב: קניתי) לְהָקִים שֵׁם־הַמֵּת עַל־נַחֲלָתוֹ: וַיֹּאמֶר
הַגֹּאֵל א"ת ב"ש - כתר לֹא אוּכַל לִגְאָל־ (כתיב: לגאול) לִי פֶּן־אַשְׁחִית אֶת־נַחֲלָתִי
גְּאַל א"ת ב"ש - כתר לְךָ אַתָּה אֶת־גְּאֻלָּתִי כִּי לֹא־אוּכַל לִגְאֹל א"ת ב"ש - כתר: וְזֹאת
לְפָנִים בְּיִשְׂרָאֵל עַל־הַגְּאוּלָּה מ"ה וְעַל־הַתְּמוּרָה לְקַיֵּם כָּל ילי דָּבָר ראה שָׁלַף
אִישׁ נַעֲלוֹ וְנָתַן אבג יתץ, ושר, אהבת חנם לְרֵעֵהוּ וְזֹאת הַתְּעוּדָה בְּיִשְׂרָאֵל: וַיֹּאמֶר
הַגֹּאֵל א"ת ב"ש - כתר לְבֹעַז קְנֵה־לָךְ וַיִּשְׁלֹף נַעֲלוֹ: וַיֹּאמֶר בֹּעַז לַזְּקֵנִים וְכָל ילי
הָעָם עֵדִים אַתֶּם הַיּוֹם נגד, מזבח, זן כִּי קָנִיתִי אֶת־כָּל ילי אֲשֶׁר לֶאֱלִימֶלֶךְ וְאֵת
כָּל ילי אֲשֶׁר לְכִלְיוֹן וּמַחְלוֹן מנד מִיַּד נָעֳמִי: וְגַם אֶת־רוּת הַמֹּאֲבִיָּה אֵשֶׁת
מַחְלוֹן מנד קָנִיתִי לִי לְאִשָּׁה לְהָקִים שֵׁם־הַמֵּת עַל־נַחֲלָתוֹ וְלֹא־יִכָּרֵת שֵׁם־
הַמֵּת מֵעִם אֶחָיו וּמִשַּׁעַר מְקוֹמוֹ עֵדִים אַתֶּם הַיּוֹם נגד, מזבח, זן: וַיֹּאמְרוּ כָּל ילי
הָעָם אֲשֶׁר־בַּשַּׁעַר וְהַזְּקֵנִים עֵדִים יִתֵּן יְהֹוָה אהדונהי אֶת־הָאִשָּׁה הַבָּאָה
אֶל־בֵּיתֶךָ כְּרָחֵל וּכְלֵאָה אֲשֶׁר בָּנוּ שְׁתֵּיהֶם אֶת־בֵּית ב"פ ראה יִשְׂרָאֵל
וַעֲשֵׂה־חַיִל ומב בְּאֶפְרָתָה וּקְרָא־שֵׁם בְּבֵית ב"פ ראה לָחֶם ג"פ יהו"ה: וִיהִי בֵיתְךָ
כְּבֵית ב"פ ראה פֶּרֶץ אֲשֶׁר־יָלְדָה תָמָר לִיהוּדָה מִן־הַזֶּרַע אֲשֶׁר יִתֵּן
יְהֹוָה אהדונהי לְךָ מִן־הַנַּעֲרָה הַזֹּאת: וַיִּקַּח חעם בֹּעַז אֶת־רוּת וַתְּהִי־לוֹ לְאִשָּׁה
וַיָּבֹא אֵלֶיהָ וַיִּתֵּן יְהֹוָה אהדונהי לָהּ הֵרָיוֹן וַתֵּלֶד בֵּן: וַתֹּאמַרְנָה הַנָּשִׁים
אֶל־נָעֳמִי בָּרוּךְ יְהֹוָה אהדונהי אֲשֶׁר לֹא הִשְׁבִּית לָךְ גֹּאֵל א"ת ב"ש - כתר הַיּוֹם
נגד, מזבח, זן וְיִקָּרֵא שְׁמוֹ בְּיִשְׂרָאֵל: וְהָיָה יהוה, יהה לָךְ לְמֵשִׁיב נֶפֶשׁ וּלְכַלְכֵּל
אֶת־שֵׂיבָתֵךְ כִּי כַלָּתֵךְ אֲשֶׁר־אֲהֵבַתֶךְ יְלָדַתּוּ אֲשֶׁר־הִיא טוֹבָה אכא לָךְ
מִשִּׁבְעָה בָּנִים: וַתִּקַּח נָעֳמִי אֶת־הַיֶּלֶד וַתְּשִׁתֵהוּ בְחֵיקָהּ וַתְּהִי־לוֹ לְאֹמֶנֶת:
וַתִּקְרֶאנָה לוֹ הַשְּׁכֵנוֹת שֵׁם לֵאמֹר יֻלַּד־בֵּן לְנָעֳמִי וַתִּקְרֶאנָה שְׁמוֹ עוֹבֵד הוּא
אֲבִי־יִשַׁי אֲבִי דָוִד: וְאֵלֶּה תּוֹלְדוֹת פָּרֶץ פֶּרֶץ הוֹלִיד אֶת־חֶצְרוֹן: וְחֶצְרוֹן
הוֹלִיד אֶת־רָם וְרָם הוֹלִיד אֶת־עַמִּינָדָב: וְעַמִּינָדָב הוֹלִיד אֶת־נַחְשׁוֹן
וְנַחְשׁוֹן הוֹלִיד אֶת שַׂלְמָה: וְשַׂלְמוֹן הוֹלִיד אֶת־בֹּעַז וּבֹעַז הוֹלִיד אֶת עוֹבֵד:

וְעֹבֵד הוֹלִיד (הֻדָ–HuDa)
אֶת־יִשָׁי וְיִשַׁי הוֹלִיד אֶת דָּוִד:

EICHA-LAMENTATIONS

אֵיכָה יָשְׁבָה בָדָד הָעִיר ערי, סנזחף, סנדלפון
רַבָּתִי עָם הָיְתָה כְּאַלְמָנָה רַבָּתִי בַגּוֹיִם שָׂרָתִי בַּמְּדִינוֹת הָיְתָה לָמַס:

בָּכוֹ תִבְכֶּה בַּלַּיְלָה מלה וְדִמְעָתָהּ עַל לֶחֱיָהּ אֵין־לָהּ מְנַחֵם מִכָּל ילי אֹהֲבֶיהָ
כָּל ילי רֵעֶיהָ בָּגְדוּ בָהּ הָיוּ לָהּ לְאֹיְבִים׃ גָּלְתָה יְהוּדָה מֵעֹנִי ריבוע מ״ה וּמֵרֹב
עֲבֹדָה הִיא יָשְׁבָה בַגּוֹיִם לֹא מָצְאָה מָנוֹחַ כָּל ילי רֹדְפֶיהָ הִשִּׂיגוּהָ בֵּין
הַמְּצָרִים מצר׃ לָמָּה לָנֶצַח תִּשְׁכָּחֵנוּ תַּעַזְבֵנוּ לְאֹרֶךְ יָמִים נלך׃
הֲשִׁיבֵנוּ יְהֹוָהאדניאהדונהי אֵלֶיךָ וְנָשׁוּבָה (כתיב: ונשוב) חַדֵּשׁ יָמֵינוּ כְּקֶדֶם׃

כִּי אִם יוהך (אֻמָ–U Ma)

מָאֹס מְאַסְתָּנוּ קָצַפְתָּ עָלֵינוּ עַד־מְאֹד׃

הֲשִׁיבֵנוּ יְהֹוָהאדניאהדונהי אֵלֶיךָ וְנָשׁוּבָה (כתיב: ונשוב) חַדֵּשׁ יָמֵינוּ כְּקֶדֶם׃

KOHELET-ECCLESIASTES

דִּבְרֵי קֹהֶלֶת בֶּן־דָּוִד מֶלֶךְ בִּירוּשָׁלָםִ׃ הֲבֵל הֲבָלִים אָמַר קֹהֶלֶת
הֲבֵל הֲבָלִים הַכֹּל ילי הָבֶל׃ מַה יִּתְרוֹן לָאָדָם מ״ה בְּכָל ילי, לכב
עֲמָלוֹ שֶׁיַּעֲמֹל תַּחַת הַשָּׁמֶשׁ׃ וְיֹתֵר מֵהֵמָּה בְּנִי הִזָּהֵר עֲשׂוֹת
סְפָרִים הַרְבֵּה אֵין קֵץ מנק וְלַהַג הַרְבֵּה יְגִעַת בָּשָׂר׃ סוֹף דָּבָר ראה
הַכֹּל ילי נִשְׁמָע אֶת־הָאֱלֹהִים מום, ילה יְרָא וְאֶת מִצְוֹתָיו שְׁמוֹר כִּי־זֶה
כָּל ילי הָאָדָם מ״ה׃ כִּי אֶת־כָּל ילי מַעֲשֶׂה הָאֱלֹהִים מום, ילה יָבִא
בְמִשְׁפָּט עַל כָּל עמם, ילי נֶעְלָם אִם יוהך טוֹב והו וְאִם יוהך רָע׃

סוֹף דָּבָר ראה (דֻרָ–DuRa)

הַכֹּל ילי נִשְׁמָע

אֶת־הָאֱלֹהִים מום, ילה יְרָא וְאֶת־מִצְוֹתָיו שְׁמוֹר כִּי־זֶה כָּל ילי הָאָדָם מ״ה׃

YEHUSHUA - JOSHUA

וַיְהִי אַחֲרֵי מוֹת מֹשֶׁה מהש עֶבֶד יְהֹוָהאדניאהדונהי וַיֹּאמֶר יְהֹוָהאדניאהדונהי
אֶל־יְהוֹשֻׁעַ בִּן־נוּן מְשָׁרֵת מֹשֶׁה מהש לֵאמֹר׃ מֹשֶׁה מהש עַבְדִּי מֵת
וְעַתָּה קוּם עֲבֹר אֶת־הַיַּרְדֵּן הַזֶּה והו אַתָּה וְכָל ילי הָעָם הַזֶּה והו
אֶל הָאָרֶץ אלהים דההין אֲשֶׁר אָנֹכִי איע נֹתֵן ושר, אבג יתץ, אהבת חנם לָהֶם
לִבְנֵי יִשְׂרָאֵל׃ כָּל ילי מָקוֹם אֲשֶׁר תִּדְרֹךְ כַּף רַגְלְכֶם בּוֹ לָכֶם נְתַתִּיו
כַּאֲשֶׁר דִּבַּרְתִּי אֶל־מֹשֶׁה מהש׃ וַיַּעֲבֹד יִשְׂרָאֵל אֶת־יְהֹוָהאדניאהדונהי
כֹּל ילי יְמֵי יְהוֹשֻׁעַ וְכֹל ילי יְמֵי הַזְּקֵנִים אֲשֶׁר הֶאֱרִיכוּ יָמִים נלך אַחֲרֵי יְהוֹשֻׁעַ
וַאֲשֶׁר יָדְעוּ אֵת כָּל ילי מַעֲשֵׂה יְהֹוָהאדניאהדונהי אֲשֶׁר עָשָׂה לְיִשְׂרָאֵל׃

וְאֶת־עַצְמוֹת יוֹסֵף ציון אֲשֶׁר־הֶעֱלוּ בְנֵי־יִשְׂרָאֵל מִמִּצְרַיִם מצר
קָבְרוּ בִשְׁכֶם בְּחֶלְקַת הַשָּׂדֶה אֲשֶׁר קָנָה יַעֲקֹב יאהדונהי אידהנויה
מֵאֵת בְּנֵי־חֲמוֹר אֲבִי־שְׁכֶם בְּמֵאָה קְשִׂיטָה וַיִּהְיוּ לִבְנֵי־יוֹסֵף ציון לְנַחֲלָה׃

וְאֶלְעָזָר בֶּן־ (בְּנָ–VuNA)

אַהֲרֹן מֵת וַיִּקְבְּרוּ אֹתוֹ בְּגִבְעַת פִּינְחָס בְּנוֹ אֲשֶׁר נִתַּן־לוֹ בְּהַר אֶפְרָיִם׃

SHOFTIM - JUDGES

וַיְהִי אַחֲרֵי מוֹת יְהוֹשֻׁעַ וַיִּשְׁאֲלוּ בְּנֵי יִשְׂרָאֵל בַּיהֹוָהאדנייאהדונהי לֵאמֹר
מִי ילי יַעֲלֶה־לָּנוּ אֶל־הַכְּנַעֲנִי בַּתְּחִלָּה לְהִלָּחֶם בּוֹ׃ וַיֹּאמֶר יְהֹוָהאדנייאהדונהי
יְהוּדָה יַעֲלֶה הִנֵּה נָתַתִּי אֶת־הָאָרֶץ אלהים דההין בְּיָדוֹ׃ וַיֹּאמֶר יְהוּדָה
לְשִׁמְעוֹן אָחִיו עֲלֵה אִתִּי בְגוֹרָלִי וְנִלָּחֲמָה בַּכְּנַעֲנִי וְהָלַכְתִּי גַם־אֲנִי אני
אִתְּךָ בְּגוֹרָלֶךָ וַיֵּלֶךְ אִתּוֹ שִׁמְעוֹן׃ וַיַּעֲשׂוּ־כֵן בְּנֵי בִנְיָמִן וַיִּשְׂאוּ
נָשִׁים לְמִסְפָּרָם מִן־הַמְּחֹלְלוֹת אֲשֶׁר גָּזָלוּ וַיֵּלְכוּ וַיָּשׁוּבוּ אֶל נַחֲלָתָם
וַיִּבְנוּ אֶת־הֶעָרִים וַיֵּשְׁבוּ בָּהֶם׃ וַיִּתְהַלְּכוּ מִשָּׁם בְּנֵי־יִשְׂרָאֵל
בָּעֵת הַהִיא אִישׁ לְשִׁבְטוֹ וּלְמִשְׁפַּחְתּוֹ וַיֵּצְאוּ מִשָּׁם אִישׁ לְנַחֲלָתוֹ׃

בַּיָּמִים נלך הָהֵם (הָמָ–HuMA)

אֵין מֶלֶךְ בְּיִשְׂרָאֵל אִישׁ הַיָּשָׁר בְּעֵינָיו יַעֲשֶׂה׃

SHMUEL - SAMUEL

וַיְהִי אִישׁ אֶחָד אהבה, דאגה מִן־הָרָמָתַיִם צוֹפִים מֵהַר אֶפְרָיִם
וּשְׁמוֹ אֶלְקָנָה בֶּן־יְרֹחָם בֶּן־אֱלִיהוּא בֶּן־תֹּחוּ בֶן־צוּף אֶפְרָתִי׃
וְלוֹ שְׁתֵּי נָשִׁים שֵׁם אַחַת חַנָּה וְשֵׁם הַשֵּׁנִית פְּנִנָּה וַיְהִי לִפְנִנָּה יְלָדִים
וּלְחַנָּה אֵין יְלָדִים׃ וְעָלָה הָאִישׁ הַהוּא מֵעִירוֹ מִיָּמִים נלך יָמִימָה
לְהִשְׁתַּחֲוֺת וְלִזְבֹּחַ לַיהֹוָהאדנייאהדונהי צְבָאוֹת בְּשִׁלֹה וְשָׁם שְׁנֵי בְנֵי־עֵלִי
חָפְנִי וּפִנְחָס כֹּהֲנִים לַיהֹוָהאדנייאהדונהי׃ הַכֹּל ילי נָתַן אֲרַוְנָה הַמֶּלֶךְ לַמֶּלֶךְ וַיֹּאמֶר
אֲרַוְנָה אֶל הַמֶּלֶךְ יְהֹוָהאדנייאהדונהי אֱלֹהֶיךָ יִרְצֶךָ׃ וַיֹּאמֶר הַמֶּלֶךְ אֶל־אֲרַוְנָה
לֹא כִּי־קָנוֹ אֶקְנֶה מֵאוֹתְךָ בִּמְחִיר וְלֹא אַעֲלֶה לַיהֹוָהאדנייאהדונהי אֱלֹהַי דמב, ילה
עֹלוֹת חִנָּם וַיִּקֶן דָּוִד אֶת־הַגֹּרֶן וְאֶת־הַבָּקָר בְּכֶסֶף שְׁקָלִים חֲמִשִּׁים׃

וַיִּבֶן שָׁם (שְׁמָ–ShuMA)

דָּוִד מִזְבֵּחַ לַיהֹוָהאדנייאהדונהי וַיַּעַל עֹלוֹת וּשְׁלָמִים וַיֵּעָתֵר
יְהֹוָהאדנייאהדונהי לָאָרֶץ וַתֵּעָצַר הַמַּגֵּפָה מֵעַל עלם יִשְׂרָאֵל׃

MELACHIM - KINGS

וְהַמֶּלֶךְ דָּוִד זָקֵן בָּא בַּיָּמִים נלך וַיְכַסֻּהוּ בַּבְּגָדִים וְלֹא יִחַם לוֹ:
וַיֹּאמְרוּ לוֹ עֲבָדָיו יְבַקְשׁוּ לַאדֹנִי הַמֶּלֶךְ נַעֲרָה בְתוּלָה וְעָמְדָה
לִפְנֵי חכמה, בינה הַמֶּלֶךְ וּתְהִי־לוֹ סֹכֶנֶת וְשָׁכְבָה בְחֵיקֶךָ וְחַם לַאדֹנִי
הַמֶּלֶךְ: וַיְבַקְשׁוּ נַעֲרָה יָפָה בְּכֹל ילי לכב גְּבוּל יִשְׂרָאֵל וַיִּמְצְאוּ
אֶת־אֲבִישַׁג הַשּׁוּנַמִּית וַיָּבִאוּ אֹתָהּ לַמֶּלֶךְ: וַיְדַבֵּר אִתּוֹ טֹבוֹת
וַיִּתֵּן אֶת־כִּסְאוֹ מִמַּעַל עלם כִּסֵּא הַמְּלָכִים אֲשֶׁר אִתּוֹ בְּבָבֶל: וְשִׁנָּא אֵת בִּגְדֵי
כִלְאוֹ וְאָכַל לֶחֶם ג״פ יהו״ה תָּמִיד נתה, קס״א קנ״א קמ״ג לְפָנָיו כָּל ילי יְמֵי חַיָּו:

וַאֲרֻחָתוֹ אֲרֻחַת (אֶת־ U TA)

תָּמִיד נתה, קס״א קנ״א קמ״ג נִתְּנָה לּוֹ מֵאֵת הַמֶּלֶךְ דְּבַר־יוֹם בְּיוֹמוֹ כֹּל ילי יְמֵי חַיָּו:

YISHAYAHU - ISAIAH

חֲזוֹן יְשַׁעְיָהוּ בֶן־אָמוֹץ אֲשֶׁר חָזָה עַל־יְהוּדָה וִירוּשָׁלָםִ בִּימֵי עֻזִּיָּהוּ יוֹתָם
אָחָז יְחִזְקִיָּהוּ מַלְכֵי נלך יְהוּדָה: שִׁמְעוּ שָׁמַיִם כוזו, י״פ טל וְהַאֲזִינִי אֶרֶץ כִּי
יְהֹוָה יאהדונהי דִּבֵּר ראה בָּנִים גִּדַּלְתִּי וְרוֹמַמְתִּי וְהֵם פָּשְׁעוּ בִי:
יָדַע שׁוֹר ושר, אבג יתץ, אהבת חנם קֹנֵהוּ וַחֲמוֹר אֵבוּס בְּעָלָיו יִשְׂרָאֵל לֹא יָדַע
עַמִּי לֹא הִתְבּוֹנָן: כִּי כַאֲשֶׁר הַשָּׁמַיִם כוזו, י״פ טל הַחֲדָשִׁים וְהָאָרֶץ אלהים דההין
הַחֲדָשָׁה אֲשֶׁר אֲנִי אני עֹשֶׂה עֹמְדִים לְפָנַי חכמה, בינה נְאֻם־יְהֹוָה יאהדונהי כֵּן
יַעֲמֹד זַרְעֲכֶם וְשִׁמְכֶם: וְהָיָה יהוה, יהה מִדֵּי־חֹדֶשׁ בְּחָדְשׁוֹ וּמִדֵּי שַׁבָּת
בְּשַׁבַּתּוֹ יָבוֹא כָל ילי בָּשָׂר לְהִשְׁתַּחֲוֺת לְפָנַי חכמה, בינה אָמַר יְהֹוָה יאהדונהי:

וְיָצְאוּ וְרָאוּ (וְ־ VuVA)

בְּפִגְרֵי הָאֲנָשִׁים הַפֹּשְׁעִים בִּי כִּי תוֹלַעְתָּם לֹא תָמוּת וְאִשָּׁם לֹא תִכְבֶּה
וְהָיוּ דֵרָאוֹן לְכָל יה אדני בָּשָׂר: וְהָיָה יהוה, יהה מִדֵּי־חֹדֶשׁ בְּחָדְשׁוֹ וּמִדֵּי שַׁבָּת
בְּשַׁבַּתּוֹ יָבוֹא כָל ילי בָּשָׂר לְהִשְׁתַּחֲוֺת לְפָנַי חכמה, בינה אָמַר יְהֹוָה יאהדונהי:

YIRMIYAHU - JEREMIAH

דִּבְרֵי יִרְמְיָהוּ בֶּן־חִלְקִיָּהוּ מִן־הַכֹּהֲנִים אֲשֶׁר בַּעֲנָתוֹת בְּאֶרֶץ בִּנְיָמִן:
אֲשֶׁר הָיָה ההה יהה דְבַר ראה יְהֹוָה יאהדונהי אֵלָיו בִּימֵי יֹאשִׁיָּהוּ בֶן־אָמוֹן
מֶלֶךְ יְהוּדָה בִּשְׁלֹשׁ־עֶשְׂרֵה שָׁנָה לְמָלְכוֹ: וַיְהִי בִּימֵי יְהוֹיָקִים
בֶּן־יֹאשִׁיָּהוּ מֶלֶךְ יְהוּדָה עַד־תֹּם עַשְׁתֵּי עֶשְׂרֵה שָׁנָה לְצִדְקִיָּהוּ
בֶן־יֹאשִׁיָּהוּ מֶלֶךְ יְהוּדָה עַד־ גְּלוֹת יְרוּשָׁלַםִ בַּחֹדֶשׁ הַחֲמִישִׁי:

וַיְדַבֵּר אִתּוֹ טֹבוֹת וַיִּתֵּן אֶת־כִּסְאוֹ מִמַּעַל עלם לְכִסֵּא הַמְּלָכִים (כתיב: מלכים)
אֲשֶׁר אִתּוֹ בְּבָבֶל: וְשִׁנָּה אֵת בִּגְדֵי והו כִלְאוֹ וְאָכַל לֶחֶם ג"פ יהו"ה לְפָנָיו
תָּמִיד נתה, קס"א קנ"א קמ"ג כָּל ילי יְמֵי חַיָּו:

וַאֲרֻחָתוֹ אֲרֻחַת (אֶתָ–U Ta)

תָּמִיד נתה, קס"א קנ"א קמ"ג נִתְּנָה לּוֹ מֵאֵת מֶלֶךְ־בָּבֶל
דְּבַר־יוֹם בְּיוֹמוֹ עַד־יוֹם נגד, מזבח, זן מוֹתוֹ כֹּל ילי יְמֵי חַיָּיו:

YECHEZKEL - EZEKIEL

וַיְהִי בִּשְׁלֹשִׁים שָׁנָה בָּרְבִיעִי בַּחֲמִשָּׁה לַחֹדֶשׁ וַאֲנִי אני בְתוֹךְ־הַגּוֹלָה
עַל־נְהַר־כְּבָר נִפְתְּחוּ הַשָּׁמַיִם כוזו, י"פ טל וָאֶרְאֶה מַרְאוֹת אֱלֹהִים מום, ילה:
בַּחֲמִשָּׁה לַחֹדֶשׁ הִיא הַשָּׁנָה הַחֲמִישִׁית לְגָלוּת הַמֶּלֶךְ יוֹיָכִין: הָיֹה יהה
הָיָה יהה דְבַר ראה יְהֹוָהאדני אהדונהי אֶל־יְחֶזְקֵאל בֶּן־בּוּזִי הַכֹּהֵן מלה בְּאֶרֶץ
כַּשְׂדִּים עַל־נְהַר־כְּבָר וַתְּהִי עָלָיו שָׁם יַד־יְהֹוָהאדני אהדונהי: וָאֵרֶא וְהִנֵּה רוּחַ
סְעָרָה בָּאָה מִן־הַצָּפוֹן עָנָן גָּדוֹל להח, מבה וְאֵשׁ מִתְלַקַּחַת וְנֹגַהּ לוֹ סָבִיב
וּמִתּוֹכָהּ כְּעֵין ריבוע מ"ה הַחַשְׁמַל מִתּוֹךְ הָאֵשׁ: וּמִתּוֹכָהּ דְּמוּת אַרְבַּע חַיּוֹת
וְזֶה מַרְאֵיהֶן דְּמוּת אָדָם מ"ה לָהֵנָּה: וְאַרְבָּעָה פָנִים לְאֶחָת וְאַרְבַּע כְּנָפַיִם
לְאַחַת לָהֶם: וְרַגְלֵיהֶם רֶגֶל יְשָׁרָה וְכַף רַגְלֵיהֶם כְּכַף רֶגֶל עֵגֶל וְנֹצְצִים
כְּעֵין ריבוע מ"ה נְחֹשֶׁת קָלָל: וִידֵי (כתיב: וידו) אָדָם מ"ה מִתַּחַת כַּנְפֵיהֶם עַל
אַרְבַּעַת רִבְעֵיהֶם וּפְנֵיהֶם וְכַנְפֵיהֶם לְאַרְבַּעְתָּם: חֹבְרֹת אִשָּׁה אֶל־אֲחוֹתָהּ
כַּנְפֵיהֶם לֹא־יִסַּבּוּ בְלֶכְתָּן אִישׁ אֶל־עֵבֶר פָּנָיו יֵלֵכוּ: וּדְמוּת פְּנֵיהֶם
פְּנֵי חכמה, בינה אָדָם מ"ה וּפְנֵי חכמה, בינה אַרְיֵה רי"ו אֶל הַיָּמִין לְאַרְבַּעְתָּם וּפְנֵי־
שׁוֹר מֵהַשְּׂמֹאול לְאַרְבַּעְתָּן וּפְנֵי חכמה, בינה נֶשֶׁר לְאַרְבַּעְתָּן: וּפְנֵיהֶם וְכַנְפֵיהֶם
פְּרֻדוֹת מִלְמָעְלָה לְאִישׁ שְׁתַּיִם חֹבְרוֹת אִישׁ וּשְׁתַּיִם מְכַסּוֹת אֵת גְּוִיֹתֵיהֶנָה:
וְאִישׁ אֶל־עֵבֶר פָּנָיו יֵלֵכוּ אֶל אֲשֶׁר יִהְיֶה ייי שָׁמָּה הָרוּחַ לָלֶכֶת יֵלֵכוּ לֹא
יִסַּבּוּ בְּלֶכְתָּן: וּדְמוּת הַחַיּוֹת מַרְאֵיהֶם כְּגַחֲלֵי־אֵשׁ בֹּעֲרוֹת כְּמַרְאֵה
הַלַּפִּדִים הִיא מִתְהַלֶּכֶת בֵּין הַחַיּוֹת וְנֹגַהּ לָאֵשׁ וּמִן־הָאֵשׁ יוֹצֵא בָרָק:
וְהַחַיּוֹת רָצוֹא וָשׁוֹב כְּמַרְאֵה הַבָּזָק: וָאֵרֶא הַחַיּוֹת וְהִנֵּה אוֹפַן
אֶחָד אהבה, דאגה בָּאָרֶץ אֵצֶל הַחַיּוֹת לְאַרְבַּעַת פָּנָיו: מַרְאֵה ראה הָאוֹפַנִּים
וּמַעֲשֵׂיהֶם כְּעֵין ריבוע מ"ה תַּרְשִׁישׁ וּדְמוּת אֶחָד אהבה, דאגה
לְאַרְבַּעְתָּן וּמַרְאֵיהֶם וּמַעֲשֵׂיהֶם כַּאֲשֶׁר יִהְיֶה ייי הָאוֹפַן בְּתוֹךְ הָאוֹפָן:

עַל־אַרְבַּעַת רִבְעֵיהֶן בְּלֶכְתָּם יֵלֵכוּ לֹא יִסַּבּוּ בְּלֶכְתָּן׃ וְגַבֵּיהֶן וְגֹבַהּ לָהֶם
וְיִרְאָה רי״ו, גבורה לָהֶם וְגַבֹּתָם מְלֵאֹת עֵינַיִם סָבִיב לְאַרְבַּעְתָּן׃ וּבְלֶכֶת הַחַיּוֹת
יֵלְכוּ הָאוֹפַנִּים אֶצְלָם וּבְהִנָּשֵׂא הַחַיּוֹת מֵעַל עלם הָאָרֶץ אלהים דההין יִנָּשְׂאוּ
הָאוֹפַנִּים׃ עַל אֲשֶׁר יִהְיֶה יי״י שָׁם הָרוּחַ לָלֶכֶת יֵלֵכוּ שָׁמָּה הָרוּחַ לָלֶכֶת
וְהָאוֹפַנִּים יִנָּשְׂאוּ לְעֻמָּתָם כִּי רוּחַ הַחַיָּה בָּאוֹפַנִּים׃ בְּלֶכְתָּם יֵלֵכוּ וּבְעָמְדָם
יַעֲמֹדוּ וּבְהִנָּשְׂאָם מֵעַל עלם הָאָרֶץ אלהים דההין יִנָּשְׂאוּ הָאוֹפַנִּים לְעֻמָּתָם כִּי
רוּחַ הַחַיָּה בָּאוֹפַנִּים׃ וּדְמוּת עַל־רָאשֵׁי הַחַיָּה רָקִיעַ כְּעֵין ריבוע מ״ה הַקֶּרַח
הַנּוֹרָא נָטוּי עַל־רָאשֵׁיהֶם מִלְמָעְלָה׃ וְתַחַת הָרָקִיעַ כַּנְפֵיהֶם יְשָׁרוֹת אִשָּׁה
אֶל אֲחוֹתָהּ לְאִישׁ שְׁתַּיִם מְכַסּוֹת לָהֵנָּה וּלְאִישׁ שְׁתַּיִם מְכַסּוֹת לָהֵנָּה אֵת
גְּוִיֹּתֵיהֶם׃ וָאֶשְׁמַע אֶת־קוֹל כַּנְפֵיהֶם כְּקוֹל מַיִם ילי רַבִּים כְּקוֹל־שַׁדַּי
בְּלֶכְתָּם קוֹל הֲמֻלָּה כְּקוֹל מַחֲנֶה בְּעָמְדָם תְּרַפֶּינָה כַנְפֵיהֶן׃ וַיְהִי־קוֹל
מֵעַל עלם לָרָקִיעַ אֲשֶׁר עַל־רֹאשָׁם בְּעָמְדָם תְּרַפֶּינָה כַנְפֵיהֶן׃ וּמִמַּעַל עלם
לָרָקִיעַ אֲשֶׁר עַל־רֹאשָׁם כְּמַרְאֵה אֶבֶן־סַפִּיר דְּמוּת כִּסֵּא וְעַל דְּמוּת
הַכִּסֵּא דְּמוּת כְּמַרְאֵה אָדָם מ״ה עָלָיו מִלְמָעְלָה׃ וָאֵרֶא כְּעֵין ריבוע מ״ה
חַשְׁמַל כְּמַרְאֵה אֵשׁ בֵּית ב״פ ראה לָהּ סָבִיב מִמַּרְאֵה מָתְנָיו וּלְמָעְלָה
וּמִמַּרְאֵה מָתְנָיו וּלְמַטָּה רָאִיתִי כְּמַרְאֵה אֵשׁ וְנֹגַהּ לוֹ סָבִיב׃
כְּמַרְאֵה הַקֶּשֶׁת אֲשֶׁר יִהְיֶה יי״י בֶעָנָן בְּיוֹם נגד, מזבח, זן הַגֶּשֶׁם כֵּן מַרְאֵה ראה
הַנֹּגַהּ סָבִיב הוּא מַרְאֵה ראה דְּמוּת כְּבוֹד־יְהֹוָהאדני יאהדונהי וָאֶרְאֶה וָאֶפֹּל
עַל־פָּנַי וחכמה, בינה וָאֶשְׁמַע קוֹל מְדַבֵּר ראה׃ וַתִּשָּׂאֵנִי רוּחַ וָאֶשְׁמַע אַחֲרַי קוֹל
רַעַשׁ גָּדוֹל להח, מבה בָּרוּךְ כְּבוֹד־יְהֹוָהאדני יאהדונהי מִמְּקוֹמוֹ עסמ״ב׃ וּפְאַת־נֶגְבָּה
חֲמֵשׁ מֵאוֹת וְאַרְבַּעַת אֲלָפִים מִדָּה וּשְׁעָרִים כתר שְׁלֹשָׁה שַׁעַר שִׁמְעוֹן
אֶחָד אהבה, דאגה שַׁעַר יִשָּׂשכָר אֶחָד אהבה, דאגה שַׁעַר זְבוּלֻן אֶחָד אהבה, דאגה׃
פְּאַת־יָמָּה חֲמֵשׁ מֵאוֹת וְאַרְבַּעַת אֲלָפִים שַׁעֲרֵיהֶם שְׁלֹשָׁה שַׁעַר
גָּד אֶחָד אהבה, דאגה שַׁעַר אָשֵׁר אֶחָד אהבה, דאגה שַׁעַר נַפְתָּלִי אֶחָד אהבה, דאגה׃

סָבִיב שְׁמֹנָה פוי (שֻׁהָ–ShuHa)

עָשָׂר אָלֶף וְשֵׁם־הָעִיר ערי, סנזווך, סנדלפון מִיּוֹם נגד, מזבח, זן יְהֹוָהאדני יאהדונהי | שָׁמָּה׃

TREI ASAR – THE TWELVE PROPHETS

דְּבַר ראה יְהֹוָהאדני יאהדונהי אֲשֶׁר הָיָה יהה אֶל־הוֹשֵׁעַ בֶּן־בְּאֵרִי בִּימֵי עֻזִּיָּה יוֹתָם
אָחָז יְחִזְקִיָּה מַלְכֵי נלך יְהוּדָה וּבִימֵי יָרָבְעָם בֶּן־יוֹאָשׁ מֶלֶךְ יִשְׂרָאֵל׃

תְּחִלַּת דִּבֶּר ראה יְהֹוָה יאהדונהי בְּהוֹשֵׁעַ וַיֹּאמֶר יְהֹוָה יאהדונהי אֶל־הוֹשֵׁעַ לֵךְ
קַח־לְךָ אֵשֶׁת זְנוּנִים וְיַלְדֵי זְנוּנִים כִּי־זָנֹה תִזְנֶה הָאָרֶץ אלהים דההין מֵאַחֲרֵי
יְהֹוָה יאהדונהי: וַיֵּלֶךְ וַיִּקַּח וזעם אֶת־גֹּמֶר בַּת־דִּבְלָיִם וַתַּהַר וַתֵּלֶד־לוֹ בֵּן:
הַמַּשָּׂא אֲשֶׁר חָזָה חֲבַקּוּק הַנָּבִיא: עַד־אָנָה יְהֹוָה יאהדונהי שִׁוַּעְתִּי וְלֹא
תִשְׁמָע אֶזְעַק אֵלֶיךָ חָמָס וְלֹא תוֹשִׁיעַ: לָמָּה תַרְאֵנִי אָוֶן וְעָמָל תַּבִּיט וְשֹׁד
וְחָמָס לְנֶגְדִּי וַיְהִי רִיב וּמָדוֹן יִשָּׂא: וַיהֹוָה יאהדונהי בְּהֵיכַל אדני, ללה קָדְשׁוֹ הַס
מִפָּנָיו כָּל ילי הָאָרֶץ אלהים דההין: תְּפִלָּה לַחֲבַקּוּק הַנָּבִיא עַל שִׁגְיֹנוֹת:
יְהֹוָה יאהדונהי שָׁמַעְתִּי שִׁמְעֲךָ יָרֵאתִי יְהֹוָה יאהדונהי פָּעָלְךָ בְּקֶרֶב שָׁנִים
חַיֵּיהוּ בְּקֶרֶב שָׁנִים תּוֹדִיעַ בְּרֹגֶז רַחֵם אברהם, רמ״ח תִּזְכּוֹר: אֱלוֹהַּ מִתֵּימָן
יָבוֹא וְקָדוֹשׁ מֵהַר־פָּארָן סֶלָה כִּסָּה שָׁמַיִם כוזו, י״פ טל הוֹדוֹ אהיה וּתְהִלָּתוֹ
מָלְאָה הָאָרֶץ אלהים דההין: וְנֹגַהּ כָּאוֹר רז, אין סוף תִּהְיֶה קַרְנַיִם מִיָּדוֹ לוֹ וְשָׁם
חֶבְיוֹן עֻזֹּה: לְפָנָיו יֵלֶךְ דָּבֶר ראה וְיֵצֵא רֶשֶׁף לְרַגְלָיו: עָמַד | וַיְמֹדֶד אֶרֶץ
רָאָה ראה וַיַּתֵּר גּוֹיִם וַיִּתְפֹּצְצוּ הַרְרֵי־עַד שַׁחוּ גִּבְעוֹת עוֹלָם הֲלִיכוֹת עוֹלָם
לוֹ: תַּחַת אָוֶן רָאִיתִי אָהֳלֵי כוּשָׁן יִרְגְּזוּן יְרִיעוֹת אֶרֶץ מִדְיָן: הֲבִנְהָרִים חָרָה
יְהֹוָה יאהדונהי אִם יוהך בַּנְּהָרִים אַפֶּךָ אִם יוהך בַּיָּם ילי עֶבְרָתֶךָ כִּי תִרְכַּב עַל־
סוּסֶיךָ מַרְכְּבֹתֶיךָ יְשׁוּעָה: עֶרְיָה תֵעוֹר קַשְׁתֶּךָ שְׁבֻעוֹת מַטּוֹת אֹמֶר סֶלָה
נְהָרוֹת תְּבַקַּע־אָרֶץ: רָאוּךָ יָחִילוּ הָרִים זֶרֶם מַיִם ילי עָבָר נָתַן תְּהוֹם קוֹלוֹ
רוֹם יָדֵיהוּ נָשָׂא: שֶׁמֶשׁ יָרֵחַ עָמַד זְבֻלָה לְאוֹר רז, אין סוף חִצֶּיךָ יְהַלֵּכוּ לְנֹגַהּ
בְּרַק חֲנִיתֶךָ: בְּזַעַם תִּצְעַד־אָרֶץ בְּאַף תָּדוּשׁ גּוֹיִם: יָצָאתָ לְיֵשַׁע עַמֶּךָ
לְיֵשַׁע אֶת־מְשִׁיחֶךָ מָחַצְתָּ רֹּאשׁ מִבֵּית ב״פ ראה רָשָׁע עָרוֹת יְסוֹד ההע
עַד־צַוָּאר סֶלָה: נָקַבְתָּ בְמַטָּיו רֹאשׁ פְּרָזָיו (כתיב: פרזו) יִסְעֲרוּ לַהֲפִיצֵנִי
עֲלִיצֻתָם כְּמוֹ־לֶאֱכֹל עָנִי בַּמִּסְתָּר: דָּרַכְתָּ בַיָּם ילי סוּסֶיךָ חֹמֶר מַיִם ילי
רַבִּים: שָׁמַעְתִּי וַתִּרְגַּז בִּטְנִי לְקוֹל צָלְלוּ שְׂפָתַי יָבוֹא רָקָב בַּעֲצָמַי
וְתַחְתַּי אֶרְגָּז אֲשֶׁר אָנוּחַ לְיוֹם נגד, מזבח, זן צָרָה אלהים דההין לַעֲלוֹת
לְעַם עלם יְגוּדֶנּוּ: כִּי־תְאֵנָה לֹא־תִפְרָח וְאֵין יְבוּל בַּגְּפָנִים כִּחֵשׁ
מַעֲשֵׂה־זַיִת וּשְׁדֵמוֹת לֹא־עָשָׂה אֹכֶל גָּזַר מִמִּכְלָה צֹאן וְאֵין בָּקָר בָּרְפָתִים:
וַאֲנִי אני בַּיהֹוָה יאהדונהי אֶעְלוֹזָה אָגִילָה בֵּאלֹהֵי דמב, ילה יִשְׁעִי:
יֱהֹוִה יאהדונהי אֲדֹנָי חֵילִי וַיָּשֶׂם רַגְלַי כָּאַיָּלוֹת וְעַל בָּמוֹתַי יַדְרִכֵנִי לַמְנַצֵּחַ
בִּנְגִינוֹתָי: זִכְרוּ תּוֹרַת מֹשֶׁה מהש עַבְדִּי אֲשֶׁר צִוִּיתִי אוֹתוֹ בְחֹרֵב עַל־כָּל ילי
יִשְׂרָאֵל חֻקִּים וּמִשְׁפָּטִים: הִנֵּה אָנֹכִי איע שֹׁלֵחַ לָכֶם אֵת אֵלִיָּה הַנָּבִיא
לִפְנֵי חכמה, בינה בּוֹא יוֹם נגד, מזבח, זן יְהֹוָה יאהדונהי הַגָּדוֹל להח, מבה וְהַנּוֹרָא:

וְהֵשִׁיב לֵב (לֵבָ–LuVA)
אָבוֹת עַל־בָּנִים וְלֵב בָּנִים עַל־אֲבוֹתָם פֶּן־אָבוֹא וְהִכֵּיתִי אֶת־
הָאָרֶץ אלהים דההין חֵרֶם׃ הִנֵּה אָנֹכִי איע שֹׁלֵחַ לָכֶם אֵת אֵלִיָּה הַנָּבִיא
לִפְנֵי חכמה, בינה בּוֹא יוֹם נגד, מזבח, זן יְהֹוָהאדניאהדונהי הַגָּדוֹל להח, מבה וְהַנּוֹרָא׃

Here we say *Kaddish Al Yisrael* (on pg. 444-446)

TEHILIM - PSALMS

אַשְׁרֵי־הָאִישׁ אֲשֶׁר לֹא הָלַךְ בַּעֲצַת רְשָׁעִים וּבְדֶרֶךְ חַטָּאִים לֹא עָמָד
וּבְמוֹשַׁב לֵצִים לֹא יָשָׁב׃ כִּי אִם יהך בְּתוֹרַת יְהֹוָהאדניאהדונהי חֶפְצוֹ וּבְתוֹרָתוֹ
יֶהְגֶּה יוֹמָם וָלָיְלָה מלה׃ וְהָיָה יהוה, יהה כְּעֵץ שָׁתוּל עַל־פַּלְגֵי מָיִם ילי אֲשֶׁר פִּרְיוֹ
יִתֵּן בְּעִתּוֹ וְעָלֵהוּ לֹא־יִבּוֹל וְכֹל ילי אֲשֶׁר־יַעֲשֶׂה יַצְלִיחַ׃ לֹא־כֵן הָרְשָׁעִים כִּי
אִם כַּמֹּץ אֲשֶׁר־תִּדְּפֶנּוּ רוּחַ׃ עַל־כֵּן לֹא־יָקֻמוּ רְשָׁעִים בַּמִּשְׁפָּט וְחַטָּאִים
בַּעֲדַת צַדִּיקִים׃ כִּי־יוֹדֵעַ יְהֹוָהאדניאהדונהי דֶּרֶךְ צַדִּיקִים וְדֶרֶךְ רְשָׁעִים
תֹּאבֵד׃ הַלְלוּיָהּ הַלְלוּ אֵל בְּקָדְשׁוֹ הַלְלוּהוּ בִּרְקִיעַ עֻזּוֹ׃ הַלְלוּהוּ בִגְבוּרֹתָיו
הַלְלוּהוּ כְּרֹב גֻּדְלוֹ׃ הַלְלוּהוּ בְּתֵקַע שׁוֹפָר הַלְלוּהוּ בְּנֵבֶל וְכִנּוֹר׃
הַלְלוּהוּ בְתֹף וּמָחוֹל הַלְלוּהוּ בְּמִנִּים וְעוּגָב׃ הַלְלוּהוּ בְצִלְצְלֵי שָׁמַע הַלְלוּהוּ
בְּצִלְצְלֵי תְרוּעָה׃ כֹּל ילי הַנְּשָׁמָה (הֻהָ–HuHA) תְּהַלֵּל ר״ת כהת יָהּ הַלְלוּיָהּ׃

IYOV - JOB

אִישׁ הָיָה ההה יהה בְאֶרֶץ־עוּץ אִיּוֹב שְׁמוֹ וְהָיָה יהוה, יהה הָאִישׁ הַהוּא תָּם
וְיָשָׁר וִירֵא אֱלֹהִים מום, ילה וְסָר מֵרָע׃ וַיִּוָּלְדוּ לוֹ שִׁבְעָה בָנִים וְשָׁלוֹשׁ בָּנוֹת׃
וַיְהִי מִקְנֵהוּ שִׁבְעַת אַלְפֵי־צֹאן וּשְׁלֹשֶׁת אַלְפֵי גְמַלִּים וַחֲמֵשׁ מֵאוֹת
צֶמֶד־בָּקָר וַחֲמֵשׁ מֵאוֹת אֲתוֹנוֹת וַעֲבֻדָּה רַבָּה מְאֹד וַיְהִי הָאִישׁ הַהוּא
גָּדוֹל להח, מבה מִכָּל ילי בְּנֵי־ קֶדֶם׃ וְלֹא נִמְצָא נָשִׁים יָפוֹת כִּבְנוֹת אִיּוֹב
בְּכָל ילי לכב הָאָרֶץ אלהים דההין וַיִּתֵּן לָהֶם אֲבִיהֶם נַחֲלָה בְּתוֹךְ אֲחֵיהֶם׃ וַיְחִי
אִיּוֹב אַחֲרֵי־זֹאת מֵאָה וְאַרְבָּעִים שָׁנָה וַיַּרְא (כתיב: ויראה) אֶת־בָּנָיו
וְאֶת־בְּנֵי בָנָיו אַרְבָּעָה דֹּרוֹת׃ וַיָּמָת אִיּוֹב (אֻבָ–U VA) זָקֵן וּשְׂבַע יָמִים נלך׃

MISHLEI - PROVERBS

מִשְׁלֵי שְׁלֹמֹה בֶן־דָּוִד מֶלֶךְ יִשְׂרָאֵל: לָדַעַת חָכְמָה וּמוּסָר לְהָבִין אִמְרֵי בִינָה וחיים: לָקַחַת מוּסַר הַשְׂכֵּל צֶדֶק וּמִשְׁפָּט וּמֵישָׁרִים: אֵשֶׁת־חַיִל ומב מִי יכלי יִמְצָא וְרָחֹק מִפְּנִינִים מִכְרָהּ: בָּטַח בָּהּ לֵב בַּעְלָהּ וְשָׁלָל לֹא יֶחְסָר: גְּמָלַתְהוּ טוֹב והו וְלֹא־רָע כֹּל יכלי יְמֵי חַיֶּיהָ: דָּרְשָׁה צֶמֶר מצר וּפִשְׁתִּים וַתַּעַשׂ בְּחֵפֶץ כַּפֶּיהָ: הָיְתָה כָּאֳנִיּוֹת סוֹחֵר מִמֶּרְחָק תָּבִיא לַחְמָהּ: וַתָּקָם | בְּעוֹד לַיְלָה מלה וַתִּתֵּן ב"פ כהת טֶרֶף לְבֵיתָהּ וְחֹק לְנַעֲרֹתֶיהָ: זָמְמָה שָׂדֶה וַתִּקָּחֵהוּ מִפְּרִי כַפֶּיהָ נָטְעָה (כתיב: נטע) כָּרֶם: חָגְרָה בְעוֹז מָתְנֶיהָ וַתְּאַמֵּץ זְרֹעוֹתֶיהָ: טָעֲמָה כִּי־טוֹב והו סַחְרָהּ לֹא־יִכְבֶּה בַלַּיְלָה (כתיב: בליל) נֵרָהּ: יָדֶיהָ שִׁלְּחָה בַכִּישׁוֹר וְכַפֶּיהָ תָּמְכוּ פָלֶךְ: כַּפָּהּ פָּרְשָׂה לֶעָנִי וְיָדֶיהָ שִׁלְּחָה לָאֶבְיוֹן: לֹא־תִירָא לְבֵיתָהּ מִשָּׁלֶג כִּי כָל יכלי בֵּיתָהּ לָבֻשׁ שָׁנִים: מַרְבַדִּים עָשְׂתָה־לָּהּ שֵׁשׁ וְאַרְגָּמָן לְבוּשָׁהּ: נוֹדָע בַּשְּׁעָרִים כתר בַּעְלָהּ בְּשִׁבְתּוֹ עִם־זִקְנֵי־אָרֶץ: סָדִין עָשְׂתָה וַתִּמְכֹּר וַחֲגוֹר נָתְנָה לַכְּנַעֲנִי: עֹז־וְהָדָר לְבוּשָׁהּ וַתִּשְׂחַק לְיוֹם נגד, מזבח, זן אַחֲרוֹן: פִּיהָ פָּתְחָה בְחָכְמָה וְתוֹרַת־חֶסֶד ע"ב, ריבוע יהוה עַל־לְשׁוֹנָהּ: צוֹפִיָּה הֲלִיכוֹת (כתיב: הילכות) בֵּיתָהּ וְלֶחֶם ג"פ יהו"ה עַצְלוּת לֹא תֹאכֵל: קָמוּ בָנֶיהָ וַיְאַשְּׁרוּהָ בַּעְלָהּ וַיְהַלְלָהּ: רַבּוֹת בָּנוֹת עָשׂוּ חָיִל ומב וְאַתְּ עָלִית עַל־כֻּלָּנָה: שֶׁקֶר הַחֵן מוחי וְהֶבֶל הַיֹּפִי אִשָּׁה יִרְאַת־יְהֹוָהאדניאהדונהי הִיא תִתְהַלָּל: תְּנוּ־לָהּ (לָהּ–LuHa) מִפְּרִי יָדֶיהָ וִיהַלְלוּהָ בַשְּׁעָרִים כתר מַעֲשֶׂיהָ:

DANIEL - DANIEL

בִּשְׁנַת שָׁלוֹשׁ לְמַלְכוּת יְהוֹיָקִים מֶלֶךְ־יְהוּדָה בָּא נְבוּכַדְנֶאצַּר מֶלֶךְ־בָּבֶל יְרוּשָׁלִַם וַיָּצַר עָלֶיהָ: וַיִּתֵּן אֲדֹנָי בְּיָדוֹ אֶת־יְהוֹיָקִים מֶלֶךְ־יְהוּדָה וּמִקְצָת כְּלֵי בֵית ב"פ ראה הָאֱלֹהִים מום, ילה וַיְבִיאֵם אֶרֶץ־שִׁנְעָר בֵּית ב"פ ראה אֱלֹהָיו ילה וְאֶת־הַכֵּלִים הֵבִיא בֵּית ב"פ ראה אוֹצַר אֱלֹהָיו ילה: וַיֹּאמֶר הַמֶּלֶךְ לְאַשְׁפְּנַז רַב סָרִיסָיו לְהָבִיא מִבְּנֵי יִשְׂרָאֵל וּמִזֶּרַע הַמְּלוּכָה וּמִן־הַפַּרְתְּמִים: וּמֵעֵת הוּסַר הַתָּמִיד נתה, קס"א קנ"א קמ"ג וְלָתֵת שִׁקּוּץ שֹׁמֵם יָמִים נלך אֶלֶף מָאתַיִם וְתִשְׁעִים: אַשְׁרֵי הַמְחַכֶּה וְיַגִּיעַ לְיָמִים נלך אֶלֶף שְׁלֹשׁ מֵאוֹת שְׁלֹשִׁים וַחֲמִשָּׁה: וְאַתָּה לֵךְ (לְכָה–LuCHA) לַקֵּץ מנק וְתָנוּחַ וְתַעֲמֹד לְגֹרָלְךָ לְקֵץ מנק הַיָּמִין:

DIVREI HAYAMIM - CHRONICLES

אָדָם מ״ה שֵׁת אֱנוֹשׁ: קֵינָן מַהֲלַלְאֵל יָרֶד: חֲנוֹךְ מְתוּשֶׁלַח לָמֶךְ: לִמְלֹאות
דְּבַר ראה יְהֹוָאדניהיאהדונהי בְּפִי יִרְמְיָהוּ עַד־רָצְתָה הָאָרֶץ אלהים דההין
אֶת־שַׁבְּתוֹתֶיהָ כָּל ילי יְמֵי הָשַּׁמָּה שָׁבָתָה לְמַלֹּאות שִׁבְעִים שָׁנָה: וּבִשְׁנַת
אַחַת לְכוֹרֶשׁ מֶלֶךְ פָּרַס לִכְלוֹת דְּבַר ראה יְהֹוָאדניהיאהדונהי בְּפִי יִרְמְיָהוּ הֵעִיר
יְהֹוָאדניהיאהדונהי אֶת־רוּחַ כּוֹרֶשׁ מֶלֶךְ־פָּרַס וַיַּעֲבֶר־ רפ״ח קוֹל בְּכָל ילי לכב
מַלְכוּתוֹ וְגַם־בְּמִכְתָּב לֵאמֹר: כֹּה היי אָמַר (אֳרָ–U RA) כּוֹרֶשׁ מֶלֶךְ פָּרַס
כָּל ילי מַמְלְכוֹת הָאָרֶץ אלהים דההין נָתַן לִי יְהֹוָאדניהיאהדונהי אֱלֹהֵי דמב, ילה
הַשָּׁמַיִם כוזו, י״פ טל וְהוּא־פָקַד עָלַי לִבְנוֹת־לוֹ בַיִת ב״פ ראה בִּירוּשָׁלַםִ
אֲשֶׁר בִּיהוּדָה מִי־בָכֶם מִכָּל ילי עַמּוֹ יְהֹוָאדניהיאהדונהי אֱלֹהָיו ילה עִמּוֹ וְיָעַל:

EZRA VENECHEMIA – EZRA AND NEHEMIAH

וּבִשְׁנַת אַחַת לְכוֹרֶשׁ מֶלֶךְ פָּרַס לִכְלוֹת דְּבַר ראה יְהֹוָאדניהיאהדונהי מִפִּי יִרְמְיָה
הֵעִיר ערי, סנדלפון יְהֹוָאדניהיאהדונהי אֶת־רוּחַ כֹּרֶשׁ מֶלֶךְ־פָּרַס וַיַּעֲבֶר רפ״ח
קוֹל בְּכָל ילי לכב מַלְכוּתוֹ וְגַם־בְּמִכְתָּב לֵאמֹר: כֹּה היי אָמַר כֹּרֶשׁ מֶלֶךְ פָּרַס
כֹּל ילי מַמְלְכוֹת הָאָרֶץ אלהים דההין נָתַן לִי יְהֹוָאדניהיאהדונהי אֱלֹהֵי דמב, ילה
הַשָּׁמָיִם כוזו, י״פ טל וְהוּא־פָקַד עָלַי לִבְנוֹת־לוֹ בַיִת ב״פ ראה בִּירוּשָׁלַםִ אֲשֶׁר
בִּיהוּדָה: מִי־בָכֶם מִכָּל ילי עַמּוֹ יְהִי אֱלֹהָיו ילה עִמּוֹ וְיַעַל לִירוּשָׁלַםִ אֲשֶׁר
בִּיהוּדָה וְיִבֶן אֶת־בֵּית ב״פ ראה יְהֹוָאדניהיאהדונהי אֱלֹהֵי דמב, ילה יִשְׂרָאֵל הוּא
הָאֱלֹהִים מום, ילה אֲשֶׁר בִּירוּשָׁלָםִ: זָכְרָה לָהֶם אֱלֹהָי דמב, ילה עַל גָּאֳלֵי
הַכְּהֻנָּה וּבְרִית הַכְּהֻנָּה וְהַלְוִיִּם: וְטִהַרְתִּים מִכָּל ילי נֵכָר וָאַעֲמִידָה מִשְׁמָרוֹת
לַכֹּהֲנִים וְלַלְוִיִּם אִישׁ בִּמְלַאכְתּוֹ: וּלְקֻרְבַּן הָעֵצִים (הֻמָ–HUMA) בְּעִתִּים
מְזֻמָּנוֹת וְלַבִּכּוּרִים זָכְרָה־לִּי אֱלֹהַי דמב, ילה לְטוֹבָה אכא:

Here we say *Kaddish Al Yisrael* (on pg. 444-446)

SPECIAL MEDITATION FOR SPIRITUAL MEMORY

Rav Chaim Vital writes (Gate of Divine Inspiration, pg. 87), "One *Yichud* (unification) that augments the memory of every person is the secret of the two Names of *Yud* and *Hei* spelled out with *Yud* and with *Hei*. Their letters are combined together, one letter from each at a time, as follows:

ייוודדההיה ייוודדהההי

The time for this meditation is every morning at dawn.

MORNING BLESSINGS

You should say the Morning Blessings from midnight onward. And you should be aware to say all of the blessings as soon as you rise after midnight, and if you don't say them completely upon rising after midnight, you are preventing the abundance of the Upper World and the *Mochin* from infusing the Upper *Partzufim*. And you also cause the *klipot* to remain attached in the upper places. Also, the *klipot's* power spreads into your *Nefesh*, *Ruach*, *Neshamah*, *Chaya*, *Yechida*, and your senses. Using your senses now, together with the *klipot*, attached, you become drained of energy instead of grasping the opportunity to use the power to remove and cancel the *klipot*. And this is one of the reasons that other kinds of misfortune and chaos occur in our lives, Heaven Forbid, and for this reason it is important to say all the Morning Blessings when you rise at midnight, even if you plan to go to sleep afterwards, this does not apply to sleeping during the day – as there is no negative energy attached to daytime sleep. When you rise after midnight, or do not sleep at all and begin studying after midnight, you should also say the Morning Blessings (excluding the Torah Blessings, which will be said at dawn). As it is mentioned in the *Zohar, Vayakhel* 14-25: "Rav Elazar and Rav Yossi were studying from the beginning of the night, when midnight came they heard the cry of the rooster and they did say the Morning Blessings." (*Nahar Shalom*, pg. 88)

MODEH ANI

Every night, when our souls ascend to the Upper Worlds, a powerful force attempts to stop us from awakening and seeing the light of a new day. This force resides within each one of us. It is our negative side, or, what the kabbalists call our "Evil Inclination," fueled by our negative behavior from the previous day. However, the Creator gives us another chance each day to change and reveal the Light that we failed to reveal the day before. The connection of *Modeh Ani* allows us to take advantage of this opportunity. This sequence of Aramaic letters arouses our appreciation for the return of our soul to our body. This act of appreciation helps to strengthen and protect all the blessings we receive.

When you wake up, even though your hands are not clean, you can still say the verse "*modeh ani*" since it does not contain one of the Holy Names.

מוֹדֶה modeh (Women say: מוֹדָה moda) אֲנִי ani אנ"י לְפָנֶיךָ lefanecha ס"ג מ"ה ב"ן

מֶלֶךְ melech חַי chai וְקַיָּם vekayam שֶׁהֶחֱזַרְתָּ shehechezarta בִּי bi

נִשְׁמָתִי nishmati בְּחֶמְלָה bechemla. רַבָּה raba אֱמוּנָתֶךָ emunatecha:

MORNING BLESSINGS

MODEH ANI

I give thanks before You, living and existing King,
for restoring my soul to me, compassionately. Great is Your trustworthiness. (*Beresheet Rabba, Ch 68*)

WASHING OF THE HANDS

When we sleep at night, many negative forces latch onto our body. When our soul returns and reconnects with our body, it removes most of that negativity, but not from our hands. By washing our hands each morning upon waking, we accomplish three important objectives:
1) To cleanse and wash away all negative forces that cling to our hands during the night;
2) To connect ourselves to the cause and seed level of reality (proactive) and not just the effect (reactive);
3) To detach ourselves from the energy of *ani* (poor) and connect ourselves to the energy of *ashir* (rich).

Wash your hands in the water of *Chesed* (mercy) to remove the filth of the *klipa* that is attached to the 5 *Gevurot* (judgments) מנצפך that are revealed by the ten fingers of the hands of *Zeir Anpin* of *Asiyah*. **First,** hold the washing vessel in your right hand and fill it with water, and then hand it over to the left hand. **Then,** pour the water from the left onto the right and then pour water from the right onto the left. This process should be repeated a second and a third time. In a way that every hand would be washed three times. You should not wash one hand three times in a row, but alternate between right and left and in doing so the impure spirit that is called "*Shiv'ta* **(do not pronounce this name)** the daughter of a king" jumps from one hand to the other until it is completely removed from the hands. And if you don't follow this order, this impure spirit is not removed. Before the blessing, you should open the palms of your hands like someone who wants to receive something, and meditate to raise *Asiyah* by the 42-Letter Name of *Yetzirah*, which is the numerical value of three hands:

Right hand (*HaGedola*) יהוה אלהינו יהוה, the secret of the first half of the Name יוד ואו דלת הא אלף
Left hand (*HaChazaka*) כוזו במוכסז כוזו, the secret of the last half of the Name ואו אלף ואו הא אלף
Middle Hand (*Rama*) יהוה יוד הא ואו הא Is the root of the Name itself and from it spreads those three hands and therefore it is in the middle. And by these three hands of *Yetzirah* we raise *Asiyah*.

The washing of the hands is the *tikkun* of the Inner Light, its interior and exterior (*Netzach, Hod, Yesod*) of *Asiyah*. **The blessing** is the *tikkun* of the Surrounding Light of the exterior (*Netzach, Hod, Yesod*) of *Asiyah*. 13 words correspond to the Thirteen Attributes of *Asiyah*.

Wash your hands, go to the bathroom as necessary, and then wash your hands again. The way to wash our hands: Hold the washing vessel in your right hand and fill it with water, and then hand it over to your left hand. Then, pour the water from the left over the right and then pour water from the right onto the left. That process should be repeated a second and a third time. You should not wash them three times in a row, but alternate between right and left. Rub your hands together 3 times and raise them to the level of the eyes and say the blessing before drying the hands.

בָּרוּךְ baruch (אל) אַתָּה Ata (רחום) יְהֹוָהאדניאהדונהי Adonai (וחנון)
אֱלֹהֵינוּ Elohenu ילה (ארך) מֶלֶךְ melech (אפים) הָעוֹלָם ha'olam (ורב חסד)
אֲשֶׁר asher (ואמת) קִדְּשָׁנוּ kideshanu (נצר חסד) בְּמִצְוֹתָיו bemitzvotav (לאלפים)
וְצִוָּנוּ vetzivanu (נשא עון) עַל al (ופשע) נְטִילַת netilat (וחטאה) יָדָיִם yadayim (ונקה)

The last three words of this blessing are *Al Netilat Yadayim*: The first letter from each of these three words spells *ani* ענ״י, Aramaic for "a poor person," and has the numerical value as the Holy Name *Mem Hei* (יוד הא ואו הא). The last 2 letters of each of these 3 words, *Ayin Lamed* על, *Lamed Tav* לת, and *Yud Mem* ים, have the same numerical value as the word *ashir* עשיר, meaning "a rich person."

WASHING OF THE HANDS

Blessed are You, Lord, our God, the King of the world,
Who has sanctified us with His commandments and obliges us with the washing of the hands.

ASHER YATZAR

Reciting *Asher Yatzar* after each time we have been to the bathroom connects us to the original spiritual DNA and blueprint of a human being. We may wake up in the morning feeling depleted of spiritual energy, depressed, fearful, moody, or even full of dread for the day to come. Through the power of *Asher Yatzar*, we inject the Light of Creation into our immune system; strengthening and boosting it so that we become filled with Light and spiritually recharged for the entire day.

In this section, there are 45 words, which are equal to the numerical value of the word *Adam* (human being) and the same numerical value of the name *Mem-Hei*, which was created by *Chochmah*. The word *Chochmah* is divided to two other words which mean strength (*Ko'ach*) to the *Mem-Hei*.

You should meditate on the Holy Name *Mem-Hei*:

יוד הא ואו הא

The blessing is the *tikkun* of Surrounding Light of the interior (*Netzach, Hod, Yesod*) of *Asiyah*.

(*Abba* of *Asiyah*) בָּרוּךְ baruch אַתָּה Ata יְהֹוָהאדניאהדונהי Adonai

אֱלֹהֵינוּ Elohenu ילה מֶלֶךְ melech הָעוֹלָם ha'olam אֲשֶׁר asher יָצַר yatzar

אֶת et הָאָדָם ha'adam מ"ה בְּחָכְמָה bechochma במילוי תרי"ג (מצוות).

וּבָרָא uvara קנ"א ב"ן, יהוה אלהים יהוה אדני, מילוי קס"א וס"ג, מ"ה ברבוע וע"ב ע"ה

בוֹ vo נְקָבִים nekavim נְקָבִים nekavim. וַחֲלוּלִים chalulim

וַחֲלוּלִים chalulim אברהם, וז"פ אל, רי"ו ול"ב נתיבות החכמה, רמ"ח (אברים), עסמ"ב וט"ז אותיות

פשוטות. גָּלוּי galuy וְיָדוּעַ veyadu'a לִפְנֵי lifnei כִסֵּא chise כְבוֹדֶךָ chevodecha

שֶׁאִם she'im לכב ב"ן, יוהך, מ"א אותיות דפשוט, דמילוי ודמילוי דמילוי דאהיה ע"ה

יִסָּתֵם yisatem אֶחָד echad אהבה, דאגה מֵהֶם mehem אוֹ oh אִם im יוהך, מ"א

אותיות דפשוט, דמילוי ודמילוי דמילוי דאהיה ע"ה יִפָּתֵחַ yipate'ach אֶחָד echad אהבה, דאגה

מֵהֶם mehem אִי ei אֶפְשָׁר efshar לְהִתְקַיֵּם lehitkayem אֲפִלּוּ afilu

שָׁעָה sha'a אַחַת echat. בָּרוּךְ baruch אַתָּה Ata יְהֹוָהאדניאהדונהי Adonai

רוֹפֵא rofe כָל chol ילי בָשָׂר basar וּמַפְלִיא umafli לַעֲשׂוֹת la'asot:

ASHER YATZAR

Blessed are You, Lord, our God, the King of the world, Who made man with wisdom and created in him many openings and many cavities. It is obvious and known before Your Throne of Glory that should any one of them become blocked or should any one of them break open, then it would be impossible to remain alive for even one hour. Blessed are You, Lord, the Healer of all flesh and Who amazes by what He does.

Elohai Neshamah: connecting with our soul

Kabbalah teaches us that there are five main levels of our soul: *Nefesh, Ruach, Neshamah, Chaya* and *Yechida*. In our day-to-day lives, most of us are not fully connected to all five levels. An umbilical-like cord constantly runs through the five levels of the soul, feeding us the minimum amount of Light we need to keep the "pilot light" glimmering in our soul. We recite *Elohai Neshamah* every morning to connect our conscious mind to the five levels of our soul so that we can awaken our true purpose and meaning in life.

The name of a person is not merely a word; it is also the spiritual connection to the soul. Each letter of a name is part of the spiritual genetic alphabet that infuses the soul with the particular form of energy that the name creates. The power of this blessing is that it tunnels through the Upper Worlds and creates a connection to all five parts of our soul. We deepen our connection to this prayer by combining our Hebrew name with the word *Neshamah* (soul). To merge your name with *Neshamah*, from right to left; **On weekdays,** insert the first letter of your name followed by the first letter of *Neshamah.* Then insert the second letter of your name followed by the second letter of *Neshamah,* and so on. **On Shabbat**, insert the first letter of *Neshamah* followed by the first letter of your name. Then insert the second letter of your *Neshamah* followed by the second letter of name, and so on. Meditate on the entire sequence of letters before connecting to the prayer. For example, with the name *Yehuda,* the combinations will look as follows:

Not every person merits the part of the soul called *Neshamah*, however, we all still have a part of the soul of Adam (the first man) that encompasses all of Creation.

In this blessing, there are 47 words, which are equal to the numerical value of:

יאהדונהי

(Pause here) ילה ; דמב ,ע"ב מילוי Elohai אֱלֹהַי *(Ima of Asiyah)*

(five aspects of the collective *Atzilut*, *Beriah*, *Yetzirah* and *Asiyah*) neshama נְשָׁמָה

◆(*Chayah* from *Atzilut*) tehora טְהוֹרָה (in the soul of *Adam*) bi בִּי shenatata שֶׁנָּתַתָּ

Ata אַתָּה ◆(*Neshamah* from *Beriah*) verata בְרָאתָהּ Ata אַתָּה

nefachta נְפַחְתָּהּ Ata אַתָּה ◆(*Ruach* from *Yetzirah*) yetzarta יְצַרְתָּהּ

meshamera מְשַׁמְּרָהּ veAta וְאַתָּה ◆(*Nefesh* from *Asiyah*) bi בִּי

litela לִטְּלָהּ atid עָתִיד veAta וְאַתָּה ◆שדי bekirbi בְּקִרְבִּי

◆lavo לָבֹא le'atid לֶעָתִיד bi בִּי ulhachazira וּלְהַחֲזִירָהּ mimeni מִמֶּנִּי

Elohai Neshamah

My God,

the soul that You have given in me is pure. You have formed it. You have created it. You have breathed it into me and You preserve it within me. You shall eventually take it away from me yet return it to me in the coming future.

כָּל kol ילי זְמַן zeman שֶׁהַנְּשָׁמָה shehaneshamah בְּקִרְבִּי vekirbi שדי

מוֹדֶה modeh אֲנִי ani אני לְפָנֶיךָ lefanecha ס״ג מ״ה ב״ן

יְהֹוָה יאהדונהי Adonai אֱלֹהַי Elohai מילוי ע״ב, דמב ; ילה וֵאלֹהֵי velohei

לכב ; מילוי ע״ב, דמב ; ילה אֲבוֹתַי avotai רִבּוֹן ribon יהוה ע״ב ס״ג מ״ה ב״ן

כָּל kol ילי הַמַּעֲשִׂים hama'asim. אֲדוֹן adon אני כָּל kol ילי

הַנְּשָׁמוֹת haneshamot. בָּרוּךְ baruch אַתָּה Ata יְהֹוָה יאהדונהי Adonai

הַמַּחֲזִיר hamachazir נְשָׁמוֹת neshamot לִפְגָרִים lifgarim מֵתִים metim:

THE EIGHTEEN BLESSINGS

The purpose of the Eighteen Blessings is to reconnect our soul to our physical body after it has been almost totally disconnected during the previous night's sleep. All of us are blessed with various gifts that, most of the time we do not appreciate, such as the connection of our soul to our body. Unfortunately, most of us only start to appreciate our gifts once we have lost them. Through the power of these Eighteen Blessings, we can inject a proactive energy force of appreciation, which, in turn, protects and preserves all that we hold dear.

The Eighteen Blessings correspond to *Yesod* of *Asiyah*. With these blessings, we draw great abundance and great illumination to the three upper *Sefirot* of *Asiyah*, and by that, their external part is blessed and receives this great Light and the external becomes equal to the internal.

THE FIRST BLESSING - DISTINGUISHES BETWEEN DAY AND NIGHT

The greatest gift we have as human beings is the power of free will. The phrase "distinguishing between day and night" refers to the ability we have to choose the Light of the Creator over darkness or good over evil. By saying this blessing, we are given clarity to see these two opposing forces that are usually concealed from us.

The First Blessing is in the three *Partzufim* of *Keter*: external, middle and internal of Direct Light of the middle *Partzuf* of *Zeir Anpin* of *Asiyah* of *Atzilut*, and of Lower *Asiyah*.

בָּרוּךְ baruch אַתָּה Ata יְהֹוָה יאהדונהי Adonai אֱלֹהֵינוּ Elohenu ילה

מֶלֶךְ melech הָעוֹלָם ha'olam הַנּוֹתֵן hanoten אבגיתץ, ושר

לַשֶּׂכְוִי lasechvi שכוי ע״ה = מלאך גבריאל בִּינָה vina ע״ה חיים, אהיה אהיה יהוה ;

ר״ת מילוי ס״ג (sweetening the night's judgment) וס״ת = ללה, אדני לְהַבְחִין lehavchin

בֵּין ben יוֹם yom ע״ה נגד, מזבח, זן, אל יהוה וּבֵין uven לָיְלָה layla מלה ; ר״ת = ג״פ יהוה:

As long as the soul is within me, I am grateful to You, Lord, my God and the God of my fathers, the Governor of all actions. The Master of all souls. Blessed are You, Lord, Who restores souls to dead corpses.

THE EIGHTEEN BLESSINGS - THE FIRST BLESSING

Blessed are You, Lord, our God,

the King of the world, Who gives the rooster the understanding to distinguish between day and night.

THE SECOND BLESSING - GIVES SIGHT TO THE BLIND

King David said: "*We have eyes, but see not. We have ears, but hear not.*" Too often, we are blinded by a lucrative opportunity or we fail to anticipate the chaos of an impending situation. The real power of this blessing is that it helps heighten our senses of perception and intuition so that we can see the truths that are normally concealed from us.

The Second Blessing is in the three *Partzufim* of *Keter*: external, middle and internal of Returning Light of the middle *Partzuf* of *Zeir Anpin* of *Asiyah* of *Atzilut*, and of Lower *Asiyah*.

baruch בָּרוּךְ Ata אַתָּה Adonai יְהֹוָאדניאהדונהי Elohenu אֱלֹהֵינוּ ילה
melech מֶלֶךְ ha'olam הָעוֹלָם poke'ach פּוֹקֵחַ ivrim עִוְרִים:

THE THIRD BLESSING - RELEASES THOSE WHO ARE BOUND

Often we become prisoners of our jobs, our mortgage payments, our relationships, our careers, or even other people's perceptions of us. In essence, to one degree or another, everyone is a prisoner, held captive by his *Desire to Receive for the Self Alone*. The energy that emanates from this blessing has the power to release us from the clutches of this powerful and self-destructive desire.

The Third Blessing is in the three of *Partzufim* of *Chochmah*: external, middle and internal of Direct Light of the middle *Partzuf* of *Zeir Anpin* of *Asiyah* of *Atzilut*, and of Lower *Asiyah*.

baruch בָּרוּךְ Ata אַתָּה Adonai יְהֹוָאדניאהדונהי Elohenu אֱלֹהֵינוּ ילה
melech מֶלֶךְ ha'olam הָעוֹלָם matir מַתִּיר asurim אֲסוּרִים:

THE FOURTH BLESSING – STRAIGHTENS THOSE WHO ARE BENT OVER

The inner meaning of this blessing pertains to the often skewed view we have of the world and the people around us. Our self-centered ego distorts our perception of reality to the point where everyone else appears crooked, imperfect, and wrong. This particular sequence of Aramaic letters has the power to imbue us with acceptance and understanding so that we can transform the negative part of our character which perceives others as bent.

The Fourth Blessing is in the three *Partzufim* of *Chochmah*: external, middle and internal of Returning Light of the middle *Partzuf* of *Zeir Anpin* of *Asiyah* of *Atzilut*, and of Lower *Asiyah*.

baruch בָּרוּךְ Ata אַתָּה Adonai יְהֹוָאדניאהדונהי Elohenu אֱלֹהֵינוּ ילה
melech מֶלֶךְ ha'olam הָעוֹלָם zokef זוֹקֵף kefufim כְּפוּפִים:

THE SECOND BLESSING

Blessed are You, Lord, our God, King of the world, Who gives sight to the blind.

THE THIRD BLESSING

Blessed are You, Lord, our God, King of the world, Who releases those who are bound.

THE FOURTH BLESSING

Blessed are You, Lord, our God, King of the world, Who straightens those who are bent over.

THE FIFTH BLESSING - CLOTHES THE NAKED

Kabbalah explains that the body is the clothing of the soul. Just as a negative person cannot change his character by donning an expensive suit, we cannot bring about personal change or lasting fulfillment without connecting to a world beyond our body consciousness. The sequence of letters in this blessing gives us the power to rise above our body consciousness and connect with our soul consciousness.

The Fifth Blessing is in the three *Partzufim* of *Binah*: external, middle and internal of Direct Light of the middle *Partzuf* of *Zeir Anpin* of *Asiyah* of *Atzilut*, and of Lower *Asiyah*. At the end of the blessing meditate to draw 378 illuminations from the Face of *Arich Anpin* to the Face of *Chashmal* of *Zeir* and *Nukva* of *Atzilut* which is the secret of *malbush* (*Malbush* means clothing which has the same numerical value of *Chashmal* – electricity).

בָּרוּךְ baruch אַתָּה Ata יְהֹוָהאדניאהדונהי Adonai אֱלֹהֵינוּ Elohenu ילה
מֶלֶךְ melech הָעוֹלָם ha'olam מַלְבִּישׁ malbish עֲרוּמִּים arumim:

THE SIXTH BLESSING - GIVES STRENGTH TO THE WEARY

We often try to affect positive change within ourselves. We attempt to face down our fears, rid ourselves of anger, and overcome our jealousies. But Satan, a negative intelligence, battles us from the inside, and can prevent these changes from happening. The sequence of letters in this blessing gives us that extra help and energy we need to defeat Satan.

The Sixth Blessing is in the three *Partzufim* of *Binah*: external, middle and internal of Returning Light of the middle *Partzuf* of *Zeir Anpin* of *Asiyah* of *Atzilut*, and of Lower *Asiyah*. At the end of the blessing meditate to draw 378 illuminations from the Face of *Arich Anpin* to the Face of *Chashmal* of *Zeir* and *Nukva* of *Atzilut* which is the secret of *malbush* (*Malbush* means clothing which has the same numerical value of *Chashmal* – electricity).

בָּרוּךְ baruch אַתָּה Ata יְהֹוָהאדניאהדונהי Adonai אֱלֹהֵינוּ Elohenu ילה מֶלֶךְ melech
הָעוֹלָם ha'olam הַנּוֹתֵן hanoten אבגיתץ, ושר לַיָּעֵף laya'ef כֹּחַ ko'ach נלך:

THE SEVENTH BLESSING - KEEPS THE LAND OVER THE WATER

The kabbalists teach that before the creation of the world, water filled all of reality and existence. Water is a physical expression of the energy force of mercy and the Lightforce of the Creator, also known as the *Desire to Share*. Physical matter has the inherent essence of the *Desire to Receive*, represented by the creation of the land on our planet. God created a delicate balance between the *Desire to Share* and the *Desire to Receive*, manifested in the balance between the water and the land. This blessing helps us achieve and maintain this balance.

THE FIFTH BLESSING

Blessed are You, Lord, our God, King of the world, Who clothes the naked.

THE SIXTH BLESSING

Blessed are You, Lord, our God, King of the world, Who gives strength to the weary.

The Seventh Blessing is in the three *Partzufim* of *Chesed*: external, middle and internal of Direct Light of the middle *Partzuf* of *Zeir Anpin* of *Asiyah* of *Atzilut*, and of Lower *Asiyah*.

בָּרוּךְ baruch אַתָּה Ata יְהֹוָהאדניאהדונהי Adonai אֱלֹהֵינוּ Elohenu ילה

מֶלֶךְ melech הָעוֹלָם ha'olam רוֹקַע roka הָאָרֶץ ha'aretz אלהים דההין ע"ה

עַל al הַמָּיִם hamayim:

THE EIGHTH BLESSING - PROVIDES FOR THE FOOTSTEPS OF MAN

When a person embarks on a spiritual path, he or she will inevitably face obstacles and challenges along the way. This particular sequence of Aramaic letters gives us the power of certainty, to know that the spiritual path we are on is the correct one, even when the road before us is temporarily dim.

The Eighth Blessing is in the three *Partzufim* of *Chesed*: external, middle and internal of Returning Light of the middle *Partzuf* of *Zeir Anpin* of *Asiyah* of *Atzilut*, and of Lower *Asiyah*.

בָּרוּךְ baruch אַתָּה Ata יְהֹוָהאדניאהדונהי Adonai אֱלֹהֵינוּ Elohenu ילה

מֶלֶךְ melech הָעוֹלָם ha'olam הַמֵּכִין hamechin מִצְעֲדֵי mitz'adei גָבֶר gaver:

THE NINTH BLESSING - PROVIDES FOR ALL MY NEEDS

This ancient sequence of letters ensures that we receive what our soul truly desires and not what our short-term reactive impulses cause us to crave.

The Ninth Blessing is in the Three *Partzufim* of *Gevurah*: external, middle and internal of Direct Light of the middle *Partzuf* of *Zeir Anpin* of *Asiyah* of *Atzilut*, and of Lower *Asiyah*.

בָּרוּךְ baruch אַתָּה Ata יְהֹוָהאדניאהדונהי Adonai אֱלֹהֵינוּ Elohenu ילה

מֶלֶךְ melech הָעוֹלָם ha'olam שֶׁעָשָׂה she'asa שֶׁעָ (ש"ע נהורין דפנים עליונים

להמתיק דינֵי ש"ה דלהלן) = אלף למד אלף למד [אל א' = יהוה ד' אותיות והכולל ואל ב' = ייא" דס"ג)]

שָׂה = אלהים דיודין וה' אותיות אלהים לִי li כָּל kol ילי צָרְכִּי tzorki:

THE SEVENTH BLESSING

Blessed are You, Lord, our God, King of the world, Who keeps land over the water.

THE EIGHTH BLESSING

Blessed are You, Lord, our God, King of the world, Who provides for the footsteps of man.

THE NINTH BLESSING

Blessed are You, Lord, our God, King of the world, Who provides for all my needs.

THE TENTH BLESSING - STRENGTHENS ISRAEL WITH MIGHT

In Aramaic, the word for "strength" is *Gevurah*. *Gevurah* has the same numerical value (216) as the three-letter sequences of the 72 Names of God (72 x 3 = 216), which helps us achieve mind over matter and overcome our reactive nature. Another secret can be found in the last three words of the blessing. The first three letters of the last three words (*Alef* א, *Yud* י, and *Bet* ב) have the same numerical value (13) as the Aramaic word for *Ahavah* (אהבה) which means "love." If we have love in our lives, we will always have the ability to tap into the power of the 72 Names of God.

The Tenth Blessing is in the three *Partzufim* of *Gevurah*: external, middle and internal of Returning Light of the middle *Partzuf* of *Zeir Anpin* of *Asiyah* of *Atzilut*, and of Lower *Asiyah*.

בָּרוּךְ baruch אַתָּה Ata יְהֹוָהאדניאהדונהי Adonai אֱלֹהֵינוּ Elohenu ילה

מֶלֶךְ melech הָעוֹלָם ha'olam אוֹזֵר ozer יִשְׂרָאֵל Yisrael

בִּגְבוּרָה bigvura ריו ; ר"ת = אהבה, אחד, דאגה:

THE ELEVENTH BLESSING - CROWNS ISRAEL WITH SPLENDOR

The word for "splendor" in Aramaic is *Tifara*, from the root *Tiferet*. *Tiferet* is the *Sefirah* or the specific dimension that connects the Upper Worlds to our physical world. The sequence of letters that make up this blessing gives us the ability to capture and store the Light—like a portable battery that can fuel us—even after we close the Siddur.

The Eleventh Blessing is in the three *Partzufim* of *Tiferet*: external, middle and internal of Direct Light of the middle *Partzuf* of *Zeir Anpin* of *Asiyah* of *Atzilut*, and of Lower *Asiyah*.

בָּרוּךְ baruch אַתָּה Ata יְהֹוָהאדניאהדונהי Adonai אֱלֹהֵינוּ Elohenu ילה

מֶלֶךְ melech הָעוֹלָם ha'olam עוֹטֵר oter יִשְׂרָאֵל Yisrael בְּתִפְאָרָה betifara:

THE TWELFTH BLESSING - DID NOT MAKE ME A GENTILE/GENTILE WOMAN

On the surface level, this blessing appears to be discriminatory. Kabbalistically, the word gentile has nothing to do with a person's religious affiliation. Rather, it is a code word which represents someone who does not have a powerful and intense *Desire to Receive*. This blessing ignites our desire for spiritual growth, inner change, and positive transformation.

THE TENTH BLESSING

Blessed are You, Lord, our God, King of the world, Who strengthens Israel with might.

THE ELEVENTH BLESSING

Blessed are You, Lord, our God, King of the world, Who crowns Israel with splendor.

The Twelfth Blessing is in the three *Partzufim* of *Tiferet*: external, middle and internal of Returning Light of the middle *Partzuf* of *Zeir Anpin* of *Asiyah* of *Atzilut*, and of Lower *Asiyah*.

בָּרוּךְ baruch אַתָּה Ata יְהֹוָהאדניאהדונהי Adonai אֱלֹהֵינוּ Elohenu ילה

מֶלֶךְ melech הָעוֹלָם ha'olam שֶׁלֹּא shelo עָשַׂנִי asani גּוֹי goi:

Women say: בָּרוּךְ baruch אַתָּה Ata יְהֹוָהאדניאהדונהי Adonai אֱלֹהֵינוּ Elohenu ילה

מֶלֶךְ melech הָעוֹלָם ha'olam שֶׁלֹּא shelo עָשַׂנִי asani גּוֹיָה goya:

THE THIRTEENTH BLESSING -DID NOT MAKE ME A SLAVE/MAIDSERVANT

This blessing gives us the support we need so that we are not governed and held captive by our reactive nature and the material world.

The Thirteenth Blessing is in the three *Partzufim* of *Netzach*: external, middle and internal of Direct Light of the middle *Partzuf* of *Zeir Anpin* of *Asiyah* of *Atzilut*, and of Lower *Asiyah*.

בָּרוּךְ baruch אַתָּה Ata יְהֹוָהאדניאהדונהי Adonai אֱלֹהֵינוּ Elohenu ילה

מֶלֶךְ melech הָעוֹלָם ha'olam שֶׁלֹּא shelo עָשַׂנִי asani עֶבֶד aved:

Women say: בָּרוּךְ baruch אַתָּה Ata יְהֹוָהאדניאהדונהי Adonai אֱלֹהֵינוּ Elohenu ילה

מֶלֶךְ melech הָעוֹלָם ha'olam שֶׁלֹּא shelo עָשַׂנִי asani שִׁפְחָה shifcha:

THE FOURTEENTH BLESSING – DID NOT MAKE ME A WOMAN/ MADE ME ACCORDING TO HIS WILL

Although this blessing appears to be chauvinistic, it is not. Kabbalistically, the inherent energy of the dimension of *Zeir Anpin* (comprising the Sefirot of *Chesed* to *Yesod*)--the pipeline through which the Light flows from the Upper Worlds into our world--is masculine. *Malchut*, our world has an inherent feminine energy. This prayer ignites appreciation for our ability to generate spiritual Light through the two energy forces of male and female, and helps the two halves of the soul--male and female--to unite.

The Fourteenth Blessing is in the three *Partzufim* of *Netzach*: external, middle and internal of Returning Light of the middle *Partzuf* of *Zeir Anpin* of *Asiyah* of *Atzilut*, and of Lower *Asiyah*.

בָּרוּךְ baruch אַתָּה Ata יְהֹוָהאדניאהדונהי Adonai אֱלֹהֵינוּ Elohenu ילה

מֶלֶךְ melech הָעוֹלָם ha'olam שֶׁלֹּא shelo עָשַׂנִי asani אִשָּׁה isha:

Women say: בָּרוּךְ baruch שֶׁעָשַׂנִי she'asani כִּרְצוֹנוֹ kirtzono:

THE TWELFTH BLESSING

Blessed are You, Lord, our God, King of the world, Who did not make me a gentile / gentile woman.

THE THIRTEENTH BLESSING

Blessed are You, Lord, our God, King of the world, Who did not make me a slave / maidservant.

THE FOURTEENTH BLESSING

Blessed are You, Lord, our God, King of the world, Who did not make me a woman. /
Blessed is He Who made me according to His Will.

THE FIFTEENTH BLESSING - REMOVES THE BOND OF SLEEP FROM MY EYES

Kabbalists have said that humanity has been asleep for 2000 years. Unfortunately, some people live their entire lives asleep. They never raise their level of consciousness, and fail to affect true inner change. The Aramaic letters in this blessing help to awaken us from that coma.

The Fifteenth Blessing is in the three *Partzufim* of *Hod*: external, middle and internal of Direct Light of the middle *Partzuf* of *Zeir Anpin* of *Asiyah* of *Atzilut*, and of Lower *Asiyah*.

בָּרוּךְ baruch אַתָּה Ata יְהֹוָואדהיאהדונהי Adonai אֱלֹהֵינוּ Elohenu ילה

מֶלֶךְ melech הָעוֹלָם ha'olam הַמַּעֲבִיר hama'avir חֶבְלֵי chevlei

שֵׁנָה shena מֵעֵינַי me'enai ריבוע מ"ה וּתְנוּמָה utnuma מֵעַפְעַפָּי me'afapai:

This blessing does not end here but in the end of the next section ("*gomel chasadim tovim le'amo Yisrael*"), so that is why we don't answer *AMEN* here.

VIHI RATZON

This prayer helps us to remove the forces of negativity that lie within us.

Vihi Ratzon removes the control of the *chitzoniyim* (negative external forces) from the internal aspect.

וִיהִי vihi רָצוֹן ratzon מהש ע"ה, ע"ב בריבוע קס"א ע"ה, אל שדי ע"ה מִלְּפָנֶיךָ milfanecha

ס"ג מ"ה ב"ן יְהֹוָואדהיאהדונהי Adonai אֱלֹהַי Elohai מילוי ע"ב, דמב ; ילה

וֵאלֹהֵי velohei לכב ; מילוי ע"ב, דמב ; ילה אֲבוֹתַי avotai שֶׁתַּרְגִּילֵנִי shetargileni

בְּתוֹרָתֶךָ betoratecha• וְתַדְבִּיקֵנִי vetadbikeni בְּמִצְוֹתֶיךָ bemitzvoteicha•

וְאַל ve'al תְּבִיאֵנִי tevi'eni לִידֵי lidei חֵטְא chet• וְלֹא velo לִידֵי lidei

עָוֹן avon• וְלֹא velo לִידֵי lidei נִסָּיוֹן nisayon• וְלֹא velo לִידֵי lidei

בִּזָּיוֹן vizayon• וְתַרְחִיקֵנִי vetarchikeni מִיֵּצֶר miyetzer הָרָע hara•

וְתַדְבִּיקֵנִי vetadbikeni בְּיֵצֶר beyetzer הַטּוֹב hatov והו• וְכוֹף vechof אֶת et

יִצְרִי yitzri לְהִשְׁתַּעְבֶּד lehisht'abed לָךְ lach• וּתְנֵנִי utneni הַיּוֹם hayom

ע"ה נגד, מזבח, זן, אל יהוה וּבְכָל uvchol ב"ן, לכב יוֹם yom ע"ה נגד, מזבח, זן, אל יהוה

THE FIFTEENTH BLESSING

Blessed are You, Lord,
our God, King of the world, Who removes the bonds of sleep from my eyes and slumber from my eyelids.

VIHI RATZON

And may it be Your will, Lord, our God and God of our fathers, that You accustom me to Your Torah and cause me to cleave to Your precepts, and do not bring me to the hands of sin, iniquity, temptation, nor shame. And cause me to distance myself from the Evil Inclination, and cling me to the Good Inclination, and compel my will to be subservient to You. Grant me this day and every day,

לְחֵן lechen מוזי, מילוי מ"ה בריבוע וּלְחֶסֶד ulchesed ע"ב, ריבוע יהוה
וּלְרַחֲמִים ulrachamim בְּעֵינֶיךָ be'enecha ע"ה קס"א ; ריבוע מ"ה
וּבְעֵינֵי uv'enei ריבוע מ"ה כָּל chol ילי רוֹאַי •ro'ai וְגָמְלֵנִי vegomleni
וַחֲסָדִים chasadim טוֹבִים •tovim בָּרוּךְ baruch אַתָּה Ata יְהֹוָאֲדֹנָיאהדונהי Adonai
גּוֹמֵל gomel חֲסָדִים chasadim טוֹבִים tovim לְעַמּוֹ le'amo יִשְׂרָאֵל :Yisrael

YEHI RATZON

Too often we attract negative people and unfavorable situations into our lives. We find ourselves in the wrong place at the wrong time. We do business with the wrong people. Here, we gain the ability to remove all external negative events from intruding into our lives. We also remove eleven distinct areas of negativity that can invade our environment.

Yehi Ratzon removes the control of the *chitzoniyim* (negative external forces) from the external aspect. In this section we mention 11 aspects corresponding to the 11 incenses of the *Ketoret*.

יְהִי yehi רָצוֹן ratzon מהש ע"ה, ע"ב בריבוע קס"א ע"ה, אל שדי ע"ה מִלְּפָנֶיךָ milfanecha
ס"ג מ"ה ב"ן יְהֹוָאֲדֹנָיאהדונהי Adonai אֱלֹהַי Elohai מילוי ע"ב, דמב ; ילה וֵאלֹהֵי velohei
לכב ; מילוי ע"ב, דמב ; ילה אֲבוֹתַי avotai שֶׁתַּצִּילֵנִי shetatzileni הַיּוֹם hayom
ע"ה נגד, מזבח, זן, אל יהוה וּבְכָל uvchol ב"ן, לכב יוֹם yom ע"ה נגד, מזבח, זן, אל יהוה
וָיוֹם vayom ע"ה נגד, מזבח, זן, אל יהוה מֵעַזֵּי me'azei אלהים ע"ה, אהיה אדני ע"ה
פָּנִים •fanim וּמֵעַזּוּת ume'azut פָּנִים •panim מֵאָדָם me'adam רָע •ra
מִיֵּצֶר miyetzer רָע •ra מֵחָבֵר mechaver רָע •ra מִשָּׁכֵן mishachen רָע •ra
מִפֶּגַע mipega רָע •ra מֵעַיִן me'ayin ריבוע מ"ה הָרָע •hara
וּמִלָּשׁוֹן umilashon הָרָע •hara מִדִּין midin קָשֶׁה •kashe
וּמִבַּעַל umiba'al דִּין din קָשֶׁה •kashe בֵּין ben שֶׁהוּא shehu
בֶּן ven בְּרִית •berit וּבֵין uven שֶׁאֵינוֹ she'eno בֶּן ven בְּרִית :berit

---

grace, loving kindness, and mercy in Your sight and in the sight of all that behold me, and bestow upon me loving kindness. Blessed are You, Lord, Who bestows loving kindness on His people Israel.

YEHI RATZON

May it be Your will, Lord our God and God of our forefathers, to save me this day and every day from an arrogant man and from arrogance, from an evil man, from the Evil Inclination, from an evil companion, from an evil neighbor, from an evil happening, from evil eye, and from evil speech, from harsh judgment, and a harsh opponent, whether he be a son of the covenant or not a son of the covenant.

BLESSINGS OF THE *TORAH*

The next three blessings are known as *Birkot haTorah* (Blessings of the Torah).

THE SIXTEENTH BLESSING - TEACHINGS OF THE TORAH

The kabbalists teach that without a connection to the *Torah*, we do not stand a chance affecting genuine positive change in our lives or in the world around us. According to Kabbalah, reference to the *Torah* refers to spiritual work and spiritual study, and to using spiritual tools. This blessing connects us to the inner essence of the *Torah* giving us the energy and fuel we need to ignite all the other blessings we have recited, and to imbue our lives with passion and spiritual energy.

The Sixteenth Blessing has two aspects:
1) The aspect of the *Mitzva* of *Esek* ("involved") of the *Torah* which is in *Zeir Anpin* of *Atzilut*.
2) The aspect that is in the three *Partzufim* of *Hod*: the external, middle and internal of Returning Light of the middle *Partzuf* of *Zeir Anpin* of *Asiyah* of *Atzilut*, and of Lower *Asiyah* (as in the other blessings). While saying this blessing, you should meditate on both aspects, and while saying the words *"asher kideshanu..."* you should also meditate to draw the *Tzelems* into *Chochmah, Binah, Da'at* of *Zeir Anpin* of *Atzilut*, as we meditate on the other precepts of the *Torah*.

בָּרוּךְ baruch אַתָּה Ata יְהֹוָאדניאהדונהי Adonai אֱלֹהֵינוּ Elohenu ילה

מֶלֶךְ melech הָעוֹלָם ha'olam אֲשֶׁר asher קִדְּשָׁנוּ kideshanu

בְּמִצְוֹתָיו bemitzvotav וְצִוָּנוּ vetzivanu עַל al דִּבְרֵי divrei ראה תוֹרָה torah:

According to the Ari:
We answer AMEN after this blessing, as this is a separate blessing from the next one.

THE SEVENTEENTH BLESSING - TEACHES *TORAH* TO THE NATION

We say this blessing with the consciousness to help everyone make a connection to the energy of the *Torah*. This is our opportunity to genuinely care about others and to share the Light of the Creator - one of the most powerful ways to transform our reactive nature into a proactive one.

The Seventeenth Blessing is in the three *Partzufim* of *Yesod*: external, middle and internal of Direct Light of the middle *Partzuf* of *Zeir Anpin* of *Asiyah* of *Atzilut*, and of Lower *Asiyah*.

וְהַעֲרֶב veha'arev נָא na יְהֹוָאדניאהדונהי Adonai אֱלֹהֵינוּ Elohenu ילה

אֶת et דִּבְרֵי divrei ראה תוֹרָתְךָ toratcha בְּפִינוּ befinu

וּבְפִיפִיּוֹת uv'fifiyot עַמְּךָ amecha בֵּית bet ב"פ ראה יִשְׂרָאֵל Yisrael.

BLESSINGS OF THE *TORAH*

THE SIXTEENTH BLESSING

Blessed are You, Lord, our God, King of the world,
Who has sanctified us with His commandments and obliged us regarding the teachings of the Torah.

THE SEVENTEENTH BLESSING

And sweeten for us, Lord,
our God, the words of Your Torah in our mouths and the mouths of Your Nation, the House of Israel.

וְנִהְיֶה venih'ye אֲנַחְנוּ anachnu וְצֶאֱצָאֵינוּ vetze'etza'enu

(You should meditate for your children to be righteous, connected to the *Torah* and to the Light)

וְצֶאֱצָאֵי vetze'etza'ei צֶאֱצָאֵינוּ tze'etza'enu וְצֶאֱצָאֵי vetze'etza'ei

עַמְּךָ amecha בֵּית bet ב"פ ראה יִשְׂרָאֵל Yisrael כֻּלָּנוּ kulanu

יוֹדְעֵי yod'ei שְׁמֶךָ shemecha וְלוֹמְדֵי velomdei תוֹרָתֶךָ toratcha

לִשְׁמָהּ lishma. בָּרוּךְ baruch אַתָּה Ata יְהֹוָה אהדונהי Adonai

הַמְלַמֵּד hamelamed תּוֹרָה torah לְעַמּוֹ le'amo יִשְׂרָאֵל Yisrael:

THE EIGHTEENTH BLESSING - GIVES THE TORAH

The Aramaic word *chai* חי ("life") has the numerical value of 18. This blessing connects us to the Tree of Life, (*Etz HaChayim* – עץ החיים) the dimension where only fulfillment, order, and endless bliss exist.

The Eighteenth Blessing is in the three *Partzufim* of *Yesod*: external, middle and internal of Returning Light of the middle *Partzuf* of *Zeir Anpin* of *Asiyah* of *Atzilut*, and of Lower *Asiyah*.

בָּרוּךְ baruch אַתָּה Ata יְהֹוָה אהדונהי Adonai אֱלֹהֵינוּ Elohenu ילה

מֶלֶךְ melech הָעוֹלָם ha'olam אֲשֶׁר asher בָּחַר bachar

בָּנוּ banu מִכָּל mikol ילי הָעַמִּים ha'amim וְנָתַן venatan

לָנוּ lanu אלהים, אהיה אדני אֶת et תּוֹרָתוֹ torato. בָּרוּךְ baruch

אַתָּה Ata יְהֹוָה אהדונהי Adonai נוֹתֵן noten אבגית"ץ, ושר הַתּוֹרָה hatorah:

THE BLESSING OF THE *KOHANIM*

Finishing the Eighteen Blessings, we make an immediate connection to the *Torah*. The verses that we recite are the blessings of the priests (*Kohanim*). In ancient times, when the *Kohen* blessed the congregation in the Temple, he used the formula *Yud, Yud, Yud* ייי one of the 72 Names of God. Each of the following three sentences begins with a *Yud*. When we recite this prayer, we activate and reveal tremendous powers of healing in our lives.

And may we and our offspring, and the offspring of our offspring, and the offspring of all Your Nation, the House of Israel, all of us know Your Names and be learners of Your Torah for its own sake. Blessed are You, Lord, Who teaches the Torah to His Nation, Israel.

THE EIGHTEENTH BLESSING

Blessed are You, Lord, our God, King of the world, Who has chosen us from among all the nations and has given us His Torah. Blessed are You, Lord, Who gives the Torah.

וַיְדַבֵּר vaydaber ראה יְהֹוָהאדניאהדונהי Adonai אֶל־ el מֹשֶׁה Moshe

מהש, ע"ב בריבוע קס"א, אל שדי, ד"פ אלהים ע"ה לֵּאמֹר lemor: דַּבֵּר daber ראה

אֶל־ el אַהֲרֹן Aharon וְאֶל־ ve'el בָּנָיו banav לֵאמֹר lemor

כֹּה ko היי תְבָרְכוּ tevarchu יהוה ריבוע יהוה ריבוע מ"ה

אֶת־ et בְּנֵי benei יִשְׂרָאֵל Yisrael אָמוֹר amor לָהֶם lahem:

The initials of the three verses give us the Holy Name: ייי.
In this section, there are 15 words, which are equal to the numerical value of the Holy Name: ההה.

(Right – *Chesed*)

יְבָרֶכְךָ yevarechecha יְהֹוָהאדניאהדונהי Adonai וְיִשְׁמְרֶךָ veyishmerecha

ר"ת = יהוה ; וס"ת = מ"ה:

(Left - *Gevurah*)

יָאֵר ya'er כף ויו זין ויו יְהֹוָהאדניאהדונהי Adonai | פָּנָיו panav

אֵלֶיךָ elecha וִיחֻנֶּךָּ vichuneka מנד ; יהה אותיות בפסוק:

(Central – *Tiferet*)

יִשָּׂא yisa יְהֹוָהאדניאהדונהי Adonai | פָּנָיו panav אֵלֶיךָ elecha

וְיָשֵׂם veyasem לְךָ lecha שָׁלוֹם shalom האא תיבות בפסוק:

(*Malchut*)

וְשָׂמוּ vesamu אֶת־ et שְׁמִי shemi עַל־ al בְּנֵי benei יִשְׂרָאֵל Yisrael

וַאֲנִי va'ani אני אֲבָרְכֵם avarchem:

Shacharit Prayer can be found on pg. 208 and *Talit* order can be found on pg. 214.

THE BLESSING OF THE *KOHANIM*

"And the Lord spoke to Moses and said:
Speak to Aaron and his sons saying: So shall you bless the Children of Israel,
Say to them: May the Lord bless you and protect you.
May the Lord enlighten His countenance for you and give you grace.
May the Lord lift His countenance towards you and give you peace.
And they shall place My Name upon the Children of Israel and I shall bless them." (Numbers 6:22-27)

AMAR RABBI SHIMON

The essence of this passage from the *Zohar, Noah,* 122-127 concerns the hands. Since the hands are the tools with which we carry out life's actions, the forces of darkness latch onto them in order to influence our deeds. We can infuse our hands with the positive energy that dwells in the Upper Worlds so that they bring blessing and good fortune to all our endeavors.

אֲמַר amar רַבִּי Rabbi שִׁמְעוֹן Shimon אֲרֵימַת aremat יְדַאי yedai

בִּצְלוֹתִין bitzlotin לְעֵילָא, le'ela דְּכַד dechad רְעוּתָא re'uta עִלָּאָה, ila'a

לְעֵילָא le'ela לְעֵילָא, le'ela קַיְּימָא kayma עַל al הַהוּא hahu

רְעוּתָא, re'uta דְּלָא dela אִתְיְדַע, ityeda וְלָא velo אִתְפַּס itpas כְּלָל kelal

לְעָלְמִין, le'almin רֵישָׁא reisha דְּסָתִים desatim יַתִּיר yatir לְעֵילָא, le'eila

וְהַהוּא vehahu רֵישָׁא resha אַפֵּיק apek מַאי mai דְּאַפֵּיק, de'apek וְלָא vela

יְדִיעַ, yedi'a וְנָהִיר venaher מַאי mai דְּנָהִיר, denaher כֹּלָּא kola

בִּסְתִימוּ. bistimu רְעוּ re'o דְּמַחֲשָׁבָה demachashava עִלָּאָה ila'a

לְמִרְדַּף lemirdaf אֲבַתְרֵיהּ, avatrei וּלְאִתְנְהָרָא ule'itnehara מִנֵּיהּ. minei

וְחַד chad פְּרִיסוּ perisu אִתְפְּרֵיס, itpereis וּמִגּוֹ umigo הַהוּא hahu

פְּרִיסָא, perisa בִּרְדִיפוּ birdifu דְּהַהִיא dehahi מַחֲשָׁבָה machashava

עִלָּאָה, ila'a מָטֵי matei וְלָא vela מָטֵי. matei עַד ad

הַהוּא hahu פְּרִיסָא perisa נָהִיר naher מַה ma דְּנָהִיר. denaher

וּכְדֵין uchden אִיהוּ ihu מַחֲשָׁבָה machashava עִלָּאָה, ila'a

נָהִיר naher בִּנְהִירוּ binhiru סָתִים satim דְּלָא dela יְדִיעַ, yedi'a

וְהַהוּא vehahu מַחֲשָׁבָה machashava לָא la יָדַע. yada

AMAR RABBI SHIMON

Rav Shimon said: "I raise my hands on high to pray. When the Supernal desire at the highest point Above, is established upon the forever unknown and ungraspable desire, it becomes the most concealed Head Above. And that Head emanates all that He emanates and all that is unknown. And He illuminates all that he illuminates in a concealed manner. The desire of the Supernal Thought runs after it to be illuminated from it. But a veil spreads and from its spreading and the running after it, it is allowed to reach - and to not reach - the Light. The Light shines upward toward the veil. Therefore the Supernal Thought shines with Unrevealed Illumination, and with Light unknown to the 'Mind (Moach) of air.' And the Thought itself is considered unknown.

כְּדֵין keden בָּטַשׁ batash הַאי hai נְהִירוּ nehiru דְּמַחֲשָׁבָה demachashava

דְּלָא dela אִתְיְידַע ityeda, בִּנְהִירוּ binhiru דְּפַרְסָא defarsa

דְּקַיְּימָא dekayma, דְּנָהִיר denaheir מִמַּה mima דְּלָא dela יְדִיעַ yedi'a

וְלָא vela אִתְיְידַע ityeda, וְלָא vela אִתְגַּלְיָיא itgalya. וּכְדֵין uchden דָא da

נְהִירוּ nehiru דְּמַחֲשָׁבָה demachashava דְּלָא dela אִתְיְידַע ityeda

בָּטַשׁ batash בִּנְהִירוּ binhiru דְּפַרְיסָא difrisa, וְנַהֲרִין venaharin

כַּחֲדָא kachada, וְאִתְעֲבִידוּ ve'it'avidu תֵּשַׁע tesha הֵיכָלִין hechalin.

וְהֵיכָלִין vehechalin, לָאו lav אִינּוּן inun נְהוֹרִין nehorin, וְלָאו velav

אִינּוּן inun רוּחִין ruchin, וְלָאו velav אִינּוּן inun נִשְׁמָתִין nishmatin וְלָא vela

אִית it מַאן man דְּקַיְּימָא dekayma בְּהוֹ beho. רְעוּתָא re'uta, דְּכָל dechol

תֵּשַׁע tesha נְהוֹרִין nehorin, דְּקַיְּימֵי dekaymei כֻּלְּהוֹ kolho

בְּמַחֲשָׁבָה bemachashava, דְּאִיהוּ de'ihu חַד chad מִנַּיְיהוּ minayhu

בְּחוּשְׁבְּנָא bechushbena כֻּלְּהוֹ kolho לְמִרְדַּף lemirdaf בַּתְרַיְיהוּ batrayhu,

בְּשַׁעֲתָא besha'ata דְּקַיְּימֵי dekaymei בְּמַחֲשָׁבָה bemach'shava וְלָא vela

מִתְדַּבְּקָן mitdabkan וְלָא vela אִתְיְידָעוּ ityeda'u, וְאִלֵּין ve'ilen לָא la

קַיְּימֵי kaymei לָא la בִּרְעוּתָא bir'uta, וְלָא vela בְּמַחֲשָׁבָה bemachashava

עִלָּאָה ila'a תָּפְסִין tafsin בָּהּ ba וְלָא vela תָּפְסִין tafsin.

Then, the illumination of the Unknown Thought hits upon the illumination of the veil that stands and shines of what is unknown, what is not known, and what is unrevealed. Thus, the illumination of the Thought that is not known hits upon the veil's illumination, and they shine together. And from them, nine Chambers are made. These Chambers are not Light. And they are neither Ruchot nor Neshamot, and nobody can understand what they are. The desire of all nine Lights is standing in the Thought and is also considered one of Them. And all desire to pursue them while the nine Lights are located in the Thought. Nevertheless, the Chambers are not attained and not known because they are not established as either an aspect of desire or as an aspect of Supernal Thought. They grasp and do not grasp.

בְּאִלֵּין be'ilen קָיְימֵי kaymei כָּל kol רָזֵי razei דִּמְהֵימְנוּתָא dim'hemenuta,
וְכָל vechol אִינּוּן inun נְהוֹרִין nehorin מֵרָזָא meraza
דְּמַחֲשָׁבָה demachashava עִלָּאָה ila'a כֻּלְּהוּ kolho אִקְרוּן ikrun אֵין en
סוֹף sof. עַד ad הָכָא hacha מָטוֹ mato נְהוֹרִין nehorin וְלָא vela
מָטוֹן maton, וְלָא vela אִתְיְידָעוּ ityeda'u, לָאו lav הָכָא hacha
רְעוּתָא re'uta, וְלָא vela מַחֲשָׁבָה machashava. כַּד kad נָהִיר naher
מַחֲשָׁבָה machashava, וְלָא vela אִתְיְידַע ityeda מִמַּאן miman
דְּנָהִיר denaher, כְּדֵין keden אִתְלַבַּשׁ itlabesh וְאַסְתִּים ve'astim גּוֹ go
בִּינָה bina, וְנָהִיר venaher לְמַאן leman דְּנָהִיר denaher וְאָעִיל ve'ael דָּא da
בְּדָא beda, עַד ad דְּאִתְכְּלִילוּ de'itkelilu כֻּלְּהוּ kolho כַּחֲדָא kachada.
וּבְרָזָא uv'raza דְקָרְבְּנָא dekorbana כַּד kad סָלֵיק salek, כֹּלָּא kola
אִתְקַשַּׁר itkashar דָּא da בְּדָא beda, וְנָהִיר venaher דָּא da בְּדָא beda,
כְּדֵין keden קָיְימֵי kaymei כֻּלְּהוּ kolho בִּסְלִיקוּ bisliku,
וּמַחֲשָׁבָה umachashava אִתְעַטַּר it'atar בְּאֵין be'en סוֹף sof.
הַהוּא hahu נְהִירוּ nehiru דְּאִתְנְהִיר de'itneher מִנֵּיהּ minei
מַחֲשָׁבָה machashava עִלָּאָה ila'a, אִקְרֵי ikrei אֵין en סוֹף sof.
וּמִנֵּיהּ uminei אִשְׁתְּכַח ishtechach וְקָיְימָא vekayma וְנָהִיר venaher
לְמַאן leman דְּנָהִיר denaher, וְעַל ve'al דָּא da כֹּלָּא kola
קָאִים ka'em. זַכָּאָה zaka'a חוּלָקֵיהוֹן chulakehon דְּצַדִּיקַיָּיא detzadikaya
בְּעָלְמָא be'alma דֵּין den וּבְעָלְמָא uve'alma דְּאָתֵי de'atei.

With these all the secrets of Faith are based upon. And all of these Lights come from the secret of the supernal Thought and all are called the Ein Sof. Because the Lights reach and do not reach, and are not known, there is neither desire nor thought at this point. When Unknown Thought shines from its source, it shines upon whom She shines, and they enter each other until they are as one. Returning to the secret of the sacrifice: when it is raised, all are enmeshed within one another and shine one upon the other. Now all the stages are in the secret of the 'Ascending' and, when it ascends to the Unknown Head, Thought is crowned by the Ein Sof. This illumination that the supernal thought illuminates from is called Ein Sof. And from there it comes. It is established and shines upon whom It shines. And all is based upon this. Happy are the righteous in this world and the World to Come.

PETICHAT ELIYAHU HANAVI – THE OPENING OF ELIJAH THE PROPHET

Reciting these paragraphs can help you open your heart to spiritual wisdom.

וִיהִי vihi נֹעַם no'am אֲדֹנָי Adonai ללה אֱלֹהֵינוּ Elohenu ילה עָלֵינוּ alenu
וּמַעֲשֵׂה uma'ase יָדֵינוּ yadenu כּוֹנְנָה konena עָלֵינוּ alenu
וּמַעֲשֵׂה uma'ase יָדֵינוּ yadenu כּוֹנְנֵהוּ konenehu:
פָּתַח patach אֵלִיָּהוּ Eliyahu לכב הַנָּבִיא hanavi, זָכוּר zachur ע"ב קס"א,
יהי אור ע"ה (סוד המשכת השפע מן ד' שמות ליסוד הנקרא זכור) לְטוֹב letov והו ;
זכור לטוב = בוזפף, סנדלפון, ערי ; אליהו הנביא זכור לטוב = ת' כנגד ת' כוונות הס"א וְאָמַר ve'amar:
רִבּוֹן ribon יהוה ע"ב ס"ג מ"ה ב"ן עָלְמִין almin דְּאַנְתְּ de'ant הוּא hu וְחָד chad
וְלָא vela בְחֻשְׁבָּן bechushban, אַנְתְּ ant הוּא hu עִלָּאָה ila'a עַל al כָּל kol
ילי ; עמם עִלָּאִין ila'in, סְתִימָא setima עַל al כָּל kol ילי ; עמם סְתִימִין setimin,
לֵית let מַחֲשָׁבָה machashava תְּפִיסָא tefisa בָּךְ bach כְּלָל kelal. אַנְתְּ ant
הוּא hu דְּאַפַּקְתְּ de'apakt עֶשֶׂר eser תִּקּוּנִין tikunin, וְקָרֵינָן vekarenan
לוֹן lon עֶשֶׂר eser סְפִירָן sefiran, לְאַנְהָגָא le'anhaga בְּהוֹן behon
עָלְמִין almin סְתִימִין setimin דְּלָא dela אִתְגַּלְיָן itgalyan וְעָלְמִין ve'almin
דְּאִתְגַּלְיָן de'itgalyan. וּבְהוֹן uv'hon אִתְכַּסִּיאַת itkasi'at מִבְּנֵי mibenei
נָשָׁא nasha. וְאַנְתְּ ve'ant הוּא hu דְּקָשִׁיר dekashir לוֹן lon וּמְיַחֵד umyached
לוֹן lon. וּבְגִין uvgin דְּאַנְתְּ de'ant מִלְּגָאו milgav כָּל kol ילי מָאן man
דְּאַפְרִישׁ de'afrish חַד chad מִן min חַבְרֵיהּ chavrei מֵאִלֵּין me'ilen
עֶשֶׂר eser, אִתְחַשִׁיב itchashiv לֵיהּ lei כְּאִלּוּ ke'ilu אַפְרִישׁ afrish בָּךְ bach.

PETICHAT ELIYAHU HANAVI

"And may the pleasantness of the Lord, our God, be upon us and may He establish the workof our hands for us and may the work of our hands establish Him" (Psalms 90:17). Elijah opened, saying: Master of the worlds, You are One without enumeration. You are above all high ones, the most concealed of all. No thought can grasp You at all. You are the one that produced the ten emanations. And we named them ten Sefirot, to conduct with them obscure worlds that are not revealed, and revealed worlds. And through them, You are screened from human beings. And You are the One who connects them and unites them. And because you are from within, thus, anyone who separates these ten one from the other, to give dominance to that one alone, it is considered for him, as if he separates in You.

וְאִלֵּין ve'ilen עֶשֶׂר eser סְפִירָן sefiran אִינּוּן inun אָזְלִין azlin
כְּסִדְרָן kesidran, וְחַד chad אָרִיךְ arich, וְחַד vechad קָצַר katzer,
וְחַד vechad בֵּינוֹנִי benoni. וְאַנְתְּ ve'ant הוּא hu דְּאַנְהִיג de'anhig לוֹן lon,
וְלֵית velet מַאן man דְּאַנְהִיג de'anhig לָךְ lach. לָא la לְעֵילָּא le'ela,
וְלָא vela לְתַתָּא letata, וְלָא vela מִכָּל mikol ילי סִטְרָא sitra.
לְבוּשִׁין levushin תַּקַּנְתְּ takant לוֹן lon, דְּמִנַּיְהוּ deminayhu פַּרְחִין farchin
נִשְׁמָתִין nishmatin לִבְנֵי livnei נָשָׁא nasha. וְכַמָּה vechama גּוּפִין gufin
תַּקַּנְתְּ takant לוֹן lon, דְּאִתְקְרִיאוּ de'itkeri'u גּוּפָא gufa לְגַבֵּי legabei
לְבוּשִׁין levushin דִּמְכַסְיָן dim'chasyan עֲלֵיהוֹן alehon. וְאִתְקְרִיאוּ ve'itkeri'u
בְּתִקּוּנָא betikuna דָא da, חֶסֶד Chesed ע"ב, ריבוע יהוה דְּרוֹעָא dero'a
יְמִינָא yemina, גְּבוּרָה Gevurah רי"ו דְּרוֹעָא dero'a שְׂמָאלָא semala,
תִּפְאֶרֶת Tiferet גּוּפָא gufa, נֶצַח Netzach וְהוֹד veHod ההה תְּרֵין teren
שׁוֹקִין shokin, יְסוֹד Yesod ההע סִיּוּמָא siyuma דְּגוּפָא degufa אוֹת ot
בְּרִית berit קֹדֶשׁ kodesh. מַלְכוּת Malchut פֶּה pe מילה ; וע"ה אלהים, אהיה אדני.
תּוֹרָה torah שֶׁבְּעַל shebe'al פֶּה pe מילה ; וע"ה אלהים, אהיה אדני קָרֵינָן karenan
לָהּ la. חָכְמָה Chochmah במילוי = תרי"ג (מצוות) מוֹחָא mocha, אִיהוּ ihu
מַחֲשָׁבָה mach'shava מִלְּגָאו milgav, בִּינָה Binah ע"ה חיים, אהיה אהיה יהוה
לִבָּא liba וּבָהּ uva הַלֵּב halev מֵבִין mevin וְעַל ve'al אִלֵּין ilen תְּרֵין teren
כְּתִיב ketiv: הַנִּסְתָּרֹת hanistarot לַיהוָהאדניאהדונהי ladonai אֱלֹהֵינוּ Elohenu ילה

And these ten Sefirot follow their order, the one is long, and one, is short. And the one is average. And You conduct them, and there is no other who will lead You, neither Above, nor Below, nor in any other side. You prepared garments, from which the Neshamot fly to the human beings and you prepared several bodies. And they are named bodies in relation to the clothing, in which they are attired. The Sefirot are named by this emendation, Chesed being the right arm, Gevurah being the left arm. Tiferet means the body. Netzach and Hod, the two thighs, Yesod the final part of the body, the sign of the Holy Covenant, Malchut, the mouth, we call it the Oral Torah. Chochmah is the brain, the thought within. Binah is the heart, and through it, the heart understands. And about these two, it is written, "The secret things belong to the Lord our God" (Deuteronomy 29:28).

כֶּתֶר Keter יהוה מלך יהוה מלך יהוה ימלוך לעולם ועד (באתב"ש גאל) עֶלְיוֹן elyon, אִיהוּ ihu

כֶּתֶר keter יהוה מלך יהוה מלך יהוה ימלוך לעולם ועד (באתב"ש גאל) מַלְכוּת malchut.

וַעֲלֵיהּ ve'alei פהל אִתְּמַר itmar: מַגִּיד magid מֵרֵאשִׁית mereshit

אַחֲרִית acharit. וְאִיהוּ ve'ihu קַרְקַפְתָּא karkafta דִתְפִלֵּי ditfilei.

מִלְּגָאו milgav אִיהוּ ihu אוֹת ot יו"ד Yud וְאוֹת ve'ot הֵ"א He וְאוֹת ve'ot

וָא"ו Vav וְאוֹת ve'ot הֵ"א He, דְּאִיהוּ de'ihu אֹרַח orach אֲצִילוּת atzilut,

אִיהוּ ihu שַׁקְיוּ shakyu דְּאִילָנָא de'ilana בִּדְרוֹעוֹי bidro'oy וְעַנְפּוֹי ve'anpoy,

כְּמַיָּא kemaya דְּאַשְׁקֵי de'ashkei לְאִילָנָא le'ilana וְאִתְרַבֵּי ve'itrabei

בְּהַהוּא behahu שַׁקְיוּ shakyu. רִבּוֹן ribon יהוה ע"ב ס"ג מ"ה ב"ן עָלְמִין almin,

אַנְתְּ ant הוּא hu עִלַּת ilat הָעִלּוֹת ha'ilot, וְסִבַּת vesibat הַסִּבּוֹת hasibot,

דְּאַשְׁקֵי de'ashkei לְאִילָנָא le'ilana בְּהַהוּא behahu נְבִיעוּ nevi'u,

וְהַהוּא vehahu נְבִיעוּ nevi'u אִיהוּ ihu כְּנִשְׁמְתָא kenishmeta לְגוּפָא legufa,

דְּאִיהִי de'ihi חַיִּים chayim אהיה אהיה יהוה, בינה ע"ה לְגוּפָא legufa. וּבָךְ uvach

לֵית let דִּמְיוֹן dimyon, וְלֵית velet דְּיוּקְנָא diyukna, מִכָּל mikol יכי

מָה ma מ"ה דִּלְגָאו dilgav וּלְבַר ulvar. וּבָרָאתָ uvarata שְׁמַיָּא shemaya

וְאַרְעָא ve'ar'a, וְאַפַּקְתְּ ve'apakt מִנְּהוֹן minehon שִׁמְשָׁא shimsha

וְסִיהֲרָא vesihara וְכֹכְבַיָּא vechochvaya וּמַזָּלֵי umazalei. וּבְאַרְעָא uve'ar'a,

אִילָנִין ilanin וּדְשָׁאִין udsha'in וְגִנְּתָא veginta דְעֵדֶן de'eden וְעִשְׂבִּין ve'isbin

וְחֵיוָן vechevan וְעוֹפִין ve'ofin וְנוּנִין venunin וּבְעִירִין uv'irin וּבְנֵי uvnei

נָשָׁא nasha. לְאִשְׁתְּמוֹדְעָא le'ishtemode'a בְּהוֹן behon עִלָּאִין ila'in,

וְאֵיךְ ve'ech יִתְנַהֲגוּן yitnahagun בְּהוֹן behon עִלָּאִין ila'in וְתַתָּאִין vetata'in.

The Supernal Keter is the crown of Malchut. And about this is said, "Declaring the end from the beginning" (Isaiah 46:10). And that is the skull of the Tefilin. Within is Yud-Vav-Dalet, Hei-Alef, Vav-Alef-Vav, Hei-Alef, which is in the path of Atzilut. It is the watering of the tree in its arms and branches, as waters that water that tree and it multiplies by this watering. Master of the Worlds, You are the Cause of all Causes, and the Reason for all Reasons, that waters the tree by that stream, and that spring is like a soul to the body, that is the life of the body. And to Yourself there is no likeness nor form inside or outside. And You created heavens and earth and produced from them sun and moon and stars and constellations. And in the earth, trees and grasses, and the Garden of Eden, and plants, and animals and fowl and fish and human beings, through them to acknowledge the high ones, and how the higher and lower ones behave.

וְאֵיךְ ve'ech אִשְׁתְּמוֹדְעָן ishtemode'an מֵעִלָּאֵי me'ila'ei וְתַתָּאֵי vetata'ei.
וְלֵית velet דְּיָדַע deyada בָּךְ bach כְּלָל kelal, וּבַר uvar יצחק, ד"פ ב"ן
מִנָּךְ minach לֵית let יִחוּדָא yichuda בְּעִלָּאֵי be'ila'ei וְתַתָּאֵי vetata'ei,
וְאַנְתְּ ve'ant אִשְׁתְּמוֹדַע ishtemoda אָדוֹן adon אני עַל al כֹּלָּא kola.
וְכָל vechol ילי סְפִירָן sefiran, כָּל kol ילי וְחַד chad אִית it לֵיהּ lei שֵׁם shem
יְדִיעַ yedi'a, וּבְהוֹן uvhon אִתְקְרִיאוּ itkeri'u מַלְאָכַיָּא mal'achaya.
וְאַנְתְּ ve'ant לֵית let לָךְ lach שֵׁם shem יְדִיעַ yedi'a, דְּאַנְתְּ de'ant הוּא hu
מְמַלֵּא memale כָּל kol ילי שְׁמָהָן shemahan, וְאַנְתְּ ve'ant הוּא hu
שְׁלִימוּ shelimu דְּכֻלְּהוּ dechulhu, וְכַד vechad אַנְתְּ ant תִּסְתַּלַּק tistalak
מִנְּהוֹן minehon אִשְׁתְּאָרוּ ishte'aru כֻּלְּהוּ kulehu שְׁמָהָן shemahan
כְּגוּפָא kegufa בְּלָא bela נִשְׁמָתָא nishmata. אַנְתְּ ant חַכִּים chakim
וְלָאו velav בְּחָכְמָה beChochmah במילוי = תרי"ג (מצוות) יְדִיעָא yedi'a. אַנְתְּ ant
הוּא hu מֵבִין mevin, וְלָאו velav מִבִּינָה miBinah ע"ה חיים, אהיה אהיה יהוה
יְדִיעָא yedi'a. לֵית let לָךְ lach אֲתַר atar יְדִיעָא yedi'a.
אֶלָּא ela לְאִשְׁתְּמוֹדְעָא le'ishtemode'a תָּקְפָּךְ tukfach וְחֵילָךְ vechelach
לִבְנֵי livnei נָשָׁא nasha, וּלְאַחֲזָאָה ule'achza'a לוֹן lon, אֵיךְ ech
אִתְנְהִיג itnehig עָלְמָא alma בְּדִינָא vedina וּבְרַחֲמֵי uvrachamei,
דְּאִינוּן de'inun צֶדֶק tzedek וּמִשְׁפָּט umishpat ע"ה ה"פ אלהים
כְּפוּם kefum עוֹבָדֵיהוֹן ovadehon דִּבְנֵי divnei נָשָׁא nasha.

And how the lower ones recognize to attain from the higher ones; and in you, there is absolutely nobody who is knowledgeable. And besides your unification, there is no such unique unity in the upper and lower ones, and You are recognized as the Master over all. Each of the Sefirot has a recognizable name, of its own. And by them the angels are named. Yet you have no known name, You are He, who fills all the names. And it is You who completes them all. And when You are gone from them, all the names remain as body without a soul. You are wise, but not with known wisdom. You understand, but not with any known understanding. And You do not occupy any known place so that human beings should perceive His strength and might and to show them how the world conducted with justice and mercy that are righteousness and just trial, according to the deeds of the lower ones.

דִּין, din אִיהוּ ihu גְּבוּרָה gevurah ר"ו מִשְׁפָּט mishpat ע"ה ה"פ אלהים

עַמּוּדָא amuda דְּאֶמְצָעִיתָא de'emtza'ita. צֶדֶק tzedek, מַלְכוּתָא malchuta

קַדִּישָׁא kadisha. מֹאזְנֵי moznei צֶדֶק tzedek, תְּרֵין teren סַמְכֵי samchei

קְשׁוֹט keshot. הִין hin צֶדֶק, tzedek אוֹת ot בְּרִית berit. כֹּלָּא kula

לְאַחֲזָאָה le'achza'a אֵיךְ ech אִתְנְהִיג itnehig עָלְמָא alma. אֲבָל aval

לָאו lav דְּאִית de'it לָךְ lach צֶדֶק tzedek יְדִיעָא yedi'a דְּאִיהוּ de'ihu

דִּין, din וְלָאו velav מִשְׁפָּט mishpat ע"ה ה"פ אלהים יְדִיעָא yedi'a דְּאִיהוּ de'ihu

רַחֲמֵי, rachamei וְלָאו velav מִכָּל mikol ילי אִלֵּין ilen מִדּוֹת midot

כְּלָל kelal. קוּם kum רִבִּי Ribi שִׁמְעוֹן Shimon וְיִתְחַדְּשׁוּן veyitchadeshun

מִלִּין milin עַל al יְדָךְ, yedach דְּהָא deha רְשׁוּתָא reshuta

אִית it לָךְ lach לְגַלָּאָה legala'a רָזִין razin טְמִירִין temirin עַל al

יְדָךְ yedach מָה ma מ"ה דְּלָא dela אִתְיְהִיב ityehiv רְשׁוּ reshu

לְגַלָּאָה legala'a לְשׁוּם leshum בַּר bar נָשׁ nash עַד ad כְּעַן ke'an. קָם kam

רִבִּי Ribi שִׁמְעוֹן, Shim'on פָּתַח patach וְאָמַר ve'amar: לְךָ lecha

יְהֹוָה(אדניאהדונהי) Adonai הַגְּדֻלָּה haGedula וְהַגְּבוּרָה vehaGevurah ר"ו

וְהַתִּפְאֶרֶת vehaTiferet וְהַנֵּצַח vehaNetzach וְהַהוֹד vehaHod ההה כִּי ki

כֹל chol ילי בַּשָּׁמַיִם bashamayim י"פ טל, י"פ כוזו וּבָאָרֶץ uva'aretz לְךָ lecha

יְהֹוָה(אדניאהדונהי) Adonai הַמַּמְלָכָה hamamlacha וגו' vegomer, עִלָּאִין ila'in

שִׁמְעוּ shema'u, אִינוּן inun דְּמִיכִין demichin דְּחֶבְרוֹן deChevron

וְרַעְיָא veRaya מְהֵימְנָא Mehemna, אִתְעָרוּ it'aru מִשְּׁנַתְכוֹן mishenatchon.

Judgement is Gevurah, judicial trial is the Central Column, Righteousness - the holy Malchut; just scales are two supports of truth. A truly measured hin is this sign of the covenant of Yesod. All to show the leadership of the world, but it is not as if there is certain justice that is strictly judgmental, and not a certain just trial that is strictly of mercy, and or of any of these attributes, at all. Rise, Rabbi Shimon and let new ideas come through you, as you have permission, that through you obscure mysteries will be revealed, because permission was not granted to any person until now to reveal them. Rabbi Shimon rose, opened and said, "Yours, Lord, is the greatness, and the power..." (I Chronicles 29:11). Listen, Supreme Ones, they who rest in Chevron, and the Faithful Shepherd, be shaken off from your sleep.

הָקִיצוּ hakitzu וְרַנְּנוּ veranenu שֹׁכְנֵי shochnei עָפָר afar, אִלֵּין ilen אִנּוּן inun

צַדִּיקַיָּא tzadikaya, דְּאִנּוּן de'inun מִסִּטְרָא misitra דְּהַהוּא dehahu

דְּאִתְּמַר de'itmar בָּהּ ba: אֲנִי ani אני יְשֵׁנָה yeshena וְלִבִּי velibi עֵר er,

וְלָאו velav אִנּוּן inun מֵתִים metim, וּבְגִין uvgin דָּא da

אִתְּמַר itmar בְּהוֹן vehon הָקִיצוּ hakitzu וְרַנְּנוּ veranenu וְגוֹ' vegomer.

רַעְיָא Raya מְהֵימְנָא Mehemna, אַנְתְּ ant וַאֲבָהָן va'avahan, הָקִיצוּ hakitzu

וְרַנְּנוּ veranenu לְאִתְעֲרוּתָא le'it'aruta דִּשְׁכִינְתָּא dish'chinta דְּאִיהִי de'ihi

יְשֵׁנָה yeshena בְּגָלוּתָא vegaluta. דְּעַד de'ad כְּעַן ke'an צַדִּיקַיָּא tzadikaya

כֻּלְּהוּ kulhu דְּמִיכִין demichin וְשִׁנְתָּא veshinta בְּחוֹרֵיהוֹן vechorehon.

מִיָּד miyad יָהִיבַת yahivat שְׁכִינְתָּא shechinta תְּלַת telat קָלִין kalin

לְגַבֵּי legabei רַעְיָא Raya מְהֵימְנָא Meheimna וְיֵימָא veyima לֵיהּ lei

קוּם kum רַעְיָא Raya מְהֵימְנָא Mehemna, דְּהָא deha עֲלָךְ alach

אִתְּמַר itmar קוֹל kol | דּוֹדִי dodi דוֹפֵק dofek מנק לְגַבָּאי legabai,

בְּאַרְבַּע be'arba אַתְוָן atvan דִּילֵיהּ dilei. וְיֵימָא veyima בְּהוֹן vehon

פִּתְחִי־ pitchi לִי li אֲחֹתִי achoti רַעְיָתִי rayati יוֹנָתִי yonati תַמָּתִי tamati.

דְּהָא deha תַּם־ tam עֲוֹנֵךְ avonech בַּת־ bat צִיּוֹן Tziyon יוסף, ו' הויות, קנאה

לֹא lo יוֹסִיף yosif לְהַגְלוֹתֵךְ lehaglotech. שֶׁרֹּאשִׁי sheroshi נִמְלָא־ nimla

טָל tal יוד הא ואו, כוזו מַאי mai נִמְלָא nimla טָל tal יוד הא ואו, כוזו.

"Awake and sing, you, that dwell in dust" (Isaiah 26:19). It is those righteous that are from this aspect about which is said, "I sleep, but my heart wakes" (Song of Songs 5:2). And they are not dead, therefore it says about them, "Awake and sing..." Faithful Shepherd, you and the Patriarchs, awake and sing to the waking of the Shechinah that sleeps in exile, as up to now all the righteous are sleeping, and the sleep is in the caverns. Instantly, the Shechinah emits three sounds towards the Faithful Shepherd, and says to him 'Rise, faithful Shepherd. As about you it was said, "hark, my beloved is knocking" (Ibid.) by me, with His four letters. And he will say with them, "Open to me, my sister, my love, my dove, my undefiled" (Ibid.). Since, 'The punishment of your iniquity is accomplished, daughter of Zion; he will no more carry you away into exile" (Lamentations 4:22). 'For my head is filled with dew" (Song of Songs 5:2). He asks, 'What is that which means 'Filled with dew'?

אלא ela אמר amar קודשא kudsha בריך berich הוא hu,

אנת ant וחשבת chashavt דמיומא demiyoma דאתחרב de'itcharav

בי bei מקדשא makdesha דעאלנא de'alna בביתא beveta דילי dili

ועאלנא ve'alna בישובא veyishuva, לאו lav הכי hachi, דלא dela

עאלנא alna כל kol ילי זמנא zimna דאנת de'ant בגלותא begaluta,

הרי harei לך lach סימנא simana שראשי sheroshi נמלא nimla

טל tal יוד הא ואו, כוזו. ה"א He, שכינתא shechinta בגלותא begaluta,

שלימו shelimu דילה dila וחיים vechayim אהיה אהיה יהוה, בינה ע"ה דילה dila,

איהו ihu טל tal יוד הא ואו, כוזו. ודא veda איהו ihu אות ot יו"ד Yod

ואות ve'ot ה"א He ואות ve'ot וא"ו Vav. ואות ve'ot ה"א He איהי ihi

שכינתא shechinta, דלא dela מחושבן mechushban ט"ל tal יוד הא ואו, כוזו.

אלא ela יו"ד Yod ה"א He וא"ו Vav, דסליקו disliku אתון atvan

לחושבן lechushban ט"ל tal יוד הא ואו, כוזו. דאיהו de'ihu מליא malya

לשכינתא lishchinta, מנביעו minevi'u דכל dechol ילי מקורין mekorin

עלאין ilai'n. מיד miyad קם kam רעיא Raya מהימנא Mehemna,

ואבהן va'avahan קדישין kadishin עמיה imei. עד ad כאן kan רזא raza

דיחודא deyichuda. ברוך baruch יהוהאדניאהדונהי Adonai לעולם le'olam

ריבוע דס"ג וי' אותיות דס"ג אמן amen יאהדונהי ואמן ve'amen יאהדונהי ; ר"ת לאו.

But the Holy One, blessed be He, said, You think that from the day of the Temple's destruction, I entered My own abode, and I entered the settlement? Not so, as I have not entered as you are in exile. And here is your proof, "For my head is filled with dew". Hei-Alef is the Shechinah, and she is in exile. Her perfection, and her life is dew (Heb. tal = 39), and that is Yud-Vav-Dalet, Hei-Alef, Vav-Alef-Vav numerically tal (= 39). And the Hei-Alef, the Shechinah, was not in the reckoning of tal, only the Yud-Vav-Dalet, Hei-Alef, Vav-Alef-Vav, which amount to tal. And it is He, who fills the Shechinah from the fountain of all the Supernal sources. The Faithful Shepherd immediately rose up, and the holy Patriarchs with him. Up to here the mysteries of unification. "Blessed be the Lord forever, Amen and Amen!" (Psalms 89:53)

וִיהֵא veyehe רַעֲוָא ra'ava מִן min קֳדָם kodam עַתִּיקָא atika

קַדִּישָׁא kadisha דְּכָל dechol ילי קַדִּישִׁין kadishin טְמִירָא temira

דְּכָל dechol ילי טְמִירִין temirin סְתִימָא setima דְּכֹלָּא dechola,

דְּיִתְמְשָׁךְ deyitmeshach טַלָּא tala עִילָּאָה ila'a מִנֵּיה minei לְמַלְיָא lemalya

רֵישֵׁיהּ reshei דִּזְעֵיר dize'ir אַנְפִּין anpin וּלְהַטִּיל ulehatil לַחֲקַל lachakal

אהיה יהוה יהוה אדני, מנוזם (שמו של משיח) תַּפּוּחִין tapuchin קַדִּישִׁין kadishin

בִּנְהִירוּ binhiru דְּאַנְפִּין de'anpin בְּרַעֲוָא bera'ava וּבְחֶדְוָותָא ubchedvata

דְּכֹלָּא dechola. וְיִתְמְשָׁךְ veyitmeshach מִן min קֳדָם kodam עַתִּיקָא atika

קַדִּישָׁא kadisha דְּכָל dechol ילי קַדִּישִׁין kadishin טְמִירָא temira

דְּכָל dechol ילי טְמִירִין temirin סְתִימָא setima דְּכֹלָּא dechola.

רְעוּתָא re'uta וְרַחֲמֵי verachamei וְחִנָּא china וְחִסְדָּא vechisda

בִּנְהִירוּ binhiru עִילָּאָה ila'a בִּרְעוּתָא bire'uta וְחֶדְוָה vechedva

עָלַי alai וְעַל ve'al כָּל kol ילי ; עמם בְּנֵי benei בֵיתִי veti ב"פ ראה וְעַל ve'al

כָּל kol ילי ; עמם בְּנֵי benei יִשְׂרָאֵל Yisrael עַמֵּיהּ amei. וְיִפְרְקִינָן veyifrekinan

מִכָּל mikol ילי עַקְתִין aktin בִּישִׁין bishin דְּיֵיתוּן deyetun לְעַלְמָא le'alma.

וְיַזְמִין veyazmin וְיִתְיְהִיב veyityehiv לָנָא lana וּלְכָל ulchol יה אדני

נַפְשָׁתָנָא nafshatana וְחִנָּא china וְחִסְדָּא vechisda וְחַיֵּי vechayei

אֲרִיכֵי arichei וּמְזוֹנֵי umzonei רְוִיחֵי revichei וְרַחֲמֵי verachamei מִן min

קֳדָמֵיהּ kodamei. אָמֵן amen יאהדונהי כֵּן ken יְהִי yehi רָצוֹן ratzon

מהש ע"ה, ע"ב בריבוע וקס"א ע"ה, אל שדי ע"ה אָמֵן amen יאהדונהי וְאָמֵן ve'amen יאהדונהי:

And may it be pleasing before the holy of holiest Atika, the hidden of all and the most concealed, that a supernal dew will be drawn from him to fulfill the head of Zeir Anpin, and to drop to Chakal Tapuchin Kadishin from this shining face with desire and happiness for all. And also will be drawn from the holy of holiest Atika, the hidden of all and the most concealed willingly, mercy, grace, kindness, with supernal illumination with desire and happiness, for me and for my household, and for all of Your people, Yisrael. And he will save us from all negative incidents that exist in our world. And he will bring and give us and all the rest of the people, grace and kindness, long life and sustenance, welfare and mercy from before him. Amen shall it be. Amen and Amen.

יְדִיד yedid נֶפֶשׁ nefesh אָב av הָרַחֲמָן harachaman • מְשׁוֹךְ meshoch

עַבְדָּךְ avdach פוי, אל אדני אֶל el רְצוֹנָךְ retzonach • יָרוּץ yarutz

עַבְדָּךְ avdach פוי, אל אדני כְּמוֹ kemo אַיָּל ayal • יִשְׁתַּחֲוֶה yishtachave אֶל el

מוּל mul הֲדָרָךְ hadarach ב"פ יבק, ס"ג קס"א • יֶעֱרַב ye'erav לוֹ lo

יְדִידוּתָךְ yedidutach ר"ת ילי • מִנֹּפֶת minofet צוּף tzuf וְכָל vechol טָעַם ta'am:

הָדוּר hadur נָאֶה na'e זִיו ziv הָעוֹלָם ha'olam • נַפְשִׁי nafshi

חוֹלַת cholat אַהֲבָתָךְ ahavatach • אָנָּא ana ב"ן אֵל El ייא"י (מילוי דס"ג)

נָא na רְפָא refa נָא na לָהּ la (11-Letter Name for healing) •

בְּהַרְאוֹת behar'ot לָהּ la נֹעַם no'am זִיוָךְ zivach • אָז az תִּתְחַזֵּק titchazek

וְתִתְרַפֵּא vetitrape • וְהָיְתָה vehayta לָהּ la שִׂמְחַת simchat עוֹלָם olam:

וָתִיק vatik יֶהֱמוּ yehemu רַחֲמֶיךָ rachamecha • וְחוּסָה vechusa

נָא na עַל al בֵּן ben אֲהוּבָךְ ahuvach • כִּי ki זֶה ze

כַּמָּה chame נִכְסוֹף nichsof נִכְסַף nichsaf • לִרְאוֹת lir'ot

בְּתִפְאֶרֶת betiferet עֻזָּךְ uzach • אָנָּא ana ב"ן אֵלִי Eli חֶמְדַּת chemdat

לִבִּי libi • חוּשָׁה chusha נָא na וְאַל ve'al תִּתְעַלָּם tit'alam:

הִגָּלֶה higale נָא na וּפְרוֹשׂ ufros חָבִיב chaviv הוי • עָלַי alai אֶת et סֻכַּת sukat

שְׁלוֹמָךְ shelomach • תָּאִיר ta'ir אֶרֶץ eretz מִכְּבוֹדָךְ mikevodach ב"ן, לכב •

נָגִילָה nagila וְנִשְׂמְחָה venismecha בָךְ vach • מַהֵר maher אֱהוֹב ahuv

כִּי ki בָא va מוֹעֵד mo'ed • וְחָנֵּנוּ vechonenu כִּימֵי kimei עוֹלָם olam:

י *Beloved of the soul, Compassionate Father, draw Your servant to Your desire. Your servant will run like a hart, he will bow before Your majesty. Your friendship will be sweeter than the dripping of the honeycomb and any taste.* ה *Majestic, Beautiful, Radiance of the world, my soul pines for Your love. Please, God, heal her, by showing her the pleasantness of Your radiance. Then she will be strengthened and healed, and she will have the gladness of the world.* ו *All Worthy One, may Your mercy be aroused and please take pity on the sons of Your beloved, because it is so very long that I have yearned intensely, speedily to see the splendor of Your strength. Only these my heart desired, so please take pity and do not conceal Yourself.* ה *Reveal and spread upon me, my Beloved, the shelter of Your peace. Illuminate the world with Your glory that we may rejoice and be glad with You. Hasten, show love, for time has come, and show us grace as in day of old.*

LESHEM YICHUD

לְשֵׁם leshem יִחוּד yichud קוּדְשָׁא kudsha בְּרִיךְ berich הוּא hu
וּשְׁכִינְתֵּיהּ ush'chintei (יאהדונהי) בִּדְחִילוּ bid'chilu וּרְחִימוּ ur'chimu
(יאההויהה), וּרְחִימוּ ur'chimu וּדְחִילוּ ud'chilu (איההייוהה), לְיַחֲדָא leyachada
שֵׁם shem יוּ"ד yud קֵי kei בְּוָא"ו bevav קֵי kei בְּיִחוּדָא beyichuda
שְׁלִים shelim (יהוה) בְּשֵׁם beshem כָּל kol ילי יִשְׂרָאֵל Yisrael,
הֲרֵינִי hareni מְקַבֵּל mekabel עָלַי alai אֱלֹהוּתוֹ Elohuto יִתְבָּרַךְ yitbarach
וְיִרְאָתוֹ veyira'to וְאַהֲבָתוֹ ve'ahavato וְהִנְנִי vehineni עֶבֶד eved
לְהַשֵּׁם leHashem יִתְבָּרַךְ yitbarach, וַהֲרֵינִי vehareni מְקַיֵּם mekayem
מִצְוַת mitzvat וְאָהַבְתָּ ve'ahavta ב"פ אור, ב"פ רז, ב"פ א"ס לְרֵעֲךָ lere'acha
כָּמוֹךָ kamocha וַהֲרֵינִי vehareni אוֹהֵב ohev אֶת et כָּל kol ילי אָדָם adam
מִיִּשְׂרָאֵל miYisrael כְּנַפְשִׁי kenafshi, וַהֲרֵינִי vehareni מְכַוֵּין mechaven
לְקַיֵּם lekayem מִצְוַת mitzvat צִיצִית tzitzit וּמִצְוַת umitzvat תַּלְמוּד talmud
תּוֹרָה torah, וַהֲרֵינִי vehareni מְכַוֵּין mechaven לְקַיֵּם lekayem
מִצְוַת mitzvat קְרִיאַת keri'at שְׁמַע Shema וּתְפִלַּת utfilat שַׁחֲרִית shacharit,
הֵם hem וְהַמִּצְוֹת vehamitzvot הַנִּלְוֹת hanilvot וְהַכְּלוּלוֹת vehakelulot
בָּהֶם bahem, וַאֲנִי va'ani אני מְכַוֵּין mechaven בְּכָל bakol ב"ן, לכב
לַעֲשׂוֹת la'asot נַחַת nachat רוּחַ ru'ach לְיוֹצְרֵנוּ leyotzrenu שֶׁלֹּא shelo
עַל al מְנָת menat לְקַבֵּל lekabel פְּרָס peras בְּשׁוּם beshum צַד tzad,
וַאֲנִי va'ani אני מְכַוֵּין mechaven בְּכָל bakol ב"ן, לכב לָדַעַת leda'at
רַבִּי Rabbi שִׁמְעוֹן Shimon בֶּן ben יוֹחַאי Yochai הַקָּדוֹשׁ hakadosh,

---

LESHEM YICHUD

For the sake of the unification between the Holy Blessed One and His Shechinah, with fear and love and with love and fear, in order to unify the Name Yud-Kei and Vav-Kei in perfect unity, and in the name of all Israel, I hereby accept upon myself His divinity, blessed be He, and the love of Him and the fear of Him, and I hereby declare myself a servant to God blessed be He. And I hereby accept upon myself the obligatory commandment of "Love your fellow as you do yourself." And I hereby declare that I love each one of Israel with my soul. And I am hereby prepared to fulfill the obligatory precept of wearing the Tzitzit, Studying Torah. And I am hereby prepared to fulfill the obligatory precept of The Shema and the prayer of Shacharit and all the precepts that are concerned with it. And I meditate to bring satisfaction to our maker, not for the sake of receiving any prize. And all my intention is according to the holy Rabbi Shimon Bar Yochai.

וְהֲרֵינִי vehareni מְקַבֵּל mekabel עָלַי alai כֹּל kol ילי תרי"ג taryag
מִצְוֹת mitzvot דְּאוֹרַיְיתָא de'orayta וּמִצְוֹת umitzvot דְּרַבָּנָן derabanan
הֵם hem וְעַנְפֵיהֶם ve'anfehem. וְאַתָּה veAta הָאֵל haEl לאה ; ייא"י (מילוי דס"ג)
הַטּוֹב hatov והו בְּרוֹב berov י"פ אהיה רַחֲמֶיךָ rachamecha
תַּצִּילֵנוּ tatzilenu מִיֵּצֶר miyetzer הָרָע hara וּתְזַכֵּנוּ ut'zakenu
לְעָבְדְךָ le'ovdecha פוי, אל אדני בֶּאֱמֶת be'emet אהיה פעמים אהיה, ז"פ ס"ג
אָמֵן amen יאהדונהי כֵּן ken יְהִי yehi רָצוֹן ratzon מהש ע"ה, ע"ב בריבוע וקס"א ע"ה,
אל שדי ע"ה. וִיהִי vihi נֹעַם no'am אֲדֹנָי Adonai ללה אֱלֹהֵינוּ Elohenu ילה
עָלֵינוּ alenu וּמַעֲשֵׂה uma'ase יָדֵינוּ yadenu כּוֹנְנָה konena
עָלֵינוּ alenu וּמַעֲשֵׂה uma'ase יָדֵינוּ yadenu כּוֹנְנֵהוּ konenehu:

יְהִי yehi רָצוֹן ratzon מהש ע"ה, ע"ב בריבוע וקס"א ע"ה, אל שדי ע"ה
מִלְּפָנֶיךָ milfanecha ס"ג מ"ה ב"ן יְהֹוָהאדנייאהדונהי Adonai
אֱלֹהֵינוּ Elohenu ילה וֵאלֹהֵי velohei לכב ; מילוי ע"ב, דמב ; ילה
אֲבוֹתֵינוּ avotenu שֶׁתַּכְנִיעַ shetachni'a כָּל kol ילי
הַמְקַטְרְגִים hamekatregim וְכָל vechol ילי הַקְּלִיפּוֹת hakelipot
הַחִיצוֹנִים hachitzonim הַמְשׁוֹטְטִים hameshotetim בָּעוֹלָם ba'olam
וּמְעַכְּבִים ume'akvim תְּפִלָּתִי tefilati לַעֲלוֹת la'alot לְפָנֶיךָ lefanecha ס"ג מ"ה ב"ן
כִּי ki אַתָּה Ata יוֹדֵעַ yode'a שֶׁרְצוֹנִי shertzoni לַעֲשׂוֹת la'asot
רְצוֹנְךָ retzoncha, אַךְ ach אהיה שְׂאוֹר se'or שֶׁבְּעִיסָּה shebe'isa
מְעַכֵּב me'akev אוֹתִי oti, לָכֵן lachen גְּעוֹר ge'or בָּהֶם bahem שֶׁאַל she'al
יְזִיקוּנִי yezikuni וְאַל ve'al יְעַכְּבוּ ye'akvu אֶת et תְּפִלָּתִי tefilati

---

And I hereby accept upon myself all the 613 precepts of the Torah and the sages and its outcomes. And You, the good God, with your mighty mercy will save us from the evil inclination and allow us the privilege of serving you with truth Amen, so may His will be. "May the pleasantness of the Lord, our God, be upon us and may He establish the work of our hands for us and may the work of our hands establish Him." (Psalms 90:17)

May it be pleasing before You, Lord, my God and God of my forefathers, that You would subjugate all the denouncers and the external klipot that exist in the world, and they deferred my prayer to come before You. And You know that my only desire is to follow your desire, but the leaven in the dough deferred me. So castigate them so they would not harm me and they would not defer my prayer,

וְאַל ve'al יִשְׁלְטוּ yishletu בִּי bi לֹא lo בְּגוּפִי begufi וְלֹא velo

בְּנִשְׁמָתִי benishmati, וְשֶׁתְּהֵא veshetehe תְּפִלָּתִי tefilati רְצוּיָה retzuya

וּמְקוּבֶּלֶת umkubelet לְפָנֶיךָ lefanecha ס״ג מ״ה ב״ן אָמֵן amen יאהדונהי כֵּן ken

יְהִי yehi רָצוֹן ratzon מהש ע״ה, ע״ב בריבוע וקס״א ע״ה, אל שדי ע״ה:

הֲרֵינִי hareni מְכַוֵּין mechaven בִּתְפִלָּתִי bitfilati כְּאִילוּ ke'ilu

אֲנִי ani אני עוֹמֵד omed בִּירוּשָׁלַיִם birushalayim בְּבֵית bevet ב״פ ראה

הַמִּקְדָּשׁ hamikdash וּמְכַוֵּין umchaven כְּנֶגֶד keneged מזבח, זן, אל יהוה בֵּית bet

ב״פ ראה קֹדֶשׁ kodesh הַקֳּדָשִׁים hakodashim כְּמוֹ kemo שֶׁנֶּאֱמַר shene'emar:

וְהִתְפַּלְלוּ vehitpalelu אֶל el הַמָּקוֹם hamakom הַזֶּה haze והו:

יְהִי yehi רָצוֹן ratzon מהש ע״ה, ע״ב בריבוע וקס״א ע״ה, אל שדי ע״ה

מִלְּפָנֶיךָ milfanecha ס״ג מ״ה ב״ן יְהֹוָהאדניאהדונהי Adonai אֱלֹהֵינוּ Elohenu ילה

וֵאלֹהֵי velohei לכב ; מילוי ע״ב, דמב ; ילה אֲבוֹתֵינוּ avotenu שֶׁיְּהֵא sheyehe לִבִּי libi

נָכוֹן nachon וּמָסוּר umasur בְּיָדִי beyadi שֶׁלֹּא shelo אֶשְׁכָּחֶךָ eshkachecha:

RIBON ALMA

Rabbi Shimon says in the *Zohar, Idra Rabba* 303: "*The soul of man is taken from the higher levels downward to Malchut. By that, it causes everything to be in single union. Whoever interrupts this union from the world is as if he severs the above mentioned soul, and indicates that another soul exists besides this one. As a result he and his memory will disappear from this world for generations upon generations.*" Saying "*Ribon Alma*" before the prayer protects us from doing intellectual mistakes throughout our spiritual work.

רִבּוֹן ribon עָלְמָא alma יְהֵא yehe רַעֲוָא ra'ava קָמָךְ kamach לְמֵיהַב lemehav

לָן lan חֵילָא chela לְאִתְעָרָא le'it'ara בִּיקָרָךְ vikarach וּלְמֶעְבַּד ulme'ebad

רְעוּתָךְ re'utach וּלְסַדְּרָא ulesadara כֹּלָּא chola כִּדְקָא kedeka יָאוּת ya'ut.

---

and they would not control me, not my body and not my soul.
And my prayer would be accepted by You, Amen, so may His will be.

I hereby meditate in my prayer
as if I am standing in the temple in Jerusalem, and tuned against the Holy of Holies. As it says: "and they shall pray toward this place" (I kings 8:35). May it be pleasing before You, Lord, my God and God of my forefathers, that my heart will be founded and devoted by me so I will not forget You.

RIBON ALMA

Master of the World, may it be pleasing before You
to give us strength, to stir ourself to honor You, to do Your will and to put everything in the right direction.

leshava'a לְשַׁוָּאָה yad'in יָדְעִין anan אֲנַן delet דְּלֵית gav גַּב al עַל ve'af וְאַף

ra'ava רַעֲוָא yehe יְהֵא ,chola כֹּלָּא letakana לְתַקָּנָא veliba וְלִבָּא re'uta רְעוּתָא

dilan דִּילָן utzelota וּצְלוֹתָא vemilin בְּמִלִּין detitre'ei דְּתִתְרְעֵי kamach קַמָּךְ

ya'ut יָאוּת kideka כִּדְקָא dil'ela דִּלְעֵלָּא tikuna תִּקּוּנָא letakana לְתַקָּנָא

ila'in עִלָּאִין veruchin וְרוּחִין ila'in עִלָּאִין hechalin הֵיכָלִין ulehevo וְלֶהֱווֹ

verucha בְּרוּחָא verucha וְרוּחָא behechala בְּהֵיכָלָא hechala הֵיכָלָא ayle עָיְלֵי

kideka כִּדְקָא beduchtayho בְּדוּכְתַּיְהוּ demitchaberan דְּמִתְחַבְּרָן ad עַד

da דָּא ve'ishtelimu וְאִשְׁתְּלִימוּ ,besheyafa בְּשַׁיָּפָא sheyafa שַׁיָּפָא ,chazei חָזֵי

,chad חַד inun אִנּוּן ad עַד veda בְּדָא da דָּא ve'ityachadu וְאִתְיַחֲדוּ veda בְּדָא

nishmeta נִשְׁמְתָא ucheden וּכְדֵין •veda בְּדָא da דָּא venaharin וְנָהֲרִין

lon לוֹן venaher וְנָהֵר mile'ela מִלְּעֵלָּא atya אַתְיָא dechola דְּכֹלָּא ila'a עִלָּאָה

bishlemu בִּשְׁלִימוּ vutzinin בּוּצִינִין kolehu כֻּלְּהוּ nehirin נְהִירִין velehevu וְלֶהֱווּ

ila'a עִלָּאָה nehora נְהוֹרָא dehahu דְּהַהוּא ad עַד ,chazei חָזֵי kideka כִּדְקָא

kodesh קֹדֶשׁ legabei לְגַבֵּי a'el אָעֵיל vechola וְכֹלָּא ,ite'ar אִתְּעַר

kevera כְּבֵירָא ve'itmalya וְאִתְמַלְיָא ve'itbarcha וְאִתְבָּרְכָא kodashim קָדָשִׁים

vecholho וְכֻלְּהוּ faskin פָּסְקִין vela וְלָא nav'in נָבְעִין demayin דְּמַיִין

dela דְּלָא vehahu וְהַהוּא •vetata וְתַתָּא le'ela לְעֵלָּא mitbarchan מִתְבָּרְכָן

re'uta רְעוּתָא ,bechushbena בְּחֻשְׁבְּנָא a'el אָעֵיל vela וְלָא ityeda אִתְיְדַע

lego לְגוֹ lego לְגוֹ basim בָּסִים ,le'almin לְעָלְמִין itpas אִתְפַּס dela דְּלָא

re'uta רְעוּתָא hahu הַהוּא ityeda אִתְיְדַע vela וְלָא ,begavayho בְּגַוַּיְהוּ

And although we do not know how to be mindful and to direct our heart, to correct everything, may it be pleasing before You, that our words and prayer will be accepted to correct the Supernal tikkun in the right direction, so the Supernal chambers and the Supernal souls are elevated, one chamber penetrates the other, and one soul the other, until they all rest in their proper places as is suitiable. One organ is within the other and one complements the other. The elements merge until they become one and shine within each other. Consequently, this most Supernal soul descends and shines on them, and all the candles (Sefirot) are becomingly lit in all their perfection, until this Supernal Light is aroused and all the chambers enter the Holy of Holies, and it is blessed and filled like a well of spring water that never ceases to flow, and all the Upper and Lower are blessed. The innermost of secrets that cannot be conceived and is taken account, it is a desire that can never be grasped, is sweetened deep within the Sefirot, and its desire cannot be conceived

וְלָא vela אִיתְפַּס itpas לְמִנְדַּע, leminda וּכְדֵין ucheden כֹּלָּא kola רְעוּתָא re'uta
וְחָדָא chada עַד ad אֵין en סוֹף sof וְכֹלָּא vechola אִיהוּ ihu בִּשְׁלֵימוּ vishlemu
מִלְּתַתָּא miletata וּמִגּוֹ umigo לְגּוֹ lego עַד ad דְּאִתְעֲבֵד de'it'aved כֹּלָּא kola
וְחַד, chad וְאִתְמַלְיָאה ve'itmali'a כֹּלָּא kola וְאִשְׁלֵם ve'ashlem כֹּלָּא kola
וְאִתְנְהִיר ve'itnahir וְאִתְבַּסֵּם ve'itbasem כֹּלָּא kola כִּדְקָא kideka יָאוּת. ya'ut

רִבּוֹן ribon עָלְמָא alma יְהֵא yehe רְעוּתָךְ re'utach עִם im עַמָּךְ amach
יִשְׂרָאֵל Yisrael לְעָלַם. le'alam וּפֻרְקַן ufurkan יְמִינָךְ yeminach אַחֲזֵי achazei
לְעַמָּךְ le'amach בְּבֵית bevet מַקְדְּשָׁךְ makdeshach וּלְאַמְטוּיֵי ule'amtuyei
לַנָא lana מִטּוּב mituv נְהוֹרָךְ nehorach וּלְקַבְּלָא ulekabela צְלוֹתָנָא tzelotana
בְּרַחֲמֵי. berachmei יְהֵא yehe רַעֲוָא ra'ava קֳמָךְ kamach דִּתֶהֱוֵי detehevei
סָעֵד sa'ed וְסָמֵיךְ vesmech לַן lan דְּנֵימָא denema מִלִּין milin בְּאֹרַח be'orach
מֵישׁוֹר. mishor בְּתִקּוּנָא betikuna דִּלְעֵלָּא dil'ela בְּתִקּוּנִין betikunin
דְּמַלְכָּא demalka קַדִּישָׁא kadisha וּמַטְרוֹנִיתָא umatronita קַדִּישָׁא kadisha
וּלְמֶעְבַּד uleme'ebad יִחוּדָא yichuda שְׁלִים shelim לְאַשְׁלָפָא le'ashalfa
לְהַהִיא lehahi נִשְׁמְתָא nishmeta דְּכֹל dechol חַיֵּי chayei מִדַּרְגָּא midarga
לְדַרְגָּא ledarga עַד ad סוֹפָא sofa דְּכָל dechol דַּרְגִּין. dargin
בְּגִין begin דִּיהֱוֵי dihevei הַהִיא hahi נִשְׁמְתָא nishmeta
מִשְׁתַּכְחָא mishtechacha בְּכֹלָּא bechola וּמִתְפַּשְּׁטָא umitpasheta
בְּכֹלָּא bechola דְּהָא deha עֵלָּא ela וְתַתָּא vetata תְּלַיִן telayin
בְּהַאי behai נִשְׁמְתָא nishmeta וּמִתְקַיְּמֵי umitkayemei בָּהּ: va:

---

or directed at knowing him. Thus, all the levels up to Ein Sof (The Endless World) unite into one, and everything is perfected from Above, Below, and within. All the levels are filled with his Light, all reach completion and all shine because of him and are suitably sweetened as it should be.

Master of the World, May Your desire be with Your nation Israel forever. The redemption of Your Right may You show to Your nation in Your Temple. May You fill us with the best of Your enlightenment and may You receive our prayers with mercy. May it be pleasing before You to assist and support us to say the words in the right way, for the Supernal tikkun and the tkkun of the holy King and the holy Matron. So it will create a complete unification which will draw out this soul which gives life to all from one height to another, all the way to the end of all levels. Because of the existence of this soul in everything and its extention in everything, Above and Below idepend on this soul and exist because of it.

ADON OLAM

The two words *Adon Olam* (אדון עולם) are equal to the numerical value of the Aramaic words *Ein Sof* (207), meaning the "Endless World"—our true origin. *Adon Olam* is also the numeric value of the Aramaic word *Or*, which means "Light." The actual words *Adon Olam* translate into English as "Master of the Universe." Through this prayer, we want to arouse a sense of awe and wonderment toward the knowledge and understanding of the spiritual system and the order and perfection of the world and of the Light of the Creator.

אֲדוֹן adon אני עוֹלָם olam אור, רז, א״ס אֲשֶׁר asher מָלַךְ malach.

בְּטֶרֶם beterem כָּל kol ילי יְצִיר yetzir נִבְרָא nivra: לְעֵת le'et נַעֲשָׂה na'asa

בְחֶפְצוֹ vecheftzo כֹּל kol ילי. אֲזַי azai מֶלֶךְ melech שְׁמוֹ shemo מהש ע״ה,

ע״ב בריבוע וקס״א ע״ה, אל שדי ע״ה נִקְרָא nikra: וְאַחֲרֵי ve'acharei כִּכְלוֹת kichlot

הַכֹּל hakol ילי. לְבַדּוֹ levado מ״ב יִמְלוֹךְ yimloch נוֹרָא nora:

וְהוּא vehu הָיָה haya יהה וְהוּא vehu הֹוֶה hove. וְהוּא vehu יִהְיֶה yihye ייי

בְּתִפְאָרָה betifara: וְהוּא vehu אֶחָד echad אהבה, דאגה וְאֵין ve'en שֵׁנִי sheni.

לְהַמְשִׁילוֹ lehamshilo וּלְהַחְבִּירָה ulhachbira: בְּלִי beli רֵאשִׁית resheet

בְּלִי beli תַכְלִית tachlit. וְלוֹ velo הָעֹז ha'oz וְהַמִּשְׂרָה vehamisra: בְּלִי beli

עֵרֶךְ erech בְּלִי beli דִמְיוֹן dimyon. בְּלִי beli שִׁנּוּי shinuy וּתְמוּרָה utmura:

בְּלִי beli חִבּוּר chibur בְּלִי beli פֵּרוּד perud. גְּדוֹל gedol להח ; עם ד׳ אותיות =

מבה, יזל, אום כֹּחַ ko'ach וּגְבוּרָה ugvurah רי״י: וְהוּא vehu אֵלִי Eli וְחַי vechai

גֹּאֲלִי go'ali. וְצוּר vetzur אלהים דההין ע״ה חֶבְלִי chevli בְּיוֹם beyom ע״ה נגד,

מזבח, זן, אל יהוה צָרָה tzara אלהים דההין: וְהוּא vehu נִסִּי nisi וּמָנוּסִי umanusi.

מְנָת menat כּוֹסִי kosi בְּיוֹם beyom ע״ה נגד, מזבח, זן, אל יהוה אֶקְרָא ekra:

ADON OLAM

Master of the Universe, Who reigned before any form was created and, when everything was made according to His will, His Name was proclaimed as King. And after everything has expired, He, the Awesome One, shall reign alone. He was, He is, and He shall remain in splendor. He is One and there is no other to compare to Him or to declare as His equal. Without beginning, without conclusion, His is the power and dominion, unfathomable and unimaginable, unchanging and irreplaceable. He is without connections or separation. His strength and valor are great. He is my God and my living Redeemer; the forbearance of pain in time of distress. He is my banner, my refuge, and the portion of my cup on the day that I call out.

וְהוּא vehu רוֹפֵא rofe וְהוּא vehu מַרְפֵּא marpe• וְהוּא vehu צוֹפֶה tzofe

וְהוּא vehu עֶזְרָה ezra: בְּיָדוֹ beyado אַפְקִיד afkid רוּחִי ruchi

ר"ת = קנ"א ב"ן, יהוה אלהים יהוה אדני, מילוי קס"א וס"ג, מ"ה ברבוע וע"ב ע"ה• בְּעֵת be'et

אִישַׁן ishan וְאָעִירָה ve'a'ira: וְעִם ve'im רוּחִי ruchi גְּוִיָּתִי geviyati•

אֲדֹנָי Adonai ללה לִי li וְלֹא velo אִירָא ira: בְּמִקְדָּשׁוֹ bemikdasho

תָּגֵל tagel נַפְשִׁי nafshi• מְשִׁיחֵנוּ meshichenu יִשְׁלַח yishlach מְהֵרָה mehera:

וְאָז ve'az נָשִׁיר nashir בְּבֵית bevet ב"פ ראה קָדְשִׁי kodshi•

אָמֵן amen יאהדונהי אָמֵן amen יאהדונהי שֵׁם shem הַנּוֹרָא hanora:

THE SMALL TALIT

The connection of the small *Talit* (*Talit katan* or *Tzitzit*) refers to a garment worn underneath the shirt. The small *Talit* creates a protective security shield around the wearer's skin and body so that evil forces cannot infiltrate or penetrate them. Our skin has the energy of *Malchut*, which is connected to the one percent realm. The small *Talit* controls the energy field around the skin and protects it.

It says in the *Zohar* that the *Tzitzit* is a talisman which covers and protects the wearer from all evil spirits and negative angels. Rabbenu Bachye says that the precept of the *Tzitzit* is linked to the Resurrection of the Dead. The *Tzitzit* represents the Surrounding Light, and for that reason, the *Talit* needs to be large in order to cover the head and the body, back and front, all the way down to the chest. The small *Talit* represents the Surrounding Light of *Katnut*.

If you do not use a *Talit* for the prayers you should only recite this blessing.
If you slept with a small *Talit* you should touch the *Tzitzit* first.

בָּרוּךְ baruch אַתָּה Ata יְהֹוָאדניאהדונהי Adonai אֱלֹהֵינוּ Elohenu ילה

מֶלֶךְ melech הָעוֹלָם ha'olam אֲשֶׁר asher קִדְּשָׁנוּ kideshanu

בְּמִצְוֹתָיו bemitzvotav וְצִוָּנוּ vetzivanu עַל al מִצְוַת mitzvat צִיצִית tzitzit:

He is a healer and a remedy. He watches and He helps. In His Hands, I surrender my spirit when I sleep and when I awaken. With my spirit shall my body remain. The Lord is with me, I shall not fear. In His Temple shall my spirit rejoice. He shall send our Mashiach speedily. Then we shall sing in His Temple: Amen, Amen, the Awesome Name.

THE SMALL TALIT

Blessed are You, Lord, our God, the King of the Earth,
Who has sanctified us with His commandments and obliged us with the commandment of Tzitzit.

THE TALIT

The *Talit* is a shawl that is draped over the shoulders of the wearer, over his clothes. It surrounds him with a spiritual protective layer of illumination. The four corners of the *Talit*, with their tassels, connect us to the four corners of the universe and to the quantum level of our world, helping us gain control over our lives. The *Talit* connects us to the Surrounding Light—our soul's potential. Generally, only married men wear it, because the energy awakened by the *Talit* is manifested through the man's connection with his wife.

LESHEM YICHUD

LeShem Yichud is a spark plug that activates the next series of prayers and actions, joining the Upper Worlds with our physical world.

לְשֵׁם leshem יִחוּד yichud קוּדְשָׁא kudsha בְּרִיךְ berich הוּא hu
וּשְׁכִינְתֵּיהּ ush'chintei (יאהדונהי) בִּדְחִילוּ bid'chilu וּרְחִימוּ ur'chimu
(יאההויהה), וּרְחִימוּ ur'chimu וּדְחִילוּ ud'chilu (איההיוהה), לְיַחֲדָא leyachada
שֵׁם shem יו"ד yud קֵ"י kei בְּוָא"ו bevav קֵ"י kei בְּיִחוּדָא beyichuda
שְׁלִים shelim (יהוה) בְּשֵׁם beshem כָּל kol ילי יִשְׂרָאֵל Yisrael, הֲרֵינִי hareni
מוּכָן muchan לִלְבּוֹשׁ lilvosh טַלִּית talit מְצֻיֶּצֶת metzuyetzet
כְּהִלְכָתָהּ kehilchata כְּמוֹ kemo שֶׁצִּוָּנוּ shetzivanu יְהֹוָהאדניהאהדונהי Adonai
אֱלֹהֵינוּ Elohenu ילה בְּתוֹרָתוֹ vetorato הַקְּדוֹשָׁה hakedosha: וְעָשׂוּ ve'asu
לָהֶם lahem צִיצִת tzitzit עַל־ al כַּנְפֵי kanfei בִגְדֵיהֶם vigdehem, כְּדֵי kedei
לַעֲשׂוֹת la'asot נַחַת nachat רוּחַ ru'ach לְיוֹצְרִי leyotzri וְלַעֲשׂוֹת vela'asot
רְצוֹן retzon מהש ע"ה, ע"ב בריבוע וקס"א ע"ה, אל שדי ע"ה בּוֹרְאִי bor'i, וַהֲרֵינִי vehareni
מוּכָן muchan לְבָרֵךְ levarech עַל al עֲטִיפַת atifat הַטַּלִּית hatalit
כְּתִקּוּן ketikkun רז"ל razal, וַהֲרֵינִי vehareni מְכַוֵּין mechaven לִפְטוֹר liftor
בִּבְרָכָה bivracha זוֹ zo גַּם gam טַלִּית talit הַקָּטָן hakatan שֶׁעָלַי she'alai.

THE TALIT
LESHEM YICHUD

For the sake of the unification between The Holy Blessed One and His Shechinah, with fear and love and with love and fear, in order to unify the Name Yud-Kei and Vav-Kei in perfect unity, and in the name of all Israel, I am hereby prepared to wear a Talit with Tzitzit, according to the law and as we were commanded by the Lord, our God, in His holy Torah: "And they made for themselves Tzitzit on the corners of their clothes." (Numbers 15:38) *In order to give pleasure to my Maker and to fulfill the wish of my Creator, I am hereby prepared to bless upon the enwrapping with the Talit, as was established by our Sages of blessed memory. I hereby intend to exempt the small Talit that I am wearing, with this blessing.*

וִיהִי vihi נֹעַם no'am אֲדֹנָי Adonai ללה אֱלֹהֵינוּ Elohenu ילה
עָלֵינוּ alenu וּמַעֲשֵׂה uma'ase יָדֵינוּ yadenu כּוֹנְנָה konena
עָלֵינוּ alenu וּמַעֲשֵׂה uma'ase יָדֵינוּ yadenu כּוֹנְנֵהוּ konenehu:

***Wrapping the Talit*:** After the blessing, you wrap the *Talit* over your head, leaving your face uncovered and the four corners falling on your chest. Then you grab the two right side *Tzitzits* and throws them over your left shoulder so they drape at the back – then you wait a bit, then take hold of the two left side *Tzitzits* and throw them over your left shoulder, draping them to the back in a way that the four *Tzitzits* will be hanging over your left shoulder towards and down the back. You should wait like that for about four seconds, before allowing the *Talit* to drop down, so it can hang comfortably and loosely over both shoulders with two *Tzitzits* in the front and two in the back.

The *Talit* is the aspect of the Surrounding Light of *Gadlut*.
The *Talit* is the *tikkun* of the external part (*Netzach, Hod, Yesod*) of *Yetzirah*.
The blessing is the *tikkun* of the Surrounding Light, and
The wearing of the *Talit* is the *tikkun* of the Inner Light.

בָּרוּךְ baruch אַתָּה Ata יְהֹוָהאדניאהדונהי Adonai אֱלֹהֵינוּ Eelohenu ילה מֶלֶךְ melech
הָעוֹלָם ha'olam אֲשֶׁר asher קִדְּשָׁנוּ kideshanu בְּמִצְוֹתָיו bemitzvotav
וְצִוָּנוּ vetzivanu לְהִתְעַטֵּף lehit'atef בְּצִיצִית betzitzit ר"ת ל"ב נתיבות החכמה:

Yichud of the *Talit*: At first, you should meditate on the *Yichud* (unification) of *Zeir Anpin*, which is: יהוה, which has the numerical value of 32 paths of wisdom (ל"ב נתיבות החכמה). In particular, you should meditate to connect the letters יה, which are *Abba* and *Ima*, with the letter ו, which is *Zeir Anpin*, so that it becomes the Surrounding Light which is the *Talit*. Then, you should meditate to connect the letter ו (*Zeir Anpin*) with the last letter ה, to draw the Surrounding Light to the letter ה, which is the *Tzitzit*.

VA'ANI

COMMUNICATING WITH THE THREE PILLARS OF PRAYER (ABRAHAM, ISAAC AND JACOB)

There are three forces present in the universe that are required to generate power, be it physical or spiritual. These forces are the Right Column positive, sharing energy, of which Abraham is the channel; the Left Column receiving, negative energy, of which Isaac is the channel, and the Central Column of balance, resistance, of which Jacob is the channel. The ancient kabbalists explain that Abraham, Isaac and Jacob are the foundation of every prayer. Their names are transmitters that activate and give power to all blessings and prayers that we perform throughout this Siddur.

"May the pleasantness of the Lord our God be upon us and may He establish the work of our hands for us and may the work of our hands establish Him." (Psalms 90:17)

Blessed are You, Lord, our God, the King of the World,
Who has sanctified us with His commandments and obliged us with enwrapping ourselves with Talit.

You should say the verse below while entering the temple, standing at the doorpost:

Abraham (Right)

וַאֲנִי va'ani אני בְּרֹב berov י"פ אהיה וְחַסְדְּךָ chasdecha אבג'יתץ

אָבוֹא avo בֵּיתֶךָ vetecha ב"פ ראה

Isaac (Left)

אֶשְׁתַּחֲוֶה eshtachave י"פ ע"ב אֶל־ el הֵיכַל hechal ללה, אדני ; ר"ת = יהוה

קָדְשְׁךָ kodshecha

Jacob (Central)

בְּיִרְאָתֶךָ beyir'atecha:

Then bow down and enter.

Right

יְהֹוָהאדניאהדונהי Adonai צְבָאוֹת Tzeva'ot פני שכינה עִמָּנוּ imanu

מִשְׂגָּב־ misgav ריבוע ס"ג, קס"א ע"ה וד' אותיות משה, מהש, ריבוע ע"ב וקס"א, אל שדי,

לָנוּ lanu ד"פ אלהים ע"ה אֱלֹהֵי Elohei אלהים, אהיה אדני מילוי ע"ב, דמב ; ילה

יַעֲקֹב Ya'akov ז' הויות, יאהדונהי אידהנויה סֶלָה sela:

Left

יְהֹוָהאדניאהדונהי Adonai צְבָאוֹת Tzeva'ot פני שכינה אַשְׁרֵי ashrei

אָדָם adam מ"ה ; ה' צבאות אשרי אדם = תפארת בֹּטֵחַ bote'ach

בָּךְ bach אדם בוטח בך = אמן (יאהדונהי) ע"ה ; בוטח בך = מילוי ע"ב ע"ה:

Central

יְהֹוָהאדניאהדונהי Adonai הוֹשִׁיעָה hoshi'a יהוה וש"ע נהורין הַמֶּלֶךְ hamelech ר"ת יהה

יַעֲנֵנוּ ya'anenu בְיוֹם veyom ע"ה נגד, מזבח, זן, אל יהוה קָרְאֵנוּ kor'enu

ר"ת יב"ק, אלהים יהוה, אהיה אדני יהוה ; ס"ת = ב"ן ועם אות כ' דהמלך = ע"ב:

VA'ANI

"And I, with the profusion of Your kindness,
come to Your House and bow towards Your Holy Ark, in awe of You." (Psalms 5:8)

"The Lord of Hosts, joyful is one who trusts in You." (Psalms 84:13)
"The Lord of Hosts is with us. The God of Jacob is a refuge for us, Selah.
Lord redeem us. The King shall answer us on the day we call Him." (Psalms 46:12)

ESH TAMID - MEDITATION TO CONTROL OUR THOUGHTS

Our brain is a receiver and there are two transmitting stations that send signals/thoughts to our brain. One source is the Light and the other is Satan. These verses disrupt and override any negative thoughts that might enter our minds.

Each verse is recited seven times:

אֵשׁ esh תָּמִיד tamid ע"ה קס"א קנ"א קמ"ג תּוּקַד tukad עַל־ al

הַמִּזְבֵּחַ hamizbe'ach נגד, זן, אל יהוה לֹא lo תִכְבֶּה tichbe:

Recite seven times

סֵעֲפִים se'afim שָׂנֵאתִי saneti וְתוֹרָתְךָ vetoratcha אָהָבְתִּי ahavti:

Recite seven times

לֵב lev טָהוֹר tahor י"פ אכא בְּרָא־ bera

קנ"א ב"ן, יהוה אלהים יהוה אדני, מילוי קס"א וס"ג, מ"ה ברבוע וע"ב ע"ה

לב טהור ברא = קס"א קנ"א קמ"ג

לִי li אֱלֹהִים Elohim אהיה אדני ; ילה ; לי אלהים = ריבוע אדני

וְרוּחַ veru'ach נָכוֹן nachon חַדֵּשׁ chadesh י"ב הויות, קס"א קנ"א בְּקִרְבִּי bekirbi שדי:

Recite seven times

AYIN LAMED MEM

This three-letter combination of the 72 Names of God gives us control over unwanted thoughts such as worry, pessimism, and obsessive or compulsive ideas. Besides using this meditation in the morning prayers, we can use it throughout the day as needed.

You should meditate on the Holy Name:

עלם

This helps to control your thoughts.

ESH TAMID

"And the Eternal Fire shall burn upon the Altar and shall never extinguish." (Leviticus 6:6)
"I hate scattered thoughts but Your Torah, I love." (Psalms 119:113)
"Create for me a pure heart, God, and renew a correct spirit within me." (Psalms 51:12)

THE MORNING PRAYER

You should be very careful not to speak, even a single word, during the prayers and meditations. According to Kabbalah, there are three distinct energy forces that govern three specific times of the day: Right Column (Abraham): morning, Left Column (Isaac): afternoon, and Central Column (Jacob): evening. The prayers of *Shacharit* correspond to the Right Column (Abraham)—sharing, merciful, positive energy. Too often we awake in a bad mood, and this negative state of mind remains with us throughout the day. To counteract this negativity, we have the connection of *Shacharit*, which imbues us with the energy of happiness and vitality, motivating us to reveal Light throughout the day.

LESHEM YICHUD

לְשֵׁם leshem יִחוּד yichud קוּדְשָׁא kudsha בְּרִיךְ berich הוּא hu

וּשְׁכִינְתֵּיהּ ush'chintei (יאהדונהי) בִּדְחִילוּ bid'chilu וּרְחִימוּ ur'chimu

(יאההויהה) וּרְחִימוּ ur'chimu וּדְחִילוּ ud'chilu (איההויהה) לְיַחֲדָא leyachda

שֵׁם shem יוּ"ד yud קֵ"י kei בְּוָא"ו bevav קֵ"י kei בְּיִחוּדָא beyichuda

שְׁלִים shelim (יהוה) בְּשֵׁם beshem כָּל kol ילי יִשְׂרָאֵל Yisrael,

הִנֵּה hine אֲנַחְנוּ anachnu בָּאִים ba'im לְהִתְפַּלֵּל lehitpalel תְּפִלַּת tefilat

שַׁחֲרִית shacharit שֶׁל shel (**on Shabbat add:** שַׁבָּת Shabbat קוֹדֶשׁ kodesh וְ ve)

שָׁבוּעוֹת Shavuot שֶׁתִּקֵּן shetiken אַבְרָהָם Avraham ח"פ אל,

ר"ו ול"ב נתיבות החכמה, רמ"ח (אברים), עסמ"ב וט"ז אותיות פשוטות אָבִינוּ avinu עָלָיו alav

הַשָּׁלוֹם hashalom עִם im כָּל kol ילי הַמִּצְוֹת hamitzvot הַכְּלוּלוֹת hakelulot

בָּהּ ba לְתַקֵּן letaken אֶת et שׁוֹרְשָׁהּ shorsha בְּמָקוֹם bemakom

עֶלְיוֹן elyon לַעֲשׂוֹת la'asot נַחַת nachat רוּחַ ru'ach לְיוֹצְרֵנוּ leyotzrenu

וְלַעֲשׂוֹת vela'asot רְצוֹן retzon מהש ע"ה, ע"ב בריבוע וקס"א ע"ה, אל שדי ע"ה

בּוֹרְאֵנוּ bor'enu. וִיהִי vihi נֹעַם no'am אֲדֹנָי Adonai ללה

אֱלֹהֵינוּ elohenu ילה עָלֵינוּ alenu וּמַעֲשֵׂה uma'ase יָדֵינוּ yadenu כּוֹנְנָה konena

עָלֵינוּ alenu וּמַעֲשֵׂה uma'ase יָדֵינוּ yadenu כּוֹנְנֵהוּ konenehu:

THE MORNING PRAYER - LESHEM YICHUD

For the sake of the unification of The Holy Blessed One and His Shechinah, with fear and love and with love and fear, in order to unify the Name Yud-Kei and Vav-Kei in perfect unity, and in the name of Israel, we have hereby come to pray the (**on Shabbat add:** *the Holy Shabbat and*) *Shavuot Morning Prayer, established by Abraham, our forefather, may peace be upon him, with all its commandments, to correct its root in the supernal place, to bring satisfaction to our Maker, and to fulfill the wish of our Creator. "And the pleasantness of the Lord, our God, be upon us and may He establish the work of our hands for us and may the work of our hands establish Him."* (Psalms 90:17)

A COMMITMENT FOR LOVE AND UNITY - ELEVATING OUR CONSCIOUSNESS

A thin, weak string cannot lift a treasure chest. However, when we weave together many thin strings, we form a rope. By uniting ourselves with the rest of the world through making a Commitment for Love, we can pull down the greatest spiritual treasures, even though we might not be worthy or strong enough to accomplish this individually.

Regarding the danger of deviation, the Kaf-Hachayim says: "In a place of deviation, the blessing removes itself, and people who had disagreements end up with damage and accidents to their bodies as well as their wealth. Those who care for themselves should stay away from any deviation."

The *Ari* writes in the Gate of Meditations: before you start your connections and prayers, you should accept within yourself the precept of "love your fellow as you do yourself." Meaning, you must meditate to love all people who are doing spiritual work as if they are part of your soul, so that your prayers will be included and elevated with the universal prayer and bring results. It is especially important to have love for the *Chaverim* (people who dedicate their lives to spiritual work) and to recognize that praying for others enables and allows our prayers to be accepted.

הֲרֵינִי hareni מְקַבֵּל mekabel עָלַי alai מִצְוַת mitzvat עֲשֵׂה ase שֶׁל shel

וְאָהַבְתָּ ve'ahavta ב"פ אור, ב"פ רז, ב"פ א"ס לְרֵעֲךָ lere'acha כָּמוֹךָ kamocha•

וַהֲרֵינִי vehareni אוֹהֵב ohev אֶת et כָּל kol ילי אֶחָד echad אהבה, דאגה

מִבְּנֵי mibenei יִשְׂרָאֵל Yisrael כְּנַפְשִׁי kenafshi וּמְאוֹדִי ume'odi•

וַהֲרֵינִי vehareni מְזַמֵּן mezamen פֶּה pe מילה ; ע"ה אלהים, אהיה אדני

שֶׁלִּי sheli לְהִתְפַּלֵּל lehitpalel לִפְנֵי lifnei מֶלֶךְ melech מַלְכֵי malchei

הַמְּלָכִים hamelachim הַקָּדוֹשׁ hakadosh בָּרוּךְ baruch הוּא hu:

THE BINDING OF ISAAC

By reciting this verse, which describes Abraham binding Isaac, we connect to the power of mercy. Simultaneously, we bind our judgment as part of our internal cleansing, and we receive help to bind the negative thoughts of people who come against us in judgment.

A COMMITMENT FOR LOVE
ELEVATING OUR CONSCIOUSNESS

I hereby accept upon myself the obligatory commandment of "Love your fellow as you do yourself." I hereby declare that I love each one of Israel with my soul and my strength. And I hereby prepare my mouth to pray before the King of all Kings, The Holy Blessed One.

אֱלֹהֵינוּ Elohenu ילה וֵאלֹהֵי velohei לכב ; מילוי ע"ב, דמב ; ילה אֲבוֹתֵינוּ avotenu

זָכְרֵנוּ zochrenu בְּזִכְרוֹן bezichron ע"ב קס"א ונש"ב טוֹב tov והו

מִלְּפָנֶיךָ milfanecha ס"ג מ"ה ב"ן וּפָקְדֵנוּ ufokdenu בִּפְקֻדַּת bifkudat

יְשׁוּעָה yeshu'a וְרַחֲמִים verachamim מִשְּׁמֵי mishmei שְׁמֵי shemei

קֶדֶם kedem◆ וּזְכָר uzchor לָנוּ lanu אלהים, אהיה אדני יְהֹוָהאדניאהדונהי Adonai

אֱלֹהֵינוּ Elohenu ילה אַהֲבַת ahavat הַקַּדְמוֹנִים hakadmonim

אַבְרָהָם Avraham וז"פ אל, רי"ו ול"ב נתיבות החכמה, רמ"ח (אברים), עסמ"ב וט"ז אותיות פשוטות

יִצְחָק Yitzchak ד"פ ב"ן וְיִשְׂרָאֵל veYisrael עֲבָדֶיךָ ◆avadecha

אֶת et הַבְּרִית haberit וְאֶת ve'et הַחֶסֶד hachesed ע"ב, ריבוע יהוה

וְאֶת ve'et הַשְּׁבוּעָה hashevu'a שֶׁנִּשְׁבַּעְתָּ shenishbata לְאַבְרָהָם le'Avraham

וז"פ אל, רי"ו ול"ב נתיבות החכמה, רמ"ח (אברים), עסמ"ב וט"ז אותיות פשוטות

אָבִינוּ avinu בְּהַר behar הַמּוֹרִיָּה ◆haMoriya וְאֶת ve'et הָעֲקֵדָה ha'akeda

שֶׁעָקַד she'akad אֶת et יִצְחָק Yitzchak ד"פ ב"ן בְּנוֹ beno עַל al גַּבֵּי gabei

הַמִּזְבֵּחַ hamizbe'ach נגד, זן, אל יהוה כַּכָּתוּב kakatuv בְּתוֹרָתָךְ :betoratach

THE PORTION CONCERNING THE BINDING

Reciting the portion concerning the Binding of Isaac every day allows us to atone for all our sins and create a shield of protection against all sickness, which cancels death from humanity.

THE BINDING OF ISAAC

Our God and the God of our forefathers, remember us favorably before You, and evoke for us the remembrance of salvation and mercy, from the earliest and the highest Heavens. And remember, for our sake, Lord, our God, the love of the ancients: Your servants, Abraham, Isaac, and Israel. And remember, also the Covenant, the compassion, and the oath that You pledged to Abraham, our forefather, on Mount Moriah, when he bound his son, Isaac, upon the altar, as it is related in Your Torah:

וַיְהִי vayehi אַחַר achar הַדְּבָרִים hadevarim הָאֵלֶּה ha'ele

וְהָאֱלֹהִים vehaElohim אהיה אדני ; ילה נִסָּה nisa אֶת־ et אַבְרָהָם Avraham

וז"פ אל, רי"ו ול"ב נתיבות החכמה, רמ"ח (אברים), עסמ"ב וט"ז אותיות פשוטות וַיֹּאמֶר vayomer

אֵלָיו elav אַבְרָהָם Avraham וז"פ אל, רי"ו ול"ב נתיבות החכמה, רמ"ח (אברים),

עסמ"ב וט"ז אותיות פשוטות וַיֹּאמֶר vayomer הִנֵּנִי hineni: וַיֹּאמֶר vayomer קַח־ kach

נָא na אֶת־ et בִּנְךָ bincha אֶת־ et יְחִידְךָ yechidcha אֲשֶׁר־ asher

אָהַבְתָּ ahavta אֶת־ et יִצְחָק Yitzchak ד"פ ב"ן וְלֶךְ־ velech לְךָ lecha

אֶל־ el אֶרֶץ eretz הַמֹּרִיָּה haMoriya וְהַעֲלֵהוּ veha'alehu שָׁם sham

לְעֹלָה le'ola עַל al אַחַד achad אהבה, דאגה הֶהָרִים heharim אֲשֶׁר asher

אֹמַר omar אֵלֶיךָ elecha: וַיַּשְׁכֵּם vayashkem אַבְרָהָם Avraham וז"פ אל,

רי"ו ול"ב נתיבות החכמה, רמ"ח (אברים), עסמ"ב וט"ז אותיות פשוטות בַּבֹּקֶר baboker

וַיַּחֲבֹשׁ vayachavosh אֶת־ et חֲמֹרוֹ chamoro וַיִּקַּח vayikach ויעם אֶת־ et

שְׁנֵי shenei נְעָרָיו ne'arav אִתּוֹ ito וְאֵת ve'et יִצְחָק Yitzchak ד"פ ב"ן בְּנוֹ beno

וַיְבַקַּע vayevaka עֲצֵי atzei עֹלָה ola וַיָּקָם vayakom וַיֵּלֶךְ vayelech כלי

אֶל־ el הַמָּקוֹם hamakom אֲשֶׁר־ asher אָמַר־ amar לוֹ lo

הָאֱלֹהִים haElohim אהיה אדני ; ילה: בַּיּוֹם bayom ע"ה נגד, מזבח, זן, אל יהוה

הַשְּׁלִישִׁי hashelishi וַיִּשָּׂא vayisa אַבְרָהָם Avraham וז"פ אל, רי"ו ול"ב נתיבות החכמה,

רמ"ח (אברים), עסמ"ב וט"ז אותיות פשוטות אֶת־ et עֵינָיו enav ריבוע מ"ה

וַיַּרְא vayar אֶת־ et הַמָּקוֹם hamakom מֵרָחֹק merachok שדי:

THE PORTION CONCERNING THE BINDING

"And it came to be that after those events, God tested Abraham and said to him: 'Abraham' and he replied: 'Here I am'. And He said: 'Please take your son, your only one, whom you love; Isaac, and go to the land of Moriah. Place him as a burnt-offering upon one of the mountains that I shall tell you.' And Abraham rose early in the morning, saddled his donkey, and took two lads with him, together with his son, Isaac. Abraham split wood for the offering then got up and went towards the place of which God told him. On the third day, Abraham lifted his eyes and saw the place from afar.

וַיֹּאמֶר vayomer אַבְרָהָם avraham ו"פ אל, רי"ו ול"ב נתיבות החכמה, רמ"ח (אברים),
עסמ"ב וט"ז אותיות פשוטות אֶל־ el נְעָרָיו ne'arav שְׁבוּ־ shevu לָכֶם lachem פֹּה po
מילה (להכניע הקליפות בסוד החמור) ; ע"ה אלהים, אהיה אדני עִם־ im הַחֲמוֹר hachamor
וַאֲנִי va'ani אני וְהַנַּעַר vehana'ar נֵלְכָה nelcha עַד־ ad כֹּה ko
וְנִשְׁתַּחֲוֶה venishtachave וְנָשׁוּבָה venashuva אֲלֵיכֶם alechem: וַיִּקַּח vayikach
ועם אַבְרָהָם Avraham ו"פ אל, רי"ו ול"ב נתיבות החכמה, רמ"ח (אברים), עסמ"ב וט"ז אותיות פשוטות
אֶת־ et עֲצֵי atzei הָעֹלָה ha'ola וַיָּשֶׂם vayasem עַל־ al יִצְחָק Yitzchak ד"פ ב"ן
בְּנוֹ beno וַיִּקַּח vayikach ועם בְּיָדוֹ beyado אֶת־ et הָאֵשׁ ha'esh שאה
וְאֶת־ ve'et הַמַּאֲכֶלֶת hama'achelet וַיֵּלְכוּ vayelchu שְׁנֵיהֶם sheneihem
יַחְדָּו yachdav: וַיֹּאמֶר vayomer יִצְחָק Yitzchak ד"פ ב"ן אֶל־ el
אַבְרָהָם Avraham ו"פ אל, רי"ו ול"ב נתיבות החכמה, רמ"ח (אברים), עסמ"ב וט"ז אותיות פשוטות
אָבִיו aviv וַיֹּאמֶר vayomer אָבִי avi וַיֹּאמֶר vayomer הִנֶּנִּי hineni בְנִי veni
וַיֹּאמֶר vayomer הִנֵּה hine הָאֵשׁ ha'esh שאה וְהָעֵצִים veha'etzim וְאַיֵּה ve'aye
הַשֶּׂה hase לְעֹלָה le'ola: וַיֹּאמֶר vayomer אַבְרָהָם Avraham ו"פ אל, רי"ו ול"ב
נתיבות החכמה, רמ"ח (אברים), עסמ"ב וט"ז אותיות פשוטות אֱלֹהִים Elohim אהיה אדני ; ילה
יִרְאֶה־ yir'eh רי"ו לּוֹ lo הַשֶּׂה hase לְעֹלָה le'ola בְּנִי beni ר"ת הבל (למתק או"ח
ע"מ לתקן עון הבל שחטא בראיה) וַיֵּלְכוּ vayelchu שְׁנֵיהֶם sheneihem יַחְדָּו yachdav:
וַיָּבֹאוּ vayavo'u אֶל־ el הַמָּקוֹם hamakom אֲשֶׁר asher אָמַר־ amar לוֹ lo
הָאֱלֹהִים haElohim אהיה אדני ; ילה וַיִּבֶן vayiven שָׁם sham אַבְרָהָם Avraham
ו"פ אל, רי"ו ול"ב נתיבות החכמה, רמ"ח (אברים), עסמ"ב וט"ז אותיות פשוטות אֶת־ et
הַמִּזְבֵּחַ hamizbe'ach נגד, זן, אל יהוה וַיַּעֲרֹךְ vaya'aroch אֶת־ et הָעֵצִים ha'etzim
וַיַּעֲקֹד vaya'akod אֶת־ et יִצְחָק Yitzchak ד"פ ב"ן בְּנוֹ beno וַיָּשֶׂם vayasem

---

And Abraham said to his lads: Stay here with the donkey, while I and my son go until there, where we shall prostrate ourselves then return to you. And Abraham took the wood for the burnt-offering and placed it upon Isaac, his son. He took in his hand the fire and the knife as they went together. And Isaac said to his father: 'My father.' and he said: 'Here I am, my son.' And Isaac said: 'Behold the fire and the wood, but where is the lamb for the burnt-offering?' And Abraham said: 'God shall show the lamb for the burnt-offering, my son.' And they went together. And they came to the place God showed him, There, Abraham built an Altar and arranged the wood. He bound his son, Isaac, and placed

אֹתוֹ oto עַל־ al הַמִּזְבֵּחַ hamizbe'ach נגד, זן, אל יהוה מִמַּעַל mima'al עלם

לָעֵצִים la'etzim: וַיִּשְׁלַח vayishlach אַבְרָהָם Avraham וז"פ אל, רי"ו ול"ב נתיבות

החכמה, רמ"ח (אברים), עסמ"ב וט"ז אותיות פשוטות אֶת־ et יָדוֹ yado וַיִּקַּח vayikach וזעם

אֶת־ et הַמַּאֲכֶלֶת hama'achelet לִשְׁחֹט lishchot אֶת־ et בְּנוֹ beno:

וַיִּקְרָא vayikra עם ה' אותיות = ב"פ קס"א אֵלָיו elav מַלְאַךְ mal'ach

יְהֹוָהאדניאהדונהי Adonai מִן־ min הַשָּׁמַיִם hashamayim י"פ טל, י"פ כוזו ; ר"ת מ"ה

וַיֹּאמַר vayomer אַבְרָהָם Avraham | וז"פ אל, רי"ו ול"ב נתיבות החכמה, רמ"ח (אברים),

עסמ"ב וט"ז אותיות פשוטות אַבְרָהָם Avraham וז"פ אל, רי"ו ול"ב נתיבות החכמה, רמ"ח (אברים),

עסמ"ב וט"ז אותיות פשוטות וַיֹּאמֶר vayomer הִנֵּנִי hineni: וַיֹּאמֶר vayomer אַל־ al

תִּשְׁלַח tishlach יָדְךָ yadcha אֶל־ el הַנַּעַר hana'ar וְאַל־ ve'al תַּעַשׂ ta'as

לוֹ lo מְאוּמָה me'uma כִּי ki | עַתָּה ata יָדַעְתִּי yadati כִּי־ ki יְרֵא yere

אֱלֹהִים Elohim אהיה אדני ; ילה אַתָּה Ata וְלֹא velo חָשַׂכְתָּ chasachta אֶת־ et

בִּנְךָ bincha אֶת־ et יְחִידְךָ yechidcha מִמֶּנִּי mimeni: וַיִּשָּׂא vayisa

אַבְרָהָם Avraham וז"פ אל, רי"ו ול"ב נתיבות החכמה, רמ"ח (אברים), עסמ"ב וט"ז אותיות פשוטות

אֶת־ et עֵינָיו enav ריבוע מ"ה וַיַּרְא vayar וְהִנֵּה־ vehine אַיִל ayil אַחַר achar

נֶאֱחַז ne'echaz בַּסְּבַךְ basevach בְּקַרְנָיו bekarnav כשאומר נאחז בסבך בקרניו

יכוין לתיבות שאחר סבך הם עגל, והשטן בעבור קיטרוג העגל היה מרחיק האיל, כדי שישחט יצחק.

ומיכאל (= הנה איל, נגא) אחר נאחז בקרניו (= שס"ח סממני הקטורת) הכניע את השטן

וַיֵּלֶךְ vayelech כלי אַבְרָהָם Avraham וז"פ אל, רי"ו ול"ב נתיבות החכמה,

רמ"ח (אברים), עסמ"ב וט"ז אותיות פשוטות וַיִּקַּח vayikach וזעם אֶת־ et

הָאַיִל ha'ayil וַיַּעֲלֵהוּ vaya'alehu לְעֹלָה le'ola תַּחַת tachat בְּנוֹ beno:

וַיִּקְרָא vayikra עם ה' אותיות = ב"פ קס"א אַבְרָהָם Avraham וז"פ אל, רי"ו ול"ב נתיבות

החכמה, רמ"ח (אברים), עסמ"ב וט"ז אותיות פשוטות שֵׁם־ shem הַמָּקוֹם hamakom

---

him upon the altar, on top of the wood. And Abraham reached out with his hand and took the knife to slaughter his son. The Angel of the Lord called to him from the Heavens and said: 'Abraham, Abraham.' And he said: 'Here I am.' And He said: 'Do not send your hand forth against the lad and do not do anything to him, for I now know that you fear God and you did not withhold your son from Me.' And Abraham lifted his eyes and saw and beheld a ram, entangled in a bush by his horns. Abraham went forth and took the ram; he burnt it as an offering, instead of his son. And Abraham called the name of this place

הַהוּא hahu יְהֹוָאדניאהדונהי Adonai | יִרְאֶה yir'e רי"ו אֲשֶׁר asher

יֵאָמֵר ye'amer הַיּוֹם hayom ע"ה נגד, מזבח, זן, אל יהוה בְּהַר behar

יְהֹוָאדניאהדונהי Adonai יֵרָאֶה yera'e רי"ו: וַיִּקְרָא vayikra עם ה' אותיות = ב"פ קס"א

מַלְאַךְ mal'ach יְהֹוָאדניאהדונהי Adonai אֶל־ el אַבְרָהָם Avraham ח"פ אל,

רי"ו ול"ב נתיבות החכמה, רמ"ח (אברים), עסמ"ב וט"ז אותיות פשוטות שֵׁנִית shenit מִן־ min

הַשָּׁמָיִם hashamayim י"פ טל, י"פ כוזו ; ר"ת מ"ה: וַיֹּאמֶר vayomer בִּי bi

נִשְׁבַּעְתִּי nishbati נְאֻם־ ne'um יְהֹוָאדניאהדונהי Adonai כִּי ki יַעַן ya'an

אֲשֶׁר asher עָשִׂיתָ asita אֶת־ et הַדָּבָר hadavar ראה הַזֶּה haze והו וְלֹא velo

חָשַׂכְתָּ chasachta אֶת־ et בִּנְךָ bincha אֶת־ et יְחִידֶךָ yechidecha: כִּי־ ki

בָרֵךְ varech אֲבָרֶכְךָ avarechecha וְהַרְבָּה veharba אַרְבֶּה arbe יצחק, ד"פ ב"ן

אֶת־ et זַרְעֲךָ zar'acha כְּכוֹכְבֵי kechochvei הַשָּׁמַיִם hashamayim י"פ טל, י"פ כוזו

וְכַחוֹל vechachol אֲשֶׁר asher עַל־ al שְׂפַת sefat הַיָּם hayam ילי

וְיִרַשׁ veyirash זַרְעֲךָ zar'acha אֵת et שַׁעַר sha'ar אֹיְבָיו oyvav:

וְהִתְבָּרְכוּ vehitbarchu יהוה ריבוע יהוה ריבוע מ"ה בְזַרְעֲךָ vezaracha

כֹּל kol ילי גּוֹיֵי goyei הָאָרֶץ ha'aretz אלהים דההין ע"ה עֵקֶב ekev ב"פ מום

אֲשֶׁר asher שָׁמַעְתָּ shamata בְּקֹלִי bekoli: וַיָּשָׁב vayashov

אַבְרָהָם Avraham ח"פ אל, רי"ו ול"ב נתיבות החכמה, רמ"ח (אברים), עסמ"ב וט"ז אותיות פשוטות

אֶל־ el נְעָרָיו ne'arav וַיָּקֻמוּ vayakumu וַיֵּלְכוּ vayelchu יַחְדָּו yachdav

אֶל־ el בְּאֵר Be'er קנ"א ב"ן, יהוה אלהים יהוה אדני, מילוי קס"א וס"ג, מ"ה ברבוע וע"ב ע"ה

שָׁבַע Shava וַיֵּשֶׁב vayeshev אַבְרָהָם Avraham ח"פ אל,

רי"ו ול"ב נתיבות החכמה, רמ"ח (אברים), עסמ"ב וט"ז אותיות פשוטות בִּבְאֵר biVe'er

קנ"א ב"ן, יהוה אלהים יהוה אדני, מילוי קס"א וס"ג, מ"ה ברבוע וע"ב ע"ה שָׁבַע Shava:

---

as: Lord shall see, when what is said on the Mount of the Lord shall be seen. Then the Angel of the Lord called to Abraham a second time from the Heavens, and said: 'I have sworn upon My Being, proclaimed the Lord, that since you have done this thing and you did not withhold your son, your only one, I shall surely bless you and I shall greatly multiply your seed, like the stars of the sky and the sand upon the seashore. Your seed shall inherit the gate of his enemies. All nations of the world shall be blessed by your seed, because you have listened to My Voice.' And Abraham returned to his lads. They got up and went to Be'er Sheva. And Abraham resided in Be'er Sheva." (Genesis 22:1-19)

RIBONO SHEL OLAM

Light can never be revealed without a Vessel. *Ribono Shel Olam* helps us build our personal Vessel to draw all the Light that Abraham generated by virtue of his actions.

רִבּוֹנוֹ ribono שֶׁל shel עוֹלָם olam. כְּמוֹ kemo שֶׁכָּבַשׁ shekavash
אַבְרָהָם Avraham ו"פ אל, רי"ו ול"ב נתיבות החכמה, רמ"ח (אברים), עסמ"ב וט"ז אותיות פשוטות
אָבִינוּ avinu אֶת et רַחֲמָיו rachamav לַעֲשׂוֹת la'asot רְצוֹנְךָ retzoncha
בְּלֵבָב belevav בוכו שָׁלֵם shalem. כֵּן ken יִכְבְּשׁוּ yichbeshu
רַחֲמֶיךָ rachamecha אֶת et כַּעַסְךָ ka'asecha. וְיִגֹּלוּ veyigolu
רַחֲמֶיךָ rachamecha עַל al מִדּוֹתֶיךָ midotecha. וְתִתְנַהֵג vetitnaheg
עִמָּנוּ imanu ריבוע דס"ג, קס"א ע"ה וד' אותיות יְהֹוָהאדניאהדונהי Adonai אֱלֹהֵינוּ Elohenu
ילה בְּמִדַּת bemidat הַחֶסֶד hachesed ע"ב, ריבוע יהוה וּבְמִדַּת uvmidat
הָרַחֲמִים harachamim. וְתִכָּנֵס vetikanes לָנוּ lanu אלהים, אהיה אדני
לִפְנִים lifnim מִשּׁוּרַת mishurat הַדִּין hadin. וּבְטוּבְךָ uvtuvcha לאו
הַגָּדוֹל hagadol להח ; עם ד' אותיות = מבה, יזל, אום יָשׁוּב yashuv חֲרוֹן charon
אַפְּךָ apach מֵעַמְּךָ me'amach וּמֵעִירְךָ ume'irach וּמֵאַרְצְךָ ume'artzach
וּמִנַּחֲלָתָךְ uminachalatach. וְקַיֵּם vekayem לָנוּ lanu אלהים, אהיה אדני
יְהֹוָהאדניאהדונהי Adonai אֱלֹהֵינוּ Elohenu ילה אֶת et הַדָּבָר hadavar ראה
שֶׁהִבְטַחְתָּנוּ shehivtachtanu בְּתוֹרָתָךְ betoratach עַל al יְדֵי yedei
מֹשֶׁה Moshe מהש, ע"ב בריבוע וקס"א, אל שדי, ד"פ אלהים ע"ה עַבְדָּךְ avdach פוי, אל אדני
כָּאָמוּר ka'amur: וְזָכַרְתִּי vezacharti אֶת־ et בְּרִיתִי beriti
יַעֲקוֹב Yaakov ז' הויות, יאהדונהי אידהנויה וְאַף ve'af אֶת־ et בְּרִיתִי beriti

---

RIBONO SHEL OLAM

Master of the Universe, just as Abraham, our father, suppressed his compassion to wholeheartedly fulfill Your will, so may Your compassion suppress Your wrath and may Your compassion reveal itself above Your other attributes. Behave with us, Lord, our God, according to the attributes of kindness and of compassion; for our sake, act towards us from beyond the framework of strict judgment. By Your great benevolence, Your anger shall be retracted from Your Nation, Your City, Your Land, and Your Heritage. Fulfill for us, Lord, our God, what You have promised to us in Your Torah, through Moses, Your servant, as it states: "I shall remember My Covenant with Jacob and My Covenant

יִצְחָק Yitzchak ד"פ ב"ן וְאַף ve'af אֶת־ et בְּרִיתִי beriti

אַבְרָהָם Avraham וז"פ אל, רי"ו ול"ב נתיבות החכמה, רמ"ח (אברים), עסמ"ב וט"ז אותיות פשוטות

אֶזְכֹּר ezkor וְהָאָרֶץ veha'aretz אלהים דההין ע"ה אֶזְכֹּר. ezkor וְנֶאֱמַר vene'emar:

וְאַף־ ve'af גַּם־ gam זֹאת zot בִּהְיוֹתָם bihyotam בְּאֶרֶץ be'eretz

אֹיְבֵיהֶם oyvehem לֹא־ lo מְאַסְתִּים me'astim וְלֹא־ velo גְעַלְתִּים ge'altim

לְכַלֹּתָם lechalotam לְהָפֵר lehafer בְּרִיתִי beriti אִתָּם itam כִּי ki אֲנִי ani אני

יְהֹוָה יאהדונהי Adonai אֱלֹהֵיהֶם Elohehem ילה: וְזָכַרְתִּי vezacharti

לָהֶם lahem בְּרִית berit רִאשֹׁנִים rishonim אֲשֶׁר asher הוֹצֵאתִי־ hotzeti

אֹתָם otam מֵאֶרֶץ me'eretz מִצְרַיִם Mitzrayim מצר לְעֵינֵי le'enei ריבוע מ"ה

הַגּוֹיִם hagoyim לִהְיוֹת lihyot לָהֶם lahem לֵאלֹהִים lelohim אהיה אדני ; ילה

אֲנִי ani אני יְהֹוָה יאהדונהי Adonai. וְנֶאֱמַר vene'emar: וְשָׁב veshav

יְהֹוָה יאהדונהי Adonai אֱלֹהֶיךָ Elohecha ילה אֶת־ et שְׁבוּתְךָ shevutcha

וְרִחֲמֶךָ verichamecha וְשָׁב veshav וְקִבֶּצְךָ vekibetzcha מִכָּל־ mikol ילי

הָעַמִּים ha'amim אֲשֶׁר asher הֱפִיצְךָ hefitz'cha יְהֹוָה יאהדונהי Adonai

אֱלֹהֶיךָ Elohecha ילה שָׁמָּה shama: אִם־ im יוהך, מ"א אותיות דפשוט,

דמילוי ודמילוי דמילוי דאהיה ע"ה יִהְיֶה yih'ye ייי נִדַּחֲךָ nidachacha בִּקְצֵה biktze

הַשָּׁמָיִם hashamayim י"פ טל, י"פ כוזו מִשָּׁם misham יְקַבֶּצְךָ yekabetzcha

יְהֹוָה יאהדונהי Adonai אֱלֹהֶיךָ Elohecha ילה וּמִשָּׁם umisham

יִקָּחֶךָ yikachecha: וֶהֱבִיאֲךָ vehevi'acha יְהֹוָה יאהדונהי Adonai

אֱלֹהֶיךָ Elohecha ילה אֶל־ el הָאָרֶץ ha'aretz אלהים דההין ע"ה אֲשֶׁר־ asher

---

with Isaac and even My Covenant with Abraham, I shall remember, and also the Land, I shall remember." (Leviticus 26:42) And as it also states: "And despite Israel's inequities, when they were to be in the land of their enemies, I did not despise them nor loathe them such as to destroy them and nullify My Covenant with them, because I am the Lord, their God. And for their sake, I shall remember the covenant of the first generation that I had brought out of the land of Egypt for the nations to behold, in order to be God unto them. I am the Lord." (Leviticus 26:44-45) And as it also states: "And the Lord shall bring you back from captivity and shall have mercy upon you. And He shall again gather you from among all nations where the Lord, your God, had dispersed you. If you have been forsaken at the end of the Heavens, then from there the Lord, your God, shall gather you and, from there, He shall fetch you. And the Lord, your God, shall lead you to the Land which

יָרְשׁוּ yarshu אֲבֹתֶיךָ avotecha וִירִשְׁתָּהּ virishta וְהֵיטִבְךָ vehetivcha
וְהִרְבְּךָ vehirbecha מֵאֲבֹתֶיךָ: me'avotecha וְנֶאֱמַר vene'emar עַל al
יְדֵי yedei נְבִיאֶךָ: nevi'echa יְהֹוָואדֹנָיאהדונהי Adonai חָנֵּנוּ chonenu
לְךָ lecha קִוִּינוּ kivinu הֱיֵה heye יהה זְרֹעָם zero'am לַבְּקָרִים labekarim
(reference to the "Ten martyrs of the kingdom") אַף־ af יְשׁוּעָתֵנוּ yeshu'atenu
בְּעֵת be'et צָרָה tzara אלהים דההין. וְנֶאֱמַר: vene'emar וְעֵת־ ve'et
צָרָה tzara אלהים דההין הִיא hee לְיַעֲקֹב leYaakov י הויות, יאהדונהי אידהנויה
וּמִמֶּנָּה umimena יִוָּשֵׁעַ. yivashe'a וְנֶאֱמַר: vene'emar בְּכָל־ bechol ב"ן, לכב
צָרָתָם | tzaratam לוֹ lo (כתיב: לא) צָר tzar וּמַלְאַךְ umal'ach
פָּנָיו panav הוֹשִׁיעָם hoshi'am בְּאַהֲבָתוֹ be'ahavato וּבְחֶמְלָתוֹ uvchemlato
הוּא hu גְאָלָם ge'alam וַיְנַטְּלֵם vaynatlem וַיְנַשְּׂאֵם vaynas'em
כָּל־ kol ילי יְמֵי yemei עוֹלָם. olam וְנֶאֱמַר: vene'emar

THE THIRTEEN ATTRIBUTES

The *Thirteen Attributes* are 13 virtues or properties that reflect the 13 different aspects of our daily relationship with the Creator. They work like a mirror. If we perform a negative action in our world, the mirror reflects this negative energy back onto us. As we attempt to transform our reactive nature into a proactive one, this direct feedback from the world of *Yetzirah* helps to guide and correct us. The number 13 also represents "one above the 12 signs of the zodiac." The 12 astrological signs dictate our instinctive, reactive behaviors. The number 13 gives us control over the 12 signs, thus giving us control over our reactive nature.

An astrological chart is best understood as a DNA blueprint of a person's soul, revealing what the person came into this world to do, and what he or she needs to correct and transform in this lifetime. We are supposed to use the positive aspects of our astrological sign to overcome and transform all the negative aspects imbued in our inner character. It is important to understand that our personal astrological profile is not the *cause* of our nature; it is the *effect*. We are handed a particular DNA blueprint based on our past-life track record. This past-life behavior—and the subsequent spiritual credits and debits that it produced—dictated the time and sign under which we were born. Astrology is merely the mechanism by which we acquire the required traits necessary for our inner growth and change.

---

your forefathers have inherited, and you shall inherit it. He shall benefit you and multiply your numbers over that of your forefathers." (Deuteronomy 30:3-5) And it is also said, through Your prophets: "Lord, be gracious to us, for we have hoped for You. Be their strong Arm in the mornings and also our salvation in times of trouble." (Isaiah 33:2) And as it is said: "It is a time of trouble for Jacob, but he shall be saved from it." (Jeremiah 30:7) Also: "God was distressed by their distress, so the angels that are before Him, redeemed them. With His love and His compassion, He had saved them. He took them and carried them throughout eternity." (Isaiah 33:9) And it is said:

(1) אל מִי־ mi יל״י אֵל El יי״א (מילוי דס״ג) כָּמוֹךָ kamocha

(2) רחום נֹשֵׂא nose עָוֹן avon

(3) וחנון וְעֹבֵר ve'over עַל־ al פֶּשַׁע pesha

(4) ארך לִשְׁאֵרִית lish'erit נַחֲלָתוֹ nachalato

(5) אפים לֹא־ lo הֶחֱזִיק hechezik לָעַד la'ad ב״פ ב״ן אַפּוֹ apo

(6) ורב חסד כִּי־ ki חָפֵץ chafetz חֶסֶד chesed ע״ב, ריבוע יהוה הוּא hu:

(7) ואמת יָשׁוּב yashuv יְרַחֲמֵנוּ yerachamenu

(8) נצר חסד יִכְבֹּשׁ yichbosh עֲוֹנֹתֵינוּ avonotenu

(9) לאלפים וְתַשְׁלִיךְ vetashlich בִּמְצֻלוֹת bimtzulot

יָם yam ילי כָּל־ kol ילי חַטֹּאותָם chatotam:

(10) נשא עון תִּתֵּן titen ב״פ כהת אֱמֶת emet אהיה פעמים אהיה, ז״פ ס״ג

לְיַעֲקֹב leYaakov ז' הויות, יאהדונהי אידהנויה (חיבור ז״א ומלכות)

(11) ופשע חֶסֶד chesed ע״ב, ריבוע יהוה לְאַבְרָהָם leAvraham

ח״פ אל, רי״ו ול״ב נתיבות החכמה, רמ״ח (אברים), עסמ״ב וט״ז אותיות פשוטות

(12) וחטאה אֲשֶׁר־ asher נִשְׁבַּעְתָּ nishbata לַאֲבֹתֵינוּ la'avotenu

(13) ונקה מִימֵי mimei קֶדֶם kedem:

THE THIRTEEN ATTRIBUTES

"1) Who is a God like You? 2) Who bears iniquity. 3) And overlooks sin. 4) For the remnant of His heritage. 5) He did not retain His anger forever. 6) For He desires kindness. 7) He shall again have mercy over us. 8) And suppress our iniquities. 9) You shall cast into the depths of the sea all their sins. 10) You grant truth to Jacob. 11) and kindness to Abraham. 12) As You have vowed to our forefathers. 13) From the earliest days." (Micah 7:18-20)

וְנֶאֱמַר vene'emar: וַהֲבִיאוֹתִים vahavi'otim אֶל־ el הַר har
קָדְשִׁי kodshi וְשִׂמַּחְתִּים vesimachtim בְּבֵית bevet ב"פ ראה
תְּפִלָּתִי tefilati עוֹלֹתֵיהֶם olotehem וְזִבְחֵיהֶם vezivchehem לְרָצוֹן leratzon
מהש ע"ה, ע"ב בריבוע וקס"א ע"ה, אל שדי ע"ה עַל־ al מִזְבְּחִי mizbechi כִּי ki
בֵיתִי veti ב"פ ראה בֵּית־ bet ב"פ ראה תְּפִלָּה tefila באתב"ש אִוכְצַ, ב"ן אדני
ונקודה ע"ה = יוד הי וו הה יִקָּרֵא yikare לְכָל lechol יה אדני הָעַמִּים ha'amim ר"ת ילה:

ELU DEVARIM

אֵלּוּ elu דְּבָרִים devarim ראה שֶׁאֵין she'en לָהֶם lahem שִׁעוּר shi'ur:
הַפֵּאָה hape'a וְהַבִּכּוּרִים vehabikurim וְהָרֵאָיוֹן vehare'ayon וּגְמִילוּת ugmilut
חֲסָדִים chasadim וְתַלְמוּד vetalmud תּוֹרָה torah. אֵלּוּ elu
דְּבָרִים devarim ראה שֶׁאָדָם she'adam מ"ה עוֹשֶׂה ose אוֹתָם otam,
אוֹכֵל ochel מִפֵּירוֹתֵיהֶם miperotehem בָּעוֹלָם ba'olam הַזֶּה haze והו
וְהַקֶּרֶן vehakeren קַיֶּמֶת kayemet לוֹ lo לְעוֹלָם le'olam ריבוע דס"ג וי' אותיות דס"ג
הַבָּא haba. וְאֵלּוּ ve'elu הֵן hen. כִּבּוּד kibud אָב av וָאֵם va'em.
וּגְמִילוּת ugmilut חֲסָדִים chasadim. וּבִקּוּר uvikur חוֹלִים cholim וחולה =
מ"ה עם ד' אותיות. וְהַכְנָסַת vehachnasat אוֹרְחִים orchim. וְהַשְׁכָּמַת vehashkamat
בֵּית bet ב"פ ראה הַכְּנֶסֶת hakeneset. וַהֲבָאַת vahava'at שָׁלוֹם shalom בֵּין ben
אָדָם adam מ"ה לַחֲבֵירוֹ lachavero. וּבֵין uven אִישׁ ish לְאִשְׁתּוֹ le'ishto.
וְתַלְמוּד vetalmud תּוֹרָה torah כְּנֶגֶד keneged מזבח, זן, אל יהוה כֻּלָּם kulam:

And it is also said: "I have brought them to My Holy Mountain and have rejoiced them in My House of Prayer. Their burnt-offerings and their sacrifices shall be accepted upon My Altar, for My House shall be called: 'My House of Prayer' for all nations." (Isaiah 56:7)

ELU DEVARIM

"The following items have no set measure: the corner of the field, the first fruit, the viewing-offering, giving kindness, and the study of Torah. The following things one person can do and benefit from their fruit, both in this world and, as the capital remains intact for him, in the World to Come. And these are: Honoring the father and mother, Bestowing kindness, Visiting the sick, Showing hospitality to guests, Arriving early at the synagogue, Bringing peace between man and his fellow and between man and his wife, and the study of Torah is equivalent to them all." (Pe'ah Ch.1:1, Shabbat 127a)

LE'OLAM YEHE ADAM

It is important to maintain a sense of awe of the Creator and to have a healthy fear of disconnecting from the Light by behaving dishonestly, whether we are alone or among others. Awe helps us realize that it is our opponent—*Satan*—who is attempting to control our behavior, and not our true nature.

לְעוֹלָם le'olam ריבוע דס"ג וי' אותיות דס"ג יְהֵא yehe אָדָם adam יְרֵא yere
שָׁמַיִם shamayim י"פ טל, י"פ כוזו בַּסֵּתֶר baseter ב"פ מצר כְּבַגָּלוּי kevagalui•
וּמוֹדֶה umode עַל al הָאֱמֶת ha'emet אהיה פעמים אהיה, ז"פ ס"ג•
וְדוֹבֵר vedover אֱמֶת emet אהיה פעמים אהיה, ז"פ ס"ג בִּלְבָבוֹ bilvavo•
וְיַשְׁכֵּם veyashkim וְיֹאמַר veyomar: רִבּוֹן ribon יהוה ע"ב ס"ג מ"ה ב"ן
הָעוֹלָמִים ha'olamim וַאֲדוֹנֵי va'adonei הָאֲדוֹנִים ha'adonim• לֹא lo עַל־ al
צִדְקוֹתֵינוּ tzidkotenu אֲנַחְנוּ anachnu מַפִּילִים mapilim תַחֲנוּנֵינוּ tachanunenu
לְפָנֶיךָ lefanecha ס"ג מ"ה ב"ן כִּי ki עַל־ al רַחֲמֶיךָ rachamecha הָרַבִּים harabim:
אֲדֹנָי Adonai | לכה שְׁמָעָה shema'a אֲדֹנָי Adonai | לכה סְלָחָה selacha
אֲדֹנָי Adonai לכה הַקְשִׁיבָה hakshiva וַעֲשֵׂה va'ase אַל־ al תְּאַחַר te'achar
לְמַעַנְךָ lema'ancha אֱלֹהַי Elohai מילוי ע"ב, דמב ; ילה כִּי־ ki שִׁמְךָ shimcha
נִקְרָא nikra עַל־ al עִירְךָ ircha וְעַל־ ve'al עַמֶּךָ amecha: מָה ma מ"ה
אֲנַחְנוּ anachnu מָה ma מ"ה חַיֵּינוּ chayenu• מָה ma מ"ה חַסְדֵּנוּ chasdenu
מָה ma מ"ה צִדְקוֹתֵינוּ tzidkotenu• מָה ma מ"ה כֹּחֵנוּ kochenu מָה ma מ"ה
גְּבוּרָתֵנוּ gevuratenu• מָה ma מ"ה נֹּאמַר nomar לְפָנֶיךָ lefanecha ס"ג מ"ה ב"ן
יְהֹוָהאדניאהדונהי Adonai אֱלֹהֵינוּ Elohenu ילה וֵאלֹהֵי velohei לכב ; מילוי ע"ב, דמב ; ילה
אֲבוֹתֵינוּ avotenu הֲלֹא halo כָּל kol ילי הַגִּבּוֹרִים hagiborim כְּאַיִן ke'ayin
לְפָנֶיךָ lefanecha ס"ג מ"ה ב"ן• וְאַנְשֵׁי ve'anshei הַשֵּׁם hashem כְּלֹא kelo הָיוּ hayu•

LE'OLAM YEHE ADAM

You should always have fear of the Heavens in private and in public and should admit to truth and speak truth in your heart. You should rise early and say: Ruler of the worlds, Master of all Masters, "do not present our pleas before You because of our righteousness but because of Your abundant compassion. Lord, hear us. Lord, forgive us. Lord, listen and act and do not delay. My God, do so for Your sake, for Your Name is invoked upon Your City and upon Your Nation." (Daniel 9:18-19) *What is our worth and to what avail are our lives, our righteousness, our strength, and our valor? What can we say before You, Lord, our God and the God of our forefathers? All the powerful ones are as nothing before You. Those men of fame are now as if they had never existed.*

וַחֲכָמִים vachachamim כִּבְלִי kivli מַדָּע mada וּנְבוֹנִים unvonim

כִּבְלִי kivli הַשְׂכֵּל haskel• כִּי ki כָּל־ chol ילי מַעֲשֵׂינוּ ma'asenu

תֹהוּ tohu וִימֵי vimei חַיֵּינוּ chayenu הֶבֶל hevel

לְפָנֶיךָ lefanecha ס"ג מ"ה ב"ן: וּמוֹתַר umotar הָאָדָם ha'adam מ"ה מִן־ min

הַבְּהֵמָה habehema ב"ן אָיִן ayin כִּי ki הַכֹּל hakol ילי הָבֶל havel:

LEVAD HANESHAMAH (EXEPT FOR THAT PURE SOUL)

The only thing of genuine value and importance is our soul, for the soul is an actual part of God. If we make the mistake of forgetting that everyone around us is also part of the Creator, we immediately disconnect ourselves from the Light. *Levad HaNeshamah* helps us value and appreciate the godliness in all creatures and respect the spiritual essence of our world.

לְבַד levad הַנְּשָׁמָה haneshamah הַטְּהוֹרָה hatehora שֶׁהִיא shehi

עֲתִידָה atida לִתֵּן liten דִּין din וְחֶשְׁבּוֹן vecheshbon לִפְנֵי lifnei כִּסֵּא chise

כְּבוֹדֶךָ chevodecha ב"ן, לכב וְכָל vechol ילי הַגּוֹיִם hagoyim כְּאַיִן ke'ayin

נֶגְדֶּךָ negdecha מזבח, זן, אל יהוה שֶׁנֶּאֱמַר shene'emar: הֵן hen גּוֹיִם goyim

כְּמַר kemar מִדְּלִי midli וּכְשַׁחַק uch'shachak מֹאזְנַיִם moznayim

נֶחְשָׁבוּ nechshavu הֵן hen אִיִּים iyim כַּדַּק kadak יִטּוֹל yitol:

AVAL

We are all descendants of Abraham, Isaac, and Jacob. These great biblical patriarchs came into this world and created a spiritual architecture with them as conduits, connecting with specific aspects of the Light, so that you and I and all the people of the world can tap into the same energy that they themselves embodied. It is because of the merit of these spiritual giants that we may now make the highest possible spiritual connections.

All the wise men are as if without any knowledge and all the sensible ones, as if without intelligence. All of our deeds are chaotic and the days of our lives arevain before You. (Tana Devei Rabbi Eliezar Ch. 21) *And man is not superior to beasts, for all is vanity.* (Ecclesiastes 3:19)

LEVAD HANESHAMAH

Except For that pure soul

that is destined to stand in judgment and be accountable before Your Throne of Glory. The nations are as nothing before You, as it is said: "Truly all nations are as a drop in a bucket and are considered as the dust upon the scales. He removes the lands as easily as dust." (Isaiah 40:15)

אֲבָל aval אֲנַחְנוּ anachnu עַמְּךָ amecha בְּנֵי benei בְרִיתֶךָ veritecha בְּנֵי benei

אַבְרָהָם Avraham ו"פ אל, רי"ו ול"ב נתיבות החכמה, רמ"ח (אברים), עסמ"ב וט"ז אותיות פשוטות

אֹהַבְךָ ohavecha שֶׁנִּשְׁבַּעְתָּ shenishbata לוֹ lo בְּהַר behar

הַמּוֹרִיָּה haMoriya. זֶרַע zera יִצְחָק Yitzchak ד"פ ב"ן עֲקֵדְךָ akedecha

שֶׁנֶּעֱקַד shene'ekad עַל־ al גַּבֵּי gabei הַמִּזְבֵּחַ hamizbe'ach נגד, זן, אל יהוה

עֲדַת adat יַעֲקֹב Yaakov ז' הויות, יאהדונהי אידהנויה בִּנְךָ bincha

בְּכוֹרֶךָ vechorecha. שֶׁמֵּאַהֲבָתְךָ sheme'ahavatcha שֶׁאָהַבְתָּ she'ahavta

אוֹתוֹ oto וּמִשִּׂמְחָתְךָ umisimchatcha שֶׁשָּׂמַחְתָּ shesamachta בּוֹ bo

קָרָאתָ karata אוֹתוֹ oto יִשְׂרָאֵל Yisrael וִישֻׁרוּן vishurun:

LEFICHACH

Lefichach awakens a sense of appreciation, ensures our good fortune, and protects all that we hold dear. There is nothing spiritually wrong with striving for bigger and better things in life, but it is our soul consciousness, not our body consciousness, that will determine whether we receive inner happiness and contentment or dissatisfaction and frustration. The deeper message is that we must be happy with our lot in life whatever it may look like, because that experience of happiness and appreciation is exactly what we need to achieve our spiritual growth.

לְפִיכָךְ lefichach אֲנַחְנוּ anachnu חַיָּבִים chayavim לְהוֹדוֹת lehodot לָךְ lach

וּלְשַׁבְּחָךְ ulshabechach וּלְפָאֲרָךְ ulfa'arach וּלְרוֹמְמָךְ ulromemach

וְלִתֵּן veliten שִׁיר shir שֶׁבַח shevach וְהוֹדָאָה vehoda'a לְשִׁמְךָ leshimcha

הַגָּדוֹל hagadol להח ; עם ד' אותיות = מבה, יזל, אום וְחַיָּבִים vechayavim

אֲנַחְנוּ anachnu לוֹמַר lomar לְפָנֶיךָ lefanecha ס"ג מ"ה ב"ן שִׁירָה shira

בְּכָל־ bechol ב"ן, לכב יוֹם yom ע"ה נגד, מזבח, זן. אל יהוה תָּמִיד tamid ע"ה קס"א קנ"א קמ"ג.

AVAL

But we are Your Nation, the members of Your Covenant: the Children of Abraham, who had loved You and to whom You had sworn upon Mount Moriah; the Offspring of Isaac, Your bound one, who was bound upon the altar; and the Congregation of Jacob, Your son, Your firstborn, that out of the love and joy You had for him, You had rejoiced in him and called him Israel and also Yeshurun.

LEFICHACH

Consequently, we have an obligation to give thanks to You, to praise, glorify, and exalt You, and give a song of praise and gratitude to Your great Name. We are obligated to say before You, daily and forever,

אַשְׁרֵנוּ ashrenu מַה ma מ״ה טּוֹב tov והו וְחֶלְקֵנוּ chelkenu

וּמַה uma מ״ה נָּעִים na'im גּוֹרָלֵנוּ goralenu• וּמַה uma מ״ה

יָּפָה yafa מְאֹד me'od יְרֻשָּׁתֵנוּ yerushatenu• אַשְׁרֵנוּ ashrenu

שֶׁאֲנַחְנוּ she'anachnu מַשְׁכִּימִים mashkimim וּמַעֲרִיבִים uma'arivim

בְּבָתֵּי bevatei כְּנֵסִיּוֹת chenesiyot וּבְבָתֵּי uvevatei מִדְרָשׁוֹת midrashot•

וּמְיַחֲדִים umyachadim שִׁמְךָ shimcha בְּכָל bechol ב״ן, לכב

יוֹם yom ע״ה נגד, מזבח, זן, אל יהוה תָּמִיד tamid ע״ה נתה, קס״א קנ״א קמ״ג

אוֹמְרִים omrim פַּעֲמַיִם pa'amayim בְּאַהֲבָה be'ahava אחד, דאגה:

SMALL SHEMA

This version of the *Shema* acts as a rocket booster, helping to launch us into *Shacharit*, the morning connection. First we scan the meditations that precede the *Shema* to prepare our internal Vessel. When we recite the *Shema*, we unite the Upper Worlds with the physical world. We acknowledge that there is only one Creator, one Source, and that the past, the present and the future are one. We overlay our physical reality with the Tree of Life Reality, creating a bridge with your consciousness, meditating that all is one.

Inside the *Shema* are two large Aramaic letters: *Ayin* ע and *Dalet* ד. Together, they spell the Aramaic word for "witness," עד. The Light is a witness to all we do, and we are always accountable for our actions, even if we think nobody saw us perform them. This is the law of Cause and Effect.

On *Shabbat* we skip the medition and continue on page 236.

First, meditate in general, on the first *Yichud* of the four *Yichuds* of the Name: יהוה, and in particular, to awaken the letter ה, and then to connect it with the letter ו. Then connect the letter י and the letter ה together in the following order: *Hei* (ה), *Hei-Vav* (ה"ו), then *Yud-Hei* (י"ה), which adds up to 31, the secret of "יא" of the Name ס"ג. It is good to meditate on this *Yichud* before reciting any *Shema* because it acts as a replacement for the times that you may have missed reading the *Shema*. This *Yichud* has the same ability to create a Supernal connection like the reading of the *Shema* - to raise *Zeir* and *Nukva* together for the *Zivug* of *Abba* and *Ima*.

---

how fortunate we are; how good is our lot; how pleasant is our destiny; and how beautiful is our inheritance. We are joyful for being able to rise early and return late, in and from the synagogues and houses of study, and to proclaim the unity of Your Name, daily and forever, and we say twice, lovingly:

Shema - שְׁמַע

General Meditation: שְׁם ע — to draw the energy from the seven lower *Sefirot* of *Ima* to the *Nukva*, which enables the *Nukva* to elevate the *Mayin Nukvin* (awakening from Below).
Particular Meditation: שׁם = יהוה + שׁדי and five times the letters י and ד of ב״ן = ע [The letter *Hei* (ה) is formed by the letters *Dalet* (ד) and *Yud* (י), so in ב״ן we have four times the letter ה plus another time the letters י and ד from יוד of ב״ן.]. Also the three letters ו (18) that are left from ב״ן, plus ב״ן itself (52) equals ע (70).

Yisrael – יִשְׂרָאֵל

General Meditation: שׂ״ר אל — to draw energy from *Chesed* and *Gevurah* of *Abba* to *Zeir Anpin*, to do his action in the secret of *Mayin Duchrin* (awakening from Above).

Particular Meditation: (the rearranged letters of the word *Yisrael*) – שׂר אלי

ש״ר = מילוי דשד״י (ין לת וד),

אלי = מ״א אותיות שבאהיה דאלפין פשוט ומלא ומלא דמלא

(אהיה אלף הא יוד הא אלף למד פא הא אלף יוד ואו דלת הא אלף).

Meditate to draw the Surrounding Light of *Ima* and the Inner Light of *Abba* of *Katnut* into *Zeir Anpin*.

Adonai Elohenu Adonai - יְהוָה אֱלֹהֵינוּ יְהוָה

General Meditation: to draw energy to *Abba*, *Ima* and *Da'at* from *Arich Anpin*,
Particular Meditation: ע״ב (יוד הי ויו הי) קס״א (אלף הי יוד הי) ע״ב (יוד הי וי הי)

Echad – אֶחָד

(The secret of the complete *Yichud-Unification*)

The letters *Alef* א and *Chet* ח from *Echad* אחד are *Zeir Anpin* and the letter *Dalet* ד is *Nukva*.
You should meditate to devote your soul for the sanctification of the Holy Name, thereby elevating your *Nefesh*, *Ruach*, *Neshamah* and *Neshamah* of *Neshamah* with *Zeir Anpin* and *Nukva* (using the Names: ע״ב and ס״ג) to *Abba* and *Ima* as the secret of *Mayin Nukvin*, and by that energy, *Abba* and *Ima* will be unified in the secret of the Name: יאהדונהי״ה.
Also meditate to draw out the Surrounding Light of *Katnut* of *Abba* and the Inner Six Edges of *Gadlut* of *Ima* into *Zeir Anpin*. The Drop, which is ע״ב, is drawn out from the Internal of *Arich Anpin*, and descends to *Yesod* of *Ima*, where it becomes: ע״ב ס״ג מ״ה ב״ן, and the four spelled out אהיה (אלף הי יוד הי, אלף הי יוד הי, אלף הא יוד הא, אלף הה יוד הה) become Her clothing. As a result, *Zeir Anpin* now has four spelled out יה״ו (יוד הי ויו, יוד הי ואו, יוד הא ואו, יוד הה וו), four spelled out אה״י (אלף הי יוד, אלף הי יוד, אלף הא יוד, אלף הה יוד) and the Inner Six Edges of *Gadlut* of *Ima*.
Also meditate on the Name: אל״ף ה״י וי״ו ה״י, which is the entire *Mochin* in the secret of *Da'at*.
And also meditate (according to the Ramchal) on the four spelled out *Alef* (אלף=111) of the Name: אהי״ה that is equal to the word *Midat (444)*, making the *Keter* for *Leah*.

Baruch Shem Kevod Malchuto Le'olam Va'ed
בָּרוּךְ שֵׁם כְּבוֹד מַלְכוּתוֹ לְעוֹלָם וָעֶד

Baruch Shem Kevod – *Chochmah*, *Binah*, *Da'at* of *Leah;*
Malchuto – Her *Keter*; ***Le'olam*** – the rest of Her *Partzuf*;
Va'ed – the four היה (4 times 20 equal to *Va'ed*=80) will make the *Keter* for *Rachel*.
And the four spelled out היה (הי יוד הי, הי יוד הי, הא יוד הא, הה יוד הה) will make the rest of Her body.

שְׁמַע shema ע׳ רבתי יִשְׂרָאֵל Yisrael יְהֹוָהאדניאהדונהי Adonai

אֱלֹהֵינוּ Elohenu ילה יְהֹוָהאדניאהדונהי Adonai | אֶחָד echad ד׳ רבתי ; אהבה, דאגה:

(Whisper :) יוזו אותיות בָּרוּךְ baruch שֵׁם shem כְּבוֹד kevod מַלְכוּתוֹ malchuto,

לְעוֹלָם le'olam ריבוע דס״ג וי׳ אותיות דס״ג וָעֶד va'ed:

ATA HU

The following *Ata Hu* occupies the metaphysical realm—*Ein Sof* (the Endless World)—that existed before our world was created. The second *Ata Hu* dwells in our physical world, which, was created after the universe came into being. This knowledge helps to reinforce that there is only one Light which encompasses both the spiritual and physical domains.

אַתָּה Ata הוּא hu אֶחָד echad אהבה, דאגה קוֹדֶם kodem עמם

שֶׁבָּרָאתָ shebarata הָעוֹלָם ha'olam וְאַתָּה veAta הוּא hu אֶחָד echad

אהבה, דאגה לְאַחַר le'achar שֶׁבָּרָאתָ shebarata הָעוֹלָם ha'olam. אַתָּה Ata

הוּא hu אֵל El ייא״י (מילוי דס״ג) בָּעוֹלָם ba'olam הַזֶּה haze והו וְאַתָּה veAta

הוּא hu אֵל El ייא״י (מילוי דס״ג) בָּעוֹלָם ba'olam הַבָּא haba. וְאַתָּה־ veAta

הוּא hu וּשְׁנוֹתֶיךָ ushnotecha לֹא lo יִתָּמּוּ yitamu: קַדֵּשׁ kadesh

שִׁמְךָ shemach בְּעוֹלָמָךְ be'olamach עַל al עַם am מְקַדְּשֵׁי mekadshei

שְׁמֶךָ shemecha. וּבִישׁוּעָתְךָ uvishu'atcha מַלְכֵּנוּ malkenu תָּרוּם tarum

וְתַגְבִּיהַּ vetagbiha קַרְנֵנוּ karnenu. וְתוֹשִׁיעֵנוּ vetoshi'enu בְּקָרוֹב vekarov

לְמַעַן lema'an שְׁמֶךָ shemecha. בָּרוּךְ baruch הַמְקַדֵּשׁ hamekadesh

שְׁמוֹ shemo מהש ע״ה, ע״ב בריבוע וקס״א ע״ה, אל שדי ע״ה בָּרַבִּים varabim:

SMALL SHEMA

"Hear Israel, the Lord our God, The Lord is One." (Deuteronomy 6:4)

"Blessed is the Name of Glory, whose Kingdom is forever and for eternity." (Pesachim 56a)

ATA HU

You are One before You had created the world and You are One after You had created the world. You are Divine in this world and You are Divine in the World to Come. It is You, and Your years are Endless. (Psalms 102:28) *Sanctify Your Name, in Your world, upon the nation which sanctifies Your Name. With Your salvation, our King, You shall raise and exalt our worth. Redeem us soon for the sake of Your Name. Blessed is He, Who sanctifies His Name upon the masses.*

אַתָּה Ata הוּא hu יְהֹוָהאדניאהדונהי Adonai הָאֱלֹהִים haElohim
אהיה אדני ; ילה ; ר"ת אהיה בַּשָּׁמַיִם bashamayim י"פ טל, י"פ כוזו מִמַּעַל mima'al עלם
וְעַל ve'al הָאָרֶץ ha'aretz אלהים דההין ע"ה מִתָּחַת mitachat בִּשְׁמֵי bishmei
הַשָּׁמַיִם hashamayim י"פ טל, י"פ כוזו הָעֶלְיוֹנִים ha'elyonim
וְהַתַּחְתּוֹנִים vehatachtonim. אַתָּה Ata הוּא hu רִאשׁוֹן rishon וְאַתָּה veAta
הוּא hu אַחֲרוֹן acharon וּמִבַּלְעָדֶיךָ umibal'adecha אֵין en אֱלֹהִים Elohim
אהיה אדני ; ילה. קַבֵּץ kabetz נְפוּצוֹת nefutzot קֹוֶיךָ kovecha מֵאַרְבַּע me'arba
כַּנְפוֹת kanfot הָאָרֶץ ha'aretz אלהים דההין ע"ה ; ר"ת = אדני. יַכִּירוּ yakiru
וְיֵדְעוּ veyedu כָּל־ chol ילי בָּאֵי ba'ei עוֹלָם olam כִּי ki אַתָּה Ata הוּא hu
הָאֱלֹהִים haElohim אהיה אדני ; ילה לְבַדְּךָ levadecha לְכֹל lechol יה אדני
מַמְלְכוֹת mamlechot הָאָרֶץ ha'aretz אלהים דההין ע"ה אַתָּה Ata עָשִׂיתָ asita
אֶת־ et הַשָּׁמַיִם hashamayim י"פ טל, י"פ כוזו וְאֶת־ ve'et הָאָרֶץ ha'aretz
אלהים דההין ע"ה: אֶת et הַיָּם hayam ילי וְאֵת ve'et כָּל־ kol ילי אֲשֶׁר־ asher
בָּם bam מ"ב וּמִי umi ילי בְּכָל vechol ב"ן, לכב מַעֲשֵׂה ma'ase יָדֶיךָ yadecha
בָּעֶלְיוֹנִים ba'elyonim וּבַתַּחְתּוֹנִים uvatachtonim שֶׁיֹּאמַר sheyomar לְךָ lach
מַה־ ma מ"ה תַּעֲשֶׂה ta'ase וּמַה uma מ"ה תִּפְעָל tif'al. אָבִינוּ avinu
שֶׁבַּשָּׁמַיִם shebashamayim י"פ טל, י"פ כוזו חַי chay וְקַיָּם vekayam עֲשֵׂה ase
עִמָּנוּ imanu ריבוע ס"ג, קס"א ע"ה וד' אותיות חֶסֶד chesed ע"ב, ריבוע יהוה
בַּעֲבוּר ba'avur כְּבוֹד kevod שִׁמְךָ shimcha הַגָּדוֹל hagadol להח ; עם ד' אותיות –
מבה, יזל, אום הַגִּבּוֹר hagibor וְהַנּוֹרָא vehanora שֶׁנִּקְרָא shenikra עָלֵינוּ alenu

---

You are the Lord, the God in the Heavens Above and upon the earth Below. In the lights of the Heavens Above and the Earth Below, You are first and You are last and apart from You there is no other God. Gather the dispersed of those who have hope in You from the four corners of the earth. Let all humanity come to recognize and to know that it is You alone Who is God of all the kingdoms of the Earth. You have made the Heavens, the Earth, the sea, and all that they contain. And who among all those who Your hands have made Above and Below can tell You what to do and how to perform? Our Father in the Heavens, Who lives and Who exists, bestow kindness to us for the sake of the glory of Your great, powerful, and awesome Name, that has been invoked upon us.

וְקַיֵּם vekayem לָנוּ lanu אלהים, אהיה אדני יְהֹוָאדנייאהדונהי Adonai
אֱלֹהֵינוּ Elohenu ילה אֶת et הַדָּבָר hadavar ראה שֶׁהִבְטַחְתָּנוּ shehivtachtanu
עַל al יְדֵי yedei צְפַנְיָה Tzefanya חוֹזָךְ chozach כָּאָמוּר ka'amur: בָּעֵת ba'et
הַהִיא hahi אָבִיא avi אֶתְכֶם etchem וּבָעֵת uva'et קַבְּצִי kabetzi
אֶתְכֶם etchem כִּי ki אֶתֵּן eten אֶתְכֶם etchem לְשֵׁם leshem
וְלִתְהִלָּה velitehila ע״ה אמת, אהיה פעמים אהיה, ז״פ ס״ג בְּכֹל bechol ב״ן, לכב עַמֵּי amei
הָאָרֶץ ha'aretz אלהים דההין ע״ה בְּשׁוּבִי beshuvi אֶת־ et שְׁבוּתֵיכֶם shevutechem
לְעֵינֵיכֶם le'enechem ריבוע דמ״ה אָמַר amar יְהֹוָאדנייאהדונהי Adonai:

THE SACRIFICES – *KORBANOT*

The word *Korbanot* means "sacrifices." *Korbanot* comes from the Aramaic word *krav*, meaning "war," and also from the Aramaic word *kiruv*, meaning "to bring close." Obviously, we no longer bring physical sacrifices to a Temple, but through this connection, we can still go to war against Satan and bring ourselves closer to the Upper Worlds. By reciting the *Korbanot* prayers with an open mind and trusting heart, we are generating the same amount of power as if we were carrying out all the proper actions in the Temple.

THE OLAH (GRAIN) SACRIFICE

According to the *Zohar* (*Zohar Chadash* 41d), we say this section to cleanse the night of negative thoughts.

וַיְדַבֵּר vaydaber ראה יְהֹוָאדנייאהדונהי Adonai אֶל־ el מֹשֶׁה Moshe
מהש, ע״ב בריבוע וקס״א, אל שדי לֵּאמֹר lemor: צַו tzav פוי, אל אדני אֶת־ et
אַהֲרֹן Aharon וְאֶת־ ve'et בָּנָיו banav לֵאמֹר lemor זֹאת zot תּוֹרַת torat
הָעֹלָה ha'ola הִוא hee הָעֹלָה ha'ola עַל al מוֹקְדָה mokda עַל־ al
הַמִּזְבֵּחַ hamizbe'ach נגד, זן, אל יהוה כָּל־ kol ילי הַלַּיְלָה halayla מלה עַד־ ad

---

May You fulfill for us, Lord, our God, what You have promised us through Tzefaniah, Your seer, as it was said: "At that time, I shall bring you and, at that time, I shall gather you. Because I shall give you fame and praise from among all the nations of the world. I shall return you from captivity before your own eyes. says the Lord." (*Tzefaniah 3:20*)

THE SACRIFICES – KORBANOT - THE OLAH (GRAIN) SACRIFICE

"And the Lord spoke to Moses and said: Command Aaron and his sons, saying, this is the law of the burnt-offering. It is the burnt-offering that is burnt upon the Altar, throughout the night until

הַבֹּקֶר haboker וְאֵשׁ ve'esh הַמִּזְבֵּחַ hamizbe'ach נגד, זן, אל יהוה תּוּקַד tukad
בּוֹ: bo וְלָבַשׁ velavash הַכֹּהֵן hakohen מלה מִדּוֹ mido בַד vad
וּמִכְנְסֵי־ umichnesei בַד vad יִלְבַּשׁ yilbash עַל־ al בְּשָׂרוֹ besaro
וְהֵרִים veherim אֶת־ et הַדֶּשֶׁן hadeshen אֲשֶׁר asher תֹּאכַל tochal
הָאֵשׁ ha'esh שאה אֶת־ et הָעֹלָה ha'ola עַל־ al הַמִּזְבֵּחַ hamizbe'ach
נגד, זן, אל יהוה וְשָׂמוֹ vesamo אֵצֶל etzel הַמִּזְבֵּחַ hamizbe'ach נגד, זן, אל יהוה:
וּפָשַׁט ufashat אֶת־ et בְּגָדָיו begadav וְלָבַשׁ velavash בְּגָדִים begadim
אֲחֵרִים acherim וְהוֹצִיא vehotzi אֶת־ et הַדֶּשֶׁן hadeshen אֶל־ el
מִחוּץ michutz לַמַּחֲנֶה lamachane אֶל־ el מָקוֹם makom טָהוֹר tahor י"פ אכא:
וְהָאֵשׁ veha'esh שאה עַל־ al הַמִּזְבֵּחַ hamizbe'ach נגד, זן, אל יהוה תּוּקַד־ tukad
בּוֹ bo לֹא lo תִכְבֶּה tichbe וּבִעֵר uvi'er עָלֶיהָ aleha פהל הַכֹּהֵן hakohen מלה
עֵצִים etzim בַּבֹּקֶר baboker בַּבֹּקֶר baboker וְעָרַךְ ve'arach עָלֶיהָ aleha פהל
הָעֹלָה ha'ola וְהִקְטִיר vehiktir עָלֶיהָ aleha פהל חֶלְבֵי chelvei
הַשְּׁלָמִים hashelamim: אֵשׁ esh תָּמִיד tamid ע"ה קס"א קנ"א קמ"ג (מילואי אהיה)
תּוּקַד tukad עַל־ al הַמִּזְבֵּחַ hamizbe'ach נגד, זן, אל יהוה לֹא lo תִכְבֶּה: tichbe

THE TAMID – (DAILY) OFFERING

The second sacrifice is the daily offering. The Aramaic word *olat* עולת, meaning "elevated," can be rearranged to spell *tola* תולע, a negative force that is awakened each morning. By adding the word *olat*, as in *Olat Tamid*, we uproot and nullify the negative forces of the morning. *Olat* has the same numeric value (506) as the first sentence in the *Ana Beko'ach*, which corresponds to the *Sefirah* of *Chesed*, which is mercy. It also represents the seed level of our soul - a realm where separation and negativity do not exist. By changing the letters in *tola* to *olat* and meditating on the first sentence of the *Ana Beko'ach*, we remove the negative force and return to the seed of unconditional love and oneness.

By saying this section, we raise the inner part of the three Upper Sefirot of *Asiyah* to the Upper Level. This is the secret of the *Tamid* Offering, to bring closer the Upper and the Lower, and to elevate the Lower all the way up (Writings of the Ari: Gates of Meditation Vol. 1 Ch. 3).

---

the morning, and the fire of the Altar shall be kept burning thereon. The Kohen shall put on his linen garment; his linen trousers he shall wear on his flesh. He shall remove the ashes when the fire has consumed the offering on the Altar; he shall place them beside it. He shall then take off his clothes, put on other garments, and carry the ashes outside the camp to a clean place. And the fire on the Altar shall remain burning and shall not be extinguished. The Kohen shall place wood upon it early in the morning. He shall lay the offering upon it and shall burn the fat as incense of the peace-offerings. The eternal fire shall burn upon the Altar and not be extinguished." (Leviticus 6:1-6)

There is a *tola'at* (worm) in the Holy Side which is the secret of *Chesed* that increases and reveals and shines every morning. And similar to that, there is another *Tola* in the *klipa* (The Impure Side). This negative worm awakens every morning to destroy the world, and God, with mercy, reveals the worm of the Pure Side which is the Light of *Chesed* (that is mentioned above). And this is the secret of the *Tamid* (Daily Offering) that is called "*Olat HaTamid*," as the word *olat* has the same letters as *tola*, just in a different order. Through the *Olat HaTamid* that is recited every morning, the *tola* of the Impure Side will surrender. In this section you should meditate to purify the Worlds and to prepare them to receive the abundance from the aspect of *Shabbat*, even though they are purified from the aspect of the weekdays.

וַיְדַבֵּר vaydaber ראה יְהֹוָאדהנויאהדונהי Adonai אֶל־ el מֹשֶׁה Moshe

מהש, ע״ב בריבוע וקס״א, אל שדי לֵּאמֹר lemor: צַו tzav פוי, אל אדני אֶת־ et בְּנֵי benei

יִשְׂרָאֵל Yisrael וְאָמַרְתָּ ve'amarta אֲלֵהֶם alehem אֶת־ et קָרְבָּנִי korbani

לַחְמִי lachmi לְאִשַּׁי le'ishai רֵיחַ re'ach נִיחֹחִי nichochi תִּשְׁמְרוּ tishmeru

לְהַקְרִיב lehakriv לִי li בְּמוֹעֲדוֹ bemo'ado: וְאָמַרְתָּ ve'amarta לָהֶם lahem

זֶה ze הָאִשֶּׁה ha'ishe אֲשֶׁר asher תַּקְרִיבוּ takrivu לַיהֹוָאדהנויאהדונהי ladonai

כְּבָשִׂים kevasim בְּנֵי־ benei שָׁנָה shana תְמִימִם temimim שְׁנַיִם shenayim

לַיּוֹם layom ע״ה נגד, מזבח, זן, אל יהוה עֹלָה ola ר״ת עשל תָּמִיד tamid ע״ה קס״א קנ״א קמ״ג:

אֶת־ et הַכֶּבֶשׂ hakeves אֶחָד echad אהבה, דאגה תַּעֲשֶׂה ta'ase בַבֹּקֶר vaboker

וְאֵת ve'et הַכֶּבֶשׂ hakeves הַשֵּׁנִי hasheni תַּעֲשֶׂה ta'ase בֵּין ben

הָעַרְבָּיִם ha'arbayim: וַעֲשִׂירִית va'asirit הָאֵיפָה ha'efa סֹלֶת solet

לְמִנְחָה lemincha ע״ה ב״פ ב״ן בְּלוּלָה belula בְּשֶׁמֶן beshemen

כָּתִית katit רְבִיעִת revi'it הַהִין hahin: עֹלַת olat ושר, אבגית״ץ

(Meditate here to surrender the *klipa* named *Tola* using the Name: אבגית״ץ)

תָּמִיד tamid ע״ה קס״א קנ״א קמ״ג הָעֲשֻׂיָה ha'asuya בְּהַר behar סִינַי Sinai נמם, ה׳

הויות (ה׳ גבורות) לְרֵיחַ lere'ach נִיחֹחַ nicho'ach אִשֶּׁה ishe לַיהֹוָאדהנויאהדונהי ladonai:

THE TAMID – (DAILY) OFFERING

"And the Lord spoke to Moses and said, Command the Children of Israel and say to them, My offering, the bread of My fire-offering, My pleasing fragrance, you shall take care to sacrifice to Me at its specified time. And you shall say to them: This is the fire-offering that you shall sacrifice to God, perfect one-year-old sheep, two per day, as a regular daily offering; one sheep you shall do in the morning and the second sheep you shall do in the late afternoon. And one tenth of ephah of fine flour, for a meal-offering, mixed with one quarter of a hin of pressed oil. This is a regular burnt-offering that is made at Mount Sinai as a pleasing fragrance and as a fire-offering before the Lord.

וְנִסְכּוֹ venisko רְבִיעִת revi'it הַהִין hahin לַכֶּבֶשׂ lakeves

הָאֶחָד ha'echad אהבה, דאגה בַּקֹּדֶשׁ bakodesh הַסֵּךְ hasech

נֶסֶךְ nesech שֵׁכָר shechar י״פ ב״ן לַיהֹוָהאדניאהדונהי ladonai:

וְאֵת ve'et הַכֶּבֶשׂ hakeves הַשֵּׁנִי hasheni תַּעֲשֶׂה ta'ase בֵּין ben

הָעַרְבָּיִם ha'arbayim כְּמִנְחַת keminchat הַבֹּקֶר haboker וּכְנִסְכּוֹ uchnisko

תַּעֲשֶׂה ta'ase אִשֵּׁה ishe (elevation to *Yetzirah*) רֵיחַ re'ach (elevation to *Beriah*)

נִיחֹחַ nicho'ach (elevation to *Atzilut*) לַיהֹוָהאדניאהדונהי ladonai (elevation to the Endless World):

THE INCENSE

These verses from the *Torah* and the *Talmud* speak about the 11 herbs and spices that were used in the Temple. These herbs and spices were used for one purpose: to help us remove the force of death from every area of our lives. This is one of the few prayers whose sole goal is the eradication of death. The *Zohar* teaches us that whoever has judgment pursuing him needs to connect to this incense. The 11 herbs and spices connect to 11 Lights that sustain the *klipot* (shells of negativity).When we uproot the 11 Lights from the *klipot* through the power of the incense, the *klipot* lose their life-force and die. In addition to bringing the 11 spices to the Temple, the people brought resin, wine, and other items with metaphysical properties to help battle the Angel of Death.

It says in the *Zohar*: "Come and see, whoever is pursued by judgment is in need of incense and must repent before his master, for incense helps judgment to disappear from him." The 11 herbs and spices correspond to the 11 holy illuminations that revive the *klipa*. By elevating them, the *klipa* will die. Through these 11 herbs, the *klipot* are pushed away and the energy-point that was giving them life is removed. And since the Pure Side and its livelihood disappear, the *klipot* is left with no life. Thus the secret of the incense is that it cleanses the force of plague and cancels it. The incense kills the Angel of Death and takes away his power to kill.

אַתָּה Ata הוּא hu יְהֹוָהאדניאהדונהי Adonai אֱלֹהֵינוּ Elohenu ילה שֶׁהִקְטִירוּ shehiktiru

אֲבוֹתֵינוּ avotenu לְפָנֶיךָ lefanecha ס״ג מ״ה ב״ן אֶת et קְטֹרֶת ketoret

י״א פעמים אדני (הנבררים מהקליפות ע״י י״א הסממנים) ; קטרת - הק׳ באתב״ש ד׳ = תרי״ג (מצוות)

הַסַּמִּים hasamim ע״ה קנ״א, אדני אלהים בִּזְמַן bizman

שֶׁבֵּית shebet ב״פ ראה הַמִּקְדָּשׁ hamikdash קַיָּם kayam

כַּאֲשֶׁר ka'asher צִוִּיתָ tzivita אוֹתָם otam עַל al יַד yad מֹשֶׁה Moshe מהש,

ע״ב בריבוע וקס״א, אל שדי נְבִיאָךְ nevia'ch כַּכָּתוּב kakatuv בְּתוֹרָתָךְ betoratach:

Its libation is one quarter of a hin for the one sheep in the Sanctuary, pour a libation of old wine before the Lord. The second sheep you shall do in the afternoon like the meal-offering of the morning; its libation you shall do as a fire-offering of a fragrance which is pleasing to the Lord." (Numbers 28:1-8)

THE INCENSE

It is You, Lord, our God, before whom our forefathers burned the incense spices, during the time when the Temple existed, as You had commanded them through Moses, Your Prophet, and as it is written in Your Torah:

THE PORTION OF THE INCENSE

To raise the *Sefirot* from all of *Nogah* of *Atzilut*, *Beriah*, *Yetzirah* and *Asiyah*.

וַיֹּאמֶר vayomer יְהֹוָה אדניאהדונהי Adonai אֶל־ el מֹשֶׁה Moshe

מהש, ע"ב בריבוע וקס"א, אל שדי קַח־ kach לְךָ lecha סַמִּים samim (***Tiferet, Netzach***)

ע"ה קנ"א, אדני אלהים נָטָף nataf | (***Hod***) וּשְׁחֵלֶת ushchelet (***Yesod***) וְחֶלְבְּנָה vechelbena

(***Malchut***) ע"ה פוי, אל אדני סַמִּים samim (***Keter, Chochmah, Binah, Chesed, Gevurah***)

ע"ה קנ"א, אדני אלהים וּלְבֹנָה ulvona זַכָּה zaka (**Surrounding Light**) בַּד bad בְּבַד bevad

יִהְיֶה yih'ye ייי: וְעָשִׂיתָ ve'asita אֹתָהּ ota קְטֹרֶת ketoret י"א פעמים אדני (הנבררים

מהקליפות ע"י י"א הסממנים); קטרת – הק' באתב"ש ד' = תרי"ג (מצוות) רֹקַח rokach מַעֲשֵׂה ma'ase

רוֹקֵחַ roke'ach שדי מְמֻלָּח memulach טָהוֹר tahor י"פ אכא קֹדֶשׁ kodesh

ס"ת רוזש בכוזו לגרש החיצונים ויועיל לזכירה: וְשָׁחַקְתָּ veshachakta מִמֶּנָּה mimena

הָדֵק hadek וְנָתַתָּה venatata מִמֶּנָּה mimena לִפְנֵי lifnei הָעֵדֻת ha'edut

בְּאֹהֶל be'ohel מוֹעֵד mo'ed אֲשֶׁר asher אִוָּעֵד iva'ed לְךָ lecha שָׁמָּה shama

קֹדֶשׁ kodesh קָדָשִׁים kadashim תִּהְיֶה tihye לָכֶם lachem. וְנֶאֱמַר vene'emar:

וְהִקְטִיר vehiktir עָלָיו alav אַהֲרֹן Aharon קְטֹרֶת ketoret י"א פעמים אדני

(הנבררים מהקליפות ע"י י"א הסממנים) ; קטרת – הק' באתב"ש ד' = תרי"ג (מצוות) סַמִּים samim

ע"ה קנ"א, אדני אלהים בַּבֹּקֶר baboker בַּבֹּקֶר baboker בְּהֵיטִיבוֹ behetivo

אֶת־ et הַנֵּרֹת hanerot יַקְטִירֶנָּה yaktirena: וּבְהַעֲלֹת uveha'alot

אַהֲרֹן Aharon אֶת־ et הַנֵּרֹת hanerot בֵּין ben הָעַרְבַּיִם ha'arbayim

ר"ת אהבה, דאגה, אחד יַקְטִירֶנָּה yaktirena קְטֹרֶת ketoret י"א פעמים אדני

(הנבררים מהקליפות ע"י י"א הסממנים) ; קטרת – הק' באתב"ש ד' = תרי"ג (מצוות) תָּמִיד tamid

ע"ה קס"א קנ"א קמ"ג לִפְנֵי lifnei יְהֹוָה אדניאהדונהי Adonai לְדֹרֹתֵיכֶם ledorotechem:

THE PORTION OF THE INCENSE

"And the Lord said to Moses: Take for yourself spices, balsam sap, onycha, galbanum, and pure frankincense, each of equal weight. You shall prepare it as an incense compound: the work of a spice-mixer, well-blended, pure, and holy. You shall grind some of it fine and place it before the Testimony in the Tabernacle of Meeting, in which I shall meet with you. It shall be the Holy of Holies unto you." (Exodus 30:34-36) *And God also said: "Aaron shall burn upon the Altar incense spices early each morning when he prepares the candles. And when Aaron raises the candles at sundown, he shall burn the incense spices as a continual incense-offering before the Lord throughout all your generations."* (Exodus 30:7-8)

THE WORKINGS OF THE INCENSE

The filling of the incense has two purposes: First, to remove the *klipot* in order to stop them from going up along with the elevation of the Worlds, and second, to draw Light to *Asiyah*. So meditate to raise the sparks of Light from all of the *Nogah* of *Azilut*, *Beriah*, *Yetzirah* and *Asiyah*.

Count the incense using your right hand, one by one, and don't skip even one, as it is said: "If one omits one of all the ingredients, he is liable to receive the penalty of death." And therefore, you should be careful not to skip any of them, because reciting this paragraph is a substitute for the actual burning of the incense.

תנו tanu רבנן rabanan פטום pitum הקטרת haketoret י״א פעמים אדני
(הנבררים מהקליפות ע״י י״א הסממנים) קטרת - הק׳ באתב״ש ד׳ = תרי״ג (מצוות);
פטום הקטרת = יהוה יהוה מצפצ יה אדני אל אלהים מצפצ (ז׳ מרגלאין דשבת):
כיצד ketzad. שלש shelosh מאות me'ot המספר = ש, אלהים דיודין
וששים veshishim המספר = מילוי הש׳ (יז) ושמונה ushmona מנים manim היו hayu
בה va. שלש shelosh מאות me'ot המספר = ש, אלהים דיודין וששים veshishim
המספר = מילוי הש׳ (יז) וחמשה vachamisha כמנין keminyan ימות yemot
החמה hachama מנה mane ע״ה פוי, אל אדני בכל bechol ב״ן, לכב
יום yom ע״ה נגד, מזבח, זן, אל יהוה. מחציתו machatzito בבקר baboker
ומחציתו umachatzito בערב ba'erev. ושלשה ushlosha מנים manim
יתרים yeterim קס״א, קנ״א וקמ״ג שמהם shemehem מכניס machnis כהן kohen מלה
גדול gadol להח ; עם ד׳ אותיות = מבה, יזל, אום ונוטל venotel מהם mehem
מלא melo חפניו chofnav ביום beyom ע״ה נגד, מזבח, זן, אל יהוה הכפורים hakipurim
מחזירן machaziran למכתשת lamachteshet בערב be'erev
יום yom ע״ה נגד, מזבח, זן, אל יהוה הכפורים hakipurim כדי kedei לקים lekayem
מצות mitzvat דקה daka מן min הדקה hadaka. ואחד ve'achad אהבה, דאגה
עשר asar סמנים samanim היו hayu בה va. ואלו ve'elu הן hen:

THE WORKINGS OF THE INCENSE

Our Sages have taught: How was the compounding of the incense done? Three hundred and sixty-eight portions were contained therein. These corresponded to the number of days in the solar year, one portion for each day: Half of it in the morning and half at sundown. As for the remaining three portions, the High Priest, on Yom Kippur, filled both his hands with them. On the Eve of Yom Kippur, he would take them back to the mortar to fulfill the requirement that they should be very finely ground. Each portion contained eleven spices:

1) הַצֳּרִי haTzori (*Keter*) מצפצ, אלהים דיודין, י"פ ייי• 2) וְהַצִּפֹּרֶן vehaTziporen (*Yesod*)
יהוה אדני אהיה שדי• 3) וְהַחֶלְבְּנָה vehaChelbena (*Malchut*) ע"ה פוי, אל אדני•
4) וְהַלְּבוֹנָה vehaLevona (**Surrounding Light** – שהוא אור לבן והוא יוזידי הנקרא אדון יוזיד)
מִשְׁקַל mishkal שִׁבְעִים shiv'im שִׁבְעִים shiv'im מָנֶה mane ע"ה פוי, אל אדני•
5) מוֹר Mor (*Chesed*)• 6) וּקְצִיעָה uKtzi'ah רהע (***Gevurah*** – "כי מצפון תפתח הרעה",
והגבורה סוד רווז צפון)• 7) וְשִׁבֹּלֶת veShibolet נֵרְדְּ Nerd (*Tiferet*)•
8) וְכַרְכֹּם veCharkom (*Netzach*) מוזוזך, סנדלפון, ערי• מִשְׁקַל mishkal שִׁשָּׁה shisha
עָשָׂר asar שִׁשָּׁה shisha עָשָׂר asar מָנֶה mane ע"ה פוי, אל אדני• 9) הַקֹּשְׁטְ Kosht
(*Chochmah*) שְׁנֵים sheneim עָשָׂר asar• 10) קִלּוּפָה Kilufa (*Binah*) שְׁלֹשָׁה shelosha•
11) קִנָּמוֹן Kinamon (*Hod*) ר"ת ג"פ ק' (בסוד קדוש קדוש קדוש) תִּשְׁעָה tish'ah•
בּוֹרִית borit כַּרְשִׁינָא karshina תִּשְׁעָה tish'ah קַבִּין kabin• יֵין yen מיכ, י"פ האא
קַפְרִיסִין Kafrisin סְאִין se'in תְּלַת telat וְקַבִּין vekabin תְּלָתָא telata אהיה קבין
וְאִם ve'im יוהך, מ"א אותיות דפשוט, דמילוי ודמילוי דמילוי דאהיה ע"ה לֹא lo מָצָא matza
יֵין yen מיכ, י"פ האא קַפְרִיסִין Kafrisin מֵבִיא mevi וַחֲמַר chamar חִוַּר chivar
עַתִּיק atik• מֶלַח melach סְדוֹמִית Sedomit רוֹבַע rova• מַעֲלֶה ma'ale
עָשָׁן ashan כָּל kol ילי שֶׁהוּא shehu• רִבִּי Ribi נָתָן Natan הַבַּבְלִי haBavli
אוֹמֵר omer: אַף af מִכִּפַּת mikipat הַיַּרְדֵּן haYarden י' הויות וד' אותיות כָּל kol ילי
שֶׁהִיא shehi• אִם im יוהך, מ"א אותיות דפשוט, דמילוי ודמילוי דמילוי דאהיה ע"ה נָתַן natan
בָּהּ ba דְּבַשׁ devash שו' (דשופר) וי"ד (האווזז) = ש"ך דינין דגדלות פְּסָלָהּ pesala•
וְאִם ve'im יוהך, מ"א אותיות דפשוט, דמילוי ודמילוי דמילוי דאהיה ע"ה חִסֵּר chiser
אַחַת achat מִכָּל־ mikol ילי סַמְמָנֶיהָ samemaneha חַיָּב chayav מִיתָה mita:

---

1) Balsam. 2) Onycha. 3) Galbanum. 4) Frankincense; the weight of seventy portions each. 5) Myrrh. 6) Cassia. 7) Spikenard. 8) And Saffron; the weight of sixteen portions each. 9) Twelve portions of Costus. 10) Three of aromatic Bark 11) Nine of Cinnamon. Further, nine kavs of Lye of Carsina. And three kavs and three se'ehs of Cyprus wine. And if one should not find any Cyprus wine, he should bring an old white wine. And a quarter of the salt of Sodom. And a small measure of a smoke raising herb. Rabbi Natan, the Babylonian, advised also, a small amount of Jordan resin. If he added to it honey, he would make it defective. If he omits even one of all its herbs, he would be liable to death.

רַבָּן Raban שִׁמְעוֹן Shimon בֶּן ben גַּמְלִיאֵל Gamli'el אוֹמֵר omer:
הַצֳּרִי haTzori מצפצ, אלהים דיודין, י"פ ייי אֵינוֹ eno אֶלָּא ela שְׂרָף seraf
הַנּוֹטֵף hanotef מֵעֲצֵי me'atzei הַקְּטָף haketaf. בּוֹרִית borit
כַּרְשִׁינָא karshina לָמָּה lema הִיא hee בָאָה va'a. כְּדֵי kedei
לְשַׁפּוֹת leshapot בָּהּ ba אֶת et הַצִּפֹּרֶן haTziporen יהוה אדני אהיה שדי
כְּדֵי kedei שֶׁתְּהֵא shetehe נָאָה na'a. יֵין yen ע' (כנגד ע' אומות העולם התלויים בסמאל), מ"כ, י"פ האא
קַפְרִיסִין Kafrisin לָמָּה lema הוּא hu בָא va. כְּדֵי kedei
לִשְׁרוֹת lishrot בּוֹ bo אֶת et הַצִּפֹּרֶן haTziporen יהוה אדני אהיה שדי
כְּדֵי kedei שֶׁתְּהֵא shetehe עַזָּה aza. וַהֲלֹא vahalo מֵי mei ילי רַגְלַיִם raglayim
יָפִין yafin לָהּ la אֶלָּא ela שֶׁאֵין she'en מַכְנִיסִין machnisin מֵי mei ילי
רַגְלַיִם raglayim בַּמִּקְדָּשׁ bamikdash מִפְּנֵי mipenei הַכָּבוֹד hakavod לאו:
תַּנְיָא tanya. רִבִּי Ribi נָתָן Natan אוֹמֵר omer: כְּשֶׁהוּא keshehu
שׁוֹחֵק shochek אוֹמֵר omer הָדֵק hadek הֵיטֵב hetev. הֵיטֵב hetev
הָדֵק hadek. מִפְּנֵי mipenei שֶׁהַקּוֹל shehakol יָפֶה yafe לַבְּשָׂמִים labesamim.
פִּטְּמָהּ pitema לַחֲצָאִין lachatza'in כְּשֵׁרָה keshera. לְשָׁלִישׁ leshalish
וּלְרָבִיעַ ulravi'a לֹא lo שָׁמַעְנוּ shamanu. אָמַר amar רִבִּי Ribi
יְהוּדָה Yehuda: זֶה ze הַכְּלָל hakelal. אִם im יוהך, מ"א אותיות דפשוט, דמילוי
ודמילוי דמילוי דאהיה ע"ה כְּמִדָּתָהּ kemidata כְּשֵׁרָה keshera לַחֲצָאִין lachatza'in.
וְאִם ve'im יוהך, מ"א אותיות דפשוט, דמילוי ודמילוי דמילוי דאהיה ע"ה וְחִסֵּר chiser
אַחַת achat מִכָּל־ mikol ילי סַמְמָנֶיהָ samemaneha חַיָּב chayav מִיתָה mita:

Rabban Shimon ben Gamliel says: The balsam was a sap that only seeped from the balsam trees. For what purpose was the lye of Carsina added? In order to rub the Onycha with it to make it pleasant looking. For what purpose was the Cyprus wine added? In order to steep in it the Onycha. Urine is more appropriate for this, but urine is not brought into the Temple out of respect. It was taught that Rabbi Natan said: When he ground, he said: 'Grind it fine, grind it fine.' This is because voice is beneficial to the spices. If he compounds half the amount it is still valid, yet regarding a third or a quarter, we have no information. Rabbi Yehuda said: This is the general rule: If it is in its correct proportions, then half is valid. Yet if he omits one of all its spices, he is liable to death.

תָּנֵי tanei בַּר Var קַפָּרָא Kapara: אַחַת achat לְשִׁשִּׁים leshishim אוֹ o
לְשִׁבְעִים leshiv'im שָׁנָה shana הָיְתָה hayta בָּאָה va'a שֶׁל shel
שִׁירַיִם shirayim לַחֲצָאִין lachatza'in. וְעוֹד ve'od תָּנֵי tanei בַּר Var
קַפָּרָא Kapara: אִלּוּ ilu הָיָה haya יהה נוֹתֵן noten אבגיתץ, ושר בָּהּ ba
קָרְטוֹב kortov שֶׁל shel דְּבַשׁ devash שו' (דשופר) וי"ד (האוזז) = ש"ך דינין דגדלות
אֵין en אָדָם adam מ"ה יָכוֹל yachol לַעֲמוֹד la'amod מִפְּנֵי mipenei
רֵיחָהּ recha. וְלָמָּה velama אֵין en מְעָרְבִין me'arvin בָּהּ ba דְּבַשׁ devash
שו' (דשופר) וי"ד (האוזז) = ש"ך דינין דגדלות מִפְּנֵי mipenei שֶׁהַתּוֹרָה shehatorah
אָמְרָה amra: כִּי ki כָל chol ילי שְׂאֹר se'or ג' מוזין דאלהים דקטנות
(ש' = אלהים דיודין ; א' כללות שם אלהים ; ר' = ריבוע אלהים) וְכָל vechol ילי דְּבַשׁ devash
שו' (דשופר) וי"ד (האוזז) = ש"ך דינין דגדלות לֹא lo תַקְטִירוּ taktiru מִמֶּנּוּ mimenu
שכן הם בחינת דינין דקטנות ודגדלות לכן נאסרה הקרבתן אִשֶּׁה ishe לַיהֹוָה יאהדונהי ladonai:

Right

יְהֹוָה יאהדונהי Adonai צְבָאוֹת Tzeva'ot פני שכינה עִמָּנוּ imanu
ריבוע דס"ג, קס"א ע"ה וד' אותיות מִשְׂגָּב misgav משה, מהש, ע"ב בריבוע וקס"א, אל שדי,
ד"פ אלהים ע"ה לָנוּ lanu אלהים, אהיה אדני אֱלֹהֵי Elohei מילוי ע"ב, דמב ; ילה
יַעֲקֹב Yaakov ד' הויות, יאהדונהי אידהנויה סֶלָה sela:

Left

יְהֹוָה יאהדונהי Adonai צְבָאוֹת Tzeva'ot פני שכינה אַשְׁרֵי ashrei
אָדָם adam מ"ה ; יהוה צבאות אשרי אדם = תפארת בֹּטֵחַ bote'ach
בָּךְ bach אדם בוטח בך = אמן (יאהדונהי) ע"ה ; בוטח בך = מילוי ע"ב ע"ה:

Bar Kappara taught that once every sixty or seventy years the leftovers would accumulate to half the measure. Bar Kappara also taught that if one would add to it a Kortov of honey, no man would withstand its smell. Why is honey not mixed with it? Because the Torah had stipulated: Because any leaven or honey, you must not burn any of it as burnt-offering to the Lord. (*Kritut 6; Yerushalmi, Yoma: ch.4*)
(Right) *"The Lord of Hosts is with us, our strength is the God of Jacob, Selah."* (*Psalms 46:12*)
(Left) *"The Lord of Hosts, joyful is one who trusts in You."* (*Psalms 84:13*)

Central

יְהֹוָה (אדני אהדונהי) Adonai הוֹשִׁיעָה hoshi'a יהוה וש"ע נהורין הַמֶּלֶךְ hamelech ר"ת יהה

יַעֲנֵנוּ ya'anenu בְיוֹם veyom ע"ה נגד, מזבח, זן, אל יהוה

קָרְאֵנוּ kor'enu ר"ת יב"ק, אלהים יהוה, אהיה אדני יהוה ; ס"ת = ב"ן ועם כף דהמלך = ע"ב:

וְעָרְבָה ve'arva לַיהֹוָה (אדני אהדונהי) ladonai

מִנְחַת minchat יְהוּדָה Yehuda וִירוּשָׁלָםִ virushalaim

כִּימֵי kimei עוֹלָם olam וּכְשָׁנִים uch'shanim קַדְמֹנִיּוֹת kadmoniyot:

The Order of the Altar Service Ritual

We recite all the activities and actions that were performed in the Temple. Utilizing the energy transference of the Aramaic letters, it is as though we are actually performing these rites and rituals ourselves. The organs of the animals that were used as sacrifices in the Temple represent our internal organs and when we recite the words of these specific sacrifices, we bring healing and order to our lives.

אַבַּיֵּי Abayei◆ (pause here) הֲוָה hava מְסַדֵּר mesader סֵדֶר seder

הַמַּעֲרָכָה hama'aracha מִשְּׁמָא mishema דִגְמָרָא digmara וְאַלִּבָּא ve'aliba

דְאַבָּא deAba שָׁאוּל Sha'ul◆ מַעֲרָכָה ma'aracha גְּדוֹלָה gedola

קוֹדֶמֶת kodemet לְמַעֲרָכָה lema'aracha שְׁנִיָּה sheniya שֶׁל shel

קְטֹרֶת ketoret י"א פעמים אדני (הנבררים מהקליפות ע"י י"א הסממנים) ; קטרת - הק' באתב"ש ד' = תרי"ג (מצוות)◆ וּמַעֲרָכָה uma'aracha שְׁנִיָּה sheniya שֶׁל shel קְטֹרֶת ketoret

י"א פעמים אדני (הנבררים מהקליפות ע"י י"א הסממנים) ; קטרת - הק' באתב"ש ד' = תרי"ג (מצוות)

קוֹדֶמֶת kodemet לְסִדּוּר lesidur שְׁנֵי shenei גְּזִירֵי gezirei עֵצִים etzim◆

(Central) *"Lord save us. The King shall answer us the day we call."* (Psalms 20:10) *"May the Lord find the offering of Yehuda and Jerusalem pleasing as He had always done and as in the years of old."* (Malachi 3:4)

The Order of the Altar Service Ritual

Abayei, he listed the order of the ritual according to the Gemara and Abba Shaul. The large pyre order preceded the second pyre order of incense. The second pyre of incense preceded the arrangement of the two wooden logs.

וְסִדּוּר vesidur שְׁנֵי shenei גְּזִירֵי gezirei עֵצִים etzim קוֹדֵם kodem עמם

לְדִשּׁוּן ledishun מִזְבֵּחַ mizbe'ach נגד, זן, אל יהוה הַפְּנִימִי hapenimi ◆

וְדִשּׁוּן vedishun מִזְבֵּחַ mizbe'ach נגד, זן, אל יהוה הַפְּנִימִי hapenimi

קוֹדֵם kodem עמם לַהֲטָבַת lahatavat חָמֵשׁ chamesh נֵרוֹת nerot ◆

וַהֲטָבַת vahatavat חָמֵשׁ chamesh נֵרוֹת nerot קוֹדֶמֶת kodemet

לְדַם ledam הַתָּמִיד hatamid ע"ה קס"א קנ"א קמ"ג ◆ וְדַם vedam

הַתָּמִיד hatamid ע"ה קס"א קנ"א קמ"ג קוֹדֵם kodem עמם

לַהֲטָבַת lahatavat שְׁתֵּי shetei נֵרוֹת nerot ◆ וַהֲטָבַת vahatavat

שְׁתֵּי shetei נֵרוֹת nerot קוֹדֶמֶת kodemet לִקְטֹרֶת liktoret י"א פעמים אדני

(הנבררים מהקליפות ע"י י"א הסממנים) ; קטרת - הק' באתב"ש ד' = תרי"ג (מצוות) ◆ וּקְטֹרֶת uktoret

י"א פעמים אדני (הנבררים מהקליפות ע"י י"א הסממנים) ; קטרת - הק' באתב"ש ד' = תרי"ג (מצוות)

לְאֵבָרִים le'evarim ◆ וְאֵבָרִים ve'evarim לְמִנְחָה lemincha ע"ה ב"פ ב"ן

וּמִנְחָה umincha ע"ה ב"פ ב"ן לַחֲבִתִּין lachavitin ◆ וַחֲבִתִּין vachavitin

לִנְסָכִין linsachin ◆ וּנְסָכִין unsachin לְמוּסָפִין lemusafin ◆ וּמוּסָפִין umusafin

לְבָזִיכִין levazichin ◆ וּבָזִיכִין uvazichin קוֹדְמִין kodmin לְתָמִיד letamid

ע"ה קס"א קנ"א קמ"ג שֶׁל shel בֵּין ben הָעַרְבַּיִם ha'arbayim ◆ שֶׁנֶּאֱמַר shene'emar:

וְעָרַךְ ve'arach עָלֶיהָ aleha פהל הָעֹלָה ha'ola וְהִקְטִיר vehiktir

עָלֶיהָ aleha פהל חֶלְבֵי chelvei הַשְּׁלָמִים hashelamim ◆ עָלֶיהָ aleha פהל

הַשְׁלֵם hashlem כָּל־ kol ילי הַקָּרְבָּנוֹת hakorbanot כֻּלָּם kulam:

The arrangement of two wooden logs preceded the removal of ashes from the inner Altar. The removal of ashes from the inner Altar preceded the preparation of the five candles. The preparation of the five candles preceded the blood of the daily offering. The blood of the daily offering preceded the preparation of the two candles. The preparation of the two candles preceded the incense. The incense preceded the limbs and the limbs preceded the meal-offerings. The meal-offerings preceded the baked-offerings. The baked-offerings preceded the wine libations. The wine libations preceded the Musaf sacrifices. The Musaf sacrifices preceded the daily offering at sundown. As was said, He set the burnt-offerings on it as incense. And upon it, you shall complete all of the sacrifices. (Yoma 33a)

ANA BEKO'ACH

The *Ana Beko'ach* is perhaps the most powerful prayer in the entire universe. Second-century Kabbalist Rav Nachunya ben HaKana was the first sage to reveal this combination of 42 letters, which encompass the power of Creation.

The *Ana Beko'ach* is a unique formula, built of 42 letters written in seven sentences, that gives us the ability to transcend this physical world with all its limitations. It is known as the 42-letter Name of God. The *Ana Beko'ach* can literally remove all friction, barriers, and obstacles associated with our physical existence. It injects order into chaos, removes Satan's influence from our nature, generates financial sustenance, arouses unity with and love for others, and provides healing energy to the body and soul. We recite or scan the *Ana Beko'ach* every day, as many times as we want.

There are four elements that we connect to, using the *Ana Beko'ach*. They are:

1) **SEVEN SENTENCES** - The seven sentences correspond to the seven *Sefirot*, from *Chesed* to *Malchut*. Although there are ten *Sefirot* in total, only the lower seven exert influence in our physical world. By connecting to these seven, we seize control over this physical world.

2) **LETTERS OF THE MONTH** - Abraham the Patriarch revealed the astrological secrets of the Aramaic letters and of the signs of the zodiac in his kabbalistic treatise, *The Book of Formation* (*Sefer Yetzirah*). Each month of the year is governed by a planet, and each planet has a corresponding verse in the *Ana Beko'ach*; therefore, we also meditate upon the planet and the Aramaic letter that created both the planet and the zodiac sign of that month. In doing so, we connect to the positive energy of each planet and not to its negative influence. For example, the Aramaic letter *Zayin* created the sign of Gemini, *Sivan.* Gemini is governed by the planet Mercury. The Aramaic letter that gave birth to Mercury is *Resh*; therefore, each day during the month of *Sivan*, we meditate upon the the letters *Zayin* and *Resh* following the recital and meditation of the first verse of the *Ana Beko'ach*.

The Month and the Letters		The Astrological Sign And the Letter		The Planet And the Letter		Ana Beko'ach meditation
Sivan	רז	Gemini	ז	Mercury	ר	יגלפזק

3) **CORRECTION OF THE SOUL - TIKKUN HANEFESH** - Throughout history, kabbalists have used this healing meditation twice a day, seven days a week, to regenerate and revitalize all the organs of the body. When we reach the sentence in the *Ana Beko'ach* that governs the particular month we are in, we stop and meditate on the letters of the month, and then do the *Tikkun HaNefesh.* (See pg. 581) Using the chart as a guide, hold your right hand over the particular part of the body to which you are channeling energy. Look at the Aramaic letter combination for the specific area of the body that you are focusing on, and allow the Light to penetrate through your right hand, into that part of the body.

4) **ANGELS OF THE DAY** - Angels are distinct packets of spiritual energy that act as a transportation system for our prayers. They carry our words and thoughts to the Upper Worlds. There is a line of *Ana Beko'ach* for each day of the week, and there are unique angels that govern each day. (See pg. 582-584)

Chesed, Sunday *(Alef Bet Gimel Yud Tav Tzadik)* אבג יתץ

אָנָּא ana בְּכֹחַ beko'ach• גְּדוּלַּת gedulat יְמִינְךָ yeminecha•

תַּתִּיר tatir צְרוּרָה tzerura:

Gevurah, Monday *(Kuf Resh Ayin Sin Tet Nun)* קרע שטן

קַבֵּל kabel רִנַּת rinat• עַמְּךָ amecha שַׂגְּבֵנוּ sagevenu•

טַהֲרֵנוּ taharenu נוֹרָא nora:

Tiferet, Tuesday *(Nun Gimel Dalet Yud Kaf Shin)* נגד יכש

נָא na גִבּוֹר gibor• דּוֹרְשֵׁי dorshei יִחוּדְךָ yichudecha•

כְּבָבַת kevavat שָׁמְרֵם shomrem:

Netzach, Wednesday *(Bet Tet Resh Tzadik Tav Gimel)* בטר צתג

בָּרְכֵם barchem טַהֲרֵם taharem• רַחֲמֵי rachamei צִדְקָתְךָ tzidkatecha•

תָּמִיד tamid גָּמְלֵם gomlem:

Hod, Thursday *(Chet Kuf Bet Tet Nun Ayin)* חקב טנע

חֲסִין chasin קָדוֹשׁ kadosh• בְּרוֹב berov טוּבְךָ tuvcha•

נַהֵל nahel עֲדָתֶךָ adatecha:

ANA BEKO'ACH

Chesed, Sunday אבג יתץ

We beseech You, with the power of Your great right, undo this entanglement.

Gevurah, Monday קרע שטן

Accept the singing of Your Nation. Strengthen and purify us, Awesome One.

Tiferet, Tuesday נגד יכש

Please, Mighty One, those who seek Your unity, guard them like the pupil of the eye.

Netzach, Wednesday בטר צתג

Bless them. Purify them. Your compassionate righteousness always grant them.

Hod, Thursday חקב טנע

Invincible and Mighty One, with the abundance of Your goodness, govern Your congregation.

Yesod, Friday *(Yud Gimel Lamed Pei Zayin Kuf)* יג"ל פז"ק

•pene פְּנֵה le'amecha לְעַמְּךָ •ge'e גֵּאֶה yachid יָחִיד

:kedushatecha קְדֻשָּׁתֶךָ zochrei זוֹכְרֵי

Malchut, Saturday *(Shin Kuf Vav Tzadik Yud Tav)* שק"ו צי"ת

•tza'akatenu צַעֲקָתֵנוּ ushma וּשְׁמַע •kabel קַבֵּל shav'atenu שַׁוְעָתֵנוּ

:ta'alumot תַּעֲלוּמוֹת yode'a יוֹדֵעַ

BARUCH SHEM KEVOD

Whispering this final verse brings all the Light from the Upper Worlds into our physical existence.

malchuto מַלְכוּתוֹ kevod כְּבוֹד shem שֵׁם baruch בָּרוּךְ יו"ד אותיות :(Whisper)

:va'ed וָעֶד ריבוע ס"ג וי' אותיות דס"ג le'olam לְעוֹלָם

RIBON HAOLAMIM

God has given us specific instructions regarding the sacrifices that were to be carried out in the *Beit HaMikdash* (Holy Temple of Jerusalem). Because of the destruction of the Temple, we are not able to carry out those instructions. Here, we ask God to allow us to use the power of these Aramaic letters as a replacement for those sacrifices.

tzivitanu צִוִּיתָנוּ Ata אַתָּה ha'olamim הָעוֹלָמִים ע"ב ס"ג מ"ה ב"ן יהוה ribon רִבּוֹן

ע"ה קס"א קנ"א קמ"ג hatamid הַתָּמִיד korban קָרְבַּן lehakriv לְהַקְרִיב

Kohanim כֹּהֲנִים velihiyot וְלִהְיוֹת •bemo'ado בְּמוֹעֲדוֹ

beduchanam בְּדוּכָנָם uLeviyim וּלְוִיִּם ba'avodatam בַּעֲבוֹדָתָם

ve'ata וְעַתָּה •bema'amadam בְּמַעֲמָדָם veYisrael וְיִשְׂרָאֵל

hamikdash הַמִּקְדָּשׁ ב"פ ראה bet בֵּית charev חָרֵב ba'avonoteinu בַּעֲוֹנוֹתֵינוּ

Yesod, Friday יג"ל פז"ק

Sole and proud One, turn to Your people, those who remember Your sanctity.

Malchut, Saturday שק"ו צי"ת

Accept our cry and hear our wail, You that knows all that is hidden.

BARUCH SHEM KEVOD

"Blessed is the Name of Glory. His Kingdom is forever and for eternity." (Pesachim 56a)

RIBON HAOLAMIM

Master of all Worlds, You have commanded us to sacrifice the daily offering at its appointed time, that the Kohens shall do their service, the Levites shall be on their platforms, and the Israelites shall be in their situations. Yet now, due to our sins, the Temple has been destroyed

וּבָטַל uvutal הַתָּמִיד hatamid ע"ה קס"א קנ"א קמ"ג וְאֵין ve'en
לָנוּ lanu אלהים, אהיה אדני לֹא lo כֹּהֵן Chohen מלה
בַּעֲבוֹדָתוֹ ba'avodato• וְלֹא velo לֵוִי Levi בְּדוּכָנוֹ beduchano•
וְלֹא velo יִשְׂרָאֵל Yisrael בְּמַעֲמָדוֹ bema'amado• וְאַתָּה veAta
אָמַרְתָּ amarta: וּנְשַׁלְּמָה un'shalma פָרִים farim שְׂפָתֵינוּ sefatenu:
לָכֵן lachen יְהִי yehi רָצוֹן ratzon מהש ע"ה, ע"ב בריבוע וקס"א ע"ה, אל שדי ע"ה
מִלְּפָנֶיךָ milfanecha ס"ג מ"ה ב"ן יְהֹוָהאדניאהדונהי Adonai אֱלֹהֵינוּ Elohenu ילה
וֵאלֹהֵי velohei לכב ; מילוי ע"ב, דמב ; ילה אֲבוֹתֵינוּ avotenu שֶׁיְּהֵא sheyehe
זֶה ze שִׂיחַ si'ach שִׂפְתוֹתֵינוּ siftotenu חָשׁוּב chashuv וּמְקֻבָּל um'kubal
וּמְרוּצֶּה um'rutze לְפָנֶיךָ lefanecha ס"ג מ"ה ב"ן כְּאִלּוּ ke'ilu הִקְרַבְנוּ hikravnu
קָרְבַּן korban הַתָּמִיד hatamid ע"ה קס"א קנ"א קמ"ג בְּמוֹעֲדוֹ bemo'ado
וְעָמַדְנוּ ve'amadnu עַל al מַעֲמָדוֹ ma'amado כְּמוֹ kemo שֶׁנֶּאֱמַר shene'emar:
וּנְשַׁלְּמָה un'shalma פָרִים farim שְׂפָתֵינוּ sefatenu• וְנֶאֱמַר vene'emar:
וְשָׁחַט veshachat אֹתוֹ oto עַל al יֶרֶךְ yerech הַמִּזְבֵּחַ hamizbe'ach נגד, זן, אל יהוה
צָפֹנָה tzafona יה פעמים יה וע"ה ע"ב ס"ג מ"ה ב"ן, הברכה (מכוון למאמרם ז"ל הרוצה להעשיר יצפין)
לִפְנֵי lifnei יְהֹוָהאדניאהדונהי Adonai וְזָרְקוּ vezarku ס"ת יהוה
בְּנֵי benei אַהֲרֹן Aharon הַכֹּהֲנִים hakohanim אֶת־ et דָּמוֹ damo
עַל־ al הַמִּזְבֵּחַ hamizbe'ach נגד, זן, אל יהוה סָבִיב saviv:
וְנֶאֱמַר vene'emar: זֹאת zot הַתּוֹרָה hatorah לָעֹלָה la'ola
לַמִּנְחָה lamincha ע"ה ב"פ ב"ן וְלַחַטָּאת velachatat וְלָאָשָׁם vela'asham
וְלַמִּלּוּאִים velamilu'im וּלְזֶבַח ulzevach הַשְּׁלָמִים hashelamim:

---

and the daily offering has ceased. We now have no Kohen to do his service; No Levite to stand his platform; and no Israelite in his situation. But we asked: "May we compensate for the bull-offerings with our lips?" (Hosea 14:3) Therefore, may it be Your will, Lord, our God and the God of our fathers, that those words that come out of our lips shall be worthy, acceptable and favorable before You, as if we had sacrificed our daily offering at its appointed time and as if we had stood at that occasion, as it was said: "May we compensate for the bull-offerings with our lips?" (Hosea 14:3) And as it was also said: "And he shall slaughter it on the northern side of the Altar before the Lord. Aaron's sons, the Kohens, shall sprinkle its blood upon the Altar, all around." (Leviticus 1:11) And: "This is the law regarding the burnt-offering, the meal-offering, the sin-offering, the guilt-offering, the inauguration-offering, and the peace-offering." (Leviticus 1:11)

THE POWER OF PEACE

It is important to connect to all levels of the Torah during the day; therefore, we read these verses from the *Mishnah*, followed by verses from the *Gemara* (both are aspects of the *Talmud*). This specific section from the *Talmud* helps to imbue us with the power of truth, unity and peace because it is the only chapter containing no debate or opposing views about the interpretations of the Torah.

Meditate here to elevate, *Netzach*, *Hod*, *Yesod* of *Asiyah* into *Chesed*, *Gevurah*, *Tiferet;* and then to elevate *Malchut* into *Netzach*, *Hod*, *Yesod*; and then to elevate the Sparks of Light that are in the *klipa* into *Malchut*.

We say this section here because it is the only chapter in the entire *Mishnah* where all the opinions are in agreement, and is why this chapter is called: "*Halacha Pesuka*," meaning unargumental law. Now, while the worlds are elevated, we need the power of peace, not of disagreement.

FIRST MISHNAH

By saying this *Mishnah*, the Internal aspect of *Netzach* of *Asiyah* rises and becomes External to the External part of *Chesed* of *Asiyah*.

אֵיזֶהוּ ezehu מְקוֹמָן mekoman שֶׁל shel זְבָחִים zevachim• קָדְשֵׁי kodshei
קָדָשִׁים kodashim שְׁחִיטָתָן shechitatan בַּצָּפוֹן batzafon• פַּר par
וְשָׂעִיר vesa'ir שֶׁל shel יוֹם yom ע״ה נגד, מזבח, זן, אל יהוה הַכִּפּוּרִים hakipurim
שְׁחִיטָתָן shechitatan בַּצָּפוֹן batzafon וְקִבּוּל vekibul דָּמָן daman בִּכְלֵי bichlei
שָׁרֵת sharet בַּצָּפוֹן batzafon• וְדָמָן vedaman טָעוּן ta'un הַזָּיָה hazaya עַל al
בֵּין ben הַבַּדִּים habadim וְעַל ve'al הַפָּרֹכֶת haparochet וְעַל ve'al
מִזְבַּח mizbach נגד, זן, אל יהוה הַזָּהָב hazahav והו• מַתָּנָה matana נתה, קס״א קנ״א קמ״ג
אַחַת achat מֵהֶן mehen מְעַכֶּבֶת me'akevet• שְׁיָרֵי shiyerei הַדָּם hadam
הָיָה haya יהה שׁוֹפֵךְ shofech עַל al יְסוֹד yesod ההע מַעֲרָבִי ma'aravi
שֶׁל shel מִזְבֵּחַ mizbe'ach נגד, זן, אל יהוה הַחִיצוֹן hachitzon• אִם im יוהך,
מ״א אותיות דפשוט, דמילוי ודמילוי דמילוי דאהיה ע״ה לֹא lo נָתַן natan לֹא lo עִכֵּב ikev:

THE POWER OF PEACE
FIRST MISHNAH

Where is the location of sacrifices? The most holy are slaughtered on the North side. The bull and male goat of Yom Kippur are slaughtered on the North side; their blood is received in service vessels on the North side. Their blood is required to be sprinkled between the poles, on the curtain, and on the Golden Altar. The absence of one of them hinders. He pours the leftover blood on the western foundation of the outer Altar; if he does not pour, he did not hinder.

SECOND MISHNAH

By saying this *Mishnah*, the Internal aspect of *Hod* of *Asiyah* rises and becomes External to the External part of *Gevurah* of *Asiyah*.

פָּרִים parim הַנִּשְׂרָפִים hanisrafim וּשְׂעִירִים us'irim הַנִּשְׂרָפִים hanisrafim
שְׁחִיטָתָן shechitatan בַּצָּפוֹן batzafon• וְקִבּוּל vekibul דָּמָן daman
בִּכְלֵי bichlei שָׁרֵת sharet בַּצָּפוֹן batzafon• וְדָמָן vedaman טָעוּן ta'un
הַזָּיָה hazaya עַל al הַפָּרֹכֶת haparochet וְעַל ve'al מִזְבַּח mizbach נג"ד, זן, אל יהוה
הַזָּהָב hazahav והו• מַתָּנָה matana נתה, קס"א קנ"א קמ"ג אַחַת achat
מֵהֶן mehen מְעַכֶּבֶת me'akevet• שְׁיָרֵי shiyrei הַדָּם hadam הָיָה haya יהה
שׁוֹפֵךְ shofech עַל al יְסוֹד yesod ההע מַעֲרָבִי ma'aravi שֶׁל shel
מִזְבֵּחַ mizbe'ach נג"ד, זן, אל יהוה הַחִיצוֹן hachitzon• אִם im יוהך,
מ"א אותיות דפשוט, דמילוי ודמילוי דמילוי דאהיה ע"ה לֹא lo נָתַן natan לֹא lo עִכֵּב ikev•
אֵלּוּ elu וָאֵלּוּ va'elu נִשְׂרָפִין nisrafin בְּבֵית bevet ב"פ ראה הַדֶּשֶׁן hadeshen:

THIRD MISHNAH

By saying this *Mishnah*, the Internal aspect of *Yesod* of *Asiyah* rises and becomes External to the External part of *Tiferet* of *Asiyah*. Here, we complete *Chesed*, *Gevurah*, *Tiferet* of *Asiyah*.

וְחַטֹּאת chatot הַצִּבּוּר hatzibur וְהַיָּחִיד vehayachid אֵלּוּ elu הֵן hen
חַטֹּאת chatot הַצִּבּוּר hatzibur: שְׂעִירֵי se'irei רָאשֵׁי rashei
חֳדָשִׁים chodashim וְשֶׁל veshel מוֹעֲדוֹת mo'adot• שְׁחִיטָתָן shechitatan
בַּצָּפוֹן batzafon• וְקִבּוּל vekibul דָּמָן daman בִּכְלֵי bichlei שָׁרֵת sharet
בַּצָּפוֹן batzafon• וְדָמָן vedaman טָעוּן ta'un אַרְבַּע arba מַתָּנוֹת matanot

---

SECOND MISHNAH

Bulls and male goats that are to be burned are slaughtered on the North side. Their blood is received in service vessels on the North side. Their blood requires sprinkling upon the curtain and upon the Golden Altar. The absence of one of them hinders. He pours the leftover blood upon the Western foundation of the outer Altar; if he did not pour, he did not hinder. These and the preceding offerings are burned in ash repositories.

THIRD *MISHNAH*

The communal and the personal sin-offerings are the communal sin-offerings: The male goats of Rosh Chodesh and of the festivals: these are slaughtered on the North side. And their blood is received in service vessels in the North side. Their blood requires four poured portions

עַל al אַרְבַּע arba קְרָנוֹת •keranot כֵּיצַד •keitzad עָלָה ala
בַּכֶּבֶשׁ bakevesh וּפָנָה ufana ע"ב ס"ג לַסּוֹבֵב lasovev וּבָא uva לוֹ lo
לְקֶרֶן lekeren דְּרוֹמִית deromit מִזְרָחִית •mizrachit מִזְרָחִית mizrachit
צְפוֹנִית •tzefonit צְפוֹנִית tzefonit מַעֲרָבִית •ma'aravit מַעֲרָבִית ma'aravit
דְּרוֹמִית •deromit שְׁיָרֵי shiyrei הַדָּם hadam הָיָה haya יהה
שׁוֹפֵךְ shofech עַל al יְסוֹד yesod ההע הַדְּרוֹמִי •haderomi
וְנֶאֱכָלִין vene'echalin לִפְנִים lifnim מִן min הַקְּלָעִים hakela'im
לְזִכְרֵי lezichrei כְהֻנָּה chehuna בְּכָל bechol ב"ן, לכב מַאֲכָל •ma'achal
לְיוֹם leyom ע"ה נגד, מזבח, זן, אל יהוה וְלַיְלָה valayla מלה עַד־ ad חֲצוֹת :chatzot

FOURTH MISHNAH - THE OLAH (BURNT) OFFERING

You say this *Mishnah* for the entirety of *Asiyah*.

הָעוֹלָה ha'ola קֹדֶשׁ kodesh קָדָשִׁים kodashim שְׁחִיטָתָהּ shechitata
בַּצָּפוֹן •batzafon וְקִבּוּל vekibul דָּמָהּ dama בִּכְלֵי bichlei
שָׁרֵת sharet בַּצָּפוֹן •batzafon וְדָמָהּ vedama טָעוּן ta'un שְׁתֵּי shetei
מַתָּנוֹת matanot שֶׁהֵן shehen אַרְבַּע •arba וּטְעוּנָה ute'una
הֶפְשֵׁט hefshet וְנִתּוּחַ venitu'ach וְכָלִיל vechalil לָאִשִּׁים :la'ishim

FIFTH MISHNAH - THE ASHAM (GUILT) OFFERINGS

By saying this *Mishnah*, the Internal aspect of the Right Column of *Malchut* of *Asiyah* rises and becomes External to the External aspect of *Netzach* of *Asiyah*.

זִבְחֵי zivchei שַׁלְמֵי shalmei צִבּוּר tzibur וַאֲשָׁמוֹת •va'ashamot
אֵלּוּ elu הֵן hen אֲשָׁמוֹת :ashamot אֲשַׁם asham גְּזֵלוֹת •gezelot

---

upon the four corners of the Altar. How: He ascends the ramp, then turns to the Surrounding ledge; then goes to the Southeastern corner, the Northeastern, the Northwestern, and the Southwestern corner. He pours the leftover blood on the Southern foundation. These are eaten within the curtains by the males of the Kohens, in every meal for one day and one night, until midnight.

FOURTH MISHNAH - THE OLAH (BURNT) OFFERING

The burnt-offering belongs to the most holy.

It is slaughtered in the north and its blood is received in service vessels in the North. Its blood requires two four-part portions. It requires flaying, dismemberment, and complete consumption by fire.

FIFTH MISHNAH - THE ASHAM (GUILT) OFFERINGS

The communal peace-offerings and guilt-offerings; These are the guilt-offerings: The guilt-offerings for thefts,

אֲשַׁם asham מְעִילוֹת me'ilot• אֲשַׁם asham שִׁפְחָה shifcha וַחֲרוּפָה charufa•
אֲשַׁם asham נָזִיר nazir• אֲשַׁם asham מְצוֹרָע metzora• אָשָׁם asham
תָּלוּי taluy• שְׁחִיטָתָן shechitatan בַּצָּפוֹן batzafon• וְקִבּוּל vekibul דָּמָן daman
בִּכְלֵי bichlei שָׁרֵת sharet בַּצָּפוֹן batzafon• וְדָמָן vedaman
טָעוּן ta'un שְׁתֵּי shetei מַתָּנוֹת matanot שֶׁהֵן shehen אַרְבַּע arba•
וְנֶאֱכָלִין vene'echalin לִפְנִים lifnim מִן min הַקְּלָעִים hakela'im
לְזִכְרֵי lezichrei כְהֻנָּה chehuna בְּכָל bechol ב"ן, לכב מַאֲכָל ma'achal
לְיוֹם leyom ע"ה נגד, מזבח, זן, אל יהוה וָלַיְלָה valayla מלה עַד־ ad וַחֲצוֹת chatzot:

SIXTH MISHNAH - THE TODA (THANKS) OFFERINGS

By saying this *Mishnah*, the Internal aspect of the Left Column of *Malchut* of *Asiyah* rises and becomes External to the External aspect of *Hod* of *Asiyah*.

הַתּוֹדָה hatoda וְאֵיל ve'el נָזִיר nazir קָדָשִׁים kodashim קַלִּים kalim•
שְׁחִיטָתָן shechitatan בְּכָל bechol ב"ן, לכב מָקוֹם makom בָּעֲזָרָה ba'azara
וְדָמָן vedaman טָעוּן ta'un שְׁתֵּי shetei מַתָּנוֹת matanot שֶׁהֵן shehen
אַרְבַּע arba• וְנֶאֱכָלִין vene'echalin בְּכָל bechol ב"ן, לכב הָעִיר ha'ir
מזוהר, סנדלפון, ערי לְכָל־ lechol יה אדני אָדָם adam מ"ה בְּכָל־ bechol ב"ן, לכב
מַאֲכָל ma'achal לְיוֹם leyom ע"ה נגד, מזבח, זן, אל יהוה וָלַיְלָה valayla מלה עַד־ ad
וַחֲצוֹת chatzot• הַמּוּרָם hamuram מֵהֶם mehem כַּיּוֹצֵא kayotze בָהֶם vahem
אֶלָּא ela שֶׁהַמּוּרָם shehamuram נֶאֱכָל ne'echal לַכֹּהֲנִים lakohanim
לִנְשֵׁיהֶם linshehem וְלִבְנֵיהֶם velivnehem וּלְעַבְדֵיהֶם ul'avdehem:

---

for misuses of sacred objects, for being with a married maid servant, of the Nazir, of a leper, and of a doubtful transgression. These are slaughtered on the North side and their blood is received in service vessels on the North side. Their blood requires two four-part portions. They are eaten within the curtains by the male Kohens, in every meal for one day and for one night, until midnight.

SIXTH MISHNAH - THE TODA (THANKS) OFFERINGS

The thanks-offering and the Nazir's ram are of minor sanctity. They are slaughtered anywhere in the courtyard. Their blood requires two four-part portions. They are eaten throughout the city by any person, in every meal for one day and for one night until midnight. That part which is set aside is treated in the same manner, except that this portion is eaten by the Kohens, their wives, their sons, and their slaves.

SEVENTH MISHNAH - THE SHELAMIM (PEACE) OFFERINGS

By saying this *Mishnah*, the Internal aspect of the Central Column of *Malchut* of *Asiyah* rises and becomes External to the External aspect of *Yesod* of *Asiyah*.

שְׁלָמִים shelamim קָדָשִׁים kodashim קַלִּים •kalim שְׁחִיטָתָן shechitatan
בְּכָל bechol ב"ן, לכב מָקוֹם makom בָּעֲזָרָה •ba'azara וְדָמָן vedaman
טָעוּן ta'un שְׁתֵּי shetei מַתָּנוֹת matanot שֶׁהֵן shehen אַרְבַּע •arba
וְנֶאֱכָלִין vene'echalin בְּכָל bechol ב"ן, לכב הָעִיר ha'ir מזוהר, סנדלפון, ערי
לְכָל־ lechol יה אדני אָדָם adam מ"ה בְּכָל־ bechol ב"ן, לכב מַאֲכָל ma'achal
לִשְׁנֵי lishnei יָמִים yamim נלך וְלַיְלָה velayla מלה אֶחָד echad אהבה, דאגה•
הַמּוּרָם hamuram מֵהֶם mehem כַּיּוֹצֵא kayotze בָהֶם vahem
אֶלָּא ela שֶׁהַמּוּרָם shehamuram נֶאֱכָל ne'echal לַכֹּהֲנִים lakohanim
לִנְשֵׁיהֶם linshehem וְלִבְנֵיהֶם velivnehem וּלְעַבְדֵיהֶם :ul'avdehem

THE FINAL MISHNAH

With this final *Mishnah*, we have the power to elevate the entire world of *Asiyah*. Any souls, or Light, that are trapped inside the *klipot* are also elevated by this verse. Because this specific section contains no debate or opposing views, it creates a thread of unity; it is only through this unity that we have the ability to elevate to the World of Formation (*Yetzirah*).

By saying this *Mishnah*, the Internal aspect (which was in the *klipa*) rises and becomes External to the External aspect of *Malchut* of *Asiyah*. And with this, you complete all of *Asiyah*.

הַבְּכוֹר habechor וְהַמַּעֲשֵׂר vehama'aser וְהַפֶּסַח vehapesach קָדָשִׁים kodashim
קַלִּים •kalim שְׁחִיטָתָן shechitatan בְּכָל bechol ב"ן, לכב מָקוֹם makom
בָּעֲזָרָה ba'azara וְדָמָן vedaman טָעוּן ta'un מַתָּנָה matana נתה, קס"א קנ"א קמ"ג
אַחַת •echat וּבִלְבַד uvilvad שֶׁיִּתֵּן sheyiten כְּנֶגֶד keneged מזבח, זן, אל יהוה
הַיְסוֹד hayesod ההע• שִׁנָּה shina בַּאֲכִילָתָן •va'achilatan

---

SEVENTH MISHNAH - THE SHELAMIM (PEACE) OFFERINGS

The peace-offerings are of lesser sanctity. They are slaughtered anywhere in the courtyard. Their blood requires two four-part portions. They are eaten throughout the city by any person, in every meal, for two days and one night. That part which is set aside is treated in the same manner, except that this portion is eaten by the Kohens, their wives, their sons, and their slaves.

THE FINAL MISHNAH

The firstborn animal, the tithes of cattle, and the Pesach-offering are of minor sanctity. They are slaughtered anywhere in the courtyard. Their blood requires one poured portion, provided that this is poured against the base of the Altar. They differ in the way that they are eaten:

הַבְּכוֹר habechor נֶאֱכָל ne'echal לַכֹּהֲנִים lakohanim. וְהַמַּעֲשֵׂר vehama'aser

לְכָל־ lechol יה אדני אָדָם adam מ"ה. וְנֶאֱכָלִין vene'echalin

בְּכָל־ bechol ב"ן, לכב הָעִיר ha'ir סוזפר, סנדלפון, ערי

בְּכָל־ bechol ב"ן, לכב מַאֲכָל ma'achal לִשְׁנֵי lishnei יָמִים yamim נלך

וְלַיְלָה velayla מלה אֶחָד echad אהבה, דאגה. הַפֶּסַח hapesach אֵינוֹ eno

נֶאֱכָל ne'echal אֶלָּא ela בַּלַּיְלָה valayla מלה. וְאֵינוֹ ve'eno נֶאֱכָל ne'echal

אֶלָּא ela עַד ad וְחֲצוֹת chatzot. וְאֵינוֹ ve'eno נֶאֱכָל ne'echal אֶלָּא ela

לִמְנוּיָו limnuyav. וְאֵינוֹ ve'eno נֶאֱכָל ne'echal אֶלָּא ela צָלִי tzali:

RIBI YISHMAEL

Ribi Yishmael acts as a link in the chain of *Sefirot*. It connects us to 13 *Sefirot*—ten in the World of Action (*Asiyah*) and three in the next level up, the World of Formation (*Yetzirah*). It is good to count the 13 *Sefirot* of *Asiyah* with the fingers of the right hand.

רִבִּי Ribi יִשְׁמָעֵאל Yishmael אוֹמֵר omer, בִּשְׁלֹשׁ bish'losh עֶשְׂרֵה esre

מִדּוֹת midot הַתּוֹרָה hatorah נִדְרֶשֶׁת nidreshet. 1) מִקַּל mikal נמם

וָחוֹמֶר vachomer. 2) מִגְּזֵרָה migezera שָׁוָה shava. 3) מִבִּנְיַן mibinyan אָב av

וְכָתוּב vechatuv אֶחָד echad אהבה, דאגה. וּמִבִּנְיַן umibinyan אָב av

וּשְׁנֵי ushenei כְתוּבִים chetuvim. 4) מִכְּלָל mikelal וּפְרָט ufrat.

5) מִפְּרָט miperat וּכְלָל uchlal. 6) כְּלָל kelal וּפְרָט ufrat וּכְלָל uchlal

אִי ei אַתָּה Ata דָן dan אֶלָּא ela כְּעֵין ke'en הַפְּרָט haperat.

The firstborn animal may be eaten by the Kohen, and the tithe may be eaten by anyone. They are eaten throughout the city, in any meal for two days and one night. The Pesach-offering may be eaten only during that night, only until midnight, and may only be eaten by those who contributed to it. It may only be eaten roasted.

RIBI YISHMAEL

"Rabbi Yishmael says: By thirteen attributes is the Torah taught: 1) From lenient law and from strict law. 2) From similarity of words. 3) From a general principle derived from one verse and from a general principle derived from two verses. 4) From a general statement followed by a specific statement. 5) From a specific statement followed by a generality. 6) From a general statement, followed by a specific statement, followed by a generally: then you may only infer what is similar to the specification.

7) מִכְּלָל mikelal שֶׁהוּא shehu צָרִיךְ tzarich לִפְרָט lifrat•
וּמִפְּרָט umiperat שֶׁהוּא shehu צָרִיךְ tzarich לִכְלָל lichlal•
8) וְכָל vechol ילי דָּבָר davar ראה שֶׁהָיָה shehaya יהה בִּכְלָל bichlal
וְיָצָא veyatza מִן־ min הַכְּלָל hakelal לְלַמֵּד lelamed• לֹא lo לְלַמֵּד lelamed
עַל al עַצְמוֹ atzmo יָצָא yatza אֶלָּא ela לְלַמֵּד lelamed עַל al הַכְּלָל hakelal
כֻּלּוֹ kulo יָצָא yatza: 9) וְכָל vechol ילי דָּבָר davar ראה שֶׁהָיָה shehaya יהה
בִּכְלָל bichlal• וְיָצָא veyatza לִטְעוֹן lit'on טָעוּן ta'un אַחֵר acher
שֶׁהוּא shehu כְעִנְיָנוֹ che'inyano• יָצָא yatza לְהָקֵל lehakel וְלֹא velo
לְהַחֲמִיר lehachmir: 10) וְכָל vechol ילי דָּבָר davar ראה שֶׁהָיָה shehaya יהה
בִּכְלָל bichlal וְיָצָא veyatza לִטְעוֹן lit'on טָעוּן ta'un אַחֵר acher שֶׁלֹּא shelo
כְעִנְיָנוֹ che'inyano יָצָא yatza לְהָקֵל lehakel וּלְהַחֲמִיר ul'hachmir:
11) וְכָל vechol ילי דָּבָר davar ראה שֶׁהָיָה shehaya יהה בִּכְלָל bichlal
וְיָצָא veyatza לִדּוֹן lidon בְּדָבָר bedavar ראה חָדָשׁ chadash י"ב הויות, קס"א קנ"א
אִי ei אַתָּה Ata יָכוֹל yachol לְהַחֲזִירוֹ lehachaziro לִכְלָלוֹ lichlalo עַד ad
שֶׁיַּחֲזִירֶנּוּ sheyachazirenu הַכָּתוּב hakatuv לִכְלָלוֹ lichlalo בְּפֵירוּשׁ beferush:
12) וְדָבָר vedavar ראה הַלָּמֵד halamed מֵעִנְיָנוֹ me'inyano וְדָבָר vedavar ראה
הַלָּמֵד halamed מִסּוֹפוֹ misofo: 13) וְכֵן vechan (וְכָאן) שְׁנֵי shenei
כְתוּבִים chetuvim הַמַּכְחִישִׁים hamach'chishim זֶה ze אֶת et זֶה ze
עַד ad שֶׁיָּבֹא sheyavo הַכָּתוּב hakatuv הַשְּׁלִישִׁי hashelishi
וְיַכְרִיעַ veyachri'a בֵּינֵיהֶם benehem:

---

7) From a general statement that requires a specific statement that, in turn, requires a general statement to explain it. 8) Anything that was part of a general statement which was then singled out from the general statement, to teach something. It was not to teach about itself that it was singled out, but to teach about the entire general statement. 9) Anything that was part of a general statement, which was later singled outto discuss another claim to its context. It was singled out in order to be more lenient and not more stringent. 10) Anything that was part of a general statement and was later singled out in order to discuss another claim out of its context. It was singled out in order to be more lenient and not more stringent. 11) Anything that was part of a general statement and was singled out in order to discuss a new concept, you cannot return it to its general context, unless the text returns it, explicitly, to its general context. 12) A matter that is learned from its context and a matter that is derived from its end. 13) And also from two verses that contradict each other, until a third one comes along and reconciles them. (Torat Kohanim Portion of Vayikra.)

יְהוּדָה Yehuda בֶּן ven תֵּימָא Tema אוֹמֵר: omer הֱוֵי hevei עַז az

כַּנָּמֵר kanamer וְקַל vekal נמם (שהם ה' גבורות) כַּנֶּשֶׁר kanesher וְרָץ veratz

כַּצְּבִי katzevi וְגִבּוֹר vegibor כָּאֲרִי ka'ari לַעֲשׂוֹת la'asot רְצוֹן retzon

מהש ע"ה, ע"ב בריבוע וקס"א ע"ה, אל שדי ע"ה אָבִיךָ avicha שֶׁבַּשָּׁמַיִם shebashamayim

י"פ טל, י"פ כוזו: הוּא hu הָיָה haya יהה אוֹמֵר: omer עַז az פָּנִים panim

לַגֵּיהִנָּם laGehinom וּבֹשֶׁת uvoshet פָּנִים panim לְגַן leGan עֵדֶן Eden:

YEHI RATZON

Even though, according to Kabbalah, the Temple still exists in the spiritual reality of the Endless World, its physical structure is missing, leaving our physical world incomplete. This prayer helps set in motion and accelerate the eventual reconstruction of the physical Temple.

יְהִי yehi רָצוֹן ratzon מהש ע"ה, ע"ב בריבוע וקס"א ע"ה, אל שדי ע"ה

מִלְּפָנֶיךָ milfanecha ס"ג מ"ה ב"ן יְהֹוָהאדניאהדונהי Adonai אֱלֹהֵינוּ Elohenu ילה

וֵאלֹהֵי velohei לכב ; מילוי ע"ב, דמב ; ילה אֲבוֹתֵינוּ avotenu

שֶׁתִּבְנֶה shetivne בֵּית bet ב"פ ראה הַמִּקְדָּשׁ hamikdash

בִּמְהֵרָה bim'hera בְּיָמֵינוּ veyamenu. וְתֵן veten חֶלְקֵנוּ chelkenu

בְּתוֹרָתָךְ betoratach לַעֲשׂוֹת la'asot חֻקֵּי chukei רְצוֹנָךְ retzonach

וּלְעָבְדָךְ ul'ovdach פוי, אל אדני בְּלֵבָב belevav בוכי שָׁלֵם shalem:

You should be careful not to speak or even to pause too long here, and you should proceed to *Hodu* right after the *Kaddish*.

KADDISH AL YISRAEL

Kaddish, in general, means to elevate the worlds in the secret of the Column. There is one column that connects the worlds to each other and stands in the middle of each palace. And by this column, each palace rises to the upper one and becomes one with it (as is mentioned in the *Zohar*). This column is the *Kaddish*. The secret of *Kaddish Al Yisrael* is that it elevates us from the World of *Asiyah* (ב"ן) to the World of *Yetzirah* (מ"ה).

Yehuda Ben Tema says: Be courageous like a tiger and light as an eagle and run like a deer and be strong like a lion to thus fulfill the will of Your Father in Heaven. He used to frequently say: An insolent person goes to Hell and a modest person to the Garden of Eden. (Avot Ch. 5)

YEHI RATZON

May it be Your will, Lord, our God and the God of our forefathers, that You shall build the Temple speedily in our days. And that You may place our lot in Your Torah, so that we may fulfill the laws of Your desires and worship You wholeheartedly.

יִתְגַּדַּל yitgadal וְיִתְקַדַּשׁ veyitkadash שדי ומילוי שדי ; י"א אותיות כמנין ו"ה

שְׁמֵיהּ shemei (שם י"ה דע"ב) רַבָּא raba קנ"א ב"ן, יהוה אלהים יהוה אדני,

מילוי קס"א וס"ג, מ"ה ברבוע וע"ב ע"ה ; ר"ת = ו"פ אלהים ; ס"ת = ג"פ יב"ק: אָמֵן amen אידהנויה.

בְּעָלְמָא be'alma דִּי di בְרָא vera כִּרְעוּתֵיהּ chir'utei.

וְיַמְלִיךְ veyamlich מַלְכוּתֵיהּ malchutei. וְיַצְמַח veyatzmach

פּוּרְקָנֵיהּ purkanei. וִיקָרֵב vikarev מְשִׁיחֵיהּ meshichei: אָמֵן amen אידהנויה.

בְּחַיֵּיכוֹן bechayechon וּבְיוֹמֵיכוֹן uvyomeichon וּבְחַיֵּי uvchayei

דְכָל dechol ילי בֵּית bet ב"פ ראה יִשְׂרָאֵל Yisrael בַּעֲגָלָא ba'agala

וּבִזְמַן uvizman קָרִיב kariv וְאִמְרוּ ve'imru אָמֵן amen: אָמֵן amen אידהנויה.

The congregation and the *chazan* say the following:

28 words (until *be'alma*) meditate: מילוי דמילוי דס"ג (יוד ויו דלת הי יוד ואו אלף ואו הי יוד)

28 letters (until *almaya*) meditate: מילוי דמילוי דמ"ה (יוד ואו דלת הא אלף ואו אלף ואו הא אלף)

יְהֵא yehe שְׁמֵיהּ shemei (שם י"ה דס"ג) רַבָּא raba קנ"א ב"ן,

יהוה אלהים יהוה אדני, מילוי קס"א וס"ג, מ"ה ברבוע וע"ב ע"ה מְבָרַךְ mevarach,

לְעָלַם le'alam לְעָלְמֵי le'almei עָלְמַיָּא almaya. יִתְבָּרַךְ yitbarach.

Seven words with six letters each (שם בן מ"ב) meditate:
יהוה - יוד הי ויו הי - מילוי דמילוי דס"ג (יוד ויו דלת הי יוד ואו אלף ואו הי יוד)
Also, seven times the letter *Vav* (שם בן מ"ב) meditate:
יהוה - יוד הי ואו הי - מילוי דמילוי דמ"ה (יוד ואו דלת הא אלף ואו אלף ואו הא אלף).

וְיִשְׁתַּבַּח veyishtabach י"פ ע"ב יהוה אל אבג יתץ.

וְיִתְפָּאַר veyitpa'ar הי נו יה קרע שטן. וְיִתְרוֹמַם veyitromam וה כוזו נגד יכש.

וְיִתְנַשֵּׂא veyitnase במוכסז בטר צתג. וְיִתְהַדָּר veyit'hadar כוזו יה חקב טנע.

וְיִתְעַלֶּה veyit'ale וה יוד ה יגל פזק. וְיִתְהַלָּל veyit'halal א ואו הא שקו צית.

שְׁמֵיהּ shemei (שם י"ה דמ"ה) דְּקוּדְשָׁא dekudsha בְּרִיךְ verich הוּא hu:

אָמֵן amen אידהנויה.

KADDISH AL YISRAEL

May His great Name be more exalted and sanctified. (Amen) In the world that He created according to His will, and may His Kingdom reign. And may He cause His redemption to sprout and may He bring the Mashiach closer. (Amen) In your lifetimes and in your days and in the lifetime of all the House of Israel, speedily and in the near future, and you shall say Amen. (Amen) May His great Name be blessed forever and for all eternity. Blessed and lauded, and glorified, and exalted, and extolled, and honored, and uplifted, and praised be the Name of the Holy Blessed One. (Amen)

לְעֵלָּא le'ela מִן min כָּל kol ילי בִּרְכָתָא birchata• שִׁירָתָא shirata•
תֻּשְׁבְּחָתָא tishbechata וְנֶחֱמָתָא venechamata• דַּאֲמִירָן da'amiran
בְּעָלְמָא be'alma וְאִמְרוּ ve'imru אָמֵן amen: אָמֵן amen אידהנויה.
עַל al יִשְׂרָאֵל Yisrael וְעַל ve'al רַבָּנָן rabanan וְעַל ve'al
תַּלְמִידֵיהוֹן talmidehon וְעַל ve'al כָּל kol ילי ; עמם תַּלְמִידֵי talmidei
תַּלְמִידֵיהוֹן talmidehon• דְּעָסְקִין de'askin בְּאוֹרַיְתָא be'orayta
קַדִּשְׁתָּא kadishta• דִּי di בְּאַתְרָא ve'atra הָדֵין haden וְדִי vedi
בְּכָל vechol ב"ן, לכב אֲתַר atar וַאֲתַר ve'atar• יְהֵא yehe
לָנָא lana וּלְהוֹן ul'hon וּלְכוֹן ul'chon חִנָּא china וְחִסְדָּא vechisda
וְרַחֲמֵי verachamei• מִן min קֳדָם kadam מָארֵי marei שְׁמַיָּא shemaya
וְאַרְעָא ve'ar'a וְאִמְרוּ ve'imru אָמֵן amen: אָמֵן amen אידהנויה.
יְהֵא yehe שְׁלָמָא shelama רַבָּא raba קנ"א ב"ן, יהוה אלהים יהוה אדני, מילוי קס"א וס"ג,
מ"ה ברבוע וע"ב ע"ה מִן min שְׁמַיָּא shemaya• וְחַיִּים chayim אהיה אהיה יהוה, בינה ע"ה
וְשָׂבָע vesava וִישׁוּעָה vishu'a וְנֶחָמָה venechama וְשֵׁיזָבָא veshezava
וּרְפוּאָה urfu'a וּגְאֻלָּה ug'ula וּסְלִיחָה uslicha וְכַפָּרָה vechapara
וְרֵיוַח verevach וְהַצָּלָה vehatzala• לָנוּ lanu אלהים, אהיה אדני וּלְכָל ulchol יה אדני
עַמּוֹ amo יִשְׂרָאֵל Yisrael וְאִמְרוּ ve'imru אָמֵן amen: אָמֵן amen אידהנויה.

Take three steps backwards and say:

עֹשֶׂה ose שָׁלוֹם shalom בִּמְרוֹמָיו bimromav ע"ב, ריבוע יהוה• הוּא hu
בְּרַחֲמָיו berachamav יַעֲשֶׂה ya'ase שָׁלוֹם shalom עָלֵינוּ alenu ר"ת ש"ע נהורין•
וְעַל ve'al כָּל kol ילי ; עמם עַמּוֹ amo יִשְׂרָאֵל Yisrael וְאִמְרוּ ve'imru אָמֵן amen:
אָמֵן amen אידהנויה•

Above all blessings, songs, praises, and words of consolation that may be said in the world, and you shall say, Amen. (Amen) Upon Israel, His Sages, their disciples, and all the students of their disciples who occupy themselves with the Holy Torah, in this place and in each and every location, may there be for us, for them, and for all, grace, kindness, and compassion from the Master of the Heavens and Earth, and you shall say Amen. (Amen) May there be abundant peace from Heaven, life, contentment, salvation, consolation, deliverance, healing, redemption, pardon, atonement, comfort, and relief for us and for His entire Nation, Israel, and you shall say, Amen. (Amen) He, Who makes peace in His High Places, with His compassion He shall make peace for us and for His entire Nation, Israel. And you shall say, Amen. (Amen)

HODU, EL NEKAMOT AND AROMIMCHA

The power of the *Kaddish* lies in its ability to elevate us to the Upper Worlds. But the initial launch from our physical world – *Asiyah* - requires an additional thrust. The ancient sages gave us three prayers, *Hodu, El Nekamot* and *Aromimcha*, for this purpose. This initial launch stage occurs in the World of Action (*Asiyah*).

HODU

Our *klipot's* sole nourishment comes from our world (*Malchut* or *Asiyah*), and consequently, the *klipot* try to prevent our world of *Malchut*, the World of Action (*Asiyah*), from rising to the World of Formation (*Yetzirah*), because that movement would disconnect them from their only source of Light. *Hodu* cuts off the *klipot's* oxygen supply, helping us break away from the *klipot's* gravitational pull.

We say *Hodu* to empower *Malchut* of *Yetzirah*, which is included in *Hechal Kodesh HaKodashim* of *Asiyah* in order to break the power of the *klipot* that prevents *Asiyah* from rising to *Yetzirah*. From *Hodu* to *baruch Elohim* (pg.253), there are 295 words which is the numerical value of *Elohim* spelled out with *Hei* (אלף למד הה יוד מם). And therefore, you should not add or omit any of the words. This prayer praises the sun on its trail when it comes to shine upon the world. So is *Yisrael* praising God with the sun, as it says: "You should be seen together with the sun" (Psalms 72:5).

הוֹדוּ hodu אהיה לַיהֹוָואדני־אהדונהי ladonai קִרְאוּ kir'u בִשְׁמוֹ vishmo מהש ע"ה,

ע"ב בריבוע וקס"א ע"ה, אל שדי ע"ה ; לאו הוֹדִיעוּ hodi'u בָעַמִּים va'amim

עֲלִילוֹתָיו alilotav: שִׁירוּ shiru לוֹ lo זַמְּרוּ־ zameru לוֹ lo שִׂיחוּ sichu

בְּכָל־ bechol ב"ן, לכב נִפְלְאוֹתָיו nifle'otav: הִתְהַלְלוּ hit'halelu בְּשֵׁם beshem

קָדְשׁוֹ kodsho יִשְׂמַח yismach משיח לֵב lev מְבַקְשֵׁי mevakshei

יְהֹוָואדני־אהדונהי Adonai: דִּרְשׁוּ dirshu יְהֹוָואדני־אהדונהי Adonai וְעֻזּוֹ ve'uzo

בַּקְּשׁוּ bakeshu פָנָיו fanav תָּמִיד tamid ע"ה קס"א קנ"א קמ"ג:

זִכְרוּ zichru נִפְלְאוֹתָיו nifle'otav אֲשֶׁר asher עָשָׂה asa מֹפְתָיו moftav

וּמִשְׁפְּטֵי־ umishpetei פִיהוּ fihu: זֶרַע zera יִשְׂרָאֵל Yisrael

עַבְדּוֹ avdo בְּנֵי benei יַעֲקֹב Yaakov י' הויות, יאהדונהי אידהנויה

בְּחִירָיו bechirav: הוּא hu יְהֹוָואדני־אהדונהי Adonai אֱלֹהֵינוּ Elohenu ילה

בְּכָל־ bechol ב"ן, לכב הָאָרֶץ ha'aretz אלהים דההין ע"ה מִשְׁפָּטָיו mishpatav:

HODU, EL NEKAMOT AND AROMIMCHA

HODU

'Be grateful to the Lord Call out His Name and make His deeds known among nations. Sing to Him, chant to Him, and speak of all His wonders. Be proud of His Holy Name. The heart of those who seek the Lord and His power shall rejoice. Constantly seek His presence. Remember the wonders that He has performed, His miracles, and the law that He uttered. You are the seed of Israel, His servant, and the sons of Jacob, His Chosen Ones. He is the Lord, our God. His judgments cover the whole Earth.

זִכְרוּ zichru לְעוֹלָם le'olam ריבוע דס"ג וי' אותיות ס"ג בְּרִיתוֹ berito דָּבָר davar ראה
צִוָּה tziva לְאֶלֶף le'elef המספר אֶלֶף = אלף למד שין דלת יוד ע"ה דּוֹר dor: אֲשֶׁר asher
כָּרַת karat אֶת־ et אַבְרָהָם Avraham וז"פ אל, רי"ו ול"ב נתיבות החכמה, רמ"ח (אברים),
עסמ"ב וט"ז אותיות פשוטות וּשְׁבוּעָתוֹ ush'vu'ato לְיִצְחָק leYitzchak ד"פ ב"ן:
וַיַּעֲמִידֶהָ vaya'amideha לְיַעֲקֹב leYaakov י' הויות, יאהדונהי אידהנויה לְחֹק lechok
לְיִשְׂרָאֵל leYisrael בְּרִית berit עוֹלָם olam: לֵאמֹר lemor לְךָ lecha
אֶתֵּן eten אֶרֶץ־ eretz כְּנָעַן Kena'an חֶבֶל chevel נַחֲלַתְכֶם nachalatchem:
בִּהְיוֹתְכֶם bih'yotchem מְתֵי metei מִסְפָּר mispar כִּמְעַט kim'at
וְגָרִים vegarim בָּהּ ba: וַיִּתְהַלְּכוּ vayit'halchu ניצוצות קדושה מִגּוֹי migoi אֶל־ el
גּוֹי goi וּמִמַּמְלָכָה umimamlacha אֶל־ el עַם am אַחֵר acher: לֹא־ lo
הִנִּיחַ hini'ach לְאִישׁ le'ish לְעָשְׁקָם le'oshkam ר"ת ללה, אדני וַיּוֹכַח vayochach
עֲלֵיהֶם alehem מְלָכִים melachim: אַל־ al תִּגְּעוּ tige'u בִּמְשִׁיחָי bimshichai
וּבִנְבִיאַי uvinvi'ai אַל־ al תָּרֵעוּ tare'u: שִׁירוּ shiru לַיהֹוָהאדניאהדונהי ladonai
כָּל־ kol ילי הָאָרֶץ ha'aretz אלהים דההין ע"ה בַּשְּׂרוּ baseru מִיּוֹם־ miyom
ע"ה נגד, מזבח, זן, אל יהוה אֶל־ el יוֹם yom ע"ה נגד, מזבח, זן, אל יהוה יְשׁוּעָתוֹ yeshu'ato:
סַפְּרוּ saperu בַגּוֹיִם vagoyim (properly enunciate the letter *Alef* in the word "et") אֶת־ et
כְּבוֹדוֹ kevodo בְּכָל bechol ב"ן, לכב הָעַמִּים ha'amim נִפְלְאוֹתָיו nifle'otav:
כִּי ki גָדוֹל gadol להח ; עם ד' אותיות = מבה, יזל, אום יְהֹוָהאדניאהדונהי Adonai
וּמְהֻלָּל um'hulal ס"ת ללה, אדני מְאֹד me'od וְנוֹרָא venora הוּא hu עַל־ al
כָּל־ kol ילי ; עמם אֱלֹהִים Elohim אהיה אדני ; ילה כִּי ki כָּל־ kol ילי
אֱלֹהֵי elohei מילוי ע"ב, דמב ; ילה הָעַמִּים ha'amim אֱלִילִים elilim (pause here)

Remember His Covenant always. That which He concluded with Abraham, vowed to Isaac, established for Jacob as a statute, and for Israel as an eternal Covenant: To you I give the land of Canaan, the share of your heritage, where you were only a few and were lost strangers in it. They wandered from one nation to another and from one kingdom to another. Yet He did not allow any one to harm them; He admonished kings because of them: Do not touch My anointed ones and do not cause distress to My prophets. Sing to the Lord all of Earth and proclaim daily His salvation. Relate His glory among the nations and His wonders among all peoples: For the Lord is great and most praised; He is awesome above and beyond all deities. For the gods of all nations are only deities

וַיהֹוָאדנִיאהדונהי vadonai שָׁמַיִם shamayim י״פ טל, י״פ כוזו עָשָׂה asa: הוֹד hod ההה
וְהָדָר vehadar לְפָנָיו lefanav עֹז oz וְחֶדְוָה vechedva בִּמְקֹמוֹ: bimkomo
הָבוּ havu אוזד, אהבה, דאגה לַיהֹוָאדנִיאהדונהי ladonai מִשְׁפְּחוֹת mishpechot
עַמִּים amim הָבוּ havu אוזד, אהבה, דאגה לַיהֹוָאדנִיאהדונהי ladonai כָּבוֹד kavod
וָעֹז: va'oz הָבוּ havu אוזד, אהבה, דאגה לַיהֹוָאדנִיאהדונהי ladonai כְּבוֹד kevod
שְׁמוֹ shemo מהש ע״ה, ע״ב בריבוע וקס״א ע״ה, אל שדי ע״ה ; הבו יהוה כבוד שמו = אדם דוד משיוז
שְׂאוּ se'u מִנְחָה mincha ע״ה ב״פ ב״ן וּבֹאוּ uvo'u לְפָנָיו lefanav
הִשְׁתַּחֲווּ hishtachavu לַיהֹוָאדנִיאהדונהי ladonai בְּהַדְרַת behadrat
קֹדֶשׁ kodesh ר״ת למפרע קבלה (היינו שביום שבת צריך ללמוד קבלה):
חִילוּ chilu מִלְּפָנָיו milfanav כָּל־ kol ילי הָאָרֶץ ha'aretz אלהים דההין ע״ה
אַף־ af תִּכּוֹן tikon תֵּבֵל tevel ב״פ רי״ו בַּל־ bal תִּמּוֹט: timot
יִשְׂמְחוּ yismechu הַשָּׁמַיִם hashamayim י״פ טל, י״פ כוזו וְתָגֵל vetagel אותיות גלות
(שכשתהיה גאולה תהא שמוזה) הָאָרֶץ ha'aretz אלהים דההין ע״ה ; ר״ת יהוה ; ס״ת = ריבוע דס״ג
וְיֹאמְרוּ veyomru בַגּוֹיִם vagoyim יְהֹוָאדנִיאהדונהי Adonai מָלָךְ malach
ר״ת יבמ, ב״ן: יִרְעַם yir'am הַיָּם hayam ילי וּמְלוֹאוֹ umlo'o ר״ת יה״ו, אהיה ;
ס״ת מום, אלהים, אהיה אדני יַעֲלֹץ ya'alotz הַשָּׂדֶה hasade וְכָל־ vechol ילי
אֲשֶׁר־ asher בּוֹ: bo אָז az יְרַנְּנוּ yeranenu עֲצֵי atzei הַיָּעַר haya'ar
בוזוזך, סנדלפון, ערי מִלִּפְנֵי milifnei יְהֹוָאדנִיאהדונהי Adonai כִּי־ ki בָא va
לִשְׁפֹּט lishpot אֶת־ et הָאָרֶץ ha'aretz אלהים דההין ע״ה ; ר״ת לאה: הוֹדוּ hodu אהיה
לַיהֹוָאדנִיאהדונהי ladonai כִּי ki טוֹב tov והו ; כי טוב = יהוה אהיה, אום, מבה, יזל כִּי ki
לְעוֹלָם le'olam ריבוע דס״ג וי׳ אותיות דס״ג וְחַסְדּוֹ chasdo ג׳ הויות (מולא עילאה) ; ר״ת = נגה:

---

and the Lord made the Heavens. Majesty and magnificence are His presence; power and joy are His place. Render the Lord you families of nations, render the Lord honor and power. Render the Lord honor befitting His Name, bring a gift and come before Him with splendor of holiness. Tremble before Him, all dwellers of Earth, so that the world will be built and will not collapse. Heaven will rejoice and the Earth will be happy. Let the nations say: the Lord reigns! Let the sea and all therein roar; let the field and all therein exult. Then shall the forest sing before the Lord, because He has come to judge the Earth. Be grateful to the Lord for He is good; for His kindness goes on forever.

וְאִמְרוּ ve'imru הוֹשִׁיעֵנוּ hoshi'enu אֱלֹהֵי Elohei מילוי ע"ב, דמב ; ילה
יִשְׁעֵנוּ yish'enu וְקַבְּצֵנוּ vekabetzenu וְהַצִּילֵנוּ vehatzilenu מִן min
הַגּוֹיִם hagoyim לְהוֹדוֹת lehodot לְשֵׁם leshem קָדְשֶׁךָ kodshecha
לְהִשְׁתַּבֵּחַ lehishtabe'ach בִּתְהִלָּתֶךָ: bit'hilatecha בָּרוּךְ baruch
יְהֹוָהאדניאהדונהי Adonai אֱלֹהֵי Elohei מילוי ע"ב, דמב ; ילה יִשְׂרָאֵל Yisrael
יהוה אלהי ישראל = תרי"ג (מצוות) ; ס"ת = אדני מִן min הָעוֹלָם ha'olam וְעַד ve'ad
הָעוֹלָם ha'olam וַיֹּאמְרוּ vayomru כָּל chol ילי הָעָם ha'am אָמֵן amen יאהדונהי
וְהַלֵּל vehalel ללה, אדני לַיהֹוָהאדניאהדונהי ladonai: רוֹמְמוּ romemu
יְהֹוָהאדניאהדונהי Adonai אֱלֹהֵינוּ Elohenu ילה וְהִשְׁתַּחֲווּ vehishtachavu
לַהֲדֹם lahadom רַגְלָיו raglav קָדוֹשׁ kadosh הוּא hu: רוֹמְמוּ romemu
יְהֹוָהאדניאהדונהי Adonai אֱלֹהֵינוּ Elohenu ילה וְהִשְׁתַּחֲווּ vehishtachavu
לְהַר lehar קָדְשׁוֹ kodsho כִּי ki קָדוֹשׁ kadosh יְהֹוָהאדניאהדונהי Adonai
אֱלֹהֵינוּ Elohenu ילה: וְהוּא vehu רַחוּם rachum יְכַפֵּר yechaper ר"ת רי"ו
עָוֹן avon (***Abba* of the *klipa***) וְלֹא velo יַשְׁחִית yashchit (***Ima* of the *klipa***)
וְהִרְבָּה vehirba לְהָשִׁיב lehashiv אַפּוֹ apo (***Zeir* of the *klipa***) וְלֹא velo
יָעִיר ya'ir כָּל kol ילי חֲמָתוֹ chamato (***Nukva* of the *klipa***): אַתָּה Ata
יְהֹוָהאדניאהדונהי Adonai לֹא lo תִכְלָא tichla רַחֲמֶיךָ rachamecha מִמֶּנִּי mimeni
חַסְדְּךָ chasdecha ר"ת = אברהם, ח"פ אל, רי"ו ול"ב נתיבות החכמה, רמ"ח (אברים), עסמ"ב וט"ז
אותיות פשוטות וַאֲמִתְּךָ va'amitecha תָּמִיד tamid ע"ה קס"א קנ"א קמ"ג יִצְּרוּנִי yitzeruni:
זְכֹר zechor ע"ב קס"א, יהי אור ע"ה (סוד המשכת השפע מן ד' שמות ליסוד הנקרא זכור)
רַחֲמֶיךָ rachamecha יְהֹוָהאדניאהדונהי Adonai וַחֲסָדֶיךָ vachasadecha כִּי ki

---

And say: Save us, God of our salvation; gather us and save us from all nations, to give thanks to Your Holy Name, and to be glorified in saying Your praise. Blessed is the Lord, the God of Israel, from this world to the world to come! The whole nation says 'Amen' and gives praise to the Lord." (I Chronicles 16:8-36) "Exult the Lord, our God, and prostrate yourselves at His footrest, for He is sacred." (Psalms 99:5) "Exult the Lord, our God, and prostrate yourselves at His holy Mountain, for the Lord, our God, is Holy." (Psalms 99:9) "He is merciful, forgives iniquities, and does not destroy. He frequently contains His anger and does not release all His wrath." (Psalms 78:38) "And You, Lord, do not withhold Your mercy from me. May Your kindness and truth always protect me." (Psalms 40:12) "Remember Your mercy and kindness, Lord,

מֵעוֹלָם me'olam הֵמָּה hema עמם: תְּנוּ tenu עֹז oz לֵאלֹהִים lelohim אהיה אדני ; ילה

עַל־ al יִשְׂרָאֵל Yisrael גַּאֲוָתוֹ ga'avato וְעֻזּוֹ ve'uzo בַּשְּׁחָקִים bashechakim:

נוֹרָא nora אֱלֹהִים Elohim אהיה אדני ; ילה מִמִּקְדָּשֶׁיךָ mimikdashecha

אֵל El ייא״י (מילוי דס״ג) יִשְׂרָאֵל Yisrael אל ישראל = כ״ב הויות (כ״א דתפילין וא׳ דטלית)

הוּא hu נֹתֵן noten אבג״יתץ, ושר עֹז oz וְתַעֲצֻמוֹת veta'atzumot לָעָם la'am עלם

בָּרוּךְ baruch אֱלֹהִים Elohim אהיה אדני ; ילה ; ס״ת מילוי שדי (ין לת וד) ; ברוך אלהים = שדי:

EL NEKAMOT

The Name *Yud, Hei, Vav,* and *Hei* appear in this connection eleven times. The power of eleven removes the dominance of the *klipot*. There are ten *Sefirot* between our world and the Endless World. The eleventh connection is designed to give the *klipot* their nourishment so they won't try to rob us of ours. When we initiate this giving of Light, we gain control over the *klipot*. Additional support is available to us by virtue of ten spiritual giants who lived and died so they could assist us. These ten righteous souls were the incarnation of the ten brothers who sold Joseph (son of the biblical Patriarch Jacob), into slavery. In their last incarnation, Joseph's brothers were brutally murdered, but they possessed the power to leave the confines of their physical bodies so they suffered no pain. By reflecting on their actions, we can get an additional surge of power to help us lift off from the physical world.

From here until the *Aromimcha*, the Holy Name: יהוה appears eleven times in order to sort the *klipot* that are attached to the 11 curtains. When you say *El Nekamot*, you should meditate that God should avenge (*Nekama* - but the deeper meaning is to elevate, which comes from the same root - *Lehakim*) the deaths of the Ten Martyrs. When we recite *El Nekamot* it gives the Ten Martyrs' souls strength to be able to collect the sparks of the souls that are captured inside the *klipa* of *Asiyah*.

אֵל El ייא״י (מילוי דס״ג) נְקָמוֹת nekamot יְהֹוָהאדניאהדונהי Adonai ר״ת אני

אֵל El ייא״י (מילוי דס״ג) נְקָמוֹת nekamot מנק ; ר״ת = יב״ק, אלהים יהוה, אהיה אדני יהוה

הוֹפִיעַ hofi'a: הִנָּשֵׂא hinase שֹׁפֵט shofet הָאָרֶץ ha'aretz אלהים דההין ע״ה

הָשֵׁב hashev ר״ת = שדי ע״ה גְּמוּל gemul עַל־ al גֵּאִים ge'im:

---

for they are eternal." (Psalms 25:6)

"Give power to God, for His majesty is over Israel and His power is in the Heavens. God, You are awesome in Your Temples, God of Israel. He gives powers and might to the nation, blessed is God." (Psalms 68:35-36)

EL NEKAMOT

"You are the God of retributions, Lord.

God of retributions appear. Arise, Judge of the world. Repay the arrogant with their due." (Psalms 94:1-2)

לַיהֹוָה יאהדונהי ladonai הַיְשׁוּעָה hayeshu'a עַל־ al עַמְּךָ amecha

בִרְכָתֶךָ virchatecha סֶּלָה sela: יְהֹוָה יאהדונהי Adonai צְבָאוֹת Tzeva'ot פני שכינה

עִמָּנוּ imanu ריבוע ס"ג, קס"א ע"ה וד' אותיות מִשְׂגָּב־ misgav משה, מהש, ע"ב בריבוע וקס"א,

אל שדי, ד"פ אלהים ע"ה לָנוּ lanu אלהים, אהיה אדני אֱלֹהֵי Elohei מילוי ע"ב, דמב ; ילה

יַעֲקֹב Ya'akov ו' הויות, יאהדונהי אידהנויה סֶלָה sela: יְהֹוָה יאהדונהי Adonai

צְבָאוֹת Tzeva'ot פני שכינה אַשְׁרֵי ashrei אָדָם adam מ"ה ; יהוה צבאות אשרי אדם = תפארת

בֹּטֵחַ bote'ach בָּךְ: bach אדם בוטח בך = אמן ע"ה = יאהדונהי ע"ה ; בוטח בך = מילוי ע"ב ע"ה:

יְהֹוָה יאהדונהי Adonai הוֹשִׁיעָה hoshi'a יהוה ושו"ע נהורין הַמֶּלֶךְ: hamelech ר"ת יהה

יַעֲנֵנוּ ya'anenu בְיוֹם veyom ע"ה נגד, מזבח, זן, אל יהוה קָרְאֵנוּ kore'nu ר"ת יב"ק,

אלהים יהוה, אהיה אדני יהוה ; ס"ת ב"ן ועם כ' דהמלך = ע"ב: הוֹשִׁיעָה hoshi'a יהוה ושו"ע נהורין

אֶת־ et עַמֶּךָ amecha ס"ת כהת, משיח בן דוד ע"ה וּבָרֵךְ uvarech אֶת־ et

נַחֲלָתֶךָ nachalatecha וּרְעֵם ur'em וְנַשְּׂאֵם venas'em עַד־ ad הָעוֹלָם ha'olam:

נַפְשֵׁנוּ nafshenu (properly enunciate the letter *Chet* in the word "chiketa") חִכְּתָה chiketa

כהת, משיח בן דוד ע"ה לַיהֹוָה יאהדונהי ladonai (יוד הה וו הה) ; ר"ת שם נוזל

עֶזְרֵנוּ ezrenu וּמָגִנֵּנוּ umaginenu הוּא hu: כִּי־ ki בוֹ vo יִשְׂמַח yismach משיח

לִבֵּנוּ libenu כִּי ki בְשֵׁם veshem קָדְשׁוֹ kodsho בָטָחְנוּ vatachnu: יְהִי־ yehi

חַסְדְּךָ chasdecha יְהֹוָה יאהדונהי Adonai עָלֵינוּ alenu כַּאֲשֶׁר ka'asher

יִחַלְנוּ yichalnu סאל, אמן (יאהדונהי) לָךְ lach: הַרְאֵנוּ har'enu יְהֹוָה יאהדונהי Adonai

חַסְדֶּךָ chasdecha וְיֶשְׁעֲךָ veyesh'acha תִּתֶּן־ titen ב"פ כהת לָנוּ lanu אלהים, אהיה אדני:

Salvation belongs to the Lord and Your blessing is upon Your Nation, Selah." (Psalms 3:9) *"The Lord of Hosts is with us, and our strength is the God of Jacob, Selah."* (Psalms 46:12) *"The Lord of Hosts, joyful is the man that trusts in You."* (Psalms 84:13) *"Lord, redeem us. The King shall answer us upon the day we call Him."* (Psalms 20:10) *"Redeem Your Nation and bless Your inheritance, provide for them and uplift them forever."* (Psalms 28:9) *"Our soul has awaited Lord. He is our help and our shield. God, in Him our heart rejoices because we have trusted in His Holy Name. Lord, may Your kindness be upon us for we have placed our trust in You."* (Psalms 33:20-22) *"Show us Your kindness, Lord, and grant us Your salvation."* (Psalms 85:8)

קוּמָה kuma קנ״א (מקוה) עֶזְרָתָה ezrata לָּנוּ lanu אלהים, אהיה אדני וּפְדֵנוּ ufdenu
לְמַעַן lema'an חַסְדֶּךָ chasdecha: אָנֹכִי anochi יְהֹוָהאדניאהדונהי Adonai
אֱלֹהֶיךָ Elohecha ילה הַמַּעַלְךָ hama'alcha מֵאֶרֶץ me'eretz מִצְרָיִם mitz'rayim
מצר הַרְחֶב־ harchev פִּיךָ picha וַאֲמַלְאֵהוּ va'amal'ehu: אַשְׁרֵי ashrei
הָעָם ha'am שֶׁכָּכָה shekacha משה, מהש, ע״ב בריבוע וקס״א, אל שדי, ד״פ אלהים ע״ה
לּוֹ lo אַשְׁרֵי ashrei הָעָם ha'am ר״ת לאה שֶׁיְהֹוָהאדניאהדונהי sheAdonai
אֱלֹהָיו Elohav ילה: וַאֲנִי va'ani אני בְּחַסְדְּךָ bechasdecha בָטַחְתִּי vatachti
יָגֵל yagel להח לִבִּי libi בִּישׁוּעָתֶךָ bishu'atecha ר״ת = ב״ן אָשִׁירָה ashira
לַיהֹוָהאדניאהדונהי ladonai כִּי ki גָמַל gamal עָלָי alai ס״ת ילי:

AROMIMCHA

When we do negative actions, we give our Light to the *klipa* – especially those in *Asiyah* - thereby preventing *Asiyah* from elevating. Because of this spiritual heaviness, we need to get rid of the *klipa* so *Asiyah* will be able to ascend to the World of Formation. Whereas the prayer *Hodu* disconnects us from the *klipa*, *Aromimcha* helps to retrieve and elevate the sparks of Light that are still trapped inside the *klipa*. When we separate these sparks of Light from the *klipa*, the *klipa* loses all its power and let go of *Asiyah*. The word *aromimcha* means "praise" but also "raise up," in reference to the lifting up of the sparks from the *klipa*. *Aromimcha* contain 92 words, which connects us to the power of the word "*Amen*" (equals 91 plus 1 for the word itself).

In this Psalm there are ten times the Name: יהוה which correspond to the Ten *Sefirot*. And there are 92 words, which is the numerical value of יהוה אדני (plus 1 for the word itself). *Aromimcha* is comprised of words of gratitude of the souls and the sparks of *Asiyah* that were saved and rose from the *klipot* of *Asiyah*, to become *Mayin Nukvin*. These souls thank God for raising them from *She'ol*.

אֲרוֹמִמְךָ aromimcha

ענין נצוצי הקדושה העולים ויוצאים מקליפות דעשיה הנקרא נפש יְהֹוָהאדניאהדונהי Adonai *(Keter)*
כִּי ki דִלִּיתָנִי dilitani וְלֹא־ velo שִׂמַּחְתָּ simach'ta אֹיְבַי oyvai לִי li:

"Arise and help us! Redeem us for the sake of Your kindness!" (Psalms 44:27) *"I am the Lord, your God, Who took you out of the land of Egypt. Open your mouth wide and I shall fill it."* (Psalms 81:11) *"Joyful is the nation for whom all this is true; happy is the nation that the Lord is their God."* (Psalms 144:15) *"And I have trusted in Your kindness, therefore my heart shall rejoice in Your salvation. I shall sing for the Lord, for He has rewarded me."* (Psalms 13:6)

AROMIMCHA

"I exalt You, Lord, for having uplifted me and did not rejoice my enemies on my account.

יְהֹוָאֵדִנָיאהדונהי (Chochmah) Adonai אֱלֹהָי Elohai מילוי ע"ב, דמב ; ילה שִׁוַּעְתִּי shivati

אֵלֶיךָ elecha וַתִּרְפָּאֵנִי vatirpa'eni: יְהֹוָאֵדִנָיאהדונהי Adonai *(Binah)*

הֶעֱלִיתָ he'elita מִן־ min שְׁאוֹל she'ol נַפְשִׁי nafshi (elevation of the souls from *Asiyah*)

חִיִּיתַנִי chiyitani ס"ת ילי מִיָּרְדִי־ miyordi (כתיב: מיורדי) בוֹר vor: זַמְּרוּ zameru

לַיהֹוָאֵדִנָיאהדונהי ladonai *(Chesed)* חֲסִידָיו chasidav וְהוֹדוּ vehodu אהיה

לְזֵכֶר lezecher קָדְשׁוֹ kodsho: כִּי ki רֶגַע rega ג"פ אלהים וה' אותיות שבכל שם אלהים

בְּאַפּוֹ be'apo ס"ת = אלהים, אהיה אדני ; ועם ם = דוזיים = ריבוע אדני

וְחַיִּים chayim אהיה אהיה יהוה, בינה ע"ה בִּרְצוֹנוֹ birtzono כי רגע באפו וחיים ברצונו = שין דלת יוד

בָּעֶרֶב ba'erev יָלִין yalin בֶּכִי bechi ר"ת י"ד (כנגד מספר אותיות יהוה אלהינו יהוה,

וכן מספר האותיות כוזו במוכסז כוזו) וְלַבֹּקֶר velaboker רִנָּה rina בערב ילין בכי ולבקר רנה =

מטטרון שר הפנים: וַאֲנִי va'ani אני אָמַרְתִּי amarti בְשַׁלְוִי veshalvi בַּל־ bal

אֶמּוֹט emot לְעוֹלָם le'olam ריבוע ס"ג וי' אותיות דס"ג: יְהֹוָאֵדִנָיאהדונהי Adonai *(Gevurah)*

בִּרְצוֹנְךָ birtzoncha הֶעֱמַדְתָּה he'emadeta לְהַרְרִי lehareri עֹז oz

הִסְתַּרְתָּ histarta פָנֶיךָ fanecha ס"ג מ"ה ב"ן הָיִיתִי hayiti נִבְהָל nivhal:

אֵלֶיךָ elecha יְהֹוָאֵדִנָיאהדונהי Adonai *(Tiferet)* אֶקְרָא ekra וְאֶל ve'el

יְהֹוָאֵדִנָיאהדונהי Adonai *(Netzach)* אֶתְחַנָּן etchanan: מַה־ ma מ"ה בֶּצַע betza

בְּדָמִי bedami בְּרִדְתִּי berideti אֶל el ס"ת ילי שָׁחַת shachat הֲיוֹדְךָ hayodcha

עָפָר afar הֲיַגִּיד hayagid ייז, כ"ב אותיות פשוטות (= אכא) וה' אותיות סופיות (מנצפך)

אֲמִתֶּךָ amitecha: שְׁמַע־ shema יְהֹוָאֵדִנָיאהדונהי Adonai *(Hod)* וְחָנֵּנִי vechoneni

יְהֹוָאֵדִנָיאהדונהי Adonai *(Yesod)* הֱיֵה־ heyeh יהה עֹזֵר ozer לִי li מוזי:

Lord, my God,I cried out to You, and You healed me. Lord, You raised my spirit from She'ol (Hell), and kept me alive when I sunk into the pit. Sing to the Lord, you, His pious ones, and give thanks to His Holy Name. For there is quietude in His anger and there is life in His will. In the evening, one may lie down crying yet be singing in the morning. When I was tranquil, I said that I shall never fall. Lord, You upported my mountain with strength; when You hid Your ountenance, I was frightened. It is to You, Lord, that I call, and to the Lord that I plead. What gain is there in spilling my blood; to be lowered into my grave? Does the dust give thanks to You, does it proclaim Your Truth? Lord, hear me and be gracious to me. Lord, be my helper.

הָפַכְתָּ hafachta מִסְפְּדִי mispedi לְמָחוֹל lemachol לִי li ס"ת ילי

פִּתַּחְתָּ pitachta שַׂקִּי saki וַתְּאַזְּרֵנִי vate'azreni שִׂמְחָה simcha:

לְמַעַן lema'an יְזַמֶּרְךָ yezamercha כָבוֹד chavod וְלֹא velo יִדֹּם yidom (pause)

יְהֹוָהאדניאהדונהי Adonai *(Malchut)* ר"ת = אלהים, אהיה אדני אֱלֹהַי Elohai

מילוי ע"ב, דמב ; ילה לְעוֹלָם le'olam ריבוע ס"ג וי' אותיות דס"ג אוֹדֶךָּ odeka:

ADONAI MELECH

This prayer transcends the concept of time, space, and motion, as well as the illusions of the five senses. The phrase "The Lord is King, the Lord has reigned, the Lord shall reign forever and for eternity" unifies past, present, and future, into one whole, so that when we recite *Adonai Melech* (The Lord is King) with the consciousness of transformation, we can correct mistakes we made in the past, while creating a better future and accomplishing it in the present. When we live in the present, we can correct the past and affect our future.

Angels are distinct energy forces that act as a transportation system for our prayers. This connection is so powerful that even the angels remain and sing along with us, instead of just carrying our words and thoughts to the Upper Worlds.

According to the Book of *Hechalot*: "There is one angel that stands every morning in the middle of heaven, and sings the verses of '*Adonai Melech*,' and all the troops in the Upper Worlds sing with him all the way until *Barechu*." Because the angels sing *Adonai Melech* while standing, so do we.

Say these verses while standing.

חכמה-חסד ם ן בינה-גבורה ץ

יְהֹוָהאדניאהדונהי Adonai מֶלֶךְ melech יְהֹוָהאדניאהדונהי Adonai מָלָךְ malach

דעת-תפארת ף ך

יְהֹוָהאדניאהדונהי Adonai | יִמְלֹךְ yimloch (מֶלֶךְ מָלַךְ יִמְלֹךְ = מנצפך, סנדלפון, ערי)

יהוה דעת-תפארת

לְעֹלָם le'olam ריבוע דס"ג וי' אותיות דס"ג ; ר"ת ייל וָעֶד va'ed:

You have turned my mourning into a celebration for me.
You have undone my sackcloth and have girded me with joy. So that
grace shall sing for You and never be silenced, Lord, my God, I shall forever thank You." (Psalms 30:2-13)

ADONAI MELECH

The Lord is King, the Lord has reigned, the Lord shall reign forever and for eternity.

נצח ס ן הוד ץ

יְהֹוָה יאהדונהי Adonai מֶלֶךְ melech יְהֹוָה יאהדונהי Adonai מָלָךְ malach

יסוד ף ך

יְהֹוָה יאהדונהי Adonai | יִמְלֹךְ yimloch (מֶלֶךְ מָלָךְ יִמְלֹךְ = מנצפך, סנדלפון, ע״רי)

יהוה יסוד

לְעֹלָם le'olam ריבוע דס״ג ו״ אותיות דס״ג ; ר״ת ייל וָעֶד va'ed:

וְהָיָה vehaya יהוה ; יהה יְהֹוָה יאהדונהי Adonai לְמֶלֶךְ lemelech

עַל־ al כָּל kol ילי ; עמם הָאָרֶץ ha'aretz אלהים דההין ע״ה בַּיּוֹם bayom

ע״ה נגד, מזבח, זן, אל יהוה הַהוּא hahu יִהְיֶה yih'ye ייי יְהֹוָה יאהדונהי Adonai

אֶחָד echad אהבה, דאגה וּשְׁמוֹ ushmo מהש ע״ה, ע״ב בריבוע וקס״א, אל שדי ע״ה

אֶחָד echad אהבה, דאגה (בסוד אבא ואמא ואריך אנפין דעולם העשיה):

הוֹשִׁיעֵנוּ hoshi'enu | יְהֹוָה יאהדונהי Adonai אֱלֹהֵינוּ Elohenu ילה

וְקַבְּצֵנוּ vekabetzenu מִן min הַגּוֹיִם hagoyim לְהוֹדוֹת lehodot לְשֵׁם leshem

קָדְשֶׁךָ kodshecha לְהִשְׁתַּבֵּחַ lehishtabe'ach בִּתְהִלָּתֶךָ bit'hilatecha:

בָּרוּךְ baruch יְהֹוָה יאהדונהי Adonai | אֱלֹהֵי Elohei מילוי ע״ב, דמב ; ילה

יִשְׂרָאֵל Yisrael ס״ת = אדני ; יהוה אלהי ישראל = תרי״ג (מצוות) מִן־ min הָעוֹלָם ha'olam

וְעַד ve'ad הָעוֹלָם ha'olam וְאָמַר ve'amar כָּל־ kol ילי הָעָם ha'am

אָמֵן amen יאהדונהי הַלְלוּיָהּ haleluya אלהים, אהיה אדני ; ללה:

כֹּל kol ילי הַנְּשָׁמָה haneshama תְּהַלֵּל tehalel ר״ת כהת, משיח בן דוד ע״ה

יָהּ Yah הַלְלוּיָהּ haleluya אלהים, אהיה אדני ; ללה:

The Lord is King, the Lord has reigned, the Lord shall reign forever and for eternity.
"And the Lord has always been King over the whole earth.
And upon that day, the Lord shall be One and His Name One." (Zecharyah 14:9)

HOSHI'ENU

"Save us, Lord, our God, and gather us from amongst the nations to give thanks to Your Holy Name and be glorified in Your praise. Blessed is the Lord, the God of Israel, from this world to the World to Come, and the whole nation said: Amen, Praise the Lord." (Psalms 106:47-48)
"Every soul will praise the Lord, Praise the Lord!" (Psalms 150:6)

LAMNATZE'ACH

In this Psalm there are 13 verses corresponding to the Thirteen Atributes of Mercy and, six times the Name: יהוה corresponding to the Six Edges of *Zeir Anpin*. Meditate for the first *Ma'amar* (Utterance) of Creation: בראשית ברא אלהים את השמים ואת הארץ.

(א-אל) לַמְנַצֵּחַ lamnatze'ach מִזְמוֹר mizmor לְדָוִד leDavid:

(ב-רחום) הַשָּׁמַיִם hashamayim י״פ טל, י״פ כוזו מְסַפְּרִים mesaperim כְּבוֹד kevod

אֵל El ייא״י (מילוי דס״ג) ; ר״ת מכאל (מיכאל = ננא) ; כבוד אל = ס״ג (יוד הי ואו הי - דעת דנוקבא)

וּמַעֲשֵׂה uma'ase יָדָיו yadav מַגִּיד magid הָרָקִיעַ haraki'a:

(ג-וחנון) יוֹם yom ע״ה נגד, מזבח, זן, אל יהוה לְיוֹם leyom ע״ה נגד, מזבח, זן, אל יהוה

יַבִּיעַ yabi'a אֹמֶר omer וְלַיְלָה velayla מלה לְּלַיְלָה lelayla מלה

יְחַוֶּה־ yechave דָּעַת da'at: (ד-ארך) אֵין־ en אֹמֶר omer וְאֵין ve'en

דְּבָרִים devarim ראה בְּלִי beli נִשְׁמָע nishma קוֹלָם kolam:

(ה-אפים) בְּכָל־ bechol ב״ן, לכב הָאָרֶץ ha'aretz אלהים דההין ע״ה

יָצָא yatza קַוָּם kavam וּבִקְצֵה uviktze תֵבֵל tevel ב״פ רי״ו

מִלֵּיהֶם milehem לַשֶּׁמֶשׁ lashemesh שָׂם־ sam אֹהֶל ohel בָּהֶם bahem:

(ו-ורב חסד) וְהוּא vehu כְּחָתָן kechatan יֹצֵא yotze מֵחֻפָּתוֹ mechupato

יָשִׂישׂ yasis כְּגִבּוֹר kegibor לָרוּץ larutz אֹרַח orach:

(ז-ואמת) מִקְצֵה miktze הַשָּׁמַיִם hashamayim י״פ טל, י״פ כוזו

מוֹצָאוֹ motza'o וּתְקוּפָתוֹ utkufato עַל־ al קְצוֹתָם ketzotam

וְאֵין ve'en נִסְתָּר nistar ב״פ מצר מֵחַמָּתוֹ mechamato:

LAMNATZE'ACH

"1) To the conductor, a song of David:

2) The heavens declare the glory of God and the expanse of the sky tells of His handiwork. 3) Day following day brings expressions of praise, and night following night bespeaks wisdom. 4) There is no speech and there are no words, their sound is unheard. 5) Their line goes forth throughout the earth, and their words reach the farthest ends of the land. He had set up a tent in their midst. 6) And He is like a groom coming forth from his bridal tent, rejoicing like a warrior to run the course. 7) The end of the Heavens is its source and its circuit is to their other end. Nothing is hidden from its heat.

The kabbalists wrote: This Psalm has a great and magnificent ability of protection. From here on we have six consecutive verses of five words each, and the second word of each verse is: יהוה. You should count the words with your right hand fingers in the following way: say the first word and put your thumb down, then say the second word which is יהוה and keep the index finger up, then say the third word and put the middle finger down, then the fourth word and put the ring finger down, and while saying the fifth word put the little finger down. And while doing so meditate that the Creator will straighten those who are bent over and also, that all your spiritual enemies will surrender and you would defeat them.

(וז-נצר וחסד) תּוֹרַת torat יְהֹוָהאדניאהדונהי Adonai ***(Chesed)*** תְּמִימָה temima

מְשִׁיבַת meshivat נָפֶשׁ nafesh עֵדוּת edut יְהֹוָהאדניאהדונהי Adonai ***(Gevurah)***

נֶאֱמָנָה ne'emana מַחְכִּימַת machkimat פֶּתִי peti: (ט-לאלפים) פִּקּוּדֵי pikudei מנק

יְהֹוָהאדניאהדונהי Adonai ***(Tiferet)*** יְשָׁרִים yesharim מְשַׂמְּחֵי־ mesamchei

לֵב lev מִצְוַת mitzvat יְהֹוָהאדניאהדונהי Adonai ***(Netzach)*** בָּרָה bara

מְאִירַת me'irat עֵינָיִם enayim ריבוע מ"ה: (י-נשא עון) יִרְאַת yir'at

יְהֹוָהאדניאהדונהי Adonai ***(Hod)*** טְהוֹרָה tehora עוֹמֶדֶת omedet

לָעַד la'ad ב"פ ב"ן מִשְׁפְּטֵי־ mishpetei יוהוואדניאהדונהי Adonai ***(Yesod)***

אֱמֶת emet אהיה פעמים אהיה, ז"פ ס"ג צָדְקוּ tzadku יַחְדָּו yachdav:

(י"א-ופשע) הַנֶּחֱמָדִים hanechemadim מִזָּהָב mizahav וּמִפַּז umipaz רָב rav

וּמְתוּקִים umtukim מִדְּבַשׁ midevash שו"ר דשופר ועם י"ד האוזן הרי ש"ך דינין דגדלות

וְנֹפֶת venofet צוּפִים tzufim: גַּם־ gam עַבְדְּךָ avdecha פוי, אל אדני

נִזְהָר nizhar בָּהֶם bahem בְּשָׁמְרָם beshomram עֵקֶב ekev ב"פ מום רָב rav:

---

8) *The Torah of the Lord* (Chesed) *is perfect and restores the soul.*
The testimony of the Lord (Gevurah) *is trustworthy, making the simple wise.*

9) *The orders of the Lord* (Tiferet) *are upright and they gladden the heart.*
The commandment of the Lord (Netzach) *is clear and enlightens the eyes.*

10) *The fear of the Lord* (Hod) *is pure and endures forever.*
The judgments of the Lord (Yesod) *are true and altogether righteous.*

11) *They are more desirable than gold and many precious stones, and sweeter than honey and the dripping of the combs. Even Your servant is careful of them, for in observing them there is great reward.*

(י"ב-וזוטאה) שְׁגִיאוֹת shegi'ot מִי־ mi יל"י יָבִין yavin מִנִּסְתָּרוֹת ministarot

נַקֵּנִי nakeni: (י"ג-ונקה) גַּם gam מִזֵּדִים mizedim חֲשֹׂךְ chasoch

שך נצוצות של ו' המלכים עַבְדֶּךָ avdecha פו"י, אל אדנ"י אַל־ al יִמְשְׁלוּ־ yimshelu

בִי vi אָז az אֵיתָם etam וְנִקֵּיתִי veniketi מִפֶּשַׁע mipesha רָב rav:

מ"ב אותיות בפסוק

יִהְיוּ yih'yu אל (ייא"י מילוי דס"ג) לְרָצוֹן leratzon מהש ע"ה, ע"ב בריבוע וקס"א ע"ה, אל שד"י ע"ה

אִמְרֵי־ imrei פִי fi ר"ת המספר אֶלֶף = אלף למד שין דלת יוד ע"ה

וְהֶגְיוֹן vehegyon לִבִּי libi לְפָנֶיךָ lefanecha ס"ג מ"ה ב"ן יְהֹוָהאדניאהדונהי Adonai

צוּרִי tzuri וְגֹאֲלִי vego'ali:

RANENU

There are 22 verses in this Psalm, indicating a connection to the 22 letters of the Aramaic alphabet. Because the Aramaic letters are the actual instruments of Creation, this prayer helps to inject order and the power of Creation into chaotic areas in our lives that need rejuvenation. Human beings are built from a four-letter genetic alphabet (A, T, C, and G) found in our DNA, with each letter representing a different chemical. The letters combine to create a set of instructions to build a human being. According to Kabbalah, the universe is built from the 22-letter genetic alphabet of the Aramaic letters, with each of the 22 letters representing a particular energy force; these forces combine in various sequences to create our universe.

In the next two Psalms there are great and deep secrets, so be cautious to say them meticulously. Because if one of the words is missing or is swallowed one would lose great goodness.

In this Psalm there are 161 words like the numerical value of the Name: אלף הי יוד הי. Also there are 22 verses corresponding to the 22 letters of the Aramaic alphabet which is the numerical value of the Name: **אכא** from the 72 Names of God.

Also meditate for the second *Ma'amar* (Utterance) of Creation: **יהי אור** ("and God said: Let there be light" - The Light was first created for the righteous and then concealed for the future to come.)

---

12) Yet, You, Who can discern mistakes, from unperceived faults cleanse me. 13) And, also from intentional sins, restrain Your servant. Let them not control me; then I shall be perfect and cleansed of great transgressions. May the words of my mouth and the thoughts of my heart find favor before You, Lord, my Rock and my Redeemer." (Psalms 19)

רַנְּנוּ ranenu צַדִּיקִים tzadikim

Meditate on the Name: אהיה דיודין (אלף הי יוד הי), because it is a correction to remove anger.

בַּיהֹוָאדנָיאהדונהי badonai לַיְשָׁרִים laysharim נָאוָה nava תְהִלָּה tehila

הוֹדוּ hodu אהיה לַיהֹוָאדנָיאהדונהי ladonai ע"ה אמת, אהיה פעמים אהיה, ד"פ ס"ג:

בְּכִנּוֹר bechinor ס"ת אלף למד יהוה בְּנֵבֶל benevel עָשׂוֹר asor ר"ת ע"ב, ריבוע יהוה

זַמְּרוּ zameru לוֹ lo ר"ת מילוי ס"ג (וד י או י) ; ס"ת = רמ"ב [רלב (עסמ"ב) וי' אותיות אלף הי יוד הי]:

שִׁירוּ־ shiru לוֹ lo שִׁיר shir חָדָשׁ chadash י"ב הויות, קס"א קנ"א

הֵיטִיבוּ hetivu נַגֵּן nagen בִּתְרוּעָה bitru'a: כִּי־ ki יָשָׁר yashar

דְּבַר־ devar ראה יְהֹוָאדנָיאהדונהי Adonai וְכָל־ vechol ילי מַעֲשֵׂהוּ ma'asehu

בֶּאֱמוּנָה be'emuna ר"ת ומב: אֹהֵב ohev צְדָקָה tzedaka ע"ה ריבוע אלהים

וּמִשְׁפָּט umishpat ע"ה ה"פ אלהים חֶסֶד chesed ע"ב, ריבוע יהוה יְהֹוָאדנָיאהדונהי Adonai

מָלְאָה mal'a הָאָרֶץ ha'aretz אלהים דההין ע"ה: בִּדְבַר bidvar ראה

יְהֹוָאדנָיאהדונהי Adonai שָׁמַיִם shamayim י"פ טל, י"פ כוזו נַעֲשׂוּ na'asu

וּבְרוּחַ uvru'ach פִּיו piv כָּל־ kol ילי צְבָאָם tzeva'am: כֹּנֵס kones כַּנֵּד kaned

מֵי mei ילי הַיָּם hayam ילי נֹתֵן noten אבגיתץ, ושר בְּאוֹצָרוֹת be'otzarot

תְּהוֹמוֹת tehomot: יִירְאוּ yir'u מֵיְהֹוָאדנָיאהדונהי meAdonai כָּל־ kol ילי

הָאָרֶץ ha'aretz אלהים דההין ע"ה מִמֶּנּוּ mimenu יָגוּרוּ yaguru כָּל kol ילי

יֹשְׁבֵי yoshvei תֵבֵל tevel ב"פ רי"ו: כִּי ki הוּא hu אָמַר amar וַיֶּהִי vayehi

הוּא־ hu צִוָּה tziva וַיַּעֲמֹד vaya'amod: יְהֹוָאדנָיאהדונהי Adonai הֵפִיר hefir

עֲצַת־ atzat גּוֹיִם goyim הֵנִיא heni מַחְשְׁבוֹת machshevot עַמִּים amim:

RANENU

"Sing joyfully, righteous ones for the Lord, because it is for the upright that praise is fitting. Give thanks to the Lord with a harp, and with the ten-stringed lyre play melodies to Him. Sing a new song to Him and play well with the sound of trumpets, for the word of the Lord is upright and, all His deeds He did with faithfulness. He loves charity and justice, and the kindness of the Lord fills the Earth. By the Word of the Lord, the Heavens were made, by the Breath of His Mouth, all their hosts. He gathers the waters of the sea like a wall and He places the deep waters in vaults. All the Earth will be fearful of the Lord and of Him will be, in dread, all the inhabitants of the world. For He spoke and it came to be, He commanded and it stood firm. The Lord annuls the counsel of the nations and He balks the designs of peoples.

עֲצַת atzat יְהֹוָ(אדני)ה יאהדונהי Adonai לְעוֹלָם le'olam ריבוע ס"ג י' ס"ג אותיות דס"ג

תַּעֲמֹד ta'amod מַחְשְׁבוֹת machshevot לִבּוֹ libo לְדֹר ledor וָדֹר vador ר"ו:

אַשְׁרֵי ashrei הַגּוֹי hagoi אֲשֶׁר־ asher יְהֹוָ(אדני)ה יאהדונהי Adonai

אֱלֹהָיו Elohav ילה הָעָם ha'am בָּחַר bachar לְנַחֲלָה lenachala לוֹ lo:

מִשָּׁמַיִם mishamayim י"פ טל, י"פ כוזו הִבִּיט hibit יְהֹוָ(אדני)ה יאהדונהי Adonai

רָאָה ra'a ראה אֶת־ et כָּל־ kol ילי בְּנֵי benei הָאָדָם ha'adam מ"ה:

מִמְּכוֹן־ mimechon שִׁבְתּוֹ shivto הִשְׁגִּיחַ hishgi'ach אֶל el כָּל־ kol ילי

יֹשְׁבֵי yoshvei הָאָרֶץ ha'aretz אלהים דההין ע"ה: הַיֹּצֵר hayotzer יַחַד yachad

לִבָּם libam הַמֵּבִין hamevin אֶל־ el כָּל־ kol ילי מַעֲשֵׂיהֶם ma'asehem:

אֵין־ en הַמֶּלֶךְ hamelech נוֹשָׁע nosha בְּרָב־ berov חָיִל chayil ומב גִּבּוֹר gibor

לֹא־ lo יִנָּצֵל yinatzel בְּרָב־ berov כֹּחַ ko'ach: שֶׁקֶר sheker הַסּוּס hasus

ריבוע אדני, כוק לִתְשׁוּעָה litshu'a וּבְרֹב uvrov י"פ אהיה וְחֵילוֹ chelo לֹא lo

יְמַלֵּט yemalet: הִנֵּה hine עֵין en ריבוע מ"ה יְהֹוָ(אדני)ה יאהדונהי Adonai

אֶל־ el ננא יְרֵאָיו yere'av לַמְיַחֲלִים lamyachalim לְחַסְדּוֹ lechasdo ג' הויות = מזלא

(להמשיך הארה ממזלא עילאה): לְהַצִּיל lehatzil מִמָּוֶת mimavet נַפְשָׁם nafsham

וּלְחַיּוֹתָם ulchayotam בָּרָעָב bara'av: נַפְשֵׁנוּ nafshenu (צריך להדגיש הויות)

חִכְּתָה chiketa כהת, משיח בן דוד ע"ה לַיהֹוָ(אדני)ה יאהדונהי ladonai (יוד הה וו הה);

ר"ת שם נוזל עֶזְרֵנוּ ezrenu וּמָגִנֵּנוּ umaginenu הוּא hu: כִּי־ ki בוֹ vo

יִשְׂמַח yismach משיח לִבֵּנוּ libenu כִּי ki בְּשֵׁם veshem קָדְשׁוֹ kodsho

בָטָחְנוּ vatachnu: יְהִי־ yehi חַסְדְּךָ chasdecha יְהֹוָ(אדני)ה יאהדונהי Adonai

עָלֵינוּ alenu כַּאֲשֶׁר ka'asher יִחַלְנוּ yichalnu סאל, אמן (יאהדונהי) לָךְ lach:

The counsel of the Lord will endure forever and the designs of His heart throughout the generations. Praiseworthy is the nation whose God is the Lord, the people which He chose for His own heritage. From His dwelling place, the Lord looks down and He sees all the inhabitants of the earth. He fashions their hearts into oneness and He comprehends all their deeds. A king is not saved by a great army nor is a hero rescued by great strength. A horse is a false savior, despite its great strength, it provides no escape. Behold, the Eye of the Lord is on those who fear Him, upon those who await His kindness. to rescue their soul from death and to sustain them in famine. Our soul waited for the Lord for He is our help and our shield; for, in Him, will our hearts be glad; for in His Holy Name, we trusted. May Your kindness, Lord, be upon us just as we awaited You." (Psalms 33).

LEDAVID

In this Psalm there are 161 words like the numerical value of the Name: אלף הי יוד הי. Also there are 22 verses correspond to the 22 letters of the Aramaic alphabet which is the numerical value of the Name: אכא from the 72 Names of God. And each verse begins with one of the letters of the alphabet in consecutive order (with one exception, the letter ו *Vav* does not appear. Instead, at the end there is an extra verse starting with the letter פ *Pei* which in *Atbash* is the letter *Vav*).

Also meditate for the third *Ma'amar* (Utterance) of Creation: יהי רקיע ("and God said: Let there be an expanse" - The expanse separated the water under the expanse from the water above it.)

לְדָוִד leDavid

בְּשַׁנּוֹתוֹ beshanoto אֶת־ et טַעְמוֹ ta'mo לִפְנֵי lifnei אֲבִימֶלֶךְ Avimelech

(אבינו שבשמים) וַיְגָרְשֵׁהוּ vay'garshehu (לסמא"ל) וַיֵּלַךְ vayelach כלי:

אֲבָרְכָה avarcha אֶת־ et יְהֹוָה יאהדונהי Adonai בְּכָל־ bechol ב"ן, לכב עֵת et

תָּמִיד tamid ע"ה קס"א קנ"א קמ"ג תְּהִלָּתוֹ tehilato בְּפִי befi:

בַּיהֹוָה יאהדונהי badonai תִּתְהַלֵּל tit'halel נַפְשִׁי nafshi

יִשְׁמְעוּ yishme'u עֲנָוִים anavim וְיִשְׂמָחוּ veyismachu:

גַּדְּלוּ gadelu לַיהֹוָה יאהדונהי ladonai אִתִּי iti וּנְרוֹמְמָה unromema

שְׁמוֹ shemo מהש ע"ה, ע"ב בריבוע וקס"א ע"ה, אל שדי ע"ה יַחְדָּו yachdav:

דָּרַשְׁתִּי darashti אֶת־ et יְהֹוָה יאהדונהי Adonai וְעָנָנִי ve'anani

ר"ת ודאי, אהיה (ובשם זה עלה משה למרום והוא מגן ממלאכי חבלה) ; ס"ת = כהת, משיח בן דוד ע"ה

וּמִכָּל־ umikol ילי מְגוּרוֹתַי megurotai הִצִּילָנִי hitzilani נתה:

הִבִּיטוּ hibitu אֵלָיו elav וְנָהָרוּ venaharu

וּפְנֵיהֶם ufnehem אַל־ al יֶחְפָּרוּ yechparu:

זֶה ze עָנִי ani ריבוע מ"ה קָרָא kara וַיהֹוָה יאהדונהי vadonai

שָׁמֵעַ shame'a וּמִכָּל־ umikol ילי צָרוֹתָיו tzarotav הוֹשִׁיעוֹ hoshi'o:

LEDAVID

'From David, when he disguised his sanity before Abimelech, who drove him out and he left. I bless the Lord at all times; His praise is always in my mouth. In God does my soul glory, may humble ones hear and be glad. Declare the greatness of the Lord with me and let us exalt His Name together. I sought out the Lord and He answered me and from all my fears, He delivered me. They look to Him and become radiant and their faces were not shamed. This poor man calls and the Lord hears and from all his troubles He saved him.

חֹנֶה chone מַלְאַךְ־ mal'ach יְהֹוָהאדניאהדונהי Adonai

סָבִיב saviv לִירֵאָיו lire'av וַיְחַלְּצֵם vay'chaletzem:

טַעֲמוּ ta'amu וּרְאוּ ur'u כִּי־ ki טוֹב tov והו ; כי טוב = יהוה אהיה, אום, מבה, יזל

יְהֹוָהאדניאהדונהי Adonai אַשְׁרֵי ashrei הַגֶּבֶר hagever יֶחֱסֶה־ yechese בּוֹ bo:

יְראוּ yir'u אֶת־ et יְהֹוָהאדניאהדונהי Adonai קְדשָׁיו kedoshav

כִּי־ ki אֵין en מַחְסוֹר machsor לִירֵאָיו lire'av:

כְּפִירִים kefirim רָשׁוּ rashu וְרָעֵבוּ vera'evu וְדֹרְשֵׁי vedorshei

יְהֹוָהאדניאהדונהי Adonai לֹא־ lo יַחְסְרוּ yachseru כָל־ chol ילי טוֹב tov והו:

לְכוּ־ lechu בָנִים vanim שִׁמְעוּ־ shim'u לִי li

יִרְאַת yir'at יְהֹוָהאדניאהדונהי Adonai אֲלַמֶּדְכֶם alamedchem:

מִי־ mi ילי הָאִישׁ ha'ish הֶחָפֵץ hechafetz חַיִּים chayim אהיה אהיה יהוה, בינה ע"ה

אֹהֵב ohev יָמִים yamim נלך לִרְאוֹת lir'ot טוֹב tov והו:

נְצֹר netzor לְשׁוֹנְךָ leshoncha מֵרָע mera

וּשְׂפָתֶיךָ usfatecha מִדַּבֵּר midaber ראה מִרְמָה mirma:

סוּר sur מֵרָע mera וַעֲשֵׂה־ va'aseh טוֹב tov והו

בַּקֵּשׁ bakesh שָׁלוֹם shalom וְרָדְפֵהוּ verodfehu:

עֵינֵי enei ריבוע מ"ה יְהֹוָהאדניאהדונהי Adonai אֶל־ el צַדִּיקִים tzadikim עלם

וְאָזְנָיו ve'oznav יוד הי ואו הה אֶל־ el שַׁוְעָתָם shavatam:

The angel of the Lord encamps around those who fear Him and releases them. Taste and see that the Lord is good; joyful is the man who takes refuge in Him. Fear the Lord all His holy ones, for those who fear Him shall not lack anything. Young lions may want and hunger, but those who seek the Lord shall not lack any good. Go, sons, heed me and I shall teach you the fear of the Lord. Who is the man who desires life and who loves days of seeing good? Guard your tongue from evil and your lips from speaking deceit. Turn away from evil and do good, seek peace and pursue it. The Eyes of the Lord are toward the righteous and His Ears to their cry.

פְּנֵי penei וחכמה בינה (the face of anger) יְהֹוָה אהדונהי Adonai

בְּעֹשֵׂי be'osei רָע ra לְהַכְרִית lehachrit מֵאֶרֶץ me'eretz זִכְרָם zichram מצר

(including the everlasting Luz bone, while He saves all the bones of the righteous):

צָעֲקוּ tza'aku וַיהֹוָה אהדונהי vadonai שָׁמֵעַ shame'a

וּמִכָּל־ umikol ילי צָרוֹתָם tzarotam הִצִּילָם hitzilam:

קָרוֹב karov יְהֹוָה אהדונהי Adonai לְנִשְׁבְּרֵי־ lenishberei לֵב lev

(the seven kings who died) וְאֶת־ ve'et דַּכְּאֵי־ dakei רוּחַ ru'ach יוֹשִׁיעַ yoshia:

רַבּוֹת rabot רָעוֹת ra'ot צַדִּיק tzadik

וּמִכֻּלָּם umikulam יַצִּילֶנּוּ yatzilenu יְהֹוָה אהדונהי Adonai:

שֹׁמֵר shomer כָּל־ kol ילי עַצְמוֹתָיו atzmotav

אַחַת achat מֵהֵנָּה mehena לֹא lo נִשְׁבָּרָה nishbara:

תְּמוֹתֵת temotet רָשָׁע rasha רָעָה ra'a רהע

וְשֹׂנְאֵי veson'ei צַדִּיק tzadik יֶאְשָׁמוּ yeshamu:

פּוֹדֶה pode יְהֹוָה אהדונהי Adonai נֶפֶשׁ nefesh עֲבָדָיו avadav

וְלֹא velo יֶאְשְׁמוּ ye'eshemu כָּל kol ילי הַחוֹסִים hachosim בּוֹ bo:

TEFILA LEMOSHE

This prayer gives us the ability to connect to the consciousness of Moses, the greatest prophet that ever lived. Moses was the epitome of pure sharing, with unconditional love and caring for others. It was this attribute, along with his close, profound relationship with God that gave him all his power.

The Face (the Face of anger) of the Lord is against evildoers, to cut off their memory from the Earth (including the everlasting Luz bone, while He saves all the bones of the righteous). They cried out and the Lord heeds; from all their troubles, He rescued them. The Lord is close to the brokenhearted (the seven kings who died) and He saves those who are crushed in spirit. Many are the mishaps of the righteous, but, from them all, the Lord rescues him. He guards all His bones such that not even one of them was broken. You shall bring an evil death-blow upon the wicked and those who hate the righteous shall be condemned. The Lord redeems the souls of His servants, and all those who seek refuge in Him shall not be condemned." (Psalms 34)

Meditate for the fourth *Ma'amar* (Utterance) of Creation:
יקוו המים מתחת השמים אל מקום אחד ותראה היבשה ("and God said: Let the water under the sky be gathered to one place, and let dry ground appear" – as it says (hereinafter): "May Your works be seen upon Your servants" – 'Your works', meaning the revelation of the land.)

תְּפִלָּה tefila בא"ת ב"ש אֻכְּצַ = ב"ן אדני וניקודה ע"ה יוד הי וו הה לְמֹשֶׁה leMoshe

מהש, ע"ב בריבוע וקס"א, אל שדי, ד"פ אלהים ע"ה אִישׁ ish הָאֱלֹהִים haElohim ילה ;

ר"ת לאה (רומז לז"א כבוד ישראל המזווג עם לאה) ; ס"ת משה (כלת משה)

אֲדֹנָי Adonai ללה מָעוֹן ma'on אַתָּה Ata הָיִיתָ hayita לָּנוּ lanu אלהים, אהיה אדני

בְּדֹר bedor ר"ת הבל (שהוא משה גלגול הבל שמתגלגל בכל דור להורות בני דורו) וָדֹר vador רי"ו:

בְּטֶרֶם beterem הָרִים harim יֻלָּדוּ yuladu וַתְּחוֹלֵל vatecholel אֶרֶץ eretz

וְתֵבֵל vetevel ב"פ רי"ו וּמֵעוֹלָם ume'olam עַד־ ad עוֹלָם olam

אַתָּה Ata אֵל el ייא" (מילוי דס"ג): תָּשֵׁב tashev אֱנוֹשׁ enosh עַד־ ad

דַּכָּא daka וַתֹּאמֶר vatomer שׁוּבוּ shuvu בְנֵי־ venei אָדָם adam מ"ה:

כִּי ki אֶלֶף elef מספר אֶלֶף = אלף למד שין דלת יוד ע"ה שָׁנִים shanim

בְּעֵינֶיךָ be'enecha ע"ה קס"א ; ריבוע מ"ה כְּיוֹם keyom ע"ה נגד, מזבח, זן, אל יהוה

אֶתְמוֹל etmol כִּי ki יַעֲבֹר ya'avor וְאַשְׁמוּרָה ve'ashmura בַלָּיְלָה valayla מלה:

זְרַמְתָּם zeramtam שֵׁנָה shena יִהְיוּ yih'yu אל (ייא" מילוי דס"ג)

בַּבֹּקֶר baboker כֶּחָצִיר kechatzir יַחֲלֹף yachalof: בַּבֹּקֶר baboker יָצִיץ yatzitz

וְחָלָף vechalaf לָעֶרֶב la'erev יְמוֹלֵל yemolel וְיָבֵשׁ veyavesh: כִּי־ ki

כָלִינוּ chalinu בְאַפֶּךָ ve'apecha וּבַחֲמָתְךָ uvachamat'cha נִבְהָלְנוּ nivhalnu:

TEFILA LEMOSHE

"A prayer of Moses, the man of God:

God, You have been a dwelling place for us in all generations, before the mountains were born and You had not yet fashioned the earth and the inhabited land. Forever and for eternity, You are God. You reduce man to a pulp and You say: Repent you sons of man. Because a thousand years in Your eyes are but a bygone yesterday and like a watch in the night. You flood them away and they become sleep-like, by morning they are like grass that withers. In the morning it blossoms and becomes rejuvenated, by evening it is cut down and brittle. We are consumed by Your fury and we are confounded by Your wrath.

שַׁתָּה shata (כתיב שת) עֲוֺנֹתֵינוּ avonotenu לְנֶגְדֶּךָ lenegdecha עֲלֻמֵנוּ alumenu
לִמְאוֹר lim'or פָּנֶיךָ panecha ס״ג מ״ה ב״ן: כִּי ki כָל chol ילי יָמֵינוּ yamenu
פָּנוּ panu בְעֶבְרָתֶךָ ve'evratecha כִּלִּינוּ kilinu שָׁנֵינוּ shanenu כְמוֹ־ chemo
הֶגֶה: hege יְמֵי־ yemei שְׁנוֹתֵינוּ shenotenu בָהֶם vahem שִׁבְעִים shiv'im
שָׁנָה shana וְאִם ve'im יוהך, מ״א אותיות דפשוט, דמילוי ודמילוי דמילוי דאהיה ע״ה
בִּגְבוּרֹת bigvurot שְׁמוֹנִים shemonim שָׁנָה shana וְרָהְבָּם verahbam
עָמָל amal וָאָוֶן va'aven כִּי־ ki גָז gaz חִישׁ chish וַנָּעֻפָה: vana'ufa מִי־ mi ילי
יוֹדֵעַ yode'a עֹז oz אַפֶּךָ apecha וּכְיִרְאָתְךָ uch'yir'atcha עֶבְרָתֶךָ: evratecha
לִמְנוֹת limnot יָמֵינוּ yamenu כֵּן ken הוֹדַע hoda וְנָבִא venavi לְבַב levav בוכו
חָכְמָה chochma במילוי = תרי״ג (מצוות): שׁוּבָה shuva הוש יְהֹוָהאדניאהדונהי Adonai
עַד־ ad מָתָי matai וְהִנָּחֵם vehinachem עַל־ al עֲבָדֶיךָ avadecha דמב, מילוי דע״ב:
שַׂבְּעֵנוּ sabe'enu בַבֹּקֶר vaboker חַסְדֶּךָ chasdecha וּנְרַנְּנָה unranena
וְנִשְׂמְחָה venismecha בְּכָל־ bechol ב״ן, לכב יָמֵינוּ: yamenu שַׂמְּחֵנוּ samchenu
כִּימוֹת kimot עִנִּיתָנוּ initanu שְׁנוֹת shenot רָאִינוּ ra'inu רָעָה ra'a רהע:
יֵרָאֶה yera'e ריי אֶל־ el עֲבָדֶיךָ avadecha פָעֳלֶךָ fa'olecha וַהֲדָרְךָ vahadarcha
עַל־ al בְּנֵיהֶם: benehem וִיהִי vihi נֹעַם no'am (נעם עליון) אֲדֹנָי Adonai ללה
אֱלֹהֵינוּ Elohenu ילה עָלֵינוּ alenu וּמַעֲשֵׂה uma'ase יָדֵינוּ yadenu
כּוֹנְנָה konena עָלֵינוּ alenu וּמַעֲשֵׂה uma'ase יָדֵינוּ yadenu כּוֹנְנֵהוּ: konenehu

---

You have set our iniquities before Yourself, our immaturity before the Light of Your countenance. For all our days passed by because of Your anger. We consumed our years like a fleeting thought. The days of our years among them are seventy years, and if with strength, eighty years, their proudest success is but toil and pain, for it is cut off swiftly and we fly away. Who knows the power of Your fury? As You are feared, so is Your anger. According to the count of our days so may You teach us, and then we shall acquire a heart of wisdom. Return Lord, for how much longer? Relent concerning Your servants. Satisfy us in the morning with Your kindness, then we shall sing out and rejoice throughout our days. Gladden us according to the day that You had afflicted us, the years when we saw evil. May Your works be seen upon Your servants and Your majesty upon their children. And may the pleasantness of the Lord, our God, be upon us and may He establish the work of our hands for us and may the work of our hands establish Him." (Psalms 90)

YOSHEV

Every positive action creates positive angels, and every negative action creates negative angels. Angels are distinct forces of spiritual energy. Negative angels or energy forces disrupt our lives in many ways. For example, oftentimes people do not understand what we are trying to say to them, or we do not fully understand what is being said to us. It is as though an unseen interference creates confusion and sends mixed signals. Miscommunication eventually leads to misunderstanding, which in turn can lead to fights, arguments, and, all too often, a lot of pain. At other times, things go wrong; no matter what we do, nothing seems to turn things around.

Meditate for the fifth *Ma'amar* (Utterance) of Creation: תדשא הארץ דשא ("and God said: Let the land produce vegetation" – vegetation was created to sustain all creatures and they should dwell in its shade.)

יֹשֵׁב yoshev בְּסֵתֶר beseter ב״פ מצר עֶלְיוֹן elyon בְּצֵל betzel שַׁדַּי Shadai

יִתְלוֹנָן yitlonan: אֹמַר omar לַיהֹוָהאדניאהדונהי ladonai מַחְסִי machsi

וּמְצוּדָתִי umtzudati אֱלֹהַי Elohai מילוי דע״ב, דמב ; ילה ; ר״ת אום, מבה, יזל

אֶבְטַח־ evtach סיט בּוֹ bo: כִּי ki הוּא hu יַצִּילְךָ yatzilcha

מִפַּח mipach ר״ת מיה יָקוּשׁ yakush מִדֶּבֶר midever הַוּוֹת havot:

בְּאֶבְרָתוֹ be'evrato יָסֶךְ yasech לָךְ lach וְתַחַת־ vetachat כְּנָפָיו kenafav

תֶּחְסֶה techse צִנָּה tzina וְסֹחֵרָה vesochera אֲמִתּוֹ amito: לֹא־ lo תִירָא tira

מִפַּחַד mipachad לָיְלָה layla מלה מֵחֵץ mechetz יָעוּף ya'uf יוֹמָם yomam:

מִדֶּבֶר midever בָּאֹפֶל ba'ofel יַהֲלֹךְ yahaloch מִקֶּטֶב miketev יָשׁוּד yashud

צָהֳרָיִם tzahorayim: יִפֹּל yipol מִצִּדְּךָ mitzidecha אֶלֶף elef מספר אֶלֶף = אלף למד שין

דלת יוד ע״ה וּרְבָבָה urvava מִימִינֶךָ miminecha אֵלֶיךָ elecha לֹא lo יִגָּשׁ yigash:

YOSHEV

"One who finds refuge in the Supreme One and dwells in the shade of Shaddai, I say of the Lord: He is my refuge and my fortress, my God in Whom I put my trust. For He shall rescue you from the snare of the trap and from destructive pestilence. He shall cover you with his pinion and you shall find refuge under his wings. His truth is a shield and armor. You shall not fear the terror of the nights, of the arrow that flies by day, of pestilence that moves in the darkness or of the destruction that strikes at noon. A thousand will fall at your side and ten thousand at your right, yet they will not approach you.

רַק rak בְּעֵינֶיךָ be'enecha ע"ה קס"א ; ריבוע מ"ה תַבִּיט tabit וְשִׁלֻּמַת veshilumat
רְשָׁעִים resha'im תִּרְאֶה: tir'e כִּי־ ki אַתָּה Ata יְהֹוָהאדני אהדונהי Adonai
מַחְסִי. machsi עֶלְיוֹן elyon שַׂמְתָּ samta מְעוֹנֶךָ me'onecha וזעם:
לֹא־ lo תְאֻנֶּה te'une אֵלֶיךָ elecha רָעָה ra'a רהע (לילית) וְנֶגַע venega (סמאל)
לֹא־ lo יִקְרַב yikrav בְּאָהֳלֶךָ: be'aholecha כִּי ki מַלְאָכָיו mal'achav
יְצַוֶּה־ yetzave לָּךְ lach ס"ת שם קדוש יוהך לִשְׁמָרְךָ lishmorcha
בְּכָל־ bechol ב"ן, לכב דְּרָכֶיךָ derachecha ס"ת שם קדוש ככך:
עַל־ al כַּפַּיִם kapayim ע"ה קנ"א, אדני אלהים יִשָּׂאוּנְךָ yisa'uncha פֶּן־ pen
תִּגֹּף tigof בָּאֶבֶן ba'even (לילית) רַגְלֶךָ: raglecha עַל־ al שַׁחַל shachal (דכורא)
וָפֶתֶן vafeten (נוקבא) תִּדְרֹךְ tidroch תִּרְמֹס tirmos כְּפִיר kefir (יסוד דקליפה)
וְתַנִּין: vetanin כִּי ki בִי vi שם בן מ"ב חָשַׁק chashak וַאֲפַלְּטֵהוּ va'afaltehu
(ע"י שם ב"ט העולה למנין יה"ו ביסוד וכן למנין אהיה ומסוגל לשמירה) אֲשַׂגְּבֵהוּ asagvehu
כִּי־ ki יָדַע yada שְׁמִי shemi ר"ת אכיש (ע"י שם ב"ט ברוך דוד מאכיש) ; ר"ת יכש:
יִקְרָאֵנִי yikra'eni וְאֶעֱנֵהוּ ve'e'enehu עִמּוֹ־ imo אָנֹכִי anochi
בְצָרָה vetzara אלהים דההין אֲחַלְּצֵהוּ achaltzehu וַאֲכַבְּדֵהוּ: va'achabdehu

We say the last verse of this Psalm twice in order to have 130 words, which is the numerical value of the Name: יוד יוד הא יוד הא ואו יוד הא ואו הא which has the power to chase those negative entities (which are mentioned here) away.

אֹרֶךְ orech יָמִים yamim נלך
אַשְׂבִּיעֵהוּ asbi'ehu וְאַרְאֵהוּ ve'arehu בִּישׁוּעָתִי: bishu'ati אֹרֶךְ orech
יָמִים yamim נלך אַשְׂבִּיעֵהוּ asbi'ehu וְאַרְאֵהוּ ve'arehu בִּישׁוּעָתִי: bishu'ati

---

You shall merely look with your eyes and see the retribution of the wicked. Because You are, Lord, my refuge. You have placed Your dwelling place in the highest Place. No evil will befall you nor will any plague come near your tent. He will charge His angels to you to protect you in all your ways. They will carry you on their palms lest you strike your foot against a stone. You will tread upon the lion and the viper, you will trample the young lion and the serpent. For he has yearned for Me and I will deliver him. I will elevate him because he knows My Name. He will call upon Me and I will answer him. I am with him in distress. I will release him and I will honor him. With long life I will satiate him and I will show him My salvation. With long life I will satiate him and I will show him My salvation." (Psalms 91)

MIZMOR SHIRU

According to Kabbalah, people will sometimes reincarnate into animals as part of their *tikkun* (correction) process. By reciting this Psalm with that in mind, we are helping to elevate their souls.

Meditate for the seventh *Ma'amar* (Utterance) of Creation: ישרצו המים ("and God said: Let the water teem" – as it says in this psalm: "The sea in its fullness will roar".)

מִזְמוֹר mizmor שִׁירוּ shiru לַיהֹוָהאדניאהדונהי ladonai שִׁיר shir חָדָשׁ chadash
י"ב הויות, קס"א קנ"א (שנתחדשו בחידוש היום) כִּי־ ki נִפְלָאוֹת nifla'ot עָשָׂה asa
הוֹשִׁיעָה hoshi'a יהוה וש"ע נהורין לּוֹ lo יְמִינוֹ yemino ר"ת יכה וּזְרוֹעַ uzro'a
קָדְשׁוֹ kodsho: הוֹדִיעַ hodi'a יְהֹוָהאדניאהדונהי Adonai יְשׁוּעָתוֹ yeshu'ato ר"ת הי"י
לְעֵינֵי le'enei ריבוע מ"ה הַגּוֹיִם hagoyim גִּלָּה gila צִדְקָתוֹ tzidkato: זָכַר zachar
חַסְדּוֹ chasdo ג' הויות, מזלא (להמשיך הארה ממזלא עילאה) וֶאֱמוּנָתוֹ ve'emunato
לְבֵית levet ב"פ ראה יִשְׂרָאֵל Yisrael רָאוּ ra'u כָל־ chol ילי אַפְסֵי־ afsei
אָרֶץ aretz אֵת et יְשׁוּעַת yeshu'at אֱלֹהֵינוּ Elohenu ילה: הָרִיעוּ hari'u
אלהים דאלפין לַיהֹוָהאדניאהדונהי ladonai כָּל־ kol ילי הָאָרֶץ ha'aretz אלהים דההין ע"ה ;
ר"ת הלכה ; ס"ת ע"ה = ריבוע אדני פִּצְחוּ pitzchu להח וְרַנְּנוּ veranenu וְזַמֵּרוּ vezameru:
זַמְּרוּ zameru לַיהֹוָהאדניאהדונהי ladonai בְּכִנּוֹר bechinor בְּכִנּוֹר bechinor
וְקוֹל vekol זִמְרָה zimra: בַּחֲצֹצְרוֹת bachatzotzrot וְקוֹל vekol שׁוֹפָר shofar
הָרִיעוּ hari'u אלהים דאלפין לִפְנֵי lifnei הַמֶּלֶךְ hamelech יְהֹוָהאדניאהדונהי Adonai:
יִרְעַם yir'am הַיָּם hayam ילי וּמְלֹאוֹ umlo'o תֵּבֵל tevel ב"פ רי"ו וְיֹשְׁבֵי veyoshvei
בָהּ va: נְהָרוֹת neharot יִמְחֲאוּ־ yimcha'u כָף chaf יַחַד yachad
הָרִים harim יְרַנֵּנוּ yeranenu: לִפְנֵי־ lifnei יְהֹוָהאדניאהדונהי Adonai
כִּי ki בָא va לִשְׁפֹּט lishpot הָאָרֶץ ha'aretz אלהים דההין ע"ה יִשְׁפֹּט־ yishpot
תֵּבֵל tevel ב"פ רי"ו בְּצֶדֶק betzedek וְעַמִּים ve'amim בְּמֵישָׁרִים bemesharim:

MIZMOR SHIRU

"A Psalm. Sing to the Lord a new song for He has done wonders. His right Hand and His holy Arm helped Him. The Lord had made known His salvation; in sight of the nations He revealed His righteousness. He recalled His kindness and faithfulness to the House of Israel. All the ends of the Earth have seen the salvation of our God. Call out to the Lord all the inhabitants of the Earth. Open your mouths in joyous songs and play melodies. Play melodies to the Lord on a harp. With harp and sound of chanted praise. With trumpets and Shofar sounds, call out before the King, the Lord. The sea in its fullness will roar, the world and those who dwell therein. Rivers will clap hands, mountains will exult together before the Lord, for He will have arrived to judge the earth. He will judge the world with righteousness and peoples with fairness." (Psalms 98)

SHIR LAMA'ALOT

This configuration of Aramaic letters helps to awaken an inner realization that nothing of substance can be achieved in this physical world without the help of the Creator. Alone, we can do nothing. The Satan, our ego, will do everything in its power to convince us that we are the sole architects of our success. This connection helps us recognize the profound truth that the Creator's hand can always be found within our good fortune.

In this praise, the word *Shomer* (guard, or derivatives of it) is mentioned six times. This stands for the letter *Vav* (ו=6) of the Name: יהוה. Also, meditate for the eighth *Ma'amar* (Utterance) of Creation: תוצא הארץ נפש חיה ("and God said: Let the land produce living creatures").

שִׁיר shir לַמַּעֲלוֹת lama'alot (מלמד שמלכות נקנית בכל מעלות) אֶשָּׂא esa

עֵינַי enai ריבוע מ״ה אֶל־ el הֶהָרִים heharim (האבות שנקראים הרים)

מֵאַיִן me'ayin (א״א) יָבֹא yavo עֶזְרִי ezri: עֶזְרִי ezri מֵעִם me'im

יְהֹוָהאדניאהדונהי Adonai עֹשֵׂה ose שָׁמַיִם shamayim י״פ טל, י״פ כוזו וָאָרֶץ va'aretz:

אַל־ al יִתֵּן yiten לַמּוֹט lamot רַגְלֶךָ raglecha אַל־ al יָנוּם yanum

שֹׁמְרֶךָ shomrecha: הִנֵּה hine לֹא־ lo יָנוּם yanum וְלֹא velo ר״ת = דמב, מילוי דע״ב

יִישָׁן yishan ש״ע נהורין דא״א שׁוֹמֵר shomer כ״א ההויות שבתפילין יִשְׂרָאֵל Yisrael:

יְהֹוָהאדניאהדונהי Adonai שֹׁמְרֶךָ shomrecha יְהֹוָהאדניאהדונהי Adonai צִלְּךָ tzilecha

עַל־ al יַד yad יְמִינֶךָ yeminecha הי״: יוֹמָם yomam הַשֶּׁמֶשׁ hashemesh

לֹא־ lo יַכֶּכָּה yakeka ר״ת ילה וְיָרֵחַ veyare'ach בַּלָּיְלָה balayla מלה:

יְהֹוָהאדניאהדונהי Adonai יִשְׁמָרְךָ yishmorcha מִכָּל־ mikol ילי

רָע ra יִשְׁמֹר yishmor אֶת־ et נַפְשֶׁךָ nafshecha מיכ:

יְהֹוָהאדניאהדונהי Adonai יִשְׁמָר־ yishmor צֵאתְךָ tzet'cha וּבוֹאֶךָ uvo'echa

מֵעַתָּה me'ata וְעַד־ ve'ad עוֹלָם olam והו:

SHIR LAMA'ALOT

"A Song of Acents: I raise my eyes to the mountains, where will my help come from? My help comes from the Lord, Who made the Heavens and the Earth. He will not allow your foot to be moved. Your Keeper will not slumber. Behold, He neither slumbers nor sleeps, the Keeper of Israel. The Lord is your Keeper. The Lord is your shade upon your right hand. By day the sun will not harm you, nor will the moon at night. The Lord will protect you from all evil. He will keep your soul. The Lord will guard your departure and your arrival, from now till eternity." (Psalms 121)

SHIR HAMA'ALOT LEDAVID

These verses connect us to the ancient Holy Temple. According to Kabbalah, the Holy Temple is the energy center and source of all spiritual Light for the whole world, similar to a nuclear power plant that provides electrical energy for an entire city. The land of Israel is the energy center of the planet; Jerusalem is the energy center of Israel; the physical Temple was the energy center of Jerusalem; and the Holy of Holies, inside the Temple, was the ultimate energy center for the Temple and thus for the entire physical world. When the Temple was standing, it acted as a generator that chugged along 24 hours a day to produce all the spiritual Light and energy we needed. With its destruction, the power lines were severed. The Aramaic letters in this connection re-establish the lines of communication with the spiritual essence of the Temple, giving us the ability to capture this energy for our personal lives.

This praise was said by King David for his kingdom, as everything was in one unification – "justice and peace kissed each other." And that's the meaning of: "I shall request good for you."

samachti שָׂמַחְתִּי leDavid לְדָוִד hama'alot הַמַּעֲלוֹת shir שִׁיר

:נלך nelech נֵלֵךְ׃ Adonai יהוהאדניאהדונהי יְהֹוָה ב״פ ראה bet בֵּית li לִי be'omrim בְּאֹמְרִים

bish'arayich בִּשְׁעָרַיִךְ׃ רהע ר״ת raglenu רַגְלֵינוּ hayu הָיוּ omdot עֹמְדוֹת

ke'ir כְּעִיר habenuya הַבְּנוּיָה Yerushalayim יְרוּשָׁלַםִ :Yerushalayim יְרוּשָׁלַםִ

shesham שֶׁשָּׁם :yachdav יַחְדָּו la לָּהּ shechubera שֶׁחֻבְּרָה־ בן זקף, סנדלפון, ערי

edut עֵדוּת Yah יָהּ shivtei שִׁבְטֵי־ shevatim שְׁבָטִים alu עָלוּ

:Adonai יהוהאדניאהדונהי יְהֹוָה׃ leshem לְשֵׁם lehodot לְהֹדוֹת leYisrael לְיִשְׂרָאֵל

ע״ה ה״פ אלהים lemishpat לְמִשְׁפָּט chis'ot כִסְאוֹת yashvu יָשְׁבוּ shama שָׁמָּה ki כִּי

shelom שְׁלוֹם sha'alu שַׁאֲלוּ :David דָּוִד׃ ב״פ ראה levet לְבֵית kis'ot כִּסְאוֹת

yehi יְהִי־ :ohavayich אֹהֲבָיִךְ׃ yishlayu יִשְׁלָיוּ Yerushalayim יְרוּשָׁלָםִ

:be'armenotayich בְּאַרְמְנוֹתָיִךְ׃ shalva שַׁלְוָה bechelech בְּחֵילֵךְ shalom שָׁלוֹם

shalom שָׁלוֹם na נָּא adabera אֲדַבְּרָה־ vere'ai וְרֵעָי achai אַחַי lema'an לְמַעַן

Adonai יהוהאדניאהדונהי יְהֹוָה ראה ב״פ bet בֵּית lema'an לְמַעַן :bach בָּךְ׃

:lach לָךְ׃ והו tov טוֹב avaksha אֲבַקְשָׁה ילה Elohenu אֱלֹהֵינוּ

SHIR HAMA'ALOT LEDAVID

"A Song of Ascents by David: I rejoiced when they said to me: Let us go to the House of the Lord. Our legs stood immobile within your gates, Jerusalem. The built-up Jerusalem is like a city that has been united together. For there the tribes ascend the tribes of God, who are testimony for Israel, to give thanks to the Name of the Lord. For there sat thrones of judgments, thrones of the House of David, they have prayed for the peace of Jerusalem, those who love you will be serene. May there be peace within your walls, and serenity within your palaces. For the sake of my brothers and my comrades, I shall speak of peace on your behalf. For the sake of the House of the Lord, I shall request good for you." (Psalms 122)

SHIR HAMA'ALOT ELECHA

All of humanity is considered to be one unified soul, which has the nature of receiving. The Light of the Creator has many dimensions, one of which expresses itself in our physical realm as the *Shechinah*, which has the nature of sharing and imparting. Joining the unified soul with the *Shechinah* is like the union of a bride and groom. The words that compose this Psalm help us to unite with the *Shechinah* and thereby to reach ultimate fulfillment.

This praise is said by the lower *Yisrael* for the sake of the Bride. Therefore, in the word "*hayoshevi*" there is an extra letter *Hei* (ה - *Malchut*) as it is the last letter of the Name: יהוה - which is the Bride.

שִׁיר shir הַמַּעֲלוֹת hama'alot אֵלֶיךָ eleicha נָשָׂאתִי nasati אֶת־ et

עֵינַי einai ריבוע מ"ה הַיֹּשְׁבִי hayoshvi בַּשָּׁמָיִם bashamayim י"פ טל, י"פ כוזו:

הִנֵּה hine כְעֵינֵי che'enei ריבוע מ"ה עֲבָדִים avadim אֶל־ el יַד yad

אֲדוֹנֵיהֶם adonehem כְּעֵינֵי ke'enei ריבוע מ"ה שִׁפְחָה shifcha אֶל־ el יַד yad

גְּבִרְתָּהּ gevirta כֵּן ken עֵינֵינוּ enenu ריבוע מ"ה אֶל־ el יְהֹוָה יאהדונהי Adonai

אֱלֹהֵינוּ Elohenu ילה עַד ad שֶׁיְּחָנֵּנוּ sheyechonenu: חָנֵּנוּ chonenu

יְהֹוָה יאהדונהי Adonai חָנֵּנוּ chonenu כִּי־ ki רַב rav שָׂבַעְנוּ savanu בוּז vuz:

רַבַּת rabat שָׂבְעָה־ sav'a לָּהּ la נַפְשֵׁנוּ nafshenu הַלַּעַג hala'ag

הַשַּׁאֲנַנִּים hasha'ananim הַבּוּז habuz לִגְאֵי lige'ei יוֹנִים yonim (כתיב לגאיונים):

SHIR HAMA'ALOT LEDAVID

Here we make our connection to the Final Redemption – the end of all chaos and spiritual darkness. Two thousand years ago, Kabbalist Rav Shimon bar Yochai said that when the wisdom of the *Zohar* becomes the property of the people (as it is now) and the secrets of the Torah are learned by everyone, young and old (as you are doing now), it will be the sign that the age of the Final Redemption is upon us.

This following praise speaks of The Final Redemption. It is also connects us to the above mentioned Bride that escapes its distress that were pursueing her from the Other Side, and entered the holy side, when *Shabbat* starts.

SHIR HAMA'ALOT ELECHA

"A Song of Ascents: To You I raised my eyes, You Who dwell in the Heavens. Behold! Like the eyes of servants unto their master's hand, Like the eyes of a maid unto her mistress's hand, so are our eyes unto the Lord, our God, until He will favor us. Favor us, Lord, favor us, for we are fully sated with contempt. Our soul is fully sated with the mockery of the complacent ones, with the contempt of the arrogant." (Psalms 123)

Meditate for the ninth *Ma'amar* (Utterance) of Creation: נעשה אדם ("and God said: Let us make man" – as it says in this psalm "had the Lord not been with us" – God image is within us).

שִׁיר shir הַמַּעֲלוֹת hama'alot לְדָוִד leDavid לוּלֵי lulei יְהֹוָהאדנייאהדונהי Adonai

שֶׁהָיָה shehaya יהה לָנוּ lanu אלהים, אהיה אדני יֹאמַר־ yomar נָא na

יִשְׂרָאֵל: Yisrael לוּלֵי lulei יְהֹוָהאדנייאהדונהי Adonai ר"ת ילי שֶׁהָיָה shehaya יהה

לָנוּ lanu אלהים, אהיה אדני בְּקוּם bekum עָלֵינוּ alenu אָדָם adam (אדם בליעל ס"מ):

אֲזַי azai חַיִּים chayim אהיה אהיה יהוה, בינה ע"ה בְּלָעוּנוּ bela'unu בַּחֲרוֹת bacharot

אַפָּם apam (נוקבא דס"מ) בָּנוּ: banu אֲזַי azai הַמַּיִם hamayim שְׁטָפוּנוּ shetafunu

(לילית וכת דלהון) נַחְלָה nachla עָבַר avar עַל־ al נַפְשֵׁנוּ: nafshenu אֲזַי azai

עָבַר avar עַל־ al נַפְשֵׁנוּ nafshenu הַמַּיִם hamayim הַזֵּידוֹנִים: hazeidonim

בָּרוּךְ baruch יְהֹוָהאדנייאהדונהי Adonai שֶׁלֹּא shelo נְתָנָנוּ netananu

טֶרֶף teref לְשִׁנֵּיהֶם: leshinehem נַפְשֵׁנוּ nafshenu כְּצִפּוֹר ketzipor

נִמְלְטָה nimleta מִפַּח mipach יוֹקְשִׁים yokshim הַפַּח hapach נִשְׁבָּר nishbar

וַאֲנַחְנוּ va'anachnu נִמְלָטְנוּ: nimlatnu עֶזְרֵנוּ ezrenu בְּשֵׁם beshem

יְהֹוָהאדנייאהדונהי Adonai עֹשֵׂה ose שָׁמַיִם shamayim י"פ טל, י"פ כוזו וָאָרֶץ: va'aretz

HALELUYA

King David says, "We have eyes, but see not. We have ears, but hear not." (Psalms 115:6) Far too often, our five senses and rational mind provide us with only a limited view of reality. Even science tells us that we utilize less than 10 percent of our brain capacity. Kabbalah asks, "Where is the remaining 90 percent?" This prayer helps to awaken our dormant capacities and strengthens our perception. We achieve a heightened sense of awareness and superior intuition.

In the following Psalm we have 20 verses for the 13 Attributes and the seven voices, and we also have 165 words for the Name: אלף הי יוד הי (וד' אותיות השורש). Meditate for the sixth *Ma'amar* (Utterance) of Creation: יהי מאורות ("and God said: Let there be lights" – the stars were created to serve God in His courtyards – the world).

SHIR HAMA'ALOT LEDAVID

"A Song of Ascents by David: Had the Lord not been with us, let Israel declare now! Had the Lord not been with us when a man rises up against us, then they would have swallowed us up alive when their anger was kindled against us. Then the waters would have washed us away, the currents would have surged against our soul, then they would have surged across our soul, the treacherous waters. Blessed is the Lord, Who did not allow us to be as prey for their teeth. Our soul escaped like a bird from the hunters' snare. The snare broke and we escaped. Our help is from the Name of the Lord, Maker of the Heavens and the Earth." (Psalms 124)

הַלְלוּיָהּ haleluya אלהים, אהיה אדני ; ללה הַלְלוּ halelu אֶת־ et שֵׁם shem

יְהֹוָה Adonai עַבְדֵי avdei הַלְלוּ halelu יְהֹוָה Adonai:

שֶׁעֹמְדִים she'omdim בְּבֵית bevet ב״פ ראה יְהֹוָה Adonai

בְּחַצְרוֹת bechatzrot בֵּית bet ב״פ ראה אֱלֹהֵינוּ Elohenu ילה: הַלְלוּיָהּ haleluya

אלהים, אהיה אדני ; ללה כִּי־ ki טוֹב tov והו ; יהוה אהיה, אום, מבה, יזל

יְהֹוָה Adonai זַמְּרוּ zameru לִשְׁמוֹ lishmo מהש ע״ה, ע״ב בריבוע וקס״א ע״ה,

אל שדי ע״ה כִּי ki נָעִים na'im: כִּי־ ki יַעֲקֹב Yaakov ו׳ הויות, יאהדונהי אידהנויה

בָּחַר bachar לוֹ lo יָהּ Yah יִשְׂרָאֵל Yisrael לִסְגֻלָּתוֹ lisgulato: כִּי ki

אֲנִי ani אני יָדַעְתִּי yadati כִּי־ ki גָדוֹל gadol להח, עם ד׳ אותיות - מבה, יזל, אום

יְהֹוָה Adonai וַאֲדֹנֵינוּ va'adonenu מִכָּל־ mikol ילי

אֱלֹהִים Elohim אהיה אדני ; ילה: כֹּל kol ילי אֲשֶׁר־ asher חָפֵץ chafetz

יְהֹוָה Adonai עָשָׂה asa בַּשָּׁמַיִם bashamayim י״פ טל, י״פ כוזו

וּבָאָרֶץ uva'aretz בַּיַּמִּים bayamim נלך וְכָל־ vechol תְּהוֹמוֹת tehomot:

מַעֲלֶה ma'ale נְשִׂאִים nesi'im מִקְצֵה miktze הָאָרֶץ ha'aretz אלהים דההין ע״ה

בְּרָקִים berakim לַמָּטָר lamatar עָשָׂה asa מוֹצֵא־ motze רוּחַ rua'ch

מֵאוֹצְרוֹתָיו me'otzrotav: שֶׁהִכָּה shehika בְּכוֹרֵי bechorei מִצְרָיִם Mitzrayim

מצר מֵאָדָם me'adam מ״ה עַד־ ad בְּהֵמָה behema ב״ן: שָׁלַח shalach אֹתוֹת otot

וּמֹפְתִים umoftim בְּתוֹכֵכִי betochechi מִצְרָיִם Mitzrayim מצר בְּפַרְעֹה beFar'o

וּבְכָל־ uvchol ב״ן, לכב עֲבָדָיו avadav: שֶׁהִכָּה shehika גּוֹיִם goyim

רַבִּים rabim וְהָרַג veharag מְלָכִים melachim עֲצוּמִים atzumim:

HALELUYA

"Praise the Lord! Praise the Name of the Lord, praise the Name of the Lord, you servants of the Lord, you who stand in the House of the Lord, in the courtyards of the House of our God. Praise God, for the Lord is good. Sing to His Name for it is pleasant, for God selected Jacob for His own, Israel as His treasure. For I know that the Lord, our God, is greater than all heavenly powers. Whatever the Lord wished for, He did in the Heavens and the Earth, in the seas and all the depths. He raises clouds from the ends of the Earth; He made lightning bolts for the rain; He brings forth winds from His treasuries. It was He Who smote the firstborn of Egypt, from man to beast. He sent signs and wonders into your midst, Egypt, upon Pharaoh and upon all his servants. It was He Who smote many nations and slew mighty kings:

לְסִיחוֹן leSichon מֶלֶךְ melech הָאֱמֹרִי haEmori וּלְעוֹג ul'Og מֶלֶךְ melech

הַבָּשָׁן haBashan וּלְכֹל ulchol יה אדני מַמְלְכוֹת mamlechot כְּנָעַן Kena'an:

וְנָתַן venatan אַרְצָם artzam נַחֲלָה nachala נַחֲלָה nachala לְיִשְׂרָאֵל leYisrael

עַמּוֹ amo: יְהֹוָהאדניאהדונהי Adonai שִׁמְךָ shimcha לְעוֹלָם le'olam

ריבוע דס"ג י' אותיות דס"ג יְהֹוָהאדניאהדונהי Adonai זִכְרְךָ zichrecha לְדֹר־ ledor ר"ת יזל

וָדֹר vador רי"ו: כִּי ki יָדִין yadin יְהֹוָהאדניאהדונהי Adonai עַמּוֹ amo

וְעַל־ ve'al עֲבָדָיו avadav יִתְנֶחָם yitnecham: עֲצַבֵּי atzabei הַגּוֹיִם hagoyim

כֶּסֶף kesef וְזָהָב vezahav מַעֲשֵׂה ma'ase יְדֵי yedei אָדָם adam:

פֶּה pe מילה, וע"ה אלהים, אהיה אדני לָהֶם lahem וְלֹא velo יְדַבֵּרוּ yedaberu

עֵינַיִם enayim ריבוע מ"ה לָהֶם lahem וְלֹא velo יִרְאוּ yir'u: אָזְנַיִם oznayim

יוד הי ואו הה לָהֶם lahem וְלֹא velo יַאֲזִינוּ ya'azinu אַף af אֵין־ en יֶשׁ־ yesh

רוּחַ ru'ach בְּפִיהֶם befihem: כְּמוֹהֶם kemohem יִהְיוּ yih'yu אל (ייא"י מילוי דס"ג)

עֹשֵׂיהֶם osehem כֹּל kol ילי אֲשֶׁר־ asher בֹּטֵחַ bote'ach בָּהֶם bahem:

בֵּית bet ב"פ ראה יִשְׂרָאֵל Yisrael בָּרְכוּ barchu יהוה ריבוע יהוה ריבוע מ"ה אֶת־ et

יְהֹוָהאדניאהדונהי Adonai בֵּית bet ב"פ ראה אַהֲרֹן Aharon בָּרְכוּ barchu יהוה ריבוע

יהוה ריבוע מ"ה אֶת־ et יְהֹוָהאדניאהדונהי Adonai: בֵּית bet ב"פ ראה הַלֵּוִי haLevi

בָּרְכוּ barchu יהוה ריבוע יהוה ריבוע מ"ה אֶת־ et יְהֹוָהאדניאהדונהי Adonai

יִרְאֵי yir'ei יְהֹוָהאדניאהדונהי Adonai בָּרְכוּ barchu יהוה ריבוע יהוה ריבוע מ"ה

אֶת־ et יְהֹוָהאדניאהדונהי Adonai: בָּרוּךְ baruch יְהֹוָהאדניאהדונהי Adonai

מִצִּיּוֹן miTziyon יוסף, ו' הויות, קנאה שֹׁכֵן shochen יְרוּשָׁלָיִם Yerushalayim

הַלְלוּיָהּ haleluya אלהים, אהיה אדני ; ללה:

Sichon, the king of the Emorites, Og, the king of the Bashan, and all the kingdoms of Canaan and presented their land as a heritage, a heritage for Israel, His nation. The Lord is Your Name forever. The Lord is your memorial throughout the generations. When the Lord will judge the nations, He will relent concerning His servants. The idols of the nations are silver and gold, human handiwork. They have mouths, but they do not speak. They have eyes, but they do not see. They have ears, but they do not heed; neither is there any breath in their mouths. Like them shall their makers become and everyone who trusts in them. House of Israel, bless the Lord. House of Aaron, bless the Lord. House of Levi, bless the Lord. Those who fear the Lord, bless the Lord. Blessed is the Lord from Zion, He who dwells in Jerusalem, Praise the Lord!" (Psalms 135)

HODU

The following Psalm has 26 verses which connect us to the Name: יהוה. It also connects us to the 26 Angels (one for each verse – in consecutive order of the Aramaic alphabet). Meditate for the tenth *Ma'amar* (Utterance) of Creation: פרו ורבו ("and God said: Be fruitful and become numerous" – for the righteous to be born and thank the Creator.

אדריאל י

הוֹדוּ hodu אהיה לַיהֹוָה ladonai אהדונהי כִּי ki טוֹב tov והו ;

כי טוב = יהוה אהיה = אום, מבה, יזל

כִּי ki לְעוֹלָם le'olam ריבוע דס"ג וי"ו אותיות דס"ג וְחַסְדּוֹ chasdo

ג' הויות, מזלא (להמשיך הארה ממזלא עילאה) ; ר"ת = נגה : יוד

ברכיאל

הוֹדוּ hodu אהיה לֵאלֹהֵי lelohei מילוי דע"ב, דמב ; ילה

הָאֱלֹהִים haElohim אהיה אדני ; ילה

כִּי ki לְעוֹלָם le'olam ריבוע דס"ג וי"ו אותיות דס"ג וְחַסְדּוֹ chasdo

ג' הויות, מזלא (להמשיך הארה ממזלא עילאה) ; ר"ת = נגה : יוד

גועיאל

הוֹדוּ hodu אהיה לַאֲדֹנֵי la'adonei הָאֲדֹנִים ha'adonim

כִּי ki לְעוֹלָם le'olam ריבוע דס"ג וי"ו אותיות דס"ג וְחַסְדּוֹ chasdo

ג' הויות, מזלא (להמשיך הארה ממזלא עילאה) ; ר"ת = נגה : יוד

דורשיאל

לְעֹשֵׂה le'ose נִפְלָאוֹת nifla'ot גְּדֹלוֹת gedolot לְבַדּוֹ levado מ"ב בסוד שם בן מ"ב

כִּי ki לְעוֹלָם le'olam ריבוע דס"ג וי"ו אותיות דס"ג וְחַסְדּוֹ chasdo

ג' הויות, מזלא (להמשיך הארה ממזלא עילאה) ; ר"ת = נגה : יוד

הדריאל

לְעֹשֵׂה le'ose הַשָּׁמַיִם hashamayim י"פ טל, י"פ כוזו בִּתְבוּנָה bitvuna

כִּי ki לְעוֹלָם le'olam ריבוע דס"ג וי"ו אותיות דס"ג וְחַסְדּוֹ chasdo

ג' הויות, מזלא (להמשיך הארה ממזלא עילאה) ; ר"ת = נגה : יוד

HODU

"Give thanks to the Lord for He is good, for His kindness endures forever.
Give thanks to the Lord of all the heavenly powers, for His kindness endures forever.
Give thanks to the Master of all masters, for His kindness endures forever.
To the One Who alone performs great wonders, for His kindness endures forever.
To the One Who made the heavens with understanding, for His kindness endures forever.

וועדיאל

hamayim הַמָּיִם al עַל־ אלהים דההין ע"ה ha'aretz הָאָרֶץ leroka לְרֹקַע

chasdo חַסְדּוֹ ריבוע דס"ג וי' אותיות דס"ג le'olam לְעוֹלָם ki כִּי

ג' הויות = מזלא (להמשיך הארה ממזלא עילאה) ; ר"ת = נגה : יוד

זבדיאל

gedolim גְּדֹלִים רז, אין סוף orim אוֹרִים le'ose לְעֹשֵׂה

chasdo חַסְדּוֹ ריבוע דס"ג וי' אותיות דס"ג le'olam לְעוֹלָם ki כִּי

ג' הויות = מזלא (להמשיך הארה ממזלא עילאה) ; ר"ת = נגה : יוד

וזניאל

hashemesh הַשֶּׁמֶשׁ et אֶת־

ע"ה נגד, מזבח, זן, אל יהוה bayom בַּיּוֹם lememshelet לְמֶמְשֶׁלֶת

chasdo חַסְדּוֹ ריבוע דס"ג וי' אותיות דס"ג le'olam לְעוֹלָם ki כִּי

ג' הויות, מזלא (להמשיך הארה ממזלא עילאה) ; ר"ת = נגה : יוד

טהוריאל

vechochavim וְכוֹכָבִים hayare'ach הַיָּרֵחַ et אֶת־

מלה balayla בַּלָּיְלָה lememshelot לְמֶמְשְׁלוֹת

chasdo חַסְדּוֹ ריבוע דס"ג וי' אותיות דס"ג le'olam לְעוֹלָם ki כִּי

ג' הויות, מזלא (להמשיך הארה ממזלא עילאה) ; ר"ת = נגה : יוד

ידידיאל

bivchorehem בִּבְכוֹרֵיהֶם מצר Mitzrayim מִצְרַיִם lemake לְמַכֵּה

chasdo חַסְדּוֹ ריבוע דס"ג וי' אותיות דס"ג le'olam לְעוֹלָם ki כִּי

ג' הויות, מזלא (להמשיך הארה ממזלא עילאה) ; ר"ת = נגה : יוד

To the One Who spreads out the earth upon the waters, for His kindness endures forever. To the One Who made great Lights, for His kindness endures forever. The sun for the reign of the day, for His kindness endures forever. The moon and the stars for the reign of the night, for His kindness endures forever. To the One Who smote Egypt through their firstborn, for His kindness endures forever.

ה

כרוביאל

וַיּוֹצֵא vayotze יִשְׂרָאֵל Yisrael מִתּוֹכָם mitocham

כִּי ki לְעוֹלָם le'olam ריבוע דס"ג וי' אותיות דס"ג חַסְדּוֹ chasdo

ג' הויות, מזלא (להמשיך הארה ממזלא עילאה) ; ר"ת = נגה : הָיָ

להטיאל

בְּיָד beyad חֲזָקָה chazaka וּבִזְרוֹעַ uvizro'a נְטוּיָה netuya

כִּי ki לְעוֹלָם le'olam ריבוע דס"ג וי' אותיות דס"ג חַסְדּוֹ chasdo

ג' הויות, מזלא (להמשיך הארה ממזלא עילאה) ; ר"ת = נגה : הָיָ

מהגביאל

לְגֹזֵר legozer יַם־ yam ילי סוּף Suf לִגְזָרִים ligzarim

כִּי ki לְעוֹלָם le'olam ריבוע דס"ג וי' אותיות דס"ג חַסְדּוֹ chasdo

ג' הויות, מזלא (להמשיך הארה ממזלא עילאה) ; ר"ת = נגה : הָיָ

נוריאל

וְהֶעֱבִיר vehe'evir יִשְׂרָאֵל Yisrael בְּתוֹכוֹ betocho

כִּי ki לְעוֹלָם le'olam ריבוע דס"ג וי' אותיות דס"ג חַסְדּוֹ chasdo

ג' הויות, מזלא (להמשיך הארה ממזלא עילאה) ; ר"ת = נגה : הָיָ

נוצציאל

וְנִעֵר veni'er פַּרְעֹה Par'o וְחֵילוֹ vecheilo בְיַם־ veyam ילי סוּף Suf

כִּי ki לְעוֹלָם le'olam ריבוע דס"ג וי' אותיות דס"ג חַסְדּוֹ chasdo

ג' הויות, מזלא (להמשיך הארה ממזלא עילאה) ; ר"ת = נגה : הָיָ

And Who took Israel out of their midst, for His kindness endures forever.
With a strong Hand and with an outstretched Arm, for His kindness endures forever.
To the One Who divided the Sea of Reeds into parts, for His kindness endures forever.
And Who caused Israel to pass through It, For His kindness endures forever.
And threw Pharaoh and his army into the Sea of Reeds, for His kindness endures forever.

ו

נוּדִיאֵל

לְמוֹלִיךְ lemolich עַמּוֹ amo בַּמִּדְבָּר bamidbar

כִּי ki לְעוֹלָם le'olam ריבוע דס"ג וי' אותיות דס"ג חַסְדּוֹ chasdo

ג' הויות, מזלא (להמשיך הארה ממזלא עילאה) ; ר"ת = נגה : וְיָוְ

סרעיאל

לְמַכֵּה lemake מְלָכִים melachim גְּדֹלִים gedolim

כִּי ki לְעוֹלָם le'olam ריבוע דס"ג וי' אותיות דס"ג חַסְדּוֹ chasdo

ג' הויות, מזלא (להמשיך הארה ממזלא עילאה) ; ר"ת = נגה : וְיָוְ

עשאל

וַיַּהֲרֹג vayaharog מְלָכִים melachim אַדִּירִים adirim הרי

כִּי ki לְעוֹלָם le'olam ריבוע דס"ג וי' אותיות דס"ג חַסְדּוֹ chasdo

ג' הויות, מזלא (להמשיך הארה ממזלא עילאה) ; ר"ת = נגה : וְיָוְ

פקדיאל

לְסִיחוֹן leSichon מֶלֶךְ melech הָאֱמֹרִי haEmori

כִּי ki לְעוֹלָם le'olam ריבוע דס"ג וי' אותיות דס"ג חַסְדּוֹ chasdo

ג' הויות, מזלא (להמשיך הארה ממזלא עילאה) ; ר"ת = נגה : וְיָוְ

צרופיאל

וּלְעוֹג ulOg מֶלֶךְ melech הַבָּשָׁן haBashan

כִּי ki לְעוֹלָם le'olam ריבוע דס"ג וי' אותיות דס"ג חַסְדּוֹ chasdo

ג' הויות, מזלא (להמשיך הארה ממזלא עילאה) ; ר"ת = נגה : וְיָוְ

קדושיאל

וְנָתַן venatan אַרְצָם artzam לְנַחֲלָה lenachala

כִּי ki לְעוֹלָם le'olam ריבוע דס"ג וי' אותיות דס"ג חַסְדּוֹ chasdo

ג' הויות, מזלא (להמשיך הארה ממזלא עילאה) ; ר"ת = נגה : וְיָוְ

To the One Who led His nation, through the wilderness, for His kindness endures forever.
To the One Who smite kings, for His kindness endures forever.
And slew mighty kings, for His kindness endures forever.
Sichon, the king of the Emorites, for His kindness endures forever.
And to Og, the king of Bashan, for His kindness endures forever.
And presented their land as a heritage, for His kindness endures forever.

ה

רוממיאל

נַחֲלָה nachala לְיִשְׂרָאֵל leYisrael עַבְדּוֹ avdo

כִּי ki לְעוֹלָם le'olam ריבוע דס"ג וי' אותיות דס"ג חַסְדּוֹ chasdo

ג' הויות, מזלא (להמשיך הארה ממזלא עילאה) ; ר"ת = נגה : הָיָ

שומריאל

שֶׁבְּשִׁפְלֵנוּ shebshiflenu זָכַר zachar לָנוּ lanu אלהים, אהיה אדני

כִּי ki לְעוֹלָם le'olam ריבוע דס"ג וי' אותיות דס"ג חַסְדּוֹ chasdo

ג' הויות, מזלא (להמשיך הארה ממזלא עילאה) ; ר"ת = נגה : הָיָ

שמריאל

וַיִּפְרְקֵנוּ vayifrekenu מִצָּרֵינוּ mitzarenu

כִּי ki לְעוֹלָם le'olam ריבוע דס"ג וי' אותיות דס"ג חַסְדּוֹ chasdo

ג' הויות, מזלא (להמשיך הארה ממזלא עילאה) ; ר"ת = נגה : הָיָ

תומכיאל

נֹתֵן noten אבג יתץ , ושר לֶחֶם lechem ג' הויות לְכָל־ lechol יה אדני בָּשָׂר basar

ר"ת = יב"ק, אלהים יהוה, אהיה אדני יהוה

כִּי ki לְעוֹלָם le'olam ריבוע דס"ג וי' אותיות דס"ג חַסְדּוֹ chasdo

ג' הויות, מזלא (להמשיך הארה ממזלא עילאה) ; ר"ת = נגה : הָיָ

תהפיאל

הוֹדוּ hodu אהיה לְאֵל leEl ייא"י (מילוי דס"ג) הַשָּׁמָיִם hashamayim י"פ טל, י"פ כוזו

כִּי ki לְעוֹלָם le'olam ריבוע דס"ג וי' אותיות דס"ג חַסְדּוֹ chasdo

ג' הויות, מזלא (להמשיך הארה ממזלא עילאה) ; ר"ת = נגה : הָיָ

LeChai Olamiim

This prayer contains 22 sentences, each starting with one of the 22 Aramaic letters in alphabetical order. Whenever we find a connection to the number 22, it is our opportunity to draw upon the creative and DNA-like powers of the Aramaic letters to transform our reactive nature and become proactive, creating order out of chaos.

A heritage for Israel, His servant, for His kindness endures forever.
In our lowliness He remembered us, for His kindness endures forever.
And released us from our tormentors, for His kindness endures forever.
He gives nourishment to all flesh, For His kindness endures forever.
Give thanks to the God of the Heavens, for His kindness endures forever." (Psalms 136)

הָאַדֶּרֶת ha'aderet וְהָאֱמוּנָה veha'emuna לְחַי lechai עוֹלָמִים olamim

הַבִּינָה habina וְהַבְּרָכָה vehaberacha לְחַי lechai עוֹלָמִים olamim

בִּינָה ע״ה = אהיה אהיה יהוה = ווֹיים

הַגַּאֲוָה haga'ava וְהַגְּדֻלָּה vehagedula לְחַי lechai עוֹלָמִים olamim

הַדֵּעָה hade'a וְהַדִּבּוּר vehadibur לְחַי lechai עוֹלָמִים olamim

הַהוֹד hahod ההה וְהֶהָדָר vehehadar לְחַי lechai עוֹלָמִים olamim

הַוַּעַד hava'ad וְהַוָּתִיקוּת vehavatikut לְחַי lechai עוֹלָמִים olamim

הַזַּךְ hazach ייז וְהַזֹּהַר vehazohar לְחַי lechai עוֹלָמִים olamim

הַחַיִל hachayil ומב וְהַחֹסֶן vehachosen לְחַי lechai עוֹלָמִים olamim

הַטֶּכֶס hateches וְהַטֹּהַר vehatohar לְחַי lechai עוֹלָמִים olamim

הַיִּחוּד hayichud וְהַיִּרְאָה vehayir'a רי״ו לְחַי lechai עוֹלָמִים olamim

הַכֶּתֶר haketer וְהַכָּבוֹד vehakavod לאו לְחַי lechai עוֹלָמִים olamim

כתר = ה׳ מלך ה׳ מלך ה׳ ימלוך לעולם ועד ובאתב״ש גאל

הַלֶּקַח halekach וְהַלִּבּוּב vehalibuv לְחַי lechai עוֹלָמִים olamim

הַמְּלוּכָה hamelucha וְהַמֶּמְשָׁלָה vehamemshala לְחַי lechai עוֹלָמִים olamim

הַנּוֹי hanoy וְהַנֵּצַח vehanetzach לְחַי lechai עוֹלָמִים olamim

---

LECHAI OLAMIM

The strength and faithfulness *to the One Who lives eternally*
The discernment and blessing *to the One Who lives eternally*
The grandeur and greatness *to the One Who lives eternally*
The wisdom and speech *to the One Who lives eternally*
The glory and majesty *to the One Who lives eternally*
The convocation and authority *to the One Who lives eternally*
The refinement and radiance *to the One Who lives eternally*
The accomplishment and power *to the One Who lives eternally*
The adornment and purity *to the One Who lives eternally*
The oneness and reverence *to the One Who lives eternally*
The crown and honor *to the One Who lives eternally*
The study and insight *to the One Who lives eternally*
The kingship and dominion *to the One Who lives eternally*
The beauty and triumph *to the One Who lives eternally*

הַסִּגּוּי hasiguy וְהַשֶּׂגֶב vehasegev לְחַי lechai עוֹלָמִים olamim

הָעֹז ha'oz וְהָעֲנָוָה veha'anava לְחַי lechai עוֹלָמִים olamim

הַפְּדוּת hapedut וְהַפְּאֵר vehape'er לְחַי lechai עוֹלָמִים olamim

הַצְּבִי hatzevi וְהַצֶּדֶק vehatzedek לְחַי lechai עוֹלָמִים olamim

הַקְּרִיאָה hakeri'a וְהַקְּדֻשָּׁה vehakedusha לְחַי lechai עוֹלָמִים olamim

הָרֹן haron וְהָרוֹמֵמוּת veharomemot לְחַי lechai עוֹלָמִים olamim

הַשִּׁיר hashir וְהַשֶּׁבַח vehashevach לְחַי lechai עוֹלָמִים olamim

הַתְּהִלָּה hatehila וְהַתִּפְאֶרֶת vehatiferet לְחַי lechai עוֹלָמִים olamim

תהלה ע"ה = אמת, אהיה פעמים אהיה, ז"פ ס"ג

כִּי ki גָבַר gavar עָלֵינוּ alenu חַסְדּוֹ chasdo ג' הויות, מזלא (להמשיך הארה ממזלא עילאה)
וֶאֱמֶת ve'emet אהיה פעמים אהיה, ז"פ ס"ג יְהֹוָהאדנייאהדונהי Adonai
לְעוֹלָם le'olam ריבוע דס"ג וי' אותיות דס"ג הַלְלוּיָהּ haleluya אלהים, אהיה אדני ; ללה:
בָּרוּךְ baruch שֶׁנָּתַן shenatan לְעַמּוֹ le'amo יִשְׂרָאֵל Yisrael אֶת et
יוֹם yom ע"ה נגד, מזבח, זן, אל יהוה (On Shabbat add: הַשַּׁבָּת haShabbat הַזֶּה hazeh והו
וְאֶת ve'et יוֹם yom ע"ה נגד, מזבח, זן, אל יהוה) וְחַג chag שָׁבוּעוֹת Shavuot
הַזֶּה hazeh והו. אֶת et יוֹם yom ע"ה נגד, מזבח, זן, אל יהוה
טוֹב tov והו מִקְרָא mikra קֹדֶשׁ kodesh הַזֶּה hazeh והו.

The eminence and supremacy to the One Who lives eternally
The might and modesty to the One Who lives eternally
The redemption and splendor to the One Who lives eternally
The desire and righteousness to the One Who lives eternally
The summons and sanctity to the One Who lives eternally
The exultation and exaltation to the One Who lives eternally
The song and praise to the One Who lives eternally
The lauding and magnificence to the One Who lives eternally

"For His compassion has overwhelmed us and the truth of the Lord is forever. Praise the Lord!" (Psalms 117:2) *Blessed is the One who gave His nation Israel this day of* (**on Shabbat:** *Shabbat and the day of*) *Shavuot holiday, and this good day of Holy Convocation.*

BARUCH SHE'AMAR

From here ("*Baruch She'amar*") until "*Chei Ha'olamim*" (pg. 335) you are in the World of *Yetzirah*.

When saying *Baruch She'amar* you should stand and hold the two front *Tzitziot* and meditate to create equality between *Asiyah* and *Yetzirah* since the purification of *Yetzirah* is done by the *Talit*. Thirteen times the word "*Baruch*" corresponding to the Thirteen Attributes of *Yetzirah*.

(1) אל (Keter) בָּרוּךְ baruch שֶׁאָמַר she'amar וְהָיָה vehaya יהה
הָעוֹלָם ha'olam• בְּשָׁוֶה – *Olam Asiyah* is now equal to *Olam Yetzirah*

(2) רחום (Chochmah) בָּרוּךְ baruch הוּא hu•

(3) וחנון (Binah) בָּרוּךְ baruch אוֹמֵר omer וְעֹשֶׂה ve'ose•

(4) ארך בָּרוּךְ baruch גּוֹזֵר gozer וּמְקַיֵּם umkayem•

(5) אפים בָּרוּךְ baruch עֹשֶׂה ose בְרֵאשִׁית vereshit•

(6) ורב חסד בָּרוּךְ baruch מְרַחֵם merachem אברהם, ח"פ אל, רי"ו ול"ב נתיבות החכמה,
רמ"ח (אברים), עסמ"ב וט"ז אותיות פשוטות עַל al הָאָרֶץ ha'aretz אלהים דההין ע"ה

(7) ואמת בָּרוּךְ baruch מְרַחֵם merachem אברהם, ח"פ אל, רי"ו ול"ב נתיבות החכמה,
רמ"ח (אברים), עסמ"ב וט"ז אותיות פשוטות עַל al הַבְּרִיּוֹת haberiyot•

(8) נצר חסד בָּרוּךְ baruch מְשַׁלֵּם meshalem שָׂכָר sachar י"פ ב"ן
טוֹב tov והו לִירֵאָיו lire'av•

(9) לאלפים בָּרוּךְ baruch חַי chai לָעַד la'ad ב"פ ב"ן
וְקַיָּם vekayam לָנֶצַח lanetzach•

(10) נשא עון בָּרוּךְ baruch פּוֹדֶה pode וּמַצִּיל umatzil•

(11) ופשע בָּרוּךְ baruch שְׁמוֹ shemo מהש ע"ה, ע"ב בריבוע וקס"א ע"ה, אל שדי ע"ה•

BARUCH SHE'AMAR

1) Blessed is the One Who spoke and the world came into being. 2) Blessed be He. 3) Blessed is the One Who says and does. 4) Blessed is the One Who decrees and fulfills. 5) Blessed is the One Who instigates Creation. 6) Blessed is the One Who is compassionate to the world. 7) Blessed is the One Who is compassionate to all creatures. 8) Blessed is the One Who repays well those who fear Him. 9) Blessed is the One Who lives forever and exists for eternity. 10) Blessed is the One Who redeems and saves. 11) Blessed is His Name.

(12) ווטאה בָּרוּךְ baruch אַתָּה Ata יְהֹוָהאדניאהדונהי Adonai

אֱלֹהֵינוּ Elohenu ילה מֶלֶךְ melech הָעוֹלָם ha'olam

הָאֵל haEl לאה ; ״יא״ (מילוי דס״ג) אָב av

הָרַחֲמָן harachman הַמְּהֻלָּל hamehulal בְּפֶה befe פ״ז

(מנין התיבות בברוך שאמר - בסוד ״כתם טהור פז״) עַמּוֹ amo•

מְשֻׁבָּח meshubach וּמְפֹאָר umfo'ar בִּלְשׁוֹן bilshon

חֲסִידָיו chasidav וַעֲבָדָיו va'avadav• וּבְשִׁירֵי uvshirei

דָּוִד David עַבְדָּךְ avdach פוי, אל אדני נְהַלֶּלְךָ nehalelach

יְהֹוָהאדניאהדונהי Adonai אֱלֹהֵינוּ Elohenu ילה בִּשְׁבָחוֹת bishvachot

וּבִזְמִירוֹת uvizmirot• וּנְגַדֶּלְךָ ungadelach וּנְשַׁבֵּחֲךָ unshabchach

וּנְפָאֶרְךָ unfa'arach וְנַמְלִיכְךָ venamlichach וְנַזְכִּיר venazkir

שִׁמְךָ shimcha מַלְכֵּנוּ malkenu אֱלֹהֵינוּ Elohenu ילה

יָחִיד yachid חֵי chei (לפי האריז״ל, חַי לפי הרש״ש)

הָעוֹלָמִים ha'olamim• מֶלֶךְ melech מְשֻׁבָּח meshubach

וּמְפֹאָר um'fo'ar עֲדֵי adei עַד ad

שְׁמוֹ shemo מהש ע״ה, ע״ב בריבוע וקס״א ע״ה, אל שדי ע״ה

הַגָּדוֹל hagadol להח ; עם ד׳ אותיות = מבה, יזל, אום•

(13) ונקה בָּרוּךְ baruch אַתָּה Ata יְהֹוָהאדני(יְהֹוָהאדני)אהדונהי Adonai

מֶלֶךְ melech מְהֻלָּל mehulal בַּתִּשְׁבָּחוֹת batishbachot:

---

12) Blessed are You, Lord, our God, the King of the world. The God, the compassionate Father, Who is lauded by the mouths of His Nation and Who is praised and glorified by the tongues of His righteous and His servants. With the songs of David, Your servant, We shall laud You, Lord, our God. With praises and songs, we shall exult and praise You, glorify You, and proclaim You, King. We shall mention Your Name our King, our God, Unique One and life of the worlds; the King Who is praised and glorified. And forever is His Name great. 13) Blessed are You, Lord, the King Who is extolled with praises.

MIZMOR SHIR LEYOM HASHABBAT

The *Zohar* says that the following two paragraphs were recited by Adam during the first Shabbat in the Garden of Eden. The terms *Adam* and *Garden of Eden* are code words. Adam is the name given to the one unified soul that encompasses all the souls of humanity that have ever or will ever come to this world. The Garden of Eden was a realm of pure Light and positive energy. The Aramaic letters that compose this paragraph represent specific energy forces that nourished and fulfilled this unified soul called Adam. This paragraph is merely the "formula" that defines these forces. The letters also act as antennas that draw these forces into our lives, thereby giving us a taste of the "Garden of Eden."

The first paragraph connects to the realm of *Malchut*, our physical universe of chaos and darkness. The second refers to the level of *Zeir Anpin*, the Upper Worlds of pure positivity and fulfillment. The sole purpose of joining these two worlds is to remove all the chaos and darkness from our existence.

In the first paragraph we have 112 words (יב"ק, אלהים + יהוה, אהיה + אדני + יהוה) and 16 verses – corresponding to the nine dots of *Malchut* (as *Malchut* does not have a consistent dot but She is included in all the other nine dots) and the seven voices of the given *Torah*.

מִזְמוֹר mizmor שִׁיר shir לְיוֹם leyom ע"ה נגד, מזבח, זן, אל יהוה הַשַּׁבָּת haShabbat

Initials of *LeMoshe* (למשה)

טוֹב tov והו לְהֹדוֹת lehodot ר"ת ט"ל לַיהֹוָאדהנויאהדונהי ladonai

וּלְזַמֵּר ulzamer לְשִׁמְךָ leshimcha עֶלְיוֹן elyon: לְהַגִּיד lehagid בַּבֹּקֶר baboker

חַסְדֶּךָ chasdecha וֶאֱמוּנָתְךָ ve'emunat'cha בַּלֵּילוֹת balelot: עֲלֵי־ alei

עָשׂוֹר asor וַעֲלֵי־ va'alei נָבֶל navel עֲלֵי alei הִגָּיוֹן higayon בְּכִנּוֹר bechinor:

כִּי ki שִׂמַּחְתַּנִי simachtani יְהֹוָאדהנויאהדונהי Adonai בְּפָעֳלֶךָ befa'olecha

בְּמַעֲשֵׂי bema'asei יָדֶיךָ yadecha אֲרַנֵּן aranen: מַה־ ma מ"ה גָּדְלוּ gadlu

מַעֲשֶׂיךָ ma'asecha יְהֹוָאדהנויאהדונהי Adonai מְאֹד me'od עָמְקוּ amku

מַחְשְׁבֹ(ו)תֶיךָ machshevotecha **(Superiour *Keter*)** יוזו: אִישׁ ish בַּעַר ba'ar

לֹא lo יֵדָע yeda וּכְסִיל uchsil לֹא־ lo יָבִין yavin אֶת־ et זֹאת zot:

MIZMOR SHIR LEYOM HASHABBAT

"A Psalm, a song for the day of Shabbat: It is good to say thanks to You, the Lord, and to sing Your Name, Exalted One. To relate Your kindness in the morning and Your faithfulness in the evenings upon ten-stringed instrument and lyre, with singing accompanied by a harp. Because You have made me happy, Lord, with Your deeds, for the work of Your Hands, I shall sing joyously. How great are Your deeds, Lord, and how greatly profound are Your thoughts. A boor cannot know nor can a fool understand this.

(ע״ב שמות) כוונות הקדושה esev עֵשֶׂב kemo כְּמוֹ resha'im רְשָׁעִים bifro'ach בִּפְרֹחַ
(The souls of the wicked are judged now to see if they are worthy to be elevated from *Gehenom*)
aven אָוֶן po'alei פֹּעֲלֵי ילי kol כָּל־ vayatzitzu וַיָּצִיצוּ
lehishamdam לְהִשָּׁמְדָם (The *klipa* that wants to be elevated with the Holiness)
marom מָרוֹם ve'ata וְאַתָּה :(but it is not allowed to go up) ad עַד adei עֲדֵי־
hine הִנֵּה ki כִּי :Adonai יְהֹוָה יאהדונהי ריבוע דס״ג י׳ אותיות דס״ג le'olam לְעֹלָם
oyvecha אֹיְבֶיךָ hine הִנֵּה ki כִּי־ Adonai יְהֹוָה יאהדונהי oyvecha אֹיְבֶיךָ
:(The *klipa*) aven אָוֶן po'alei פֹּעֲלֵי ילי kol כָּל־ yitpardu יִתְפָּרְדוּ yovedu יֹאבֵדוּ
baloti בַּלֹּתִי karni קַרְנִי kir'em כִּרְאֵים (The Holiness) vatarem וַתָּרֶם
דמ״ה ריבוע eni עֵינִי vatabet וַתַּבֵּט :ra'anan רַעֲנָן beshemen בְּשֶׁמֶן
mere'im מְרֵעִים alai עָלַי bakamim בַּקָּמִים beshurai בְּשׁוּרָי
(The soul of the righteous that is elevated now) :יוד הי ואו הה oznai אָזְנָי tishmana תִּשְׁמַעְנָה
קרח ס״ת yifrach יִפְרָח katamar כַּתָּמָר דלעיל כלה באי ג״פ tzadik צַדִּיק
:yisge יִשְׂגֶּה baLevanon בַּלְּבָנוֹן ke'erez כְּאֶרֶז (meditate to elevate the soul of *Korach*)
Adonai יְהֹוָה יאהדונהי ראה ב״פ bevet בְּבֵית shetulim שְׁתוּלִים
od עוֹד :yafrichu יַפְרִיחוּ ילה Elohenu אֱלֹהֵינוּ bechatzrot בְּחַצְרוֹת
vera'ananim וְרַעֲנַנִּים deshenim דְּשֵׁנִים beseva בְּשֵׂיבָה yenuvun יְנוּבוּן
yashar יָשָׁר ki כִּי־ lehagid לְהַגִּיד :(דס״ג) מילוי (ייא״י) אל yih'yu יִהְיוּ
:bo בּוֹ (כתיב: עלתה) avlata עַוְלָתָה velo וְלֹא־ tzuri צוּרִי Adonai יְהֹוָה יאהדונהי

When the wicked bloom (from Gehenom) *like grass and all doers of iniquity blossom in order to destroy them forever. And You are exalted forever, Lord. For behold, Your enemies, Lord! For behold, Your enemies shall perish and all the doers of iniquity* (those are the *klipot*) *shall be dispersed. And You shall lift up* (the Holiness) *my worth like an ox and I will be drenched with fresh oil. And my eyes will see my foes and my ears will hear those who rise up to harm me. A righteous man will flourish like a palm leaf, like a cedar in the Lebanon, he will grow tall. They are planted in the House of the Lord, they shall flourish in the courtyards of our God. They will still be fruitful in old age, vigorous and fresh they shall be. To declare that the Lord is just, my rock in Whom there is no wrong."* (Psalms 92).

ADONAI MALACH

In this Psalm there are 45 words correspond to the Holy Name: (מ"ה (יוד הא ואו הא

ge'ut גֵּאוּת malach מָלָךְ (*Zeir Anpin*) Adonai יְהֻוָהאדניאהדונהי

(410 cords of *Arich Anpin* - where *Zeir Anpin* is elevated on *Shabbat* and he is clothing them)

hit'azar הִתְאַזָּר oz עֹז Adonai יְהֻוָהאדניאהדונהי lavesh לָבֵשׁ lavesh לָבֵשׁ

רי"ו ב"פ tevel תֵּבֵל tikon תִּכּוֹן אדני אהיה ,אלהים = ר"ת af אַף־

ומב me'az מֵאָז kis'acha כִּסְאֲךָ nachon נָכוֹן :timot תִּמּוֹט bal בַּל־

neharot נְהָרוֹת nas'u נָשְׂאוּ :קנ"א, אדני אלהים = ר"ת Ata אָתָּה me'olam מֵעוֹלָם

(410 cords of *Arich Anpin* -
Which draw Light from the sea of *Chochmah* -מוזא סתימא דא"א- on *Shabbat* to *Zeir Anpin*)

neharot נְהָרוֹת קין = ר"ת nas'u נָשְׂאוּ Adonai יְהֻוָהאדניאהדונהי

:דני ר"ת dochyam דָּכְיָם neharot נְהָרוֹת yis'u יִשְׂאוּ kolam קוֹלָם

ערי ,סנדלפון ,מןזוךך = ר"ת rabim רַבִּים mayim מַיִם (410 cords) mikolot מִקֹּלוֹת

ילי yam יָם mishberei מִשְׁבְּרֵי־ הרי adirim אַדִּירִים (לעשות בה מ"ן שהם ה"ג - *Ima*)

Arich Anpin [has 221 *Ribo* (tens of thousands) illuminations],
He is giving 150 *Ribo* (tens of thousands) illuminations to *Zeir Anpin*.
Initials of אמי (my mother) because, *Zeir Anpin* first goes up and takes *Mochin* from *Ima* (mother).

:Adonai יְהֻוָהאדניאהדונהי bamarom בַּמָּרוֹם הרי adir אַדִּיר

Initials of אבי (my father), because *Zeir Anpin* later goes up and takes *Mochin* from *Abba* (Father).

ADONAI MALACH

The Lord has reigned. He clothed Himself with pride. The Lord clothed Himself and girded Himself with might. He also established the world firmly so that it will not collapse. Your throne has been established ever since, You have been forever. The rivers have lifted the Lord, the rivers have raised their voices. The rivers will raise their powerful waves. More than the roars of many waters and the powerful waves of the sea, You are immense in the high places, Lord.

עֵדֹתֶיךָ edotecha נֶאֶמְנוּ ne'emnu מְאֹד me'od ר״ת = קין לְבֵיתְךָ levetcha

ב״פ ראה נַאֲוָה na'ava קֹדֶשׁ kodesh יְהֹוָאדנָיאהדונהי Adonai לְאֹרֶךְ le'orech

יָמִים yamim נלך ; ר״ת ילי ; ס״ת אדני ; ה' לאורך ימים = ש״ע נהורים עם האותיות׃

YEHI CHEVOD

We find 18 verses in this connection, with 18 times the power of *Yud, Hei, Vav,* and *Hei.* The significance of 18 is found within the power of the *Mezuzah.* The kabbalists teach that the *Mezuzah*, which contains a piece of parchment bearing the Aramaic letters *Shin, Dalet, Yud* שדי, or *Shaddai* - a powerful Name of God that brings us protection from negative forces, should be placed at each doorway. A doorway or entranceway is the beginning, or seed level of a room. Negative forces cling to all entryways, infecting the seed with negativity. The *Mezuzah* not only cancels this negative force but also transforms the negative energy into positive energy.

Another secret of *Shin, Dalet, Yud* is its a connection to another 72 Name of God, one that gives us the ability to eradicate all forms of negativity: The next letter after *Shin* ש in the Aramaic alphabet is *Tav* ת. The next letter to *Dalet* ד is *Hei* ה. The next letter after *Yud* י is *Kaf* כ. Placed side by side and in reverse order, these letters spell *Kaf, Hei, Tav* כהת. This three-letter sequence has the power to defuse negative energy, and was used to destroy the evil *Haman* in Persia during Purim, 2500 years ago.

When you say the 18 verses of *Yehi Chevod*, you should meditate on the 18 letters of the six combinations of the Name *Shaddai* שדי that exist in the central Vessels of *Zeir Anpin* of *Yetzirah*, and also meditate on the 18 times the Name: יהוה appears in this section, because they are equal to the two letters *Tet* ט in the Name of the Angel Ma-tat-ron מטטרון **(Do not pronounce)** which is in *Zeir Anpin* of *Yetzirah*. You should meditate that the *Tet* (9) corresponds to *Tikkunei Dikna* of *Zeir Anpin* of *Yetzirah* (nine of Direct Light and nine of Returning Light).

The numerical value of the acronym of the 18 verses of *Yehi Chevod* adds up to 686. The numerical value of the last letter of each of the 18 verses is 602, plus 18 (*Yesod – Chai* - ח״י) adds up to 620. The number of words in *Yehi Chevod* is 138 (with the *Kolel*). You should also meditate to draw ע״ב, ס״ג, מ״ה, ב״ן with קס״א, קמ״ג, קנ״א (which adds up to 686 – with the *Kolel* - and is equal to the numerical value of the word *Porat*), to "*Ben Porat Yosef* " which is *Yesod – Chai* (18) *Almin*. Thereby creating the *Keter* (620) of *Nukva* (which is called: *Chakal* חק״ל, which adds up to 138).The *Keter* itself will be built later by the 22 letters of the *Ashrei*.

Your testimonies are extremely trustworthy.
Your House is the holy sanctuary. The Lord will be there for long days." (Psalms 93)

(Keter–ש) יְהִי yehi כְּבוֹד chevod יְהֹוָ֖האדניאהדונהי Adonai (ארך)

כבוד יהוה = יוד הי ואו הה לְעוֹלָם le'olam ריבוע ס"ג וי' אותיות דס"ג יִשְׂמַח yismach משיח ;

לעולם ישמח ע"ה = ריבוע קס"א יְהֹוָ֖האדניאהדונהי Adonai (אפים) בְּמַעֲשָׂיו bema'asav

יהוה במעשיו ע"ה = קס"א קנ"א קמ"ג ; הושע ; ר"ת הפסוק = אמן (יאהדונהי) ע"ה: (Keter–ד) יְהִי yehi

שֵׁם shem יְהֹוָ֖האדניאהדונהי Adonai (ורב וחסד) מְבֹרָךְ mevorach ר"ת =

ריבוע ע"ב וריבוע ס"ג ; יהוה מברך = רפ"ח (להעלות רפ"ח ניצוצות שנפלו לקליפה דמשם באים התולאים)

מֵעַתָּה me'ata וְעַד־ ve'ad עוֹלָם olam ילי:

(Chochmah–י) מִמִּזְרַח־ mimizrach שֶׁמֶשׁ shemesh עַד־ ad ר"ת קדוש

מְבוֹאוֹ mevo'o מְהֻלָּל mehulal שֵׁם shem יְהֹוָ֖האדניאהדונהי Adonai (נשא עון):

(Chochmah–ש) רָם ram עַל־ al כָּל kol ילי ; עמם גּוֹיִם goyim

יְהֹוָ֖האדניאהדונהי Adonai (ופשע) עַל al הַשָּׁמַיִם hashamayim י"פ טל, י"פ כוזו ;

ר"ת ושמל כְּבוֹדוֹ kevodo: (Binah–י) יְהֹוָ֖האדניאהדונהי Adonai (ונקה) שִׁמְךָ shimcha

לְעוֹלָם le'olam ריבוע ס"ג וי' אותיות דס"ג יְהֹוָ֖האדניאהדונהי Adonai (פוקד)

זִכְרְךָ zichrecha לְדֹר־ ledor ר"ת יזל וָדֹר vador רי"ו:

(Binah–ד) יְהֹוָ֖האדניאהדונהי Adonai (על שלשים) בַּשָּׁמַיִם bashamayim י"פ טל, י"פ כוזו

הֵכִין hechin כִּסְאוֹ kis'o וּמַלְכוּתוֹ umalchuto בַּכֹּל bakol ב"ן, לכב

מָשָׁלָה mashala מבה: (Chesed–ד) יִשְׂמְחוּ yismechu הַשָּׁמַיִם hashamayim

י"פ טל, י"פ כוזו וְתָגֵל vetagel אותיות גלות (כשתהיה גאולה תהא שמחה) הָאָרֶץ ha'aretz

אלהים דההין ע"ה ; ר"ת יהוה וס"ת ריבוע דס"ג וְיֹאמְרוּ veyomru בַגּוֹיִם vagoyim

יְהֹוָ֖האדניאהדונהי Adonai (ועל רבעים) מָלָךְ malach ר"ת יבמ, ב"ן:

YEHI CHEVOD

"May the glory of the Lord last forever. May the Lord rejoice in His works." (Psalms 104:31) "May the Name of the Lord be blessed from now and for all eternity. From the sun's rising until its setting the Lord's Name is praised. The Lord is high above all nations. His glory is above the heavens." (Psalms 113:2-4) "Lord, Your Name is forever. Lord, Your fame is for every generation." (Psalms 135:13) "The Lord established His Throne in the heavens, and His kingdom rules over everything." (Psalms 103:19) "Let the heavens rejoice and let the earth be glad and let them proclaim among the nations: The Lord has reigned. (I Chronicles 16:31)

(*Chesed*–ש) יְהֹוָאדניאהדונהי Adonai (ארך) מֶלֶךְ melech

יְהֹוָאדניאהדונהי Adonai (אפים) מָלָךְ malach יְהֹוָאדניאהדונהי Adonai (ורב וחסד) |

יִמְלֹךְ yimloch מלך מלך ימלך = בוזוך, סנדלפון, ערי לְעֹלָם le'olam ריבוע ס"ג וי' אותיות דס"ג

ר"ת י"ל וָעֶד va'ed: (*Gevurah*–י) יְהֹוָאדניאהדונהי Adonai (נושא עון) מֶלֶךְ melech

עוֹלָם olam וָעֶד va'ed ר"ת = כוק, ריבוע אדני אָבְדוּ avdu גּוֹיִם goyim

מֵאַרְצוֹ me'artzo ס"ת = ב"ן: (*Gevurah*–ד) יְהֹוָאדניאהדונהי Adonai (ופשע)

הֵפִיר hefir עֲצַת־ atzat גּוֹיִם goyim הֵנִיא heni מַחְשְׁבוֹת machshevot

עַמִּים amim: (*Tiferet*–י) רַבּוֹת rabot מַחֲשָׁבוֹת machashavot בְּלֶב־ belev

אִישׁ ish וַעֲצַת va'atzat יְהֹוָאדניאהדונהי Adonai (ונקה) הִיא hee

תָקוּם takum כ"א הויות: (*Tiferet*–ש) עֲצַת atzat יְהֹוָאדניאהדונהי Adonai (פוקד)

לְעוֹלָם le'olam ריבוע ס"ג וי' אותיות דס"ג תַּעֲמֹד ta'amod מַחְשְׁבוֹת machshevot

לִבּוֹ libo לְדֹר ledor וָדֹר vador רי"ו: (*Netzach*–י) כִּי ki הוּא hu

אָמַר amar וַיֶּהִי vayehi הוּא־ hu צִוָּה tziva וַיַּעֲמֹד vaya'amod:

(*Netzach*–ש) כִּי־ ki בָּחַר vachar יְהֹוָאדניאהדונהי Adonai (על שלשים)

בְּצִיּוֹן beTziyon יוסף, ו' הויות, קנאה אִוָּהּ iva וזבו לְמוֹשָׁב lemoshav לוֹ lo:

(*Hod*–ד) כִּי־ ki יַעֲקֹב Yaakov ד' הויות, יאהדונהי אידהנויה בָּחַר bachar לוֹ lo יָהּ Yah

יִשְׂרָאֵל Yisrael לִסְגֻלָּתוֹ lisgulato: (*Hod*–י) כִּי ki לֹא־ lo יִטֹּשׁ yitosh

יְהֹוָאדניאהדונהי Adonai (ועל רבעים) עַמּוֹ amo וְנַחֲלָתוֹ venachalato לֹא lo

יַעֲזֹב ya'azov: (*Yesod*–ד) וְהוּא vehu רַחוּם rachum יְכַפֵּר yechaper ר"ת רי"ו

"The Lord reigns, the Lord has reigned. The Lord shall reign forever and ever. The Lord is King forever and ever. Nations have perished from His land." (Psalms 10:16) *"The Lord has disrupted the conspiracy of peoples and thwarted the plans of nations."* (Psalms 33:10) *"Many are the thoughts in the heart of man, but it is the purpose of the Lord that takes place."* (Proverbs 19:21) *"The purpose of the Lord shall endure forever and the thoughts of His Heart, for all generations."* (Psalms 33:11) *"Because He said and it came to be, He commanded and it was established."* (Psalms 33:9) *"For the Lord chose Zion as His desired dwelling place."* (Psalms 132:13) *"For God chose Jacob for Himself and Israel as His treasure."* (Psalms 135:4) *"For the Lord shall not forsake His people nor shall He abandon His heritage."* (Psalms 94:14) *"And He is merciful, forgives*

עָוֹן avon (**Abba** of the **klipa**) וְלֹא־ velo יַשְׁחִית yashchit (**Ima** of the **klipa**)

וְהִרְבָּה vehirba לְהָשִׁיב lehashiv אַפּוֹ apo (**Zeir** of the **klipa**)

וְלֹא־ velo יָעִיר ya'ir כָּל־ kol ילי חֲמָתוֹ chamato (**Nukva of the klipa**):

(ש־יסוד) יְהֹוָהאדניאהדונהי Adonai הוֹשִׁיעָה hoshi'a יהוה וש"ע נהורין

הַמֶּלֶךְ hamelech ר"ת יהה יַעֲנֵנוּ ya'anenu בְיוֹם veyom ע"ה נגד, מזבח, זן אל יהוה

קָרְאֵנוּ kor'enu ר"ת יב"ק, אלהים יהוה, אהיה אדני יהוה ; ס"ת ב"ן ועם כ' דהמלך = ע"ב:

Then without any interruption you should immediately start the two verses of *Ashrei* to make *Keter* to *Nukva* from the 22 letters of *Ashrei* (as mentioned before *Yehi Chevod*).

THE ASHREI

Twenty-one of the twenty-two letters of the Aramaic alphabet are encoded in the *Ashrei* in their correct order from *Alef* to *Tav*. King David, the author, left out the Aramaic letter *Nun* from this prayer, because *Nun* is the first letter in the Aramaic word *nefilah*, which means "falling." Falling refers to a spiritual decline, as in falling into the *klipa*. Feelings of doubt, depression, worry, and uncertainty are consequences of spiritual falling. Because the Aramaic letters are the actual instruments of Creation, this prayer helps to inject order and the power of Creation into our lives, without the energy of falling.

In this Psalm there are ten times the Name: יהוה for the Ten *Sefirot*. This Psalm is written according to the order of the *Alef Bet*, but the letter *Nun* is omitted to prevent falling.

אַשְׁרֵי ashrei (סוד הכתר) יוֹשְׁבֵי yoshvei בֵיתֶךָ vetecha ב"פ ראה

עוֹד od יְהַלְלוּךָ yehalelucha סֶּלָה sela: אַשְׁרֵי ashrei הָעָם ha'am

שֶׁכָּכָה shekacha מהש, משה, ע"ב בריבוע וקס"א, אל שדי, ד"פ אלהים ע"ה כּוֹ lo

אַשְׁרֵי ashrei הָעָם ha'am ר"ת לאה שֶׁיְהֹוָהאדניאהדונהי she'Adonai (**Keter**)

אֱלֹהָיו Elohav ילה: תְּהִלָּה tehila ע"ה אמת, אהיה פעמים אהיה, ז"פ ס"ג לְדָוִד leDavid

אֲרוֹמִמְךָ aromimcha אֱלוֹהַי Elohai הַמֶּלֶךְ hamelech וַאֲבָרְכָה va'avarcha

שִׁמְךָ shimcha לְעוֹלָם le'olam ריבוע דס"ג וי' אותיות דס"ג וָעֶד va'ed:

---

iniquity, and does not destroy; He frequently diverts His anger and does not arouse all His wrath." (Psalms 70:38) *"Lord save us. The King shall answer on the day that we call Him."* (Psalms 20:10)

THE ASHREI

"Joyful are those who dwell in Your House, they shall praise You, Selah." (Psalms 84:5) *"Joyful is the nation that this is theirs and joyful the nation that the Lord is their God."* (Psalms 145:15) *"A Praise of David:*
א *I shall exalt You, my God, the King, and I shall bless Your Name forever and for eternity.*

בְּכָל־ bechol ב״ן, לכב יוֹם yom ע״ה נגד, מזבח, זן אל יהוה
אֲבָרְכֶךָּ avarcheka וַאֲהַלְלָה va'ahalela מ״ה יהוה שִׁמְךָ shimcha
לְעוֹלָם le'olam ריבוע דס״ג וי׳ אותיות דס״ג וָעֶד va'ed:

גָּדוֹל gadol להח ; עם ד׳ אותיות = מבה, יזל, אום
יְהֹוָהאדניאהדונהי Adonai (*Chochmah*) וּמְהֻלָּל umhulal אדני, ללה
מְאֹד me'od וְלִגְדֻלָּתוֹ veligdulato והו אֵין en חֵקֶר cheker:

דּוֹר dor לְדוֹר ledor יְשַׁבַּח yeshabach מַעֲשֶׂיךָ ma'asecha ר״ת דלים
וּגְבוּרֹתֶיךָ ugvurotecha יַגִּידוּ yagidu ייז, כ״ב אותיות פשוטות (=אכא) וה׳ אותיות סופיות מןץףך:

הֲדַר hadar כְּבוֹד kevod הוֹדֶךָ hodecha וְדִבְרֵי vedivrei
נִפְלְאוֹתֶיךָ nifle'otecha ר״ת אלהים, אהיה אדני
אָשִׂיחָה asicha ר״ת הפסוק = פ״ז (בסוד כתם טהור פז):

וֶעֱזוּז ve'ezuz נוֹרְאוֹתֶיךָ no'rotecha יֹאמֵרוּ yomeru וּגְדוּלָּתְךָ ugdulatcha
(כתיב: וגדלותיך) ר״ת = ע״ב, ריבוע יהוה אֲסַפְּרֶנָּה asaperena ס״ת = ייא״י (מילוי דס״ג):

זֵכֶר zecher רַב־ rav טוּבְךָ tuvcha לאו יַבִּיעוּ yabi'u
וְצִדְקָתְךָ vetzidkatcha יְרַנֵּנוּ yeranenu ס״ת = ב״ן, יבמ, לכב ; ר״ת הפסוק = רי״ו יהוה:

חַנּוּן chanun וְרַחוּם verachum יְהֹוָהאדניאהדונהי Adonai (*Binah*)
חנון ורחום יהוה = עשל אֶרֶךְ erech ס״ת = ס״ג ב״ן אַפַּיִם apayim ר״ת = יהוה
וּגְדָל־ ugdal (כתיב: וגדול) וָחֶסֶד chased ע״ב, ריבוע יהוה:

ב *I shall bless You every day and I shall praise Your Name forever and for eternity.*
ג *The Lord is great and exceedingly praised. His greatness is unfathomable.*
ד *One generation and the next shall praise Your deeds and tell of Your might.*
ה *The brilliance of Your splendid glory and the wonders of Your acts, I shall speak of.*
ו *They shall speak of the might of Your awesome acts and I shall tell of Your greatness.*
ז *They shall express the remembrance of Your abundant goodness, and Your righteousness they shall joyfully proclaim.* חו *The Lord is merciful and compassionate, slow to anger and great in kindness.*

טוֹב־ tov והו יְהֹוָהאדניאהדונהי Adonai (*Chesed*) לַכֹּל lakol

יה אדני ; ס"ת ל"ו (מילוי ד"ס"ג) וְרַחֲמָיו verachamav עַל־ al

כָּל kol ילי ; עמם ; ר"ת ריבוע ב"ן ע"ה מַעֲשָׂיו ma'asav ס"ת ע"ב, ריבוע יהוה:

יוֹדוּךָ yoducha יְהֹוָהאדניאהדונהי Adonai (*Gevurah*) כָּל־ kol ילי מַעֲשֶׂיךָ ma'asecha

וַחֲסִידֶיךָ vachasidecha ר"ת אלהים, אהיה אדני יְבָרְכוּכָה yevarchucha ס"ת = מ"ה:

כְּבוֹד kevod מַלְכוּתְךָ malchutcha יֹאמֵרוּ yomeru וּגְבוּרָתְךָ ugvuratcha

יְדַבֵּרוּ yedaberu ר"ת הפסוק = אלהים, אהיה אדני ; ס"ת = ב"ן, יבמ, לכב:

לְהוֹדִיעַ lehodi'a לִבְנֵי livnei הָאָדָם ha'adam ר"ת ללה, אדני

גְּבוּרֹתָיו gevurotav וּכְבוֹד uchvod הֲדַר hadar

מַלְכוּתוֹ malchuto ר"ת מ"ה וס"ת = רי"ו ; ר"ת הפסוק ע"ה = ק"כ צירופי אלהים:

מַלְכוּתְךָ malchutcha מַלְכוּת malchut כָּל־ kol ילי עֹלָמִים olamim

וּמֶמְשַׁלְתְּךָ umemshaltecha בְּכָל־ bechol ב"ן, לכב דּוֹר dor וָדֹר vador רי"ו:

סוֹמֵךְ somech ריבוע אדני יְהֹוָהאדניאהדונהי Adonai (*Tiferet*)

לְכָל־ lechol יה אדני ; סומך אדני לכל ר"ת סאל, אמן (יאהדונהי) הַנֹּפְלִים hanoflim

וְזוֹקֵף vezokef לְכָל־ lechol יה אדני הַכְּפוּפִים haketufim נמם:

עֵינֵי־ enei ריבוע דמ"ה כֹל chol ילי אֵלֶיךָ elecha יְשַׂבֵּרוּ yesaberu וְאַתָּה veAta

נוֹתֵן־ noten אבג"יתץ, ושר לָהֶם lahem אֶת־ et אָכְלָם ochlam בְּעִתּוֹ be'ito:

ט *The Lord is good to all, His compassion extends over all His acts.*
י *All that You have made shall thank You, God, and Your pious ones shall bless You.*
כ *They shall speak of the glory of Your Kingdom and talk of Your mighty deeds.*
ל *His mighty deeds He makes known to man and the glory of His splendid Kingdom.*
מ *Yours is the Kingdom of all worlds and Your reign extends to each and every generation.*
ס *The Lord supports all those who fell and holds upright all those who are bent over.*
ע *The eyes of all look hopefully towards You, and You give them their food at its proper time.*

POTE'ACH ET YADECHA

We connect to the letters *Pei, Alef,* and *Yud* by opening our hands and holding our palms skyward. Our consciousness is focused on receiving sustenance and financial prosperity from the Light through our actions of tithing and sharing, our *Desire to Receive for the Sake of Sharing*. In doing so, we also acknowledge that the sustenance we receive comes from a higher source and is not of our own doing. According to the sages, if we do not meditate on this idea at this juncture, we must repeat the prayer.

פתוז (שע״ז נהורין למ״ה ולס״ה)

יוד הי ויו הי יוד הי ויו הי (וז׳ וזיוורתי)
אלף למד אלף למד (ש״ע)
יוד הא ואו הא (לז״א)
אדני (ולנוקבא)

פותוז את ידך ר״ת פאי
ג׳ימ׳ יאהדונהי זו״ן
וזכמה דז״א ו״ק
יסוד דנוק׳

פּוֹתֵחַ pote'ach אֶת et יָדֶךָ yadecha ר״ת פאי וס״ת וזתך עם ג׳ אותיות = דִּיקָרְנוֹסָא

ובאתב״ש הוא סאל, פאי, אמן, יאהדונהי ; ועוד יכוין שם וזתך בשילוב יהוה – יְוָזהְתְוּכָהָ

מצפץ מצפץ מווזין דפנים דאוזור אלהים אלהים
להמשיך פ״ו אורות לכל מילוי דכל

אוזור דפרצופי נה״י ווזג״ת
דפרצוף וזג״ת דיצירה דז״א
לף מד י וד ם
אלף למד הי יוד מם

וזתך
סאל יאהדונהי

ואוזור דפרצופי נה״י ווזג״ת
דיצירה דרוזל הנקראת לאה
לף מד י וד ם
אלף למד הי יוד מם

וּמַשְׂבִּיעַ umasbi'a וזתך עם ג׳ אותיות = דִּיקָרְנוֹסָא

ובא״ת ב״ש הוא סאל, אמן, יאהדונהי ; ועוד יכוין שם וזתך בשילוב יהוה – יְוָזהְתְוּכָהָ

מצפץ מצפץ מווזין דפנים דאוזור אלהים אלהים
להמשיך פ״ו אורות לכל מילוי דכל

אוזור דפרצופי נה״י ווזג״ת
דפרצוף נה״י דיצירה דז״א
לף מד י וד ם
אלף למד הי יוד מם

וזתך

ואוזור דפרצופי נה״י ווזג״ת
דיצירה דרוזל הנקראת לאה
לף מד י וד ם
אלף למד הי יוד מם

לְכָל־ lechol יה אדני (להמשיך מווזין ד־יה אל הנוקבא שהיא אדני)

חַי chai כל וזי = אהיה אהיה יהוה, בינה ע״ה, וזיים

רָצוֹן ratzon מהש ע״ה, ע״ב בריבוע וקס״א ע״ה, אל שדי ע״ה ; ר״ת רוזל שהיא המלכות הצריכה לשפע

יוד יוד הי יוד הי ויו יוד הי ויו הי יסוד דאבא
אלף הי יוד הי יסוד דאימא
להמתיק רוזל וב׳ דמעין שך פר

Also meditate to draw abundance and sustenance and blessing to all the worlds from the *ratzon* mentioned above. You should meditate and focus on this verse because it is the essence of prosperity, and that God is intervening and sustaining and supporting all of Creation.

POTE'ACH ET YADECHA

פ *Open Your Hands and satisfy every living thing with desire.*

צַדִּיק tzadik יהוה אהדונהי Adonai (*Yesod*) בְּכָל bechol ב״ן, לכב

דְּרָכָיו derachav וְחָסִיד vechasid בְּכָל bechol ב״ן, לכב מַעֲשָׂיו ma'asav יבמ, ב״ן:

קָרוֹב karov יְהֹוָה אהדונהי Adonai (*Malchut*) לְכָל־ lechol יה אדני

קֹרְאָיו kor'av לְכֹל lechol יה אדני אֲשֶׁר asher

יִקְרָאֻהוּ yikra'uhu בֶאֱמֶת ve'emet אהיה פעמים אהיה, ז״פ ס״ג:

רְצוֹן retzon מהש ע״ה, ע״ב בריבוע וקס״א ע״ה, אל שדי ע״ה יְרֵאָיו yere'av יַעֲשֶׂה ya'ase

ר״ת רי״ וְאֶת־ ve'et שַׁוְעָתָם shav'atam יִשְׁמַע yishma וְיוֹשִׁיעֵם veyoshi'em:

שׁוֹמֵר shomer כ״א הויות שבתפילין יְהֹוָה אהדונהי Adonai (*Netzach*)

אֶת־ et כָּל־ kol ילי אֹהֲבָיו ohavav ר״ת אכא

וְאֵת ve'et כָּל־ kol ילי הָרְשָׁעִים haresha'im יַשְׁמִיד yashmid:

תְּהִלַּת tehilat יְהֹוָה אהדונהי Adonai (*Hod*) יְדַבֶּר yedaber ראה פִּי pi

וִיבָרֵךְ vivarech ע״ב ס״ג מ״ה ב״ן, הברכה (למתק את ז׳ המלכים שמתו) כָּל kol ילי

בָּשָׂר basar שֵׁם shem קָדְשׁוֹ kodsho לְעוֹלָם le'olam ריבוע ס״ג וי׳ אותיות דס״ג

וָעֶד va'ed: וַאֲנַחְנוּ va'anachnu נְבָרֵךְ nevarech יָהּ ya מֵעַתָּה me'ata

וְעַד־ ve'ad עוֹלָם olam הַלְלוּיָהּ haleluya אלהים, אהיה אדני ; ללה:

THE FIVE PSALMS

At the beginning and end of each Psalm, we find the word *Haleluyah*, meaning "Praise the Lord." As Kabbalah always says, God does not need our praise. The word is a code; these ten *Haleuyahs* link us to the Ten *Sefirot*. They help us ascend to the top of the World of Formation, *Yetzirah*.

צ *The Lord is righteous in all His ways and virtuous in all His deeds.*
ק *The Lord is close to all who call Him, and only to those who call Him truthfully.*
ר *He shall fulfill the will of those who fear Him; He hears their wailing and saves them.*
ש *The Lord protects all who love Him and He destroys the wicked.*
ת *My lips utter the praise of the Lord and all flesh shall bless His Holy Name, forever and for eternity."*
(Psalms 145) *"And we shall bless the Lord forever and for eternity. Praise the Lord!"* (Psalms 115:18)

Ten times *Haleluyah* is the *tikkun* of the Ten *Sefirot* of *Beriah* in *Yetzirah*

THE FIRST PSALM – MALCHUT AND YESOD

This first Psalm contains *Yud, Hei, Vav,* and *Hei,* the Tetragrammaton (יהוה), nine times. This nine is linked to the upper nine *Sefirot*, from *Yesod* to *Keter*. The energy of our realm, the World of *Malchut*, is receiving. Like the moon, *Malchut* has no Light of its own and draws its Light from the upper nine dimensions through our spiritual actions of transformation.

(Malchut of Yetzirah) הַלְלוּיָהּ haleluya אלהים, אהיה אדני ; ללה הַלְלִי haleli

נַפְשִׁי nafshi אֶת־ et יְהֹוָהאדני יאהדונהי Adonai ***(Keter)***: אֲהַלְלָה ahalela מ״ה יהוה

יְהֹוָהאדני יאהדונהי Adonai ***(Chochmah)*** בְּחַיָּי bechayai אֲזַמְּרָה azamra

לֵאלֹהַי lelohai מילוי ע״ב, דמב ; ילה בְּעוֹדִי be'odi ר״ת וס״ת הפסוק = אמן (יאהדונהי):

אַל־ al תִּבְטְחוּ tivtechu בִנְדִיבִים vindivim בְּבֶן־ beven אָדָם adam

שֶׁאֵין she'en לוֹ lo תְשׁוּעָה teshu'a: תֵּצֵא tetze רוּחוֹ rucho יָשֻׁב yashuv

לְאַדְמָתוֹ le'admato בַּיּוֹם bayom ע״ה נגד, מזבח, זן אל יהוה הַהוּא hahu

אָבְדוּ avdu עֶשְׁתֹּנֹתָיו eshtonotav: אַשְׁרֵי ashrei שֶׁאֵל sheEl ייא״י (מילוי דס״ג)

יַעֲקֹב Ya'akov ז׳ הויות, יאהדונהי אידהנויה בְּעֶזְרוֹ be'ezro שִׂבְרוֹ sivro

עַל al יְהֹוָהאדני יאהדונהי Adonai ***(Binah)*** אֱלֹהָיו Elohav ילה: עֹשֶׂה ose

שָׁמַיִם shamayim י״פ טל, י״פ כוזו וָאָרֶץ va'aretz אֶת־ et הַיָּם hayam ילי

וְאֶת־ ve'et כָּל־ kol ילי אֲשֶׁר־ asher בָּם bam שם בן מ״ב הַשֹּׁמֵר hashomer

אֱמֶת emet אהיה פעמים אהיה, ז״פ ס״ג לְעוֹלָם le'olam ריבוע ס״ג וי׳ אותיות דס״ג:

עֹשֶׂה ose מִשְׁפָּט mishpat ע״ה ה״פ אלהים לַעֲשׁוּקִים la'ashukim נֹתֵן noten

אבגיתץ, ושר לֶחֶם lechem ג׳ הויות לָרְעֵבִים lare'evim יְהֹוָהאדני יאהדונהי Adonai

(Chesed) מַתִּיר matir אֲסוּרִים asurim: יְהֹוָהאדני יאהדונהי Adonai ***(Gevurah)***

פֹּקֵחַ poke'ach מ״ה קמ״ג עִוְרִים ivrim יְהֹוָהאדני יאהדונהי Adonai ***(Tiferet)*** זֹקֵף zokef

כְּפוּפִים kefufim יְהֹוָהאדני יאהדונהי Adonai ***(Netzach)*** אֹהֵב ohev צַדִּיקִים tzadikim:

THE FIVE PSALMS - THE FIRST PSALM

"Praise the Lord! My soul praises the Lord! I shall praise the Lord while I am still alive; I shall play melodies to my God while I exist. Do not place your trust in nobles; not in a man who has no means of salvation. His breath leaves him and he returns to his earth. Upon that day, his plans perish. Fortunate is the one whom the God of Jacob comes to his aid, and who rests his hope on the Lord, his God. He creates the heavens and the earth, the sea, and all that they contain. The One Who guards truth forever; Who acts justly toward the oppressed; Who gives bread to the hungry. The Lord releases those who are imprisoned. The Lord gives sight to the blind. The Lord stands upright those who are bent over. The Lord loves the righteous.

יְהֹוָהאדֹנָי אהדונהי Adonai (Hod) שֹׁמֵר shomer אֶת־ et גֵּרִים gerim ר"ת = שדי

יָתוֹם yatom יוסף (ויהי יוסף יפה תואר ויפה מראה) וְאַלְמָנָה ve'almana

יְעוֹדֵד ye'oded ר"ת = יהוה וְדֶרֶךְ vederech ב"פ יב"ק, ע"ב קס"א רְשָׁעִים resha'im

יְעַוֵּת ye'avet ר"ת רי"ו: יִמְלֹךְ yimloch יוהוואדנהי יאהדונהי Adonai (Yesod)

לְעוֹלָם le'olam ריבוע ס"ג וי' אותיות דס"ג אֱלֹהַיִךְ Elohayich ילה צִיּוֹן Tziyon

יוסף, ו' הויות, קנאה לְדֹר ledor וָדֹר vador רי"ו ; ר"ת אצלו (רמז שמלכות אצל ז"א

אע"פ שאין הויה כנגדה) (Yesod of Yetzirah) הַלְלוּיָהּ haleluya אלהים, אהיה אדני ; ללה:

THE SECOND PSALM – THE NEXT 2 SEFIROT

The power of this Psalm helps us balance our acts of judgment and mercy towards other people.

This Psalm contains the Name: יהוה five times, which corresponds to the five *Chasadim* (mercy) through which the five *Gevurot* (judgment) are sweetened. This Psalm contains 139 words (with the *Kolel)* which adds up to the numerical value of *ko'ach* (strength), and *Yabok* (יב"ק = יהוה + אלהים - a code for sweetening judgment).

הַלְלוּיָהּ haleluya אלהים, אהיה אדני ; ללה כִּי־ ki טוֹב tov והו ; כי טוב =

יהוה אהיה, אום, מבה, יזל (Yesod) זַמְּרָה zamera אֱלֹהֵינוּ Elohenu ילה (Hod) כִּי־ ki

נָעִים na'im (Netzach) נָאוָה nava תְהִלָּה tehila ע"ה אמת, אהיה פעמים אהיה, ז"פ ס"ג:

בּוֹנֵה bone ס"ג יְרוּשָׁלַיִם Yerushalayim יְהֹוָהאדֹנָי אהדונהי Adonai (First Chesed)

נִדְחֵי nidchei ע"ב, ריבוע יהוה יִשְׂרָאֵל Yisrael יְכַנֵּס yechanes:

הָרֹפֵא harofe לִשְׁבוּרֵי lishvurei לֵב lev ר"ת ללה, אדני

The Lord watches over the converts and gives encouragement to the orphan and the widow, But He twists the way of the wicked. The Lord shall reign forever, your God, for each and every generation, Zion. Praise the Lord!" (Psalms 146)

THE SECOND PSALM

"Praise the Lord! For it is good to play melodies to our God, for it is pleasant and beautiful to praise Him. The Lord builds Jerusalem. He shall gather the scattered of Israel. He is healer of the brokenhearted

UMECHABESH LE'ATZVOTAM

According to the *Zohar*, this verse releases the energy of immortality, hastening its arrival. By releasing the energy of immortality into our spiritual atmosphere, we are helping to empower medical researchers, biologists, geneticists, and all other scientists in their quest to find the secrets to longevity, anti-aging, and the regeneration of human cells and organs.

וּמְחַבֵּשׁ umechabesh לְעַצְּבוֹתָם le'atzvotam:

מוֹנֶה mone מִסְפָּר mispar לַכּוֹכָבִים lakochavim לְכֻלָּם lechulam

שֵׁמוֹת shemot יִקְרָא yikra: גָּדוֹל gadol להח ; עם ד' אותיות = מבה, יזל, אום

אֲדוֹנֵינוּ adonenu וְרַב־ verav כֹּחַ ko'ach ע"ב ס"ג מ"ה ב"ן, וד' כוללים

לִתְבוּנָתוֹ litvunato אֵין en מִסְפָּר mispar: מְעוֹדֵד me'oded עֲנָוִים anavim

יְהֹוָהאדניאהדונהי Adonai ***(Second Chesed)*** מַשְׁפִּיל mashpil רְשָׁעִים resha'im

עֲדֵי־ adei אָרֶץ aretz: עֱנוּ enu לַיהֹוָהאדניאהדונהי ladonai ***(Third Chesed)***

בְּתוֹדָה betoda זַמְּרוּ zameru לֵאלֹהֵינוּ lelohenu ילה בְכִנּוֹר vechinor:

הַמְכַסֶּה ham'chase שָׁמַיִם shamayim י"פ טל, י"פ כוזו בְּעָבִים be'avim

הַמֵּכִין hamechin לָאָרֶץ la'aretz מָטָר matar ר"ת מלה הַמַּצְמִיחַ hamatzmi'ach

הָרִים harim חָצִיר chatzir: נוֹתֵן noten אבגיתץ, ושר לִבְהֵמָה livhema ב"ן

לַחְמָהּ lachma לִבְנֵי livnei עֹרֵב orev אֲשֶׁר asher יִקְרָאוּ yikra'u:

לֹא lo בִגְבוּרַת vigvurat הַסּוּס hasus ריבוע אדני, כוק יֶחְפָּץ yechpatz

לֹא־ lo בְשׁוֹקֵי veshokei הָאִישׁ ha'ish ***(Netzach and Hod)*** יִרְצֶה yirtze:

UMECHABESH LE'ATZVOTAM

And He tends to their grief. He sets the numbers of stars and calls them by their names. Our Master is great and exceedingly powerful. His understanding is limitless. The Lord gives strength to the humble, and lowers the wicked down to earth. Raise your voices to the Lord with gratitude. Play melodies with a harp to our God. He covers the heavens with clouds. He prepares rain for the earth; He causes mountains to grow grass. He provides the beasts with food and for the young ravens that call out. He does not desire the strength of the horse nor does He want the thighs of man.

רוֹצֶה rotze יְהֹוָהאדניאהדונהי Adonai **(*Fourth Chesed*)** אֶת־ et יְרֵאָיו yere'av

אֶת־ et הַמְיַחֲלִים ham'yachalim ייי לְחַסְדּוֹ lechasdo ג' הויות, מזלא

(להמשיך הארה ממזלא עילאה): שַׁבְּחִי shabechi יְרוּשָׁלַםִ Yerushalayim אֶת־ et

יְהֹוָהאדניאהדונהי Adonai **(*Fifth Chesed*)** הַלְלִי haleli אֱלֹהַיִךְ Elohayich ילה

צִיּוֹן Tziyon יוסף, ו' הויות, קנאה: כִּי־ ki חִזַּק chizak בְּרִיחֵי berichei פהל

שְׁעָרָיִךְ she'arayich בֵּרַךְ berach בָּנַיִךְ banayich בְּקִרְבֵּךְ bekirbech:

הַשָּׂם־ hasam גְּבוּלֵךְ gevulech שָׁלוֹם shalom חֵלֶב chelev חִטִּים chitim

יַשְׂבִּיעֵךְ yasbi'ech: הַשֹּׁלֵחַ hashole'ach אִמְרָתוֹ imrato אָרֶץ aretz ר"ת האא

עַד־ ad מְהֵרָה mehera יָרוּץ yarutz דְּבָרוֹ devaro ראה:

הַנֹּתֵן hanoten אבג יתץ, ושר שֶׁלֶג sheleg אלף אלף אלף אלף ד"ג אהיה כַּצָּמֶר katzamer מצר

כְּפוֹר kefor כָּאֵפֶר ka'efer יְפַזֵּר yefazer: מַשְׁלִיךְ mashlich קַרְחוֹ karcho

כְפִתִּים chefitim לִפְנֵי lifnei קָרָתוֹ karato מִי mi ילי יַעֲמֹד ya'amod:

יִשְׁלַח yishlach דְּבָרוֹ devaro ראה וְיַמְסֵם veyamsem יַשֵּׁב yashev רוּחוֹ rucho

יִזְּלוּ־ yizelu מָיִם mayim: מַגִּיד magid דְּבָרָיו devarav ראה (כתיב: דברו)

לְיַעֲקֹב leYaakov ז' הויות, יאהדונהי אידהנויה חֻקָּיו chukav וּמִשְׁפָּטָיו umishpatav

לְיִשְׂרָאֵל leYisrael **(*Hod*)**: לֹא lo עָשָׂה asa כֵן chen לְכָל־ lechol יה אדני

גּוֹי goy וּמִשְׁפָּטִים umishpatim בַּל־ bal ל"ב נתיבות הקדושה וכנגדם ב"ל בס"א (בלעם ובלק)

ר"ת = סמאל יְדָעוּם yeda'um **(*Hod*)** הַלְלוּיָהּ haleluya אלהים, אהיה אדני ; ללה:

The Lord only wants those who fear Him and those who place their hopes in His kindness. Praise the Lord, Jerusalem, and laud your God, Zion, for He has strengthened the bolts of your gates and blessed your children within. He sets peace at your borders. He satiates you with the best of wheat. He sends out His messages to the earth and His words travel very fast. He sends down snow as if it was wool and He scatters frost as if ash. He tosses His hail as if crumbs of bread. Who can stand up to His cold? He sends forth His word and melts it. He makes His wind blow and His waters to flow. He teaches His words to Jacob; His statutes and laws to Israel. He has not done so for any other nation. He informed them not of the laws. Praise the Lord!" (Psalms 147)

THE THIRD PSALM (DAILY HALEL) – TIFERET AND GEVURAH

In this Psalm, we offer thanks to the Creator, but what we are actually doing is acknowledging that we are not really entitled to anything - that our gifts in this life far outweigh our efforts. This does not come from the standpoint of having low self-worth, but rather from a combined sense of humility and appreciation for everything we receive in life.

You should be very careful with this Psalm and say it slowly with genuine deep meditation because here the sages said: "My part should be with those who say the *Halel* everyday." There are 14 verses for the word *yad* (hand) whose numerical value is 14, connecting us to *Yad Rama* (Central Column) and *Yad Chazaka* (Left Column).

(***Tiferet* of *Yetzirah***) הַלְלוּיָהּ haleluya אלהים, אהיה אדני ; ללה הַלְלוּ halelu (***Asiyah***)

אֶת־ et יְהֹוָאדהנויאהדונהי Adonai ר"ת אהיה מִן־ min הַשָּׁמַיִם hashamayim

י"פ טל, י"פ כוזו ; ר"ת מ"ה הַלְלוּהוּ haleluhu (***Yetzirah***) בַּמְּרוֹמִים bameromim:

הַלְלוּהוּ haleluhu (***Beriah***) כָל chol ילי מַלְאָכָיו mal'achav הַלְלוּהוּ haleluhu

(***Atzilut***) כָּל kol ילי צְבָאָו tzeva'av ר"ת הפסוק = ע"ב ס"ג מ"ה ; ס"ת הפסוק = אהיה ס"ג:

הַלְלוּהוּ haleluhu שֶׁמֶשׁ shemesh וְיָרֵחַ veyare'ach הַלְלוּהוּ haleluhu כָּל kol ילי

כּוֹכְבֵי kochvei אוֹר or רז, אין סוף: הַלְלוּהוּ haleluhu שְׁמֵי shemei

הַשָּׁמָיִם hashamayim י"פ טל, י"פ כוזו וְהַמַּיִם vehamayim אֲשֶׁר asher מֵעַל me'al

עלם הַשָּׁמָיִם hashamayim י"פ טל, י"פ כוזו ; ר"ת מ"ה: יְהַלְלוּ yehalelu אֶת־ et

שֵׁם shem יְהֹוָאדהנויאהדונהי Adonai כִּי ki הוּא hu צִוָּה tziva וְנִבְרָאוּ venivra'u:

וַיַּעֲמִידֵם vaya'amidem לָעַד la'ad ב"פ ב"ן לְעוֹלָם le'olam ריבוע ס"ג וי' אותיות דס"ג

חָק־ chok נָתַן natan וְלֹא velo ס"ת קנ"א (אלף הה יוד הה, מקוה), אדני אלהים

יַעֲבוֹר ya'avor רפ"ח (להעלות רפ"ח ניצוצות שנפלו לקליפה דמשם באים התחלואים):

THE THIRD PSALM

"Praise the Lord! Praise the Lord from the Heavens; praise Him in the high places; praise Him, all His angels; praise Him, all His Hosts. Praise Him, sun and moon; praise Him, all stars of Light; praise Him, the Highest Heavens, and the water that is above the Heavens. They praise the Name of the Lord, for He commanded and they were created. And He erected them forever and ever; He set laws that cannot be transgressed.

הַלְלוּ halelu אֶת־ et יְהֹוָהאדניאהדונהי Adonai מִן min הָאָרֶץ ha'aretz אלהים דההין ע״ה

תַּנִּינִים taninim וְכָל־ vechol ילי תְּהֹמוֹת tehomot: אֵשׁ esh וּבָרָד uvarad

שֶׁלֶג sheleg אלף אלף אלף דג׳ אהיה וְקִיטוֹר vekitor רוּחַ ru'ach סְעָרָה se'ara

עֹשָׂה osa דְבָרוֹ devaro ראה: הֶהָרִים heharim וְכָל־ vechol ילי גְּבָעוֹת geva'ot

עֵץ etz פְּרִי peri וְכָל vechol ילי אֲרָזִים arazim: הַחַיָּה hachaya וְכָל־ vechol ילי

בְּהֵמָה behema ב״ן רֶמֶשׂ remes וְצִפּוֹר vetzipor כָּנָף kanaf ע״ה קנ״א, אדני אלהים:

מַלְכֵי malchei אֶרֶץ eretz וְכָל־ vechol ילי לְאֻמִּים le'umim שָׂרִים sarim

וְכָל־ vechol ילי שֹׁפְטֵי shoftei אָרֶץ aretz: בַּחוּרִים bachurim וְגַם־ vegam

בְּתוּלוֹת betulot זְקֵנִים zekenim עִם־ im נְעָרִים ne'arim: יְהַלְלוּ yehalelu

אֶת־ et שֵׁם shem יְהֹוָהאדניאהדונהי Adonai כִּי־ ki נִשְׂגָּב nisgav

שְׁמוֹ shemo מהש ע״ה, ע״ב בריבוע וקס״א ע״ה, אל שדי ע״ה לְבַדּוֹ levado שם בן מ״ב

הוֹדוֹ hodo אהיה עַל־ al אֶרֶץ eretz וְשָׁמָיִם veshamayim י״פ טל, י״פ כוזו:

וַיָּרֶם vayarem קֶרֶן keren לְעַמּוֹ le'amo תְּהִלָּה tehila ע״ה אמת, אהיה פעמים אהיה, ז״פ ס״ג

לְכָל lechol יה אדני חֲסִידָיו chasidav לִבְנֵי livnei יִשְׂרָאֵל Yisrael

עַם־ am קְרֹבוֹ kerovo (*Gevurah* of *Yetzirah*) הַלְלוּיָהּ haleluya אלהים, אהיה אדני ; ללה:

THE FOURTH PSALM (SHIRU) - CHESED

This Psalm is comprised of nine verses referring to nine "skies" that separate the Upper Worlds from the Lower World. This idea of separation is a direct reference to the concept of time and its relationship to Cause and Effect. Through these verses, we manipulate time and shorten the distance between Cause and Effect.

To allow us to express our uniquely human trait of free will, time is inserted into the Cause and Effect process. This space gives Satan, our ego, and our limiting selfish thoughts the opportunity to challenge us. Satan makes us believe that we get away with our negative actions. He makes us believe that life is unfair and that good behavior goes unrewarded. Changing ourselves and our belief systems becomes more challenging. Now that we are approaching the end of days, the Final Correction, we can shorten the separation between Cause and Effect and reap the rewards of our positive behavior much more quickly. Likewise, our negative actions will produce a much quicker payback. The result in both situations is accelerated change on our part.

Praise the Lord from the Earth. Great fish and depths, fire and hail, snow and steam, and stormy wind do His bidding. The mountains and the hills, fruit trees and all the cedars, wild beasts and all cattle, creeping things and winged birds; Kings of the Earth and all nations, princes and all the judges of the Earth; Young men and maidens, old along with the young: they all praise the Name of the Lord, for His Name alone is powerful; His splendor is over the Earth and Heavens. And He praises the word of His nation, a praise for all His pious ones, for the children of Israel, the nation that is close to Him. Praise the Lord!" (Psalm 148)

There are 61 words in this Psalm like the numerical value of the Names: *Alef Gimel Lamed Alef* (אגלא) (35, also equals to *Alef Lamed Dalet* אלד) plus יהוה (26), to give us protection from Evil Eye.

(**Chesed of Yetzirah**) הַלְלוּיָהּ haleluya אלהים, אהיה אדני ; ללה שִׁירוּ shiru
לַיהֹוָה יאהדונהי ladonai שִׁיר shir חָדָשׁ chadash י"ב הויות, קס"א קנ"א
תְּהִלָּתוֹ tehilato בִּקְהַל bik'hal חֲסִידִים chasidim: יִשְׂמַח yismach משיח
יִשְׂרָאֵל Yisrael בְּעֹשָׂיו be'osav בְּנֵי benei צִיּוֹן Tziyon יוסף, ו' הויות, קנאה
יָגִילוּ yagilu בְמַלְכָּם vemalkam: יְהַלְלוּ yehalelu שְׁמוֹ shemo מהש ע"ה,
ע"ב בריבוע וקס"א ע"ה, אל שדי ע"ה בְמָחוֹל vemachol בְּתֹף betof וְכִנּוֹר vechinor
יְזַמְּרוּ yezameru לוֹ lo: כִּי ki רוֹצֶה rotze יְהֹוָה יאהדונהי Adonai
בְּעַמּוֹ be'amo ר"ת = ע"ב ס"ג מ"ה ב"ן, הברכה (למתק את ז' המלכים שמתו) ; ס"ת יהוה
יְפָאֵר yefa'er עֲנָוִים anavim בִּישׁוּעָה bishu'a פוי, אל אדני ; ר"ת הפסוק = שדי:
יַעְלְזוּ yalezu ג"פ אם (אותיות דפשוט, דמילוי ודמילוי דמילוי דג"פ אהיה) חֲסִידִים chasidim
בְּכָבוֹד bechavod בוכו, ובאתב"ש הוא שם שלשפ"ק הממתק את ג' אם דלעיל (והוא עולה למנין
עסמ"ב קס"א קנ"א קמ"ג וג"פ אם הנ"ל) יְרַנְּנוּ yeranenu עַל־ al מִשְׁכְּבוֹתָם mishkevotam:
רוֹמְמוֹת romemot אֵל El ייא"י (מילוי דס"ג) בִּגְרוֹנָם bigronam
ר"ת = קנ"א ב"ן, יהוה אלהים יהוה אדני, מילוי קס"א וס"ג, מ"ה ברבוע וע"ב ע"ה
וְחֶרֶב vecherev רי"ו פִּיפִיּוֹת pifiyot בְּיָדָם beyadam: לַעֲשׂוֹת la'asot
נְקָמָה nekama מנק בַּגּוֹיִם bagoyim תּוֹכֵחוֹת tochechot בַּלְאֻמִּים bale'umim:
לֶאְסֹר lesor מַלְכֵיהֶם malchehem בְּזִקִּים bezikim וְנִכְבְּדֵיהֶם venichbedehem
בְּכַבְלֵי bechavlei בַרְזֶל varzel ר"ת בלהה רחל זלפה לאה: לַעֲשׂוֹת la'asot
בָּהֶם bahem מִשְׁפָּט mishpat ע"ה ה"פ אלהים כָּתוּב katuv הָדָר hadar הוּא hu
לְכָל־ lechol יה אדני חֲסִידָיו chasidav הַלְלוּיָהּ haleluya אלהים, אהיה אדני ; ללה:

THE FOURTH PSALM

"Praise the Lord! Sing to the Lord a new song. His praise is in the gathering of the pious. Israel shall rejoice with its Maker, the children of Zion shall exult with their King. They shall praise His Name with dance. With drum and harp they shall play melodies to Him. For the Lord favors His nation; He glorifies the humble with redemption. The pious shall be merry with His Glory and shall joyously sing upon their beds. The high praises of God are in their thoughts and a double-edged sword is in their hands to bring vengeance upon the nations, retributions upon the peoples, to bind their kings in chains, and their nobles in iron shackles, to administer to them justice that is written. Glory for all His pious ones, Praise the Lord!" (Psalms 149)

THE FIFTH PSALM (HALELU EL) – THE THREE UPPER SEFIROT

The six verses found here connect us to Ma-tat-ron (**do not pronounce**), the highest of all the angels. The Aramaic word for Ma-tat-ron contains six letters—*Mem, Tet, Tet, Reish, Vav,* final *Nun.* Each verse in this connection helps form the name. Because Ma-tat-ron controls all the angels in the spiritual world, he can help give us control over our physical world and assist us in accomplishing our spiritual work.

This Psalm has six verses for the six letters of the Angel מטטרו״ן (**do not pronounce**) of *Yetzirah* to raise *Asiyah* in it. The Angel סנדלפו״ן (**do not pronounce**) has seven letters and for this reason we repeat the sixth verse to complete the seventh. Also we say this Psalm to connect to the three Upper *Sefirot* of *Yetzirah*. It includes all the Ten *Sefirot* of *Yetzirah* with the secret of the Ten *Haleluyas*.

אל (יא״י מילוי דס״ג) אותיות בפסוק הַלְלוּיָהּ haleluya **(*Keter*)** אלהים, אהיה אדני ; ללה

הַלְלוּ־ halelu אֵל El יא״י (מילוי דס״ג) בְּקָדְשׁוֹ bekodsho

הַלְלוּהוּ haleluhu **(*Chochmah*)** בִּרְקִיעַ birki'a עֻזּוֹ uzo ס״ת = ע״ב ב״ן:

הַלְלוּהוּ haleluhu **(*Binah*)** בִּגְבוּרֹתָיו vigvurotav הַלְלוּהוּ haleluhu **(*Chesed*)**

כְּרֹב kerov גֻּדְלוֹ gudlo: הַלְלוּהוּ haleluhu **(*Gevurah*)** בְּתֵקַע beteka

שׁוֹפָר shofar הַלְלוּהוּ haleluhu **(*Tiferet*)** בְּנֵבֶל benevel וְכִנּוֹר vechinor:

הַלְלוּהוּ haleluhu **(*Netzach*)** בְתֹף betof וּמָחוֹל umachol הַלְלוּהוּ haleluhu **(*Hod*)**

בְּמִנִּים beminim וְעֻגָב ve'ugav: הַלְלוּהוּ haleluhu **(*Yesod*)** בְּצִלְצְלֵי־ vetziltzelei

שָׁמַע shama הַלְלוּהוּ haleluhu **(*Malchut*)** בְּצִלְצְלֵי betziltzelei תְרוּעָה teru'a:

כֹּל kol ילי הַנְּשָׁמָה haneshamah תְּהַלֵּל tehalel ר״ת כהת, משיח בן דוד ע״ה

יָהּ Yah הַלְלוּיָהּ haleluya אלהים, אהיה אדני ; ללה:

כֹּל kol ילי הַנְּשָׁמָה haneshamah תְּהַלֵּל tehalel ר״ת כהת, משיח בן דוד ע״ה

יָהּ Yah הַלְלוּיָהּ haleluya אלהים, אהיה אדני ; ללה:

THE FIFTH PSALM

"Praise the Lord! Praise Him in His Sanctuary; praise Him in the firmaments of His might; praise Him by His valorous deeds; praise Him according to His bountiful greatness; praise Him with blowing the Shofar; praise Him with lyre and harp; praise Him with drum and dance; praise Him with instruments and pipe; Praise Him with the sound of cymbals; praise Him with reverberating sounds. All the souls praise God. Praise Him! All the souls praise God. Praise Him!" (Psalms 150)

BARUCH

Each of these four verses is a conduit to the four letters in *Yud, Hei, Vav*, and *Hei* (יהוה), helping us make the jump to the upper part of the World of Formation – *Atzilut* of *Yetzirah*.

י

בָּרוּךְ baruch יְהֹוָהאדניאהדונהי Adonai לְעוֹלָם le'olam ריבוע דס"ג וי' אותיות דס"ג

אָמֵן amen יאהדונהי וְאָמֵן ve'amen יאהדונהי ; ר"ת לאו:

ה

בָּרוּךְ baruch יְהֹוָהאדניאהדונהי Adonai מִצִּיּוֹן miTziyon יוסף, ו' הויות, קנאה

שֹׁכֵן shochen יְרוּשָׁלָיִם Yerushalayim הַלְלוּיָהּ haleluya אלהים, אהיה אדני ; ללה:

ו

בָּרוּךְ baruch יְהֹוָהאדניאהדונהי Adonai אֱלֹהִים Elohim אהיה אדני ; ילה

אֱלֹהֵי Elohei מילוי דע"ב, דמב ; ילה יִשְׂרָאֵל Yisrael

עֹשֵׂה ose נִפְלָאוֹת nifla'ot לְבַדּוֹ levado שם בן מ"ב:

ה

וּבָרוּךְ uvaruch שֵׁם shem כְּבוֹדוֹ kevodo לְעוֹלָם le'olam ריבוע דס"ג וי' אותיות דס"ג

וְיִמָּלֵא veyimale כְבוֹדוֹ chevodo אֶת־ et כָּל־ kol ילי

הָאָרֶץ ha'aretz אלהים דההין ע"ה אָמֵן amen יאהדונהי וְאָמֵן ve'amen יאהדונהי:

BARUCH

"Blessed is the Lord forever, Amen and Amen." (Psalms 89:53) *"Blessed is the Lord from Zion, He Who dwells in Jerusalem. Praise the Lord!"* (Psalms 135:21) *"Blessed is the Lord, our God, the God of Israel, Who alone performs wonders. And blessed is the Name of His glory, forever. May His glory fill the entire world, Amen and Amen."* (Psalms 72:18-19)

VAY'VARECH DAVID - THE HIGHEST POINT OF THE WORLD OF FORMATION *(YETZIRAH)*

The kabbalists teach us that there are two prerequisites for activating the power of a prayer:
1) Understanding the inner significance of the prayer, and
2) Certainty that the prayer will produce the Light and energy that it is designed to generate.
This next prayer imbues us with the power of certainty. *Vadai* ודאי (certainty) is created by the first letter of each of the first four words of this prayer. Everyone who recites this prayer arouses an intense feeling of certainty in their life. If we are not certain that the prayer will work, it won't. Satan's job is to fill us with uncertainty every chance he gets, even as we read these words. This prayer combats our doubts and uncertainties, and fills us with conviction and certitude.

Tikkun of *Atzilut* of *Yetzirah*.
Until the Song of the Sea we have ten times the Name: יהוה, five for *Chasadim* and five for *Gevurot*.

Stand when reciting "*vayvarech David.*"

וַיְבָרֶךְ vay'varech ע"ב ס"ג מ"ה ב"ן, הברכה (למתק את ז' המלכים שמתו) דָּוִיד David

אֶת־ et יְהֹוָאֲדֹנָיאהדונהי Adonai **(*First Chesed*)** ר"ת ודאי (=אהיה) (בשם זה עלה משה למרום

והוא מגן ממלאכי חבלה) לְעֵינֵי le'enei ריבוע מ"ה כָּל kol ילי הַקָּהָל hakahal

וַיֹּאמֶר vayomer דָּוִיד David ר"ת = אדני בָּרוּךְ baruch אַתָּה Ata

יְהֹוָאֲדֹנָיאהדונהי Adonai **(*Second Chesed*)** אֱלֹהֵי Elohei מילוי ע"ב, דמב ; ילה

יִשְׂרָאֵל Yisrael יהוה אלהי ישראל = תרי"ג (מצוות) אָבִינוּ avinu מֵעוֹלָם me'olam

וְעַד־ ve'ad עוֹלָם olam: לְךָ lecha יְהֹוָאֲדֹנָיאהדונהי Adonai **(*Third Chesed*)**

הַגְּדֻלָּה hagedula וְהַגְּבוּרָה vchagevura רי"ו וְהַתִּפְאֶרֶת vehatiferet

וְהַנֵּצַח vehanetzach וְהַהוֹד vehahod ההה כִּי־ ki כֹל chol ילי

בַּשָּׁמַיִם bashamayim י"פ טל, י"פ כוזו וּבָאָרֶץ uva'aretz לְךָ lecha

יְהֹוָאֲדֹנָיאהדונהי Adonai **(*Fourth Chesed*)** הַמַּמְלָכָה hamamlacha

וְהַמִּתְנַשֵּׂא vehamitnase לְכֹל lechol יה אדני לְרֹאשׁ lerosh ריבוע אלהים ואלהים דיודין

ע"ה: וְהָעֹשֶׁר veha'osher וְהַכָּבוֹד vehakavod לאו מִלְּפָנֶיךָ milfanecha ס"ג מ"ה ב"ן

VAY'VARECH DAVID

'Then David blessed the Lord before the eyes of the whole congregation. David said: Blessed are You, Lord, the God of Israel, our Father, forever until eternity. Yours, Lord, are the greatness, the power, the glory, the victory, and the splendor. Everything in the Heavens and Earth is Yours. Yours, Lord, is the kingship; You are over all those who ascend to lead. The riches and honors are before You;

וְאַתָּה veAta מוֹשֵׁל moshel בַּכֹּל bakol ב"ן, לכב ; ר"ת ומב

וּבְיָדְךָ uvyadcha כֹּחַ ko'ach וּגְבוּרָה ugvura רי"ו ; ר"ת בוכו (אהיה)

וּבְיָדְךָ uvyadcha לְגַדֵּל legadel וּלְחַזֵּק ulchazek פהל לַכֹּל lakol יה אדני:

וְעַתָּה ve'ata אֱלֹהֵינוּ Elohenu ילה מוֹדִים modim כנגד מאה ברכות שתיקן דוד לאמרם כל יום אֲנַחְנוּ anachnu לָךְ lach וּמְהַלְלִים um'halelim לְשֵׁם leshem

תִּפְאַרְתֶּךָ tifartecha: וִיבָרְכוּ vivarchu יהוה ריבוע יהוה ריבוע מ"ה שֵׁם shem

כְּבוֹדֶךָ kevodecha ב"ן, לכב וּמְרוֹמָם umromam עַל־ al כָּל־ kol ילי ; עמם

בְּרָכָה beracha וּתְהִלָּה ut'hila ע"ה אמת, אהיה פעמים אהיה, ז"פ ס"ג:

אַתָּה־ Ata הוּא hu יְהֹוָאֲדֹנָיאהדונהי Adonai (*Fifth Chesed*) לְבַדֶּךָ levadecha

אַתָּ ata עָשִׂיתָ asita אֶת־ et הַשָּׁמַיִם hashamayim י"פ טל, י"פ כוזו שְׁמֵי shemei

הַשָּׁמַיִם hashamayim י"פ טל, י"פ כוזו וְכָל־ vechol ילי צְבָאָם tzeva'am

הָאָרֶץ ha'aretz אלהים דההין ע"ה וְכָל־ vechol ילי אֲשֶׁר asher עָלֶיהָ aleha פהל

הַיַּמִּים hayamim נלך וְכָל־ vechol ילי אֲשֶׁר asher בָּהֶם bahem

וְאַתָּה veAta מְחַיֶּה mechaye ס"ג אֶת־ et כֻּלָּם kulam וּצְבָא utzva

הַשָּׁמַיִם hashamayim י"פ טל, י"פ כוזו לְךָ lecha מִשְׁתַּחֲוִים mishtachavim ר"ת מלה:

אַתָּה־ Ata הוּא hu יְהֹוָאֲדֹנָיאהדונהי Adonai (*First Gevurah*) הָאֱלֹהִים haElohim

אהיה אדני ; ילה ; ר"ת אהיה (stand until here) אֲשֶׁר asher בָּחַרְתָּ bacharta

בְּאַבְרָם beAvram וְהוֹצֵאתוֹ vehotzeto מֵאוּר meUr כַּשְׂדִּים Kasdim

וְשַׂמְתָּ vesamta שְׁמוֹ shemo מהש ע"ה, ע"ב בריבוע וקס"א ע"ה, אל שדי ע"ה

אַבְרָהָם Avraham וז"פ אל, רי"ו ול"ב נתיבות הוזכמה, רמ"וז (אברים), עסמ"ב וט"ז אותיות פשוטות:

You rule over everything. In Your Hand are powers and might. And it is in Your Hand to make great and to give strength to all. Now, our God, we are grateful to You and praise the Name of Your splendors." (I Chronicles 29:10-13) "And they shall bless the Name of Your glory, which is exalted above all blessing and praise. It is You, alone, Who is the Lord. You made the Heavens, the highest Heavens and all their hosts, the Earth and all that is upon it, the seas and all that they contain, and You sustain life in them all. And the hosts of the Heavens prostrate themselves before You It is You, Lord, the God, Who chose Abram and brought him out of Ur of the Chaldeans and made his name Abraham.

וּמָצָאתָ umatzata אֶת־ et לְבָבוֹ levavo נֶאֱמָן ne'eman לְפָנֶיךָ lefanecha

ס"ג מ"ה ב"ן וְכָרוֹת vecharot עִמּוֹ imo הַבְּרִית haberit לָתֵת latet אֶת־ et

אֶרֶץ eretz הַכְּנַעֲנִי haKena'ani הַחִתִּי haChiti הָאֱמֹרִי haEmori

וְהַפְּרִזִּי vehaPerizi וְהַיְבוּסִי vehaYevusi וְהַגִּרְגָּשִׁי vehaGirgashi לָתֵת latet

לְזַרְעוֹ lezar'o וַתָּקֶם vatakem אֶת־ et דְּבָרֶיךָ devarecha ראה כִּי ki

צַדִּיק tzadik אָתָּה Ata: וַתֵּרֶא vatere אֶת־ et עֳנִי oni ריבוע מ"ה

אֲבֹתֵינוּ avotenu בְּמִצְרָיִם beMitzrayim מצר וְאֶת־ ve'et זַעֲקָתָם za'akatam

שָׁמַעְתָּ shamata עַל־ al יַם־ Yam יל"י סוּף Suf: וַתִּתֵּן vatiten ב"פ כהת

אֹתֹת otot וּמֹפְתִים umoftim בְּפַרְעֹה beFar'oh וּבְכָל־ uvchol ב"ן, לכב

עֲבָדָיו avadav וּבְכָל־ uvchol ב"ן, לכב עַם am אַרְצוֹ artzo כִּי ki יָדַעְתָּ yadata

כִּי ki הֵזִידוּ hezidu עֲלֵיהֶם alehem וַתַּעַשׂ־ vata'as לְךָ lecha שֵׁם shem

כְּהַיּוֹם kehayom ע"ה נגד, מזבח, זן אל יהוה הַזֶּה haze והו: וְהַיָּם vehayam יל"י

בָּקַעְתָּ bakata לִפְנֵיהֶם lifnehem וַיַּעַבְרוּ vaya'avru בְתוֹךְ־ vetoch

הַיָּם hayam יל"י בַּיַּבָּשָׁה bayabasha וְאֶת־ ve'et רֹדְפֵיהֶם rodfehem

הִשְׁלַכְתָּ hishlachta בִמְצוֹלֹת vimtzolot ר"ת רהב (שרו של מצרים) כְּמוֹ־ kemo

אֶבֶן even ר"ת = אהיה בְּמַיִם bemayim עַזִּים azim ר"ת ע"ב, ריבוע יהוה:

You found his heart faithful before You, and You established the Covenant with him to give the land of the Canaanite, the Hittite, the Amorite, the Perizzite, the Jebusite, and the Girgashite - to give it to his descendants. You have kept Your promise, for You are righteous. You saw the afflictions of our forefathers in Egypt and You heard their cries at the Sea of Reeds. You performed signs and wonders against Pharaoh, all his servants, and all the people of his land, for You knew that they had sinned willfully against our forefathers. You thereby made for Yourself a Name as it is to this day. You then split the sea before them so that they crossed mid-sea, on dry land; their pursuers You cast into the depths, like a stone in turbulent waters." (Nechamiah 9:5-11)

VAYOSHA

When said with enormous happiness, "*vayosha*" has the power to remove negativity and make our *tikkun* process much easier. The *tikkun* process refers to the personal corrections that each person has come into this world to make. The corrections we must make are based on our negative, reactive behavior from this life and from past lives. *Tikkun* can include areas of finance, relationships, and health among others. We can identify our *tikkun* in all areas of our life by noticing where we experience the most difficulties.

וַיּוֹשַׁע vayosha יְהֹוָה(אדני)אהדונהי Adonai **(*Second Gevurah*)** בַּיּוֹם bayom

ע״ה נגד, מזבח, זן, אל יהוה ; ר״ת = וה״ו הַהוּא hahu אֶת־ et יִשְׂרָאֵל Yisrael

מִיַּד miyad מִצְרָיִם Mitzrayim מצר ; ר״ת = אמן (יאהדונהי) וַיַּרְא vayar

יִשְׂרָאֵל Yisrael אֶת־ et מִצְרַיִם Mitzrayim מצר מֵת met עַל־ al

שְׂפַת sefat הַיָּם hayam ילי : וַיַּרְא vayar יִשְׂרָאֵל Yisrael אֶת־ et

הַיָּד hayad והו הַגְּדֹלָה hagedola ר״ת אהיה אֲשֶׁר asher עָשָׂה asa

יְהֹוָה(אדני)אהדונהי Adonai **(*Third Gevurah*)** בְּמִצְרַיִם beMitzrayim מצר

וַיִּירְאוּ vayir'u הָעָם ha'am אֶת־ et יְהֹוָה(אדני)אהדונהי Adonai **(*Fourth Gevurah*)**

וַיַּאֲמִינוּ vaya'aminu בַּיהֹוָה(אדני)אהדונהי badonai **(*Fifth Gevurah*)** ; ר״ת איוב

וּבְמֹשֶׁה uvMoshe מהש, ע״ב בריבוע וקס״א, אל שדי, ד״פ אלהים ע״ה עַבְדּוֹ avdo:

THE 72 NAMES OF GOD

This chart shows the 72 Names of God. Moses used these sequences and formulas to connect to the true laws of nature—miracles and wonders—and remove all the obstacles that prevent mankind from connecting to them. This is how the Red Sea was split (Exodus 14:19-21). The splitting of the Red Sea is an expression of connection to the 99 Percent Realm where miracles are the norm. Simply by scanning these configurations of letters, we connect to our true nature and power. We become more proactive and move closer to the true purpose of our soul.

VAYOSHA

"And on that day, the Lord saved Israel from the hand of Egypt, and Israel saw the Egyptians dead at the seashore. Israel beheld the great Hand that the Lord had wrought against Egypt; and the people feared the Lord; they believed in the Lord and in Moses, His servant." (Exodus 14:30-31)

To scan: Begin at upper right (A-1) and scan each row right to left, ending in lower left (I-8).

←

8	7	6	5	4	3	2	1	
כהת	אכא	ללה	מהש	עלם	סיט	ילי	והו	A
הקם	הרי	מבה	יזל	ההע	לאו	אלד	הזי	B
חהו	מלה	ייי	נלך	פהל	לוו	כלי	לאו	C
ושר	לכב	אום	ריי	שאה	ירת	האא	נתה	D
ייז	רהע	חעם	אני	מנד	כוק	להח	יחו	E
מיה	עשל	ערי	סאל	ילה	וול	מיך	ההה	F
פוי	מבה	נית	ננא	עמם	החש	דני	והו	G
מחי	ענו	יהה	ומב	מצר	הרח	ייל	נמם	H
מום	היי	יבמ	ראה	חבו	איע	מנק	דמב	I

SONG OF THE SEA - AZ YASHIR MOSHE

Moses and the Israelites sang this song after the splitting of the Red Sea. It is the song of the soul. Unfortunately, we lose touch with our soul when we are caught up in the material world. This prayer helps to awaken the memory and power of the original song that resides in the depths of our soul; because when we are connected to our soul, we can achieve anything.

Eighteen times the Name of God (יהוה or אדני) for the eighteen blessings of the Worlds of *Yetzirah*. You should meditate that these eighteen are the numerical value of the two letters *Tet* ט in Ma-tat-ron **(do not pronounce)** which is in *Zeir Anpin* of *Yetzirah*, as well as meditate on the nine *tikkuns* of *Zeir Anpin* of *Yetzirah*, nine of Direct Light and nine of Returning Light. (The same way we meditated in *Yehi Chevod* on pg. 137) You should also imagine that you crossed the Red Sea on that day. Saying it with happiness will cleanse all of our transgressions.

אָז az יָשִׁיר־ yashir מֹשֶׁה Moshe מהש, ע״ב בריבוע וקס״א, אל שדי, ד״פ אלהים ע״ה

וּבְנֵי uvnei יִשְׂרָאֵל Yisrael ר״ת ע״ה נגד, מזבח, זן אל יהוה אֶת־ et הַשִּׁירָה hashira

הַזֹּאת hazot לַיהוָהאדניאהדונהי ladonai (ארך) וַיֹּאמְרוּ vayomru לֵאמֹר lemor

אָשִׁירָה ashira לַיהוָהאדניאהדונהי ladonai (אפים) כִּי־ ki גָאֹה ga'o גָּאָה ga'a

סוּס sus ריבוע אדני, כוק וְרֹכְבוֹ verochvo רָמָה rama בַיָּם vayam ילי:

עָזִּי ozi אלהים ע״ה, אהיה אדני ע״ה וְזִמְרָת vezimrat יָהּ Yah וַיְהִי־ vayehi לִי li

לִישׁוּעָה lishu'a זֶה ze אֵלִי Eli וְאַנְוֵהוּ ve'anvehu (Meditate on the Holy Name: יְהוֹאֵלוֹ

יהואל, לכב) אֱלֹהֵי Elohei מילוי ע״ב, דמב ; ילה אָבִי avi וַאֲרֹמְמֶנְהוּ va'aromemenhu:

SONG OF THE SEA - AZ YASHIR MOSHE

Moses and the Children of Israel sang this song to the Lord: I sing to the Lord because He became most exalted and flung the horse and its rider into the sea. My strength and my praise are God; He became my salvation. This is my God and I shall glorify Him, the God of my father; and I shall exalt Him

יְהֹוָה(אדני)יאהדונהי Adonai (ורב וחסד) אִישׁ ish מִלְחָמָה milchama

יְהֹוָה(אדני)יאהדונהי Adonai (נֹשֵׂא עָוֹן) שְׁמוֹ shemo מהש ע"ה, ע"ב בריבוע וקס"א ע"ה, אל שדי ע"ה:

מַרְכְּבֹת markevot פַּרְעֹה Par'oh וְחֵילוֹ vechelo יָרָה yara בַיָּם vayam ילי

וּמִבְחַר umivchar שָׁלִשָׁיו shalishav טֻבְּעוּ tube'u בְיַם־ veYam ילי סוּף Suf:

תְּהֹמֹת tehomot יְכַסְיֻמוּ yechasyumu יָרְדוּ yardu בִמְצוֹלֹת vimtzolot

כְּמוֹ־ kemo אָבֶן aven ר"ת = אהיה: יְמִינְךָ yemincha יְהֹוָה(אדני)יאהדונהי Adonai

(ופשע) נֶאְדָּרִי ne'edari בַּכֹּחַ bako'ach ר"ת = ע"ב, ריבוע יהוה וס"ת = יגל

יְמִינְךָ yemincha יְהֹוָה(אדני)יאהדונהי Adonai (ונקה) תִּרְעַץ tir'atz אוֹיֵב oyev

צרעת איוב (בזמנא דמלכא משיחא): וּבְרֹב uvrov י"פ אהיה גְּאוֹנְךָ ge'oncha

תַּהֲרֹס taharos קָמֶיךָ kamecha (בימי גוג ומגוג) תְּשַׁלַּח te'shalach

חֲרֹנְךָ charoncha יֹאכְלֵמוֹ yochlemo כַּקַּשׁ kakash (בעת תחיית המתים):

וּבְרוּחַ uvru'ach אַפֶּיךָ apecha נֶעֶרְמוּ ne'ermu מַיִם mayim ר"ת אמן (יאהדונהי)

נִצְּבוּ nitzevu כְמוֹ־ chemo נֵד ned ר"ת ק"כ צירופי אלהים נֹזְלִים nozlim

קָפְאוּ kaf'u תְהֹמֹת tehomot בְּלֶב־ belev יָם yam ילי: אָמַר amar אוֹיֵב oyev

אֶרְדֹּף erdof אַשִּׂיג asig אֲחַלֵּק achalek שָׁלָל shalal תִּמְלָאֵמוֹ timla'emo

נַפְשִׁי nafshi אָרִיק arik חַרְבִּי charbi רי"י תּוֹרִישֵׁמוֹ torishemo יָדִי yadi:

נָשַׁפְתָּ nashafta בְרוּחֲךָ veruchacha ר"ת ב"ן כִּסָּמוֹ kisamo יָם yam ילי

צָלְלוּ tzalelu כַּעוֹפֶרֶת ka'oferet בְּמַיִם bemayim אַדִּירִים adirim הרי ; ר"ת קמ"ג:

The Lord is the Master of war – The Lord is His Name. The chariots of Pharaoh and his army, He cast into the sea and his select officers were sunk into the Sea of Reeds. The deep waters covered them and they sunk into the depths like a stone. Your right, Lord, is immensely powerful; Your right, Lord, smashes the enemy. With Your great ingenuity, You demolish those who rise against You. You send forth Your wrath and it consumes them like straw. And with the wing of Your anger, the waters were filled up; the flowing waters stood like a wall and the deep waters froze in the heart of the sea. The enemy said: I shall pursue, overtake, and divide the spoils. I shall satisfy my desires with them. I shall unsheathe my sword and my hand shall impoverish them. You blew with Your wind and the sea covered them. They sank like lead in the mighty waters.

מִי־ mi ילי כָמֹכָה chamocha בָּאֵלִם ba'elim יְהֹוָאדנָי־אהדונהי Adonai (פוקד)

ר"ת = ע"ב, ריבוע יהוה ; ס"ת מ"ה מִי mi ילי כָּמֹכָה kamocha נֶאְדָּר ne'edar

בַּקֹּדֶשׁ bakodesh ר"ת = יבק, אלהים יהוה, אהיה אדני יהוה נוֹרָא nora תְהִלֹּת tehilot

עֹשֵׂה ose פֶלֶא fele: נָטִיתָ natita יְמִינְךָ yemincha תִּבְלָעֵמוֹ tivla'emo

ר"ת נית (זו מות) אָרֶץ aretz: נָחִיתָ nachita בְחַסְדְּךָ vechasdecha ר"ת ב"ן עַם־ am

זוּ zu גָּאָלְתָּ ga'alta נֵהַלְתָּ nehalta בְעָזְּךָ ve'ozcha אֶל־ el נְוֵה neve

קָדְשֶׁךָ kodshecha ר"ת קנ"א ב"ן, יהוה אלהים יהוה אדני, מילוי קס"א וס"ג, מ"ה ברבוע וע"ב ע"ה:

שָׁמְעוּ sham'u עַמִּים amim יִרְגָּזוּן yirgazun חִיל chil ומב אָחַז achaz

יֹשְׁבֵי yoshvei פְּלָשֶׁת Pelashet (כוּוזוֹת ישמעאל): אָז az נִבְהֲלוּ nivhalu

אַלּוּפֵי alufei אֱדוֹם Edom (כוּוזוֹת עשו) אֵילֵי elei מוֹאָב Mo'av

יֹאחֲזֵמוֹ yochazemo רָעַד ra'ad (כוּוזוֹת שאר כל השרים שהם נכנעים תוזתיהם)

נָמֹגוּ namogu כֹּל kol ילי יֹשְׁבֵי yoshvei כְנָעַן Chena'an:

תִּפֹּל tipol עֲלֵיהֶם alehem אֵימָתָה emata וָפַחַד vafachad ר"ת שם קדוש תעא"ו

בִּגְדֹל bigdol זְרוֹעֲךָ zero'acha יִדְּמוּ yidemu כָּאָבֶן ka'aven ר"ת = טל (יוד הא ואו)

עַד־ ad יַעֲבֹר ya'avor עַמְּךָ amecha יְהֹוָאדנָי־אהדונהי Adonai (עַל שלשים)

עַד־ ad יַעֲבֹר ya'avor עַם־ am זוּ zu קָנִיתָ kanita: תְּבִאֵמוֹ tevi'emo

וְתִטָּעֵמוֹ vetita'emo בְּהַר behar נַחֲלָתְךָ nachalatcha ר"ת ב"ן מָכוֹן machon

לְשִׁבְתְּךָ leshivtecha פָּעַלְתָּ pa'alta יְהֹוָאדנָי־אהדונהי Adonai (ועל רבעים) ר"ת

ע"ה = קס"א מִקְּדָשׁ mikedash אֲדֹנָי Adonai (ארך) כּוֹנְנוּ konenu יָדֶיךָ yadecha:

Who among the deities is like You, Lord; Who is like You, awesome in holiness, tremendous in praise, and Who works wonders! You stretched out Your right and the earth swallowed them. With Your kindness, You governed this nation that You redeemed. You led them with Your strength to Your holy Sanctuary. Nations heard and trembled. Terror seized the dwellers of Philistia. Then the leaders of Edom were frightened. The mighty ones of Moab were panic-stricken and the dwellers of Canaan withered away. Dread and fear fell upon them, by the greatness of Your arm. They became still, like stones, until Your nation crossed over, the Lord, until the nation that You adopted crossed over Bring them and settle them in the mountains of Your heritage, in that place of Your dwelling which You have made, Lord. Your Hands established the Temple of the Lord.

A 72 Name of God is encoded in this connection: *Yud, Yud, Lamed* ייל. This formula gives us the power of certainty and us the ability to let go, especially in the face of adversity. When things are going well, most of us find it easy to accept the idea of a Creator and a Cause and Effect principle at work in our universe. But when we face a sudden obstacle or stressful situation, we just as readily doubt the existence of a Creator and the teachings of Kabbalah. The kabbalists teach us that absolutely everything is a test. If we can maintain certainty in the Light when adversity strikes, we will pass the test and the Light will work for us 100% of the time. Satan's mission is to flood our minds with uncertainty. The *Yud, Yud, Lamed* wipes out all uncertainties, giving us the strength to recognize and pass our tests. A test will produce negative consequences only if we fail to recognize that the hardship is a test—and if we doubt the existence of the Creator.

יְהֹוָאדהנהי Adonai (אפים) | יִמְלֹךְ yimloch לְעֹלָם le'olam

ריבוע ס"ג וי' אותיות דס"ג ; ר"ת ייל וָעֶד va'ed: יְהֹוָאדהנהי Adonai (ורב וחסד) |

יִמְלֹךְ yimloch לְעֹלָם le'olam ריבוע ס"ג וי' אותיות דס"ג ; ר"ת ייל וָעֶד va'ed:

יְהֹוָאדהנהי Adonai (נשא עון) מַלְכוּתֵיהּ malchutei קָאֵים ka'em

לְעָלַם le'alam וּלְעָלְמֵי ul'almei עָלְמַיָּא almaya: כִּי ki בָא va סוּס sus ריבוע

אדני, כוק פַּרְעֹה Par'oh בְּרִכְבּוֹ berichbo וּבְפָרָשָׁיו uvfarashav בַּיָּם bayam ילי

וַיָּשֶׁב vayashev יְהֹוָאדהנהי Adonai (ופשע) עֲלֵהֶם alehem אֶת־ et מֵי mei

ילי הַיָּם hayam ילי וּבְנֵי uvnei יִשְׂרָאֵל Yisrael הָלְכוּ halchu בַיַּבָּשָׁה vayabasha

בְּתוֹךְ betoch הַיָּם hayam ילי: כִּי ki לַיהֹוָאדהנהי ladonai (ונקה)

הַמְּלוּכָה hamelucha ר"ת כלה (רמז למלכות שהיא הכלה) וּמוֹשֵׁל umoshel

בַּגּוֹיִם bagoyim: וְעָלוּ ve'alu מוֹשִׁעִים moshi'im בְּהַר behar צִיּוֹן Tziyon

יוסף, ו' הויות, קנאה לִשְׁפֹּט lishpot אֶת־ et הַר har עֵשָׂו Esav וְהָיְתָה vehayta

לַיהֹוָאדהנהי ladonai (פוקד) הַמְּלוּכָה hamelucha: וְהָיָה vehaya יהוה ; יהה

יְהֹוָאדהנהי Adonai (על שלשים) לְמֶלֶךְ lemelech עַל־ al כָּל kol ילי ; עמם

הָאָרֶץ ha'aretz אלהים דההין ע"ה בַּיּוֹם bayom ע"ה נגד, מזבח, זן אל יהוה הַהוּא hahu

יִהְיֶה yihye ייי יְהֹוָאדהנהי Adonai (ועל רבעים) אֶחָד echad אהבה, דאגה

וּשְׁמוֹ ushmo מהש ע"ה, ע"ב בריבוע וקס"א ע"ה, אל שדי ע"ה אֶחָד echad אהבה, דאגה:

The Lord shall reign forever and for eternity. The Lord shall reign forever and for eternity." (Exodus 15:1-18) *Lord your kingdom will reign forever and eternity. "For when Pharaoh's horses, chariots, and cavalry came into the sea, Lord turned the water upon them; and the Children of Israel walked upon the dry land within the sea."* (Exodus 15:19) *"For the Kingdom belongs to the Lord and He rules over the nations."* (Psalms 22:29) *"And deliverers shall ascend Mount Zion to seek retribution from Mount Esav, and then the entire universe shall recognize the Kingship of the Lord."* (Obadiah 1:21) *"And the Lord shall then be King over the whole earth and upon that day the Lord shall be One and His Name One."* (Zechariah 14:9)

NISHMAT KOL CHAI

There is always extra energy being released into our physical world during a holiday or on Shabbat. This particular connection builds up our internal Vessel so that we have both the capability to draw in this extra force and the capacity to handle what we draw in.

This praise is precious and exalted and you should say it in a pleasant manner. The kabbalists say that when a person goes through some trouble, problem or any danger - making a vow to say "*Nishmat Kol Chai*" will give that person great assistance.

If you forget and skip "*Nishmat Kol Chai*" and already say the blessing of "*Yishtabach*", as long as you didn't start the next blessing "*Yotzer Or*", you can go back and say "*Nishmat Kol Chai*". But if you start "*Yotzer Or*", you should complete it after the end of the prayer without the blessing of "*Yishtabach*".

נִשְׁמַת nishmat כָּל kol ילי וְחַי chai

ר"ת נכוז כמס' ג' הויות יהוה יהוה יהוה

On *Shabbat* meditate to receive the extra soul called: *Nefesh*
from the aspect of the day of *Shabbat*

The three above mentioned יהוה are the three *Mochin* - *Chochmah, Binah, Da'at* - that are in the Surrounding of the letter *Mem* (מ) of the *Tzelem* (צל"ם) of *Abba*, as the *Mochin* from *Ima* already entered *Zeir Anpin*. So right now *Zeir Anpin* has all his Surrounding for *Abba* and *Ima* [of the letter *Mem* (מ) of the *Tzelem* (צל"ם)] and that is why we can now receive the extra soul of *Shabbat*.

כָּל וְחַי = חיים, אהיה אהיה יהוה

תמורת תפילין הנקרא חיי המלך, והוא נשמה, כי בינה הוא בחינת נשמה.

אטמון = ק"ו, ב"פ ב"ן (יוד הה וו הה) עם ב' כוללים.

קול = ר"ת ועשה לו כתנת פסים (להתיר הקול).

אלף הי יוד הי

אלף הא יוד הא

אלף הה יוד הה

ס"ת ועשה לו כתנת פסים עולה למנין קס"א קמ"ג קנ"א (עם ד' תיבות ועשה לו כתנת פסים).

גם יכוין: פסי"ם נוטריקון פסקו"ן סגרו"ן יהוא"ל מטטרו"ן

פַּסְקוֹן (בניקוד ה' שפתי תפתח)

סָגָרוֹן (יכוין ס"ג ורנו כנפי החיות וניקו' ניקו' רָנוּ שָׁמַיִם)

יְהַוְאֵל (according to the Rashash) לכב (יוצא מפסוק זה אלי וְאַנְוֵהוּ הוא וניקודו)

מְטַטְרוֹן (בניקוד ר"ת הִנֵּה אָנֹכִי שֹׁלֵחַ מַלְאָךְ לְפָנֶיךָ)

תְּבָרֵךְ tevarech אֶת et שִׁמְךָ shimcha יְהֹוָהאדניאהדונהי Adonai אֱלֹהֵינוּ Elohenu ילה

וְרוּחַ veru'ach כָּל kol ילי בָּשָׂר basar תְּפָאֵר tefa'er וּתְרוֹמֵם utromem

זִכְרְךָ zichrecha מַלְכֵּנוּ malkenu תָּמִיד tamid ע"ה קס"א קנ"א קמ"ג (מילואי אהיה).

NISHMAT KOL CHAI

The soul of every living thing shall bless Your Name Lord, our God, and the spirit of all flesh shall always glorify and exalt Your remembrance, our King.

מִן min הָעוֹלָם ha'olam וְעַד ve'ad הָעוֹלָם ha'olam אַתָּה ata

אֵל El ייא״י (מילוי דס״ג). וּמִבַּלְעָדֶיךָ umibal'adecha אֵין en לָנוּ lanu אלהים, אהיה אדני

מֶלֶךְ melech גּוֹאֵל go'el וּמוֹשִׁיעַ umoshi'a. פּוֹדֶה pode וּמַצִּיל umatzil.

וְעוֹנֶה ve'one וּמְרַחֵם umrachem אברהם, ח״פ אל, רי״ו ול״ב נתיבות החכמה, רמ״ח (אברים),

עסמ״ב וט״ז אותיות פשוטות. בְּכָל bechol ב״ן, לכב עֵת et צָרָה tzara אלהים דההין

וְצוּקָה vetzuka. אֵין en לָנוּ lanu אלהים, אהיה אדני מֶלֶךְ melech

עוֹזֵר ozer וְסוֹמֵךְ vesomech ריבוע אדני, כוק אֶלָּא ela אַתָּה ata:

אֱלֹהֵי Elohei מילוי דע״ב, דמב ; ילה הָרִאשׁוֹנִים harishonim

וְהָאַחֲרוֹנִים veha'acharonim. אֱלוֹהַּ Eloha מ״ב כָּל kol ילי בְּרִיּוֹת beriyot.

אֲדוֹן adon אני כָּל kol ילי תּוֹלָדוֹת toladot. הַמְהֻלָּל hamehulal

בְּכָל bechol ב״ן, לכב הַתִּשְׁבָּחוֹת hatishbachot. הַמְנַהֵג hamenaheg

עוֹלָמוֹ olamo בְּחֶסֶד bechesed ע״ב, ריבוע יהוה וּבְרִיּוֹתָיו uvriyotav

בְּרַחֲמִים berachamim מצפצ, אלהים דיודין, י״פ ייי. וַיהֹוָהאדנילאהדונהי vadonai

אֱלֹהִים Elohim אהיה אדני ; ילה אֱמֶת emet אהיה פעמים אהיה, ז״פ ס״ג

לֹא lo יָנוּם yanum וְלֹא velo יִישָׁן yishan ש״ע נהורין רא״א.

הַמְעוֹרֵר hame'orer יְשֵׁנִים yeshenim וְהַמֵּקִיץ vehamekitz נִרְדָּמִים nirdamim.

מְחַיֵּה mechaye ס״ג מֵתִים metim. וְרוֹפֵא verofe חוֹלִים cholim חולה =

מ״ה עם ד׳ אותיות. פּוֹקֵחַ poke'ach עִוְרִים ivrim. וְזוֹקֵף vezokef כְּפוּפִים kefufim.

הַמֵּשִׂיחַ hamesi'ach אִלְּמִים ilmim. וְהַמְפַעְנֵחַ vehamfa'ane'ach

נֶעֱלָמִים ne'elamim. וּלְךָ ulcha לְבַדְּךָ levadcha אֲנַחְנוּ anachnu

מוֹדִים modim כנגד מאה ברכות שתיקן דוד לאמרם כל יום:

From this world to the World to Come, You are God. And apart from You, we have no king, redeemer, or savior. He Who liberates, rescues, sustains, answers and is merciful in every time of distress and anguish, we have no king, helper or supporter but You, God of the first and of the last, God of all creatures, Master of all generations, Who is extolled through a multitude of praises, and Who guides His world with kindness and His creatures with mercy. And the Lord, God, is true and He neither slumbers nor sleeps. He Who arouses the ones who sleep, and awakens the slumberers. He Who resurrects the dead, and heals the sick. He gives sight to the blind and straightens the ones who are bent. He makes the mute speak and uncovers the hidden. And to You alone, we give thanks.

וְאִלּוּ ve'ilu פִינוּ finu מָלֵא male שִׁירָה shira כַּיָּם kayam יכ"י♦

וּלְשׁוֹנֵנוּ ulshonenu רִנָּה rina כַּהֲמוֹן kahamon גַּלָּיו galav♦

וְשִׂפְתוֹתֵינוּ vesiftoteinu שֶׁבַח shevach כְּמֶרְחֲבֵי kemerchavei רָקִיעַ raki'a♦

וְעֵינֵינוּ ve'enenu ריבוע מ"ה מְאִירוֹת me'irot כַּשֶּׁמֶשׁ kashemesh

וְכַיָּרֵחַ vechayare'ach♦ וְיָדֵינוּ veyadenu פְרוּשׂוֹת ferusot כְּנִשְׁרֵי kenishrei

שָׁמָיִם shamayim י"פ טל, י"פ כוזו♦ וְרַגְלֵינוּ veragleinu קַלּוֹת kalot

כָּאַיָּלוֹת ka'ayalot♦ אֵין en אֲנַחְנוּ anachnu מַסְפִּיקִין maspikin

לְהוֹדוֹת lehodot לְךָ lecha יְהֹוָהאדניאהדונהי Adonai אֱלֹהֵינוּ Elohenu ילה♦

וּלְבָרֵךְ ulvarech אֶת et שְׁמֶךָ shimcha מַלְכֵּנוּ malkenu♦ עַל al

אַחַת achat מֵאֶלֶף me'elef מספר אֶלֶף = אלף למד שין דלת יוד ע"ה אַלְפֵי alfei

אֲלָפִים alafim וְרוֹב verov רִבֵּי ribei רְבָבוֹת revavot פְעָמִים pe'amim♦

הַטּוֹבוֹת hatovot נִסִּים nisim וְנִפְלָאוֹת venifla'ot שֶׁעָשִׂיתָ she'asita

עִמָּנוּ imanu ריבוע ס"ג, קס"א ע"ה וד' אותיות וְעִם ve'im אֲבוֹתֵינוּ avotenu♦

מִלְּפָנִים milfanim מִמִּצְרַיִם miMitzrayim מצר גְּאַלְתָּנוּ ge'altanu

יְהֹוָהאדניאהדונהי Adonai אֱלֹהֵינוּ Elohenu ילה♦ מִבֵּית mibet ב"פ ראה

עֲבָדִים avadim פְּדִיתָנוּ peditanu♦ בְּרָעָב bera'av זַנְתָּנוּ zantanu♦

וּבְשָׂבָע uvsava כִּלְכַּלְתָּנוּ kilkaltanu♦ מֵחֶרֶב mecherev הִצַּלְתָּנוּ hitzaltanu♦

מִדֶּבֶר midever מִלַּטְתָּנוּ milatetanu♦ וּמֵחֳלָאִים umechola'im רָעִים ra'im

וְרַבִּים verabim דִּלִּיתָנוּ dilitanu: עַד ad הֵנָּה hena עֲזָרוּנוּ azarunu

רַחֲמֶיךָ rachamecha וְלֹא velo עֲזָבוּנוּ azavunu חֲסָדֶיךָ chasadecha♦

Were our mouth as full of song as the sea and our tongue as full of joyous song as its multitude of waves, and our lips as full of praise as the breadth of the firmament, and our eyes as brilliant as the sun and the moon, and our hands as outspread as eagles of the skies and our legs as swift as hinds, We still cannot thank You enough, Lord, our God, and bless Your Name, our King, for even one of the thousands upon thousands of thousands and of the myriad upon myriad of myriad of favors, miracles and wonders that You performed for our ancestors and for us. From within Egypt, You have redeemed us, Lord, our God, and liberated us from the house of bondage. In famine You nourished us and in plenty, You sustained us. From the sword You saved us and from plague You let us escape and from severe numerous and enduring diseases, You spared us. Until now Your mercy has helped us and Your kindness has not forsaken us.

עַל al כֵּן ken אֵבָרִים evarim שֶׁפִּלַּגְתָּ shepilagta בָּנוּ banu.
וְרוּחַ veru'ach וּנְשָׁמָה unshama שֶׁנָּפַחְתָּ shenafachta בְּאַפֵּינוּ be'apenu.
וְלָשׁוֹן velashon אֲשֶׁר asher שַׂמְתָּ samta בְּפִינוּ befinu.
הֵן hen הֵם hem, יוֹדוּ yodu וִיבָרְכוּ vivarchu יהוה ריבוע יהוה ריבוע מ״ה.
וִישַׁבְּחוּ vishabechu. וִיפָאֲרוּ vifa'aru. אֶת et שִׁמְךָ shimcha מַלְכֵּנוּ malkenu
תָּמִיד tamid ע״ה קס״א קנ״א קמ״ג. כִּי ki כָל chol ילי פֶּה pe מילה ; וע״ה אלהים, אהיה אדני
לְךָ lecha יוֹדֶה yode. וְכָל vechol ילי לָשׁוֹן lashon לְךָ lecha
תְּשַׁבֵּחַ te'shabe'ach. וְכָל vechol ילי עַיִן ayin ריבוע מ״ה לְךָ lecha תְּצַפֶּה tetzape.
וְכָל vechol ילי בֶּרֶךְ berech לְךָ lecha תִכְרַע tichra.
וְכָל vechol ילי קוֹמָה koma לְפָנֶיךָ lefanecha ס״ג מ״ה ב״ן תִשְׁתַּחֲוֶה tishtachave.
וְהַלְּבָבוֹת vehalevavot יִירָאוּךָ yira'ucha וְהַקֶּרֶב vehakerev
וְהַכְּלָיוֹת vehakelayot יְזַמְּרוּ yezameru לִשְׁמֶךָ lishmecha. כַּדָּבָר kadavar ראה
שֶׁנֶּאֱמַר shene'emar: כָּל kol ילי עַצְמוֹתַי atzmotai תֹּאמַרְנָה tomarna
יְהֹוָהאדניאהדונהי Adonai מִי mi ילי כָמוֹךָ chamocha מַצִּיל matzil עָנִי ani ריבוע מ״ה
מֵחָזָק mechazak פהל מִמֶּנּוּ mimenu וְעָנִי ve'ani ריבוע מ״ה וְאֶבְיוֹן ve'evyon
מִגֹּזְלוֹ migozlo: שַׁוְעַת shavat עֲנִיִּים aniyim עין = ריבוע מ״ה אַתָּה ata
תִּשְׁמַע tishma. צַעֲקַת tza'akat הַדַּל hadal תַּקְשִׁיב takshiv וְתוֹשִׁיעַ vetoshi'a.
וְכָתוּב vechatuv: רַנְּנוּ ranenu צַדִּיקִים tzadikim בַּיהֹוָהאדניאהדונהי badonai
לַיְשָׁרִים laysharim נָאוָה nava תְהִלָּה tehila ע״ה אמת, אהיה פעמים אהיה, ז״פ ס״ג:

Therefore, organs that You have spread within us, and spirit and soul that You have breathed into our nostrils, and the tongue that You placed in our mouth, it is they that shall thank, bless, praise, and glorify Your Name, our King, forever. For every mouth shall offer thanks to You and every tongue shall say praise to You, And every eye shall look towards You. And every knee shall bend to You. And every erect form shall prostrate itself before You. And the hearts shall fear You. And the inner organs and the kidneys shall sing to Your Name, as it is written: All my bones shall say. Lord, who is like You? "You save the poor man from one stronger than he, and the poor and the destitute from one who wants to rob him." (Psalms 35:10) *You hear the outcry of the poor and You listen to the screams of the destitute and You save. And it is written: "Sing joyfully, righteous ones, before the Lord, for the upright praise is befitting."* (Psalms 33:1)

Isaac and Rivka

Isaac the Patriarch successfully prayed for his wife Rivka to have a baby. All of us, especially at this juncture, pray for others who are in need of financial, health, personal, or emotional sustenance. The only way our own prayers will be answered is for us to pray for others with a genuine heart.

The next four verses correspond to the four pillars that carry the Throne of *Beriah* which the Ten *Sefirot* of *Atzilut* stand on. Also, the four verses stand for the Throne of *Beriah* itself which includes the three Patriarchs (*Chesed, Gevurah, Tiferet*) and King David (*Malchut*).

Right Avraham	מיכאל בְּפִי befi	קדמיאל יְשָׁרִים yesharim	פדאל תִּתְרוֹמָם titromam:
Left Yitzchak	גבריאל וּבְשִׂפְתֵי uvsiftei	צדקיאל צַדִּיקִים tzadikim	חסדיאל תִּתְבָּרַךְ titbarach:
East Yaakov	רפאל וּבִלְשׁוֹן uvilshon	רזיאל חֲסִידִים chasidim	סטטרויה תִּתְקַדָּשׁ titkadash:
Fourth David	נוריאל וּבְקֶרֶב uvkerev	יופיאל קְדוֹשִׁים kedoshim	ענאל תִּתְהַלָּל tit'halal:

בְּמִקְהֲלוֹת bemikhalot רִבְבוֹת rivevot עַמְּךָ amcha בֵּית bet ב"פ ראה
יִשְׂרָאֵל Yisrael. שֶׁכֵּן sheken חוֹבַת chovat כָּל kol ילי הַיְצוּרִים hayetzurim
לְפָנֶיךָ lefanecha ס"ג מ"ה ב"ן יְהֹוָהאדניאהדונהי Adonai אֱלֹהֵינוּ Elohenu ילה
וֵאלֹהֵי velohei לכב ; מילוי דע"ב, דמ"ב ; ילה אֲבוֹתֵינוּ avotenu
לְהוֹדוֹת lehodot. לְהַלֵּל lehalel אדני, ללה. לְשַׁבֵּחַ leshabe'ach.
לְפָאֵר lefa'er. לְרוֹמֵם leromem. לְהַדֵּר lehader. וּלְנַצֵּחַ ulnatze'ach.
עַל al כָּל kol ילי ; עמם דִּבְרֵי divrei ראה שִׁירוֹת shirot וְתִשְׁבְּחוֹת vetishbachot
דָּוִד David בֶּן ben יִשַׁי Yishai עַבְדְּךָ avdecha פוי, אל אדני מְשִׁיחֶךָ meshichecha:

Isaac and Rivka

By the mouths of the upright, You shall be exalted.
And by the lips of the righteous, You shall be blessed.
And by the tongues of the pious, You shall be sanctified.
And among the holy ones, You shall be lauded.

And in the assemblies of the myriad of Your nation, the House of Israel, for such is the duty of all the creatures before You, Lord, our God and the God of our forefathers, to thank and to laud, to praise, glorify, exalt, adore and to render triumphant even beyond all expressions of the songs and praises of David, the son of Ishai, Your servant, Your anointed.

Yishtabach

Now that we have split the Red Sea, our next level of connection is the World of Creation (*Beriah*). The first word, *Yishtabach* ישתבח has a numerical value of 720, or ten times the 72 Names of God (10 x 72). By reciting *Yishtabach*, we receive the power of King Solomon, that of wisdom. Solomon שלמה is encoded in the next group of words and letters as shown below. Also, the first letters of each of the last five lines of this prayer spell out the name Abraham. Abraham denotes the power of sharing. We use the power of Solomon and Abraham—wisdom and sharing—to help us make the jump to the World of Creation.

The praise of *Yishtabach* is immense and awesome. It consists of 13 praises for the 13 Attributes of *Beriah* and the 13 *Sefirot* of *Yetzirah*. You should say the words slowly and gently and count them with the fingers of your right hand. Be careful not to stop between counting the 13 for any reason. And if you have to stop for any reason, you should go back and count them again from the beginning ("*ki lecha na'e*") in order to say them in one breath as mentioned in the *Zohar*.

וּבְכֵן uvchen ע״ב, ריבוע יהוה

יִשְׁתַּבַּח yishtabach י״פ ע״ב שִׁמְךָ shimcha לָעַד la'ad ב״פ ב״ן מַלְכֵּנוּ malkenu

הָאֵל haEl לאה ; ייא״י (מילוי דס״ג) הַמֶּלֶךְ: hamelech **(*King Solomon*)**

הַגָּדוֹל hagadol להח ; עם ד׳ אותיות = מבה, יזל, אום וְהַקָּדוֹשׁ vehakadosh

בַּשָּׁמַיִם bashamayim י״פ טל, י״פ כוזו וּבָאָרֶץ uva'aretz: כִּי ki לְךָ lecha נָאֶה na'e

יְהֹוָֹאדהנּהי Adonai אֱלֹהֵינוּ Elohenu ילה וֵאלֹהֵי velohei לכב ; מילוי ע״ב, דמב ; ילה

אֲבוֹתֵינוּ avotenu לְעוֹלָם le'olam ריבוע ס״ג ו׳ אותיות דס״ג וָעֶד va'ed:

1) שִׁיר shir (אל) 2) וּשְׁבָחָה ushvacha (רחום). 3) הַלֵּל halel (וחנון) ללה, אדני

4) וְזִמְרָה vezimra (ארך). 5) עֹז oz (אפים) 6) וּמֶמְשָׁלָה umemshala (ורב חסד).

7) נֶצַח netzach (ואמת). 8) גְּדֻלָּה gedula (נצר חסד). 9) גְּבוּרָה gevura

10) תְּהִלָּה tehila (לאלפים) רי״ו. (נשא עון) ע״ה אמת, אהיה פעמים אהיה, ז״פ ס״ג.

11) וְתִפְאֶרֶת vetif'eret (ופשע). 12) קְדֻשָּׁה kedusha (וחטאה).

Yishtabach

And so,

may Your Name be praised forever, our King, the God, the great and holy King, Who is in the Heavens and on the Earth. For to You are befitting, Lord, our God and the God of our forefathers, 1) song 2) and praise 3) exultation 4) and melody 5) power 6) and dominion 7) eternity 8) greatness 9) valor 10) praise 11) and glory 12) holiness

13) וּמַלְכוּת umalchut (וְנַקֵּה). בְּרָכוֹת berachot וְהוֹדָאוֹת vehoda'ot

לְשִׁמְךָ leshimcha הַגָּדוֹל hagadol לההו ; עם ד' אותיות = מבה, יזל, אום

וְהַקָּדוֹשׁ vehakadosh. וּמֵעוֹלָם ume'olam וְעַד ve'ad עוֹלָם olam

אַתָּה Ata אֵל El ייא"י (מילוי דס"ג). בָּרוּךְ baruch אַתָּה Ata

יְהֹוָאדהֹנָהי (יְהֹוָאדניה) יאהדונהי Adonai מֶלֶךְ melech גָּדוֹל gadol לההו ; עם ד' אותיות =

מבה, יזל, אום וּמְהֻלָּל umehulal בַּתִּשְׁבָּחוֹת batishbachot. אֵל El ייא"י (מילוי דס"ג)

הַהוֹדָאוֹת hahoda'ot. אֲדוֹן adon אני הַנִּפְלָאוֹת hanifla'ot. בּוֹרֵא bore

כָּל kol ילי הַנְּשָׁמוֹת haneshamot. רִבּוֹן ribon יהוה ע"ב ס"ג מ"ה ב"ן כָּל kol ילי

הַמַּעֲשִׂים hama'asim. הַבּוֹחֵר habocher בְּשִׁירֵי beshirei זִמְרָה zimra.

מֶלֶךְ melech **(*Abraham*)** אֵל El ייא"י (מילוי דס"ג)

וְחַי chei (לפי הרש"ש, וַחֵי לפי האריז"ל) הָעוֹלָמִים ha'olamim: אָמֵן amen יאהדונהי.

HALF KADDISH

The secret of this half *Kaddish* is that it elevates us from *Yetzirah* (מ"ה) to *Beriah* (ס"ג).

יִתְגַּדַּל yitgadal וְיִתְקַדַּשׁ veyitkadash שדי ומילוי שדי ; י"א אותיות כמנין ו"ה

שְׁמֵיהּ shemei (שם י"ה דע"ב) רַבָּא raba קנ"א ב"ן, יהוה אלהים יהוה אדני,

מילוי קס"א וס"ג, מ"ה ברבוע וע"ב ע"ה ; ר"ת = ו"פ אלהים ; ס"ת = ג"פ יב"ק: אָמֵן amen אידהנויה.

בְּעָלְמָא be'alma דִּי di בְרָא vera כִרְעוּתֵיהּ chir'utei.

וְיַמְלִיךְ veyamlich מַלְכוּתֵיהּ mal'chutei. וְיַצְמַח veyatzmach

פּוּרְקָנֵיהּ purkanei. וִיקָרֵב vikarev מְשִׁיחֵיהּ meshichei: אָמֵן amen אידהנויה.

---

13) and sovereignty. Blessings and thanksgiving to Your great and Holy Name from this world to the World to Come. You are God. Blessed are You, Lord, King, Who is great and lauded with praise. God of thanksgiving. Master of the wonders. Creator of the souls. Master of all deeds. One Who chooses melodious songs of praise. The King, the God Who gives life to all the worlds, Amen.

HALF KADDISH

May His great Name be more exalted and sanctified. (Amen)

In the world that He created according to His will, and may His Kingdom reign. And may He cause His redemption to sprout and may He bring the Mashiach closer. (Amen)

בְּחַיֵּיכוֹן bechayechon וּבְיוֹמֵיכוֹן uvyomechon וּבְחַיֵּי uvchayei

דְכָל dechol ילי בֵּית bet ב"פ ראה יִשְׂרָאֵל Yisrael בַּעֲגָלָא ba'agala

וּבִזְמַן uvizman קָרִיב kariv וְאִמְרוּ ve'imru אָמֵן amen: אָמֵן amen אידהנויה.

The congregation and the *chazan* say the following:

28 words (until *be'alma*) meditate: מילוי דמילוי דע"ב (יוד ויו דלת הי יוד ויו יוד ויו הי יוד)

28 letters (until *almaya*) meditate: מילוי דמילוי דס"ג (יוד ויו דלת הי יוד ואו אלף ואו הי יוד)

יְהֵא yehe שְׁמֵיהּ shemei (שם י"ה דס"ג) רַבָּא raba קנ"א ב"ן,

יהוה אלהים יהוה אדני, מילוי קס"א וס"ג, מ"ה ברבוע וע"ב ע"ה מְבָרַךְ mevarach

לְעָלַם le'alam לְעָלְמֵי le'almei עָלְמַיָּא almaya. יִתְבָּרַךְ yitbarach.

Seven words with six letters each (שם בן מ"ב) meditate:
יהוה + יוד הי ויו הי + מילוי דמילוי דע"ב (יוד ויו דלת הי יוד ויו יוד ויו הי יוד)
Also, seven times the letter *Vav* (שם בן מ"ב) meditate:
יהוה + יוד הי ואו הי + מילוי דמילוי דס"ג (יוד ויו דלת הי יוד ואו אלף ואו הי יוד).

וְיִשְׁתַּבַּח veyishtabach י"פ ע"ב יהוה אל אבג יתץ.

וְיִתְפָּאַר veyitpa'ar הי נו יה קרע שטן. וְיִתְרוֹמַם veyitromam וה כוזו נגד יכש.

וְיִתְנַשֵּׂא veyitnase במוכסז בטר צתג. וְיִתְהַדָּר veyit'hadar כוזו יה חקב טנע.

וְיִתְעַלֶּה veyit'ale וה יוד ה יגל פזק. וְיִתְהַלָּל veyit'halal א ואו הא שקו צית.

שְׁמֵיהּ shemei (שם י"ה דמ"ה) דְּקוּדְשָׁא dekudsha בְּרִיךְ verich הוּא hu:

אָמֵן amen אידהנויה.

לְעֵלָּא le'ela מִן min כָּל kol ילי בִּרְכָתָא birchata. שִׁירָתָא shirata.

תִּשְׁבְּחָתָא tishbechata וְנֶחָמָתָא venechamata. דַּאֲמִירָן da'amiran

בְּעָלְמָא be'alma וְאִמְרוּ ve'imru אָמֵן amen: אָמֵן amen אידהנויה.

In your lifetimes and in your days and in the lifetime of all the House of Israel, speedily and in the near future, and you should say, Amen. (Amen) *May His great Name be blessed forever and for all eternity blessed and lauded, and glorified and exalted, and extolled and honored, and uplifted and praised be, the Name of the Holy Blessed One.* (Amen) *Above all blessings, songs, praises, and words of consolation that may be said in the world, and you shall say, Amen.* (Amen)

BARCHU

When we enter the World of Creation *(Beriah)*, we recite the *Barchu* (you should bless). This powerful connection brings back the part of our soul that left us while we slept. Even if a person remains awake, a part of his soul still leaves during the night. There are five words in the *Barchu* that connect us to the five parts of our soul. Each part of the soul is connected to one of the five worlds.

The *chazan* says:

בָּרְכוּ barchu יהוה ריבוע יהוה ריבוע מ״ה אֶת et יְהֹוָהאדניאהדונהי Adonai

הַמְּבוֹרָךְ hamevorach ס״ת כהת, משיח בן דוד ע״ה:

While the *chazan* says the verse "*barchu*", the congregation says "*yishtabach*" as follows (The *chazan* will say "*yishtabach*" as the congregation replies "*baruch*" as below):

יִשְׁתַּבַּח yishtabach י״פ ע״ב וְיִתְפָּאַר veyitpa'ar שְׁמוֹ shemo מהש ע״ה, ע״ב בריבוע וקס״א ע״ה, אל שדי ע״ה שֶׁל shel מֶלֶךְ melech מַלְכֵי malchei הַמְּלָכִים hamelachim הַקָּדוֹשׁ hakadosh בָּרוּךְ baruch הוּא hu שֶׁהוּא shehu רִאשׁוֹן rishon וְהוּא vehu אַחֲרוֹן acharon וּמִבַּלְעָדָיו umibal'adav אֵין en אֱלֹהִים Elohim אהיה אדני ; ילה. יְהִי yehi שֵׁם shem יְהֹוָהאדניאהדונהי Adonai מְבֹרָךְ mevorach ר״ת ריבוע ע״ב וריבוע ס״ג יהוה מברך = רפ״ח (להעלות רפ״ח ניצוצות שנפלו לקליפה דמשם באים התחלואים) מֵעַתָּה me'ata וְעַד־ ve'ad עוֹלָם olam ילי: וּמְרוֹמַם umromam עַל־ al כָּל־ kol ילי ; עמם בְּרָכָה beracha וּתְהִלָּה ut'hila ע״ה אמת, אהיה פעמים אהיה, ז״פ ס״ג:

When we reply "*baruch Adonai hamevorach le'olam va'ed*" we receive the five parts of the soul (*Nefesh, Ruach, Neshamah, Chayah* and *Yechidah*) that left us during the last night's sleep.

First the congregation replies the following, and then the *chazan* repeats it:

Nefosh בָּרוּךְ baruch *Ruach* יְהֹוָהאדניאהדונהי Adonai *Neshamah* הַמְּבוֹרָךְ hamevorach

Chayah לְעוֹלָם le'olam ריבוע ס״ג ו׳ אותיות דס״ג *Yechidah* וָעֶד va'ed:

BARCHU

Bless the Lord, the Blessed One.

Praised and exalted is the Name of the King of all Kings, the Holy Blessed One, Who is first and Who is last and without Whom, there is no God. Let the Name of the Lord be blessed from now till all eternity, above all blessings and praise. Blessed be the Lord, the Blessed One, forever and for eternity.

THE WORLD OF CREATION – *BERIAH*

The beginning verse states: *yotzer or uvore choshech* (forms light and creates darkness). This refers to the concept of Light and darkness, good and evil. A 50/50 split between good and evil gives us the free will to choose either Light or darkness.

From here (“*yotzer or*”) until “*ga'al Yisrael*” (pg. 363) you are in the World of *Beriah*.

Hechal Livnat Hasapir (the Sapphire Stone Chamber) - *Yesod* of *Zeir Anpin* in *Beriah*.

In the following paragraph there are sixty words which correspond to the sixty mighty ones (they protect the *Malchut* of *Atzilut* when it ascends to *Beriah*). The minister in this *Hechal* is the angel *Adarhani-el*-אדרהניאל (**do not pronounce this name**) and the spirit of this *Hechal* is יאהדונהי.

בָּרוּךְ baruch אַתָּה Ata יְהֹוָהאדניאהדונהי Adonai אֱלֹהֵינוּ Elohenu ילה

מֶלֶךְ melech הָעוֹלָם ha'olam יוֹצֵר yotzer אוֹר or רז, אין סוף

וּבוֹרֵא uvore חֹשֶׁךְ choshech חשך נצוצות של ז' המלכים. עֹשֶׂה ose שָׁלוֹם shalom

וּבוֹרֵא uvore אֶת et הַכֹּל hakol ילי: הַכֹּל hakol ילי יוֹדוּךְ yoducha

וְהַכֹּל vehakol ילי יְשַׁבְּחוּךְ yeshabechucha וְהַכֹּל vehakol ילי יֹאמְרוּ yomru

אֵין en קָדוֹשׁ kadosh כַּיהֹוָהאדניאהדונהי kadonai הַכֹּל hakol ילי

יְרוֹמְמוּךְ yeromemucha סֶּלָה sela יוֹצֵר yotzer הַכֹּל hakol ילי.

הָאֵל haEl לאה ; אל (ייא" מילוי דס"ג) הַפּוֹתֵחַ hapote'ach בְּכָל bechol ב"ן, לכב יוֹם yom

ע"ה נגד, מזבח, זן, אל יהוה דַּלְתוֹת daltot שַׁעֲרֵי sha'arei מִזְרָח mizrach.

וּבוֹקֵעַ uvoke'a חַלּוֹנֵי chalonei רָקִיעַ raki'a. מוֹצִיא motzi חַמָּה chama

מִמְּקוֹמָהּ mimekoma וּלְבָנָה ulvana מִמְּכוֹן mimechon שִׁבְתָּהּ shivta.

וּמֵאִיר ume'ir לָעוֹלָם le'olam ריבוע ס"ג י' אותיות דס"ג כֻּלּוֹ kulo וּלְיוֹשְׁבָיו ulyoshvav

שֶׁבָּרָא shebara קנ"א ב"ן, יהוה אלהים יהוה אדני, מילוי קס"א וס"ג, מ"ה ברבוע ע"ב ע"ה

בְּמִדַּת bemidat הָרַחֲמִים harachamim:

THE WORLD OF CREATION

Blessed are You, Lord, our God, King of the Universe, “Who forms Light and creates darkness, makes peace, and creates everything.” (Isaiah 45:7) *Everything gives thanks to You. Everything praises You. Everyone says that there is none as holy as the Lord. Everyone exalts You, Selah! He, Who forms everything. The God Who opens daily the doors of the gateways of the east and Who splits the windows of the firmament. Who removes the sun from its place and the moon from the place of its rest. Who illuminates the whole world and its inhabitants which He created with His attribute of mercy.*

הַמֵּאִיר hame'ir לָאָרֶץ la'aretz וְלַדָּרִים veladarim עָלֶיהָ aleha פהל

בְּרַחֲמִים berachamim מצפצ, אלהים דיודין, י"פ ייי. וּבְטוּבוֹ uvtuvo (שהוא החסד אור גנוז בו)

מְחַדֵּשׁ mechadesh י"ב הויות, קס"א קנ"א בְּכָל bechol ב"ן, לכב יוֹם yom ע"ה נגד, מזבח, זן,

תָּמִיד tamid ע"ה קס"א קנ"א קמ"ג מַעֲשֵׂה ma'ase בְרֵאשִׁית vereshit ר"ת מ"ב:

מָה ma מ"ה רַבּוּ rabu מַעֲשֶׂיךָ ma'asecha יְהֹוָהאדניאהדונהי Adonai

כֻּלָּם kulam בְּחָכְמָה bechochma במילוי = תרי"ג (מצוות) עָשִׂיתָ asita

All the actions come (as potential of potential) from *Abba* which encloses the Endless Light, and done (as actual of potential) by *Ima* which encloses *Abba* - *Abba* says and *Ima* does.

מָלְאָה mal'a הָאָרֶץ ha'aretz אלהים דההין ע"ה קִנְיָנֶךָ kinyanecha

The Holy Animals and the *Ofanim* of "*Hechal Livnat Hasapir*".

הַמֶּלֶךְ hamelech הַמְרוֹמָם hameromam

לְבַדּוֹ levado מ"ב מֵאָז me'az ומב ; לבדו מאז ע"ה = אמן (יאהדונהי)

Malchut* of *Beriah (where *Asiyah* and *Yetzirah* are included in Her now) goes up from "*Hechal Kodesh HaKodashim*" of *Yetzirah* to "*Hechal Livnat Hasapir*" of *Beriah*. **Meditate** to connect *Malchut* and *Yesod* of *Beriah*, and to draw the *Neshamah* from the Upper *Da'at* of *Beriah* for Them.

הַמְשֻׁבָּח hameshubach וְהַמְפֹאָר vehamefo'ar

וְהַמִּתְנַשֵּׂא vehamitnase מִימוֹת mimot עוֹלָם olam:

אֱלֹהֵי Elohei מילוי דע"ב, דמב ; ילה עוֹלָם olam בְּרַחֲמֶיךָ berachamecha

הָרַבִּים harabim רַחֵם rachem אברהם, וז"פ אל, רי"ו ול"ב נתיבות החכמה,

רמ"ח (אברים), עסמ"ב וט"ז אותיות פשוטות עָלֵינוּ alenu. אֲדוֹן adon אני עֻזֵּנוּ uzenu.

צוּר tzur אלהים דההין ע"ה מִשְׂגַּבֵּנוּ misgabenu.

מָגֵן magen ג"פ אל (יי"א מילוי דס"ג) ; ר"ת מיכאל גבריאל נוריאל יִשְׁעֵנוּ yish'enu.

מִשְׂגָּב misgav מוה, מהש, ע"ב בריבוע קס"א, אל שדי, ד"פ אלהים ע"ה בַּעֲדֵנוּ ba'adenu:

On Shabbat: *Hechal Ratzon* (the Desire Chamber) - *Tiferet* of *Zeir Anpin* in *Beriah*.

And, with His goodness, He renews, every day and always, the works of creation. How manifold are Your works, Lord, You have made them all with wisdom and the world is filled with Your possessions. The King, Who was exalted alone from the beginning. The One Who is praised, glorified and extolled from the beginning of time. God of the world, with Your plentiful compassions take pity over us. Master of our strength, shield of our redemption and Who is strength for us.

אֵין en עֲרוֹךְ aroch לְךָ lecha וְאֵין ve'en זוּלָתְךָ zulatach• אֶפֶס efes

בִּלְתְּךָ biltach וּמִי umi ילי דּוֹמֶה dome לָךְ: lach אֵין en עֲרוֹךְ aroch לְךָ lecha

יְהֹוָהאדניה Adonai אֱלֹהֵינוּ Elohenu ילה בָּעוֹלָם ba'olam הַזֶּה haze והו•

וְאֵין ve'en זוּלָתְךָ zulatach מַלְכֵּנוּ malkenu לְחַיֵּי lechayei

הָעוֹלָם ha'olam הַבָּא :haba אֶפֶס efes בִּלְתְּךָ biltach גּוֹאֲלֵנוּ go'alenu

לִימוֹת limot הַמָּשִׁיחַ •hamashi'ach וּמִי umi ילי דּוֹמֶה dome

לָךְ lach מוֹשִׁיעֵנוּ moshi'enu לִתְחִיַּת lit'chiyat הַמֵּתִים :hametim

EL ADON

We find the 22 letters of the Aramaic alphabet encoded into this prayer. The first letter in each of the first 22 words is the alphabet in its correct order. Because the Aramaic letters are the actual instruments of Creation, this prayer helps to inject order and the power of creation into our lives.

> **On Shabbat:** *Hechal Ahavah* (the Love Chamber) - *Chesed* of *Zeir Anpin* in *Beriah*. **Meditate** to draw additional Holiness of *Shabbat* (from the aspect of the day – male) to *Nukva* of *Zeir Anpin* of *Beriah* so She will have a new Name: אל אלף דלת נון יוד (702=*Shabbat*). Also **Meditate** to elevate "*Hechal Ahavah*" (*Chesed*) of *Zeir Anpin* of *Beriah* to the Upper "*Hechal Ahavah*" (*Chesed*) of *Abba* and *Ima* of *Beriah*, in order to draw the extra Holiness of *Shabbat*.

Hechal Etzem Hashamayim (the Heaven's Embodiment Chamber) - *Hod* of *Zeir Anpin* in *Beriah*.

א אֵל El ייא״י (מילוי ד״סג) ב אָדוֹן adon אני

ג עַל al ד כָּל kol ילי ; עמם ה הַמַּעֲשִׂים •hama'asim

ו בָּרוּךְ: baruch ז וּמְבוֹרָךְ: umvorach

ח בְּפִי befi ט כָּל chol ילי ; עמם י הַנְּשָׁמָה •haneshama

There is no comparison to You, there is nothing except for You, for who is like You? There is no comparison to You, Lord, our God, in this world And there will be nothing except for You, our King, in the life of the World to Come. There will be nothing without You, our Redeemer in the days of the Mashiach. And who will be like You, our Savior, at the resurrection of the dead?

EL ADON

א *God, Master over all the works.* ב *Blessed One Who is blessed by the mouth of every soul.*

והו ילי סיט עלם

גָּדְלוֹ godlo וְטוּבוֹ vetuvo מָלֵא male עוֹלָם olam •

מהש ללה אכא כהת

דַּעַת da'at וּתְבוּנָה utvuna סוֹבְבִים sovevim הוֹדוֹ hodo אהיה:

הזי אלד לאו ההע

הַמִּתְגָּאֶה hamitga'e עַל al וְחַיּוֹת chayot הַקֹּדֶשׁ hakodesh •

יזל מבה הרי הקם

וְנֶהְדָּר venehdar בְּכָבוֹד bechavod בוכו עַל al הַמֶּרְכָּבָה hamerkava •

לאו כלי לוו פהל

זְכוּת zechut וּמִישׁוֹר umishor לִפְנֵי lifnei כִּסְאוֹ chis'o •

נלך ייי מלה חהו

חֶסֶד chesed ע"ב, ריבוע יהוה וְרַחֲמִים verachamim מָלֵא male כְּבוֹדוֹ chevodo:

נתה האא ירת שאה

טוֹבִים tovim מְאוֹרוֹת me'orot שֶׁבָּרָאָם shebera'am אֱלֹהֵינוּ Elohenu ילה •

ריי אום

יְצָרָם yetzaram בְּדַעַת beda'at

לכב ושר

בְּבִינָה bevina ע"ה אהיה אהיה יהוה, חיים וּבְהַשְׂכֵּל uv'haskel •

יחו להח כוק מנד

כֹּחַ ko'ach וּגְבוּרָה ugvura רי"ו נָתַן natan בָּהֶם bahem •

אני חעם רהע ייז

לִהְיוֹת lih'yot מוֹשְׁלִים moshlim בְּקֶרֶב bekerev תֵּבֵל tevel ב"פ רי"ו:

ההה מיכ וול ילה

מְלֵאִים mele'im זִיו ziv וּמְפִיקִים umfikim נֹגַהּ noga דני •

ג His greatness and His goodness fill the world. ד Wisdom and insight surround His glory. ה He Who is exalted over the holy Beasts. ו And splendors in glory over the Chariot. ז Merit and fairness are before His Throne. ח Kindness and mercy fill His glory. ט Good are the luminaries that our God had created. י With insight, and with discernment. He had fashioned them with knowledge. כ He bestowed upon them strength and power, ל To be dominant within the world. מ They are full of brilliance and radiate brightness.

נָאֶה na'e זִיוָם zivam בְּכָל bechol ב"ן, לכב הָעוֹלָם ha'olam ✦

שְׂמֵחִים semechim בְּצֵאתָם betzetam שָׂשִׂים sasim בְּבוֹאָם bevo'am ✦

עוֹשִׂים osim בְּאֵימָה be'ema ר"ת ע"ב (יוד הי ויו הי), ריבוע יהוה (י יה יהו יהוה)

רְצוֹן retzon מהש ע"ה, ע"ב בריבוע וקס"א ע"ה, אל שדי ע"ה קוֹנֵיהֶם konehem ⁘

פְּאֵר pe'er וְכָבוֹד vechavod נוֹתְנִים notnim לִשְׁמוֹ lishmo

מהש ע"ה, ע"ב בריבוע וקס"א ע"ה, אל שדי ע"ה

צָהֳלָה tzahola וְרִנָּה verina לְזֵכֶר lezecher מַלְכוּתוֹ malchuto ✦

קָרָא kara לַשֶּׁמֶשׁ lashemesh וַיִּזְרַח vayizrach אוֹר or רז, אין סוף ✦

רָאָה ra'a ראה וְהִתְקִין vehitkin צוּרַת tzurat הַלְּבָנָה halevana ⁘

שֶׁבַח shevach נוֹתְנִים notnim לוֹ lo כָּל kol ילי צְבָא tzeva מָרוֹם marom ✦

תִּפְאֶרֶת tiferet וּגְדוּלָּה ugdula *(Beriah)* שְׂרָפִים serafim

(Yetzirah) וְחַיּוֹת vechayot *(Asiyah)* וְאוֹפַנֵּי ve'ofanei הַקֹּדֶשׁ hakodesh ⁘

נ *Their brilliance is beautiful all around the world.* ס *Glad as they go forth and exultant as they return.* ע *They do with awe their Creator's will.* פ *All the hosts above bestow praise to Him.* צ *Jubilation and merry song upon the mention of His reign.* ק *He called out to the sun and it glowed with light.* ר *He saw and fashioned the form of the moon.* ש *Splendor and glory they give to His Name.* ת *Splendor and greatness by the Seraphs, Beasts And the holy Ofans.*

On *Shabbat* we add:

LAEL ASHER

Each of us is imbued with the Creator's DNA. These verses help us awaken all of the Godlike features within us so that we can achieve fulfillment and control over our lives.

לָאֵל laEl ייא״י (מילוי דס״ג) אֲשֶׁר asher שָׁבַת shavat מִכָּל mikol הַמַּעֲשִׂים hama'asim

וּבַיּוֹם uvayom ע״ה נגד, מזבח, זן, אל יהוה הַשְּׁבִיעִי hashevi'i נִתְעַלָּה nit'ala

Meditate that *Zeir Anpin* that was "sitting" in *Yetzirah*, is now elevating to *Beriah*.

As for now, the five *Tzelem* (of *Netzach, Hod, Yesod* of *Yisrael Saba* and *Tevunah*) which is called צ, the five *Tzelem* (of *Chesed, Gevurah, Tiferet* of *Yisrael Saba* and *Tevunah*) which is called ל, and the five *Tzelem* (of *Chochmah, Binah, Da'at* of *Yisrael Saba* and *Tevunah*) which is called ם, (and is also called: *Nefesh, Ruach, Neshamah, Chayah, Yechidah,* of *Neshamah*), already entered to the five *Partzufim* of *Netzach, Hod, Yesod,* and to the five *Partzufim* of *Chesed, Gevurah, Tiferet* and to the five *Partzufim* of *Chochmah, Binah, Da'at* of *Binah* of *Zeir Anpin* – which is called – *Gadlut Alef* (First Adulthood - which is not considered as an elevation for *Zeir Anpin*). **Also meditate** for *Yaakov* and *Rachel* which They are now enclosing *Netzach, Hod, Yesod* of *Binah* of *Zeir Anpin* (which is *Netzach, Hod, Yesod* of *Yisrael Saba* and *Tevunah*).

וַיָּשַׁב veyashav עַל al כִּסֵּא kise כְבוֹדוֹ chevodo. תִּפְאֶרֶת tiferet

עָטָה ata לְיוֹם leyom ע״ה נגד, מזבח, זן, אל יהוה הַמְּנוּחָה hamenucha.

עֹנֶג oneg ר״ת עדן נהר גן קָרָא kara לְיוֹם leyom ע״ה נגד, מזבח, זן, אל יהוה

הַשַּׁבָּת haShabbat: זֶה ze שִׁיר shir שֶׁבַח shevach שֶׁל shel

יוֹם yom ע״ה נגד, מזבח, זן, אל יהוה הַשְּׁבִיעִי hashevi'i שֶׁבּוֹ shebo שָׁבַת shavat

אֵל El ייא״י (מילוי דס״ג) מִכָּל mikol ילי מְלַאכְתּוֹ melachto.

וְיוֹם veyom ע״ה נגד, מזבח, זן, אל יהוה הַשְּׁבִיעִי hashevi'i מְשַׁבֵּחַ meshabe'ach

וְאוֹמֵר ve'omer: מִזְמוֹר mizmor שִׁיר shir לְיוֹם leyom ע״ה נגד, מזבח, זן, אל יהוה

הַשַּׁבָּת haShabbat ר״ת למשה: לְפִיכָךְ lefichach יְפָאֲרוּ yefa'aru

לָאֵל laEl ייא״י (מילוי דס״ג) כָּל kol ילי יְצוּרָיו yetzurav. שֶׁבַח shevach וִיקָר vikar

וּגְדֻלָּה ugdula וְכָבוֹד vechavod יִתְּנוּ yitenu לַמֶּלֶךְ lamelech יוֹצֵר yotzer

כֹּל kol ילי. הַמַּנְחִיל hamanchil מְנוּחָה menucha לְעַמּוֹ le'amo יִשְׂרָאֵל Yisrael

בְּיוֹם beyom ע״ה נגד, מזבח, זן, אל יהוה שַׁבַּת Shabbat קֹדֶשׁ kodesh.

LAEL ASHER

To the God Who rested from all the works and Who, on the Seventh Day, was elevated and sat on the Throne of His glory. With splendor He enwrapped the Day of Rest, He declared the Shabbat Day a delight. This is the song of praise of the Shabbat Day on which God rested from all His work. And the Seventh Day praises and says: A psalm, a song for the Shabbat Day. It is good to give thanks to the Lord. Therefore, let all that He had fashioned glorify and bless God. Praise, honor, greatness and glory, let them render to God, the King, Who fashioned everything. He Who gives a heritage of contentment to His People, Israel, in His holiness, on the Day of Shabbat.

שִׁמְךָ shimcha יְהֹוָאדהנה Adonai אֱלֹהֵינוּ Elohenu ילה יִתְקַדֵּשׁ yitkadash
שין דלת יוד• וְזִכְרְךָ vezichrecha יִתְפָּאַר yitpa'ar מַלְכֵּנוּ malkenu
בַּשָּׁמַיִם bashamayim י״פ טל, י״פ כוזו מִמַּעַל mima'al עלם וְעַל ve'al הָאָרֶץ ha'aretz
אלהים דההין ע״ה מִתָּחַת •mitachat עַל al כָּל kol ילי ; עמם שֶׁבַח shevach
מַעֲשֵׂה ma'ase יָדֶיךָ •yadecha וְעַל ve'al מְאוֹרֵי me'orei אוֹר or רז, אין סוף
שֶׁיָּצַרְתָּ sheyatzarta הֵמָּה hema יְפָאֲרוּךָ yefa'arucha סֶּלָה :sela

TITBARACH LANETZACH

The last Name of the 72 Names of God—*Mem, Vav,* final *Mem* מום appears in this connection. This Name means "blemish" or "imperfection." If we are on this planet, we still have at least one imperfection, if not countless more. This connection helps us to correct these blemishes.

תִּתְבָּרַךְ titbarach לָנֶצַח lanetzach צוּרֵנוּ tzurenu מַלְכֵּנוּ malkenu
וְגוֹאֲלֵנוּ vego'alenu בּוֹרֵא bore קְדוֹשִׁים kedoshim יִשְׁתַּבַּח yishtabach
י״פ ע״ב ; ר״ת יב״ק, אלהים יהוה, אהיה אדני יהוה שִׁמְךָ shimcha לָעַד la'ad ב״פ ב״ן
מַלְכֵּנוּ malkenu יוֹצֵר yotzer מְשָׁרְתִים meshartim וַאֲשֶׁר va'asher
מְשָׁרְתָיו meshartav ר״ת מום, אלהים כֻּלָּם kulam עוֹמְדִים omdim
כלם עומדים = י׳ הויות בְּרוּם berum עוֹלָם olam ר״ת ע״ב, ריבוע יהוה ;
ברום עולם ע״ה = קס״א קנ״א קמ״ג עם ג׳ כוללים (לא כולל האהיה עצמם) וּמַשְׁמִיעִים umashmi'im
בְּיִרְאָה beyir'a רי״ו יַחַד yachad בְּקוֹל ,bekol דִּבְרֵי divrei ראה
אֱלֹהִים Elohim אהיה אדני ; ילה וְחַיִּים chayim אהיה אהיה יהוה, בינה ע״ה וּמֶלֶךְ umelech
עוֹלָם •olam כֻּלָּם kulam אֲהוּבִים •ahuvim כֻּלָּם kulam בְּרוּרִים •berurim
כֻּלָּם kulam גִּבּוֹרִים giborim ר״ת אבג• כֻּלָּם kulam קְדוֹשִׁים •kedoshim

---

May Your Name, Lord, our God, be sanctified and may Your remembrance, our King, be glorified in the heaven above and upon the earth below. May You be blessed, our Savior, beyond all the praises of Your handiwork. And beyond the brilliant luminaries that You had formed, may they glorify You, Selah!

TITBARACH LANETZACH

May You be eternally blessed, our Rock, our King, and our Redeemer, Creator of the holy angels. May Your Name be praised forever, our King, Who forms ministering angels. And Whose ministering angels stand in the heights of the world and loudly proclaim, with reverence and in unison, the words of the living God and the King of the Universe. They are all-beloved. They are all-pure. They are all-powerful. They are all-holy.

כֻּלָּם kulam עוֹשִׂים osim בְּאֵימָה be'ema ר"ת ע"ב, ריבוע יהוה

וּבְיִרְאָה uvyir'a רי"ו רְצוֹן retzon מהש ע"ה, ע"ב בריבוע וקס"א ע"ה, אל שדי ע"ה

קוֹנֵיהֶם konehem וְכֻלָּם vechulam פּוֹתְחִים potchim אֶת et

פִּיהֶם pihem בִּקְדוּשָּׁה bikdusha וּבְטָהֳרָה uvtahora בְּשִׁירָה beshira

וּבְזִמְרָה uvzimra וּמְבָרְכִין umvarchin• וּמְשַׁבְּחִין umshabechin•

וּמְפָאֲרִין umfa'arin• וּמַקְדִּישִׁין umakdishin• וּמַעֲרִיצִין uma'aritzin•

וּמַמְלִיכִין umamlichin ר"ת ז' ווין בסוד שם בן מ"ב ; ס"ת = מצפצ, אלהים דיודין, י"פ ייי•

ET SHEM

The word *reshut* רשות is found inside this connection. *Reshut* has the same numerical value (906) as the initials of the words comprising the last sentence in the *Ana Beko'ach* (*Shav'atenu Kabel Ushma Tza'akatenu Yode'a Ta'alumot*) - שקו צית. This specific sequence correlates to our physical world, *Malchut*.

אֶת־ et שֵׁם shem הָאֵל haEl לאה ; אל (יא"י מילוי דס"ג) הַמֶּלֶךְ: hamelech

הַגָּדוֹל hagadol להח ; עם ד' אותיות = מבה, יזל, אום הַגִּבּוֹר hagibor וְהַנּוֹרָא vehanora

ר"ת = יהוה קָדוֹשׁ kadosh הוּא hu• וְכֻלָּם vechulam מְקַבְּלִים mekabelim

עֲלֵיהֶם alehem עֹל ol מַלְכוּת malchut שָׁמַיִם shamayim י"פ טל, י"פ כוזו זֶה ze

מִזֶּה mize• וְנוֹתְנִים venotnim רְשׁוּת reshut שקו צית זֶה ze לָזֶה laze•

לְהַקְדִּישׁ lehakdish לְיוֹצְרָם leyotzram בְּנַחַת benachat רוּחַ ru'ach•

בְּשָׂפָה besafa בְרוּרָה verura בשפה ברורה ע"ה = לשון הקודש וּבִנְעִימָה uvin'ima•

קְדוּשָּׁה kedusha כֻּלָּם kulam כְּאֶחָד ke'echad אהבה, דאגה

עוֹנִים onim בְּאֵימָה be'ema• וְאוֹמְרִים ve'omrim בְּיִרְאָה beyir'a רי"ו:

They all execute, with reverence and with awe, the will of their Maker. They all open their mouths with holiness and with purity, and give song and melody. They bless, praise, glorify, sanctify, revere, and enthrone.

ET SHEM

The Name of God, the King, the great, powerful and awesome One, for He is Holy.

They all accept upon themselves the yoke of the Heavenly Kingdom, one from another. And they give leave to one another and they consent to sanctify their Creator. And in a calm spirit, with a clear expression, and pleasantly, they proclaim sanctity, with reverence. And they all say in unison and in awe:

KADOSH, KADOSH, KADOSH

This phrase translates into "Holy, Holy, Holy," but it does not refer to what we normally consider the word "holy" to mean (sacred, blessed, or sanctified). Rather, it signifies the concept of *whole* or "wholly", as in the quantum wholeness of reality that is unified and interconnected. Repeating the word "holy" three times also connects us to the Right (positive), Left (negative), and Central Columns (neutral). This prayer instills within us the awareness that although we may have imperfections, we still have the Divine Spark of Light within us. Our soul is part of God.

It is good to recite this verse according to its intonations (*te'amim*).

קָדוֹשׁ kadosh | **(Right)** קָדוֹשׁ kadosh **(Left)** קָדוֹשׁ kadosh **(Central)**

יְהֹוָהאדניאהדונהי Adonai צְבָאוֹת Tzeva'ot פני שכינה

מְלֹא melo כָל־ chol ילי הָאָרֶץ ha'aretz אלהים דההין ע״ה כְּבוֹדוֹ kevodo׃

וְהָאוֹפַנִּים veha'ofanim וְחַיּוֹת vechayot הַקֹּדֶשׁ hakodesh

בְּרַעַשׁ bera'ash גָּדוֹל gadol להוז ; עם ד׳ אותיות = מבה, יזל, אום

מִתְנַשְּׂאִים mitnase'im לְעֻמַּת le'umat הַשְּׂרָפִים haserafim

לְעֻמָּתָם le'umatam מְשַׁבְּחִים meshabchim וְאוֹמְרִים ve'omrim׃

בָּרוּךְ baruch כְּבוֹד kevod יְהֹוָהאדניאהדונהי Adonai ; כבוד יהוה = יוד הי ואו הה

מִמְּקוֹמוֹ mimekomo עסמ״ב, הברכה (למתק את ז׳ המלכים שמתו)

ר״ת = ע״ב, ריבוע יהוה ; ר״ת מיכ, י״פ האא׃

LAEL BARUCH

Hechal Nogah (the Brightness Chamber) - *Netzach* of *Zeir Anpin* in *Beriah*.

לָאֵל laEl ייא״י (מילוי דס״ג) בָּרוּךְ baruch• נְעִימוֹת ne'imot יִתֵּנוּ yitenu•

לַמֶּלֶךְ lamelech אֵל El ייא״י (מילוי דס״ג) חַי chai וְקַיָּם vekayam•

זְמִירוֹת zemirot יֹאמֵרוּ yomeru• וְתִשְׁבָּחוֹת vetishbachot יַשְׁמִיעוּ yashmi'u•

KADOSH, KADOSH, KADOSH

"Holy, Holy, Holy
Is the Lord of Hosts. The world is full with His glory." (Isaiah 6:3)
"The Offanim and all the Holy Beasts soar with thunderous voice toward the Seraphs who stand opposite them, and give praise and say: Blessed is the glory of the Lord from His place." (Ezekiel 3:12)

LAEL BARUCH

To the blessed God, they give their melodies.
To the King, the living and everlasting God, they shall sing hymns and proclaim praises.

SEVEN VERSES

Each of these seven verses connects to a different heavenly body. Four thousand years ago, Abraham the Patriarch revealed that there were seven key heavenly bodies that could be seen with the naked eye - the sun, the moon, Mars, Mercury, Saturn, Venus and Jupiter. These are the ones with a direct influence over our physical world and they correspond to the seven lower *Sefirot*. According to Abraham, the upper three dimensions (*Sefirot*) do not directly influence our world.

מ"ב levado לְבַדּוֹ hu הוּא ki כִּי

♦vekadosh וְקָדוֹשׁ (*Chochmah*) marom מָרוֹם (*Keter*)

:**corresponding to the seven planets** – כנגד ז' כוכבי לכת

(Sun)	gevurot גְּבוּרוֹת	po'el פּוֹעֵל	(*Binah*)
(Moon)	chadashot חֲדָשׁוֹת	ose עוֹשֶׂה	(*Chesed*)
(Mars)	milchamot מִלְחָמוֹת	ba'al בַּעַל	(*Gevurah*)
(Mercury)	tzedakot צְדָקוֹת	zore'a זוֹרֵעַ	(*Tiferet*)
	(*Resh Tav Bet Gimel Dalet Kaf Pei*)	ר ת ב ג ד כ פ	
(Saturn)	yeshu'ot יְשׁוּעוֹת	matzmi'ach מַצְמִיחַ	(*Netzach*)
(Venus)	refu'ot רְפוּאוֹת	bore בּוֹרֵא	(*Hod*)
(Jupiter)	tehilot תְּהִלּוֹת	nora נוֹרָא	(*Yesod*)
	♦hanifla'ot הַנִּפְלָאוֹת	אני adon אֲדוֹן	(*Malchut*)

MA'ASE BERESHEET

Hechal Zechut (the Merit Chamber) - *Gevurah* of *Zeir Anpin* in *Beriah*.

Be aware at all times that every new day is a renewal of all of Creation. Too often, we live life either in the past or the future, letting the present slip away. Real spiritual growth occurs in the present. This prayer helps to instill this consciousness within us. In the present, we proactively deal with the effects we have created in the past and through our actions, we plant seeds for our future. If we miss the opportunities that the present offers us, we will find ourselves on a reactive wheel with no control over our lives.

SEVEN VERSES

(Keter) *For He above is lofty* (Chochmah) *and holy.*

(Binah)	*He performs mighty deeds.*	(Sun)	(Chesed)	*Makes new things.*	(Moon)
(Gevurah)	*Master of wars.*	(Mars)	(Tiferet)	*Sows righteousness.*	(Mercury)
(Netzach)	*Brings about salvation.*	(Saturn)	(Hod)	*Creates remedies.*	(Venus)
(Yesod)	*Awesome in praises.*	(Jupiter)	(Malchut)	*He, in His goodness.*	

הַמְחַדֵּשׁ hamechadesh (י"ב הויות, קס"א קנ"א) בְּטוּבוֹ betuvo בְּכָל־ bechol (ב"ן, לכב)

יוֹם yom (ע"ה נגד, מזבח, זן, אל יהוה) תָּמִיד tamid (ע"ה קס"א קנ"א קמ"ג).

מַעֲשֵׂה ma'ase בְרֵאשִׁית vereshit (ר"ת מ"ב). כָּאָמוּר ka'amur:

לְעֹשֵׂה le'ose אוֹרִים orim (רז, אין סוף) גְּדֹלִים gedolim כִּי ki

לְעוֹלָם le'olam (ריבוע ס"ג וי' אותיות דס"ג) חַסְדּוֹ chasdo (ג' הויות, מילוי ; ר"ת = נגה):

בָּרוּךְ baruch אַתָּה Ata יְהֹוָהאדניאהדונהי Adonai יוֹצֵר yotzer הַמְּאוֹרוֹת hame'orot:

AHAVAT OLAM

Hechal Ahavah (the Love Chamber) - *Chesed* of *Zeir Anpin* in *Beriah*.

The purpose of this prayer is to inspire within us a love for the world and for other people.

אַהֲבַת ahavat עוֹלָם olam (on Shabbat we say "*Ahava Raba*" instead of "*Ahavat Olam*"):

אַהֲבָה ahava (אחד, דאגה) רַבָּה raba) אֲהַבְתָּנוּ ahavtanu (ר"ת ע"ב, ריבוע יהוה)

יְהֹוָהאדניאהדונהי Adonai אֱלֹהֵינוּ Elohenu (ילה) חֶמְלָה chemla גְּדוֹלָה gedola

וִיתֵרָה vitera חָמַלְתָּ chamalta עָלֵינוּ alenu. אָבִינוּ avinu מַלְכֵּנוּ malkenu

בַּעֲבוּר ba'avur שִׁמְךָ shimcha הַגָּדוֹל hagadol (להח ; עם ד' אותיות = מבה, יזל, אום)

וּבַעֲבוּר uva'avur אֲבוֹתֵינוּ avotenu שֶׁבָּטְחוּ shebatchu בָךְ vach

וַתְּלַמְּדֵמוֹ vatelamdemo חֻקֵּי chukei חַיִּים chayim (אהיה אהיה יהוה, בינה ע"ה)

לַעֲשׂוֹת la'asot רְצוֹנְךָ retzoncha בְּלֵבָב belevav (בוכו) שָׁלֵם shalem.

כֵּן ken תְּחָנֵּנוּ techonenu אָבִינוּ avinu אָב av הָרַחֲמָן harachaman.

MA'ASE BERESHEET

Renews, every day and forever, the work of Creation as it is stated: "To the One Who makes the great luminaries, for His kindness is forever." (Psalms 136:7) Blessed are You, Lord, Maker of luminaries.

AHAVA RABA

You have loved us an abundant love, Lord, our God.

Great and abundant compassion You have bestowed upon us. our Father, our King, for the sake of Your great Name and for the sake of our forefathers who trusted in You. Teach life-giving precepts so we may fulfill Your will, wholeheartedly, so shall you be gracious to us, our Father, merciful Father.

הַמְרַחֵם hamerachem אברהם, וח"פ אל, רי"ו ול"ב נתיבות החכמה, רמ"ח (אברים),

עסמ"ב וט"ז אותיות פשוטות רַחֵם rachem אברהם, וח"פ אל, רי"ו ול"ב נתיבות החכמה, רמ"ח (אברים),

עסמ"ב וט"ז אותיות פשוטות נָא na עָלֵינוּ alenu וְתֵן veten בְּלִבֵּנוּ belibenu

בִּינָה vina ע"ה אהיה אהיה יהוה, חיים לְהָבִין lehavin• לְהַשְׂכִּיל lehaskil•

לִשְׁמוֹעַ lishmo'a• לִלְמוֹד lilmod וּלְלַמֵּד ulelamed• לִשְׁמוֹר lishmor

וְלַעֲשׂוֹת vela'asot וּלְקַיֵּם ulkayem אֶת־ et כָּל־ kol ילי דִּבְרֵי divrei ראה

תַּלְמוּד talmud תּוֹרָתְךָ toratecha בְּאַהֲבָה be'ahava אחד, דאגה• וְהָאֵר veha'er

עֵינֵינוּ enenu ריבוע מ"ה בְּתוֹרָתֶךָ betoratecha• וְדַבֵּק vedabek

לִבֵּנוּ libenu בְּמִצְוֹתֶיךָ vemitzvotecha• וְיַחֵד veyached לְבָבֵנוּ levavenu

לְאַהֲבָה le'ahava אחד, דאגה וּלְיִרְאָה ulyir'a רי"ו אֶת־ et שְׁמֶךָ shemecha•

וְלֹא velo נֵבוֹשׁ nevosh וְלֹא velo נִכָּלֵם nikalem וְלֹא velo נִכָּשֵׁל nikashel

לְעוֹלָם le'olam ריבוע ס"ג וי' אותיות דס"ג וָעֶד va'ed• כִּי ki בְּשֵׁם veshem

קָדְשְׁךָ kodshecha הַגָּדוֹל hagadol להח ; עם ד' אותיות = מבה, יזל, הום

וְהַנּוֹרָא vehanora בָּטָחְנוּ vatachnu• נָגִילָה nagila וְנִשְׂמְחָה venismecha

בִּישׁוּעָתֶךָ vishu'atecha• וְרַחֲמֶיךָ verachamecha יְהֹוָאדנָיאהדונהי Adonai

אֱלֹהֵינוּ Elohenu ילה וַחֲסָדֶיךָ vachasadecha הָרַבִּים harabim

אַל al יַעַזְבוּנוּ ya'azvunu נֶצַח netzach סֶלָה sela וָעֶד va'ed•

Gather the four corners of the *Talit* in your left hand and hold them against your heart until after reciting the words "*la'ad ule'olmei olamim*" on pg. 348.

מַהֵר maher וְהָבֵא vehave עָלֵינוּ alenu בְּרָכָה beracha

וְשָׁלוֹם veshalom מְהֵרָה mehera מֵאַרְבַּע me'arba כַּנְפוֹת kanfot

הָאָרֶץ ha'aretz אלהים דההין ע"ה ; ר"ת = אדני•

Be merciful to us, merciful One. Place understanding in our hearts so we may understand, discern, hear, study, teach, keep, do, and fulfill all the words of the teachings of Your Torah in love. Enlighten our eyes with Your Torah. Bond our hearts with Your commandments. Unify our hearts to love and fear Your Name; then we shall be neither ashamed nor humiliated; nor shall we fail ever and for all eternity. Because we have placed our trust in Your great and awesome Name. May we rejoice and be happy in Your salvation. May Your compassion never leave us, Lord, our God, nor Your many kindnesses, Selah, forever. Hurry and bring upon us blessing and peace, speedily, from the four corners of the Earth.

tzavarenu צַוָּארֵנוּ עלם me'al מֵעַל hagoyim הַגּוֹיִם ol עוֹל ushvor וּשְׁבוֹר
♦le'artzenu לְאַרְצֵנוּ komemiyut קוֹמְמִיּוּת mehera מְהֵרָה veholichenu וְהוֹלִיכֵנוּ
ר"ת פאי, אמן Ata אַתָּה yeshu'ot יְשׁוּעוֹת po'el פּוֹעֵל (ייא" (במילוי דס"ג El אֵל ki כִּי
♦velashon וְלָשׁוֹן am עַם ילי mikol מִכָּל־ vacharta בָחַרְתָּ uvanu וּבָנוּ (יאהדונהי)

VEKERAVTANU MALKENU

Saying *Vekeravtanu Malkenu* reminds us of and gives us a direct connection to Mount Sinai and the energy of immortality.

malkenu מַלְכֵּנוּ vekeravtanu וְקֵרַבְתָּנוּ

LESHIMCHA HAGADOL

This phrase gives us the power to remove all doubt and uncertainty from our lives.

Without the power of certainty, all our prayers are rendered ineffective. The kabbalists explain that uncertainty is the seed of all evil in the world: about us, about the existence of God, about our destiny and about our ability to overcome challenges. Because our consciousness creates our reality, our uncertainty inevitably leads to chaos. When we destroy our doubt, all that can remain is positivity and certainty in the Light. The word *Amalek* עמלק has the same numerical value as the Aramaic word for "uncertainty" and "doubt", ספק (240). *Amalek* refers to the doubts and uncertainties that infect us, causing disunity and hatred among people. A story in the Bible recounts how God ordered the Israelites to go and slaughter all the men, women, and children of the nation of *Amalek*. The *Zohar* explains that in this passage is a code for the key to destroying our doubt. God was really telling the Israelites to slaughter the uncertainty within them.

מבה, יזל, אום = עם ד' אותיות ; להח hagadol הַגָּדוֹל leshimcha לְשִׁמְךָ

BE'AHAVA LEHODOT LACH

We are now gaining the strength to refrain from any kind of evil speech or gossip about other people. Spiritualy, evil speech is considered one of the most serious negative actions a person can commit— even more serious than murder. With murder, say the sages, one person only dies once. When we gossip about someone spiritually, three people die – the speaker, the listener and whoever is spoken of. And not only that, every time the gossip spreads from one person to another we kill that person again. Speech has tremendous power. When we speak ill of others, not only do we hurt and damage their lives, but the harm spills over into the person listening to the gossip, as well as into our own lives. The *Talmud* teaches that the destruction of the Temple occurred because of evil speech and hatred between people. If we do not refrain from speaking ill about our fellow man, others will not be able to refrain from speaking ill of us. The kabbalists teach us that evil speech is one of the spiritual causes of the most negative force in our physical world, *hatred for no reason.*

lach לָךְ lehodot לְהוֹדוֹת אחד, דאגה be'ahava בְּאַהֲבָה

Break the yoke of the nations from our necks and quickly lead us, proudly upright, to our land. For You are God, Who works salvation. You chose us from among all nations and tongues.

VEKERAVTANU MALKENU - *And brought us close, our King,*
LESHIMCHA HAGADOL - *To Your great Name*
BE'AHAVA LEHODOT LACH - *To lovingly express our gratitude,*

וּלְיַחֶדְךָ ulyachedcha וּלְאַהֲבָה ul'ahava אהבה, דאגה אֶת־ et שִׁמְךָ shimcha:

ר״ת הברכה עולה למנין ל״ב נתיבות החכמה

בָּרוּךְ baruch אַתָּה Ata יְהֹוָהאדניאהדונהי Adonai

הַבּוֹחֵר habocher בְּעַמּוֹ be'amo יִשְׂרָאֵל Yisrael בְּאַהֲבָה be'ahava אהבה, דאגה

ר״ת שם קדוש ביב (באתב״ש שמש):

THE SHEMA

The *Shema* is one of the most powerful tools to draw the energy of healing to our lives. The true power of the *Shema* is unleashed when we meditate upon others who need healing energy while reciting it.
The first verse of the *Shema* channels the energy of *Zeir Anpin*, or the Upper Worlds.
The second verse refers to our world, the World of *Malchut*.
There are a total of 248 words in this prayer, and these 248 words transmit healing energy to the 248 parts of the human body and its soul. The first paragraph of the *Shema* is built of 42 words, connecting us to the 42-Letter Name of God in the *Ana Beko'ach*. The second paragraph is composed of 72 words that connect us to The 72 Names of God. The third paragraph contains 50 words that link us to The 50 Gates of Binah, which helps us rise above the 50 Gates of Negativity.The final paragraph of the *Shema* has 72 words, which also connects us to The 72 Names of God, but through a different letter combination than that which is used in the second paragraph.

1) In order to receive the Light of the *Shema*, you have to accept upon yourself the precept of: "Love your neighbor as yourself," and see yourself together with all the souls that are part of the original Adam.
2) You need to meditate to connect to the precept of the Reading of *Shema* twice a day.
3) Before saying the *Shema* you should cover your eyes with the right hand (while saying the words "*Shema Yisrael ... le'olam va'ed*",) and hold the four *tzitziot* with the left hand and place them on your heart.
4) You should read the *Shema* with deep meditation, saying it with the intonations. It is necessary to be careful with the pronunciation of all the letters. Every word that ends with the same letter that the next word begins with must be pronounced on its own and not lead into the next word e.g. *bechol levavcha*. *Bechol* ends with a *Lamed* and *levavcha* begins with a *Lamed*. Each of these words must be pronounced separately so that both *Lameds* are heard. And therefore we add a special symbol ( ) on top of each place.

First, meditate in general, on the first *Yichud* of the four *Yichuds* of the Name: יהוה, and in particular, to awaken the letter ה, and then to connect it with the letter ו. Then connect the letter י and the letter ה together in the following order: *Hei* (ה), *Hei-Vav* (ו״ה), then *Yud-Hei* (ה״י), which adds up to 31, the secret of ״יא״ of the Name ס״ג. It is good to meditate on this *Yichud* before reciting any *Shema* because it acts as a replacement for the times that you may have missed reading the *Shema*. This *Yichud* has the same ability to create a Supernal connection like the reading of the *Shema* - to raise *Zeir* and *Nukva* together for the *Zivug* of *Abba* and *Ima*.

---

to unify You, and to love Your Name.
Blessed are You, Lord, Who has chosen His Nation Israel, with love.

(According to the Ramchal, the elevation of the *Mochin* during this *Shema* is the same as during the *Shema* of *Shacharit* of weekdays, except that *Zeir Anpin* is elevated to *Netzach, Hod, Yesod* of *Ima*.)

Shema – שְׁמַע

The reason for saying here the *Shema* is to awaken the *Mochin* (brains/energy) for *Ze'ir Anpin*. We need to do so in *Beriah*, because in *Atzilut* we are not able to do that anymore.
General Meditation: שם ע — to draw the energy from the seven lower *Sefirot* of *Ima* to the *Nukva*, which enables the *Nukva* to elevate the *Mayin Nukvin* (awakening from Below).
Particular Meditation: שם = יהוה + שדי and five times the letters י and ד of ב"ן = ע [The letter *Hei* (ה) is formed by the letters *Dalet* (ד) and *Yud* (י), so in ב"ן we have four times the letter ה plus another time the letters י and ד from יוד of ב"ן.]. Also the three letters ו (18) that are left from ב"ן, plus ב"ן itself (52) equals ע (70).

Yisrael – יִשְׂרָאֵל

General Meditation: שיר אל — to draw energy from *Chesed* and *Gevurah* of *Abba* to *Zeir Anpin*, to do his action in the secret of *Mayin Duchrin* (awakening from Above).

Particular Meditation: (the rearranged letters of the word *Yisrael*) – שר אלי

י"ה דאלהים דמוח חכמה בהכאה (יו"ד פעמים ה"י) = ש',

י"ה דאלהים דמוח בינה בהכאה (יו"ד פעמים ה"ה) = ר',

י"ה דאלהים דמוח דחסדים דדעת (יו"ד ה"א), וי"ה דאלהים דמוח דגבורות דדעת (י"ה) = אל"י.

Also meditate to draw the Surrounding Light of *Abba* of *Katnut* into *Zeir Anpin*.

Adonai Elohenu Adonai - יְהוָה אֱלֹהֵינוּ יְהוָה

General Meditation: to draw energy to *Abba*, *Ima* and *Da'at* from *Arich Anpin*,

Particular Meditation: ע"ב (יוד הי ויו הי) קס"א (אלף הי יוד הי) ע"ב (יוד הי ו הי).

Echad – אֶחָד

(The secret of the complete *Yichud-Unification*)

The letters *Alef* א and *Chet* ח from *Echad* אחד are *Zeir Anpin* and the letter *Dalet* ד is *Nukva*.
You should meditate to devote your soul for the sanctification of the Holy Name, thereby elevating your *Nefesh*, *Ruach*, *Neshamah* and *Neshamah* of *Neshamah* with *Zeir Anpin* and *Nukva* (using the Names: ע"ב and ס"ג) to *Abba* and *Ima* as the secret of *Mayin Nukvin*, and by that energy, *Abba* and *Ima* will be unified in the secret of the Name: יאהדויה"ה.
Also meditate to draw out the Inner Six Edges of *Gadlut* of *Ima* into *Zeir Anpin*. The Drop, which is ע"ב, is drawn out from the external of *Atik,* and descends to *Yesod* of *Ima*, where it becomes: ע"ב ס"ג מ"ה ב"ן, and the four spelled out אהיה (אלף הי יוד הי, אלף הא יוד הא, אלף הה יוד הה) become Her clothing. <u>As a result</u>, *Zeir Anpin* now has four spelled out יה"ו (יוד הי ויו, יוד הי ואו, יוד הא ואו, יוד הה וו), four spelled out אה"י (אלף הי יוד, אלף הי יוד, אלף הא יוד, אלף הה יוד) and the Inner Six Edges of *Gadlut* of *Ima*.
Also meditate on the Name: אל"ף ה"י וי"ו ה"י, which is the entire *Mochin* in the secret of *Da'at*.
And also meditate (according to the Ramchal) on the four spelled out *Alef* (אלף=111) of the Name: אהי"ה that is equal to the word *Midat (444)*, making the *Keter* for *Leah*.

Baruch Shem - בָּרוּךְ שֵׁם כְּבוֹד מַלְכוּתוֹ לְעוֹלָם וָעֶד

Baruch Shem Kevod – *Chochmah*, *Binah*, *Da'at* of *Leah;*

Malchuto – Her *Keter*; ***Le'olam*** – the rest of Her *Partzuf*;

Va'ed – the four היה (4 times 20 equal to *Va'ed*=80) will make the *Keter* for *Rachel*.

And the four spelled out היה (הי יוד הי, הי יוד הי, הא יוד הא, הה יוד הה) will make the rest of Her body.

שְׁמַע shema ע' רבתי יִשְׂרָאֵל Yisrael יְהֹוָואדניאהדונהי Adonai

אֱלֹהֵינוּ Elohenu ילה יְהֹוָואדניאהדונהי Adonai | אֶחָד echad ד' רבתי ; אהבה, דאגה:

(: Whisper) יוזו אותיות בָּרוּךְ baruch שֵׁם shem כְּבוֹד kevod מַלְכוּתוֹ malchuto,

לְעוֹלָם le'olam ריבוע דס"ג וי' אותיות דס"ג וָעֶד va'ed:

***Yud, Chochmah,* head** – 42 words corresponding to the Holy 42-Letter Name of God.

א ב

וְאָהַבְתָּ ve'ahavta ב"פ אור, ב"פ רז, ב"פ אין סוף ; (יכוין לקיים מ"ע של אהבת ה') אֵת et

ג י

יְהֹוָואדניאהדונהי Adonai אֱלֹהֶיךָ Elohecha ילה ; ס"ת כהת, משיח בן דוד ע"ה

ת צ ק ר

בְּכָל־ bechol ב"ן, לכב לְבָבְךָ levavcha וּבְכָל־ uvchol ב"ן, לכב נַפְשְׁךָ nafshecha

ע ש ט נ

וּבְכָל־ uvchol ב"ן, לכב מְאֹדֶךָ me'odecha: וְהָיוּ vehayu הַדְּבָרִים hadevarim

נ ג ד י כ

הָאֵלֶּה ha'ele אֲשֶׁר asher אָנֹכִי anochi מְצַוְּךָ metzavecha הַיּוֹם hayom

ש ב ט

ע"ה נגד, מזבח, זן, אל יהוה (pause here) עַל al לְבָבֶךָ levavecha: וְשִׁנַּנְתָּם veshinantam

ר צ ת ג

לְבָנֶיךָ levanecha וְדִבַּרְתָּ vedibarta בָּם bam מ"ב בְּשִׁבְתְּךָ beshivtecha

חו ק ב

בְּבֵיתֶךָ bevetecha ב"פ ראה וּבְלֶכְתְּךָ uvlechtecha בַדֶּרֶךְ vaderech

ט נ

ב"פ יב"ק, ס"ג, קס"א וּבְשָׁכְבְּךָ uvshochbecha וּבְקוּמֶךָ uvkumecha:

ע י ג ל

וּקְשַׁרְתָּם ukshartam לְאוֹת le'ot עַל־ al יָדֶךָ yadecha

THE SHEMA

"Hear Israel, the Lord our God. The Lord is One." (Deuteronomy 6:4)

"Blessed is the glorious Name, His Kingdom is forever and for eternity." (Pesachim 56a)

"And you shall love the Lord, your God, with all your heart and with all your soul and with all that you possess. Let those words that I command you today be upon your heart. And you shall teach them to your children and you shall speak of them while you sit in your home and while you walk on your way and when you lie down and when you rise. You shall bind them as a sign upon your hand

פ ז ק ש

וְהָיוּ vehayu לְטֹטָפֹת letotafot בֵּין ben עֵינֶיךָ enecha

ק י

ע״ה קס״א ; ריבוע מ״ה: וּכְתַבְתָּם uchtavtam עַל־ al

צ י ת

מְזֻזוֹת mezuzot נ״ת (וז מות) בֵּיתֶךָ betecha ב״פ ראה וּבִשְׁעָרֶיךָ: uvish'arecha

VEHAYA IM SHAMO'A

***Hei, Binah,* arms and body** – 72 words corresponding to the 72 Names of God.

והו ילי

וְהָיָה vehaya יהוה ; יהה אִם־ im יוה״ך, מ״א אותיות דפשוט, דמילוי ודמילוי דמילוי דאהיה ע״ה

סיט עלם מהש ללה אכא

שָׁמֹעַ shamo'a תִּשְׁמְעוּ tishme'u אֶל־ el מִצְוֺתַי mitzvotai אֲשֶׁר asher

כהת הזי אלד לאו

אָנֹכִי anochi מְצַוֶּה metzave אֶתְכֶם etchem הַיּוֹם hayom ע״ה נגד, מזבח, זן, אל יהוה

ההע יזל מבה

(pause here) לְאַהֲבָה le'ahava אחד, דאגה אֶת־ et יְהֹוָהאדניאהדונהי Adonai

הרי הקם

אֱלֹהֵיכֶם Elohechem ילה (enunciate the letter *Ayin* in the word "*ul'ovdo*") וּלְעָבְדוֹ ul'ovdo

לאו כלי לוו

בְּכָל bechol ב״ן, לכב לְבַבְכֶם levavchem וּבְכָל־ uvchol ב״ן, לכב

פהל נלך ייי מלה

נַפְשְׁכֶם: nafshechem וְנָתַתִּי venatati מְטַר־ metar אַרְצְכֶם artzechem

ווהו נתה האא ירת שאה

בְּעִתּוֹ be'ito יוֹרֶה yore וּמַלְקוֹשׁ umalkosh וְאָסַפְתָּ ve'asafta דְגָנֶךָ deganecha

רייי אום לכב ושר

וְתִירֹשְׁךָ vetiroshcha וְיִצְהָרֶךָ: veyitz'harecha וְנָתַתִּי venatati עֵשֶׂב esev ע״ב שמות

---

and they shall be as frontlets between your eyes.
And you shall write them upon the doorposts of your house and your gates." (Deuteronomy 6:5-9)

VEHAYA IM SHAMO'A

"And it shall come to be that if you shall listen to My commandments that I am commanding you with today to love the Lord, your God, and to serve Him with all your heart and with all your soul, then I shall send rain upon your land in its proper time, both early rain and late rain. You shall then gather your grain and your wine and your oil. And I shall give grass

יוזו להוו כוק מנד

בְּשָׂדְךָ besadcha לִבְהֶמְתֶּךָ livhemtecha וְאָכַלְתָּ ve'achalta וְשָׂבָעְתָּ: vesavata

אני וזעם רהע ייז ההה

הִשָּׁמְרוּ hishamru לָכֶם lachem פֶּן־ pen יִפְתֶּה yifte לְבַבְכֶם levavchem

מיכ וול ילה סאל

וְסַרְתֶּם vesartem וַעֲבַדְתֶּם va'avadetem אֱלֹהִים elohim אֲחֵרִים acherim

ערי עשל

משה (העומד נגד הקליפות) וְהִשְׁתַּחֲוִיתֶם vehishtachavitem לָהֶם: lahem

מיה והו דני החש

וְחָרָה vechara (pause here) אַף־ af יְהֹוָה יאהדונהי Adonai בָּכֶם bachem

עמם ננא נית מבה

וְעָצַר ve'atzar אֶת־ et הַשָּׁמַיִם hashamayim י״פ טל, י״פ כוזו וְלֹא־ velo

פוי נמם ייל הרוח מצר

יִהְיֶה yihye ייי מָטָר matar וְהָאֲדָמָה veha'adama לֹא lo תִתֵּן titen ב״פ כהת

ומב יהה ענו מחי דמב

אֶת־ et יְבוּלָהּ yevula וַאֲבַדְתֶּם va'avadetem מְהֵרָה mehera מֵעַל me'al עלם

מנק איע חבו

הָאָרֶץ ha'aretz אלהים דההין ע״ה הַטֹּבָה hatova אֲשֶׁר asher

ראה יבמ היי

יְהֹוָה יאהדונהי Adonai נֹתֵן noten אבג יתץ, ושר לָכֶם: lachem **Vav, Zeir Anpin**

מום א

וְשַׂמְתֶּם vesamtem **stomach** – 50 words corresponding to the 50 Gates of *Binah* אֶת־ et

ה י ה א ה

דְּבָרַי devarai ראה אֵלֶּה ele עַל־ al לְבַבְכֶם levavchem וְעַל־ ve'al

י ה א ה

נַפְשְׁכֶם nafshechem וּקְשַׁרְתֶּם ukshartem אֹתָם otam לְאוֹת le'ot ר״ת לאו

---

in your field for your cattle. And you shall eat and you shall be satiated. Be careful lest your heart be seduced and you may turn away and serve alien deities and prostrate yourself before them. And the wrath of the Lord shall be upon you and He shall stop the Heavens and there shall be no more rain and the earth shall not give forth its crop. And you shall quickly perish from the good land that the Lord has given you. And you shall place those words of Mine upon your heart and upon your soul and you shall bind them as a sign

י ה א
עַל־ al יְדְכֶם yedchem וְהָיוּ vehayu

ה י ה
לְטוֹטָפֹת letotafot בֵּין ben עֵינֵיכֶם enechem ריבוע מ״ה:

א ה י ה
וְלִמַּדְתֶּם velimadetem אֹתָם otam אֶת־ et בְּנֵיכֶם benechem

א ה י
לְדַבֵּר ledaber ראה בָּם bam שם בן מ״ב בְּשִׁבְתְּךָ beshivtecha

ה א ה
בְּבֵיתֶךָ bevetecha ב״פ ראה וּבְלֶכְתְּךָ uvlechtecha בַדֶּרֶךְ vaderech ב״פ יב״ק, ס״ג קס״א

י ה א ה
וּבְשָׁכְבְּךָ uvshochbecha וּבְקוּמֶךָ: uvkumecha וּכְתַבְתָּם uchtavtam עַל־ al

י ה א ה
מְזוּזוֹת mezuzot בֵּיתֶךָ betecha ב״פ ראה וּבִשְׁעָרֶיךָ: uvish'arecha לְמַעַן lema'an

י ה א ה
יִרְבּוּ yirbu יְמֵיכֶם yemechem ר״ת י״ל וִימֵי vimei בְנֵיכֶם venechem

י ה אהיה
עַל al הָאֲדָמָה ha'adama אֲשֶׁר asher (enunciate the letter *Ayin* in the word "*nishba*")

אהיה אהיה
נִשְׁבַּע nishba יכוין לשבועת המבול יְהֹוָהאדניּיאהדונהי Adonai

אהיה אהיה אהיה אהיה
לַאֲבֹתֵיכֶם la'avotechem לָתֵת latet לָהֶם lahem כִּימֵי kimei

אהיה אהיה אהיה
הַשָּׁמַיִם hashamayim י״פ טל, י״פ כוזו עַל־ al הָאָרֶץ ha'aretz אלהים דההין ע״ה:

---

upon your hands and they shall be as frontlets between your eyes. And you shall teach them to your children and speak of them while you sit at home and while you walk on your way and when you lie down and when you rise. You shall write them upon the doorposts of your house and upon your gates. This is so that your days shall be numerous and so shall the days of your children upon the Earth that the Lord had sworn to your fathers to give them as the days of the Heavens upon the Earth." (Deuteronomy 11:13-21)

Vayomer

Hei, Malchut, legs and reproductive organs,

72 words corresponding to the 72 Names of God in direct order (according to the Ramchal).

(ווו) ויאמר vayomer (ייי) יהוה יאהדונהי Adonai (סכט) אל־ el (עאם) משה Moshe

מהש, ע"ב בריבוע וקס"א, אל שדי, ד"פ אלהים ע"ה (מבש) לאמר lemor: (ליה) דבר daber ראה (אנא) אל־ el

(כמות) בני benei (הוזי) ישראל Yisrael (אנד) ואמרת ve'amarta (להו) אלהם alehem (המע) ועשו ve'asu

(יצל) להם lahem (מרה) ציצת tzitzit (היי) על־ al (הממ) כנפי kanfei (לוו) בגדיהם vigdehem

(כבי) לדרתם ledorotam (ליו) ונתנו venatnu (פנל) על־ al (נמך) ציצת tzitzit

(יוזי) הכנף hakanaf ע"ה קנ"א, אדני אלהים (מנה) פתיל petil י"פ ב"ן (וזהו) תכלת techelet:

(ניה) והיה vehaya יהוה ; יהה (השא) לכם lachem (ירת) לציצת letzitzit (שאה) וראיתם ur'item (רלי) אתו oto

You should pass the *tzitziot* over the eyes and kiss them, then repeat this procedure.

(אום) וזכרתם uzchartem (ליב) את־ et (והר) כל־ kol ילי (ייו) מצות mitzvot (לההו) יהוה יאהדונהי Adonai

(כעק) ועשיתם va'asitem (מנד) אתם otam (אני) ולא־ velo (וזום) תתורו taturu (רהע) אחרי acharei

(יוזו) לבבכם levavchem (השה) ואחרי ve'acharei (מככ) עיניכם enechem ריבוע מ"ה

You should pass the *Tzitziot* over the eyes and then kiss them.

Doing so (kissing the *tzitzit* and passing it over the eyes), is a great support and assistance for the soul to be protected from any transgression. And you should meditate on the precept: "not to follow negative sexual thoughts of the heart and the sights of the eyes for prostitution."

Vayomer

"And the Lord spoke to Moses and said: Speak to the Children of Israel and say to them that they should make for themselves Tzitzit, on the corners of their garments, throughout all their generations. And they must place upon the Tzitzit, of each corner, a blue strand. And this shall be to you as a Tzitzit: you shall see it and remember the commandments of the Lord and fulfill them. And you shall not stray after your hearts and your eyes,

וול ייה סאל ערי עאל

אֲשֶׁר־ asher אַתֶּם atem זֹנִים zonim אַחֲרֵיהֶם acharehem: לְמַעַן lema'an

מתה והו דלי היש עלם

תִּזְכְּרוּ tizkeru וַעֲשִׂיתֶם va'asitem אֶת־ et כָּל־ kol ילי מִצְוֹתָי mitzvotai

נהא נות מלה

וִהְיִיתֶם vihyitem קְדֹשִׁים kedoshim לֵאלֹהֵיכֶם lelohechem ילה:

פאי נקם ירל הבוז

אֲנִי ani אני יְהֹוָה Adonai יאהדונהי אֱלֹהֵיכֶם Elohechem ילה אֲשֶׁר asher

מזר והב יאה עלו

הוֹצֵאתִי hotzeti אֶתְכֶם etchem מֵאֶרֶץ me'eretz מִצְרַיִם Mitzrayim מצר

You should meditate to remember the exodus from *Mitzrayim* (Egypt).

מוי דהב מכק

לִהְיוֹת lihyot לָכֶם lachem לֵאלֹהִים lelohim אהיה אדני ; ילה

אלע וזהו רלה

אֲנִי ani אני יְהֹוָה Adonai יאהדונהי אֱלֹהֵיכֶם Elohechem ילה:

Be careful to complete this paragraph together with the *chazan* and the congregation, and say the word "*emet*" out loud. The *chazan* should say the word "*emet*" in silence.

יוד הי ויו אֱמֶת emet אהיה פעמים אהיה, ז"פ ס"ג.

The congregation should be silent, listen and hear the words "*Adonai Elohechem emet*" spoken by the *chazan*. If you did not complete the paragraph together with the *chazan* you should repeat the last three words on your own. With these three words the *Shema* is completed.

ייט הלי

יְהֹוָה Adonai יאהדונהי אֱלֹהֵיכֶם Elohechem ילה:

מוהם

אֱמֶת emet אהיה פעמים אהיה, ז"פ ס"ג.

VEYATZIV

Before the *Amidah*, signifying the World of Emanation *(Atzilut)*, we come across various connections. The Aramaic word *Emet* אמת appears four times on two occasions. The Ari says that the four appearances of the word *emet*, occuring on two occasions, for a total of eight times, refers to the four Exiles and to the four Redemptions of the Israelites that have occurred in history. This word means "truth." When a small degree of untruthfulness lies in our hearts, it is difficult to succeed in our spiritual work. This prayer has the power to remove all falsehoods and open our hearts to truth.

---

after which you adulterate. This is so that you shall remember to fulfill all My commandments and thereby be holy before your God. I am the Lord, your God, Who brought you out of the land of Egypt to be your God. I, the Lord, your God, Is true." (Numbers 15:37-41) *the Lord, your God, is true!*

We find another code in the word *Emet* אמת:

In Aramaic, this word begins with the letter *Alef* א, the first letter of the alphabet. The second letter in *Emet* is *Mem* מ, the middle of the alphabet. The last letter in *Emet* is *Tav* ת, the last letter of the alphabet. A person of truth has the power of the entire alphabet, which, in essence, is the power of the entire universe.

Hechal Ratzon (the Desire Chamber) - *Tiferet* of *Zeir Anpin* in *Beriah*.

א' של אמת וי"ה ווין = אמן (יאהדונהי) וְיַצִּיב veyatziv• וְנָכוֹן venachon• וְקַיָּם vekayam•
וְיָשָׁר veyashar• וְנֶאֱמָן vene'eman• וְאָהוּב ve'ahuv• וְחָבִיב vechaviv הזי•
וְנֶחְמָד venechmad• וְנָעִים vena'im• וְנוֹרָא venora• וְאַדִּיר ve'adir הרי•
וּמְתוּקָּן umtukan• וּמְקֻבָּל umkubal• וְטוֹב vetov והו• וְיָפֶה veyafe•
יכוין ט"ו ווין גימ' יה, הווין עצמן ו, ור"ת הדבר הרי יהוה הַדָּבָר hadavar ראה
הַזֶּה haze והו עָלֵינוּ alenu לְעוֹלָם le'olam ריבוע ס"ג וי' אותיות דס"ג וָעֶד va'ed:•

יוד הי ואו אֱמֶת emet אהיה פעמים אהיה, ז"פ ס"ג אֱלֹהֵי Elohei מילוי ע"ב, דמב ; ילה
עוֹלָם olam מַלְכֵּנוּ malkenu• צוּר tzur אלהים דההין ע"ה יַעֲקֹב Ya'akov
ז' הויות, יאהדונהי אידהנויה מָגֵן magen ג"פ אל (ייא" מילוי דס"ג) ; ר"ת מיכאל גבריאל נוריאל
יִשְׁעֵנוּ yish'enu• לְדוֹר ledor וָדוֹר vador רי"ו הוּא hu קַיָּם kayam
וּשְׁמוֹ ushmo מהש ע"ה, ע"ב בריבוע וקס"א ע"ה, אל שדי ע"ה קַיָּם kayam וְכִסְאוֹ vechis'o
נָכוֹן nachon וּמַלְכוּתוֹ umalchuto וֶאֱמוּנָתוֹ ve'emunato לָעַד la'ad ב"פ ב"ן ; ר"ת לוו
קַיֶּמֶת kayemet:• וּדְבָרָיו udvarav וְחָיִים chayim אהיה אהיה יהוה, בינה ע"ה
וְקַיָּמִים vekayamim וְנֶאֱמָנִים vene'emanim וְנֶחֱמָדִים venechemadim לָעַד la'ad
ב"פ ב"ן (kiss the *Tzitziot*, pass them over the eyes then release) וּלְעוֹלְמֵי ul'olmei עוֹלָמִים olamim•

VEYATZIV

And He is established, and correct, and lasting, and straightforward, and trustworthy, and beloved, and dear, and desirable, and pleasant, and awesome, and powerful and proper, and accepted, and good, and beautiful. This is to us, forever and ever. It is true that the God of the World is our King, the Rock of Jacob and the Shield of our salvation. For every generation He endures and His Name endures. His Throne is established; His sovereignty and His faithfulness endure forever. His words are alive, enduring, trustworthy and pleasant for all eternity.

עַל al אֲבוֹתֵינוּ avotenu • עָלֵינוּ alenu וְעַל ve'al בָּנֵינוּ banenu וְעַל ve'al

דּוֹרוֹתֵינוּ dorotenu וְעַל ve'al כָּל־ kol ילי ; עמם דּוֹרוֹת dorot זֶרַע zera

יִשְׂרָאֵל Yisrael עֲבָדֶיךָ avadecha : עַל al הָרִאשׁוֹנִים harishonim וְעַל ve'al

הָאַחֲרוֹנִים ha'acharonim דָּבָר davar ראה טוֹב tov והו וְקַיָּם vekayam •

יוד הא ואו בֶּאֱמֶת be'emet אהיה פעמים אהיה, ז"פ ס"ג וּבֶאֱמוּנָה uve'emuna חוֹק chok

וְלֹא velo יַעֲבוֹר ya'avor רפ"ח (להעלות רפ"ח ניצוצות שנפלו לקליפה דמשם באים התחלואים) •

יוד הה וו אֱמֶת emet אהיה פעמים אהיה, ז"פ ס"ג שֶׁאַתָּה sheAta

הוּא hu יְהֹוָאדהנויאהדונהי Adonai אֱלֹהֵינוּ Elohenu ילה

וֵאלֹהֵי velohei לכב ; מילוי ע"ב, דמב ; ילה אֲבוֹתֵינוּ avotenu •

מַלְכֵּנוּ malkenu מֶלֶךְ melech אֲבוֹתֵינוּ avotenu גּוֹאֲלֵנוּ go'alenu

גּוֹאֵל go'el אֲבוֹתֵינוּ avotenu • יוֹצְרֵנוּ yotzrenu צוּר tzur אלהים דההין ע"ה

יְשׁוּעָתֵנוּ yeshu'atenu • פּוֹדֵנוּ podenu וּמַצִּילֵנוּ umatzilenu ר"ת = אלהים, אהיה אדני

MEM, HEI, SHIN

The letters *Mem* מ, *Hei* ה, and *Shin* ש unleash the force of healing.

When we close our eyes and visualize these three letters emitting rays of Light, we awaken healing energy from the Upper Worlds and from within ourselves. We can meditate to bathe our entire body in a flood of white Light and to send this energy to others in need of healing. These letters, rearranged, spell out the name of Moses מהש = משה, who reached the highest level of connection to the Light of the Creator.

מֵעוֹלָם me'olam הוּא hu שִׁמְךָ shemecha

ר"ת מהש, משה, ע"ב בריבוע וקס"א, אל שדי

וְאֵין ve'en לָנוּ lanu אלהים, אהיה אדני עוֹד od

אֱלֹהִים Elohim אהיה אדני ; ילה זוּלָתְךָ zulatcha סֶלָה sela :

This is upon us and upon our sons and upon our future generations and upon all the future generations of the descendants of Israel, Your servants. Upon the earlier and upon the later ones, this is a good and an everlasting thing. With truth and with faith, this is an unbreakable decree. It is true that You are the Lord, our God and the God of our fathers, our King and the King of our fathers, our Redeemer and the Redeemer of our fathers, our Maker and the Rock of our salvation. Our Redeemer and Rescuer.

MEM HEI SHIN

Your Name is of eternity, and we have no other God but You. Selah.

EZRAT

Ayin, Alef, and *Alef,* עאא, the first letters of the first three words of this prayer, have a numerical value of 72. The number 72 is also a code for the concept of mercy and the *Sefirah* of *Chesed.* We learn from this connection that we were meant to live our lives with genuine mercy for others in order to activate the power of the 72 Names of God. If, for some reason, we are not generating results from our prayers, it is only for one reason: we are not treating the people in our life with true mercy. Kabbalah teaches us that even if we are justified in our anger and our refusal to forgive, we must have mercy in our hearts and in our actions towards both our friends and our enemies.

עֶזְרַת ezrat מיכאל מלכיאל שׁנדיאל, יהוה פעמים יהוה ע״ה אֲבוֹתֵינוּ avotenu אַתָּה Ata

ר״ת = ע״ב, ריבוע יהוה הוּא hu מֵעוֹלָם me'olam• מָגֵן magen ג״פ אל (ייא״י מילוי דס״ג) ;

ר״ת מיכאל גבריאל נוריאל וּמוֹשִׁיעַ umoshi'a לָהֶם lahem וְלִבְנֵיהֶם velivnehem

אַחֲרֵיהֶם acharehem בְּכָל bechol ב״ן, לכב דּוֹר dor וָדוֹר vador רי״ו•

בְּרוּם berum עוֹלָם olam ר״ת ע״ב, ריבוע יהוה ; ברום עולם ע״ה = קס״א קנ״א קמ״ג

עם ג׳ כוללים (לא כולל האהיה עצמם) מוֹשָׁבֶךָ moshavecha• וּמִשְׁפָּטֶיךָ umishpatecha

וְצִדְקָתְךָ vetzidkatcha עַד ad אַפְסֵי afsei אָרֶץ aretz:

אהיה אֱמֶת emet אהיה פעמים אהיה, ז״פ ס״ג אַשְׁרֵי ashrei

אִישׁ ish שֶׁיִּשְׁמַע sheyishma לְמִצְוֹתֶיךָ lemitzvotecha•

וְתוֹרָתְךָ vetoratcha וּדְבָרְךָ udvarcha יָשִׂים yasim עַל al לִבּוֹ libo:

אהיה אֱמֶת emet אהיה פעמים אהיה, ז״פ ס״ג שֶׁאַתָּה sheAta הוּא hu

אָדוֹן adon אני לְעַמֶּךָ le'amecha• וּמֶלֶךְ umelech גִּבּוֹר gibor

לָרִיב lariv רִיבָם rivam לְאָבוֹת le'avot וּבָנִים uvanim:

EZRAT

You have always been the aid for our forefathers, a shield and a savior for them and their children after them in every generation. In the heights of the world is Your abode and Your laws and justice extend to the ends of the Earth. It is true that a man who abides by Your commandments is joyful while he sets Your Torah and Your teachings upon his heart. It is true that You are a Master of Your people and a valorous King, Who fights for their cause, be it the fathers or the sons.

אהיה אֱמֶת emet אהיה פעמים אהיה, ז"פ ס"ג אַתָּה Ata הוּא hu רִאשׁוֹן rishon

וְאַתָּה veAta הוּא hu אַחֲרוֹן acharon. וּמִבַּלְעָדֶיךָ umibal'adecha אֵין en

לָנוּ lanu אלהים, אהיה אדני מֶלֶךְ melech גּוֹאֵל go'el וּמוֹשִׁיעַ umoshi'a:

אהיה אֱמֶת emet אהיה פעמים אהיה, ז"פ ס"ג מִמִּצְרַיִם miMitzrayim מצר

גְּאַלְתָּנוּ ge'altanu יְהֹוָהאדניאהדונהי Adonai אֱלֹהֵינוּ Elohenu ילה. וּמִבֵּית mibet

ב"פ ראה עֲבָדִים avadim פְּדִיתָנוּ peditanu. כָּל־ kol ילי בְּכוֹרֵיהֶם bechorehem

הָרַגְתָּ haragta וּבְכוֹרְךָ uvchorcha יִשְׂרָאֵל Yisrael גָּאָלְתָּ ga'alta.

וְיַם־ veYam ילי סוּף Suf לָהֶם lahem בָּקַעְתָּ bakata. וְזֵדִים vezedim

טִבַּעְתָּ tibata. וִידִידִים vididim עָבְרוּ avru יָם yam ילי. וַיְכַסּוּ vayechasu

מַיִם mayim צָרֵיהֶם tzarehem אֶחָד echad אהבה, דאגה מֵהֶם mehem לֹא lo

נוֹתָר notar: עַל al זֹאת zot שִׁבְּחוּ shibechu אֲהוּבִים ahuvim

וְרוֹמְמוּ veromemu לָאֵל laEl ייא"י (מילוי דס"ג) וְנָתְנוּ venatnu יְדִידִים yedidim

זְמִירוֹת zemirot שִׁירוֹת shirot וְתִשְׁבָּחוֹת vetishbachot בְּרָכוֹת berachot

וְהוֹדָאוֹת vehoda'ot לַמֶּלֶךְ lamelech אֵל El ייא"י (מילוי דס"ג) וְחַי chai וְקַיָּם vekayam.

רָם ram וְנִשָּׂא venisa גָּדוֹל gadol להח ; עם ד' אותיות = מבה, יזל, אום וְנוֹרָא venora.

מַשְׁפִּיל mashpil גֵּאִים ge'im עֲדֵי adei אָרֶץ aretz. מַגְבִּיהַּ magbiha

שְׁפָלִים shefalim עַד ad מָרוֹם marom. מוֹצִיא motzi אֲסִירִים asirim.

פּוֹדֶה pode עֲנָוִים anavim. עוֹזֵר ozer דַּלִּים dalim הָעוֹנֶה ha'one

לְעַמּוֹ le'amo יִשְׂרָאֵל Yisrael בְּעֵת be'et שַׁוְּעָם shave'am אֵלָיו elav.

Ozer Dalim: poverty removes the transgressions of a person and through that the Creator gives mercy to His creation. And therefore you should meditate to make yourself poor in the eyes of the *Shechinah* and be concerned that the *Shechinah* is in exile together with the Children of Israel.

It is true that You are first and You are last and apart from You we have no King Who redeems and saves. It is true that You have redeemed us from Egypt, Lord, our God, and from a house of slaves did You redeem us. You killed all their firstborn and You saved Your firstborn Israel. You split the Sea of Reeds for them. And You drowned the tyrants while Your beloved crossed the sea. The waters then covered their enemies and not one of them was spared. For this, the beloved ones praised and exalted God. And the dear ones offered melodies, songs, lyrics and praises, blessings and thanks to the King, to the living and lasting God. Who is Supernal and uplifted, powerful and awesome and Who degrades the arrogant to the ground; Who raises the meek to great heights; Who frees the imprisoned, redeems the humble and helps the needy; He, Who answers the Children of Israel when they cry out to Him.

TEHILOT

We now begin to elevate to the World of Emanation (*Atzilut*). Accordingly, we rise and stand to ignite the engines of our soul. To prepare ourselves for this launch, we must eliminate any hatred or ill feelings that we harbor for others from our minds.

Hechal Kodesh HaKodashim (the Holy of Holies Chamber) – of *Zeir Anpin* in *Beriah*.

תְּהִלּוֹת tehilot לָאֵל laEl ייא״ (מילוי דס״ג) עֶלְיוֹן elyon גּוֹאֲלָם go'alam

בָּרוּךְ baruch הוּא hu וּמְבוֹרָךְ umvorach. מֹשֶׁה Moshe מהש, ע״ב בריבוע וקס״א,

אל שדי, ד״פ אלהים ע״ה וּבְנֵי uvnei יִשְׂרָאֵל Yisrael ר״ת ע״ה נגד, מזבח, זן, אל יהוה

לְךָ lecha עָנוּ anu שִׁירָה shira בְּשִׂמְחָה besimcha רַבָּה raba וְאָמְרוּ ve'amru

כֻּלָּם chulam: מִי mi ילי כָמֹכָה chamocha בָּאֵלִם ba'elim

יְהֹוָהאדניאהדונהי Adonai ; ר״ת = ע״ב, ריבוע יהוה ; ס״ת מ״ה מִי mi ילי כָּמֹכָה kamocha

נֶאְדָּר ne'edar בַּקֹּדֶשׁ bakodesh ר״ת = יב״ק, אלהים יהוה, אהיה אדני יהוה נוֹרָא nora

תְהִלֹּת tehilot עֹשֵׂה ose פֶלֶא fele: שִׁירָה shira חֲדָשָׁה chadasha

שִׁבְּחוּ shibechu גְאוּלִים ge'ulim לְשִׁמְךָ leshimcha הַגָּדוֹל hagadol להח ; עם ד׳

אותיות = מבה, יזל, הום עַל al שְׂפַת sefat הַיָּם hayam ילי יַחַד yachad כֻּלָּם kulam

הוֹדוּ hodu אהיה וְהִמְלִיכוּ vehimlichu וְאָמְרוּ ve'amru: יְהֹוָהאדניאהדונהי Adonai |

יִמְלֹךְ yimloch לְעֹלָם le'olam ריבוע ס״ג ו׳ אותיות דס״ג ; ר״ת ייל וָעֶד va'ed:

וְנֶאֱמַר vene'emar גֹּאֲלֵנוּ go'alenu יְהֹוָהאדניאהדונהי Adonai צְבָאוֹת Tzeva'ot פני שכינה

שְׁמוֹ shemo מהש ע״ה, ע״ב בריבוע וקס״א ע״ה, אל שדי ע״ה קְדוֹשׁ kedosh יִשְׂרָאֵל Yisrael:

בָּרוּךְ baruch אַתָּה Ata יְהֹוָהאדניאהדונהי Adonai גָּאַל ga'al כתר יִשְׂרָאֵל Yisrael:

Begin the *Amidah* immediately without any interruption, not even one breath. Doing so prevents separation between *Yesod* (awakened by the words "*ga'al Yisrael*") and *Malchut* (awakened by the word "*Adonai*"). Your reward is great. You receive protection from negativity and from making mistakes. This action also helps to correct the transgression of spilling one's seed.

TEHILOT

Praises to the Supreme God, Who is their redeemer. Blessed is He Who is blessed. Moses and the Children of Israel raised their voice in song to You, with great joy, and they all said: "Who is like You among the deities, Lord? Who is like You, mighty in holiness, awesome in praises, and Who works wonders?" (Exodus 15:11) *With a new song did the redeemed praise Your great Name by the seashore. All of them in unison gave thanks and accepted Your sovereignty and they said, "the Lord shall reign forever and ever."* (Exodus 15:18) *And it is said: "Our redeemer, the Lord of hosts is His Name, the holy One of Israel."* (Isaiah 47:4) *Blessed are You, Lord, Who redeemed Israel.*

Malchut of *Atzilut* is included now in *Hechal Kodesh HaKodashim* of *Beriah*.

When *Shavuot* (second day) falls on *Shabbat* scan the following:

The Format of the Ascension in *Shacharit* of *Shabbat*

In the silent connection of *Shachrit* of *Shabbat*, the *Mochin* from the Supernal *Abba* and *Ima* are starting to enter into *Zeir Anpin*. **Meditate**, that the letter צ of the *Tzelem* enter the five *Partzufim* of *Netzach, Hod, Yesod* of *Chochmah* of *Zeir Anpin* (which is called: *Nefesh, Ruach, Neshamah, Chayah, Yechidah* of *Nefesh* of *Chayah*).**So now**, *Keter, Chochmah, Binah, Da'at* of *Zeir Anpin* are elevated to *Netzach, Hod, Yesod* of the Supernal *Abba* and *Ima*, and *Chesed, Gevurah, Tiferet* of *Zeir Anpin* are elevated to *Chochmah, Binah, Da'at* of *Yisrael Saba* and *Tevunah* and *Netzach, Hod, Yesod* of *Zeir Anpin* are elevated to *Chesed, Gevurah, Tiferet* of *Yisrael Saba* and *Tevunah*, and *Yaakov* and *Rachel* (that are standing in *Netzach, Hod, Yesod* of *Binah* of *Zeir Anpin*, which means, *Netzach, Hod, Yesod* of *Yisrael Saba* and *Tevunah*) are elevated to *Chesed, Gevurah, Tiferet* of *Binah* of *Zeir Anpin* (which means *Chesed, Gevurah, Tiferet* of *Yisrael Saba* and *Tevunah*). **So now**, *Netzach, Hod, Yesod* of *Zeir Anpin* become *Mochin* (*Keter, Chochmah, Binah, Da'at*) for *Yaakov* and *Rachel*.

In the Silent connection - when saying "*Baruch*" meditate to draw the Six Edges (*Chesed, Gevurah, Tiferet, Netzach, Hod, Yesod* of *Keter, Chochmah, Binah, Da'at* of *Netzach, Hod, Yesod* of the Internal of Supernal *Ima*) that were drawn by the *Shema* (to *Keter, Chochmah, Binah, Da'at, Chesed, Gevurah, Tiferet* of *Zeir Anpin*); **to** *Chesed, Gevurah, Tiferet, Netzach, Hod, Yesod* of *Keter, Chochmah, Binah, Da'at* of *Netzach, Hod, Yesod* of *Chochmah* of the Internal of *Zeir Anpin*. **When saying "*Ata*" meditate to draw** *Keter, Chochmah, Binah, Da'at* of *Keter, Chochmah, Binah, Da'at* to the Three Upper *Sefirot* of *Zeir Anpin* and push down the Six Edges (of *Tevunah*) to the Six Edges of *Zeir Anpin*. **When saying "*Adonai*" meditate to draw** *Chochmah, Chesed, Netzach, Binah, Gevurah, Hod, Da'at, Tiferet, Yesod* (in three columns) of *Keter, Chochmah, Binah, Da'at* of *Netzach, Hod, Yesod* of the Internal of Supernal *Abba* to *Zeir Anpin* by the two stages of standing upright.

In the repetition of *Shachrit* of *Shabbat*, *Zeir Anpin* and *Leah* rise in *Chesed, Gevurah, Tiferet* of Supernal *Abba* and *Ima*. **Meditate**, that the letter ל of the *Tzelem* (five *Tzelamim* of *Chesed, Gevurah, Tiferet* of the Supernal *Abba* and *Ima*) enters the five *Partzufim* of *Chesed, Gevurah, Tiferet* of *Chochmah* of *Zeir Anpin* (which is called: *Nefesh, Ruach, Neshamah, Chayah, Yechidah* of *Ruach* of *Chayah*). **So now**, *Keter, Chochmah, Binah, Da'at* of *Zeir Anpin* are elevated to *Chesed, Gevurah, Tiferet* of the Supernal *Abba* and *Ima*, and *Chesed, Gevurah, Tiferet* of *Zeir Anpin* are elevated to *Netzach, Hod, Yesod* of the Supernal *Abba* and *Ima*, and *Netzach, Hod, Yesod* of *Zeir Anpin* are elevated to *Keter, Chochmah, Binah, Da'at* of *Yisrael Saba* and *Tevunah*, and *Yaakov* and *Rachel* (that are standing in *Chesed, Gevurah, Tiferet* of *Binah* of *Zeir Anpin*, which means, *Chesed, Gevurah, Tiferet* of *Yisrael Saba* and *Tevunah*) are elevated to *Keter, Chochmah, Binah, Da'at* of *Binah* of *Zeir Anpin* (which means *Keter, Chochmah, Binah, Da'at* of *Yisrael Saba* and *Tevunah*). **So now**, *Netzach, Hod, Yesod* of *Binah Zeir Anpin* become *Mochin - Keter, Chochmah, Binah, Da'at* – for *Yaakov* and *Rachel*.

In the repetition - when saying "*Baruch*" meditate to draw the Six Edges (*Chesed, Gevurah, Tiferet, Netzach, Hod, Yesod* of *Keter, Chochmah, Binah, Da'at* of *Chesed, Gevurah, Tiferet* of the Internal of Supernal *Ima*) that were drawn by the *Shema* (to *Keter, Chochmah, Binah, Da'at, Chesed, Gevurah, Tiferet* of *Zeir Anpin*); **to** *Chesed, Gevurah, Tiferet, Netzach, Hod, Yesod* of *Keter, Chochmah, Binah, Da'at* of *Chesed, Gevurah, Tiferet* of *Chochmah* of the Internal of *Zeir Anpin*. **When saying "*Ata*" meditate to draw** *Keter, Chochmah, Binah, Da'at* of *Keter, Chochmah, Binah, Da'at* to the Three Upper *Sefirot* of *Zeir Anpin* and push down the Six Edges (of *Tevunah*) to the Six Edges of *Zeir Anpin*. **When saying "*Adonai*" meditate to draw** *Chochmah, Chesed, Netzach*, and *Binah, Gevurah, Hod*, and *Da'at, Tiferet, Yesod* (in three columns) of *Keter, Chochmah, Binah, Da'at* of *Chesed, Gevurah, Tiferet* of the Internal of Supernal *Abba* to *Zeir Anpin* by the two stages of standing upright.

Meditate to receive the extra soul called: *Ruach*

from the aspect of the day of *Shabbat*.

אֲדֹנָי Adonai ללה (pause here) שְׂפָתַי sefatai תִּפְתָּח tiftach וּפִי ufi יַגִּיד yagid

תְּהִלָּתֶךָ tehilatecha ייז (כ"ב אותיות פשוטות [=אכא] וה' אותיות סופיות מנצפך) ס"ת = בוכו:

THE FIRST BLESSING - INVOKES THE SHIELD OF ABRAHAM.

Abraham is the channel of the Right Column energy of positivity, sharing, and mercy. Sharing actions can protect us from all forms of negativity.

Chesed that becomes *Chochmah*

In this section there are 42 words, the secret of the 42-Letter Name of God and therefore it begins with the letter *Bet* (2) and ends with the letter *Mem* (40).

Bend your knees at *"baruch"*, bow at *"Ata"* and straighten up at *"Adonai"*.

א ב

בָּרוּךְ baruch אַתָּה Ata א-ת (אותיות הא"ב המסמלות את השפע המגיע) לה' המלכות

ג י

יְהֹוָאדנייאהדונהי Adonai (יא) אֱלֹהֵינוּ Elohenu ילה

ת צ

וֵאלֹהֵי velohei לכב ; מילוי ע"ב, דמב ; ילה אֲבוֹתֵינוּ avotenu•

ק ר

אֱלֹהֵי Elohei מילוי ע"ב, דמב ; ילה אַבְרָהָם Avraham (*Chochmah*)

וו"פ אל, רי"ו ול"ב נתיבות החכמה, רמ"ח (אברים), עסמ"ב וט"ז אותיות פשוטות

ע ש

אֱלֹהֵי Elohei מילוי ע"ב, דמב ; ילה יִצְחָק Yitzchak (*Binah*) ד"פ ב"ן

ט נ

וֵאלֹהֵי velohei לכב ; מילוי ע"ב, דמב ; ילה יַעֲקֹב Yaakov (*Da'at*) ז' הויות, יאהדונהי אידהנויה

THE AMIDAH

"My Lord, open my lips, and my mouth shall relate Your praise." (Psalms 51:17)

THE FIRST BLESSING

Blessed are You, Lord,

our God and God of our forefathers: the God of Abraham, the God of Isaac, and the God of Jacob.

נ ג

הָאֵל haEl לאה ; ייא״ (מילוי דס״ג) הַגָּדוֹל hagadol האל הגדול = סיט ; גדול = להח

ד י

עם ד׳ אותיות = מבה, יזל, הום הַגִּבּוֹר hagibor ר״ת ההה וְהַנּוֹרָא vehanora♦

כ ש

אֵל El ייא״ (מילוי דס״ג) ; ר״ת ע״ב, ריבוע יהוה עֶלְיוֹן elyon♦

ב ט ר צ ת

גּוֹמֵל gomel חֲסָדִים chasadim טוֹבִים tovim♦ קוֹנֵה kone הַכֹּל hakol ילי

ג ח ק ב

וְזוֹכֵר vezocher חַסְדֵי chasdei אָבוֹת avot♦ וּמֵבִיא umevi

ט נ ע י

גּוֹאֵל go'el לִבְנֵי livnei בְנֵיהֶם venehem לְמַעַן lema'an

ג ל

שְׁמוֹ shemo מהש ע״ה, ע״ב בריבוע וקס״א ע״ה, אל שדי ע״ה בְּאַהֲבָה be'ahava אחד, דאגה♦

When saying the word "*be'ahava*" you should meditate to devote your soul to sanctify the Holy Name and accept upon yourself the four forms of death.

פ ז ק ש

מֶלֶךְ melech עוֹזֵר ozer וּמוֹשִׁיעַ umoshi'a וּמָגֵן umagen

ג״פ אל (ייא״ מילוי דס״ג) ; ר״ת מיכאל גבריאל נוריאל♦

Bend your knees at "*baruch*", bow at "*Ata*" and straighten up at "*Adonai*".

אהיה יהו אלף הי יוד הי (on Shabbat: יְהוָה)

ק ו צ

בָּרוּךְ baruch אַתָּה Ata יְהֹוָהאדני(יְהֹוָהאדני)יאהדונהי Adonai (הד)

י ת

מָגֵן magen ג״פ אל (ייא״ מילוי דס״ג) ; ר״ת מיכאל גבריאל נוריאל אַבְרָהָם Avraham

ח״פ אל, רי״ו ול״ב נתיבות החכמה, רמ״ח (אברים), עסמ״ב וט״ז אותיות פשוטות♦

The great, mighty and awesome God.
The Supernal God, Who bestows beneficial kindness and creates everything.
Who recalls the kindness of the forefathers and brings a Redeemer to their descendants for the sake of His Name, lovingly. King, Helper, Savior and Shield. Blessed are You, Lord, the shield of Abraham.

THE SECOND BLESSING

THE ENERGY OF ISAAC IGNITES THE POWER FOR THE RESURRECTION OF THE DEAD.

Whereas Abraham represents the power of sharing, Isaac represents the Left Column energy of judgment. Judgment shortens the *tikkun* process and paves the way for our eventual resurrection.

Gevurah that becomes *Binah*.

In this section there are 49 words corresponding to the 49 gates of the Pure System in *Binah*.

אַתָּה Ata גִּבּוֹר gibor לְעוֹלָם le'olam ריבוע ס"ג וי' אותיות דס"ג אֲדֹנָי Adonai ללה

(ר"ת אַגְלָא והוא שם גדול ואמיץ, ובו היה יהודה מתגבר על אויביו. ע"ה אלד, בוכו).

מְחַיֵּה mechaye ס"ג מֵתִים metim אַתָּה Ata• רַב rav לְהוֹשִׁיעַ lehoshi'a•

מוֹרִיד morid הַטָּל hatal יוד הא ואו, כוזו, מספר אותיות דמילואי עסמ"ב ; ר"ת מ"ה:

If you mistakenly say "*Mashiv haru'ach*", and realize this before the end of the blessing ("*baruch Ata Adonai*"), you should return to the beginning of the blessing ("*Ata gibor*") and continue as usual. But if you only realize this after the end of the blessing, you should start the *Amidah* from the beginning.

מְכַלְכֵּל mechalkel חַיִּים chayim אהיה אהיה יהוה, בינה ע"ה בְּחֶסֶד bechesed

ע"ב, ריבוע יהוה• מְחַיֵּה mechaye ס"ג מֵתִים metim בְּרַחֲמִים berachamim

(במוכסז) מצפצ, אלהים דההין, י"פ ייי רַבִּים rabim (טלא דעתיק)• סוֹמֵךְ somech

(אכדטם) כוק, ריבוע אדני נוֹפְלִים noflim (זו"ן)• וְרוֹפֵא verofe חוֹלִים cholim

חולה = מ"ה וד' אותיות• וּמַתִּיר umatir אֲסוּרִים asurim• וּמְקַיֵּם umekayem

אֱמוּנָתוֹ emunato לִישֵׁנֵי lishenei עָפָר afar• מִי mi ילי כָּמוֹךָ chamocha

בַּעַל ba'al גְּבוּרוֹת gevurot (you should enunciate the letter *Ayin* in the word *"ba'al"*)

וּמִי umi ילי דּוֹמֶה dome לָּךְ lach• מֶלֶךְ melech מֵמִית memit

וּמְחַיֶּה umchaye ס"ג (יוד הי ואו הי) וּמַצְמִיחַ umatzmi'ach יְשׁוּעָה yeshu'a:

THE SECOND BLESSING

You are mighty forever, Lord. You resurrect the dead and are very capable of redeeming.
Who causes dew to fall.

You sustain life with kindness and resurrect the dead with great compassion. You support those who have fallen, heal the sick, release the imprisoned, and fulfill Your faithful words to those who are asleep in the dust. Who is like You, Master of might, and Who can compare to You, King, Who causes death, Who gives life, and Who sprouts salvation?

וְנֶאֱמָן vene'eman אַתָּה Ata לְהַחֲיוֹת lehachayot מֵתִים metim:

אהיה יהו אלף הי יוד הי (on Shabbat: יְהֹוִה)

בָּרוּךְ baruch אַתָּה Ata יְהֹוָואדִהֹנָהי(יְהֹוָואדִנָהי)יאהדונהי Adonai

מְחַיֵּה mechaye ס"ג (יוד הי ואו הי) הַמֵּתִים hametim ר"ת מ"ה וס"ת מ"ה:

NAKDISHACH – THE KEDUSHA

The congregation recites this prayer together.

Saying the *Kedusha* (Holiness) we meditate to bring the holiness of the Creator among us. As it says: "*Venikdashti betoch Benei Israel*" (God is hallowed among the children of Israel).

נַקְדִּישָׁךְ nakdishach וְנַעֲרִיצָךְ vena'aritzach.

כְּנוֹעַם keno'am שִׂיחַ si'ach סוֹד sod מיכ, י"פ האא שַׂרְפֵי sarfei

קֹדֶשׁ kodesh הַמְשַׁלְּשִׁים hameshaleshim לְךָ lecha קְדֻשָּׁה kedusha.

וְכֵן vechen כָּתוּב katuv עַל al יַד yad נְבִיאָךְ nevi'ach. וְקָרָא vekara

זֶה ze אֶל־ el זֶה ze י"ב פרקין דיעקב מאירים לי"ב פרקין דרוזל וְאָמַר ve'amar:

קָדוֹשׁ kadosh | קָדוֹשׁ kadosh קָדוֹשׁ kadosh (סוד ג' רישין דעתיקא קדישא)

יְהֹוָואדִהֹנָהיאהדונהי Adonai צְבָאוֹת Tzeva'ot פני שכינה מְלֹא melo כָל־ chol ילי

הָאָרֶץ ha'aretz אלהים דההין ע"ה כְּבוֹדוֹ kevodo:

לְעֻמָּתָם le'umatam מְשַׁבְּחִים meshabechim וְאוֹמְרִים ve'omrim:

(או"א) בָּרוּךְ baruch כְּבוֹד־ kevod יְהֹוָואדִהֹנָהיאהדונהי Adonai ; כבוד ה' = יוד הי ואו הה

מִמְּקוֹמוֹ mimekomo עסמ"ב, הברכה (למתק את ז' המלכים שמתו) ; ר"ת ע"ב, ריבוע יהוה ; ר"ת מיכ:

וּבְדִבְרֵי uvdivrei קָדְשָׁךְ kodshach כָּתוּב katuv לֵאמֹר lemor:

(זו"ן) יִמְלֹךְ yimloch קדוש ברוך ימלך ר"ת יב"ק, אלהים יהוה, אהיה אדני יהוה

יְהֹוָואדִהֹנָהיאהדונהי Adonai לְעוֹלָם le'olam ריבוע ס"ג וי' אותיות דס"ג אֱלֹהַיִךְ Elohayich ילה

צִיּוֹן Tziyon יוסף, ו' הויות, קנאה לְדֹר ledor וָדֹר vador ר"י ; ר"ת אצלו (מלכות אצל ז"א – ו)

הַלְלוּיָהּ haleluya אלהים, אהיה אדני ; ללה:

And You are faithful to resurrecting the dead. Blessed are You, Lord, Who resurrects the dead.

NAKDISHACH

We sanctify You and we revere You, according to the pleasant words of the counsel of the Holy Angels, who recite Holy before You three times, as it is written by Your Prophet: "And each called to the other and said: Holy, Holy, Holy, Is the Lord of Hosts, the entire world is filled with His glory." (Isaiah 6:3) Facing them they give praise and say: "Blessed is the glory of the Lord from His Place." (Ezekiel 3:12) And in Your Holy Words, it is written as follows: "The Lord, your God, shall reign forever, for each and for every generation. Zion, Praise the Lord!" (Psalms 146:10)

THE THIRD BLESSING

This blessing connects us to Jacob, the Central Column and the power of restriction. Jacob is our channel for connecting mercy with judgment. By restricting our reactive behavior, we are blocking our Desire to Receive for the Self Alone. Jacob also gives us the power to balance our acts of mercy and judgment toward other people in our lives.

Tiferet that becomes _Da'at_ (14 words).

אַתָּה Ata קָדוֹשׁ kadosh וְשִׁמְךָ veshimcha קָדוֹשׁ kadosh ר״ת = אור, רז, אין סוף ♦

וּקְדוֹשִׁים ukdoshim בְּכָל־ bechol ב״ן, לכב יוֹם yom ע״ה נגד, מזבח, זן, אל יהוה

יְהַלְלוּךָ yehalelucha סֶּלָה sela:♦

אה״ה יהו אלף הא יוד הא (on Shabbat: מצפצ)

בָּרוּךְ baruch אַתָּה Ata יְהֹוָאדִהֹנָי (יְהֹוָאדֹנָי) יאהדונהי Adonai

הָאֵל haEl לאה ; ייא״י (מילוי דס״ג) הַקָּדוֹשׁ hakadosh י״פ מ״ה (יוד הא ואו הא):♦

Meditate here on the Name: יאהדונהי, as it can help to remove anger.

THE MIDDLE BLESSING

The middle blessing connects us to the true essence of *Shavuot*. *Shavuot* is our connection to immortality and this blessing is our opportunity to choose the seed we wish to plant for immortality. The power of the letters in the Fourth Blessing is in their ability to automatically choose the correct seed we need and not necessarily the seed we want.

אַתָּה Ata בְּחַרְתָּנוּ vechartanu מִכָּל mikol ילי הָעַמִּים ha'amim ♦

אָהַבְתָּ ahavta אוֹתָנוּ otanu וְרָצִיתָ veratzita בָּנוּ banu ♦

וְרוֹמַמְתָּנוּ veromamtanu מִכָּל mikol ילי הַלְּשׁוֹנוֹת haleshonot ♦

וְקִדַּשְׁתָּנוּ vekidashtanu בְּמִצְוֹתֶיךָ bemitzvotecha ♦ וְקֵרַבְתָּנוּ vekeravtanu

מַלְכֵּנוּ malkenu לַעֲבוֹדָתֶךָ la'avodatecha ♦ וְשִׁמְךָ veshimcha הַגָּדוֹל hagadol

להח ; ועם ד׳ אותיות = מבה, יזל, אום וְהַקָּדוֹשׁ vehakadosh עָלֵינוּ alenu קָרָאתָ karata:♦

THE THIRD BLESSING

You are holy, and Your Name is holy, and the Holy Ones praise You every day, for you are God, the Holy King Selah. Blessed are You, Lord, the Holy God.

THE MIDDLE BLESSING

You had chosen us from among all the nations. You had loved us and have found favor in us. You had exalted us above all the tongues and You had sanctified us with Your commandments. You drew us close, our King, to Your service and proclaimed Your great and Holy Name upon us.

וַתִּתֶּן vatiten ב"פ כהת לָנוּ lanu אלהים, אהיה אדני יְהֹוָאדנהיאהדונהי Adonai

אֱלֹהֵינוּ Elohenu ילה בְּאַהֲבָה be'ahava אחד, דאגה (On Shabbat add:

שַׁבָּתוֹת shabbatot לִמְנוּחָה limnucha ו) מוֹעֲדִים mo'adim לְשִׂמְחָה lesimcha.

חַגִּים chagim וּזְמַנִּים uzmanim לְשָׂשׂוֹן lesason. אֶת et

יוֹם yom ע"ה נגד, מזבח, זן, אל יהוה (On Shabbat add: הַשַּׁבָּת hashabat הַזֶּה hazeh והו.

וְאֶת ve'et יוֹם yom ע"ה נגד, מזבח, זן, אל יהוה) חַג chag הַשָּׁבוּעוֹת haShavuot

הַזֶּה hazeh והו. אֶת et יוֹם yom ע"ה נגד, מזבח, זן, אל יהוה טוֹב tov והו

מִקְרָא mikra קֹדֶשׁ kodesh הַזֶּה hazeh והו. זְמַן zeman מַתַּן matan

תּוֹרָתֵנוּ toratenu. בְּאַהֲבָה be'ahava אחד, דאגה מִקְרָא mikra

קֹדֶשׁ kodesh. זֵכֶר zecher לִיצִיאַת litzi'at מִצְרָיִם Mitzrayim מצר.

אֱלֹהֵינוּ elhenu ילה וֵאלֹהֵי vElohei לכב ; מילוי ע"ב, דמב ; ילה אֲבוֹתֵינוּ avotenu

יַעֲלֶה ya'ale וְיָבֹא veyavo וְיַגִּיעַ veyagi'a וְיֵרָאֶה veyera'e ריו וְיֵרָצֶה veyeratze

וְיִשָּׁמַע veyishama וְיִפָּקֵד veyipaked וְיִזָּכֵר veyizacher ר"ת = מ"ב

זִכְרוֹנֵנוּ zichronenu וְזִכְרוֹן vezichron ע"ב קס"א ונש"ב אֲבוֹתֵינוּ avotenu.

זִכְרוֹן zichron ע"ב קס"א ונש"ב יְרוּשָׁלַיִם Yerushalayim עִירָךְ irach.

וְזִכְרוֹן vezichron ע"ב קס"א ונש"ב מָשִׁיחַ mashi'ach בֶּן ben דָּוִד David ע"ה כהת ;

בן דוד = אדני ע"ה עַבְדָּךְ avdach פוי, אל אדני. וְזִכְרוֹן vezichron ע"ב קס"א ונש"ב כָּל kol ילי

עַמְּךָ amecha בֵּית bet ב"פ ראה יִשְׂרָאֵל Yisra'el לְפָנֶיךָ lefanecha ס"ג מ"ה ב"ן

לִפְלֵיטָה lifleta לְטוֹבָה letova אכא. לְחֵן lechen מילוי דמ"ה בריבוע ; מוחי

לְחֶסֶד lechesed ע"ב, ריבוע יהוה וּלְרַחֲמִים ulrachamim.

And may You give us, Lord, our God, with love (**on Shabbat add:** *Shabbat for rest and) holidays for happiness, festivals and time of joy, this day* (**on Shabbat add:** *of Shabbat and this day) of the Shavuot Holiday, and this good day of Holy Convocation, The time we received our Torah with love, a Holy Convocation, a remembrance of the exit from Egypt.*

Our God and the God of our fathers,
may it rise and come and arrive and appear and find favor and be heard and be considered and be remembered, our remembrance and the remembrance of our fathers, the remembrance of Jerusalem, Your city, and the remembrance of Mashiach Ben David, Your servant, and the remembrance of Your entire Nation,

לְחַיִּים lechayim אהיה אהיה יהוה, בינה ע״ה טוֹבִים tovim וּלְשָׁלוֹם ulshalom•

בְּיוֹם beyom ע״ה נגד, מזבח, זן, אל יהוה (On Shabbat add: הַשַּׁבָּת hashabat הַזֶּה hazeh והו•

וּבְיוֹם uvyom ע״ה נגד, מזבח, זן, אל יהוה) חַג chag הַשָּׁבוּעוֹת haShavuot הַזֶּה hazeh

והו בְּיוֹם beyom ע״ה נגד, מזבח, זן, אל יהוה טוֹב tov והו מִקְרָא mikra קֹדֶשׁ kodesh

הַזֶּה hazeh והו• לְרַחֵם lerachem אברהם, וח״פ אל, רי״ו ול״ב נתיבות החכמה, רמ״ח (אברים),

עסמ״ב וט״ז אותיות פשוטות בּוֹ bo עָלֵינוּ alenu וּלְהוֹשִׁיעֵנוּ ulhoshi'enu•

זָכְרֵנוּ zochrenu **(from *Zeir Anpin*)** יְהֹוָהאדניאהדונהי Adonai אֱלֹהֵינוּ Elohenu ילה

בּוֹ bo לְטוֹבָה letova אכא• וּפָקְדֵנוּ ufokdenu **(from *Nukva*)** בוֹ vo

לִבְרָכָה livracha• וְהוֹשִׁיעֵנוּ vehoshi'enu **(from *Da'at*)** בוֹ vo לְחַיִּים lechayim

אהיה אהיה יהוה, בינה ע״ה טוֹבִים tovim• בִּדְבַר bidvar ראה יְשׁוּעָה yeshu'a

וְרַחֲמִים verachamim• חוּס chus וְחָנֵּנוּ vechanenu וַחֲמוֹל vachamol

וְרַחֵם verachem אברהם, וח״פ אל, רי״ו ול״ב נתיבות החכמה, רמ״ח (אברים), עסמ״ב וט״ז אותיות פשוטות

עָלֵינוּ alenu• וְהוֹשִׁיעֵנוּ vehoshi'enu כִּי ki אֵלֶיךָ elecha עֵינֵינוּ enenu ריבוע מ״ה•

כִּי ki אֵל El יא״י מֶלֶךְ melech חַנּוּן chanun וְרַחוּם verachum אָתָּה Ata:

וְהַשִּׂיאֵנוּ vehashsyenu יְהֹוָהאדניאהדונהי Adonai אֱלֹהֵינוּ Elohenu ילה•

אֶת et בִּרְכַּת birkat מוֹעֲדֶיךָ mo'adecha לְחַיִּים lechayim אהיה אהיה יהוה, בינה ע״ה

בְּשִׂמְחָה besimcha וּבְשָׁלוֹם uvshalom• כַּאֲשֶׁר ka'asher רָצִיתָ ratzita

וְאָמַרְתָּ ve'amarta לְבָרְכֵנוּ levarchenu• כֵּן ken תְּבָרְכֵנוּ tevarchenu

סֶלָה selah:

---

*the House of Israel, before You for deliverance, for good, for grace, kindness and compassion, for a good life and for peace on this Day of (***on Shabbat say:** *Shabbat and on this Day of) the Shavuot Holiday, on this good Day of Holy Convocation, to take pity on us and to save us. Remember us, Lord, our God, on it for good and consider us, on it, for blessing and deliver us on it for a good life with the words of deliverance and mercy. Take pity and be gracious to us and have mercy and be compassionate with us and save us, for our eyes turn to You, because You are God, King Who is gracious and compassionate. And give us, Lord, our God Your blessing of Your*

MEKADESH ISRAEL AND THE TIMES

(On Shabbat add: אֱלֹהֵינוּ Elohenu ילה וֵאלֹהֵי veElohei לכב ; מילוי ע"ב, דמב ; ילה
אֲבוֹתֵינוּ avotenu רְצֵה retze נָא na בִמְנוּחָתֵינוּ vimnuchatenu)
קַדְּשֵׁנוּ kadshenu בְּמִצְוֹתֶיךָ vemitzvotecha. תֵּן ten וְחֶלְקֵנוּ chelkenu
בְּתוֹרָתָךְ vetoratach. שַׂבְּעֵנוּ sabe'enu מִטּוּבָךְ mituvach לאו.
שַׂמֵּחַ same'ach נַפְשֵׁנוּ nafshenu בִּישׁוּעָתָךְ bishu'atach.
וְטַהֵר vetaher לִבֵּנוּ libenu לְעָבְדְּךָ le'ovdecha פוי, אל יהוה בֶּאֱמֶת ve'emet
אהיה פעמים אהיה, ז"פ ס"ג. וְהַנְחִילֵנוּ vehanchilenu יְהֹוָהאדניאהדונהי Adonai
אֱלֹהֵינוּ Elohenu ילה (On Shabbat add: בְּאַהֲבָה be'ahava אחד, דאגה
וּבְרָצוֹן uvratzon מהש ע"ה, ע"ב בריבוע וקס"א ע"ה, אל שדי) בְּשִׂמְחָה vesimcha
וּבְשָׂשׂוֹן uvsason (On Shabbat add: שַׁבְּתוֹת shabatot ו) מוֹעֲדֵי mo'adei
קָדְשֶׁךָ kodshecha, וְיִשְׂמְחוּ veyismechu בְךָ vecha כָּל kol ילי יִשְׂרָאֵל Yisrael
מְקַדְּשֵׁי mekadshei שְׁמֶךָ shemecha. בָּרוּךְ baruch אַתָּה Ata
יְהֹוָהאדניאהדונהי Adonai
אהיה יהו אלף הה יוד הה (on Shabbat: יה אדני)
מְקַדֵּשׁ mekadesh (On Shabbat add: הַשַּׁבָּת hashabat וְ ve) יִשְׂרָאֵל Yisrael
וְהַזְּמַנִּים vehazemanim:

THE FINAL THREE BLESSINGS

Through the merit of Moses, Aaron and Joseph, who are our channels for the final three blessings, we are able to bring down all the spiritual energy that we aroused with our prayers and blessings.

THE FIFTH BLESSING

During this blessing, referring to Moses, we should always meditate to try to know exactly what God wants from us in our life, as signified by the phrase, "Let it be the will of God." We ask God to guide us toward the work we came to Earth to do. The Creator cannot just accept the work that we want to do; we must carry out the work we were destined to do.

---

holidays for happy and peaceful life. As You desired and said to bless us. So You shall bless us Selah.

MEKADESH ISRAEL AND THE TIMES

(**on Shabbat:** *Our God and the God of our forefathers, please desire our rest.)*

Sanctify us with Your commandments and place our lot in Your Torah and satiate us from Your goodness and gladden our spirits with Your salvation. and purify our heart so as to serve You truly. And grant us, Lord, our God, (**on Shabbat:** *with love and favor,) with happiness and joy*

Netzach

Meditate for the Supernal Desire (*Keter*) that is called *Metzach HaRatzon* (the Forehead of the Desire).

רְצֵה retze אלף למד הה יוד מם

Meditate here to transform misfortune and tragedy (צרה) into desire and acceptance (רצה).

יְהֹוָהאדניאהדונהי Adonai אֱלֹהֵינוּ Elohenu ילה בְּעַמְּךָ be'amecha יִשְׂרָאֵל Yisrael

וְלִתְפִלָּתָם velitfilatam שְׁעֵה she'e• וְהָשֵׁב vehashev הָעֲבוֹדָה ha'avoda

לִדְבִיר lidvir רי"ו בֵּיתֶךָ betecha ב"פ ראה• וְאִשֵּׁי ve'ishei יִשְׂרָאֵל Yisrael

וּתְפִלָּתָם utfilatam מְהֵרָה mehera בְּאַהֲבָה be'ahava אוזר, דאגה

תְקַבֵּל tekabel בְּרָצוֹן beratzon מהש ע"ה, ע"ב בריבוע וקס"א ע"ה, אל שדי ע"ה•

וּתְהִי ut'hi לְרָצוֹן leratzon מהש ע"ה, ע"ב בריבוע וקס"א ע"ה, אל שדי ע"ה

תָּמִיד tamid ע"ה קס"א קנ"א קמ"ג עֲבוֹדַת avodat יִשְׂרָאֵל Yisrael עַמֶּךָ amecha:

וְאַתָּה veAta בְּרַחֲמֶיךָ verachamecha הָרַבִּים harabim•

תַחְפֹּץ tachpotz בָּנוּ banu וְתִרְצֵנוּ vetirtzenu וְתֶחֱזֶינָה vetechezena

עֵינֵינוּ enenu ריבוע מ"ה בְּשׁוּבְךָ beshuvcha לְצִיּוֹן leTziyon יוסף, ו' הויות, קנאה

בְּרַחֲמִים berachamim מצפצ, אלהים דיודין, י"פ ייי:

אהיה יהו אלף למד הי יוד מם (on Shabbat: אל)

בָּרוּךְ baruch אַתָּה Ata יְהֹוָהאדניאהדונהי Adonai

הַמַּחֲזִיר hamachazir שְׁכִינָתוֹ shechinato לְצִיּוֹן leTziyon יוסף, ו' הויות, קנאה:

---

*(**on Shabbat:** Shabbatot and) the holidays, and all Israel, who sanctify Your Name will be joyful with You. Blessed are You, Lord, who sanctifies (**on Shabbat:** the Sabbath) and Israel and the Times.*

THE FINAL THREE BLESSINGS

THE FIFTH BLESSING

Find favor, Lord, our God,
in Your People, Israel, and turn to their prayer.
Restore the service to the inner sanctuary of Your Temple. Accept the offerings of Israel and their prayer with favor, speedily, and with love. May the service of Your People Israel always be favorable to You.

THE SIXTH BLESSING

This blessing is our thank you. Kabbalistically, the biggest 'thank you' we can give the Creator is to do exactly what we are supposed to do in terms of our spiritual work.

Hod

Bow your entire body at "*modem*" and straighten up at *'Adonai'*.

מוֹדִים modim מאה ברכות שתיקן דוד לאמרם כל יום אֲנַחְנוּ anachnu לָךְ lach

שָׁאַתָּה sheAta הוּא hu יְהֹוָהאדניאהדונהי Adonai (וג) אֱלֹהֵינוּ Elohenu ילה

וֵאלֹהֵי velohei לכב ; מילוי ע"ב, דמב ; ילה אֲבוֹתֵינוּ avotenu לְעוֹלָם le'olam

ריבוע ס"ג וי' אותיות דס"ג וָעֶד •va'ed צוּרֵנוּ tzurenu צוּר tzur אלהים דההין ע"ה

וְחַיֵּינוּ chayenu וּמָגֵן umagen ג"פ אל (ייא" מילוי דס"ג) ; ר"ת מיכאל גבריאל נוריאל

יִשְׁעֵנוּ yish'enu אַתָּה Ata הוּא •hu לְדוֹר ledor וָדוֹר vador רי"ו נוֹדֶה node

לְךָ lecha וּנְסַפֵּר unsaper תְּהִלָּתֶךָ •tehilatecha עַל־ al וְחַיֵּינוּ chayenu

הַמְּסוּרִים hamesurim בְּיָדֶךָ •beyadecha וְעַל ve'al נִשְׁמוֹתֵינוּ nishmotenu

הַפְּקוּדוֹת hapekudot לָךְ •lach וְעַל־ ve'al נִסֶּיךָ nisecha שֶׁבְּכָל shebechol

ב"ן, לכב יוֹם yom ע"ה נגד, מזבח, זן, אל יהוה עִמָּנוּ imanu ריבוע ס"ג, קס"א ע"ה וד' אותיות

וְעַל ve'al נִפְלְאוֹתֶיךָ nifle'otecha וְטוֹבוֹתֶיךָ vetovotecha שֶׁבְּכָל shebechol

ב"ן, לכב עֵת •et עֶרֶב erev וָבֹקֶר vavoker וְצָהֳרָיִם •vetzahorayim הַטּוֹב hatov

והו כִּי־ ki לֹא־ lo כָלוּ chalu רַחֲמֶיךָ •rachamecha הַמְרַחֵם hamerachem

אברהם, וז"פ אל, רי"ו ול"ב נתיבות החכמה, רמ"ח (אברים), עסמ"ב וט"ז אותיות פשוטות כִּי־ ki לֹא lo

תַמּוּ tamu חֲסָדֶיךָ chasadecha כִּי ki מֵעוֹלָם me'olam קִוִּינוּ kivinu לָךְ lach:

And You in Your great compassion take delight in us and are pleased with us. May our eyes witness Your return to Zion with compassion. Blessed are You, Lord, Who returns His Shechinah to Zion.

THE SIXTH BLESSING

We give thanks to You, for it is You, Lord, Who is our God and God of our forefathers, forever and for all eternity. You are our Rock, the Rock of our lives, and the Shield of our salvation. From one generation to another, we shall give thanks to You and we shall tell of Your praise. For our lives that are entrusted in Your hands, for our souls that are in Your care, for Your miracles that are with us every day, and for Your wonders and Your favors that are with us at all times:

MODIM DERABANAN

This prayer is recited by the congregation in the repetition when the *chazan* says "*modim*."

In this section there are 44 words which is the same numerical value as the Name: ריבוע אהיה (א אה אהי אהיה).

מוֹדִים modim מאה ברכות שתיקן דוד לאמרם כל יום אֲנַחְנוּ anachnu לָךְ lach

שָׁאַתָּה sheAta הוּא hu יְהֹוָהאדניאהדונהי Adonai אֱלֹהֵינוּ Elohenu ילה

וֵאלֹהֵי velohei לכב ; מילוי ע"ב, דמב ; ילה אֲבוֹתֵינוּ avotenu

אֱלֹהֵי Elohei מילוי ע"ב, דמב ; ילה כָּל chol ילי בָּשָׂר basar. יוֹצְרֵנוּ yotzrenu

יוֹצֵר yotzer בְּרֵאשִׁית bereshit. בְּרָכוֹת berachot וְהוֹדָאוֹת vehoda'ot

לְשִׁמְךָ leshimcha הַגָּדוֹל hagadol להח ; עם ד' אותיות = מבה, יזל, אום

וְהַקָּדוֹשׁ vehakadosh עַל al שֶׁהֶחֱיִיתָנוּ shehecheyitanu וְקִיַּמְתָּנוּ vekiyamtanu.

כֵּן ken תְּחַיֵּינוּ techayenu וּתְחָנֵּנוּ utchonenu. וְתֶאֱסוֹף vete'esof

גָּלֻיּוֹתֵינוּ galuyoteinu לְחַצְרוֹת lechatzrot קָדְשֶׁךָ kodshecha. לִשְׁמוֹר lishmor

חֻקֶּיךָ chukecha וְלַעֲשׂוֹת vela'asot רְצוֹנָךְ retzoncha. וּלְעָבְדָךְ ul'ovdecha

פוי, אל אדני בְּלֵבָב belevav בוכו שָׁלֵם shalem. עַל al שֶׁאֲנַחְנוּ she'anachnu

מוֹדִים modim לָךְ lach. בָּרוּךְ baruch אֵל El ייא"י (מילוי דס"ג) הַהוֹדָאוֹת hahoda'ot:

וְעַל ve'al כֻּלָּם kulam יִתְבָּרַךְ yitbarach וְיִתְרוֹמָם veyitromam

וְיִתְנַשֵּׂא veyitnase תָּמִיד tamid ע"ה קס"א קנ"א קמ"ג שִׁמְךָ shimcha

מַלְכֵּנוּ malkenu לְעוֹלָם le'olam ריבוע ס"ג וי' אותיות דס"ג וָעֶד va'ed.

וְכָל־ vechol ילי הַחַיִּים hachayim אהיה אהיה יהוה, בינה ע"ה יוֹדוּךָ yoducha סֶּלָה sela:

וִיהַלְלוּ vihalelu וִיבָרְכוּ vivarchu יהוה ריבוע יהוה ריבוע מ"ה

אֶת־ et שִׁמְךָ shimcha הַגָּדוֹל hagadol להח ; עם ד' אותיות = מבה, יזל, אום

---

evening, morning and afternoon. You are the good One, for Your compassion has never ceased. You are the compassionate One, for Your kindness has never ended, for we have always placed our hope in You.

MODIM DERABANAN

We give thanks to You, for it is You Lord, our God and God of our forefathers, the God of all flesh, our Maker and the Former of all Creation. Blessings and thanks to Your great and Holy Name for giving us life and for preserving us. So may You continue to give us life, be gracious to us, and gather our exiles to the courtyards of Your Sanctuary, so that we may keep Your laws, fulfill Your will, and serve You wholeheartedly. For this, we thank You. Bless the God of thanksgiving.

בֶּאֱמֶת be'emet אהיה פעמים אהיה, ז"פ ס"ג לְעוֹלָם le'olam ריבוע ס"ג וי' אותיות דס"ג
כִּי ki טוֹב tov והו ; כי טוב = יהוה אהיה, אום, מבה, יזל.
הָאֵל haEl לאה ; ייא"י (מילוי דס"ג) יְשׁוּעָתֵנוּ yeshu'atenu וְעֶזְרָתֵנוּ ve'ezratenu
סֶלָה sela. הָאֵל haEl לאה ; ייא"י (מילוי דס"ג) הַטּוֹב hatov והו:

Bend your knees at *"baruch"*, bow at *"Ata"* and straighten up at *"Adonai"*.

אהיה יהו אלף למד הה יוד מם (on Shabbat: אלהים)

בָּרוּךְ baruch אַתָּה Ata יְהֹוָהאדניאהדונהי Adonai (הי) הַטּוֹב hatov והו
שִׁמְךָ shimcha וּלְךָ ulcha נָאֶה na'e לְהוֹדוֹת lehodot ס"ת כהת, משיח בן דוד ע"ה:

BLESSING OF THE *KOHANIM*

During the repetition we say the blessing of the *Kohanim*. The Kohen is a channel for the Right Column energy of sharing and therefore also for healing. Because the Light revealed through this blessing is stronger than we can handle, we cover our eyes to prevent looking directly at this awesome healing Light.

If there is no *Kohen* present, the *chazan* should say:

אֱלֹהֵינוּ Elohenu ילה וֵאלֹהֵי velohei לכב ; מילוי ע"ב, דמב ; ילה אֲבוֹתֵינוּ avotenu,
בָּרְכֵנוּ barchenu בַּבְּרָכָה baberacha הַמְשֻׁלֶּשֶׁת hameshuleshet בַּתּוֹרָה batora
הַכְּתוּבָה haketuva עַל al יְדֵי yedei מֹשֶׁה Moshe מהש, ע"ב בריבוע וקס"א, אל שדי,
עַבְדֶּךָ avdecha ד"פ אלהים ע"ה פוי, אל אדני הָאֲמוּרָה ha'amura מִפִּי mipi אַהֲרֹן Aharon
וּבָנָיו uvanav כֹּהֲנִים kohanim עַם am קְדוֹשֶׁךָ kedoshecha, כָּאָמוּר ka'amur:

Then the *chazan* will continue from *"yevarechecha Adonai..."* until *"veyasem lecha Shalom"* (on the next page).

After the congregation answers *Amen*, the *chazan* will say *"Kohanim"*. Then the *Kohanim* will recite the following in silence:

יְהִי yehi רָצוֹן ratzon מהש ע"ה, ע"ב בריבוע וקס"א ע"ה, אל שדי ע"ה מִלְּפָנֶיךָ milfanecha
ס"ג מ"ה ב"ן יְהֹוָהאדניאהדונהי Adonai אֱלֹהֵינוּ Elohenu ילה וֵאלֹהֵי velohei
לכב ; מילוי ע"ב, דמב ; ילה אֲבוֹתֵינוּ avotenu, שֶׁתְּהֵא shetihye בְּרָכָה beracha זוֹ zo
שֶׁצִּוִּיתָנוּ shetzivitanu לְבָרֵךְ levarech אֶת et עַמְּךָ amecha יִשְׂרָאֵל Yisrael
בְּרָכָה beracha שְׁלֵמָה shelema וְלֹא velo יִהְיֶה yihye ייי בָּהּ ba
מִכְשׁוֹל michshol וְעָוֹן ve'avon מֵעַתָּה me'ata וְעַד ve'ad עוֹלָם olam:

And for all those things, may Your Name be always blessed, exalted and extolled, our King, forever and ever, and all the living shall thank You, Selah. And they shall praise and bless Your Great Name, sincerely and forever, for It is good, the God of our salvation and our help, Selah, the good God. Blessed are You, Lord, whose Name is good, and to You it is befitting to give thanks.

The *Kohanim* say the following blessing facing the Ark and when they reach the word "*vetzivanu*," they should turn clockwise and face the congregation and continue the blessing. If there is only one *Kohen*, the *chazan* should not call him but instead the *Kohen* should say the following blessing right away.

בָּרוּךְ baruch אַתָּה Ata יְהֹוָה יאהדונהי Adonai אֱלֹהֵינוּ Elohenu ילה
מֶלֶךְ melech הָעוֹלָם ha'olam אֲשֶׁר asher קִדְּשָׁנוּ kideshanu
בִּקְדֻשָּׁתוֹ bikdushato שֶׁל shel אַהֲרֹן Aharon וְצִוָּנוּ vetzivanu
לְבָרֵךְ levarech אֶת et עַמּוֹ amo יִשְׂרָאֵל Yisrael בְּאַהֲבָה be'ahava אחד, דאגה:

The *chazan* prompts the *Kohanim* by reciting one word at a time (even if there is only one *Kohen* present). And the congregation answers: "*Amen*" (or "*ken yehi ratzon*" in case the *chazan* reciting it) after each verse.

The initials of the three verses give us the Holy Name: ייי.
In this section, there are 15 words, which are equal to the numerical value of the Holy Name: ההה.

(Right – *Chesed*)

יְבָרֶכְךָ yevarechecha יְהֹוָה יאהדונהי Adonai וְיִשְׁמְרֶךָ veyishmerecha
ר"ת = יהוה ; וס"ת = מ"ה:

(Left - *Gevurah*)

יָאֵר ya'er כף ויו זין ויו יְהֹוָה יאהדונהי Adonai | פָּנָיו panav אֵלֶיךָ elecha
וִיחֻנֶּךָּ vichuneka מנ"ד ; יהה אותיות בפסוק:

(Central – *Tiferet*)

יִשָּׂא yisa יְהֹוָה יאהדונהי Adonai | פָּנָיו panav אֵלֶיךָ elecha
וְיָשֵׂם veyasem לְךָ lecha שָׁלוֹם shalom האא תיבות בפסוק:

(*Malchut*)

(וְשָׂמוּ vesamu אֶת־ et שְׁמִי shemi עַל־ al בְּנֵי benei יִשְׂרָאֵל Yisrael
וַאֲנִי va'ani אני אֲבָרְכֵם avarchem:)

The *Kohanim* add in silence:

רִבּוֹן ribon יהוה ע"ב ס"ג מ"ה ב"ן הָעוֹלָמִים ha'olamim,
עָשִׂינוּ asinu מַה ma מ"ה שֶׁגָּזַרְתָּ shegazarta עָלֵינוּ alenu, עֲשֵׂה ase אַתָּה Ata
מַה ma מ"ה שֶׁהִבְטַחְתָּנוּ shehivtachtanu: הַשְׁקִיפָה hashkifa מִמְּעוֹן mime'on
קָדְשְׁךָ kodshecha מִן־ min הַשָּׁמַיִם hashamayim י"פ טל, י"פ כוזו ; ר"ת מ"ה
וּבָרֵךְ uvarech אֶת־ et עַמְּךָ amecha אֶת־ et יִשְׂרָאֵל Yisrael:

BLESSING OF THE *KOHANIM*

Our God and the God of our forefathers, bless us with the triple blessing written in the Torah by Moses, Your servant, and said by Aaron and his sons the Kohanim, Your Holy People, as it says: May it be your will Lord, our God and the God of our forefathers, that this blessing with which You commanded us to bless Your People, Israel, be a perfect blessing, and may it not contain any hindrance or iniquity from now until eternity.

In this section there are 22 words, which is the numerical value of the Holy Name: **אכא** You should medidtate on the following when the *chazan* says the first word of each verse:

Yevarechecha (first verse): **אֵל נָא קְרַב תְּשׁוּעַת מְצַפֶּיךָ** (ר"ת אנקתם)

Ya'er (second verse): **פּוֹדֶךְ סַר תּוֹצִיאֵם מִמַּאסָר** (ר"ת פסתם)

Yisa (third verse): **פְּדֵה סוֹעִים פְּתַח סוֹמִים יִשְׁעֲךָ מְצַפִּים** (ר"ת פספסים)

דַּלֵּה יוֹקְשִׁים וְקַבֵּץ נְפוּצִים סָמוֹךְ יָהּ מִפַּלְטֵנוּ (ר"ת דיונסים)

(whisper:) יו"ד אותיות בפסוק **בָּרוּךְ** baruch **שֵׁם** shem **כְּבוֹד** kevod **מַלְכוּתוֹ** malchuto, **לְעוֹלָם** le'olam ריבוע ס"ג וי' אותיות דס"ג **וָעֶד** va'ed:

If you had a bad dream that is causing you distress, say the following while the *Kohanim* say their blessing:

רִבּוֹנוֹ ribono **שֶׁל** shel **עוֹלָם** olam **אֲנִי** ani אני **שֶׁלְּךָ** shelcha **וַחֲלוֹמוֹתַי** vechalomotai
שֶׁלָּךְ shelcha. **חֲלוֹם** chalom **חָלַמְתִּי** chalamti **וְאֵינִי** ve'eni **יוֹדֵעַ** yode'a **מַה** ma מ"ה
הוּא hu. **בֵּין** ben **שֶׁחָלַמְתִּי** shechalamti **אֲנִי** ani אני **לְעַצְמִי** le'atzmi **וּבֵין** uven
שֶׁחָלְמוּ shechalmu **לִי** li **אֲחֵרִים** acherim, **וּבֵין** uven **שֶׁאֲנִי** she'ani אני **חָלַמְתִּי** chalamti
עַל al **אֲחֵרִים** acherim, **אִם** im יוהך, מ"א אותיות אהיה בפשוטו במילואו ובמילוי דמילואו ע"ה
טוֹבִים tovim **הֵם** hem **חַזְּקֵם** chazkem **וְאַמְּצֵם** ve'amtzem **כַּחֲלוֹמוֹתָיו** kachalomotav
שֶׁל shel **יוֹסֵף** Yosef קנאה, ו' הויות, ציון **הַצַּדִּיק** hatzadik, **וְאִם** ve'im יוהך, מ"א אותיות אהיה
בפשוטו במילואו ובמילוי דמילואו ע"ה **צְרִיכִים** tzerichim **רְפוּאָה** refu'a **רְפָאֵם** refa'em
כְּמֵי kemei ילי **מָרָה** mara **עַל** al **יְדֵי** yedei **מֹשֶׁה** Moshe מהש, ע"ב בריבוע וקס"א, אל שדי,
ד"פ אלהים ע"ה **רַבֵּינוּ** rabenu **עָלָיו** alav **הַשָּׁלוֹם** hashalom, **וּכְמֵי** uchmei ילי
יְרִיחוֹ Yericho **עַל** al **יְדֵי** yedei **אֱלִישָׁע** Elisha, **וּכְמִרְיָם** ucheMiryam
מִצָּרַעְתָּהּ mitzarata, **וּכְנַעֲמָן** ucheNa'aman **מִצָּרַעְתּוֹ** mitzarato, **וּכְחִזְקִיָּהוּ** ucheChizkiyahu
מֵחָלְיוֹ mecholyo. **וּכְשֵׁם** uchshem **שֶׁהָפַכְתָּ** shehafachta **קִלְלַת** kilelat **בִּלְעָם** Bil'am
הָרָשָׁע harasha **לִבְרָכָה** livracha, **כֵּן** ken **הֲפוֹךְ** hafoch **כָּל** kol ילי **חֲלוֹמוֹתַי** chalomotai
עָלַי alai **וְעַל** ve'al **כָּל** kol ילי ; עמם **יִשְׂרָאֵל** Yisrael **לְטוֹבָה** letova אכא
וְלִבְרָכָה velivracha **וְתִרְצֵנִי** vetirtzeni **בְּרַחֲמֶיךָ** berachamecha **הָרַבִּים** harabim.
מ"ב אותיות בפסוק **יִהְיוּ** yihyu אל (יא"י מילוי דס"ג) **לְרָצוֹן** leratzon מהש ע"ה, ע"ב בריבוע וקס"א
ע"ה, אל שדי ע"ה **אִמְרֵי-** imrei **פִי** fi ר"ת אֶלֶף = אלף למד שין דלת יוד ע"ה **וְהֶגְיוֹן** vehegyon
לִבִּי libi **לְפָנֶיךָ** lefanecha ס"ג מ"ה ב"ן יְהֹוָהאדהנויאהדונהי Adonai **צוּרִי** tzuri **וְגוֹאֲלִי** vego'ali.

Blessed are You, Lord, our God, King of the universe,
Who has sanctified us with the sanctity of Aaron, and has commanded us to bless His People, Israel, with love.
(Right) *May the Lord bless you and protect you. (Amen)*
(Left) *May the Lord shine His Countenance upon you and be gracious to you. (Amen).*
(Central) *May the Lord lift His Face towards you and give you peace. (Amen)*
(And they shall place My Name upon the Children of Israel and I shall bless them). (Numbers 6:24-27)
Master of the world, we have done what you have decreed for us. Now, You do as you promised us: "Gaze down from your holy abode, from the heaven, and bless your people, Yisrael" (Devarim 26,15)

THE FINAL BLESSING

We are emanating the energy of peace to the entire world. We also make it our intent to use our mouths only for good. Kabbalistically, the power of words and speech is unimaginable. We hope to use that power wisely, which is perhaps one of the most difficult tasks we have to carry out.

Yesod

שִׂים sim שָׁלוֹם shalom

טוֹבָה tova אכא וּבְרָכָה uvracha חַיִּים chayim אהיה אהיה יהוה, בינה ע״ה וְחֵן chen

מילוי דמ״ה בריבוע, מוזי וָחֶסֶד vachesed ע״ב, ריבוע יהוה צְדָקָה tzedaka ע״ה ריבוע אלהים

וְרַחֲמִים verachamim עָלֵינוּ alenu וְעַל־ ve'al כָּל־ kol ילי ; עמם

יִשְׂרָאֵל Yisrael עַמֶּךָ amecha וּבָרְכֵנוּ uvarchenu אָבִינוּ avinu כֻּלָּנוּ kulanu

כְּאֶחָד ke'echad אהבה, דאגה בְּאוֹר be'or רז, א״ס פָּנֶיךָ panecha ס״ג מ״ה ב״ן כִּי ki

בְאוֹר ve'or רז, א״ס פָּנֶיךָ panecha ס״ג מ״ה ב״ן נָתַתָּ natata לָּנוּ lanu אלהים, אהיה אדני

יְהֹוָהאדניאהדונהי Adonai אֱלֹהֵינוּ Elohenu ילה תּוֹרָה torah וְחַיִּים vechayim

אהיה אהיה יהוה, בינה ע״ה. אַהֲבָה ahava אחד, דאגה וָחֶסֶד vachesed ע״ב, ריבוע יהוה.

צְדָקָה tzedaka ע״ה ריבוע אלהים וְרַחֲמִים verachamim. בְּרָכָה beracha

וְשָׁלוֹם veshalom. וְטוֹב vetov והו בְּעֵינֶיךָ־ be'enecha ע״ה קס״א ; ריבוע מ״ה

לְבָרְכֵנוּ levarchenu וּלְבָרֵךְ ulvarech אֶת et כָּל־ kol ילי עַמְּךָ amecha

יִשְׂרָאֵל Yisrael בְּרוֹב־ berov י״פ אהיה עֹז oz וְשָׁלוֹם veshalom:

אהיה יהו אלף למד הא יוד מם (on Shabbat: מצפצ)

בָּרוּךְ baruch אַתָּה Ata יְהֹוָהאדניאהדונהי Adonai

הַמְּבָרֵךְ hamevarech אֶת et עַמּוֹ amo יִשְׂרָאֵל Yisrael

ר״ת = אלהים (אילהויהם = יב״ק) בַּשָּׁלוֹם bashalom. אָמֵן amen יאהדונהי.

Master of the World! I am Yours and my dreams are Yours. I had a dream, but I do not know its meaning: whether I had dreamt about myself, or whether others dreamt about me, or whether I had dreamt about others. If they [my dreams] are good, then strengthen them and invigorate them, like the dreams of Joseph, the righteous one. If they require healing, then remedy them like the waters of Marah at the hands of Moses, our master, may peace be upon him, like the waters of Jericho at the hands of Elisha and like Miriam from her leprosy, like Na'aman from his leprosy, and like Chizkiyahu from his illness. And just as You have converted the curse of the wicked Bilaam into blessings, so, too, change my dreams, for my sake and for the sake of all Israel, into good and into blessing. Favor me with Your bountiful compassions. "May the utterances of my mouth and the thoughts oef my heart find favor before You, Lord, my Rock and my Redeemer." (Psalms 19:15)

YIH'YU LERATZON

There are 42 letters in the verse in the secret of *Ana Beko'ach*.

יִהְיוּ yih'yu אל (ייא״י מילוי דס״ג) לְרָצוֹן leratzon מהש ע״ה, ע״ב בריבוע וקס״א ע״ה, אל שדי ע״ה
אִמְרֵי־ imrei פִי fi ר״ת אֶלֶף = אלף למד שין דלת יוד ע״ה וְהֶגְיוֹן vehegyon לִבִּי libi
לְפָנֶיךָ lefanecha ס״ג מ״ה ב״ן יְהֹוָהאדניאהדונהי Adonai צוּרִי tzuri וְגֹאֲלִי vego'ali:

ELOHAI NETZOR

אֱלֹהַי Elohai מילוי ע״ב, דמב ; ילה נְצוֹר netzor לְשׁוֹנִי leshoni מֵרָע mera•
וּשְׂפָתוֹתַי vesiftotai מִדַּבֵּר midaber ראה מִרְמָה mirma• וְלִמְקַלְלַי velimkalelai
נַפְשִׁי nafshi תִדּוֹם tidom• וְנַפְשִׁי venafshi כֶּעָפָר ke'afar
לַכֹּל lakol יה אדני תִּהְיֶה tih'ye• פְּתַח petach לִבִּי libi בְּתוֹרָתֶךָ betoratecha•
וְאַחֲרֵי ve'acharei מִצְוֹתֶיךָ mitzvotecha תִּרְדּוֹף tirdof נַפְשִׁי nafshi•
וְכָל־ vechol ילי הַקָּמִים hakamim עָלַי alai לְרָעָה lera'a• רהע מְהֵרָה mehera
הָפֵר hafer עֲצָתָם atzatam וְקַלְקֵל vekalkel מַחֲשְׁבוֹתָם machshevotam•
עֲשֵׂה ase לְמַעַן lema'an שְׁמָךְ shemach• עֲשֵׂה ase לְמַעַן lema'an
יְמִינָךְ yeminach• עֲשֵׂה ase לְמַעַן lema'an תּוֹרָתָךְ toratach• עֲשֵׂה ase
לְמַעַן lema'an קְדֻשָּׁתָךְ kedushatach• ר״ת הפסוק = מ״ה יהוה לְמַעַן lema'an
יֵחָלְצוּן yechaltzun יְדִידֶיךָ yedidecha ר״ת ילי הוֹשִׁיעָה hoshi'a יהוה וש״ע נהורין
יְמִינְךָ yemincha וַעֲנֵנִי va'aneni (כתיב: ועננו) ר״ת אל (ייא״י מילוי דס״ג):

Before we recite the next verse ("*yih'yu leratzon*") we have an opportunity to strengthen our connection to our soul using our name. Each person has a verse in the *Torah* that connects to their name. Either their name is in the verse, or the first and last letters of the name correspond to the first or last letters of a verse. For example, the name Yehuda begins with a *Yud* and ends with a *Hei*. Before we end the *Amidah*, we state that our name will always be remembered when our soul leaves this world.

THE FINAL BLESSING

Place peace, goodness, blessing, life, grace, kindness, righteousness, and mercy upon us and upon all of Israel, Your People. Bless us all as one, our Father, with the Light of Your Countenance, because it is with the Light of Your Countenance that You, Lord, our God, have given us Torah and life, love and kindness, righteousness and mercy, blessing and peace. May it be good in Your Eyes to bless us and to bless Your entire Nation, Israel, with abundant power and with peace.Blessed are You, Lord, Who blesses His Nation, Israel, with peace, Amen.

YIH'YU LERATZON

"May the utterances of my mouth and the thoughts of my heart find favor before You, Lord, my Rock and my Redeemer." (Psalms 19:15)

YIH'YU LERATZON (THE SECOND)

There are 42 letters in the verse in the secret of *Ana Beko'ach*.

יִהְיוּ yih'yu אל (ייא״ מילוי דס״ג) לְרָצוֹן leratzon מהש ע״ה, ע״ב בריבוע וקס״א ע״ה, אל שדי ע״ה
אִמְרֵי־ imrei פִי fi ר״ת אֱלֶף = אלף למד שין דלת יוד ע״ה וְהֶגְיוֹן vehegyon לִבִּי libi
לְפָנֶיךָ lefanecha ס״ג מ״ה ב״ן יְהֹוָה Adonai צוּרִי tzuri וְגֹאֲלִי vego'ali:

OSE SHALOM

You take three steps backward;

עֹשֶׂה ose שָׁלוֹם shalom

Left
You turn to the left and say:

בִּמְרוֹמָיו bimromav ר״ת ע״ב, ריבוע יהוה
הוּא hu בְּרַחֲמָיו verachamav יַעֲשֶׂה ya'ase

Right
You turn to the right and say:

שָׁלוֹם shalom עָלֵינוּ alenu ר״ת ש״ע נהורין
וְעַל ve'al כָּל־ kol ילי ; עמם עַמּוֹ amo יִשְׂרָאֵל Yisrael

Center
You face the center and say:

וְאִמְרוּ ve'imru אָמֵן amen יאהדונהי:

יְהִי yehi רָצוֹן ratzon מהש ע״ה, ע״ב בריבוע וקס״א ע״ה, אל שדי ע״ה
מִלְּפָנֶיךָ milfanecha ס״ג מ״ה ב״ן יְהֹוָה Adonai אֱלֹהֵינוּ Elohenu ילה
וֵאלֹהֵי velohei לכב ; מילוי ע״ב, דמב ; ילה אֲבוֹתֵינוּ avotenu, שֶׁתִּבְנֶה shetivne
בֵּית bet ב״פ ראה הַמִּקְדָּשׁ hamikdash בִּמְהֵרָה bimhera בְיָמֵינוּ veyamenu
וְתֵן veten חֶלְקֵנוּ chelkenu בְּתוֹרָתָךְ betoratach לַעֲשׂוֹת la'asot חֻקֵּי chukei
רְצוֹנָךְ retzonach וּלְעָבְדָךְ ul'ovdach פוי, אל אדני בְּלֵבָב belevav בוכו שָׁלֵם shalem.

You take three steps forward.

ELOHAI NETZOR

My God, guard my tongue from evil and my lips from speaking deceit. To those who curse me, let my spirit remain silent, and let my spirit be as dust for everyone. Open my heart toYour Torah and let my heart pursue Your commandments. All those who rise against me to do me harm, speedily nullify their plans and disturb their thoughts. Do so for the sake of Your Name. Do so for the sake of Your Right. Do so for the sake of Your Torah. Do so for the sake of Your Holiness, "So that Your loved ones may be saved. Redeem Your right and answer me." (Psalms 60:7)

YIH'YU LERATZON (THE SECOND)

"May the utterances of my mouth
and the thoughts of my heart find favor before You, Lord, my Rock and my Redeemer." (Psalms 19:15)

THE HALEL

The word *Halel* has the same numerical value (65) as *Lamed, Lamed, Hei* ללה, the 72 Name of God for dreams. Sixty five is also the numerical value of both the word *hakeli* הכלי, which means the Vessel, and the Aramaic word אדני *Adonai*, the Name of God that corresponds to our physical world of *Malchut*. The *Halel* helps us lift off from this physical world to make our connections to the holidays. The seven parts of the *Halel* correspond to the seven *Sefirot* that directly influence our world.

בָּרוּךְ baruch אַתָּה Ata יְהֹוָאדהויאהדונהי Adonai אֱלֹהֵינוּ Elohenu ילה

מֶלֶךְ melech הָעוֹלָם ha'olam אֲשֶׁר asher קִדְּשָׁנוּ kideshanu

בְּמִצְוֹתָיו bemitzvotav וְצִוָּנוּ vetzivanu לִקְרוֹא likro

אֶת et הַהַלֵּל hahalel ללה, אדני ; ר"ת לאה:

CHESED – HALELUYA

"God lifts me up from dust." This verse signifies the ability for positive change to occur at any moment. The first step is letting go of our ego. If we tune out those whispers and maintain total certainty that the Light can dramatically alter our situation instantly, we will ignite the power of this connection.

In this Psalm there are 58 words which is the numerical value of the Holy Name: אל יהוה ע"ה.

הַלְלוּיָהּ haleluya אלהים, אהיה אדני ; ללה הַלְלוּ halelu עַבְדֵי avdei

יְהֹוָאדהויאהדונהי Adonai הַלְלוּ halelu אֶת־ et שֵׁם shem יְהֹוָאדהויאהדונהי Adonai:

יְהִי yehi שֵׁם shem יְהֹוָאדהויאהדונהי Adonai מְבֹרָךְ mevorach ר"ת ריבוע ע"ב ריבוע ס"ג

יהוה מברך = רפ"ח (להעלות רפ"ח ניצוצות שנפלו לקליפה דמשם באים התולואים) מֵעַתָּה me'ata

וְעַד־ ve'ad עוֹלָם olam ילי: מִמִּזְרַח mimizrach שֶׁמֶשׁ shemesh עַד־ ad

ר"ת קדוש מְבוֹאוֹ mevo'o מְהֻלָּל mehulal שֵׁם shem יְהֹוָאדהויאהדונהי Adonai:

רָם ram עַל־ al כָּל־ kol ילי ; עמם גּוֹיִם goyim יְהֹוָאדהויאהדונהי Adonai

עַל al הַשָּׁמַיִם hashamayim י"פ טל, י"פ כוזו ; ר"ת וזשמל כְּבוֹדוֹ kevodo:

THE HALEL

Blessed are You, Lord, our God, King of the world,
Who has sanctified us with His commandments and obliged us to complete the Halel.

CHESED – HALELUYA

"Praise the Lord, You servants of the Lord. Praise the Name of the Lord. May the Name of the Lord be blessed from now and forever. From the rising of the sun until its setting, God's Name is praised. God is high above all nations, His glory is above the Heavens.

מי mi ילי כיהוהאדנייאהדונהי kadonai אלהינו Elohenu ילה
המגביהי hamagbihi לשבת lashavet: המשפילי hamashpili לראות lir'ot
בשמים bashamayim י״פ טל, י״פ כוזו ובארץ uva'aretz:
מקימי mekimi מעפר me'afar דל dal מאשפת me'ashpot ירים yarim
אביון evyon: להושיבי lehoshivi עם־ im נדיבים nedivim עם im
נדיבי nedivei עמו amo: מושיבי moshivi עקרת akeret הבית habayit
ב״פ ראה ; עקרת הבית היא רוזל אם־ em יוהך, מ״א אותיות דפשוט, דמילוי ודמילוי דמילוי דאהיה ע״ה
הבנים habanim שמחה semecha הללויה haleluya אלהים, אהיה אדני ; ללה:

GEVURAH - BETZET YISRAEL

"Yehuda was holy," refers to the head of the Tribe of Yehuda, a man named Nachshon ben Aminadav. Nachshon was the first person to demonstrate complete certainty when he entered the Red Sea during the Exodus. He overcame his reactive fears and doubts and continued into the water until it reached his nostrils, whereupon it rushed into his throat and began choking him. At that precise moment, Satan attempted to bombard him with fear and uncertainty. Even when miracles are supposed to happen, the slightest doubt can prevent them from occurring. But Nachshon ben Aminadav didn't waver. A split second later, he was breathing fresh air as the waters of the Red Sea climbed toward the Heavens.

In this Psalm there are 52 words which correspond to the Holy Name: יוד הה וו הה (בוזינת נוקבא).

בצאת betzet ישראל Yisrael ממצרים miMitzrayim מצר בית bet ב״פ ראה
יעקב Yaakov ו׳ הויות, יאהדונהי אידהנויה מעם me'am לעז lo'ez: היתה hayta
יהודה Yehuda לקדשו lekadsho ישראל Yisrael ממשלותיו mamshelotav:
הים hayam ילי ראה ra'a ראה וינס vayanos הירדן haYarden י׳ הויות וד׳ אותיות
יסב yisov לאחור le'achor: ההרים heharim רקדו rakdu כאילים che'elim
גבעות geva'ot כבני־ kivnei צאן tzon: מה־ ma מ״ה לך lecha הים hayam ילי
כי ki תנוס tanus הירדן haYarden י׳ הויות וד׳ אותיות תסב tisov לאחור le'achor:

Who is like the Lord, our God, Who dwells so high, Who looks down upon the Heavens and the earth? He raises the poor from the dust and uplifts the pauper from the trash heap. He seats them together with the noblemen, with the nobility of His Nation. He seats the mistress of the house, the mother of the children, happily. Praise the Lord!" (Psalms 113)

GEVURAH - BETZET YISRAEL

"When Israel left Egypt and the House of Jacob from among a foreign nation, Judah then became sanctified to Him and Israel was His Dominion. The sea saw and fled, the Jordan turned backward. The mountains skipped like rams, and the hills like young lambs. What ails you sea, that you flee? Jordan, that you turn backward?

הֶהָרִים heharim תִּרְקְדוּ tirkedu כְאֵילִים che'elim גְּבָעוֹת geva'ot

כִּבְנֵי־ kivnei צֹאן tzon: מִלִּפְנֵי milifnei אָדוֹן adon אני חוּלִי chuli אָרֶץ aretz

מִלִּפְנֵי milifnei אֱלוֹהַּ Eloha שם בן מ"ב יַעֲקֹב Yaakov ד׳ הויות, יאהדונהי אידהנויה:

הַהֹפְכִי hahofchi הַצּוּר hatzur אלהים דההין ע"ה אֲגַם־ agam ריבוע אהיה = דם

(ומהפכו למים) מָיִם mayim חַלָּמִישׁ chalamish לְמַעְיְנוֹ־ lema'yno מָיִם mayim:

TIFERET - LO LANU

Rav Yehuda Ashlag reminds us that despite whatever we are able to achieve spiritually on our own, we still can never truly earn or merit the Light that glimmers within us. Our physical body may not deserve anything in this world, but the Creator gave us the spark of Light that sustains our soul and is our essence. This spark of Light is known by the code word *Name*, from the verse: *"Do it for Your Name!"* In reality, we are asking the Creator to give us Light for the God-like part of us—our soul. To ensure that we receive the Creator's Light with this prayer, we must mirror our request through actions. We do that when we recognize the spark of Light within others. Even our worst enemy is imbued with a spark of the Light of God. The more we recognize this, the more blessings and good fortune we receive in our own life.

לֹא lo לָנוּ lanu אלהים אהיה אדני יְהֹוָהאדניאהדונהי Adonai לֹא lo לָנוּ lanu

אלהים אהיה אדני כִּי־ ki לְשִׁמְךָ leshimcha תֵּן ten כָּבוֹד kavod

עַל־ al חַסְדְּךָ chasdecha עַל al אֲמִתֶּךָ amitecha: לָמָּה lama יֹאמְרוּ yomru

הַגּוֹיִם hagoyim אַיֵּה־ aye נָא na אֱלֹהֵיהֶם Elohehem ילה: וֵאלֹהֵינוּ velohenu

ילה בַשָּׁמָיִם vashamayim י"פ טל, י"פ כוזו כֹּל kol ילי אֲשֶׁר asher חָפֵץ chafetz

עָשָׂה asa: עֲצַבֵּיהֶם atzabehem כֶּסֶף kesef וְזָהָב vezahav מַעֲשֵׂה ma'ase

יְדֵי yedei אָדָם adam מ"ה: פֶּה־ pe מילה ; ע"ה אלהים, אהיה אדני לָהֶם lahem

וְלֹא velo יְדַבֵּרוּ yedaberu עֵינַיִם enayim ריבוע דמ"ה לָהֶם lahem

וְלֹא velo יִרְאוּ yir'u: אָזְנַיִם oznayim יוד הי ואו הה לָהֶם lahem וְלֹא velo

יִשְׁמָעוּ yishma'u אַף af לָהֶם lahem וְלֹא velo יְרִיחוּן yerichun:

Mountains, that you skip like rams? Hills, like young lambs? Before the Lord tremble, Earth, before the God of Jacob, Who turns the rock into a lake of water, the flint into a flowing fountain." (Psalms 113)

TIFERET - LO LANU

Not for our sake, Lord, not for our sake, but for the sake of Your Name give glory, for the sake of Your kindness and Your truth. Why should the nations say: Where is their God? Our God is in the Heavens. He formed all that He desired. Their idols are of silver and gold, the work of the hands of man. They have mouths but cannot speak. They have eyes but cannot see. They have noses but cannot smell.

יְדֵיהֶם yedehem וְלֹא velo יְמִישׁוּן yemishun רַגְלֵיהֶם raglehem

וְלֹא velo יְהַלֵּכוּ yehalechu לֹא־ lo יֶהְגּוּ yehgu בִּגְרוֹנָם: bigronam

כְּמוֹהֶם kemohem יִהְיוּ yih'yu ייא״י (מילוי דס״ג) עֹשֵׂיהֶם osehem

כֹּל kol ילי אֲשֶׁר־ asher בֹּטֵחַ bote'ach בָּהֶם: bahem יִשְׂרָאֵל Yisrael

בְּטַח betach בַּיהֹוָהאדניאהדונהי badonai עֶזְרָם ezram וּמָגִנָּם umaginam

הוּא: hu בֵּית bet ב״פ ראה אַהֲרֹן Aharon בִּטְחוּ bitchu

בַּיהֹוָהאדניאהדונהי badonai עֶזְרָם ezram וּמָגִנָּם umaginam הוּא: hu יִרְאֵי yir'ei

יְהֹוָהאדניאהדונהי Adonai בִּטְחוּ bitchu בַּיהֹוָהאדניאהדונהי badonai עֶזְרָם ezram

יי״ז (כ״ב אותיות פשוטות (=אכא) ועוד ה׳ אותיות מנצפך) וּמָגִנָּם umaginam הוּא: hu

NETZACH – ADONAI ZECHARANU

"*The Heavens were given to God, but the land was given to the people.*" The Creator separated from this world so that we could become creators and express the godliness that is part of all of us. This paragraph gives us the strength to become true creators in our own lives. A tiny candle glimmering on a blazing sunlit day contributes little. But even the darkness of a large stadium responds to the light of a single candle. In this realm of darkness in which we find ourselves, one candle takes on tremendous value and worth.

When our own actions are those of sharing and revealing Light, we achieve oneness with the Creator through similarity of form. This oneness enables us to become true creators in our own lives.

יְהֹוָהאדניאהדונהי Adonai זְכָרָנוּ zecharanu יְבָרֵךְ yevarech עסמ״ב, הברכה

(למתק את ז׳ המלכים שמתו) יְבָרֵךְ yevarech עסמ״ב, הברכה (למתק את ז׳ המלכים שמתו) ; ר״ת ייז

אֶת־ et בֵּית bet ב״פ ראה יִשְׂרָאֵל Yisrael יְבָרֵךְ yevarech עסמ״ב, הברכה

(למתק את ז׳ המלכים שמתו) אֶת־ et בֵּית bet ב״פ ראה אַהֲרֹן: Aharon

יְבָרֵךְ yevarech עסמ״ב, הברכה (למתק את ז׳ המלכים שמתו) יִרְאֵי yir'ei

יְהֹוָהאדניאהדונהי Adonai ר״ת ייי הַקְּטַנִּים haketanim עִם im הַגְּדֹלִים: hagedolim

---

Their hands cannot touch, their legs cannot walk. They utter no sounds from their throats. May their makers be like them and whoever trusts in them. Israel, place your trust in the Lord. He is your Helper and Protector. House of Aaron, place your trust in the Lord. He is your Helper and Protector. Those who fear the Lord, place your trust in the Lord. He is your Helper and Protector." (Psalms 115:1-11)

NETZACH – ADONAI ZECHARANU

"The Lord Who remembers us, blesses. He blesses the House of Israel. He blesses the House of Aaron. He blesses those who fear the Lord, the small as well as the great.

יֹסֵף yosef יְהֹוָ‍אדהנויאהדונהי Adonai עֲלֵיכֶם alechem עֲלֵיכֶם alechem

וְעַל ve'al בְּנֵיכֶם :benechem בְּרוּכִים beruchim אַתֶּם atem

לַיהֹוָ‍אדהנויאהדונהי ladonai עֹשֵׂה ose שָׁמַיִם shamayim י״פ טל, י״פ כוזו

וָאָרֶץ :va'aretz הַשָּׁמַיִם hashamayim י״פ טל, י״פ כוזו שָׁמַיִם shamayim י״פ טל, י״פ כוזו

לַיהֹוָ‍אדהנויאהדונהי ladonai וְהָאָרֶץ veha'aretz אלהים דההין ע״ה נָתַן natan

לִבְנֵי־ livnei אָדָם adam מ״ה: לֹא lo הַמֵּתִים hametim יְהַלְלוּ־ yehalelu

יָהּ Yah וְלֹא velo כָּל kol ילי יֹרְדֵי yordei דוּמָה :duma וַאֲנַחְנוּ va'anachnu

נְבָרֵךְ nevarech יָהּ Yah מֵעַתָּה me'ata וְעַד־ ve'ad עוֹלָם olam

הַלְלוּיָהּ haleluya אלהים, אהיה אדני ; ללה:

HOD– AHAVTI

Rav Elimelech, a great 18th century Kabbalist, teaches us that while we pray, Satan, our Opponent, often comes to us to say: "Why are you bothering to stand here and pray? You don't really want to change. It's too difficult. So why bother with all this complicated spiritual work? Given all the negative actions you have already performed, your personal situation is hopeless." This prayer shuts down Satan's negative and destructive influence and helps us understand that it doesn't matter what we did previously. From this moment forward, we can change and transform our nature if we really want to.

"God protects and saves the fools." The smartest men can make the biggest mistakes. If we think we really know it all, if our egos tell us that we are brilliant people, then we really are fools and the Light will never reach us. But those people who can admit that there is always something to learn are acknowledging that we are all fools, in a proactive manner. God will protect them and take them to even higher levels of fulfillment.

אָהַבְתִּי ahavti כִּי־ ki יִשְׁמַע yishma יְהֹוָ‍אדהנויאהדונהי Adonai

אֶת־ et קוֹלִי koli תַּחֲנוּנָי :tachanunai כִּי־ ki הִטָּה hita

אָזְנוֹ ozno יוד הי ואו הה לִי li וּבְיָמַי uvyamai אֶקְרָא :ekra

אֲפָפוּנִי afafuni חֶבְלֵי־ chevlei מָוֶת mavet וּמְצָרֵי umtzarei שְׁאוֹל she'ol

מְצָאוּנִי metza'uni צָרָה tzara אלהים דההין וְיָגוֹן veyagon אֶמְצָא :emtza

---

May the Lord increase you more and more, you and your children. Blessed are you Lord, Creator of Heaven and Earth. The Heavens are the Heavens of the Lord, and the Earth He gave to mankind. The dead do not praise the Lord, nor do those who descend to the grave. But we will bless the Lord from now and forever. Praise the Lord." (Psalms 115:12-end)

HOD– AHAVTI

"I wanted that the Lord would listen to my voice and to my supplications and turn His Ear towards me and that all my days I would call upon Him. Pangs of death have surrounded me and the misery of the grave has found me. I found trouble and sorrow.

וּבְשֵׁם uvshem יְהֹוָהאדניאהדונהי Adonai אֶקְרָא ekra ושר, אבגיתץ
אָנָּה ana יְהֹוָהאדניאהדונהי Adonai מַלְּטָה maleta נַפְשִׁי nafshi:
חַנּוּן chanun יְהֹוָהאדניאהדונהי Adonai וְצַדִּיק vetzadik וֵאלֹהֵינוּ velohenu ילה
מְרַחֵם merachem אברהם, ו"פ אל, רי"ו ול"ב נתיבות החכמה, רמ"ח (אברים), עסמ"ב וט"ז אותיות
פשוטות: שֹׁמֵר shomer פְּתָאִים peta'im יְהֹוָהאדניאהדונהי Adonai דַּלּוֹתִי daloti
וְלִי veli יְהוֹשִׁיעַ yehoshi'a: שׁוּבִי shuvi נַפְשִׁי nafshi לִמְנוּחָיְכִי limnuchaychi
כִּי ki יְהֹוָהאדניאהדונהי Adonai גָּמַל gamal עָלָיְכִי alaychi: כִּי ki
חִלַּצְתָּ chilatzta נַפְשִׁי nafshi מִמָּוֶת mimavet אֶת־ et עֵינִי eni ריבוע מ"ה
מִן־ min דִּמְעָה dim'a אֶת־ et רַגְלִי ragli מִדֶּחִי midechi:
אֶתְהַלֵּךְ ethalech לִפְנֵי lifnei יְהֹוָהאדניאהדונהי Adonai בְּאַרְצוֹת be'artzot
הַחַיִּים hachayim אהיה אהיה יהוה, בינה ע"ה: הֶאֱמַנְתִּי he'emanti כִּי ki
אֲדַבֵּר adaber ראה אֲנִי ani אני עָנִיתִי aniti מְאֹד me'od: אֲנִי ani אני
אָמַרְתִּי amarti בְחָפְזִי vechofzi כָּל kol ילי הָאָדָם ha'adam מ"ה כֹּזֵב kozev:

YESOD - MA ASHIV

In the following paragraph, we find the verse *Ana Hashem*, which acknowledges that the Creator is our only true spiritual master and asks the Creator to give us signs, teachers, directions, and pathways that will lead us to the Light.

מָה־ ma מ"ה אָשִׁיב ashiv לַיהֹוָהאדניאהדונהי ladonai כָּל־ kol ילי
תַּגְמוּלוֹהִי tagmulohi עָלָי alai: כּוֹס־ kos אלהים, אהיה אדני
במילוי (כף וו סמך) = עסמ"ב, הברכה (למתק את ז' המלכים שמתו) יְשׁוּעוֹת yeshu'ot
אֶשָּׂא esa וּבְשֵׁם uvshem יְהֹוָהאדניאהדונהי Adonai אֶקְרָא ekra:

Then I called the Name of the Lord: Please, God, rescue my soul. For our Lord is gracious and righteous; our Lord is merciful. The Lord watches over the simple people. I became destitute and He saved me. Return, my soul, to your peacefulness, for the Lord has dealt kindly with you. For You have salvaged my soul from death, my eyes from tears, and my feet from stumbling. I shall walk before the Lord in the land of the living. I believed even as I spoke, when I was greatly impoverished, and I said in my haste, all men are treacherous." (Psalms 116:1-11)

YESOD - MA ASHIV

"How can I repay the Lord for all that He has bestowed upon me? I raise a cup of salvation and call out in the Name of the Lord.

נְדָרַי nedarai לַיהֹוָאדהנויאהדונהי ladonai אֲשַׁלֵּם ashalem נֶגְדָה־ negda
נגד, מזבח, זן, אל יהוה נָּא na לְכָל־ lechol יה אדני עַמּוֹ amo: יָקָר yakar
בְּעֵינֵי be'enei ריבוע דמ"ה יְהֹוָאדהנויאהדונהי Adonai הַמָּוְתָה hamavta
לַחֲסִידָיו lachasidav: אָנָּה ana יְהֹוָאדהנויאהדונהי Adonai כִּי־ ki אֲנִי ani אני
עַבְדֶּךָ avdecha פוי, אל אדני אֲנִי־ ani אני עַבְדְּךָ avdecha פוי, אל אדני
בֶּן־ ben אֲמָתֶךָ amatecha פִּתַּחְתָּ pitachta לְמוֹסֵרָי lemoserai: לְךָ־ lecha
אֶזְבַּח ezbach זֶבַח zevach תּוֹדָה toda וּבְשֵׁם uvshem יְהֹוָאדהנויאהדונהי Adonai
אֶקְרָא ekra: נְדָרַי nedarai לַיהֹוָאדהנויאהדונהי ladonai אֲשַׁלֵּם ashalem
נֶגְדָה־ negda נגד, מזבח, זן, אל יהוה נָּא na לְכָל־ lechol יה אדני עַמּוֹ amo:
בְּחַצְרוֹת bechatzrot בֵּית bet ב"פ ראה יְהֹוָאדהנויאהדונהי Adonai בְּתוֹכֵכִי betochechi
יְרוּשָׁלָיִם Yerushalayim הַלְלוּיָהּ haleluya אלהים, אהיה אדני ; ללה:

MALCHUT - HALELU

"All the nations of the world should praise God." Each nation, according to Kabbalah, has its own path to the Light. But there is only one Creator who gives Light to all of us. For this reason, "*Love your neighbor as yourself*" applies to all the nations of the world. We must treat all people with dignity. There is war between nations and chaos in society only because of the lack of compassion and sensitivity between people.

הַלְלוּ halelu אֶת־ et יְהֹוָאדהנויאהדונהי Adonai כָּל־ kol ילי גּוֹיִם goyim
שַׁבְּחוּהוּ shabechuhu כָּל־ kol ילי הָאֻמִּים ha'umim: כִּי ki גָבַר gavar
עָלֵינוּ alenu חַסְדּוֹ chasdo ג' הויות, מזלא (להמשיך הארה ממזלא עילאה)
וֶאֱמֶת־ ve'emet אהיה פעמים אהיה, ז"פ ס"ג יְהֹוָאדהנויאהדונהי Adonai
לְעוֹלָם le'olam ריבוע דס"ג ו' אותיות דס"ג הַלְלוּיָהּ haleluya אלהים, אהיה אדני ; ללה:

I shall pay my vows to the Lord before all His People. It is difficult in the Eyes of the Lord, the death of His pious ones. Please, Lord, I am Your servant. I am Your servant, then a son of Your handmaid. You have untied my bonds. To You I shall sacrifice a thanksgiving-offering and call out in the Name of the Lord. I shall pay my vows to the Lord, before all His People, in the courtyards of the Lord, within Jerusalem. Praise the Lord." (Psalms 116:12-end)

MALCHUT - HALELU

"Praise the Lord, all you people, Exalt Him, all you people. For His kindness has overwhelmed us and the truth of the Lord is eternal, Praise the Lord." (Psalms 117)

MALCHUT – HODU

The next four verses connect us to the four spiritual worlds, represented by the four different combinations of the *Yud, Hei, Vav,* and *Hei.* Each of these different combinations of letters is a transformer that channels currents of spiritual energy from various levels of the *Ten Sfirot* to our physical realm. Spiritually speaking, some people are connected to the Highest Worlds, while others are connected to the Middle and Lower Realms. The only way for humanity to achieve true unity is for each of us to let go of our ego and accept the fact that no one is higher or lower than anyone else; only our connections are different.

The *Talmud* reinforces this concept. We learn that a mosquito is actually on a much higher spiritual level than a man who isn't pursuing his spiritual work. A mosquito comes into this world to bite. As we all know, the mosquito does his job quite effectively. We came here to achieve a spiritual transformation. We give too much importance to a person's physical status in this world. However, whether one is an executive or a factory worker – if they are both doing their spiritual work, they are on the same level according to the Creator. Some people are never happy with where they are. Part of their work is to appreciate that they are doing their spiritual work. They should realize that they're on the same spiritual level as not only the people they envy but also the people they consider to be on a lower level than themselves. They are all working on spiritual tranformation.

Chochmah **(ע"ב – יוד הי ויו הי, קס"א –אלף הי יוד הי)**

הוֹדוּ hodu אהיה לַיהֹוָֽהאדניאהדונהי ladonai כִּי־ ki טוֹב tov והו

כי טוב = יהוה אהיה, אום, מבה, יזל

כִּי ki לְעוֹלָם le'olam ריבוע ס"ג וי' אותיות דס"ג חַסְדּוֹ chasdo

ג' הויות, מזלא (להמשיך הארה ממזלא עילאה) ; ר"ת = נגה:

Binah **(ס"ג – יוד הי ואו הי, קס"א – אלף הי יוד הי)**

יֹאמַר־ yomar נָא na יִשְׂרָאֵל Yisrael

כִּי ki לְעוֹלָם le'olam ריבוע ס"ג וי' אותיות דס"ג חַסְדּוֹ chasdo

ג' הויות, מזלא (להמשיך הארה ממזלא עילאה) ; ר"ת = נגה:

Zeir Anpin **(מ"ה – יוד הא ואו הא, קמ"ג – אלף הא יוד הא)**

יֹאמְרוּ־ yomru נָא na בֵית־ vet ב"פ ראה אַהֲרֹן Aharon

כִּי ki לְעוֹלָם le'olam ריבוע ס"ג וי' אותיות דס"ג חַסְדּוֹ chasdo

ג' הויות, מזלא (להמשיך הארה ממזלא עילאה) ; ר"ת = נגה:

Malchut **(ב"ן – יוד הה וו הה, קנ"א – אלף הה יוד הה)**

יֹאמְרוּ־ yomru נָא na יִרְאֵי yir'ei יְהֹוָֽהאדניאהדונהי Adonai

כִּי ki לְעוֹלָם le'olam ריבוע ס"ג וי' אותיות דס"ג חַסְדּוֹ chasdo

ג' הויות, מזלא (להמשיך הארה ממזלא עילאה) ; ר"ת = נגה:

MALCHUT – HODU

"Give thanks to the Lord for He is good, for His kindness is forever.
Let Israel say so now, for His kindness is forever.
Let the House of Aaron say so now, for His kindness is forever.
Let those who fear the Lord say so now, for His kindness is forever.

MIN HAMETZAR

"*From the straits I called upon God.*" Unfortunately, most of us call upon the Creator when we are in dire straits. Kabbalah teaches that we also need to call upon the Creator during good times and recognize the Light's influence in all of our good fortune. The *Zohar* teaches us that if we create a spiritual opening within ourselves no wider than the eye of a needle, God will answer us and open the Supernal Gates for us. Whatever its size, this opening for spirituality must be a complete opening where there can be no doubt or uncertainty.

א׳ ארך — מִן min הַמֵּצַר hametzar מצר קָרָאתִי karati יָּהּ Yah

ב׳ אפים — עָנָנִי anani בַמֶּרְחָב vamerchav יָּהּ: Yah

ג׳ ורב וחסד — יְהֹוָה (אדני אהדונהי) Adonai לִי li לֹא lo אִירָא ira

ד׳ נשא עון — מַה ma מ״ה יַּעֲשֶׂה ya'ase לִי li אָדָם adam מ״ה:

ה׳ ופשע — יְהֹוָה (אדני אהדונהי) Adonai לִי li בְּעֹזְרָי be'ozrai

ו׳ ונקה — וַאֲנִי va'ani אני אֶרְאֶה er'e בְשֹׂנְאָי: veson'ai

ז׳ פוקד — טוֹב tov והו לַחֲסוֹת lachasot בַּיהֹוָה (אדני אהדונהי) badonai

ח׳ על שלשים — מִבְּטֹחַ mibetoach בָּאָדָם ba'adam מ״ה:

ט׳ ועל רבעים — טוֹב tov והו לַחֲסוֹת lachasot בַּיהֹוָה (אדני אהדונהי) badonai

מִבְּטֹחַ mibetoa'ch בִּנְדִיבִים bindivim כָּל־ kol ילי גּוֹיִם goyim

סְבָבוּנִי sevavuni בְּשֵׁם beshem יְהֹוָה (אדני אהדונהי) Adonai כִּי ki אֲמִילַם: amilam

סַבּוּנִי sabuni גַם־ gam סְבָבוּנִי sevavuni בְּשֵׁם beshem יְהֹוָה (אדני אהדונהי) Adonai

כִּי ki אֲמִילַם: amilam סַבּוּנִי sabuni כִדְבוֹרִים chidvorim דֹּעֲכוּ do'achu

כְּאֵשׁ ke'esh קוֹצִים kotzim בְּשֵׁם beshem יְהֹוָה (אדני אהדונהי) Adonai

כִּי ki אֲמִילַם: amilam דָּחֹה dacho דְחִיתַנִי dechitani לִנְפֹּל linpol

וַיהֹוָה (אדני אהדונהי) vadonai עֲזָרָנִי: azarani עָזִּי ozi אלהים ע״ה, אהיה אדני ע״ה

וְזִמְרָת vezimrat יָהּ Yah וַיְהִי־ vay'hi לִי li לִישׁוּעָה: lishu'a

---

MIN HAMETZAR

Greatly from my distress I called out to the Lord. Patient Lord answered me in His expansiveness. The Lord is with me, I shall not fear those who bear iniquities. What can man do to me? And sins, the Lord shall come to my rescue and cleanses. And I shall look upon my enemies. It is good to take refuge in the Lord rather than to trust in man. It is better to take refuge in the Lord than to trust in noblemen. All the nations surrounded me. In the Name of the Lord, I shall cut them down. They surrounded me again and again. In the Name of the Lord, I shall cut them down. They surrounded me like bees, but are extinguished like a fire on thorns. With the Name of the Lord, I shall cut them down. They pushed me time and again to fall and the Lord came to my aid. The strength and cutting power of God were for me a salvation.

קוֹל kol רִנָּה rina וִישׁוּעָה vishua בְּאָהֳלֵי be'aholei צַדִּיקִים tzadikim

יְמִין yemin יְהֹוָאדניאהדונהי Adonai עֹשָׂה osa חָיִל chayil ומב:

יְמִין yemin יְהֹוָאדניאהדונהי Adonai רוֹמֵמָה romema ר״ת רי״י יְמִין yemin

יְהֹוָאדניאהדונהי Adonai עֹשָׂה osa רהע חָיִל chayil ומב: לֹא lo אָמוּת amut

כִּי ki אֶחְיֶה echye וַאֲסַפֵּר va'asaper מַעֲשֵׂי ma'asei יָהּ Yah:

יַסֹּר yasor יִסְּרַנִּי yisrani יָּהּ Yah ר״ת ייי וְלַמָּוֶת velamavet לֹא lo

נְתָנָנִי netanani: פִּתְחוּ pitchu לִי li שַׁעֲרֵי sha'arei צֶדֶק tzedek אָבֹא avo

בָם vam שם בן מ״ב אוֹדֶה ode יָהּ Yah: זֶה zeh הַשַּׁעַר hasha'ar

לַיהֹוָאדניאהדונהי ladonai צַדִּיקִים tzadikim יָבֹאוּ yavo'u בוֹ vo:

ODCHA

We have four verses that connect us to the four letters of the Tetragrammaton. Each verse is recited twice.

Yud – Chochmah - י

אוֹדְךָ odcha כִּי ki עֲנִיתָנִי anitani וַתְּהִי vatehi לִי li לִישׁוּעָה lishua: 2x

Hei – Binah - ה

אֶבֶן even מָאֲסוּ ma'asu הַבּוֹנִים habonim הָיְתָה hayta

לְרֹאשׁ lerosh ריבוע אלהים ואלהים דיודין ע״ה פִּנָּה pina ע״ב ס״ג ; ר״ת פהל: 2x

Vav – Zeir Anpin - ו

מֵאֵת me'et יְהֹוָאדניאהדונהי Adonai הָיְתָה hayta זֹּאת zot

הִיא hee נִפְלָאת niflat בְּעֵינֵינוּ be'enenu ריבוע דמ״ה: 2x

Hei – Malchut - ה

זֶה ze הַיּוֹם hayom ע״ה נגד, מזבח, זן, אל יהוה עָשָׂה asa יְהֹוָאדניאהדונהי Adonai

נָגִילָה nagila וְנִשְׂמְחָה venismecha מלה בוֹ vo: 2x

The sound of song and salvation is in the tents of the righteous. The right of the Lord does mighty things. The right of the Lord is raised. The right of the Lord does mighty things. I shall not die, but rather I shall live and tell of the deeds of God. God has chastised me again and again, but He has not surrendered me to death. Open for me the gates of righteousness. I will go through them and give thanks to God. This is the Gate of the Lord, the righteous may go through It.

ODCHA

I am grateful to You, for You have answered me and have become my salvation.
The stone that was rejected by the builders has become the main cornerstone.
This came about from the Lord, it is wondrous in our eyes.
The Lord has made this day let us be glad and rejoice in it.

ANA

These four verses offer us a different pathway to connect to the Light. The numeric equivalent of the word אנא (*Ana*) is 52, which is also the numerical value of the Name of God that connects to our physical realm of *Malchut*.

You should meditate that *Malchut*, which is: ב״ן, receives from *Chochmah* which is: ע״ב.

אָנָּא ana ב״ן (יוד הה וו הה) יְהֹוָאדנהיאהדונהי Adonai (יוד הי ויו הי)

הוֹשִׁיעָה hoshi'a יהוה וש״ע נהורין נָּא na:

You should meditate that *Malchut*, which is: ב״ן, receives from *Binah* which is: ס״ג.

אָנָּא ana ב״ן (יוד הה וו הה) יְהֹוָאדנהיאהדונהי Adonai (יוד הי ואו הי)

הוֹשִׁיעָה hoshi'a יהוה וש״ע נהורין נָּא na:

You should meditate that *Malchut*, which is ב״ן, receives from *Zeir Anpin* which is: מ״ה.

אָנָּא ana ב״ן (יוד הה וו הה) יְהֹוָאדנהיאהדונהי Adonai (יוד הא ואו הא)

הַצְלִיחָה hatzlicha נָּא na:

Meditate that *Malchut*, which is ב״ן, receives from all the above mentioned: ע״ב, ס״ג, מ״ה.

אָנָּא ana ב״ן (יוד הה וו הה) יְהֹוָאדנהיאהדונהי Adonai

(יוד הי ויו הי, יוד הי ואו הי, יוד הא ואו הא) הַצְלִיחָה hatzlicha נָּא na:

BARUCH HABA

We have four verses that connect us to the four letters of the Tetragrammaton. Each verse is recited twice.

Yud – Chochmah - י

בָּרוּךְ baruch הַבָּא haba בְּשֵׁם beshem יְהֹוָאדנהיאהדונהי Adonai

בֵּרַכְנוּכֶם berachnuchem מִבֵּית mibet ב״פ ראה יְהֹוָאדנהיאהדונהי Adonai: 2x

Hei – Binah - ה

אֵל El ייא״י (מילוי דס״ג) יְהֹוָאדנהיאהדונהי Adonai וַיָּאֶר vaya'er כף ויו זין ויו

לָנוּ lanu אלהים, אהיה אדני אִסְרוּ־ isru חַג chag בַּעֲבֹתִים ba'avotim

עַד־ ad קַרְנוֹת karnot הַמִּזְבֵּחַ hamizbe'ach נגד, זן, אל יהוה: 2x

---

ANA

We beseech You, Lord, save us now. We beseech You, Lord, save us now.
We beseech You, Lord, give us success now. We beseech You, Lord, give us success now.

BARUCH HABA

Blessed is the one who comes in the Name of the Lord. We bless you from The House of the Lord.
The Lord is God, He illuminates for us. Tie the holiday-offering with ropes till the corners of the Altar.

***Vav – Zeir Anpin* - ו**

ve'odeka וְאוֹדֶךָּ Ata אַתָּה Eli אֵלִי

2x :aromemeka אֲרוֹמְמֶךָּ ילה ; דמב ,דע״ב מילוי Elohai אֱלֹהַי

***Hei – Malchut* - ה**

והו tov טוֹב ki כִּי ladonai לַיהֹוָהאדניאהדונהי אהיה hodu הוֹדוּ

כי טוב = יהוה אהיה, אום, מבה, יזל

chasdo חַסְדּוֹ דס״ג אותיות וי׳ ס״ג ריבוע le'olam לְעוֹלָם ki כִּי

2x : ג׳ הויות, מזלא (להמשיך הארה ממזלא עילאה) ; ר״ת = נגה

ילי kol כָּל ילה Elohenu אֱלֹהֵינוּ Adonai יְהֹוָהאדניאהדונהי yehalelucha יְהַלְלוּךָ

osei עוֹשֵׂי vetzadikim וְצַדִּיקִים vachasidecha וַחֲסִידֶיךָ ma'asecha מַעֲשֶׂיךָ

Yisrael יִשְׂרָאֵל ראה ב״פ bet בֵּית ve'amcha וְעַמְּךָ retzonecha רְצוֹנֶךָ

מ״ה ריבוע יהוה ריבוע יהוה vivarchu וִיבָרְכוּ yodu יוֹדוּ berina בְּרִנָּה kulam כֻּלָּם

,ב״ן kevodecha כְּבוֹדֶךָ shem שֵׁם et אֶת vifa'aru וִיפָאֲרוּ vishabchu וִישַׁבְּחוּ

ulshimcha וּלְשִׁמְךָ .lehodot לְהוֹדוֹת והו tov טוֹב lecha לְךָ ki כִּי .לכב

olam עוֹלָם ve'ad וְעַד ume'olam וּמֵעוֹלָם .lezamer לְזַמֵּר na'im נָעִים

Ata אַתָּה baruch בָּרוּךְ :(מילוי דס״ג) ייא״י El אֵל Ata אַתָּה

.batishbachot בַּתִּשְׁבָּחוֹת mehulal מְהֻלָּל melech מֶלֶךְ Adonai יְהֹוָהאדניאהדונהי

:יאהדונהי amen אָמֵן

You are my God and I thank You, my God, and I shall exalt You.

Be grateful to the Lord for He is good. For His kindness is forever." (Psalms 118)

All Your deeds and all Your pious ones shall praise You, Lord, our God, and the righteous ones who do Your will, as well as Your nation, the House of Israel. They shall all joyously give thanks, bless, praise and glorify the Name of Your glory, because to You it is good to give thanks, and to Your Name, it is pleasing to sing. And from this world until the next, You are God. Blessed are You, Lord, a King Who is extolled in praises. Amen.

Recite this verse three times to connect to the Light of protection.

וְאַבְרָהָם veAvraham וז"פ אל, רי"ו ול"ב נתיבות החכמה, רמ"ח (אברים), עסמ"ב וט"ז אותיות פשוטות
זָקֵן zaken בָּא ba בַּיָּמִים bayamim נלך וַיהֹוָ‍אדהנהי‍ אהדונהי vadonai בֵּרַךְ berach אֶת־ et
אַבְרָהָם Avraham וז"פ אל, רי"ו ול"ב נתיבות החכמה, רמ"ח (אברים), עסמ"ב וט"ז אותיות פשוטות
בַּכֹּל bakol ב"ן, לכב:

Meditate on the Name of the Angel (וְבַדְיָה) derived from the above mentioned verse.

יִשְׁמְרֵנִי yishmereni וִיחַיֵּנִי viychayeni, כֵּן ken יְהִי yehi רָצוֹן ratzon
מהש ע"ה, ע"ב בריבוע וקס"א ע"ה, אל שדי ע"ה מִלְּפָנֶיךָ milfanecha ס"ג מ"ה ב"ן
אֱלֹהִים Elohim אהיה אדני ; ילה חַיִּים chayim אהיה אהיה יהוה, בינה ע"ה וּמֶלֶךְ umelech
עוֹלָם olam אֲשֶׁר asher בְּיָדוֹ beyado נֶפֶשׁ nefesh כָּל kol ילי חָי chai אָמֵן amen
יאהדונהי כֵּן ken יְהִי yehi רָצוֹן ratzon מהש ע"ה, ע"ב בריבוע וקס"א ע"ה, אל שדי ע"ה:

KADDISH TITKABAL

יִתְגַּדַּל yitgadal וְיִתְקַדַּשׁ veyitkadash שדי ומילוי שדי ; י"א אותיות כמנין ו"ה
שְׁמֵיהּ shemei (שם י"ה דע"ב) רַבָּא raba קנ"א ב"ן, יהוה אלהים יהוה אדני,
מילוי קס"א וס"ג, מ"ה ברבוע וע"ב ע"ה ; ר"ת = ו"פ אלהים ; ס"ת = ג"פ יב"ק: אָמֵן amen אידהנויה.
בְּעָלְמָא be'alma דִּי di בְרָא vera כִּרְעוּתֵיהּ chir'utei.
וְיַמְלִיךְ veyamlich מַלְכוּתֵיהּ mal'chutei. וְיַצְמַח veyatzmach
פּוּרְקָנֵיהּ purkanei. וִיקָרֵב vikarev מְשִׁיחֵיהּ meshichei: אָמֵן amen אידהנויה.
בְּחַיֵּיכוֹן bechayechon וּבְיוֹמֵיכוֹן uvyomechon וּבְחַיֵּי uvchayei
דְכָל dechol ילי בֵּית bet ב"פ ראה יִשְׂרָאֵל Yisrael בַּעֲגָלָא ba'agala
וּבִזְמַן uvizman קָרִיב kariv וְאִמְרוּ ve'imru אָמֵן amen: אָמֵן amen אידהנויה.

"And Abraham was old, and ripe in age, and God has blessed Abraham with everything." (Genesis 24:1) *May He preserve me and enliven me. And may it so be pleasing before You the God of life and the King of the world, in Whose Hands lie the spirit of all that lives. Amen, may it so be His pleasure.*

KADDISH TITKABAL

May His great Name be more exalted and sanctified. (Amen)
In the world that He created according to His will, and may His kingdom reign. And may He cause His redemption to sprout and may He bring the Mashiach closer. (Amen) *In your lifetimes and in your days and in the lifetime of all the House of Israel, speedily and in the near future, and you shall say, Amen.* (Amen)

The congregation and the *chazan* say the following:

28 words (until *be'alma*) and 28 letters (until *almaya*)

יְהֵא yehe שְׁמֵיהּ shemei (שם י״ה דס״ג) רַבָּא raba קנ״א ב״ן, יהוה אלהים יהוה אדני, מילוי קס״א וס״ג, מ״ה ברבוע וע״ב ע״ה מְבָרַךְ mevarach, לְעָלַם le'alam לְעָלְמֵי le'almei עָלְמַיָּא almaya• יִתְבָּרַךְ yitbarach•

Seven words with six letters each (שם בן מ״ב) – and, seven times the letter *Vav* (שם בן מ״ב)

וְיִשְׁתַּבַּח veyishtabach י״פ ע״ב יהוה אל אבג יתץ•

וְיִתְפָּאַר veyitpa'ar הי נו יה קרע שטן• וְיִתְרוֹמַם veyitromam וה כוזו נגד יכש•

וְיִתְנַשֵּׂא veyitnase במוכסז בטר צתג• וְיִתְהַדָּר veyit'hadar כוזו יה וקב טנע•

וְיִתְעַלֶּה veyit'ale וה יוד ה יגל פזק• וְיִתְהַלָּל veyit'halal א ואו הא שקו צית•

שְׁמֵיהּ shemei (שם י״ה דמ״ה) דְּקוּדְשָׁא dekudsha בְּרִיךְ verich הוּא hu:

אָמֵן amen אידהנויה•

לְעֵלָּא le'ela מִן min כָּל kol ילי בִּרְכָתָא birchata• שִׁירָתָא shirata• תֻּשְׁבְּחָתָא tishbechata וְנֶחָמָתָא venechamata• דַּאֲמִירָן da'amiran בְּעָלְמָא be'alma וְאִמְרוּ ve'imru אָמֵן amen: אָמֵן amen אידהנויה.

תִּתְקַבַּל titkabal צְלוֹתָנָא tzelotana וּבָעוּתָנָא uva'utana עִם im צְלוֹתְהוֹן tzelotehon וּבָעוּתְהוֹן uva'utehon דְּכָל dechol ילי בֵּית bet ב״פ ראה יִשְׂרָאֵל Yisrael קֳדָם kadam אֲבוּנָא avuna דְּבִשְׁמַיָּא devishmaya וְאִמְרוּ ve'imru אָמֵן amen: אָמֵן amen אידהנויה•

May His great Name be blessed forever and for all eternity. Blessed and lauded, and glorified, and exalted, and extolled, and honored, and uplifted, and praised be the Name of the Holy Blessed One (Amen) *Above all blessings, songs, praises, and words of consolation that may be said in the world, and you shall say, Amen.* (Amen) *May our prayers and pleas be accepted, together with the prayers and pleas of the entire House of Israel, before our Father in Heaven, and you say, Amen.* (Amen)

יְהֵא yehe שְׁלָמָא shelama רַבָּא raba קנ"א ב"ן, יהוה אלהים יהוה אדני, מילוי קס"א וס"ג,

מ"ה ברבוע וע"ב ע"ה מִן min שְׁמַיָּא shemaya• וְחַיִּים chayim אהיה אהיה יהוה, בינה ע"ה

וְשָׂבָע vesava וִישׁוּעָה vishu'a וְנֶחָמָה venechama וְשֵׁיזָבָא veshezava

וּרְפוּאָה urfu'a וּגְאֻלָּה ug'ula וּסְלִיחָה uslicha וְכַפָּרָה vechapara

וְרֵיוַח verevach וְהַצָּלָה vehatzala• לָנוּ lanu אלהים, אהיה אדני וּלְכָל ulchol יה אדני

עַמּוֹ amo יִשְׂרָאֵל Yisrael וְאִמְרוּ ve'imru אָמֵן amen: אָמֵן amen אידהנויה.

Take three steps backwards and say:

עוֹשֶׂה ose שָׁלוֹם shalom

בִּמְרוֹמָיו bimromav ע"ב, ריבוע יהוה• הוּא hu בְּרַחֲמָיו berachamav

יַעֲשֶׂה ya'ase שָׁלוֹם shalom עָלֵינוּ alenu ר"ת ש"ע נהורין•

וְעַל ve'al כָּל kol ילי ; עמם עַמּוֹ amo יִשְׂרָאֵל Yisrael וְאִמְרוּ ve'imru אָמֵן amen:

אָמֵן amen אידהנויה•

May there be abundant peace from heaven; Life, contentment, salvation, consolation, deliverance, healing, redemption, pardon, atonement, comfort, and relief. For us and for His entire nation, Israel, and you shall say, Amen. (Amen) *He, Who makes peace in His high places, He, in His compassion, shall make peace upon us And upon His entire nation, Israel, and you shall say, Amen.* (Amen)

Before we open the Ark we say:
On *Shabbat* we start here:

אַתָּה Ata הָרְאֵתָ hor'eta לָדַעַת lada'at כִּי ki יְהֹוָהאדניאהדונהי Adonai הוּא hu

הָאֱלֹהִים haElohim אהיה אדני ; ילה ; ה' הוא האלקים = ענו ע"ג ; ר"ת יהה אֵין en עוֹד od

מִלְּבַדּוֹ milvado מ"ב: אֵין־ en כָּמוֹךָ kamocha בָאֱלֹהִים vaElohim אהיה אדני ; ילה

אֲדֹנָי Adonai ללה וְאֵין ve'en כְּמַעֲשֶׂיךָ: kema'asecha

When *Shavuot* falls on weekdays we start here:

יְהִי yehi יְהֹוָהאדניאהדונהי Adonai אֱלֹהֵינוּ Elohenu ילה עִמָּנוּ imanu ריבוע ס"ג, קס"א

כַּאֲשֶׁר ka'asher ע"ה וד' אותיות הָיָה haya יהה עִם־ im אֲבֹתֵינוּ avotenu אַל־ al

יַעַזְבֵנוּ ya'azvenu וְאַל־ ve'al יִטְּשֵׁנוּ: yiteshenu הוֹשִׁיעָה hoshi'a יהוה וש"ע נהורין

אֶת־ et עַמֶּךָ amecha ס"ת כהת, משיח בן דוד ע"ה וּבָרֵךְ uvarech אֶת־ et

נַחֲלָתֶךָ nachalatecha וּרְעֵם ur'em וְנַשְּׂאֵם venas'em עַד־ ad הָעוֹלָם: ha'olam

וַיְהִי vay'hi בִּנְסֹעַ binso'a הָאָרֹן ha'aron וַיֹּאמֶר vayomer מֹשֶׁה Moshe מהש,

ע"ב בריבוע קס"א, אל שדי, ד"פ אלהים ע"ה קוּמָה kuma קנ"א (מקוה) | יְהֹוָהאדניאהדונהי Adonai

וְיָפֻצוּ veyafutzu אֹיְבֶיךָ oyvecha וְיָנֻסוּ veyanusu מְשַׂנְאֶיךָ mesanecha

מִפָּנֶיךָ mipanecha ס"ג מ"ה ב"ן: קוּמָה kuma קנ"א (מקוה) יְהֹוָהאדניאהדונהי Adonai

לִמְנוּחָתֶךָ limnuchatecha אַתָּה Ata וַאֲרוֹן va'aron עֻזֶּךָ: uzecha

כֹּהֲנֶיךָ kohanecha יִלְבְּשׁוּ־ yilbeshu צֶדֶק tzedek וַחֲסִידֶיךָ vachasidecha

יְרַנֵּנוּ: yeranenu בַּעֲבוּר ba'avur דָּוִד David עַבְדֶּךָ avdecha פוי, אל אדני

אַל־ al תָּשֵׁב tashev פְּנֵי penei חכמה בינה מְשִׁיחֶךָ: meshichecha

---

"You have shown to be known that the Lord is your God and there is none beside Him." (Deuteronomy 4:35) *"There is none like You among the deities Lord and there is nothing like Your works."* (Psalms 86:8) *"May the Lord, our God, be with us as He was with our forefathers. May He not abandon or forsake us."* (1 Kings 8:57) *"Save Your people and bless Your heritage. Lead them and uplift them forever."* (Psalms 28:9) *When the Ark traveled forward, Moses would say: Arise, Lord. Let Your enemies be scattered and let those who hate You flee before You."* (Numbers 10:35) *"Arise Lord to Your resting place, You and the Ark of Your strength. Your priests don justice and your pious once shall sing. For the sake of David, Your servant, do not turn Your countenance away from Your anointed one."* (Psalms 132:8-10)

OPENING OF THE ARK

Drawing the Light of *Chochmah*.

Rabbi Shimon Bar Yochai says: "While the Ark is open, we should prepare ourselves with awe. Everyone should arouse an inner sense of wonder, as if we are actually standing on Mount Sinai, trembling as we behold the overwhelming expression of Light. Silent we stand, focused solely on the opportunity of hearing each sacred word of the scroll. When we take out the Torah in public to read, all the Gates of Mercy in Heaven are open, and we awaken a love from above."

וַיְהִי vayhi בִּנְסֹעַ binso'a הָאָרֹן ha'aron וַיֹּאמֶר vayomer מֹשֶׁה Moshe

מהש, ע"ב בריבוע וקס"א, אל שדי, ד"פ אלהים ע"ה קוּמָה kuma קנ"א (מקוה) |

יְהֹוָהאדניאהדונהי Adonai וְיָפֻצוּ veyafutzu אֹיְבֶיךָ oyvecha וְיָנֻסוּ veyanusu

מְשַׂנְאֶיךָ mesan'echa מִפָּנֶיךָ mipanecha ס"ג מ"ה ב"ן: כִּי ki

מִצִּיּוֹן miTziyon יוסף, ו' הויות, קנאה תֵּצֵא tetze תוֹרָה torah וּדְבַר udvar ראה

יְהֹוָהאדניאהדונהי Adonai מִירוּשָׁלָם mirushalaim: בָּרוּךְ baruch שֶׁנָּתַן shenatan

תּוֹרָה torah לְעַמּוֹ le'amo יִשְׂרָאֵל Yisrael בִּקְדֻשָּׁתוֹ bikdushato.

THE THIRTEEN ATTRIBUTES

The 13 Attributes are 13 virtues or properties that reflect 13 aspects of our relationship with the Creator. These 13 Attributes are how we interact with God in our daily lives, whether we know it or not. They work like a mirror.

When we look into a mirror and smile, the image smiles back. When we look into a mirror and curse, the image curses back. If we perform a negative action in our world, the mirror reflects negative energy at us. There are 13 Attributes that have these reflecting properties within us. As we attempt to transform our reactive nature into proactive, this direct feedback guides and corrects us.

The number 13 also represents one above the 12 signs of the zodiac. The 12 signs control our find instinctive, reactive nature. The number 13 gives us control over the 12 signs, which, in essence, gives us control over our behavior.

OPENING OF THE ARK

"When the Ark traveled forward, Moses would say: Arise, Lord. Let Your enemies be scattered and let those who hate You flee before You." (Numbers 10:35) *"Because out of Zion shall the Torah emerge, and the Word of the Lord from Jerusalem."* (Isaiah 2:3) *Blessed is He Who gave the Torah to His Nation, Israel, due to His Holiness.*

On *Shabbat* we skip the 13 Attributes.

We recite the verse three times:

יהוה אדני אהדונהי Adonai | יהוה אדני אהדונהי Adonai

(1 אל el ייא״ מילוי דס״ג (Keter) (2 רחום rachum (Chochmah) (3 וחנון vechanun

(4 ארך erech (5 אפים apayim (6 ורב verav חסד chesed ע״ב, ריבוע יהוה

(7 ואמת ve'emet אהיה פעמים אהיה, ז״פ ס״ג: (8 נצר notzer חסד chesed ע״ב, ריבוע יהוה

(9 לאלפים la'alafim ר״ת שם נוזל (10 נשא nose עון avon (11 ופשע vafesha

(12 וחטאה vechata'a (13 ונקה venake קס״א (אלף הי יוד הי)

וע״י שם זה יכוין לברר ולנקות את נצוצי הקדושה שנפלו עם הקיטרוגים, להעלותם לשורשם:

THE PRAYER FROM THE ARI (THE PERSONAL WISH)

It is through the merit of Kabbalist Rav Isaac Luria (the Ari), that we have an opportunity to make a personal wish on Shavuot to effect change for the entire year. All too often, we ask for what we want instead of asking for what we really need to help us grow spiritually. Only through growth and inner transformation can we achieve lasting fulfillment as opposed to instant and momentary gratification.

רבונו ribono של shel עולם olam, מלא male משאלותי mishalotai

לטובה letova אכא, והפק vehafek רצוני retzoni, ותן veten שאלתי she'elati

ומחול umchol כל kol ילי עונותי avonotai ועונות va'avonot

בני benei ביתי beti ב״פ ראה, מחילה mechila בחסד bechesed ע״ב, ריבוע יהוה,

מחילה mechila ברחמים berachamim מצפץ, אלהים דיודין, י״פ ייי,

וטהרני vetahareni מהפשעים mehapsha'im והחטאים vehachata'im.

וזכרני vezochreni ברצון beratzon מהש ע״ה, ע״ב בריבוע וקס״א ע״ה, אל שדי ע״ה

טוב tov והו מלפניך milfanecha ס״ג מ״ה ב״ן ופקדני ufokdeni

בפקדת bifkudat ישועה yeshu'a ורחמים verachamim,

THE THIRTEEN ATTRIBUTES

"Lord, Lord, (1) God (Keter) (2) Compassionate (Chochmah) (3) Gracious (4) Greatly (5) Patient (6) Abounding with kindness (7) and truth (8) He keeps kindness (9) for the thousands (10) He bears iniquities (11) and sin (12) and transgression (13) and cleanses." (Exodus 34:6-7)

THE PRAYER FROM THE ARI (THE PERSONAL WISH)

Master of the world,

fulfill my requests favorably and bring out my desire and give me my request and forgive all my sins and the sins of the members of my household and forgiveness through favor, a forgiveness through mercy. Purify me from sins and crimes. And remember me favorably before You and visit me with redemption and mercy.

וְזָכְרֵנִי vezochreni לְחַיִּים lechayim אהיה אהיה יהוה, בינה ע״ה טוֹבִים tovim
וַאֲרוּכִים ve'arukim, וּפַרְנָסָה ufarnasa טוֹבָה tova אכא וְכַלְכָּלָה vechalkala,
וְלֶחֶם velechem ג״פ יהוה לֶאֱכוֹל le'echol וּבֶגֶד uveged לִלְבּוֹשׁ lilbosh,
וְעוֹשֶׁר ve'osher וְכָבוֹד vechavod וַאֲרִיכוּת ve'arichut יָמִים yamim נלך
בְּתוֹרָתֶךָ betoratecha וּבְמִצְוֹתֶיךָ vevemitzotecha, וְהָפֵק vehafek תְּעָלָה te'ala
וּרְפוּאָה urfu'a לְכָל lechol יה אדני מַכְאוֹבֵי mach'ovei לִבֵּנוּ libenu,
וּתְבָרֵךְ utvarech מַעֲשֵׂי ma'asei יָדֵינוּ yadenu, וּגְזוֹר ugzor עָלֵינוּ alenu
גְּזֵרוֹת gezerot טוֹבוֹת tovot וּבַטֵּל uvatel מֵעָלֵינוּ me'alenu כָּל kol ילי
גְּזֵרוֹת gezerot קָשׁוֹת kashot וְרָעוֹת veraot. אָמֵן יאהדונהי amen כֵּן ken יְהִי yehi
רָצוֹן ratzon מהש ע״ה, ע״ב בריבוע וקס״א ע״ה, אל שדי ע״ה. יִהְיוּ yihyu אל (ייא״י מילוי דס״ג)
לְרָצוֹן leratzon מהש ע״ה, ע״ב בריבוע וקס״א ע״ה, אל שדי ע״ה אִמְרֵי imrei
פִּי fi ר״ת אֶלֶף = אלף למד ⊥ שין דלת יוד ע״ה וְהֶגְיוֹן vehegyon לִבִּי libi
לְפָנֶיךָ lefanecha ס״ג מ״ה ב״ן יְהֹוָאדהיאהדונהי Adonai צוּרִי tzuri וְגֹאֲלִי vego'ali:

BERICH SHEMEI

This section is taken directly from the *Zohar* and appears in its original Aramaic. The *Berich Shemei* works like a time machine that literally transports our soul to Mount Sinai, when Moses received the tablets. By revisiting the exact time and place of the revelation, we are able to draw down aspects of the original Light through the reading of the Torah. The *Berich Shemei* contains 130 words. Adam was separated from his wife, Eve, for 130 years during which time he sinned. Each word in the prayer helps to correct one of those years. Each of us was included in the soul of Adam. We are Adam. Adam is merely the code name of the unified soul that includes every human being who has and will ever walk this planet.

בְּרִיךְ berich שְׁמֵיהּ shemei דְּמָארֵי demarei עָלְמָא alma
בְּרִיךְ berich כִּתְרָךְ kitrach וְאַתְרָךְ ve'atrach. יְהֵא yehe
רְעוּתָךְ re'utach עִם im עַמָּךְ amach יִשְׂרָאֵל Yisrael לְעָלַם le'alam.

Remember me for a good and long life and with good sustenance and with earnings and with bread to eat and with clothes to wear and with wealth, honor, and long days in the study of Your Torah and in fulfilling Your commandments. Send cure and healing to all the pains of our hearts and bless our handiwork, Amen, may it so be Your will. Sentence us with good verdicts and cancel for us all evil and hard verdicts. "And may the words of my mouth and the thoughts of my heart be favorable to You, Lord, my Rock and my Redeemer." (Psalms 19:15)

BERICH SHEMEI

Blessed is the Name of the Master of the World.

Blessed are Your Crown and Your Location. May Your desire be with Your Nation, Israel, forever.

וּפוּרְקַן ufurkan יְמִינָךְ yeminach אַחֲזֵי achzei לְעַמָּךְ le'amach

בְּבֵית bevet ב"פ ראה מַקְדְּשָׁךְ ♦mikdashach לְאַמְטוּיֵי le'amtuye לָנָא lana

מִטּוּב mituv נְהוֹרָךְ ♦nehorach וּלְקַבֵּל ulkabel צְלוֹתָנָא tzelotana

בְּרַחֲמִין ♦berachamin יְהֵא yehe רַעֲוָא ra'ava קֳדָמָךְ kodamach

דְּתוֹרִיךְ detorich לָן lan חַיִּין chayin בְּטִיבוּ ♦betivu וְלֶהֱוֵי velehevei אֲנָא ana ב"ן

עַבְדָּךְ avdach פוי, אל אדני פְּקִידָא pekida בְּגוֹ bego צַדִּיקַיָּא ♦tzadikaya

לְמִרְחַם lemircham אברהם, וז"פ אל, רי"ו ול"ב נתיבות החכמה, רמ"ח (אברים), עסמ"ב וט"ז אותיות

פשוטות עָלַי alai וּלְמִנְטַר ulmintar יָתִי yati וְיַת veyat כָּל kal ילי

דִּילִי dili וְדִי vedi לְעַמָּךְ le'amach יִשְׂרָאֵל ♦Yisrael אַנְתְּ ant הוּא hu

זָן zan נגד, מזבח, אל יהוה לְכֹלָּא lechola וּמְפַרְנֵס umfarnes לְכֹלָּא ♦lechola

אַנְתְּ ant הוּא hu שַׁלִּיט shalit עַל al כֹּלָּא ♦kola אַנְתְּ ant הוּא hu

דְּשַׁלִּיט deshalit עַל al מַלְכַיָּא malchaya וּמַלְכוּתָא umalchuta דִּילָךְ dilach

הִיא ♦hee אֲנָא ana ב"ן עַבְדָּא avda דְקוּדְשָׁא dekudsha בְּרִיךְ berich

הוּא hu דְּסָגִידְנָא desagidna קַמֵּהּ kame וּמִן umin קַמֵּהּ kame דִּיקַר dikar

אוֹרַיְתֵהּ orayte בְּכָל־ bechol ב"ן, לכב עִדָּן idan וְעִדָּן ♦ve'idan

לָא la עַל al אֱנָשׁ enash רְחִיצְנָא ♦rachitzna וְלָא vela עַל al בַּר bar

אֱלָהִין elahin ילה סָמִיכְנָא ♦samichna אֶלָּא ela בֶּאֱלָהָא be'elaha

דִשְׁמַיָּא ♦dishmaya דְּהוּא dehu אֱלָהָא elaha קְשׁוֹט ♦keshot

וְאוֹרַיְתֵהּ ve'orayte קְשׁוֹט keshot וּנְבִיאוֹהִי unvi'ohi קְשׁוֹט ♦keshot

וּמַסְגֵּא umasgei לְמֶעְבַּד lemebad טַבְוָן tavevan וּקְשׁוֹט ♦ukshot

---

The redemption of Your Right may You show to Your Nation in Your Temple. May You fill us with the best of Your enlightenment, and may You receive our prayers with mercy. May it be pleasing before You to lengthen our lives with good. And I, Your servant, shall be remembered together with the righteous ones. Have mercy on me and protect me, and all that I have, and all that belongs to Your Nation, Israel. You are the One Who nourishes all and provides all with their livelihood. You are the One Who controls everything. You have control over kings, and their kingdoms are Yours. I am the servant of the Holy Blessed One, as I prostrate myself before Him and before the glory of His Torah, at each and every moment. I put not my trust in any man, and I have no faith in the sons of the gods. My trust and faith are only in the God in Heaven, Who is the true God; His Torah is true; His prophets are true; and He abundantly performs compassion and truth.

בֵּיהּ bei אֲנָא ana ב"ן רָחִיץ rachitz וְלִשְׁמֵהּ velishme יַקִּירָא yakira
קַדִּישָׁא kadisha אֲנָא ana ב"ן אֵמַר emar תֻּשְׁבְּחָן tushbechan. יְהֵא yehe
רַעֲוָא ra'ava קֳדָמָךְ kodamach דְּתִפְתַּח detiftach לִבָּאִי liba'i
בְּאוֹרָיְתָךְ be'oraytach. (וְתִיהַב vetihav לִי li בְּנִין benin דִּכְרִין dichrin
דְּעָבְדִין de'avdin רְעוּתָךְ re'utach.) וְתַשְׁלִים vetashlim מִשְׁאֲלִין mish'alin
דְּלִבָּאִי deliba'i וְלִבָּא veliba דְּכָל dechol ילי עַמָּךְ amach יִשְׂרָאֵל Yisrael
לְטַב letav וּלְחַיִּין ulchayin וְלִשְׁלָם velishlam אָמֵן amen יאהדונהי:

TAKING OUT THE TORAH FROM THE ARK

The *Torah* is taken out to give us all a chance to make a personal connection with it, either by kissing or touching it. Sometimes, people rush to make their connection, pushing, crowding, and shoving others aside as they try to touch the scroll. Spiritually, these actions reflect energy opposite to that of the *Torah*. The *Torah* connection is not just physical. Connections to the *Torah* are made by way of a spiritual state of mind, which includes tolerance and care for others. One cannot be in the right spiritual frame of mind if he is rude to another individual.

בָּרוּךְ baruch הַמָּקוֹם hamakom שֶׁנָּתַן shenatan תּוֹרָה torah לְעַמּוֹ le'amo
יִשְׂרָאֵל Yisrael בָּרוּךְ baruch הוּא hu: אַשְׁרֵי ashrei הָעָם ha'am
שֶׁכָּכָה shekacha משה, מהש, ע"ב בריבוע קס"א, אל שדי, ד"פ אלהים ע"ה לוֹ lo אַשְׁרֵי ashrei
הָעָם ha'am ר"ת לאה שֶׁיְהֹוָה sheAdonai יאהדונהי אֱלֹהָיו Elohav ילה:

Before the *Torah* is carried to the *bimah* (podium), the *chazan* says:

גַּדְּלוּ gadelu לַיהֹוָה ladonai יאהדונהי אִתִּי iti וּנְרוֹמְמָה uneromema
שְׁמוֹ shemo מהש ע"ה, ע"ב בריבוע וקס"א ע"ה, אל שדי ע"ה יַחְדָּו yachdav:

In Him, I trust and I say praises
to His Holy and precious Name. May it be pleasing before You that You shall open my heart with Your Torah (and that You may give me male sons, who shall fulfill Your desire). And may You fulfill the requests of my heart and the heart of Your entire Nation, Israel, for good, for life, and for peace. Amen.

TAKING OUT THE TORAH FROM THE ARK

Blessed is the Providence Who had given the Torah to His nation, Israel,
Blessed is He. "Joyfull is the nationthat this is so for them, joyfull is the nation that the Lord is their God." *(Psalms 144:15)* *"Proclaim the Lord's greatness with me and let us exalt His Name together."* *(Psalms 34:4)*

Then the congregation says the following while the *Torah* is carried to the *bimah*:

לְךָ lecha יְהֹוָה יאהדונהי Adonai הַגְּדֻלָּה hagedula וְהַגְּבוּרָה vehagevura רי"ו
וְהַתִּפְאֶרֶת vehatiferet וְהַנֵּצַח vehanetzach וְהַהוֹד vehahod ההה כִּי־ ki
כֹל chol ילי בַּשָּׁמַיִם bashamayim י"פ טל, י"פ כוזו וּבָאָרֶץ uva'aretz לְךָ lecha
יְהֹוָה יאהדונהי Adonai הַמַּמְלָכָה hamamlacha וְהַמִּתְנַשֵּׂא vehamitnase
לְכֹל lechol יה אדני לְרֹאשׁ lerosh ריבוע אלהים ואלהים דיודין ע"ה: רוֹמְמוּ romemu
יְהֹוָה יאהדונהי Adonai אֱלֹהֵינוּ Elohenu ילה וְהִשְׁתַּחֲווּ vehishtachavu
לַהֲדֹם lahadom רַגְלָיו raglav קָדוֹשׁ kadosh הוּא hu: רוֹמְמוּ romemu
יְהֹוָה יאהדונהי Adonai אֱלֹהֵינוּ Elohenu ילה וְהִשְׁתַּחֲווּ vehishtachavu לְהַר lehar
קָדְשׁוֹ kodsho כִּי־ ki קָדוֹשׁ kadosh יְהֹוָה יאהדונהי Adonai אֱלֹהֵינוּ Elohenu ילה:

Some add this section:

אֵין־ en קָדוֹשׁ kadosh כַּיהֹוָה יאהדונהי kadonai כִּי ki אֵין en בִּלְתֶּךָ biltecha
וְאֵין ve'en צוּר tzur אלהים דההין ע"ה כֵּאלֹהֵינוּ kelohenu ילה: כִּי ki מִי mi ילי
אֱלוֹהַּ Eloha מ"ב מִבַּלְעֲדֵי mibal'adei יְהֹוָה יאהדונהי Adonai וּמִי umi ילי צוּר tzur
אלהים דההין ע"ה זוּלָתִי zulati אֱלֹהֵינוּ Elohenu ילה: תּוֹרָה torah צִוָּה־ tziva לָנוּ lanu
אלהים, אהיה אדני מֹשֶׁה Moshe מהש, ע"ב בריבוע וקס"א, אל שדי, ד"פ אלהים ע"ה
מוֹרָשָׁה morasha קְהִלַּת kehilat יַעֲקֹב Yaakov ז' הויות, יאהדונהי אידהנויה:
עֵץ־ etz חַיִּים chayim אהיה אהיה יהוה, בינה ע"ה הִיא hee
לַמַּחֲזִיקִים lamachazikim ר"ת להח בָּהּ ba וְתֹמְכֶיהָ vetomcheha מְאֻשָּׁר me'ushar:
דְּרָכֶיהָ deracheha דַּרְכֵי־ darchei נֹעַם no'am וְכָל־ vechol ילי
נְתִיבוֹתֶיהָ netivoteha שָׁלוֹם shalom: שָׁלוֹם shalom רָב rav
לְאֹהֲבֵי le'ohavei תוֹרָתֶךָ toratecha וְאֵין־ ve'en לָמוֹ lamo מִכְשׁוֹל michshol:

"Yours, Lord, is the greatness, the strength, the splendor, the triumph, and the glory, and everything in the Heavens and the Earth. Yours, Lord, is the Kingdom and the sovereignty over every leader." (I Chronicles 29:11) *"Exalt the Lord, our God, and prostrate yourselves at His footstool, is holy. Exalt the Lord, our God, and prostrate yourselves at His Holy mountain because the Lord, our God, is Holy."* (Psalms 99:9)

"There is none as holy as the Lord, because there is none other beside You. There is no Rock like our God." (I Samuel 2:2) *"For Who is God beside the Lord? Who is a Rock, other than our God?"* (Psalms 18:32) *"The Torah that Moses commanded us with is a heritage for the congregation of Jacob."* (Deuteronomy 33:4) *"It is a tree of life to those who hold on to it, and those who support it are happy."* (Proverb 3:18) *"Its ways are the way of pleasantness and all its paths lead to peace."* (Proverbs 3:17) *"Abundance of peace for those who love Your Torah and for them there is no obstacle."* (Psalms 119:165)

יְהֹוָהאדניאהדונהי Adonai עֹז oz לְעַמּוֹ le'amo יִתֵּן yiten יְהֹוָהאדניאהדונהי Adonai
יְבָרֵךְ yevarech ע"ב ס"ג מ"ה ב"ן, הברכה (למתק את ז' המלכים שמתו) אֶת־ et עַמּוֹ amo
בַשָּׁלוֹם vashalom ר"ת ע"ב, ריבוע יהוה: כִּי ki שֵׁם shem יְהֹוָהאדניאהדונהי Adonai
אֶקְרָא ekra הָבוּ havu אוזר, אהבה, דאגה גֹדֶל godel לֵאלֹהֵינוּ lelohenu ילה:
הַכֹּל hakol ילי תְּנוּ tenu עֹז oz לֵאלֹהִים lelohim אהיה אדני ; ילה
וּתְנוּ utnu כָבוֹד chavod לַתּוֹרָה latorah:

RAISING THE TORAH

After the scroll is placed on the *bimah* (the podium), a person is called up to raise the Torah for the congregation to see the specific section we will be reading from the Torah Scroll. As we raise the Torah, we meditate to also raise our level of consciousness. We should look at the parchment to try to see the first letter of that week's reading. We should also attempt to find the first letter of our Hebrew name within the text. You can use the *Talit* to help yourself focus (if you don't have a *Talit* you can use your finger).

וְזֹאת vezot הַתּוֹרָה hatorah אֲשֶׁר־ asher שָׂם sam מֹשֶׁה Moshe
מהש, ע"ב בריבוע וקס"א, אל שדי, ד"פ אלהים ע"ה לִפְנֵי lifnei בְּנֵי benei יִשְׂרָאֵל Yisrael:
אֵל El ייא"י (מילוי דס"ג) שַׁדַּי Shadai אל שדי = משה, מהש, ע"ב בריבוע וקס"א, ד"פ אלהים ע"ה
אֱמֶת emet אהיה פעמים אהיה, ז"פ ס"ג וּמֹשֶׁה uMoshe מהש, ע"ב בריבוע וקס"א, אל שדי,
ד"פ אלהים ע"ה אֱמֶת emet אהיה פעמים אהיה, ז"פ ס"ג וְתוֹרָתוֹ vetorato
אֱמֶת emet אהיה פעמים אהיה, ז"פ ס"ג: תּוֹרָה torah צִוָּה־ tziva
לָנוּ lanu אלהים, אהיה אדני מֹשֶׁה Moshe מהש, ע"ב בריבוע וקס"א, אל שדי, ד"פ אלהים ע"ה
מוֹרָשָׁה morasha קְהִלַּת kehilat יַעֲקֹב Yaakov ז' הויות, יאהדונהי אידהנויה:
הָאֵל haEl ייא"י (מילוי דס"ג) תָּמִים tamim דַּרְכּוֹ darko אִמְרַת imrat
יְהֹוָהאדניאהדונהי Adonai צְרוּפָה tzerufa מָגֵן magen ג"פ אל (ייא"י מילוי דס"ג)
ר"ת מיכאל גבריאל נוריאל הוּא hu לְכֹל lechol יה אדני הַחוֹסִים hachosim בּוֹ bo:

"The Lord give might to his people, The Lord will bless his nation with peace." (Psalms 29:11) *"When I call out the Name of the Lord, proclaim greatness to our God."* (Dutoronomy 32:3) *"All should attribute power to God."* (Psalms 68:35) *And give honor to the Torah.*

RAISING THE TORAH

"And this is the Torah that Moses placed before the Children of Israel." (Deuteronomy 4:44)

God is true and Moses is true and His Torah is true. "The Torah, which Moses commanded us with, is a heritage for the Congregation of Jacob." (Deuteronomy 33:4) *"God! His ways are perfect. Lord's statement is pure. He is the Shield for all who take refuge in Him"* (II Samuel 22:31)

The *Torah* reading for *Shavuot* can be found on page 573.

The *chazan* says:

בֵּית bet ב"פ ראה אַהֲרֹן Aharon בָּרְכוּ barchu יהוה ריבוע יהוה ריבוע מ"ה אֶת et
ה' Hashem הַמְבֹרָךְ hamevorach, כֹּהֵן kohen מלה קְרַב kerav וְכַהֵן vechahen מלה.

The one who goes up to the *Torah* ("the ole"), holds the Scroll with both his hands, and says:

יְהֹוָהאדניאהדונהי Adonai עִמָּכֶם imachem:

The congregation replies:

יְבָרֶכְךָ yevarchecha ה' Hashem:

The *ole* continues:

(ויכוין "ברכו את ה' המבורך" - מ"ב ור"ך שהם שמאל וימין):

רַבָּנָן rabanan: בָּרְכוּ barchu יהוה ריבוע יהוה ריבוע מ"ה אֶת et
יְהֹוָהאדניאהדונהי Adonai הַמְבֹרָךְ: hamevorach ס"ת כהת, משיח בן דוד ע"ה.

The congregation then replies:

Nefesh בָּרוּךְ: baruch *Ruach* יְהֹוָהאדניאהדונהי Adonai *Neshamah* הַמְבוֹרָךְ: hamevorach
Chayah לְעוֹלָם le'olam ריבוע ס"ג ו' אותיות דס"ג *Yechidah* וָעֶד va'ed:

The *ole* repeats this line after the congregation:

Nefesh בָּרוּךְ: baruch *Ruach* יְהֹוָהאדניאהדונהי Adonai *Neshamah* הַמְבוֹרָךְ: hamevorach
Chayah לְעוֹלָם le'olam ריבוע ס"ג ו' אותיות דס"ג *Yechidah* וָעֶד va'ed:

THE READING

(The House of Aaron, bless the Lord, the Blessed One. Kohen, come close and stand and do your priestly duty.)
May the Lord be with you! May the Lord bless you!
Masters, Bless the Lord, the Blessed One.
Blessed is the Lord, the Blessed One, forever and for eternity.

And then says the following blessing:

בָּרוּךְ baruch אַתָּה Ata יְהֹוָהאדניאהדונהי Adonai אֱלֹהֵינוּ Elohenu ילה
מֶלֶךְ melech הָעוֹלָם ha'olam אֲשֶׁר asher בָּחַר־ bachar בָּנוּ banu
מִכָּל־ mikol ילי הָעַמִּים ha'amim וְנָתַן־ venatan לָנוּ lanu אלהים, אהיה אדני
אֶת et תּוֹרָתוֹ torato. בָּרוּךְ baruch אַתָּה Ata יְהֹוָהאדניאהדונהי Adonai
נוֹתֵן noten אבג יתץ, ושר הַתּוֹרָה hatorah.

After the reading, the *ole* says the following blessing:

בָּרוּךְ baruch אַתָּה Ata יְהֹוָהאדניאהדונהי Adonai אֱלֹהֵינוּ Elohenu ילה
מֶלֶךְ melech הָעוֹלָם ha'olam אֲשֶׁר asher נָתַן natan לָנוּ lanu אלהים, אהיה אדני
אֶת et תּוֹרָתוֹ torato תּוֹרַת־ torat אֱמֶת emet אהיה פעמים אהיה, ז"פ ס"ג
וְחַיֵּי vechayei עוֹלָם olam נָטַע nata בְּתוֹכֵנוּ betochenu. בָּרוּךְ baruch
אַתָּה Ata יְהֹוָהאדניאהדונהי Adonai נוֹתֵן noten אבג יתץ, ושר הַתּוֹרָה hatorah.

BLESSING OF HAGOMEL

אוֹדֶה ode יְהֹוָהאדניאהדונהי Adonai בְּכָל־ bechol ב"ן, לכב לֵבָב levav בוכו
בְּסוֹד besod מיכ, י"פ האא יְשָׁרִים yesharim וְעֵדָה ve'eda סיט:

בָּרוּךְ baruch אַתָּה Ata יְהֹוָהאדניאהדונהי Adonai אֱלֹהֵינוּ Elohenu ילה
מֶלֶךְ melech הָעוֹלָם ha'olam הַגּוֹמֵל hagomel לְחַיָּבִים lechayavim
טוֹבוֹת tovot, שֶׁגְּמָלַנִי shegemalani כָּל kol ילי טוּב tuv והו.

The congregation answers: אָמֵן amen יאהדונהי And then the congregation recites:

הָאֵל haEl לאה ; ייא"י (מילוי דס"ג) שֶׁגְּמָלְךָ shegemalach כָּל kol ילי טוּב tuv והו.
הוּא hu יִגְמָלְךָ yigmolcha כָּל kol ילי טוּב tuv והו סֶלָה sela.

The person who says "Hagomel" recites silently:

אָמֵן amen יאהדונהי כֵּן ken יְהִי yehi רָצוֹן ratzon מהש ע"ה, ע"ב בריבוע וקס"א ע"ה, אל שדי ע"ה.

Blessed are You, Lord, our God, the King of the World,
Who chose us from among the nations and gave us His Torah. Blessed are You, Lord, Who gives the Torah.
Blessed are You, Lord, our God, King of the World, Who gave us His Torah,
the Torah of truth, and implanted within us eternal life. Blessed are You, Lord, Who gives the Torah.

BLESSING OF HAGOMEL

"I give thank to the Lord whole heartedly, in the conceal of the upright and congregation." (Psalms 111:1)
Blessed are You, Lord, our God, King of the World, Who gives goodness to the guilty, Who bestows upon me all that is good. The God, Who bestows upon you all the best, he will bestow upon you all the best, Selah. Amen, so shall it be desired.

HALF KADDISH

יִתְגַּדַּל yitgadal וְיִתְקַדַּשׁ veyitkadash שדי ומילוי שדי ; י"א אותיות כמנין ו"ה

שְׁמֵיהּ shemei (שם י"ה דע"ב) רַבָּא raba קנ"א ב"ן, יהוה אלהים יהוה אדני,

מילוי קס"א וס"ג, מ"ה ברבוע וע"ב ע"ה ; ר"ת = ו"פ אלהים ; ס"ת = ג"פ יב"ק: אָמֵן amen אידהנויה.

בְּעָלְמָא be'alma דִּי di בְרָא vera כִּרְעוּתֵיהּ kir'utei.

וְיַמְלִיךְ veyamlich מַלְכוּתֵיהּ mal'chutei. וְיַצְמַח veyatzmach

פּוּרְקָנֵיהּ purkanei. וִיקָרֵב vikarev מְשִׁיחֵיהּ meshichei: אָמֵן amen אידהנויה.

בְּחַיֵּיכוֹן bechayechon וּבְיוֹמֵיכוֹן uvyomechon וּבְחַיֵּי uvchayei

דְכָל dechol ילי בֵּית bet ב"פ ראה יִשְׂרָאֵל Yisrael בַּעֲגָלָא ba'agala

וּבִזְמַן uvizman קָרִיב kariv וְאִמְרוּ ve'imru אָמֵן amen: אָמֵן amen אידהנויה.

The congregation and the *chazan* say the following:

28 words (until *be'alma*) – and 28 letters (until *almaya*)

יְהֵא yehe שְׁמֵיהּ shemei (שם י"ה דס"ג) רַבָּא raba קנ"א ב"ן,

יהוה אלהים יהוה אדני, מילוי קס"א וס"ג, מ"ה ברבוע וע"ב ע"ה מְבָרַךְ mevarach,

לְעָלַם le'alam לְעָלְמֵי le'almei עָלְמַיָּא almaya. יִתְבָּרַךְ yitbarach.

Seven words with six letters each (שם ב"ן מ"ב). Also, seven times the letter Vav (שם ב"ן מ"ב).

וְיִשְׁתַּבַּח veyishtabach י"פ ע"ב יהוה אל אבג יתץ.

וְיִתְפָּאַר veyitpa'ar הי נו יה קרע שטן. וְיִתְרוֹמַם veyitromam וה כוזו נגד יכש.

וְיִתְנַשֵּׂא veyitnase במוכסז בטר צתג. וְיִתְהַדָּר veyit'hadar כוזו יה וזקב טנע.

וְיִתְעַלֶּה veyit'ale וה יוד ה יגל פזק. וְיִתְהַלָּל veyit'halal א ואו הא שקו צית.

שְׁמֵיהּ shemei (שם י"ה דמ"ה) דְּקוּדְשָׁא dekudsha בְּרִיךְ verich הוּא hu:

אָמֵן amen אידהנויה.

HALF KADDISH

May His great Name be more exalted and sanctified. (Amen) *In the world that He created according to His will, and may His kingdom reign. And may He cause His redemption to sprout and may He bring the Mashiach closer.* (Amen) *In your lifetimes and in your days and in the lifetime of all the House of Israel, speedily and in the near future, and you should say, Amen.* (Amen) *May His great Name be blessed forever and for all eternity blessed and lauded, and glorified and exalted, And extolled and honored, and uplifted and praised, be the Name of the Holy Blessed One.* (Amen)

לְעֵלָּא le'ela מִן min כָּל kol יל״י בִּרְכָתָא birchata• שִׁירָתָא shirata•
תֻּשְׁבְּחָתָא tishbechata וְנֶחֱמָתָא venechamata• דַּאֲמִירָן da'amiran
בְּעָלְמָא be'alma וְאִמְרוּ ve'imru אָמֵן amen: אָמֵן amen אירהנויה.

BLESSING OF THE HAFTARAH

The *Maftir* (the *ole* for *Maftir*) recite this blessing before the reading of the *Haftarah*. It is recommended to read the *Haftarah* individually (along with the reader), as it is not a full connection to hear it only by the reader.

There is a level far higher than divine inspiration, called prophecy. Many great people throughout history have received divine inspiration. This refers to the acquiring of knowledge or hidden secrets of life that would normally be beyond the accessibility of the average person. Further, the receiver of this knowledge understands it perfectly, without inaccuracy. In prophecy, a person attains a complete bond and attachment to the Creator. Kabbalist Rav Moshe Chaim Luzzatto explains that even prophecy must come through an intermediary, which acts as a lens through which one sees the vision. Attaining this level is a gradual, step-by-step process of elevation.The words in this blessing prepare us, the Vessel, for a powerful connection to the wisdom of the prophets in the Haftorah, the reading after the Torah. Making this connection helps us become prophets.

בָּרוּךְ baruch אַתָּה Ata יְהֹוָואדֹנָיאהדונהי Adonai אֱלֹהֵינוּ Elohenu ילה
מֶלֶךְ melech הָעוֹלָם ha'olam אֲשֶׁר asher בָּחַר bachar
בִּנְבִיאִים binvi'im טוֹבִים tovim וְרָצָה veratza בְדִבְרֵיהֶם vedivrehem
הַנֶּאֱמָרִים hane'emarim בֶּאֱמֶת be'emet אהיה פעמים אהיה, ז״פ ס״ג•
בָּרוּךְ baruch אַתָּה Ata יְהֹוָואדֹנָיאהדונהי Adonai הַבּוֹחֵר habocher
בַּתּוֹרָה batorah וּבְמֹשֶׁה uvMoshe מהש, ע״ב בריבוע קס״א, אל שדי, ד״פ אלהים ע״ה
עַבְדּוֹ avdo וּבְיִשְׂרָאֵל uvYisrael עַמּוֹ amo וּבִנְבִיאֵי uvinvi'ei
הָאֱמֶת ha'emet אהיה פעמים אהיה, ז״פ ס״ג וְהַצֶּדֶק vehatzedek:

Above all blessings, songs, praises, and words of consolation that may be said in the world, and you shall say, Amen. *(Amen)*

BLESSING OF THE HAFTARAH

Blessed are You, Lord, our God, the King of the world, Who had chosen good prophets and Who was pleased with their words that were uttered with truth. Blessed are You, Lord, who chose the Torah and Moses, His servant, and Israel, His Nation, and the prophets of truth and righteousness.

BLESSING AFTER THE HAFTARAH

The reader says these blessings after the reading of the *Haftarah*:

בָּרוּךְ baruch אַתָּה Ata יְהֹוָהאדניאהדונהי Adonai אֱלֹהֵינוּ Elohenu ילה
מֶלֶךְ melech הָעוֹלָם ha'olam צוּר tzur אלהים דההין ע"ה כָּל kol ילי
הָעוֹלָמִים ha'olamim צַדִּיק tzadik בְּכָל bechol ב"ן, לכב הַדּוֹרוֹת hadorot
הָאֵל haEl לאה ; ייא"י (מילוי דס"ג) הַנֶּאֱמָן hane'eman הָאוֹמֵר ha'omer
וְעֹשֶׂה ve'ose, הַמְדַבֵּר hamedaber ראה וּמְקַיֵּם umkayem, כִּי ki כָּל chol ילי
דְּבָרָיו devarav ראה אֱמֶת emet אהיה פעמים אהיה, ז"פ ס"ג וָצֶדֶק vatzedek:
נֶאֱמָן ne'eman אַתָּה Ata הוּא hu יְהֹוָהאדניאהדונהי Adonai אֱלֹהֵינוּ Elohenu ילה
וְנֶאֱמָנִים vene'emanim דְּבָרֶיךָ devarecha ראה וְדָבָר vedavar ראה אֶחָד echad
אהבה, דאגה מִדְּבָרֶיךָ midevarecha ראה אָחוֹר achor לֹא lo יָשׁוּב yashuv
רֵיקָם rekam כִּי ki אֵל El ייא"י (מילוי דס"ג) מֶלֶךְ melech נֶאֱמָן ne'eman
וְרַחֲמָן verachaman אָתָּה Ata. בָּרוּךְ baruch אַתָּה Ata יְהֹוָהאדניאהדונהי Adonai
הָאֵל haEl לאה ; ייא"י הַנֶּאֱמָן hane'eman בְּכָל bechol ב"ן, לכב דְּבָרָיו devarav ראה:

רַחֵם rachem אברהם, וז"פ אל, רי"ו ול"ב נתיבות החכמה, רמ"ח (אברים), עסמ"ב וט"ז אותיות פשוטות
עַל al צִיּוֹן Tziyon יוסף, ו' הויות, קנאה כִּי ki הִיא hee בֵּית bet ב"פ ראה וְחַיֵּינוּ chayenu
וְלַעֲלוּבַת vela'aluvat נֶפֶשׁ nefesh תּוֹשִׁיעַ toshi'a בִּמְהֵרָה bimhera
בְּיָמֵינוּ beyamenu. בָּרוּךְ baruch אַתָּה Ata יְהֹוָהאדניאהדונהי Adonai
מְשַׂמֵּחַ mesame'ach צִיּוֹן Tziyon יוסף, ו' הויות, קנאה בְּבָנֶיהָ bevaneha:

BLESSING AFTER THE HAFTARAH

Blessed are You, Lord, our God, King of the world, rock of all eternities, righteous in all generations. The trustworthy God Who says and does, Who speaks and fulfills, for all of His words are true and just. Trustworthy are You, Lord, our God, and trustworthy are Your words, and not one of Your words is turned back to its origin unfulfilled, for You, God, are a trustworthy and a compassionate King. Blessed are You, Lord, the God Who is trustworthy in all His words. Have mercy on Zion, for it is the house of our livelihood, and to the one whose spirit is humiliated bring salvation speedily in our days. Blessed are You, Lord, Who gladdens Zion with her sons.

שַׂמְּחֵנוּ samchenu יְהֹוָ֘ה֘ אדני אהדונהי Adonai אֱלֹהֵינוּ Elohenu ילה

בְּאֵלִיָּהוּ beEliyahu לכב הַנָּבִיא hanavi עַבְדֶּךָ avdecha פוי, אל אדני

וּבְמַלְכוּת uvmalchut בֵּית bet ב"פ ראה דָּוִד David מְשִׁיחֶךָ meshichecha,

בִּמְהֵרָה bimhera יָבֹא yavo וְיָגֵל veyagel להחו לִבֵּנוּ libenu,

עַל al כִּסְאוֹ kis'o לֹא lo יֵשֵׁב yeshev זָר zar וְלֹא velo

יִנְחֲלוּ yinchalu עוֹד od אֲחֵרִים acherim אֶת et כְּבוֹדוֹ kevodo,

כִּי ki בְשֵׁם veshem קָדְשְׁךָ kodshecha נִשְׁבַּעְתָּ nishbata לוֹ lo,

שֶׁלֹּא shelo יִכְבֶּה yichbe נֵרוֹ nero לְעוֹלָם le'olam ריבוע ס"ג י' אותיות דס"ג

וָעֶד vaed. בָּרוּךְ baruch אַתָּה Ata יְהֹוָ֘ה֘ אדני אהדונהי Adonai

מָגֵן magen ג"פ אל (ייא" מילוי דס"ג) ; ר"ת מיכאל גבריאל נוריאל דָּוִד David:

עַל al הַתּוֹרָה hatorah וְעַל ve'al הָעֲבוֹדָה ha'avoda

וְעַל ve'al הַנְּבִיאִים hanevi'im וְעַל ve'al יוֹם yom ע"ה נגד, מזבח, זן, אל יהוה

(on Shabbat add: הַשַּׁבָּת haShabbat הַזֶּה haze והו וְעַל ve'al יוֹם yom ע"ה נגד, מזבח, זן, אל יהוה)

חַג chag הַשָּׁבוּעוֹת haShavuot הַזֶּה hazeh והו. וְעַל ve'al

יוֹם yom ע"ה נגד, מזבח, זן, אל יהוה טוֹב tov והו מִקְרָא mikra קֹדֶשׁ kodesh

הַזֶּה haze והו. שֶׁנָּתַתָּ shenatata לָּנוּ lanu אלהים, אהיה אדני יְהֹוָ֘ה֘ אדני אהדונהי Adonai

אֱלֹהֵינוּ Elohenu ילה (on Shabbat add: לִקְדֻשָּׁה likdusha וְלִמְנוּחָה velimnucha)

לְכָבוֹד lechavod וּלְתִפְאָרֶת ultifaret:

---

*Gladden us, Lord, our God, through Eliyahu the prophet, Your servant, and with the Kingdom of the House of David, Your anointed, may he come speedily and cause our hearts to exult. On his throne let no stranger sit, nor let others inherit his honor anymore, For by Your Holy Name, You swore to him that his candlelight will never be extinguished for eternity. Blessed are You, Lord, the Shield of David. For the Torah and for the Prophets and for this day of (*On Shabbat: *Shabbat and on this day of) Holiday of Matzot and on this good day of holy convocation that You, Lord our God, had given us (*On Shabbat: *for holiness and contentment,) for honor and for splendor.*

עַל al הַכֹּל hakol ילי יְהֹוָואדהנויאהדונהי Adonai אֱלֹהֵינוּ Elohenu ילה אֲנַחְנוּ anachnu

מוֹדִים modim כנגד מאה ברכות שתיקן דוד לאמרם כל יום לָךְ lach

וּמְבָרְכִים umvarchim אוֹתָךְ otach יִתְבָּרַךְ yitbarach שִׁמְךָ shimcha בְּפִי befi

כָּל kol ילי חַי chai כל חי = אהיה אהיה יהוה, בינה ע"ה, חיים תָּמִיד tamid ע"ה קס"א קנ"א קמ"ג

לְעוֹלָם le'olam ריבוע ס"ג וי' אותיות דס"ג וָעֶד va'ed.

בָּרוּךְ baruch אַתָּה Ata יְהֹוָואדהנויאהדונהי Adonai מְקַדֵּשׁ mekadesh

(on Shabbat add: הַשַּׁבָּת hashabat וְ ve) יִשְׂרָאֵל Yisrael וְהַזְּמַנִּים vehazemanim:

"Amen" is said by the one who said the blessing together with the congregation:

אָמֵן יאהדונהי amen.

YIZKOR - PRAYER FOR THE DECEASED

A few special times during the year, we have the opportunity to help elevate the souls of loved ones who have left us. The Seventh Day of *Pesach* is one of those times. We can take the Light that we are receiving and use it to help a loved one's soul ascend higher and more easily into the Upper Worlds. There is also a metaphysical void left in our life when a loved one passes on. Part of the Light that they automatically share with us is now missing. *Yizkor* helps to fill this void with their spiritual energy by making contact with the soul in the Upper World.

The Ari use the short version of this "Prayer for the Deceased". He used to say that sometimes the words that exist in the long version are not actually helping to elevate the soul of the deceased, but disturb the process of the elevation.

הַמְרַחֵם hamerachem אברהם, וז"פ אל, רי"ו ול"ב נתיבות החכמה, רמ"ח (אברים), עסמ"ב וט"ז אותיות פשוטות עַל al כָּל kol ילי ; עמם בְּרִיּוֹתָיו beriyotav הוּא hu יָחוּס yachus וְיַחֲמוֹל veyachamol וִירַחֵם virachem אברהם, וז"פ אל, רי"ו ול"ב נתיבות החכמה, רמ"ח (אברים), עסמ"ב וט"ז אותיות פשוטות עַל al נֶפֶשׁ nefesh רוּחַ ru'ach וּנְשָׁמָה uneshamah שֶׁל shel (the deceased's name and their father's name) רוּחַ ru'ach יְהֹוָואדהנויאהדונהי Adonai רוח ה' = י"פ יוה תְּנִיחֶנּוּ tenichenu (for woman: תְּנִיחֶנָּה tenichena) בְּגַן beGan עֵדֶן Eden:

For all of this we are grateful to You,
*Lord our God, and bless we You.May Your Name be blessed by the mouth of all the living always and for all eternity. And Your word, our King, is true and exists forever. Blessed are You Lord, King over the whole earth who sanctifies (**On Shabbat:** the Shabbat and) Israel and the Times. Amen!*

***YIZKOR* - PRAYER FOR THE DECEASED**

May the One Who is merciful to all that
He had created take pity and spare and be merciful on the Nefesh, Ruach and Neshamah of (Name), *the son/daughter of* (the father's Name). *May the Spirit of God place him/her in the Garden of Eden.*

The Ashrei

Twenty-one of the twenty-two letters of the Aramaic alphabet are encoded in the *Ashrei* in their correct order from *Alef* to *Tav*. King David, the author, left out the Aramaic letter *Nun* from this prayer, because *Nun* is the first letter in the Aramaic word *nefilah*, which means "falling." Falling refers to a spiritual decline, as in falling into the *klipa*. Feelings of doubt, depression, worry, and uncertainty are consequences of spiritual falling. Because the Aramaic letters are the actual instruments of Creation, this prayer helps to inject order and the power of Creation into our lives, without the energy of falling.

In this Psalm there are ten times the Name: יהוה for the Ten *Sefirot*. This Psalm is written according to the order of the *Alef Bet*, but the letter *Nun* is omitted to prevent falling.

אַשְׁרֵי ashrei (סוד הכתר) יוֹשְׁבֵי yoshvei בֵיתֶךָ vetecha ב״פ ראה

עוֹד od יְהַלְלוּךָ yehalelucha סֶּלָה sela: אַשְׁרֵי ashrei הָעָם ha'am

שֶׁכָּכָה shekacha מהש, משה, ע״ב בריבוע וקס״א, אל שדי, ד״פ אלהים ע״ה לוֹ lo

אַשְׁרֵי ashrei הָעָם ha'am ר״ת לאה שֶׁיְהֹוָהאדֹנָיאהדונהי she'Adonai (***Keter***)

אֱלֹהָיו Elohav ילה: תְּהִלָּה tehila ע״ה אמת, אהיה פעמים אהיה, ז״פ ס״ג לְדָוִד leDavid

אֲרוֹמִמְךָ aromimcha אֱלוֹהַי Elohai הַמֶּלֶךְ hamelech וַאֲבָרְכָה va'avarcha

שִׁמְךָ shimcha לְעוֹלָם le'olam ריבוע דס״ג ו׳ אותיות דס״ג וָעֶד va'ed:

בְּכָל־ bechol ב״ן, לכב יוֹם yom ע״ה נגד, מזבח, זן אל יהוה

אֲבָרְכֶךָּ avarcheka וַאֲהַלְלָה va'ahalela מ״ה יהוה שִׁמְךָ shimcha

לְעוֹלָם le'olam ריבוע דס״ג ו׳ אותיות דס״ג וָעֶד va'ed:

גָּדוֹל gadol להח ; עם ד׳ אותיות = מבה, יזל, אום

יְהֹוָהאדֹנָיאהדונהי Adonai (***Chochmah***) וּמְהֻלָּל umhulal אדני, ללה

מְאֹד me'od וְלִגְדֻלָּתוֹ veligdulato והו אֵין en חֵקֶר cheker:

The Ashrei

"Joyful are those who dwell in Your House, they shall praise You, Selah." (Psalms 84:5)
"Joyful is the nation that this is theirs and joyful the nation that the Lord is their God." (Psalms 144:15)
"A praise of David.

א *I shall exalt You, my God, the King, and I shall bless Your Name forever and for eternity.*
ב *I shall bless You every day and I shall praise Your Name forever and for eternity.*
ג *The Lord is great and exceedingly praised. His greatness is unfathomable.*

דּוֹר dor לְדוֹר ledor יְשַׁבַּח yeshabach מַעֲשֶׂיךָ ma'asecha ר"ת דלים

וּגְבוּרֹתֶיךָ ugvurotecha יַגִּידוּ yagidu ייז, כ"ב אותיות פשוטות (=אכא) וה' אותיות סופיות בוןזחך:

הֲדַר hadar כְּבוֹד kevod הוֹדֶךָ hodecha וְדִבְרֵי vedivrei

נִפְלְאוֹתֶיךָ nifle'otecha ר"ת אלהים, אהיה אדני

אָשִׂיחָה asicha ר"ת הפסוק = פ"ז (בסוד כתם טהור פז):

וֶעֱזוּז ve'ezuz נוֹרְאֹתֶיךָ nor'otecha יֹאמֵרוּ yomeru וּגְדוּלָּתְךָ ugdulatcha

(כתיב: וגדלותיך) ר"ת = ע"ב, ריבוע יהוה אֲסַפְּרֶנָּה asaprena ס"ת = "יאי" (מילוי דס"ג):

זֵכֶר zecher רַב־ rav טוּבְךָ tuvcha לאו יַבִּיעוּ yabi'u

וְצִדְקָתְךָ vetzidkatcha יְרַנֵּנוּ yeranenu ס"ת = ב"ן, יבמ, לכב ; ר"ת הפסוק = רי"ו יהוה:

חַנּוּן chanun וְרַחוּם verachum יְהֹוָהאדניאהדונהי Adonai (Binah)

חנון ורחום יהוה = עשל אֶרֶךְ erech ס"ת = ס"ג ב"ן אַפַּיִם apayim ר"ת = יהוה

וּגְדָל־ ugdal (כתיב: וגדול) וָחֶסֶד chased ע"ב, ריבוע יהוה:

טוֹב־ tov והו יְהֹוָהאדניאהדונהי Adonai (Chesed) לַכֹּל lakol

יה אדני ; ס"ת ל"ו (מילוי דס"ג) וְרַחֲמָיו verachamav עַל־ al

כָּל kol ילי ; עמם ; ר"ת ריבוע ב"ן ע"ה מַעֲשָׂיו ma'asav ס"ת ע"ב, ריבוע יהוה:

ד *One generation and the next shall praise Your deeds and tell of Your might.*
ה *The brilliance of Your splendid glory and the wonders of Your acts, I shall speak of.*
ו *They shall speak of the might of Your awesome acts and I shall tell of Your greatness.*
ז *They shall express the remembrance of Your abundant goodness, and Your righteousness they shall joyfully proclaim.* חו *The Lord is merciful and compassionate, slow to anger and great in kindness.*
ט *The Lord is good to all, His compassion extends over all His acts.*

יוֹדוּךָ yoducha יְהֹוָאדֹנָיאהדונהי Adonai (*Gevurah*) כָּל־ kol ילי מַעֲשֶׂיךָ ma'asecha

וַחֲסִידֶיךָ vachasidecha ר״ת אלהים, אהיה אדני יְבָרְכוּכָה yevarchucha ס״ת = מ״ה:

כְּבוֹד kevod מַלְכוּתְךָ malchutcha יֹאמֵרוּ yomeru וּגְבוּרָתְךָ ugvuratcha

יְדַבֵּרוּ yedaberu ר״ת הפסוק = אלהים, אהיה אדני ; ס״ת = ב״ן, יבמ, לכב:

לְהוֹדִיעַ lehodi'a לִבְנֵי livnei הָאָדָם ha'adam ר״ת ללה, אדני

גְּבוּרֹתָיו gevurotav וּכְבוֹד uchvod הֲדַר hadar

מַלְכוּתוֹ malchuto ר״ת מ״ה וס״ת = רי״ו ; ר״ת הפסוק ע״ה = ק״כ צירופי אלהים:

מַלְכוּתְךָ malchutcha מַלְכוּת malchut כָּל־ kol ילי עֹלָמִים olamim

וּמֶמְשַׁלְתְּךָ umemshaltecha בְּכָל־ bechol ב״ן, לכב דּוֹר dor וָדֹר vador רי״ו:

סוֹמֵךְ somech ריבוע אדני יְהֹוָאדֹנָיאהדונהי Adonai (*Tiferet*)

לְכָל־ lechol יה אדני ; סומך אדני לכל ר״ת סאל, אמן (יאהדונהי) הַנֹּפְלִים hanoflim

וְזוֹקֵף vezokef לְכָל־ lechol יה אדני הַכְּפוּפִים hakefufim נמם:

עֵינֵי־ enei ריבוע דמ״ה כֹל chol ילי אֵלֶיךָ elecha יְשַׂבֵּרוּ yesaberu וְאַתָּה veAta

נוֹתֵן־ noten אבגיתץ, ושר לָהֶם lahem אֶת־ et אָכְלָם ochlam בְּעִתּוֹ be'ito:

י *All that You have made shall thank You, Lord, and Your pious ones shall bless You.*

כ *They shall speak of the glory of Your Kingdom and talk of Your mighty deeds.*

ל *His mighty deeds He makes known to man and the glory of His splendid Kingdom.*

מ *Yours is the Kingdom of all worlds and Your reign extends to each and every generation.*

ס *The Lord supports all those who fell and holds upright all those who are bent over.*

ע *The eyes of all look hopefully towards You, and You give them their food at its proper time.*

POTE'ACH ET YADECHA

We connect to the letters *Pei, Alef,* and *Yud* by opening our hands and holding our palms skyward. Our consciousness is focused on receiving sustenance and financial prosperity from the Light through our actions of personal tithing and sharing, our *Desire to Receive for the Sake of Sharing.* In doing so, we also acknowledge that the sustenance we receive comes from a higher source and is not of our own doing. According to the sages, if we do not meditate on this idea at this juncture, we must repeat the prayer.

פתוז (שע״ז נהורין למ״ה ולס״ה)

יוד הי ויו הי יוד הי ויו הי (וז׳ וזיוורתי)
אלף למד אלף למד (ש״ע)
יוד הא ואו הא (כז״א)
אדני (ולנוקבא)

פותוז את ידך ר״ת פאי
גימ׳ יאהדונהי זו״ן
וזכמה דז״א ו״ק
יסוד דנוק׳

פּוֹתֵחַ pote'ach אֶת et יָדֶךָ yadecha ר״ת פאי וס״ת וזתך עם ג׳ אותיות = דִּיקַרְנוֹסָא

ובאתב״ש הוא סאל, פאי, אמן, יאהדונהי ; ועוד יכוין שם וזתך בשילוב יהוה - יְוֹהֲהִתְוֹכֵהָ

Drawing abundance and sustenance from *Chochmah* of *Zeir Anpin*

יוד הי ויו הי יוד ויו דלת הי יוד ויו יוד ויו הי יוד
וזתך סאל יאהדונהי

וּמַשְׂבִּיעַ umasbi'a וזתך עם ג׳ אותיות = דִּיקַרְנוֹסָא

ובא״ת ב״ש הוא סאל, אמן, יאהדונהי ; ועוד יכוין שם וזתך בשילוב יהוה – יְוֹהֲהִתְוֹכֵהָ

Drawing abundance and sustenance from *Chochmah* of *Zeir Anpin*

יוד הי ויו הי יוד ויו דלת הי יוד ויו יוד ויו הי יוד

לְכָל־ lechol יה אדני (להמשיך מווזין ד-יה אל הנוקבא שהיא אדני)

וַזִי chai כל וזי = אהיה אהיה יהוה, בינה ע״ה, וזיים

רָצוֹן ratzon מהש ע״ה, ע״ב בריבוע וקס״א ע״ה, אל שדי ע״ה
ר״ת רוזל שהיא המלכות הצריכה לשפע

יוד יוד הי יוד הי ויו יוד הי ויו הי יסוד דאבא
אלף הי יוד הי יסוד דאימא
להמתיק רוזל וב׳ דמעין שך פר

Also meditate to draw abundance and sustenance and blessing to all the worlds from the *ratzon* mentioned above. You should meditate and focus on this verse because it is the essence of prosperity, and that God is intervening and sustaining and supporting all of Creation.

POTE'ACH ET YADECHA

פ *Open Your Hands and satisfy every living thing with desire.*

צַדִּיק tzadik יְה�ֹוָהאדנּיאהדונהי Adonai (*Yesod*) בְּכָל bechol ב"ן, לכב

דְּרָכָיו derachav וְחָסִיד vechasid בְּכָל bechol ב"ן, לכב מַעֲשָׂיו ma'asav יבמ, ב"ן:

קָרוֹב karov יְהֹוָהאדנּיאהדונהי Adonai (*Malchut*) לְכָל־ lechol יה אדני

קֹרְאָיו kor'av לְכֹל lechol יה אדני אֲשֶׁר asher

יִקְרָאֻהוּ yikra'uhu בֶאֱמֶת ve'emet אהיה פעמים אהיה, ז"פ ס"ג:

רְצוֹן retzon מהש ע"ה, ע"ב בריבוע וקס"א ע"ה, אל שדי ע"ה יְרֵאָיו yere'av יַעֲשֶׂה ya'ase

ר"ת רי"י וְאֶת־ ve'et שַׁוְעָתָם shav'atam יִשְׁמַע yishma וְיוֹשִׁיעֵם veyoshi'em:

שׁוֹמֵר shomer כ"א הויות שבתפילין יְהֹוָהאדנּיאהדונהי Adonai (*Netzach*)

אֶת־ et כָּל־ kol ילי אֹהֲבָיו ohavav ר"ת אכא

וְאֵת ve'et כָּל־ kol ילי הָרְשָׁעִים haresha'im יַשְׁמִיד yashmid:

תְּהִלַּת tehilat יְהֹוָהאדנּיאהדונהי Adonai (*Hod*) יְדַבֶּר yedaber ראה פִּי pi

וִיבָרֵךְ vivarech ע"ב ס"ג מ"ה ב"ן, הברכה (למתק את ז' המלכים שמתו) כָּל kol ילי

בָּשָׂר basar שֵׁם shem קָדְשׁוֹ kodsho לְעוֹלָם le'olam ריבוע ס"ג ו' אותיות דס"ג

וָעֶד va'ed: וַאֲנַחְנוּ va'anachnu נְבָרֵךְ nevarech יָהּ Yah מֵעַתָּה me'ata

וְעַד־ ve'ad עוֹלָם olam הַלְלוּיָהּ haleluya אלהים, אהיה אדני ; ללה:

RETURNING THE TORAH TO THE ARK

Before we return the *Torah* back to the Ark we recite the following verse twice:

יִמְלֹךְ yimloch יְהֹוָהאדנּיאהדונהי Adonai | לְעוֹלָם le'olam ריבוע ס"ג י' אותיות דס"ג

אֱלֹהַיִךְ Elohayich ילה צִיּוֹן Tziyon יוסף, ו' הויות, קנאה לְדֹר ledor

וָדֹר vador רי"ו ; ר"ת אצלו (רמז שמלכות אצל ז"א) הַלְלוּיָהּ haleluya אלהים = אהיה אדני ; ללה:

צ *The Lord is righteous in all His ways and virtuous in all His deeds.*
ק *The Lord is close to all who call Him, only to those who call Him truthfully.*
ר *He shall fulfill the will of those who fear Him; He hears their wailing and saves them.*
ש *The Lord protects all who love Him and He destroys the wicked.*
ת *My lips utter the praise of the Lord and all flesh shall bless His holy Name, forever and for eternity."*
(Psalms 145) "And we shall bless the Lord forever and for eternity. Praise the Lord!" (Psalms 115:18)

RETURNING THE TORAH TO THE ARK

"The Lord will reign forever, your God, Zion, for each and every generation, Praise the Lord!" (Psalms 146:10)

מִזְמוֹר mizmor לְדָוִד leDavid הָבוּ havu אוזד, אהבה, דאגה

לַיהֹוָהאדניאהדונהי ladonai בְּנֵי benei ר"ת הבל אֵלִים elim הבו יהוה בני אלים = יעקב

הָבוּ havu אוזד, אהבה, דאגה לַיהֹוָהאדניאהדונהי ladonai כָּבוֹד kavod וָעֹז va'oz:

הָבוּ havu אוזד, אהבה, דאגה לַיהֹוָהאדניאהדונהי ladonai כְּבוֹד kevod שְׁמוֹ shemo

מהש ע"ה, ע"ב בריבוע וקס"א ע"ה, אל שדי ע"ה ; הבו יהוה כבוד שמו = אדם דוד משיח

הִשְׁתַּחֲווּ hishtachavu לַיהֹוָהאדניאהדונהי ladonai בְּהַדְרַת־ behadrat ר"ת הבל

קֹדֶשׁ kodesh ר"ת למפרע קבלה (שביום שבת צריך ללמוד קבלה): קוֹל kol

יְהֹוָהאדניאהדונהי Adonai עַל־ al הַמָּיִם hamayim ר"ת = אלף למד (וזסד – ואל שני רמוז

במילה בהמשך). אֵל־ El ייא"י (מילוי דס"ג) הַכָּבוֹד hakavod לאו הִרְעִים hir'im ה"פ אדני

(להמתיק שכ"ה דינים) יְהֹוָהאדניאהדונהי Adonai עַל־ al מַיִם mayim רַבִּים rabim

ר"ת הרעים (שכ"ה דינים – ושני השכ"ה דינים נמתקים ע"י שני שמות א"ל הרמוזים לעיל):

קוֹל־ kol יְהֹוָהאדניאהדונהי Adonai בַּכֹּחַ bako'ach ר"ת יב"ק, אלהים יהוה, אהיה אדני יהוה

קוֹל kol יְהֹוָהאדניאהדונהי Adonai בֶּהָדָר behadar ר"ת יב"ק, אלהים יהוה, אהיה אדני יהוה:

קוֹל kol יְהֹוָהאדניאהדונהי Adonai שֹׁבֵר shover אֲרָזִים arazim וַיְשַׁבֵּר vayshaber

יְהֹוָהאדניאהדונהי Adonai אֶת־ et אַרְזֵי arzei הַלְּבָנוֹן haLevanon ר"ת האא:

וַיַּרְקִידֵם vayarkidem כְּמוֹ־ kemo עֵגֶל egel לְבָנוֹן Levanon

וְשִׂרְיֹן veSiryon כְּמוֹ kemo בֶן־ ven רְאֵמִים re'emim: קוֹל־ kol

יְהֹוָהאדניאהדונהי Adonai חֹצֵב chotzev ס"ת הב"ל לַהֲבוֹת lahavot אֵשׁ esh:

קוֹל kol יוהוואדניאהדונהי Adonai יָחִיל yachil ס"ת ללה, אדני מִדְבָּר midbar

יָחִיל yachil יְהֹוָהאדניאהדונהי Adonai מִדְבַּר midbar קָדֵשׁ kadesh ר"ת = קין:

A Psalm of David: Render to the Lord, you sons of the powerful ones, render to the Lord honor and might. Render to the Lord honor worthy of His Name, prostrate yourselves before the Lord in the glory of His Holiness. The Voice of the Lord is upon the waters, The God of glory had thundered, Lord is upon vast waters. The Voice of the Lord is powerful. The Voice of the Lord is majesty. The Voice of the Lord breaks cedars, the Lord breaks the cedars of Lebanon. He makes them dance around like a calf, Lebanon and Sirion like a wild young ox. The Voice of the Lord cleaves the flames of fire. The Voice of the Lord convulses the wilderness; the Lord convulses the wilderness of Kadesh.

קוֹל kol יְהֹוָהאדניאהדונהי Adonai יְחוֹלֵל yecholel אַיָּלוֹת ayalot
וַיֶּחֱשֹׂף vayechesof יְעָרוֹת ye'arot וּבְהֵיכָלוֹ uvhechalo כֻּלּוֹ kulo אֹמֵר omer
כָּבוֹד kavod: יְהֹוָהאדניאהדונהי Adonai לַמַּבּוּל lamabul יָשָׁב yashav
ר"ת ילי וס"ת הבל וַיֵּשֶׁב vayeshev יְהֹוָהאדניאהדונהי Adonai מֶלֶךְ melech
לְעוֹלָם le'olam ריבוע ס"ג י' אותיות דס"ג: יְהֹוָהאדניאהדונהי Adonai עֹז oz
לְעַמּוֹ le'amo יִתֵּן yiten יְהֹוָהאדניאהדונהי Adonai יְבָרֵךְ yevarech עסמ"ב, הברכה
(למתק את ז' המלכים שמתו) אֶת־ et עַמּוֹ amo בַשָּׁלוֹם vashalom ר"ת ע"ב, ריבוע יהוה:

שׁוּבָה shuva הוזש לִמְעוֹנָךְ limonach וּשְׁכוֹן ushchon בְּבֵית bevet ב"פ ראה
מַאֲוָיָךְ ma'avayach. כִּי ki כָל chol ילי פֶּה pe מילה ע"ה, אלהים, אהיה אדני
וְכָל vechol ילי לָשׁוֹן lashon יִתְּנוּ yitenu הוֹד hod ההה וְהָדָר vehadar
לְמַלְכוּתָךְ lemalchutach: וּבְנֻחֹה uvnucho יֹאמַר yomar שׁוּבָה shuva הוזש
יְהֹוָהאדניאהדונהי Adonai רִבְבוֹת rivevot אַלְפֵי alfei יִשְׂרָאֵל Yisrael:
הֲשִׁיבֵנוּ hashivenu יְהֹוָהאדניאהדונהי Adonai | אֵלֶיךָ elecha וְנָשׁוּבָה venashuva
(כתיב: ונשוב) חַדֵּשׁ chadesh י"ב הויות, קס"א קנ"א יָמֵינוּ yamenu כְּקֶדֶם kekedem:

HALF KADDISH

יִתְגַּדַּל yitgadal וְיִתְקַדַּשׁ veyitkadash שדי ומילוי שדי ; י"א אותיות כמנין ו"ה
שְׁמֵיהּ shemei (שם י"ה דע"ב) רַבָּא raba קנ"א ב"ן, יהוה אלהים יהוה אדני,
מילוי קס"א וס"ג, מ"ה ברבוע וע"ב ע"ה ; ר"ת = ו"פ אלהים ; ס"ת = ג"פ יב"ק: אָמֵן amen אידהנויה.

The Voice of the Lord frightens the hinds and strips the forests bare, and in His Temple all proclaim His Glory. The Lord sat at the deluge, and the Lord sits as King forever. The Lord gives might to His people. The Lord will bless His people with peace." (Psalms 29)
"Return to Your dwelling Place and reside in Your desirable House because every mouth and every tongue proclaim the majesty and the splendor of Your reign. And when It rested, he would say: Return, Lord, to the myriad thousands of Israel." (Numbers 10:36)
"Bring us back to You, Lord, and we shall return, renew our days as of old." (Lamentations 5:21)

HALF KADDISH

May His great Name be more exalted and sanctified. (Amen)

בְּעָלְמָא be'alma דִּי di בְרָא vera כִּרְעוּתֵיהּ kir'utei.

וְיַמְלִיךְ veyamlich מַלְכוּתֵיהּ mal'chutei. וְיַצְמַח veyatzmach

פּוּרְקָנֵיהּ purkanei. וִיקָרֵב vikarev מְשִׁיחֵיהּ meshichei: אָמֵן amen אירהנויה.

בְּחַיֵּיכוֹן bechayechon וּבְיוֹמֵיכוֹן uvyomechon וּבְחַיֵּי uvchayei

דְּכָל dechol ילי בֵּית bet ב"פ ראה יִשְׂרָאֵל Yisrael בַּעֲגָלָא ba'agala

וּבִזְמַן uvizman קָרִיב kariv וְאִמְרוּ ve'imru אָמֵן amen: אָמֵן amen אירהנויה.

The congregation and the *chazan* say the following:

28 words (until *be'alma*) and 28 letters (until *almaya*)

יְהֵא yehe שְׁמֵיהּ shemei (שם י"ה דס"ג) רַבָּא raba קנ"א ב"ן,

יהוה אלהים יהוה אדני, מילוי קס"א וס"ג, מ"ה ברבוע וע"ב ע"ה מְבָרַךְ mevarach,

לְעָלַם le'alam לְעָלְמֵי le'almei עָלְמַיָּא almaya. יִתְבָּרַךְ yitbarach.

Seven words with six letters each (שם בן מ"ב) and seven times the letter Vav (שם בן מ"ב)

וְיִשְׁתַּבַּח veyishtabach י"פ ע"ב יהוה אל אבג יתץ.

וְיִתְפָּאַר veyitpa'ar הי נו יה קרע שטן. וְיִתְרוֹמַם veyitromam וה כוזו נגד יכש.

וְיִתְנַשֵּׂא veyitnase במוכסז בטר צתג. וְיִתְהַדָּר veyit'hadar כוזו יה וזקב טנע.

וְיִתְעַלֶּה veyit'ale וה יוד ה יגל פזק. וְיִתְהַלָּל veyit'halal א ואו הא שקו צית.

שְׁמֵיהּ shemei (שם י"ה דמ"ה) דְּקוּדְשָׁא dekudsha בְּרִיךְ verich הוּא hu:

אָמֵן amen אירהנויה.

לְעֵלָּא le'ela מִן min כָּל kol ילי בִּרְכָתָא birchata. שִׁירָתָא shirata.

תִּשְׁבְּחָתָא tishbechata וְנֶחָמָתָא venechamata. דַּאֲמִירָן da'amiran

בְּעָלְמָא be'alma וְאִמְרוּ ve'imru אָמֵן amen: אָמֵן amen אירהנויה.

In the world that He created according to His will, and may His kingdom reign. And may He cause His redemption to sprout and may He bring the Mashiach closer. (Amen) In your lifetimes and in your days and in the lifetime of all the House of Israel, speedily and in the near future, and you should say, Amen. (Amen) May His great Name be blessed forever and for all eternity blessed and lauded, and glorified and exalted, and extolled and honored, and uplifted and praised, be the Name of the Holy Blessed One. (Amen) Above all blessings, songs, praises, and words of consolation that may be said in the world, and you shall say, Amen. (Amen)

MUSAF OF SHAVUOT

אֲדֹנָי Adonai ללה (pause here) שְׂפָתַי sefatai תִּפְתָּח tiftach וּפִי ufi יַגִּיד yagid

ייז (כ״ב אותיות פשוטות [=אכא] וה׳ אותיות סופיות במוףך) תְּהִלָּתֶךָ tehilatecha ס״ת = בוכו:

THE FIRST BLESSING - INVOKES THE SHIELD OF ABRAHAM.

Abraham is the channel of the Right Column energy of positivity, sharing, and mercy. Sharing actions can protect us from all forms of negativity.

Chesed that becomes *Chochmah*

In this section there are 42 words, the secret of the 42-Letter Name of God and therefore it begins with the letter *Bet* (2) and ends with the letter *Mem* (40).

Bend your knees at *"baruch"*, bow at *"Ata"* and straighten up at *"Adonai"*.

א ב

בָּרוּךְ baruch אַתָּה Ata א-ת (אותיות הא״ב המסמלות את השפע המגיע) לה׳ המלכות

ג י

יְהֹוָהאדניאהדונהי Adonai (יא) אֱלֹהֵינוּ Elohenu ילה

ת צ

וֵאלֹהֵי velohei לכב ; מילוי ע״ב, דמב ; ילה אֲבוֹתֵינוּ avotenu.

ק ר

אֱלֹהֵי Elohei מילוי ע״ב, דמב ; ילה אַבְרָהָם Avraham (*Chochmah*)

וז״פ אל, רי״ו ול״ב נתיבות הוזכמה, רמ״וז (אברים), עסמ״ב וט״ז אותיות פשוטות

ע ש

אֱלֹהֵי Elohei מילוי ע״ב, דמב ; ילה יִצְחָק Yitzchak (*Binah*) ד״פ ב״ן

ט נ

וֵאלֹהֵי velohei לכב ; מילוי ע״ב, דמב ; ילה יַעֲקֹב Yaakov (*Da'at*) ז׳ הויות, יאהדונהי אידהנויה

MUSAF OF SHAVUOT

THE AMIDAH

"My Lord, open my lips, and my mouth shall relate Your praise." (Psalms 51:17)

THE FIRST BLESSING

Blessed are You, Lord,

our God and God of our forefathers:the God of Abraham, the God of Isaac, and the God of Jacob.

נ ג

הָאֵל haEl לאה ; ייא״ (מילוי דס״ג) הַגָּדוֹל hagadol האל הגדול = סיט ; גדול = להח

ד י

עם ד׳ אותיות = מבה, יזל, אום הַגִּבּוֹר hagibor ר״ת ההה וְהַנּוֹרָא vehanora•

כ ש

אֵל El ייא״ (מילוי דס״ג) ; ר״ת ע״ב, ריבוע יהוה עֶלְיוֹן elyon•

ב ט ר צ ת

גּוֹמֵל gomel חֲסָדִים chasadim טוֹבִים tovim• קוֹנֵה kone הַכֹּל hakol ילי

ג ח ק ב

וְזוֹכֵר vezocher חַסְדֵי chasdei אָבוֹת avot• וּמֵבִיא umevi

ט נ ע י

גּוֹאֵל go'el לִבְנֵי livnei בְנֵיהֶם venehem לְמַעַן lema'an

ג ל

שְׁמוֹ shemo מהש ע״ה, ע״ב בריבוע וקס״א ע״ה, אל שדי ע״ה בְּאַהֲבָה be'ahava אחד, דאגה:

When saying the word "*be'ahava*" you should meditate to devote your soul to sanctify the Holy Name and accept upon yourself the four forms of death.

פ ז ק ש

מֶלֶךְ melech עוֹזֵר ozer וּמוֹשִׁיעַ umoshi'a וּמָגֵן umagen

ג״פ אל (ייא״ מילוי דס״ג) ; ר״ת מיכאל גבריאל נוריאל:

Bend your knees at "*baruch*", bow at "*Ata*" and straighten up at "*Adonai*".

אהיה יהו אלף הי יוד הי (on Shabbat: יְהֹוָה)

ק ו צ

בָּרוּךְ baruch אַתָּה Ata יְהֹוָהאדני (יְהֹוָהאֱדֹנָי) יאהדונהי Adonai (הד)

י ת

מָגֵן magen ג״פ אל (ייא״ מילוי דס״ג) ; ר״ת מיכאל גבריאל נוריאל אַבְרָהָם Avraham

וז״פ אל, רי״ו ול״ב נתיבות החכמה, רמ״ח (אברים), עסמ״ב וט״ז אותיות פשוטות:

The great, mighty and awesome God.

The Supernal God, Who bestows beneficial kindness and creates everything. Who recalls the kindness of the forefathers and brings a Redeemer to their descendants for the sake of His Name, lovingly. King, Helper, Savior and Shield. Blessed are You, Lord, the shield of Abraham.

THE SECOND BLESSING

THE ENERGY OF ISAAC IGNITES THE POWER FOR THE RESURRECTION OF THE DEAD.

Whereas Abraham represents the power of sharing, Isaac represents the Left Column energy of judgment. Judgment shortens the *tikkun* process and paves the way for our eventual resurrection.

Gevurah that becomes *Binah*.

In this section there are 49 words corresponding to the 49 gates of the Pure System in *Binah*.

אַתָּה Ata גִּבּוֹר gibor לְעוֹלָם le'olam ריבוע ס"ג וי' אותיות דס"ג אֲדֹנָי Adonai ללה

(ר"ת אַגְלָא והוא שם גדול ואמיץ, ובו היה יהודה מתגבר על אויביו. ע"ה אלד, בוכו).

מְחַיֵּה mechaye ס"ג מֵתִים metim אַתָּה Ata• רַב rav לְהוֹשִׁיעַ lehoshi'a•

מוֹרִיד morid הַטָּל hatal יוד הא ואו, כוזו, מספר אותיות דמילואי עסמ"ב ; ר"ת מ"ה:

If you mistakenly say "*Mashiv haru'ach*", and realize this before the end of the blessing ("*baruch Ata Adonai*"), you should return to the beginning of the blessing ("*Ata gibor*") and continue as usual. But if you only realize this after the end of the blessing, you should start the *Amidah* from the beginning.

מְכַלְכֵּל mechalkel חַיִּים chayim אהיה אהיה יהוה, בינה ע"ה בְּחֶסֶד bechesed

ע"ב, ריבוע יהוה• מְחַיֵּה mechaye ס"ג מֵתִים metim בְּרַחֲמִים berachamim

(בְּמוֹכסז) מצפצ, אלהים דההין, י"פ ייי רַבִּים rabim (טלא דעתיק)• סוֹמֵךְ somech

(אכדטם) כוק, ריבוע אדני נוֹפְלִים noflim (זו"ן)• וְרוֹפֵא verofe חוֹלִים cholim

חולה = מ"ה וד' אותיות• וּמַתִּיר umatir אֲסוּרִים asurim• וּמְקַיֵּם umekayem

אֱמוּנָתוֹ emunato לִישֵׁנֵי lishenei עָפָר afar• מִי mi ילי כָּמוֹךָ chamocha

בַּעַל ba'al גְּבוּרוֹת gevurot (you should enunciate the letter *Ayin* in the word "*ba'al*")

וּמִי umi ילי דּוֹמֶה dome לָךְ lach• מֶלֶךְ melech מֵמִית memit

וּמְחַיֶּה umchaye ס"ג (יוד הי ואו הי) וּמַצְמִיחַ umatzmi'ach יְשׁוּעָה yeshu'a:

וְנֶאֱמָן vene'eman אַתָּה Ata לְהַחֲיוֹת lehachayot מֵתִים metim:

אהיה יהו אלף הי יוד הי (on Shabbat: יְהֹוָה)

בָּרוּךְ baruch אַתָּה Ata יְהֹוָהאדה(יְהֹוָהאדני)יאהדונהי Adonai

מְחַיֵּה mechaye ס"ג (יוד הי ואו הי) הַמֵּתִים hametim ר"ת מ"ה וס"ת מ"ה:

THE SECOND BLESSING

You are mighty forever, Lord.

You resurrect the dead and are very capable of redeeming. Who causes dew to fall. You sustain life with kindness and resurrect the dead with great compassion. You support those who have fallen, heal the sick, release the imprisoned, and fulfill Your faithful words to those who are asleep in the dust. Who is like You, Master of might, and Who can compare to You, King, Who causes death, Who gives life, and Who sprouts salvation? And You are faithful to resurrecting the dead. Blessed are You, Lord, Who resurrects the dead.

THE KEDUSHA OF KETER

The congregation recites this prayer together.

Keter is the highest level in the spiritual atmosphere. As we reach this high point in our connections, we stand with both legs together. It is also one of the most powerful prayers to help us connect to the seed level of life before there was any differentiation between the cells of the body. Our meditations during this time increase the production of stem cells in our body.

Lifting a heavy chest filled with vast treasures is impossible if you use just a single string: The string will snap because it is too weak. However, if we unite and combine numerous strings, we will eventually build a rope. A rope can easily lift the treasure chest. By combining and uniting the congregation's prayers, we become a united force, capable of pulling down the most valuable spiritual treasures. Furthermore, this unity helps people who are not well-versed or knowledgeable in the connections. By uniting and meditating as one soul, we all receive the benefit because of the powerof unity, regardless of our knowledge and understanding. This prayer occurs in between the second and third blessings. It signifies the Central Column that unites the Left and Right Columns.

In this prayer the angels speak to each other, saying: "*Kadosh, Kadosh, Kadosh*" ("Holy, Holy, Holy"). When we recite these three words, we stand with our feet stand together as one. With each utterance of *Kadosh*, we jump a little higher in the air. Jumping is an act of restriction and it defies the force of gravity. Spiritually, gravity has the energy of the Desire to Receive for the Self Alone. It is the reactive force of our planet, always pulling everything toward itself.

The Secret of the *Kedusha* from the Ramchal:

We (humans) say *Kedusha* (Holiness) only from the power of the holiness of the angels. Because our way of making the Unification is to recite the "Shema" and the angles do so by the *Kedusha*. But even the correction of the angels is done by us. Because the angels' holiness originated from Abba and Ima they are protected from the negativity, as *Abba* and Ima do not allow the negativity to come closer, even to the external aspect of the angels.

For us, the negativity can grab hold onto the external aspect, which is the body. All of this is for now, during the *tikkun* process. But at the end of the *tikkun* process, even the body will be corrected and holy, so even the angels will draw their *Kedusha* from us. So for now, we say the *Kedusha* from the power of the angels, as we don't have the power to do it ourselves and we need to take it from the correction of the angels and by that we receive a small illumination, even for the body. This illumination is not strong enough to remove the negative forces totally but can only receive the holiness that is available now.

So one should meditate, for the congregation prayer, to be as *Malchut* (you), which is now uniting with *Chesed*, *Gevurah* and *Tiferet* (the congregation). So then the awakening will rise up to *Arich Anpin* to draw the abundance of holiness to *Malchut* and from *Her* to us.

Also scan here the 24 Holy Names – the Adornments of the Bride - on page IV
and meditate for the Holy Unification between *Keter* of *Zeir Anpin* and *Keter* of *Nukva*.

Saying the *Kedusha* (holiness) we meditate to bring the holiness of the Creator among us. As it says: "*Venikdashti betoch Benei Israel*" (God is hallowed among the children of Israel).

כֶּתֶר keter ה' מלך ה' מלך ה' ימלוך לעולם ועד ובאתב"ש גאל יִתְּנוּ yitnu לְךָ lecha

יְהֹוָה אדני אהדונהי Adonai אֱלֹהֵינוּ Elohenu ילה (*Zeir* and *Nukva*) מַלְאָכִים mal'achim

הֲמוֹנֵי hamonei מַעְלָה ma'la (*Abba* and *Ima*) עִם im עַמְּךָ amecha יִשְׂרָאֵל Yisrael

קְבוּצֵי kevutzei מַטָּה mata (by the Righteous). יַחַד yachad כֻּלָּם kulam

קְדֻשָּׁה kedusha לְךָ lecha יְשַׁלֵּשׁוּ yeshaleshu כַּדָּבָר kadavar ראה

הָאָמוּר ha'amur עַל al יַד yad נְבִיאָךְ nevi'ach וְקָרָא vekara

זֶה ze אֶל־ el זֶה ze י"ב פרקין דיעקב מאירין אל י"ב פרקין דרחל וְאָמַר ve'amar:

Meditate to elevate *Malchut* to *Chesed*, *Gevurah*, *Tiferet* of Supernal *Ima*.

(*Chesed*) קָדוֹשׁ kadosh | **(*Gevurah*)** קָדוֹשׁ kadosh **(*Tiferet*)** קָדוֹשׁ kadosh

יְהֹוָה אדני אהדונהי Adonai צְבָאוֹת Tzeva'ot פני שכינה מְלֹא melo כָל־ chol ילי

הָאָרֶץ ha'aretz אלהים דההין ע"ה כְּבוֹדוֹ kevodo:

כְּבוֹדוֹ kevodo מָלֵא male עוֹלָם olam וּמְשָׁרְתָיו umshartav שׁוֹאֲלִים sho'alim

On *Shabbat*: Meditate to receive the extra soul called: *Neshamah*
from the aspect of the day of *Shabbat*.

Da'at	***Chochmah***	***Binah***
Thirteenth *Mazal* (וְנַקֵּה)	***Abba***	***Ima***
אַ	יֵּ	הּ ayeh

מְקוֹם mekom כְּבוֹדוֹ kevodo

Malchut (which is called כבוד ו' – the honor of *Zeir Anpin*)
is in *Chochmah, Binah, Da'at* (also known as איה – *Ayeh*, as mention above).

לְהַעֲרִיצוֹ leha'aritzo איה מקום כבודו להעריצו ר"ת = אמן (יאהדונהי)

לְעֻמָּתָם le'umatam מְשַׁבְּחִים meshabechim וְאוֹמְרִים ve'omrim:

(או"א) בָּרוּךְ baruch כְּבוֹד־ kevod יְהֹוָה אדני אהדונהי Adonai ; כבוד ה' = יוד הי ואו הה

מִמְּקוֹמוֹ mimekomo עסמ"ב, הברכה (למתק את ז' המלכים שמתו) ; ר"ת ע"ב, ריבוע יהוה ; ר"ת מיכ:

Kedusha of Keter

A crown they will give to You, Lord,
our God, the angels of the multitudes above, together with Your nation, Israel, who are assembled below. Together they will all recite the holiness three times, as the word spoken by Your prophet: "And each calls the other and says: Holy, Holy, Holy is the Lord of Hosts; the whole earth is filled with His glory." (Isaiah 6:3) *His glory fills the world and His servants ask: Where is the place of His glory to adore Him? Facing one another, they praise and say: "Blessed is the glory of the Lord from His place."* (Ezekiel 3:12)

מִמְּקוֹמוֹ mimekomo עסמ"ב, הברכה (למתק את ז' המלכים שמתו) הוּא hu יִפֶן yifen

בְּרַחֲמָיו berachamav לְעַמּוֹ le'amo הַמְיַחֲדִים hameyachadim שְׁמוֹ shemo מהש ע"ה,

ע"ב בריבוע וקס"א ע"ה, אל שדי ע"ה עֶרֶב erev וָבֹקֶר vavoker בְּכָל bechol ב"ן, לכב

יוֹם yom ע"ה נגד, מזבח, זן, אל יהוה תָּמִיד tamid ע"ה קס"א קנ"א קמ"ג

אוֹמְרִים omrim פַּעֲמַיִם pa'amayim בְּאַהֲבָה be'ahava אחד, דאגה:

Meditate, to devote your soul for the sanctification of the Holy Name, as well as to elevate your *Neshamah of Neshamah*, by the Name ע"ב, to become *Mayin Duchrin* to *Zeir Anpin* and to elevate your *Neshamah*, by the Name ס"ג, to become *Mayin Mayin* to so They can be unified in *Ima* (**on *Shabbat***: *Zeir Anpin* in *Abba* and *Nukva* in *Ima*) in the secret of the Complete Unification.

שְׁמַע shema ע' רבתי יִשְׂרָאֵל Yisrael יְהֹוָהאדניאהדונהי Adonai אֱלֹהֵינוּ Elohenu ילה

יְהֹוָהאדניאהדונהי Adonai | אֶחָד echad ד' רבתי ; אהבה, דאגה:

הוּא hu אֱלֹהֵינוּ Elohenu ילה. הוּא hu אָבִינוּ avinu. הוּא hu מַלְכֵּנוּ malkenu.

הוּא hu מוֹשִׁיעֵנוּ moshi'enu. הוּא hu יוֹשִׁיעֵנוּ yoshi'enu וְיִגְאָלֵנוּ veyigalenu

שֵׁנִית shenit. וְיַשְׁמִיעֵנוּ veyashmi'enu בְּרַחֲמָיו berachamav לְעֵינֵי le'enei ריבוע מ"ה

כָּל kol ילי וחַי chai כל חי = אהיה אהיה יהוה, בינה ע"ה, חיים לֵאמֹר lemor.

הֵן hen גָּאַלְתִּי ga'alti אֶתְכֶם et'chem אַחֲרִית acharit כְּרֵאשִׁית kereshit

לִהְיוֹת lih'yot לָכֶם lachem לֵאלֹהִים lelohim אהיה אדני ; ילה.

אֲנִי ani אני יְהֹוָהאדניאהדונהי Adonai אֱלֹהֵיכֶם Elohechem ילה:

וּבְדִבְרֵי uvdivrei קָדְשְׁךָ kodshach כָּתוּב katuv לֵאמֹר lemor:

(זו"ן) יִמְלֹךְ yimloch קדוש ברוך ימלך ר"ת יב"ק, אלהים יהוה, אהיה אדני יהוה

יְהֹוָהאדניאהדונהי Adonai לְעוֹלָם le'olam ריבוע ס"ג וי' אותיות דס"ג אֱלֹהַיִךְ Elohayich ילה

צִיּוֹן Tziyon יוסף, ו' הויות, קנאה לְדֹר ledor וָדֹר vador רי"ו ; ר"ת אצלו (מלכות אצל ז"א – ו)

הַלְלוּיָהּ haleluya אלהים, אהיה אדני ; ללה:

From His place, may He turn with compassion to His nation, who, evening and morning, twice each day, proclaims with constancy the Oneness of His Name, saying with love: "Hear Israel, the Lord is our God, the Lord is One." (Deuteronomy 6:4) *He is our God. He is our Father. He is our King. He is our Savior. He will save and redeem us again and will let us hear, through His compassion to the eyes of all the living, and will say: Behold I have redeemed you in later times as I have in earlier times, in order to be a God for you. I am the Lord, your God. And in Your holy writings, the following is written: "The Lord will reign forever, your God, Zion, from one generation to the other, praise the Lord!"* (Psalms 146:10)

THE THIRD BLESSING

This blessing connects us to Jacob, the Central Column and the power of restriction. Jacob is our channel for connecting mercy with judgment. By restricting our reactive behavior, we are blocking our Desire to Receive for the Self Alone. Jacob also gives us the power to balance our acts of mercy and judgment toward other people in our lives.

Tiferet* that becomes *Da'at (14 words).

אַתָּה Ata קָדוֹשׁ kadosh וְשִׁמְךָ veshimcha קָדוֹשׁ kadosh ר״ת = אור, רז, אין סוף ◆

וּקְדוֹשִׁים ukdoshim בְּכָל־ bechol ב״ן, לכב יוֹם yom ע״ה נגד, מזבח, זן, אל יהוה

יְהַלְלוּךָ yehaleluch סֶלָה sela:

אה״ה יהו אלף הא יוד הא (on Shabbat: מצפצ)

בָּרוּךְ baruch אַתָּה Ata יְהֹוָהאדהנויה (יְהֹוָהאדהנויה) יאהדונהי Adonai

הָאֵל haEl לאה ; ייא״י (מילוי דס״ג) הַקָּדוֹשׁ hakadosh י״פ מ״ה (יוד הא ואו הא):

Meditate here on the Name: יאהדונהי, as it can help to remove anger.

THE MIDDLE BLESSING

The middle blessing connects us to the true essence of *Shavuot*. *Shavuot* is our connection to immortality and this blessing is our opportunity to choose the seed we wish to plant for immortality. The power of the letters in the Fourth Blessing is in their ability to automatically choose the correct seed we need and not necessarily the seed we want.

אַתָּה Ata בְּחַרְתָּנוּ vechartanu מִכָּל mikol ילי הָעַמִּים ha'amim ◆

אָהַבְתָּ ahavta אוֹתָנוּ otanu וְרָצִיתָ veratzita בָּנוּ banu ◆

וְרוֹמַמְתָּנוּ veromamtanu מִכָּל mikol ילי הַלְּשׁוֹנוֹת haleshonot ◆

וְקִדַּשְׁתָּנוּ vekidashtanu בְּמִצְוֹתֶיךָ bemitzvotecha ◆ וְקֵרַבְתָּנוּ vekeravtanu

מַלְכֵּנוּ malkenu לַעֲבוֹדָתֶךָ la'avodatecha ◆ וְשִׁמְךָ veshimcha הַגָּדוֹל hagadol

להח ; ועם ד׳ אותיות = מבה, יזל, אום וְהַקָּדוֹשׁ vehakadosh עָלֵינוּ alenu קָרָאתָ karata:

THE THIRD BLESSING

You are holy, and Your Name is holy.
and the holy ones praise You every day, Selah. Blessed are You, Lord, the Holy God.

THE MIDDLE BLESSING

You had chosen us from among all the nations. You had loved us and have found favor in us. You had exalted us above all the tongues and You had sanctified us with Your commandments. You drew us close, our King, to Your service and proclaimed Your great and Holy Name upon us.

וַתִּתֶּן vatiten ב"פ כהת לָנוּ lanu אלהים, אהיה אדני יְהֹוָהאדנייאהדונהי Adonai
אֱלֹהֵינוּ Elohenu ילה בְּאַהֲבָה be'ahava אחד, דאגה (On Shabbat add:
שַׁבָּתוֹת shabbatot לִמְנוּחָה limnucha ו u) מוֹעֲדִים mo'adim לְשִׂמְחָה lesimcha.
חַגִּים chagim וּזְמַנִּים uzmanim לְשָׂשׂוֹן lesason. אֶת et
יוֹם yom ע"ה נגד, מזבח, זן, אל יהוה (On Shabbat add: הַשַּׁבָּת hashabat הַזֶּה hazeh והו.
וְאֶת ve'et יוֹם yom ע"ה נגד, מזבח, זן, אל יהוה) חַג chag הַשָּׁבוּעוֹת haShavuot
הַזֶּה hazeh והו. אֶת et יוֹם yom ע"ה נגד, מזבח, זן, אל יהוה טוֹב tov והו
מִקְרָא mikra קֹדֶשׁ kodesh הַזֶּה hazeh והו. זְמַן zeman
חֵרוּתֵנוּ cherutenu. בְּאַהֲבָה be'ahava אחד, דאגה מִקְרָא mikra
קֹדֶשׁ kodesh. זֵכֶר zecher לִיצִיאַת litzi'at מִצְרָיִם Mitzrayim מצר.

אֱלֹהֵינוּ Elohenu ילה וֵאלֹהֵי vElohei לכב; מילוי ע"ב, דמב; ילה אֲבוֹתֵינוּ avotenu
מִפְּנֵי mipnei חֲטָאֵינוּ chataenu גָּלִינוּ galinu מֵאַרְצֵנוּ me'artzenu.
וְנִתְרַחַקְנוּ venitrachaknu מֵעַל me'al עלם אַדְמָתֵנוּ admatenu. וְאֵין ve'en
אֲנַחְנוּ anachnu יְכוֹלִים yecholim לַעֲלוֹת la'alot וְלֵרָאוֹת veleraot
וּלְהִשְׁתַּחֲוֺת ulhishtachavot לְפָנֶיךָ lefanecha ס"ג מ"ה ב"ן בְּבֵית bevet ב"פ ראה
בְּחִירָתָךְ bechiratach בִּנְוֵה binveh הֲדָרָךְ hadarach ב"פ יב"ק, קס"א ס"ג
בַּבַּיִת babayit ב"פ ראה הַגָּדוֹל hagadol להח; עם ד' אותיות = מבה, יזל, אום
וְהַקָּדוֹשׁ vehakadosh שֶׁנִּקְרָא shenikra שִׁמְךָ shimcha עָלָיו alav מִפְּנֵי mipnei
הַיָּד hayad והו שֶׁנִּשְׁתַּלְּחָה shenishtalcha בְּמִקְדָּשָׁךְ bemikdashach:

YHI RATZON

This prayer connects to the desire to see the Holy Temple rebuilt. Even though, according to Kabbalah, the temple still exists on a spiritual level, the physical structure is missing, leaving our world incomplete. This prayer helps set in motion and accelerate the eventual construction of the physical temple.

And may You give us, Lord, our God, with love (**on Shabbat add:** *Shabbat for rest and) holidays for happiness, festivals and time of joy, this day* (**on Shabbat add:** *of Shabbat and this day) of the Shavuot Holiday, and this good day of Holy Convocation, the time we received our Torah with love, a Holy Convocation, a remembrance of the exit from Egypt.*

Our God and the God of our fathers, because of our sins we are in exile from our land. We are far from our land. And we cannot come to pilgrim, be seen and bow before You, in Your house of choice. Your house of glory, the big and Holy house called after Your Name, because of the hand that ruined Your Temple.

יְהִי yehi רָצוֹן ratzon מִלְּפָנֶיךָ milfanecha יְהֹוָהאדניאהדונהי Adonai
אֱלֹהֵינוּ Elohenu ילה וֵאלֹהֵי vElohei לכב; מילוי ע"ב = דמב; ילה אֲבוֹתֵינוּ avotenu•
מֶלֶךְ melech רַחֲמָן rachaman• שֶׁתָּשׁוּב shetashuv וּתְרַחֵם utrachem ג"פ רי"ו;
אברהם, וז"פ אל, רי"ו ול"ב נתיבות החכמה, רמ"ח (איברים), עסמ"ב וט"ז אותיות פשוטות עָלֵינוּ alenu•
וְעַל ve'al מִקְדָּשְׁךָ mikdashcha בְּרַחֲמֶיךָ berachamecha הָרַבִּים harabim•
וְתִבְנֵהוּ vetivnehu מְהֵרָה mehera• וּתְגַדֵּל utgadel כְּבוֹדוֹ kevodo•
אָבִינוּ avinu• מַלְכֵּנוּ malkenu• אֱלֹהֵינוּ Elohenu ילה• גַּלֵּה gale כְּבוֹד kevod
מַלְכוּתְךָ malchutcha עָלֵינוּ alenu מְהֵרָה mehera• וְהוֹפַע vehofa
וְהִנָּשֵׂא vehinase עָלֵינוּ alenu לְעֵינֵי le'enei ריבוע מ"ה כָּל kol ילי
חַי chai כל חי = חיים, אהיה אהיהיהוה, בינה ע"ה• וְקָרֵב vekarev פְּזוּרֵינוּ pezurenu
מִבֵּין miben הַגּוֹיִם hagoyim• וּנְפוּצוֹתֵינוּ unfutzotenu כַּנֵּס kanes
מִיַּרְכְּתֵי miyarketei אָרֶץ aretz• וַהֲבִיאֵנוּ vahavi'enu יְהֹוָהאדניאהדונהי Adonai
אֱלֹהֵינוּ Elohenu ילה לְצִיּוֹן leTziyon יוסף, ו' הויות, קנאה עִירְךָ irach בְּרִנָּה berina•
וְלִירוּשָׁלַיִם velirushalayim עִיר ir ערי, מנצפך, סנדלפון מִקְדָּשְׁךָ mikdashcha
בְּשִׂמְחַת besimchat עוֹלָם olam• אָנָּא ana ב"ן, לכב אֱלֹהֵינוּ Elohenu ילה
וְשָׁם vesham נַעֲשֶׂה na'ase לְפָנֶיךָ lefanecha ס"ג מ"ה ב"ן אֶת et קָרְבְּנוֹת korbenot
חוֹבוֹתֵינוּ chovotenu• תְּמִידִים temidim כְּסִדְרָם kesidram• וּמוּסָפִים umusafim
כְּהִלְכָתָם kehilchatam• (On weekdays we say: אֶת et מוּסַף musaf יוסף)
(On Shabbat we say: אֶת et מוּסְפֵי musfei יוֹם yom ע"ה נגד, מזבח, זן, אל יהוה
הַשַּׁבָּת hashabat הַזֶּה hazeh והו• וְאֶת ve'et) יוֹם yom ע"ה נגד, מזבח, זן, אל יהוה
חַג chag הַשָּׁבוּעוֹת haShavuot הַזֶּה haze והו

May it be Your will, Lord, our God, God of our forefathers, compassionate King, that You again have mercy upon us and upon Your Sanctuary, in Your abundant compassion, and may You rebuild it speedily and make great its glory. Our Father, our King, our God, Reveal the glory of Your Kingdom over us speedily and appear and be exalted over us, before the eyes of all the living. Draw near our scattered from among the nations, and gather our dispersed from the ends of the earth. And bring us, Lord, our God, to Zion, Your city, with joyous song, and to Jerusalem, city of Your Sanctuary, in everlasting joy. Please, our God – and there we shall perform before You our obligatory sacrifices: the daily-offerings in their proper order and the Musaf-offerings according to their prescribed laws. The Musaf-offerings (**on Shabbat we say:** *Musaf-offerings of this day of Shabbat and of) this day of the Shavuot Holiday.*

אֶת et יוֹם yom ע״ה נגד, מזבח, זן, אל יהוה טוֹב tov והו מִקְרָא mikra קֹדֶשׁ kodesh
הַזֶּה haze והו • נַעֲשֶׂה na'ase וְנַקְרִיב venakriv לְפָנֶיךָ lefanecha ס״ג מ״ה ב״ן
בְּאַהֲבָה be'ahava אחד, דאגה כְּמִצְוַת kemitzvat רְצוֹנָךְ retzonach כְּמוֹ kemo
שֶׁכָּתַבְתָּ shekatavta עָלֵינוּ alenu בְּתוֹרָתָךְ betoratach עַל al יְדֵי yedei
מֹשֶׁה Moshe מהש, ע״ב בריבוע וקס״א, אל שדי, ד״פ אלהים ע״ה עַבְדָּךְ avdecha פוי, אל יהוה:

אֱלֹהֵינוּ Elohenu ילה וֵאלֹהֵי vElohei לכב; מילוי ע״ב, דמב; ילה אֲבוֹתֵינוּ avotenu,
מֶלֶךְ melech רַחֲמָן rachaman רַחֵם rachem אברהם, וז״פ אל, רי״ו ול״ב נתיבות החכמה, רמ״ח
(איברים), עסמ״ב וט״ז אותיות פשוטות עָלֵינוּ alenu • טוֹב tov והו וּמֵטִיב umetiv
הִדָּרֵשׁ hidaresh לָנוּ lanu אלהים, אדני אהיה • שׁוּבָה shuva הוזש עָלֵינוּ alenu
בַּהֲמוֹן bahamon רַחֲמֶיךָ rachamecha • בִּגְלַל biglal אָבוֹת avot שֶׁעָשׂוּ she'asu
רְצוֹנֶךָ retzonecha • בְּנֵה bene בֵּיתְךָ vetcha ב״פ ראה כְּבַתְּחִלָּה kevatechila •
כּוֹנֵן konen כוק בֵּית bet ב״פ ראה מִקְדָּשְׁךָ mikdashcha עַל al מְכוֹנוֹ mechono •
הַרְאֵנוּ harenu בְּבִנְיָנוֹ bevinyano • שַׂמְּחֵנוּ samchenu בְּתִיקּוּנוֹ betikuno •
וְהָשֵׁב vehashev שְׁכִינָתְךָ shechinatcha לְתוֹכוֹ letocho, וְהָשֵׁב vehashev
כֹּהֲנִים Kohanim לַעֲבוֹדָתָם la'avodatam, וּלְוִיִּם uLviyim לְדוּכָנָם leduchanam
לְשִׁירָם leshiram וּלְזִמְרָם ulzimram • וְהָשֵׁב vehashev יִשְׂרָאֵל Yisrael
לִנְוֵיהֶם linvehem • וְשָׁם vesham נַעֲלֶה na'ale וְנֵרָאֶה venerae
וְנִשְׁתַּחֲוֶה venishtachave לְפָנֶיךָ lefanecha ס״ג מ״ה ב״ן, בְּשָׁלֹשׁ beshalosh
פַּעֲמֵי pe'amei רְגָלֵינוּ regalenu בְּכָל bechol יה אדני שָׁנָה shana וְשָׁנָה veshana •

The good day of holy convocation.
we shall prepare and offer before You, with love, according to the commandment
of Your will, as You wrote for us in Your Torah, through Moshe, Your servant.

Our God and the God of our fathers, Compassionate King, have mercy upon us. Good and Kind, seek us. Return to us with Your mass compassion. Because of Your fathers who obeyed Your will. Build Your house as before. And bring back the Tamale to its place. Show us its rebuilding. Let us be happy with its restoration. Bring Your Shechinah, and bring back the Kohanim to their works, the Lveites to their stand, their singing and chanting. Bring Israel back to their dwelling place. There we shall come to bow before You, each year, during the three pilgrimage.

כַּכָּתוּב kakatuv בַּתּוֹרָה batora: שָׁלֹשׁ shalosh פְּעָמִים pe'amim
בַּשָּׁנָה bashana יֵרָאֶה yera'e ריו כָּל chol יכי זְכוּרְךָ zechurcha אֶת et
פְּנֵי penei חכמה בינה יְהֹוָהאדניאהדונהי Adonai אֱלֹהֶיךָ Elohecha ילה
בַּמָּקוֹם bamakom אֲשֶׁר asher יִבְחָר yivchar בְּחַג bechag הַמַּצּוֹת hamatzot
וּבְחַג uvchag הַשָּׁבוּעוֹת hashavu'ot וּבְחַג uvchag הַסֻּכּוֹת hasukot וְלֹא velo
יֵרָאֶה yera'e ריו אֶת et פְּנֵי penei חכמה בינה יְהֹוָהאדניאהדונהי Adonai רֵיקָם rekam:
אִישׁ ish כְּמַתְּנַת kematnat יָדוֹ yado כְּבִרְכַּת kevirkat
יְהֹוָהאדניאהדונהי Adonai אֱלֹהֶיךָ Elohecha ילה אֲשֶׁר asher נָתַן natan לָךְ lach:
וְהַשִּׂיאֵנוּ vehasi'enu יְהֹוָהאדניאהדונהי Adonai אֱלֹהֵינוּ Elohenu ילה.
אֶת et בִּרְכַּת birkat מוֹעֲדֶיךָ mo'adecha לְחַיִּים lechayim אהיה אהיה יהוה, בינה ע"ה
בְּשִׂמְחָה besimcha וּבְשָׁלוֹם uvshalom. כַּאֲשֶׁר ka'asher רָצִיתָ ratzita
וְאָמַרְתָּ ve'amarta לְבָרְכֵנוּ levarchenu. כֵּן ken תְּבָרְכֵנוּ tevarchenu
סֶלָה selah:

MEKADESH ISRAEL AND THE TIME

(On Shabbat add: אֱלֹהֵינוּ Elohenu ילה וֵאלֹהֵי veElohei לכב ; מילוי ע"ב, דמב ; ילה
אֲבוֹתֵינוּ avotenu רְצֵה retze נָא na בִּמְנוּחָתֵינוּ vimnuchatenu)
קַדְּשֵׁנוּ kadshenu בְּמִצְוֹתֶיךָ vemitzvotecha. תֵּן ten וְחֶלְקֵנוּ chelkenu
בְּתוֹרָתֶךָ vetoratach. שַׂבְּעֵנוּ sabe'enu מִטּוּבָךְ mituvach לאו.

As stated in the Torah: "Three times a year all your remembrance shall see the face of the Lord, your God, at the place of His choice on the holiday of the Matzot, on the holiday of Shavuot and the holiday of Sukkot, and no one should see the face of the Lord empty handed. Each person with his present as blessed by what the Lord, your God, gave you." (Deuteronomy 16:16-17)

And give us, Lord, our God Your blessing of Your holidays for happy and peaceful life. As You desired and said to bless us. So You shall bless us Selah.

MEKADESH ISRAEL AND THE TIME

(**on Shabbat:** *Our God and the God of our forefathers, please desire our rest.)*

Sanctify us with Your commandments and place our lot in Your Torah and satiate us from Your goodness

שַׂמֵּחַ same'ach נַפְשֵׁנוּ nafshenu בִּישׁוּעָתֶךָ bishu'atach.

וְטַהֵר vetaher לִבֵּנוּ libenu לְעָבְדְּךָ le'ovdecha פוי, אל יהוה בֶּאֱמֶת ve'emet

אהיה פעמים אהיה, ז"פ ס"ג. וְהַנְחִילֵנוּ vehanchilenu יְהֹוָהאדניאהדונהי Adonai

אֱלֹהֵינוּ Elohenu ילה (On Shabbat add: בְּאַהֲבָה be'ahava אחד, דאגה

וּבְרָצוֹן uvratzon מהש ע"ה, ע"ב בריבוע וקס"א ע"ה, אל שדי) בְּשִׂמְחָה vesimcha

וּבְשָׂשׂוֹן uvsason (On Shabbat add: שַׁבָּתוֹת shabatot ו) מוֹעֲדֵי mo'adei

קָדְשֶׁךָ kodshecha, וְיִשְׂמְחוּ veyismechu בְךָ vecha כָּל kol ילי יִשְׂרָאֵל Yisrael

מְקַדְּשֵׁי mekadshei שְׁמֶךָ shemecha. בָּרוּךְ baruch אַתָּה Ata

יְהֹוָהאדניאהדונהי Adonai

אהיה יהו אלף הה יוד הה (on Shabbat: יה אדני)

מְקַדֵּשׁ mekadesh (On Shabbat add: הַשַּׁבָּת hashabat וְ ve) יִשְׂרָאֵל Yisrael

וְהַזְּמַנִּים vehazemanim:

THE FINAL THREE BLESSINGS

Through the merit of Moses, Aaron and Joseph, who are our channels for the final three blessings, we are able to bring down all the spiritual energy that we aroused with our prayers and blessings.

THE FIFTH BLESSING

During this blessing, referring to Moses, we should always meditate to try to know exactly what God wants from us in our life, as signified by the phrase, "Let it be the will of God." We ask God to guide us toward the work we came to Earth to do. The Creator cannot just accept the work that we want to do; we must carry out the work we were destined to do.

Netzach

Meditate for the Supernal Desire (*Keter*) that is called *Metzach HaRatzon* (the Forehead of the Desire).

---

*and gladden our spirits with Your salvation. and purify our heart so as to serve You truly. And grant us, Lord, our God, (***on Shabbat:*** with love and favor,) with happiness and joy (***on Shabbat:*** Shabbatot and) the holidays, and all Yisrael, who sanctify Your Name will be joyful with You. Blessed are You, Lord, who sanctifies (***on Shabbat:*** the Sabbath) and Israel and the Times.*

רְצֵה retze אלף למד הה יוד מם

Meditate here to transform misfortune and tragedy (צרה) into desire and acceptance (רצה).

יְהֹוָאדהֿנָיאהדונהי Adonai אֱלֹהֵינוּ Elohenu ילה בְּעַמְּךָ be'amecha יִשְׂרָאֵל Yisrael

וְלִתְפִלָּתָם velitfilatam שְׁעֵה she'e• וְהָשֵׁב vehashev הָעֲבוֹדָה ha'avoda

לִדְבִיר lidvir רי״ו בֵּיתֶךָ betecha ב״פ ראה• וְאִשֵּׁי ve'ishei יִשְׂרָאֵל Yisrael

וּתְפִלָּתָם utfilatam מְהֵרָה mehera בְּאַהֲבָה be'ahava אחד, דאגה

תְּקַבֵּל tekabel בְּרָצוֹן beratzon מהש ע״ה, ע״ב בריבוע וקס״א ע״ה, אל שדי ע״ה•

וּתְהִי ut'hi לְרָצוֹן leratzon מהש ע״ה, ע״ב בריבוע וקס״א ע״ה, אל שדי ע״ה

תָּמִיד tamid ע״ה קס״א קנ״א קמ״ג עֲבוֹדַת avodat יִשְׂרָאֵל Yisrael עַמֶּךָ amecha:

וְאַתָּה veAta בְּרַחֲמֶיךָ verachamecha הָרַבִּים harabim•

תַּחְפֹּץ tachpotz בָּנוּ banu וְתִרְצֵנוּ vetirtzenu

וְתֶחֱזֶינָה vetechezena עֵינֵינוּ enenu ריבוע מ״ה בְּשׁוּבְךָ beshuvcha

לְצִיּוֹן leTziyon יוסף, ו׳ הויות, קנאה בְּרַחֲמִים berachamim מצפצ, אלהים דיודין, י״פ ייי:

בָּרוּךְ baruch אַתָּה Ata

אהיה יהו אלף למד הי יוד מם (on Shabbat: אל)

יְהֹוָאדהֿנָיאהדונהי Adonai

הַמַּחֲזִיר hamachazir שְׁכִינָתוֹ shechinato לְצִיּוֹן leTziyon יוסף, ו׳ הויות, קנאה:

THE FINAL THREE BLESSINGS

THE FIFTH BLESSING

Find favor, Lord, our God, in Your people, Israel, and turn to their prayer. Restore the service to the inner sanctuary of Your Temple. Accept the offerings of Israel and their prayer with favor, speedily, and with love. May it always be favorable to You, the service of Israel Your nation.

And You in Your great compassion take delight in us and be pleased with us. May our eyes witness Your return to Zion with compassion. Blessed are You, Lord, Who returns His Shechinah to Zion.

THE SIXTH BLESSING

This blessing is our thank you. Kabbalistically, the biggest "thank you" we can give the Creator is to do exactly what we are supposed to do in terms of our spiritual work.

Hod

Bow your entire body at "*modim*" and straighten up at "*Adonai.*"

מוֹדִים modim מאה ברכות שתיקן דוד לאמרם כל יום אֲנַחְנוּ anachnu לָךְ lach

שָׁאַתָּה sheAta הוּא hu יְהֹוָהאדניאהדונהי Adonai (ונ) אֱלֹהֵינוּ Elohenu ילה

וֵאלֹהֵי velohei לכב ; מילוי ע"ב, דמב ; ילה אֲבוֹתֵינוּ avotenu לְעוֹלָם le'olam

ריבוע ס"ג וי' אותיות דס"ג וָעֶד va'ed. צוּרֵנוּ tzurenu צוּר tzur אלהים דההין ע"ה

חַיֵּינוּ chayenu וּמָגֵן umagen ג"פ אל (ייא" מילוי דס"ג) ; ר"ת מיכאל גבריאל נוריאל

יִשְׁעֵנוּ yish'enu אַתָּה Ata הוּא hu. לְדֹר ledor וָדֹר vador רי"ו נוֹדֶה node

לְךָ lecha וּנְסַפֵּר unsaper תְּהִלָּתֶךָ tehilatecha. עַל־ al חַיֵּינוּ chayenu

הַמְּסוּרִים hamesurim בְּיָדֶךָ beyadecha. וְעַל ve'al נִשְׁמוֹתֵינוּ nishmotenu

הַפְּקוּדוֹת hapekudot לָךְ lach. וְעַל־ ve'al נִסֶּיךָ nisecha שֶׁבְּכָל shebechol

ב"ן, לכב יוֹם yom ע"ה נגד, מזבח, זן, אל יהוה עִמָּנוּ imanu ריבוע ס"ג, קס"א ע"ה וד' אותיות

וְעַל ve'al נִפְלְאוֹתֶיךָ nifle'otecha וְטוֹבוֹתֶיךָ vetovotecha שֶׁבְּכָל shebechol

ב"ן, לכב עֵת et. עֶרֶב erev וָבֹקֶר vavoker וְצָהֳרָיִם vetzahorayim. הַטּוֹב hatov

והו כִּי־ ki לֹא־ lo כָלוּ chalu רַחֲמֶיךָ rachamecha. הַמְרַחֵם hamerachem

אברהם, וח"פ אל, רי"ו ול"ב נתיבות החכמה, רמ"ח (אברים), עסמ"ב וט"ז אותיות פשוטות כִּי־ ki לֹא lo

תַמּוּ tamu חֲסָדֶיךָ chasadecha כִּי ki מֵעוֹלָם me'olam קִוִּינוּ kivinu לָךְ lach:

THE SIXTH BLESSING

We give thanks to You, for it is You, Lord, Who is our God and the God of our forefathers, forever and for all eternity. You are our Rock, the Rock of our lives, and the shield of our salvation. From one generation to another, we shall give thanks to You and we shall tell of Your praise. For our lives that are entrusted in Your hands, for our souls that are in Your care, for Your miracles that are with us every day, and for Your wonders and Your favors that are with us at all times: evening, morning and afternoon. You are the good One, for Your compassion has never ceased. You are the compassionate One, for Your kindness has never ended, for we have always placed our hope in You.

MODIM DERABANAN

This prayer is recited by the congregation in the repetition when the *chazan* says "*modim.*"

In this section there are 44 words which is the same numerical value as the Name: ריבוע אהיה (א אה אהי אהיה).

מוֹדִים modim מאה ברכות שתיקן דוד לאמרם כל יום אֲנַחְנוּ anachnu לָךְ lach
שָׁאַתָּה sheAta הוּא hu יְהֹוָה(אדני)אהדונהי Adonai אֱלֹהֵינוּ Elohenu ילה
וֵאלֹהֵי velohei לכב ; מילוי ע"ב, דמב ; ילה אֲבוֹתֵינוּ avotenu
אֱלֹהֵי Elohei מילוי ע"ב, דמב ; ילה כָל chol ילי בָּשָׂר basar. יוֹצְרֵנוּ yotzrenu
יוֹצֵר yotzer בְּרֵאשִׁית bereshit. בְּרָכוֹת berachot וְהוֹדָאוֹת vehoda'ot
לְשִׁמְךָ leshimcha הַגָּדוֹל hagadol להח ; עם ד' אותיות = מבה, יזל, אום
וְהַקָּדוֹשׁ vehakadosh עַל al שֶׁהֶחֱיִיתָנוּ shehecheyitanu וְקִיַּמְתָּנוּ vekiyamtanu.
כֵּן ken תְּחַיֵּינוּ techayenu וּתְחָנֵּנוּ utchonenu. וְתֶאֱסוֹף vete'esof
גָּלֻיּוֹתֵינוּ galuyoteinu לְחַצְרוֹת lechatzrot קָדְשֶׁךָ kodshecha. לִשְׁמוֹר lishmor
חֻקֶּיךָ chukecha וְלַעֲשׂוֹת vela'asot רְצוֹנְךָ retzoncha. וּלְעָבְדְּךָ ul'ovdecha
פוי, אל אדני בְּלֵבָב belevav בוכו שָׁלֵם shalem. עַל al שֶׁאֲנַחְנוּ she'anachnu
מוֹדִים modim לָךְ lach. בָּרוּךְ baruch אֵל El ייא"י (מילוי דס"ג) הַהוֹדָאוֹת hahoda'ot:

וְעַל ve'al כֻּלָּם kulam יִתְבָּרַךְ yitbarach וְיִתְרוֹמַם veyitromam
וְיִתְנַשֵּׂא veyitnase תָּמִיד tamid ע"ה קס"א קנ"א קמ"ג שִׁמְךָ shimcha
מַלְכֵּנוּ malkenu לְעוֹלָם le'olam ריבוע ס"ג וי' אותיות דס"ג וָעֶד va'ed.
וְכָל־ vechol ילי הַחַיִּים hachayim אהיה אהיה יהוה, בינה ע"ה יוֹדוּךָ yoducha סֶּלָה sela:

וִיהַלְלוּ vihalelu וִיבָרְכוּ vivarchu יהוה ריבוע יהוה ריבוע מ"ה
אֶת־ et שִׁמְךָ shimcha הַגָּדוֹל hagadol להח ; עם ד' אותיות = מבה, יזל, אום

MODIM DERABANAN

We give thanks to You, for it is You

Who is our God and God of our forefathers, the God of all flesh, our Maker and the Former of all Creation. Blessings and thanks to Your great and Holy Name for giving us life and for preserving us. So may You continue to give us life, be gracious to us, and gather our exiles to the courtyards of Your Sanctuary, so that we may keep Your laws, fulfill Your will, and serve You wholeheartedly. For this, we thank You. Bless the God of thanksgiving.

And for all those things, may Your Name be always blessed, exalted and extolled, our King, forever and ever, and all the living shall thank You, Selah. And they shall praise and bless Your great Name,

בֶּאֱמֶת be'emet אהיה פעמים אהיה, ז"פ ס"ג לְעוֹלָם le'olam ריבוע ס"ג וי' אותיות דס"ג

כִּי ki טוֹב tov והו ; כי טוב = יהוה אהיה, אום, מבה, יזל.

הָאֵל haEl לאה ; ייא"י (מילוי דס"ג) יְשׁוּעָתֵנוּ yeshu'atenu

וְעֶזְרָתֵנוּ ve'ezratenu סֶלָה sela. הָאֵל haEl לאה ; ייא"י (מילוי דס"ג) הַטּוֹב hatov והו:

Bend your knees at "baruch", bow at "Ata" and straighten up at "Adonai".

אהיה יהו אלף למד הה יוד מם (on Shabbat: אלהים)

בָּרוּךְ baruch אַתָּה Ata יְהֹוָהאדהנויאהדונהי Adonai (הי) הַטּוֹב hatov והו

שִׁמְךָ shimcha וּלְךָ ulcha נָאֶה na'e לְהוֹדוֹת lehodot ס"ת כהת, משיח בן דוד ע"ה:

For the blessing of the *Kohanim* see page 376.

THE FINAL BLESSING

We are emanating the energy of peace to the entire world. We also make it our intent to use our mouths only for good. Kabbalistically, the power of words and speech is unimaginable. We hope to use that power wisely, which is perhaps one of the most difficult tasks we have to carry out.

Yesod

שִׂים sim שָׁלוֹם shalom

טוֹבָה tova אכא וּבְרָכָה uvracha חַיִּים chayim אהיה אהיה יהוה, בינה ע"ה

חֵן chen מילוי דמ"ה בריבוע, מוזי וָחֶסֶד vachesed ע"ב, ריבוע יהוה

צְדָקָה tzedaka ע"ה ריבוע אלהים וְרַחֲמִים verachamim עָלֵינוּ alenu

וְעַל־ ve'al כָּל־ kol ילי ; עמם יִשְׂרָאֵל Yisrael עַמֶּךָ amecha

וּבָרְכֵנוּ uvarchenu אָבִינוּ avinu כֻּלָּנוּ kulanu כְּאֶחָד ke'echad אהבה, דאגה

בְּאוֹר be'or רז, א"ס פָּנֶיךָ panecha ס"ג מ"ה ב"ן כִּי ki בְּאוֹר ve'or רז, א"ס

פָּנֶיךָ panecha ס"ג מ"ה ב"ן נָתַתָּ natata לָּנוּ lanu אלהים, אהיה אדני יְהֹוָהאדהנויאהדונהי Adonai

אֱלֹהֵינוּ Elohenu ילה תּוֹרָה torah וְחַיִּים vechayim אהיה אהיה יהוה, בינה ע"ה.

---

sincerely and forever, for It is good, the God of our salvation and our help, Selah, the good God. Blessed are You, Lord, whose Name is good and to You it is befitting to give thanks.

THE FINAL BLESSING

Place peace, goodness, blessing, life, grace, kindness, righteousness, and mercy upon us and upon all of Israel, Your people. Bless us all as one, our Father, with the Light of Your countenance, because it is with the Light of Your countenance that You, Lord, our God, have given us Torah and life,

אַהֲבָה ahava אוזר, דאגה וָחֶסֶד vachesed ע״ב, ריבוע יהוה.
צְדָקָה tzedaka ע״ה ריבוע אלהים וְרַחֲמִים verachamim. בְּרָכָה beracha
וְשָׁלוֹם veshalom. וְטוֹב vetov והו בְּעֵינֶיךָ be'enecha ע״ה קס״א ; ריבוע מ״ה
לְבָרְכֵנוּ levarchenu וּלְבָרֵךְ ulvarech אֶת et כָּל kol ילי עַמְּךָ amecha
יִשְׂרָאֵל Yisrael בְּרוֹב berov י״פ אהיה עֹז oz וְשָׁלוֹם veshalom:

בָּרוּךְ baruch אַתָּה Ata
אהיה יהו אלף למד הה יוד מם (on Shabbat: מצפצ)
יְהֹוָהאדניאהדונהי Adonai

הַמְבָרֵךְ hamevarech אֶת et עַמּוֹ amo יִשְׂרָאֵל Yisrael
ר״ת = אלהים (אילההויהם = יב״ק) בַּשָּׁלוֹם bashalom. אָמֵן amen יאהדונהי.

YIH'YU LERATZON

There are 42 letters in the verse in the secret of *Ana Beko'ach*.

יִהְיוּ yih'yu אל (ייא״י מילוי דס״ג) לְרָצוֹן leratzon מהש ע״ה, ע״ב בריבוע וקס״א ע״ה, אל שדי ע״ה
אִמְרֵי imrei פִי fi ר״ת אֶלֶף = אלף למד שין דלת יוד ע״ה וְהֶגְיוֹן vehegyon לִבִּי libi
לְפָנֶיךָ lefanecha ס״ג מ״ה ב״ן יְהֹוָהאדניאהדונהי Adonai צוּרִי tzuri וְגֹאֲלִי vego'ali:

ELOHAI NETZOR

אֱלֹהַי Elohai מילוי ע״ב, דמב ; ילה נְצוֹר netzor לְשׁוֹנִי leshoni מֵרָע mera.
וּשְׂפָתוֹתַי vesiftotai מִדַּבֵּר midaber ראה מִרְמָה mirma. וְלִמְקַלְלַי velimkalelai
נַפְשִׁי nafshi תִדּוֹם tidom. וְנַפְשִׁי venafshi כֶּעָפָר ke'afar
לַכֹּל lakol יה אדני תִּהְיֶה tihye. פְּתַח petach לִבִּי libi בְּתוֹרָתֶךָ betoratecha.

---

love and kindness, righteousness and mercy, blessing and peace. May it be good in Your eyes to bless us and to bless Your entire nation, Israel, with abundant power and with peace. Blessed are You, Lord Who blesses His nation, Israel, with peace, Amen.

YIH'YU LERATZON

"May the utterances of my mouth
and the thoughts of my heart find favor before You, Lord, my Rock and my Redeemer." (Psalms 19:15)

ELOHAI NETZOR

My God, guard my tongue from evil and my lips from speaking deceit. To those who curse me, let my spirit remain silent, and let my spirit be as dust for everyone. Open my heart in Your Torah

וְאַחֲרֵי ve'acharei מִצְוֹתֶיךָ mitzvotecha תִּרְדּוֹף tirdof נַפְשִׁי nafshi•
וְכָל־ vechol ילי הַקָּמִים hakamim עָלַי alai לְרָעָה lera'a רהע• מְהֵרָה mehera
הָפֵר hafer עֲצָתָם atzatam וְקַלְקֵל vekalkel מַחְשְׁבוֹתָם machshevotam•
עֲשֵׂה ase לְמַעַן lema'an שְׁמָךְ shemach• עֲשֵׂה ase לְמַעַן lema'an
יְמִינָךְ yeminach• עֲשֵׂה ase לְמַעַן lema'an תּוֹרָתָךְ toratach• עֲשֵׂה ase
לְמַעַן lema'an קְדֻשָּׁתָךְ kedushatach• ר"ת הפסוק = מ"ה יהוה לְמַעַן lema'an
יֵחָלְצוּן yechaltzun יְדִידֶיךָ yedidecha ר"ת ילי הוֹשִׁיעָה hoshi'a יהוה וש"ע נהורין
יְמִינְךָ yemincha וַעֲנֵנִי va'aneni (כתיב: ועננו) ר"ת אל (יי"א" מילוי דס"ג)•:

Before we recite the next verse ("*yih'yu leratzon*") we have an opportunity to strengthen our connection to our soul using our name. Each person has a verse in the *Torah* that connects to their name. Either their name is in the verse, or the first and last letters of the name correspond to the first or last letters of a verse. For example, the name Yehuda begins with a *Yud* and ends with a *Hei*. Before we end the *Amidah*, we state that our name will always be remembered when our soul leaves this world.

YIH'YU LERATZON (THE SECOND)

There are 42 letters in the verse in the secret of *Ana Beko'ach*.

יִהְיוּ yih'yu אל (יי"א" מילוי דס"ג) לְרָצוֹן leratzon מוהש ע"ה, ע"ב בריבוע וקס"א ע"ה, אל שדי ע"ה
אִמְרֵי־ imrei פִי fi ר"ת אֱלֶף = אלף למד שין דלת יוד ע"ה וְהֶגְיוֹן vehegyon לִבִּי libi
לְפָנֶיךָ lefanecha ס"ג מ"ה ב"ן יְהֹוָהאדניאהדונהי Adonai צוּרִי tzuri וְגֹאֲלִי vego'ali•:

---

and let my heart pursue Your commandments. All those who rise against me to do me harm, speedily nullify their plans and disturb their thoughts. Do so for the sake of Your Name. Do so for the sake of Your right. Do so for the sake of Your Torah. Do so for the sake of Your Holiness, "So that Your loved ones may be saved. Redeem Your right and answer me." (Psalms 60:7).

YIH'YU LERATZON (THE SECOND)

"May the utterances of my mouth
and the thoughts of my heart find favor before You, Lord, my Rock and my Redeemer." (Psalms 19:15)

OSE SHALOM

You take three steps backward;

עֹשֶׂה ose שָׁלוֹם shalom

Left

You turn to the left and say:

בִּמְרוֹמָיו bimromav ר״ת ע״ב, ריבוע יהוה

הוּא hu בְּרַחֲמָיו verachamav יַעֲשֶׂה ya'ase

Right

You turn to the right and say:

שָׁלוֹם shalom עָלֵינוּ alenu ר״ת ש״ע נהורין

Center

You face the center and say:

וְעַל ve'al כָּל־ kol ילי ; עמם עַמּוֹ amo יִשְׂרָאֵל Yisrael

וְאִמְרוּ ve'imru אָמֵן amen יאהדונהי:

יְהִי yehi רָצוֹן ratzon מהש ע״ה, ע״ב בריבוע וקס״א ע״ה, אל שדי ע״ה
מִלְּפָנֶיךָ milfanecha ס״ג מ״ה ב״ן יְהֹוָאדֹנָיאהדונהי Adonai אֱלֹהֵינוּ Elohenu ילה
וֵאלֹהֵי velohei לכב ; מילוי ע״ב, דמב ; ילה אֲבוֹתֵינוּ avotenu, שֶׁתִּבְנֶה shetivne
בֵּית bet ב״פ ראה הַמִּקְדָּשׁ hamikdash בִּמְהֵרָה bimhera בְּיָמֵינוּ veyamenu
וְתֵן veten חֶלְקֵנוּ chelkenu בְּתוֹרָתָךְ betoratach לַעֲשׂוֹת la'asot חֻקֵּי chukei
רְצוֹנָךְ retzonach וּלְעָבְדָךְ ul'ovdach פוי, אל אדני בְּלֵבָב belevav בוכו שָׁלֵם shalem.

You take three steps forward.

OSE SHALOM

He, Who makes peace in His high places, He, in His compassion,
shall make peace upon us And upon His entire nation, Israel, and you should say, Amen.

May it be pleasing before You, Lord,
our God, and the God of our forefathers, that You shall rebuild the Temple speedily, in our days, and place our lot in Your Torah, so that we may fulfill the laws of Your desire and serve You wholeheartedly.

KADDISH TITKABAL

יִתְגַּדַּל yitgadal וְיִתְקַדַּשׁ veyitkadash שדי ומילוי שדי ; י"א אותיות כמנין ו"ה

שְׁמֵיהּ shemei (שם י"ה דע"ב) רַבָּא raba קנ"א ב"ן, יהוה אלהים יהוה אדני,

מילוי קס"א וס"ג, מ"ה ברבוע וע"ב ע"ה ; ר"ת = ו"פ אלהים ; ס"ת = ג"פ יב"ק: אָמֵן amen אידהנויה.

בְּעָלְמָא be'alma דִּי di בְרָא vera כִרְעוּתֵיהּ chir'utei.

וְיַמְלִיךְ veyamlich מַלְכוּתֵיהּ mal'chutei. וְיַצְמַח veyatzmach

פּוּרְקָנֵיהּ purkanei. וִיקָרֵב vikarev מְשִׁיחֵיהּ meshichei: אָמֵן amen אידהנויה.

בְּחַיֵּיכוֹן bechayechon וּבְיוֹמֵיכוֹן uvyomechon וּבְחַיֵּי uvchayei

דְכָל dechol יאי בֵּית bet ב"פ ראה יִשְׂרָאֵל Yisrael בַּעֲגָלָא ba'agala

וּבִזְמַן uvizman קָרִיב kariv וְאִמְרוּ ve'imru אָמֵן amen: אָמֵן amen אידהנויה.

The congregation and the *chazan* say the following:

28 words (until *be'alma*) and 28 letters (until *almaya*)

יְהֵא yehe שְׁמֵיהּ shemei (שם י"ה דס"ג) רַבָּא raba קנ"א ב"ן,

יהוה אלהים יהוה אדני, מילוי קס"א וס"ג, מ"ה ברבוע וע"ב ע"ה מְבָרַךְ mevarach,

לְעָלַם le'alam לְעָלְמֵי le'almei עָלְמַיָּא almaya. יִתְבָּרַךְ yitbarach.

Seven words with six letters each (שם בן מ"ב) and, seven times the letter *Vav* (שם בן מ"ב).

וְיִשְׁתַּבַּח veyishtabach י"פ ע"ב יהוה אל אבג יתץ.

וְיִתְפָּאַר veyitpa'ar הי נו יה קרע שטן. וְיִתְרוֹמַם veyitromam וה כוזו נגד יכש.

וְיִתְנַשֵּׂא veyitnase במוכסז בטר צתג. וְיִתְהַדָּר veyit'hadar כוזו יה וזקב טנע.

וְיִתְעַלֶּה veyit'ale וה יוד ה יגל פזק. וְיִתְהַלָּל veyit'halal א ואו הא שקו צית.

שְׁמֵיהּ shemei (שם י"ה) דְּקוּדְשָׁא dekudsha בְּרִיךְ verich הוּא hu:

אָמֵן amen אידהנויה.

KADDISH TITKABAL

May His great Name be more exalted and sanctified. (Amen) In the world that He created according to His will, and may His kingdom reign. And may He cause His redemption to sprout and may He bring the Mashiach closer. (Amen) In your lifetimes and in your days and in the lifetime of all the House of Israel, speedily and in the near future, and you shall say, Amen. (Amen) May His great Name be blessed forever and for all eternity. Blessed and lauded, and glorified, and exalted, and extolled, and honored, and uplifted, and praised be the Name of the Holy Blessed One (Amen)

לְעֵלָּא le'ela מִן min כָּל kol ילי בִּרְכָתָא birchata. שִׁירָתָא shirata.
תִּשְׁבְּחָתָא tishbechata וְנֶחָמָתָא venechamata. דַּאֲמִירָן da'amiran
בְּעָלְמָא be'alma וְאִמְרוּ ve'imru אָמֵן amen: אָמֵן amen אידהנויה.

תִּתְקַבַּל titkabal צְלוֹתָנָא tzelotana וּבָעוּתָנָא uva'utana
עִם im צְלוֹתְהוֹן tzelotehon וּבָעוּתְהוֹן uva'utehon דְּכָל dechol ילי
בֵּית bet ב"פ ראה יִשְׂרָאֵל Yisrael קֳדָם kadam אֲבוּנָא avuna
דְּבִשְׁמַיָּא devishmaya וְאִמְרוּ ve'imru אָמֵן amen: אָמֵן amen אידהנויה.

יְהֵא yehe שְׁלָמָא shelama רַבָּא raba קנ"א ב"ן, יהוה אלהים יהוה אדני, מילוי קס"א וס"ג,
מ"ה ברבוע וע"ב ע"ה מִן min שְׁמַיָּא shemaya. וְחַיִּים chayim אהיה אהיה יהוה, בינה ע"ה
וְשָׂבָע vesava וִישׁוּעָה vishu'a וְנֶחָמָה venechama וְשֵׁיזָבָא veshezava
וּרְפוּאָה urfu'a וּגְאֻלָּה ug'ula וּסְלִיחָה uslicha וְכַפָּרָה vechapara
וְרֵיוַח verevach וְהַצָּלָה vehatzala. לָנוּ lanu אלהים, אהיה אדני וּלְכָל ulchol יה אדני
עַמּוֹ amo יִשְׂרָאֵל Yisrael וְאִמְרוּ ve'imru אָמֵן amen: אָמֵן amen אידהנויה.

Take three steps backwards and say:

עוֹשֶׂה ose שָׁלוֹם shalom

בִּמְרוֹמָיו bimromav ע"ב, ריבוע יהוה. הוּא hu בְּרַחֲמָיו berachamav

יַעֲשֶׂה ya'ase שָׁלוֹם shalom עָלֵינוּ alenu ר"ת ש"ע נהורין.
וְעַל ve'al כָּל kol ילי ; עמם עַמּוֹ amo יִשְׂרָאֵל Yisrael וְאִמְרוּ ve'imru אָמֵן amen:

אָמֵן amen אידהנויה.

Above all blessings, songs, praises, and words of consolation that may be said in the world, and you shall say, Amen. (Amen) May our prayers and pleas be accepted, together with the prayers and pleas of the entire House of Israel, before our Father in Heaven, and you say, Amen. (Amen) May there be abundant peace from heaven; Life, contentment, salvation, consolation, deliverance, healing, redemption, pardon, atonement, comfort, and relief. For us and for His entire nation, Israel, and you shall say, Amen. (Amen) He, Who makes peace in His high places, He, in His compassion, shall make peace upon us And upon His entire nation, Israel, and you shall say, Amen. (Amen)

KAVEH

We now connect to the World of Action, *Asiyah*. Something remarkable happens during this prayer. We have finished all our morning spiritual connections, and now would like to retain all this energy that we have worked so hard for by sealing and secure it up. *Kaveh* takes us back up through the Upper Words of Action (*Asiyah*), Formation (*Yetzirah*), Creation (*Beriah*) and Emanation (*Atzilut*) to a realm known as *Arich Anpin* (Long Face). From this realm we still elevate higher, passed the realms of Atik (Ancient), and *Adam Kadmon* (Primordial Man) until we travel into the realm of the Light of Endless Word. This journey retraces our steps through the Upper Words ensuring that we leave no openings behind for negativity to enter.

At this point, the Satan wants to prevent us from closing these openings, so he bombards us with a feeling of impatience that the prayers will be over soon. His goal is to lower our guard and weaken our concentration during this final stage so that we leave an opening for him to enter and sabotage our efforts and taint our Light with negative energy.

קַוֵּה kaveh אֶל־ el יְהֹוָהאדניאהדונהי Adonai חֲזַק chazak פהל

וְיַאֲמֵץ veya'ametz לִבֶּךָ libecha וְקַוֵּה vekave אֶל־ el יְהֹוָהאדניאהדונהי Adonai:

אֵין en קָדוֹשׁ kadosh כַּיהֹוָהאדניאהדונהי kadonai כִּי ki אֵין en בִּלְתֶּךָ biltecha

וְאֵין ve'en צוּר tzur אלהים דההין ע"ה כֵּאלֹהֵינוּ kelohenu יכה: כִּי ki

מִי mi ילי אֱלוֹהַּ Eloha שם בן מ"ב מִבַּלְעֲדֵי mibal'adei יְהֹוָהאדניאהדונהי Adonai

וּמִי umi ילי צוּר tzur אלהים דההין ע"ה זוּלָתִי zulati אֱלֹהֵינוּ Elohenu יכה:

Connection to *Olam Asiyah* (Action).

אֵין en הה כֵּאלֹהֵינוּ kelohenu יכה נוּקְבָא.

אֵין en וו כַּאדוֹנֵנוּ kadonenu ז"א.

אֵין en הה כְּמַלְכֵּנוּ kemalkenu אמא.

אֵין en יוד כְּמוֹשִׁיעֵנוּ kemoshi'enu אבא:

KAVEH

"Place hope in the Lord. Make your heart strong and courageous, and place your hope in the Lord." (Psalms 27:14). "There is none as holy as the Lord, for there is none besides You and there is no Rock to compare with our God." (I Samuel 2:2) "For who is God besides the Lord, and who is a rock besides our God?" (Psalms 18:32)

There is none like our God.

There is none like our Master. There is none like our King. There is none like our Redeemer.

Connection to *Olam Yetzirah* (Formation).

מִי ילי mi הא כֵּאלֹהֵינוּ chelohenu ילה נוקבא.

מִי ילי mi ואו כַּאדוֹנֵנוּ chadonenu ז"א.

מִי ילי mi הא כְּמַלְכֵּנוּ chemalkenu אמא.

מִי ילי mi יוד כְּמוֹשִׁיעֵנוּ chemoshi'enu אבא:

Connection to *Olam Beriah* (Creation).

אין, מי, נודה ר"ת אמן = יאהדונהי – וזיווג ז"א ומלכות.

נוֹדֶה node הי לֵאלֹהֵינוּ lelohenu ילה נוקבא.

נוֹדֶה node ואו לַאדוֹנֵנוּ ladonenu ז"א.

נוֹדֶה node הי לְמַלְכֵּנוּ lemalkenu אמא.

נוֹדֶה node יוד לְמוֹשִׁיעֵנוּ lemoshi'enu אבא:

Connection to *Olam Atzilut* (Emanation).

בָּרוּךְ baruch הי אֱלֹהֵינוּ Elohenu ילה נוקבא.

בָּרוּךְ baruch ויו אֲדוֹנֵנוּ adonenu ז"א.

בָּרוּךְ baruch הי מַלְכֵּנוּ malkenu אמא.

בָּרוּךְ baruch יוד מוֹשִׁיעֵנוּ moshi'enu אבא:

Connection to the Worlds above *Atzilut*,
Connection to *Keter* of *Arich Anpin* (Long Face).

אַתָּה Ata הוּא hu אֱלֹהֵינוּ Elohenu ילה.

Connection to the head of *Atik* (Ancient).

אַתָּה Ata הוּא hu אֲדוֹנֵנוּ adonenu.

Connection to *Adam Kadmon* (Primordial Man).

אַתָּה Ata הוּא hu מַלְכֵּנוּ malkenu.

Connection to the Endless Light, which is enclosed by *Adam Kadmon*.

אַתָּה Ata הוּא hu מוֹשִׁיעֵנוּ moshi'enu:

Who is like our God? Who is like our Master? Who is like our King? Who is like our Redeemer? We shall give thanks to our God, we shall give thanks to our Master, we shall give thanks to our King, we shall give thanks to our Redeemer. Blessed is our God. Blessed is our Master. Blessed is our King. Blessed is our Redeemer. You are our God. You are our Master. You are our King. You are our Redeemer.

אַתָּה Ata *Keneset Yisrael* (Congregation of *Yisrael*) תּוֹשִׁיעֵנוּ toshi'enu

אַתָּה Ata תָקוּם takum כ״א הויות שבתפילין תְּרַחֵם terachem ג״פ רי״ו ; אברהם, וז״פ אל,

רי״ו ול״ב נתיבות החכמה, רמ״ח (אברים), עסמ״ב וט״ז אותיות פשוטות צִיּוֹן Tziyon יוסף, ו׳ הויות, קנאה

כִּי־ ki עֵת et לְחֶנְנָהּ lechenena כִּי־ ki בָא va מוֹעֵד mo'ed:

(Some say here "The *Ketoret* portion", on pg. 241-247)

TANA DEVEI ELIYAHU

It is said that people who learn the *Torah* bring peace. Because each Hebrew letter is imbued with mystical forces, reciting words that speak about bringing peace arouses the energy of peace within the world. The Hebrew word *Shalom* inspires feelings of peace and harmony within us. If we cannot develop peace within ourselves, we cannot share peace with others, for one cannot share what he doesn't have. To conclude this connection we say that God will bless us with peace.

תָּנָא tana דְבֵי devei אֵלִיָּהוּ Eliyahu לכב: כָּל־ kol ילי הַשּׁוֹנֶה hashone

הֲלָכוֹת halachot בְּכָל־ bechol ב״ן, לכב יוֹם yom ע״ה נגד, מזבח, זן, אל יהוה

מוּבְטָח muvtach לוֹ lo שֶׁהוּא shehu בֶּן ben הָעוֹלָם ha'olam

הַבָּא haba. שֶׁנֶּאֱמַר shene'emar: הֲלִיכוֹת halichot עוֹלָם olam לוֹ lo.

אַל al תִּקְרֵי tikrei הֲלִיכוֹת halichot אֶלָּא ela הֲלָכוֹת halachot:

אָמַר amar רִבִּי Ribi אֶלְעָזָר Elazar אָמַר amar רִבִּי Ribi חֲנִינָא Chanina:

תַּלְמִידֵי talmidei חֲכָמִים chachamim מַרְבִּים marbim שָׁלוֹם shalom

בָּעוֹלָם ba'olam. שֶׁנֶּאֱמַר shene'emar: וְכָל־ vechol ילי בָּנַיִךְ banayich

לִמּוּדֵי limudei יְהֹוָהאדניאהדונהי Adonai וְרַב verav שְׁלוֹם shelom בָּנָיִךְ banayich:

אַל al תִּקְרֵי tikrei בָּנָיִךְ banayich אֶלָּא ela בּוֹנָיִךְ bonayich: יְהִי־ yehi

שָׁלוֹם shalom בְּחֵילֵךְ bechelech שַׁלְוָה shalva בְּאַרְמְנוֹתָיִךְ be'armenotayich:

You shall redeem us. You shall rise and be merciful to Zion, for the time for favor has come and it is the appointed time. (Psalms 102:14)

TANA DEVEI ELIYAHU

"It was taught in the learning House of Eliyahu that one who studies law rulings, every day, is assured to be present in the World to Come." (Megillah 28b) *It was said: "The ways of the world are His."* (Chavakuk 3:6) *Do not read it 'ways' but 'law rulings'. Rabbi Elazar said that Rabbi Chanina had said that learned scholars increase the peace in the world.* (Brachot 64a; Yvamot 122b; Kritut 28b; Tamid 32b) *As it is said: "And all your children are the students of God."* (Isaiah 54:13) *Do not read it 'your children' but 'your builders.' May there be peace in your chambers and serenity in your palaces.*

לְמַעַן lema'an אַחַי achai וְרֵעָי vere'ai אֲדַבְּרָה־ adabra נָּא na

שָׁלוֹם shalom בָּךְ: bach לְמַעַן lema'an בֵּית־ bet ב"פ ראה

יְהֹוָהאדניאהדונהי Adonai אֱלֹהֵינוּ Elohenu ילה אֲבַקְשָׁה avaksha

טוֹב tov והו לָךְ: lach וּרְאֵה ure'e ראה בָנִים vanim לְבָנֶיךָ levanecha

שָׁלוֹם shalom עַל־ al יִשְׂרָאֵל: Yisrael שָׁלוֹם shalom רָב rav

לְאֹהֲבֵי le'ohavei תוֹרָתֶךָ toratecha וְאֵין־ ve'en לָמוֹ lamo מִכְשׁוֹל: michshol

יְהֹוָהאדניאהדונהי Adonai עֹז oz לְעַמּוֹ le'amo יִתֵּן yiten יְהֹוָהאדניאהדונהי Adonai

יְבָרֵךְ yevarech ע"ב ס"ג מ"ה ב"ן, הברכה (למתק את ז' המלכים שמתו)

אֶת־ et עַמּוֹ amo בַשָּׁלוֹם vashalom ר"ת ע"ב, ריבוע יהוה:

KADDISH AL YISRAEL

This *Kaddish* helps elevate all souls in the secret of the Resurrection of Death. According to the Ari – If a person lost a parent he should say this *Kaddish* through the whole first year, even on *Shabbat* and holidays. Because, besides that the *Kaddish* helps a soul to be saved form the spiritual cleansing of *Gehenom*, this *Kaddish* also helps to elevate a soul from one spiritual level to the upper one and to enter to the Garden of Eden.

יִתְגַּדַּל yitgadal וְיִתְקַדַּשׁ veyitkadash שדי ומילוי שדי ; י"א אותיות כמנין ו"ה

שְׁמֵיהּ shemei (שם י"ה דע"ב) רַבָּא raba קנ"א ב"ן, יהוה אלהים יהוה אדני,

מילוי קס"א וס"ג, מ"ה ברבוע וע"ב ע"ה ; ר"ת = ו"פ אלהים ; ס"ת = ג"פ יב"ק: אָמֵן amen אידהנויה.

בְּעָלְמָא be'alma דִּי di בְרָא vera כִרְעוּתֵיהּ. chir'utei

וְיַמְלִיךְ veyamlich מַלְכוּתֵיהּ. malchutei וְיַצְמַח veyatzmach

פֻּרְקָנֵיהּ. purkanei וִיקָרֵב vikarev מְשִׁיחֵיהּ: meshichei אָמֵן amen אידהנויה.

"For the sake of my brothers and my friends, I shall seek peace concerning you. For the sake of the House of the Lord, our God, I shall seek well for you." (Psalms 122:7-9) *"May you witness children for your children and peace for Israel."* (Psalms 128:6) *"There is abundance of peace for those who love Your Torah and for them, there is no obstacle."* (Psalms 128:6) *"May the Lord give strength to His people may the Lord bless His nation with peace."* (Psalms 29:11)

KADDISH AL YISRAEL

May His great Name be more exalted and sanctified. (Amen)
In the world that He created according to His will, and may His Kingdom reign.
And may He cause His redemption to sprout and may He bring the Mashiach closer. (Amen)

בְּחַיֵּיכוֹן bechayechon וּבְיוֹמֵיכוֹן uvyomechon וּבְחַיֵּי uvchayei

דְכָל dechol ילי בֵּית bet ב״פ ראה יִשְׂרָאֵל Yisrael בַּעֲגָלָא ba'agala

וּבִזְמַן uvizman קָרִיב kariv וְאִמְרוּ ve'imru אָמֵן amen: אָמֵן amen אידהנויה.

The congregation and the prayer leader say the following:

28 words (until *be'alma*) and 28 letters (until *almaya*)

יְהֵא yehe שְׁמֵיהּ shemei (שם י״ה דס״ג) רַבָּא raba קנ״א ב״ן,

יהוה אלהים יהוה אדני, מילוי קס״א וס״ג, מ״ה ברבוע וע״ב ע״ה מְבָרַךְ mevarach,

לְעָלַם le'alam לְעָלְמֵי le'almei עָלְמַיָּא almaya. יִתְבָּרַךְ yitbarach.

Seven words with six letters each (שם בן מ״ב) – and also, seven times the letter Vav (שם בן מ״ב)

וְיִשְׁתַּבַּח veyishtabach י״פ ע״ב יהוה אל אבג יתץ.

וְיִתְפָּאַר veyitpa'ar הי נו יה קרע שטן. וְיִתְרוֹמַם veyitromam וה כוזו נגד יכש.

וְיִתְנַשֵּׂא veyitnase במוכסז בטר צתג. וְיִתְהַדָּר veyit'hadar כוזו יה וקב טנע.

וְיִתְעַלֶּה veyit'ale וה יוד ה יגל פזק. וְיִתְהַלָּל veyit'halal א ואו הא שקו צית.

שְׁמֵיהּ shemei (שם י״ה) דְּקוּדְשָׁא dekudsha בְּרִיךְ verich הוּא hu:

אָמֵן amen אידהנויה.

לְעֵלָּא le'ela מִן min כָּל kol ילי בִּרְכָתָא birchata. שִׁירָתָא shirata.

תֻּשְׁבְּחָתָא tishbechata וְנֶחָמָתָא venechamata. דַּאֲמִירָן da'amiran

בְּעָלְמָא be'alma וְאִמְרוּ ve'imru אָמֵן amen: אָמֵן amen אידהנויה.

In your lifetimes and in your days and in the lifetime of all the House of Israel, speedily and in the near future, and you shall say, Amen. (Amen) May His great Name be blessed forever and for all eternity. Blessed and lauded, and glorified, and exalted, and extolled, and honored, and uplifted, and praised be the Name of the Holy Blessed One. (Amen)Above all blessings, songs, praises, and words of consolation that may be said in the world, and you shall say, Amen. (Amen)

ve'al וְעַל rabanan רַבָּנָן ve'al וְעַל Yisrael יִשְׂרָאֵל al עַל

talmidei תַלְמִידֵי עמם ; ילי kol כָּל ve'al וְעַל talmidehon תַלְמִידֵיהוֹן

be'oraita בְּאוֹרַיְתָא de'askin דְּעָסְקִין •talmidehon תַלְמִידֵיהוֹן

vedi וְדִי haden הָדֵין ve'atra בְּאַתְרָא di דִּי •kadishta קַדִּישְׁתָּא

yehe יְהֵא •ve'atar וְאָתָר atar אָתָר לכב ב"ן, vechol בְּכָל

vechisda וְחִסְדָּא china וְחִנָּא ul'chon וּלְכוֹן ul'hon וּלְהוֹן lana לָנָא

shemaya שְׁמַיָּא marei מָארֵי kadam קֳדָם min מִן •verachamei וְרַחֲמֵי

.אידהנויה amen אָמֵן :amen אָמֵן ve'imru וְאִמְרוּ ve'ara וְאַרְעָא

קנ"א ב"ן, יהוה אלהים יהוה אדני, מילוי קס"א וס"ג, raba רַבָּא shelama שְׁלָמָא yehe יְהֵא

אהיה אהיה יהוה, בינה ע"ה chayim וְחַיִּים •shemaya שְׁמַיָּא min מִן מ"ה ברבוע וע"ב ע"ה

veshezava וְשֵׁיזָבָא venechama וְנֶחָמָה vishu'a וִישׁוּעָה vesava וְשָׂבָע

vechapara וְכַפָּרָה uslicha וּסְלִיחָה uge'ula וּגְאֻלָּה urefu'a וּרְפוּאָה

יה אדני ulchol וּלְכָל אלהים, אהיה אדני lanu לָנוּ •vehatzala וְהַצָּלָה verevach וְרֶוַח

.אידהנויה amen אָמֵן :amen אָמֵן ve'imru וְאִמְרוּ Yisrael יִשְׂרָאֵל amo עַמּוֹ

Take three steps backwards and say:

hu הוּא •ע"ב, ריבוע יהוה bimromav בִּמְרוֹמָיו shalom שָׁלוֹם ose עוֹשֶׂה

•ר"ת ש"ע נהורין alenu עָלֵינוּ shalom שָׁלוֹם ya'ase יַעֲשֶׂה berachamav בְּרַחֲמָיו

:amen אָמֵן ve'imru וְאִמְרוּ Yisrael יִשְׂרָאֵל amo עַמּוֹ עמם ; ילי kol כָּל ve'al וְעַל

•אידהנויה amen אָמֵן

Upon Israel, His Sages, Their disciples, and all the students of their disciples who occupy themselves with the Holy Torah, in this place and in each and every location, may there be for us, for them, and for all, grace, kindness, and compassion from the Master of the Heavens and earth, and you shall say Amen. (Amen) *May there be abundant peace from Heaven, life, contentment, salvation, consolation, deliverance, healing, redemption, pardon, atonement, comfort, and relief for us and for His entire Nation, Israel, and you shall say, Amen.* (Amen) *He, Who makes peace in His High Places, with His compassion He shall make peace for us And for His entire Nation, Israel. And you shall say, Amen.* (Amen)

BARCHU

The *chazan* (or a person who said the *Kaddish Al Yisrael*) says:

רַבָּנָן rabanan: בָּרְכוּ barchu יהוה ריבוע יהוה ריבוע מ״ה אֶת et

יְהֹוָאדהֿיאהדונהי Adonai הַמְבֹרָךְ hamevorach ס״ת כהת, משיח בן דוד ע״ה:

First the congregation replies with the following, and then the *chazan* (or a person who said the *Kaddish Al Yisrael*) repeats it:

Nefesh בָּרוּךְ baruch *Ruach* יְהֹוָאדהֿיאהדונהי Adonai *Neshamah* הַמְבֹרָךְ hamevorach

Chayah לְעוֹלָם le'olam ריבוע ס״ג ו׳ אותיות דס״ג *Yechidah* וָעֶד va'ed:

ALENU

Alenu is a cosmic sealing agent. It cements and secures all of our prayers, protecting them from any negative forces such as the *klipot*. All prayers prior to *Alenu* drew down what the kabbalists call Inner Light. *Alenu*, however, attracts Surrounding Light, which envelops our prayers with a protective force-field to block out the *klipot*.

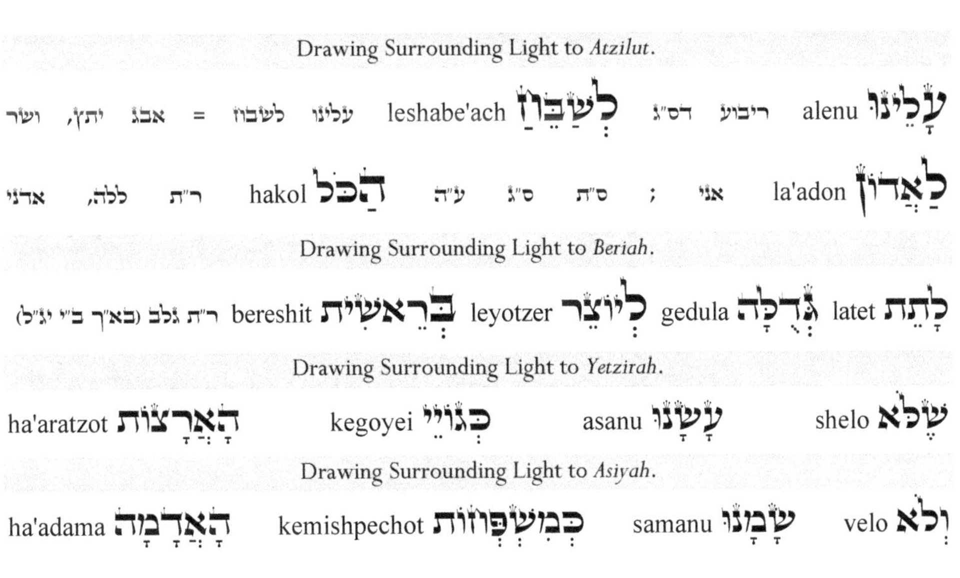

Drawing Surrounding Light to *Atzilut*.

עָלֵינוּ alenu ריבוע דס״ג לְשַׁבֵּחַ leshabe'ach עלינו לשבח = אבג יתץ, ושר

לַאֲדוֹן la'adon אני ; ס״ת ס״ג ע״ה הַכֹּל hakol ר״ת ללה, אדני

Drawing Surrounding Light to *Beriah*.

לָתֵת latet גְּדֻלָּה gedula לְיוֹצֵר leyotzer בְּרֵאשִׁית bereshit ר״ת גלב (באך ב״י יג״ל)

Drawing Surrounding Light to *Yetzirah*.

שֶׁלֹּא shelo עָשָׂנוּ asanu כְּגוֹיֵי kegoyei הָאֲרָצוֹת ha'aratzot

Drawing Surrounding Light to *Asiyah*.

וְלֹא velo שָׂמָנוּ samanu כְּמִשְׁפְּחוֹת kemishpechot הָאֲדָמָה ha'adama

---

BARCHU

Masters: Bless the Lord, the Blessed One.
Blessed be the Lord, the Blessed One, forever and for eternity.

ALENU

It is incumbent upon us to give praise to the Master of all and to attribute greatness to the Molder of Creation, for He did not make us like the nations of the lands. He did not place us like the families of the earth

שֶׁלֹּא shelo שָׂם sam וְחֶלְקֵנוּ chelkenu כָּהֶם kahem וְגוֹרָלֵנוּ vegoralenu

כְּכָל kechol הֲמוֹנָם hamonam• שֶׁהֵם shehem מִשְׁתַּחֲוִים mishtachavim

לְהֶבֶל lahevel וָרִיק varik וּמִתְפַּלְּלִים umitpalelim אֶל el אֶל el

לֹא lo יוֹשִׁיעַ Yoshi'a• (pause here, and when you say "*va'anachnu mishtachavim*" bow your entire body)

וַאֲנַחְנוּ va'anachnu מִשְׁתַּחֲוִים mishtachavim לִפְנֵי lifnei מֶלֶךְ melech

מַלְכֵי malchei הַמְּלָכִים hamelachim הַקָּדוֹשׁ hakadosh בָּרוּךְ: baruch

הוּא hu• שֶׁהוּא shehu נוֹטֶה note שָׁמַיִם shamayim י"פ טל, י"פ כוזו ; ר"ת = י"פ אדני

שבי ספירות של נוקבא דז"א וְיוֹסֵד veyosed אָרֶץ aretz• וּמוֹשַׁב umoshav

יְקָרוֹ yekaro בַּשָּׁמַיִם bashamayim י"פ טל, י"פ כוזו מִמַּעַל mima'al עלם•

וּשְׁכִינַת ush'chinat עֻזּוֹ uzo בְּגָבְהֵי begovhei מְרוֹמִים meromim•

הוּא hu אֱלֹהֵינוּ Elohenu ילה וְאֵין ve'en עוֹד od אַחֵר acher•

אֱמֶת emet אהיה פעמים אהיה, ז"פ ס"ג מַלְכֵּנוּ malkenu וְאֶפֶס ve'efes

זוּלָתוֹ zulato• כַּכָּתוּב kakatuv בַּתּוֹרָה batorah: וְיָדַעְתָּ veyadata

הַיּוֹם hayom ע"ה נגד, מזבח, זן, אל יהוה וַהֲשֵׁבֹתָ vahashevota אֶל־ el

לְבָבֶךָ levavecha ר"ת לאו כִּי ki יְהֹוָה Adonai הוּא hu

הָאֱלֹהִים haElohim אהיה אדני ; ילה ; ר"ת יהה וכן עולה למנין ענו עג"כ

בַּשָּׁמַיִם bashamayim י"פ טל, י"פ כוזו מִמַּעַל mima'al עלם ;

רמז לאור פנימי המתוזיל מלמעלה וְעַל־ ve'al הָאָרֶץ ha'aretz אלהים דההין ע"ה

מִתָּחַת mitachat רמז לאור מקיף המתוזיל מלמטה אֵין en עוֹד od:

He did not make our lot like theirs and our destiny like that of their multitudes, for they prostrate themselves to futility and emptiness and they pray to a deity that does not help. But we prostrate ourselves before the King of all Kings, the Holy Blessed One. It is He Who spreads the Heavens and establishes the earth. The Seat of His glory is in the Heaven above and the Divine Presence of His power is in the Highest of Heights. He is our God and there is no other. Our King is true and there is none beside Him. As it is written in the Torah: "And you shall know today and you shall take it to your heart that it is the Lord Who is God in the Heavens above and upon the Earth below, and there is none other." (Deuteronomy 4:39)

עַל al כֵּן ken נְקַוֶּה nekave לְּךָ lach יְהֹוָאדניאהדונהי Adonai אֱלֹהֵינוּ Elohenu
ילה לִרְאוֹת lir'ot מְהֵרָה mehera בְּתִפְאֶרֶת betiferet עֻזָּךְ uzach ס"ת כהת, משיח
בן דוד ע"ה לְהַעֲבִיר leha'avir גִּלּוּלִים gilulim מִן min הָאָרֶץ ha'aretz אלהים דההין
ע"ה וְהָאֱלִילִים veha'elilim כָּרוֹת karot יִכָּרֵתוּן •yikaretun לְתַקֵּן letaken
עוֹלָם olam בְּמַלְכוּת bemalchut שַׁדַּי •Shadai וְכָל vechol ילי בְּנֵי benei
בָשָׂר vasar יִקְרְאוּ yikre'u בִשְׁמֶךָ vishmecha לְהַפְנוֹת lehafnot אֵלֶיךָ elecha
כָּל kol ילי רִשְׁעֵי rish'ei אָרֶץ •aretz יַכִּירוּ yakiru וְיֵדְעוּ veyed'u כָּל kol ילי
יוֹשְׁבֵי yoshvei תֵבֵל tevel ב"פ רי"ו• כִּי ki לְךָ lecha תִּכְרַע tichra כָּל־ kol ילי
בֶּרֶךְ berech תִּשָּׁבַע tishava כָּל kol ילי לָשׁוֹן •lashon לְפָנֶיךָ lefanecha ס"ג מ"ה ב"ן
יְהֹוָאדניאהדונהי Adonai אֱלֹהֵינוּ Elohenu ילה יִכְרְעוּ yichre'u וְיִפֹּלוּ veyipolu
וְלִכְבוֹד velichvod שִׁמְךָ shimcha יְקָר yekar יִתֵּנוּ •yitenu וִיקַבְּלוּ vikabelu
כֻלָּם chulam אֶת et עוֹל־ ol מַלְכוּתֶךָ •malchutecha וְתִמְלוֹךְ vetimloch
עֲלֵיהֶם alehem מְהֵרָה mehera לְעוֹלָם le'olam ריבוע ס"ג ו' אותיות דס"ג וָעֶד •va'ed
כִּי ki הַמַּלְכוּת hamalchut שֶׁלְּךָ shelcha הִיא •hee וּלְעוֹלְמֵי ul'olmei
עַד ad תִּמְלוֹךְ timloch בְּכָבוֹד bechavod בוכו• כַּכָּתוּב kakatuv
בְּתוֹרָתָךְ :betoratach יְהֹוָאדניאהדונהי Adonai | יִמְלֹךְ yimloch לְעֹלָם le'olam
ריבוע ס"ג ו' אותיות דס"ג ; ר"ת יי"ל וָעֶד •va'ed וְנֶאֱמַר :vene'emar וְהָיָה vehaya יהוה ; יהה
יְהֹוָאדניאהדונהי Adonai לְמֶלֶךְ lemelech עַל־ al כָּל־ kol ילי ; עסמב
הָאָרֶץ ha'aretz אלהים דההין ע"ה בַּיּוֹם bayom ע"ה נגד, מזבח, זן, אל יהוה הַהוּא hahu
יִהְיֶה yih'ye ייי יְהֹוָאדניאהדונהי Adonai אֶחָד echad אהבה, דאגה וּשְׁמוֹ ushmo מהש
ע"ה, ע"ב בריבוע וקס"א ע"ה, אל שדי ע"ה אֶחָד echad אהבה, דאגה:

Consequently, we place our hope in You, Lord, our God, that we shall speedily see the glory of Your might, when You remove the idols from the earth and the deities shall be completely destroyed to correct the world with the kingdom of the Almighty. And all mankind shall then call out Your Name and You shall turn back to Yourself all the wicked ones of the earth. Then all the inhabitants of the world shall recognize and know that, for You, every knee bends and every tongue vows. Before You, Lord, our God, they shall kneel and fall and shall give honor to Your glorious Name. And they shall all accept the yoke of Your Kingdom and You shall reign over them, forever and ever. Because the kingdom is Yours. and forever and for eternity, You shall reign gloriously. As it is written in the Torah: "The Lord shall reign forever and ever," (Exodus 15:18) and it is also stated: "The Lord shall be King over the whole world and, on that day, the Lord shall be One and His Name One." (Zechariah 14:9)

VAYOMER

There is a specific angel that carries each prayer we make to the Upper Worlds. By reciting this additional prayer after *Alenu* we ensure that our prayers elevate into the Upper Worlds. There are four Yuds יייי within the verse "I am your God, your healer," which according to the Ari, ignite the power of healing.

וַיֹּאמֶר vayomer אִם־ im יוהך, מ"א אותיות דפשוט, דמילוי ודמילוי דמילוי דאהיה ע"ה

שָׁמוֹעַ shamo'a תִּשְׁמַע tishma לְקוֹל lekol | יְהֹוָהאדניאהדונהי Adonai

אֱלֹהֶיךָ Elohecha ילה וְהַיָּשָׁר vehayashar בְּעֵינָיו be'enav ריבוע מ"ה

תַּעֲשֶׂה ta'ase וְהַאֲזַנְתָּ veha'azanta לְמִצְוֹתָיו lemitzvotav וְשָׁמַרְתָּ veshamarta

כָּל־ kol ילי חֻקָּיו chukav כָּל־ kol ילי הַמַּחֲלָה hamachala

אֲשֶׁר־ asher שַׂמְתִּי samti בְמִצְרַיִם veMitzrayim מצר לֹא־ lo אָשִׂים asim

עָלֶיךָ alecha כִּי ki אֲנִי ani אני יְהֹוָהאדניאהדונהי Adonai

Corresponds to the four *Yuds* in the Holy Name: ע"ב (יוד הי ויו הי)

רֹפְאֶךָ rofecha ר"ת איר:

עֵץ־ etz חַיִּים chayim אהיה אהיה יהוה, בינה ע"ה הִיא hee

לַמַּחֲזִיקִים lamachazikim ר"ת להח בָּהּ ba וְתֹמְכֶיהָ vetomcheha

מְאֻשָּׁר me'ushar: דְּרָכֶיהָ deracheha דַּרְכֵי־ darchei נֹעַם no'am וְכָל־ vechol

ילי נְתִיבוֹתֶיהָ netivoteha שָׁלוֹם shalom: מִגְדַּל־ migdal עֹז oz שֵׁם shem

יְהֹוָהאדניאהדונהי Adonai בּוֹ־ bo יָרוּץ yarutz צַדִּיק tzadik וְנִשְׂגָּב venisgav:

מי"ץ	עו"י	מבט"ע
יצ"ד	ווה	גר"ג
הי"י	זדו	דצ"ב
ונ"ק	שוה	לקה

כִּי ki בִי vi מ"ב יִרְבּוּ yirbu יָמֶיךָ yamecha וְיוֹסִיפוּ veyosifu לְךָ lecha

שְׁנוֹת shenot חַיִּים chayim אהיה אהיה יהוה, בינה ע"ה:

VAYOMER

"And God said: If you shall listen to the voice of the Lord, your God, and do that which is upright in His eyes, and if you carefully heed His commandments and keep all His statutes, then all the illnesses that I had set upon Egypt, I shall not set upon you, for I am the Lord, your healer." (Exodus 15:26) *"It is a Tree of Life for those who hold on to it, and those who support it are joyful."* (Proverbs 3:18) *"Its ways are ways of pleasantness and all its pathways are of peace."* (Proverbs 3:17) *"The Name of the Lord is a tower of strength. In it, a righteous person runs and is strengthened."* (Proverbs 18:10) *"For through Me, your days shall be increased, and years of life shall be added to you."* (Proverbs 9:11)

YEHI RATZON

The following connection helps us to make sure our prayers are accepted.
It also helps us to remove jealousy and envy from within.

יְהִי yehi רָצוֹן ratzon מהש ע״ה, ע״ב בריבוע וקס״א ע״ה, אל שדי ע״ה מִלְּפָנֶיךָ milefanecha
ס״ג מ״ה ב״ן יְהֹוָאדהנויאהדונהי Adonai אֱלֹהַי Elohai מילוי ע״ב, דמב ; ילה וֵאלֹהֵי velohei לכב ;
מילוי דע״ב, דמב ; ילה אֲבוֹתַי avotai, שֶׁלֹּא shelo נִכָּשֵׁל nikashel בִּדְבַר bidvar ראה
הֲלָכָה halacha. וְלֹא velo נֹאמַר nomar עַל al טָמֵא tame טָהוֹר tahor י״פ אכא
וְלֹא velo עַל al טָהוֹר tahor י״פ אכא טָמֵא tame, וְלֹא velo עַל al אִיסּוּר isur
מוּתָּר mutar וְלֹא velo עַל al מוּתָּר mutar אִיסּוּר isur, וְלֹא velo יִכָּשְׁלוּ yikashlu
וַחֲבֵרַי chaverai בִּדְבַר bidvar ראה הֲלָכָה halacha וְאֶשְׂמַח ve'esmach אֲנִי ani אני
בָּהֶם bahem. וְלֹא velo אֶכָּשֵׁל ekashel אֲנִי ani אני בּוֹ vo וְיִשְׂמְחוּ veyismechu
הֵם hem בִּי bi, כִּי ki יְהֹוָאדהנויאהדונהי Adonai יִתֵּן yiten חָכְמָה chochmah
במילוי = תרי״ג (מצוות) מִפִּיו mipiv דַּעַת da'at וּתְבוּנָה utvuna. גַּל־ gal
עֵינַי enai ריבוע מ״ה וְאַבִּיטָה ve'abita נִפְלָאוֹת nifla'ot מִתּוֹרָתֶךָ: mitoratecha

There is an additional connection that helps us keep the Light in our consciousness the entire day. Before we close our prayer book and leave, we recite this prayer to keep the angels with us all day.

יְהֹוָאדהנויאהדונהי Adonai נְחֵנִי necheni בְצִדְקָתֶךָ vetzidkatecha לְמַעַן lema'an
שׁוֹרְרָי shorerai הַיְשַׁר hayshar (כתיב: הושר) לְפָנַי lefanai דַּרְכֶּךָ: darkecha
וְיַעֲקֹב veYaakov ז׳ הויות, יאהדונהי אידהנויה הָלַךְ halach מיה לְדַרְכּוֹ ledarko
וַיִּפְגְּעוּ vayifge'u בוֹ vo מַלְאֲכֵי mal'achei אֱלֹהִים Elohim אהיה אדני ; ילה:
וַיֹּאמֶר vayomer יַעֲקֹב Yaakov ז׳ הויות, יאהדונהי אידהנויה כַּאֲשֶׁר ka'asher
רָאָם ra'am מַחֲנֵה machane אֱלֹהִים Elohim אהיה אדני ; ילה זֶה ze וַיִּקְרָא vayikra
עם ה׳ אותיות ב״פ קס״א שֵׁם־ shem הַמָּקוֹם hamakom הַהוּא hahu מַחֲנָיִם: Machanayim

---

YEHI RATZON

May it be Your will,

Lord, my God and God of my forefathers, that we may not err in a matter of halachah, and that we may not call impure pure or pure impure, or that we may not call forbidden permitted or permitted forbidden. That my colleagues may not err in a matter of halachah and that I may rejoice in them, and that no offence may occur through me, and that my colleagues may rejoice in me. Because from his mouth Lord gives wisdom and understanding "open my eyes, so that I will see wonders from your Torah" (Psalms 119.18) *"Lord, instruct me with Your righteousness, and against my foes lead me in Your ways."* (Psalms 5:9) *"And Jacob went on his way, and the angels of God met him. And Jacob, when he saw them, said: This is the camp of God. And he called that place Machanayim."* (Genesis 32:2-3)

KIDDUSH FOR SHAVUOT DAY

All our prayers have been arousing spiritual energy from the Upper Worlds. But now we need to manifest and express this energy in our physical world so we can utilize it in a practical manner. The drinking of the wine is one of our methods for expressing this energy.

On *Shabbat* we add:

ושמרו veshamru בני־ venei ישראל yisrael את־ et השבת hashabat ר"ת ביאה
לעשות la'asot את־ et השבת hashabat לדרתם ledorotam ר"ת אהל (וו אשתו, למשוך
נשמה קדושה ולא מסט"א) ברית berit עולם olam: ביני beni ובין uven בני benei
ישראל yisrael אות ot הוא hi ר"ת ביאה לעלם le'olam ריבוע דס"ג וי' אותיות דס"ג כי־ ki
ששת sheshet ימים yamim נלך עשה asa יהוהאדנהיאהדונהי Adonai את־ et
השמים hashamayim י"פ טל, י"פ כוזו ואת־ ve'et הארץ ha'aretz אלהים דההין ע"ה
וביום uvayom ע"ה נגד, מזבח, זן, אל יהוה השביעי hashevi'i שבת shavat
וינפש vayinafash:

אלה ele מועדי moadei יהוהאדנהיאהדונהי Adonai מקראי mikra'ei קדש kodesh
אשר־ asher תקראו tikre'u אתם otam במועדם bemo'adam:
וידבר vaydaber ראה משה Moshe מהש, ע"ב בריבוע וקס"א, אל שדי, ד"פ אלהים ע"ה
את־ et מועדי mo'adei יהוהאדנהיאהדונהי Adonai אל־ el בני benei ישראל Yisrael:

On *Shabbat* we add:

על al כן ken ברך berach יהוהאדנהיאהדונהי Adonai את et
יום yom ע"ה נגד, מזבח, זן, אל יהוה השבת hashabat ויקדשהו vaykadshehu:

סברי savri מרנן maranan (we answer: לחיים lechayim)
ברוך baruch אתה Ata יהוהאדנהיאהדונהי Adonai אלהינו Elohenu מלך melech
העולם ha'olam בורא bore פרי peri הגפן hagefen:

KIDDUSH FOR SHAVUOT DAY

"And the Children of Israel shall keep the Shabbat, to make the Shabbat an eternal covenant for all their generations. Between Me and the Children of Israel, It is an eternal sign that in six days did the Lord make the Heavens and the earth and on the Seventh Day, He was refreshed. For that reason, the Lord blessed the Shabbat day and made it holy." (Exodus 31:17)

Those are the holiday of the Lord, Holy covenant you shall call them, on their time.
And Moses spoke the holidays of the lord to the children of Israel

So the Lord blessed the day of Shabbat and made it Holy.

With your permission, my masters. (And answer: *To life!*)
Blessed are You, Lord, Our God, King of the universe, Who creates the fruit of the vine.

MINCHAH OF SHAVUOT

The numerical value of the word *Minchah* (103) is also the number of sub-worlds (within the five major worlds), controlled by the Left Column energy of judgment. The purpose of the *Minchah* prayer is not simply to make a connection to the Light of the Creator, it is to quiet the energy of judgment in the world.

Isaac the Patriarch is our channel to overcome judgment. Isaac came to this world to create a path that would lead us to sweetening the judgment in our lives.

LESHEM YICHUD

לְשֵׁם leshem יִחוּד yichud קוּדְשָׁא kudsha בְּרִיךְ berich הוּא hu
וּשְׁכִינְתֵּיהּ ush'chintei (יאהדונהי) בִּדְחִילוּ bid'chilu וּרְחִימוּ ur'chimu
(יאההויהה) וּרְחִימוּ ur'chimu וּדְחִילוּ ud'chilu (איההיוהה) לְיַחֲדָא leyachda
שֵׁם shem יוּ"ד yud קֵ"י kei בְּוָא"ו bevav קֵ"י kei בְּיִחוּדָא beyichuda
שְׁלִים shelim (יהוה) בְּשֵׁם beshem כָּל kol ילי יִשְׂרָאֵל Yisrael,
הִנֵּה hine אֲנַחְנוּ anachnu בָּאִים ba'im לְהִתְפַּלֵּל lehitpalel תְּפִלַּת tefilat
מִנְחָה mincha ע"ה ב"פ ב"ן שֶׁל shel (on Shabbat add: שַׁבָּת Shabbat קוֹדֶשׁ kodesh
וְ (ve שָׁבוּעוֹת Shavuot שֶׁתִּקֵּן shetiken יִצְחָק Yitzchak ד"פ ב"ן אָבִינוּ avinu
עָלָיו alav הַשָּׁלוֹם hashalom עִם im כָּל kol ילי הַמִּצְוֹת hamitzvot
הַכְּלוּלוֹת hakelulot בָּהּ ba לְתַקֵּן letaken אֶת et שׁוֹרְשָׁהּ shorsha
בְּמָקוֹם bemakom עֶלְיוֹן elyon לַעֲשׂוֹת la'asot נַחַת nachat רוּחַ ru'ach
לְיוֹצְרֵנוּ leyotzrenu וְלַעֲשׂוֹת vela'asot רְצוֹן retzon מהש ע"ה, ע"ב בריבוע וקס"א ע"ה,
אל שדי ע"ה בּוֹרְאֵנוּ bor'enu. וִיהִי vihi נֹעַם no'am אֲדֹנָי Adonai ללה
אֱלֹהֵינוּ Elohenu ילה עָלֵינוּ alenu וּמַעֲשֵׂה uma'ase יָדֵינוּ yadenu
כּוֹנְנָה konena עָלֵינוּ alenu וּמַעֲשֵׂה uma'ase יָדֵינוּ yadenu כּוֹנְנֵהוּ konenehu:

MINCHAH OF SHAVUOT
LESHEM YICHUD

For the sake of the unification

of The Holy Blessed One and His Shechinah, with fear and love and with love and fear, in order to unify The Name Yud-Kei and Vav-Kei in perfect unity, and in the name of Israel, we have hereby come to recite the prayer of Minchah for (on Shabbat add: the holy Shabbat and) the holiday of Shavuot, established by Isaac, our forefather, may peace be upon him, With all its commandments, to correct its root in the supernal place, to bring satisfaction to our Maker,and to fulfill the wish of our Creator. "And may the pleasantness of Lord, our God, be upon us and may He establishes the work of our hands for us and may the work of our hands establish Him." (Psalms 90:17)

THE SACRIFICES – KORBANOT - THE TAMID – (DAILY) OFFERING

וַיְדַבֵּר vaydaber ראה יְהֹוָאדהנויאהדונהי Adonai אֶל־ el מֹשֶׁה Moshe

מהש, ע״ב בריבוע וקס״א, אל שדי לֵּאמֹר lemor: צַו tzav פוי, אל אדני אֶת־ et בְּנֵי benei

יִשְׂרָאֵל Yisrael וְאָמַרְתָּ ve'amarta אֲלֵהֶם alehem אֶת־ et קָרְבָּנִי korbani

לַחְמִי lachmi לְאִשַּׁי le'ishai רֵיחַ re'ach נִיחֹחִי nichochi תִּשְׁמְרוּ tishmeru

לְהַקְרִיב lehakriv לִי li בְּמוֹעֲדוֹ bemo'ado: וְאָמַרְתָּ ve'amarta לָהֶם lahem

זֶה ze הָאִשֶּׁה ha'ishe אֲשֶׁר asher תַּקְרִיבוּ takrivu לַיהֹוָאדהנויאהדונהי ladonai

כְּבָשִׂים kevasim בְּנֵי־ benei שָׁנָה shana תְמִימִם temimim שְׁנַיִם shenayim

לַיּוֹם layom ע״ה נגד, מזבח, זן, אל יהוה עֹלָה ola ר״ת עשל תָּמִיד tamid ע״ה קס״א קנ״א קמ״ג:

אֶת־ et הַכֶּבֶשׂ hakeves אֶחָד echad אהבה, דאגה תַּעֲשֶׂה ta'ase בַבֹּקֶר vaboker

וְאֵת ve'et הַכֶּבֶשׂ hakeves הַשֵּׁנִי hasheni תַּעֲשֶׂה ta'ase בֵּין ben

הָעַרְבָּיִם ha'arbayim: וַעֲשִׂירִית va'asirit הָאֵיפָה ha'efa סֹלֶת solet

לְמִנְחָה lemincha ע״ה ב״פ ב״ן בְּלוּלָה belula בְּשֶׁמֶן beshemen

כָּתִית katit רְבִיעִת revi'it הַהִין hahin: עֹלַת olat ושר, אבגיתץ

(Meditate here to surrender the *klipa* named *Tola* using the Name: אבגיתץ)

תָּמִיד tamid ע״ה קס״א קנ״א קמ״ג הָעֲשֻׂיָה ha'asuya

בְּהַר behar סִינַי Sinai נמם, ה׳ הויות (ה׳ גבורות) לְרֵיחַ lere'ach נִיחֹחַ nicho'ach

אִשֶּׁה ishe לַיהֹוָאדהנויאהדונהי ladonai: וְנִסְכּוֹ venisko רְבִיעִת revi'it

הַהִין hahin לַכֶּבֶשׂ lakeves הָאֶחָד ha'echad אהבה, דאגה בַּקֹּדֶשׁ bakodesh

הַסֵּךְ hasech נֶסֶךְ nesech שֵׁכָר shechar י״פ ב״ן לַיהֹוָאדהנויאהדונהי ladonai:

THE SACRIFICES – KORBANOT - THE TAMID – (DAILY) OFFERING

"And the Lord spoke to Moses and said, Command the Children of Israel and say to them, My offering, the bread of My fire-offering, My pleasing fragrance, you shall take care to sacrifice to Me at its specified time. And you shall say to them: This is the fire-offering that you shall sacrifice to God, perfect one-year-old sheep, two per day, as a regular daily offering; one sheep you shall do in the morning and the second sheep you shall do in the late afternoon. And one tenth of ephahof fine flour, for a meal-offering, mixed with one quarter of a hin of pressed oil. This is a regular burnt-offering that is made at Mount Sinai as a pleasing fragrance and as a fire-offering before the Lord. Its libation is one quarter of a hin for the one sheep in the Sanctuary, pour a libation of old wine before the Lord.

וְאֵת ve'et הַכֶּבֶשׂ hakeves הַשֵּׁנִי hasheni תַּעֲשֶׂה ta'ase בֵּין ben
הָעַרְבָּיִם ha'arbayim כְּמִנְחַת keminchat הַבֹּקֶר haboker וּכְנִסְכּוֹ uchnisko
תַּעֲשֶׂה ta'ase אִשֵּׁה ishe (elevation to *Yetzirah*) רֵיחַ re'ach (elevation to *Beriah*)
נִיחֹחַ nicho'ach (elevation to *Atzilut*) לַיהֹוָהאדניאהדונהי ladonai (elevation to the Endless World):

THE INCENSE

These verses from the *Torah* and the *Talmud* speak about the 11 herbs and spices that were used in the Temple. These herbs and spices were used for one purpose: to help us remove the force of death from every area of our lives. This is one of the few prayers whose sole goal is the eradication of death. The *Zohar* teaches us that whoever has judgment pursuing him needs to connect to this incense. The 11 herbs and spices connect to 11 Lights that sustain the *klipot* (shells of negativity). When we uproot the 11 Lights from the *klipot* through the power of the incense, the *klipot* lose their life-force and die. In addition to bringing the 11 spices to the Temple, the people brought resin, wine, and other items with metaphysical properties to help battle the Angel of Death.

It says in the *Zohar*: "Come and see, whoever is pursued by judgment is in need of incense and must repent before his master, for incense helps judgment to disappear from him." The 11 herbs and spices correspond to the 11 holy illuminations that revive the *klipa*. By elevating them, the *klipa* will die. Through these 11 herbs, the *klipot* are pushed away and the energy-point that was giving them life is removed. And since the Pure Side and its livelihood disappear, the *klipot* is left with no life. Thus the secret of the incense is that it cleanses the force of plague and cancels it. The incense kills the Angel of Death and takes away his power to kill.

אַתָּה Ata הוּא hu יְהֹוָהאדניאהדונהי Adonai אֱלֹהֵינוּ Elohenu ילה
שֶׁהִקְטִירוּ shehiktiru אֲבוֹתֵינוּ avotenu לְפָנֶיךָ lefanecha ס״ג מ״ה ב״ן
אֶת et קְטֹרֶת ketoret י״א פעמים אדני (הנבררים מהקליפות ע״י י״א הסממנים) ;
קטרת - הק׳ באתב״ש ד׳ = תרי״ג (מצוות) הַסַּמִּים hasamim ע״ה קנ״א, אדני אלהים
בִּזְמַן bizman שֶׁבֵּית shebet ב״פ ראה הַמִּקְדָּשׁ hamikdash קַיָּם kayam
כַּאֲשֶׁר ka'asher צִוִּיתָ tzivita אוֹתָם otam עַל־ al יַד yad מֹשֶׁה Moshe מהש,
ע״ב בריבוע וקס״א, אל שדי נְבִיאָךְ nevia'ch כַּכָּתוּב kakatuv בְּתוֹרָתָךְ betoratach:

The second sheep you shall do in the afternoon like the meal-offering of the morning; its libation you shall do as a fire-offering of a fragrance which is pleasing to the Lord." (Numbers 28:1-8)

THE INCENSE

It is You, Lord, our God, before whom our forefathers burned the incense spices, during the time when the Temple existed, as You had commanded them through Moses, Your Prophet, and as it is written in Your Torah:

THE PORTION OF THE INCENSE

To raise the *Sefirot* from all of *Nogah* of *Atzilut*, *Beriah*, *Yetzirah* and *Asiyah*.

וַיֹּאמֶר vayomer יְהֹוָה(אדני אהדונהי) Adonai אֶל־ el מֹשֶׁה Moshe

מהש, ע״ב בריבוע וקס״א, אל שדי קַח־ kach לְךָ lecha סַמִּים samim **(*Tiferet, Netzach*)**

ע״ה קנ״א, אדני אלהים נָטָף nataf | **(*Hod*)** וּשְׁחֵלֶת ushchelet **(*Yesod*)** וְחֶלְבְּנָה vechelbena

(*Malchut*) ע״ה פוי, אל אדני סַמִּים samim **(*Keter, Chochmah, Binah, Chesed, Gevurah*)**

ע״ה קנ״א, אדני אלהים וּלְבֹנָה ulvona זַכָּה zaka **(Surrounding Light)** בַּד bad בְּבַד bevad

יִהְיֶה yih'ye ייי: וְעָשִׂיתָ ve'asita אֹתָהּ ota קְטֹרֶת ketoret י״א פעמים אדני (הנבררים

מהקליפות ע״י י״א הסממנים); קטרת - הק׳ באתב״ש ד׳ = תרי״ג (מצוות) רֹקַח rokach מַעֲשֵׂה ma'ase

רוֹקֵחַ roke'ach שדי מְמֻלָּח memulach טָהוֹר tahor י״פ אכא קֹדֶשׁ kodesh

ס״ת רוחש בכוונו לגרש החיצונים ויועיל לזכירה: וְשָׁחַקְתָּ veshachakta מִמֶּנָּה mimena

הָדֵק hadek וְנָתַתָּה venatata מִמֶּנָּה mimena לִפְנֵי lifnei הָעֵדֻת ha'edut

בְּאֹהֶל be'ohel מוֹעֵד mo'ed אֲשֶׁר asher אִוָּעֵד iva'ed לְךָ lecha שָׁמָּה shama

קֹדֶשׁ kodesh קָדָשִׁים kadashim תִּהְיֶה tihye לָכֶם lachem. וְנֶאֱמַר vene'emar:

וְהִקְטִיר vehiktir עָלָיו alav אַהֲרֹן Aharon קְטֹרֶת ketoret י״א פעמים אדני

(הנבררים מהקליפות ע״י י״א הסממנים) ; קטרת - הק׳ באתב״ש ד׳ = תרי״ג (מצוות) סַמִּים samim

ע״ה קנ״א, אדני אלהים בַּבֹּקֶר baboker בַּבֹּקֶר baboker בְּהֵיטִיבוֹ behetivo

אֶת־ et הַנֵּרֹת hanerot יַקְטִירֶנָּה yaktirena: וּבְהַעֲלֹת uveha'alot

אַהֲרֹן Aharon אֶת־ et הַנֵּרֹת hanerot בֵּין ben הָעַרְבַּיִם ha'arbayim

ר״ת אהבה, דאגה, אחד יַקְטִירֶנָּה yaktirena קְטֹרֶת ketoret י״א פעמים אדני

(הנבררים מהקליפות ע״י י״א הסממנים) ; קטרת - הק׳ באתב״ש ד׳ = תרי״ג (מצוות) תָּמִיד tamid

ע״ה קס״א קנ״א קמ״ג לִפְנֵי lifnei יְהֹוָה(אדני אהדונהי) Adonai לְדֹרֹתֵיכֶם ledorotechem:

THE PORTION OF THE INCENSE

"And the Lord said to Moses: Take for yourself spices, balsam sap, onycha, galbanum, and pure frankincense, each of equal weight. You shall prepare it as an incense compound: the work of a spice-mixer, well-blended, pure, and holy. You shall grind some of it fine and place it before the Testimony in the Tabernacle of Meeting, in which I shall meet with you. It shall be the Holy of Holies unto you." (Exodus 30:34-36) *And God also said: "Aaron shall burn upon the Altar incense spices early each morning when he prepares the candles. And when Aaron raises the candles at sundown, he shall burn the incense spices as a continual incense-offering before God throughout all your generations."* (Exodus 30:7-8)

THE WORKINGS OF THE INCENSE

The filling of the incense has two purposes: First, to remove the *klipot* in order to stop them from going up along with the elevation of the Worlds, and second, to draw Light to *Asiyah*. So meditate to raise the sparks of Light from all of the *Nogah* of *Azilut*, *Beriah*, *Yetzirah* and *Asiyah*.

Count the incense using your right hand, one by one, and don't skip even one, as it is said: "If one omits one of all the ingredients, he is liable to receive the penalty of death." And therefore, you should be careful not to skip any of them, because reciting this paragraph is a substitute for the actual burning of the incense.

תָּנוּ tanu רַבָּנָן rabanan פִּטּוּם pitum הַקְּטֹרֶת haketoret י"א פעמים אדני
(הנבררים מהקליפות ע"י י"א הסממנים) קטרת - הק' באתב"ש ד' = תרי"ג (מצוות);
פטום הקטרת = יְהֹוָה יֱהֹוִה מצפצ יה אדני אל אלהים מצפצ (ו' מרגלאין דשבת):
כֵּיצַד ketzad. שְׁלֹשׁ shelosh מֵאוֹת me'ot המספר = ש', אלהים דיודין
וְשִׁשִּׁים veshishim המספר = מילוי הש' (ין) וּשְׁמוֹנָה ushmona מָנִים manim הָיוּ hayu
בָהּ va. שְׁלֹשׁ shelosh מֵאוֹת me'ot המספר = ש', אלהים דיודין וְשִׁשִּׁים veshishim
המספר = מילוי הש' (ין) וַחֲמִשָּׁה vachamisha כְּמִנְיַן keminyan יְמוֹת yemot
הַחַמָּה hachama מָנֶה mane ע"ה פוי, אל אדני בְּכָל bechol ב"ן, לכב
יוֹם yom ע"ה נגד, מזבח, זן, אל יהוה. מַחֲצִיתוֹ machatzito בַּבֹּקֶר baboker
וּמַחֲצִיתוֹ umachatzito בָּעֶרֶב ba'erev. וּשְׁלֹשָׁה ushlosha מָנִים manim
יְתֵרִים yeterim קס"א, קנ"א וקמ"ג שֶׁמֵּהֶם shemehem מַכְנִיס machnis כֹּהֵן kohen מלה
גָּדוֹל gadol להח ; עם ד' אותיות = מבה, יזל, אום וְנוֹטֵל venotel מֵהֶם mehem
מְלֹא melo חָפְנָיו chofnav בְּיוֹם beyom ע"ה נגד, מזבח, זן, אל יהוה הַכִּפּוּרִים hakipurim
מַחֲזִירָן machaziran לְמַכְתֶּשֶׁת lamachteshet בְּעֶרֶב be'erev
יוֹם yom ע"ה נגד, מזבח, זן, אל יהוה הַכִּפּוּרִים hakipurim כְּדֵי kedei לְקַיֵּם lekayem
מִצְוַת mitzvat דַּקָּה daka מִן min הַדַּקָּה hadaka. וְאַחַד ve'achad אהבה, דאגה
עֲשָׂר asar סַמָּנִים samanim הָיוּ hayu בָהּ va. וְאֵלּוּ ve'elu הֵן hen:

THE WORKINGS OF THE INCENSE

Our Sages have taught: How was the compounding of the incense done? Three hundred and sixty-eight portions were contained therein. These corresponded to the number of days in the solar year, one portion for each day: Half of it in the morning and half at sundown. As for the remaining three portions, the High Priest, on Yom Kippur, filled both his hands with them. On the Eve of Yom Kippur, he would take them back to the mortar to fulfill the requirement that they should be very finely ground. Each portion contained eleven spices:

1) הַצֳּרִי haTzori **(*Keter*)** מצפצ, אלהים דיודין, י"פ ייי. 2) וְהַצִּפֹּרֶן vehaTziporen **(*Yesod*)**
יהוה אדני אהיה שדי. 3) וְהַחֶלְבְּנָה vehaChelbena **(*Malchut*)** ע"ה פוי, אל אדני.
4) וְהַלְּבוֹנָה vehaLevona **(Surrounding Light** – שהוא אור לבן והוא יוזידי הנקרא אדון יוזיד)
מִשְׁקַל mishkal שִׁבְעִים shiv'im שִׁבְעִים shiv'im מָנֶה mane ע"ה פוי, אל אדני.
5) מוֹר Mor **(*Chesed*)**. 6) וּקְצִיעָה uKtzi'ah רהע **(*Gevurah*** – "כי מצפון תפתח הרעה",
והגבורה סוד רווז צפון). 7) וְשִׁבֹּלֶת veShibolet נֵרְדְּ Nerd **(*Tiferet*)**.
8) וְכַרְכֹּם veCharkom **(*Netzach*)** בוזוהר, סנדלפון, ערי. מִשְׁקַל mishkal שִׁשָּׁה shisha
עָשָׂר asar שִׁשָּׁה shisha עָשָׂר asar מָנֶה mane ע"ה פוי, אל אדני. 9) קֹשְׁטְ Kosht
(*Chochmah*) שְׁנֵים sheneim עָשָׂר asar. 10) קִלּוּפָה Kilufa **(*Binah*)** שְׁלֹשָׁה shelosha.
11) קִנָּמוֹן Kinamon ***(Hod)*** ר"ת ג"פ ק' (בסוד קדוש קדוש קדוש) תִּשְׁעָה tish'ah.
בּוֹרִית borit כַּרְשִׁינָא karshina תִּשְׁעָה tish'ah קַבִּין kabin. יֵין yen מיכ, י"פ האא
קַפְרִיסִין Kafrisin סְאִין se'in תְּלַת telat וְקַבִּין vekabin תְּלָתָא telata אהיה קבין
וְאִם ve'im יוהך, מ"א אותיות דפשוט, דמילוי ודמילוי דמילוי דאהיה ע"ה לֹא lo מָצָא matza
יֵין yen מיכ, י"פ האא קַפְרִיסִין Kafrisin מֵבִיא mevi חֲמַר chamar חִוָּר chivar
עַתִּיק atik. מֶלַח melach סְדוֹמִית Sedomit רוֹבַע rova. מַעֲלֶה ma'ale
עָשָׁן ashan כָּל kol ילי שֶׁהוּא shehu. רִבִּי Ribi נָתָן Natan הַבַּבְלִי haBavli
אוֹמֵר omer: אַף af מִכִּפַּת mikipat הַיַּרְדֵּן haYarden י' הויות וד' אותיות כָּל kol ילי
שֶׁהִיא shehi. אִם im יוהך, מ"א אותיות דפשוט, דמילוי ודמילוי דמילוי דאהיה ע"ה נָתַן natan
בָּהּ ba דְּבַשׁ devash שו' (דשופר) וי"ד (האוזז) = ש"ך דינין דגדלות פְּסָלָהּ pesala.
וְאִם ve'im יוהך, מ"א אותיות דפשוט, דמילוי ודמילוי דמילוי דאהיה ע"ה חִסַּר chiser
אַחַת achat מִכָּל־ mikol ילי סַמְמָנֶיהָ samemaneha חַיָּב chayav מִיתָה mita:

---

1) Balsam. 2) Onycha. 3) Galbanum. 4) Frankincense; the weight of seventy portions each. 5) Myrrh. 6) Cassia. 7) Spikenard. 8) And Saffron; the weight of sixteen portions each. 9) Twelve portions of Costus. 10) Three of aromatic Bark 11) Nine of Cinnamon. Further, nine kavs of Lye of Carsina. And three kavs and three se'ehs of Cyprus wine. And if one should not find any Cyprus wine, he should bring an old white wine. And a quarter of the salt of Sodom. And a small measure of a smoke raising herb. Rabbi Natan, the Babylonian, advised also, a small amount of Jordan resin. If he added to it honey, he would make it defective. If he omits even one of all its herbs, he would be liable to death.

רַבָּן Raban שִׁמְעוֹן Shimon בֶּן ben גַּמְלִיאֵל Gamli'el אוֹמֵר omer:
הַצֳּרִי haTzori מצפצ, אלהים דיודין, י"פ ייי אֵינוֹ eno אֶלָּא ela שְׂרָף seraf
הַנּוֹטֵף hanotef מֵעֲצֵי me'atzei הַקְּטָף haketaf. בּוֹרִית borit
כַּרְשִׁינָא karshina לְמָה lema הִיא hee בָּאָה va'a. כְּדֵי kedei
לְשַׁפּוֹת leshapot בָּהּ ba אֶת et הַצִּפּוֹרֶן haTziporen יהוה אדני אהיה שדי
כְּדֵי kedei שֶׁתְּהֵא shetehe נָאָה na'a. יֵין yen ע' (כנגד ע' אומות העולם התלויים בסמאל),
מ"כ, י"פ האא קַפְרִיסִין Kafrisin לְמָה lema הוּא hu בָּא va. כְּדֵי kedei
לִשְׁרוֹת lishrot בּוֹ bo אֶת et הַצִּפּוֹרֶן haTziporen יהוה אדני אהיה שדי
כְּדֵי kedei שֶׁתְּהֵא shetehe עַזָּה aza. וַהֲלֹא vahalo מֵי mei ילי רַגְלַיִם raglayim
יָפִין yafin לָהּ la אֶלָּא ela שֶׁאֵין she'en מַכְנִיסִין machnisin מֵי mei ילי
רַגְלַיִם raglayim בַּמִּקְדָּשׁ bamikdash מִפְּנֵי mipenei הַכָּבוֹד hakavod לאו:
תַּנְיָא tanya. רִבִּי Ribi נָתָן Natan אוֹמֵר omer: כְּשֶׁהוּא keshehu
שׁוֹחֵק shochek אוֹמֵר omer הָדֵק hadek הֵיטֵב hetev. הֵיטֵב hetev
הָדֵק hadek. מִפְּנֵי mipenei שֶׁהַקּוֹל shehakol יָפֶה yafe לַבְּשָׂמִים labesamim.
פִּטְּמָהּ pitema לַחֲצָאִין lachatza'in כְּשֵׁרָה keshera. לְשָׁלִישׁ leshalish
וּלְרָבִיעַ ulravi'a לֹא lo שָׁמַעְנוּ shamanu. אָמַר amar רִבִּי Ribi
יְהוּדָה Yehuda: זֶה ze הַכְּלָל hakelal. אִם im יוהך, מ"א אותיות דפשוט, דמילוי
ודמילוי דמילוי דאהיה ע"ה כְּמִדָּתָהּ kemidata כְּשֵׁרָה keshera לַחֲצָאִין lachatza'in.
וְאִם ve'im יוהך, מ"א אותיות דפשוט, דמילוי ודמילוי דמילוי דאהיה ע"ה חִסֵּר chiser
אַחַת achat מִכָּל־ mikol סַמְמָנֶיהָ ילי samemaneha חַיָּב chayav מִיתָה mita:

Rabban Shimon ben Gamliel says: The balsam was a sap that only seeped from the balsam trees. For what purpose was the lye of Carsina added? In order to rub the Onycha with it to make it pleasant looking. For what purpose was the Cyprus wine added? In order to steep in it the Onycha. Urine is more appropriate for this, but urine is not brought into the Temple out of respect. It was taught that Rabbi Natan said: When he ground, he said: 'Grind it fine, grind it fine.' This is because voice is beneficial to the spices. If he compounds half the amount it is still valid, yet regarding a third or a quarter, we have no information. Rabbi Yehuda said: This is the general rule: If it is in its correct proportions, then half is valid. Yet if he omits one of all its spices, he is liable to death.

תָּנֵי tanei בַּר Var קַפָּרָא Kapara: אַחַת achat לְשִׁשִּׁים leshishim אוֹ o
לְשִׁבְעִים leshiv'im שָׁנָה shana הָיְתָה hayta בָּאָה va'a שֶׁל shel
שִׁירַיִם shirayim לַחֲצָאִין lachatza'in. וְעוֹד ve'od תָּנֵי tanei בַּר Var
קַפָּרָא Kapara: אִלּוּ ilu הָיָה haya יהה נוֹתֵן noten אבגיתץ, ושר בָּהּ ba
קָרְטוֹב kortov שֶׁל shel דְּבַשׁ devash שו' (דשופר) וי"ד (האווז) = ש"ך דינין דגדלות
אֵין en אָדָם adam מ"ה יָכוֹל yachol לַעֲמוֹד la'amod מִפְּנֵי mipenei
רֵיחָהּ recha. וְלָמָּה velama אֵין en מְעָרְבִין me'arvin בָּהּ ba דְּבַשׁ devash
שו' (דשופר) וי"ד (האווז) = ש"ך דינין דגדלות מִפְּנֵי mipenei שֶׁהַתּוֹרָה shehatorah
אָמְרָה amra: כִּי ki כָּל־ chol ילי שְׂאֹר se'or ג' מוחין דאלהים דקטנות
(ש' = אלהים דיודין ; א' כללות שם אלהים ; ר' = ריבוע אלהים) וְכָל־ vechol ילי דְּבַשׁ devash
שו' (דשופר) וי"ד (האווז) = ש"ך דינין דגדלות לֹא־ lo תַקְטִירוּ taktiru מִמֶּנּוּ mimenu
שכן הם בחינת דינין דקטנות ודגדלות לכן נאסרה הקרבתן אִשֶּׁה ishe לַיהֹוָהאדניאהדונהי ladonai:

Right

יְהֹוָהאדניאהדונהי Adonai צְבָאוֹת Tzeva'ot פני שכינה עִמָּנוּ imanu
ריבוע דס"ג, קס"א ע"ה וד' אותיות מִשְׂגָּב־ misgav משה, מהש, ע"ב בריבוע וקס"א, אל שדי,
ד"פ אלהים ע"ה לָנוּ lanu אלהים, אהיה אדני אֱלֹהֵי Elohei מילוי ע"ב, דמב ; ילה
יַעֲקֹב Yaakov ו' הויות, יאהדונהי אידהנויה סֶלָה sela:

Left

יְהֹוָהאדניאהדונהי Adonai צְבָאוֹת Tzeva'ot פני שכינה אַשְׁרֵי ashrei
אָדָם adam מ"ה ; יהוה צבאות אשרי אדם = תפארת בֹּטֵחַ bote'ach
בָּךְ bach אדם בוטח בך = אמן (יאהדונהי) ע"ה ; בוטח בך = מילוי ע"ב ע"ה:

Bar Kappara taught that once every sixty or seventy years the leftovers would accumulate to half the measure. Bar Kappara also taught that if one would add to it a Kortov of honey, no man would withstand its smell. Why is honey not mixed with it? Because the Torah had stipulated: Because any leaven or honey, you must not burn any of it as burnt-offering to the Lord. (Kritut 6; Yerushalmi, Yoma: ch.4)
(Right) *"The Lord of Hosts is with us, our strength is the God of Jacob, Selah."* (Psalms 46:12)
(Left) *"The Lord of Hosts, joyful is one who trusts in You."* (Psalms 84:13)

Central

יְהֹוָואדניאהדונהי Adonai הוֹשִׁיעָה hoshi'a יהוה וש״ע נהורין הַמֶּלֶךְ hamelech ר״ת יהה
יַעֲנֵנוּ ya'anenu בְּיוֹם veyom ע״ה נגד, מזבח, זן, אל יהוה
קָרְאֵנוּ kor'enu ר״ת יב״ק, אלהים יהוה, אהיה אדני יהוה ; ס״ת = ב״ן ועם כף דהמלך = ע״ב:
וְעָרְבָה ve'arva לַיהֹוָואדניאהדונהי ladonai
מִנְחַת minchat יְהוּדָה Yehuda וִירוּשָׁלָם virushalaim
כִּימֵי kimei עוֹלָם olam וּכְשָׁנִים uch'shanim קַדְמֹנִיּוֹת kadmoniyot:

ANA BEKO'ACH (to learn more about the *Ana Beko'ach* go to pg. 249)

The *Ana Beko'ach* is perhaps the most powerful prayer in the entire universe. Second-century Kabbalist Rav Nachunya ben HaKana was the first sage to reveal this combination of 42 letters, which encompass the power of Creation.

Chesed, Sunday ***(Alef Bet Gimel Yud Tav Tzadik)*** אבג יתץ

אָנָּא ana בְּכֹחַ beko'ach• גְּדוּלַּת gedulat יְמִינְךָ yeminecha•
תַּתִּיר tatir צְרוּרָה tzerura:

Gevurah, Monday ***(Kuf Resh Ayin Sin Tet Nun)*** קרע שטן

קַבֵּל kabel רִנַּת rinat• עַמְּךָ amecha שַׂגְּבֵנוּ sagevenu•
טַהֲרֵנוּ taharenu נוֹרָא nora:

Tiferet, Tuesday ***(Nun Gimel Dalet Yud Kaf Shin)*** נגד יכש

נָא na גִּבּוֹר gibor• דּוֹרְשֵׁי dorshei יִחוּדְךָ yichudecha•
כְּבָבַת kevavat שָׁמְרֵם shomrem:

(Central) *"Lotd save us. The King shall answer us the day we call."* (Psalms 20:10) *"May the Lord find the offering of Yehuda and Jerusalem pleasing as He had always done and as in the years of old."* (Malachi 3:4)

ANA BEKO'ACH

Chesed, Sunday אבג יתץ

We beseech You, with the power of Your great right, undo this entanglement.

Gevurah, Monday קרע שטן

Accept the singing of Your Nation. Strengthen and purify us, Awesome One.

Tiferet, Tuesday נגד יכש

Please, Mighty One, those who seek Your unity, guard them like the pupil of the eye.

Netzach, Wednesday *(Bet Tet Resh Tzadik Tav Gimel)* בטר צתג

בָּרְכֵם barchem טַהֲרֵם taharem◆ רַחֲמֵי rachamei צִדְקָתְךָ tzidkatecha◆

תָּמִיד tamid גָּמְלֵם gomlem:

Hod, Thursday *(Chet Kuf Bet Tet Nun Ayin)* חקב טנע

חֲסִין chasin קָדוֹשׁ kadosh◆ בְּרוֹב berov טוּבְךָ tuvcha◆

נַהֵל nahel עֲדָתֶךָ adatecha:

Yesod, Friday *(Yud Gimel Lamed Pei Zayin Kuf)* יגל פזק

יָחִיד yachid גֵּאֶה ge'e◆ לְעַמְּךָ le'amecha פְּנֵה pene◆

זוֹכְרֵי zochrei קְדוּשָּׁתֶךָ kedushatecha:

Malchut, Saturday *(Shin Kuf Vav Tzadik Yud Tav)* שקו צית

שַׁוְעָתֵנוּ shav'atenu קַבֵּל kabel◆ וּשְׁמַע ushma צַעֲקָתֵנוּ tza'akatenu◆

יוֹדֵעַ yode'a תַּעֲלוּמוֹת ta'alumot:

BARUCH SHEM KEVOD

(Whisper): יו״ו אותיות בָּרוּךְ baruch שֵׁם shem כְּבוֹד kevod מַלְכוּתוֹ malchuto

לְעוֹלָם le'olam ריבוע ס״ג ו׳ אותיות דס״ג וָעֶד va'ed:

Netzach, Wednesday בטר צתג

Bless them. Purify them. Your compassionate righteousness always grant them.

Hod, Thursday חקב טנע

Invincible and Mighty One, with the abundance of Your goodness, govern Your congregation.

Yesod, Friday יגל פזק

Sole and proud One, turn to Your people, those who remember Your sanctity.

Malchut, Saturday שקו צית

Accept our cry and hear our wail, You that knows all that is hidden.

BARUCH SHEM KEVOD

"Blessed is the Name of Glory. His Kingdom is forever and for eternity." (*Pesachim 56a*)

THE ASHREI

Twenty-one of the twenty-two letters of the Aramaic alphabet are encoded in the *Ashrei* in their correct order from *Alef* to *Tav*. King David, the author, left out the Aramaic letter *Nun* from this prayer, because *Nun* is the first letter in the Aramaic word *nefilah*, which means "falling." Falling refers to a spiritual decline, as in falling into the *klipa*. Feelings of doubt, depression, worry, and uncertainty are consequences of spiritual falling. Because the Aramaic letters are the actual instruments of Creation, this prayer helps to inject order and the power of Creation into our lives, without the energy of falling.

In this Psalm there are ten times the Name: יהוה for the Ten *Sefirot*. This Psalm is written according to the order of the *Alef Bet*, but the letter *Nun* is omitted to prevent falling.

אַשְׁרֵי ashrei (סוד הכתר) יוֹשְׁבֵי yoshvei בֵיתֶךָ vetecha ב"פ ראה

עוֹד od יְהַלְלוּךָ yehalelucha סֶּלָה sela: אַשְׁרֵי ashrei הָעָם ha'am

שֶׁכָּכָה shekacha מהש, משה, ע"ב בריבוע וקס"א, אל שדי, ד"פ אלהים ע"ה לוֹ lo

אַשְׁרֵי ashrei הָעָם ha'am ר"ת לאה שֶׁיְהֹוָאדהֹנָי אהדונהי she'Adonai (*Keter*)

אֱלֹהָיו Elohav ילה: תְּהִלָּה tehila ע"ה אמת, אהיה פעמים אהיה, ז"פ ס"ג לְדָוִד leDavid

אֲרוֹמִמְךָ aromimcha אֱלוֹהַי Elohai הַמֶּלֶךְ hamelech וַאֲבָרְכָה va'avarcha

שִׁמְךָ shimcha לְעוֹלָם le'olam ריבוע ס"ג ו' אותיות ס"ג וָעֶד va'ed:

בְּכָל bechol ב"ן, לכב יוֹם yom ע"ה נגד, מזבח, זן אל יהוה

אֲבָרְכֶךָּ avarcheka וַאֲהַלְלָה va'ahalela מ"ה יהוה שִׁמְךָ shimcha

לְעוֹלָם le'olam ריבוע ס"ג ו' אותיות ס"ג וָעֶד va'ed:

גָּדוֹל gadol להח ; עם ד' אותיות = מבה, יזל, אום

יְהֹוָאדהֹנָי אהדונהי Adonai (*Chochmah*) וּמְהֻלָּל umhulal אדני, ללה

מְאֹד me'od וְלִגְדֻלָּתוֹ veligdulato והו אֵין en חֵקֶר cheker:

THE ASHREI

"Joyful are those who dwell in Your House, they shall praise You, Selah." (Psalms 84:5) *"Joyful is the nation that this is theirs and joyful the nation that the Lord is their God."* (Psalms 145:15) *"A praise of David:*

א *I shall exalt You, my God, the King, and I shall bless Your Name forever and for eternity.*

ב *I shall bless You every day and I shall praise Your Name forever and for eternity.*

ג *The Lord is great and exceedingly praised. His greatness is unfathomable.*

דּוֹר dor לְדוֹר ledor יְשַׁבַּח yeshabach מַעֲשֶׂיךָ ma'asecha ר"ת דלים

וּגְבוּרֹתֶיךָ ugvurotecha יַגִּידוּ yagidu יי"ו, כ"ב אותיות פשוטות (=אכא) וה' אותיות סופיות בםןףך:

הֲדַר hadar כְּבוֹד kevod הוֹדֶךָ hodecha וְדִבְרֵי vedivrei

נִפְלְאוֹתֶיךָ nifle'otecha ר"ת אלהים, אהיה אדני

אָשִׂיחָה asicha ר"ת הפסוק = פ"ז (בסוד) כתם טהור פז):

וֶעֱזוּז ve'ezuz נוֹרְאוֹתֶיךָ no'rotecha יֹאמֵרוּ yomeru וּגְדוּלָּתְךָ ugdulatcha

(כתיב : וגדלותיך) ר"ת = ע"ב, ריבוע יהוה אֲסַפְּרֶנָּה asaperena ס"ת = ייא"י (מילוי דס"ג):

זֵכֶר zecher רַב־ rav טוּבְךָ tuvcha לאו יַבִּיעוּ yabi'u

וְצִדְקָתְךָ vetzidkatcha יְרַנֵּנוּ yeranenu ס"ת = ב"ן, יבמ, לכב ; ר"ת הפסוק = רי"ו יהוה:

חַנּוּן chanun וְרַחוּם verachum יְהֹוָהאדניאהדונהי Adonai (Binah)

חנון ורחום יהוה = עשל אֶרֶךְ erech ס"ת = ס"ג ב"ן אַפַּיִם apayim ר"ת = יהוה

וּגְדָל־ ugdal (כתיב : וגדול) וָחֶסֶד chased ע"ב, ריבוע יהוה:

טוֹב־ tov והו יְהֹוָהאדניאהדונהי Adonai (Chesed) לַכֹּל lakol

יה אדני ; ס"ת ל"ו (מילוי דס"ג) וְרַחֲמָיו verachamav עַל־ al

כָּל kol ילי ; עמם ; ר"ת ריבוע ב"ן ע"ה מַעֲשָׂיו ma'asav ס"ת ע"ב, ריבוע יהוה:

ד *One generation and the next shall praise Your deeds and tell of Your might.*
ה *The brilliance of Your splendid glory and the wonders of Your acts, I shall speak of.*
ו *They shall speak of the might of Your awesome acts and I shall tell of Your greatness.*
ז *They shall express the remembrance of Your abundant goodness, and Your righteousness they shall joyfully proclaim.* ח *The Lord is merciful and compassionate, slow to anger and great in kindness.*
ט *The Lord is good to all, His compassion extends over all His acts.*

יוֹדוּךָ yoducha יְהֹוָה יאהדונהי Adonai (*Gevurah*) כָּל־ kol ילי מַעֲשֶׂיךָ ma'asecha

וַחֲסִידֶיךָ vachasidecha ר"ת אלהים, אהיה אדני יְבָרְכוּכָה yevarchucha ס"ת = מ"ה:

כְּבוֹד kevod מַלְכוּתְךָ malchutcha יֹאמֵרוּ yomeru וּגְבוּרָתְךָ ugvuratcha

יְדַבֵּרוּ yedaberu ר"ת הפסוק = אלהים, אהיה אדני ; ס"ת = ב"ן, יבמ, לכב:

לְהוֹדִיעַ lehodi'a לִבְנֵי livnei הָאָדָם ha'adam ר"ת ללה, אדני

גְּבוּרֹתָיו gevurotav וּכְבוֹד uchvod הֲדַר hadar

מַלְכוּתוֹ malchuto ר"ת מ"ה וס"ת = רי"ו ; ר"ת הפסוק ע"ה = ק"כ צירופי אלהים:

מַלְכוּתְךָ malchutcha מַלְכוּת malchut כָּל־ kol ילי עֹלָמִים olamim

וּמֶמְשַׁלְתְּךָ umemshaltecha בְּכָל־ bechol ב"ן, לכב דּוֹר dor וָדֹר vador רי"ו:

סוֹמֵךְ somech ריבוע אדני יְהֹוָה יאהדונהי Adonai (*Tiferet*)

לְכָל־ lechol יה אדני ; סומך אדני לכל ר"ת סאל, אמן (יאהדונהי) הַנֹּפְלִים hanoflim

וְזוֹקֵף vezokef לְכָל־ lechol יה אדני הַכְּפוּפִים hakefufim נמם:

עֵינֵי־ enei ריבוע דמ"ה כֹל chol ילי אֵלֶיךָ elecha יְשַׂבֵּרוּ yesaberu וְאַתָּה veAta

נוֹתֵן־ noten אבגיתץ, ושר לָהֶם lahem אֶת־ et אָכְלָם ochlam בְּעִתּוֹ be'ito:

י *All that You have made shall thank You, Lord, and Your pious ones shall bless You.*

כ *They shall speak of the glory of Your Kingdom and talk of Your mighty deeds.*

ל *His mighty deeds He makes known to man and the glory of His splendid Kingdom.*

מ *Yours is the Kingdom of all worlds and Your reign extends to each and every generation.*

ס *The Lord supports all those who fell and holds upright all those who are bent over.*

ע *The eyes of all look hopefully towards You, and You give them their food at its proper time.*

POTE'ACH ET YADECHA

We connect to the letters *Pei, Alef,* and *Yud* by opening our hands and holding our palms skyward. Our consciousness is focused on receiving sustenance and financial prosperity from the Light through our actions of tithing and sharing, our *Desire to Receive for the Sake of Sharing*. In doing so, we also acknowledge that the sustenance we receive comes from a higher source and is not of our own doing. According to the sages, if we do not meditate on this idea at this juncture, we must repeat the prayer.

פתוז (שע"ז נהורין למ"ה ולס"ה)

פותוז את ידך ר"ת פאי	יוד הי ויו הי יוד הי ויו הי (וז' וזיוורתי)
גימ' יאהדונהי זו"ן	אלף למד אלף למד (ש"ע)
וזכמה דז"א ו"ק	יוד הא ואו הא (לז"א)
יסוד דנוק'	אדני (ולנוקבא)

פּוֹתֵחַ pote'ach אֶת et יָדֶךָ yadecha ר"ת פאי וס"ת וזתך עם ג' אותיות = דִיקַרְנוֹסָא

ובאתב"ש הוא סאל, פאי, אמן, יאהדונהי ; ועוד יכוין שם וזתך בשילוב יהוה – יְוֹזְהַתְוֹכָה

אלף למד הי יוד מם אלף למד הי יוד מם מווזין דפנים דאוזור אלהים אלהים

להמשיך פ"ו אורות לכל מילוי דכל

ואוזור דפרצופי נה"י וזג"ת	וזתך	אוזור דפרצופי נה"י וזג"ת
דיצירה דרוזל הנקראת לאה		דפרצוף וזג"ת דיצירה דז"א
לף מד י וד ם		לף מד י וד ם
אלף למד הי יוד מם	סאל יאהדונהי	אלף למד הי יוד מם

וּמַשְׂבִּיעַ umasbi'a וזתך עם ג' אותיות = דִיקַרְנוֹסָא

ובא"ת ב"ש הוא סאל, אמן, יאהדונהי ; ועוד יכוין שם וזתך בשילוב יהוה – יְוֹזְהַתְוֹכָה

אלף למד הי יוד מם אלף למד הי יוד מם מווזין דפנים דאוזור אלהים אלהים

להמשיך פ"ו אורות לכל מילוי דכל

ואוזור דפרצופי נה"י וזג"ת	וזתך	אוזור דפרצופי נה"י וזג"ת
דיצירה דרוזל הנקראת לאה		דפרצוף נה"י דיצירה דז"א
לף מד י וד ם		לף מד י וד ם
אלף למד הי יוד מם		אלף למד הי יוד מם

לְכָל־ lechol יה אדני (להמשיך מווזין ד–יה אל הנוקבא שהיא אדני)

וזַי chai כל וזי = אהיה אהיה יהוה, בינה ע"ה, וזיים

רָצוֹן ratzon מהש ע"ה, ע"ב בריבוע וקס"א ע"ה, אל שדי ע"ה ; ר"ת רוזל שהיא המלכות הצריכה לשפע

יוד יוד הי יוד הי ויו יוד הי ויו הי יסוד דאבא

אלף הי יוד הי יסוד דאימא

להמתיק רוזל וב' דמעין שך פר

We should also meditate to draw abundance and sustenance and blessing to all the worlds from the *ratzon* mentioned above. We should meditate and focus on this verse because it is the essence of prosperity, and meditate that God is intervening and sustaining and supporting all of Creation.

POTE'ACH ET YADECHA

פ *Open Your Hands and satisfy every living thing with desire.*

צַדִּיק tzadik יֹוהֹוָוהאדֹנָיאהדונהי Adonai (*Yesod*) בְּכָל bechol ב״ן, לכב
דְּרָכָיו derachav וְחָסִיד vechasid בְּכָל bechol ב״ן, לכב מַעֲשָׂיו ma'asav יבמ, ב״ן:

קָרוֹב karov יְהֹוָהאדֹנָיאהדונהי Adonai (*Malchut*) לְכָל־ lechol יה אדני
קֹרְאָיו kor'av לְכֹל lechol יה אדני אֲשֶׁר asher
יִקְרָאֻהוּ yikra'uhu בֶאֱמֶת ve'emet אהיה פעמים אהיה, ז״פ ס״ג:

רְצוֹן retzon מהש ע״ה, ע״ב בריבוע וקס״א ע״ה, אל שדי ע״ה יְרֵאָיו yere'av יַעֲשֶׂה ya'ase
ר״ת רי״ וְאֶת־ ve'et שַׁוְעָתָם shav'atam יִשְׁמַע yishma וְיוֹשִׁיעֵם veyoshi'em:

שׁוֹמֵר shomer כ״א הויות שבתפילין יְהֹוָהאדֹנָיאהדונהי Adonai (*Netzach*)
אֶת־ et כָּל־ kol ילי אֹהֲבָיו ohavav ר״ת אכא
וְאֵת ve'et כָּל־ kol ילי הָרְשָׁעִים haresha'im יַשְׁמִיד yashmid:

תְּהִלַּת tehilat יְהֹוָהאדֹנָיאהדונהי Adonai (*Hod*) יְדַבֶּר yedaber ראה
פִּי pi וִיבָרֵךְ vivarech ע״ב ס״ג מ״ה ב״ן, הברכה (למתק את ז׳ המלכים שמתו)
כָּל kol ילי בָּשָׂר basar שֵׁם shem קָדְשׁוֹ kodsho
לְעוֹלָם le'olam ריבוע ס״ג וי׳ אותיות דס״ג וָעֶד va'ed:

וַאֲנַחְנוּ va'anachnu נְבָרֵךְ nevarech יָהּ Yah מֵעַתָּה me'ata
וְעַד־ ve'ad עוֹלָם olam הַלְלוּיָהּ haleluya אלהים, אהיה אדני ; ללה:

צ *The Lord is righteous in all His ways and virtuous in all His deeds.*
ק *The Lord is close to all who call Him, and only to those who call Him truthfully.*
ר *He shall fulfill the will of those who fear Him; He hears their wailing and saves them.*
ש *The Lord protects all who love Him and He destroys the wicked.*
ת *My lips utter the praise of the Lord and all flesh shall bless His Holy Name, forever and for eternity."*
(Psalms 145) "And we shall bless the Lord forever and for eternity. Praise the Lord!" (Psalms 115:18)

UVA LETZIYON

This prayer is our connection to redemption. The prayer starts, "And a redeemer should come to *Zion*." The redeemer is a reference to the *Mashiach*. Kabbalistically, the *Mashiach* is not a righteous person who will come and save us and bring about *world peace*. *Mashiach* is a state of spirituality and consciousness that every individual can achieve. No one is coming to save us and do the work for us. We must each achieve our own level of spiritual growth and fulfillment, our personal *Mashiach*, and when a critical mass of people have reached this state, the global *Mashiach* will appear for humanity.

וּבָא uva לְצִיּוֹן leTziyon יוסף, ו׳ הויות, קנאה גּוֹאֵל go'el וּלְשָׁבֵי ulshavei פֶשַׁע fesha

בְּיַעֲקֹב beYaakov ו׳ הויות, יאהדונהי אידהנויה נְאֻם ne'um יְהֹוָהאדניאהדונהי Adonai:

וַאֲנִי va'ani אני ; ר״ת גוף בניו (שירדו לחיצונים בעון הוצאת ז״ל, ויחזרו לגוף אוצר הנשמות, ויבוא גואל)

זֹאת zot בְּרִיתִי beriti אוֹתָם otam אָמַר amar יְהֹוָהאדניאהדונהי Adonai

רוּחִי ruchi אֲשֶׁר asher עָלֶיךָ alecha וּדְבָרַי udvarai אֲשֶׁר־ asher

שַׂמְתִּי samti בְּפִיךָ beficha לֹא־ lo יָמוּשׁוּ yamushu מִפִּיךָ mipicha

וּמִפִּי umipi זַרְעֲךָ zar'acha וּמִפִּי umipi זֶרַע zera זַרְעֲךָ zar'acha

אָמַר amar יְהֹוָהאדניאהדונהי Adonai מֵעַתָּה me'ata וְעַד־ ve'ad עוֹלָם olam:

וְאַתָּה veAta קָדוֹשׁ kadosh יוֹשֵׁב yoshev תְּהִלּוֹת tehilot יִשְׂרָאֵל Yisrael:

וְקָרָא vekara זֶה ze אֶל־ el זֶה ze י״ב פרקין דיעקב מאירין ל״ב פרקין דרוח״ל וְאָמַר ve'amar:

On *Shabbat* Meditate on the letters *Tav* ת and *Tzadik* צ from: אבג״יתץ, which helps spiritual remembering.

קָדוֹשׁ kadosh | (*Chesed*) קָדוֹשׁ kadosh (*Gevurah*) קָדוֹשׁ kadosh (*Tiferet*)

יְהֹוָהאדניאהדונהי Adonai צְבָאוֹת Tzeva'ot פני שכינה מְלֹא melo

כָל־ chol ילי הָאָרֶץ ha'aretz אלהים דההין ע״ה כְּבוֹדוֹ kevodo:

וּמְקַבְּלִין umkabelin דֵּין den מִן min דֵּין den וְאָמְרִין ve'amrin.

קַדִּישׁ kadish ב״פ אור, ב״פ רז, ב״פ א״ס בִּשְׁמֵי bishmei מְרוֹמָא meroma

עִלָּאָה ila'a בֵּית bet ב״פ ראה שְׁכִינְתֵּהּ shechinte.

UVA LETZIYON

"A redeemer shall come to Zion and to those who shall turn away from sin from amongst [the House of] Jacob, so says the Lord. And as for Me, this is My Covenant with them, says the Lord. My spirit, which is upon you, and My words, that I have put in your mouth, shall not depart from your mouths, the mouths of your children, or the mouths of your children's children, says the Lord, from now and forever." (Isaiah 59:20-21) *"And You are holy and await the praises of Israel. And one called to the other and said: Holy, Holy, Holy is the Lord of Hosts, the whole earth is filled with His glory."* (Isaiah 6:3) *And they receive consent from one another and say: Holy in the Highest Heavens is the abode of His Shechinah.*

קַדִּישׁ kadish ב״פ אור, ב״פ רז, ב״פ א״ס עַל־ al אַרְעָא ara עוֹבַד ovad

גְּבוּרְתֵּהּ gevurte • קַדִּישׁ kadish ב״פ אור, ב״פ רז, ב״פ א״ס לְעָלַם le'alam

וּלְעָלְמֵי ule'almei עָלְמַיָּא almaya : יְהֹוָאֲדֹנָיאהדונהי Adonai צְבָאוֹת Tzeva'ot

פני שכינה מַלְיָא malya כָל chol ילי אַרְעָא ar'a זִיו ziv יְקָרֵהּ yekare :

וַתִּשָּׂאֵנִי vatisa'eni רוּחַ ru'ach וָאֶשְׁמַע va'eshma אַחֲרַי acharai קוֹל kol

רַעַשׁ ra'ash גָּדוֹל gadol להח ; עם ד׳ אותיות = מבה, יזל, אום בָּרוּךְ baruch

כְּבוֹד kevod יְהֹוָאֲדֹנָיאהדונהי Adonai כבוד יהוה = יוד הי ואו הה מִמְּקוֹמוֹ mimekomo

עסמ״ב, הברכה (למתק את ז׳ המלכים שמתו) ; ר״ת = ע״ב, ריבוע יהוה ; ר״ת מיכ, י״פ האא :

וּנְטָלַתְנִי untalatni רוּחָא rucha • וּשְׁמָעִית ushma'it בַּתְרַי batrai קַל kal

נמם (ה׳ גבורות) זִיעַ zi'a שַׂגִּיא sagi דִּמְשַׁבְּחִין dim'shabechin וְאָמְרִין ve'amrin

בְּרִיךְ berich יְקָרָא yekara דַּיהֹוָאֲדֹנָיאהדונהי dadonai מֵאֲתַר me'atar

בֵּית bet ב״פ ראה שְׁכִינְתֵּהּ shechinte • יְהֹוָאֲדֹנָיאהדונהי Adonai | יִמְלֹךְ yimloch

לְעֹלָם le'olam ריבוע ס״ג ו׳ אותיות דס״ג ; ר״ת ייל וָעֶד va'ed : יְהֹוָאֲדֹנָיאהדונהי Adonai

מַלְכוּתֵהּ malchute קָאֵם ka'im לְעָלַם le'alam וּלְעָלְמֵי ule'almei

עָלְמַיָּא almaya : יְהֹוָאֲדֹנָיאהדונהי Adonai אֱלֹהֵי Elohei מילוי ע״ב, דמב ; ילה

אַבְרָהָם Avraham וו״פ אל, רי״ו ול״ב נתיבות החכמה, רמ״ח (אברים), עסמ״ב וט״ז אותיות פשוטות

יִצְחָק Yitzchak ד״פ ב״ן וְיִשְׂרָאֵל veYisrael אֲבֹתֵינוּ avotenu

שָׁמְרָה־ shomrah זֹּאת zot לְעוֹלָם le'olam ריבוע ס״ג ו׳ אותיות דס״ג

לְיֵצֶר leyetzer מַחְשְׁבוֹת mach'shevot לְבַב levav בוכו

עַמֶּךָ amecha וְהָכֵן vehachen לְבָבָם levavam אֵלֶיךָ elecha :

Holy, upon the Earth, is the work of His valor. Holy, forever and for all eternity, is the Lord of Hosts, the entire Earth is filled with the splendor of His glory. "And a wind carried me and from behind me I heard a great thunderous voice giving praise: Blessed is the glory of the Lord from His abode." (Ezikiel 3:12) And saying: Blessed is the glory of the Lord from the place of residence of His Shechinah. "The Lord shall reign forever and ever" (Exodus 15:18) The Lord, His Kingdom is established forever and for eternity. "The Lord, God of Abraham, Isaac, and Israel - our forefathers - safeguard this forever for the sake of the thoughts in the hearts of Your Nation, and direct their hearts toward You!" (I Chronicles 29:18)

וְהוּא vehu רַחוּם rachum יְכַפֵּר yechaper ר״ת רי״ו עָוֺן avon (*Abba* of the *klipa*)

וְלֹא velo יַשְׁחִית yashchit (*Ima* of the *klipa*) וְהִרְבָּה vehirba לְהָשִׁיב lehashiv

אַפּוֹ apo (*Zeir* of the *klipa*) וְלֹא־ velo יָעִיר ya'ir כָּל־ kol ילי וַחֲמָתוֹ chamato

(*Nukva* of the *klipa*): כִּי־ ki אַתָּה Ata אֲדֹנָי Adonai ללה טוֹב tov והו

וְסַלָּח vesalach יהוה ע״ב וְרַב־ verav (*Yitzchak*) חֶסֶד chesed (*Avraham*) ע״ב, ריבוע יהוה

לְכָל־ lechol יה אדני קֹרְאֶיךָ kor'echa (*Yaakov*): צִדְקָתְךָ tzidkat'cha צֶדֶק tzedek

לְעוֹלָם le'olam ריבוע ס״ג וי׳ אותיות דס״ג וְתוֹרָתְךָ vetorat'cha אֱמֶת emet

אהיה פעמים אהיה, ז״פ ס״ג: תִּתֵּן titen ב״פ כהת אֱמֶת emet אהיה פעמים אהיה, ז״פ ס״ג

לְיַעֲקֹב leYaakov ד׳ הויות, יאהדונהי אידהנויה חֶסֶד chesed ע״ב, ריבוע יהוה

לְאַבְרָהָם leAvraham וח״פ אל, רי״ו ול״ב נתיבות החכמה, רמ״ח (אברים), עסמ״ב וט״ז אותיות פשוטות

אֲשֶׁר־ asher נִשְׁבַּעְתָּ nishbata לַאֲבֹתֵינוּ la'avotenu מִימֵי mimei קֶדֶם kedem:

בָּרוּךְ baruch אֲדֹנָי Adonai ללה יוֹם yom ע״ה נגד, מזבח, ון אל יהוה יוֹם yom

ע״ה נגד, מזבח, ון אל יהוה יַעֲמָס־ ya'amos ר״ת ייי לָנוּ lanu אלהים, אהיה אדני ; ר״ת ייל

הָאֵל haEl לאה ; אל (ייא״י מילוי דס״ג) ; ר״ת ילה יְשׁוּעָתֵנוּ yeshu'atenu סֶלָה sela:

יְהֹוָהאדניאהדונהי Adonai צְבָאוֹת Tzeva'ot פני שכינה עִמָּנוּ imanu

ריבוע ס״ג, קס״א ע״ה וד׳ אותיות מִשְׂגָּב־ misgav מהש, ע״ב בריבוע וקס״א, אל שדי, ד״פ אלהים ע״ה

לָנוּ lanu אלהים, אהיה אדני אֱלֹהֵי Elohei מילוי ע״ב, דמב ; ילה יַעֲקֹב Yaakov

ד׳ הויות, יאהדונהי אידהנויה סֶלָה sela: יְהֹוָהאדניאהדונהי Adonai צְבָאוֹת Tzeva'ot פני שכינה

אַשְׁרֵי ashrei אָדָם adam מ״ה ; יהוה צבאות אשרי אדם = תפארת בֹּטֵחַ bote'ach

בָּךְ bach אדם בוטח בך = אמן (יאהדונהי) ע״ה ; בוטח בך = מילוי ע״ב ע״ה:

"And He is merciful and forgives iniquities and shall not destroy, and He frequently thwarts His wrath and will never arouse all His anger." (Psalms 78:38) *"Because You, Lord, are good and forgiving and abound in kindness to all who call to You."* (Psalms 86:5) *"Your righteousness is an everlasting justice, and Your Torah is true."* (Psalms 119:142) *"You give truth to Jacob and kindness to Abraham, as You have vowed to our forefathers since the earliest days."* (Michah 7:20) *"Blessed is the Lord, Who heaps burdens upon us each and every day, the God of our salvation. Selah."* (Psalms 68:20) *"The Lord of Hosts is with us; the God of Jacob is our strength. Selah."* (Psalms 46:12) *"Lord of Hosts, joyful is the man who trusts in You."* (Psalms 84:13)

יְהֹוָה יאהדונהי Adonai הוֹשִׁיעָה hoshi'a יהוה וש"ע נהורין הַמֶּלֶךְ hamelech ר"ת יהה

יַעֲנֵנוּ ya'anenu בְיוֹם- veyom ע"ה נגד, מזבח, זן, אל יהוה קָרְאֵנוּ kor'enu

ר"ת יב"ק, אלהים יהוה, אהיה אדני יהוה וס"ת ב"ן ועם אות כ' דהמלך = ע"ב:

BARUCH ELOHENU

Reciting the next verse ("*baruch Elohenu*") with genuine happiness and a trusting heart will generate extra Light in our lives and our *tikkun* process will be much easier. Meditate to *devote your soul to sanctify the Holy Name* (*Kedushat HaShem*).

בָּרוּךְ baruch אֱלֹהֵינוּ Elohenu ילה שֶׁבְּרָאָנוּ shebera'anu לִכְבוֹדוֹ lichvodo

וְהִבְדִּילָנוּ vehivdilanu מִן min הַתּוֹעִים hato'im (connecting to the right information)

וְנָתַן venatan לָנוּ lanu אלהים, אהיה אדני תּוֹרַת torat אֱמֶת emet אהיה פעמים אהיה, ז"פ ס"ג

וְחַיֵּי vechayei עוֹלָם olam נָטַע nata בְּתוֹכֵנוּ betochenu. הוּא hu יִפְתַּח yiftach

לִבֵּנוּ libenu בְּתוֹרָתוֹ betorato. וְיָשִׂים veyasim בְּלִבֵּנוּ belibenu אַהֲבָתוֹ ahavato

וְיִרְאָתוֹ veyir'ato לַעֲשׂוֹת la'asot רְצוֹנוֹ retzono וּלְעָבְדוֹ ule'ovdo

בְּלֵבָב belevav בוכו שָׁלֵם shalem. לֹא lo נִיגַע niga לָרִיק larik

(Meditate here to be protected from night emission, so that the spiritual effort will not go to negativity [*Rik* and *Behala*]. Also meditate to have righteous children following the way of the Light)

וְלֹא velo נֵלֵד neled לַבֶּהָלָה labehala. יְהִי yehi רָצוֹן ratzon מהש ע"ה,

ע"ב בריבוע וקס"א ע"ה, אל שדי ע"ה מִלְּפָנֶיךָ milfanecha ס"ג מ"ה ב"ן יְהֹוָה יאהדונהי Adonai

אֱלֹהֵינוּ Elohenu ילה וֵאלֹהֵי velohei לכב ; מילוי ע"ב, דמב ; ילה אֲבוֹתֵינוּ avotenu

שֶׁנִּשְׁמוֹר shenishmor חֻקֶּיךָ chukecha וּמִצְוֹתֶיךָ umitzvotecha

בָּעוֹלָם ba'olam הַזֶּה haze והו. וְנִזְכֶּה venizke וְנִחְיֶה venichye וְנִירַשׁ venirash

טוֹבָה tova אכא וּבְרָכָה uvracha לְחַיֵּי lechayei הָעוֹלָם ha'olam הַבָּא haba:

"Lord, save us. The King shall answer us on the day when we call him." (Psalms 20:10)

BARUCH ELOHENU

Blessed is our God, Who created us for the sake of His glory, Who separated us from those who have been led astray, Who gave us the Torah of truth, and Who implanted within us eternal life. May He open our hearts with His Torah, and place within our hearts love for Him and fear of Him, to fulfill His will and to serve Him wholeheartedly. May we not toil in vain, and may we not give birth to panic. May it be Your will, Lord, our God and God of our forefathers, that we should keep Your statutes and Your commandments in this world, and may we merit, live, and attain goodness and blessing for the life in the World to Come.

לְמַעַן lema'an יְזַמֶּרְךָ yezamercha כָבוֹד chavod וְלֹא velo יִדֹּם yidom

יְהֹוָואדניאהדונהי Adonai ר"ת = אלהים, אהיה אדני אֱלֹהַי Elohai מילוי ע"ב, דמב ; ילה

לְעוֹלָם le'olam ריבוע ס"ג וי' אותיות דס"ג אוֹדֶךָּ odeka: יְהֹוָואדניאהדונהי Adonai

חָפֵץ chafetz לְמַעַן lema'an צִדְקוֹ tzidko יַגְדִּיל yagdil תּוֹרָה torah ר"ת צ"ת

וְיַאְדִּיר veya'adir ר"ת = אבגית"ץ, ושר: וְיִבְטְחוּ veyivtechu בְךָ vecha יוֹדְעֵי yod'ei

שְׁמֶךָ shemecha כִּי ki ר"ת יכש לֹא lo עָזַבְתָּ azavta דֹרְשֶׁיךָ dorshecha

יְהֹוָואדניאהדונהי Adonai ס"ת כהת, משיח בן דוד ע"ה: יְהֹוָואדניאהדונהי Adonai

אֲדֹנֵינוּ adonenu מָה־ ma מ"ה אַדִּיר adir הרי שִׁמְךָ shimcha בְּכָל־ bechol

הָאָרֶץ ha'aretz אלהים דההין ע"ה: בי"ן, לכב ; ומב חִזְקוּ chizku וְיַאֲמֵץ veya'ametz

לְבַבְכֶם levavchem כָּל kol ילי הַמְיַחֲלִים hameyachalim לַיהֹוָואדניאהדונהי ladonai:

On *Shabbat* we continue with Half Kaddish below.

On weekdays we continue with "*Tikon Tefilati*" on page 483.

HALF KADDISH

יִתְגַּדַּל yitgadal וְיִתְקַדַּשׁ veyitkadash שדי ומילוי שדי ; י"א אותיות כמנין ו"ה

שְׁמֵיהּ shemei (שם י"ה דע"ב) רַבָּא raba קנ"א ב"ן, יהוה אלהים יהוה אדני,

מילוי קס"א וס"ג, מ"ה ברבוע וע"ב ע"ה ; ר"ת = ו"פ אלהים ; ס"ת = ג"פ יב"ק: אָמֵן amen אידהנויה.

בְּעָלְמָא be'alma דִּי di בְרָא vera כִּרְעוּתֵיהּ kir'utei.

וְיַמְלִיךְ veyamlich מַלְכוּתֵיהּ mal'chutei. וְיַצְמַח veyatzmach

---

"So that glory should make melodies to You and not be silent, Lord, my God, I shall forever thank You." (Psalms 30:13) *"Lord desires righteousness: He makes the Torah great and powerful."* (Isaiah 42:21) *"And they shall place their trust in You, all those who know Your Name, for You have not abandoned those who seek You, Lord."* (Psalms 9:11) *"Lord, our Master, how mighty is Your Name throughout the world."* (Psalms 8:2) *Be strong and your hearts be courageous, all you, who place your hope in the Lord.*

HALF KADDISH

May His great Name be more exalted and sanctified. (Amen)
In the world that He created according to His will, and may His kingdom reign.
And may He cause His redemption to sprout and may He bring the Mashiach closer. (Amen)

פּוּרְקָנֵיהּ purkanei• וִיקָרֵב vikarev מְשִׁיחֵיהּ meshichei: אָמֵן amen אידהנויה•

בְּחַיֵּיכוֹן bechayechon וּבְיוֹמֵיכוֹן uvyomechon וּבְחַיֵּי uvchayei

דְּכָל dechol ילי בֵּית bet ב"פ ראה יִשְׂרָאֵל Yisrael בַּעֲגָלָא ba'agala

וּבִזְמַן uvizman קָרִיב kariv וְאִמְרוּ ve'imru אָמֵן amen: אָמֵן amen אידהנויה•

The congregation and the *chazan* say the following:

28 words (until *be'alma*) and 28 letters (until *almaya*)

יְהֵא yehe שְׁמֵיהּ shemei (שם י"ה דס"ג) רַבָּא raba קנ"א ב"ן,

יהוה אלהים יהוה אדני, מילוי קס"א וס"ג, מ"ה ברבוע וע"ב ע"ה מְבָרַךְ mevarach,

לְעָלַם le'alam לְעָלְמֵי le'almei עָלְמַיָּא almaya• יִתְבָּרַךְ yitbarach•

Seven words with six letters each (שם בן מ"ב) and also, seven times the letter Vav (שם בן מ"ב).

וְיִשְׁתַּבַּח veyishtabach י"פ ע"ב יהוה אל אבג יתץ•

וְיִתְפָּאַר veyitpa'ar הי נו יה קרע שטן• וְיִתְרוֹמַם veyitromam וה כוזו נגד יכש•

וְיִתְנַשֵּׂא veyitnase במוכסז בטר צתג• וְיִתְהַדָּר veyit'hadar כוזו יה וקב טנע•

וְיִתְעַלֶּה veyit'ale וה יוד ה יגל פזק• וְיִתְהַלָּל veyit'halal א ואו הא שקו צית•

שְׁמֵיהּ shemei (שם י"ה דמ"ה) דְּקוּדְשָׁא dekudsha בְּרִיךְ verich הוּא hu:

אָמֵן amen אידהנויה•

לְעֵלָּא le'ela מִן min כָּל kol ילי בִּרְכָתָא birchata• שִׁירָתָא shirata•

תֻּשְׁבְּחָתָא tishbechata וְנֶחֱמָתָא venechamata• דַּאֲמִירָן da'amiran

בְּעָלְמָא be'alma וְאִמְרוּ ve'imru אָמֵן amen: אָמֵן amen אידהנויה.

In your lifetimes and in your days and in the lifetime of all the House of Israel, speedily and in the near future, and you shall say, Amen. (Amen) May His great Name be blessed forever and for all eternity. Blessed and lauded, and glorified, and exalted, and extolled, and honored, and uplifted, and praised be the Name of the Holy Blessed One (Amen) Above all blessings, songs, praises, and words of consolation that may be said in the world, and you shall say, Amen. (Amen)

VA'ANI TEFILATI

Va'ani Tefilati helps to remove all the judgment that will confront us in the coming week. While we recite *Va'ani Tefilati*, our intent and objective should be to convert all judgments headed our way into acts of mercy.

This verse should be said while standing even if there is no *Torah* scroll presents.

The *chazan* should put on a *Talit* before starting *Va'ani Tefilati* because this time is called "*Et Ratzon*" (time of satisfaction and acceptance) as the Light of *Mitzcha Dera'ava* (the Forehead of the desire) is revealed. Meditate on the letter י from שקוצית as *Zeir Anpin* is being elevated to the 500 *nimin* (cords) of *Dikna* of *Arich Anpin* (during the rest of the week - *Zeir Anpin* receives this illumination from a long distance), and He encloses these 500 *nimin* (represented by the Name: יוד הי ויו הי).

Adonai יהואדני אהדונהי יְהֹוָה lecha לְךָ tefilati תְפִלָּתִי־ אני va'ani וַאֲנִי

יוד הי ויו הי

Meditate to draw to *Zeir Anpin* the illumination of the 500 *nimin* of *Arich Anpin*.

עֵת et י"פ יהוה וי"פ אהיה רָצוֹן ratzon מהש ע"ה, ע"ב בריבוע וקס"א ע"ה, אל שדי ע"ה

Meditate to draw illumination from *Chesed* of *Atik Yomin* to the *Yesod* of *Atik Yomin* (which is enclosed by the Forehead of *Arich Anpin*), and to lower all the above mentioned illuminations to *Tiferet* of *Dikna* of *Arich Anpin*, which is the eighth *Mazal* ("*notzer chesed*" - *notzer* has the same letters as *ratzon*-desire), as this is where *Zeir Anpin* is going up in *Minchah* of *Shabbat*. Now, meditate to draw all the above mentioned illuminations to the Three Upper *Sefirot* of *Zeir Anpin* (which are in the place of *Keter, Chochmah, Binah, Da'at* of Supernal *Abba* and *Ima*). So first meditate to split and reveal the Three Upper *Sefirot* of Supernal *Abba* and *Ima* and only then to split the essence of the Three Upper *Sefirot* of *Zeir Anpin*, and by doing so, *Netzach, Hod, Yesod* of *Abba* and *Ima* (which are inside *Chochmah, Binah, Da'at* of *Zeir Anpin*, and where *Chochmah, Binah, Da'at* of *Beriah* were elevated) are split. **Then the *Mochin*** that used to be covered by *Netzach, Hod, Yesod* of Supernal *Abba* and *Ima* and inside the Forhead of *Zeir Anpin*, **are revealed** and They are illuminated in *Chochmah, Binah, Da'at* of the essence of *Zeir Anpin*. All the above processes sweeten the judgment that is revealed in the Forehead of *Zeir Anpin* and make it like *Mitzcha Dera'ava* - the Forehead of *Atik Yomin*.

***Five Gevurot* (Judgments)**

אהיה יהוה אהיה יהוה
אהיה יהוה
אהיה יהוה אהיה יהוה

***Five Chasadim* (Mercies)**

אהיה יהוה אהיה יהוה
אהיה יהוה
אהיה יהוה אהיה יהוה

chasdecha וַחְסְדֶּךָ berov בְּרָב־ ילה ; אהיה אדני Elohim אֱלֹהִים

:yishecha יִשְׁעֶךָ אהיה פעמים אהיה, ז"פ ס"ג be'emet בֶּאֱמֶת aneni עֲנֵנִי

VA'ANI TEFILATI

"As for me, may my prayer to You, Lord, be a time of desire.
God, with the abundance of Your kindness, answer me with the truth of Your salvation." (Psalms 69:14)

Second time:

וַאֲנִי va'ani אני תְפִלָּתִי־ tefilati

To connect *Malchut* to *Zeir Anpin*

לְךָ lecha יְהֹוָהאדנייאהדונהי Adonai

Even though *Malchut* is not ascending to *Dikna* of *Arich Anpin*, you should meditate to draw the above mentioned illumination (*Mitzcha Dera'ava*) to *Malchut*. So now, meditate to draw illumination from *Chesed* of *Atik Yomin* to the *Yesod* of *Atik Yomi*n and then to the Forehead of *Arich Anpin* and together with the illumination of the eighth *Mazal* to *Chochmah* and *Binah* of *Yaakov* and *Rachel*. Doing so causes Their *Mochin* (the following Names below, equal to the word "*et*" - 470) and the soul of *Nukva* (the four letters of the Name: יְהֹוָה as follow) to be revealed (all together – the *Mochin* [470] and the soul [4] – equal *Da'at* – 474). And these *Mochin* are illuminating in the Forehead of *Yaakov* and *Rachel* and are sweetening the judgment in Their Forehead by the illumination of the Forehead of *Atik Yomin* (*Mitzcha Dera'ava*).

עֵת et י"פ יהוה וי"פ אהיה רָצוֹן ratzon מהש ע"ה, ע"ב בריבוע וקס"א ע"ה, אל שדי ע"ה

יְהֹוָה

י יה יהו יהוה

י יה יהו יהוה

יוד יוד הא יוד הא ואו יוד הא ואו הא

יוד יוד הה יוד הה וו יוד הה וו הה

יוד הה וו הה

אֱלֹהִים Elohim אהיה אדני ; ילה בְּרָב־ berov חַסְדֶּךָ chasdecha

עֲנֵנִי aneni בֶּאֱמֶת be'emet אהיה פעמים אהיה, ז"פ ס"ג יִשְׁעֶךָ yishecha:

Meditate that now, during *Minchah* of *Shabbat* (after the repetition of *Musaf*), *Zeir* and *Nukva* are ascending to *Keter* of Supernal *Abba* and *Ima*. And *Beriah* ascended and enclosed the space of the essence of *Zeir Anpin*, to draw great Light to *Beriah* so we can receive the illumination of the *Torah*.

VA'ANI TEFILATI

"As for me, may my prayer to You, Lord, be a time of desire. God, with the abundance of Your kindness, answer me with the truth of Your salvation." (Psalms 69:14)

OPENING OF THE ARK

Drawing the Light of *Chochmah.*

Rabbi Shimon Bar Yochai says: "While the Ark is open, we should prepare ourselves with awe. Everyone should arouse an inner sense of wonder, as if we are actually standing on Mount Sinai, trembling as we behold the overwhelming expression of Light. Silent we stand, focused solely on the opportunity of hearing each sacred word of the scroll. When we take out the Torah in public to read, all the Gates of Mercy in Heaven are open, and we awaken a love from Above."

וַיְהִי vay'hi בִּנְסֹעַ binso'a הָאָרֹן ha'aron וַיֹּאמֶר vayomer מֹשֶׁה Moshe

מהש, ע״ב בריבוע וקס״א, אל שדי, ד״פ אלהים ע״ה קוּמָה kuma קנ״א (מקוה) |

יְהֹוָאדהנויאהדונהי Adonai וְיָפֻצוּ veyafutzu אֹיְבֶיךָ oyvecha וְיָנֻסוּ veyanusu

מְשַׂנְאֶיךָ mesan'echa מִפָּנֶיךָ mipanecha ס״ג מ״ה ב״ן: כִּי ki

מִצִּיּוֹן miTziyon יוסף, ו׳ הויות, קנאה תֵּצֵא tetze תוֹרָה torah וּדְבַר udvar ראה

יְהֹוָאדהנויאהדונהי Adonai מִירוּשָׁלָם mirushalaim: בָּרוּךְ baruch שֶׁנָּתַן shenatan

תּוֹרָה torah לְעַמּוֹ le'amo יִשְׂרָאֵל Yisrael בִּקְדֻשָּׁתוֹ bikdushato•

BERICH SHEMEI

This section is taken directly from the *Zohar* and appears in its original Aramaic. The *Berich Shemei* works like a time machine that literally transports our soul to Mount Sinai, when Moses received the tablets. By revisiting the exact time and place of the revelation, we are able to draw down aspects of the original Light through the reading of the Torah. The *Berich Shemei* contains 130 words. Adam was separated from his wife, Eve, for 130 years during which time he sinned. Each word in the prayer helps to correct one of those years. Each of us was included in the soul of Adam. We are Adam. Adam is merely the code name of the unified soul that includes every human being who has and will ever walk this planet.

בְּרִיךְ berich שְׁמֵיהּ shemei דְּמָארֵי demarei עָלְמָא alma בְּרִיךְ berich

כִּתְרָךְ kitrach וְאַתְרָךְ ve'atrach• יְהֵא yehe רְעוּתָךְ re'utach עִם im

עַמָּךְ amach יִשְׂרָאֵל Yisrael לְעָלַם le'alam• וּפוּרְקַן ufurkan יְמִינָךְ yeminach

אַחְזֵי achzei לְעַמָּךְ le'amach בְּבֵית bevet ב״פ ראה מִקְדְּשָׁךְ mikdashach•

OPENING OF THE ARK

"When the Ark traveled forward, Moses would say: Arise, Lord. Let Your enemies be scattered and let those who hate You flee before You." (Numbers 10:35) *"Because out of Zion shall the Torah emerge, and the Word of the Lord from Jerusalem."* (Isaiah 2:3) *Blessed is He Who gave the Torah to His Nation, Israel, due to His Holiness.*

BERICH SHEMEI

Blessed is the Name

of the Master of the world. Blessed are Your Crown and Your Location. May Your desire be with Your Nation, Israel, forever. The redemption of Your Right may You show to Your Nation in Your Temple.

לְאַמְטוּיֵי le'amtuye לָנָא lana מִטּוּב mituv נְהוֹרָךְ •nehorach וּלְקַבֵּל ulkabel

צְלוֹתָנָא tzelotana בְּרַחֲמִין •berachamin יְהֵא yehe רַעֲוָא ra'ava

קֳדָמָךְ kodamach דְּתוֹרִיךְ detorich לָן lan וְחַיִּין chayin בְּטִיבוּ •betivu

וְלֶהֱוֵי velehevei אֲנָא ana ב"ן עַבְדָּךְ avdach פוי, אל אדני פְּקִידָא pekida

בְּגוֹ bego צַדִּיקַיָּא •tzadikaya לְמִרְחַם lemircham אברהם, ו"פ אל, רי"ו ול"ב נתיבות

החכמה, רמ"ח (אברים), עסמ"ב וט"ז אותיות פשוטות עָלַי alai וּלְמִנְטַר ulmintar יָתִי yati

וְיַת veyat כָּל kal ילי דִּלִי dili וְדִי vedi לְעַמָּךְ le'amach יִשְׂרָאֵל •Yisrael

אַנְתְּ ant הוּא hu זָן zan נגד, מזבח, אל יהוה לְכֹלָּא lechola וּמְפַרְנֵס umfarnes

לְכֹלָּא •lechola אַנְתְּ ant הוּא hu שַׁלִּיט shalit עַל al כֹּלָּא •kola אַנְתְּ ant

הוּא hu דְּשַׁלִּיט deshalit עַל al מַלְכַיָּא malchaya וּמַלְכוּתָא umalchuta

דִּילָךְ dilach הִיא •hee אֲנָא ana ב"ן עַבְדָּא avda דְקוּדְשָׁא dekudsha

בְּרִיךְ berich הוּא hu דְּסָגִידְנָא desagidna קַמֵּהּ kame וּמִן umin קַמֵּהּ kame

דִּיקַר dikar אוֹרַיְתֵהּ orayte בְּכָל bechol ב"ן, לכב עִידָּן idan וְעִידָּן •ve'idan

לָא la עַל al אֱנָשׁ enash רְחִיצְנָא •rachitzna וְלָא vela עַל al

בַּר bar אֱלָהִין elahin ילה סָמִיכְנָא •samichna אֶלָּא ela בֶּאֱלָהָא be'elaha

דִשְׁמַיָּא •dishmaya דְּהוּא dehu אֱלָהָא elaha קְשׁוֹט •keshot

וְאוֹרַיְתֵהּ ve'orayte קְשׁוֹט keshot וּנְבִיאוֹהִי unvi'ohi קְשׁוֹט •keshot

וּמַסְגֵּא umasgei לְמֶעְבַּד lemebad טַבְוָן tavevan וּקְשׁוֹט •ukshot

בֵּיהּ bei אֲנָא ana ב"ן רָחִיץ rachitz וְלִשְׁמֵהּ velishme יַקִּירָא yakira

קַדִּישָׁא kadisha אֲנָא ana ב"ן אֵמַר emar תֻּשְׁבְּחָן •tushbechan

---

May You fill us with the best of Your enlightenment, and may You receive our prayers with mercy. May it be pleasing before You to lengthen our lives with good. And I, Your servant, shall be remembered together with the righteous ones. Have mercy on me and protect me, and all that I have, and all that belongs to Your Nation, Israel. You are the One Who nourishes all and provides all with their livelihood. You are the One Who controls everything. You have control over kings, and their kingdoms are Yours. I am the servant of the Holy Blessed One, as I prostrate myself before Him and before the glory of His Torah, at each and every moment. I put not my trust in any man, and I have no faith in the sons of the gods. My trust and faith are only in the God in Heaven, Who is the true God; His Torah is true; His prophets are true; and He abundantly performs compassion and truth. In Him, I trust and I say praises to His Holy and precious Name.

יְהֵא yehe רַעֲוָא ra'ava קֳדָמָךְ kodamach דְּתִפְתַּח detiftach לִבָּאִי liba'i
בְּאוֹרַיְתָךְ be'oraytach (וְתִיהַב vetihav לִי li בְּנִין benin דִּכְרִין dichrin
דְּעָבְדִין de'avdin רְעוּתָךְ re'utach) וְתַשְׁלִים vetashlim מִשְׁאֲלִין mish'alin
דְּלִבָּאִי deliba'i וְלִבָּא veliba דְּכָל dechol ילי עַמָּךְ amach יִשְׂרָאֵל Yisrael
לְטַב letav וּלְחַיִּין ulchayin וְלִשְׁלָם velishlam אָמֵן amen יאהדונהי:

TAKING OUT THE TORAH FROM THE ARK

The *Torah* is taken out to give us all a chance to make a personal connection with it, either by kissing or touching it. Sometimes, people rush to make their connection, pushing, crowding, and shoving others aside as they try to touch the scroll. Spiritually, these actions reflect energy opposite to that of the *Torah*. The *Torah* connection is not just physical. Connections to the *Torah* are made by way of a spiritual state of mind, which includes tolerance and care for others. One cannot be in the right spiritual frame of mind if he is rude to another individual.

Before the *Torah* is carried to the *bimah* (podium), the *chazan* says:

גַּדְּלוּ gadelu לַיהֹוָהאדניאהדונהי ladonai אִתִּי iti וּנְרוֹמְמָה uneromema
שְׁמוֹ shemo מהש ע"ה, ע"ב בריבוע וקס"א ע"ה, אל שדי ע"ה יַחְדָּו yachdav:

Then the congregation says the following while the *Torah* is carried to the *bimah*:

לְךָ lecha יְהֹוָהאדניאהדונהי Adonai הַגְּדֻלָּה hagedula וְהַגְּבוּרָה vehagevura רי"ו
וְהַתִּפְאֶרֶת vehatiferet וְהַנֵּצַח vehanetzach וְהַהוֹד vehahod ההה כִּי ki
כֹל chol ילי בַּשָּׁמַיִם bashamayim י"פ טל, י"פ כוזו וּבָאָרֶץ uva'aretz לְךָ lecha
יְהֹוָהאדניאהדונהי Adonai הַמַּמְלָכָה hamamlacha וְהַמִּתְנַשֵּׂא vehamitnase
לְכֹל lechol יה אדני לְרֹאשׁ lerosh ריבוע אלהים ואלהים דיודין ע"ה: רוֹמְמוּ romemu
יְהֹוָהאדניאהדונהי Adonai אֱלֹהֵינוּ Elohenu ילה וְהִשְׁתַּחֲווּ vehishtachavu
לַהֲדֹם lahadom רַגְלָיו raglav קָדוֹשׁ kadosh הוּא hu: רוֹמְמוּ romemu
יְהֹוָהאדניאהדונהי Adonai אֱלֹהֵינוּ Elohenu ילה וְהִשְׁתַּחֲווּ vehishtachavu לְהַר lehar
קָדְשׁוֹ kodsho כִּי ki קָדוֹשׁ kadosh יְהֹוָהאדניאהדונהי Adonai אֱלֹהֵינוּ Elohenu ילה:

May it be pleasing before You that You shall open my heart with Your Torah (and that You may give me male sons, who shall fulfill Your desire). And may You fulfill the requests of my heart and the heart of Your entire Nation, Israel, for good, for life, and for peace. Amen.

TAKING OUT THE TORAH FROM THE ARK

"Proclaim the Lord's greatness with me and let us exalt His Name together." (Psalms 34:4) "Yours, Lord, is the greatness, the strength, the splendor, the triumph, and the glory, and everything in the Heavens and the earth. Yours, Lord, is the Kingdom and the sovereignty over every leader." (I Chronicles 29:11) "Exalt the Lord, our God, and prostrate yourselves at His footstool, is holy. Exalt the Lord, our God, and prostrate yourselves at His holy mountain because the Lord, our God, is holy." (Psalms 99:9)

Some add this section:

אין en קדוש kadosh כיהוה יאהדונהי kadonai כי ki אין en בלתך biltecha

ואין ve'en צור tzur אלהים דההין ע"ה כאלהינו kelohenu ילה: כי ki מי mi ילי

אלוה Eloha מ"ב מבלעדי mibal'adei יהוה יאהדונהי Adonai ומי umi ילי צור tzur

אלהים דההין ע"ה זולתי zulati אלהינו Elohenu ילה: תורה torah צוה tziva לנו lanu

אלהים, אהיה אדני משה Moshe מהש, ע"ב בריבוע וקס"א, אל שדי, ד"פ אלהים ע"ה

מורשה morasha קהלת kehilat יעקב Yaakov ז' הויות, יאהדונהי אידהנויה: עץ etz

חיים chayim אהיה אהיה יהוה, בינה ע"ה היא hee למחזיקים lamachazikim ר"ת להח

בה ba ותמכיה vetomcheha מאשר me'ushar: דרכיה deracheha

דרכי darchei נעם no'am וכל vechol ילי נתיבותיה netivoteha שלום shalom:

שלום shalom רב rav לאהבי le'ohavei תורתך toratecha ואין ve'en למו lamo

מכשול michshol: יהוה יאהדונהי Adonai עז oz לעמו le'amo יתן yiten

יהוה יאהדונהי Adonai יברך yevarech עסמ"ב, הברכה (למתק את ז' המלכים שמתו)

את et עמו amo בשלום vashalom ר"ת ע"ב, ריבוע יהוה:

כי ki שם shem יהוה יאהדונהי Adonai אקרא ekra הבו havu אחד, אהבה, דאגה

גדל godel לאלהינו lelohenu ילה: הכל hakol ילי תנו tenu עז oz

לאלהים lelohim אהיה אדני ; ילה ותנו utnu כבוד chavod לתורה latorah:

RAISING THE TORAH

After the scroll is placed on the *bimah* (the podium), a person is called up to raise the Torah for the congregation to see the specific section we will be reading from the Torah Scroll. As we raise the Torah, we meditate to also raise our level of consciousness. We should look at the parchment to try to see the first letter of that week's reading. We should also attempt to find the first letter of our Hebrew name within the text. You can use the *Talit* to help yourself focus (if you don't have a *Talit* you can use your finger).

"There is none as holy as the Lord, because there is none other beside You. There is no Rock like our God." (I Samuel 2:2) "For Who is God beside the Lord? Who is a Rock, other than our God?" (Psalms 18:32) "The Torah that Moses commanded us with is a heritage for the congregation of Jacob." (Deuteronomy 33:4) "It is a tree of life to those who hold on to it, and those who support it are happy." (Proverb 3:18) "Its ways are the way of pleasantness and all its paths lead to peace." (Proverbs 3:17) "Abundance of peace for those who love Your Torah and for them there is no obstacle." (Psalms 119:165) "The Lord give might to his people, The Lord will bless his nation with peace." (Psalms 29:11) "When I call out the Name of the Lord, proclaim greatness to our God." (Dutoronomy 32:3) "All should attribute power to God and give honor to the Torah." (Psalms 68:35)

וְזֹאת vezot הַתּוֹרָה hatorah אֲשֶׁר־ asher שָׂם sam מֹשֶׁה Moshe
מהש, ע״ב בריבוע וקס״א, אל שדי, ד״פ אלהים ע״ה לִפְנֵי lifnei בְּנֵי benei יִשְׂרָאֵל Yisrael:
אֵל El ייא״י (מילוי דס״ג) שַׁדַּי Shadai אל שדי = מושה, מהש, ע״ב בריבוע וקס״א, ד״פ אלהים ע״ה
אֱמֶת emet אהיה פעמים אהיה, ז״פ ס״ג וּמֹשֶׁה uMoshe מהש, ע״ב בריבוע וקס״א, אל שדי,
ד״פ אלהים ע״ה אֱמֶת emet אהיה פעמים אהיה, ז״פ ס״ג וְתוֹרָתוֹ vetorato
אֱמֶת emet אהיה פעמים אהיה, ז״פ ס״ג: תּוֹרָה torah צִוָּה־ tziva
לָנוּ lanu אלהים, אהיה אדני מֹשֶׁה Moshe מהש, ע״ב בריבוע וקס״א, אל שדי, ד״פ אלהים ע״ה
מוֹרָשָׁה morasha קְהִלַּת kehilat יַעֲקֹב Yaakov ז׳ הויות, יאהדונהי אידהנויה:
הָאֵל haEl ייא״י (מילוי דס״ג) תָּמִים tamim דַּרְכּוֹ darko אִמְרַת imrat
יְהֹוָהאדניאהדונהי Adonai צְרוּפָה tzerufa מָגֵן magen ג״פ אל (ייא״י מילוי דס״ג)
ר״ת מיכאל גבריאל נוריאל הוּא hu לְכֹל lechol יה אדני הַחֹסִים hachosim בּוֹ bo:

THE READING

To maximize the power of the connection, we must think to share all the energy we're receiving with everyone else. We should become channels for sharing spiritual Light. If we think only about ourselves, it is like blowing a fuse. No current will flow, even though the plug is connected into the socket. When you are called up (the *ole*) to recite the blessing before the *Torah* reading, you must visually connect with the letters of the *Torah* to ignite the power of his words. A blessing is recited before and after each of the readings. The first blessing is equivalent to plugging a wire (our soul) into a wall socket (the *Torah*). The last blessing draws the spiritual current to us to bring the Light into our lives.

Meditation for the people that go to the *Torah* during *Minchah*

The above mentioned Three Upper *Sefirot* (*Chochmah, Binah, Da'at* of *Zeir Anpin*) are now revealing the illumination of Supernal *Abba* inside Them and this illumination (*Yesod* of *Abba*) is going out. The three people that go up to the *Torah* during *Minchah* are: The first corresponds to *Chochmah*, the second corresponds to *Binah* and the third corresponds to *Da'at* (and as the sixth *Aliya* of *Shabbat* morning *Torah* reading is more significant because it is the aspect of *Yesod*, you should try to get the third *Aliya* of *Minchah*, which corresponds to *Da'at*, and is also for the correction of the *Yesod*.)

We call three people to the *Torah* and we do not read less than ten verses. We read from the portion that is read the following *Shabbat* (even if the following *Shabbat* falls on a holiday, we read the next *Shabbat's* portion and not of the holiday).

RAISING THE TORAH

"And this is the Torah that Moses placed before the Children of Israel." (Deuteronomy 4:44)

God is true and Moses is true and His Torah is true. "The Torah, which Moses commanded us with, is a heritage for the Congregation of Jacob." (Deuteronomy 33:4) *"God! His ways are perfect. Lord's statement is pure. He is the Shield for all who take refuge in Him"* (II Samuel 22:31)

The *chazan* says:

בֵּית bet ב"פ ראה אַהֲרֹן Aharon בָּרְכוּ barchu יהוה ריבוע יהוה ריבוע מ"ה אֶת et
ה' Hashem הַמְּבֹרָךְ, hamevorach כֹּהֵן kohen מלה קְרַב kerav וְכַהֵן vechahen מלה.

The one who goes up to the *Torah* (*"the ole"*), holds the Scroll with both his hands, and says:

יְהֹוָאדהנויאהדונהי Adonai עִמָּכֶם imachem:

The congregation replies:

יְבָרֶכְךָ yevarchecha ה' Hashem:

The *ole* continues:

(ויכוין "ברכו את ה' המבורך" - מ"ב ור"ך שהם שמאל וימין):

רַבָּנָן rabanan: בָּרְכוּ barchu יהוה ריבוע יהוה ריבוע מ"ה אֶת et
יְהֹוָאדהנויאהדונהי Adonai הַמְּבֹרָךְ hamevorach ס"ת כהת, משיח בן דוד ע"ה.

The congregation then replies:

Nefesh בָּרוּךְ baruch *Ruach* יְהֹוָאדהנויאהדונהי Adonai *Neshamah* הַמְּבוֹרָךְ hamevorach
Chayah לְעוֹלָם le'olam ריבוע ס"ג וי' אותיות דס"ג *Yechidah* וָעֶד va'ed:

The *ole* repeats the line after the congregation:

Nefesh בָּרוּךְ baruch *Ruach* יְהֹוָאדהנויאהדונהי Adonai *Neshamah* הַמְּבוֹרָךְ hamevorach
Chayah לְעוֹלָם le'olam ריבוע ס"ג וי' אותיות דס"ג *Yechidah* וָעֶד va'ed:

And then says the following blessing:

בָּרוּךְ baruch אַתָּה Ata יְהֹוָאדהנויאהדונהי Adonai אֱלֹהֵינוּ Elohenu ילה
מֶלֶךְ melech הָעוֹלָם ha'olam אֲשֶׁר asher בָּחַר־ bachar בָּנוּ banu
מִכָּל־ mikol ילי הָעַמִּים ha'amim וְנָתַן־ venatan לָנוּ lanu אלהים, אהיה אדני
אֶת et תּוֹרָתוֹ torato. בָּרוּךְ baruch אַתָּה Ata יְהֹוָאדהנויאהדונהי Adonai
נוֹתֵן noten אבג יתץ, ושר הַתּוֹרָה hatorah.

THE READING

(The House of Aaron, bless the Lord, the Blessed One. Kohen, come close and stand and do your priestly duty.)
May the Lord be with you! May the Lord bless you!
Masters, Bless the Lord, the Blessed One. Blessed is the Lord, the Blessed One, forever and for eternity.
Blessed are You, Lord, our God, the King of the World,
Who chose us from among the nations and gave us His Torah. Blessed are You, Lord, Who gives the Torah.

After the reading, the *ole* says the following blessing:

בָּרוּךְ baruch אַתָּה Ata יְהֹוָואדניאהדונהי Adonai אֱלֹהֵינוּ Elohenu ילה
מֶלֶךְ melech הָעוֹלָם ha'olam אֲשֶׁר asher נָתַן natan לָנוּ lanu אלהים, אהיה אדני
אֶת et תּוֹרָתוֹ torato תּוֹרַת־ torat אֱמֶת emet אהיה פעמים אהיה, ז"פ ס"ג
וְחַיֵּי vechayei עוֹלָם olam נָטַע nata בְּתוֹכֵנוּ betochenu• בָּרוּךְ baruch
אַתָּה Ata יְהֹוָואדניאהדונהי Adonai נוֹתֵן noten אבג יתץ, ושר הַתּוֹרָה hatorah•

RETURNING THE TORAH TO THE ARK

Before the *Torah* is carried back to the ark, the *chazan* says:

יְהַלְלוּ yehalelu אֶת־ et שֵׁם shem יְהֹוָואדניאהדונהי Adonai כִּי־ ki נִשְׂגָּב nisgav
שְׁמוֹ shemo מהש ע"ה, ע"ב בריבוע וקס"א ע"ה, אל שדי ע"ה לְבַדּוֹ levado מ"ב

Then the congregation says while carrrying the *Torah* back to the Ark:

הוֹדוֹ hodo אהיה עַל־ al אֶרֶץ eretz וְשָׁמָיִם veshamayim י"פ טל, י"פ כוזו:
וַיָּרֶם vayarem קֶרֶן keren לְעַמּוֹ le'amo תְּהִלָּה tehila ע"ה אמת, אהיה פעמים אהיה,
ז"פ ס"ג לְכָל־ lechol יה אדני וַחֲסִידָיו chasidav לִבְנֵי livnei יִשְׂרָאֵל Yisrael
עַם־ am קְרֹבוֹ kerovo הַלְלוּיָהּ haleluya אלהים, אהיה אדני ; ללה:

Then the *chazan* says:

יְהֹוָואדניאהדונהי Adonai הוּא hu הָאֱלֹהִים haElohim
אהיה אדני ; ילה ; ר"ת יהה ועולה למנין ענו עם ג' כוללים:
יְהֹוָואדניאהדונהי Adonai הוּא hu הָאֱלֹהִים haElohim
אהיה אדני ; ילה ; ר"ת יהה ועולה למנין ענו עם ג' כוללים:

בַּשָּׁמַיִם bashamayim י"פ טל, י"פ כוזו מִמַּעַל mima'al עלם וְעַל־ ve'al
הָאָרֶץ ha'aretz אלהים דההין ע"ה מִתָּחַת mitachat אֵין en עוֹד od:

Blessed are You, Lord, our God, King of the World, Who gave us His Torah, the Torah of truth, and implanted within us eternal life. Blessed are You, Lord, Who gives the Torah.

RETURNING THE TORAH TO THE ARK

"Praise be the name of the Lord, His name alone is exalted His glory on heaven and earth. He raised funds to his nation, praise to his Chassidim, people of Israel his close nation, praise the Lord." (Psalms 148:13-14) *"The Lord is the God! The Lord is the God! In the Heavens above and on the Earth below, there is no other."* (Deuteronomy 4:39)

אֵין en כָּמוֹךָ kamocha בָאֱלֹהִים vaElohim אהיה אדני ; ילה אֲדֹנָי Adonai ללה

וְאֵין ve'en כְּמַעֲשֶׂיךָ kema'asecha: וּבְנֻחֹה uvnucho יֹאמַר yomar שׁוּבָה shuva

הוזש יְהֹוָ֘ה֘אדני֘יאהדונהי Adonai רִבְבוֹת rivevot אַלְפֵי alfei יִשְׂרָאֵל Yisrael:

הֲשִׁיבֵנוּ hashivenu יְהֹוָ֘ה֘אדני֘יאהדונהי Adonai | אֵלֶיךָ elecha וְנָשׁוּבָה venashuva

(כתיב : ונשוב) חַדֵּשׁ chadesh י״ב הויות, קס״א קנ״א יָמֵינוּ yamenu כְּקֶדֶם kekedem:

ר״ת הפסוק = נפש רוח נשמה חיה יחידה ע״ה

תִּכּוֹן tikon תְּפִלָּתִי tefilati קְטֹרֶת ketoret י״א פעמים אדני לְפָנֶיךָ lefanecha ס״ג מ״ה ב״ן

מַשְׂאַת mas'at כַּפַּי kapai מִנְחַת־ minchat עָרֶב arev: הַקְשִׁיבָה hakshiva

לְקוֹל lekol שַׁוְעִי shave'i מַלְכִּי malki וֵאלֹהָי velohai לכב ; מילוי ע״ב, דמ״ב ; ילה

כִּי־ ki אֵלֶיךָ elecha אֶתְפַּלָּל etpalal:

HALF KADDISH

יִתְגַּדַּל yitgadal וְיִתְקַדַּשׁ veyitkadash ש״די ומילוי ש״די ; י״א אותיות כמנין ו״ה

שְׁמֵיהּ shemei (שם י״ה דע״ב) רַבָּא raba קנ״א ב״ן, יהוה אלהים יהוה אדני,

מילוי קס״א וס״ג, מ״ה ברבוע וע״ב ע״ה ; ר״ת = ו״פ אלהים ; ס״ת = ג״פ יב״ק: אָמֵן amen אידהנויה.

בְּעָלְמָא be'alma דִּי di בְרָא vera כִּרְעוּתֵיהּ kir'utei.

וְיַמְלִיךְ veyamlich מַלְכוּתֵיהּ malchutei. וְיַצְמַח veyatzmach

פּוּרְקָנֵיהּ purkanei. וִיקָרֵב vikarev מְשִׁיחֵיהּ meshichei: אָמֵן amen אידהנויה.

"There is none like You among the gods, Lord, and there is nothing like Your handiwork." (Psalms 86:8) "And when the Ark rested, Moses would say, Return, Lord, to the tens of thousands of Israel." (Numbers 10:36) "Bring us back, Lord, and we shall return. Renew our days as of old." (Lamentataion 5:21) "Let my prayer be set before You as the incense offering, the lifting up of my hand as the afternoon meal offering." (Psalms 141:2) "Listen to the sound of my outcry, my King, My God for it is to You I am praying." (Psalms 5:3)

HALF KADDISH

May His great Name be more exalted and sanctified. (Amen)

In the world that He created according to His will, and may His kingdom reign.

And may He cause His redemption to sprout and may He bring the Mashiach closer. (Amen)

בְּחַיֵּיכוֹן bechayechon וּבְיוֹמֵיכוֹן uvyomechon וּבְחַיֵּי uvchayei

דְּכָל dechol ילי בֵּית bet ב״פ ראה יִשְׂרָאֵל Yisrael בַּעֲגָלָא ba'agala

וּבִזְמַן uvizman קָרִיב kariv וְאִמְרוּ ve'imru אָמֵן amen: אָמֵן amen אידהנויה.

The congregation and the *chazan* say the following:

28 words (until *be'alma*) and 28 letters (until *almaya*)

יְהֵא yehe שְׁמֵיהּ shemei (שם י״ה דס״ג) רַבָּא raba קנ״א ב״ן,

יהוה אלהים יהוה אדני, מילוי קס״א וס״ג, מ״ה ברבוע וע״ב ע״ה מְבָרַךְ mevarach,

לְעָלַם le'alam לְעָלְמֵי le'almei עָלְמַיָּא almaya. יִתְבָּרַךְ yitbarach.

Seven words with six letters each (שם בן מ״ב) and seven times the letter Vav (שם בן מ״ב)

וְיִשְׁתַּבַּח veyishtabach י״פ ע״ב יהוה אל אבג יתץ.

וְיִתְפָּאַר veyitpa'ar הי נו יה קרע שטן. וְיִתְרוֹמַם veyitromam וה כוזו נגד יכש.

וְיִתְנַשֵּׂא veyitnase במוכסז בטר צתג. וְיִתְהַדָּר veyit'hadar כוזו יה וקב טנע.

וְיִתְעַלֶּה veyit'ale וה יוד ה יגל פזק. וְיִתְהַלָּל veyit'halal א ואו הא שקו צית.

שְׁמֵיהּ shemei (שם י״ה דמ״ה) דְּקוּדְשָׁא dekudsha בְּרִיךְ verich הוּא hu:

אָמֵן amen אידהנויה.

לְעֵלָּא le'ela מִן min כָּל kol ילי בִּרְכָתָא birchata. שִׁירָתָא shirata.

תֻּשְׁבְּחָתָא tishbechata וְנֶחָמָתָא venechamata. דַּאֲמִירָן da'amiran

בְּעָלְמָא be'alma וְאִמְרוּ ve'imru אָמֵן amen: אָמֵן amen אידהנויה.

In your lifetimes and in your days and in the lifetime of all the House of Israel, speedily and in the near future, and you should say, Amen. (Amen) *May His great Name be blessed forever and for all eternity blessed and lauded, and glorified and exalted, And extolled and honored, and uplifted and praised, be the Name of the Holy Blessed One.* (Amen) *Above all blessings, songs, praises, and words of consolation that may be said in the world, and you shall say, Amen.* (Amen)

THE AMIDAH

When we begin the connection, we take three steps backward, signifying our leaving this physical world. Then we take three steps forward to begin the *Amidah*. The three steps are:

1. Stepping into the land of Israel – to enter the first spiritual circle.
2. Stepping into the city of Jerusalem – to enter the second spiritual circle.
3. Stepping inside the Holy of Holies – to enter the innermost circle.

Before we recite the first verse of the *Amidah*, we ask: "*God, open my lips and let my mouth speak,*" thereby asking the Light to speak for us so that we can receive what we need and not just what we want. All too often, what we want from life is not necessarily the desire of the soul, which is what we actually need to fulfill us. By asking the Light to speak through us, we ensure that our connection will bring us genuine fulfillment and opportunities for spiritual growth and change.

The Format of the Ascension in *Minchah* of *Shabbat*

In the silent *Amidah*, *Zeir Anpin* (which means *Yisrael* and *Leah*), elevates to *Netzach, Hod, Yesod* of *Dikna* in its three *tikkunim* (corrections -which are the thirteenth *tikkun*, twelfth *tikkun* and eleventh *tikkun*), which means that the five *Tzelamim* of *Netzach, Hod, Yesod* of *Dikna* (which is the letter צ of the *Tzelem*), expand in the five *Partzufim* of *Netzach, Hod, Yesod* of *Keter* of *Zeir Anpin* (and it is called *Nefesh, Ruach, Neshamah, Chayah, Yachidah* of *Nefesh* of *Yechidah*) **So now,** *Keter, Chochmah, Binah* of *Zeir Anpin* are elevated to *Netzach, Hod, Yesod* of *Dikna*, and *Chesed, Gevurah, Tiferet* of *Zeir Anpin* are elevated to *Keter, Chochmah, Binah* of Supernal *Abba* and *Ima* and *Netzach, Hod, Yesod* of *Zeir Anpin* are elevated to *Chesed, Gevurah, Tiferet* of Supernal *Abba* and *Ima*. And *Yaakov* and *Rachel* (which are standing in *Netzach, Hod, Yesod* of *Chochmah* of *Zeir Anpin*, which means *Netzach, Hod, Yesod* of Supernal *Abba* and *Ima*) are elevated to *Chesed, Gevurah, Tiferet* of *Chochmah* of *Zeir Anpin* (which means to *Chesed, Gevurah, Tiferet* of Supernal *Abba* and *Ima*, and where *Netzach, Hod, Yesod* of *Zeir Anpin* are elevated now in *Minchah*). And *Netzach, Hod, Yesod* of *Zeir Anpin* become *Mochin* for *Chochmah, Binah, Da'at* of *Yaakov* and *Rachel*.

In the repetition, *Zeir Anpin* (which means *Yisrael* and *Leah*), elevates to *Chesed, Gevurah, Tiferet* of *Dikna* in its three *tikkunim* (corrections -which are the tenth *tikkun*, ninth *tikkun* and eighth *tikkun*), which means that the five *Tzelamim* of *Chesed, Gevurah, Tiferet* of *Dikna* of *Arich Anpin* (which is the letter ל of the *Tzelem*), expand in the five *Partzufim* of *Chesed, Gevurah, Tiferet* of *Keter* of *Zeir Anpin* (and it is called *Nefesh, Ruach, Neshamah, Chayah, Yachidah* of *Ruach* of *Yechidah*) **So now,** *Keter, Chochmah, Binah* of *Zeir Anpin* are elevated to *Chesed, Gevurah, Tiferet* of *Dikna*, and *Chesed, Gevurah, Tiferet* of *Zeir Anpin* are elevated to *Netzach, Hod, Yesod* of *Dikna*, and *Netzach, Hod, Yesod* of *Zeir Anpin* are elevated to *Chochmah, Binah, Da'at* of Supernal *Abba* and *Ima*. And *Yaakov* and *Rachel* (which are standing in *Chesed, Gevurah, Tiferet* of *Chochmah* of *Zeir Anpin*, which means *Chesed, Gevurah, Tiferet* of Supernal *Abba* and *Ima*) are elevated to *Keter, Chochmah, Binah* of *Chochmah* of *Zeir Anpin* (which means to *Keter, Chochmah, Binah* of Supernal *Abba* and *Ima*, and where *Netzach, Hod, Yesod* of *Zeir Anpin* are elevated now in the repetition of *Minchah*). And *Netzach, Hod, Yesod* of *Zeir Anpin* become *Mochin* for *Chochmah, Binah, Da'at* of *Yaakov* and *Rachel*.

אֲדֹנָי Adonai ללה (pause here) שְׂפָתַי sefatai תִּפְתָּח tiftach וּפִי ufi יַגִּיד yagid

ייז (כ״ב אותיות פשוטות [=אכא] וה׳ אותיות סופיות בןךםףץ) תְּהִלָּתֶךָ tehilatecha ס״ת = בוכו:

THE FIRST BLESSING - INVOKES THE SHIELD OF ABRAHAM.

Abraham is the channel of the Right Column energy of positivity, sharing, and mercy. Sharing actions can protect us from all forms of negativity.

Chesed that becomes *Chochmah*

In this section there are 42 words, the secret of the 42-Letter Name of God and therefore it begins with the letter *Bet* (2) and ends with the letter *Mem* (40).

Bend your knees at *"baruch"*, bow at *"Ata"* and straighten up at *"Adonai"*.

א ב

בָּרוּךְ baruch אַתָּה Ata א-ת (אותיות הא״ב המסמלות את השפע המגיע) לה׳ המלכות

ג י

יְהֹוָאדהנהי Adonai יאהדונהי (יא) אֱלֹהֵינוּ Elohenu ילה

ת צ

וֵאלֹהֵי velohei לכב ; מילוי ע״ב, דמב ; ילה אֲבוֹתֵינוּ avotenu.

ק ר

אֱלֹהֵי Elohei מילוי ע״ב, דמב ; ילה אַבְרָהָם Avraham (*Chochmah*)

ו״פ אל, רי״ו ול״ב נתיבות החכמה, רמ״ח (אברים), עסמ״ב וט״ז אותיות פשוטות

ע ש

אֱלֹהֵי Elohei מילוי ע״ב, דמב ; ילה יִצְחָק Yitzchak (*Binah*) ד״פ ב״ן

ט נ

וֵאלֹהֵי velohei לכב ; מילוי ע״ב, דמב ; ילה יַעֲקֹב Yaakov (*Da'at*) ז׳ הויות, יאהדונהי אידהנויה

THE AMIDAH

"My Lord, open my lips, and my mouth shall relate Your praise." (Psalms 51:17)

THE FIRST BLESSING

Blessed are You, Lord,
our God and God of our forefathers: the God of Abraham, the God of Isaac, and the God of Jacob.

ג ג

הָאֵל haEl לאה ; ייא״ (מילוי דס״ג) הַגָּדוֹל hagadol האל הגדול = סיט ; גדול = להח

ד י

עם ד׳ אותיות = מבה, יזל, אום הַגִּבּוֹר hagibor ר״ת ההה וְהַנּוֹרָא vehanora.

כ ש

אֵל El ייא״ (מילוי דס״ג) ; ר״ת ע״ב, ריבוע יהוה עֶלְיוֹן elyon.

ב ט ר צ ת

גּוֹמֵל gomel חֲסָדִים chasadim טוֹבִים tovim. קוֹנֵה kone הַכֹּל hakol יכי

ג ח ק ב

וְזוֹכֵר vezocher חַסְדֵי chasdei אָבוֹת avot. וּמֵבִיא umevi

ט נ ע י

גּוֹאֵל go'el לִבְנֵי livnei בְנֵיהֶם venehem לְמַעַן lema'an

ג ל

שְׁמוֹ shemo מהש ע״ה, ע״ב בריבוע וקס״א ע״ה, אל שדי ע״ה בְּאַהֲבָה be'ahava אחד, דאגה:

When saying the word *"be'ahava"* you should meditate to devote your soul to sanctify the Holy Name and accept upon yourself the four forms of death.

פ ז ק ש

מֶלֶךְ melech עוֹזֵר ozer וּמוֹשִׁיעַ umoshi'a וּמָגֵן umagen

ג״פ אל (ייא״ מילוי דס״ג) ; ר״ת מיכאל גבריאל נוריאל:

Bend your knees at *"baruch"*, bow at *"Ata"* and straighten up at *"Adonai"*.

אהיה יהו אלף הי יוד הי (on Shabbat: יְהֹוָה)

ק ו צ

בָּרוּךְ baruch אַתָּה Ata יְהֹוָאדהֹנָיאהדונהי (יְהֹוָהאֱהֹיֶה) Adonai (הד)

י ת

מָגֵן magen ג״פ אל (ייא״ מילוי דס״ג) ; ר״ת מיכאל גבריאל נוריאל אַבְרָהָם Avraham

וז״פ אל, רי״ו ול״ב נתיבות החכמה, רמ״ח (אברים), עסמ״ב וט״ז אותיות פשוטות:

The great, mighty and awesome God.
The Supernal God, Who bestows beneficial kindness and creates everything.
Who recalls the kindness of the forefathers and brings a Redeemer to their descendants for the sake of His Name, lovingly. King, Helper, Savior and Shield. Blessed are You, Lord, the shield of Abraham.

THE SECOND BLESSING

THE ENERGY OF ISAAC IGNITES THE POWER FOR THE RESURRECTION OF THE DEAD.

Whereas Abraham represents the power of sharing, Isaac represents the Left Column energy of judgment. Judgment shortens the *Tikkun* process and paves the way for our eventual resurrection.

Gevurah that becomes *Binah*.

In this section there are 49 words corresponding to the 49 gates of the Pure System in *Binah*.

אַתָּה Ata גִּבּוֹר gibor לְעוֹלָם le'olam ריבוע ס״ג וי׳ אותיות דס״ג אֲדֹנָי Adonai ללה

(ר״ת אֲגְלָא והוא שם גדול ואמיץ, ובו היה יהודה מתגבר על אויביו. ע״ה אלד, בוכו).

מְחַיֵּה mechaye ס״ג מֵתִים metim אַתָּה Ata• רַב rav לְהוֹשִׁיעַ lehoshi'a•

מוֹרִיד morid הַטָּל hatal יוד הא ואו, כוזו, מספר אותיות דמילואי עסמ״ב ; ר״ת מ״ה:

If you mistakenly say "*Mashiv haru'ach*", and realize this before the end of the blessing ("*baruch Ata Adonai*"), you should return to the beginning of the blessing ("*Ata gibor*") and continue as usual. But if you only realize this after the end of the blessing, you should start the *Amidah* from the beginning.

מְכַלְכֵּל mechalkel חַיִּים chayim אהיה אהיה יהוה, בינה ע״ה בְּחֶסֶד bechesed

ע״ב, ריבוע יהוה• מְחַיֵּה mechaye ס״ג מֵתִים metim בְּרַחֲמִים berachamim

(במוכסז) מצפצ, אלהים דההין, י״פ ייי רַבִּים rabim (טלא דעתיק)• סוֹמֵךְ somech

(אכדטם) כוק, ריבוע אדני נוֹפְלִים noflim (זו״ן)• וְרוֹפֵא verofe חוֹלִים cholim

וחולה = מ״ה וד׳ אותיות• וּמַתִּיר umatir אֲסוּרִים asurim• וּמְקַיֵּם umekayem

אֱמוּנָתוֹ emunato לִישֵׁנֵי lishenei עָפָר afar• מִי mi ילי כָּמוֹךָ chamocha

(you should enunciate the letter *Ayin* in the word *"ba'al"*) בַּעַל ba'al גְּבוּרוֹת gevurot

וּמִי umi ילי דּוֹמֶה dome לָּךְ lach• מֶלֶךְ melech מֵמִית memit

וּמְחַיֶּה umchaye ס״ג (יוד הי ואו הי) וּמַצְמִיחַ umatzmi'ach יְשׁוּעָה yeshu'a:

וְנֶאֱמָן vene'eman אַתָּה Ata לְהַחֲיוֹת lehachayot מֵתִים metim:

אהיה יהו אלף הי יוד הי (on Shabbat: יֱהֹוִה)

בָּרוּךְ baruch אַתָּה Ata יְהֹוָאדהנהי(יְהֹוָאדהִי)יאהדונהי Adonai

מְחַיֵּה mechaye ס״ג (יוד הי ואו הי) הַמֵּתִים hametim ר״ת מ״ה וס״ת מ״ה:

THE SECOND BLESSING

You are mighty forever, Lord.

You resurrect the dead and are very capable of redeeming. Who causes dew to fall. You sustain life with kindness and resurrect the dead with great compassion. You support those who have fallen, heal the sick, release the imprisoned, and fulfill Your faithful words to those who are asleep in the dust. Who is like You, Master of might, and Who can compare to You, King, Who causes death, Who gives life, and Who sprouts salvation? And You are faithful to resurrecting the dead. Blessed are You, Lord, Who resurrects the dead.

NAKDISHACH – THE KEDUSHA

The congregation recites this prayer together.

Saying the *Kedusha* (holiness) we meditate to bring the holiness of the Creator among us. As it says: "*Venikdashti betoch Benei Israel*" (God is hallowed among the children of Israel).

נַקְדִּישָׁךְ nakdishach וְנַעֲרִיצָךְ vena'aritzach.

כְּנוֹעַם keno'am שִׂיחַ si'ach סוֹד sod מ״כ, י״פ האא שַׂרְפֵי sarfei

קֹדֶשׁ kodesh הַמְשַׁלְּשִׁים hameshaleshim לְךָ lecha קְדֻשָּׁה kedusha.

וְכֵן vechen כָּתוּב katuv עַל al יַד yad נְבִיאָךְ nevi'ach. וְקָרָא vekara

זֶה ze אֶל־ el זֶה ze י״ב פרקין דיעקב מאירים ל״ב פרקין דרוזל וְאָמַר ve'amar:

קָדוֹשׁ kadosh | קָדוֹשׁ kadosh קָדוֹשׁ kadosh (סוד ג' רישין דעתיקא קדישא)

יְהֹוָהאדניאהדונהי Adonai צְבָאוֹת Tzeva'ot פני שכינה מְלֹא melo כָל־ chol ילי

הָאָרֶץ ha'aretz אלהים דההין ע״ה כְּבוֹדוֹ kevodo:

לְעֻמָּתָם le'umatam מְשַׁבְּחִים meshabechim וְאוֹמְרִים ve'omrim:

(או״א) בָּרוּךְ baruch כְּבוֹד־ kevod יְהֹוָהאדניאהדונהי Adonai ; כבוד ה' = יוד הי ואו הה

מִמְּקוֹמוֹ mimekomo עסמ״ב, הברכה (למתק את ז' המלכים שמתו) ; ר״ת ע״ב, ריבוע יהוה ; ר״ת מ״כ:

וּבְדִבְרֵי uvdivrei קָדְשָׁךְ kodshach כָּתוּב katuv לֵאמֹר lemor:

(זו״ן) יִמְלֹךְ yimloch קדוש ברוך ימלך ר״ת יב״ק, אלהים יהוה, אהיה אדני יהוה

יְהֹוָהאדניאהדונהי Adonai לְעוֹלָם le'olam ריבוע ס״ג וי' אותיות דס״ג אֱלֹהַיִךְ Elohayich ילה

צִיּוֹן Tziyon יוסף, ו' הויות, קנאה לְדֹר ledor וָדֹר vador רי״ו ; ר״ת אצלו (מלכות אצל ז״א – ו)

הַלְלוּיָהּ haleluya אלהים, אהיה אדני ; ללה:

NAKDISHACH

We sanctify You and we revere You, according to the pleasant words of the counsel of the Holy Angels, who recite Holy before You three times, as it is written by Your Prophet: "And each called to the other and said: Holy, Holy, Holy, Is the Lord of Hosts, the entire world is filled with His glory." (Isaiah 6:3) Facing them they give praise and say: "Blessed is the glory of the Lord from His Place." (Ezekiel 3:12) And in Your Holy Words, it is written as follows: "The Lord, your God, shall reign forever, for each and for every generation. Zion, Praise the Lord!" (Psalms 146:10)

THE THIRD BLESSING

This blessing connects us to Jacob, the Central Column and the power of restriction. Jacob is our channel for connecting mercy with judgment. By restricting our reactive behavior, we are blocking our Desire to Receive for the Self Alone. Jacob also gives us the power to balance our acts of mercy and judgment toward other people in our lives.

Tiferet* that becomes *Da'at (14 words).

אַתָּה Ata קָדוֹשׁ kadosh וְשִׁמְךָ veshimcha קָדוֹשׁ kadosh ר״ת = אור, רז, אין סוף •

וּקְדוֹשִׁים ukdoshim בְּכָל־ bechol ב״ן, לכב יוֹם yom ע״ה נגד, מזבח, זן, אל יהוה

יְהַלְלוּךָ yehalelucha סֶּלָה sela •:

אה״ה יהו אלף הא יוד הא (on Shabbat: מצפצ)

בָּרוּךְ baruch אַתָּה Ata יְהֹוָהאדני(יְהֹוָהאדני)יאהדונהי Adonai

הָאֵל haEl לאה ; ייא״י (מילוי דס״ג) הַקָּדוֹשׁ hakadosh י״פ מ״ה (יוד הא ואו הא) •:

Meditate here on the Name: יאהדונהי, as it can help to remove anger.

THE MIDDLE BLESSING

The middle blessing connects us to the true essence of *Shavuot*. *Shavuot* is our connection to immortality and this blessing is our opportunity to choose the seed we wish to plant for immortality. The power of the letters in the Fourth Blessing is in their ability to automatically choose the correct seed we need and not necessarily the seed we want.

אַתָּה Ata בְּחַרְתָּנוּ vechartanu מִכָּל mikol ילי הָעַמִּים ha'amim •

אָהַבְתָּ ahavta אוֹתָנוּ otanu וְרָצִיתָ veratzita בָּנוּ banu •

וְרוֹמַמְתָּנוּ veromamtanu מִכָּל mikol ילי הַלְּשׁוֹנוֹת haleshonot •

וְקִדַּשְׁתָּנוּ vekidashtanu בְּמִצְוֹתֶיךָ bemitzvotecha • וְקֵרַבְתָּנוּ vekeravtanu

מַלְכֵּנוּ malkenu לַעֲבוֹדָתֶךָ la'avodatecha • וְשִׁמְךָ veshimcha הַגָּדוֹל hagadol

להוז ; ועם ד׳ אותיות = מבה, יזל, אום וְהַקָּדוֹשׁ vehakadosh עָלֵינוּ alenu קָרָאתָ karata •:

THE THIRD BLESSING

You are holy, and Your Name is holy, and the Holy Ones praise You every day, for you are God, the Holy King Selah. Blessed are You, Lord, the Holy God.

THE MIDDLE BLESSING

You had chosen us from among all the nations. You had loved us and have found favor in us. You had exalted us above all the tongues and You had sanctified us with Your commandments. You drew us close, our King, to Your service and proclaimed Your great and Holy Name upon us.

וַתִּתֶּן vatiten ב"פ כהת לָנוּ lanu אלהים, אהיה אדני יְהֹוָאדהנָיאהדונהי Adonai

אֱלֹהֵינוּ Elohenu ילה בְּאַהֲבָה be'ahava אחד, דאגה (On Shabbat add:

שַׁבָּתוֹת shabbatot לִמְנוּחָה limnucha ו u) מוֹעֲדִים mo'adim לְשִׂמְחָה lesimcha.

חַגִּים chagim וּזְמַנִּים uzmanim לְשָׂשׂוֹן lesason. אֶת et

יוֹם yom ע"ה נגד, מזבח, זן, אל יהוה (On Shabbat add: הַשַּׁבָּת hashabat הַזֶּה hazeh והו.

וְאֶת ve'et יוֹם yom ע"ה נגד, מזבח, זן, אל יהוה) חַג chag הַשָּׁבוּעוֹת haShavuot

הַזֶּה hazeh והו. אֶת et יוֹם yom ע"ה נגד, מזבח, זן, אל יהוה טוֹב tov והו

מִקְרָא mikra קֹדֶשׁ kodesh הַזֶּה hazeh והו. זְמַן zeman

חֵרוּתֵנוּ cherutenu. בְּאַהֲבָה be'ahava אחד, דאגה מִקְרָא mikra

קֹדֶשׁ kodesh. זֵכֶר zecher לִיצִיאַת litzi'at מִצְרָיִם Mitzrayim מצר.

אֱלֹהֵינוּ elhenu ילה וֵאלֹהֵי vElohei לכב ; מילוי ע"ב, דמב ; ילה אֲבוֹתֵינוּ avotenu

יַעֲלֶה ya'ale וְיָבֹא veyavo וְיַגִּיעַ veyagi'a וְיֵרָאֶה veyera'e רי"ו וְיֵרָצֶה veyeratze

וְיִשָּׁמַע veyishama וְיִפָּקֵד veyipaked וְיִזָּכֵר veyizacher ר"ת = מ"ב

זִכְרוֹנֵנוּ zichronenu וְזִכְרוֹן vezichron ע"ב קס"א ונש"ב אֲבוֹתֵינוּ avotenu.

זִכְרוֹן zichron ע"ב קס"א ונש"ב יְרוּשָׁלַיִם Yerushalayim עִירָךְ irach.

וְזִכְרוֹן vezichron ע"ב קס"א ונש"ב מָשִׁיחַ mashi'ach בֶּן ben דָּוִד David ע"ה כהת ;

בן דוד = אדני ע"ה עַבְדָּךְ avdach פוי, אל אדני. וְזִכְרוֹן vezichron ע"ב קס"א ונש"ב כָּל kol ילי

עַמְּךָ amecha בֵּית bet ב"פ ראה יִשְׂרָאֵל Yisra'el לְפָנֶיךָ lefanecha ס"ג מ"ה ב"ן

לִפְלֵיטָה lifleta לְטוֹבָה letova אכא. לְחֵן lechen מילוי דמ"ה בריבוע ; מוחי

לְחֶסֶד lechesed ע"ב, ריבוע יהוה וּלְרַחֲמִים ulrachamim.

---

*And may You give us, Lord, our God, with love (***on Shabbat add:** *Shabbat for rest and) holidays for happiness, festivals and time of joy, this day (***on Shabbat add:** *of Shabbat and this day) of the shavuot Holiday, and this good day of Holy Convocation, the time we received our Torah with love, a Holy Convocation, a remembrance of the exit from Egypt.*

Our God and the God of our fathers,

may it rise and come and arrive and appear and find favor and be heard and be considered and be remembered, our remembrance and the remembrance of our fathers, the remembrance of Jerusalem, Your city, and the remembrance of Mashiach Ben David, Your servant, and the remembrance of Your entire Nation, the House of Israel, before You for deliverance, for good, for grace, kindness and compassion,

לְחַיִּים lechayim אהיה אהיה יהוה, בינה ע"ה טוֹבִים tovim וּלְשָׁלוֹם ulshalom.

בְּיוֹם beyom ע"ה נגד, מזבח, זן, אל יהוה (**On Shabbat add:** הַשַּׁבָּת hashabat הַזֶּה hazeh והו.

וּבְיוֹם uvyom ע"ה נגד, מזבח, זן, אל יהוה) חַג chag הַשָּׁבוּעוֹת haShavuot הַזֶּה hazeh

והו בְּיוֹם beyom ע"ה נגד, מזבח, זן, אל יהוה טוֹב tov והו מִקְרָא mikra קֹדֶשׁ kodesh

הַזֶּה hazeh והו. לְרַחֵם lerachem אברהם, וז"פ אל, רי"ו ול"ב נתיבות החכמה, רמ"ח (אברים),

עסמ"ב וט"ז אותיות פשוטות בּוֹ bo עָלֵינוּ alenu וּלְהוֹשִׁיעֵנוּ ulhoshi'enu.

זָכְרֵנוּ zochrenu **(from *Zeir Anpin*)** יְהֹוָהאדניאהדונהי Adonai אֱלֹהֵינוּ Elohenu ילה

בּוֹ bo לְטוֹבָה letova אכא. וּפָקְדֵנוּ ufokdenu **(from *Nukva*)** בוֹ vo

לִבְרָכָה livracha. וְהוֹשִׁיעֵנוּ vehoshi'enu **(from *Da'at*)** בוֹ vo לְחַיִּים lechayim

אהיה אהיה יהוה, בינה ע"ה טוֹבִים tovim. בִּדְבַר bidvar ראה יְשׁוּעָה yeshu'a

וְרַחֲמִים verachamim. חוּס chus וְחָנֵּנוּ vechanenu וַחֲמוֹל vachamol

וְרַחֵם verachem אברהם, וז"פ אל, רי"ו ול"ב נתיבות החכמה, רמ"ח (אברים), עסמ"ב וט"ז אותיות פשוטות

עָלֵינוּ alenu. וְהוֹשִׁיעֵנוּ vehoshi'enu כִּי ki אֵלֶיךָ elecha עֵינֵינוּ enenu ריבוע מ"ה.

כִּי ki אֵל El יא"י מֶלֶךְ melech חַנּוּן chanun וְרַחוּם verachum אָתָּה Ata:

וְהַשִּׂיאֵנוּ vehashsyenu יְהֹוָהאדניאהדונהי Adonai אֱלֹהֵינוּ Elohenu ילה.

אֶת et בִּרְכַּת birkat מוֹעֲדֶיךָ mo'adecha לְחַיִּים lechayim אהיה אהיה יהוה, בינה ע"ה

בְּשִׂמְחָה besimcha וּבְשָׁלוֹם uvshalom. כַּאֲשֶׁר ka'asher רָצִיתָ ratzita

וְאָמַרְתָּ ve'amarta לְבָרְכֵנוּ levarchenu. כֵּן ken תְּבָרְכֵנוּ tevarchenu

סֶלָה selah:

---

for a good life and for peace on this Day of (**on Shabbat say:** *Shabbat and on this Day of*) *the Shavuot, Holiday on this good Day of Holy Convocation, to take pity on us and to save us. Remember us, Lord, our God, on it for good and consider us, on it, for blessing and deliver us on it for a good life with the words of deliverance and mercy. Take pity and be gracious to us and have mercy and be compassionate with us and save us, for our eyes turn to You, because You are God, King Who is gracious and compassionate. And give us, Lord, our God Your blessing of Your holidays for happy and peaceful life. As You desired and said to bless us. So You shall bless us Selah.*

MEKADESH ISRAEL AND THE TIMES

(On Shabbat add: אֱלֹהֵינוּ Elohenu ילה וֵאלֹהֵי veElohei לכב ; מילוי ע״ב, דמב ; ילה

אֲבוֹתֵינוּ avotenu רְצֵה retze נָא na בִמְנוּחָתֵינוּ vimnuchatenu)

קַדְּשֵׁנוּ kadshenu בְּמִצְוֹתֶיךָ vemitzvotecha• תֵּן ten וְחֶלְקֵנוּ chelkenu

בְּתוֹרָתָךְ vetoratach• שַׂבְּעֵנוּ sabe'enu מִטּוּבָךְ mituvach לאו•

שַׂמֵּחַ same'ach נַפְשֵׁנוּ nafshenu בִּישׁוּעָתָךְ bishu'atach•

וְטַהֵר vetaher לִבֵּנוּ libenu לְעָבְדְּךָ le'ovdecha פוי, אל יהוה בֶּאֱמֶת ve'emet

אהיה פעמים אהיה, ז״פ ס״ג• וְהַנְחִילֵנוּ vehanchilenu יְהֹוָאדהיאהדונהי Adonai

אֱלֹהֵינוּ Elohenu ילה (On Shabbat add: בְּאַהֲבָה be'ahava אחד, דאגה

וּבְרָצוֹן uvratzon מהש ע״ה, ע״ב בריבוע וקס״א ע״ה, אל שדי) בְּשִׂמְחָה vesimcha

וּבְשָׂשׂוֹן uvsason (On Shabbat add: שַׁבָּתוֹת shabatot ו) מוֹעֲדֵי mo'adei

קָדְשֶׁךָ kodshecha, וְיִשְׂמְחוּ veyismechu בְךָ vecha כָּל kol ילי יִשְׂרָאֵל Yisrael

מְקַדְּשֵׁי mekadshei שְׁמֶךָ shemecha• בָּרוּךְ baruch אַתָּה Ata

יְהֹוָאדהיאהדונהי Adonai

אהיה יהו אלף הה יוד הה (on Shabbat: יה אדני)

מְקַדֵּשׁ mekadesh (On Shabbat add: הַשַּׁבָּת hashabat וְ ve) יִשְׂרָאֵל Yisrael

וְהַזְּמַנִּים vehazemanim:

THE FINAL THREE BLESSINGS

Through the merit of Moses, Aaron and Joseph, who are our channels for the final three blessings, we are able to bring down all the spiritual energy that we aroused with our prayers and blessings.

THE FIFTH BLESSING

During this blessing, referring to Moses, we should always meditate to try to know exactly what God wants from us in our life, as signified by the phrase, "Let it be the will of God." We ask God to guide us toward the work we came to Earth to do. The Creator cannot just accept the work that we want to do; we must carry out the work we were destined to do.

MEKADESH ISRAEL AND THE TIMES

(**on Shabbat:** *Our God and the God of our forefathers, please desire our rest.)*

Sanctify us with Your commandments and place our lot in Your Torah and satiate us from Your goodness and gladden our spirits with Your salvation. and purify our heart so as to serve You truly. And grant us, Lord, our God, (**on Shabbat:** *with love and favor,) with happiness and joy* (**on Shabbat:** *Shabbatot and) the holidays, and all Yisrael, who sanctify Your Name will be joyful with You. Blessed are You, Lord, who sanctifies* (**on Shabbat:** *the Sabbath) and Israel and the Times.*

Netzach

Meditate for the Supernal Desire (*Keter*) that is called *metzach haratzon* (the Forehead of the Desire).

רְצֵה retze אלף למד הה יוד מם

Meditate here to transform misfortune and tragedy (צָרָה) into desire and acceptance (רְצֵה).

יְהֹוָאדהיאהדונהי Adonai אֱלֹהֵינוּ Elohenu ילה בְּעַמְּךָ be'amecha יִשְׂרָאֵל Yisrael

וְלִתְפִלָּתָם velitfilatam שְׁעֵה she'e. וְהָשֵׁב vehashev הָעֲבוֹדָה ha'avoda

לִדְבִיר lidvir רי״ו בֵּיתֶךָ betecha ב״פ ראה. וְאִשֵּׁי ve'ishei יִשְׂרָאֵל Yisrael

וּתְפִלָּתָם utfilatam מְהֵרָה mehera בְּאַהֲבָה be'ahava אחד, דאגה

תְקַבֵּל tekabel בְּרָצוֹן beratzon מהש ע״ה, ע״ב בריבוע וקס״א ע״ה, אל שדי ע״ה.

וּתְהִי ut'hi לְרָצוֹן leratzon מהש ע״ה, ע״ב בריבוע וקס״א ע״ה, אל שדי ע״ה

תָּמִיד tamid ע״ה קס״א קנ״א קמ״ג עֲבוֹדַת avodat יִשְׂרָאֵל Yisrael עַמֶּךָ amecha:

וְאַתָּה veAta בְּרַחֲמֶיךָ verachamecha הָרַבִּים harabim.

תַּחְפֹּץ tachpotz בָּנוּ banu וְתִרְצֵנוּ vetirtzenu וְתֶחֱזֶינָה vetechezena

עֵינֵינוּ enenu ריבוע מ״ה בְּשׁוּבְךָ beshuvcha לְצִיּוֹן leTziyon יוסף, ו׳ הויות, קנאה

בְּרַחֲמִים berachamim מצפצ, אלהים דיודין, י״פ ייי:

אהיה יהו אלף למד הי יוד מם (on Shabbat: אל)

בָּרוּךְ baruch אַתָּה Ata יְהֹוָאדהיאהדונהי Adonai

הַמַּחֲזִיר hamachazir שְׁכִינָתוֹ shechinato לְצִיּוֹן leTziyon יוסף, ו׳ הויות, קנאה:

THE FINAL THREE BLESSINGS

THE FIFTH BLESSING

Find favor, Lord, our God,
in Your People, Israel, and turn to their prayer.

Restore the service to the inner sanctuary of Your Temple. Accept the offerings of Israel and their prayer with favor, speedily, and with love. May the service of Your People Israel always be favorable to You.

And You in Your great compassion take delight in us and are pleased with us. May our eyes witness Your return to Zion with compassion. Blessed are You, Lord, Who returns His Shechinah to Zion.

THE SIXTH BLESSING

This blessing is our thank you. Kabbalistically, the biggest "thank you" we can give the Creator is to do exactly what we are supposed to do in terms of our spiritual work.

Hod

Bow your entire body at "*modim*" and straighten up at *'Adonai'*.

מוֹדִים modim מאה ברכות שתיקן דוד לאמרם כל יום אֲנַחְנוּ anachnu לָךְ lach

שֶׁאַתָּה sheAta הוּא hu יְהֹוָהאדנייאהדונהי Adonai (ונ) אֱלֹהֵינוּ Elohenu ילה

וֵאלֹהֵי velohei לכב ; מילוי ע"ב, דמב ; ילה אֲבוֹתֵינוּ avotenu לְעוֹלָם le'olam

ריבוע ס"ג וי' אותיות דס"ג וָעֶד ◆va'ed צוּרֵנוּ tzurenu צוּר tzur אלהים דההין ע"ה

וְחַיֵּינוּ chayenu וּמָגֵן umagen ג"פ אל (ייא" מילוי דס"ג) ; ר"ת מיכאל גבריאל נוריאל

יִשְׁעֵנוּ yish'enu אַתָּה Ata הוּא ◆hu לְדוֹר ledor וָדוֹר vador רי"ו נוֹדֶה node

לְךָ lecha וּנְסַפֵּר unsaper תְּהִלָּתֶךָ ◆tehilatecha עַל al חַיֵּינוּ chayenu

הַמְּסוּרִים hamesurim בְּיָדֶךָ ◆beyadecha וְעַל ve'al נִשְׁמוֹתֵינוּ nishmotenu

הַפְּקוּדוֹת hapekudot לָךְ ◆lach וְעַל ve'al נִסֶּיךָ nisecha שֶׁבְּכָל shebechol

ב"ן, לכב יוֹם yom ע"ה נגד, מזבח, זן, אל יהוה עִמָּנוּ imanu ריבוע ס"ג, קס"א ע"ה וד' אותיות

וְעַל ve'al נִפְלְאוֹתֶיךָ nifle'otecha וְטוֹבוֹתֶיךָ vetovotecha שֶׁבְּכָל shebechol

ב"ן, לכב עֵת ◆et עֶרֶב erev וָבֹקֶר vavoker וְצָהֳרָיִם ◆vetzahorayim הַטּוֹב hatov

והו כִּי ki לֹא lo כָלוּ chalu רַחֲמֶיךָ ◆rachamecha הַמְרַחֵם hamerachem

אברהם, ח"פ אל, רי"ו ול"ב נתיבות החכמה, רמ"ח (אברים), עסמ"ב וט"ז אותיות פשוטות כִּי ki לֹא lo

תַמּוּ tamu חֲסָדֶיךָ chasadecha כִּי ki מֵעוֹלָם me'olam קִוִּינוּ kivinu לָךְ lach:

THE SIXTH BLESSING

We give thanks to You, for it is You, Lord, Who is our God and God of our forefathers, forever and for all eternity. You are our Rock, the Rock of our lives, and the Shield of our salvation. From one generation to another, we shall give thanks to You and we shall tell of Your praise. For our lives that are entrusted in Your hands, for our souls that are in Your care, for Your miracles that are with us every day, and for Your wonders and Your favors that are with us at all times: evening, morning and afternoon. You are the good One, for Your compassion has never ceased. You are the compassionate One, for Your kindness has never ended, for we have always placed our hope in You.

MODIM DERABANAN

This prayer is recited by the congregation in the repetition when the *chazan* says "*modim*."

In this section there are 44 words which is the same numerical value as the Name: ריבוע אהיה (א אה אהי אהיה).

מוֹדִים modim מאה ברכות שתיקן דוד לאמרם כל יום אֲנַחְנוּ anachnu לָךְ lach

שָׁאַתָּה sheAta הוּא hu יְהֹוָאדהנויאהדונהי Adonai אֱלֹהֵינוּ Elohenu ילה

וֵאלֹהֵי velohei לכב ; מילוי ע"ב, דמב ; ילה אֲבוֹתֵינוּ avotenu

אֱלֹהֵי Elohei מילוי ע"ב, דמב ; ילה כָּל chol ילי בָּשָׂר basar. יוֹצְרֵנוּ yotzrenu

יוֹצֵר yotzer בְּרֵאשִׁית bereshit. בְּרָכוֹת berachot וְהוֹדָאוֹת vehoda'ot

לְשִׁמְךָ leshimcha הַגָּדוֹל hagadol להח ; עם ד' אותיות = מבה, יזל, אום

וְהַקָּדוֹשׁ vehakadosh עַל al שֶׁהֶחֱיִיתָנוּ shehecheyitanu וְקִיַּמְתָּנוּ vekiyamtanu.

כֵּן ken תְּחַיֵּנוּ techayenu וּתְחָנֵּנוּ utchonenu. וְתֶאֱסוֹף vete'esof

גָּלֻיּוֹתֵינוּ galuyoteinu לְחַצְרוֹת lechatzrot קָדְשֶׁךָ kodshecha. לִשְׁמֹר lishmor

חֻקֶּיךָ chukecha וְלַעֲשׂוֹת vela'asot רְצוֹנְךָ retzoncha. וּלְעָבְדְךָ ul'ovdecha

פוי, אל אדני בְּלֵבָב belevav בוכו שָׁלֵם shalem. עַל al שֶׁאֲנַחְנוּ she'anachnu

מוֹדִים modim לָךְ lach. בָּרוּךְ baruch אֵל El ייא"י (מילוי דס"ג) הַהוֹדָאוֹת hahoda'ot:

וְעַל ve'al כֻּלָּם kulam יִתְבָּרַךְ yitbarach וְיִתְרוֹמָם veyitromam

וְיִתְנַשֵּׂא veyitnase תָּמִיד tamid ע"ה קס"א קנ"א קמ"ג שִׁמְךָ shimcha

מַלְכֵּנוּ malkenu לְעוֹלָם le'olam ריבוע ס"ג ו' אותיות דס"ג וָעֶד va'ed.

וְכָל־ vechol ילי הַחַיִּים hachayim אהיה אהיה יהוה, בינה ע"ה יוֹדוּךָ yoducha סֶּלָה sela:

וִיהַלְלוּ vihalelu וִיבָרְכוּ vivarchu יהוה ריבוע יהוה ריבוע מ"ה

אֶת־ et שִׁמְךָ shimcha הַגָּדוֹל hagadol להח ; עם ד' אותיות = מבה, יזל, אום

MODIM DERABANAN

We give thanks to You, for it is You Lord,

our God and God of our forefathers, the God of all flesh, our Maker and the Former of all Creation. Blessings and thanks to Your great and Holy Name for giving us life and for preserving us. So may You continue to give us life, be gracious to us, and gather our exiles to the courtyards of Your Sanctuary, so that we may keep Your laws, fulfill Your will, and serve You wholeheartedly. For this, we thank You. Bless the God of thanksgiving.

And for all those things, may Your Name be always blessed, exalted and extolled, our King, forever and ever, and all the living shall thank You, Selah. And they shall praise and bless Your Great Name,

בֶּאֱמֶת be'emet אהיה פעמים אהיה, ז"פ ס"ג לְעוֹלָם le'olam ריבוע ס"ג וי' אותיות דס"ג
כִּי ki טוֹב tov והו ; כי טוב = יהוה אהיה, אום, מבה, יזל.
הָאֵל haEl לאה ; ייא" (מילוי דס"ג) יְשׁוּעָתֵנוּ yeshu'atenu וְעֶזְרָתֵנוּ ve'ezratenu
סֶלָה sela. הָאֵל haEl לאה ; ייא" (מילוי דס"ג) הַטּוֹב hatov והו:

Bend your knees at "baruch", bow at "Ata" and straighten up at "Adonai".

אהיה יהו אלף למד הה יוד מם (on Shabbat: אלהים)

בָּרוּךְ baruch אַתָּה Ata יְהֹוָהאדהנויאהדונהי Adonai (הי) הַטּוֹב hatov והו
שִׁמְךָ shimcha וּלְךָ ulcha נָאֶה na'e לְהוֹדוֹת lehodot ס"ת כהת, משיח בן דוד ע"ה:

THE FINAL BLESSING

We are emanating the energy of peace to the entire world. We also make it our intent to use our mouths only for good. Kabbalistically, the power of words and speech is unimaginable. We hope to use that power wisely, which is perhaps one of the most difficult tasks we have to carry out.

Yesod

שִׂים sim שָׁלוֹם shalom

טוֹבָה tova אכא וּבְרָכָה uvracha וְחַיִּים chayim אהיה אהיה יהוה, בינה ע"ה
חֵן chen מילוי דמ"ה בריבוע, מוזי וָחֶסֶד vachesed ע"ב, ריבוע יהוה
צְדָקָה tzedaka ע"ה ריבוע אלהים וְרַחֲמִים verachamim עָלֵינוּ alenu וְעַל־ ve'al
כָּל־ kol ילי ; עמם יִשְׂרָאֵל Yisrael עַמֶּךָ amecha וּבָרְכֵנוּ uvarchenu
אָבִינוּ avinu כֻּלָּנוּ kulanu כְּאֶחָד ke'echad אהבה, דאגה בְּאוֹר be'or רז, א"ס
פָּנֶיךָ panecha ס"ג מ"ה ב"ן כִּי ki בְאוֹר ve'or רז, א"ס פָּנֶיךָ panecha ס"ג מ"ה ב"ן
נָתַתָּ natata לָּנוּ lanu אלהים, אהיה אדני יְהֹוָהאדהנויאהדונהי Adonai
אֱלֹהֵינוּ Elohenu ילה תּוֹרָה torah וְחַיִּים vechayim אהיה אהיה יהוה, בינה ע"ה.

---

sincerely and forever, for It is good, the God of our salvation and our help, Selah, the good God. Blessed are You, Lord, whose Name is good, and to You it is befitting to give thanks.

THE FINAL BLESSING

Place peace, goodness, blessing, life, grace, kindness, righteousness, and mercy upon us and upon all of Israel, Your People. Bless us all as one, our Father, with the Light of Your Countenance, because it is with the Light of Your Countenance that You, Lord, our God, have given us Torah and life,

אַהֲבָה ahava אחד, דאגה וָחֶסֶד vachesed ע״ב, ריבוע יהוה◆
צְדָקָה tzedaka ע״ה ריבוע אלהים וְרַחֲמִים verachamim◆ בְּרָכָה beracha
וְשָׁלוֹם veshalom◆ וְטוֹב vetov והו בְּעֵינֶיךָ be'enecha ע״ה קס״א ; ריבוע מ״ה
לְבָרְכֵנוּ levarchenu וּלְבָרֵךְ ulvarech אֶת et כָּל kol ילי עַמְּךָ amecha
יִשְׂרָאֵל Yisrael בְּרוֹב berov י״פ אהיה עֹז oz וְשָׁלוֹם veshalom:

בָּרוּךְ baruch אַתָּה Ata

אהיה יהו אלף למד הא יוד מם (on Shabbat: מצפצ)

יְהֹוָהאדניאהדונהי Adonai

הַמְּבָרֵךְ hamevarech אֶת et עַמּוֹ amo יִשְׂרָאֵל Yisrael
ר״ת = אלהים = (אילהויהם = יב״ק) בַּשָּׁלוֹם bashalom◆ אָמֵן amen יאהדונהי◆

YIH'YU LERATZON

There are 42 letters in the verse in the secret of *Ana Beko'ach*.

יִהְיוּ yih'yu אל (ייא״י מילוי דס״ג) לְרָצוֹן leratzon מהש ע״ה, ע״ב בריבוע וקס״א ע״ה, אל שדי ע״ה
אִמְרֵי imrei פִי fi ר״ת אֶלֶף = אלף למד שין דלת יוד ע״ה וְהֶגְיוֹן vehegyon לִבִּי libi
לְפָנֶיךָ lefanecha ס״ג מ״ה ב״ן יְהֹוָהאדניאהדונהי Adonai צוּרִי tzuri וְגֹאֲלִי vego'ali:

ELOHAI NETZOR

אֱלֹהַי Elohai מילוי ע״ב, דמב ; ילה נְצוֹר netzor לְשׁוֹנִי leshoni מֵרָע mera◆
וּשְׂפָתוֹתַי vesiftotai מִדַּבֵּר midaber ראה מִרְמָה mirma◆ וְלִמְקַלְלַי velimkalelai
נַפְשִׁי nafshi תִדּוֹם tidom◆ וְנַפְשִׁי venafshi כֶּעָפָר ke'afar
לַכֹּל lakol יה אדני תִּהְיֶה tih'ye◆ פְּתַח petach לִבִּי libi בְּתוֹרָתֶךָ betoratecha◆

---

love and kindness, righteousness and mercy, blessing and peace. May it be good in Your Eyes to bless us and to bless Your entire Nation, Israel, with abundant power and with peace. Blessed are You, Lord, Who blesses His Nation, Israel, with peace, Amen.

YIH'YU LERATZON

"May the utterances of my mouth
and the thoughts of my heart find favor before You, Lord, my Rock and my Redeemer." (Psalms 19:15)

ELOHAI NETZOR

My God, guard my tongue from evil and my lips from speaking deceit. To those who curse me, let my spirit remain silent, and let my spirit be as dust for everyone. Open my heart toYour Torah

וְאַחֲרֵי ve'acharei מִצְוֹתֶיךָ mitzvotecha תִּרְדּוֹף tirdof נַפְשִׁי nafshi.

וְכָל־ vechol ילי הַקָּמִים hakamim עָלַי alai לְרָעָה lera'a רהע. מְהֵרָה mehera

הָפֵר hafer עֲצָתָם atzatam וְקַלְקֵל vekalkel מַחֲשְׁבוֹתָם machshevotam.

עֲשֵׂה ase לְמַעַן lema'an שְׁמָךְ shemach. עֲשֵׂה ase לְמַעַן lema'an

יְמִינָךְ yeminach. עֲשֵׂה ase לְמַעַן lema'an תּוֹרָתָךְ toratach. עֲשֵׂה ase

לְמַעַן lema'an קְדוּשָּׁתָךְ kedushatach. ר"ת הפסוק = מ"ה יהוה לְמַעַן lema'an

יֵחָלְצוּן yechaltzun יְדִידֶיךָ yedidecha ר"ת ילי הוֹשִׁיעָה hoshi'a יהוה וש"ע נהורין

יְמִינְךָ yemincha וַעֲנֵנִי va'aneni (כתיב: ועננו) ר"ת אל (יי"א מילוי דס"ג):

Before we recite the next verse ("*yih'yu leratzon*") we have an opportunity to strengthen our connection to our soul using our name. Each person has a verse in the *Torah* that connects to their name. Either their name is in the verse, or the first and last letters of the name correspond to the first or last letters of a verse. For example, the name Yehuda begins with a *Yud* and ends with a *Hei*. Before we end the *Amidah*, we state that our name will always be remembered when our soul leaves this world.

YIH'YU LERATZON (THE SECOND)

There are 42 letters in the verse in the secret of *Ana Beko'ach*.

יִהְיוּ yih'yu אל (יי"א מילוי דס"ג) לְרָצוֹן leratzon מהש ע"ה, ע"ב בריבוע וקס"א ע"ה, אל שדי ע"ה

אִמְרֵי־ imrei פִי fi ר"ת אֶלֶף – אלף למד שין דלת יוד ע"ה וְהֶגְיוֹן vehegyon לִבִּי libi

לְפָנֶיךָ lefanecha ס"ג מ"ה ב"ן יְהֹוָהאדניאהדונהי Adonai צוּרִי tzuri וְגֹאֲלִי vego'ali:

---

and let my heart pursue Your commandments. All those who rise against me to do me harm, speedily nullify their plans and disturb their thoughts. Do so for the sake of Your Name. Do so for the sake of Your Right. Do so for the sake of Your Torah. Do so for the sake of Your Holiness, "So that Your loved ones may be saved. Redeem Your right and answer me." (Psalms 60:7)

YIH'YU LERATZON (THE SECOND)

"May the utterances of my mouth
and the thoughts of my heart find favor before You, Lord, my Rock and my Redeemer." (Psalms 19:15)

OSE SHALOM

You take three steps backward;

עֹשֶׂה ose שָׁלוֹם shalom

Left
You turn to the left and say:

בִּמְרוֹמָיו bimromav ר"ת ע"ב, ריבוע יהוה

הוּא hu בְּרַחֲמָיו verachamav יַעֲשֶׂה ya'ase

Right
You turn to the right and say:

שָׁלוֹם shalom עָלֵינוּ alenu ר"ת ש"ע נהורין

Center
You face the center and say:

וְעַל ve'al כָּל־ kol ילי ; עמם עַמּוֹ amo יִשְׂרָאֵל Yisrael

וְאִמְרוּ ve'imru אָמֵן amen יאהדונהי:

יְהִי yehi רָצוֹן ratzon מהש ע"ה, ע"ב בריבוע וקס"א ע"ה, אל שדי ע"ה
מִלְּפָנֶיךָ milfanecha ס"ג מ"ה ב"ן יְהֹוָהאדניאהדונהי Adonai אֱלֹהֵינוּ Elohenu ילה
וֵאלֹהֵי velohei לכב ; מילוי ע"ב, דמב ; ילה אֲבוֹתֵינוּ avotenu, שֶׁתִּבְנֶה shetivne
בֵּית bet ב"פ ראה הַמִּקְדָּשׁ hamikdash בִּמְהֵרָה bimhera בְּיָמֵינוּ veyamenu
וְתֵן veten חֶלְקֵנוּ chelkenu בְּתוֹרָתָךְ betoratach לַעֲשׂוֹת la'asot חֻקֵּי chukei
רְצוֹנָךְ retzonach וּלְעָבְדָךְ ul'ovdach פוי, אל אדני בְּלֵבָב belevav בוכו שָׁלֵם shalem.

You take three steps forward.

OSE SHALOM

He, Who makes peace in His high places, He,
in His compassion, shall make peace upon us And upon His entire nation, Israel, and you shall say, Amen.

May it be pleasing before You,
Lord, our God and God of our forefathers, that You shall rebuild the Temple speedily, in our days, and place our lot in Your Torah, so that we may fulfill the laws of Your desire and serve You wholeheartedly.

KADDISH TITKABAL

יִתְגַּדַּל yitgadal וְיִתְקַדַּשׁ veyitkadash שד״י ומילוי שד״י ; י״א אותיות כמנין ו״ה

שְׁמֵיהּ shemei (שם י״ה דע״ב) רַבָּא raba קנ״א ב״ן, יהוה אלהים יהוה אדני,

מילוי קס״א וס״ג, מ״ה ברבוע וע״ב ע״ה ; ר״ת = ו״פ אלהים ; ס״ת = ג״פ יב״ק: אָמֵן amen אידהנויה.

בְּעָלְמָא be'alma דִּי di בְרָא vera כִּרְעוּתֵיהּ kir'utei.

וְיַמְלִיךְ veyamlich מַלְכוּתֵיהּ malchutei. וְיַצְמַח veyatzmach

פּוּרְקָנֵיהּ purkanei. וִיקָרֵב vikarev מְשִׁיחֵיהּ meshichei: אָמֵן amen אידהנויה.

בְּחַיֵּיכוֹן bechayechon וּבְיוֹמֵיכוֹן uvyomechon וּבְחַיֵּי uvchayei

דְכָל dechol ילי בֵּית bet ב״פ ראה יִשְׂרָאֵל Yisrael בַּעֲגָלָא ba'agala

וּבִזְמַן uvizman קָרִיב kariv וְאִמְרוּ ve'imru אָמֵן amen: אָמֵן amen אידהנויה.

The congregation and the *chazan* say the following:

28 words (until *be'alma*) and 28 letters (until *almaya*)

יְהֵא yehe שְׁמֵיהּ shemei (שם י״ה דס״ג) רַבָּא raba קנ״א ב״ן,

יהוה אלהים יהוה אדני, מילוי קס״א וס״ג, מ״ה ברבוע וע״ב ע״ה מְבָרַךְ mevarach,

לְעָלַם le'alam לְעָלְמֵי le'almei עָלְמַיָּא almaya. יִתְבָּרַךְ yitbarach.

Seven words with six letters each (שם בן מ״ב) and also, seven times the letter Vav (שם בן מ״ב):

וְיִשְׁתַּבַּח veyishtabach י״פ ע״ב יהוה אל אבג יתץ.

וְיִתְפָּאַר veyitpa'ar הי נו יה קרע שטן. וְיִתְרוֹמַם veyitromam וה כוזו נגד יכש.

וְיִתְנַשֵּׂא veyitnase במוכסז בטר צתג. וְיִתְהַדָּר veyit'hadar כוזו יה וקב טנע.

וְיִתְעַלֶּה veyit'ale וה יוד ה יגל פזק. וְיִתְהַלָּל veyit'halal א ואו הא שקו צית.

שְׁמֵיהּ shemei (שם י״ה דמ״ה) דְּקוּדְשָׁא dekudsha בְּרִיךְ verich הוּא hu:

אָמֵן amen אידהנויה.

KADDISH TITKABAL

May His great Name be more exalted and sanctified. (Amen)

In the world that He created according to His will, and may His Kingdom reign. And may He cause His redemption to sprout and may He bring the Mashiach closer. (Amen) *In your lifetimes and in your days and in the lifetime of all the House of Israel, speedily and in the near future, and you shall say, Amen.* (Amen) *May His great Name be blessed forever and for all eternity. Blessed and lauded, and glorified, and exalted, and extolled, and honored, and uplifted, and praised be the Name of the Holy Blessed One.* (Amen)

לְעֵלָּא le'ela מִן min כָּל kol ילי בִּרְכָתָא birchata• שִׁירָתָא shirata•
תֻּשְׁבְּחָתָא tishbechata וְנֶחֱמָתָא venechamata• דַּאֲמִירָן da'amiran
בְּעָלְמָא be'alma וְאִמְרוּ ve'imru אָמֵן amen: אָמֵן amen אידהנויה.

תִּתְקַבַּל titkabal צְלוֹתָנָא tzelotana וּבָעוּתָנָא uva'utana
עִם im צְלוֹתְהוֹן tzelotehon וּבָעוּתְהוֹן uva'utehon דְּכָל dechol ילי
בֵּית bet ב"פ ראה יִשְׂרָאֵל Yisrael קֳדָם kadam אֲבוּנָא avuna
דְּבִשְׁמַיָּא devishmaya וְאִמְרוּ ve'imru אָמֵן amen: אָמֵן amen אידהנויה.

יְהֵא yehe שְׁלָמָא shelama רַבָּא raba קנ"א ב"ן, יהוה אלהים יהוה אדני, מילוי קס"א וס"ג,
מ"ה ברבוע וע"ב ע"ה מִן min שְׁמַיָּא shemaya• וְחַיִּים chayim אהיה אהיה יהוה, בינה ע"ה
וְשָׂבָע vesava וִישׁוּעָה vishu'a וְנֶחָמָה venechama וְשֵׁיזָבָא veshezava
וּרְפוּאָה urfu'a וּגְאֻלָּה ug'ula וּסְלִיחָה uslicha וְכַפָּרָה vechapara
וְרֵיוַח verevach וְהַצָּלָה vehatzala• לָנוּ lanu אלהים, אהיה אדני וּלְכָל ulchol יה אדני
עַמּוֹ amo יִשְׂרָאֵל Yisrael וְאִמְרוּ ve'imru אָמֵן amen: אָמֵן amen אידהנויה.

Take three steps backwards and say:

עוֹשֶׂה ose שָׁלוֹם shalom

בִּמְרוֹמָיו bimromav ע"ב, ריבוע יהוה. הוּא hu בְּרַחֲמָיו berachamav
יַעֲשֶׂה ya'ase שָׁלוֹם shalom עָלֵינוּ alenu ר"ת ש"ע נהורין.
וְעַל ve'al כָּל kol ילי ; עמם עַמּוֹ amo יִשְׂרָאֵל Yisrael וְאִמְרוּ ve'imru אָמֵן amen:
אָמֵן amen אידהנויה.

Above all blessings, songs, praises, and words of consolation that may be said in the world, and you shall say, Amen. (Amen) May our prayers and pleas be accepted, together with the prayers and pleas of the entire House of Israel, before our Father in heaven, and you say, Amen. (Amen) May there be abundant peace from heaven. Life, contentment, salvation, consolation, deliverance, healing, redemption, pardon, atonement, comfort, and relief. For us and for His entire nation, Israel, and you shall say, Amen. (Amen) He, Who makes peace in His high places, He, in His compassion, shall make peace upon us And upon His entire nation, Israel, and you shall say, Amen. (Amen)

When *Shavuot* (second day) falls on *Shabbat* we add the following.

HALELUYA

According to the *Alef Bet* (bringing order to our life).

הַלְלוּיָהּ haleluya אלהים, אהיה אדני ; ילה ; ללה אוֹדֶה ode יְהֹוָה‎אדני‎אהדונהי Adonai

בְּכָל־ bechol ב״ן, לכב לֵבָב levav בוכו בְּסוֹד besod מיכ, י״פ האא יְשָׁרִים yesharim

וְעֵדָה ve'eda סיט: גְּדֹלִים gedolim מַעֲשֵׂי ma'asei יְהֹוָה‎אדני‎אהדונהי Adonai

דְּרוּשִׁים derushim לְכָל־ lechol יה אדני חֶפְצֵיהֶם cheftzehem:

הוֹד־ hod ההה וְהָדָר vehadar פָּעֳלוֹ pa'olo וְצִדְקָתוֹ vetzidkato עֹמֶדֶת omedet

לָעַד la'ad ב״פ ב״ן: זֵכֶר zecher עָשָׂה asa לְנִפְלְאֹתָיו lenifle'otav חַנּוּן chanun

וְרַחוּם verachum יְהֹוָה‎אדני‎אהדונהי Adonai חנון ורחום יהוה = עשל: טֶרֶף teref נָתַן natan

לִירֵאָיו lire'av יִזְכֹּר yizkor לְעוֹלָם le'olam ריבוע ס״ג וי׳ אותיות דס״ג בְּרִיתוֹ berito:

כֹּחַ ko'ach מַעֲשָׂיו ma'asav הִגִּיד higid לְעַמּוֹ le'amo לָתֵת latet לָהֶם lahem

נַחֲלַת nachalat גּוֹיִם goyim: מַעֲשֵׂי ma'asei יָדָיו yadav

אֱמֶת emet אהיה פעמים אהיה, ז״פ ס״ג וּמִשְׁפָּט umishpat ע״ה ה״פ אלהים

נֶאֱמָנִים ne'emanim כָּל־ kol ילי פִּקּוּדָיו pikudav מנק: סְמוּכִים semuchim

לָעַד la'ad ב״פ ב״ן לְעוֹלָם le'olam ריבוע ס״ג וי׳ אותיות דס״ג עֲשׂוּיִם asuyim

בֶּאֱמֶת be'emet אהיה פעמים אהיה, ז״פ ס״ג וְיָשָׁר veyashar: פְּדוּת pedut שָׁלַח shalach

לְעַמּוֹ le'amo צִוָּה־ tziva לְעוֹלָם le'olam ריבוע ס״ג וי׳ אותיות דס״ג בְּרִיתוֹ berito

קָדוֹשׁ kadosh וְנוֹרָא venora שְׁמוֹ shemo ע״ב בריבוע קס״א ע״ה, אל שדי ע״ה, מהש ע״ה:

HALELUYA

'Praise the Lord!

א *I will give thanks to the Lord with my whole heart,* ב *in the council of the upright, and in the congregation.* ג *The works of the Lord are great,* ד *sought out of all them that have delight therein.* ה *His work is glory and majesty;* ו *and His righteousness endures forever.* ז *He has made a memorial for His wonderful works;* ח *the Lord is gracious and full of compassion.* ט *He has given food to those that fear Him;* י *He will ever be mindful of His covenant.* כ *He has declared to His people the power of His works,* ל *in giving them the heritage of the nations.* מ *The works of His hands are truth and justice;* נ *all His precepts are sure.* ס *They are established for ever and ever,* ע *they are done in truth and uprightness.* פ *He has sent redemption unto His people;* צ *He has commanded His covenant for ever;* ק *Holy and awesome is His Name.*

רֵאשִׁית reshit וְחָכְמָה chochmah במילוי = תרי"ג (מצוות) יִרְאַת yir'at
יְהֹוָהאדניאהדונהי Adonai שֵׂכֶל sechel טוֹב tov והו לְכָל־ lechol יה אדני
עֹשֵׂיהֶם osehem תְּהִלָּתוֹ tehilato עֹמֶדֶת omedet לָעַד la'ad ב"פ ב"ן:

SHIR HAMA'ALOT LEDAVID

These verses connect us to the ancient Holy Temple. According to Kabbalah, the Holy Temple is the energy center and source of all spiritual Light for the whole world, similar to a nuclear power plant that provides electrical energy for an entire city. The land of Israel is the energy center of the planet; Jerusalem is the energy center of Israel; the physical Temple was the energy center of Jerusalem; and the Holy of Holies, inside the Temple, was the ultimate energy center for the Temple and thus for the entire physical world. When the Temple was standing, it acted as a generator that chugged along 24 hours a day to produce all the spiritual Light and energy we needed. With its destruction, the power lines were severed. The Aramaic letters in this connection re-establish the lines of communication with the spiritual essence of the Temple, giving us the ability to capture this energy for our personal lives.

This praise was said by King David for his kingdom, as everything was in one unification – "justice and peace kissed each other." And that's the meaning of: "I shall request good for you."

שִׁיר shir הַמַּעֲלוֹת hama'alot לְדָוִד leDavid שָׂמַחְתִּי samachti
בְּאֹמְרִים be'omrim לִי li בֵּית bet ב"פ ראה יְהֹוָהאדניאהדונהי Adonai נֵלֵךְ nelech נלך:
עֹמְדוֹת omdot הָיוּ hayu רַגְלֵינוּ raglenu ר"ת רהע בִּשְׁעָרַיִךְ bish'arayich
יְרוּשָׁלָםִ Yerushalayim: יְרוּשָׁלַםִ Yerushalayim הַבְּנוּיָה habenuya
כְּעִיר ke'ir בזוהר, סנדלפון, ערי שֶׁחֻבְּרָה־ shechubera לָּהּ la יַחְדָּו yachdav:
שֶׁשָּׁם shesham עָלוּ alu שְׁבָטִים shevatim שִׁבְטֵי־ shivtei יָהּ Yah עֵדוּת edut
לְיִשְׂרָאֵל leYisrael לְהֹדוֹת lehodot לְשֵׁם leshem יְהֹוָהאדניאהדונהי Adonai:

ר *The fear of the Lord is the beginning of wisdom;*
ש *a good understanding have all they that do thereafter;* ת *His praise endures for ever."* (Psalms 111)

SHIR HAMA'ALOT LEDAVID

"A Song of Ascents by David:

I rejoiced when they said to me: Let us go to the House of the Lord. Our legs stood immobile within your gates, Jerusalem. The built-up Jerusalem is like a city that has been united together. For there the tribes ascend the tribes of God, who are testimony for Israel, to give thanks to the Name of the Lord. For there sat thrones of judgments, thrones of the House of David, they have prayed for the peace of

כִּי ki שָׁמָּה shama יָשְׁבוּ yashvu כִסְאוֹת chis'ot לְמִשְׁפָּט lemishpat ע״ה ה״פ אלהים
כִּסְאוֹת kis'ot לְבֵית levet ב״פ ראה דָּוִיד David: שַׁאֲלוּ sha'alu שְׁלוֹם shelom
יְרוּשָׁלָםִ Yerushalayim יִשְׁלָיוּ yishlayu אֹהֲבָיִךְ ohavayich: יְהִי־ yehi
שָׁלוֹם shalom בְּחֵילֵךְ bechelech שַׁלְוָה shalva בְּאַרְמְנוֹתָיִךְ be'armenotayich:
לְמַעַן lema'an אַחַי achai וְרֵעָי vere'ai אֲדַבְּרָה־ adabera נָּא na שָׁלוֹם shalom
בָּךְ bach: לְמַעַן lema'an בֵּית bet ב״פ ראה יְהֹוָה(אדני)אהדונהי Adonai
אֱלֹהֵינוּ Elohenu ילה אֲבַקְשָׁה avaksha טוֹב tov והו לָךְ lach:

KADDISH YEHE SHELAMA

יִתְגַּדַּל yitgadal וְיִתְקַדַּשׁ veyitkadash שדי ומילוי שדי ; י״א אותיות כמנין ו״ה
שְׁמֵיהּ shemei (שם י״ה דע״ב) רַבָּא raba קנ״א ב״ן, יהוה אלהים יהוה אדני,
מילוי קס״א וס״ג, מ״ה ברבוע וע״ב ע״ה ; ר״ת = ו״פ אלהים ; ס״ת = ג״פ יב״ק: אָמֵן amen אידהנויה.

בְּעָלְמָא be'alma דִּי di בְרָא vera כִּרְעוּתֵיהּ kir'utei.
וְיַמְלִיךְ veyamlich מַלְכוּתֵיהּ malchutei. וְיַצְמַח veyatzmach
פּוּרְקָנֵיהּ purkanei. וִיקָרֵב vikarev מְשִׁיחֵיהּ meshichei: אָמֵן amen אידהנויה.

בְּחַיֵּיכוֹן bechayechon וּבְיוֹמֵיכוֹן uvyomechon וּבְחַיֵּי uvchayei
דְכָל dechol ילי בֵּית bet ב״פ ראה יִשְׂרָאֵל Yisrael בַּעֲגָלָא ba'agala
וּבִזְמַן uvizman קָרִיב kariv וְאִמְרוּ ve'imru אָמֵן amen: אָמֵן amen אידהנויה.

Jerusalem, those who love you will be serene. May there be peace within your walls, and serenity within your palaces. For the sake of my brothers and my comrades, I shall speak of peace on your behalf. For the sake of the House of the Lord, I shall request good for you." (Psalms 122)

KADDISH YEHE SHELAMA

May His great Name be more exalted and sanctified. (Amen)

In the world that He created according to His will, and may His kingdom reign. And may He cause His redemption to sprout and may He bring the Mashiach closer. (Amen) *In your lifetimes and in your days and in the lifetime of all the House of Israel, speedily and in the near future, and you shall say, Amen.* (Amen)

The congregation and the *chazan* say the following:

28 words (until *be'alma*) and 28 letters (until *almaya*)

יְהֵא yehe שְׁמֵיהּ shemei (שׁם י״ה דס״ג) רַבָּא raba קנ״א ב״ן,

יהוה אלהים יהוה אדני, מילוי קס״א וס״ג, מ״ה ברבוע וע״ב ע״ה מְבָרַךְ mevarach,

לְעָלַם le'alam לְעָלְמֵי le'almei עָלְמַיָּא almaya. יִתְבָּרַךְ yitbarach.

Seven words with six letters each (שם בן מ״ב) and also, seven times the letter Vav (שם בן מ״ב):

וְיִשְׁתַּבַּח veyishtabach י״פ ע״ב יהוה אל אבג יתץ.

וְיִתְפָּאַר veyitpa'ar הי גו יה קרע שטן. וְיִתְרוֹמַם veyitromam וה כוזו נגד יכש.

וְיִתְנַשֵּׂא veyitnase במוכסז בטר צתג. וְיִתְהַדָּר veyit'hadar כוזו יה וזקב טנע.

וְיִתְעַלֶּה veyit'ale וה יוד ה יגל פזק. וְיִתְהַלָּל veyit'halal א ואו הא שקו צית.

שְׁמֵיהּ shemei (שׁם י״ה דמ״ה) דְּקוּדְשָׁא dekudsha בְּרִיךְ verich הוּא hu:

אָמֵן amen אידהנויה.

לְעֵלָּא le'ela מִן min כָּל kol יל״י בִּרְכָתָא birchata. שִׁירָתָא shirata.

תֻּשְׁבְּחָתָא tishbechata וְנֶחָמָתָא venechamata. דַּאֲמִירָן da'amiran

בְּעָלְמָא be'alma וְאִמְרוּ ve'imru אָמֵן amen: אָמֵן amen אידהנויה.

יְהֵא yehe שְׁלָמָא shelama רַבָּא raba קנ״א ב״ן, יהוה אלהים יהוה אדני, מילוי קס״א וס״ג,

מ״ה ברבוע וע״ב ע״ה מִן min שְׁמַיָּא shemaya. וְחַיִּים chayim אהיה אהיה יהוה, בינה ע״ה

וְשָׂבָע vesava וִישׁוּעָה vishu'a וְנֶחָמָה venechama וְשֵׁיזָבָא veshezava

וּרְפוּאָה urefu'a וּגְאֻלָּה uge'ula וּסְלִיחָה uslicha וְכַפָּרָה vechapara

וְרֵיוַח verevach וְהַצָּלָה vehatzala. לָנוּ lanu אלהים, אהיה אדני וּלְכָל ulchol יה אדני

עַמּוֹ amo יִשְׂרָאֵל Yisrael וְאִמְרוּ ve'imru אָמֵן amen: אָמֵן amen אידהנויה.

May His great Name be blessed forever and for all eternity. Blessed and lauded, and glorified, and exalted, and extolled, and honored, and uplifted, and praised be the Name of the Holy Blessed One. (Amen) *Above all blessings, songs, praises, and words of consolation that may be said in the world, and you shall say, Amen.* (Amen) *May there be abundant peace from heaven, life, contentment, salvation, consolation, deliverance, healing, redemption, pardon, atonement, comfort, and relief. For us and for His entire nation, Israel, and you shall say, Amen.* (Amen)

Take three steps backwards and say:

עוֹשֶׂה ose שָׁלוֹם shalom בִּמְרוֹמָיו bimromav ע״ב, ריבוע יהוה. הוּא hu

בְּרַחֲמָיו berachamav יַעֲשֶׂה ya'ase שָׁלוֹם shalom עָלֵינוּ alenu ר״ת ש״ע נהורין.

וְעַל ve'al כָּל kol ילי ; עמם עַמּוֹ amo יִשְׂרָאֵל Yisrael וְאִמְרוּ ve'imru אָמֵן amen:

אָמֵן amen אידהנויה.

ALENU

Drawing Surrounding Light in order to be protected from the *klipot* (negative side).

עָלֵינוּ alenu ריבוע דס״ג לְשַׁבֵּחַ leshabe'ach עלינו לשבח = אבג יתץ, ושר

לַאֲדוֹן la'adon אני ; ס״ת ס״ג ע״ה הַכֹּל hakol ר״ת לכה, אדני

לָתֵת latet גְּדֻלָּה gedula לְיוֹצֵר leyotzer בְּרֵאשִׁית bereshit ר״ת גלב (באך ב״י יג״ל)

שֶׁלֹּא shelo עָשָׂנוּ asanu כְּגוֹיֵי kegoyei הָאֲרָצוֹת ha'aratzot

וְלֹא velo שָׂמָנוּ samanu כְּמִשְׁפְּחוֹת kemishpechot הָאֲדָמָה ha'adama

שֶׁלֹּא shelo שָׂם sam חֶלְקֵנוּ chelkenu כָּהֶם kahem וְגוֹרָלֵנוּ vegoralenu

כְּכָל kechol הֲמוֹנָם hamonam. שֶׁהֵם shehem מִשְׁתַּחֲוִים mishtachavim

לְהֶבֶל lahevel וָרִיק varik וּמִתְפַּלְּלִים umitpalelim אֶל el אֵל el

לֹא lo יוֹשִׁיעַ Yoshi'a. (pause here, and when you say "*va'anchnu mishtachavim*" bow your entire body)

וַאֲנַחְנוּ va'anachnu מִשְׁתַּחֲוִים mishtachavim לִפְנֵי lifnei מֶלֶךְ melech

מַלְכֵי malchei הַמְּלָכִים hamelachim הַקָּדוֹשׁ hakadosh בָּרוּךְ baruch

הוּא hu. שֶׁהוּא shehu נוֹטֶה note שָׁמַיִם shamayim י״פ טל, י״פ כוזו ;

ר״ת = י״פ אדני שבי ספירות של נוקבא דז״א וְיוֹסֵד veyosed אֶרֶץ aretz.

He, Who makes peace in His high places, with His compassion
He shall make peace for us and for His entire nation, Israel. And you shall say, Amen. (Amen)

ALENU

It is incumbent upon us to give praise to the Master of all and to attribute greatness to the Molder of Creation, for He did not make us like the nations of the lands. He did not place us like the families of the earth He did not make our lot like theirs and our destiny like that of their multitudes, for they prostrate themselves to futility and emptiness and they pray to a deity that does not help. But we prostrate ourselves before the King of all Kings, the Holy Blessed One. It is He Who spreads the Heavens and establishes the earth.

וּמוֹשַׁב umoshav יְקָרוֹ yekaro בַּשָּׁמַיִם bashamayim י"פ טל, י"פ כוזו
מִמַּעַל mima'al עלם. וּשְׁכִינַת ush'chinat עֻזּוֹ uzo בְּגָבְהֵי begovhei
מְרוֹמִים meromim. הוּא hu אֱלֹהֵינוּ eloheinu ילה וְאֵין ve'ein עוֹד od
אַחֵר acher. אֱמֶת emet אהיה פעמים אהיה, ז"פ ס"ג מַלְכֵּנוּ malkenu וְאֶפֶס ve'efes
זוּלָתוֹ zulato. כַּכָּתוּב kakatuv בַּתּוֹרָה batorah: וְיָדַעְתָּ veyadata
הַיּוֹם hayom ע"ה נגד, מזבח, זן, אל יהוה וַהֲשֵׁבֹתָ vahashevota אֶל־ el
לְבָבֶךָ lvavecha ר"ת לאו כִּי ki יְהֹוָהאדניאהדונהי Adonai הוּא hu
הָאֱלֹהִים haElohim אהיה אדני ; ילה ; ר"ת יהה וכן עולה למנין ענו עג"כ
בַּשָּׁמַיִם bashamayim י"פ טל, י"פ כוזו מִמַּעַל mima'al עלם ;
רמז לאור פנימי המתוז"ל מלמעלה וְעַל־ ve'al הָאָרֶץ ha'aretz אלהים דההין ע"ה
מִתָּחַת mitachat רמז לאור מקיף המתוז"ל מלמטה אֵין en עוֹד od:

עַל al כֵּן ken נְקַוֶּה nekave לְּךָ lach יְהֹוָהאדניאהדונהי Adonai
אֱלֹהֵינוּ Elohenu ילה לִרְאוֹת lir'ot מְהֵרָה mehera בְּתִפְאֶרֶת betiferet
עֻזָּךְ uzach ס"ת כהת, משיח בן דוד ע"ה לְהַעֲבִיר leha'avir גִּלּוּלִים gilulim
מִן min הָאָרֶץ ha'aretz אלהים דההין ע"ה וְהָאֱלִילִים veha'elilim
כָּרוֹת karot יִכָּרֵתוּן yikaretun. לְתַקֵּן letaken עוֹלָם olam
בְּמַלְכוּת bemalchut שַׁדַּי Shadai. וְכָל vechol ילי בְּנֵי benei
בָשָׂר vasar יִקְרְאוּ yikre'u בִשְׁמֶךָ vishmecha לְהַפְנוֹת lehafnot
אֵלֶיךָ eleicha כָּל kol ילי רִשְׁעֵי rish'ei אֶרֶץ aretz.

The Seat of His glory is in the Heaven above and the Divine Presence of His power is in the Highest of Heights. He is our God and there is no other. Our King is true and there is none beside Him. As it is written in the Torah: "And you shall know today and you shall take it to your heart that it is the Lord Who is God in the Heavens above and upon the Earth below, and there is none other". (Deuteronomy 4:39) Consequently, we place our hope in You, Lord, our God, that we shall speedily see the glory of Your might, when You remove the idols from the earth and the deities shall be completely destroyed to correct the world with the kingdom of the Almighty. And all mankind shall then call out Your Name and You shall turn back to Yourself all the wicked ones of the earth.

יַכִּירוּ yakiru וְיֵדְעוּ veyed'u כָּל kol ילי יוֹשְׁבֵי yoshvei תֵבֵל tevel ב״פ רי״ו.

כִּי ki לְךָ lecha תִּכְרַע tichra כָּל־ kol ילי בֶּרֶךְ berech תִּשָּׁבַע tishava

כָּל kol ילי לָשׁוֹן lashon. לְפָנֶיךָ lefanecha ס״ג מ״ה ב״ן יְהֹוָה יאהדונהי Adonai

אֱלֹהֵינוּ Elohenu ילה יִכְרְעוּ yichre'u וְיִפֹּלוּ veyipolu וְלִכְבוֹד velichvod

שִׁמְךָ shimcha יְקָר yekar יִתֵּנוּ yitenu. וִיקַבְּלוּ vikabelu כֻלָּם chulam אֶת et

עוֹל־ ol מַלְכוּתֶךָ malchutecha. וְתִמְלוֹךְ vetimloch עֲלֵיהֶם alehem

מְהֵרָה mehera לְעוֹלָם le'olam ריבוע ס״ג וי׳ אותיות דס״ג וָעֶד va'ed. כִּי ki

הַמַּלְכוּת hamalchut שֶׁלְּךָ shelcha הִיא hee. וּלְעוֹלְמֵי ul'olmei

עַד ad תִּמְלוֹךְ timloch בְּכָבוֹד bechavod בוכו. כַּכָּתוּב kakatuv

בְּתוֹרָתָךְ betoratach: יְהֹוָה יאהדונהי Adonai | יִמְלֹךְ yimloch לְעֹלָם le'olam

ריבוע ס״ג וי׳ אותיות דס״ג ; ר״ת ייל וָעֶד va'ed. וְנֶאֱמַר vene'emar: וְהָיָה vehaya יהוה ; יהה

יְהֹוָה יאהדונהי Adonai לְמֶלֶךְ lemelech עַל־ al כָּל־ kol ילי ; עמם

הָאָרֶץ ha'aretz אלהים דההין ע״ה בַּיּוֹם bayom ע״ה נגד, מזבח, זן, אל יהוה

הַהוּא hahu יִהְיֶה yih'ye ייי יְהֹוָה יאהדונהי Adonai אֶחָד echad אהבה, דאגה

וּשְׁמוֹ ushmo מהש ע״ה, ע״ב בריבוע וקס״א ע״ה, אל שדי ע״ה אֶחָד echad אהבה, דאגה:

Then all the inhabitants of the world shall recognize and know that, for You, every knee bends and every tongue vows. Before You, Lord, our God, they shall kneel and fall and shall give honor to Your glorious Name. And they shall all accept the yoke of Your Kingdom and You shall reign over them, forever and ever. Because the kingdom is Yours. and forever and for eternity, You shall reign gloriously. As it is written in the Torah: "The Lord shall reign forever and ever," (Exodus 15:18) and it is also stated: "The Lord shall be King over the whole world and, on that day, the Lord shall be One and His Name One." (Zechariah 14:9)

ARVIT OF MOTZA'EI SHAVUOT

In the evening prayer of *Arvit*, we connect to Jacob the Patriarch, who is the channel for Central Column energy. He helps us connect the two energies of Judgment and Mercy in a balanced way. It is said that the whole world was created only for Jacob, who embodies truth: "Give truth to Jacob" *(Michah 7:20)*. To activate the power of our prayer, and specifically the power of the prayer of *Arvit*, we must be truthful with others and, most importantly, with ourselves.

LESHEM YICHUD

לְשֵׁם leshem יִחוּד yichud קוּדְשָׁא kudsha בְּרִיךְ berich הוּא hu

וּשְׁכִינְתֵּיהּ ush'chintei (יאהדונהי) בִּדְחִילוּ bid'chilu וּרְחִימוּ ur'chimu

(יאההויהה) וּרְחִימוּ ur'chimu וּדְחִילוּ ud'chilu (איההיוהה) לְיַחֲדָא leyachda

שֵׁם shem יוּ״ד yud קֵ״י kei בְּוָא״ו bevav קֵ״י kei בְּיִחוּדָא beyichuda

שְׁלִים shelim (יהוה) בְּשֵׁם beshem כָּל kol ילי יִשְׂרָאֵל Yisrael,

הִנֵּה hine אֲנַחְנוּ anachnu בָּאִים ba'im לְהִתְפַּלֵּל lehitpalel תְּפִלַּת tefilat

עַרְבִית arvit שֶׁתִּקֵּן shetiken יַעֲקֹב Yaakov ו׳ הויות, יאהדונהי אידהנויה אָבִינוּ avinu

עָלָיו alav הַשָּׁלוֹם hashalom עִם im כָּל kol ילי הַמִּצְוֺת hamitzvot

הַכְּלוּלוֹת hakelulot בָּהּ ba לְתַקֵּן letaken אֶת et שׁוֹרְשָׁהּ shorsha

בְּמָקוֹם bemakom עֶלְיוֹן elyon לַעֲשׂוֹת la'asot נַחַת nachat רוּחַ ru'ach

לְיוֹצְרֵנוּ leyotzrenu וְלַעֲשׂוֹת vela'asot רְצוֹן retzon מהש ע״ה, ע״ב בריבוע וקס״א ע״ה,

אל שדי ע״ה בּוֹרְאֵינוּ bor'enu. וִיהִי vihi נֹעַם no'am אֲדֹנָי Adonai ללה

אֱלֹהֵינוּ Elohenu ילה עָלֵינוּ alenu וּמַעֲשֵׂה uma'ase יָדֵינוּ yadenu

כּוֹנְנָה konena עָלֵינוּ alenu וּמַעֲשֵׂה uma'ase יָדֵינוּ yadenu כּוֹנְנֵהוּ konenehu:

ARVIT OF MOTZA'EI SHAVUOT - LESHEM YICHUD

For the sake of unification of The Holy Blessed One and His Shechinah, with fear and love and with love and fear, in order to unify The Name Yud-Kei and Vav-Kei in perfect unity, and in the name of Israel, we have hereby come to recite the prayer of Arvit, established by Jacob, our forefather, may peace be upon him, With all its commandments, to correct its root in the supernal place, to bring satisfaction to our Maker, and to fulfill the wish of our Creator. "And may the pleasantness of Lord, our God, be upon us and may He establish the work of our hands for us and may the work of our hands establish Him." (Psalms 90:17)

Right

יְהֹוָ‍אדניאהדונהי Adonai צְבָאוֹת Tzeva'ot פני שכינה עִמָּנוּ imanu

ריבוע ס"ג, קס"א ע"ה וד' אותיות מִשְׂגָּב misgav מושה, מהש, ריבוע ע"ב וקס"א, אל שדי,

ד"פ אלהים ע"ה לָנוּ lanu אלהים, אהיה אדני אֱלֹהֵי Elohei מילוי ע"ב, דמב ; ילה

יַעֲקֹב Yaakov ו' הויות, יאהדונהי אידהנויה סֶלָה sela:

Left

יְהֹוָ‍אדניאהדונהי Adonai צְבָאוֹת Tzeva'ot פני שכינה אַשְׁרֵי ashrei

אָדָם adam מ"ה ; ה' צבאות אשרי אדם = תפארת בֹּטֵחַ bote'ach

בָּךְ bach אדם בוטח בך = אמן (יאהדונהי) ע"ה ; בוטח בך = מילוי ע"ב ע"ה:

Central

יְהֹוָ‍אדניאהדונהי Adonai הוֹשִׁיעָה hoshi'a יהוה וש"ע נהורין הַמֶּלֶךְ hamelech ר"ת יהה

יַעֲנֵנוּ ya'anenu בְיוֹם veyom ע"ה נגד, מזבח, זן, אל יהוה קָרְאֵנוּ kor'enu

ר"ת יב"ק, אלהים יהוה, אהיה אדני יהוה ; ס"ת = ב"ן ועם אות כ' דהמלך = ע"ב:

HALF KADDISH

יִתְגַּדַּל yitgadal וְיִתְקַדַּשׁ veyitkadash שדי ומילוי שדי ; י"א אותיות כמנין ו"ה

שְׁמֵיהּ shemei (שם י"ה דע"ב) רַבָּא raba קנ"א ב"ן, יהוה אלהים יהוה אדני,

מילוי קס"א וס"ג, מ"ה ברבוע וע"ב ע"ה ; ר"ת = ו"פ אלהים ; ס"ת = ג"פ יב"ק: אָמֵן amen אידהנויה.

בְּעָלְמָא be'alma דִּי di בְרָא vera כִּרְעוּתֵיהּ chir'utei.

וְיַמְלִיךְ veyamlich מַלְכוּתֵיהּ mal'chutei. וְיַצְמַח veyatzmach

פּוּרְקָנֵיהּ purkanei. וִיקָרֵב vikarev מְשִׁיחֵיהּ meshichei: אָמֵן amen אידהנויה.

"The Lord of Hosts, joyful is one who trusts in You." (Psalms 84:13)
"The Lord of Hosts is with us. The God of Jacob is a refuge for us, Selah.
Lord redeem us. The King shall answer us on the day we call Him." (Psalms 20:10)

HALF KADDISH

May His great Name be more exalted and sanctified. (Amen)
In the world that He created according to His will, and may His Kingdom reign.
And may He cause His redemption to sprout and may He bring the Mashiach closer. (Amen)

בְּחַיֵּיכוֹן bechayechon וּבְיוֹמֵיכוֹן uvyomechon וּבְחַיֵּי uvchayei

דְּכָל dechol ילי בֵּית bet ב"פ ראה יִשְׂרָאֵל Yisrael בַּעֲגָלָא ba'agala

וּבִזְמַן uvizman קָרִיב kariv וְאִמְרוּ ve'imru אָמֵן amen: אָמֵן amen אידהנויה.

The congregation and the *chazan* say the following:

28 words (until *be'alma*) – meditate:

מילוי דמילוי דע"ב (יוד ויו דלת הי יוד ויו יוד ויו הי יוד)

28 letters (until *almaya*) – meditate:

מילוי דמילוי דס"ג (יוד ויו דלת הי יוד ואו אלף ואו הי יוד)

יְהֵא yehe שְׁמֵיהּ shemei (שם י"ה דס"ג) רַבָּא raba קנ"א ב"ן,

יהוה אלהים יהוה אדני, מילוי קס"א וס"ג, מ"ה ברבוע וע"ב ע"ה מְבָרַךְ: mevarach

לְעָלַם le'alam לְעָלְמֵי le'almei עָלְמַיָּא almaya. יִתְבָּרַךְ yitbarach.

Seven words with six letters each (שם בן מ"ב) – meditate:

יהוה - יוד הי ויו הי - מילוי דמילוי דע"ב (יוד ויו דלת הי יוד ויו יוד ויו הי יוד)

Also, seven times the letter Vav (שם בן מ"ב) – meditate:

יהוה - יוד הי ואו הי - מילוי דמילוי דס"ג (יוד ויו דלת הי יוד ואו אלף ואו הי יוד).

וְיִשְׁתַּבַּח veyishtabach י"פ ע"ב יהוה אל אבג יתץ.

וְיִתְפָּאַר veyitpa'ar הי גו יה קרע שטן. וְיִתְרוֹמַם veyitromam וה כוזו נגד יכש.

וְיִתְנַשֵּׂא veyitnase במוכסז בטר צתג. וְיִתְהַדָּר veyit'hadar כוזו יה וזקב טנע.

וְיִתְעַלֶּה veyit'ale וה יוד ה יגל פזק. וְיִתְהַלָּל veyit'halal א ואו הא שקו צית.

שְׁמֵיהּ shemei (שם י"ה דמ"ה) דְּקוּדְשָׁא dekudsha בְּרִיךְ verich הוּא hu:

אָמֵן amen אידהנויה.

לְעֵלָּא le'ela מִן min כָּל kol ילי בִּרְכָתָא birchata. שִׁירָתָא shirata.

תֻּשְׁבְּחָתָא tishbechata וְנֶחָמָתָא venechamata. דַּאֲמִירָן da'amiran

בְּעָלְמָא be'alma וְאִמְרוּ ve'imru אָמֵן amen: אָמֵן amen אידהנויה.

In your lifetimes and in your days and in the lifetime of all the House of Israel, speedily and in the near future, and you should say, Amen. (Amen) May His great Name be blessed forever and for all eternity blessed and lauded, and glorified and exalted, and extolled and honored, and uplifted and praised be, the Name of the Holy Blessed One. (Amen) Above all blessings, songs, praises, and words of consolation that may be said in the world, and you shall say, Amen. (Amen)

VEHU RACHUM

"*Vehu Rachum*" contains thirteen words. The number thirteen denotes the Thirteen Attributes of Mercy, which, in this instance, we recite to cool down the fires of hell for all who reside there.

There are 13 words corresponding to the 13 Atributes of Mercy of *Arich Anpin*.

וְהוּא vehu רַחוּם rachum יְכַפֵּר yechaper ר"ת רי"ו עָוֺן avon (*Abba of the klipa*)

וְלֹא velo יַשְׁחִית yashchit (*Ima of the klipa*) וְהִרְבָּה vehirba לְהָשִׁיב lehashiv

אַפּוֹ apo (*Zeir of the klipa*) וְלֹא velo יָעִיר ya'ir כָּל kol ילי חֲמָתוֹ chamato

(*Nukva of the klipa*): יְהֹוָהאדניאהדונהי Adonai הוֹשִׁיעָה hoshi'a יהוה וש"ע נהורין

הַמֶּלֶךְ hamelech ר"ת יהה יַעֲנֵנוּ ya'anenu בְיוֹם veyom ע"ה נגד, מזבח, זן אל יהוה

קָרְאֵנוּ kor'enu ר"ת יב"ק, אלהים יהוה, אהיה אדני יהוה ; ס"ת ב"ן ועם כ' דהמלך = ע"ב:

BARCHU

The *chazan* says:

בָּרְכוּ barchu יהוה ריבוע יהוה ריבוע מ"ה אֶת et יְהֹוָהאדניאהדונהי Adonai

הַמְבוֹרָךְ hamevorach ס"ת כהת, משיח בן דוד ע"ה:

First the congregation replies the following, and then the *chazan* repeats it:

Nefesh בָּרוּךְ baruch *Ruach* יְהֹוָהאדניאהדונהי Adonai *Neshamah* הַמְבוֹרָךְ hamevorach

Chayah לְעוֹלָם le'olam ריבוע ס"ג וי' אותיות דס"ג *Yechidah* וָעֶד va'ed:

VEHU RACHUM

And He is merciful,

forgives iniquity, and does not destroy; He frequently diverts His anger and does not arouse all His wrath." (Psalms 70:38) *"Lord save us. The King shall answer on the day that we call Him."* (Psalms 20:10)

BARCHU

Bless the Lord, the Blessed One.

Blessed be the Lord, the Blessed One, forever and for eternity.

HAMA'ARIV ARAVIM – FIRST CHAMBER – LIVNAT HASAPIR

In the time of *Arvit*, we have an opportunity to connect to four different "Chambers" in the House of the King - Chamber of Sapphire Stone (*Livnat Hasapir*), Chamber of Love (*Ahavah*), Chamber of Desire (*Ratzon*), and the Chamber of Holy of Holies (*Kodesh HaKodeshim*). Each Chamber connects us to another level in the spiritual plane. The blessing connecting us to the First Chamber, *Livnat Hasapir*, contains 53 words, which is also the numerical value of the word gan גַּן, meaning "garden," therefore connecting us to the Garden of Eden of our world.

Hechal Livnat Hasapir (the Sapphire Stone Chamber) of *Nukva* in *Beriah*.

בָּרוּךְ baruch אַתָּה Ata יְהֹוָהאדניאהדונהי Adonai אֱלֹהֵינוּ Elohenu ילה

מֶלֶךְ melech הָעוֹלָם ha'olam אֲשֶׁר asher בִּדְבָרוֹ bidvaro מַעֲרִיב ma'ariv

עֲרָבִים aravim בְּחָכְמָה bechochmah (*Atzilut*) במילוי = תרי"ג (מצוות)•

פּוֹתֵחַ pote'ach שְׁעָרִים she'arim כתר בִּתְבוּנָה bitvuna •(*Beriah*)

מְשַׁנֶּה meshane עִתִּים itim (*Yetzirah*) וּמַחֲלִיף umachalif אֶת et

הַזְּמַנִּים hazemanim (*Asiyah*) וּמְסַדֵּר umsader אֶת et הַכּוֹכָבִים hakochavim

(*The Seven Planets*)• בְּמִשְׁמְרוֹתֵיהֶם bemishmerotehem בָּרָקִיעַ baraki'a

כִּרְצוֹנוֹ kirtzono• בּוֹרֵא bore יוֹמָם yomam וָלָיְלָה valayla •מלה גּוֹלֵל golel

אוֹר or רז, אין סוף מִפְּנֵי mipenei חֹשֶׁךְ choshech שך נצוצות של ז' המלכים

וְחֹשֶׁךְ vechoshech שך נצוצות של ז' המלכים מִפְּנֵי mipenei אוֹר or רז, אין סוף•

הַמַּעֲבִיר hama'avir יוֹם yom ע"ה נגד, מזבח, זן, אל יהוה וּמֵבִיא umevi לָיְלָה layla

•מלה וּמַבְדִּיל umavdil בֵּין ben יוֹם yom ע"ה נגד, מזבח, זן, אל יהוה וּבֵין uven

לָיְלָה layla •מלה יְהֹוָהאדניאהדונהי Adonai צְבָאוֹת Tzeva'ot פני שכינה שְׁמוֹ shemo

מהש ע"ה, ע"ב בריבוע וקס"א ע"ה, אל שדי ע"ה יְהֹוָהאדניאהדונהי Adonai• בָּרוּךְ baruch

אַתָּה Ata יְהֹוָהאדניאהדונהי Adonai הַמַּעֲרִיב hama'ariv עֲרָבִים aravim:

HAMA'ARIV ARAVIM – FIRST CHAMBER – LIVNAT HASAPIR

Blessed are You, Lord, our God, King of the universe,

Who brings with His words evenings with wisdom. He opens gates with understanding. He changes the seasons and varies the times and arranges the stars in their constellations in the sky, according to His will. He creates day and night and rolls Light away from before darkness, and darkness from before Light. He is the One Who causes the day to pass and brings on night and separates between day and night. Lord of Hosts, His Name is the Lord. Blessed are You, Lord, who brings on evenings.

AHAVAT OLAM – SECOND CHAMBER - LOVE

This blessing connects us to the Second Chamber, *Ahavah* (Love) and its purpose is to inspire us with a renewed love for others and for the world.

Hechal Ahavah (the Love Chamber) of *Nukva* in *Beriah*.
The following paragraph has 50 words corresponding to the 50 Gates of *Binah*.

אַהֲבַת ahavat עוֹלָם olam בֵּית bet ב"פ ראה יִשְׂרָאֵל Yisrael עַמְּךָ amecha

אָהָבְתָּ ♦ahavta תּוֹרָה torah (*Atzilut*) וּמִצְוֹת umitzvot (*Beriah*) חֻקִּים chukim

(*Yetzirah*) וּמִשְׁפָּטִים umishpatim (*Asiyah*) אוֹתָנוּ otanu לִמַּדְתָּ ♦limadeta

עַל al כֵּן ken יְהֹוָה אהדונהי Adonai אֱלֹהֵינוּ Elohenu ילה

בְּשָׁכְבֵנוּ beshochvenu וּבְקוּמֵנוּ uvkumenu נָשִׂיחַ nasi'ach בְּחֻקֶּיךָ bechukecha

וְנִשְׂמַח venismach וְנַעֲלוֹז vena'aloz בְּדִבְרֵי bedivrei תַלְמוּד talmud

תּוֹרָתֶךָ toratecha וּמִצְוֹתֶיךָ umitzvotecha וְחֻקּוֹתֶיךָ vechukotecha

לְעוֹלָם le'olam ריבוע דס"ג וי' אותיות דס"ג וָעֶד ♦va'ed כִּי ki הֵם hem

חַיֵּינוּ chayenu וְאֹרֶךְ ve'orech יָמֵינוּ yamenu וּבָהֶם uvahem נֶהְגֶּה nehge

יוֹמָם yomam וָלַיְלָה valayla מלה♦ וְאַהֲבָתְךָ ve'ahavatcha לֹא lo תָסוּר tasur

מִמֶּנּוּ mimenu לְעוֹלָמִים ♦le'olamim בָּרוּךְ baruch אַתָּה Ata

יְהֹוָה אהדונהי Adonai אוֹהֵב ohev אֶת et עַמּוֹ amo יִשְׂרָאֵל Yisrael:

THE SHEMA (to learn more about the *Shema* go to pg. 351)

The *Shema* is one of the most powerful tools to draw the energy of healing to our lives. The true power of the *Shema* is unleashed when we recite this prayer while meditating on others who need healing energy.

1) In order to receive the Light of the *Shema*, you have to accept upon yourself the precept of: "Love your neighbor as yourself," and see yourself united with all the souls that comprise the Original Adam.
2) You need to meditate to connect to the precept of the Reciting of *Shema* twice a day.
3) Before saying the *Shema* you should cover your eyes with your right hand (saying the words "*Shema Yisrael ... le'olam va'ed*".) And you should read the *Shema* with deep meditation, chanting it with the intonations. It is necessary to be careful with the pronunciation of all the letters.

AHAVAT OLAM – SECOND CHAMBER - LOVE

With eternal love, You have loved Your Nation, the House of Israel.
Torah, commandments, statutes, and laws, You have taught us. Therefore, Lord, our God, when we lie down and when we rise up, we shall discuss Your statutes and we shall rejoice and exult in the words of the teachings of Your Torah, Your commandments, and Your statutes, forever and ever. They are our lifetimes and the length of our days; with them we shall direct ourselves day and night. And Your love, You shall never remove from us. Blessed are You, Lord, Who loves His Nation, Israel.

First, meditate in general, on the first *Yichud* of the four *Yichuds* of the Name: יהוה, and in particular, to awaken the letter ה, and then to connect it with the letter ו. Then connect the letter י and the letter ה together in the following order: *Hei* (ה), *Hei-Vav* (ה"ו), then *Yud-Hei* (י"ה), which adds up to 31, the secret of "יא" of the Name ס"ג. It is good to meditate on this *Yichud* before reciting any *Shema* because it acts as a replacement for the times that you may have missed reading the *Shema*. This *Yichud* has the same ability to create a Supernal connection like the reading of the *Shema* - to raise *Zeir* and *Nukva* together for the *Zivug* of *Abba* and *Ima*.

Shema – שְׁמַע

General Meditation: שם ע — to draw the energy from the seven lower *Sefirot* of *Ima* to the *Nukva*, which enables the *Nukva* to elevate the *Mayin Nukvin* (awakening from Below). **Particular Meditation:** שם = יהוה + שדי and five times the letters י and ד of ב"ן = ע [The letter *Hei* (ה) is formed by the letters *Dalet* (ד) and *Yud* (י), so in ב"ן we have four times the letter ה plus another time the letters י and ד from יוד of ב"ן.]. Also the three letters ו (18) - that are left from ב"ן, plus ב"ן itself (52) equals ע (70).

Yisrael – יִשְׂרָאֵל

General Meditation: שיר אל — to draw energy from *Chesed* and *Gevurah* of *Abba* to *Zeir Anpin*, to do his action in the secret of *Mayin Duchrin* (awakening from Above).

Particular Meditation: (the rearranged letters of the word *Yisrael*) – שר אלי

אלהים דיודין (אלף למד הי יוד מם) = ש',

רבוע אלהים (א אל אלה אלהי אלהים) = ר',

מ"א אותיות רבוע אלהים במילואו (אלף אלף למד אלף למד הי אלף למד הי יוד אלף למד הי יוד מם) = אל"י.

Also meditate to draw the Inner *Mochin* of *Abba* of *Katnut* into *Zeir Anpin*.

Adonai Elohenu Adonai - יהוה אלהינו יהוה

General Meditation: to draw energy to *Abba*, *Ima* and *Da'at* from *Arich Anpin*,

Particular Meditation: ע"ב (יוד הי ויו הי) קס"א (אלף הי יוד הי) ע"ב (יוד הי וי הי).

Echad – אֶחָד

(The secret of the complete *Yichud-Unification*)

The letters *Alef* א and *Chet* ח from *Echad* אחד are *Zeir Anpin* and the letter *Dalet* ד is *Nukva*. **You should meditate** to devote your soul for the sanctification of the Holy Name, thereby elevating your *Nefesh*, *Ruach*, *Neshamah* and *Neshamah* of *Neshamah* with *Zeir Anpin* and *Nukva* (using the Names: ע"ב and ס"ג) to *Abba* and *Ima* as the secret of *Mayin Nukvin*, and by that energy, *Abba* and *Ima* will be unified in the secret of the Name: יאהדויה"ה. **Also meditate** to draw out the Inner Six Edges of *Gadlut* of *Ima* into *Zeir Anpin*. The Drop, which is ע"ב, is drawn out from the external of *Arich Anpin*, and descends to *Yesod* of *Ima*, where it becomes: ע"ב ס"ג מ"ה ב"ן, and the four spelled out אהיה (אלף הי יוד הי, אלף הי יוד הי, אלף הא יוד הא, אלף הה יוד הה) become Her clothing. As a result, *Zeir Anpin* now has four spelled out יה"ו (יוד הי ויו, יוד הי ואו, יוד הא ואו, יוד הה וו), four spelled out אה"י (אלף הי יוד, אלף הי יוד, אלף הא יוד, אלף הה יוד) and the Inner Six Edges of *Gadlut* of *Ima*. **Also meditate** on the Name: אל"ף ה"י וי"ו ה"י, which is the entire *Mochin* in the secret of *Da'at*. **And also meditate** (according to the Ramchal) on the four spelled out *Alef* (אלף=111) of the Name: אהי"ה that is equal to the word *Midat (444)*, making the *Keter* for *Leah*.

Baruch Shem - בָּרוּךְ שֵׁם כְּבוֹד מַלְכוּתוֹ לְעוֹלָם וָעֶד

Baruch Shem Kevod – *Chochmah*, *Binah*, *Da'at* of *Leah*;

Malchuto – Her *Keter*; ***Le'olam*** – the rest of Her *Partzuf*;

Va'ed – the four היה (4 times 20 equal to *Va'ed*=80) will make the *Keter* for *Rachel* .

And the four spelled out היה (הי יוד הי, הי יוד הי, הא יוד הא, הה יוד הה) will make the rest of Her body.

שְׁמַע shema ע' רבתי יִשְׂרָאֵל Yisrael יְהֹוָהאדני יאהדונהי Adonai

אֱלֹהֵינוּ Elohenu ילה יְהֹוָהאדני יאהדונהי Adonai | אֶחָד echad ד' רבתי ; אהבה, דאגה:

(Whisper :) יוזו אותיות בָּרוּךְ baruch שֵׁם shem כְּבוֹד kevod מַלְכוּתוֹ malchuto,

לְעוֹלָם le'olam ריבוע דס"ג וי' אותיות דס"ג וָעֶד va'ed:

***Yud, Chochmah,* head** – 42 words corresponding to the Holy 42-Letter Name of God.

א ב

וְאָהַבְתָּ ve'ahavta ב"פ אור, ב"פ רז, ב"פ אין סוף ; (יכוין לקיים מ"ע של אהבת ה') אֵת et

ג י

יְהֹוָהאדני יאהדונהי Adonai אֱלֹהֶיךָ Elohecha ילה ; ס"ת כהת, משיח בן דוד ע"ה

ת צ ק ר

בְּכָל־ bechol ב"ן, לכב לְבָבְךָ levavcha וּבְכָל־ uvchol ב"ן, לכב נַפְשְׁךָ nafshecha

ע ש ט נ

וּבְכָל־ uvchol ב"ן, לכב מְאֹדֶךָ me'odecha: וְהָיוּ vehayu הַדְּבָרִים hadevarim

נ ג ד י כ

הָאֵלֶּה ha'ele אֲשֶׁר asher אָנֹכִי anochi מְצַוְּךָ metzavecha הַיּוֹם hayom

ש ב ט

ע"ה נגד, מזבח, זן, אל יהוה (pause here) עַל al לְבָבֶךָ levavecha: וְשִׁנַּנְתָּם veshinantam

ר צ ת ג

לְבָנֶיךָ levanecha וְדִבַּרְתָּ vedibarta בָּם bam מ"ב בְּשִׁבְתְּךָ beshivtecha

חז ק ב

בְּבֵיתֶךָ bevetecha ב"פ ראה וּבְלֶכְתְּךָ uvlechtecha בַדֶּרֶךְ vadcrech

ט נ

ב"פ יב"ק, ס"ג קס"א וּבְשָׁכְבְּךָ uvshochbecha וּבְקוּמֶךָ uvkumecha:

ע י ג ל

וּקְשַׁרְתָּם ukshartam לְאוֹת le'ot עַל־ al יָדֶךָ yadecha

THE SHEMA

"Hear Israel, the Lord our God. The Lord is One." (Deuteronomy 6:4)

"Blessed is the glorious Name, His Kingdom is forever and for eternity." (Pesachim 56a)

"And you shall love the Lord, your God, with all your heart and with all your soul and with all that you possess. Let those words that I command you today be upon your heart. And you shall teach them to your children and you shall speak of them while you sit in your home and while you walk on your way and when you lie down and when you rise. You shall bind them as a sign upon your hand

פ וְהָיוּ vehayu ז לְטֹטָפֹת letotafot ק בֵּין ben ש עֵינֶיךָ enecha

ע"ה קס"א ; ריבוע מ"ה: ק וּכְתַבְתָּם uchtavtam ו עַל־ al

צ מְזֻזוֹת mezuzot ג"ת (זו מות) י בֵּיתֶךָ betecha ב"פ ראה ת וּבִשְׁעָרֶיךָ uvish'arecha:

VEHAYA IM SHAMO'A

***Hei, Binah,* arms and body** – 72 words corresponding to the 72 Names of God.

והו וְהָיָה vehaya יהוה ; יהה ילי אִם־ im יוה"ך, מ"א אותיות דפשוט, דמילוי ודמילוי דמילוי דאהיה ע"ה

סיט שָׁמֹעַ shamo'a עלם תִּשְׁמְעוּ tishme'u מהש אֶל־ el ללה מִצְוֺתַי mitzvotai אכא אֲשֶׁר asher

כהת אָנֹכִי anochi הזי מְצַוֶּה metzave אלד אֶתְכֶם etchem לאו הַיּוֹם hayom ע"ה נגד, מזבח, זן, אל יהוה

(pause here) ההע לְאַהֲבָה le'ahava אחד, דאגה יזל אֶת־ et מבה יְהוָֹאדהנויאהדונהי Adonai

הרי אֱלֹהֵיכֶם Elohechem ילה (enunciate the letter *Ayin* in the word "*ul'ovdo*") הקם וּלְעָבְדוֹ ul'ovdo

לאו בְּכָל bechol ב"ן, לכב כלי לְבַבְכֶם levavchem לוו וּבְכָל־ uvchol ב"ן, לכב

פהל נַפְשְׁכֶם nafshechem: נלך וְנָתַתִּי venatati ייי מְטַר־ metar מלה אַרְצְכֶם artzechem

ווהו בְּעִתּוֹ be'ito נתה יוֹרֶה yore האא וּמַלְקוֹשׁ umalkosh ירת וְאָסַפְתָּ ve'asafta שאה דְגָנֶךָ deganecha

ריי וְתִירֹשְׁךָ vetiroshcha אום וְיִצְהָרֶךָ veyitz'harecha: לכב וְנָתַתִּי venatati ושר עֵשֶׂב esev ע"ב שמות

---

and they shall be as frontlets between your eyes.
And you shall write them upon the doorposts of your house and your gates." (Deuteronomy 6:5-9)

VEHAYA IM SHAMO'A

"And it shall come to be that if you shall listen to My commandments that I am commanding you with today to love the Lord, your God, and to serve Him with all your heart and with all your soul, then I shall send rain upon your land in its proper time, both early rain and late rain. You shall then gather your grain and your wine and your oil. And I shall give grass

יוזו להוו כוק מנד
בְּשָׂדְךָ besadcha לִבְהֶמְתֶּךָ livhemtecha וְאָכַלְתָּ ve'achalta וְשָׂבָעְתָּ vesavata:

אני וזעם רהע ייז ההה
הִשָּׁמְרוּ hishamru לָכֶם lachem פֶּן־ pen יִפְתֶּה yifte לְבַבְכֶם levavchem

מיכ וול ילה סאל
וְסַרְתֶּם vesartem וַעֲבַדְתֶּם va'avadetem אֱלֹהִים elohim אֲחֵרִים acherim

ערי עשל
משה (העומד נגד הקליפות) וְהִשְׁתַּחֲוִיתֶם vehishtachavitem לָהֶם lahem:

מיה והו דני הוזש
וְחָרָה vechara (pause here) אַף־ af יְהֹוָהאדניאהדונהי Adonai בָּכֶם bachem

עמם ננא נית מבה
וְעָצַר ve'atzar אֶת־ et הַשָּׁמַיִם hashamayim י"פ טל, י"פ כוזו וְלֹא־ velo

פוי נמם ייל הרוז מצר
יִהְיֶה yihye ייי מָטָר matar וְהָאֲדָמָה veha'adama לֹא lo תִתֵּן titen ב"פ כהת

ומב יהה ענו מוזי דמב
אֶת־ et יְבוּלָהּ yevula וַאֲבַדְתֶּם va'avadetem מְהֵרָה mehera מֵעַל me'al עלם

מנק איע וזבו
הָאָרֶץ ha'aretz אלהים דההין ע"ה הַטֹּבָה hatova אֲשֶׁר asher

ראה יבמ היי
יְהֹוָהאדניאהדונהי Adonai נֹתֵן noten אבג יתץ, ושר לָכֶם lachem: *Vav, Zeir Anpin*

מום
וְשַׂמְתֶּם vesamtem **stomach** – 50 words corresponding to the 50 Gates of *Binah*

א ה י ה א
אֶת־ et דְּבָרַי devarai ראה אֵלֶּה ele עַל־ al לְבַבְכֶם levavchem

ה י ה א
וְעַל־ ve'al נַפְשְׁכֶם nafshechem וּקְשַׁרְתֶּם ukshartem אֹתָם otam

---

in your field for your cattle. And you shall eat and you shall be satiated. Be careful lest your heart be seduced and you may turn away and serve alien deities and prostrate yourself before them. And the wrath of the Lord shall be upon you and He shall stop the Heavens and there shall be no more rain and the earth shall not give forth its crop. And you shall quickly perish from the good land that the Lord has given you. And you shall place those words of Mine upon your heart and upon your soul and you shall bind them

לְאוֹת le'ot ר״ת לאו עַל־ al יֶדְכֶם yedchem וְהָיוּ vehayu

לְטוֹטָפֹת letotafot בֵּין ben עֵינֵיכֶם enechem ריבוע מ״ה:

וְלִמַּדְתֶּם velimadetem אֹתָם otam אֶת־ et בְּנֵיכֶם benechem

לְדַבֵּר ledaber ראה בָּם bam שׂם בן מ״ב בְּשִׁבְתְּךָ beshivtecha

בְּבֵיתֶךָ bevetecha ב״פ ראה וּבְלֶכְתְּךָ uvlechtecha בַדֶּרֶךְ vaderech ב״פ יב״ק, ס״ג קס״א

וּבְשָׁכְבְּךָ uvshochbecha וּבְקוּמֶךָ uvkumecha: וּכְתַבְתָּם uchtavtam עַל־ al

מְזוּזוֹת mezuzot בֵּיתֶךָ betecha ב״פ ראה וּבִשְׁעָרֶיךָ uvish'arecha: לְמַעַן lema'an

יִרְבּוּ yirbu יְמֵיכֶם yemechem ר״ת יי״ל וִימֵי vimei בְנֵיכֶם venechem

עַל al הָאֲדָמָה ha'adama אֲשֶׁר asher (enunciate the letter *Ayin* in the word "*nishba*")

נִשְׁבַּע nishba יכוין לשבועת המבול יְהֹוָהאדניאהדונהי Adonai

לַאֲבֹתֵיכֶם la'avotechem לָתֵת latet לָהֶם lahem כִּימֵי kimei

הַשָּׁמַיִם hashamayim י״פ טל, י״פ כוזו עַל־ al הָאָרֶץ ha'aretz אלהים דההין ע״ה:

---

as a sign upon your hands and they shall be as frontlets between your eyes. And you shall teach them to your children and speak of them while you sit at home and while you walk on your way and when you lie down and when you rise. You shall write them upon the doorposts of your house and upon your gates. This is so that your days shall be numerous and so shall the days of your children upon the Earth that the Lord had sworn to your fathers to give them as the days of the Heavens upon the Earth." (Deuteronomy 11:13-21)

VAYOMER

Hei, Malchut, legs and reproductive organs,

72 words corresponding to the 72 Names of God in direct order (according to the Ramchal).

וו ייי סבט עאם

וַיֹּאמֶר vayomer · יְהֹוָהאדניאהדונהי Adonai · אֶל־ el · מֹשֶׁה Moshe

מבש ליה אנא

מהש, ע״ב בריבוע וקס״א, אל שדי, ד״פ אלהים ע״ה · לֵּאמֹר lemor: · דַּבֵּר daber · ראה · אֶל־ el

כמות הוזי אנד להו המע

בְּנֵי benei · יִשְׂרָאֵל Yisrael · וְאָמַרְתָּ ve'amarta · אֲלֵהֶם alehem · וְעָשׂוּ ve'asu

יצל מרה היי המם לוו

לָהֶם lahem · צִיצִת tzitzit · עַל־ al · כַּנְפֵי kanfei · בִגְדֵיהֶם vigdehem

כבי ליו פנל נמך

לְדֹרֹתָם ledorotam · וְנָתְנוּ venatnu · עַל־ al · צִיצִת tzitzit

יוזי מנה וזהו

הַכָּנָף hakanaf · ע״ה קנ״א, אדני אלהים · פְּתִיל petil · י״פ ב״ן · תְּכֵלֶת techelet:

נזה השא ירת שאה רלי

וְהָיָה vehaya · יהוה ; יהה · לָכֶם lachem · לְצִיצִת letzitzit · וּרְאִיתֶם ur'item · אֹתוֹ oto

אום ליב והר ייו להוו

וּזְכַרְתֶּם uzchartem · אֶת־ et · כָּל־ kol · יכי · מִצְוֹת mitzvot · יְהֹוָהאדניאהדונהי Adonai

כעק מנד אני וזום רהע

וַעֲשִׂיתֶם va'asitem · אֹתָם otam · וְלֹא־ velo · תָתוּרוּ taturu · אַחֲרֵי acharei

יוזז השה מככ

לְבַבְכֶם levavchem · וְאַחֲרֵי ve'acharei · עֵינֵיכֶם enechem · ריבוע מ״ה

You should meditate on the precept:
"not to follow negative sexual thoughts of the heart and the sights of the eyes for prostitution."

VAYOMER

"And the Lord spoke to Moses and said,
Speak to the Children of Israel and say to them that they should make for themselves Tzitzit, on the corners of their garments, throughout all their generations. And they must place upon the Tzitzit, of each corner, a blue strand. And this shall be to you as a Tzitzit: you shall see it and remember the commandments of the Lord and fulfill them. And you shall not stray after your hearts and your eyes,

You should meditate to remember the exodus from *Mitzrayim* (Egypt).

לִהְיוֹת lihyot לָכֶם lachem לֵאלֹהִים lelohim אהיה אדני ; ילה

אֲנִי ani אני יְהֹוָה Adonai אֱלֹהֵיכֶם Elohechem ילה:

Be careful to complete this paragraph together with the *chazan* and the congregation, and say the word *"emet"* out loud. The *chazan* should say the word *"emet"* in silence.

אֱמֶת emet אהיה פעמים אהיה, ז"פ ס"ג.

The congregation should be silent, listen and hear the words *"Adonai Elohechem emet"* spoken by the *chazan*. If you did not complete the paragraph together with the *chazan* you should repeat the last three words on your own. With these three words the *Shema* is completed.

יְהֹוָה Adonai אֱלֹהֵיכֶם Elohechem ילה:

אֱמֶת emet אהיה פעמים אהיה, ז"פ ס"ג.

---

after which you adulterate. This is so that you shall remember to fulfill all My commandments and thereby be holy before your God. I am the Lord, your God, Who brought you out of the land of Egypt to be your God. I, the Lord, your God, Is true." (Numbers 15:37-41) *the Lord, your God, is true!*

VE'EMUNA – THIRD CHAMBER – RATZON

Ve'emuna connects us to the Third Chamber in the House of the King: *Ratzon,* or desire. Before we can connect to any form of spiritual energy, we need to feel a want or desire. Desire is the vessel that draws spiritual Light. A small desire draws a small amount of Light. A large desire draws a large amount.

Hechal Ratzon (the Desire Chamber) of *Nukva* in *Beriah*.

וֶאֱמוּנָה ve'emuna (בחינת לילה) כָּל kol ילי זֹאת zot וְקַיָּם vekayam עָלֵינוּ alenu,
כִּי ki הוּא hu יְהֹוָהאדניאהדונהי Adonai אֱלֹהֵינוּ Elohenu ילה וְאֵין ve'en
זוּלָתוֹ zulato. וַאֲנַחְנוּ va'anachnu יִשְׂרָאֵל Yisrael עַמּוֹ amo.
הַפּוֹדֵנוּ hapodenu מִיַּד miyad מְלָכִים melachim. הַגּוֹאֲלֵנוּ hago'alenu
מַלְכֵּנוּ malkenu מִכַּף mikaf כָּל kol ילי עָרִיצִים aritzim.
הָאֵל haEl לאה ; ייא״ (מילוי דס״ג) הַנִּפְרָע hanifra לָנוּ lanu אלהים, אהיה אדני
מִצָּרֵינוּ mitzarenu. הַמְשַׁלֵּם hameshalem גְּמוּל gemul לְכָל lechol יה אדני
אוֹיְבֵי oyvei נַפְשֵׁנוּ nafshenu: הַשָּׂם hasam נַפְשֵׁנוּ nafshenu
בַּחַיִּים bachayim אהיה אהיה יהוה, בינה ע״ה וְלֹא velo נָתַן natan לַמּוֹט lamot
רַגְלֵנוּ raglenu. הַמַּדְרִיכֵנוּ hamadrichenu עַל al בָּמוֹת bamot
אוֹיְבֵינוּ oyvenu. וַיָּרֶם vayarem קַרְנֵנוּ karnenu עַל al כָּל kol ילי ; עמם
שׂוֹנְאֵינוּ son'enu. הָאֵל haEl לאה ; ייא״ (מילוי דס״ג) הָעוֹשֶׂה ha'ose
לָנוּ lanu אלהים, אהיה אדני נִסִּים nisim וּנְקָמָה unkama בְּפַרְעֹה beFar'o.
בְּאוֹתוֹת be'otot וּבְמוֹפְתִים uvmoftim בְּאַדְמַת be'admat בְּנֵי benei
חָם Cham. הַמַּכֶּה hamake בְּעֶבְרָתוֹ ve'evrato כָּל kol ילי
בְּכוֹרֵי bechorei מִצְרַיִם Mitzrayim מצר. וַיּוֹצֵא vayotzi אֶת et
עַמּוֹ amo יִשְׂרָאֵל Yisrael מִתּוֹכָם mitocham לְחֵרוּת lecherut עוֹלָם olam.

VE'EMUNA – THIRD CHAMBER - RATZON

And trustworthy. All this and He are set upon us because He is the Lord, our God, and there is none other. And we are Israel, His Nation. He redeems us from the hands of kings. He is our King, Who delivers us from the reach of tyrants; The God, Who avenges us against our enemies. He pays our mortal enemies their due. He Who keeps us alive and does not allow our feet to falter; He Who lets us walk upon the plains of our foes. He Who raises our worth over all our enemies. He is God, Who wrought for us retribution against Pharaoh, with signs and wonders, in the land of the children of Cham. He Who struck down with His anger at the first-born of Egypt, and brought out His Nation, Israel, from amongst them to everlasting freedom.

הַמַּעֲבִיר hama'avir בָּנָיו banav

בֵּין ben גִּזְרֵי gizrei יַם yam ילי סוּף Suf. וְאֶת ve'et רוֹדְפֵיהֶם rodfehem

וְאֶת ve'et שׂוֹנְאֵיהֶם son'ehem בִּתְהוֹמוֹת bitehomot טִבַּע tiba. רָאוּ ra'u

בָנִים vanim אֶת et גְּבוּרָתוֹ gevurato שִׁבְּחוּ shibechu וְהוֹדוּ vehodu אהיה

לִשְׁמוֹ lishmo מהש ע"ה, ע"ב בריבוע וקס"א ע"ה, אל שדי ע"ה. וּמַלְכוּתוֹ umalchuto

בְּרָצוֹן beratzon מהש ע"ה, ע"ב בריבוע וקס"א ע"ה, אל שדי ע"ה קִבְּלוּ kibelu

עֲלֵיהֶם alehem. מֹשֶׁה Moshe מהש, ע"ב בריבוע וקס"א, אל שדי, ד"פ אלהים ע"ה

וּבְנֵי uvnei יִשְׂרָאֵל Yisrael ר"ת ע"ה נגד, מזבח, זן, אל יהוה לְךָ lecha עָנוּ anu

שִׁירָה shira בְּשִׂמְחָה besimcha רַבָּה raba וְאָמְרוּ ve'amru כֻלָּם chulam:

מִי־ mi ילי כָמֹכָה chamocha בָּאֵלִם ba'elim יְהֹוָהאדניאהדונהי Adonai

ר"ת ע"ב, ריבוע יהוה ; ס"ת מ"ה מִי mi ילי כָּמֹכָה kamocha נֶאְדָּר nedar

בַּקֹּדֶשׁ bakodesh ר"ת יב"ק, אלהים יהוה, אהיה אדני יהוה נוֹרָא nora תְהִלֹּת tehilot

עֹשֵׂה ose פֶלֶא fele: מַלְכוּתְךָ malchutcha יְהֹוָהאדניאהדונהי Adonai

אֱלֹהֵינוּ Elohenu ילה רָאוּ ra'u בָנֶיךָ vanecha עַל־ al הַיָּם hayam ילי

יַחַד yachad כֻּלָּם kulam הוֹדוּ hodu אהיה וְהִמְלִיכוּ vehimlichu

וְאָמְרוּ ve'amru: יְהֹוָהאדניאהדונהי Adonai | יִמְלֹךְ yimloch לְעֹלָם le'olam

ריבוע ס"ג וי' אותיות דס"ג ; ר"ת ייל וָעֶד va'ed. וְנֶאֱמַר vene'emar: כִּי־ ki פָדָה fada

יְהֹוָהאדניאהדונהי Adonai אֶת־ et יַעֲקֹב Yaakov ד' הויות, יאהדונהי אידהנויה

וּגְאָלוֹ ug'alo מִיַּד miyad חָזָק chazak פהל מִמֶּנּוּ mimenu: בָּרוּךְ baruch

אַתָּה Ata יְהֹוָהאדניאהדונהי Adonai גָּאַל ga'al באתב"ש כתר יִשְׂרָאֵל Yisrael:

He Who caused His Children to pass between the sections of the Sea of Reeds, while their pursuers and their enemies, He drowned in the depths. The Children saw His might and they praised and gave thanks to His Name; they accepted His sovereignty over them willingly. Moses and the Children of Israel raised their voices in song to Him, with great joy, and they all said, as one "Who is like You among the gods, Lord? Who is like You, awesome in holiness, tremendous in praise and Who works wonders?" (Exodus 15:11) Our Children saw Your Kingdom, Lord, our God, upon the sea, and they all in unison gave thanks to You and accepted Your sovereignty and said: "The Lord shall reign forever and ever." (Exodus 15:18) And it is stated: "For the Lord has delivered Jacob and redeemed him from the hand of one that is stronger than he." (Jeremiah 31:10) Blessed are You, Lord, Who redeemed Israel.

HASHKIVENU – FOURTH CHAMBER – HOLY OF HOLIES

The Fourth Chamber is *Kodesh HaKodeshim*, the Holy of Holies, which is our link to the next level that we reach through the *Amidah*.

Hechal Kodesh HaKodashim (the Holy of Holies Chamber) of *Nukva* in *Beriah*.

הַשְׁכִּיבֵנוּ hashkivenu אָבִינוּ avinu לְשָׁלוֹם leshalom ר"ת לאה

וְהַעֲמִידֵנוּ veha'amidenu מַלְכֵּנוּ malkenu לְחַיִּים lechayim אהיה אהיה יהוה, בינה ע"ה

טוֹבִים tovim וּלְשָׁלוֹם ulshalom וּפְרוֹשׂ ufros עָלֵינוּ alenu

סֻכַּת sukat סוכה = סאל, אמן (יאהדונהי) שְׁלוֹמֶךָ shelomecha וְתַקְּנֵנוּ vetakenenu

מַלְכֵּנוּ malkenu בְּעֵצָה be'etza טוֹבָה tova אכא מִלְּפָנֶיךָ milfanecha ס"ג מ"ה ב"ן

וְהוֹשִׁיעֵנוּ vehoshi'enu מְהֵרָה mehera לְמַעַן lema'an שְׁמֶךָ shemecha

וְהָגֵן vehagen בַּעֲדֵנוּ ba'adenu. וְהָסֵר vehaser מֵעָלֵינוּ me'alenu מַכַּת makat

אוֹיֵב oyev. דֶּבֶר dever. וְחֶרֶב cherev. וְחוֹלִי choli וחולי = מ"ה עם ד' אותיות.

צָרָה tzara אלהים דההין. רָעָה ra'a רהע. רָעָב ra'av. וְיָגוֹן veyagon.

וּמַשְׁחִית umashchit. וּמַגֵּפָה umagefa. שְׁבוֹר shevor וְהָסֵר vehaser

הַשָּׂטָן hasatan מִלְּפָנֵינוּ milfanenu וּמֵאַחֲרֵינוּ ume'acharenu. וּבְצֵל uvtzel

כְּנָפֶיךָ kenafecha תַּסְתִּירֵנוּ tastirenu. וּשְׁמוֹר ushmor צֵאתֵנוּ tzetenu

וּבוֹאֵנוּ uvo'enu לְחַיִּים lechayim אהיה אהיה יהוה, בינה ע"ה טוֹבִים tovim

וּלְשָׁלוֹם ulshalom מֵעַתָּה me'ata וְעַד ve'ad עוֹלָם olam: כִּי ki אֵל El ייא"י

(מילוי דס"ג) שׁוֹמְרֵנוּ shomrenu כ"א הויות שבתפילין וּמַצִּילֵנוּ umatzilenu אָתָּה Ata

מִכָּל mikol ילי דָּבָר davar ראה רָע ra וּמִפַּחַד umipachad לַיְלָה layla מלה.

בָּרוּךְ baruch אַתָּה Ata יְהֹוָהאדניאהדונהי Adonai שׁוֹמֵר shomer כ"א הויות שבתפילין

אֶת et עַמּוֹ amo יִשְׂרָאֵל Yisrael לָעַד la'ad ב"פ ב"ן. אָמֵן amen יאהדונהי:

HASHKIVENU – FOURTH CHAMBER – HOLY OF HOLIES

Lay us down in peace, Father, and stand us up, our King, for good life and for peace. Spread over us Your protection of peace. Set us straight with good counsel from You and save us speedily for the sake of Your Name. And remove from us the blow of our enemy, pestilence, sword, illness, distress, evil, famine, sorrow, ruin, and plague. Destroy and remove Satan from before us and from behind us. Hide us in the shade of Your Wings and watch over our goings and our comings, for a good life and for peace, from now and until eternity. For You, God, are our Guardian and our Rescuer from all evil things and from the terror of the night. Blessed are You, Lord, Who guards His Nation, Israel, forever. Amen!

HALF KADDISH

יִתְגַּדַּל yitgadal וְיִתְקַדַּשׁ veyitkadash שדי ומילוי שדי ; י"א אותיות כמנין ו"ה

שְׁמֵיהּ shemei (שם י"ה דע"ב) רַבָּא raba קנ"א ב"ן, יהוה אלהים יהוה אדני,

מילוי קס"א וס"ג, מ"ה ברבוע וע"ב ע"ה ; ר"ת = ו"פ אלהים ; ס"ת = ג"פ יב"ק: אָמֵן amen אידהנויה.

בְּעָלְמָא be'alma דִּי di בְרָא vera כִּרְעוּתֵיהּ chir'utei.

וְיַמְלִיךְ veyamlich מַלְכוּתֵיהּ malchutei. וְיַצְמַח veyatzmach

פּוּרְקָנֵיהּ purkanei. וִיקָרֵב vikarev מְשִׁיחֵיהּ meshichei: אָמֵן amen אידהנויה.

בְּחַיֵּיכוֹן bechayechon וּבְיוֹמֵיכוֹן uvyomechon וּבְחַיֵּי uvchayei

דְכָל dechol ילי בֵּית bet ב"פ ראה יִשְׂרָאֵל Yisrael בַּעֲגָלָא ba'agala

וּבִזְמַן uvizman קָרִיב kariv וְאִמְרוּ ve'imru אָמֵן amen: אָמֵן amen אידהנויה.

The congregation and the *chazan* say the following:

28 words (until *be'alma*) – meditate: מילוי דמילוי דע"ב (יוד ויו דלת הי יוד ויו יוד ויו הי יוד)

28 letters (until *almaya*) - meditate: מילוי דמילוי דע"ב (יוד ויו דלת הי יוד ויו יוד ויו הי יוד)

יְהֵא yehe שְׁמֵיהּ shemei (שם י"ה דס"ג) רַבָּא raba קנ"א ב"ן,

יהוה אלהים יהוה אדני, מילוי קס"א וס"ג, מ"ה ברבוע וע"ב ע"ה מְבָרַךְ mevarach,

לְעָלַם le'alam לְעָלְמֵי le'almei עָלְמַיָּא almaya. יִתְבָּרַךְ yitbarach.

HALF KADDISH

May His great Name be more exalted and sanctified. (Amen)

In the world that He created according to His will, and may His kingdom reign. And may He cause His redemption to sprout and may He bring the Mashiach closer. (Amen) In your lifetimes and in your days and in the lifetime of all the House of Israel, speedily and in the near future, and you should say, Amen. (Amen) May His great Name be blessed forever and for all eternity blessed

Seven words with six letters each (שֵׁם בֶּן מ״ב) – meditate:

יהוה ✦ יוד הי ויו הי ✦ מילוי דמילוי דע״ב (יוד ויו דלת הי יוד ויו יוד ויו הי יוד)

Also, seven times the letter Vav (שֵׁם בֶּן מ״ב) – meditate:

יהוה ✦ יוד הי ויו הי ✦ מילוי דמילוי דע״ב (יוד ויו דלת הי יוד ויו יוד ויו הי יוד).

וְיִשְׁתַּבַּח veyishtabach י״פ ע״ב יהוה אל אבג יתץ.

וְיִתְפָּאַר veyitpa'ar הי נו יה קרע שטן. וְיִתְרוֹמַם veyitromam וה כוזו נגד יכש.

וְיִתְנַשֵּׂא veyitnase במוכסז בטר צתג. וְיִתְהַדָּר veyit'hadar כוזו יה וזקב טנע.

וְיִתְעַלֶּה veyit'ale וה יוד ה יגל פזק. וְיִתְהַלָּל veyit'halal א ואו הא שקו צית.

שְׁמֵיהּ shemei (שם י״ה דמ״ה) דְּקוּדְשָׁא dekudsha בְּרִיךְ verich הוּא hu:

אָמֵן amen אידהנויה.

לְעֵלָּא le'ela מִן min כָּל kol ילי בִּרְכָתָא birchata. שִׁירָתָא shirata.

תִּשְׁבְּחָתָא tishbechata וְנֶחָמָתָא venechamata. דַּאֲמִירָן da'amiran

בְּעָלְמָא be'alma וְאִמְרוּ ve'imru אָמֵן amen: אָמֵן amen אידהנויה.

THE AMIDAH

When we begin the connection, we take three steps backward, signifying our leaving this physical world. Then we take three steps forward to begin the *Amidah*. The three steps are:

1. Stepping into the land of Israel – to enter the first spiritual circle.
2. Stepping into the city of Jerusalem – to enter the second spiritual circle.
3. Stepping inside the Holy of Holies – to enter the innermost circle.

Before we recite the first verse of the *Amidah*, we ask: "*God, open my lips and let my mouth speak,*" thereby asking the Light to speak for us so that we can receive what we need and not just what we want. All too often, what we want from life is not necessarily the desire of the soul, which is what we actually need to fulfill us. By asking the Light to speak through us, we ensure that our connection will bring us genuine fulfillment and opportunities for spiritual growth and change.

---

and lauded, and glorified and exalted, And extolled and honored, and uplifted and praised, be the Name of the Holy Blessed One. (Amen) Above all blessings, songs, praises, and words of consolation that may be said in the world, and you shall say, Amen. (Amen)

אֲדֹנָי Adonai ללה (pause here) שְׂפָתַי sefatai תִּפְתָּח tiftach וּפִי ufi יַגִּיד yagid

ייז (כ"ב אותיות פשוטות [=אכא] וה' אותיות סופיות מנצפך) תְּהִלָּתֶךָ tehilatecha ס"ת = בוכו:

THE FIRST BLESSING - INVOKES THE SHIELD OF ABRAHAM.

Abraham is the channel of the Right Column energy of positivity, sharing, and mercy. Sharing actions can protect us from all forms of negativity.

Chesed that becomes *Chochmah*

In this section there are 42 words, the secret of the 42-Letter Name of God and therefore it begins with the letter *Bet* (2) and ends with the letter *Mem* (40).

Bend your knees at *"baruch"*, bow at *"Ata"* and straighten up at *"Adonai"*.

א ב

בָּרוּךְ baruch אַתָּה Ata א-ת (אותיות הא"ב המסמלות את השפע המגיע) לה' המלכות

ג י

יְהֹוָאדהנויאהדונהי Adonai (יא) אֱלֹהֵינוּ Elohenu ילה

ת צ

וֵאלֹהֵי velohei לכב ; מילוי ע"ב, דמב ; ילה אֲבוֹתֵינוּ avotenu•

ק ר

אֱלֹהֵי Elohei מילוי ע"ב, דמב ; ילה אַבְרָהָם Avraham (*Chochmah*)

וז"פ אל, רי"ו ול"ב נתיבות החכמה, רמ"ח (אברים), עסמ"ב וט"ז אותיות פשוטות

ע ש

אֱלֹהֵי Elohei מילוי ע"ב, דמב ; ילה יִצְחָק Yitzchak (*Binah*) ד"פ ב"ן

ט נ

וֵאלֹהֵי velohei לכב ; מילוי ע"ב, דמב ; ילה יַעֲקֹב Yaakov (*Da'at*) ו' הויות, יאהדונהי אידהנויה

THE AMIDAH

'My Lord, open my lips, and my mouth shall relate Your praise." (Psalms 51:17)

THE FIRST BLESSING

Blessed are You, Lord,

our God and God of our forefathers: the God of Abraham, the God of Isaac, and the God of Jacob.

ג ג

הָאֵל haEl לאה ; ייא״ (מילוי דס״ג) הַגָּדוֹל hagadol האל הגדול = סיט ; גדול = להח

ד י

עם ד׳ אותיות = מבה, יזל, הום הַגִּבּוֹר hagibor ר״ת ההה וְהַנּוֹרָא vehanora.

כ ש

אֵל El ייא״ (מילוי דס״ג) ; ר״ת ע״ב, ריבוע יהוה עֶלְיוֹן elyon.

ב ט ר צ ת

גּוֹמֵל gomel חֲסָדִים chasadim טוֹבִים tovim. קוֹנֵה kone הַכֹּל hakol ילי

ג ח ק ב

וְזוֹכֵר vezocher חַסְדֵי chasdei אָבוֹת avot. וּמֵבִיא umevi

ט נ ע י

גּוֹאֵל go'el לִבְנֵי livnei בְנֵיהֶם venehem לְמַעַן lema'an

ג ל

שְׁמוֹ shemo מהש ע״ה, ע״ב בריבוע וקס״א ע״ה, אל שדי ע״ה בְּאַהֲבָה be'ahava אחד, דאגה:

When saying the word *"be'ahava"* you should meditate to devote your soul to sanctify the Holy Name and accept upon yourself the four forms of death.

פ ז ק ש

מֶלֶךְ melech עוֹזֵר ozer וּמוֹשִׁיעַ umoshi'a וּמָגֵן umagen

ג״פ אל (ייא״ מילוי דס״ג) ; ר״ת מיכאל גבריאל נוריאל:

Bend your knees at *"baruch"*, bow at *"Ata"* and straighten up at *"Adonai"*.

ק ו צ

בָּרוּךְ baruch אַתָּה Ata יְהֵוָהאדנָיה (יְהֵוָהאדֵנָיה) יאהדונהי Adonai (הד׳)

י ת

מָגֵן magen ג״פ אל (ייא״ מילוי דס״ג) ; ר״ת מיכאל גבריאל נוריאל אַבְרָהָם Avraham

ח״פ אל, רי״ו ול״ב נתיבות החכמה, רמ״ח (אברים), עסמ״ב וט״ז אותיות פשוטות:

The great, mighty and awesome God.
The Supernal God, Who bestows beneficial kindness and creates everything. Who recalls the kindness of the forefathers and brings a Redeemer to their descendants for the sake of His Name, lovingly. King, Helper, Savior and Shield. Blessed are You, Lord, the shield of Abraham.

THE SECOND BLESSING

THE ENERGY OF ISAAC IGNITES THE POWER FOR THE RESURRECTION OF THE DEAD.

Whereas Abraham represents the power of sharing, Isaac represents the Left Column energy of judgment. Judgment shortens the *tikkun* process and paves the way for our eventual resurrection.

Gevurah that becomes *Binah*.

In this section there are 49 words corresponding to the 49 gates of the Pure System in *Binah*.

אַתָּה Ata גִּבּוֹר gibor לְעוֹלָם le'olam ריבוע ס"ג וי' אותיות דס"ג אֲדֹנָי Adonai ללה

(ר"ת אֲגְלָא והוא שם גדול ואמיץ, ובו היה יהודה מתגבר על אויביו. ע"ה אלד, בוכו).

מְחַיֵּה mechaye ס"ג מֵתִים metim אַתָּה Ata• רַב rav לְהוֹשִׁיעַ lehoshi'a•

מוֹרִיד morid הַטָּל hatal יוד הא ואו, כוזו, מספר אותיות דמילואי עסמ"ב ; ר"ת מ"ה :

If you mistakenly say "*Mashiv haru'ach*", and realize this before the end of the blessing ("*baruch Ata Adonai*"), you should return to the beginning of the blessing ("*Ata gibor*") and continue as usual. But if you only realize this after the end of the blessing, you should start the *Amidah* from the beginning.

מְכַלְכֵּל mechalkel חַיִּים chayim אהיה אהיה יהוה, בינה ע"ה בְּחֶסֶד bechesed

ע"ב, ריבוע יהוה• מְחַיֵּה mechaye ס"ג מֵתִים metim בְּרַחֲמִים berachamim

(במוכסז) מצפצ, אלהים דההין, י"פ ייי רַבִּים rabim (טלא דעתיק)• סוֹמֵךְ somech

(אכדטם) כוק, ריבוע אדני נוֹפְלִים noflim (זו"ן)• וְרוֹפֵא verofe חוֹלִים cholim

חולה = מ"ה וד' אותיות• וּמַתִּיר umatir אֲסוּרִים asurim• וּמְקַיֵּם umekayem

אֱמוּנָתוֹ emunato לִישֵׁנֵי lishenei עָפָר afar• מִי mi ילי כָּמוֹךָ chamocha

בַּעַל ba'al גְּבוּרוֹת gevurot (you should enunciate the letter *Ayin* in the word "*ba'al*")

וּמִי umi ילי דּוֹמֶה dome לָּךְ lach• מֶלֶךְ melech מֵמִית memit

וּמְחַיֶּה umchaye ס"ג (יוד הי ואו הי) וּמַצְמִיחַ umatzmi'ach יְשׁוּעָה yeshu'a:

וְנֶאֱמָן vene'eman אַתָּה Ata לְהַחֲיוֹת lehachayot מֵתִים metim:

בָּרוּךְ baruch אַתָּה Ata יְהֹוָהאדנהי(יְהֹוָהאדנהי)יאהדונהי Adonai

מְחַיֵּה mechaye ס"ג (יוד הי ואו הי) הַמֵּתִים hametim ר"ת מ"ה וס"ת מ"ה:

THE SECOND BLESSING

You are mighty forever, Lord.

You resurrect the dead and are very capable of redeeming. Who causes dew to fall. You sustain life with kindness and resurrect the dead with great compassion. You support those who have fallen, heal the sick, release the imprisoned, and fulfill Your faithful words to those who are asleep in the dust. Who is like You, Master of might, and Who can compare to You, King, Who causes death, Who gives life, and Who sprouts salvation? And You are faithful to resurrecting the dead. Blessed are You, Lord, Who resurrects the dead.

THE THIRD BLESSING

This blessing connects us to Jacob, the Central Column and the power of restriction. Jacob is our channel for connecting mercy with judgment. By restricting our reactive behavior, we are blocking our Desire to Receive for the Self Alone. Jacob also gives us the power to balance our acts of mercy and judgment toward other people in our lives.

Tiferet that becomes *Da'at* (14 words).

אַתָּה Ata קָדוֹשׁ kadosh וְשִׁמְךָ veshimcha קָדוֹשׁ kadosh ר"ת = אור, רז, אין סוף •

וּקְדוֹשִׁים ukdoshim בְּכָל־ bechol ב"ן, לכב יוֹם yom ע"ה נגד, מזבח, זן, אל יהוה

יְהַלְלוּךָ yehalelucha סֶּלָה sela:

בָּרוּךְ baruch אַתָּה Ata יְהֹוָ‍ואדה‍יאהדונהי Adonai

הָאֵל haEl לאה ; ייא" (מילוי דס"ג) הַקָּדוֹשׁ hakadosh י"פ מ"ה (יוד הא ואו הא):

Meditate here on the Name: **יאהדונהי**, as it can help to remove anger.

THIRTEEN MIDDLE BLESSINGS

There are thirteen blessings in the middle of the *Amidah* that connect us to the Thirteen Attributes.

THE FIRST (FOURTH) BLESSING

This blessing helps us transform information into knowledge by helping us internalize everything that we learn.

Chochmah

In this blessing there are 17 words, the same numerical value as the word *tov* (good) in the secret of *Etz HaDa'at Tov vaRa*, (Tree of Knowledge Good and Evil), where we connect only to the *Tov*.

אַתָּה Ata חוֹנֵן chonen לְאָדָם le'adam מ"ה דַּעַת da'at •

וּמְלַמֵּד umlamed לֶאֱנוֹשׁ le'enosh בִּינָה bina ע"ה אהיה אהיה יהוה, חיים •

THE THIRD BLESSING

You are holy, and Your Name is holy, and the Holy Ones praise You every day, for you are God, the Holy King Selah. Blessed are You, Lord, the Holy God.

THIRTEEN MIDDLE BLESSINGS

THE FIRST (FOURTH) BLESSING

You graciously grant knowledge to man and understanding to humanity.

On *Motza'ei Shabbat* **(Saturday night)** and on *Motza'ei Chag* we add the following:

ATAH CHONANTANU

This connection helps us differentiate good from evil during the week. All too often we attract the wrong people and embrace the wrong opportunities in our life. This connection gives us the sixth sense to perceive the long-term consequences.

אַתָּה Ata חוֹנַנְתָּנוּ chonantanu יְהֹוָהאדניאהדונהי Adonai אֱלֹהֵינוּ Elohenu ילה
מַדָּע mada וְהַשְׂכֵּל vehaskel, אַתָּה Ata אָמַרְתָּ amarta לְהַבְדִּיל lehavdil
בֵּין ben קוֹדֶשׁ kodesh לְחוֹל lechol וּבֵין uven אוֹר or רז, א״ס
לְחוֹשֶׁךְ lechoshech וּבֵין uven יִשְׂרָאֵל Yisrael לָעַמִּים la'amim,
וּבֵין uven יוֹם yom ע״ה נגד, מזבח, זן, אל יהוה הַשְּׁבִיעִי hashevi'i לְשֵׁשֶׁת lesheshet
יְמֵי yemei הַמַּעֲשֶׂה hama'ase. כְּשֵׁם keshem שֶׁהִבְדַּלְתָּנוּ shehivdaltanu
יְהֹוָהאדניאהדונהי Adonai אֱלֹהֵינוּ Elohenu ילה מֵעַמֵּי me'amei
הָאֲרָצוֹת ha'aratzot וּמִמִּשְׁפְּחוֹת umimishpechot הָאֲדָמָה ha'adama,
כַּךְ kach פְּדֵנוּ pedenu וְהַצִּילֵנוּ vehatzilenu מִשָּׂטָן misatan רָע ra
וּמִפֶּגַע umipega רָע ra, וּמִכָּל umikol ילי גְּזֵרוֹת gezerot קָשׁוֹת kashot
וְרָעוֹת vera'ot הַמִּתְרַגְּשׁוֹת hamitrageshot לָבֹא lavo בָּעוֹלָם ba'olam:

וְחָנֵּנוּ vechonenu מֵאִתְּךָ me'itecha חָכְמָה chochmah במילוי = תרי״ג (מצוות)
בִּינָה binah ע״ה אהיה אהיה יהוה, חיים וָדָעַת vada'at ר״ת חבו:
בָּרוּךְ baruch אַתָּה Ata יְהֹוָהאדניאהדונהי Adonai חוֹנֵן chonen הַדָּעַת hada'at:

You have graciously granted us, Lord our God, knowledge and intelegence. You commanded us to separate between the holy and non-holy, between Light and darkness, between Israel and the nations and between the seventh day and the six days of Creation. Just as You separated us, Lord our God, from the nations of the lands and from the families of earth, so may You redeem us and rescue us from any evil adversary, from any mishap, and from all types of harsh and evil decrees which enthusiastically come to the world.

Graciously grant us, from Yourself,
wisdom, understanding and knowledge. Blessed are You, Lord, Who graciously grants knowledge.

THE SECOND (FIFTH) BLESSING

This blessing keeps us in the Light. Everyone at one time or another succumbs to the doubt and uncertainty that the Satan constantly implants in us. If we make the unfortunate mistake of stepping back and falling away from the Light, we do not want the Creator to mirror our actions and step away from us. Instead, we want Him to catch us. In the box below there are certain lines that we can recite and meditate on for others who may be stepping back. The war against the Satan is the oldest war known to man. And the only way to defeat the Satan is to unite, share, help and pray for each other.

Binah

In this blessing there are 15 words, as the powerful action of *Teshuva* (repentance) raises 15 levels on the way to *Kise Hakavod* (the Throne of Honor). It goes through seven *Reki'im* (firmaments), seven *Avirim* (air), and another firmament on top of the Holy Animals (together this adds up to 15). Also, there are 15 words in the two main verses of Isaiah the Prophet and King David that speak of *Teshuva* (*Isaiah 55:7*; *Psalms 32:5*). The number 15 is also the secret of the Name: יה.

הֲשִׁיבֵנוּ hashivenu אָבִינוּ avinu לְתוֹרָתֶךָ letoratecha (וסד שבה - יְהֹוָהאדהיאהדונהי)

וְקָרְבֵנוּ vekarvenu מַלְכֵּנוּ malkenu לַעֲבוֹדָתֶךָ la'avodatecha

וְהַחֲזִירֵנוּ vehachazirenu בִּתְשׁוּבָה bitshuva שְׁלֵמָה shelema

לְפָנֶיךָ lefanecha ס״ג מ״ה ב״ן:

> If you want to pray for another and help them in their spiritual process say:
>
> יְהִי yehi רָצוֹן ratzon מהש ע״ה, ע״ב בריבוע וקס״א ע״ה, אל שדי ע״ה
>
> מִלְּפָנֶיךָ milfanecha ס״ג מ״ה ב״ן יְהֹוָהאדהיאהדונהי Adonai אֱלֹהַי Elohai מילוי ע״ב, דמב; ילה
>
> וֵאלֹהֵי velohei לכב; מילוי ע״ב, דמב; ילה אֲבוֹתַי avotai שֶׁתַּחְתּוֹר shetachtor
>
> חֲתִירָה chatira מִתַּחַת mitachat כִּסֵּא kise כְּבוֹדֶךָ kevodecha וּתְקַבֵּל utkabel
>
> בִּתְשׁוּבָה bitshuva אֶת et (*the person's name and his/her father's name*) כִּי ki יְמִינְךָ yemincha
>
> יְהֹוָהאדהיאהדונהי Adonai פְּשׁוּטָה peshuta לְקַבֵּל lekabel שָׁבִים shavim

בָּרוּךְ baruch אַתָּה Ata יְהֹוָהאדהיאהדונהי Adonai

הָרוֹצֶה harotze בִּתְשׁוּבָה bitshuva:

THE SECOND (FIFTH) BLESSING

Bring us back, our Father, to Your Torah,
and bring us close, our King, to Your service, and cause us to return with perfect repentance before You.

> *May it be pleasing before You, Lord, my God and God of my forefathers, that You shall dig deep beneath the Throne of Your glory and accept as repentant* (the person's name and his/her father' name) *because Your Right Hand, Lord, extends outwards to receive those who repent.*

Blessed are You, Lord, Who desires repentance.

THE THIRD (SIXTH) BLESSING

This blessing helps us achieve true forgiveness. We have the power to cleanse ourselves of our negative behavior and hurtful actions toward others through forgiveness. This blessing does not mean we plead for forgiveness and our slate is wiped clean. Forgiveness refers to the methodologies for washing away the residue that comes from our iniquities. There are two ways to wash away the residue: physical and spiritual. We collect physical residue when we are in denial of our misdeeds and the laws of cause and effect. We cleanse ourselves when we experience any kind of pain, whether it is financial, emotional, or physical. If we choose to cleanse spiritually, we forgo the physical cleansing. We do so by arousing the pain in ourselves that we caused to others. We feel the other person; and with a truthful heart, recite this prayer experiencing the hurt and heartache we inflicted on others. This form of spiritual cleansing prevents us from having to cleanse physically.

Chesed

In this blessing there are 21 words which is the numerical value of the Holy Name: אהיה.

סְלַח selach יהוה ע״ב לָנוּ lanu אלהים, אהיה אדני אָבִינוּ avinu ר״ת סאל, אמן (יאהדונהי)

כִּי ki חָטָאנוּ chatanu. מְחוֹל mechol לָנוּ lanu אלהים, אהיה אדני ; מחול לנו ע״ה =

קס״א וי׳ אותיות מַלְכֵּנוּ malkenu כִּי ki פָשָׁעְנוּ fashanu. כִּי ki אֵל El ייא״י (מילוי דס״ג)

טוֹב tov והו וְסַלָּח vesalach יהוה ע״ב אָתָּה Ata: בָּרוּךְ baruch אַתָּה Ata

יְהֹוָאדנָהי יאהדונהי Adonai חַנּוּן chanun הַמַּרְבֶּה hamarbe לִסְלוֹחַ lislo'ach:

THE FOURTH (SEVENTH) BLESSING

This blessing helps us achieve redemption after we are spiritually cleansed.

Gevurah

רְאֵה re'e ראה נָא na בְעָנְיֵנוּ ve'onyenu ר״ת רנ״ב (אברים באשה, כנגד הגבורה)

וְרִיבָה veriva רִיבֵנוּ rivenu. וּמַהֵר umaher לְגָאֳלֵנוּ lega'olenu

גְּאֻלָּה ge'ula מ״ה שְׁלֵמָה shelema לְמַעַן lema'an שְׁמֶךָ shemecha

כִּי ki אֵל El ייא״י (מילוי דס״ג) גּוֹאֵל go'el וְחָזָק chazak פהל אָתָּה Ata:

בָּרוּךְ baruch אַתָּה Ata יְהֹוָאדנָהי יאהדונהי Adonai גּוֹאֵל go'el יִשְׂרָאֵל Yisrael:

THE FIFTH (EIGHTH) BLESSING

This blessing gives us the power to heal every part of our body. All healing originates from the Light of the Creator. Accepting and understanding this truth opens us to receive this Light. We should also think of sharing this healing energy with others.

THE THIRD (SIXTH) BLESSING

Forgive us, our Father, for we have transgressed. Pardon us, our King, for we have sinned, because You are a good and forgiving God. Blessed are You, Lord, Who is gracious and forgives magnanimously.

THE FOURTH (SEVENTH) BLESSING

Behold our poverty and take up our fight; hurry to redeem us with a complete redemption for the sake of Your Name, because You are a powerful and a redeeming God. Blessed are You, Lord, Who redeems Israel.

Tiferet

רְפָאֵנוּ refa'enu יְהֹוָה יאהדונהי Adonai וְנֵרָפֵא venerafe ר"ת רי"ו.

הוֹשִׁיעֵנוּ hoshi'enu וְנִוָּשֵׁעָה venivashe'a כִּי ki תְהִלָּתֵנוּ tehilatenu

אַתָּה Ata ר"ת = ב"פ רי"ו. וְהַעֲלֵה veha'ale אֲרוּכָה arucha וּמַרְפֵּא umarpe

לְכָל־ lechol יה אדני תַּחֲלוּאֵינוּ .tachalu'enu וּלְכָל־ ulchol יה אדני

מַכְאוֹבֵינוּ mach'ovenu וּלְכָל־ ulchol יה אדני מַכּוֹתֵינוּ .makotenu

To pray for healing for yourself and/or others add the following, in the parentheses below, insert the names:

יְהִי yehi רָצוֹן ratzon מהש ע"ה, ע"ב בריבוע וקס"א ע"ה, אל שדי ע"ה

מִלְּפָנֶיךָ milfanecha ס"ג מ"ה ב"ן יְהֹוָה יאהדונהי Adonai אֱלֹהַי Elohai מילוי ע"ב, דמב ; ילה

וֵאלֹהֵי velohei לכב ; מילוי ע"ב, דמב ; ילה אֲבוֹתַי avotai שֶׁתִּרְפָּאֵנִי shetirpa'eni

(וְתִרְפָּא vetirpa (insert the person's name) בֶּן ben (Women: בַּת bat) (insert their mother's name))

רְפוּאָה refu'a שְׁלֵמָה shelema רְפוּאַת refu'at הַנֶּפֶשׁ hanefesh

וּרְפוּאַת urfu'at הַגּוּף ,haguf כְּדֵי kedei שֶׁאֶהְיֶה she'ehye חָזָק chazak פהל

(Women: חֲזָקָה chazaka פהל) בִּבְרִיאוּת ,bivri'ut וְאַמִּיץ ve'amitz

(Women: וְאַמִּיצַת ve'amitzat) כֹּחַ ,ko'ach בְּמָאתַיִם bematayim וְאַרְבָּעִים ve'arba'im

וּשְׁמוֹנָה ushmona רמ"ח (אברים), אברהם, ח"פ אל, רי"ו ול"ב נתיבות החכמה, עסמ"ב וט"ז אותיות

פשוטות (Women: בְּמָאתַיִם bematayim וַחֲמִשִּׁים vechamishim וּשְׁנַיִם ushnayim)

אֵבָרִים evarim וּשְׁלֹשׁ ushlosh מֵאוֹת me'ot המספר = ש = אלהים דיודין

וְשִׁשִּׁים veshishim המספר = מילוי הש' (ין) וַחֲמִשָּׁה vachamisha גִּידִים gidim שֶׁל shel

נִשְׁמָתִי nishmati וְגוּפִי ,vegufi לְקִיּוּם lekiyum תּוֹרָתְךָ toratcha הַקְּדוֹשָׁה .hakedosha

כִּי ki אֵל El ייא"י (במילוי דס"ג) רוֹפֵא rofe רַחֲמָן rachaman וְנֶאֱמָן vene'eman

אָתָּה :Ata בָּרוּךְ baruch אַתָּה Ata יְהֹוָה יאהדונהי Adonai רוֹפֵא rofe

חוֹלֵי cholei חולה = מ"ה (יוד הא ואו הא) וד' אותיות עַמּוֹ amo יִשְׂרָאֵל Yisrael

ר"ת רפ"ח (להעלות הניצוצות שנפלו לקליפה דמשם באים החולאים):

THE FIFTH (EIGHTH) BLESSING

Heal us, Lord, and we shall heal. Save us and we shall be saved.

For You are our praise. Bring cure and healing to all our ailments, to all our pains, and to all our wounds.

May it be pleasing before You, Lord, my God and God of my forefathers, that You would heal me (and the person's name and their mother's name*) completely with healing of the spirit and healing of the body, so that I shall be strong in health and vigorous in my strength in all 248 (*a woman says: *252) organs and 365 sinews of my soul and my body, so that I shall be able to keep Your Holy Torah.*

Because You are a healing,

compassionate, and trustworthy God, blessed are You, Lord, Who heals the sick of His People, Israel.

THE SIXTH (NINTH) BLESSING

This blessing draws sustenance and prosperity for the entire globe and provides us with personal sustenance. We would like all of our years to be filled with dew and rain, the sustaining lifeblood of our world.

Netzach

If you mistakenly say "*barech alenu*" instead of "*barchenu*", and realize this before the end of the *Amidah* ("*yihyu leratzon*" – the second one), then you should return and say "*barchenu*" and continue as usual. If you realize this later, you should start the *Amidah* from the beginning.

בָּרְכֵנוּ barchenu יְהֹוָהאדניאהדונהי Adonai אֱלֹהֵינוּ Elohenu ילה בְּכָל־ bechol
לכב, ב״ן מַעֲשֵׂי ma'asei יָדֵינוּ yadenu• וּבָרֵךְ uvarech שְׁנָתֵנוּ shenatenu
בְּטַלְלֵי betalelei רָצוֹן ratzon מהש ע״ה, ע״ב בריבוע וקס״א ע״ה, אל שדי ע״ה
בְּרָכָה beracha וּנְדָבָה undava בינה (וע״ה אהיה אהיה יהוה, חיים)• וּתְהִי utehi
אַחֲרִיתָהּ acharita וְחַיִּים chayim אהיה אהיה יהוה, בינה ע״ה וְשָׂבָע vesava
וְשָׁלוֹם veshalom כַּשָּׁנִים kashanim הַטּוֹבוֹת hatovot לִבְרָכָה livracha•

If you want to pray for sustenance you can add:

יְהִי yehi רָצוֹן ratzon מהש ע״ה, ע״ב בריבוע וקס״א ע״ה, אל שדי ע״ה מִלְּפָנֶיךָ milfanecha
ס״ג מ״ה ב״ן יְהֹוָהאדניאהדונהי Adonai אֱלֹהֵינוּ Elohenu ילה וֵאלֹהֵי velohei
לכב ; מילוי ע״ב, דמב ; ילה אֲבוֹתֵינוּ avotenu שֶׁתִּתֵּן shetiten ב״פ כהת לִי li
וּלְכָל ulchol יה אדני הַסְּמוּכִים hasemuchim עַל al שׁוּלְחָנִי shulchani הַיּוֹם hayom
ע״ה נגד, מזבח, זן, אל יהוה וּבְכָל uvchol ב״ן, לכב יוֹם yom ע״ה נגד, מזבח, זן, אל יהוה
מְזוֹנוֹתַי mezonotai וּמְזוֹנוֹתֵיהֶם umzonotehem בְּכָבוֹד bechavod בוכו וְלֹא velo
בְּבִזּוּי bevizui בְּהֶיתֵּר beheter וְלֹא velo בְּאִיסּוּר be'isur בִּזְכוּת bizchut
שִׁמְךָ shimcha הַגָּדוֹל hagadol להח ; עם ד׳ אותיות = מבה, יזל, אום
(Do not pronounce this name: דִּיקַרְנוֹסָא וחתך עם ג׳ אותיות - ובאתב״ש סאל, אמן, יאהדונהי)

THE SIXTH (NINTH) BLESSING

During the summer:

Bless us, Lord, our God, in all our endeavors, and bless our years with the dews of good will, blessing, and benevolence. May its conclusion be life, contentment, and peace, as with other years for blessing.

May it be pleasing before You, Lord, my God and God of my forefathers, that You would provide for me and for my household, today and everyday, mine and their nourishment, with dignity and not with shame, in a permissible but not a forbidden manner, by virtue of your great name

הַיּוֹצֵא hayotze מִפָּסוּק mipasuk: וַהֲרִיקֹתִי vaharikoti לָכֶם lachem
בְּרָכָה beracha עַד־ ad בְּלִי־ beli דָי dai וּמִפָּסוּק umipasuk: נְסָה nesa
עָלֵינוּ alenu אוֹר or רז, אין סוף פָּנֶיךָ panecha ס״ג מ״ה ב״ן יְהֹוָהאדנ״יאהדונה״י Adonai
וְאַל ve'al תַּצְרִיכֵנוּ tatzrichenu לִידֵי lidei מַתְּנוֹת matnot בָּשָׂר basar
וָדָם vadam כִּי ki אִם im ייהך, מ״א אותיות אהיה בפשוטו ומילואו ומילוי דמילואו ע״ה
מִיָּדְךָ miyadcha הַמְּלֵאָה hamele'a וּמֵאוֹצַר ume'otzar מַתְּנַת matnat וְחִנָּם chinam
תְּכַלְכְּלֵנִי techalkelni וְתַשְׁפִּיעֵנִי vetashpi'eni אָמֵן amen יאהדונה״י סֶלָה sela.

כִּי ki אֵל El ייא״י (מילוי דס״ג) טוֹב tov והו וּמֵטִיב umetiv
אַתָּה Ata וּמְבָרֵךְ umvarech הַשָּׁנִים hashanim: בָּרוּךְ baruch
אַתָּה Ata יְהֹוָהאדנ״יאהדונה״י Adonai מְבָרֵךְ mevarech הַשָּׁנִים hashanim:

THE SEVENTH (TENTH) BLESSING

This blessing gives us the power to positively influence all of humanity. Kabbalah teaches that each individual affects the whole. We affect the world, and the rest of the world affects us, even though we cannot perceive this relationship with our five senses. We call this relationship quantum consciousness.

Hod

תְּקַע teka ב״פ בוזוך וי׳ אותיות בְּשׁוֹפָר beshofar גָּדוֹל gadol להוו ; עם ד׳ אותיות =
מבה, יזל, אום לְחֵרוּתֵנוּ lecherutenu. וְשָׂא vesa נֵס nes מ״ה אדנ״י לְקַבֵּץ lekabetz
גָּלֻיּוֹתֵינוּ galuyotenu. וְקַבְּצֵנוּ vekabetzenu יַחַד yachad מֵאַרְבַּע me'arba
כַּנְפוֹת kanfot וזבו (בסגולתו להוציא ניצוצות מן הקליפות) ויכוין וְזִבּוּ עם נקודותיו = ע״ב, ריבוע יהוה
הָאָרֶץ ha'aretz אלהים דההין ע״ה ; ר״ת = אדנ״י לְאַרְצֵנוּ lc'artzenu:

The following is recited throughout the entire year:
The following meditation helps us to release and redeem all the remaining sparks of Light we have lost through our irresponsible actions (especially sexual misconduct):

---

that comes from the verse: "pour down for you blessing until there be no room to suffice for it" (Malachi 3:10) and from the verse: "Raise up over us the light of Your countenance, Lord" (Psalms 4:7), and we will not require the gifts of flesh and blood, but only from your hand which is full, and from the treasure of the free gift you shall support and nurish me. Amen. Sela.

for You are a good and a beneficent God and You bless the years. Blessed are You, Lord, Who blesses the years.

THE SEVENTH (TENTH) BLESSING

Blow a great Shofar for our freedom and raise a banner to gather our exiles, and gather us speedily from all four corners of the Earth to our Land.

יְהִי yehi רָצוֹן ratzon מהש ע״ה, ע״ב בריבוע וקס״א ע״ה, אל שדי ע״ה מִלְּפָנֶיךָ milfanecha
ס״ג מ״ה ב״ן יְהֹוָואדניאהדונהי Adonai אֱלֹהַי Elohai מילוי ע״ב, דמב ; ילה
וֵאלֹהֵי velohei לכב ; מילוי ע״ב, דמב ; ילה אֲבוֹתַי avotai שֶׁכָּל shekol ילי טִיפָּה tipa
וְטִיפָּה vetipa שֶׁל shel קֶרִי keri שֶׁיָּצָא sheyatza מִמֶּנִּי mimeni לְבַטָּלָה levatala
וּמִכָּל umikol ילי יִשְׂרָאֵל Yisrael בִּכְלָל bichlal וּבִפְרָט uvifrat שֶׁלֹּא shelo
בִּמְקוֹם bimkom מִצְוָה mitzva בֵּין ben בְּאוֹנֶס be'ones בֵּין ben בְּרָצוֹן beratzon
מהש ע״ה, ע״ב בריבוע וקס״א ע״ה, אל שדי ע״ה בֵּין ben בְּשׁוֹגֵג beshogeg בֵּין ben
בְּמֵזִיד bemezid, בֵּין ben בְּהִרְהוּר behirhur וּבֵין uven בְּמַעֲשֶׂה bema'ase,
בֵּין ben בְּגִלְגּוּל begilgul זֶה ze בֵּין ben בְּגִלְגּוּל begilgul אַחֵר acher
וְנִבְלַע venivla בַּקְּלִיפּוֹת bakelipot, שֶׁתָּקִיא shetaki הַקְּלִיפּוֹת hakelipot
הַנִּיצוֹצוֹת hanitzotzot קֶרִי keri שֶׁנִּבְלְעוּ shenivle'u בָּהּ ba בִּזְכוּת bizechut
שִׁמְךָ shimcha הַגָּדוֹל hagadol להח ; עם ד׳ אותיות = מבה, יזל, הום הַיּוֹצֵא hayotze
מִפָּסוּק mipasuk: חַיִל chayil ומב בָּלַע bala וַיְקִאֶנּוּ vayki'enu ר״ת וזבו ו-ילי
מִבִּטְנוֹ mibitno יֹרִשֶׁנּוּ yorishenu אֵל El ייא״י (מילוי דס״ג) ; ס״ת ויל וּבִזְכוּת uvizechut
שִׁמְךָ shimcha הַגָּדוֹל hagadol להח ; עם ד׳ אותיות = מבה, יזל, הום יוהבוה
שֶׁתַּחֲזִירֵם shetachazirem לִמְקוֹם limkom קְדוּשָּׁה kedusha
וְהַטּוֹב vehatov והו בְּעֵינֶיךָ be'enecha קס״א ע״ה ; ריבוע מ״ה עֲשֵׂה ase.

You should meditate to correct the thought that caused the loss of the sparks of Light. Also meditate on the Names that control our thoughts for each of the six days of the week as follow:

Day	Name	Meditation	World
Sunday	יְהֶוֶה	על צבא כף ואו זין ואו טפטפיה א מן אהיה דמרגלא ושם:	*Beriah*.
Monday	יֱהֱוִה	על מגן כף ואו זין ואו טפטפיה ה מן אהיה דמרגלא ושם:	*Yetzirah*.
Tuesday	מצפץ	צוה פוזד כף ואו זין ואו טפטפיה י מן אהיה דמרגלא ושם:	*Asiyah*.
Wednesday	אל	צוה פוזד כף ואו זין ואו טפטפיה י מן יהו דמרגלא ושם:	*Asiyah*.
Thursday	אלהים	על מגן כף ואו זין ואו טפטפיה ה מן יהו דמרגלא ושם:	*Yetzirah*.
Friday	מצפץ	על צבא כף ואו זין ואו טפטפיה ו מן יהו דמרגלא ושם:	*Beriah*.

Each of these Names (על צבא, כף ואו זין ואו, טפטפיה), adds up to 193, which is the same numerical value as the word *zokef* (raise). These Names raise the Holy Spark from the *Chitzoniyim*. Also, when you say the words "*mekabetz nidchei*" (in the continuation of the blessing), which adds up to 304 – the same numerical value of *Shin*, *Dalet* (demon), you should meditate to collect all the lost sparks and cancel out the power of the negative forces.

May it be pleasing before You, Lord, my God and God of my forefathers, that every drop and drop of keri that came out of me for vain, and from all of Yisrael in general, and especially not as a cause of precept, if it was coerced or willfully, with intention or without, by passing thought or by an action, in this lifetime or in previous, and it was swallowed by the klipa, that the klipa will vomit all the sparks of keri that was swollen by it, by virtue of your great name that comes from the verse:"He swallowed up wealth and vomited it out, and from his belly God will cast it." (Job 20:15), and by the virtue of your great name you will return them to the holy place, and do what is good in Your eyes.

בָּרוּךְ baruch אַתָּה Ata יְהֹוָואדֹנָיאהדונהי Adonai ; יכוין וזבו בשילוב יהוה כוזו: יְוָזְהֲבָוּוּה
מְקַבֵּץ mekabetz ע״ב ס״ג מ״ה ב״ן, הברכה (למתק את ז' המלכים שמתו)
נִדְחֵי nidchei ע״ב, ריבוע יהוה עַמּוֹ amo וזבו יִשְׂרָאֵל Yisrael:

THE EIGHTH (ELEVENTH) BLESSING

This blessing helps us to balance judgment with mercy. As mercy is time, we can use it to change ourselves before judgment occurs.

Yesod

הָשִׁיבָה hashiva שׁוֹפְטֵינוּ shoftenu כְּבָרִאשׁוֹנָה kevarishona.
וְיוֹעֲצֵינוּ veyo'atzenu כְּבַתְּחִלָּה kevatechila ר״ת שכ״ה (דינים זכרים שביסוד) ויהוה (הממתקם).
וְהָסֵר vehaser מִמֶּנּוּ mimenu יָגוֹן yagon (סמאל) וַאֲנָחָה va'anacha (לילית).
וּמְלוֹךְ umloch עָלֵינוּ aleinu מְהֵרָה mehera אַתָּה Ata
יְהֹוָואדֹנָיאהדונהי Adonai לְבַדְּךָ levadcha. בְּחֶסֶד bechesed ע״ב, ריבוע יהוה
וּבְרַחֲמִים uvrachamim מצפצ, אלהים דיודין, י״פ ייי ; להמתיק ברחמים דיני צדק ומשפט
בְּצֶדֶק betzedek וּבְמִשְׁפָּט uvmishpat ע״ה = ה״פ אלהים: בָּרוּךְ baruch אַתָּה Ata
יְהֹוָואדֹנָיאהדונהי Adonai מֶלֶךְ melech אוֹהֵב ohev ממתיק דיני
צְדָקָה tzedaka ע״ה ריבוע אלהים וּמִשְׁפָּט umishpat ע״ה ה״פ אלהים:

THE NINTH (TWELFTH) BLESSING

This blessing helps us remove all forms of negativity, whether it comes from people, situations or even the negative energy of the Angel of Death [(**do not pronounce these names**) *Sa-ma-el* (male aspect) and*Li-li-th* (female aspect), which are encoded here], by using the Holy Name: *Shadai* שדי, which is encoded mathematically into the last four words of this blessing and also appears inside a *Mezuzah* for the same purpose.

Blessed are You, Lord, Who gathers the displaced of His Nation, Israel.

THE EIGHTH (ELEVENTH) BLESSING

Restore our judges, as at first, and our mentors, as in the beginning. Remove from us sorrow and moaning. Reign over us soon, You alone, Lord, with kindness and compassion, with righteousness and justice. Blessed are You, Lord, the King Who loves righteousness and justice.

Keter

לַמִּינִים laminim וְלַמַּלְשִׁינִים velamalshinim אַל al תְּהִי tehi תִקְוָה tikva

וְכָל vechol ילי הַזֵּדִים hazedim כְּרֶגַע kerega ג"פ אלהים עם ט"ו אותיות פשוטות

יֹאבֵדוּ yovedu• וְכָל־ vechol ילי אוֹיְבֶיךָ oyvecha (סמאל)

וְכָל־ vechol ילי שׂוֹנְאֶיךָ son'echa (לילית) מְהֵרָה mehera יִכָּרֵתוּ yikaretu•

וּמַלְכוּת umalchut הָרִשְׁעָה harish'a מְהֵרָה mehera תְעַקֵּר te'aker

וּתְשַׁבֵּר utshaber וּתְכַלֵּם utchalem וְתַכְנִיעֵם vetachni'em בִּמְהֵרָה bimhera

בְיָמֵינוּ veyamenu: בָּרוּךְ baruch אַתָּה Ata יְהֹוָהאדני(יהוהאדני)יאהדונהי Adonai

שׁוֹבֵר shover אוֹיְבִים oyvim וּמַכְנִיעַ umachni'a זֵדִים zedim ר"ת = שדי:

The Tenth (thirteenth) Blessing

This blessing surrounds us with total positivity to help us always be at the right place at the right time. It also helps attract only positive people into our lives.

Yesod

עַל al הַצַּדִּיקִים hatzadikim צדיק יסוד עולם וְעַל ve'al הַחֲסִידִים hachasidim

וְעַל ve'al שְׁאֵרִית she'erit עַמְּךָ amecha בֵּית bet ב"פ ראה יִשְׂרָאֵל Yisrael•

וְעַל ve'al פְּלֵיטַת peletat בֵּית bet ב"פ ראה סוֹפְרֵיהֶם sofrehem•

וְעַל ve'al גֵּרֵי gerei הַצֶּדֶק hatzedek וְעָלֵינוּ ve'alenu• יֶהֱמוּ yehemu

נָא na רַחֲמֶיךָ rachamecha יְהֹוָהאדנייאהדונהי Adonai אֱלֹהֵינוּ Elohenu ילה

וְתֵן veten שָׂכָר sachar י"פ ב"ן טוֹב tov והו לְכָל־ lechol יה אדני

הַבּוֹטְחִים habotchim בְּשִׁמְךָ beshimcha בֶּאֱמֶת be'emet אהיה פעמים אהיה, ז"פ ס"ג•

The Ninth (twelfth) Blessing

For the heretics and for the slanderers, let there be no hope.

Let all the wicked perish in an instant. And may all Your foes and all Your haters be speedily cut down. And as for the evil government, may You quickly uproot and smash it, and may You destroy and humble it, speedily in our days. Blessed are You, Lord, Who smashes foes and humbles the wicked.

The Tenth (thirteenth) Blessing

On the righteous, on the pious, on the remnants of the House of Israel, on the remnants of their writers' academies, on the righteous converts, and on us, may Your compassion be stirred, Lord, our God. And give good reward to all those who truly trust in Your Name.

וְשִׂים vesim וְחֶלְקֵנוּ chelkenu עִמָּהֶם imahem וּלְעוֹלָם ul'olam ריבוע ס"ג וי' אותיות דס"ג

לֹא lo נֵבוֹשׁ nevosh כִּי ki בְךָ vecha בָּטָחְנוּ batachnu.

וְעַל ve'al חַסְדְּךָ chasdecha הַגָּדוֹל hagadol להח ; עם ד' אותיות = מבה, יזל, אום

בֶּאֱמֶת be'emet אהיה פעמים אהיה, ז"פ ס"ג נִשְׁעָנְנוּ nish'anenu:

בָּרוּךְ baruch אַתָּה Ata יְהֹוָהאדניאהדונהי Adonai מִשְׁעָן mish'an

וּמִבְטָח umivtach לַצַּדִּיקִים latzadikim ר"ת ימול (כל מי שנימול נקרא צדיק):

THE ELEVENTH (FOURTEENTH) BLESSING

This blessing connects us to the power of Jerusalem, to the building of the Temple, and to the preparation for the *Mashiach*.

Hod

תִּשְׁכּוֹן tishkon בְּתוֹךְ betoch יְרוּשָׁלַיִם Yerushalayim עִירְךָ ircha

כַּאֲשֶׁר ka'asher דִּבַּרְתָּ dibarta ראה וְכִסֵּא vechise דָוִד David

עַבְדְּךָ avdecha פוי, אל אדני מְהֵרָה mehera בְּתוֹכָהּ vetocha תָּכִין tachin

Meditate here that *Mashiach Ben Yosef* shall not be killed by the wicked *Armilos* **(Do not pronounce).**

וּבְנֵה uvne אוֹתָהּ ota בִּנְיַן binyan עוֹלָם olam בִּמְהֵרָה bimhera

בְּיָמֵינוּ veyamenu: בָּרוּךְ baruch אַתָּה Ata יְהֹוָהאדניאהדונהי Adonai

בּוֹנֵה bone ס"ג יְרוּשָׁלָיִם Yerushalayim:

THE TWELFTH (FIFTEENTH) BLESSING

This blessing helps us achieve a personal state of *Mashiach* by transforming our reactive nature into becoming proactive. Just as there is a global *Mashiach*, each person has a personal *Mashiach* within. When enough people achieve their transformation, the way will be paved for the appearance of the global *Mashiach*.

---

and place our lot with them. And may we never be embarrassed, for it is in You that we place our trust; it is upon Your great compassion that we truly rely. Blessed are You, Lord, the support and security of the righteous.

THE ELEVENTH (FOURTEENTH) BLESSING

May You dwell in Jerusalem, Your City,

as You have promised. And may You establish the throne of David, Your servant, speedily within it and build it as an eternal structure, speedily in our days Blessed are You, Lord, Who builds Jerusalem.

Netzach

This blessing contains 20 words, which is the same number of words in *"Ki nicham Adonai Tziyon nicham kol chorvoteha..." (Isaiah 51:3)*, a verse that speaks about the Final Redemption.

אֶת et צֶמַח tzemach יהוה אהיה יהוה אדני דָּוִד David

עַבְדְּךָ avdecha פוי, אל אדני מְהֵרָה mehera תַּצְמִיחַ tatzmia'ch וְקַרְנוֹ vekarno

תָּרוּם tarum בִּישׁוּעָתֶךָ bishu'atecha. כִּי ki לִישׁוּעָתְךָ lishu'atcha

קִוִּינוּ kivinu כָּל־ kol ילי הַיּוֹם hayom ע״ה נגד, מזבח, זן, אל יהוה

You should meditate and ask here for the Final Redemption to occur right away.

בָּרוּךְ baruch אַתָּה Ata יְהֹוָהאדניאהדונהי Adonai

מַצְמִיחַ matzmi'ach קֶרֶן keren יְשׁוּעָה yeshu'a:

THE THIRTEENTH (SIXTEENTH) BLESSING

This blessing is the most important of all blessings, because here we acknowledge all of our reactive behavior. We make reference to our wrongful actions in general, and we also specify a particular incident. The section inside the box provides us with an opportunity to ask the Light for personal sustenance. The Ari states that throughout this prayer, even on fast days, we have a personal angel accompanying us. If we meditate upon this angel, all our prayers must be answered. The Thirteenth Blessing is one above the twelve zodiac signs, and it raises us above the influence of the stars and planets.

Tiferet

שְׁמַע shema קוֹלֵנוּ kolenu יְהֹוָהאדניאהדונהי Adonai (יוד הה וו הה)

אֱלֹהֵינוּ Elohenu ילה (אבג יתץ). אָב av הָרַחֲמָן harachaman רַחֵם rachem

עָלֵינוּ alenu אברהם, וז״פ אל, רי״ו ול״ב נתיבות החכמה, רמ״ח (אברים), עסמ״ב וט״ז אותיות פשוטות

(קרע שטן). וְקַבֵּל vekabel בְּרַחֲמִים berachamim מצפצ, אלהים דיודין, י״פ ייי

וּבְרָצוֹן uvratzon מהש ע״ה, ע״ב בריבוע וקס״א ע״ה, אל שדי ע״ה אֶת et

תְּפִלָּתֵנוּ tefilatenu (נגד יכש). כִּי ki אֵל El ייא״י (מילוי דס״ג)

שׁוֹמֵעַ shome'a תְּפִלּוֹת tefilot וְתַחֲנוּנִים vetachanunim אָתָּה Ata (בטר צתג).

THE TWELFTH (FIFTEENTH) BLESSING

The offspring of David, Your servant, may You speedily cause to sprout. And may You raise their worth with Your salvation, because it is for Your salvation that we have hoped all day long. Blessed are You, Lord, Who sprouts out the worth of the salvation.

THE THIRTEENTH (SIXTEENTH) BLESSING

Hear our voice, Lord, our God. Merciful Father, have mercy over us. Accept our prayer with compassion and favor, because You are God, Who hears prayers and supplications.

It is good for you to be aware, acknowledge and confess your prior negative actions and to ask for your livelihood here:

רִבּוֹנוֹ ribono שֶׁל shel עוֹלָם olam, וְחָטָאתִי chatati עָוִיתִי aviti
וּפָשַׁעְתִּי ufashati לְפָנֶיךָ lefanecha ס״ג מ״ה ב״ן יְהִי yehi רָצוֹן ratzon מהש ע״ה,
ע״ב בריבוע וקס״א ע״ה, אל שדי ע״ה מִלְּפָנֶיךָ milfanecha ס״ג מ״ה ב״ן שֶׁתִּמְחוֹל shetimchol
וְתִסְלַח vetislach יהוה ע״ב וּתְכַפֵּר utchaper לִי li עַל al כָּל kol ילי ; עמם
מַה ma מ״ה שֶׁחָטָאתִי shechatati וְשֶׁעָוִיתִי veshe'aviti וְשֶׁפָּשַׁעְתִּי veshepashati
לְפָנֶיךָ lefanecha ס״ג מ״ה ב״ן מִיּוֹם miyom ע״ה נגד, מזבח, זן, אל יהוה
שֶׁנִּבְרֵאתִי shenivreti עַד ad הַיּוֹם hayom ע״ה נגד, מזבח, זן, אל יהוה הַזֶּה haze והו
וּבִפְרַט uvifrat (mention here a specific negative action or behavior you have and ask for forgivness)
וִיהִי vihi רָצוֹן ratzon מהש ע״ה, ע״ב בריבוע וקס״א ע״ה, אל שדי ע״ה
מִלְּפָנֶיךָ milfanecha ס״ג מ״ה ב״ן יְהֹוָאדהנויאהדונהי Adonai אֱלֹהֵינוּ Elohenu ילה
וֵאלֹהֵי velohei לכב ; מילוי ע״ב, דמב ; ילה אֲבוֹתֵינוּ avotenu שֶׁתַּזְמִין shetazmin
פַּרְנָסָתֵנוּ parnasatenu וּמְזוֹנוֹתֵינוּ umzonotenu לִי li וּלְכָל ulchol יה אדני
אַנְשֵׁי anshei בֵיתִי veti ב״פ ראה הַיּוֹם hayom ע״ה נגד, מזבח, זן, אל יהוה
וּבְכָל uvchol ב״ן, לכב יוֹם yom ע״ה נגד, מזבח, זן, אל יהוה
וָיוֹם vayom ע״ה נגד, מזבח, זן, אל יהוה בְּרֵיוַח berevach וְלֹא velo
בְּצִמְצוּם vetzimtzum, בְּכָבוֹד bechavod בוכו וְלֹא velo בְּבִזּוּי bevizui,
בְּנַחַת benachat וְלֹא velo בְּצַעַר vetza'ar, וְלֹא velo אֶצְטָרֵךְ etztarech
לְמַתְּנוֹת lematenot בָּשָׂר basar וָדָם vadam וְלֹא velo לְהַלְוָאָתָם lehalva'atam,
אֶלָּא ela מִיָּדְךָ miyadcha הָרְוָחָה harchava וְהַפְּתוּחָה vehapetucha
וְהַמְּלֵאָה vehamele'a וּבִזְכוּת uvizchut שִׁמְךָ shimcha הַגָּדוֹל hagadol
להו; עם ד׳ אותיות = מבה, יזל, אום (Do not pronounce this Name): דִּיקַרְנוֹסָא וזהך עם ג׳ אותיות
- ובאתב״ש = סאל, אמן, יאהדונהי) הַמְּמֻנֶּה hamemune עַל al הַפַּרְנָסָה haparnasa:

Master of the World!

I have transgressed. I have committed iniquity and I have sinned before You. May it be Your will that You would pardon, forgive and excuse all my transgressions, and all the iniquities that I have committed, and all the sins that I have sinned before You, ever since the day I was created and until this day (and especially…). May it be pleasing before You, Lord, our God and God of my forefathers, that You would provide for my livelihood and sustenance, and that of my household, today and each and every day, with abundance and not with meagerness; with dignity and not with shame; with comfort and not with suffering; and that I may not require the gifts of flesh and blood, nor their loans, but only from Your Hand, which is generous, open, and full, and by virtue of Your great Name, which is responsible for livelihood.

malkenu מַלְכֵּנוּ ב"ן מ"ה ס"ג umilfanecha וּמִלְּפָנֶיךָ

(טנ"ע וזקב) te'shivenu תְּשִׁיבֵנוּ al אַל־ rekam רֵיקָם

:tefilatenu תְּפִלָּתֵנוּ ushma וּשְׁמַע va'anenu וַעֲנֵנוּ chonenu וְחָנֵּנוּ

pe פֶּה ילי kol כָּל־ tefilat תְּפִלַּת shome'a שׁוֹמֵעַ Ata אַתָּה ki כִּי

(פה דו"א) מילה ; וע"ה אלהים, אהיה אדני (יגל פזק)

Adonai יְהֹוָהאדניה(יהואדניה)יאהדונהי Ata אַתָּה baruch בָּרוּךְ

You should meditate here on the Holy Name: אראריתא"א

Rav Chaim Vital says: "I have found in the books of the kabbalists that person's prayer, who meditates on this Name in the blessing *shome'a tefila*, will never go unanswered."

:יוד הי וו הה = ע"ה אדני וניקודה ב"ן ,אְוּכְצְ א"ש אתב (שקו צית) tefila תְּפִלָּה shome'a שׁוֹמֵעַ

The Final Three Blessings

Through the merit of Moses, Aaron and Joseph, who are our channels for the final three blessings, we are able to bring down all the spiritual energy that we aroused with our prayers and blessings.

The Seventeenth Blessing

During this blessing, referring to Moses, we should always meditate to try to know exactly what God wants from us in our life, as signified by the phrase, "Let it be the will of God." We ask God to guide us toward the work we came to Earth to do. The Creator cannot just accept the work that we want to do; we must carry out the work we were destined to do.

Netzach

You have made requests (of daily needs) to God. Now, after asking for your needs to be met, you should praise the Creator in the last three blessings. This is like a person who has received what he needs from his Master and departs from Him. You should say "*retze*" and meditate for the Supernal Desire (*Keter*) that is called *metzach haratzon* (the Forehead of the Desire).

And from before You, our King,
do not turn us away empty-handed but be gracious,
answer us, and hear our prayer. Because You hear the prayer of every mouth.
Blessed are You, Lord, Who hears prayers.

רְצֵה retze אלף למד הה יוד מם

Meditate here to transform misfortune and tragedy (צָרָה) into desire and acceptance (רְצֵה).

יְהֹוָאדהנויאהדונהי Adonai אֱלֹהֵינוּ Elohenu ילה בְּעַמְּךָ be'amecha יִשְׂרָאֵל Yisrael

וְלִתְפִלָּתָם velitfilatam שְׁעֵה she'e. וְהָשֵׁב vehashev הָעֲבוֹדָה ha'avoda

לִדְבִיר lidvir רי״ו בֵּיתֶךָ betecha ב״פ ראה. וְאִשֵּׁי ve'ishei יִשְׂרָאֵל Yisrael

וּתְפִלָּתָם utfilatam מְהֵרָה mehera בְּאַהֲבָה be'ahava אחד, דאגה

תְקַבֵּל tekabel בְּרָצוֹן beratzon מהש ע״ה, ע״ב בריבוע וקס״א ע״ה, אל שדי ע״ה.

וּתְהִי ut'hi לְרָצוֹן leratzon מהש ע״ה, ע״ב בריבוע וקס״א ע״ה, אל שדי ע״ה

תָּמִיד tamid ע״ה קס״א קנ״א קמ״ג עֲבוֹדַת avodat יִשְׂרָאֵל Yisrael עַמֶּךָ amecha:

וְאַתָּה veAta בְּרַחֲמֶיךָ verachamecha הָרַבִּים harabim.

תַּחְפֹּץ tachpotz בָּנוּ banu וְתִרְצֵנוּ vetirtzenu וְתֶחֱזֶינָה vetechezena

עֵינֵינוּ enenu ריבוע מ״ה בְּשׁוּבְךָ beshuvcha

לְצִיּוֹן leTziyon יוסף, ו׳ הויות, קנאה בְּרַחֲמִים berachamim מצפצ, אלהים דיודין, י״פ ייי:

בָּרוּךְ baruch אַתָּה Ata יְהֹוָאדהנויאהדונהי Adonai

הַמַּחֲזִיר hamachazir שְׁכִינָתוֹ shechinato לְצִיּוֹן leTziyon יוסף, ו׳ הויות, קנאה:

THE FINAL THREE BLESSINGS
THE SEVENTEENTH BLESSING

Find favor, Lord, our God, in Your People, Israel, and turn to their prayer. Restore the service to the inner sanctuary of Your Temple. Accept the offerings of Israel and their prayer with favor, speedily, and with love. May the service of Your People Israel always be favorable to You. And You in Your great compassion take delight in us and are pleased with us. May our eyes witness Your return to Zion with compassion. Blessed are You, Lord, Who returns His Shechinah to Zion.

THE EIGHTEENTH BLESSING

This blessing is our thank you. Kabbalistically, the biggest 'thank you' we can give the Creator is to do exactly what we are supposed to do in terms of our spiritual work.

Hod

Bow your entire body at "*modem*" and straighten up at *'Adonai'*.

מוֹדִים modim מאה ברכות שתיקן דוד לאמרם כל יום אֲנַחְנוּ anachnu לָךְ lach

שָׁאַתָּה sheAta הוּא hu יְהֹוָאדהיאהדונהי Adonai (ננ) אֱלֹהֵינוּ Elohenu ילה

וֵאלֹהֵי velohei לכב ; מילוי ע״ב, דמב ; ילה אֲבוֹתֵינוּ avotenu לְעוֹלָם le'olam

ריבוע ס״ג וי׳ אותיות דס״ג וָעֶד va'ed• צוּרֵנוּ tzurenu צוּר tzur אלהים דההין ע״ה

חַיֵּינוּ chayenu וּמָגֵן umagen ג״פ אל (ייא״י מילוי דס״ג) ; ר״ת מיכאל גבריאל נוריאל

יִשְׁעֵנוּ yish'enu אַתָּה Ata הוּא hu• לְדוֹר ledor וָדוֹר vador רי״ו נוֹדֶה node

לְךָ lecha וּנְסַפֵּר unsaper תְּהִלָּתֶךָ tehilatecha• עַל־ al חַיֵּינוּ chayenu

הַמְּסוּרִים hamesurim בְּיָדֶךָ beyadecha• וְעַל ve'al נִשְׁמוֹתֵינוּ nishmotenu

הַפְּקוּדוֹת hapekudot לָךְ lach• וְעַל־ ve'al נִסֶּיךָ nisecha שֶׁבְּכָל shebechol

ב״ן, לכב יוֹם yom ע״ה נגד, מזבח, זן, אל יהוה עִמָּנוּ imanu ריבוע ס״ג, קס״א ע״ה וד׳ אותיות

וְעַל ve'al נִפְלְאוֹתֶיךָ nifle'otecha וְטוֹבוֹתֶיךָ vetovotecha שֶׁבְּכָל shebechol

ב״ן, לכב עֵת et• עֶרֶב erev וָבֹקֶר vavoker וְצָהֳרָיִם vetzahorayim• הַטּוֹב hatov

והו כִּי־ ki לֹא־ lo כָלוּ chalu רַחֲמֶיךָ rachamecha• הַמְרַחֵם hamerachem

אברהם, וח״פ אל, רי״ו ול״ב נתיבות החכמה, רמ״ח (אברים), עסמ״ב וט״ז אותיות פשוטות כִּי־ ki לֹא lo

תַמּוּ tamu חֲסָדֶיךָ chasadecha כִּי ki מֵעוֹלָם me'olam קִוִּינוּ kivinu לָךְ lach:

THE EIGHTEENTH BLESSING

We give thanks to You, for it is You, Lord, Who is our God and God of our forefathers, forever and for all eternity. You are our Rock, the Rock of our lives, and the Shield of our salvation. From one generation to another, we shall give thanks to You and we shall tell of Your praise. For our lives that are entrusted in Your hands, for our souls that are in Your care, for Your miracles that are with us every day, and for Your wonders and Your favors that are with us at all times: evening, morning and afternoon. You are the good One, for Your compassion has never ceased. You are the compassionate One, for Your kindness has never ended, for we have always placed our hope in You.

וְעַל ve'al כֻּלָּם kulam יִתְבָּרַךְ yitbarach וְיִתְרוֹמַם veyitromam

וְיִתְנַשֵּׂא veyitnase תָּמִיד tamid ע״ה קס״א קנ״א קמ״ג שִׁמְךָ shimcha

מַלְכֵּנוּ malkenu לְעוֹלָם le'olam ריבוע ס״ג וי׳ אותיות דס״ג וָעֶד va'ed.

וְכָל־ vechol ילי הַחַיִּים hachayim אהיה אהיה יהוה, בינה ע״ה יוֹדוּךָ yoducha סֶּלָה sela:

וִיהַלְלוּ vihalelu וִיבָרְכוּ vivarchu יהוה ריבוע יהוה ריבוע מ״ה אֶת־ et

שִׁמְךָ shimcha הַגָּדוֹל hagadol להח ; עם ד׳ אותיות = מבה, יזל, אום בֶּאֱמֶת be'emet

אהיה פעמים אהיה, ז״פ ס״ג לְעוֹלָם le'olam ריבוע ס״ג וי׳ אותיות דס״ג כִּי ki טוֹב tov והו ;

כי טוב = יהוה אהיה, אום, מבה, יזל. הָאֵל haEl לאה ; ייא״י (מילוי דס״ג) יְשׁוּעָתֵנוּ yeshu'atenu

וְעֶזְרָתֵנוּ ve'ezratenu סֶלָה sela. הָאֵל haEl לאה ; ייא״י (מילוי דס״ג) הַטּוֹב hatov והו:

Bend your knees at *"baruch"*, bow at *"Ata"* and straighten up at *"Adonai"*.

בָּרוּךְ baruch אַתָּה Ata יְהֹוָהאדניאהדונהי Adonai (הי) הַטּוֹב hatov והו

שִׁמְךָ shimcha וּלְךָ ulcha נָאֶה na'e לְהוֹדוֹת lehodot ס״ת כהת, משיח בן דוד ע״ה:

THE FINAL BLESSING

We are emanating the energy of peace to the entire world. We also make it our intent to use our mouths only for good. Kabbalistically, the power of words and speech is unimaginable. We hope to use that power wisely, which is perhaps one of the most difficult tasks we have to carry out.

Yesod

שִׂים sim שָׁלוֹם shalom

טוֹבָה tova אכא וּבְרָכָה uvracha חַיִּים chayim אהיה אהיה יהוה, בינה ע״ה

חֵן chen מילוי דמ״ה בריבוע, מוחי וָחֶסֶד vachesed ע״ב, ריבוע יהוה

צְדָקָה tzedaka ע״ה ריבוע אלהים וְרַחֲמִים verachamim עָלֵינוּ alenu

וְעַל־ ve'al כָּל־ kol ילי ; יִשְׂרָאֵל Yisrael עמם עַמֶּךָ amecha

---

And for all those things, may Your Name be always blessed, exalted and extolled, our King, forever and ever, and all the living shall thank You, Selah. And they shall praise and bless Your Great Name, sincerely and forever, for It is good, the God of our salvation and our help, Selah, the good God. Blessed are You, Lord, whose Name is good, and to You it is befitting to give thanks.

THE FINAL BLESSING

Place peace, goodness,
blessing, life, grace, kindness, righteousness, and mercy upon us and upon all of Israel, Your People.

וּבָרְכֵנוּ uvarchenu אָבִינוּ avinu כֻּלָּנוּ kulanu כְּאֶחָד ke'echad אהבה, דאגה

בְּאוֹר be'or רז, א"ס פָּנֶיךָ panecha ס"ג מ"ה ב"ן כִּי ki בְאוֹר ve'or רז, א"ס

פָּנֶיךָ panecha ס"ג מ"ה ב"ן נָתַתָּ natata לָנוּ lanu אלהים, אהיה אדני

יְהֹוָה יאהדונהי Adonai אֱלֹהֵינוּ Elohenu ילה תּוֹרָה torah וְחַיִּים vechayim

אהיה אהיה יהוה, בינה ע"ה. אַהֲבָה ahava אחד, דאגה וָחֶסֶד vachesed ע"ב, ריבוע יהוה.

צְדָקָה tzedaka ע"ה ריבוע אלהים וְרַחֲמִים verachamim. בְּרָכָה beracha

וְשָׁלוֹם veshalom. וְטוֹב vetov והו בְּעֵינֶיךָ be'enecha ע"ה קס"א ; ריבוע מ"ה

לְבָרְכֵנוּ levarchenu וּלְבָרֵךְ ulvarech אֶת et כָּל kol ילי עַמְּךָ amecha

יִשְׂרָאֵל Yisrael בְּרוֹב berov י"פ אהיה עֹז oz וְשָׁלוֹם veshalom:

בָּרוּךְ baruch אַתָּה Ata יְהֹוָה יאהדונהי Adonai

הַמְבָרֵךְ hamevarech אֶת et עַמּוֹ amo יִשְׂרָאֵל Yisrael

ר"ת = אלהים (אילהויהם = יב"ק) בַּשָּׁלוֹם bashalom. אָמֵן amen יאהדונהי.

YIH'YU LERATZON

There are 42 letters in the verse in the secret of *Ana Beko'ach*.

יִהְיוּ yih'yu אל (ייא" מילוי דס"ג) לְרָצוֹן leratzon מהש ע"ה, ע"ב בריבוע וקס"א ע"ה, אל שדי ע"ה

אִמְרֵי imrei פִי fi ר"ת אֶלֶף = אלף למד שין דלת יוד ע"ה וְהֶגְיוֹן vehegyon לִבִּי libi

לְפָנֶיךָ lefanecha ס"ג מ"ה ב"ן יְהֹוָה יאהדונהי Adonai צוּרִי tzuri וְגֹאֲלִי vego'ali:

Bless us all as one, our Father, with the Light of Your Countenance, because it is with the Light of Your Countenance that You, Lord, our God, have given us Torah and life, love and kindness, righteousness and mercy, blessing and peace. May it be good in Your Eyes to bless us and to bless Your entire Nation, Israel, with abundant power and with peace.Blessed are You, Lord, Who blesses His Nation, Israel, with peace, Amen.

YIH'YU LERATZON

"May the utterances of my mouth
and the thoughts of my heart find favor before You, Lord, my Rock and my Redeemer." (Psalms 19:15)

ELOHAI NETZOR

אֱלֹהַי Elohai מילוי ע"ב, דמב ; ילה נְצֹור netzor לְשׁוֹנִי leshoni מֵרָע mera⬩

וְשִׂפְתוֹתַי vesiftotai מִדַּבֵּר midaber ראה מִרְמָה mirma⬩ וְלִמְקַלְלַי velimkalelai

נַפְשִׁי nafshi תִדּוֹם tidom⬩ וְנַפְשִׁי venafshi כֶּעָפָר ke'afar

לַכֹּל lakol יה אדני תִּהְיֶה tih'ye⬩ פְּתַח petach לִבִּי libi בְּתוֹרָתֶךָ betoratecha⬩

וְאַחֲרֵי ve'acharei מִצְוֹתֶיךָ mitzvotecha תִּרְדֹּוף tirdof נַפְשִׁי nafshi⬩

וְכָל vechol ילי הַקָּמִים hakamim עָלַי alai לְרָעָה lera'a רהע⬩ מְהֵרָה mehera

הָפֵר hafer עֲצָתָם atzatam וְקַלְקֵל vekalkel מַחְשְׁבוֹתָם machshevotam⬩

עֲשֵׂה ase לְמַעַן lema'an שְׁמָךְ shemach⬩ עֲשֵׂה ase לְמַעַן lema'an

יְמִינָךְ yeminach⬩ עֲשֵׂה ase לְמַעַן lema'an תּוֹרָתָךְ toratach⬩ עֲשֵׂה ase

לְמַעַן lema'an קְדֻושָּׁתָךְ kedushatach⬩ ר"ת הפסוק = מ"ה יהוה לְמַעַן lema'an

יֵחָלְצוּן yechaltzun יְדִידֶיךָ yedidecha ר"ת ילי הוֹשִׁיעָה hoshi'a יהוה וש"ע נהורין

יְמִינְךָ yemincha וַעֲנֵנִי va'aneni (כתיב: ועננו) ר"ת אל (יי"א" מילוי דס"ג)⬩:

Before we recite the next verse ("*yih'yu leratzon*") we have an opportunity to strengthen our connection to our soul using our name. Each person has a verse in the *Torah* that connects to their name. Either their name is in the verse, or the first and last letters of the name correspond to the first or last letters of a verse.

YIH'YU LERATZON (THE SECOND)

There are 42 letters in the verse in the secret of *Ana Beko'ach*.

יִהְיוּ yih'yu אל (יי"א" מילוי דס"ג) לְרָצוֹן leratzon מהש ע"ה, ע"ב בריבוע וקס"א ע"ה, אל שדי ע"ה

אִמְרֵי imrei פִי fi ר"ת אֱלֶף = אלף למד שין דלת יוד ע"ה וְהֶגְיוֹן vehegyon לִבִּי libi

לְפָנֶיךָ lefanecha ס"ג מ"ה ב"ן יְהֹוָהאדניאהדונהי Adonai צוּרִי tzuri וְגֹאֲלִי vego'ali⬩:

ELOHAI NETZOR

My God, guard my tongue from evil and my lips from speaking deceit. To those who curse me, let my spirit remain silent, and let my spirit be as dust for everyone. Open my heart toYour Torah and let my heart pursue Your commandments. All those who rise against me to do me harm, speedily nullify their plans and disturb their thoughts. Do so for the sake of Your Name. Do so for the sake of Your Right. Do so for the sake of Your Torah. Do so for the sake of Your Holiness, "So that Your loved ones may be saved. Redeem Your right and answer me." (Psalms 60:7)

YIH'YU LERATZON (THE SECOND)

"May the utterances of my mouth
and the thoughts of my heart find favor before You, Lord, my Rock and my Redeemer." (Psalms 19:15)

OSE SHALOM

You take three steps backward;

עֹושֶׂה ose שָׁלֹום shalom

Left
You turn to the left and say:

בִּמְרֹומָיו bimromav ר"ת ע"ב, ריבוע יהוה

הוּא hu בְּרַחֲמָיו verachamav יַעֲשֶׂה ya'ase

Right
You turn to the right and say:

שָׁלֹום shalom עָלֵינוּ alenu ר"ת ש"ע נהורין

וְעַל ve'al כָּל־ kol ילי ; עמם עַמּוֹ amo יִשְׂרָאֵל Yisrael

Center
You face the center and say:

וְאִמְרוּ ve'imru אָמֵן amen יאהדונהי:

יְהִי yehi רָצוֹן ratzon מהש ע"ה, ע"ב בריבוע וקס"א ע"ה, אל שדי ע"ה
מִלְּפָנֶיךָ milfanecha ס"ג מ"ה ב"ן יְהֹוָהאדניאהדונהי Adonai אֱלֹהֵינוּ Elohenu ילה
וֵאלֹהֵי velohei לכב ; מילוי ע"ב, דמב ; ילה אֲבוֹתֵינוּ avotenu, שֶׁתִּבְנֶה shetivne
בֵּית bet ב"פ ראה הַמִּקְדָּשׁ hamikdash בִּמְהֵרָה bimhera בְיָמֵינוּ veyamenu
וְתֵן veten חֶלְקֵנוּ chelkenu בְּתוֹרָתָךְ betoratach לַעֲשׂוֹת la'asot חֻקֵּי chukei
רְצוֹנָךְ retzonach וּלְעָבְדָךְ ul'ovdach פוי, אל אדני בְּלֵבָב belevav בוכו שָׁלֵם shalem.

You take three steps forward.

OSE SHALOM

He, Who makes peace in His high places, He,
in His compassion, shall make peace upon us And upon His entire nation, Israel, and you shall say, Amen.

May it be pleasing before You,
Lord, our God and God of our forefathers, that You shall rebuild the Temple speedily, in our days, and place our lot in Your Torah, so that we may fulfill the laws of Your desire and serve You wholeheartedly.

KADDISH TITKABAL

יִתְגַּדַּל yitgadal וְיִתְקַדַּשׁ veyitkadash שד"י ומילוי שד"י ; י"א אותיות כמנין ו"ה

שְׁמֵיהּ shemei (שם י"ה דע"ב) רַבָּא raba קנ"א ב"ן, יהוה אלהים יהוה אדני,

מילוי קס"א וס"ג, מ"ה ברבוע וע"ב ע"ה ; ר"ת = ו"פ אלהים ; ס"ת = ג"פ יב"ק: אָמֵן amen אידהנויה.

בְּעָלְמָא be'alma דִּי di בְרָא vera כִרְעוּתֵיהּ chir'utei.

וְיַמְלִיךְ veyamlich מַלְכוּתֵיהּ malchutei. וְיַצְמַח veyatzmach

פּוּרְקָנֵיהּ purkanei. וִיקָרֵב vikarev מְשִׁיחֵיהּ meshichei: אָמֵן amen אידהנויה.

בְּחַיֵּיכוֹן bechayechon וּבְיוֹמֵיכוֹן uvyomechon וּבְחַיֵּי uvchayei

דְכָל dechol ילי בֵּית bet ב"פ ראה יִשְׂרָאֵל Yisrael בַּעֲגָלָא ba'agala

וּבִזְמַן uvizman קָרִיב kariv וְאִמְרוּ ve'imru אָמֵן amen: אָמֵן amen אידהנויה.

The congregation and the *chazan* say the following:

28 words (until *be'alma*) – meditate: מילוי דמילוי דע"ב (יוד ויו דלת הי יוד ויו יוד ויו הי יוד)
28 letters (until *almaya*) - meditate: מילוי דמילוי דע"ב (יוד ויו דלת הי יוד ויו יוד ויו הי יוד)

יְהֵא yehe שְׁמֵיהּ shemei (שם י"ה דס"ג) רַבָּא raba קנ"א ב"ן,

יהוה אלהים יהוה אדני, מילוי קס"א וס"ג, מ"ה ברבוע וע"ב ע"ה מְבָרַךְ mevarach,

לְעָלַם le'alam לְעָלְמֵי le'almei עָלְמַיָּא almaya. יִתְבָּרַךְ yitbarach.

Seven words with six letters each (שם בן מ"ב) – meditate:
יהוה - יוד הי ויו הי - מילוי דמילוי דע"ב (יוד ויו דלת הי יוד ויו יוד ויו הי יוד)
Also, seven times the letter Vav (שם בן מ"ב) – meditate:
יהוה - יוד הי ויו הי - מילוי דמילוי דע"ב (יוד ויו דלת הי יוד ויו יוד ויו הי יוד).

וְיִשְׁתַּבַּח veyishtabach י"פ ע"ב יהוה אל אבג יתץ.

וְיִתְפָּאַר veyitpa'ar הי גו יה קרע שטן. וְיִתְרוֹמַם veyitromam וה כוזו נגד יכש.

וְיִתְנַשֵּׂא veyitnase במוכסז בטר צתג. וְיִתְהַדָּר veyit'hadar כוזו יה וזקב טנע.

וְיִתְעַלֶּה veyit'ale וה יוד ה יגל פזק. וְיִתְהַלָּל veyit'halal א ואו הא שקו צית.

שְׁמֵיהּ shemei (שם י"ה דמ"ה) דְּקוּדְשָׁא dekudsha בְּרִיךְ verich הוּא hu:

אָמֵן amen אידהנויה.

KADDISH TITKABAL

May His great Name be more exalted and sanctified. (Amen) In the world that He created according to His will, and may His Kingdom reign. And may He cause His redemption to sprout and may He bring the Mashiach closer. (Amen) In your lifetimes and in your days and in the lifetime of all the House of Israel, speedily and in the near future, and you shall say, Amen. (Amen) May His great Name be blessed forever and for all eternity. Blessed and lauded, and glorified, and exalted, and extolled, and honored, and uplifted, and praised be the Name of the Holy Blessed One. (Amen)

לְעֵלָּא le'ela מִן min כָּל kol ילי בִּרְכָתָא birchata• שִׁירָתָא shirata•
תִּשְׁבְּחָתָא tishbechata וְנֶחָמָתָא venechamata• דַּאֲמִירָן da'amiran
בְּעָלְמָא be'alma וְאִמְרוּ ve'imru אָמֵן amen: אָמֵן amen אידהנויה.

תִּתְקַבַּל titkabal צְלוֹתָנָא tzelotana וּבָעוּתָנָא uva'utana
עִם im צְלוֹתְהוֹן tzelotehon וּבָעוּתְהוֹן uva'utehon דְּכָל dechol ילי
בֵּית bet ב"פ ראה יִשְׂרָאֵל Yisrael קֳדָם kadam אֲבוּנָא avuna
דְּבִשְׁמַיָּא devishmaya וְאִמְרוּ ve'imru אָמֵן amen: אָמֵן amen אידהנויה.

יְהֵא yehe שְׁלָמָא shelama רַבָּא raba קנ"א ב"ן, יהוה אלהים יהוה אדני, מילוי קס"א וס"ג,
מ"ה ברבוע וע"ב ע"ה מִן min שְׁמַיָּא shemaya• וְחַיִּים chayim אהיה אהיה יהוה, בינה ע"ה
וְשָׂבָע vesava וִישׁוּעָה vishu'a וְנֶחָמָה venechama וְשֵׁיזָבָא veshezava
וּרְפוּאָה urfu'a וּגְאֻלָּה ug'ula וּסְלִיחָה uslicha וְכַפָּרָה vechapara
וְרֵיוַח verevach וְהַצָּלָה vehatzala• לָנוּ lanu אלהים, אהיה אדני וּלְכָל ulchol יה אדני
עַמּוֹ amo יִשְׂרָאֵל Yisrael וְאִמְרוּ ve'imru אָמֵן amen: אָמֵן amen אידהנויה.

Take three steps backwards and say:

עוֹשֶׂה ose שָׁלוֹם shalom

בִּמְרוֹמָיו bimromav ע"ב, ריבוע יהוה• הוּא hu בְּרַחֲמָיו berachamav
יַעֲשֶׂה ya'ase שָׁלוֹם shalom עָלֵינוּ alenu ר"ת ש"ע נהורין•
וְעַל ve'al כָּל kol ילי ; עמם עַמּוֹ amo יִשְׂרָאֵל Yisrael וְאִמְרוּ ve'imru אָמֵן amen:
אָמֵן amen אידהנויה•

Above all blessings, songs, praises, and words of consolation that may be said in the world, and you shall say, Amen. (Amen) May our prayers and pleas be accepted, together with the prayers and pleas of the entire House of Israel, before our Father in Heaven, and you say, Amen. (Amen) May there be abundant peace from heaven; Life, contentment, salvation, consolation, deliverance, healing, redemption, pardon, atonement, comfort, and relief. For us and for His entire nation, Israel, and you shall say, Amen. (Amen) He, Who makes peace in His high places, He, in His compassion, shall make peace upon us And upon His entire nation, Israel, and you shall say, Amen. (Amen)

SHIR LAMA'ALOT

שִׁיר shir לַמַּעֲלוֹת lama'alot אֶשָּׂא esa עֵינַי enai ריבוע מ״ה
אֶל־ el הֶהָרִים heharim מֵאַיִן me'ayin יָבֹא yavo עֶזְרִי: ezri
עֶזְרִי ezri מֵעִם me'im יְהֹוָהאדניאהדונהי Adonai עֹשֵׂה ose שָׁמַיִם shamayim
וָאָרֶץ: va'aretz י״פ כוזו, י״פ טל אַל־ al יִתֵּן yiten לַמּוֹט lamot רַגְלֶךָ raglecha
אַל־ al יָנוּם yanum שֹׁמְרֶךָ: shomrecha הִנֵּה hine לֹא־ lo יָנוּם yanum
וְלֹא velo יִישָׁן yishan ע״ע נהורין דא״א שׁוֹמֵר shomer כ״א ההויות שבתפילין
יִשְׂרָאֵל: Yisrael יְהֹוָהאדניאהדונהי Adonai שֹׁמְרֶךָ shomrecha
יְהֹוָהאדניאהדונהי Adonai צִלְּךָ tzilecha עַל־ al יַד yad יְמִינֶךָ yeminecha היי:
יוֹמָם yomam הַשֶּׁמֶשׁ hashemesh לֹא־ lo יַכֶּכָּה yakeka ר״ת ילה
וְיָרֵחַ veyare'ach בַּלָּיְלָה balayla מלה: יְהֹוָהאדניאהדונהי Adonai
יִשְׁמָרְךָ yishmorcha מִכָּל־ mikol ילי רָע ra יִשְׁמֹר yishmor
אֶת־ et נַפְשֶׁךָ nafshecha מיכ: יְהֹוָהאדניאהדונהי Adonai יִשְׁמָר yishmor
צֵאתְךָ tzetcha וּבוֹאֶךָ uvo'echa מֵעַתָּה me'ata וְעַד־ ve'ad עוֹלָם olam וול:

KADDISH YEHE SHELAMA

יִתְגַּדַּל yitgadal וְיִתְקַדַּשׁ veyitkadash שדי ומילוי שדי ; י״א אותיות כמנין ו״ה
שְׁמֵיהּ shemei (שם י״ה דע״ב) רַבָּא raba קנ״א ב״ן, יהוה אלהים יהוה אדני,
מילוי קס״א וס״ג, מ״ה ברבוע וע״ב ע״ה ; ר״ת = ו״פ אלהים ; ס״ת = ג״פ יב״ק: אָמֵן amen אידהנויה.
בְּעָלְמָא be'alma דִּי di בְרָא vera כִּרְעוּתֵיהּ chir'utei.
וְיַמְלִיךְ veyamlich מַלְכוּתֵיהּ malchutei. וְיַצְמַח veyatzmach
פֻּרְקָנֵיהּ purkanei. וִיקָרֵב vikarev מְשִׁיחֵיהּ meshichei: אָמֵן amen אידהנויה.

SHIR LAMA'ALOT

"A Song of Ascents: I lift up my eyes to the mountains; from where will my help come? My help is from the Lord, Creator of the Heavens and the Earth. He will not allow your legs to falter. Your Guardian shall not sleep. Behold: the Guardian of Israel shall neither slumber nor sleep. The Lord is your Guardian. The Lord is your protective shade at your right hand. During the day, the sun shall not harm you, nor shall the moon, at night. The Lord shall protect you from all evil, He will guard your soul. He shall guard you when you leave and when you come, from now and for eternity." (Psalms 121)

KADDISH YEHE SHELAMA

May His great Name be more exalted and sanctified. (Amen)
In the world that He created according to His will, and may His kingdom reign.
And may He cause His redemption to sprout and may He bring the Mashiach closer. (Amen)

בְּחַיֵּיכוֹן bechayechon וּבְיוֹמֵיכוֹן uvyomechon וּבְחַיֵּי uvchayei

דְּכָל dechol ילי בֵּית bet ראה ב״פ יִשְׂרָאֵל Yisrael בַּעֲגָלָא ba'agala

וּבִזְמַן uvizman קָרִיב kariv וְאִמְרוּ ve'imru אָמֵן amen: אָמֵן amen אידהנויה.

The congregation and the *chazan* say the following:

28 words (until *be'alma*) – meditate:

מילוי דמילוי דס״ג (יוד ויו דלת הי יוד ואו אלף ואו הי יוד)

28 letters (until *almaya*) - meditate:

מילוי דמילוי דמ״ה (יוד ואו דלת הא אלף ואו אלף ואו הא אלף).

יְהֵא yehe שְׁמֵיהּ shemei (שׁם י״ה דס״ג) רַבָּא raba קנ״א ב״ן,

יהוה אלהים יהוה אדני, מילוי קס״א וס״ג, מ״ה ברבוע וע״ב ע״ה מְבָרַךְ mevarach,

לְעָלַם le'alam לְעָלְמֵי le'almei עָלְמַיָּא almaya. יִתְבָּרַךְ yitbarach.

Seven words with six letters each (שׁם בן מ״ב) – meditate:

יהוה - יוד הי ואו הי - מילוי דמילוי דס״ג (יוד ויו דלת הי יוד ואו אלף ואו הי יוד) ;

Also, seven times the letter Vav (שׁם בן מ״ב) – meditate:

יהוה - יוד הא ואו הא - מילוי דמילוי דמ״ה (יוד ואו דלת הא אלף ואו אלף ואו הא אלף).

וְיִשְׁתַּבַּח veyishtabach י״פ ע״ב יהוה אל אבג יתץ.

וְיִתְפָּאַר veyitpa'ar הי נו יה קרע שטן. וְיִתְרוֹמַם veyitromam וה כוזו נגד יכש.

וְיִתְנַשֵּׂא veyitnase במוכסז בטר צתג. וְיִתְהַדָּר veyit'hadar כוזו יה וזקב טנע.

וְיִתְעַלֶּה veyit'ale וה יוד ה יגל פזק. וְיִתְהַלָּל veyit'halal א ואו הא שקו צית.

שְׁמֵיהּ shemei (שׁם י״ה דמ״ה) דְּקוּדְשָׁא dekudsha בְּרִיךְ verich הוּא hu:

אָמֵן amen אידהנויה.

לְעֵלָּא le'ela מִן min כָּל kol ילי בִּרְכָתָא birchata. שִׁירָתָא shirata.

תֻּשְׁבְּחָתָא tishbechata וְנֶחָמָתָא venechamata. דַּאֲמִירָן da'amiran

בְּעָלְמָא be'alma וְאִמְרוּ ve'imru אָמֵן amen: אָמֵן amen אידהנויה.

In your lifetimes and in your days and in the lifetime of all the House of Israel, speedily and in the near future, and you shall say, Amen. (Amen) May His great Name be blessed forever and for all eternity. Blessed and lauded, and glorified, and exalted, and extolled, and honored, and uplifted, and praised be the Name of the Holy Blessed One. (Amen) Above all blessings, songs, praises, and words of consolation that may be said in the world, and you shall say, Amen. (Amen)

יְהֵא yehe שְׁלָמָא shelama רַבָּא raba קנ"א ב"ן, יהוה אלהים יהוה אדני, מילוי קס"א וס"ג, מ"ה ברבוע וע"ב ע"ה מִן min שְׁמַיָּא shemaya• וְחַיִּים chayim אהיה אהיה יהוה, בינה ע"ה וְשָׂבָע vesava וִישׁוּעָה vishu'a וְנֶחָמָה venechama וְשֵׁיזָבָא veshezava וּרְפוּאָה urefu'a וּגְאֻלָּה uge'ula וּסְלִיחָה uslicha וְכַפָּרָה vechapara וְרֵיוַח verevach וְהַצָּלָה vehatzala• לָנוּ lanu אלהים, אהיה אדני וּלְכָל ulchol יה אדני עַמּוֹ amo יִשְׂרָאֵל Yisrael וְאִמְרוּ ve'imru אָמֵן amen: אָמֵן amen אידהנויה.

Take three steps backwards and say:

עוֹשֶׂה ose שָׁלוֹם shalom בִּמְרוֹמָיו bimromav ע"ב, ריבוע יהוה• הוּא hu בְּרַחֲמָיו berachamav יַעֲשֶׂה ya'ase שָׁלוֹם shalom עָלֵינוּ alenu ר"ת ש"ע נהורין• וְעַל ve'al כָּל kol ילי ; עמם עַמּוֹ amo יִשְׂרָאֵל Yisrael וְאִמְרוּ ve'imru אָמֵן amen: אָמֵן amen אידהנויה•

BARCHU

The *chazan* (or a person who said the *Kaddish Yehe Shelama*) says:

רַבָּנָן rabanan: בָּרְכוּ barchu יהוה ריבוע יהוה ריבוע מ"ה אֶת et יְהֹוָהאדנימאהדונהי Adonai הַמְבוֹרָךְ: hamevorach ס"ת כהת, משיח בן דוד ע"ה:

First the congregation replies with the following, and then the *chazan* (or a person who said the "*Kaddish Yehe Shelama*") repeats it:

Nefesh בָּרוּךְ baruch *Ruach* יְהֹוָהאדנימאהדונהי Adonai *Neshamah* הַמְבוֹרָךְ hamevorach *Chayah* לְעוֹלָם le'olam ריבוע ס"ג וי' אותיות דס"ג *Yechidah* וָעֶד va'ed:

May there be abundant peace from heaven, life, contentment, salvation, consolation, deliverance, healing, redemption, pardon, atonement, comfort, and relief. For us and for His entire nation, Israel, and you shall say, Amen. (Amen) *He, Who makes peace in His high places, with His compassion He shall make peace for us and for His entire nation, Israel. And you shall say, Amen.* (Amen)

BARCHU

Masters: Bless the Lord, the Blessed One.
Blessed be the Lord, the Blessed One, forever and for eternity.

ALENU

Alenu is a cosmic sealing agent. It cements and secures all of our prayers, protecting them from any negative forces such as the *klipot*. All prayers prior to *Alenu* drew down what the kabbalists call Inner Light. *Alenu*, however, attracts Surrounding Light, which envelops our prayers with a protective force-field to block out the *klipot*.

Drawing Surrounding Light in order to be protected from the *klipot* (negative side).

עָלֵינוּ alenu ריבוע דס״ג לְשַׁבֵּחַ leshabe'ach עלינו לשבח = אבג יתץ, ושר

לַאֲדוֹן la'adon אני ; ס״ת ס״ג ע״ה הַכֹּל hakol ר״ת ללה, אדני

לָתֵת latet גְּדֻלָּה gedula לְיוֹצֵר leyotzer בְּרֵאשִׁית bereshit ר״ת גלב (באך ב״י יג״ל)

שֶׁלֹּא shelo עָשָׂנוּ asanu כְּגוֹיֵי kegoyei הָאֲרָצוֹת ha'aratzot

וְלֹא velo שָׂמָנוּ samanu כְּמִשְׁפְּחוֹת kemishpechot הָאֲדָמָה ha'adama

שֶׁלֹּא shelo שָׂם sam חֶלְקֵנוּ chelkenu כָּהֶם kahem וְגוֹרָלֵנוּ vegoralenu

כְּכָל kechol הֲמוֹנָם hamonam ◆ שֶׁהֵם shehem מִשְׁתַּחֲוִים mishtachavim

לְהֶבֶל lahevel וָרִיק varik וּמִתְפַּלְּלִים umitpalelim אֶל el אֵל el

לֹא lo יוֹשִׁיעַ Yoshi'a ◆ (pause here, and when you say "*va'anachnu mishtachavim*" bow your entire body)

וַאֲנַחְנוּ va'anachnu מִשְׁתַּחֲוִים mishtachavim לִפְנֵי lifnei מֶלֶךְ melech

מַלְכֵי malchei הַמְּלָכִים hamelachim הַקָּדוֹשׁ hakadosh בָּרוּךְ baruch

הוּא hu ◆ שֶׁהוּא shehu נוֹטֶה note שָׁמַיִם shamayim י״פ טל, י״פ כוזו ; ר״ת = י״פ אדני

שבי׳ ספירות של נוקבא דז״א וְיוֹסֵד veyosed אָרֶץ aretz ◆ וּמוֹשַׁב umoshav

יְקָרוֹ yekaro בַּשָּׁמַיִם bashamayim י״פ טל, י״פ כוזו מִמַּעַל mima'al עלם ◆

וּשְׁכִינַת ush'chinat עֻזּוֹ uzo בְּגָבְהֵי begovhei מְרוֹמִים meromim ◆

הוּא hu אֱלֹהֵינוּ Elohenu ילה וְאֵין ve'en עוֹד od אַחֵר acher ◆

ALENU

It is incumbent upon us to give praise to the Master of all and to attribute greatness to the Molder of Creation, for He did not make us like the nations of the lands. He did not place us like the families of the earth He did not make our lot like theirs and our destiny like that of their multitudes, for they prostrate themselves to futility and emptiness and they pray to a deity that does not help. But we prostrate ourselves before the King of all Kings, the Holy Blessed One. It is He Who spreads the Heavens and establishes the earth. The Seat of His glory is in the Heaven above and the Divine Presence of His power is in the Highest of Heights. He is our God and there is no other.

אֱמֶת emet אהיה פעמים אהיה, ז"פ ס"ג מַלְכֵּנוּ malkenu וְאֶפֶס ve'efes
זוּלָתוֹ zulato. כַּכָּתוּב kakatuv בַּתּוֹרָה batorah: וְיָדַעְתָּ veyadata
הַיּוֹם hayom ע"ה נגד, מזבח, זן, אל יהוה וַהֲשֵׁבֹתָ vahashevota אֶל־ el
לְבָבֶךָ levavecha ר"ת לאו כִּי ki יְהֹוָה Adonai הוּא hu
הָאֱלֹהִים haElohim אהיה אדני ; ילה ; ר"ת יהה וכן עולה למנין ענו עג"כ
בַּשָּׁמַיִם bashamayim י"פ טל, י"פ כוזו מִמַּעַל mima'al עלם ;
רמז לאור פנימי המתחזיל מלמעלה וְעַל־ ve'al הָאָרֶץ ha'aretz אלהים דההין ע"ה
מִתָּחַת mitachat רמז לאור מקיף המתחזיל מלמטה אֵין en עוֹד od:

עַל al כֵּן ken נְקַוֶּה nekave לְּךָ lach יְהֹוָה Adonai
אֱלֹהֵינוּ Elohenu ילה לִרְאוֹת lir'ot מְהֵרָה mehera בְּתִפְאֶרֶת betiferet
עֻזָּךְ uzach ס"ת כהת, משיח בן דוד ע"ה לְהַעֲבִיר leha'avir גִּלּוּלִים gilulim מִן min
הָאָרֶץ ha'aretz אלהים דההין ע"ה וְהָאֱלִילִים veha'elilim כָּרוֹת karot
יִכָּרֵתוּן yikaretun. לְתַקֵּן letaken עוֹלָם olam בְּמַלְכוּת bemalchut
שַׁדַּי Shadai. וְכָל vechol ילי בְּנֵי benei בָשָׂר vasar יִקְרְאוּ yikre'u
בִשְׁמֶךָ vishmecha לְהַפְנוֹת lehafnot אֵלֶיךָ elecha כָּל kol ילי רִשְׁעֵי rish'ei
אָרֶץ aretz. יַכִּירוּ yakiru וְיֵדְעוּ veyed'u כָּל kol ילי יוֹשְׁבֵי yoshvei
תֵבֵל tevel ב"פ רי"ו. כִּי ki לְךָ lecha תִּכְרַע tichra כָּל־ kol ילי בֶּרֶךְ berech.
תִּשָּׁבַע tishava כָּל kol ילי לָשׁוֹן lashon. לְפָנֶיךָ lefanecha ס"ג מ"ה ב"ן

Our King is true and there is none beside Him. As it is written in the Torah: "And you shall know today and you shall take it to your heart that it is the Lord Who is God in the Heavens above and upon the earth below, and there is none other". (Deuteronomy 4:39) Consequently, we place our hope in You, Lord, our God, that we shall speedily see the glory of Your might, when You remove the idols from the earth and the deities shall be completely destroyed to correct the world with the kingdom of the Almighty. And all mankind shall then call out Your Name and You shall turn back to Yourself all the wicked ones of the earth. Then all the inhabitants of the world shall recognize and know that, for You, every knee bends and every tongue vows. Before You,

יהוהאדניאהדונהי Adonai אלהינו Elohenu ילה יכרעו yichre'u ויפלו veyipolu
ולכבוד velichvod שמך shimcha יקר yekar יתנו yitenu• ויקבלו vikabelu
כלם chulam את et עול- ol מלכותך malchutecha• ותמלוך vetimloch
עליהם alehem מהרה mehera לעולם le'olam ריבוע ס"ג וי' אותיות דס"ג ועד va'ed•
כי ki המלכות hamalchut שלך shelcha היא hee• ולעולמי ul'olmei
עד ad תמלוך timloch בכבוד bechavod בוכו• ככתוב kakatuv
בתורתך betoratach: יהוהאדניאהדונהי Adonai | ימלך yimloch לעלם le'olam
ריבוע ס"ג וי' אותיות דס"ג ; ר"ת ייל ועד va'ed• ונאמר vene'emar: והיה vehaya יהוה ; יהה
יהוהאדניאהדונהי Adonai למלך lemelech על- al כל- kol ילי ; עמם
הארץ ha'aretz אלהים דההין ע"ה ביום bayom ע"ה נגד, מזבח, זן, אל יהוה ההוא hahu
יהיה yihye ייי יהוהאדניאהדונהי Adonai אחד echad אהבה, דאגה ושמו ushmo מהש
ע"ה, ע"ב בריבוע וקס"א ע"ה, אל שדי ע"ה אחד echad אהבה, דאגה:

If you prayed alone recite the following before you start *Arvit* and before "*Alenu*" instead of "*Barchu*":

אמר amar רבי Rabi עקיבא Akiva חיה chaya אחת achat עומדת omedet
ברקיע baraki'a ושמה ushma ישראל Yisrael וחקוק vechakuk על al
מצחה mitzcha ישראל Yisrael• עומדת omedet באמצע be'emtza
הרקיע haraki'a ואומרת ve'omeret: ברכו barchu יהוה ריבוע יהוה וריבוע מ"ה את et
יהוהאדניאהדונהי Adonai המבורך hamevorach ס"ת כהת, משיח בן דוד ע"ה וכל vechol
ילי גדודי gedudei מעלה mala עונים onim: ברוך baruch יהוהאדניאהדונהי Adonai
המבורך hamevorach לעולם le'olam ריבוע ס"ג וי' אותיות דס"ג ועד va'ed•

Lord, our God, they shall kneel and fall and shall give honor to Your glorious Name. And they shall all accept the yoke of Your Kingdom and You shall reign over them, forever and ever. Because the kingdom is Yours. and forever and for eternity, You shall reign gloriously. As it is written in the Torah: "The Lord shall reign forever and ever," (Exodus 15:18) and it is also stated: "The Lord shall be King over the whole world and, on that day, the Lord shall be One and His Name One." (Zechariah 14:9)

Rabbi Akiva said: Standing in Heaven, there is one animal named Israel, and Israel is engraved on her forehead, and she is standing in mid-Heaven saying: Bless the Lord, the Blessed One, and all of Heaven's armies are answering: Blessed be the Lord, the Blessed One, forever and for eternity.

HAVDALAH

To complete and close out the Shabbat or the Holiday, we do *Havdalah*, which literally meaning "separation." Many times, the people we think are our friends are actually our enemies, and the people we think are our enemies are actually our friends. If we share personal and intimate information about ourselves with our so-called friends, should they ever become our enemies, they will become the most dangerous kind of enemy we can possibly have. Therefore, knowing how to differentiate between good and evil is vital if we are to achieve a sense of peace and serenity in our life. Participating in *Havdalah* helps us gain a deeper understanding, insight, and greater awareness about what is good and bad for our personal life.

Some start here:

אָנָּא ana ב״ן יְהֹוָהאדניאהדונהי Adonai הוֹשִׁיעָה hoshi'a יהוה וש״ע נהורין נָּא na:

אָנָּא ana ב״ן יְהֹוָהאדניאהדונהי Adonai הוֹשִׁיעָה hoshi'a יהוה וש״ע נהורין נָּא na:

אָנָּא ana ב״ן יְהֹוָהאדניאהדונהי Adonai הַצְלִיחָה hatzlicha נָּא na:

אָנָּא ana ב״ן יְהֹוָהאדניאהדונהי Adonai הַצְלִיחָה hatzlicha נָּא na:

הַצְלִיחֵנוּ hatzlichenu. הַצְלִיחַ hatzli'ach דְּרָכֵינוּ derachenu. הַצְלִיחַ hatzli'ach

לִמּוּדֵינוּ limudenu. וּשְׁלַח ushlach בְּרָכָה beracha רְוָחָה revacha

וְהַצְלָחָה vehatzlacha בְּכָל bechol ב״ן, לכב מַעֲשֵׂה ma'ase יָדֵינוּ yadenu,

כִּדְכְתִיב kedichtiv: יִשָּׂא yisa בְרָכָה veracha מֵאֵת me'et ר״ת יבמ, ב״ן

יְהֹוָהאדניאהדונהי Adonai וּצְדָקָה utzdaka ע״ה ריבוע אלהים ; יהה מֵאֱלֹהֵי melohei

מילוי דע״ב, רמב ; ילה יִשְׁעוֹ yish'o שכינה ע״ה ; ס״ת יהוה: לַיְּהוּדִים layehudim מלה

הָיְתָה hayta אוֹרָה ora וְשִׂמְחָה vesimcha וְשָׂשֹׂן vesason וִיקָר vikar,

וּכְתִיב uchtiv: וַיְהִי vayhi דָוִד David לְכָל־ lechol יה אדני דְּרָכָו derachav

מַשְׂכִּיל maskil וַיהֹוָהאדניאהדונהי vadonai עִמּוֹ imo: כֵּן ken יִהְיֶה yihye ייי

עִמָּנוּ imanu ריבוע ס״ג, קס״א ע״ה וד׳ אותיות תָּמִיד tamid ע״ה קס״א קנ״א קמ״ג:

Continue "*kos yeshu'ot esa...*" on the next page.

Meditation for spiritual memory (before saying *Havdalah*):

משבענא עליך פורה שר של שכוזה שתסיר לב טפש ממני
ותשליכהו על טורי רומיא ארמימ״ס רמימ״ס מימ״ס ימ״ס מ״ס ס׳.

וְנֹחַ veNo'ach מָצָא matza חֵן chen מילוי ריבוע מ״ה, מוזי

בְּעֵינֵי be'enei ריבוע מ״ה יְהֹוָהאדניאהדונהי Adonai:

HAVDALAH

"Please, Lord, save us. Please, Lord, save us. Please, Lord, give us success. Please, Lord, give us success." (Psalms 118:25) *Give us success, make our ways successful, make our studies successful, and send blessing and tranquillity to all the work of our hands, as it was written: "He shall receive blessing from Lord and righteousness from the God of his salvation."* (Psalms 24:5) *"And to the Jews it was Light and gladness and joy and honor."* (Esther 8:16) *And it was also written: "And David was successful in all his ways and the Lord is with him. May He so be with us always."* (I Samuel 18:14)

We shouldn't add water to the *Havdalah* wine.

הִנֵּה hine אֵל el ייא״י (מילוי דס״ג) יְשׁוּעָתִי yeshu'ati אֶבְטַח evtach

וְלֹא velo אֶפְחָד efchad כִּי־ ki עָזִּי ozi אלהים ע״ה, אהיה אדני ע״ה וְזִמְרָת vezimrat

יָהּ Yah ההה יְהֹוָה יאהדונהי Adonai וַיְהִי־ vayehi לִי li לִישׁוּעָה lishu'a:

וּשְׁאַבְתֶּם־ ush'avtem מַיִם mayim בְּשָׂשׂוֹן besason מִמַּעַיְנֵי mima'aynei

הַיְשׁוּעָה hayeshu'a: לַיהֹוָה יאהדונהי ladonai הַיְשׁוּעָה hayeshu'a עַל־ al

עַמְּךָ amecha בִרְכָתֶךָ virchatecha סֶּלָה sela: יְהֹוָה יאהדונהי Adonai

צְבָאוֹת Tzeva'ot פני שכינה עִמָּנוּ imanu ריבוע ס״ג, קס״א ע״ה וד׳ אותיות

מִשְׂגָּב־ misgav מהש, ע״ב בריבוע קס״א, אל שדי, ד״פ אלהים ע״ה לָנוּ lanu אלהים, אהיה אדני

אֱלֹהֵי Elohei מילוי ע״ב, דמב ; ילה יַעֲקֹב Yaakov ו׳ הויות, יאהדונהי אידהנויה סֶלָה sela:

יְהֹוָה יאהדונהי Adonai צְבָאוֹת Tzeva'ot פני שכינה אַשְׁרֵי ashrei אָדָם adam מ״ה ;

יהוה צבאות אשרי אדם = תפארת בֹּטֵחַ bote'ach בָּךְ bach אדם בוטח בך = אמן (יאהדונהי) ע״ה;

בוטח בך = מילוי ע״ב ע״ה: יְהֹוָה יאהדונהי Adonai הוֹשִׁיעָה hoshi'a יהוה ושע נהורין

הַמֶּלֶךְ hamelech ר״ת יהה יַעֲנֵנוּ ya'anenu בְיוֹם veyom ע״ה נגד, מזבח, זן, אל יהוה

קָרְאֵנוּ kor'enu ר״ת יב״ק, אלהים יהוה = אהיה אדני יהוה ; ס״ת = ב״ן ועם כ׳ דהמלך = ע״ב:

לַיְּהוּדִים layehudim מלה הָיְתָה hay'ta אוֹרָה ora וְשִׂמְחָה vesimcha

וְשָׂשֹׂן vesason וִיקָר vikar: כֵּן ken תִּהְיֶה tihye לָנוּ lanu אלהים, אהיה אדני:

כּוֹס־ kos אלהים, אהיה אדני ; ובמילוי (כף וו סמך) = עסמ״ב, הברכה (למתק את ז׳ המלכים שמתו)

יְשׁוּעוֹת yeshu'ot אֶשָּׂא esa וּבְשֵׁם uvshem יְהֹוָה יאהדונהי Adonai אֶקְרָא ekra:

"Behold God is my salvation, I will trust and not be afraid. Indeed, the Lord is my strength and my song and He has become my salvation. You shall draw water with joy from the wells of salvation." (Isaiah 12:2-3) *"Salvation belongs to the Lord, may Your blessings be upon Your people, Selah."* (Psalms 3:9) *"The Lord of Hosts is with us, the God of Jacob is a refuge for us, Selah."* (Psalms 84:13) *"Lord of Hosts, happy is the man who trusts in You. Lord, save us; may the King answer us on the day we call."* (Psalms 20:10) *"The Judeans had radiance and happiness, joy and honor."* (Esther 8:16) *"So may it be for us. I will raise the cup of salvations and invoke the Name of the Lord."* (Psalms 116:13)

maranan מָרָנָן savri סַבְרִי

ע"ה בינה ,יהוה אהיה אהיה lechayim לְחַיִּים (: and the others reply)

BORE PERI HAGEFEN

Elohenu אֱלֹהֵינוּ (יוד הי ויו הי) Adonai יְהֹוָאהדונהי Ata אַתָּה baruch בָּרוּךְ

:hagefen הַגָּפֶן peri פְּרִי bore בּוֹרֵא ha'olam הָעוֹלָם melech מֶלֶךְ ילה

On Saturday night (*Motza'ei Shabbat*) we add the blessings over the *Besamim* and over the fire:

BORE ATZEI BESAMIM

Havdalah includes smelling the fragrance of the myrtle branch (if we don't have a myrtle branch we can use another source of natural fragrance) to fill the void created by the departure of the extra soul that was present within us throughout the Shabbat.

You should take one bundle of the three myrtles (the one that you used on *Shabbat*) and meditate that they correspond to *Nefesh, Ruach* and *Neshamah* in order to save the energy of the additional soul (from all three aspects) of *Shabbat* and that's done right now by these three myrtles and the action of smelling them. Hold the myrtles in your right hand and when you smell them inhale their fragrance deeply into your nostrils three times (corresponding to *Nefesh, Ruach* and *Neshamah*). Also meditate on the four words as follow (without pronouncing it):

רֵיחַ נִיחוֹחַ אִשֶּׁה לַיהֹוָאהדונהי:

(יוד הי ואו הי) Adonai יְהֹוָאהדונהי Ata אַתָּה baruch בָּרוּךְ

bore בּוֹרֵא ha'olam הָעוֹלָם melech מֶלֶךְ ילה Elohenu אֱלֹהֵינוּ

:vesamim בְשָׂמִים (minei מִינֵי) (isbei עִשְׂבֵי) atzei עֲצֵי

BORE ME'OREI HAESH

We then make our right hand into a fist, hiding the thumb under the four fingers and look at the *Havdalah* candle's reflection in the nails of our four fingers. The ancient Kabbalists teach us that the body of Adam was actually made of this enamel. As Shabbat concludes, negative forces and entities immediately swarm around us like hungry predators trying to rob us of our Light. The first place they strike are the fingers, specifically the fingernails. The candlelight reflected in our nails wipes them all out.

By Your leave masters, (and the others reply) *for life!*

BORE PERI HAGEFEN

Blessed are You, Lord, our God, the King of the world, Who creates the fruit of the vine.

BORE ATZEI BESAMIM

Blessed are You, Lord,

our God, the King of the world, Who creates the plants (spices) (varieties) of fragrance.

We use a special candle made of wax that is lit like a torch for the connection with this blessing. You should fold the top of the right hand fingers into your right palm and the thumb is covered underneath. And the fingers should be folded tightly towards your face and towards the candle. You should hold the right hand and the fingers up by bending your elbow and face of the fingers towards your face and then you should fold the tops of the fingers into the palm and you should straighten the back of your fingers up against the candle. Indeed your fingers should be folded down on top of the thumb as it is mentioned and you should look only at reflection of the Light that comes back from your fingernails and not at the rest of your fingers. And the reason is because in the four fingers there are 2500 outside forces that suck energy from the fingers and this is why we show it in front of the flame of the candle (that represents the *Shechinah*) to subdue them. And we bless "*bore me'orei ha'esh*" because we want to connect to their creator and not to them.

בָּרוּךְ baruch אַתָּה Ata יְהֹוָהאדניאהדונהי Adonai (יוד הא ואו הא)
אֱלֹהֵינוּ Elohenu ילה מֶלֶךְ melech הָעוֹלָם ha'olam
בּוֹרֵא bore מְאוֹרֵי me'orei הָאֵשׁ ha'esh שאה:

HAMAVDIL

The final blessing separates the good from evil, giving us the ability to distinguish between these two forces in every area of our life.

בָּרוּךְ baruch אַתָּה Ata יְהֹוָהאדניאהדונהי Adonai אֱלֹהֵינוּ Elohenu ילה
מֶלֶךְ melech הָעוֹלָם ha'olam הַמַּבְדִּיל hamavdil בֵּין ben קֹדֶשׁ kodesh
לְחוֹל lechol וּבֵין uven אוֹר or רז, א״ס לְחוֹשֶׁךְ lechoshech שך נצוצות של ז׳ המלכים
וּבֵין uven יִשְׂרָאֵל Yisrael לָעַמִּים la'amim וּבֵין uven יוֹם yom
ע״ה נגד, מזבח, זן, אל יהוה הַשְּׁבִיעִי hashevi'i לְשֵׁשֶׁת lesheshet יְמֵי yemei
הַמַּעֲשֶׂה hama'ase. בָּרוּךְ baruch אַתָּה Ata יְהֹוָהאדניאהדונהי Adonai
(יוד הה וו הה) הַמַּבְדִּיל hamavdil בֵּין ben קֹדֶשׁ kodesh לְחוֹל lechol (קליפת נגה):

After performing the *Havdalah* you should sit and drink "*revi'it*" (approximately three ounces of the wine) and then say the last blessing. If you cannot drink from the wine you should give this to somebody else that has the intention to complete his obligation to drink (instead of you) and this other person should say the last blessing. But if the other person didn't have the intention to complete his obligation to drink he should just bless "*bore pri hagefen*" and drink. There is some opinion that women shouldn't drink from the *Havdalah* wine because the Tree of Knowledge fruit was grape. And because of the sin, Eve got the blood of menstruation to differentiate her from Adam (we do not pay attention to this). But even women that pay attention to this, when they do *Havdalah* for themselves they should drink. It is better that they would do *Havdalah* on grape juice (or black beer and they should say *shehakhol*) and then drink *revi'it*.

BORE ME'OREI HAESH

Blessed are You, Lord, our God, King of the world, Who creates the luminaries of fire.

HAMAVDIL

Blessed are You, Lord, our God, King of the world, Who separates between the Holy and the mundane and between Light and darkness, and between Israel and the other nations, and between the Seventh Day and the six days of action. Blessed are You, Lord, Who separates between the Holy and the mundane.

1. *Kiddush Levanah* should be recited during the period between the seventh day after the new moon ("*Molad*") and the fifteenth day (exactly - fourteen days, eighteen hours and twenty-two minutes after the *Molad*).
2. *Kiddush Levanah* should be recited under an open and clear sky and preferably on a Saturday night (in the month of *Menchem-Av* recite it after *Tisha B'Av* and in the month of *Tishrei* recite it after *Yom Kippur*).
3. *Kiddush Levanah* should not be recited on a Friday night or the eve of a holiday unless it is the last opportunity to recite it during the above period.

The Earth is governed by the moon's monthly cycle. We bless the moon when it is blooming for the purpose of removing its negativity and its influence in our personal life, which usually occurs seven days after *Rosh Chodesh* (the New Moon). By actively blessing the moon, we seize control over it. The moon and the sun were once of equal size and brilliance, according to the *Torah*. The moon, not satisfied with its position of power, jealously denounced the sun, envious that it also merited great worth and importance. Because of this jealousy for no reason, the moon was diminished in size and was given no Light of its own. The only Light the moon radiates comes from the sun. This parable reveals our own jealousies. Many times, having certain possessions is not enough for us. Sometimes our selfish desires do not want another person to have what we have, although their possessions in no way diminish our own. The seed of this negative human trait is the moon. We are like the moon in that that we receive all of our Light from the Creator. The goal is for the moon and for us to radiate our own Light. Presently, we receive our Light from the world of *Zeir Anpin*. Eventually, by transforming our reactive nature and becoming more proactive, we will be able to connect directly to the *Sefirah* of *Binah*, which is equivalent to the moon having its own Light. This goal is called *Mashiach*.

LAMNATZE'ACH

The first connection in *Kiddush Levanah* has thirteen verses denoting the Thirteen Attributes. In addition, the number thirteen is one number above the twelve signs of the zodiac. Rising above the twelve signs of the zodiac elevates us above their sphere of influence, thereby giving us control and power over the signs of the zodiac instead of letting the constellations exert control over us. Through the science of Kabbalistic astrology, we rise above their influence to take control of our destiny. Our normal reactive behavior is a by-product of the influence of the twelve zodiac signs. To be proactive is to rise above the twelve.

In this Psalm there are: 13 verses corresponding to the 13 attributes of mercy,
And six times the Name: יהוה corresponding to the Six Edges of *Zeir Anpin*.

(א-אל) לַמְנַצֵּחַ lamnatze'ach מִזְמוֹר mizmor לְדָוִד leDavid:

(ב-רוזום) הַשָּׁמַיִם hashamayim י"פ טל, י"פ כוזו מְסַפְּרִים mesaprim כְּבוֹד kevod

אֵל El ייא"י (מילוי דס"ג) ; ר"ת מכאל (מיכאל = נ֫גא) ; כבוד אל = ס"ג (יוד הי ואו הי - דעת דנוקבא)

וּמַעֲשֵׂה uma'ase יָדָיו yadav מַגִּיד magid הָרָקִיעַ haraki'a:

(ג-וזנון) יוֹם yom ע"ה נגד, מזבוז, זן, אל יהוה לְיוֹם leyom ע"ה נגד, מזבוז, זן, אל יהוה

יַבִּיעַ yabi'a אֹמֶר omer וְלַיְלָה velayla מלה לְּלַיְלָה lelayla מלה

יְחַוֶּה־ yechave דָּעַת da'at: (ד-ארך) אֵין־ en אֹמֶר omer וְאֵין ve'en

דְּבָרִים devarim ראה בְּלִי beli נִשְׁמָע nishma קוֹלָם kolam:

LAMNATZE'ACH

1) To the conductor, a song of David. 2) The heavens declare the glory of God and the expanse of the sky tells of His handiwork. 3) Day following day brings expressions of praise, and night following night bespeaks wisdom. 4) There is no speech and there are no words, their sound is unheard.

(ה-אפים) בְּכָל־ bechol ב"ן, לכב הָאָרֶץ ha'aretz אלהים דההין ע"ה יָצָא yatza

קַוָּם kavam וּבִקְצֵה uviktze תֵּבֵל tevel ב"פ רי"ו מִלֵּיהֶם mileihem

לַשֶּׁמֶשׁ lashemesh שָׂם־ sam אֹהֶל ohel בָּהֶם bahem: (ו-ורב וחסד)

וְהוּא vehu כְּחָתָן kechatan יֹצֵא yotze מֵחֻפָּתוֹ mechupato יָשִׂישׂ yasis

כְּגִבּוֹר kegibor לָרוּץ larutz אֹרַח orach: (ז-ואמת) מִקְצֵה miktze

הַשָּׁמַיִם hashamayim י"פ טל, י"פ כוזו מוֹצָאוֹ motza'o וּתְקוּפָתוֹ utkufato עַל־ al

קְצוֹתָם ketzotam וְאֵין ve'en נִסְתָּר nistar ב"פ מצר מֵחַמָּתוֹ mechamato:

The kabbalists wrote: This Psalm has a great and magnificent ability of protection. From here on we have six consecutive verses of five words each, and the second word of each of them is: יהוה. You should count the words with your right hand fingers in the following way: say the first word and put your thumb down, then say the second word which is יהוה and keep the index finger up, then say the third word and put the middle finger down, then the fourth word and put the ring finger down, and while saying the fifth word put the little finger down. And while doing so meditate that the Creator will straighten those who are bent over and also, that all your spiritual enemies will surrender and you would defeat them.

(ח-נצר וחסד) תּוֹרַת torat יְהֹוָהאדנָיאהדונהי Adonai *(Chesed)* תְּמִימָה temima

מְשִׁיבַת meshivat נָפֶשׁ nafesh עֵדוּת edut יְהֹוָהאדנָיאהדונהי Adonai *(Gevurah)*

נֶאֱמָנָה ne'emana מַחְכִּימַת machkimat פֶּתִי peti: (ט-לאלפים) פִּקּוּדֵי pikudei מנק

יְהֹוָהאדנָיאהדונהי Adonai *(Tiferet)* יְשָׁרִים yesharim מְשַׂמְּחֵי־ mesamchei

לֵב lev מִצְוַת mitzvat יְהֹוָהאדנָיאהדונהי Adonai *(Netzach)* בָּרָה bara

מְאִירַת me'irat עֵינָיִם enayim ריבוע מ"ה: (י-נשא עון) יִרְאַת yir'at

יְהֹוָהאדנָיאהדונהי Adonai *(Hod)* טְהוֹרָה tehora עוֹמֶדֶת omedet

לָעַד la'ad ב"פ ב"ן מִשְׁפְּטֵי־ mishpetei יוהוויאדנָיהויאהדונהי Adonai *(Yesod)*

אֱמֶת emet אהיה פעמים אהיה, ד"פ ס"ג צָדְקוּ tzadku יַחְדָּו yachdav:

---

5) Their line goes forth throughout the earth,
and their words reach the farthest ends of the land. He had set up a tent in their midst.
6) And He is like a groom coming forth from his bridal tent, rejoicing like a warrior to run the course.
7) The end of the heavens is its source and its circuit is to their other end. Nothing is hidden from its heat.
8) The Torah of Lord (Chesed) *is perfect and restores the soul.*
The testimony of Lord (Gevurah) *is trustworthy, making the simple wise.*
9) The orders of Lord (Tiferet) *are upright and they gladden the heart.*
The commandment of Lord (Netzach) *is clear and enlightens the eyes.*
10) The fear of Lord (Hod) *is pure and endures forever.*
The judgments of Lord (Yesod) *are true and altogether righteous.*

(י"א-ופשע) הַנֶּחֱמָדִים hanechemadim מִזָּהָב mizahav וּמִפַּז umipaz רָב rav

וּמְתוּקִים umtukim מִדְּבַשׁ midevash שו' דשופר ועם י"ד האוזו הרי ש"ך דינין דגדלות

וְנֹפֶת venofet צוּפִים tzufim: גַּם־ gam עַבְדְּךָ avdecha פוי, אל אדני

נִזְהָר nizhar בָּהֶם bahem בְּשָׁמְרָם beshomram עֵקֶב ekev ב"פ מום רָב rav:

(י"ב-ווזטאה) שְׁגִיאוֹת shegi'ot מִי־ mi ילי יָבִין yavin מִנִּסְתָּרוֹת ministarot

נַקֵּנִי nakeni: (י"ג-ונקה) גַּם gam מִזֵּדִים mizedim חֲשֹׂךְ chasoch

ש"ך נצוצות של ה' המלכים עַבְדֶּךָ avdecha פוי, אל אדני אַל־ al יִמְשְׁלוּ־ yimshelu

בִי vi אָז az אֵיתָם etam וְנִקֵּיתִי veniketi מִפֶּשַׁע mipesha רָב rav:

מ"ב אותיות בפסוק

יִהְיוּ yihyu אל (ייא"י מילוי דס"ג) לְרָצוֹן leratzon מהש ע"ה, ע"ב בריבוע וקס"א ע"ה, אל שדי ע"ה

אִמְרֵי־ imrei פִי fi ר"ת המספר אֶלֶף = אלף למד שין דלת יוד ע"ה

וְהֶגְיוֹן vehegyon לִבִּי libi לְפָנֶיךָ lefanecha ס"ג מ"ה ב"ן יְהֹוָהאדהנויאהדונהי Adonai

צוּרִי tzuri וְגֹאֲלִי vego'ali:

צוּרִי tzuri בָּעוֹלָם ba'olam הַזֶּה haze והו וְגוֹאֲלִי vego'ali לָעוֹלָם le'olam

ריבוע ס"ג י' אותיות דס"ג הַבָּא haba: וְכָל־ vechol ילי קַרְנֵי karnei רְשָׁעִים resha'im

אֲגַדֵּעַ agade'a תְּרוֹמַמְנָה teromamna קַרְנוֹת karnot צַדִּיק tzadik:

HALELUYA

This Psalm speaks about the sun and the moon. The mere mention of the two words signifying these celestial bodies immediately gives us a connection to their inner energy. Aramaic letters are like computer keys. When we press the correct sequence of keys on a computer terminal, we can open any internal file or document. By reciting the correct sequence of Aramaic letters that spell out "moon," for example, we are opening the internal file, the inner energy of the moon, to give us a direct connection and control over the "document."

---

11) They are more desirable than gold and many precious stones, and sweeter than honey and the dripping of the combs. Even Your servant is careful of them, for in observing them there is great reward. 12) Yet, You, Who can discern mistakes, from unperceived faults cleanse me. 13) And, also from intentional sins, restrain Your servant. Let them not control me; then I shall be perfect and cleansed of great transgressions. May the words of my mouth and the thoughts of my heart find favor before You, Hashem, my Rock and my Redeemer." (Psalms 19)

He is my Rock in this world and my Redeemer in the World to Come.
I shall cut down the horns of the wicked. May the horns of the righteous be uplifted. (Psalms 75:11)

הַלְלוּיָהּ haleluya אלהים, אהיה אדני ; ללה הַלְלוּ halelu (*Asiyah*) אֶת־ et

יְהֹוָאדהנויאהדונהי Adonai ר"ת אהיה מִן־ min הַשָּׁמַיִם hashamayim

י"פ טל, י"פ כוזו ; ר"ת מ"ה הַלְלוּהוּ haleluhu (*Yetzirah*) בַּמְּרוֹמִים bamromim:

הַלְלוּהוּ haleluhu (*Beriah*) כָל chol ילי מַלְאָכָיו mal'achav הַלְלוּהוּ haleluhu

(*Atzilut*) כָּל kol ילי צְבָאָו tzeva'av ר"ת הפסוק = ע"ב ס"ג מ"ה ; ס"ת הפסוק = אהיה ס"ג:

הַלְלוּהוּ haleluhu שֶׁמֶשׁ shemesh וְיָרֵחַ veyare'ach הַלְלוּהוּ haleluhu כָּל kol ילי

כּוֹכְבֵי kochvei אוֹר or רז, אין סוף: הַלְלוּהוּ haleluhu שְׁמֵי shemei

הַשָּׁמָיִם hashamayim י"פ טל, י"פ כוזו וְהַמַּיִם vehamayim אֲשֶׁר asher מֵעַל me'al

עלם הַשָּׁמָיִם hashamayim י"פ טל, י"פ כוזו ; ר"ת מ"ה: יְהַלְלוּ yehalelu אֶת־ et

שֵׁם shem יְהֹוָאדהנויאהדונהי Adonai כִּי ki הוּא hu צִוָּה tziva וְנִבְרָאוּ venivra'u:

וַיַּעֲמִידֵם vaya'amidem לָעַד la'ad ב"פ ב"ן לְעוֹלָם le'olam ריבוע ס"ג וי' אותיות דס"ג

חָק־ chok נָתַן natan וְלֹא velo ס"ת קנ"א (אלף הה יוד הה, מקוה), אדני אלהים

יַעֲבוֹר ya'avor רפ"ח (להעלות רפ"ח ניצוצות שנפלו לקליפה דמשם באים התחלואים):

We make a visual connection to the moon to finalize and secure our control over this lunar body. Our intention is to connect to the positive aspect of the moon, while negating its negative influence. We should not attempt visual contact with the moon again for the rest of the month. Any further contact will draw only negative influences.

כִּי־ ki אֶרְאֶה er'e שָׁמֶיךָ shamecha מַעֲשֵׂה ma'ase אֶצְבְּעֹתֶיךָ etzbe'otecha

יָרֵחַ yare'ach וְכוֹכָבִים vechochavim אֲשֶׁר asher כּוֹנָנְתָּה konanta:

יְהֹוָאדהנויאהדונהי Adonai אֲדֹנֵינוּ adonenu מָה־ ma מ"ה אַדִּיר adir הרי

שִׁמְךָ shimcha בְּכָל־ bechol ב"ן, לכב ; ומב הָאָרֶץ ha'aretz אלהים דההין ע"ה:

HALELUYA

"Praise the Lord! Praise the Lord, from the heavens. Praise Him in the high places. Praise Him, all His angels. Praise Him, all His Hosts Praise Him, sun and moon. Praise Him, all stars of Light. Praise Him, highest heavens and the waters above the heavens. Let them praise the Name of Lord, for He commanded and they were created. He set laws that cannot be transgressed." (Psalms 148:1-6)

"When I behold Your heavens, the work of Your Fingers, the moon and the stars that You have established." (Psalms 8:4) *"Lord, our Master, how mighty is Your Name throughout the world."* (Psalms 8:10)

LESHEM YICHUD

We prepare ourselves for the lunar connection by interlocking the Upper Worlds (Heaven) and the Lower World (Earth).

לְשֵׁם leshem יִחוּד yichud קֻדְשָׁא kudsha בְּרִיךְ berich הוּא hu

וּשְׁכִינְתֵּיהּ ush'chintei (יאהדונהי) בִּדְחִילוּ bid'chilu וּרְחִימוּ ur'chimu

(יאהויהה), וּרְחִימוּ ur'chimu וּדְחִילוּ ud'chilu (איההיוהה), לְיַחֲדָא leyachda

שֵׁם shem יוּ"ד yud קֵ"י kei בְּוָא"ו bevav קֵ"י kei בְּיִחוּדָא beyichuda

שְׁלִים shelim (יהוה) בְּשֵׁם beshem כָּל kol ילי יִשְׂרָאֵל Yisrael.

הִנֵּה hine אֲנַחְנוּ anachnu בָּאִים ba'im לְבָרֵךְ levarech בִּרְכַּת birkat

הַלְּבָנָה halevana כְּמוֹ kemo שֶׁתִּקְּנוּ shetiknu לָנוּ lanu אלהים, אהיה אדני

רַזַ"ל razal עִם im כָּל kol ילי הַמִּצְוֹת hamitzvot הַכְּלוּלוֹת haklulot בָּהּ ba,

לְתַקֵּן letaken אֶת et שׁוֹרְשָׁהּ shorsha בְּמָקוֹם bemakom עֶלְיוֹן elyon.

וִיהִי vihi נֹעַם no'am אֲדֹנָי Adonai ללה אֱלֹהֵינוּ Elohenu ילה

עָלֵינוּ alenu וּמַעֲשֵׂה uma'ase יָדֵינוּ yadenu כּוֹנְנָה konena

עָלֵינוּ alenu וּמַעֲשֵׂה uma'ase יָדֵינוּ yadenu כּוֹנְנֵהוּ konenehu:

BARUCH ATA

This is the actual connection for the Blessing of the Moon. The prior blessings and Psalms were gradual build-ups that were necessary to lead us to this point. This verse, however, is the culmination.

בָּרוּךְ baruch אַתָּה Ata יְהֹוָהאדניאהדונהי Adonai אֱלֹהֵינוּ Elohenu ילה

מֶלֶךְ melech הָעוֹלָם ha'olam אֲשֶׁר asher בְּמַאֲמָרוֹ bema'amaro

בָּרָא bara קנ"א ב"ן, יהוה אלהים יהוה אדני, מילוי קס"א ס"ג, מ"ה ברבוע ע"ב ע"ה

שְׁחָקִים shechakim וּבְרוּחַ uvru'ach פִּיו piv כָּל kol ילי צְבָאָם tzeva'am.

LESHEM YICHUD

For the sake of unification between the Holy Blessed One and His Shechinah, with fear and love and with love and fear, in order to unify the Name Yud-Kei and Vav-Kei in perfect unity, and in the name of all Israel, we have hereby come to recite the Blessing of the Moon, as it was established for us by our Sages of blessed memory, with all the commandments contained therein, in order to rectify its source in a high place. "May the pleasantness of Lord, our God, be upon us and may He establish the work of our hands for us and may the work of our hands establish Him." (Psalms 90:17)

BARUCH ATA

Blessed are You, Lord, our God, King of the world,
Who created the Heavens with the breath of His Word and with the breath of His Mouth, all their Hosts.

וְחֹק chok וּזְמַן uzman נָתַן natan לָהֶם lahem שֶׁלֹּא shelo יְשַׁנּוּ yeshanu אֶת־ et

תַּפְקִידָם tafkidam. שָׂשִׂים sasim וּשְׂמֵחִים usmechim לַעֲשׂוֹת la'asot

רְצוֹן retzon מהש ע"ה, ע"ב בריבוע וקס"א ע"ה, אל שדי ע"ה קוֹנֵיהֶם konehem.

פּוֹעֵל po'el אֱמֶת emet אהיה פעמים אהיה, ז"פ ס"ג שֶׁפְּעֻלָּתוֹ shepulato אֱמֶת emet

אהיה פעמים אהיה, ז"פ ס"ג. וְלַלְּבָנָה velalevana אָמַר amar שֶׁתִּתְחַדֵּשׁ shetit'chadesh

י"ב הויות, קס"א קנ"א עֲטֶרֶת ateret תִּפְאֶרֶת tiferet לַעֲמוּסֵי la'amusei בָטֶן vaten.

שֶׁגַּם shegam הֵם hem עֲתִידִים atidim לְהִתְחַדֵּשׁ lehit'chadesh

י"ב הויות, קס"א קנ"א כְּמוֹתָהּ kemota וּלְפָאֵר ulfa'er לְיוֹצְרָם leyotzram עַל al

שֵׁם shem כְּבוֹד kevod מַלְכוּתוֹ malchuto. בָּרוּךְ baruch אַתָּה Ata

יְהֹוָהאדהנויאהדונהי Adonai מְחַדֵּשׁ mechadesh י"ב הויות, קס"א קנ"א חֳדָשִׁים chodashim:

This phrase is usually spoken at celebrations, such as a wedding. We wish someone "a good sign," meaning to have a control of the signs of the zodiac and connect only to positivity. The word *Tov* טוב is a code for the Name: *Vav, Hei, Vav* והו, the first Name and seed of all the 72 Names of God. Both, טוב and והו, share the same numerical value of 17. This phrase gives us the power to transform negativity into positivity by changing the DNA at the seed level of any situation.

Recite this verse three times:

בְּסִימָן besiman טוֹב tov והו תְּהִי tehi לָנוּ lanu אלהים, אהיה אדני

וּלְכָל ulchol יה אדני יִשְׂרָאֵל Yisrael:

We repeat the following verses (until "*David melech Yisrael chai vekayam*") three times.

בָּרוּךְ baruch יוֹצְרֵךְ yotzrich — ***Yetzirah*** - So *Yetzirah* will bless *Asiyah*.

בָּרוּךְ baruch עוֹשֵׂךְ osich — ***Asiyah*** – So Lower *Hei* will connect with *Vav*.

בָּרוּךְ baruch קוֹנֵךְ konich — ***Atzilut*** - So *Atzilut* will bless *Beriah*.

בָּרוּךְ baruch בּוֹרְאֵךְ bor'ich — ***Beriah*** – So Upper *Hei* will connect with *Yud*.

ר"ת יעקב (ו' הויות, יאהדונהי אידהנויה)

He gave them law and time so they would not deviate from their assignment. They rejoice and delight in doing the will of their Master. A truthful worker whose work is true. He told the moon to renew itself and to be a crown of glory to those carried in the womb, for they, too, are destined to be renewed like the moon, and shall glorify their Maker for the glory of the Name of His Kingdom. Blessed are You, Lord, Who renews the months.

May it be a good sign for us and for all of Israel.

Blessed is the One Who formed you. Blessed is the One Who made you.

Blessed is the One Who owns you. Blessed is the One Who created you

כשם keshem שאנחנו she'anachnu מרקדים merakdim

Jump three times and meditate to elevate the Worlds of *Asiyah*, *Yetzirah* and *Beriah* to *Atzilut*.

כנגדיך kenegdich ואין ve'en אנחנו anachnu יכולים yecholim לגע liga

ביך bich• כך kach אם im יוהך, מ"א אותיות דאהיה פשוט, מילואו ומילוי דמילואו ע"ה

ירקדו yerakedu אחרים acherim כנגדנו kenegdenu להזיקנו lehazikenu•

לא lo יוכלו yuchlu לגע liga בנו banu• ולא velo ישלטו yishletu בנו vanu•

ולא velo יעשו ya'asu בנו vanu שום shum רושם roshem•

(some add: יהי yehi רצון ratzon שלא shelo יהא yehe לנו lanu כאב Ke'ev שינים shinayim)

MALCHUT

We now want to protect our world of *Malchut* from all negativity because *Malchut* is the closest world to the *klipot*. We do not want *Malchut* to have any connection to these negative entities. The next verse is the same as this verse, but backwards in order to uproot the *klipot* from our life. When we uproot our *klipot*, the Light decides to whom this negativity will be transferred. If a person truly desires to change his negative nature, he can remove and transfer all his *klipot* to the evil people of our world. However, if a person avoids spiritual change and maintains his selfish, ego-driven ways, he will not only be stuck in the mire of his misery and negativity, but he will also be a potential target and lightning rod for other people's negativity.

תפל tipol עליהם alehem אימתה emata ופחד vafachad ר"ת תעאו שם קדוש

בגדל bigdol זרועך zero'acha ידמו yidemu כאבן ka'aven ר"ת טל, כוזו, יוד הא ואו:

כאבן ka'aven ידמו yidemu זרועך zero'acha בגדל bigdol

ופחד vafachad אימתה emata עליהם alehem תפל tipol:

Go back to "*baruch yotzrich*" (pg. 621) and recite all over three times.

KING DAVID

King David was the King of Israel. He is also the physical embodiment of the *Sefirah* of *Malchut*. Uttering this verse connects all of the Light that we have aroused to our world of Malchut.

דוד David מלך melech ישראל Yisrael חי chai וקים vekayam

דוד מלך חי וקיים = רפ"ח (להעלות רפ"ח ניצוצות שנפלו לקליפה דמשם באים התולואים): **3x**

And just as we dance before You yet cannot touch You,
so, too, if others should jump at us, they would be unable to touch, rule over, or leave any mark upon us.

MALCHUT

"May dread and fear fall upon them. By the greatness of Your arm, may they become as still as stone." (Exodus 16:13) *As still as stone may they become by Your arm in its greatness, and may terror and fear fall upon them.*

KING DAVID

David, King of Israel, lives and endures. (x3)

We recite the following (until "*bekirbi*") seven times – from *Chesed* to *Malchut*:

אָמֵן amen יאהדונהי אָמֵן amen יאהדונהי אָמֵן amen יאהדונהי:

נֶצַח netzach נֶצַח netzach נֶצַח netzach:

סֶלָה sela סֶלָה sela סֶלָה sela: וָעֶד va'ed וָעֶד va'ed וָעֶד va'ed:

לֵב lev טָהוֹר tahor י״פ אכא בְּרָא bera קנ״א ב״ן, יהוה אלהים יהוה אדני, מילוי קס״א ס״ג,

מ״ה ברבוע ע״ב ע״ה ; לב טהור ברא = קס״א קנ״א קמ״ג לִי li אֱלֹהִים Elohim

וְרוּחַ veru'ach נָכוֹן nachon חַדֵּשׁ chadesh י״ב הויות, קס״א קנ״א בְּקִרְבִּי bekirbi שדי:

SHIR LAMA'ALOT

שִׁיר shir לַמַּעֲלוֹת lama'alot אֶשָּׂא esa עֵינַי enai ריבוע מ״ה

אֶל־ el הֶהָרִים heharim מֵאַיִן me'ayin יָבֹא yavo עֶזְרִי ezri:

עֶזְרִי ezri מֵעִם me'im יְהֹוָה יאהדונהי Adonai עֹשֵׂה ose שָׁמַיִם shamayim

י״פ טל, י״פ כוזו וָאָרֶץ va'aretz: אַל־ al יִתֵּן yiten לַמּוֹט lamot רַגְלֶךָ raglecha

אַל־ al יָנוּם yanum שֹׁמְרֶךָ shomrecha: הִנֵּה hine לֹא־ lo יָנוּם yanum

וְלֹא velo יִישָׁן yishan ש״ע נהורין דא״א שׁוֹמֵר shomer כ״א ההויות שבתפילין

יִשְׂרָאֵל Yisrael: יְהֹוָה יאהדונהי Adonai שֹׁמְרֶךָ shomrecha

יְהֹוָה יאהדונהי Adonai צִלְּךָ tzilecha עַל־ al יַד yad יְמִינֶךָ yeminecha היי:

יוֹמָם yomam הַשֶּׁמֶשׁ hashemesh לֹא־ lo יַכֶּכָּה yakeka ר״ת ילה

וְיָרֵחַ veyare'ach בַּלָּיְלָה balayla מלה: יְהֹוָה יאהדונהי Adonai

יִשְׁמָרְךָ yishmorcha מִכָּל־ mikol ילי רָע ra יִשְׁמֹר yishmor

אֶת־ et נַפְשֶׁךָ nafshecha מיכ: יְהֹוָה יאהדונהי Adonai יִשְׁמָר yishmor

צֵאתְךָ tzetcha וּבוֹאֶךָ uvo'echa מֵעַתָּה me'ata וְעַד־ ve'ad עוֹלָם olam וול:

Amen, Amen, Amen, Eternal, Eternal, Eternal, Selah, Selah, Selah. Forever, forever, forever.
"Create a pure heart within me, God, and renew an upright spirit within me." (Psalms 51:12)

SHIR LAMA'ALOT

"A Song of Ascents: I lift up my eyes to the mountains; from where will my help come? My help is from the Lord, Creator of the Heavens and the Earth. He will not allow your legs to falter. Your Guardian shall not sleep. Behold: the Guardian of Israel shall neither slumber nor sleep. The Lord is your Guardian. The Lord is your protective shade at your right hand. During the day, the sun shall not harm you, nor shall the moon, at night. The Lord shall protect you from all evil, He will guard your soul. He shall guard you when you leave and when you come, from now and for eternity." (Psalms 121)

HALELUYA - HALELU EL BEKODSHO

This Psalm connect us to Ma-tat-ron מטטרון (**Do not pronounce**), the highest of all angels and controls all them in the spiritual world. his Name contains six Aramaic letters. Each verse in this connection helps form the Name. He can help give us control over our physical world and assist us in accomplishing our spiritual work.

אל (״יא״ מילוי דס״ג) אותיות בפסוק הַלְלוּיָהּ haleluya (*Keter*) אלהים, אהיה אדני ; ללה

הַלְלוּ־ halelu אֵל El ״יא״ (מילוי דס״ג) בְּקׇדְשׁוֹ bekodsho

הַלְלוּהוּ haleluhu (*Chochmah*) בִּרְקִיעַ birki'a עֻזּוֹ uzo ס״ת = ע״ב ב״ן:

הַלְלוּהוּ haleluhu (*Binah*) בִּגְבוּרֹתָיו vigvurotav הַלְלוּהוּ haleluhu (*Chesed*)

כְּרֹב kerov גֻּדְלוֹ gudlo: הַלְלוּהוּ haleluhu (*Gevurah*) בְּתֵקַע beteka

שׁוֹפָר shofar הַלְלוּהוּ haleluhu (*Ti'eret*) בְּנֵבֶל benevel וְכִנּוֹר vechinor:

הַלְלוּהוּ haleluhu (*Netzach*) בְּתֹף betof וּמָחוֹל umachol הַלְלוּהוּ haleluhu (*Hod*)

בְּמִנִּים beminim וְעֻגָב ve'ugav: הַלְלוּהוּ haleluhu (*Yesod*) בְּצִלְצְלֵי־ vetziltzelei

שָׁמַע shama הַלְלוּהוּ haleluhu (*Malchut*) בְּצִלְצְלֵי betziltzelei תְרוּעָה teru'a:

כֹּל kol ילי הַנְּשָׁמָה haneshama תְּהַלֵּל tehalel ר״ת כהת, משיח בן דוד ע״ה

יָהּ Yah הַלְלוּיָהּ haleluya אלהים, אהיה אדני ; ללה:

כֹּל kol ילי הַנְּשָׁמָה haneshama תְּהַלֵּל tehalel ר״ת כהת, משיח בן דוד ע״ה

יָהּ Yah הַלְלוּיָהּ haleluya אלהים, אהיה אדני ; ללה:

TANA

This verse states, "If we would be privileged to connect to the Face of the Creator once a month, this would have been enough." When we bless the moon we transform the world's negativity into positivity from a seed level, we are face-to-face with the Creator. Because we are face-to-face with the Creator, our negativity is removed.

תָּנָא tana דְּבֵי devei רִבִּי Ribi יִשְׁמָעֵאל Yishmael. אִלְמָלֵא ilmale זָכוּ zachu

בְּנֵי venei יִשְׂרָאֵל Yisrael אֶלָּא ela לְהַקְבִּיל lehakbil פְּנֵי penei וחכמה בינה

HALELUYA - HALELU EL BEKODSHO

"Praise the Lord! Praise Him in His Sanctuary; praise Him in the firmaments of His might; praise Him by His valorous deeds; praise Him according to His bountiful greatness; praise Him with blowing the Shofar; praise Him with lyre and harp; praise Him with drum and dance; praise Him with instruments and pipe; praise Him with the sound of cymbals; praise Him with reverberating sounds. All the souls praise God, Praise Him! All the souls praise God, Praise Him!" (Psalms 150)

TANA

"It was taught in the house of Rabbi Yishmael:
If the Children of Israel would be privileged but with greeting the Countenance

אֲבִיהֶם avihem שֶׁבַּשָּׁמַיִם shebashamayim י״פ טל, י״פ כוזו פַּעַם pa'am מנק
אַחַת achat בַּחֹדֶשׁ bachodesh י״ב הויות, קס״א קנ״א דַּיָּם dayam.
אָמַר amar אַבַּיֵּי Abayei הִלְכָּךְ helkach נֵימְרִינְהוּ nimrinhu מְעוֹמֵד me'omed:

We say *Kaddish Al Yisrael* (on pg.444-446) and then we continue:

VEHAYA

We request that the light of the moon be like the light of the sun once again. This is our connection to Messiah, when both the sun and moon will be two equal kings reigning in the Heavens.

וְהָיָה vehaya יהוה ; יהה אוֹר־ or רז, א״ס הַלְּבָנָה halevana כְּאוֹר ke'or רז, א״ס
הַחַמָּה hachama וְאוֹר ve'or רז, א״ס הַחַמָּה hachama יִהְיֶה yih'ye ייי
שִׁבְעָתַיִם shiv'atayim כְּאוֹר ke'or רז, א״ס שִׁבְעַת shiv'at הַיָּמִים hayamim נלך
בְּיוֹם beyom ע״ה נגד, מזבח, זן, אל יהוה חֲבֹשׁ chavosh יְהֹוָאֲדֹנָיאהדונהי Adonai אֶת־ et
שֶׁבֶר shever עַמּוֹ amo וּמַחַץ umachatz מַכָּתוֹ makato יִרְפָּא yirpa: וַתַּעְדִּי vata'adi
זָהָב zahav וָכֶסֶף vachesef וּמַלְבּוּשֵׁךְ umalbushech שֵׁשׁ shesh (כתיב: ששי)
וָמֶשִׁי vameshi וְרִקְמָה verikma סֹלֶת solet וּדְבַשׁ udvash שו׳ דשופר וי״ד האוזו =
ע״ך דינין דגדלות וָשֶׁמֶן vashemen אָכָלְתְּ achalt (כתיב: אכלתי) וַתִּיפִי vatifi
בִּמְאֹד bim'od מְאֹד me'od וַתִּצְלְחִי vatitzlechi לִמְלוּכָה limlucha:

SHALOM ALECHEM

We wish *Shalom Alechem / Alechem Shalom* to at least three people to conclude the Blessing of the Moon. *Shalom Alechem* offers peace to our neighbors. The reply of *Alechem Shalom* offers peace back. The act of reaching out to others helps to manifest the energy of "loving your neighbor." This moment is a powerful one to inject this kind of energy because we have just removed negativity from its root source (the moon), which gives us a window of opportunity to effect positive change.

Saying "*Shalom Alechem*" is to help to remove the jealousy that the moon has for the sun.

You should bless three of your freinds: שָׁלוֹם shalom עֲלֵיכֶם alechem
Each one of the three friend replies: עֲלֵיכֶם alechem שָׁלוֹם shalom:

Shake the edge of your clothing, and then meditate to remove all the *klipot* (the *klipot* always attach themselves to the edges) that was created from the jealousy of the moon and then look at your *Tzitzit*.

---

of their Father in the Heavens only once a month, it would be sufficient for them. Abbayeh said: Therefore let us recite it while we stand." (Sanhedrin 42a)

VEHAYA

"And the light of the moon shall be like the light of the sun, and the light of the sun shall be sevenfold, as the light of seven days, upon that day when Lord will set right the misfortune of His nation and will heal the wound of His blow." (Isaiah 30:26)
"And you adorned yourself with gold and silver; your dress was of linen, silk, and embroidery. You ate fine flour, honey, and oil; you became extremely beautiful and you became fit to reign." (Ezikiel 116:13)

SHALOM ALECHEM

Peace be upon you (And each one of them answers :) *Upon you is peace.*

TORAH READING FOR SHAVUOT

בַּחֹדֶשׁ י"ב הויות הַשְּׁלִישִׁי לְצֵאת ר"ת הבל בְּנֵי־יִשְׂרָאֵל מֵאֶרֶץ אלהים דאלפין
מִצְרָיִם מצר בַּיּוֹם ע"ה = נגד, זן, מזבח הַזֶּה והו בָּאוּ מִדְבַּר סִינָי נמם, ה"פ יהוה׃
וַיִּסְעוּ מֵרְפִידִים וַיָּבֹאוּ מִדְבַּר סִינַי נמם, ה"פ יהוה וַיַּחֲנוּ בַּמִּדְבָּר רמ"ח, ו"פ אל
וַיִּחַן־שָׁם יִשְׂרָאֵל נֶגֶד זן, מזבח הָהָר רבוע אלהים - ה'׃ וּמֹשֶׁה מהש, אל שדי
עָלָה אֶל־הָאֱלֹהִים מום, אהיה אדני ; ילה וַיִּקְרָא עם ה' אותיות = ב"פ קס"א אֵלָיו
יְהֹוָהאדניאהדונהי מִן־הָהָר לֵאמֹר כֹּה הי תֹאמַר לְבֵית ב"פ ראה
יַעֲקֹב ו"פ יהוה, יאהדונהי אידהנויה וְתַגֵּיד לִבְנֵי יִשְׂרָאֵל׃ אַתֶּם רְאִיתֶם אֲשֶׁר
עָשִׂיתִי לְמִצְרָיִם מצר וָאֶשָּׂא אֶתְכֶם עַל־כַּנְפֵי נְשָׁרִים וָאָבִא אֶתְכֶם אֵלָי׃
וְעַתָּה אִם־ יוהך, ע"ה מ"ב שָׁמוֹעַ תִּשְׁמְעוּ בְּקֹלִי וּשְׁמַרְתֶּם אֶת־בְּרִיתִי וִהְיִיתֶם
לִי סְגֻלָּה מִכָּל־ ילי הָעַמִּים ע"ה קס"א כִּי־לִי כָּל־ ילי הָאָרֶץ אלהים דההין ע"ה׃
וְאַתֶּם תִּהְיוּ־לִי מַמְלֶכֶת כֹּהֲנִים מלה וְגוֹי קָדוֹשׁ אֵלֶּה הַדְּבָרִים ראה
אֲשֶׁר תְּדַבֵּר ראה אֶל־בְּנֵי יִשְׂרָאֵל׃ *Levi* וַיָּבֹא מֹשֶׁה מהש, אל שדי
וַיִּקְרָא עם ה' אותיות = ב"פ קס"א לְזִקְנֵי הָעָם וַיָּשֶׂם לִפְנֵיהֶם אֵת כָּל־ ילי
הַדְּבָרִים ראה הָאֵלֶּה אֲשֶׁר צִוָּהוּ יְהֹוָהאדניאהדונהי׃ וַיַּעֲנוּ כָל־ ילי הָעָם יַחְדָּו
וַיֹּאמְרוּ כֹּל ילי אֲשֶׁר־דִּבֶּר ראה יְהֹוָהאדניאהדונהי נַעֲשֶׂה וַיָּשֶׁב מֹשֶׁה מהש, אל שדי
אֶת־דִּבְרֵי ראה הָעָם אֶל־יְהֹוָהאדניאהדונהי׃ וַיֹּאמֶר יְהֹוָהאדניאהדונהי
אֶל־מֹשֶׁה מהש, אל שדי הִנֵּה מ"ה יה אָנֹכִי איע בָּא אֵלֶיךָ אני בְּעַב הֶעָנָן
בַּעֲבוּר יִשְׁמַע הָעָם בְּדַבְּרִי ראה עִמָּךְ ה' הויות, נמם וְגַם־ יג"ל בְּךָ יַאֲמִינוּ
לְעוֹלָם וַיַּגֵּד מֹשֶׁה מהש, אל שדי אֶת־דִּבְרֵי ראה הָעָם אֶל־יְהֹוָהאדניאהדונהי׃

TORAH READING FOR SHAVUOT

"On the third month after the children of Israel exodus from the land of Egypt, on this day, they arrived at the Sinai desert. They journeyed from Rephidim and arrived at the Sinai desert and encamped in the desert, and Israel encamped there, opposite the mountain. And Moses ascended to God, and the Lord called to him from the mountain, saying: 'So shall you say to the House of Jacob, and relate to the children of Israel: "You have seen what I did to Egypt, and I have borne you on the wings of Egypt and brought you to Me. And now, if you hearken well to Me and observe my covenant, you shall beloved to Me more that all the peoples, for Mine is the entire world. And you shall be to Me a kingdom of ministers and a holy nation." These are the words that you shall speak to the children of Israel.' **LEVI** *And Moses called the elders of the people, and put before them all these words that the Lord has commanded him. And all the people responded together, saying: "Everything that the Lord has spoken, we shall do!" And Moses told the Lord the peoples words. And the Lord spoke to Moses: "Behold! I come to you in the thickness of the cloud, so that the people will pay heed when I speak to you, and they will believe in you forever, as well." And Moses told the Lord the words of the people.*

וַיֹּאמֶר יְהֹוָאדהנויאהדונהי אֶל־מֹשֶׁה מהש, אל שדי לֵךְ אֶל־הָעָם וְקִדַּשְׁתָּם
הַיּוֹם ע״ה = נגד, זן, מזבח וּמָחָר רמ״ח וְכִבְּסוּ שִׂמְלֹתָם: וְהָיוּ נְכֹנִים
לַיּוֹם ע״ה = נגד, זן, מזבח הַשְּׁלִישִׁי כִּי | בַּיּוֹם ע״ה = נגד, זן, מזבח הַשְּׁלִשִׁי יֵרֵד
יְהֹוָאדהנויאהדונהי לְעֵינֵי ריבוע מ״ה כָל־ ילי הָעָם עַל־הַר רבוע אלהים + ה׳
סִינָי נמם, ה״פ יהוה: וְהִגְבַּלְתָּ אֶת־הָעָם סָבִיב לֵאמֹר הִשָּׁמְרוּ לָכֶם עֲלוֹת
בָּהָר אור, רז וּנְגֹעַ מלוי אהיה דאלפין בְּקָצֵהוּ כָּל־ ילי הַנֹּגֵעַ מלוי אהיה דאלפין
בָּהָר אור, רז מוֹת יוּמָת: לֹא־תִגַּע בּוֹ יָד כִּי־סָקוֹל יִסָּקֵל אוֹ־יָרֹה יִיָּרֶה
אִם־ יוהך, ע״ה מ״ב בְּהֵמָה ב״ן, לכב, יבמ אִם־ יוהך, ע״ה מ״ב אִישׁ ע״ה קנ״א קס״א לֹא
יִחְיֶה בִּמְשֹׁךְ הַיֹּבֵל הֵמָּה יַעֲלוּ בָהָר אור, רז: **Israel** וַיֵּרֶד רי״י מֹשֶׁה מהש, אל שדי
מִן־הָהָר אֶל־הָעָם וַיְקַדֵּשׁ אֶת־הָעָם וַיְכַבְּסוּ שִׂמְלֹתָם: וַיֹּאמֶר אֶל־הָעָם הֱיוּ
נְכֹנִים לִשְׁלֹשֶׁת יָמִים נלך אַל־תִּגְּשׁוּ אֶל־אִשָּׁה: וַיְהִי אל, יא״י בַיּוֹם ע״ה = נגד, זן, מזבח
הַשְּׁלִישִׁי בִּהְיֹת הַבֹּקֶר וַיְהִי אל, יא״י קֹלֹת וּבְרָקִים וְעָנָן כָּבֵד עַל־הָהָר
וְקֹל נמם, רבוע מ״ה שֹׁפָר חָזָק פהל מְאֹד מ״ה וַיֶּחֱרַד כָּל־ ילי הָעָם אֲשֶׁר בַּמַּחֲנֶה:
וַיּוֹצֵא מֹשֶׁה מהש, אל שדי אֶת־הָעָם לִקְרַאת הָאֱלֹהִים מום, אהיה אדני ; ילה
מִן־הַמַּחֲנֶה וַיִּתְיַצְּבוּ בְּתַחְתִּית הָהָר: וְהַר רבוע אלהים + ה׳ סִינַי נמם, ה״פ יהוה
עָשַׁן כֻּלּוֹ מִפְּנֵי חכמה בינה אֲשֶׁר יָרַד עָלָיו יְהֹוָאדהנויאהדונהי בָּאֵשׁ אלהים דיודין ע״ה
וַיַּעַל עֲשָׁנוֹ כְּעֶשֶׁן הַכִּבְשָׁן וַיֶּחֱרַד כָּל־ ילי הָהָר מְאֹד מ״ה: וַיְהִי אל, יא״י
קוֹל ע״ב ס״ג ע״ה הַשּׁוֹפָר הוֹלֵךְ וְחָזֵק פהל מְאֹד מ״ה מֹשֶׁה מהש, אל שדי
יְדַבֵּר ראה וְהָאֱלֹהִים מום, אהיה אדני ; ילה יַעֲנֶנּוּ בְקוֹל ע״ב ס״ג ע״ה: **Fourth**

And the Lord said to Moses: "Go to the people and sanctify them today and tomorrow, and they shall wash their clothing. And they shall be ready for the third day, for on the third day the Lord shall descend in the sight of the entire people on Mount Sinai. You shall set boundaries for the people roundabout, saying: 'Beware lest you ascend the mountain or touch its edge, whoever touches the mountain shall surely die.' No hand shall touch it, for he shall surely be stoned or thrown down, whether animal or person, he shall not live. Upon an extended blast of the Shofar, they may ascend the mountain." **ISRAEL** *And Moses went down from the mountain to the people, he sanctified the people and they washed their clothing. He said to the people: "Be ready after a three-day period, do not approach a woman." And on the third day when it was morning, there were thunder and lightning and a heavy cloud on the mountain, and a very strong sound of the Shofar and the entire people that was in the camp shuddered. Moses brought the people forth toward God from the camp, and they stood at the bottom of the mountain. And Mount Sinai was completely in smoke because the Lord descended upon it in the fire, its smoke ascended like the smoke of the furnace, and the entire mountain shuddered exceedingly. The sound of the Shofar grew continually much stronger. Moses spoke, and God responded to him with a voice.* **FOURTH**

וַיֵּרֶד רי״י יְהֹוָאדניאהדונהי עַל־הַר רבוע אלהים + ה׳ סִינַי נמם, ה״פ יהוה אֶל־
רֹאשׁ ריבוע אלהים ואלהים דיודין ע״ה הָהָר רבוע אלהים + ה׳ וַיִּקְרָא עם ה׳ אותיות = ב״פ קס״א
יְהֹוָאדניאהדונהי לְמֹשֶׁה מהש, אל שדי אֶל־רֹאשׁ ריבוע אלהים ואלהים דיודין ע״ה הָהָר
וַיַּעַל מֹשֶׁה מהש, אל שדי: וַיֹּאמֶר יְהֹוָאדניאהדונהי אֶל־מֹשֶׁה מהש, אל שדי רֵד הָעֵד
בָּעָם פֶּן־יֶהֶרְסוּ אֶל־יְהֹוָאדניאהדונהי לִרְאוֹת וְנָפַל מִמֶּנּוּ רָב ע״ב ורבוע מ״ה: וְגַם יג״ל
הַכֹּהֲנִים מלה הַנִּגָּשִׁים אֶל־יְהֹוָאדניאהדונהי יִתְקַדָּשׁוּ פֶּן־יִפְרֹץ בָּהֶם
יְהֹוָאדניאהדונהי: וַיֹּאמֶר מֹשֶׁה מהש, אל שדי אֶל־יְהֹוָאדניאהדונהי לֹא־יוּכַל הָעָם
לַעֲלֹת אֶל־הַר רבוע אלהים + ה׳ סִינָי נמם, ה״פ יהוה כִּי־אַתָּה הַעֵדֹתָה בָּנוּ לֵאמֹר
ר״ת הבל הַגְבֵּל אֶת־הָהָר וְקִדַּשְׁתּוֹ: וַיֹּאמֶר אֵלָיו יְהֹוָאדניאהדונהי לֶךְ־רֵד וְעָלִיתָ
אַתָּה וְאַהֲרֹן ע״ב ורבוע ע״ב עִמָּךְ ה׳ הויות, נמם וְהַכֹּהֲנִים מלה וְהָעָם אַל־יֶהֶרְסוּ
לַעֲלֹת אֶל־יְהֹוָאדניאהדונהי פֶּן־יִפְרָץ־בָּם מ״ב: וַיֵּרֶד רי״י מֹשֶׁה מהש, אל שדי אֶל־
הָעָם וַיֹּאמֶר אֲלֵהֶם: וַיְדַבֵּר ראה אֱלֹהִים מום, אהיה אדני ; ילה אֵת כָּל־ ילי
הַדְּבָרִים ראה הָאֵלֶּה לֵאמֹר: (*Keter*) אָנֹכִי איע יְהֹוָאדניאהדונהי אֱלֹהֶיךָ ילה
אֲשֶׁר הוֹצֵאתִיךָ מֵאֶרֶץ אלהים דאלפין מִצְרַיִם מצר מִבֵּית ב״פ ראה עֲבָדִים
(*Chochmah*) לֹא־יִהְיֶה ייי לְךָ אֱלֹהִים מום, אהיה אדני ; ילה אֲחֵרִים עַל־פָּנָי וחכמה בינה:
לֹא־תַעֲשֶׂה לְךָ פֶסֶל וְכָל־ ילי תְּמוּנָה אֲשֶׁר בַּשָּׁמַיִם מִמַּעַל עלם וַאֲשֶׁר
בָּאָרֶץ אלהים דאלפין מִתָּחַת וַאֲשֶׁר בַּמַּיִם מִתַּחַת לָאָרֶץ אלהים דאלפין: לֹא־
תִשְׁתַּחֲוֶה לָהֶם וְלֹא תָעָבְדֵם כִּי אָנֹכִי איע יְהֹוָאדניאהדונהי אֱלֹהֶיךָ ילה אֵל ייא״י
קַנָּא קנ״א, מקוה פֹּקֵד רבוע ע״ב עֲוֺן ג״פ מ״ב אָבֹת עַל־בָּנִים עַל־שִׁלֵּשִׁים וְעַל־
רִבֵּעִים לְשֹׂנְאָי: וְעֹשֶׂה חֶסֶד ע״ב, ריבוע יהוה לַאֲלָפִים קס״א לְאֹהֲבַי וּלְשֹׁמְרֵי מִצְוֺתָי:

And the Lord descended upon Mount Sinai to the top of the mountain, and the Lord summoned Moses to the top of the mountain, and Moses ascended. And the Lord said to Moses: "Descend, warn the people lest they break through to the Lord to see, and a multitude of it will fall. Even the priests who approach the Lord should be prepared, lest the Lord burst forth against them." And Moses said to the Lord "The people cannot ascend Mount Sinai, for You have warned us, saying 'Bound the mountain and sanctify it.' Then the Lord said to him "Go, descend, then you shall ascend and Aaron with you, and the priests, and the people, they shall not break through to ascend to the Lord, lest He burst forth against them." And Moses descended to the people and said to them: "God spoke all these statements, saying: **Keter** *I am the Lord, your God, Who took you out of the land of Egypt, from the house of slavery.* **Chochmah** *You shall not recognize the gods of others before My presence. You shall not make yourself a carved image nor any likeness of that which is in the Heavens above or on the Earth below or in the water beneath the earth. You shall not prostrate yourself to them nor worship them, for I am the Lord, your God, a jealous God, Remembering the sin of fathers upon children to the third and fourth generations, for My enemies, but showing kindness for thousands (of generations) to those who love Me and observe My commandments.*

(*Binah*) לֹא תִשָּׂא אֶת־שֵׁם־ יהוה שדי יְהֹוָאדנָיאהדונהי אֱלֹהֶיךָ ילה לַשָּׁוְא כִּי לֹא
יְנַקֶּה יְהֹוָאדנָיאהדונהי אֵת אֲשֶׁר־יִשָּׂא אֶת־שְׁמוֹ מהש ע״ה, אל שדי ע״ה לַשָּׁוְא:
(*Chesed*) זָכוֹר ע״ב קס״א אֶת־יוֹם ע״ה = נגד, זן, מזבח הַשַּׁבָּת לְקַדְּשׁוֹ: שֵׁשֶׁת
יָמִים נלך תַּעֲבֹד וְעָשִׂיתָ כָּל־ ילי מְלַאכְתֶּךָ: וְיוֹם ע״ה = נגד, זן, מזבח הַשְּׁבִיעִי
שַׁבָּת לַיהֹוָאדנָיאהדונהי אֱלֹהֶיךָ ילה לֹא־תַעֲשֶׂה כָל־ ילי מְלָאכָה אל אדני
אַתָּה | וּבִנְךָ וּבִתֶּךָ עַבְדְּךָ פוי וַאֲמָתְךָ וּבְהֶמְתֶּךָ וְגֵרְךָ אֲשֶׁר בִּשְׁעָרֶיךָ:
כִּי שֵׁשֶׁת־יָמִים נלך עָשָׂה יְהֹוָאדנָיאהדונהי אֶת־הַשָּׁמַיִם י״פ טל, י״פ כוזו
וְאֶת־הָאָרֶץ אלהים דההין ע״ה אֶת־הַיָּם ילי וְאֶת־כָּל־ ילי אֲשֶׁר־בָּם מ״ב וַיָּנַח בַּיּוֹם
ע״ה = נגד, זן, מזבח הַשְּׁבִיעִי עַל־כֵּן בֵּרַךְ יְהֹוָאדנָיאהדונהי אֶת־יוֹם ע״ה = נגד, זן, מזבח
הַשַּׁבָּת וַיְקַדְּשֵׁהוּ: (*Gevurah*) כַּבֵּד אֶת־אָבִיךָ וְאֶת־אִמֶּךָ לְמַעַן יַאֲרִכוּן
יָמֶיךָ עַל הָאֲדָמָה אֲשֶׁר־יְהֹוָאדנָיאהדונהי אֱלֹהֶיךָ ילה נֹתֵן אבגיתץ, ושר, אהבת חנם לָךְ:
(*Tiferet*) לֹא תִרְצָח (*Netzach*) לֹא תִנְאָף (*Hod*) לֹא תִגְנֹב
(*Yesod*) לֹא־תַעֲנֶה בְרֵעֲךָ עֵד שָׁקֶר: (*Malchut*) לֹא תַחְמֹד בֵּית ב״פ ראה
רֵעֶךָ לֹא־תַחְמֹד אֵשֶׁת רֵעֶךָ וְעַבְדּוֹ וַאֲמָתוֹ וְשׁוֹרוֹ וַחֲמֹרוֹ וְכֹל ילי
אֲשֶׁר לְרֵעֶךָ: *Fifth* וְכָל־ ילי הָעָם רֹאִים אֶת־הַקּוֹלֹת וְאֶת־הַלַּפִּידִם וְאֵת
קוֹל ע״ב ס״ג ע״ה הַשֹּׁפָר וְאֶת־הָהָר עָשֵׁן וַיַּרְא אלף למד יהוה הָעָם וַיָּנֻעוּ וַיַּעַמְדוּ
מֵרָחֹק שדי: וַיֹּאמְרוּ אֶל־מֹשֶׁה מהש, אל שדי דַּבֵּר־ ראה אַתָּה עִמָּנוּ וְנִשְׁמָעָה
וְאַל־יְדַבֵּר ראה עִמָּנוּ אֱלֹהִים מום, אהיה אדני ; ילה פֶּן־נָמוּת: וַיֹּאמֶר
מֹשֶׁה מהש, אל שדי אֶל־הָעָם אַל־תִּירָאוּ כִּי לְבַעֲבוּר נַסּוֹת אֶתְכֶם בָּא
הָאֱלֹהִים מום, אהיה אדני ; ילה וּבַעֲבוּר תִּהְיֶה יִרְאָתוֹ עַל־פְּנֵיכֶם לְבִלְתִּי תֶחֱטָאוּ:

Binah *You shall not take the Name of the Lord, your God, in a vain oath, for the Lord will not absolve anyone in a vain oath.* **Chesed** *Remember the Shabbat day to sanctify it. Six days you shall work and accomplish all your tasks, but the seventh day is Shabbat to the Lord, your God, you shall not do any work, you, your son, your daughter, your salve, your maidservant, your animal, and the convert within your gates, for in six days the Lord made the Heavens and the Earth, the sea and all that is in them, and He rested on the seventh day. Therefore, the Lord blessed the Shabbat day and sanctified it.* **Gevurah** *Honor your father and your mother, so that you may live a long life upon the land that the Lord, your God, gives you.* **Tiferet** *You shall not kill.* **Netzach** *You shall not commit adultery.* **Hod** *You shall not steal.* **Yesod** *You shall not bear false witness against your neighbor.* **Malchut** *You shall not covet your neighbor's house. You shall not covet your neighbor's wife, his manservant, his maidservant, his ox, his ass, nor anything that belongs to your neighbor.* **FIFTH** *And all the people saw the thunder and the flames, the sounds of the Shofar, and the smoking mountain, the people saw and trembled and stood from afar. And they said to Moses: "You speak to us and we shall hear, let God not speak to us lest we die." And Moses said to the people 'Do not fear, for in order to elevate you has God come, and so that fear of Him shall be upon your faces so that you shall not sin."*

וַיַּעֲמֹד הָעָם מֵרָחֹק שדי וּמֹשֶׁה מהש, אל שדי נִגַּשׁ אֶל־הָעֲרָפֶל אֲשֶׁר־שָׁם
הָאֱלֹהִים מום, אהיה אדני ; ילה: וַיֹּאמֶר יְהֹוָהאדניאהדונהי אֶל־מֹשֶׁה מהש, אל שדי
כֹּה היי תֹאמַר אֶל־בְּנֵי יִשְׂרָאֵל אַתֶּם רְאִיתֶם כִּי מִן־הַשָּׁמַיִם י"פ טל, י"פ כוזו
דִּבַּרְתִּי ראה עִמָּכֶם: לֹא תַעֲשׂוּן אִתִּי אֱלֹהֵי דמב, ילה כֶסֶף וֵאלֹהֵי דמב, ילה
זָהָב לֹא תַעֲשׂוּ לָכֶם: מִזְבַּח זן, נגד אֲדָמָה תַּעֲשֶׂה־לִּי וְזָבַחְתָּ עָלָיו
אֶת־עֹלֹתֶיךָ וְאֶת־שְׁלָמֶיךָ אֶת־צֹאנְךָ וְאֶת־בְּקָרֶךָ בְּכָל־ ב"ן, לכב, יבמ
הַמָּקוֹם יהוה ברבוע, ו"פ אל אֲשֶׁר אַזְכִּיר אֶת־שְׁמִי רבוע ע"ב ורבוע ס"ג אָבוֹא
אֵלֶיךָ אני וּבֵרַכְתִּיךָ: וְאִם־ יוהך, ע"ה מ"ב מִזְבַּח זן, נגד אֲבָנִים תַּעֲשֶׂה־לִּי לֹא־
תִבְנֶה אֶתְהֶן גָּזִית כִּי חַרְבְּךָ הֵנַפְתָּ עָלֶיהָ פהל וַתְּחַלְלֶהָ: וְלֹא־תַעֲלֶה בְמַעֲלֹת
עַל־מִזְבְּחִי אֲשֶׁר לֹא־תִגָּלֶה עֶרְוָתְךָ עָלָיו:

After the reading say Half *Kaddish* (pg. 407), and then read the *Maftir* (below)

MAFTIR

וּבְיוֹם ע"ה = נגד, זן, מזבח הַבִּכּוּרִים בְּהַקְרִיבְכֶם מִנְחָה ע"ה ב"פ ב"ן חֲדָשָׁה
לַיהֹוָהאדניאהדונהי בְּשָׁבֻעֹתֵיכֶם מִקְרָא־ שם ע"ה, יהוה שדי קֹדֶשׁ יִהְיֶה ייי לָכֶם כָּל־ ילי
מְלֶאכֶת עֲבֹדָה לֹא תַעֲשׂוּ: וְהִקְרַבְתֶּם עוֹלָה לְרֵיחַ אברהם, ח"פ אל, רמ"ח נִיחֹחַ
לַיהֹוָהאדניאהדונהי פָּרִים בְּנֵי־בָקָר שְׁנַיִם אַיִל אֶחָד אהבה, דאגה שִׁבְעָה כְבָשִׂים
בְּנֵי שָׁנָה: וּמִנְחָתָם סֹלֶת בְּלוּלָה בַשָּׁמֶן י"פ טל, י"פ כוזו, ביט שְׁלֹשָׁה עֶשְׂרֹנִים
לַפָּר מוחך, ערי, סנדלפו"ן הָאֶחָד אהבה, דאגה שְׁנֵי עֶשְׂרֹנִים לָאַיִל הָאֶחָד אהבה, דאגה:
עִשָּׂרוֹן עִשָּׂרוֹן לַכֶּבֶשׂ ב"פ קס"א הָאֶחָד אהבה, דאגה לְשִׁבְעַת הַכְּבָשִׂים:

The people stood from afar and Moses approached the thick cloud where God was. And the Lord said to Moses: "So shall you say to the children of Israel, 'You have seen that I have spoken to you from heaven. You shall not make what is with Me, gods of gold, and gods of silver shall you not make for yourselves. An altar of earth shall you make for Me, and you shall slaughter upon it your elevation-offerings and your peace-offerings, your flock and your herd, wherever I cause My Name to be mentioned I shall come to you and bless you. And when you make an altar of stones for Me, do not build them of hewn stones, for you will have raised your sword over it and desecrated it. You shall not ascend My altar through steps so that your nakedness will not be uncovered upon it." (Exodus 19:1-20:23)

MAFTIR

"On the day of the first fruits, when you offer a new flour-offering to c on your holiday of Shavuot, it shall be a holy convocation to you, no service work shall be done. You shall offer an elevation-offering for u satisfying aroma to the Lord, two young bulls, one arm and seven lambs within their first year. And their meal-offering shall be fine flour mixed with oil, three tenth-ephah for each bull, two tenth-ephah for each ram, one tenth-ephah for each lamb, of the seven lambs.

שְׂעִיר עִזִּים אֶחָד אהבה, דאגה לְכַפֵּר מצפצ עֲלֵיכֶם: מִלְּבַד
עֹלַת אבגיתץ, ושר, אהבת חנם הַתָּמִיד ע״ה נתה, קס״א קנ״א קמ״ג וּמִנְחָתוֹ תַּעֲשׂוּ
תְּמִימִם יִהְיוּ־ אל לָכֶם וְנִסְכֵּיהֶם:

Say the blessing before the *Haftarah* (pg. 408) and then read the *Haftarah* (below).

HAFTARAH FOR SHAVUOT

וַיְהִי | בִּשְׁלֹשִׁים שָׁנָה בָּרְבִיעִי בַּחֲמִשָּׁה לַחֹדֶשׁ וַאֲנִי אני בְתוֹךְ־הַגּוֹלָה עַל־
נְהַר־כְּבָר נִפְתְּחוּ הַשָּׁמַיִם י״פ כוזו, י״פ טל וָאֶרְאֶה מַרְאוֹת אֱלֹהִים מום, ילה:
בַּחֲמִשָּׁה לַחֹדֶשׁ הִיא הַשָּׁנָה הַחֲמִישִׁית לְגָלוּת הַמֶּלֶךְ יוֹיָכִין: הָיֹה יהה
הָיָה יהה דְבַר־ ראה יְהֹוָהאדניאהדונהי אֶל־יְחֶזְקֵאל בֶּן־בּוּזִי הַכֹּהֵן מלה בְּאֶרֶץ
כַּשְׂדִּים עַל־נְהַר־כְּבָר וַתְּהִי עָלָיו שָׁם יַד־יְהֹוָהאדניאהדונהי: וָאֵרֶא וְהִנֵּה רוּחַ
סְעָרָה בָּאָה מִן־הַצָּפוֹן עָנָן גָּדוֹל להח, מבה וְאֵשׁ מִתְלַקַּחַת וְנֹגַהּ לוֹ סָבִיב
וּמִתּוֹכָהּ כְּעֵין ריבוע מ״ה הַחַשְׁמַל מִתּוֹךְ הָאֵשׁ: וּמִתּוֹכָהּ דְּמוּת אַרְבַּע חַיּוֹת
וְזֶה מַרְאֵיהֶן דְּמוּת אָדָם מ״ה לָהֵנָּה: וְאַרְבָּעָה פָנִים לְאֶחָת וְאַרְבַּע כְּנָפַיִם
לְאַחַת לָהֶם: וְרַגְלֵיהֶם רֶגֶל יְשָׁרָה וְכַף רַגְלֵיהֶם כְּכַף רֶגֶל עֵגֶל וְנֹצְצִים
כְּעֵין ריבוע מ״ה נְחֹשֶׁת קָלָל: וִידֵי (כתיב: וידו) אָדָם מ״ה מִתַּחַת כַּנְפֵיהֶם
עַל אַרְבַּעַת רִבְעֵיהֶם וּפְנֵיהֶם וְכַנְפֵיהֶם לְאַרְבַּעְתָּם: חֹבְרֹת אִשָּׁה
אֶל־אֲחוֹתָהּ כַּנְפֵיהֶם לֹא־יִסַּבּוּ בְלֶכְתָּן אִישׁ אֶל־עֵבֶר פָּנָיו יֵלֵכוּ:

One he-goat, to atone for you. Aside from the continual elevation-offering and its meal-offering shall you offer (them) unblemished shall they be, and their libations." (Numbers 28:26-31)

HAFTARAH FOR SHAVUOT

"And it happened in the thirtieth year in the fourth (month) on the fifth of the month, as I was among the exile by the River Kevar, the Heavens opened and I saw visions of God. On the fifth of the month, it was the fifth year of the exile of King Jeconiah. The word of the Lord had come to Ezekiel the son of Buzi, the priest, in the land of the Casdim by the River Kevar, and the hand of the Lord was upon him there. Then I looked and behold! A stormy wind was coming from the north, a great cloud with flashing fire and a brilliance surrounding it, and from its midst came a semblance of Chashmal from the midst of the fire, and from its midst a semblance of four Chayot (animals). This was their appearance: they had the semblance of a man, and four faces for each, and four wings for each of them. Their legs were a straight leg, and the sole of their feet was like the sole of a rounded foot, and they glittered like burnished bronze. And human hands were under their wings on each of their four sides, and their faces and wings were alike on the four of them. Joined to one another were their wings. They did not turn to one another as they moved, each went straight ahead.

וּדְמ֣וּת פְּנֵיהֶם֮ פְּנֵ֣י וחכמה, בינה אָדָם֒ מ"ה וּפְנֵ֨י וחכמה, בינה אַרְיֵ֤ה רי"ו אֶל־הַיָּמִין֙
לְאַרְבַּעְתָּ֔ם וּפְנֵי־ וחכמה, בינה שׁ֥וֹר מֵהַשְּׂמֹ֖אול לְאַרְבַּעְתָּ֑ן וּפְנֵי־ וחכמה, בינה נֶ֖שֶׁר
לְאַרְבַּעְתָּֽן׃ וּפְנֵיהֶ֕ם וְכַנְפֵיהֶ֥ם פְּרֻד֖וֹת מִלְמָ֑עְלָה לְאִ֗ישׁ שְׁתַּ֙יִם֙ חֹבְר֣וֹת אִ֔ישׁ
וּשְׁתַּ֣יִם מְכַסּ֔וֹת אֵ֖ת גְּוִיֹתֵיהֶֽנָה׃ וְאִ֛ישׁ אֶל־עֵ֥בֶר פָּנָ֖יו יֵלֵ֑כוּ אֶ֣ל אֲשֶׁר֩
יִֽהְיֶה־ ייי שָׁ֨מָּה הָר֤וּחַ לָלֶ֙כֶת֙ יֵלֵ֔כוּ לֹ֥א יִסַּ֖בּוּ בְּלֶכְתָּֽן׃ וּדְמ֨וּת הַחַיּ֜וֹת מַרְאֵיהֶ֣ם
כְּגַחֲלֵי־אֵ֞שׁ בֹּעֲר֨וֹת כְּמַרְאֵ֣ה הַלַּפִּדִ֔ים הִ֕יא מִתְהַלֶּ֖כֶת בֵּ֣ין הַחַיּ֑וֹת וְנֹ֣גַהּ לָאֵ֔שׁ
וּמִן־הָאֵ֖שׁ יוֹצֵ֥א בָרָֽק׃ וְהַחַיּ֖וֹת רָצ֣וֹא וָשׁ֑וֹב כְּמַרְאֵ֖ה הַבָּזָֽק׃ וָאֵ֖רֶא הַחַיּ֑וֹת
וְהִנֵּה֩ אוֹפַ֨ן אֶחָ֥ד אהבה, דאגה בָּאָ֛רֶץ אֵ֥צֶל הַחַיּ֖וֹת לְאַרְבַּ֥עַת פָּנָֽיו׃ מַרְאֵ֨ה ראה
הָאוֹפַנִּ֤ים וּמַעֲשֵׂיהֶם֙ כְּעֵ֣ין ריבוע מ"ה תַּרְשִׁ֔ישׁ וּדְמ֥וּת אֶחָ֖ד אהבה, דאגה
לְאַרְבַּעְתָּ֑ן וּמַרְאֵיהֶם֙ וּמַ֣עֲשֵׂיהֶ֔ם כַּאֲשֶׁ֛ר יִהְיֶ֥ה ייי הָאוֹפַ֖ן בְּת֥וֹךְ הָאוֹפָֽן׃
עַל־אַרְבַּ֥עַת רִבְעֵיהֶ֖ן בְּלֶכְתָּ֣ם יֵלֵ֑כוּ לֹ֥א יִסַּ֖בּוּ בְּלֶכְתָּֽן׃ וְגַ֨בֵּיהֶ֔ן וְגֹ֥בַהּ לָהֶ֖ם
וְיִרְאָ֣ה רי"ו, גבורה לָהֶ֑ם וְגַבֹּתָ֗ם מְלֵאֹ֥ת עֵינַ֛יִם סָבִ֖יב לְאַרְבַּעְתָּֽן׃ וּבְלֶ֙כֶת֙
הַֽחַיּ֔וֹת יֵלְכ֥וּ הָאוֹפַנִּ֖ים אֶצְלָ֑ם וּבְהִנָּשֵׂ֤א הַחַיּוֹת֙ מֵעַ֣ל עלם הָאָ֔רֶץ אלהים דההין
יִנָּשְׂא֖וּ הָאוֹפַנִּֽים׃ עַ֣ל אֲשֶׁר֩ יִֽהְיֶה־ ייי שָׁ֨ם הָר֤וּחַ לָלֶ֙כֶת֙ יֵלֵ֔כוּ שָׁ֥מָּה הָר֖וּחַ
לָלֶ֑כֶת וְהָאוֹפַנִּ֗ים יִנָּשְׂאוּ֙ לְעֻמָּתָ֔ם כִּ֛י ר֥וּחַ הַחַיָּ֖ה בָּאוֹפַנִּֽים׃ בְּלֶכְתָּ֣ם יֵלֵ֔כוּ
וּבְעָמְדָ֖ם יַעֲמֹ֑דוּ וּֽבְהִנָּשְׂאָ֞ם מֵעַ֣ל עלם הָאָ֗רֶץ אלהים דההין יִנָּשְׂא֤וּ
הָאוֹפַנִּים֙ לְעֻמָּתָ֔ם כִּ֛י ר֥וּחַ הַחַיָּ֖ה בָּאוֹפַנִּֽים׃ וּדְמ֨וּת עַל־רָאשֵׁ֤י
הַחַיָּה֙ רָקִ֔יעַ כְּעֵ֖ין ריבוע מ"ה הַקֶּ֣רַח הַנּוֹרָ֑א נָט֥וּי עַל־רָאשֵׁיהֶ֖ם מִלְמָֽעְלָה׃

As for the semblance of their faces, the face of a man and the face of a lion to the right of the four, the face of an ox to the left of the four and the face of an eagle to the four. And as for their faces, their wings extend upwards, for each face two joined for each and two covered their bodies. Each one went straight ahead, towards wherever there was the spirit to go, they went, they turned not as they went. And as for the appearance of the Chayot, their appearance was like fiery coals, burning like the appearance of torches, it manifested itself among the Chayot. There was a brilliance to the fire, and from the fire went forth lightning. And the Chayot ran to and fro like the appearance of Bazak. When I saw the Chayot, Behold! One Ofan was on the surface near the Chayot by its four faces. The appearance of the Ofanim and their deeds were like Tarshis with the same semblance for the four, and their appearance and their deeds like an Ofan within an Ofan. Toward their four sides, wherever they went they could go, they did not turn as they went. And they had backs, and they were tall and fearsome, and their backs were full of eyes surrounding the four of them. As the Chayot move, the Ofanim moved by them, and as the Chayot were lifted from upon the surface, the Ofanim were lifted. Wherever the spirit chose to go they went, there the spirit chose to go, the Ofanim were lifted opposite them, for the spirit of the Chayah was in the Ofanim. When they moved, they moved, and when they halted, they halted. And when they were lifted from upon the surface, the Ofanim were lifted opposite them, for the spirit of the Chayah in the Ofanim. And as for the semblance of the expanse above the heads of the Chayah, it resembled awesome ice spread out upon their heads from above.

וְתַחַת הָרָקִיעַ כַּנְפֵיהֶם יְשָׁרוֹת אִשָּׁה אֶל־אֲחוֹתָהּ לְאִישׁ שְׁתַּיִם מְכַסּוֹת
לָהֵנָּה וּלְאִישׁ שְׁתַּיִם מְכַסּוֹת לָהֵנָּה אֵת גְּוִיֹּתֵיהֶם: וָאֶשְׁמַע אֶת־קוֹל כַּנְפֵיהֶם
כְּקוֹל מַיִם רַבִּים כְּקוֹל־שַׁדַּי בְּלֶכְתָּם קוֹל הֲמֻלָּה כְּקוֹל מַחֲנֶה בְּעָמְדָם
תְּרַפֶּינָה כַנְפֵיהֶן: וַיְהִי־קוֹל מֵעַל עלם לָרָקִיעַ אֲשֶׁר עַל־רֹאשָׁם בְּעָמְדָם
תְּרַפֶּינָה כַנְפֵיהֶן: וּמִמַּעַל עלם לָרָקִיעַ אֲשֶׁר עַל־רֹאשָׁם כְּמַרְאֵה אֶבֶן־סַפִּיר
דְּמוּת כִּסֵּא וְעַל דְּמוּת הַכִּסֵּא דְּמוּת כְּמַרְאֵה אָדָם מ״ה עָלָיו מִלְמָעְלָה:
וָאֵרֶא | כְּעֵין ריבוע מ״ה חַשְׁמַל כְּמַרְאֵה־אֵשׁ בֵּית־ ב״פ ראה לָהּ סָבִיב מִמַּרְאֵה
מָתְנָיו וּלְמָעְלָה וּמִמַּרְאֵה מָתְנָיו וּלְמַטָּה רָאִיתִי כְּמַרְאֵה־אֵשׁ וְנֹגַהּ לוֹ
סָבִיב: כְּמַרְאֵה הַקֶּשֶׁת אֲשֶׁר יִהְיֶה ייי בֶעָנָן בְּיוֹם נגד, מזבח, זן הַגֶּשֶׁם כֵּן
מַרְאֵה ראה הַנֹּגַהּ סָבִיב הוּא מַרְאֵה ראה דְּמוּת כְּבוֹד־יְהֹוָהאדניאהדונהי וָאֶרְאֶה
וָאֶפֹּל עַל־פָּנַי חכמה, בינה וָאֶשְׁמַע קוֹל מְדַבֵּר ראה: וַתִּשָּׂאֵנִי רוּחַ וָאֶשְׁמַע
אַחֲרַי קוֹל רַעַשׁ גָּדוֹל להח, מבה בָּרוּךְ כְּבוֹד־יְהֹוָהאדניאהדונהי מִמְּקוֹמוֹ עסמ״ב:

Say the blessing after the *Haftarah* (pg. 409).

Beneath the expanse their wings were even, one with the other, for each (face), two covered them, and for each two covered them, their bodies. Then I heard the sound of their wings like the sound of great waters, like the sound of Shaddai as they moved, the sound of the words like the sound of a great company, when they halt they release their wings. So there was a sound from above the expanse that was upon their heads, when they halt they release their wings. Above the expanse that was upon their heads was like the appearance of sapphire stone in the likeness of a throne. And upon the likeness of the throne was a likeness like the appearance of a man upon it from above. I saw a semblance of Chashmal like the appearance of fire within it all around from the appearance of his loins and upwards, and from the appearance of his loins and downward I saw as if the appearance of fire, and it had brilliance all around. Like the appearance of the rainbow that shall be upon the cloud on a rainy day, so was the appearance of the brilliance all around. That was the appearance of the semblance of the glory of the Lord! When I saw this, I threw myself upon my face and I heard a voice speaking. And a wind lifted me up, and I heard behind me the sound of a great noise. Blessed be the Lord from His place." (Ezekiel 1:1-28, 3:12)

3 *Binah* Left Brain יֵהֵוֵהֵ	1 *Keter* Skull יָהָוָהָ	2 *Chochmah* Right Brain יַהַוַהַ
5 Left Eye יהוה יהוה יהוה יהוה יהוה	9 8 Nose יוד הי ואו הי יוד הי ואו הי	4 Right Eye יהוה יהוה יהוה יהוה יהוה
7 Left Ear יוד הי ואו הה		6 Right Ear יוד הי ואו הה
	10 Mouth יוד הי ואו הי (אהיה) אוזה"ע גיכ"ק דטלנ"ת זסשר"ץ בומ"ף	
12 *Gevurah* Left Arm יְהְוְהְ	13 *Tiferet* Body יֹהֹוֹהֹ	11 *Chesed* Right Arm יֶהֶוֶהֶ
15 *Hod* Left Leg יֻהֻוֻהֻ	16 *Yesod* Reproductive Organs יו הו וו הו	14 *Netzach* Right Leg יִהִוִהִ
	17 *Malchut* עֲטָרָה יהוהאדני	

Sunday - יוֹם א

יֶהֹוִה

יוּד הֵי וִיו הֵי יוּד הֵי וָאו הֵי

אל שדי יאולדפההייויאודההיי

אנא בכח גדולת ימינך תתיר צרורה

אבגיתץ יהוה יהוה

סמטוריה גזריאל ועניאל למואל

ר"ת סגול

Monday - יוֹם ב

יוד הי ואו הי יוד הי ואו הי יוד הא ואו הא

אל יהוה יאולדפההאאויאודההאא

קבל רנת עמך שגבנו טהרנו נורא

קרעשטן יהוה יהוה

שמעיאל ברכיאל אהניאל

ר"ת שוא

Tuesday - יוֹם ג

יוד הא ואו הא יוד הה וו הה

אל אדני יאולדפהההויודההה

נא גבור דורשי יחודך כבבת שמרם

נגדיכש יהוה יהוה

חניאל להדיאל מחניאל

ר"ת חלם

Wednesday - יום ד׳

יוד הא ואו הא יוד הה וו הה

אל אדני יאולדפההויודההה

ברכם טהרם רוזמי צדקתך תמיד גמלם

בטרצתג יהוה יהוה

וזזקיאל רהטיאל קדשיאל

ר״ת וזרק

Thursday - יום ה׳

יוד הי ואו הי יוד הי ואו הי יוד הא ואו הא

אל יהוה יאולדפההאאויאודההאא

וזסין קדוש ברוב טובך נהל עדתך

וזקבטנע יהוה יהוה

שמועאל רעמיאל קניאל

ר״ת שרק

(הקבוץ מלאכיו בר״ת שורק)

Friday - יום וו

יוד הי ויו הי יוד הי ואו הי

אל שדי יאולדפההייויאודההיי

יוזיד גאה לעמך פנה זוכרי קדושתך

יגלפזק יהוה יוהוודו

שומושויואולו רופואולו קודושויואולו

ר״ת שרק

Angels of Friday night

יוד הי ואו הי   שועתנו קבל ושמע צעקתנו יודע תעלומות

שקוצית יהוה יהוה יהוה

שמעיאל ברכיאל אהניאל

ר"ת שוא

סמטוריה גזריאל וענאל למואל

ר"ת סגול

צוריאל רזיאל יופיאל

ר"ת צירי

Angels of *Shabbat* (Saturday) Morning

יוד הי ויו הי יוד הי ויו הי

שועתנו קבל ושמע צעקתנו יודע תעלומות

שקוצית יהוה יהוה יהוה

שמעיאל ברכיאל אהניאל

ר"ת שוא

קדמיאל מלכיאל צוריאל

ר"ת קמץ

Angels of Shabbat (Saturday) Afternoon

יוד הא ואו הא יוד הא ואו הא

שועתנו קבל ושמע צעקתנו יודע תעלומות

שקוצית יהוה יהוה יהוה

שמעיאל ברכיאל אהניאל

ר"ת שוא

פדאל תלמיאל (תומיאל) וסדיאל

ר"ת פתח